ALEXIS LICHINE'S
New
Encyclopedia of
WINES & SPIRITS

Also by Alexis Lichine

WINES OF FRANCE (1951)

ALEXIS LICHINE'S GUIDE TO THE WINES AND VINEYARDS OF FRANCE (1979)

These are BORZOI BOOKS *published in New York by* ALFRED A. KNOPF

THIRD EDITION
fully revised and brought up to date
With a new appendix on the latest developments in American, French, and Italian wines

ALEXIS LICHINE'S
New Encyclopedia of
WINES &SPIRITS

IN COLLABORATION WITH

William Fifield

AND WITH THE ASSISTANCE OF

Jonathan Bartlett, Jane Stockwood, John Laird,
Samuel Perkins, and Katie Philson

NEW YORK *Alfred A. Knopf* 1981

THIS IS A BORZOI BOOK
PUBLISHED BY ALFRED A. KNOPF, INC.

Published in the United States by Alfred A. Knopf, Inc., New York, and
simultaneously in Canada by Random House of Canada Limited, Toronto. Distributed
by Random House, Inc., New York.

Library of Congress Cataloging in Publication Data
Lichine, Alexis. (Date)
Alexis Lichine's new encyclopedia of wines & spirits.

Edition published in 1979 under title: Lichine's encyclopedia of wines & spirits.
"With a new appendix on the latest developments in American, French, and Italian wines."
Bibliography: p.
Includes index.
1. Wine and wine making—Dictionaries.
I. Fifield, William.   II. Title.   III. Title: New encyclopedia of wines & spirits.
TP546.L5   1981   641.2′1′0321   80-22385
ISBN 0-394-51781-4

Manufactured in the United States of America

First Edition published November 6, 1967
Reprinted seven times
Second Edition, completely revised, enlarged and reset, published October 1974
Reprinted four times
Third Edition, fully revised and with a new appendix, published April 1981

To Sacha and Sandra,

who were raised in the Médoc—

in the hope that this will help to develop their taste

Contents

Preface

This book is written for the consumer and those in the trade whose function it is to relate the taste, traditions, and knowledge of wine, the subtle changes between one vineyard and another, and the inescapable limitations of fine wines produced from limited acreage. Such knowledge adds immeasurably to the real enjoyment of a good bottle. Also, it helps to blow away the cobwebs from a subject which, for too long, has been shrouded in mystery. Some of the people who approach wine with awe are not even sure that it is made from grapes: that is why so much importance has been given in this book to the sciences of viticulture and wine-making. Detailed information on these matters—as well as on the history, value, and serving of wine—will be found in the chapters which precede the alphabetical encyclopedic section.

It has been impossible, because of restrictions of space, to give every topic its own entry, and some subjects will be found included under an entry of greater importance. No hard and fast rules have been laid down, however. Wine is a subject of infinite flexibility, and every aspect is treated according to its individual merits and placed where it seems to fit best. It should therefore be stressed that full use must be made of the index, which in cases of doubt will quickly pinpoint all references to a particular aspect of any subject. The appendixes supply complete documentation of such matters as cooperage and bottle sizes, useful conversion tables, lists of worthy but non-classified châteaux of the Bordeaux region, and complete lists of the 1971 register of German vineyards. Any production figure quoted in the text is a mean average unless a specific figure is given as representing a typical year. These figures are naturally subject to the fluctuations of season from year to year. Any regulations quoted in the encyclopedia are in force at the time of going to press but some are liable to annual amendment.

In order to make quite clear when reference is being made to the genuine wine and when to an imitation of it, an initial capital letter is given to such wines as Sherry, Port, Burgundy, etc. only when they are legally restricted wines coming from Spain, Portugal, France, etc.

My first book, *Wines of France* (recently completely re-written and published as a new book, *Alexis Lichine's Guide to the Wines and Vineyards of France*), was so well received and widely bought that I decided to embark, in somewhat the same manner, on the wines and spirits of the world. This volume would not, however, have been possible without the particular collaboration of the following persons:

The late Herr Karl Ress, not only a great taster, but one whose sincere dedication to his beloved Rheingau was an invaluable source of information for that and other important German wine regions. His son Joachim has admirably followed in his late father's footsteps, generously contributing to this revised edition.

Dr. Franz Werner Michel of the Stabilisierungsfonds für Wein in Mainz, who has been especially helpful in seeing that all the German entries are up to date, reflecting the changes of the 1971 West German wine laws.

Mr. Peter M. F. Sichel of New York, the final member of this faithful trio, each of whom has done so much to assure the completeness of the new German entries.

Dr. Maynard Amerine, the leading oenologist of the United States, whose technical assistance has been sought by governments throughout the world. His books, reflecting his knowledge of the science of modern wine-making, are respected by such experts as Dr. Peynaud and Dr. Ribéreau-Gayon of France; and he is a wine-lover who realizes that wine is not only a science, but also one of the civilizing graces.

Monsieur Patrick Leon, the wine-buyer of Alexis Lichine & Co., who spent long hours and many late nights checking the small vineyards of France and their production, with the result that no other book published, even in France, can approach this one in the wide range of statistics surveyed.

Monsieur Claude Taittinger, who has given of his time and knowledge to ensure that the Champagne entry is as complete and authoritative as it can possibly be.

The late Monsieur François Hine, Cognac-shipper of Jarnac, whose jovial nature was as internationally esteemed as his product.

Messieurs Protin and Friedas of the Office International du Vin, Paris, who kindly offered important statistical information on the wine-producing countries around the world, and so generously supplied the many maps, once intended for publication as a separate wine atlas.

Prof. Georges Portmann of Bordeaux who, as the successor to Louis Pasteur, contributed willingly to the chapter on wine and health.

Monsieur Pierre Perromat, wine-grower and president of the I.N.A.O., whose kindness is witnessed on many pages of this book.

Monsieur Pierre Bréjoux, former inspector-general of the I.N.A.O., who personally checked the entries on his native Anjou and gave freely of his time for the preparation of entries on the recent Appellations Contrôlées.

The late Dr. Philippe Dufaye, who abandoned medicine to become a wine-grower in Châteauneuf-du-Pape, feeling that he could find a fuller and happier life dealing with the nature of the soil than with human nature.

Monsieur Georges Duboeuf, a dedicated broker who started off as a grower, and who today, with his qualifications for selecting wines and working toward the unity of the Beaujolais growers, is well on the way to becoming the outstanding personality of his famous wine region. His colleague, Monsieur Michel Brun, also provided great assistance.

The more than fifty brokers, shippers, owners, and knowledgeable friends who helped with the revision of the Bordeaux wine classification appearing on pages 117-121. Once the pressures of politics and bias are removed, reasonable men are capable of ranking with constructive good will the red wines of the Gironde. The frank opinions of these advisers have been kept privileged as promised, so as not to hinder their daily work in the Bordeaux marketplace.

Dr. Bruno Roncarati of London, who sorted out the vast array of D.O.C. Italian wines.

Miss Jane Stockwood, who has worked diligently with me over the past fifteen years, who shared my frustration when 20 per cent of the manuscript was inadvertently destroyed by a typist, and gave me a helping hand in getting the missing sections into order again. If it had not been for her, this book would never have reached the publishers.

Mr. John Laird, a willing student of wines, who gave yeoman service during the year-long revision of this book in 1974.

Mr. Sam Perkins and Mr. Martin Sinkoff, who in 1978 and 1979 assisted with its further updating, and Miss Katie Philson, who continued their work in 1980.

All those who were close to me in the original eleven years, starting in 1956, when I optimistically believed this book would be finished in 1959 and not 1967. And the many friends who waited patiently through the massive 1974 revision, which began as an updating, but ended as an expansion of most of the book.

Others, too many to name here, have given me considerable help, and these are listed on pages 676-681. I also wish to acknowledge my indebtedness to Yves Renouil and Paul de Traversay's *Dictionnaire du Vin* (Féret et Fils, Bordeaux, 1962), from which the tables on pages 46-47 and 339-340 were taken.

ALEXIS LICHINE

Introduction

I can truthfully say that since I reached the age of discretion I have consistently drunk more than most people would say was good for me. Nor do I regret it. Wine has been to me a firm friend and a wise counsellor. Often wine has shown me matters in their true perspective, and has, as though by the touch of a magic wand, reduced great disasters to small inconveniences.

Wine has lit up for me the pages of literature, and revealed in life romance lurking in the commonplace.

Wine has made me bold but not foolish; has induced me to say silly things but not to do them.

Under its influence words have often come too easily which had better not have been spoken, and letters have been written which had better not have been sent.

But if such small indiscretions standing in the debit column of wine's account were added up, they would amount to nothing in comparison with the vast accumulation on the credit side.

Duff Cooper: OLD MEN FORGET

Wine as a business is of international importance, an affair of vast ramifications. It provides a livelihood for some 37 million people throughout the world. More than 10 million hectares (nearly 25 million acres) of the earth's surface are planted in vines. Each year the world's harvest is some 300 million hectoliters (7.94 billion U.S. gallons, 6.6 billion imp.), or roughly the equivalent of 3.5 billion cases of wine. And fully one-quarter of this great quantity comes from the Common Market countries. If all the vineyards were laid low by a sudden plague, millions of people would be thrown out of work or ruined, many others would be hard-hit, and an unmanageable economic crisis would follow.

As the world becomes increasingly industrialized and standards more materialistic, as automation brings more leisure, people everywhere expect a share in the good things of life—the pleasures of civilized eating and drinking among them. It is harder now to find young men prepared to give the necessary time and devotion to the cultivation of the vine. Yet, in the cities, interest in wine, far from declining, is growing all the time.

Since the publication of the first edition of this book in 1967, interest in wines all over the world—and especially in the United States—has grown as never before. There are still those for whom drinking wine revolves around the First Classified Growths of the Médoc, which have become the most expensive red wines in the world; but for the more broad-minded recent convert, with perhaps less money to spend, this new edition gives thorough attention to the less well-known growths from nearly every wine-producing country on the globe. Though the wines of Bordeaux and some of Burgundy declined dramatically in price in 1974, the importance of the many other different wines can only continue to increase, as each nation recognizes the value of its own wines; the tremendous expansion of viticulture in California (and the expected increase in price for premium California wines) is but one example of this increasing awareness. The new West German, Italian, Spanish, and South African wine laws are another result. After having suffered the record prices of the first years of the world wine boom, the consumer can look forward to greatly improved average-quality wines achieved through the application of oenological know-how.

A bursting desire for a way of life closer to nature has impelled Americans from coast to coast to turn to vine-growing and wine-making, especially in California. New vineyards and wineries popped up in increasing numbers in newly found areas during the seventies. In this third edition I have tried to reflect these changes, both in the body of the text and in the new Appendix entitled "Recent Developments."

Thus wine, one of the first and now one of the most passionate interests of civilized man, is at once a major industry and a major pleasure of life. The figures comparing yearly *per capita* consumption in different countries vary greatly and make interesting reading. France and Italy seesaw back and forth in the lead, each with an average consumption of around 105 liters (about 27.5 U.S. gallons, 23 imp.). Argentina, with 85 liters, is fourth. Spaniards enjoy some 70 liters of their own product, but it is the neighboring Portuguese who come in third with about 95 liters *per capita*. In the course of a year, an average American will drink scarcely eight liters (less than two gallons), a little more than an Englishman, but one-fifth the consumption of a Greek, Swiss, Chilean, Austrian, or Luxembourgeois. A Russian, who used to consume very little wine, has lately seen his country's vineyards and imports expand by more than 50 per cent, and now drinks rather more wine than does the American; but the wine itself is considerably inferior in quality to that which the American puts in his glass.

As more and more people travel and acquire a taste for good wine, the civilized custom of having a bottle on the table gains ground. Will demand outrun supply? In the past half dozen years, it indeed has for some wines in certain parts of the world; hence the price spiral of the early seventies. Though some regions can still increase their vineyard acreage, Burgundy, for example, has reached its maximum; and some fine and famous areas are extraordinarily small: 2,000 hectares (5,000 acres) for the whole Chablis district. (Compare this figure with the thousands of bottles labeled Chablis to be found on restaurant tables all over the world and draw your own conclusions.)

The present cry is for more of everything, turned out faster and more cheaply. If there is one thing which does not respond to this call, it is great wine. It can be made expensively but still will not increase in quantity. It can be made in bulk but will not then be a fine wine. The best wines have always been those from comparatively nonproductive grapevines—which are pruned short in order to reduce output and channel the plant's energy into the production of superior fruit. Because the grower cannot at the same time obtain both quantity and quality, enlightened laws have been set up to limit production. That is why the statistics of this book represent the amount the soil can produce—not the amount to which an unscrupulous merchant may, accordion-like, stretch his merchandise, while his labels claim for it the geographical limitations of a vineyard, a district, or even a region to which it has no right. In these malpractices many countries have been at fault. In Italy, for instance, too often the famous growths of the north have been blended with cheaper wines coming from the south; and it will take a few years for the recently enacted laws to put a stop to such "sophistications."

At this time there is an oversupply of bulk wines coming from many parts of the world, especially Spain and certain regions of France. Since 1972 there has been an increase of 15 per cent in world production, to more than 350 million hectoliters per year (9.24 billion U.S. gallons, 7.27 imp.), which can be accounted for by the overproduction of ordinary wines. This trend can only be cut back by more judicious matching of better grape varieties to the soil and greater care in finding the proper microclimates. California is pulling ahead in this regard. Until recently, 50 per cent of its production was appropriate only for use as table grapes or raisins, but the state is beginning to grow more of the better varieties. In the interest of the consumer and the top producers of California wine, the U.S. government and the state of California are taking a well-advised hard look at the philosophy of the Appellation Contrôlée laws enacted in France and of similar laws in other Common Market countries. A strict control of place-names is needed in California, where many of the mediocre wines of the central valley and southern parts of the state seek refuge under the umbrella of quality wines produced by the best growers in the northern counties.

There have been other recent changes throughout the world regarding the sale and distribution of bulk wine. These include huge imports of Algerian wine by the Soviet Union and the sale of large quantities of Italian wine to France. Prior to the independence of Algeria, most of this country's production was used for blending with the *vin du Midi* or *vin ordinaire* of France, and for bolstering certain Burgundies. Now the Soviet Union is trying to fight vodka alcoholism with the promotion of Algerian wines, and currently the French are bringing in Italian wines, high in alcoholic content, to replace the Algerian. This has become profitable since the devaluation of the lira and since these wines can be imported duty-free as a result of the Common Market.

In this book I have set out to represent wine in terms of today. By stressing the small production of the great vineyards, I hope to be able to guide the consumer through the mazes of nomenclature and of impermissible—as against permissible and honest—blending. For the contemporary trend toward a standard product is one which creates difficulty for the wine-maker. His harvest will be different in different years. He may honestly blend them toward uniformity—but no blending vat in the world is capable of turning out a standard wine of the highest quality. Fine wines will survive if the consumer insists on higher and more regular standards. That is what this book is dedicated to.

Clearly, the average wine-drinker cannot expect to enjoy the greatest wines every day. Even if he could afford to, there would soon not be enough to go around. But the supply of sound, honest wines is fortunately not short. Bordeaux is one region which has been able to increase the size of some of its classified vineyards by as much as 30 per cent; and the American customer, who once believed he must always aim as high as Château Lafite, has learned to extend his knowledge not only to the other Classified Growths offering great quality but also to the unclassified ones and the many sound regional wines. He will be quite content if he—and the shippers—will get used to honest labeling, and if he does not expect a true Pommard for the price of an ordinary red Burgundy. Conversely, experience will teach him that for the price of a commercial Liebfraumilch (even with the 1971 West German Wine Law, a rather meaningless name), he could find a wine from a good vineyard and double his enjoyment.

As Ernest Hemingway wrote in *Death in the Afternoon*, "A person with increasing knowledge and sensory education may derive infinite enjoyment from wine."

I have tried, in what follows, to help the reader distinguish the small wine from the great, and by comparing one with the other, to educate his palate and develop his taste and his pleasure. To quote again from Hemingway: "Wine is one of the most civilized things in the world, and one of the material things of the world that has been brought to the greatest perfection and which offers a greater range of enjoyment and appreciation than, possibly, any other purely sensory thing which may be purchased."

Alexis Lichine's
New
Encyclopedia of
WINES &SPIRITS

CANADA

U.S.A.

MEXICO

COLOMBIA

PERU

BRAZIL

BOLIVIA

CHILE

URUGUAY

ARGENTINA

AUSTRALIA

NEW ZEALAND

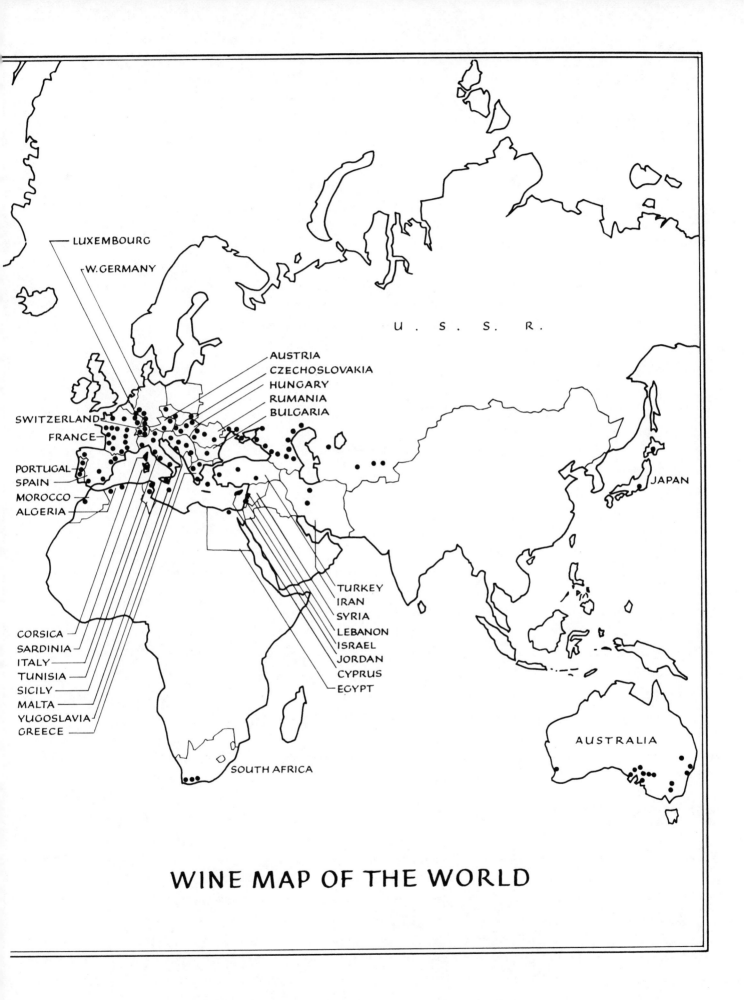

LUXEMBOURG
W. GERMANY

U . S . S . R .

AUSTRIA
CZECHOSLOVAKIA
HUNGARY
RUMANIA
BULGARIA

SWITZERLAND
FRANCE

PORTUGAL
SPAIN
MOROCCO
ALGERIA

JAPAN

TURKEY
IRAN
SYRIA
LEBANON
ISRAEL
JORDAN
CYPRUS
EGYPT

CORSICA
SARDINIA
ITALY
TUNISIA
SICILY
MALTA
YUGOSLAVIA
GREECE

AUSTRALIA

SOUTH AFRICA

WINE MAP OF THE WORLD

1 History of Wine

The history of wine is inextricably interwoven with the history of man. It has been said that civilization grew out of agriculture: when the first nomads planted seeds and waited for the crop to grow, their wandering ceased. It might be as true to say that it was with wine that civilization began, for the vine takes longer to mature than any other crop, and does not produce grapes for the *vendange* until its fourth year—after four years in one place, a nomad tribe would be well settled and already practiced in domestic arts.

We do not know when men first had wine, but it was accepted as a gift from the gods: the Egyptians attributed it to Osiris, the Greeks to Dionysos; the Armenians maintained that Noah planted the first vineyard near Erivan. Since grape seeds have been found in prehistoric caves, it is conceivable that wine is older than history—although it is unlikely that the cavemen knew how to ferment their grapes. That discovery, when it came, was probably accidental. According to one legend, a Persian king who was very fond of grapes stored some away in a great jar marked *Poison*. Some time afterward, one of the neglected beauties of his harem, tired of life, drank from the jar—and the poison was by then so delicious that, much revived, she took a cup to the king, who drank from it, took the lady back into favor, and ordained that thereafter the grapes should be allowed to ferment. However they discovered it, the Persians evidently loved wine: according to Herodotus, all important matters were discussed twice in the councils of state—once when they were drinking, and again when they were sober.

Mesopotamia and the Caucasian slopes were no doubt early sources of wine: the Libation Scene in the "Standard" panel from Ur (now in the British Museum) dates from the first half of the third millennium before Christ. In Egypt vineyards were being planted for funerary wines soon after 3000 B.C.; and legendary tales of wine-drinking in China date from much the same period. In any case, it is believed that Greece, the first European country to make wine, received the art from the East, and also, no doubt, from Egypt.

The earliest records of wine in Egypt are the sealing inscriptions on the stoppers of amphorae found in pre-Dynastic tombs. In early days, the king had his own vineyard, from which the funeral wines came, and (according to H. F. Lutz) a domestic vine-plot to provide his table wine. Vineyards belonging to important persons were given names: Rameses III (1198–1166 B.C.) developed the famous Ka-n-komet, as well as new plantations in oases. Another, more long-winded name was King Zoser's

"Praised be Horus, who is in the front of Heaven"—the wine from there was sometimes more succinctly described as "Beverage of Horus." Wine labels, on the other hand, could be models of clarity: "In the year xxx Good wine of the large irrigated terrain of the Temple of Rameses II in Per-Amon. The chief of the wine-dressers, Tutmes." Would that all labels were as honest, explicit, and simply expressed.

In the unchanging climate of Africa, vintage years were not very important. But soil matters vitally to the vine, wherever it grows, so that the Egyptians were concerned about the sites of their vineyards. The vines grew best near the Delta, where they were irrigated by the annual flooding of the Nile—but since marsh is not the land for them, the walled vineyards were planted on artificially raised plots.

The reliefs and wall-paintings in the tombs, in which so clear a picture of Egyptian life is preserved, show workers harvesting the vine with curved knives like the hand-sickles still occasionally in use, the grapes being picked by women and dropped into wicker baskets to be carried on the men's backs—or balanced on shoulder yokes—to the press. The Egyptians used fermenting vats of acacia wood, in which they trod the grapes in a compulsive rhythm, sung and clapped out by hand—this is a sight familiar to everyone who has watched the vintage on the Douro or in Spain. Nor does the parallel with modern times end there: a certain Bilgai, "Overseer of the Fortress of the sea," shamelessly recorded, on a stele, that he had assessed the people 23,568 measures of wine in excess of his due as tax-collector. Moreover, the Code of Hammurabi (Babylon, *c.* 2000 B.C.) stipulated the conditions under which wine could be bought; and a seller who gave short measure was thrown into the water—then, as now, there was fraud in the business.

We know little about the wine of the common people because they lacked the means to have themselves buried in great tombs or to have their thoughts and histories carved out in stone—probably they drank the wines made from palms and dates, and the barley beer. The wine of the royal and the rich was mainly white. The most celebrated kinds were as follows. Mareotic: grown near what was to be the city of Alexandria—a white wine, sweet and light, long-lasting, and with a fragrant bouquet. Centuries later, it was known in Rome: Horace wrote that this was the wine which fired Cleopatra. Taeniotic: Athenaeus (*c.* A.D. 200) declared that this was even better than the Mareotic—an unctuous, greenish-white wine, sweet and aromatic, and of a slightly astringent character. (He went on to say that the wine-loving Egyptians often ate boiled cabbage before a feast, and took cabbage-water to cure a hangover.) Sebennyticum: described by Pliny as being the product of three different grapes, the Thasian, the soot grape, and the pitch-pine. Egyptian wines were sealed up in amphorae of the Greek pattern—and since they were not sufficient for the people of the country, many more came in from Greece, from Phoenicia, and from Syria.

It has been reckoned that wine is mentioned 155 times in the Old Testament and 10 times in the New. In the book of Numbers it says that, at the time of the Exodus, the Hebrews regretted leaving behind the wines of Egypt: but they need not have feared, for the land of the Philistines and the Plain of Sharon were green with the vine, and Palestine came to be rich in vineyards. Indeed, vines flourished prolifically in the eastern Mediterranean countries and around the Caspian and the Black seas. In Ezekiel, Chapter 27, we read about Damascus, that great center of the wine trade: "thy merchant . . . in the wine of Helbon." The wine of Byblos was celebrated too. The Syrians and the Phoenicians sent their wine by the old caravan routes to Arabia and Egypt, to India, and as far as China; and their famous Chalybon went to the Persian kings. Vines were planted in Arabia too, and large quantities of wine—mostly red—were made there.

There are also many references to wine in the Babylonian Talmud, in their inscriptions, and in their art. The southern parts of the country were not very suitable to the vine, and here, as in the Nile Delta, plots had to be raised by human labor. But in the north, soil and climate were favorable, and at one time Babylonian wines were much esteemed, and traveled as far as Arabia. Wine was blessed and offered to Abraham by King Melchizedek (Genesis, Chapter 14): libations were made with daily burnt offerings at the Feast of the Tabernacles; and so a link is made with King Nebuchadnezzar, dedicating wines with strange names to the pagan god Marduk, and with Assurbanipal in Nineveh, making libations freely—pouring wine on cornerstones, on sacred objects, on lions killed in the hunt, or on beheaded enemies. In the voodoo ceremonies of Haiti, libations are still offered to the gods; nor is there anything surprising about this custom, since primitive gods are largely anthropomorphic—and what more natural than to offer wine to an honored guest?

The ancient Greeks also poured libations to their gods, and from Homeric times and earlier they were a wine-drinking people. Vines decorated the shield of Achilles, the gold cup of Nestor is still famous, and Odysseus and his men washed down "abundant flesh with sweet wine." The Greeks liked their wines old and watered down. These sweet wines, trodden in stone vats and matured in earthenware crocks, may have borne some resemblance to Malmsey. Hesiod, the Boeotian farmer-poet, who was writing his *Works and Days* in about 700 B.C., pruned and planted his vines in the ways that were to be followed by countless generations (*see* Classical Wines). The Pramnian and pure Maronean first described in Homer are still discussed—and regretted: some writers are of the opinion that the well-matured vintages of ancient Greece

were the quintessence of fine wine. Nobody alive is in a position to dispute this view. Yet the pitched vessels in which much of the Greek wine was stored, the mixture, with some of it, of sea water, and the addition of perfumes must have combined to produce flavors not much to our taste.

Some of the grapes which yielded the Greek wines were almost certainly transplanted to the Greek colonies in Sicily and southern Italy, and the wine would surely have been made there in the same way. Up on the mainland, the Etruscans (migrants, it has been said, from Asia Minor) were already a wine-drinking people, loving luxury and splendid banquets in which their women took a prominent part. The Etruscans' wine god was called Fufluns. In the same province of Tuscany some of the best Italian wines are made today.

Viniculture, therefore, would have been a natural heritage of the Romans. Like the Greeks, they made red, white, and amber wines; and they too could drink them "pitched and pickled," sometimes mixed with sea water or exposed in a smoky room (*fumarium*). In old age some of them would be, as Tovey said, "reduced to a syrup and rendered so muddy and thick they had to be strained through cloths and dissolved in hot water." But the *fumarium* was intended to mellow the wine by heat rather than by smoke—the principle was not unlike that of maturing Madeira near ovens—and the jars were protected by a thick coat of plaster or pitch. The Romans themselves complained of "smoky wines" when they returned from Marseille—settled about 600 B.C. by Greeks from Phocaea, and surely the first place in Gaul to have made real wine. The wines most prized in Rome were luscious, less in need of acrid preservatives—they probably resembled the Lágrima of today (*see* Classical Wines). Wine traveled in earthenware amphorae, and fragments of these jars have been found in riverbeds and along roads. Wrecked ships loaded with amphorae have been retrieved from the Mediterranean—the jars, still corked, contain a liquid that, in the years before Christ, was new wine.

Where the Romans went, conquering and colonizing, the culture of the vine went with them. Using the waters of the Rhône to make their way northward in what is now France, they are said to have planted the Picatum, a hardy grape with a slight taste of pitch. On an old wine cup found in the region, the legend reads, "Give us Aminean, not Picatum." At the end of the first century, Martial tells that this wine was being exported to Rome. When in A.D. 97 the Emperor Domitian issued an edict calling for the uprooting of many vines throughout the Empire, no doubt protecting Italian wines was one of his motives (along with encouraging agriculture and controlling surplus wine production). But it is not to be supposed that all of the vines were destroyed—the French character being what it is, orders are not much regarded; but however half-heartedly the growers carried out the order, their descendants must have been relieved when, in 280, the Emperor Probus repealed it.

When the vines were openly planted again, they spread beyond the old vineyard regions of Marseille, the Rhône Valley, and the Iberian peninsula to the northern and western regions of France and Germany, and to Britain. When Ausonius, the Bordelais professor, poet, and consul, accompanied the Emperor Valentinian to the Moselle, he compared the well-kept vines and broad rivers of France and Germany and was charmed by both. In Germany, as in France, viticulture was encouraged by Charlemagne; soon, in an age when most wine was only fit to drink when young, the Germans, storing theirs in huge casks, promoted a taste for "old Rhenish." In Alsace grapes were planted and casks of wine taken to Colmar and Strasbourg for shipment to Germany. The wine also came to England, where it was known as Osey or Aussey, and much appreciated. It is mentioned in Langland's *Piers Plowman* in the mid-fourteenth century.

With the spread of Christianity, monasteries sprang up, and royal or noble patrons endowed them with vineyards, particularly in Burgundy, where several wines, such as those of Beaune, had been known in Rome. Charlemagne himself (*c.* 800) had vines at Corton (hence the great vineyard name, Corton-Charlemagne); about 1100 the Cistercians made Clos de Vougeot and produced wine in Chablis as well. All through the early Middle Ages the Church was the principal producer. Because of their learning and their industry, the monks took the lead in viticulture: the pure wine of the grape was needed both for sacrament and for sustenance. Cluny, in Burgundy, was the great monastic center. When life there became too luxurious, the ascetic Cistercians broke away, disseminating the Gospel and the culture of the vine wherever they went, inside France and across her frontiers.

In early medieval times vines were grown in England mostly by monks in the southern counties. But wine was also imported from the Rhine and the north of France. In spite of the marriage of Henry II and Eleanor of Aquitaine (*see* Bordeaux), it was not until the beginning of the thirteenth century that Bordeaux (Gascon) wines began to come in any quantity to England, Flanders, and the Hanseatic ports. A record of wines imported for King John lists only those from places farther north—Gaillac, Auxerre, and the Rhine; there is no mention of any from Gascony.

Yet within a few years, the king was drinking the wines and granting favors and tax cuts to the burghers of Bordeaux. English merchants went over at harvest time to spend some weeks bargaining with the Bordelais. The Gascon wine was soon much loved in England, where it was known as claret; and by the early fourteenth century, the people were able to enjoy table wines from Spain and Portugal, as well as the sweet wines of Crete and Cyprus. Malvasia, or Malmsey, came originally from Greece; but when the Turks occupied the mainland, the wine was shipped from Candia (Crete) and other islands, often in the vessels of the powerful Venetians who, in the reign of Richard III, were bringing the legendary Helbon of Damascus to Western Europe. To England, they were obliged to bring with each cask ten Levantine yews to be made into bows. Inside the country also, there were strict controls. Officials boarded the merchant ships to supervise the cargoes and test the quality of the wine, and the king took his *prise* from every load. Although the wine was cheap, the common people did not drink very freely. Each town was allowed only a specified number of taverns; and no man except a peer or one with a considerable income and household was permitted to keep more than ten gallons of wine at home. Yet an Archbishop of York bought and dispensed one hundred tuns at his enthronement—wine was not, however, as strong then as it is now.

In the meantime, the wine which had come so early to the Middle East had been forbidden to the followers of Mohammed—yet the prohibition must not be taken too seriously, since certain Turks are known to have been devoted to drink. But as the power of the Moslems spread, so did the rule of abstinence; and when the practical monks of Carbonnieux wanted to sell their wine to the Turks, they labeled it *Mineral Water of Carbonnieux.* The Crusaders, however, are said to have found new vines in the lands of the Saracen and to have brought back with them sweet Muscat grapes, which they planted at the foot of the Pyrenees, and which produced Muscat de Frontignan, Lunel, and Rivesaltes. It was from the abstemious Saracens that Europe learned the art of distilling spirits.

Since in the Middle Ages all wine was drunk young, some of it must have been very acid and crude; this, especially at banquets, was made palatable by admixtures of honey and spices known as *piments,* which combined "the strength of wine, the sweetness of honey, and the perfume of aromatics." Of these liqueur-like drinks, the most celebrated were hippocras, about which poets rhapsodized, and clarry—the basis for which, clearly, was claret.

Because Burgundy was far inland and served by bad roads, its wines were little known in England and the northern capitals; but their fame grew in their own region, where the dukes and princes were often at war with the French kings. In 1395, Philip the Bold of Burgundy made laws to maintain the quality of the wines, banishing the inferior grape, Gamay, and trying to keep out the wines of other districts which might have been used to stretch the Burgundy. Having possessions in Belgium, he moved his court—and some of his wine—to Brussels. Burgundy was also appreciated by the popes during their exile at Avignon. In 1443, Nicolas Rolin, chancellor of Philip the Fair, founded the Hôtel Dieu, or Hospice, at Beaune.

The vineyards of Champagne, planted by the Romans, yielded, in the Middle Ages and for some two hundred years afterward, still red wines which were at first lumped in with those of the Île de France and sold abroad earlier than were the Gascon growths. Saint Remi, who baptized Clovis at Rheims in 496, was a vineyard-owner and patron of wine in the district. Henry VIII of England and Cardinal Wolsey bought some of the wine, which was enjoyed by the Valois kings, one of whom, Henri IV, was the first to give the name *Champagne* to the products of Rheims and Épernay.

In England, by Elizabeth I's reign, although the gentry still drank a lot of wine, the price of French wines had risen and the common people drank less of it—and more beer; Sack and Sherry were already well established (the name *Sack* was applied to wines from the Canaries and other places besides Jerez). James I loved his claret; Oliver Cromwell, who hated fun and destroyed beauty, was yet human enough to approve of good wine. Osey remained popular; but when, in 1618, the Thirty Years' War broke out, the vineyards were largely destroyed, and the trade did not flourish again for two centuries.

Charles II brought back from France a new taste for Champagne, which was fostered also by the French philosopher and wit Saint-Evremond, who was in exile in England. The wines of Rheims and Épernay were now sometimes white, or *vins gris* with a faint, evanescent foam. It was not until the last years of the century that the cellarer-monk Dom Pérignon was credited with the discovery of Champagne more or less as we know it. King Louis XIV was known to favor the red wine of Burgundy, and a keen competition developed between the growers of that district and of Champagne: doctors were asked to debate the qualities of the rival products. Under the Regency and in the reign of Louis XV, Champagne had a great success at court; and some of the big *négociants* were already becoming established, starting with Ruinart in 1729. About a century later, the sparkling wine was perfected by the addition of a sweet *liqueur de tirage* and the evolution of *dégorgement* to rid the bottles of their sediment (*see* Champagne).

Under William of Orange and his German successors, crippling duties were put on French wine; and the Methuen Treaty of 1703 gave overwhelming preference to Port—not then the fortified drink we know, but simply Portuguese table wine which was, as Englishmen complained, much inferior to Bordeaux. Many of them refused it and turned to "Florence" wine instead. The poorer people turned, regrettably and excessively, to gin. Rhenish, also, was to be had, and some Spanish table wine, as well as Sherry—by the early eighteenth century, Sack was seldom heard of. Claret, of course, was smuggled in and the rich got their share. But gradually people took to Port—perhaps the first "brandying" (which started, probably, about 1715) had something to do with it. In time, the shippers of Oporto learned to fortify and mature the wine as they do now, and by the end of the century Port was first in popularity, although Hermitage, Champagne, and Madeira were doing well. During these years, wine bottles, which had formerly been nothing more than squat jugs for holding wine taken fresh from the barrel, developed more or less the form they have now, and so, in 1781, the first Clairet to be stored in a well-rounded bottle was laid down in the cellars of Château Lafite.

When the French Revolution broke out, the vineyards were taken from the nobles and the Church and given to the people. A few years later, Napoleon secularized the vineyards of Germany—almost as great a revolution, from the point of view of the German growers. In France, ever since, the Burgundian holdings have mostly been divided into small parcels, although in Bordeaux the big estates were soon re-established. Talleyrand became the owner of Château Haut-Brion, and some sharp wits attributed his diplomatic successes at the Congress of Vi-

enna to the talents of his cook. At delicious dinners he would ply his guests with fine wines, and then play them off against each other. The chief opponent of Talleyrand was Metternich, later proud possessor of the great German vineyard Schloss Johannisberg.

By the middle of the nineteenth century, new vineyards were established in new countries: in South Africa and Australia and, most importantly, in America. When Leif Ericson crossed the Atlantic, he found a country green with wild vines and called it "Vineland." Later settlers made many experiments with transplanted European vines; finally, they discovered that, while the *Vitis vinifera* would grow in California, it was better to stick to the native species in the eastern states (*see* United States).

It was never guessed that the American vine, living independently, was developing an immunity to certain vine pests and diseases, themselves strengthened continually in the competition. But when American vines were brought to Europe a hundred years ago, the pests struck, and in the second half of the century nearly all the vineyards of Europe were decimated by the burrowing plant louse phylloxera. Indeed, the plagues swept over the world, and wine as we know it might have vanished. Luckily, the growth which brought disaster also contained the cure. American roots became immune to phylloxera, and it was found that the European varieties would grow on American root-stocks. What the final result will be, in terms of quality, of grafting onto American stocks cannot yet be determined. Some people say that the wines are better than "before phylloxera"; others deny this. The long adjustments of the vine to soil and weather, changes very gradual in all wine history, must be given their own time.

In addition to this effect of American vine on Europe is the story of wine in America itself. At first, in the Colonies, European wines were drunk. How discriminating were the drinkers, and of what kinds the wines, can be judged from records of the time. The writer Washington Irving was a famous lover of wine, and we have many of his letters and receipts for orders of hogsheads from France and Spain. There were a great number of others, but we will cite excerpts from two letters of Thomas Jefferson, a true expert, the first written in 1792 to Henry Sheaff, a Philadelphia merchant, and the second in 1817 to President James Monroe at the White House.

Burgundy. the best wines of Burgundy are Montrachet, a white wine. it is made but by two persons, to wit, Monsʳ de Clermont, & Monsieur de Sassnet. the latter rents to Monsʳ de la Tour. this costs 48 sous the bottle, new, and 3 livres when fit for drinking.

Meursault, a white wine. the best quality of it is called Goutte d'Or. it costs 6 sous the bottle new. I do not believe this will bear transportation. but the Montrachet will in a proper season.

Chambertin, Vougeau, Beaune, are red wines, of the first quality, and are the only red wines of Burgundy which will bear transportation and even these require to be moved in the best season, & not to be exposed to great heat or great cold. These cost 48 sous the bottle, new & 3 livres old. I think it next to impossible to have any of the Burgundy wines brought here in a sound state.

Champagne. the Mousseux or sparkling Champagne is never brought to a good table in France, the still, or non-mousseux is alone drunk by connoisseurs.

Bordeaux red wines. There are four crops of them more famous than all the rest. These are Chateau-Margau, Tour de Segur, Hautbrion, & De La Fite. they cost 3 livres a bottle, old: but are so engaged beforehand that it is impossible to get them. the merchants, if you desire it, will send you a wine by any of those names, & make you pay 3 livres a bottle: but I will venture to affirm that there never was a bottle of those wines sent to America by a merchant, nor is it worthwhile to seek for them; for I will defy any person to distinguish them from the wines of the next quality, to wit.

Rohan-Margau, which is made by Madame de Rohan this is what I import for myself & consider as equal to any of the four crops.

There are also the wines of Dabbadie, la Rose, Quirouen & Durfort which are reckoned as good as Madame de Rohan's. yet I have preferred hers. these wines cost 40 sous the bottle, when of the proper age for drinking.

Bordeaux white wines.

Grave. the best is called Pontac, & is made by Monsr de Lamont. it costs 18 sous a bottle.

Sauterne. this is the best white wine of France (except Champagne and Hermitage). the best of it is made by Monsr de Lur-Salur and costs at 4 years old (when fit to drink) from 20 to 24 sous the bottle. there are two other white wines made in the same neighborhood called Prignac & Barsac, esteemed by some. but the Sauterne is that preferred at Paris, & much the best in my judgment. they cost the same. a great advantage of the Sauterne is that it becomes higher flavored the day the bottle has been opened, than it is at first.

Mr. Fenwick, Consul of the U.S. at Bordeaux, is well informed on the subject of these wines, and has supplied the President and myself with them genuine & good. he would be a proper person to endeavor to get from the South of France some of the wines made there which are most excellent & very cheap, say 10 or 12 sous the bottle. those of Rousillon are the best . . .

I promised you, when I should have received and tried the wines I had ordered from France and Italy, to give you a note of the kinds which I should think worthy of your procurement. They are the following:

Vin blanc liquoreux d'Hermitage de M. Jourdan à Tains. This costs about .82 a bottle put on shipboard . . . .

There is still another wine to be named to you, which is the wine of Florence called Montepulciano, with which Appleton can best furnish you. There is a particular very best crop of it known to him, and which he has usually sent to me. He knows too from experience how to have it so bottled and packed as to ensure its bearing the passage, which in the ordinary way it does not. I have imported it through him annually 10 or 12 years and do not think I have lost 1 bottle in 100.

By the middle of the nineteenth century, tariffs between England and France had been so much lowered that the English bourgeoisie became claret-drinking people again—although Cyrus Redding, a few years earlier, had written that the English palate, coarsened by a long diet of brandied wines imported under the Methuen Treaty, could not appreciate a great growth of Bordeaux in its pure natural state, and so, especially for the English market, fine clarets were "sophisticated" with Cahors, Hermitage, Benicarlo, and even brandy. The Premiers Crus, even of the "year of the comet" (1811), were subjected to this treatment; and when Nathaniel Johnston—one of a number of foreigners who had settled into the Bordeaux wine trade—wanted to drink some of the excellent 1798 unblended, he ordered bottles of "neat Lafitte" to be kept apart for him.

But Burgundy, Redding believed, could not be successfully adulterated—because its exquisite delicacy and bouquet were inimitable. (That he should have supposed blended and over-chaptalized imitations to be unacceptable seems odd today.) Burgundy was also held by the eighteenth-century writer Barry to be too delicate a wine to travel, and it was not in fact widely known in England in his time.

It must be added that, even if Mr. Redding's strictures on the clarets prepared for England were deserved, a race of keen connoisseurs was to spring up in the second half of the century, whose rhapsodies over the great pre-phylloxera vintages of the eighteen-sixties and -seventies are still quoted today. By that time, Englishmen must have earned the right to buy their claret pure.

Also about mid-century came the first disastrous vine disease—the oïdium mildew, considered the greatest of plagues until it was followed by phylloxera.

The other momentous event was the Official Bordeaux Classification (based on earlier unofficial ratings) of the great growths of the Médoc. The age of jurisprudence in the organization of the wine trade was beginning. It was clearly necessary that place-names should be controlled in a way which would make it difficult if not impossible for an inferior wine to masquerade as a great one. The campaign, which began on the Douro to protect the good name of Port, was carried on in France through the early years of this century until, in 1936, the laws of Appellation Contrôlée were passed—models of their kind, which the other vine-growing countries of the world have only recently begun to imitate (*see* Appellation d'Origine).

Wine is getting more expensive, but the demand for it is greater than ever and, in spite of bad summers in Europe, production flourishes. The Office International du Vin, a working group of wine-growers and legislators, has assessed the production of forty-four member countries; it now amounts to nearly 300 million hectoliters (7.95 billion U.S. gallons, 6.6 billion imp.). In this age of mechanization, man has returned as never before to the wine of the soil, the drink of civilization.

NOTE: *See* Classical Wines for additional history. Also regional entries (United States, Bordeaux, Burgundy, etc.) for local history.

2 History of Spirits and Distillation

In the Middle Ages spirit was known as *aqua vitae,* a term which survives today in Swedish and Norwegian aquavit and Danish akvavit. This was symptomatic, because the name means "water of life."

In ancient Greece, Aristotle wrote: "Sea water can be rendered potable by distillation. After it has been converted into humid vapors it returns to liquid." A Greek is said to have discovered this simply by noticing how steam condensed on the inner lid of a dish.

The principal remedies of the ancients were, as we know, wine and herbs. From the time of the Egyptians great use was made of flowers, plants, and spices, cooked, macerated, or infused for pharmaceutical or culinary purposes. With wine or water, the healing perfumed liquid was preserved in airtight jars. The science of distillation, if not continuously practiced, crops up again and again in history. The distillates, as far as we know, were water and scents. The discovery of the distillation of alcohol was made by the Arabs in the early Middle Ages. The philosopher Avicenna in the tenth century produced a complete description of the alembic, but did not mention alcohol—although it must have been discovered about that time. Like alchemy, the word *alcohol* derives from the Arabic. A certain black powder was liquefied, converted to vapor, allowed to solidify again, and then used as eye-paint by the harem beauties. This was *kohl,* which is in use throughout the Arab world today. And when the spirit of wine began to be distilled, the Arabic name for this distilled powder—*Al Koh'l*—was adopted, because of the similarity of the process.

In fact, we inherited the Arabian science of distillation by way of alchemy, which played a larger part in the medieval world. The earliest name of genuine importance in distillation is that of Arnáu of Vilanova (d. 1313), a Catalan professor at the University of Montpellier. He was probably the first to write of alcohol and his treatise on wine and spirits was a handbook of the time. His pupil, Raimundo Lulio (or Raymond Lull), was a philosopher and chemist who carried on with the experiments.

Eau-de-vie, Lulio wrote, is "an emanation of the divinity, an element newly revealed to men but hid from antiquity, because the human race was then too young to need this beverage destined to revive the energies of modern decrepitude." Arnáu had been more ecstatic. To him, the liquor was the long-sought panacea, the elixir of life itself, the dream of the alchemists. Although they never found what they were looking for—the secret of transmuting base metal into gold, or the elixir of everlasting life—the alchemists discovered a great many other things by the way. They developed the science of chemistry; and

while they did not discover *aqua vitae,* they used it extensively and bequeathed its uses to us.

To the general public *aqua vitae* was a medicine and tasted like one. Another name for it was *aqua ardens—*firewater. The fruit and herbs with which the spirit was doctored helped to hide the taste as well as to heal the patients. When, later on, people began to think of brandies and liqueurs primarily as drinks, there was much experimenting with different plants to improve the flavor; and except in such favored regions as Cognac, Frenchmen were still tackling the same problem at the end of the eighteenth century. Then, in 1800, Adam invented the process of rectification or rectifying—that is, a redistillation which removed the *mauvais goût.* Unfortunately, it removed all taste, good as well as bad, and the French, who had been adding herbs and fruit concoctions to hide the nasty taste, had to restore them again to give flavor to the neutral spirit.

Aqua vitae was on sale in Italy in the Middle Ages; at about the same time, or a little earlier, it appeared in Ireland, gaelicized into *uisge beatha* and distilled from a barley beer. Variants of this name for "the water of life" persisted throughout the centuries, but in the end it was unquestionably whisky.

Scotch whisky originated in the Highlands. By the fifteenth century, it was a familiar drink there and was purely malt whisky. Gradually it seeped through to the Lowlands and the Scottish court.

The English at first preferred the fine French Cognac brandies miraculously distilled from the thin sharp wines of Charente. In early days, ships from the north used to put in at La Rochelle, principally to pick up salt. Then the inhabitants began to sell their wine as well; and afterward, to save space in the ships—and perhaps to avoid taxes—they began to boil down the wine, which traveled much better when it was thus metamorphosed. At first the idea was to restore the wine by adding water when it reached land again; but it was soon discovered to taste better as it was. A gentleman called Croix-Maron, who is supposed to have had a lot to do with the boiling down of the wine, is said to have remarked: "In cooking my wines, I have discovered their soul."

A report from 1688 says that very little wine of the Charente region could be sold abroad, but "when the white wines are converted to *eau-de-vie,* which is the customary thing, then the English and Danish fleets come to the ports of the Charente in search of it." So, by that date, the brandy of Cognac was established. The name *brandy* may well have come from the Germanic *Branntwein*—

6

burnt wine. There are mentions of "brand wine" in English in 1622 and 1650.

It is interesting that much of the early distilling was done in the house, and the politest ladies were proficient in this domestic art, as common as cooking. Scotch whisky was at first almost entirely made at home: the best was for the Highland chiefs; the crofters mashed their surplus grain into whisky. When, in that mountainous and inaccessible country, the domestic stills were banned by the Hanoverian kings, and heavy taxes and duties began to be placed on the spirit, the distillers quite naturally took to the hills.

It is estimated that of the roughly half a million gallons of Scotch whisky being made annually in 1800, the amount made legally was approximately nil. Some 300,000 illegal gallons are said to have eluded the excise men and flowed down over the border into England year after year. At one time there were two hundred illicit stills in the famous glen of Glenlivet, where perhaps the finest unblended whisky in the world is made today.

The Scottish distillers were defiant men who brewed their illegal potions quite openly. All that was necessary was to choose a defendable glen, and then go about armed to the teeth. In 1823, the English government lowered the duty on whisky in order to encourage the open and legal distillation of good spirit. Yet the illicit stills were so well established that when a daredevil named George Smith came to Glenlivet itself and set up a legal distillery, he was considered to have shown great effrontery. His memoirs tell nothing of how he made his whisky, but they do tell the secret of his success. He hired the toughest men he could find, and by standing watch in turn with them around the clock he saved his still from being burned out, the fate that befell the few others as bold as himself. Smith's foothold in Glenlivet was the beginning of the end. The sad decline in illegal distilling can be read in the statistics of illicit stills detected in Scotland: in 1834, 692; in 1835, 177; in 1854, 73; in 1864, 19; in 1874, 6. Whisky-runners were a dying race, like the romantic highwaymen of the previous century.

American whiskey (the word is spelled whisky in Canada, England, and Scotland, whiskey in the United States and Ireland) began to be made in the eighteenth century. Distilling of rye and barley grains had become so strong a habit by the year 1794 that such interferences as taxation and control were resented to the point of armed revolt—this was the year of the Whiskey Rebellion in Pennsylvania. The distillers, losing the fight, moved west in large numbers, preferring the Indians to revenue men. A few years before, in Bourbon County, Kentucky, they had started making corn whiskey: with the arrival of the refugees from the east, the trade prospered. At first corn whiskey was made to reduce the carrier's load: the packhorses winding down the narrow mountain trails of Kentucky could carry only 4 bushels of corn each; when the corn was distilled to whiskey, they could carry the equivalent of 24 bushels. This corn whiskey took the name *Bourbon* from Bourbon County.

There was another incentive for home distilling, and that was the whiskey price in Kentucky. In 1782, about

the time when the first Bourbon stills were set up, the price fixed by the court in Jefferson County, Kentucky, was 15 dollars a half-pint and 240 dollars a gallon. The Indians had already set the example, making a corn spirit they called Nohelick (the Apaches, further west in undiscovered territory, were brewing their Teeswin from boiled corn), and the settlers pitched in. The first may have been Elijah Craig. At any rate, that intrepid Baptist preacher "considered it as honorable a business as any. Even preachers did not deem it derogatory to their high calling to lend their countenance to its manufacture and engage in it themselves, or drink a little for the stomach's sake."

Adam's process of rectification eventually set off a complete revolution in the manufacture of spirits. Even Cognac (which even now is never rectified, but is pot-distilled by the ancient method derived from the alembic) changed its manner of exportation some three-quarters of a century ago as a consequence of the growing competition from rectified spirits. Traditionally shipped in barrel, it began to be exported in bottle, so that the distillers and shippers could be sure of having full control over the liquid they were selling—sent abroad in cask, it was increasingly likely that it would be stretched and adulterated at the end of its journey. One important consequence was that the brandy began to be called after the little river-town from which it was shipped, and for the first time it was known as Cognac.

Rum—the sugar-cane spirit of the West Indies—had a riotous history in those islands. It was the traditional drink of the fighting men along the sea lanes of the empire-builders—and if the sailors did not get their issue of rum, there was danger of mutiny. The blazing cane-juice brew was also the drink of the western American Colonies and, in one sense, fired them to revolt and form an independent United States—for England's taxing of rum was resented at least as bitterly as her taxing of tea. Even more romantic was the connection of rum with the pirates of the Spanish Main. In the coves of Barbados, Jamaica, and the other islands, the privateers hove to for concealment—and a fresh load of rum.

We drink—by and large—rather tamed rum today. Once again it is rectification that has brought about the revolution. By repeated redistilling, all by-products can be eliminated from any base liquid—in many a light modern rectified rum little of the lustiness of the pungent cane is left. These light rums are the Puerto Rican and Cuban—different from the heavier, pungent, sweeter liquors of Demerara and Jamaica, and more to the modern taste.

It is in the vast popularity of gin and vodka that the true effects of rectification appear. Both are, fundamentally, spirits made neutral by rectification, then—in the case of gin—reflavored. The persisting predilection for gin may be called "the vogue of the Martini." During Prohibition, complex mixtures of alcohol appeared all over North America and spread their influence over the world. These mixtures were known as cocktails. Evolving perhaps from cold punches or mint juleps, they certainly developed and multiplied as they did because illicit synthetic "bath tub" gins needed to be well-disguised by other, less disgusting flavors. Nowadays the cocktail—once so complex—grows simpler and simpler. The overwhelming preference is for the Martini—simply gin with a touch of vermouth, a concoction which is only possible when the basic ingredients are good.

Vodka is the latest craze. Originally a Russian, Polish, Balkan, Lithuanian and Estonian spirit, it is now made from grain in the United States and in England, France, and elsewhere in Europe. The Smirnoff vodka formula bought by an American firm in 1939 from a White Russian refugee started this post-war fashion.

3 Wine and Food

Matchmaking, always a diverting occupation, becomes a positive pleasure when its object is a marriage between food and wine: once complementary flavors are brought together, the two combine in a gastronomic treat infinitely more delicious than either could provide alone. A fine meal, cooked well and served so that it is as seductive to the eye as to the appetite, is a delight in itself; add a glass of wine—gleaming red or a translucent greenish-gold—and delectation will be doubled. The flavor and aroma of wine enormously enhance the taste of food; moreover, the combination induces a sense of well-being—euphoria—and stimulates the imagination. That is why, since the days of Socrates, a dinner table has been the traditional setting for good talk.

The tradition was, indeed, broken by the contemporary habit of sitting over cocktails before dinner, and hurrying out of the dining room afterward to look at television; but fortunately there is, all over the world, a reviving interest in wine, and people who plan their dinner parties with care and round out the meal with several good bottles usually see to it that the aperitifs are Sherry, dry Champagne, or dry vermouth well iced—one of the best of these is a dry Chambéry. It is a waste of time to achieve felicitous matches between the wine and food unless the drinks also complement each other: wine should be preceded (and followed) by the products of the grape, not of the grain—wine and spirits, excellent apart, do not go well together.

That wine and food *do* go well together was discovered by our remotest ancestors. In the old days, vast meals would be washed down by jugs of new wine fresh from the wood. Then, in the eighteenth century, wine began to be matured in glass bottles, and by 1800 it was no longer a refreshing drink to be gulped down: the country gentleman still ate hugely and sometimes downed his three bottles a day; but in the renaissance of fine French cuisine, in the time of Carême and the other great cooks, dinners began to be planned with finesse, and the carefully selected wines were appreciatively sniffed and sipped. Even then, and until late in the nineteenth century, meals were, by our standards, enormous and endless, with a formidable array of glasses beside each plate.

In comparison with the vigorous Victorians, we eat and even entertain sparingly; yet at a special dinner where three or more wines are served (each course planned so that the accompanying bottle may be greater than the one before) it is still possible to play the classic music of the wines: instead of draining your glass, leave a little in it to taste against the wine which comes with the next course until the best bottle arrives with the cheese.

The meal may start with a dry white wine, go on to a red one, and then an older or finer red—for instance, a Chablis, a Clairet, and an older or greater Clairet; or depending on the dishes served, there may be three red wines, beginning with the youngest and ascending to the finest, often the oldest. In France, the cheese always comes before the pudding, and the red wine is finished with this course. Then, if the host has a luscious dessert wine to offer, it will make its own counterpoint of sweetness with the sweet. Champagne (semi-sweet) and Vouvray are perfect with fruit; Sauternes or Barsac with desserts, tarts, and sweet fruits.

To offer wine is the most charming gesture of hospitality, and a host brings out for his guests the finest he has. Whether there are four wines or one, the gesture is the same. A single wine, chosen for the main dish, will be more of a success if it goes with the first course too; if, for instance, it is a Bordeaux, the meal might start with a cheese soufflé. It is worth considering, however, that a bottle of white wine and a bottle of red may be just as easy to produce as two of red. In France, where almost everybody drinks wine every day, most households content themselves on ordinary occasions with a single modest wine. A Frenchman's dinner table always shows if it is Sunday, a holiday, or a christening, because then a special bottle of good wine appears. And there will be chicken, fish, or meat for dinner according to which will best show off the qualities of that wine.

COMBINATIONS OF FOOD AND WINE

Traditionally, certain wines accompany certain dishes—Chablis and oysters go together like bread and butter—and wine-bores (of whom, unfortunately, there are plenty, since on no other subject is a little learning such a tedious thing) tend to be extremely didactic about it. Most of the rules are sound, however, since they are the result of experiment over the centuries: dry white wines taste best before red ones, the great ones taste better when they follow lesser ones of a similar type; sweet wines are not at all good with meat—all this was discovered long ago. Moreover, many wine and food partners are near relations: with the famous sausages of Lyon, no wine is so good as a fruity young Beaujolais grown in the region; and in the Loire Valley they wash down the *rillettes de tours* with local Sancerre, Vouvray, or Pouilly-Fumé.

The man who likes to make up his own mind would be

wise, then, not to reject the rules—even if they are laid down for him by wine-snobs—but to prove them for himself and to test them against his own experiments. In choosing the wine for his meal, the important consideration is, after all, that it should please *him*. He should remember, though, when he makes his experiments, that time and place must be taken into account: the light rosé which goes so well with a midday sandwich will be out of place with a fine dish at dinnertime. The author remembers drinking, on a torrid night in the Caribbean, a fine Bordeaux, followed by a great red Burgundy; and although the food suited them, the temperature did not. (Rules are only useful to those who know how to break them; and in the tropics, chilled pink or white wines are most agreeable, whatever the menu.) Conversely, the cool rosé one enjoyed on a warm day in the south of France would not do with a big steak on a cold winter's night.

Some foods clash resoundingly with some wines: a hot curry will kill a Clairet; but a white wine with a distinctive flavor (a Gewürztraminer, for example), can hold its own against the spicy taste. As for such things as anchovies, kippers, and vinegary salad dressings—they are deadly to all wines and should not be served with them.

TYPES OF WINE

Some wines are good to drink alone or with a biscuit; these are usually the very sweet Sauternes, Barsacs, and the German Beerenauslesen, Trockenbeerenauslesen, and Auslesen, or the fortified wines—Sherry, Port, Madeira. Natural still wines cannot be truly appreciated without the harmonious taste of food. A great dish needs wine to set it off; and a fine bottle is wasted when it is accompanied by a discordant series of food flavors.

TABLE WINES

These are the still beverage wines we drink with meals. They are light—from 9 per cent to 14 per cent in alcohol—and may be red, pink, or white; dry or sweet; light or heavy.

Dry white wines are traditionally associated with seafood. Chablis, as we have said before, is perfect with oysters—but so are Champagne, Muscadet, Riesling, and other dry wines; and white Burgundy is also excellent with shrimp or lobster, and with ham, veal, or chicken cooked in a white wine sauce. With poached sole, a Montrachet is magnificent; and a dry white Hermitage is so distinctive in taste that it can balance curry and other highly spiced dishes. As a general rule, it should be remembered that dry white wines are light and delicate in flavor, and so they should be accompanied by food in the same category. Rich heavy dishes will usually overpower them.

Sweet white wines, we know, are delicious with sweet fruits and puddings. At the start of a meal, the sugary content kills the taste buds and spoils the appetite; whereas at the end these same characteristics are precisely what is needed to induce a feeling of satisfaction and content. Yet in the early years of the century, Sauternes was constantly served with the fish; and even today some Frenchmen in the Bordeaux country consider that this is the wine which goes best with a rich fish such as salmon. Sauternes also complements a good *foie gras*.

Red wines are almost exclusively dry. (Some sweet red wines do exist, but they fall into much the same category as red sparkling wines—pleasant if you like that sort of thing, but not generally distinguished; and their sweetness renders them incompatible with food.) Everywhere in the world, more red wine than white is consumed; on the continent of Western Europe, *vin ordinaire* is the workingman's staple beverage.

The outstanding characteristic of red wines is their variety: white wines are either dry or sweet, still or sparkling; dry red wines range from lightness to full-bodied robustness, each with its own distinctive taste and complexities derived from differences in soil and grape variety. Clearly, the heavier the food, the heavier the wine you will want to drink with it. Fowl, veal and other light meats are excellent with light red wines—as with white; but full-blooded meats need heartier company, and game and pasta with meat sauce usually demand the sturdiest of wines. The best accompaniment for red wine is cheese; but it must not be too strong, especially if the wine is old and delicate. Because of this affinity, the finest wine always comes on with the cheese—which is always mild.

SPARKLING WINES

Most fully sparkling wines are white, but a very few are red, and they range from dry to sweet—sometimes too sweet. Sweet red sparkling wines are generally shunned by experienced wine-drinkers because many are quite mediocre, and even the best lack the distinction of their fine white counterparts. Moreover, they do not go well with food. On the other hand, the Italians, among others, have been making them for centuries and seem to enjoy them.

Champagne, of course, is far and away the best sparkling white wine. Many others have borrowed this famous place-name; but only the French wine made by the true Champagne process in the region of Champagne is entitled to bear it. And it is easy enough to distinguish the original from the imitations at the first sip. Yet many white sparkling wines are very agreeable and, like Champagne itself, these may be dry, semi-sweet, or sweet. There are people who consider Champagne to be the only drink; and certainly it is delicious late in the evening: before meals, if it is dry; with fruit or dessert at the end of a meal, if it is fairly sweet. By its devotees, it is sometimes drunk all through dinner; this is not to be recommended, yet there is no valid reason why you should not do so, as long as you do not continue a Champagne *brut* into the sweet course—and once you have tried other wines and decided that you really enjoy the Champagne most. The general opinion is, however, that when it comes to balancing the wine against the food, Champagne has too little body and too many bubbles. But there is no doubt that for launching ships, for toasting the New Year and the new bride, this bubbly wine is superlative.

FORTIFIED WINES

These may be white or red, dry or sweet. Dry Sherry (Fino or Manzanilla) is generally considered to be the perfect aperitif, particularly before a meal at which fine wines are to be served. After dinner, Port is held by many to be incomparable; yet some people prefer sweet Sherries or Madeiras. There is also a variety of lesser fortified wines, esteemed, as a rule, in their own country—the Italian Moscato, for instance, and the *vin doux naturel* of Banyuls. It is as well to know, however, that in certain parts of the world, outside Europe, fortified wines of a kind are made, cloyingly sweet and excessively alcoholic—really nothing but a substitute for cheap spirits. Naturally, nobody would think of drinking fortified wines with meals—except, perhaps, for a dry Sherry with the soup.

A FEW SIMPLE RULES

It is possible to make endless permutations and combinations of food and wines—and everyone can discover new ones for himself. He will not, however, waste good wine on unnecessary mistakes if he observes these simple rules.

Dry white wines taste best before red; and red wines are better when they are served after others of the same type but lesser quality. In the second instance, it is an elegant—and most enjoyable—practice to serve more than one red wine with a fine meal. In this case, it is a good idea to stick to the wine of one region, offering, for example, Bordeaux after Bordeaux, and Burgundy after Burgundy, rather than mixing the two. And it is advisable to serve the wines in reverse order of age—the youngest first. With wines of the same age, the lesser should come first.

Certain foods and flavors simply do not harmonize with wine. Vinegar has been mentioned; and such pungent things as onions, garlic, and fishy *hors d'oeuvres* spoil the palate for wine. Spices, curry, and mustard also have a regrettable effect, unless the wine itself has a taste so definite that it can prevail over the others.

Once these obvious pitfalls have been avoided, it is as well not to worry too much (unless you are planning a dinner party) about what to drink with what. Wine and food have a natural affinity, and in more cases than anyone would think possible, they unite with felicitous results.

4 Serving Wine

White wines are served chilled, red ones at room temperature—but a good deal of care must be expended on them before they ever reach the table.

HALVES AND MAGNUMS

Half-bottles are good buys when you want to try out a wine, or if you are in the habit of using a small quantity at a time; but only young or average wines should be bought in this way, since great wines age prematurely in small bottles and are, indeed, happier in magnums. In extra big bottles wine matures more slowly, and this, in a great wine, is a guarantee that it will eventually achieve real quality—a quickly matured wine will never attain great heights.

IN THE CELLAR

To begin with, if you have bought an old red wine which will probably have formed a sediment, let the bottle stand upright for a day or two before laying it down in the bin; in this way, the deposit stirred up on the journey will not come up into the neck. Afterward, lay the bottle flat in the rack, label upward, to be read at a glance (this applies, of course, to all table wines, red or white). Again, before bringing an old red wine out of the cellar to the table, it should be stood upright for some hours, so that the sediment may sink.

AGE AND TEMPERATURE

White wines should mostly be drunk young: the chances are that after five years many of them will lose their freshness and start oxidizing. Yet a good white Burgundy may live some years longer. (What is a young wine? In Bordeaux of good vintage, less than four years old; in red Burgundy, less than two-and-a-half years.)

White wines need to be chilled—the sweeter, the colder; but it is a mistake to freeze wines too much, since this kills the taste and destroys the character. Rather drink a fine white Burgundy under- than over-chilled. Most people now put their wine in the refrigerator. One or two hours is sufficient, as 40° to 50°F. (5° to 10°C.) is the ideal temperature for dry white wines, although an ice bucket is said to be a better cooler, because less time is required, twenty minutes being sufficient. Naturally, the time for chilling a wine largely depends on the temperature of the bottle before chilling. If you have no ice bucket, lay the bottle in a big salad bowl full of crushed

ice or ice cubes with some water. Just before you are ready to serve it, take the bottle from the freezer and pull the cork.

Pink wines, as well as white, are served chilled.

Red wines which are young and full-bodied (great young Médocs, for instance) should be uncorked several hours before dinner; a very young one may even benefit from being opened the day before—this extra time for breathing will help it to achieve some maturity and softness. In Beaujolais, extreme youth is an advantage: nine months to under three years is its age cycle; treat it like white wine, and uncork it immediately before serving. Although it need not be chilled in a cold climate, Beaujolais is better chilled in a very hot one. A Claret between five and fifteen years old should be opened about two hours before drinking; but a very old wine needs less breathing space—if it is really old and delicate (earlier than 1964), decant it at dinner: even then, it may have faded and died a little by the time you pour the second glass, whereas a younger red wine will expand and develop in the glass.

DECANTING

Wine which contains sediment a quarter of an inch or more thick should be taken up very gently, held steady in the position in which you first grasp it, and poured in one continuous movement into a clean crystal decanter, until the deposit begins to rise to the neck of the bottle—then stop at once. So that you may keep an eye on the sediment, hold the bottle in front of the light. Since the process of decanting enables the wine to breathe, there is no need to leave the stopper out. Here again, the age of the wine will determine how long it should be exposed to air before drinking. However, all red wines should be brought into the dining room a couple of hours before the meal, so that they may come up to room temperature (or become *chambrés*): to warm them suddenly before a fire or in hot water is injurious. They should not be drunk if less than about 63° to 65° F (17° to 18° C) in temperature. The purpose of a wine basket is to hold steady a bottle which may contain sediment; since in restaurants many waiters pour the wine in jerks and wave these baskets about, they are usually superfluous adjuncts to the often meaningless ritual which has grown up about wine.

OPENING

When you open a bottle of wine, cut the capsule and tinfoil below the tip with a knife; use a clean cloth to remove the mold which usually forms under the capsule; draw the cork and then carefully clean the lip of the bottle inside.

Don't choose fancy corkscrews with all kinds of levering gadgets. These are all right for young wines but not for old ones, where the cork is apt to break or crumble into powder. The best is the old-fashioned T-screw: look for one with a long stem (great wines have long corks) which is rounded—not sharp enough to cut the cork. If the cork *should* break or turn out to be old and powdery, it can be got out by leverage: insert the screw delicately, slightly sideways; set the bottle on its side, so that the pressure of the wine is against the inside face of the cork, then turn the screw gently, using some leverage to lift the bottom of the cork toward the upper side of the bottle. One occasionally finds a defect in even the finest of corks—sometimes an invisible vein which, with age, is liable to deteriorate and turn moldy (this is not the fault of the winemaker or merchant and may happen to the best wines). The wine will then have an unpleasant corky taste and smell—and the cork will smell of itself and not of the wine. In a restaurant, the waiter should smell the cork and then bring it to you; and the reason why a little wine is poured first into the glass of the host is that he may make sure the wine is not corked, before it is offered to his guests. Sometimes the infection is so slight that only the first glassful is spoiled; therefore, when you open the wine at home, it is worth putting the bottle aside to see if it will afterward be fit for you yourself to drink. In a restaurant it must, of course, be sent back at once.

SERVING

At a small dinner for four or five people, given in a private house, the bottle of wine is set on the table in front of the host, who will pour it; if the party is larger, a second bottle should be given to the hostess to pass around at her end of the table. When the wine is brought around by a servant, he serves the ladies first, starting on the right side of the host and moving, clockwise, to the lady on his left; then the men, beginning with the one sitting on the right of the hostess. Never make the mistake of leaving the wine until after the food has been served. At his own table, a host does not taste the wine first, because, having opened it himself, he knows that it is not corked.

For the order in which wines should be brought on, *see* A Few Simple Rules, p. 11.

GLASSES

Choose plain crystal to display the sparkle of the wine itself. Great wines can be ruined in small glasses; there should be room for the wine to be swirled around and for it to breathe and reveal its bouquet. The best glass is large and tulip-shaped, clear and thin, without markings, the bowl the size of an apple or orange. Different shapes exist for different wines; but this tulip glass serves equally well for all, including Champagne—in the shallow "Champagne glass" the carefully manufactured bubbles will be dissipated and the flavor lost. (Incidentally, the swizzle-stick is a negative instrument, designed as it is deliberately to destroy the sparkle which is the distinctive characteristic of Champagne and the result of years of labor. People who do not care for bubbles would do better to order a still Champagne.)

BRANDY

That served with the coffee should be poured, not into a small liqueur glass but into one big enough to be warmed in the palm of the hand and to allow the brandy (serve good Cognac, Armagnac, or marc) to be rolled around in it. For *eau-de-vie* or white spirits (such as framboise, mirabelle, quetsch, or kirsch) chill the glass first by swirling a piece of ice in it: this mellows the taste of the very alcoholic drink.

PORT

It is the custom, particularly in England, to serve Port at the end of dinner and before the coffee. Very often the ladies leave the dining room and the men remain to enjoy their wine alone. The decanter is passed clockwise.

SMOKING

In England, it is bad form to smoke with good wine. The French are less strict in some ways, and many growers smoke when they are drinking wine—between meals. The French fortunately have never adopted the American custom of smoking between courses.

5 Value and Wine

Wine is good value when you find the right bottle for the right purpose, and at the right price. A bogus Burgundy at five dollars (two pounds fifty) is expensive; a genuine Richebourg is reasonable at fifteen dollars (seven pounds fifty). A regional wine, or a shipper's Monopole (wine with a brand name, blended for consistent year-after-year quality and character by a shipper whose own name is its guarantee), may be the same price as a château-bottled Bordeaux growth; but even though the shipper's blend is a reliable one, the first is a bad buy—whereas if it were to be sold for less it would be a good one. In every case, personal choice must be considered: no wine, however honest, can be good value unless it pleases you and goes well with the food you are going to eat.

The obvious way for an amateur in wine to find out what he likes best and to learn which wines best accompany which dishes is to consult a wine merchant who knows his business and who is a man of integrity and taste as well. In England more than anywhere else, and in America, in a number of old-established houses, sound traditions of selling wine flourish—and one of their lists alone is a store of information and advice. In France, they hardly exist; people buy direct from the grower—or from the grocer; and it is not always easy, in one part of the country, to find wine from elsewhere. A village shop in Burgundy will stock the local wine but is unlikely to supply you with Bordeaux. In France, however, wine-drinking, chauvinistic as it may be, is part of a way of life; in America, it is not. Yet well-informed wine merchants do exist in the United States, and the increasing number of tourists who return from Europe or California with a new appreciation of wine is encouraging them to expand their business. The number of serious wine merchants is increasing all over the U.S.

WINE FOR THE HOUSE

Wine is bought either to be drunk within the next month or two, or to be laid down for future use. In the old days, when life was stable and people lived in houses with large cellars, it was customary to buy wines of a fine vintage, as soon as possible and at a good price, and lay them away to mature. By the time they had reached their peak, the retail price would have risen considerably and the early purchaser—or the son who succeeded him—would congratulate himself on his foresight. Nowadays, when the tendency is to live in the present rather than plan for the future—and to live also in apartments where storage space is limited—there is less laying down of wine. The small quantity that can be fitted into a modern cup-

board should be chosen with extra care: for suggestions on cellarage conditions and the contents of a model cellar, *see* Chapter Six.

INEXPENSIVE WINES

Many of the wines bought for immediate consumption will probably be unpretentious regional types: but there is every reason why these should still be sound and palatable, living honestly up to the statements on the bottle label—and some labels offer a better guarantee of validity than others. On French wines, look for the words Appellation Contrôlée; on Spanish, Denominación de Origen; on Italian, Denominazione di Origine Controllata. The better bottles from the vineyards of South Africa, Australia, and California will, at a moderate price, be good value; but they will be better value if you avoid those bearing such meaningless generic names as "South African Claret" and "Californian Burgundy" (for neither Claret nor Burgundy could come from anywhere outside the Bordeaux and Burgundy regions of France) and look instead for "varietal wines"—that is, wines named for the dominant grape variety, such as Riesling, Cabernet Sauvignon, or Pinot Noir. If the specific place of origin is also named, the wine will probably be above average in quality.

Some South American wines—notably, those from Chile—are good bargains and very agreeable to drink—as are many from Italy, Spain, and Portugal. Pleasant wines can also be found from Yugoslavia and Hungary: the best are those bearing a state seal. Look for vintages on the labels, for the date will give an indication of the amount of ageing the wine has undergone; and, if possible, choose any of these wines when they are from three to five years old.

In France and Germany, the choice becomes infinitely expanded and the price-range wider: and the first question to ask yourself about such wines is simply: "Is this what it pretends to be—is it authentic?"

FRENCH WINES

All French wines sold abroad must bear the words "Produce of France" and *Appellation Contrôlée*, signifying that it has been made in accordance with the strict laws of place-name (*see* Appellation d'Origine) and that it conforms to certain minimum standards. Since France produces about 10 million hectoliters (256 million U.S. gallons, 220 million imp.) of wine of Appellation Contrôlée in an average year, even bottles carrying this legend will vary considerably. In buying fine wines, the rule is: the more specific the place, the better the wine will be (i.e., Médoc should be better than simply Bordeaux; Margaux will be better than Médoc). The exception is the wine of Alsace, where grape variety takes precedence over place, the better bottles selling as Alsatian Riesling, Alsatian Gewürztraminer, and so on—and in rare cases bearing the vineyard as well as the grape name. Clearly, then, some detailed knowledge of geography will be invaluable in selecting wines. With French wines, for example, it is impossible to choose the bottle from the more specific place unless you know whether Saint-Julien, say, is in the Haut-Médoc (as it is) or the Haut-Médoc in Saint-Julien (which it isn't).

FINE FRENCH WINES

Apart from Champagne, the great wines of France are those from Bordeaux and Burgundy, and the finest examples carry the name of the vineyard where the grapes were grown. If you are prepared to spend the large sum demanded for some of these great wines, the surest indication that you are getting your money's worth is the guarantee on the label that the wine (if it is a Bordeaux) was bottled at the château where it was made: the French words are *Mis en Bouteilles au Château*. Burgundies bottled by the growers are rarer, since the Burgundian estates are so small (*see* Burgundy); but domaine bottling is done more than ever, due to the growing demand for wines sold directly from the estates. Failing one of these, look for the label of a reliable shipper such as Bouchard Père et Fils, Louis Jadot, Joseph Drouhin, and Louis Latour.

The system for labeling wines from other districts is much the same—except that individual vineyard names do not occur so frequently. Champagne is usually a blend of wines from that region, made by one of the big firms whose names are famous. The best carry vintage years. (Other sparkling wines are poorer value than Champagne, since none of them can compare with it, and yet taxes on sparkle put them in the same high price-range.) Wines from other regions are often blended, although some come from specific vineyards; and one such from Châteauneuf-du-Pape, Hermitage, Côtes du Rhône, or Tavel in the Rhône Valley, or from Anjou, Vouvray, or Pouilly-sur-Loire in the Loire Valley, can be not only pleasant but admirable.

GERMAN WINES

Because of their northerly climate, it is almost impossible for the Germans to make great wines inexpensively, and the finest are admittedly very dear. But, fortunately, many sound, agreeable wines do exist at prices which are not extreme. Since, however, in Germany as elsewhere, unscrupulous wine merchants are to be found, it is wise to look for a bottle named for the place of origin, the grape variety, and the date of vintage (e.g., Hattenheimer Riesling 1980er—i.e., town, grape variety, and date). The better wines will bear the name of the vineyard as well (e.g., Hattenheimer Nussbrunnen Riesling 1980er); or may omit the grape and simply read, for instance, Hattenheimer Nussbrunnen 1980er, since in many of the fine German vineyards only Riesling is grown. The next thing to look at is the name of the bottler: if one of the owners of this particular vineyard has bottled the wine, there will be a complete degree of authenticity. Certain aristocrats among the wines, such as Schloss Johannisberger, Schloss Vollrads, and Steinberger state only the name and year, and these three are always estate-bottled and almost always expensive. Buyers of the sweet Trockenbeerenauslesen Steinberger 1971 paid as much as $175 (£87) for a single bottle; this acknowledged king of the Rheingau is made in minute quantities and sold for whatever price customers are willing to bid. Schloss Johannisberger has invented a system of colored seals to distinguish the various types of estate-bottled, personally selected, and late-picked wines (*see* Rheingau), and some other vineyards have followed this example. The Spätlese and Auslese wines of the great vineyards are those which have been late-harvested and selected after the noble rot or *Edelfäule* has set in, and these, as well as the Edelbeerenauslese and especially the Trockenbeerenauslese, like the Sauternes which is harvested in the same way, will be luscious dessert wines. Yielded by grapes grown so far north, this sweetness is a *tour de force*; indeed, in some of the great years these wines, although extraordinary, may even be too sweet; whereas in lesser years they may have less than the expected sweetness.

Again, because of the harsh climate in which they are grown, vintage years in authentic German estate-bottled wines are unusually important. (The further north you carry the cultivation of the vine, the greater the variation in the seasons—and a summer without sunshine means grapes lacking in sugar. Yet a northern wine which does succeed will have more finesse than one grown in the south.)

As a rule, German wine labels carry a wealth of information—if you can understand them. It was always said that only an expert could find his way around one of these; and although in recent years the tendency has been to standardize and simplify, the labels are still confusing. The 1971 wine law has done much to help. (*See* Germany: A Wine-label Baedeker.)

Finally, there are several German wines which can usually be depended on to be of no value at all. One of these is the celebrated Liebfraumilch: the name applies to no place and used to be given to any unspecified Rheinhessen—or indeed to wines of even more indefinite origin. Moselblümchen and Zeller Schwarze Katz are in the same category, as they never exhibit the potential greatness of a Mosel.

THE GREATEST WINES

Sooner or later every amateur of wine will be tempted to taste one of the world's great growths. First, let him educate his own palate, starting with lesser wines, learning to recognize a good bottle when one comes his way, before he sits down to savor the best. A great wine must be sufficiently aged if its true excellence is to be appreciated—and it is axiomatic that it will not be cheap, especially if (as now is so often the case) it must be bought fully aged from a wine merchant. Whether it is bought young, for laying down, or later, for immediate use, it is wise to take no risks in planning such a treat, but to decide on one of the illustrious names among the acknowledged elite (Château Margaux, Chambertin, Château d'Yquem, Montrachet) and from a great year. Vintage charts, as we have said elsewhere, are not as infallible as they seem; but a great vineyard is unlikely to produce a poor wine, however bad the summer may have been, and a Chambertin or a Château Prieuré-Lichine of an offbeat year may be very good and less expensive than usual, and the fully matured fine wine of a great year will be an incomparable experience. Look for these supreme names in the First, Second, Third, Fourth, or Fifth Growths (*Premiers, Seconds, Troisièmes, Quatrièmes, Cinquièmes Crus*) of Bordeaux (*see* Médoc and Bordeaux classifications), among the Burgundian *grands vins* (*see* Burgundy), or the fine German wines (*see* Germany).

The best Californian wines come from the Napa and Sonoma valleys and other parts of the North Coast vineyard district. (*See* United States: California for names of some reliable wineries.)

WINE IN THE RESTAURANT

Getting value for your money in a restaurant is rather different from doing the same thing in a shop. In many restaurants in France, diners-out discard the list of mediocre wines at inflated prices and order the carafe Beaujolais or rosé instead—and these, incidentally, are often quite good value. This is the easier way out but it is not the answer; constructive criticism would be much more effective. Complain, complain, complain—but make allowances for the fact that the management must make a fair percentage on the bottle. A number of restaurants keep good cellars and present excellent wine lists: it is easy to find out which these are, since their reputations will be generally known; at other places, the manager may really know very little about wine, and, tactfully handled, might be willing to learn and to change his source of supply to one of the more reliable shippers or merchants. It cannot be repeated too insistently that in a restaurant the regular customer gets the wine he deserves.

VINTAGE CHARTS

As for the great years, read the vintage charts but do not let yourself be hypnotized by them: in the small space of one of these printed lists, only the broadest generalities can be included. The vintage notes in the catalogue of the first-class wine merchant will be fuller and therefore more reliable—but even those cannot possibly cite the many exceptions to every rule.

The men who devote their lives to making wine are agreed on one point: wine is a living, constantly changing complex. In any given year, it will start out "green," generally fruity, often harsh, and will mature, first in barrel

and then in bottle, until it is soft and mellow. Then (it may be years after bottling) the wine is at its peak—a state of excellence which endures for varying lengths of time. Those wines which, in the opinion of the experts, will slowly mature to greatness and hold it are given high marks on vintage charts; if a wine is marked low, it may be not unpleasant but one which should be drunk when it is young. What the marking system cannot take into account is the fact that individual wines are full of surprises. Wines from adjoining vineyards, all made by experienced and devoted men, may yet vary enormously. In Burgundy, 1947 was a fabulous year, yet many growers made poor wine because their grapes were too high in sugar and volatile acidity; 1945 was a good vintage—but not in Chablis, where the vineyards were spoiled by hail.

Once its limitations are realized, however, a chart is useful. Some notes on recent vintages follow.

RECENT VINTAGES

The factors determining quality are the soil, the climate, the grape variety, and the man who makes the wines, taking for granted that the grape varieties will be suited to the vineyards in which they are planted. When all these elements are perfectly married, the buyer will be justified in expecting value in a bottle of wine. Vintage years are important; yet overemphasis on vintage charts will not solve all the buyer's problems.

Provided the possibilities of fraud have been set aside, the expert can select in any given year the best wines from the château-bottlings of Bordeaux and the estate-bottlings of Burgundy, eliminating the failures of both nature and man. Some great vintage years will produce some disappointing wines through premature picking or faulty wine-making. Nature does not bless a large area with a uniform balance of sunshine and rain when needed.

Vintage charts at best can only generalize. In lesser years, often condemned categorically as "poor," the wine-buyer can find well-selected, good, enjoyable values, and occasionally he will find an absolute delight. This especially applies to red wines. A minimum amount of sunshine is required for white wines; otherwise, excessive acidity will throw them out of balance. In a perfect vintage, a red wine will have a higher degree of alcohol, plus an abundance of tannin. This will make for a slow-maturing wine, one which often disappoints the early drinker and requires ageing to carry it to a high level of quality where well-matured velvet will replace the harsh bitterness of tannin.

A great vintage in a red Bordeaux is one which, thanks to the abundance of sunshine, will have a high sugar content that is transformed into a high degree of alcohol. To some great years, like 1961, 1970, 1975, and 1978, vintage chart makers will, perhaps sincerely, give the highest possible rating, but they will be rating in terms of the "high" the wine will reach once it is fully matured. Sometimes such memorable vintages have an overabundance of tannin. This tannin acts like a corset, to hold the wine together over a period of years until it reaches its apex. This may only be attained at the end of some fifteen or twenty years. To drink the 1961 in 1965 might have been a disappointing experience. If you had waited until the 1970s that wine—from a great vineyard—would have been one of the most memorable experiences available to living man in the enjoyment of wines.

If one must generalize, one can say that vintage charts are much more important in white wines than in reds, since in the poor years the high acidity caused by lack of maturity is expressed in a certain greenness, and the defects of the wine are more apparent. In red wines, one must consider the district, whether its wines are generally fast or slow in maturing. Another generalization is that the greater the wine, the more slowly it matures. Bearing these facts in mind, here are the generalities, always remembering that they may be upset by the storage and the climate in which the wines will be drunk, for hot storage ages the wines prematurely and perfect cool storage will allow the wines to reach their potentials naturally.

BORDEAUX

1955—A very great year for red wines. Magnificently balanced.

In white wines this was a perfect year for those who find Sauternes over-sweet.

1956—Red wines were poor to fair.

The white Bordeaux were disappointing.

1957—Small, good vintage for red wines. This and inflation caused high prices. Vineyards that harvested late benefited from a uniquely warm October. A tendency to hardness made the wines relatively slow-maturing, harsh, and lacking roundness.

1958—Very light, fast-maturing, lacking the character to warrant keeping for any length of time. Expect faded bottles today.

1959—Was over-optimistically heralded as the year of the century. The '59s made banner headlines throughout the civilized world. This good vintage, however, was not great. The red wines were full, harmonious, and slow-maturing.

For those who like Barsacs and Sauternes 1959 is the year. Perfectly balanced, the '59s helped to re-establish a dying custom, the serving of Sauternes with desserts.

1960—A large quantity of good red wine in the Médoc, which is now fading.

1961—One of the smallest years remembered in the Médoc. The flowering during the cold and rainy month of May resulted in a diminution in production of 40 to 50 per cent in comparison with the previous year. Then a hot summer, followed by a superb September, gave us (in quality if not in quantity) the greatest red wine vintage since 1945. Taking into consideration the change in vinification methods, the wines are softer than those of 1945 but they were not at their best until 1975. This was a very great vintage, and a great success, also, in Saint-Émilion and Pomerol.

This was a good vintage for the sweet wines of Sauternes and Barsac although some were less successful be-

cause of October rains. The Sauternes produced great bottles which will last ten, twenty, or thirty years.

1962—These red wines were ready long before those of 1961.

1963—Some light and drinkable wines in the Médoc, a disaster in Saint-Émilion and Pomerol. After a rainy summer, the harvest took place in bad conditions—with a few exceptions. A year to forget.

1964—A very plentiful year for red wines. A magnificent summer was followed by an excellent September, and the grapes achieved maturity in good conditions. Certain châteaux in the Médoc waited to harvest late, but unfortunately it rained incessantly from October 8 onward. This year, which started so well, proved a disappointment in wines harvested late. However, 1964 was generally an excellent vintage in the Médoc. Very successful in Saint-Émilion and Pomerol, where the harvest finished before the rain started.

Fair for sweet white wines, but for the growers who waited until the end of October, it was a disaster because the *pourriture noble* turned to grey rot.

1965—The summer was rainy. A few vineyards harvested late under fair conditions. When well selected, there were some fair quality wines which did not last long.

1966—Uniformly a great vintage. A very dark deep color with perfect balance made these round wines outstanding. The best since 1961. Slow-maturing, they are just now starting to be ready and will last for some time.

Barsac and Sauternes—one-third very good. The remainder disappointing.

1967—Softer than the '66s, hence faster-maturing—a good vintage requiring selectivity—abundant in quantity. Pleasant to drink now. Will not last over 20 years. The Sauternes are excellent.

1968—Light, due to a rainy summer—some fairly pleasant values were found.

1969—Fairly good in the Médoc; disappointing in Saint-Émilion and Pomerol. Due to chilly rainy weather during the June flowering, the quantity was small. July and August had abundant sun followed by freakish rains in September. The quality was saved by an unusual burst of a three-week hot spell just before and during the late harvest in October.

The sweet Barsacs and Sauternes are only fair.

1970—A great vintage. Unquestionably the best since 1961, with an abundance not seen since the beginning of the century. Many of the wines will mature at different ages, and a selection should be made accordingly, with some wines to be drunk early, and some put away for drinking in the late 1970s or 1980s.

1971—A very good vintage, lighter and faster-maturing than the '70s. The reds are light but round. Some growers prefer the '71s to the '70s because of the elegance, breed, and perfect balance of the former.

The white wines are generally good, with some very exceptional highs in Sauternes, which will be delightful until the '80s. The Graves had an unusual lasting ability, amounting to 7 or 8 years.

1972—After a disastrously rainy summer, the vintage

was somewhat saved by the miracle of hot sunny weather from late September through the October harvest. The reds showed too much acidity when young, and even when mature they will not be great. These wines were originally sold in Bordeaux at ridiculously high prices, the highest on record. However, starting in 1976, the buyers who overpaid for these wines have been dumping them at a considerable loss, such that these wines have turned out to be good values, selling at reasonable prices.

Forget the light dry wines of '72; those of Barsac and Sauternes did not approach the quality of the '71s.

1973—An extremely large harvest, even more plentiful than the record produced in 1970. But, typically, the tremendous quantity meant that the wines were not of the greatest quality. The reds are round, though lacking the tannin that would give them longevity. They will be light and pleasant drinking up to the 1980s. Wines from the Médoc were more successful than those from Graves, Saint-Émilion, and Pomerol. Some of the better red wines resemble those from 1967. Most fortunately, prices dropped 40 to 50 per cent in 1976, again making the top Bordeaux good values.

The dry white wines were fair to good, the sweet ones barely average. Hail destroyed the Sauternes vineyards several times.

1974—For red wines, a fair to very good vintage, fast-maturing with deep color, good character and finish. The intermittent rains at the end of September and during the harvest contributed to the large quantity, without seriously harming the quality. The large harvest and the fact that these wines will eventually surpass the '73s make this vintage a good value.

The dry whites were good—fruity and well-balanced without an excess of acidity. Unfortunately the harvest in Sauternes was a disaster.

1975—A very great vintage for red wines; rich, harmonious, slow-maturing. The quality is the best since 1961, and it will eventually overshadow the 1960s and 1970s. Only a small quantity was produced (50 per cent less than in 1974).

Excellent dry white wines, superb sweet Barsac and Sauternes due to the good weather which prevailed in late October and early November.

1976—The dry, hot summer, which caused the most serious drought in the last 100 years, brought high hopes for a memorable vintage. The vineyards which started to pick the faster-maturing Merlots at the end of the first week of September and which were able to hold off harvesting the rest of the crop during the intermittent rains of the second half of September will produce very fine wines in abundant quantities. The better of the '76s will be enjoyable before the slow-maturing '75s from the great vineyards. Hence, the '76s compare to the '75s as the '71s do to the somewhat harder '70s. The Médoc and parts of Graves produced some relatively better wines than those of Saint-Émilion. Some growers in the Médoc have compared the tannic acid content of the '76s favorably with that of the '75s.

The dry white wines, when picked early, produced excellent results. Sauternes and Barsac were spotty due to the October rains. Rot set in before the *Botrytis cinerea* could exercise its "noble rot" process. By that time, luckily, the red wines had been harvested.

1977—The tragedy of the 1977 vintage was the spring freeze, which killed the buds and resulted in the smallest crop in 20 years. Of the Médoc, Pomerol, and St. Émilion, the Médoc was spared the greatest damage and suffered only 50 per cent loss, whereas the other two took losses of 80 per cent. The drop in quantity entailed substantial increases in price for all categories of wine. Concerning the quality: After a rainy summer, the 1977 growing cycle performed something of a miracle. At the end of a cool August, a warm, dry sunny period began, lasting until the completion of the late harvest, which took place under very good conditions at the end of October. This late hot spell produced wines dark in color, fruity, and slightly on the hard side, which will, however, mature fairly rapidly. It requires selectivity. Although different from the 1974 vintage, the 1977 can be rated in the same class, superior to the '72s; some optimists have likened it to the 1967.

The white wines are good, fresh, and fruity, their acidity giving them a pleasant freshness and lasting ability. They do not have the flatness of certain '76s and should be well rated despite the reduced quantity resulting from the March 30 freeze. Of the sweet wines of Barsac and Sauternes, only a minute quantity was produced, a few of them acceptable.

1978—A very great vintage. Relatively even in quality, with some reds superior to many '70s, 1978 will unquestionably go down as one of the memorable years of the past few decades. Very long-lasting on the palate, the '78s have beautiful color, depth of character, and good harmony and balance.

The dry whites of this year were good but not comparable to the highs achieved by the reds. Small quantities of good Barsacs and Sauternes were made, requiring careful selection.

1979—An exceptionally abundant harvest, especially for red wines. The wines are of generally very good quality, although varying widely from region to region. The wines are deep-colored, and despite their fullness they have a tendency to be soft and round. They will mature relatively quickly. They are characterized by the softer Merlot grape which ripened more completely than the harder Cabernet Sauvignon. For this reason, the wines of Pomerol and Saint-Émilion will be of very good quality. Some producers compare the '79s to '62s, others compare them to the '67s. Some even claim that the 1979 vintage is better than the 1978. The final assessment of this very fine vintage will be much more obvious in the mid-1980s.

The harvest of white wines was also abundant and the quality is generally good. The wines are well-balanced although some may lack fruit.

Above-average quantities for sweet whites. Noble rot developed well and the wines will be characteristic and fine without achieving the concentration of the '71s or the '67s.

1980—A good vintage, round and fast-maturing wines, superior to 1973 and 1974. This is the fourth consecutive vintage blessed with good weather in late September and October, resulting in a most welcome boost in quality. The very late 1980 harvest reached satisfactory maturity. The wine shows good tannins and aromas—this despite some rain during the harvest in mid-October.

In the Médoc the wines are round and soft, showing many of the qualities of the 1979s—with, however, a tendency toward quicker development. Results were less favorable in Saint-Émilion and Pomerol, which suffered a great reduction in the Merlot grape variety.

The dry white wines are fruity without excessive acidity. The good October and November were especially beneficial to the sweet wines of Sauternes and Barsac, which promise to be an excellent vintage. At Château d'Yquem, for instance, 80 percent of the harvest will be sold under its label, as opposed to 40 percent in 1979. Although possessing different characteristics, the 1980s will be of the caliber of the '71s, '76s, and '78s.

BURGUNDY

1961—A very great year for red Burgundies. Rich, tannic, and well-balanced wines with a beautiful color.

A high degree of alcohol counterbalanced by acidity gave the white Burgundies an excellent well-deserved reputation. This is now a matter of the past.

1962—Very fine, light, and well-balanced red Burgundies with a tendency toward early maturity. They were ready before the '61s.

1963—Red Burgundies were disastrous.

White Burgundies were barely drinkable but no more.

1964—In some instances the red Burgundies were better than the red Bordeaux. These well-rounded wines could be drunk fairly early, as was the case with the '62s, and had plenty of bouquet.

Though the white Burgundies were well balanced they tended to lack acidity and matured quickly.

This was a good year for Beaujolais.

1965—The floods, which spoiled many vineyards, and the lack of maturity made the red wines a disaster.

1966—Burgundies from Côte d'Or were similar to '64, being full, round, and fast-maturing.

1967—Good vintage lacking the body of the '66s.

1968—Light, disappointing wines.

1969—Great vintage in the Côte d'Or with a deep color—round, full, with lasting character. The white wines lacked the required acidity and have now faded.

1970—A good vintage, but not in same league as the '69s, which have faded.

1971—The harvest was small due to the bad weather during the flowering, followed by storms and hail. The red wines were full-bodied with good color, although sometimes lacking in finesse and not equal to the '69s.

The best vintage between 1969 and 1976.

The white wines were full-bodied; a fine vintage, although the quantity was small.

1972—In spite of the good weather during the late harvest in October, the Pinot Noir and other red wine grapes lacked maturity. Some reds have good color and balance, but on the whole are only average.

The white wines were generally disappointing.

1973—A very large harvest for the Côte d'Or; therefore, the quality was less than it could have been. Not worthy of much consideration today.

Whites better than reds, but with a tendency to fade.

1974—A rather good vintage, the reds better than the '70s, at the same level as the '71s. Fruity wines with a strong Pinot Noir character. An overabundance of production due to excessive September rains diluted the quality.

Good white wines, to be consumed rather rapidly, were produced in large quantities.

1975—Very disappointing vintage. The red wines were too light, had too little color, because of abundant rains at the beginning of September and during the harvest. In the Côte de Beaune there were certain valid exceptions. In the Côte de Nuits the wines were more successful, and a few of them were good.

The white wines were, surprisingly, of exceptionally good quality, and in many instances better than the '74s. But they will not have great longevity. They were especially good in southern Burgundy, where the wines of the Mâconnais and the Beaujolais, including the Pouilly-Fuissés, enjoyed a good vintage.

Beaujolais produced a tiny quantity of good wines amounting to 10 to 15 per cent maximum; 30 to 40 per cent was average and at least half was bad. There were a few good wines in the Crus, such as Fleurie, Brouilly, and Moulin-à-Vent.

1976—A great vintage. For Burgundy, which suffers from a lack of good vintages, '76 was an exception. The wines were full, round, deep in color and character. These were the best from the region since 1969.

The whites were full-bodied, though lacking in the acidity needed to give them freshness and the ability to last beyond 1983.

Beaujolais enjoyed its best vintage since 1961. This is especially true in the Crus. Huge world demand drove the prices of wines from this popular area to levels previously unencountered.

1977—Small in quality and large in quantity, these wines were too light, thin, and short. A few exceptional wines may be found acceptable but at prices 30 per cent higher than those of the superb '76s. The whites are good, slightly fruity wines which, although pleasant when young, will not hold, despite their acidity.

Unless one chooses a well-selected Villages or certain *crus*, Beaujolais are disappointingly light, especially for export. If the typical floweriness and fruit are to be appreciated, these wines should be consumed quickly.

Chablis suffered less than many other wine regions, but despite a near-normal harvest, the prices have doubled for these average-to-good wines.

1978—A very good year. The reds are soft and not

overly tannic.

The whites also turned out well. Excellent Chablis, Beaujolais, and Mâconnais were produced.

1979—Abundant crop of red wines. Quality is uneven, although good on the average. The wines are fruity and well-colored, but they lack depth and body. The best wines were made from older vines and those from vineyards with a limited production.

Abundant quantities of Beaujolais were produced. Here, too, quality was uneven: 20 per cent good, 20 per cent acceptable, 60 per cent poor. The situation is the same for the *crus* (Brouilly, Morgon, etc.). Rigorous selection vat by vat will enable good merchants to offer good wines.

Abundant crop of white Burgundy. Although light-bodied, the wines are well-balanced and fruity. Although not wines for laying down, they are better than the reds. The whites of Chassagne are superior to those of Puligny. The Maconnais, such as Pouilly-Fuissé, are to be judged as favorably as the other white Burgundies.

1980—The red wines had a fairly good vintage. They will be fast-maturing and above the average quality of recent years (excepting 1976), but below average in quantity. Meursault, Puligny, and Chassagne made well-balanced whites on the fruity side—a good vintage, but no more than that. Mâconnais, Pouilly-Fuissé, Saint-Véran, and others tended to be a bit acid and short.

In the Beaujolais, 1980 produced a good "typical" light vintage, though lesser wines tended to be acid and light. They should be drunk quickly. Among the nine *crus*, Moulin à Vent, Morgon, and Chénas were above the vintage average.

RHÔNE

1960—A great vintage. The only region in France that produced great-quality wines that year.

1961—Unlike any other region in France, the Rhône Valley produced a good vintage, but nothing more.

1962—A small vintage which produced flat wines lacking in character, but with some isolated successes.

1963—A very small vintage. Wine completely lacking in color. Very clearly inferior to the '62s.

1964—An average vintage.

1965—A fair vintage. The Côtes du Rhône region, unlike other parts of France, did not lack sunshine. The harvest weather was nearly ideal.

1966—A top vintage. The best since the great 1960, which was exceptional in the Rhône. Some growers claim that the great '66s even surpassed it.

1967—The Rhône, which is blessed with more good vintages than any wine district in France, outdid itself in 1967 as in 1966.

1968—A few quite pleasant wines were produced.

1969—Small in quantity and short in quality—disappointing color. The main exceptions were in the Côte Rôtie, where excellent wines were produced.

1970—A very good vintage, in quantity and quality.

1971—Fair to good.

1972—Most of the Rhône wines were disappointing, but a few were good.

1973—One of the largest harvests on record since the Second World War. But the quality was only average, since the wines lacked both acidity and fruit. Generally mediocre wines. Hail struck at Hermitage, but those wines which escaped turned out to be very good.

1974—A good vintage in general, with, unfortunately, many exceptions. Good color, good fruit, and character, in some cases an excellent lasting ability.

1975—Average quality at best, with a few highs and lows, more of the latter than the former. Châteauneuf-du-Pape was particularly disappointing.

1976—Only fair. Thirty per cent of the wine, generally from Condrieu, Côte Rôtie, and Hermitage, was of very good quality. Twenty-five per cent or so was very acceptable, and the remaining forty-five per cent—those of Châteauneuf-du-Pape and other southern Côtes du Rhône—were mediocre. Late summer rains lasted through the harvest in the south, swelling the grapes and producing weak, thin wines.

1977—The Côtes du Rhône was unquestionably one of the most favored regions in France in 1977. The sun and warm weather prevailed, producing an abundant crop of full, round, well-balanced wines which will be long-lasting both on the palate and in the cellar. This excellent quality applies to much of the vintage, and full-pleasing wines will be easy to find. Both Châteauneuf-du-Pape and Tavel had very good vintages.

1978—An excellent vintage. Châteauneuf-du-Pape and Tavel were exceptionally favored.

1979—An abundant crop of good quality, although inferior qualitatively to 1978. On the whole, the wines are well-structured and have good color. The Tavel wines are just as good as those of 1978.

1980—A good vintage, somewhat resembling 1978.

LOIRE

1969—A good vintage for all the wines of the Loire. With the exception of sweet wines, the quality of the whites is a thing of the past.

1970—A fairly good vintage for the Loire in general. Excellent in Pouilly-Fumé. These are now oxidized.

1971—Good, with excellent Muscadet, now faded.

1972—Not a good vintage. The wines were light and without character. They are now a thing of the past.

1973—A great deal of wine was made. The quality was only good and nothing more for most of the wines; but the Muscadet was quite fine, if not perfect.

1974—Fruity, well balanced wines were produced. However, they were a bit flat in that they lacked character and acidity. These wines were fine when drunk very young, less than three years old.

1975—Very good vintage. Many excellent Muscadets were produced, but some were harvested a bit too late and the grapes were thus overripe, lacking their characteristic greenness. Therefore, the latter lacked the needed acidity and freshness.

An exceptionally good vintage in the Anjou, especially in the rosés. Very good wines in Vouvray, exceptionally so in Pouilly-Fumé and Sancerre.

1976—Very good in Muscadet, especially when harvested the first days in September. France's drought brought about a premature ripening, which for these wines means a lack of acidity. Therefore, freshness, a prerequisite in Muscadet, is less obviously present in the '76s than the '75s. In other parts of the Loire such as Vouvray, Sancerre, and Pouilly-Fumé, the quantities and quality in general were good, especially for the Vouvray. For the wines of Sancerre and Pouilly-Fumé, the wines were quite good, though of a lower caliber than those of 1975. Muscadets were a little short on acid, although those who picked early enough had a very good year.

1977—Tragically small quantities were produced due to the spring freeze, especially in the Muscadet. The lack of white wines thoughout the Loire brought on a general increase in price. The quality throughout was quite good and some pleasant, drinkable wines were produced.

1978—A good vintage for Muscadet, though quantity was low. The rest of the Loire, except Sancerre (where vineyards were badly hit by hail), produced wines of a very good quality.

1979—An abundant harvest of Muscadet. Quality is good since the grapes were picked before the rains. The wines are clean and well-balanced: good fruit without excessive acidity.

Large quantities were also produced in Anjou. The Cabernet franc was, however, produced in more limited quantities and made the best wines. The Anjou harvest took place during the rain and in general the wines were thin and disappointing.

Production of Vouvray—as for the other Loire wines—was high, twice the production of 1978. Quality is poor. Fortunately, most of the wines will be processed as sparkling wines.

In Pouilly-Fumé and Sancerre, production was also large and quality is generally good. The wines are well-balanced and even charming, if somewhat light-bodied. They should be consumed young.

1980—Muscadets lacked ripeness and maturity and were therefore slightly acid; not equal to 1979. However, in Anjou, 1980 will be better than 1979.

ALSACE

1970—Only fair in quality due to the tremendous quantity produced—the largest in this century.

1971—Fair to good, ranging upward in quality from wines very high in alcoholic content, thus destroying the light, spritely, easy-to-drink characteristics of good Alsatian wines. But many small producers successful in their endeavors will look back at '71 as a highly prestigious vintage. Today it is only of academic interest.

1972—Though pleasant and typically Alsatian, most of the wines lacked depth and were slightly acid.

1973—The most abundant year in Alsace since the war. Most wines showed a certain lack of acidity, so they will not last long in bottle and should be drunk young.

1974—Well balanced, fresh despite rains throughout harvest, these should be drunk when very young.

1975—A good vintage; the wines are characteristically fruity and harmonious.

1976—As in Champagne, both the quantity and quality were high.

1977—Fair, drinkable fruity wines, a bit hard.

1978—A very good vintage, though lacking in quantity. Gewürztraminer production was especially low. The Rieslings, however, are plentiful, ripe, and good.

1979—A good abundant vintage. The wines are well-balanced.

1980—A fairly good vintage, though lacking in quantity, especially the Gewürztraminers.

CHAMPAGNE

Only when of a superior quality is the vintage indicated on the bottles of Champagne; hence the expression "a vintage year," meaning one of quality.

1966—Magnificent wines. Excellent bouquet with great finesse. Well balanced. Some 80 million bottles produced.

1967—What could have been an exceptional vintage was diminished by pouring rains between the fifth and twenty-first of September, just one week before the harvest. Non-vintage.

1968—Disastrous vintage.

1969—A good vintage, well-balanced and full-bodied. Small quantity produced.

1970—The most abundant vintage on record. The quality was good to fair.

1971—Good vintage. The small quantity produced caused high prices.

1972—Not a vintage year.

1973—A good and very plentiful vintage year.

1974—Fairly good vintage; wines without too much depth of character.

1975—A vintage year. Wines of a good quality, with a tendency toward lack of acidity.

1976—The 1976 vintage was one of significant quantity and good quality. A vintage year.

1977—Not a vintage year, although Champagne winemakers were moderately well pleased.

1978—A good-quality harvest, though bad weather at the beginning of the summer limited production. Prices are 20 percent higher than those of 1977.

1979—An abundant quantity of good quality. Some firms will produce vintage wines.

Like all white wines, sparkling or not, Champagne should be drunk fairly young, say at the most within ten to fifteen years after the harvest.

1980—Fair to good quality, disastrously small quantity, ridiculously high prices. Not a vintage year.

RHINE AND MOSEL

1959—A very great year, comparable to 1949 and 1953. High in alcohol, rich in sugar. The rare sweeter wines made history.

1960—A very large crop but below average in quality.

1961—The Mosel was good. Along the Rhine there were some disappointments.

1962—The Rheingau was favored, the Mosel was not.

1963—Large quantity but small in quality.

1964—Good vintage with many very high peaks.

1965—Uninteresting.

1966—Good, especially in the big estates, where they started picking on October 28.

1967—Mixed quality—one-third was a good vintage, of which some was great; the other two-thirds was average or downright disappointing. The difference in quality was caused by poor weather during the harvest.

1968—Light, mediocre wines.

1969—Better than 1966 and 1967, yet not great. A characteristic strong bouquet is the main quality feature of this good elegant vintage.

1970—The summer weather along the Rhine and the Mosel encouraged great expectations but, unfortunately, cool rainy weather in early October prevented the grapes from maturing properly. The larger estates waited to harvest, and in some cases the grapes were picked as late as Christmas. This exceptional delay was fortuitous, resulting in wine of great quality. In other vineyards the huge quantity harvested resulted in a leveling of quality, although generally this vintage has been most successful.

1971—One of the greatest vintages of the century, by far.

The wines have the miraculous balance of sugar and acidity that makes good German white wines among the world's very best. They will last long. In the Rheingau an astonishing 95 percent of the harvest was *Qualitätswein mit Prädikat*, the new legal phrase first applied in this year, for Kabinett, Spätlese, Auslese, etc. wines.

1972—After a rather cold summer the wines were poor, since the grapes did not ripen completely. They are pleasant and light, but nothing more.

1973—The largest harvest ever recorded in Germany. The hot and sunny summer made good quality likely, but two opposite problems made the wines less than very good. The lack of snow and rain during the previous winter damaged the vines in some areas; and then just before the picking was to commence in the fall of 1973, rain fell steadily for several days. A few unusually cold days in early December froze many grapes still on the vines at some of the great Rheingau estates, and a few growers were able to make Eiswein.

1974—Small in quality, due to mediocre weather in summer, with abundant rains then and during the harvest. A few agreeable wines to be rapidly drunk were the result. No Spätlesen or Auslesen were produced.

1975—A great year, not approaching the '71s but with a good quantity of outstanding top-quality wines. The Rheingau produced Qualitätswein in 50 percent of the harvest. The Mosel-Saar-Ruwer was very lucky this year with 45 percent Spätlesen and 15 percent Auslesen. The Palatinate and Rheinhessen areas produced 50 percent Qualitätswein and 15 percent Spätlesen.

1976—A very great year. The exceptionally hot weather which prevailed thoughout Europe had an especially positive effect in the Rheingau and the Mosel. The sugar content of the grapes was so high during the harvest, most notably in the Rheingau, that the Rieslings gave very little wine below the Spätlesen standard. In fact, one of the largest quantities of Auslesen wines, including the usually rare Beerenauslesen and Trockenbeerenauslesen, was produced—perhaps more than the market can absorb. Müller-Thurgaus and Sylvaners were more or less disappointing, having suffered in the extreme heat. Only half the normal crop was harvested in the Mosel, where the quality of the sweet wines was just as high as in the Rheingau. Sweet, perfectly balanced wines earmark this vintage, and good dry wines will be hard to find; choose them from lesser years.

1977—Of fairly low quality. For a vintage to be rated great in Germany, much sun is required, which 1977 notably lacked. For those who enjoy dry German wines, many pleasant bottles can be found.

1978—An extremely cold and wet summer created unfavorable growing conditions. The quality and quantity of the harvest were low. Along the Mosel, quantity was reduced by one-third to one-half. In the Rheingau, Rheinhessen, and Rheinpfalz, quantities were reduced, in some cases, by two-thirds. Surprisingly, the wines have turned out to be very drinkable, in some instances more so than the '77s, which they resemble.

1979—Extreme winter frosts hampered wine production; the total German harvest was below average with 8.5 million hectoliters (224.4 million U.S. gallons, 187 million imp.). The quality was generally good, with no real highs or lows. The Riesling wines best withstood the frost, especially in the Mosel, but not so in the Saar and Ruwer Valleys, where crops were very small. These wines were quite good. Young vines suffered, especially in the Rheinhessen and the Palatinate, but the small crops yielded wines of very good, although not excellent, quality. The Rheingau crop was high in quality and quantity.

1980—In the Rheingau, as in the rest of Germany, the good harvest weather was not enough to make up for the wet and cold summer that preceded. Production was less than 50 percent of the normal crop, and quality was poor. This was also the case in the Mosel. In the Saar-Ruwer, winemakers produced only 10 percent of their normal harvest, and the quality was poor.

In the Rheinhessen and Palatinate, the harvest was down by half. The quality was fair, owing to the many new *vinifera* grape varieties planted, which managed to resist the cold, wet summer weather.

6 Starting a Cellar

A wine cellar conjures up a picture of a more spacious age when men laid down their crusted Port and pre-phylloxera Claret—or when their fathers were drinking their three bottles a day and suffering from gout. A country house with ample cellars is an undeniable asset; but even the owner of a modern "2½ room" apartment can emulate Professor Saintsbury's "very inferior accommodations," if he exercises some ingenuity.

The ideal wine cellar should be roomy, airy, and dry, away from light, free from vibration, and maintaining a constant temperature of about 55°F. (13°C.). Obviously this ideal is not very often attainable, and even in France only a few cellars approach it. The next best thing is to contrive a storeplace which satisfies as many of these conditions as possible. An understanding of why these conditions are ideal and how they affect the wine is a great help.

A roomy, airy, dry place. Lack of room, of course, means simply that you will be cramped for storage space, and so you lay down less wine. Proper ventilation will ensure that the air doesn't get stale and musty, creating an atmosphere which will eventually permeate through the corks, slowly imparting a moldy taste to the wine. A certain amount of humidity is to be sought for. This prevents the corks from drying up prematurely. A good "flooring" is to cover the ground with an inch of small gravel, sprinkling a little water over it periodically. The gravel will contain the humidity. Excessive humidity is injurious to the labels but rarely to the wine. For the fortunate one owning a large cellar, it would be wise to have the bottles recorked every twenty-five to thirty years. This is the maximum expected life span of a good cork.

Away from light and free from vibration. Some of the diseases that afflict wine—such as protein casse, a precipitate formed by the presence of excess protein—react only in the presence of light. Strong light may also "bake" your wine, maderizing or oxidizing it—i.e., turning it prematurely flat, musty, and brown like Madeira in color. Vibration agitates wines and also ages them prematurely: a house near a railway is therefore a bad place for a wine cellar, although if the disturbance is not too great and the wine is placed close to the ground there may be no ill effects.

A constant temperature of about 55°F. This is almost certainly the biggest bugbear of the would-be wine-keeper. Yet wines will not be ruined by temperatures rising as high as 75°F. (24°C.), provided that the rise is gradual, although they will age faster; old wines in particular are fragile and will not keep very long above 60°F. (16°C.). Between 50° and 57°F. (10° and 14°C.) wines age normally, and although they can generally adapt themselves to an almost imperceptibly rising temperature, sudden changes will soon kill them. To keep them near hot pipes is particularly injurious; and any house where the temperature rises during the day and drops suddenly during the night is a bad wine-store. In general, red wines are less susceptible to heat than are white ones; and white wines are best kept closest to the floor in the coolest part of the cellar.

It will be perfectly obvious that a "wine cellar" need not necessarily be in the cellar. With a little ingenuity, it is often possible to convert some corner into a store for wines that are to be consumed reasonably soon. It will not then be possible to buy great wines very young—when prices are most advantageous—and keep them until they are old and mature; yet a variety of good wines can be kept on hand at all times. A hall cupboard, for instance, would do—or the space under the stairs; then you can start planning what you will put into it.

To begin with, all natural wines—that is, wines not fortified with brandy—should be stored lying on their sides, so that the wine wets the cork, keeping it from shrinking and letting air into the bottle, ruining the wine. Sherry, Port, spirits, and liqueurs can be stored standing up since the higher alcoholic content will preserve them; but since—with the exception of Vintage Port and Madeira—these do not improve in bottle, there is little point in keeping a great store on hand. As you will probably want to keep both wines and spirits in your cellar, you will need shelves on which to stand the spirits, and bins and racks in which to lay the wines.

Many wine shops have metal and wooden racks at fairly reasonable prices, and they make excellent containers for wines. As a substitute, a whisky carton, laid on its side, is a simple and effective arrangement. Special bins can also be made; these should be of stout wood, preferably in the shape of a honeycomb or lozenge to keep the bottles from rolling when one of them is removed. Clay pipes, fifteen inches around, may also be used; these provide a protective cover for the bottles and insulate them from sudden changes in temperature. The bins need not be large—one a foot and a half square will hold almost a case of wine—but unless you plan to keep large quantities of the same wine on hand, they should not be too deep either. Wines keep best when they are not disturbed, and scrambling through them to find a bottle at the bottom of the pile is restful neither for the wine nor for the searcher.

Once you have your racks or bins installed, the cellar needs very little extra equipment: the main things are a thermometer, some tags, and a cellar-book.

Of these, the thermometer is the most important, since it shows at once if the temperature of your storeplace is proper for the normal ageing of wines. Tags come in handy for identifying bottles which are laid on their sides and in helping you to find the one you want without upsetting all the others. Finally, the cellar-book. While it may seem pretentious to keep a book if you only have half a dozen bottles or at most a case of wines on hand, the book will nevertheless be useful—and a pleasure to look back on later.

Whatever book you choose, your entries in it will run true to form: the wine, its name and year; the amount purchased, from whom, and on what date; the name of the shipper, and the price paid. On the other side of the page you will want space to enter the date of drinking and your comments. It is a good idea to devote one full page to a wine, particularly if you have bought a number of bottles.

Cellars provide the most enjoyment if the selection is a balanced one with a variety from which to choose. This variety may include wines of different types, qualities, and prices. Some ideas for a "model" cellar are given below, each one balanced in its selection. In establishing a large and elaborate cellar, it is best to call in an expert wine merchant who will be familiar with the market and can secure the best values.

36-BOTTLE CELLAR

4 bottles of rosé, the all-purpose pink wine, to be served chilled. Choose a Tavel, Provence, Anjou, Côtes du Roussillon, or California rosé—not more than three years old.

4 bottles of red Burgundy, inexpensive: Mâcon, Beaujolais, Moulin-à-Vent, Fleurie—less than two or three years old.

3 bottles of red Burgundy: Pommard, Nuits-Saint-Georges, Vosne-Romanée, Clos de Vougeot, Chambolle-Musigny, Beaune, Volnay, Chambertin, less than ten years old.

4 bottles of white Burgundy: Chablis, Chassagne-Montrachet, Meursault, Pouilly-Fuissé, Mâcon, Saint-Veran, or Puligny-Montrachet, each preferably bearing a vineyard name in addition to that of the parish—such as Les Preuses, Blanchots, Vaudésir, Les Clos, Vaillon, Fourchaume, or Montée de Tonnerre for the wines of Chablis; Les Perrières, Blagny, or La Goutte d'Or for Meursault; Les Pucelles, Les Combettes, or Les Chalumeaux for Puligny-Montrachet. Vintages: less than five years old.

2 bottles of red Bordeaux: a shipper's bottling of Saint-Émilion, Saint-Estèphe, Saint-Julien, or Margaux, or preferably an inexpensive château-bottled Clairet from one of the Bourgeois Growths (Crus Bourgeois).

3 bottles of château-bottled red Bordeaux (for great occasions): Beychevelle, Cheval-Blanc, Calon-Ségur, Cos d'Estournel, Haut-Brion, Lafite, Lascombes, Latour, one of the three Léovilles, Margaux, Mouton-Rothschild, Palmer, Pichon-Longueville, Prieuré-Lichine, or Talbot. Vintages: a good vintage in the last twenty years: see chart, pp. 648-649, and the list on pp. 17-18.

2 bottles of red Italian wine such as Barolo, Valpolicella, or Chianti.

3 bottles of white Italian wine: Verdicchio or Soave.

2 bottles of Spanish red Rioja wine from a good winery such as Bodegas Bilbainos, Bodegas Marqués de Riscal, or Bodegas Marqués de Murrietta.

1 bottle of Spanish white Rioja Tarragona.

1 bottle of sweet wine—Barsac or Sauternes, either from a shipper or, preferably, a château-bottled wine such as Climens, Coutet, Filhot, Guiraud, La Tour-Blanche, Rabaud, or the very expensive Château d'Yquem. Vintages: less than ten years old.

2 bottles of young Rhine wines (less than five years old): Hattenheimer, Hochheimer, Niersteiner, Rüdesheimer, Schloss Johannisberger, Schloss Vollrads. Wines bottled by the grower at the estate are preferable. A vineyard name in addition to that of the district is likewise desirable. Labels often have the word Auslese (selected) or Spätlese (late-picking) after the name of the wine. These are usually sweeter. Avoid Liebfraumilch—the use of this name has been limited by the 1971 West German Wine Law, but there are many other, better German wines.

1 bottle of young Mosel wine less than five years old, such as Bernkasteler, Wehlener, or Zeltinger.

1 bottle of Loire Valley wine, such as Pouilly-Fumé, Sancerre, Saumur, or Vouvray—not more than five years old.

1 bottle of dry white Bordeaux from the Graves district, either from a good shipper (in which case the price should not be high) or a château-bottled Graves such as Domaine de Chevalier, Couhins, Haut-Brion Blanc, Carbonnieux, La Tour-Martillac, Olivier, or Laville-Haut-Brion.

2 bottles of Alsatian wine, such as Riesling or Gewürztraminer—less than four years old.

In the United States, the wines from the Mosel, the Loire, Graves, and Alsace could be omitted and the other selections limited to 18-20 bottles. Substitute:

8 bottles of red varietal wine from California, including Cabernet Sauvignon, Pinot Noir, and Zinfandel. The best wines come from the North Coast counties of Napa, Sonoma, Mendocino, and Monterey. (For descriptions of the best wineries see United States: California.) A few of the bottles might be from reliable producers in New York or other eastern states.

8 bottles United States dry white wine from California, New York, Ohio, or Washington. The best ones carry the grape variety names. Look for Pinot Chardonnay, Chenin Blanc, Sémillon, Johannisberg Riesling, Sauvignon Blanc, Traminer, or Delaware. If vintage-dated, the wines should not be more than a few years old (California producers may be found listed by county under United States: California. Wineries in other states are treated in the separate state entries, e.g., United States: Ohio; United States: New York).

7 Wine and Health

Wine can be considered with good reason as the most healthful and the most hygienic of all beverages.

Louis Pasteur

Wine is one of the noblest cordials in nature.

John Wesley, founder of Methodism

Wine is a food.

Oliver Wendell Holmes

The magic of wine is intrinsic and complete. It induces confidence, a sense of well-being, and euphoria, thus conditioning a moderate wine-drinking man to be happy and healthy—for good wine is a tonic in convalescence. It disposes him to relax and encourages his appetite—a process well understood in this age of psychological study, but one which can only partially be demonstrated scientifically. A laboratory rat cannot show how wine will influence a tired or debilitated man, nor would a man feel the same after a hypodermic injection of wine as he does when he holds a sparkling glassful up to the light, sniffs the bouquet, and rolls the first sip around on his tongue. The secret is not in the alcoholic content alone, for wine has virtues which other alcoholic beverages do not share. In the chemical compound wine, which awaits final analysis, there are infinitesimal esters, contributing largely to the smell, taste, and character of the whole, but too subtle to have been trapped by the chemist so far. Its main ingredients have nevertheless been long established. The astonishing thing about modern scientific research is the way it proves that wine-making traditions dating from the earliest times are, according to our lights, perfectly logical and sane. Practices which might, at first glance, seem to be dictated by superstition have taken on a new authority in the cold light of science.

The study of wine is necessarily the study both of the particular and of the general effect—of the component and the composite. In France it is held that men who drink wine are gay, men who drink beer are heavy and often slower-witted, and men who drink spirits may be hectic and are often ugly-tempered. Professor Arnozan has said:

"Wine taken every day in moderation gently excites the intellectual faculties of him who absorbs it. It ends by giving him certain special characteristics: sharpens his wits, animates, renders more amiable, confers a great facility of assimilation, producing a sort of self-confidence—such are the traits of the man who every day makes use of wine."

It is worth remembering that not only were the Greeks and Romans wine-drinking people, not only are the French, Spanish, and Italians today, but the English, during their most vivid and adventurous period, the Elizabethan Age, were wine-drinkers too.

WINE AS FOOD

Depending on its richness in sugar and alcohol, a liter of wine is equal to 600–1,000 calories. More than one hundred chemical ingredients have been isolated in wine. It contains vitamins A, B, and C; and all thirteen of the minerals established by E. J. Underwood in 1940 as necessary to human life are also present. These are: calcium, phosphorus, magnesium, sodium, potassium, chlorine, sulfur, iron, copper, manganese, zinc, iodine, and cobalt.

Vitamin B is significantly present in wine. Red wine is richer than white in many food elements because it is obtained by maceration or steeping with the skins during fermentation; this is not the case with white wine, yet studies at the University of California College of Agriculture have established that in vitamin B content there is no difference between red and white wine, nor between dry and fortified wine. In riboflavin, white wines tend to lead, some of them having two-thirds the value of fresh milk. The vitamin B complex in wines remains stable and does not deteriorate as they age; but the freezing or pasteurizing necessary to preserve unfermented grape juice destroys vitamin B, including riboflavin, the content of which may reach 120 micrograms in 100 grams, with 50 micrograms of thiamin and other elements.

Besides these vitamins and minerals, which help to maintain the body and its metabolism, are the nutritive components in the grape sugars (dextrose is valuable here), polyphenols, proteins, and alcohol. ("It has been demonstrated that natural grape sugars in wine are readily absorbed by the human system and are desirable in the diet, that the alcohol in wine is a quick source of caloric energy, that wine has a definite blood-building iron content."—*Encyclopaedia Britannica*.) Ninety-five per cent of the energy in alcohol is converted for immediate use—so Neumann said in Germany at the beginning of the century, and it has been confirmed by Atwater and Benedict. "Ethylic alcohol is absorbed directly and progressively unless the stomach is empty." (Starling.) "Carried by the blood to every part of the system, it is burned up in the tissues." (Duroy, Perrin, and Lallemand.) The nutritive value of wine has been recognized in Spain, where it is placed under the same price controls as bread. Because of the nourishing quality of the other ingredients in wine the alcoholic content is taken into the body more slowly and utilized more efficiently than when it is absorbed in a higher percentage from more potent drinks.

Research by Professor Georges Portmann of Bordeaux, president of the International Committee for the Scientific Study of Wine, and by Max Eylaud has revealed that while a small amount of alcohol can increase the vigor of the human machine by 15 per cent, a double and triple dose does not have a proportionately greater effect, and it has been found independently that in larger quantities of alcohol there is an inhibition which actually decreases its utility. The approximate 11 per cent of alcohol in natural wine is believed to be the most effective proportion. Even more surprising is the claim that alcohol as an internal disinfectant seems to be most powerful in solution in wine and even in wine-and-water. The increase of prophylactic effect with the *decrease* of proportion of alcohol remained totally baffling until very recently, when it was discovered that certain elements of wine, other than alcohol, prevent or impede the growth of the germs of certain diseases in the human body.

WINE IN WEIGHT REDUCTION

Various investigations and experiments have established in graphable figures the predictable effects of wine on the human system. Taken in dilution of about 10 to 11 per cent—the saturation of natural wine—the body oxidizes approximately half a gram of alcohol per pound of body-weight in twenty-four hours, provided that the drinks are taken at well-spaced intervals. This quantity completely disappears in the vital processes, leaving no residue in the blood, urine, or other analyzable media. It is excess alcohol, not this assimilable amount, which causes inebriation. The ideal intake, therefore, totally used by the system in restoration and in generating energy, with nothing left over, is the number of pounds of body-weight multiplied by half a gram of alcohol.

In a man of average size this comes to a rough 500 calories per day, a gram of alcohol providing 7 calories. (150 pounds of body-weight multiplied by half a gram of alcohol = 75 grams; 75 × 7 calories = 525 calories.) The average daily caloric expenditure under normal conditions is 3,000 calories; wine therefore can supply 17 per cent of the calories needed in daily life. In fact, in a great part of the world, it does—here is a laboratory experiment verified on a gigantic scale in many lands and over thousands of years, where wine has always been a chief element of diet. This vast human experiment was confirmed under closely controlled conditions by W. O. Atwater and others of the American Academy of Science. Three healthy men between the ages of twenty-five and thirty-three and conditioned by different environments, a Swede, an American, and a Canadian, one an individual accustomed to drink wine and two teetotalers, were observed in a calorimetric chamber. They were given a diet which included 72 grams of alcohol a day. The heat production and by-products of their bodies were studied. The alcohol provided 20 per cent of total calories during rest and 14 per cent during work, and was found to be capable of replacing proteins, carbohydrates, and fats, and of protecting proteins and other tissue-substances ingested

from other sources. The weight of all three men remained constant throughout the experiment.

The significance of wine in diet has been summarized as follows by Georges Portmann, professor of medicine, who is one of Europe's outstanding authorities on wine and health: "Wine can be used to replace 500 calories of fat or sugar intake in the daily diet. These calories will be completely consumed and will not add an ounce of body-weight. So employed, wine is very useful in reducing—it being understood that the food intake will be reduced by the 500 calories replaced by the wine."

Experiments in the United States and Italy have shown that wine not only replaces carbohydrate calories but in doing so reduces carbohydrate hunger, making it easier to do without the weight-producing sugar foods. Although there may be disagreement on the subject, it was shown that in lessening the type of intake and thus the food mass, alcohol has been demonstrated to lighten proportionately the work of the digestive glands.

The standard bottle of wine (three-quarters of a liter), if it is at 10 per cent of alcohol, provides 525 alcoholic calories. Considered as food alone, a bottle of natural wine a day is the desirable average for a person of normal size, although for one not engaged in manual labor, a little less wine (say half a liter) may be sufficient. While providing about one-sixth of required nourishment, it cannot add weight.

WINE IN ANOREXIA (LACK OF APPETITE)

While it has been found to reduce carbohydrate hunger, wine—dry white wine and especially red wine—excites the olfactory nerves and the taste buds, and so sharpens sluggish appetite.

Taken in the heavy-artillery concentration of the before-dinner cocktail or highball, alcohol *inhibits* appetite.

Alcohol in the dilution in which it is found in natural wine (in combination with sugars, acidity, and vitamin B_2) prompts the flow of saliva, hydrochloric acid, and gastric secretions—as, to some extent, does fruit juice. In other words, wine starts hunger and appetite into action. S. P. Lucia, professor of medicine in the University of California School of Medicine, describes what happens when too brutal a dose is taken. "If, however, the concentration of alcohol surpasses the optimum, then the albumin-coagulating action of the alcohol, the changes in osmotic pressure, and other physico-chemical alterations will induce a suppression of secretion" (*Wine as Food and Medicine*).

Tartaric and acetic acids and the tannins in dry wine, white or red, stimulate appetite quite apart from the influence of the alcohol. In order to investigate this, the acids alone in non-alcoholic solutions were fed to twenty-one men and women between twenty-two and fifty-three years of age in an experiment conducted in 1953 by the Institute of Medical Research in Oakland, California. The individuals were engaged in their regular clerical work, and on certain test days took the wine-derived acids with their meals, or even, in a few cases, in place of their meals.

After the normality of the subject's nasal passages had been established by making him breathe on a polished metal surface (which would show cloudy patches of equal size and consistency), a nose-piece was fitted on, attached by pure gum rubber tubes to a bottle from which air could be injected into his nostrils under completely controlled conditions. By this method, the exact amount of any given odor projected to the subject could be known. The odor selected for the entire experiment was a standard brand of coffee.

It was found that after a normal meal olfactory sensitivity always decreased. This was graphed. When the acids accompanied the meal olfactory sensitivity remained constant, the graph line cutting straight through the sharp zag which indicated the individual's usual loss of capacity to respond to the smell of an appetite-provoking substance. This corresponded more or less exactly with the capacity of the acids to remove the sensation of satiety usual after a large meal.

Independently, in 1955, an appetite-stimulating ingredient, apart from the acids and still incompletely understood, was isolated in red wine.

WINE AS MEDICINE

Wine serves as medicine, either as a general tonic, or as a specific in the cure of a large number of diseases. Its greatest value is probably in the way it can stimulate energy and give moral support, preparing the ground for recovery. It is an alkaline agent.

From very early times, the therapeutic and antiseptic properties of wine were known and valued. Medical papyri of ancient Egypt have preserved prescriptions in which wine played an essential part. Xenophon, in his *Anabasis*, recorded Cyrus's orders to his troops to take wine with them and, while it lasted, mix it with the unaccustomed water of foreign lands; and in the nineteenth century wine was still recommended to be mixed with the impure water that caused cholera. From Homeric days until a few centuries ago, wine was used for the cleansing and poulticing of wounds: Hippocrates advised it also as a diuretic and for cooling fevers; Galen made a list of wines and their different healing virtues. During the Middle Ages and after, the various theriacs and pharmaceutical compounds of herbs, spices, and magic animal ingredients were mixed in wine; and right up to the last century wines were employed in great quantity in hospitals and in private practice: white wines as diuretics, red Burgundy for dyspepsia, red Bordeaux for stomach trouble and diarrhea, German wines for nerves, Champagne for nausea and catarrh, Port and Sherry in convalescence. Even now, a base of wine is not unknown in medical prescriptions. Its falling from favor in many of these instances was due in the first place to American agitation against intoxicants and, secondly, to the discovery of new drugs.

Some specific curative effects of pure unadulterated wine in cardiology, neurology, geriatrics, etc., are as follows:

(1) In France the general opinion is that by their richness in tartrates, certain wines add to the intestinal secretion, although red wines with high tannin content decrease it. Such red wines have long been well known for relieving diarrhea, particularly through the influence of the tannin in red wine on the large intestine. (But this is only true of good wine, especially Bordeaux; it is not suggested that a wine which has been adulterated with coarser blends will have the same beneficial effect.) Wine is beneficial also in cases of colitis and hemorrhoids.

(2) It is indispensable in low-sodium diets: a glass of wine contains from 1.3 to 9.9 milligrams of sodium, whereas an egg contains 40 milligrams; a glass of milk, 120 milligrams; an ounce of Cheddar cheese, 210 milligrams; a slice of white bread, 215 milligrams.

(3) Regular wine-drinkers are less apt than others to develop gallstones.

(4) "It is the safest of all sedatives" (according to Haggard and Jellinek).

(5) Wine that is rich in iron counteracts iron deficiency in anemia.

WINE AS A GERM-KILLER

Wine and alcohol have always been known as germ-killers both inside and outside the body. Curiosity about the effectiveness of wine prophylactics dating back to the Romans caused a student at the University of California College of Pharmacy, John Gardner, to track down an ingredient in red wine—not the alcohol—capable of killing *Staphylococcus aureus* and other bacteria. Numbers of germs, including that of typhus, had long been known to succumb to alcohols and certain of the acids in wine. Ordinary wine is equally capable of killing the dysentery bacillus, and even in great dilution red wine has been effectively utilized in purifying polluted water. The universal use of red wine in drinking-water in the past, and throughout much of the world today, has contributed immeasurably to the preservation of human life. Even in countries where the water supply is pure, this bactericidal action is useful. Wine taken with the meal functions in the system against such germs as may have been eaten on leafy vegetables or fruit, or derived from infectious organisms present in uncooked shellfish and other foods.

A wine of nine per cent or more alcohol has been shown to delay or prevent digestive liberation of trichinosis (J. B. McNaught and G. N. Pierce, Jr.: *The Protective Action of Alcohol in Experimental Trichinosis*, American Journal of Clinical Pathology, 1939). "I should be sorry to give up the use of wine in severe forms of enteric and pneumonic fever,"—so said Sir William Osler, the distinguished Canadian physician. And wine is well known in the treatment of bronchitis and influenza.

WINE IS NOT ALL ALCOHOL, AND ALCOHOL DOES NOT NECESSARILY LEAD TO ALCOHOLISM

It is now certain that small quantities of wine stimulate and large amounts of alcohol stun. Cocktails are depressants, only appearing to be otherwise because they release the inhibitions. But natural wine is generally only one-tenth alcohol, whereas a cocktail will be 40 per cent or over. Another difference is the presence in wine of the many elements other than alcohol which have their effect. A big dose of alcohol will inhibit the flow of bile; a 10 per cent dose in natural wine will cause the flow to increase. Professor Georges Portmann once said: "Wine is a total complex—balanced, living, and in existence nowhere else. Do you know anything about food and life and think that balance and vitality count for nothing? It is the only thing man consumes that comes to him direct from the earth and alive."

Excess, not habit, in wine as in spirits, may lead to harm. In wine, where the amount of alcohol is less, the danger is less. Old theories regarding the diseases caused by alcohol are now mostly exploded; these were often caused by vitamin and food deficiencies. Bright's disease, or inflammation of the kidneys, supposed in 1827 by Bright to have been sometimes caused by alcohol, has been established as having no connection with alcohol, which actually helps the kidneys to function. If the drinker eats properly, it is only with some difficulty that heavy consumption of alcohol can cause cirrhosis of the liver; and taken in moderation alcohol has a stimulating effect on the liver. There is at present no known ailment caused by natural wine, provided it is not consumed in great excess.

8 The Vine

Grapevines belong to the botanical family *Ampelidaceae*, a family which includes such other assorted plants as the Virginia creeper (*Ampelidaceae, Parthenocissus quinquefolia*) and other climbing berry-bearing growths, but not common ivy (*Hedera helix*). Of the ten genera of the family, only one—the genus *Vitis*—is important to the wine-maker, although others are capable of producing grapes. (Wine has been attempted from grapes of the genus *Ampelocissus* but the result was light and sour and the experiment should not be repeated.) The genus *Vitis* suffices, however, for its vines are found virtually everywhere in the temperate world, growing wild generally between 35° south latitude and 50° north latitude and cultivated between 38° south and 53° north. The genus embraces two sub-genera (*Euvites* and *Muscadiniae*) and numerous species. The varieties within the species proliferate enormously.

Genus *Vitis* (sub-genus *Euvites*) species *vinifera* is responsible for all the world's great wines. Thought to have originated in Transcaucasia, *Vitis vinifera* found its most successful home in the warm Mediterranean basin where early civilization domesticated it; and from there it has been transplanted to California, Australia, North and South Africa, and South America. It has rivals as far as wine-making is concerned—but none serious—in species native to western Asia and America. None of the eastern species is of particular note for the viticultor, although a few are planted in Japan and some wines of *Vitis coignetiae* were imported into France at the height of the phylloxera influx. (Even with *Vitis vinifera* stock grafted onto them they bore an attractive distinctive fruit, which fermented into something nearer to a sweet liqueur than a wine.) Nor are the American species of vines of much importance in the development of wine, although they are used extensively in the eastern United States and Canada. Otherwise, they are useful in France and other places as root-stocks, resistant to phylloxera, onto which *Vitis vinifera* species are grafted.

The classification of the species of genus *Vitis* is open to considerable debate; botanical classifications are arbitrary things at best and scientists often disagree about them. Perhaps the most widely accepted—especially in Europe and academic American circles—is that used by Professor Branas (perhaps the world's foremost ampelographer) in his classes at the École Nationale d'Agriculture at Montpellier, in southern France. This classification divides the species as follows:

I—Sub-Genus *EUVITES*

A American Species

(1) TEMPERATE REGIONS

(EASTERN ZONE)

Vitis labrusca	Vitis aestivalis
Vitis lincecunici	Vitis bicolor

(CENTRAL ZONE)

Vitis riparia	Vitis rupestris
Vitis rubra	Vitis monticola
Vitis berlandieri	Vitis cordifolia
Vitis candicans	Vitis cinerea

(WESTERN ZONE)

Vitis Californica	Vitis Arizonica

(2) TORRID REGIONS

(FLORIDA AND THE BAHAMAS)

Vitis coriacea	Vitis gigas

(TROPICAL AND EQUATORIAL ZONES)

Vitis Bourgoeana	Vitis Cariboea

B Eastern Asian Species (incomplete)

(1) TEMPERATE REGIONS

Vitis amurensis	(Japan, Mongolia, Sakhalin Is.)
Vitis coignetiae	(Japan, Sakhalin Is., Korea)
Vitis Thunbergii	(Japan, Korea, Formosa, Southwest China)
Vitis flexuosa	(Korea, Japan, India, Nepal, Cochin-China)
Vitis Romaneti	(China)
Vitis Piasezkii	(China)
Vitis armata	(China)
Vitis Wilsonae	(China)
Vitis rutilans	(China)
Vitis Pagnucii	(China)
Vitis pentagona	(China)
Vitis Romanetia	(China)
Vitis Davidii	(China)

(2) SUB-TROPICAL REGIONS

Vitis Retordi	(Tonkin)
Vitis Balansaeana	(Tonkin)
Vitis lanata	(India, Nepal, Dekkan, Southern China, Burma)
Vitis pedicellata	(Himalayan Mountains)

C European and East and Central Asian Species

Vitis vinifera

II—Sub-Genus *MUSCADINIAE*

A North American Species

Vitis rotundifolia
Vitis Munsoniana
Vitis Popenoei

On the American side of the Atlantic, most practicing viticulturists have adopted the classification of the American scientist Bailey. Considered by Europeans to be scholastically less accurate—but extremely effective from a practical standpoint—the Bailey classification includes several variations in nomenclature and some slightly different divisions. The notable changes are in nomenclature: *Vitis riparia* becomes *Vitis vulpina*, *Vitis bicolor* is *Vitis argentifolia*. Bailey also divides *Vitis Cariboea*, recognizing two distinct species (*Vitis tilioefolia* and *Vitis sola*) where Europeans see mutations of the same one.

HYBRIDIZATION

A distinct difficulty in the classification of vines is that they can be interbred, and the result may be a new vine with some characteristics from both parents, but all the characteristics of neither; and such a hybrid may seem to be a new species altogether. In the United States, artificial hybridization has been practiced to a large degree and many of the better wines of the eastern part of the country—where for various reasons *Vitis vinifera* simply will not grow—result from efforts made over the past century and a half.

Americans are not the only people interested in hybrids. Practically every wine-growing country in the world has its viticultural stations, and the French in particular have experimented widely. The French hybrids—crosses between *Vitis vinifera* and American species or *Vitis vinifera* and hybrids—are named after the men who developed them, and some of the achievements of Baco, Seibel, and Couderc are known to vineyard owners the world over. Hybrids of varying sorts occupy large areas of vineyards in the eastern United States and Canada, in southern France, in Italy and Spain; and while they produce more than do *Vitis vinifera*, and are more resistant to disease, they give wine which is sound and reasonably priced but nothing more. Yet the search for a better hybrid continues. Throughout the world, researchers strive to perfect the cross which will combine vigor, resistance to disease, and productivity with fruit of the quality of *Vitis vinifera*. The world's great wines continue, however, to come exclusively from *Vitis vinifera*. Moreover, they continue to come, as they have for the past several centuries, from the same handful of vineyards.

FACTORS THAT DETERMINE QUALITY

Oenologists, or wine scientists, maintain that four factors determine the quality of any wine; soil, climate, vine-type, and man. Other minor factors, such as the prevailing yeasts, may enter the equation as subheadings, but these are the essentials. In order to arrive at a great wine,

they must all be linked together, each one supporting and complementing the others, each adding its indispensable qualities. In this combination the vine is of paramount importance; and next, the soil in which it grows.

Soil. The elements that make soil "noble" for wine are many and difficult to analyze. The outstanding attribute of the soil of fine wine vineyards is its obvious poverty, for vines often do their best in land where nothing else will grow. The oolitic debris of Burgundy prompted the Burgundian paradox: "If our soil weren't the richest in the world it would be the poorest"; and the scarcely fertile chalk of Champagne, the sandy gravel of Bordeaux, and the slate sections of the German Mosel Valley nourish plants whose grapes yield some of the world's greatest wines. By the same token, such rich and fertile soils as those of France's Mediterranean coastline and Italy's Po Valley produce little more than a good *vin ordinaire*.

Together with the poverty of the soil must go certain types of richness: a richness in trace elements. One of wine's greatest glories resides in the nuances of taste and aroma, and these come—at least in part—from the action and interaction of the elements that nourished the vine.

These elements, broadly speaking, are present in rock or soil in relatively small quantities. Among them may be such minerals as boron, cobalt, copper, iodine, manganese, molybdenum, nickel, selenium, vanadium, and zinc. These, if they are too concentrated, can be harmful to plant life; but they are often essential in small quantities. While tests have not been extensively performed on vines, the effects of trace elements on plant life have been dramatically demonstrated in orchards and vineyards in the United States, where even a small increase in the boron content of the soil has eliminated a defect in the flesh of apples. Similar results with other elements have been obtained in other parts of the world, such as Germany and Australia.

It is thought that trace elements affect wines by controlling the rate of growth and the processes of the vine and by modifying the enzyme complex of the growth. The soil elements that nourish the vine affect taste and aroma. The type and number of fermentation-causing yeasts can have considerable effect upon wine (*see also* Chapter Nine).

Very small transformations in soil may affect wine made from grapes grown in it, but obviously the basic essentials must be present before these trace elements can assume any importance. Vines produce their finest fruit generally in quartz, calcareous, or slate soil, and where soil composition is large-grained and consequently well-drained. This leads to riper grapes. Nitrogenous and humus materials prompt the vine to produce luxuriant foliage, but the quality of the fruit suffers. Small amounts of iron are to be found in most fine vineyards, but if there is too much the wine may be difficult to clarify and stabilize (although some experts maintain that it is the iron in the wine-making equipment rather than in the soil which causes this trouble). A plenitude of elements will be present in one degree or another, and the components and the interplay between them dictate the quality of the fruit. The result is that a prospective vineyard-owner can tell with little difficulty where the vine will grow well; to tell where it will produce with grandeur is a matter of time, trial, and a large measure of luck.

Climate. Heat and rainfall are the direct climatic influences on vines. Moderately cold rainy winters and fairly long hot summers with some—but not much—rain are the most desirable. The first cold of the late autumn or early winter encourages the vine to become dormant and allows the wood to toughen and mature; but severe cold during the winter will kill it. Sufficient summer heat is necessary to mature the fruit; and later summer sunshine, in particular, will soon mature the grape internally. Therefore, growers in cool temperate regions must harvest as late as possible, taking advantage of any late summer sun they may get. The quality of a marginal harvest may not be decided until the final week or so of the summer when a sudden burst of sunshine may produce a very pleasant wine, whereas the result of rain will be a mediocre wine at best. Most of the rain a vine gets should come during the winter and early spring, for the diseases that afflict vines are most active in hot humid weather, and in very wet years the fruit is apt to rot on the vine. Moreover, the lack of sunshine will mean that grapes do not mature so well as they would in a sunny year.·

Among the indirect climatic influences are the frequency and severity of frosts, hail, and wind. A late frost, occurring in May, just before or during the flowering of the vine, may destroy the entire year's crop; and late summer hail or a very strong wind can easily remove the grapes before the harvest. Other important factors are the proximity of water—for lakes and rivers have a tempering effect upon heat and cold—and the situation of the vineyard on the slope. For proper drainage and exposure to the sun most great vineyards are on slopes, ranging from the gently rolling near-plains of Bordeaux to the swift-plunging cliffs of the German Rhine and Mosel valleys.

Vine-type. For any specific conditions of soil and climate the right vine-type—of the thousands that exist—must be found. An example of the importance of grape variety is Burgundy, where the noble red vine is the Pinot Noir along the Côte d'Or, and the Gamay some thirty miles to the south in the Beaujolais. Even in so small a distance as this, the difference is markedly great: Gamay, on the Côte d'Or, gives ordinary wine; Pinot Noir, in the Beaujolais, produces flat and insipid wines; yet put the two where they belong, and the results may be superlative.

Man. The last major factor is man. Human error is always to be considered in human endeavor and only when man is most skillful and nature most bountiful will great wine be made. Much of the skill will be needed after the harvest; but unless the grapes are brought to proper maturity, the harvest will hardly be worth the effort. Tending these grapes is arduous and exacting work, and the conscientious grower finds little time for other pursuits.

VINEYARD PREPARATION

The preparation of a new vineyard requires the greatest care and backbreaking labor. In some sections of the world—such as the steep Rhine Valley in Germany or Portugal's River Douro—the grower may have to blast rock, build terraces, and even carry earth to his high site simply to get enough soil to nourish his vine. In parts of Europe, "trenching" is a necessity. This may be a very deep plow, but it can be more—depending upon the needs of the specific soil. The ground may be plowed so that topsoil and subsoil both benefit without the two being mixed; or both may be mixed together; or topsoil may be turned under and subsoil over, each taking the place of the other; or subsoil may be plowed without disturbing the topsoil too much. This process is often desperately complicated, because so many European vineyards are planted on slopes which cannot always be worked by tractor and sometimes not even by horses, so that man has to plod away alone. After this plowing, a cover crop is usually planted, and in one or two years the vineyard is ready for its vines. These, when they are set out, are sometimes one, more often two years old.

In California and other newer grape areas where land in most cases can be leveled, or the lower slope levels (workable by tractor) are available, it is customary to clear, plow, and plant the vines within a few days. Most soils are virgin and quite fertile, so that cover crops to enrich the soil are not necessary. Mechanization of the work allows many acres to be planted in a day by very few men. In California, the land must be fumigated to kill off oak fungus or other diseases.

PROPAGATION OF THE VINE

There are various ways in which vines can be made to reproduce, not all of them useful to the viticulturist. The original purpose of the grape was to carry seeds, and vines will reproduce by seedlings, but this is perhaps the most impracticable method for the vineyard-owner. In order that they may reproduce, vines must be pollinated; and they may or may not be pollinated by plants of the same variety. If not, the seedlings will not be of the same variety as the parent, they will be hybrids. Since the vineyard-owner is looking for an exact replica of his bearing vine, and since seedlings require such expensive extras as greenhouses and potting sheds, he leaves this to the nurseryman and hybridist.

Layering or *marcottage* was once the traditional way of propagating vines but is rarer since the phylloxera outbreak of the last century. It allows vine-shoots to establish roots of their own before being cut from the parent vine—which permits a shoot to draw nourishment from the old vine until its own roots are strong enough to support it. The usual practice was to lead one shoot—still attached to the vine—down, into the ground, then out again. The nodes along the buried section of the shoot sent forth roots while the exposed end developed foliage. When the new roots were considered fully developed, the shoot was cut from the parent. *Provignage* was a variation by which an old vine was buried with one single shoot coming forth from the ground. This shoot developed roots but also drew nourishment from the old ones as long as they lived, and the fruit had characteristics of the old vines. Neither of these methods is widespread today, because of phylloxera. In most cases, modern vines are made up of *Vitis vinifera* tops grafted onto American or hybrid roots. If either *marcottage* or *provignage* were used, it would mean establishing a vine with *Vitis vinifera* roots, and these would probably be open to attack by phylloxera—although *marcottage* has been extensively used in a part of Château Prieuré-Lichine vineyard since 1958, with no visible ill-effects. In California, however, where soil and climate are not conducive to the growth of phylloxera, 65 per cent of the vines are planted on their own roots. Similar conditions prevail in Turkey, in Asia Minor generally, and in some parts of Germany.

The only practical means of allowing vines to reproduce today is by cuttings. Vine canes—cut in the autumn or winter from the dormant vine and kept until the spring in sawdust or sand—are placed in fertile ground until the roots develop. At the end of a year or so, these roots are strong enough to support transplantation. The rooted portions, of course, are normally of American or hybrid stock, and the *Vitis vinifera*-bearing wood is grafted onto them.

Bench-grafting and field-budding or -grafting are the two methods usually found in vineyards. In bench-grafting, the two sections—scion (top of the vine—*Vitis vinifera*) and stock (root)—are joined at a nursery, and only after the graft has healed is the new vine placed in soil to develop roots. In field-budding, the stock forms the roots and is placed in its proper spot in the vineyard; the top is cut off when the bud has become established, and the scion is grafted or budded on in its place.

In California in recent years, due to the extreme demand for grapevine rootings—which has resulted from a rapid expansion in vineyard planting—a quick method of propagation has been developed and is widely used. Mature canes are cut into one-bud pieces and grown in 85°-chambers under an intermittent fine mist of water. After the buds have sprouted and grown leaves, the shoots are cut into one-bud-plus-one-leaf pieces, dipped in a growth hormone, and rooted in the mist chamber. By this method, called mist propagation, a single five-year-old vine can produce thousands of new rootings in a single year.

Whichever of these methods is chosen, the result is the same—a new vine is in existence. Four years after the vine has been planted it will start producing fruit worthy of being made into wine, although many varieties produce grapes of sorts after three years.

CARE OF THE VINE

Although this is an oversimplification, it might be said that during the first year of the vine's life the major preoccupation of the grower is to make sure that his vine develops good roots; during the second year, strong and well-placed branches; in the third year (and thereafter) that the fruit be of the best possible quality. All of these considerations will be concurrent throughout the life span of the vine, but in the early years they take on extra significance. The above-ground portions of the vine can be divided into the following parts:

The TRUNK—the body of the vine. From it come:

ARMS—or branches. These in turn, support:
1. SHOOTS—the current season's growth, including
   (a) new foliage
   (b) tendrils (slender winding shoots that twine around trellises and other supports)
   (c) watersprouts (shoots growing on wood more than one year old)
   (d) suckers (shoots which appear below the ground)
2. CANES—one-year-old matured shoots. The most important are fruit canes (or canes that will bear the current year's crop)
3. SPURS—short canes, divided into
   (a) fruit spurs (intended to bear fruit)
   (b) renewal spurs (intended to bear the next season's canes)
   (c) replacement spurs (used to replace existing branches)

Pruning and training—two technically separate but interrelated practices—are the methods the vine-grower uses to keep the vegetative parts of his vine in order and to ensure a fairly—and consistently—large quantity of good fruit. Pruning is the removal of excess portions of the vine's growth; training, the directing of the vine into conformations that will make it easy to handle and convenient to work.

Pruning. The purpose of pruning is to achieve an optimal balance between vine growth and the amount of crop. If allowed to grow without pruning, the vine will produce more grapes than it is capable of ripening, while overly severe pruning will excessively limit the overall growth of the vine. Ideally one wishes to achieve the largest amount of leaf area which will be able to ripen the largest amount of fruit to the optimum condition.

The amount of pruning performed will depend upon the fertility of the soil, the vigor of the vine, the warmth of the climate, and the amount of available water. When the weather is hot, the soil fertile, and the vine vigorous, long pruning—leaving four or more buds or "eyes" on each cane—may be used, for the vine has the energy to support large crops and plenty of foliage. Alternatively, a greater number of normal-sized spurs may be retained to allow for the extra growth. The number, length, and placement of spurs is determined by the type of training system used. In California, the espalier system (*see* below) is being used increasingly for premium-wine grape production even though an expensive trellis is required, so several canes each with fifteen to twenty eyes may be left on each vine. In regions where the weather is rather cold—such as Germany and northern France—the vine will be feebler, and gobelet training (*see* below) with short spur pruning is often adopted.

In practice, once the vine is mature and the desired shape established, one determines the amount to prune by the performance of the vine in the last season. If the crop was well balanced, one leaves the same total number of eyes on the vine as there were canes the previous year, while if the vine overproduced one year, the number of canes (and hence the amount of crop) should be reduced.

Training. The method of pruning chosen, and the conditions which dictated the pruning, will also have an effect upon the way the vine is trained. The three major methods of training are: (1) *cordon*, (2) *gobelet* or head, and (3) *espalier*.

(1) A *cordon*-trained vine has the trunk extended in a single direction, be it vertical, horizontal, or oblique.

There are numerous variations of cordon training, but the most frequently encountered consists of a trunk coming out of the ground, bent sideways to run parallel with the ground and usually supported by a wire or style. The quantity of spurs that grow up and down from this trunk may be regulated as well as the number of eyes on each spur, and the method—although requiring some skill to establish—rewards the skillful with large harvests. It is not applicable to all vine varieties and cannot normally be used for the finer—and less fruitful—types. Perhaps the most important of the cordon styles is the Guyot—one of the most widespread in the world of fine wines—which consists usually of a trunk and one arm. Canes coming forth from that arm are trained along wires. It is particularly effective for vines with infertile basal nodes and those that form small and compact bunches of grapes.

In California, the most common form of cordon is in the shape of a T with the trunk branching to form two horizontal branches.

(2) *Gobelet* (or head) training leaves a single vertical trunk terminating in several arms rising in approximately the shape of a vase or goblet (French *gobelet*). It has the particular virtue that no support is needed for the vine, and it is simple to establish and maintain. However, if the basal buds of the vine are infertile it cannot be used, and in some cases very vigorous vines tend to set their fruit badly.

(3) *Espalier* training leaves a trunk terminating in one or two arms and several canes, most often all trained in the same plane. Like the cordon-trained vine, it must have a trellis or wire for support. There are a number of variations on this system, including the decorative trellis-trained vine, so often found in formal gardens.

CYCLE OF THE VINE

The growth-cycle of the vine starts in the spring when the dormant winter stage has passed and sap begins to flow. Five to six weeks after the rising of the sap, the vine begins to produce foliage and the buds along the canes swell, bursting out of the brown scaly wood which has covered and protected them during the winter and revealing a small woolly bud. Tiny delicate leaves form, and from this point until the vine flowers—for unlike many fruits the vine does not put forth fruit and leaves at the same time—it is budding out, a time of growth before floral parts develop (French *débourrement*). The time this occurs depends mainly on the warmth of the soil, but also to a certain extent on the time chosen for pruning.

If a vine is pruned during the winter season—as most are—budding will occur naturally; but if it is pruned after the sap has begun to flow, budding will be delayed by as much as two weeks. Late pruning involves loss of a considerable amount of sap and although this sap has practically no nutrient value, growers usually feel that such a loss could only be detrimental to the vine, and so they tend to avoid late pruning. In areas where late frosts prevail, however, it can be valuable, retarding budding until the danger of frost has abated. "Green" or "summer" pruning implies the removal of succulent growth.

A variation of this used in California is called "double pruning"; the vines are pruned in the normal manner in the fall or mid-winter except that long spurs are left, four to eight buds instead of two to four buds. The apical buds are allowed to push, and the spurs are immediately cut to normal length before excessive starch reserves are used up. Using this method, second pruning may be done at leisure with no worry that growth will commence before pruning is complete, and yet the bud-push is delayed five to fourteen days.

The young shoots of the vine put forth leaves and, later, flower clusters. On each cluster is a group of tiny blossoms in the form the grape bunch will eventually take. At first each flower in the cluster is covered by a cap—which slips away, revealing the flowering parts of the vine.

In most vines, the flower consists of a cone-like female pistil and five male stamens, equally vigorous. The pistil has an ovary, style, and stigma, and the stamens are composed of filaments carrying anthers, tiny sacs of pollen. When the sacs open, pollen is discharged and the grains are trapped by the stigma, where the pollen germinates. The pollen tube grows down the style and into the ovary, where fertilization takes place.

Most *Vitis vinifera* vines are hermaphroditic and both male and female organs of the same vine are equally developed. In some other vines one set of organs may be stunted, and the vineyard-owner will need both female (to bear fruit) and male (to fertilize the female) vines. Hermaphroditic vines usually fertilize themselves—the pollen falling from the male to the female portions—but unisexual vines *must* be cross-pollinated. It is a curious fact that cross-pollination has little or no effect whatsoever upon fruit. The grape will always run true to the bearing vine, and changes will take place only in the seeds, which are of no interest to the viniculter.

The vine flowers for a period of about two weeks. During this time the weather is of the utmost importance, for on it depends the fruit the vine will yield. Failure to flower properly or completely is the condition known as *coulure* (*see* Vine Pathology *below*) and, if serious, this may mean that the plant will develop no grapes at all. At the end of a normal flowering a tiny green berry will form, growing and maturing into the grape.

The flowering (*floraison*) is followed by the slow preliminary maturing of the fruit. The grapes, green with chlorophyll, assimilate carbon in exactly the same manner as the leaves; they grow in bulk, and chemically they show very little change beyond a slight rise in acidity. The next stage, usually starting in August, is the *véraison*, when the grape changes color, turning from the early green to its final red-purplish hue, or translucent greenish-white, after which the final maturing will occur. The approximate duration of these various operations is:

Putting forth leaves	72– 75 days	
Flowering	10– 20 days	
Developing grape	40– 45 days	
Maturing grape	48– 50 days	
Total	170–190 days	

This chart is only valid for grapes of "first epoch," because different varieties of grape mature their fruit at different intervals. The most widely accepted classification of *time* of maturing is that of the Frenchman Pulliat, devised toward the end of the last century. Pulliat took the Chasselas Doré grape as a "standard," and from its cycle built up the following table.

Designation		*Time of Maturing* Before or after Chasselas Doré
"Precocious"	Very early	10 days before
First epoch	Early	about same time
Second epoch	Early mid-season	12 days after
Third epoch	Mid-season	24 days after
Fourth epoch	Late	36 days after

The system of Pulliat is not the best guide to predict the days to maturity, since it does not account for environmental influences. It does allow comparison of the relative *rate* of maturation of different varieties. A more precise determination of the time to mature is the method of Winkler and Amerine, based on the total heat summation required to mature a given variety. With knowledge of the required heat summation and weather records, the number of days to mature a given variety in a given area may be predicted.

After the *véraison* the grape starts its significant change. It has already achieved its acid, and from this point on acidity will decrease and sugar content increase. The bulk also increases, and the reaction speeds its pace as the grape approaches maturity. Full maturity is attained when no more sugar is generated, and the grapes are then ready for picking or for the second stage of going into the noble rot. In some cases there will be an increase in *apparent* sugar content after final maturation, but this is due to evaporation of water rather than to increase in sugar. (In certain parts of the world, as in the Barsac–Sauternes districts of Bordeaux and, to a much smaller extent, the Mosel and Rhine districts of Germany, the mold *Botrytis cinerea*, the noble rot, forms on the grapes, hastening the process and resulting in an extremely sweet wine.) During the ripening period of the fruit a waxy "bloom" forms on the outside, protecting the grape from sunburn and trapping the yeasts that will cause the fermentation (*see* Botrytis cinerea).

While the vine is preparing itself and producing its fruit, there are a number of maladies to which it may succumb. The most crippling of these thrive in wet weather, since they multiply faster under humid conditions and since rain washes off the chemical sprays used by the grower in an attempt to counteract or control them. Some of the more important diseases—and their antidotes—are outlined below.

VINE PATHOLOGY

The ills to which the vine is prone fall into two major categories: (1) accidents and non-parasitic maladies and (2) maladies of parasitic origin. The first group embraces afflictions caused by climate, soil, vine, and man, and the second those caused by viruses, bacteria, cryptogams, and animal parasites.

1. Accidents and Non-Parasitic Maladies

(a) *Climate*

Frost is the most important climatic danger. Although most vineyards are so situated that frosts will have a minimal effect, those that do occur can be devastating. The severe winter of 1956 in Bordeaux caused a decrease in production of as much as 90 per cent in some districts; but it is partly because such winters are so rare (1956 was the second-worst winter in the region since 1709) that growers are unprepared to cope with them. In general, winter temperatures below 5°F. (-15°C.) are dangerous for vines, and spring temperatures even a few degrees below freezing (25°F. or -4°C.) are equally critical. Many American vine-types are more resistant to cold than are *Vitis vinifera*, and the Beta grape—a crossing of *Vitis labrusca* and *Vitis riparia* found in the northern United States and Canada—can withstand temperatures as low as -4°F. (-20°C.), while *Vitis amurensis* can live at fantastically low temperatures. (At the present time, unfortunately, *Vitis amurensis* has not given useful grapes.) In exceptionally cold vineyard areas, vines may be protected from winter cold by covering them completely with soil, a practice occasionally followed in Russia, Hungary, Bulgaria, Asia Minor, and Canada. Late spring frosts are also a great hazard, but late pruning will sometimes retard flowering until the danger has passed.

In many parts of California, early spring frosts are common and can destroy the majority of a crop by killing the young shoots. In the past, growers employed oil or butane heaters in the vineyards in an attempt to prevent frost, or installed motor-driven propellers called wind machines to circulate the higher warmer air. Today the most effective method of preventing spring frost where water is available is to install overhead sprinkler systems. During a cold period, the sprinklers are turned on to maintain a constant coating of water on the vines, protecting them from freezing by the heat released when the water freezes to ice. This method, though expensive, is so effective that it is allowing vineyards to be successfully planted in areas previously unplantable due to the severity of spring or autumn frosts.

Heat, if excessive, may damage vines, although temperatures must rise above about 110°F. (43°C.) before the critical limit is reached. This kind of heat is unusual in vineyards elsewhere than in North Africa, where the hot, dry, dehydrating, sustained winds of the sirocco sometimes wreak enormous damage.

Hail scars leaves and branches and may remove vegetation, weakening the vine. Late summer hailstorms are called "harvesters" by vine-growers and may destroy or remove the entire crop. Rockets fired into hail clouds sometimes cause them to burst before they come over the vineyards, but it is not easy to do this successfully because of the height of the clouds and the speed with which they form.

Wind breaks off and cracks shoots, fruit, and vegetation; and salt winds blowing in from the sea, as sometimes happens in the Médoc—even as far as fifty miles inland—can wither the leaves.

(b) *Soil*

Drought causes vine leaves to turn yellow, and unless some manner of irrigation is installed the plant eventually degenerates or dies.

Excess moisture may drown the plant, but only after some time. If the vine is flooded for less than ten weeks, it is able to survive. This has led to flooding as a countermeasure to phylloxera; the water drowns the pest and is then drained off before the vines are affected.

Chlorosis is a yellowing of the leaves caused by a lack of chlorophyll. In Europe it is often due to an excess of calcium in the soil, which results in iron deficiency. Vines differ in degrees of resistance to it, and most *Vitis vinifera* varieties are practically unaffected. Treatment is with ferrous sulfate, on the theory that a comparative excess of calcium impedes the vine from assimilating iron, thus causing the disease. *Vitis berlandieri* is somewhat resistant and is thus used as root-stock.

Soil deficiencies are principally caused by lack of boron, potassium, or zinc. Zinc deficiency is fairly common in California and Australia, and the vine is treated with zinc; the more widespread boron deficiency is treated in various ways, either by increasing the soil's boron content or by injecting boron into the vine.

Soil toxicity comes mainly from an excess of salt. Selection of root-stock may overcome it (hybrids, particularly those from *Vitis candicans*, whose native habitat is the swamps of Mississippi, are highly resistant); or the land may be "washed" by flooding for a short period with clear water. Micro-nutrients, especially boron, are occasionally present in toxic amounts.

(c) *Vine*

Coulure is the dropping of flowers, flower clusters, or of the tiny berries during the period of their initial development; or is their failure to develop. Its most important cause is bad weather, for proper flowering can only take place under rainless, warm, sunny skies. Too rapid a growth can also cause *coulure*, in which case the vines would be better grafted onto root-stock more appropriate to their vigor.

Shot berries (*millerandage*) is the name given to grape clusters with grapes of varying sizes. If the flowering has not been complete, some or all of the grapes may remain small, green, and hard, resembling buckshot. It is an aftermath of *coulure*.

Leaf reddening (*rougeau*), if not caused by a virus, is due to a wound which interrupts the flow of sap to the roots. The wound may be on the above-ground portion of the vine—in which case the afflicted part will be removed, if possible. If it is due to wounds on the roots, potassium fertilizers sometimes have a restorative effect by translocating more potassium, especially when the root growth is restricted.

(d) *Man*

Browning (*brunissure*) is a result of overproduction, of not pruning the vine sufficiently. Brown stains appear on the leaf, which drops off; the quality of the fruit suffers, and eventually the vine may lose some of its reserves of strength and die. Decreasing the number of grape bunches may combat the malady in its early stages; but if the disease exhausts the vine too much, there is no cure.

Burning of leaves by insecticides, chemical fertilizers, or even, in some instances, by smoke from nearby factories may do damage to the vine, whether caused by the carelessness of man, or by unfavorable vineyard sites.

2. Maladies of Parasitic Origin

(a) *Viruses and Rickettsiae*

Infectious degeneration or *fan leaf* (*court noué*) is a virus disease that apparently appears only in the wake of phylloxera. Fan leaf is spread in the soil by the vector *Xiphema index*. The leaf turns yellow along its veins and in patches between them; leaves grow misshapen, shoots bifurcate and multiply laterally, and flowers form double clusters. The malady forms in "stains" or patches throughout the vineyard and spreads slowly. Its insidious character is threefold: it progressively shortens the life of the vine; it lives in the soil; there is no known treatment. It is spread and intensified by plowing, and the only present solution is to pull up affected vines and plow lightly, if at all. The progressive action means that, while a pre-phylloxera vine might have lived a hundred years, the first generation thereafter may survive only for forty years and the second for fifteen. When this life span gets down to four years there will be no more wine from that vineyard. The infected soil may be cleaned up by removing vines from infected areas, allowing the land to lie fallow until all the old roots rot, and fumigating with D.D. (dichloropropane dichloropropylene).

Pierce's disease is found in California. The leaves yellow along the veins, the edges burn, the vine puts out dwarf shoots, fruit wilts and colors prematurely, and the vine dies in from one to five years. The disease is caused by the same *rickettsiae* which cause alfalfa dwarf, and it is spread by insects, i.e., sharpshooters. Treatment: pulling up the affected vines is useless; the insect-carriers of the disease must be attacked with powerful insecticides. Other widespread virus diseases which cause considerable damage are *corky bark, yellow vein, leaf roll,* and the *mosaic complex.*

(b) *Bacteria*

Oleron's disease or *bacterial blight of vines* causes stains on leaves and flower clusters and destroys intercellular walls. European in origin, it is of little importance today outside the vineyards of South Africa. It is thought that widespread use of copper sprays and sterilization of pruning instruments have led to its disappearance in Europe.

(c) *Cryptogams or fungus diseases*

Downy (or *false*) *mildew* (in Europe known as mildew) is the most crippling fungus disease of the vine. American in origin, it is caused by *Plasmospora viticola* and attacks the green portions of the vine, but only before the *véraison*—the changing of color in the grape. On leaves, an oily stain later turning to white forms on the undersides and spreads. It also appears on shoots just below the buds, and it can attack flowers and fruit. Downy mildew needs high humidity and heat to generate, and since it is partly spread by wind, it can be devastating once it gets started. (Most American vine-types are resistant to downy mildew and American vineyards are not treated for it. The fungus is thus allowed to run rampant and this has been one of the major factors in keeping *vinifera* vines out of eastern America, although the primary problem with *vinifera* in the eastern United States is winter cold—and black rot, if not controlled, is a menace.) Treatment is by copper sulfate ($CuSO_4$), 80,000 tons of which are used annually in France to combat mildew. It is usually applied in the Bordeaux mixture, made up of varying amounts of copper sulfate, chalk, and water.

Powdery (or *true*) *mildew* (in Europe known as oïdium) also attacks only green organs. Introduced into Europe from America, it caused widespread damage in 1854, reducing the crop in France by 20 per cent. Powdery mildew limits growth, attacks leaves, and splits berries, and if untreated will kill the vine—especially the susceptible *vinifera*—in a few years. Wines made from grapes affected by this disease will have a disagreeable taste and smell, a poor color, and a low degree of alcohol. Even when only the leaves of a plant have been attacked, the ensuing wine will be tainted. Finely ground sulfur—75,000 tons of which are used annually in France—combats it.

Black rot is also of American origin. It forms stains speckled with black on green organs, and the fruit shrivels and turns brown. It is most virulent when the temperature is about 70°F. (21°C.) and when humidity is high. The treatment, which is copper sulfate, is the same as for downy mildew, and since this has little or no effect in the eastern United States, black rot is most vicious there.

Anthracnose is the only important vine disease of European origin. It forms small polygonal stains on leaves, fruit, and shoots. It develops under the same conditions as black rot, and treatment is the same as for downy mildew.

Excoriose is exceedingly rare and attacks mainly branches. Treatment is to spray with a concentrated Bordeaux mixture.

Gray rot (*pourriture grise*) is caused by the same fungus which is the noble rot responsible for the sweet white wines of Sauternes, Germany, and Hungary—*Botrytis cinerea*. At an optimum temperature of about 77°F. (25°C.),

in moist weather, and often after other diseases have weakened the vine, gray rot forms, causing stains on the leaves and alterations within the fruit. Only under certain conditions—i.e., high humidity followed by hot weather—can it become *pourriture noble* (noble rot), and in most areas and under most conditions it is simply a hazard (*see* Botrytis cinerea).

White rot (*rot blanc*) forms on ripening berries, splitting them. Prompt treatment with copper or sodium bisulfite counters it.

Brenner is a browning between the veins on basal leaves, caused by a fungus. Early sulfate treatment will counter it, and it only occurs where winters are cold and dry—the conditions of life for the fungus. It is most prevalent in Germany.

"Apoplexy" (*Esca*) gets its name from the spectacular way the vine dies in the hottest part of the summer. It is a disease found in all plants in all parts of the world and is caused by a cryptogamic growth entering the wood and liberating an enzyme that kills the wood ahead of it. Sodium arsenite seems to combat it, although the reasons are as yet unknown.

Armillaria root-rot (*pourridié*) develops on shoots, trunk, and roots, with the result that the upper roots develop at the expense of the lower and more useful ones, which remain weak. It is especially virulent in sandy soils and is often found near streams. There is no effective treatment short of pulling up the vine, disinfecting the soil, and letting it rest until all traces of the causative fungi—*Armillaria mellea* and *Rosellinia necatrix* or *Dermatophora necatrix*—have been killed.

(d) *Animal parasites*

Animal parasites differ widely from one place to another, and those found in France will not necessarily be the same as those in South Africa or California, or even in Spain. However, some of the most important are:

Phylloxera, found the world over (with the exception of the vineyards of Chile and a few isolated sections elsewhere). A burrowing vine louse native to America, phylloxera caused the greatest single viticultural disaster since the Flood, necessitated significant changes in viticulture, and started off the Great Debate among connoisseurs: is post-phylloxera wine equal to that of pre-phylloxera days? Phylloxera and the questions and problems it raised are all discussed in the encyclopedic section of this book (*see* Phylloxera).

Grape berry moths (*Eudemis*, *Cochylis*, and *Polychrosis viteana*) produce larvae which feed on grape bunches, leaving those not completely ruined open to attack from other quarters. Treatment is by arsenic or D.D.T.

Meal-moth (*Pyralis*) feeds on foliage and fruit. Arsenic and D.D.T. are the most effective insecticides.

Altise, a type of beetle, feeds on leaves, reducing them to the aspect of very fine lace. Killed with insecticides.

Cochineal (*cochnilles*) bugs, of varying sorts, attack vines—and other plants—feeding on sap and weakening the vine until it dies. Various emulsions of oil, applied both during winter and summer, are used to combat them.

Acariose, a species of mite, feeds on fruit and foliage. Destroyed by copper sprays.

Erinose (*Phytoptus vitis* or *Eriophyes vitis*) is a microscopically small mite which causes blisters on leaves, grapes, and flower clusters. Most vines are resistant to it; and those that are not are treated with the same solution as is normally used against powdery mildew.

Eelworms (*anguillules*) are nematodes, or threadlike parasitic worms, which puncture roots and form nodosities resembling those of phylloxera. *Vitis vinifera* vines are particularly susceptible, but proper choice of root-stock on which the *Vitis vinifera* will be grafted obviates much of the danger. Sterilization of the soil by D.D. is necessary if the nematodes become too numerous. Next to phylloxera this is by far the most important animal parasite.

Japanese beetles are a considerable menace in the eastern United States but have not as yet appeared in California or in Europe. D.D.T. and arsenic compounds are used to fight them.

A VINEYARD CALENDAR

In addition to the combating of diseases, there is a considerable amount of work to be done in a vineyard. The details of the labor and the time chosen for each chore will vary according to the situation of the vineyard and the traditional practice of the area. The following calendar represents a part of the seasonal division of labor at the author's Château Prieuré-Lichine in the town of Margaux in the Bordeaux region of France. Usual practice elsewhere will be very similar to that represented here, although there are slight variations even among the other vineyards in Margaux.

Autumn. In late September or October the harvest, which lasts for more than two weeks, is followed by a general cleaning-up of ditches and the turn-around spaces in the vineyard. Autumn plowing aerates the soil and covers and protects the sensitive graft zone of the plants against the cold.

Winter. Pruning continues throughout the winter. Pickets and support wires are replaced and repaired as needed and the trunks and branches attached to them.

Spring. A second plowing, for the same reasons as before; and women follow with special rakes to draw out the soil from between the plants where it cannot be reached by the plow. During budding, excess buds are removed from the vines and "suckers" growing below the graft are removed. A third plowing is done and any necessary planting of vines (April–May).

Summer. Weeds are removed and in June shoots are attached with reeds to the supporting wires. The ends of the shoots are trimmed—to curb excessive growth—and the spraying treatments against vine maladies started (there may be anything from three to eight during the course of the summer). A fourth plowing does away with summer weeds and the grapes are left to ripen.

Autumn. When the grapes reach maturity, the harvest starts. After this the cycle recommences with the cleaning-up.

9 Wine: What it is, How it is Made

Wine comes from the fermentation of grape sugar. Dandelions, parsnips, and elderberries can be made to yield a kind of "homemade wine," but properly wine comes from grapes and nothing else—and it is the natural product of grapes which have been gathered, carted to the wine shed, pressed, and left in vats until the grape sugar has fermented into alcohol. The biochemical reactions of wine fermentation are due to yeast. These microscopic plants grow in the rich natural medium of the fresh juice and produce enzymes which convert the sugar, through an intricate series of biochemical reactions, to alcohol, carbon dioxide, and other fermentation products.

The result of such a haphazard process as natural fermentation would undoubtedly be a poor vinegar, although the first wine known to man must have been just that, the historic consequence of a felicitous accident. But fine wine comes from good management rather than good luck, and over the centuries men have been learning, first by trial and error and later by scientific experiment, how to improve the technique of making it. The discoveries of Louis Pasteur (1822-95) shed new light on the scientific theories of earlier wine-makers and provided a logical explanation for many time-honored practices, some of them dating from ancient Greece and Rome. The scientists did not, in fact, add very much that was new to the practical art of wine-making, but they did show contemporary vintners *why* certain things should be done and encouraged them to use the wisest methods. And they cut out the "lows" of the poor vintage years by teaching growers how to salvage a harvest that might have been a disaster fifty years before.

THE GRAPE

The basic ingredient of wine is clearly the grape. At perfect maturity it will have certain specific characteristics, although fruit from different vine varieties will differ considerably. Skins, pulp, and—with some exceptions—seeds all donate certain qualities to the wine.

Grape skins give mainly tannins and coloring matter. The color and tannin are generally conceded to be bound in the internal portions of the skin cells. Until these cells are killed it is very difficult to remove the pigments. Several methods are available to cause cell death and cell wall collapse—heat, alcohol, or physical disintegration. The second method is usually used, in which the juice and skins are allowed to ferment together until sufficient alcohol is produced to cause the cell walls to become permeable and the color to be released. The extraction of color rises to its peak after a few days, then diminishes;

but duration of vatting time is the most important factor in coloring wines. Rosés, which are separated quickly from the skins, are vatted for a shorter time than reds, while white wines are made from grapes that have been separated from the skins at the outset. Some minor grape varieties keep the pigment in the inner layers of the skin and yield tinted juice, while a very few have colored flesh and give deep red juice. The tannins also pass from skin and pulp to juice during vatting—the essential difference between red and white wines lies more in tannin content than in color.

In some cases the skin contributes another element—an odorant which may be either agreeable or disagreeable. In many *Vitis vinifera* varieties this odorant imparts a fresh light perfume—a whiff of the grape. This is most apparent when the wine is young but tends to disappear as it ages and bouquet develops. In some eastern American vines—notably *Vitis labrusca*—the odorant gives a "foxy" scent and taste, strange and sometimes disagreeable to those brought up on European wines, and the variety is not allowed in France. Many eastern American and Canadian wine-makers keep the vatting period of their wines as short as possible to prevent this characteristic developing.

The bulk of the grape is pulp, comprising from 80 to 90 per cent of its weight. While composition of a ripe grape varies, an approximate breakdown has been given by the French scientist Jules Ventre in his *Traité de vinification pratique et rationnelle*:

COMPOSITION OF A RIPE GRAPE

Constituent	Range (per cent)	Remarks
Water	70-80	
Extract	15-30	
Carbohydrates		
Sugars	12-27	Dextrose and levulose
Pectins	0.1-1.0	Includes gums, etc.
Pentosans	0.1-0.5	Also small amounts of pentoses
Inositol	traces	
Acids, total		
Malic	0.1-0.5	Varies with region, variety, and season
Tartaric	0.2-0.8	Mainly potassium bitartrate
Citric	traces	
Tannin	0.0-0.2	
Nitrogen	0.01-0.20	Mostly proteins, amino acids, ammonia
Ash	0.2-0.6	

The skin and pulp of the grape are the important elements for the wine-maker. Seeds contain tannin and an oily resinous material that would render the wine unpalatable if released, and so care must be taken not to break the seeds in the pressing.

Another element that may figure in the constitution of wine is the stalk or stem of the grape bunches. Rich in tannin, it will be included in the materials vatted in areas giving soft wines. In most cases, however, stems are taken out before grapes and juice go to the fermenting vats, removed either by hand in the very small European wineries or by a device called a stemmer or *égrappoir*. In white wines seeds are definitely obnoxious, because of an enzyme (oenoxidase) which may impart to the unfermented grape juice (must)—and later to the wine—a brown stain, like an apple bitten into and exposed to air. This stain may take as little as an hour to develop.

HARVEST

The time chosen for the harvest (or *vendange*) has an important effect upon the quality of the wine. In the fine wine districts, the grapes are tested for maturity with great care and are picked only at the latest possible moment in the cooler regions where it is extremely difficult to obtain maturity. In the warmer areas the grapes are harvested when the sugar and acid have the proper balance to make the desired wine. Once picked, they are destemmed immediately and run off into the fermenting vats. A delay, even of little more than twelve hours, could result in serious difficulties: (1) the elements that naturally form the bouquet might oxidize in the presence of too much air, giving the wine an unpleasant aroma; (2) undesirable or unwanted bacteria or tiny sugar-flies might begin to attack the sugar, spoiling the wine.

FERMENTATION

Alcoholic fermentation is defined by Yves Renouil and Paul de Traversay as the biochemical phenomenon which causes sugar to be transformed into ethyl alcohol and carbon dioxide.

Before the experiments of Pasteur (*c.* 1857) fermentation was largely a mystery, and only in comparatively recent times have the processes of fermentation been studied at all. The list opposite shows the elements present in must and wine.

(For an up-to-date summary of the approximate amounts of these materials present in wine *see* Ribéreau-Gayon and Peynaud's *Traité d'oenologie.*)

Most of the constituents found in the must remain to some degree in the wine. The sugars are greatly depleted and usually are found only in small amounts in dry wines. However, many new products appear during the fermentation and it is these that make wine different from solutions of water, acid, and alcohol.

In plain language, the process is essentially the changing of hexose sugars—dextrose and levulose—into alcohol

Must	Wine
Water	Water
Sugars:	Sugars:
glucose	glucose
fructose	fructose
pentoses	pentoses
sucrose	
	Alcohols:
	ethanol
	glycerol
	2, 3-butanediol
	acetoin
	isoamyl
	active amyl
	isobutyl
	n-propyl
	Esters:
	ethyl acetate
	ethyl succinate
	ethyl lactate
	other esters
Acids:	Acids:
tartaric	tartaric
malic	malic
citric	citric
ascorbic	succinic
	lactic
	acetic
Minerals:	Minerals:
sodium	sodium
potassium	potassium
calcium	calcium
iron	iron
phosphorus	phosphorus
sulfur	sulfur
	copper
Nitrogenous substances:	Nitrogenous substances:
ammonia	ammonia
amino acids	amino acids
proteins	proteins
	Acetaldehyde
Phenolic substances	Phenolic substances
Color pigments	Color pigments
Vitamins	Vitamins

and carbon dioxide gas through the action of yeasts. The classic chemical expression is that of Gay-Lussac:

$$C_6H_{12}O_6 \rightarrow 2C_2H_6O + 2CO_2$$

(hexose sugar)   (ethyl alcohol)   (carbon dioxide)

While this formula remains the basic statement of the beginning and end of fermentation, it is only 90 per cent valid—10 per cent of the sugar is fermented into by-products such as glycerin, butylene glycol, aldehydes, etc.—and is actually a simplified statement of a complicated series of chemical reactions. According to Amerine and Joslyn (*Table Wines: The Technology of their Production in Cali-*

fornia), the dextrose molecule alone passes through twelve stable intermediary stages before forming alcohol. Actually decarboxylation takes place all along the way and CO_2 is given off at several places. In addition there are thirty-odd organic and inorganic substances which must be present if the process is to succeed. The Amerine-Joslyn definition of fermentation is: "Essentially a process of a series of reversible inter- and intra-molecular oxidation reductions, phosphorylations, and an irreversible decarboxylation."

YEASTS

The yeasts are responsible for the fermentation of wine sugars into ethanol in wines. A number of microorganisms are capable of accomplishing fermentation, but not all are useful to the wine-maker. Yeasts differ according to genus, species, and variety, and the combination of varieties found in one place will never be exactly the same as that found in any other.

The yeast strain *Saccharomyces cereviseae* is the workhorse of the wine-maker. (It should be noted that yeasts are classified according to morphological and physiological traits. They are broadly divided into more than twenty genera of yeasts, which are subsequently subdivided into many thousands of individual species and strains with slightly different characteristics.) Occurring in numerous mutations and variants, this strain is valued for its ability to ferment sugar more completely than can any of the others. But it is not the only yeast to contribute to fermentation; others help to develop bouquet and flavor, and it is thought that the number and type of yeasts active in fermentation have a considerable effect upon the wine. Not even the finest yeasts will make a good wine of mediocre grapes, but in providing the last nuance of quality subsidiary yeasts may play an important part. In the traditional fine wine regions, the yeasts used are those trapped by the waxy "bloom" on the outside of ripe grapes and are thus completely natural to the region.

Centuries of wine-making in Western Europe have established such large populations of desirable wine yeasts that danger of "bad" fermentation from unwanted spoilage yeasts has been greatly reduced. In newer wine regions such as California and Australia, however, there is such a great risk of spoilage by undesirable native wild yeasts that sulfur dioxide is added immediately to inhibit them and the must is inoculated with a pure culture of a desirable yeast, often imported from European wine-growing districts.

Yeast variations contribute minor amounts of "nuances" of flavors, but the climate and the choice of varieties have greatly overriding effects. The final touch of glory on a superlative wine might be the slight increase in esters caused by an ester-forming wild yeast. However, the same wine could be ruined by the same yeast if it produced too much ester. Common sense and scientific knowledge demand that in order to obtain the greatest degree of continued success yeast cultures of pure yeast of known quality should be used. The study of these organisms is not so far advanced that laboratory-procured mixed cultures can always be used with complete assurance.

To the uninitiated the rapid wine fermentation appears to be a seething cauldron and may sound like a hive of angry bees. However, this type of fermentation is rapidly disappearing. As the technical skills and mechanical equipment become available, musts are being fermented at lower temperatures, sometimes in closed tanks, and the wines may take weeks instead of days to complete their fermentations.

The yeasts multiply very rapidly in fresh must, and the usual number of live yeast cells in one milliliter of must after initial yeast growth will be above 100 million. This amount will vary with temperature and the nutrient qualities of the must.

If no yeast culture is added, then sulfur dioxide in minor amounts can be added, since wild yeast is easily inhibited by the sulfur dioxide. But, if pure yeast cultures are employed then a little sulfur dioxide may be used to inhibit the growth of wild yeast. The pure culture can be acclimatized to the sulfur dioxide and will grow vigorously in its presence without delay.

Wine yeasts ferment effectively over a wide temperature range of 50° to 90°F. (10° to 32°C.). However, white wines are usually of the best quality if fermented at the lower temperatures. Red wines are improved in quality by fermenting on the skins at slightly warmer temperatures, i.e., 65° to 85°F. (18° to 29°C.). If the temperature exceeds 100°F. (38°C.), the yeast cells may be killed, resulting in a "stuck" fermentation. This situation is carefully avoided by competent wine-makers, since quality is greatly decreased, and the fermentation is very difficult to restart.

Wines with incomplete fermentations are a big problem in some areas. The reasons for this are not always apparent but can be due to the use of yeast with low tolerance for alcohol, low nutritional value of grapes, or too high or low a fermentation temperature.

RED WINES

For red wines, grapes are fermented with their skins for varying lengths of time, depending on the type of wine, the specific characteristics of the vintage, and the traditions of the region. In Bordeaux, the old style—followed decreasingly by a very few vineyards—was to leave the wines in the fermenting vats for from three to four weeks. The modern method is to vat from nine to fourteen days, with the result that the wines are lighter, more supple, and ready to drink sooner, since they do not pick up so much tannin from the skins. (But some of the younger growers in Bordeaux are returning to the longer vatting time of three weeks.) In Burgundy the practice is totally different. Since the end of the First World War, wines have been vatted for the shortest possible time, and five to seven days is considered optimum, eight to nine days extreme.

During fermentation, the pulp and mass of color- and tannin-imparting skins float on top of the juice, forming the *chapeau* or "hat"; in a large vat, this may attain a thickness of two or three feet. Various methods exist for diffusing the elements contained in the *chapeau* throughout the wine: (1) the *chapeau* may be punched down two or three times a day; (2) a sort of chimney may be inserted into the vat, through which the wine rises and spills over to water the "hat"; (3) a false top may be put on, forcing the *chapeau* down into the seething grape juice. Pumping the wine through a thick hose affixed to the lower spigot in the vat and up over the *chapeau* on top of the vat is the method most commonly used in France.

When fermentation is over, the wine is drained off and the *chapeau* falls to the bottom of the vat. This residue is then pressed for whatever wine it still contains. The first lots of the "press wine" may be kept separate or added to the free-run juice, and the later ones will be vinified separately into ordinary wine for the workers. When drained off after vatting, the wine is put into oak barrels to age.

Wine is aged in the wood to allow it to clarify and throw off its "gross lees," and to permit it to complete any remaining physical and biochemical changes—continuation of fermentation, precipitation of various compounds, etc.—before bottling. Many of the reactions that must take place need the presence of oxygen—which comes through the pores of the wood and through the bung—of which the wine will be deprived in bottle.

In his *Etudes sur le vin*, Pasteur observed that, without oxygen, wine could not mature or outlive its early sharpness. The wine, on ageing in a wooden cask or barrel, will usually change in alcohol concentration. If the humidity is low the water will evaporate at a greater rate than the alcohol, but if the humidity is high then the alcohol will evaporate more quickly than the water. The evaporation will slightly increase the concentration of the non-volatile constituents but not enough to be noticeable in most dry wines. But oxidation of the sulfurous salt ($SO_2 + O_2 \rightarrow SO_4$) will increase the wine's acidity, as will concentration of the liquid (10 to 15 per cent) and the action of bacteria.

Initial ageing and racking

For the first year of ageing of a red wine, it is kept in a lightly bunged barrel—one that can always be kept filled. In most *chais* (wine sheds or cellars), twice weekly in winter and three times in summer, a worker will "top" the barrel to compensate for evaporation. (This is called *ouillage*, ullage.) If the level were allowed to go down there would be an air space in which undesirable bacteria could set to work creating too much volatile acidity. As the months go by, the wine, losing some of the astringency of its tannin, becomes gradually less harsh to the taste—malolactic fermentation (*see below, under* Secondary Fermentation in Red or White Wines) mitigates the bitterness. The color, growing less vivid, will by the end of the year have achieved its deepest red; the hue may be affected by variations in the wine's sulfurous acid content.

During the early phase, the wine is in repose and any particles left over from fermentation slowly settle to the bottom; after this wine is "racked"—racking is the draining or pumping of wine from one barrel into a clean sterile one, leaving the lees or sediment behind.

The ideal time for racking wine is when the moon is full, the wind in the north, and the weather clear—science supports these superstitions. Such conditions imply high atmospheric pressure, conditions in which the wine will be at its least active. (When atmospheric pressure is low, the dissolved gases coming out of solution are apt to stir up the lighter lees, which will then be less liable to stay behind in the old barrel.) However, few vineyards of any size can afford the luxury of waiting on nature to this extent. The changes due to atmospheric variations are extremely small and can be neglected with little penalty. Since most of the harmful bacteria collect in the lees, racking helps to free the wine from infection. These lees are then gathered together and, by further settling, give a small amount of wine, one of inferior quality, usually for the staff. Racking is generally done about four times during the first year—and if the wine is a small one, it is bottled at the end of that year or is sold to be served straight from the barrel. A fine wine requires more care.

Quality wines, to be barrel-aged further, are kept in the barrels usually for another year and rarely longer. During this second year of ageing the barrels are tightly bunged and put on their sides so that the bung will stay wet and seal well. Oxidation still proceeds, as the barrels allow a certain amount of air-transfer through the wood. The wine may be racked twice or three times during this period. When it is removed from the barrel it is usually fined and filtered and may be stabilized by certain treatments, depending on the standard practices of the area. Oxidation is replaced by reduction, and the bouquet begins to develop. During the second year, changes in the wine are not so noticeable. It goes on deepening in color and flavor, deriving character and mellowness from contact with the wood. There will still be some precipitation.

The wine rests in this way for another year—longer in some cases—during which time the rackings will continue; just before being bottled or shipped the wine undergoes a "fining."

Fining

Fining, or *collage*, ensures that a wine will be perfectly clear and free from any suspended particles and also helps stabilize the wine against precipitation of certain protein, color, or polyphenolic material, depending on the type of fining material used. Colloidal matter is added to the cask; it coagulates, attracting to itself any minute particles which may be floating in the wine, and the whole mass settles to the bottom. The recommended colloidals for red wines are gelatine, white of egg, blood, etc. These organic agents perform a chemical action—or one which is at once chemical and physical. Inorganic clarifiers, such as Spanish clay, with its active ingredient kaolin, and the special clay of Wyoming (bentonite), are also used, especially in California. When the sediment has settled, the wine is racked once more and bottled or shipped in barrel.

For satisfactory results, clarification should be effected at least six months after vintage, when both fermentation and malolactic fermentation (*see below, under* Secondary Fermentation in Red or White Wines) are complete. At the same time, the wine must be inert, so that there shall be no agitation of the sediment; it follows that the wine must have been adequately racked. The task will be more easily accomplished on a day when the temperature is stable.

Where wines need sulfite treatment, this should be given the day before the fining. The added sulfurous acid temporarily inhibits the active microorganisms in the wine.

In some modern French plants outside the fine wine regions fining is an almost obsolete practice, and filtration has taken its place. Filters differ in type and design, but the object is to clear the wine with the least possible exposure to the air. In other large wineries centrifuges are used to clarify rapidly the wine which is to be sold as quickly as possible (within several months of fermentation), and the procedure in these plants is to rack and centrifuge the new wine several times, put it into a cold tank (39°F., 4°C.) for a week or two, centrifuge, filter, and bottle.

Filtration in itself does no harm to a wine if the necessary competent help and the proper filters are available. Filtering is used in most modern wineries after each racking or fining and certainly before bottling. As long as the filter is made of suitable materials and the pumps used are of a non-aerating type the wines profit by this treatment.

Fining is not replaced by filtration. Fining does more than clarify a wine; it also makes a wine of improved flavor and balance and one which will remain clear in the bottle for a longer period.

WHITE WINES

It should be made clear at the outset that the methods of making dry and sweet white wines are not the same. And special cases such as Sherry, which is a fortified wine, are discussed separately in this book and are not considered here (*see* Sherry).

White wines are sweet, semi-sweet, or dry, depending on how complete is the conversion of sugar into alcohol. Sweet wines result from the fact that sugar will not normally ferment after 15 to 16 per cent of alcohol has been generated. In practice dry wines are allowed to proceed until all the sugar is fully fermented.

Sweet white wines

Sweet wines are made by four methods: (1) by using grapes so rich in sugar that all will not be converted, (2) by stopping the fermentation artificially, usually by chemical means, (3) by racking several times during fermentation, and (4) by fortifying the wine either before or during fermentation with brandy or wine alcohol. (An alternative to (4) is the addition of sugar to wine, but the results are poor and the practice is generally frowned upon.)

(1) Grapes rich enough in sugar to stop fermentation are rare. They are found mainly in the Sauternes district of France, in the German Rhine and Mosel valleys, and in a part of Hungary. In all these cases, the grapes are left on the vine until the special mold *Botrytis cinerea*—known

to the French as *pourriture noble* and to the Germans as *Edelfäule*, both meaning "noble rot"—has formed, to cause certain chemical changes. These grapes, in fact, contain not an abnormal amount of sugar—merely less water. Another way of getting the same result is to dry grapes—as is done in sections of France, Italy, and Spain; but drying can never, as does *Botrytis*, proportionately decrease acidity as well as water.

(2) The commonest way of stopping fermentation artificially is by the addition of sulfur dioxide. This invaluable chemical has the ability to kill yeasts and microorganisms, but has a lesser and later effect upon the desirable ones than on the undesirable. If it is added in large quantities, the good as well as the bad microbes will be killed and fermentation will cease altogether, leaving any remaining sugar unresolved. The danger is that too much SO_2 might stay in the wine, and impart to it the unpleasant flavor and aroma of sulfur—a fault of many mediocre sweet and semi-sweet white wines. Alternative methods are pasteurization or severe and sterilizing filtration. In all cases the ferments will be killed or removed before all sugar has been resolved.

(3) Whatever the method used, the wines must be chilled to a temperature close to 32°F. (0°C.) or lower for the treatments to be effective.

(4) Alcohol added before or during fermentation prevents or stops it, and guards all or part of the unresolved sugar. Many of the world's sweet fortified wines are made on this principle. An alternative method is also used by wine-makers, both for red and white wines. Starting with a base of grape juice, the maker adds sugar and alcohol, a concoction which some people feel should not be allowed the name of wine.

Semi-sweet wines

Of increasing popularity, especially in California and in Germany, are white table wines with one to three per cent residual sugar. These wines are low in alcohol, and are most commonly made in California by fermenting the juice dry, then sweetening with concentrate of unfermented grape juice and stabilizing either chemically or by sterile filtration.

Pressing the grapes

The significant practice in the making of all white wines is the removal of the grape juice from the skins at the earliest possible moment: grapes are crushed and pressed immediately upon arrival at the vatting shed and the juice collected in tanks or barrels to ferment. Fine white wines are made only from the "free-run" juice and that of the earliest pressings, for as pressure increases, quality decreases.

Clarification of the must

To make the highest quality of white wine in California, it is important that the juice be as free as possible from suspended solids before fermentation. The traditional practice has been to allow the solids to settle overnight, then to rack the clear juice from the sediment. In recent years, centrifuges have become increasingly popular as the most satisfactory method of white must clarification.

Fermentation and racking

White wines are fermented either in large vats (bulk method) or small barrels of about 60 U.S. gallons (50 imp.) maximum (quality French method). The exception is Germany, where great wines are fermented in large barrels. The secret of a fine white wine is in a slow, controlled fermentation at a low temperature. Oxygen plays a less important role in the maturing in wood of white wines than it does with a red, nor is oxygen necessary for the improvement of white wine.

Vats are only partially filled, for the must expands and quantities of foam and grape particles rise to the top; if the containers were filled, the must would overflow and be wasted.

However, white wine fermentation that takes place in barrels is probably of a lesser quality than that in a 1,000-gallon tank if starting with the same juice. The *only* reason for the French using barrels in their vineyards is that formerly it was all they had. It has become a tradition and it allows some, but not much, temperature control. White wines to be at their best must be protected from oxygen, and a half-full 60-gallon barrel is poor protection.

When the first tumultuous fermentation has ended, the lees begin to settle, and afterward a light racking is done—a more thorough racking would remove active as well as spent yeasts, and any further fermentation that might remain could become "stuck." In many wine regions, this first racking is extremely light, for removal of all the particles would hinder the secondary or malolactic fermentation (*see* below) which diminishes acidity. In hot areas (parts of California, for example) the contrary is true, for in making their low-acid wines great care is taken to ensure that malolactic fermentation does not start.

In addition to the periodic light rackings, fermentation is also controlled by temperature. Most growers consider that a fermentation temperature of 60° to 70°F. (16° to 21°C.) is optimum, but some prefer an even lower one. A slow, cool fermentation extracts the fruity quality of the grape and results in a wine with greater finesse than is possible if fermentation is fast.

In warmer countries where the addition of acid is permitted, malolactic fermentation is sometimes encouraged, and the wine acidity is adjusted with tartaric or citric acid to an optimum amount after the malolactic fermentation is completed. It is desirable that such fermentation be controlled, since it can occur many times during the initial fermentation or within a month afterward. There is no sure way to control it, but judicious use of sulfur dioxide and the raising of the acidity, as well as thorough rackings and early clarifications, do help. The fermentation at lower temperatures will also reduce the likelihood of a malolactic fermentation.

The fermentation temperature is usually kept as low as the vineyard can manage with its facilities. Some well-equipped California wineries ferment all their white wines at less than 60°F. (16°C.) and at an average temperature of slightly above 50°F. (10°C.). Racking can be used to reduce fermentation rates, but the danger of "sticking" the wine is always present.

Initial ageing of white wines

White wines are conserved at lower temperatures than reds. Tartrates and other dissolved substances—more noticeable in white wine than in red—precipitate best at low temperatures, and nowadays most people like their wines perfectly clear. In spite of every precaution, suspended particles of potassium bitartrate sometimes show, forming white flecks like snow and, though generally tasteless, detract from the appearance of the wine. If the wine is kept at the proper low temperature and is not bottled too early—before the particles have had a chance to precipitate—these flecks will not generally appear.

Fining and bottling

Dry white wines are bottled young—younger than sweet white wines. A year or eighteen months in the barrel often suffices for clarification, and the wines are fined, racked, and either bottled or sold in barrel. Most fine white wines of California, with the exception of Chardonnay, remain in stainless steel tanks blanketed with carbon dioxide to prevent oxidation and are stabilized and bottled as soon as possible. The fining of white wines, like the fining of reds, should be done only if taste and chemical or physical tests deem it necessary. The most common problem is the formation of a white protein cloud, a situation which is best prevented by fining with bentonite.

Unless they are kept in very new wood and have picked up a lot of wood tannin, the use of organic fining agents is questionable. There are also some new agents in use—nylon powder and very occasionally P.V.P. (polyvinylpyrrolidone). These substances help stabilize the wines against changes to brown color. Sweet white wines are now often fined with bentonite, which removes protein matter from them, helping to establish proper stabilization. Bottle-ageing is similar in principle for white and red wines: less time for dry, longer for sweet wines. In general it is the fresh, early scent of the grape that is appreciated in dry white wines, while the sweet varieties develop bouquet after several years in glass and keep far longer; some of the great ones have been known to hold their excellence for a half-century or even longer.

SECONDARY FERMENTATION IN RED OR WHITE WINES

Many wines undergo a secondary fermentation sometimes concurrent with, often after, the first. Not a sugar-alcohol process, it is called malolactic fermentation and is caused by bacteria attacking the malic acid and turning it into much weaker lactic acid and carbon dioxide gas. It is *not* responsible for Champagne and other sparkling wines. These are produced by a second sugar-alcohol fermentation, generally induced artificially, either in the bottle—Champagne process—or in enclosed tanks or vats—Charmat process (*see* Champagne *and* Charmat).

If secondary fermentation occurs before bottling, the

gas will escape and the result will simply be a wine with reduced acid strength. An extra racking will often be a good thing. In the normally high-acid wines of Switzerland, malolactic fermentation is considered of enormous importance; and the Bordeaux oenologists hold it responsible for much of the excellence of the wines of the region, both red and white. In the cases of red wines, it is a good thing to have the secondary fermentation completed soon after the first. If this does not occur, it may take place six or nine months—or even a year or more—later. There is no known process for bringing about this biological de-acidification at a given time. Once begun, however, it can be helped by the use of big butts: the reason is that a large volume of liquid will retain the heat generated by the alcoholic fermentation longer than will a small quantity. If secondary fermentation starts or continues in the bottle, the gas is confined and the wine becomes turgid and gassy, frequently unpleasant. If the bubble is a slight one, it can sometimes be eliminated by airing the wine—either by swirling it around in the glass or by pouring it from one glass to another; but if such a wine is served in a restaurant, it is best to send it back.

Recently, scientific knowledge has increased to the point where specific malolactic bacteria can be cultured in the laboratory and added to must prior to fermentation, thus inducing the malolactic fermentation to proceed along with the primary fermentation. Occasionally a bad strain of malolactic bacteria would occur in the wine, spoiling it by off-aromas and -flavor. This can sometimes be avoided now by the controlled use of a known strain—which also allows the wines to be brought to maturity sooner and avoids the occurrence of secondary fermentation in the bottles.

AGEING OF WINES

Not all wines improve with age. Some—notably the dry whites—are at their best when young. Most fine wines improve, both in barrel and in bottle, but eventually pass their prime, decline, and finally fall apart altogether. What happens to wine while it is ageing? Salts precipitate, acidity decreases, and alcohols, acids, and other components are transformed into innumerable complex compounds—esters, aldehydes, acetals, and the like. Professor E. Peynaud of the Bordeaux Oenological Station recognizes two sharp divisions in wines: (1) those such as Port, Sherry, and the sweet fortified wines in general, whose excellence comes from a process of oxidation and the formation of aldehydes, notably acetaldehyde (other oxidative changes occurring at the same time, as well as the components picked up from the barrels, give this wine an aged character); and (2) those wines which can only develop their best characteristics in the absence of air. In the case of wines of the second category, the characteristics come from the grape used; for example, Bordeaux mainly comes from the Cabernet grape, and Burgundy from the Pinot Noir. Bouquet is an important product of ageing, and this can only come about, in wines of the second category, when there is an odorant supplied by the grape, when the wine is effectively sealed from air, and when good reducing conditions are provided.

Barrel-ageing is important in hastening the clarification and stability of wines and in imparting certain characteristics donated by wood—for, once bottled, the wines can no longer be treated and cared for—but the amount of oxygen that enters the wine, and its importance, is disputed and perhaps overestimated. Bottle-ageing of fine wines is very incompletely understood, but the scientists differ from the wine-makers, maintaining that the amount of air which enters a bottle through the cork plays a very small role, if any. Professor J. Ribéreau-Gayon, of the University of Bordeaux, states in the impressive *Traité d'oenologie*: "The quantity of oxygen that normally penetrates into bottles is infinitesimal if not nil; it is improbable that an important role could be attributed to it." He supports his statement with the observation that wines age as well in hermetically sealed tubes as in corked bottles. With these matters so incompletely understood, it seems unlikely that artificial ageing, a process which has received a good deal of attention, will very soon become practical.

What is generally overlooked by the non-scientist is that there is some air in the wine when it is bottled, and this can play a role in the changes which occur. Actually 8 to 10 milliliters of air are present in the average bottle of wine. If the cork is kept wet little or no air transfer would be expected to occur, but the air already there would cause certain variations to take place. Extreme care should be taken to reduce the amount of air at the time of bottling so that bottle oxidative changes are at a minimum and reductive changes can proceed. Bottle age bouquets can be developed by artificial treatments and do show some promise for certain common wines.

EXCEPTIONAL PRACTICES

The wine-maker must always reckon with the possibility of unfavorable weather during the growing season of the vine and thus with the prospect of immature or badly matured grapes. In earlier times this spelled disaster, but today there are ways of bringing the wine up to standard. Some of these methods are:

Chaptalisation. Named after its French inventor, Dr. Chaptal, who proposed the idea around the turn of the nineteenth century, it is also called in Germany *Gallization* (after Dr. Gall) and *Anreicherung* (meaning "enrichment"). *Chaptalisation* is the addition of sugar to sugar-deficient musts—but never wines—to make certain that the wine will have an alcoholic content commensurate with its other qualities. Regular sugar (sucrose) hydrolyzes into hexose sugars (dextrose and levulose) when added to the must and ferments normally. Used discreetly, *chaptalisation* may bring the alcohol into better balance with the other constituents of the wine; but abused—as it unfortunately is in some areas—it results in "wine" being made from grape skins, sugar, and acids. *Chaptalisation* is widespread in Germany and Burgundy, and may sometimes be found as far to the south as Bordeaux—but only when specifically authorized by the government. In Burgundy, where unfortunately it is a yearly practice, some of the great wines are now allowed to be overabundantly sugared. In regions where the sun is hot enough to generate the requisite amount of sugar in the grapes, it is not necessary. In their *Dictionnaire du vin*, Messieurs Renouil and de Traversay say that *chaptalisation* could with advantage increase the alcoholic content, since the fermentation of sugar gives rise not only to alcohol but also to by-products (such as glycerol, succinic acid, etc.) which exert a considerable influence on the flavor of wine. The operation also decreases the excessive tartness of certain wines by precipitating the cream of tartar.

Chaptalisation is not legal in California.

De-acidification. When the weather is really bad, the grapes may be too high in acid as well as deficient in sugar. The common way of handling this is to blend the wine with low-acid wines, a perfectly proper procedure providing the wine is not then sold under an *appellation*, or place-name, to which it has no right. A rarer method is to add calcium carbonate. This reacts with the acids and mainly precipitates out, but calls for very careful handling and usually gives poor results.

Acidification. After an exceptionally hot summer, grapes may have too little acid, resulting in a flat and tasteless wine. This may be corrected quite legally by adding to the must either a small amount of tartaric acid (which does not improve the quality of fine wines) or the less mature—and therefore more acid—grapes from a late flowering of the vine; or by blending with high-acid wines.

De-coloration. If a white wine is tinged with red—or a pink wine is too deeply colored—fining with charcoal will remove as much of the color as desired. Unfortunately it also removes any character the wine might otherwise have had.

Concentration. Sugar deficiency may be corrected by adding concentrated must, from which some of the water has been boiled off. Alcohol-deficient wines may similarly be treated by adding wine from which some of the water has been removed by freezing. In either case, the sugar or alcohol of the must or wine will be proportionately raised. The drawbacks are that in some countries these practices are illegal, and while they increase sugar or alcohol, they also increase acidity, sometimes to the detriment of the wine.

Pasteurization. The applicability of the method of sterilization by heat is still disputed. Many experts feel that heat kills wine, although the Bordeaux oenologist Professor Ribéreau-Gayon says that this is true only under certain conditions. Pasteurization, or heating wine quickly up to a temperature of 130°F. (54°C.), effectively sterilizes wines in barrel, destroying all bacteria—but it is impracticable, if not impossible, for wines already bottled. It is also a cumbersome procedure, partly because the mechanics of it have never been satisfactorily worked out. In certain circumstances it can be very useful; but in the fine wine districts it is best avoided, since wines so treated tend to become inert. However, in sweet or semi-sweet table wines of many countries it is routine to pasteurize before bottling or during bottling. The common wines are

heated to 180°F. (82°C.) for one minute or may be bottled at 130° to 140°F. (54° to 60°C.) and then cooked slowly. Some large wineries selling competitive wines have the systems so perfected that not one bottle will spoil from yeast or bacteria out of the thousands bottled every hour unless a defective closure or something unforeseen occurs. The mechanical conditions for wine pasteurization are well understood. Recent research shows that the more rapidly the wine is heated and cooled, the less it is decreased in quality. Very rapid-flash pasteurizers are being developed, but the process is costly and still plagued with the problem of recontamination of the wine during bottling.

THE COMPOSITION OF WINE

Wine is an extraordinarily intricate and inconstant complex of different ingredients. It is because of its ability to change in many ways from the time the grape is picked until the wine is poured that wine is said to "live"—as indeed it does.

Alcohol

The most obvious, but not the most important element of wine, alcohol, derived from the fermentation of the non-alcoholic grape juice, comprises from 7 to 24 per cent of the contents by volume; most is ethyl alcohol, but some—less than 0.15 per cent—is methyl alcohol, present in wine in quantities varying between 36 and 350 milligrams per liter. In addition there are varying amounts of such higher alcohols as amyl, isoamyl, *n*-propyl, isopropyl, *n*-butyl, *sec*-butyl, isobutyl, *a*-terpineol, and perhaps *n*-hexyl, *n*-heptyl, and *sec*-nonyl.

Ethyl alcohol (*ethanol*). The degree of this essential component is decided by the amount of sugar in the must. It varies, according to the maturity of the grape, between 7 and 16 per cent of the volume (higher when extra alcohol has been added). In fine wines, the amount, which influences both quality and longevity, is of vital importance. As the acids in the wine gradually combine with the alcohol to produce esters, so the elements that compose the bouquet develop. The antiseptic properties of the ethyl alcohol help to inhibit the growth of the various bacteria and yeast disorders to which wine is prone.

Acids

Acids give freshness and tartness to the taste. An acid-deficient wine is flat; a too-acid wine undrinkable. The organic acids (malic, tartaric, etc.) are those which impart the characteristic flavor, sharp on the tip of the tongue—a sensation caused by the presence of hydrogen ions. A wine vinified from unripe grapes will have a total acidity and a low pH. In brandy, a high degree of acid is a fault, although a moderate content gives it body.

Acidity, by preventing or slowing down the development of such harmful bacteria as the mannitic (which turns wine sour), helps to preserve the wine. It affects also stability and color—the higher the acid content, the more brilliant the hue. The total acidity of a young healthy wine averages four to five grams a liter, expressed in sul-

BASIC RULES OF WINE-MAKING

Recommendations to follow

1. Cleanliness is essential. See that all equipment coming into contact with the wine is kept clean. Avoid iron utensils or copper-containing metals—certain plastics, glass, and stainless steel or wood are recommended for tools, tanks, pipes, etc., where the wine is contacted.

2. Gather the grapes in as sound a condition as the year permits, and in a suitable state of ripeness.
Bring them whole to the presses, and free of soil.

3. Pressing must be done rapidly for white musts, nor should the grapes be overpressed.
Avoid oxidation of the musts by maceration of the crushed grapes in the open air.

4. Cleanse the must—and so the wine—by the addition of a small but adequate dose of sulfurous acid. Remove the suspended solids of a white must before fermentation, either by settling, filtration, or centrifugation.

5. Control fermentations at suitable temperatures, as low as possible but not too low, otherwise the fermentation may be arrested.
With red wines, time the fermentation periods very carefully.
Beware of deterioration which may be caused by the exposure to air of the top crusts.

6. As soon as fermentation is complete, the wines should be ullaged (i.e., the barrels topped up). Never leave a broached wine in contact with air.

7. Red, rosé, and dry white wines must not retain the slightest trace of reducing sugars. (Yet in many places small amounts of residual sugars in dry white and rosé wine are tolerated or even encouraged—without excessive alcohol. It is quite possible to preserve such wines successfully by use of sorbic acid and sulfur dioxide. Many German wines have residual sugar, and this is thought of as a necessity for quality in some instances.)

Faults to be avoided

Unpleasant taste or smell.
Metallic casse (or breakdown) of the wine; deterioration, and microbial cloudiness.

Unpleasant taste of mold.
Turning sour (for mildewed wines).
Excessive, or insufficient, acidity.
Depreciation and microbial cloud, breakdown due to metal content.

Lack of freshness and fruitiness.
Excessive tannin. Colloidal cloud.
Excess of proteids.
Oxidasic breakdown, molding.

Deterioration and microbial cloud, oxidasic casse.
Excessive hydrogen sulfide formation, poor clarification.

Excess of reducing sugars, moldiness.
Scouring or excessive volatile acidity and ropiness (if the temperature is too high).

Fungoid growth, deteriorations, and microbial cloud.

Lactic acid moldiness.
Mannitic fermentation.

---

furic acid. This will be less, by about 25 per cent, than the acidity of the original must.

Three of the major acids in wine are naturally present in the grape (tartaric, malic, and citric; it is interesting that the grape is the only temperate fruit in which there is tartaric acid), and the rest are the result of fermentation. Most of the acid content is tartaric, and about 10 to 40 per cent is malic, so called because it is present in apples and supposedly responsible for the "fruitiness" of many wines. Citric acid is found in very small amounts, as are succinic, lactic, and acetic acids; there are minute traces of butyric, capric, caproic, caprylic, formic, lauric, propionic, and, in sparkling wines, carbonic. Acetic, butyric, carbonic, formic, and propionic acids are the "volatile" acids, and chemists consider volatile acidity in wines to be

of the same order as temperature in man: it is always present, but when it deviates from normal there is something wrong. The others are the "fixed" organic acids. The sum of the fixed and volatile acidity makes up the "total acidity" of the wine; that is, the titratable acidity expressed usually as grams of tartaric acid.

Tartaric acid. This is the most important of the fixed acids in wine and the one particularly associated with the grape; it is rarely found elsewhere in nature. The quantity of the acid present in the grape is decreased by respiratory combustion, during the periods of high temperature. The addition of tartaric acid to the must is allowed in cases of low acidity. At too high a concentration, however, it will impart to the wine a certain astringency, even harshness.

Recommendations to follow	*Faults to be avoided*
The high alcoholic content of the great sweet and mellow white wines helps to preserve them without much sulfur dioxide.	Secondary fermentation.
Conversely, the lesser white wines, sweet and mellow, are difficult to keep.	
To avoid giving the wines large doses of sulfur dioxide they may be sterilized before bottling.	Development and depositing of yeast.
8. Carry out rackings at the right time, and sufficiently often, either with aeration or away from air, as the case may be. Do not forget that malolactic fermentation to a certain extent may either be achieved or avoided according to the amount of acidity which the wine should retain. This operation calls, however, for constant care, particularly as regards white wines. Other factors besides acidity determine whether or not there will be malolactic fermentation. Fornachon points out that it depends on nutrients, aeration, pH, and sulfur dioxide. It is a very complex system and interactions exist, making it impossible to predict with assurance if a wine will naturally undergo a malolactic fermentation.	Excess or deficiency of acidity. Ropiness.
Filtering will assist the maturing of all wines.	
9. The wine will attain physical maturity during the first winter by means of precipitation of the various tartars. The ordinary wines, drunk a few months after the harvest, may be treated with metatartaric acid or, preferably, they may be refrigerated. Filtering will assist the maturing of all wines.	Crystalline precipitations. Colloidal cloudiness.
Clarification, without excessive use of fining agents, will help the maturation of wines.	Over-fining, making a thin wine lacking in character. Coagulation of the proteins.
10. The blending of wines can only be recommended when it is possible to marry qualities which complement each other. It is better to lower the classification of an inferior wine if these inferior qualities can only be diluted, rather than improve it by blending in a better wine and giving it the somewhat misleading classification of the superior component.	No character.
11. In order that the maker may guarantee his product, it is essential for the wine to be delivered in bottle to the consumer, and bearing a label with the bottler's guarantee, as is the case with mineral waters, soda-waters, beers, etc.	Deterioration and microbial cloud. Poor keeping qualities. A loss of authenticity.
12. Put the bottles up for sale in such a way as not to mislead the consumer.	Reprehensible labeling. (Regulatory action by the enforcing agency of the country.)

Malic acid. The principal acid in many fruits and vegetables. The quantity present in grapes at the *vendange* is of considerable importance in wine-making. While the fruit is ripening, cellular respiration causes the malic acid concentration to be lowered. Under the influence of bacteria, it undergoes lactic fermentation. The tartness of wines made after a cold summer and the sharpness of young wines are due to the malic acid which determines almost by itself the state of ripeness of the grape.

Citric acid. This occurs in all varieties of grapes, both ripe and unripe—and to a greater extent where *Botrytis cinerea* has developed. Wines made from grapes in a state of noble rot may contain as much as a gram of citric acid. Normal quantities (usually increasing somewhat during fermentation) vary between 1 and 10 grams and tend to be much lower in red wines than in white. The bacteria which cause malolactic fermentation may ferment the citric acid and produce volatile acidity. Wines vary in the amount of citric acid naturally present, and this may affect a casse formation. Amounts which may be added to wine vary from country to country.

Carbonic acid. Carbonic acid is formed by the reaction of carbon dioxide and water ($CO_2 + H_2O = H_2CO_3$). The amount of carbonic acid in wine depends upon the amount of dissolved carbon dioxide, which in still wines is usually less than 0.5 grams per liter. Carbon dioxide is produced during the decomposition of sugar in alcoholic fermentation, by the decomposition of malic acid in malolactic fermentation, and during respiration of any yeast or bacteria in the wine. It is the continual production of carbon dioxide during fermentation that limits the amount of oxygen available in the wine, inhibiting acetic acid-forming bacteria and causing the yeast to produce ethanol rather than to completely break down the sugar to carbon dioxide and water. Carbon dioxide is purposefully trapped in the bottle for Champagne production by adding extra fermentable sugar to a dry wine and sealing the bottle.

Sulfurous Acid. Sulfur dioxide (SO_2) gas, when added to wine, reacts with water to form sulfurous acid H_2SO_3. A chemical equilibrium is established between the sulfur dioxide and its hydrated forms as follows:

$$SO_2 + H_2O \leftrightarrow H_2SO_3 \leftrightarrow H^+ + HSO_3^- \leftrightarrow 2H^+ + SO_3^=$$

Sulfur dioxide is used for preserving casks of wood and, being antiseptic, is carefully added to wine, which it protects against deterioration. Sulfurous acid and sorbic acid are at present the only two antiseptics allowed under French law. The former, an anti-oxidant, is also a reducing agent.

Among the useful properties of this acid are its antiseptic qualities, effective against those microbial diseases caused by harmful yeasts and bacteria. Sulfite treatment is used to subdue too violent fermentation. Sulfurous acid has its drawbacks, however. Because it is solvent in contact with various metals and minerals, it is apt to cause ferric casse, both blue and white, and, in white wines, cuprous casse (*see* Wine Disorders *below*). It is likewise well known that wines which have been overdosed with it retain a disagreeable smell and taste of sulfur.

In the French vineyards, when a wine is to receive sulfite treatment, it (or the must) is poured into a cask in which a stick of sulfur has been burned. This old-fashioned method is not precise, since unburned sulfur is liable to remain at the bottom of the barrel and sulfur dioxide may escape through the bung. The theory that 10 grams of sulfur will produce, when burned, 20 grams of sulfur dioxide is incorrect—under favorable conditions the sulfur may make 15 grams, which will only be completely effective if put in through the bung of the cask. Barely half a stick (about 20 grams) can be burned in a cask of 225 liters: it can be estimated therefore that the sulfur burned introduces into the wine the equivalent of its own weight in sulfur dioxide.

An ordinary water solution of sulfur dioxide is saturated at about five to six per cent sulfur dioxide and cannot be further concentrated. Of course, a solution of sodium sulfite or sodium bisulfite or metabisulfite can be made more concentrated. The five to six per cent solution is extremely corrosive to metal.

Bisulfites or metabisulfites should be used in the form of pellets or crystals. In all wine-making countries, sulfite treatment is restricted in terms of free and total sulfurous acid content. Total sulfur dioxide is the aggregate of free sulfur dioxide and compound sulfur dioxide. The amount of free sulfur dioxide decreases steadily to an equilibrium level because part is combined with aldehydes, color pigments, sugars, etc. Some sulfur dioxide is oxidized to the sulfate by the oxygen in solution. The amount of free

TABLE OF WINE ACIDS

(according to J. Ribéreau-Gayon and E. Peynaud)

Name of Wine Acid	Remarks
Fixed organic	
Tartaric	
Malic	These acids come from the grape.
Citric	
Succinic	
Lactic	Produced by fermentation.
Gluconic	
Glycuronic	Eudemized grapes.
Dioxymalic	
Dioxytartaric	Oxidation of the tartaric acid.
Glycolic	
Glyoxylic	
Glyceric	Not yet studied thoroughly in wines.
Saccharic	
High fatty	
Volatile organic	
Formic	Acetic alone is always present in
Acetic	wine.
Mineral	
Hydrochloric	
Sulfuric	
Sulfurous	Authorized antiseptics.
Orthophosphoric	
Carbonic	Produced by fermentation.

Acidification Procedures Permitted in Various Wine-producing Countries

Algeria: Musts: tartaric acid, without restriction (during fermentation); citric acid: 50 grams per hectoliter maximum (after fermentation). Wines: tartaric acid forbidden; citric acid: maximum 50 grams per hectoliter, providing the original must has not been acidified at this dose.

Austria: Forbidden in principle to increase the acid content.

West
Germany: Same as Austria.

Bulgaria: Tartaric and citric acid only for the sparkling wines.

Spain: Pure citric acid, maximum 1 gram per liter; tartaric acid only in musts or wines of low acidity, but not for other usages.

U.S.: Tartaric, malic, and citric acids—within specified limits.

France: Musts: tartaric acid. Wines: citric acid, maximum 0.50 gram per liter.

sulfur is proportionate to the amount of the total once an equilibrium is reached with the combining materials (generally about two weeks). After this there is a slow loss by chemical change but the relative amounts of the total and free sulfur dioxide stay the same.

Usually sulfur dioxide is added at the time of bottling as a protection against oxidation and to combine an inactivated acetaldehyde. Over a period of years the total sulfur dioxide will become greatly reduced. However, if the wine is well made and in the bottle, little will happen because of this loss.

Volatile acidity. The primary source of volatile acidity in most wines is acetic acid. However, other acids—such as formic or sulfurous acid, or any other steam-distillable acid—do contribute. The actual smell of "acetic" wine can be attributed to ethyl acetate in many instances. The presence of these chemicals is normal, and only when they are in excess do they become objectionable. In France, volatile acidity in wine is expressed in sulfuric acid, averaging between 0.3 and 0.7 grams per liter. When this figure is exceeded, the wine is affected. In France there have from time to time been strict regulations about the degree permissible in wine to be sold: the current law lays down that a wine is spoiled at 0.9 gram per liter at the wholesale, and 1.2 grams at the retail stages. In California, the legal limits for volatile acidity are 1.10 grams per liter for white wines and 1.20 grams per liter for red wines, expressed as acetic acid.

Sugar and glycerin

In a sugar-alcohol fermentation, the most important by-product is glycerin (or glycerol). This donates some of the sweetness and smoothness to a wine and was once erroneously thought to be responsible for the "legs"—the streaks that run down the side of a glass in which wine has been swirled. (Legs are now known to be a result of ethyl alcohol.) Compounds related to glycerin and found in very small quantities are 2,3-butylene glycol, acetylmethylcarbinol, and diacetyl. Sugar will also be present—even in a completely "dry" wine. (Less than 0.2 per cent sugar is about standard for dry wines; this amount cannot be tasted, nor will it ferment further.) Some of this is hexose sugar—dextrose and levulose, of which levulose is the sweeter—and some are pentose sugars, mostly arabinose and some xylose. There are also related compounds such as rhamnose, pentosans, methyl pentosans, dihydroxymaleic acid, and pectins.

Aldehydes and esters

Aldehydes are a halfway step between alcohols and acids and are formed by the oxidation of alcohols; esters are the result of a combination of acid and alcohol. Both play an important part in wines, particularly in bouquet.

The most important wine aldehyde is acetaldehyde. In addition there are traces of formaldehyde, propionaldehyde, cinnamaldehyde, cenanthaldehyde, vanillin, methyl ethylketone, acetal, capraldehyde, and benzaldehyde—and probably furfural and acrolein, although these two have not been sufficiently established for chemists to be quite sure. In certain sweet wines—those that have been heated, such as Madeira and some imitation "sherries"—there is also a trace of hydroxymethylfurfural.

Esters fall into two groups: (1) volatile odoriferous esters usually formed from acetic acid, and (2) the neutral and acid esters of the fixed acids, mostly tartaric and malic. Ethyl acetate is by far the most prevalent ester, but others, formed from all the acids mentioned above plus those of valeric, caproic, and pelargonic acids, will be present to a greater or lesser degree.

Dry extract and ash

When wine is placed in a test tube and carefully heated, the liquid boils away, leaving salts which, when heated to high temperatures, form the ash, useful to the wine chemist in determining what is present and in what quantity. The salts include chlorides, phosphates, silicates, and sulfates; and the minerals include potassium, calcium, magnesium, sodium, iron, copper, and small amounts of boron, iodine, manganese, molybdenum, titanium, vanadium, and zinc. The type and amount of minerals present will largely depend upon the soil in which the grapes were grown, what minerals nourished the vine, and the elements which came into contact with the wine.

Nitrogen and vitamins

The most important nitrogen by-products are the amino acids, some of which disappear during fermentation or are used by yeasts to form the higher alcohols. Other amino acids are formed by the yeast. Common amino acids are alanine, arginine, aspartic acid, cystine, glutamic acid, glycine, histidine, isoleucine, leucine, lysine, methionine, proline, serine, threonine, tryptophan, tyrosine, valine, and phenylalanine. Vitamins include vitamin A, ascorbic acid, thiamin, riboflavin, pyridoxin, nicotinic acid, pantothenic acid, *p*-aminobenzoic acid, biotin, and inositol.

Phenolic substances and tannin

The phenolic constituents of wine are a complex group which include the tannins, anthocyanins, catechins, and other flavonoids, cinnamates, etc. Tannins occur primarily in the seeds and stems and contribute an astringent flavor to wines. They have antiseptic qualities, helping to inhibit noxious bacteria, and serve as anti-oxidants to protect the wine during ageing. The longer a red wine has fermented on the skins, the greater will be the tannin content and consequently the longer the wine will be able to age. During ageing, the tannins undergo complicated oxidative reactions and polymerizations with aldehydes, pigments, and other constituents, so that the harshness of the young wine is gradually reduced as the tannins combine and precipitate. These changes contribute greatly to the character and appearance of a fine aged wine.

The anthocyanins are the primary red pigments of grapes, located in the cells of the skin and released during fermentation as the skins are degraded by alcohol. Grape varieties differ as to quantity and types of anthocyanins, and therefore as to the stability of the pigment in the finished wine. During ageing, the anthocyanins complex and precipitate out, so that a very old wine may have a sediment of pigment at the bottom of the bottle and an orange-brown color, due mainly to the remaining tannin complexes.

White wines generally contain less than 350 milligrams per liter of phenols expressed as gallic acid, while red wines may contain as much as 3,000 milligrams per liter.

WINE DISORDERS

Young wine is a living thing in the sense that biochemical processes are taking place continuously. It is subject to diseases and disorders of various sorts. These may be divided into maladies caused by biological disorders and those caused by the physical environment.

(1) *Biological disorders*

Bacterial or yeast spoilage can take place under either aerobic or anaerobic conditions. In many cases it is extremely difficult to pinpoint the organism causing the trouble; the same bacteria may cause apparently different diseases under different conditions. Over the years the nomenclature of the various diseases also changes. The most common bacteria are the lactobacilli, which will ferment malic acid and also citric acid under certain conditions. These are only dangerous if the strain metabolizes undesired substances or gives off odor or flavors, or the wine is so low in acid as to become flat and unbalanced after the secondary fermentation. Some widely recognized diseases are:

Flowers of wine (flor). Flowers of wine is the name given to a particular film-forming yeast which will grow on the surface of young wines if they are exposed to air. This is not a disorder when used to produce the distinctive character of Spanish Sherry or the *vin jaune* of the French Jura. This yeast growth generally has to be encouraged and can easily be prevented by keeping the wine container full.

Mycoderma (fleur). This is a fairly harmless microbe which grows rapidly on the surface of young wine, forming a film. It is often mistaken for *flor* but under microscopic observation the difference is easily determined. This disease can also be prevented by limiting the exposure of the wine surface to the air.

Acescence (piqûre) or *acetification*. Like *fleur*, acescence is marked by the formation of a film on the surface of the wine—but of a translucent gray rather than white in many instances. *Acetobacter* causes a rapid decrease in alcohol and sugar and produces varying amounts of acetic acid and ethyl acetate which give the wine the disagreeable vinegary taste, thus ruining it. Again, this disease can be easily prevented if the wine is not subject to excess aeration by exposure of the partly full container to air and by good cellar practice.

Tourne. The wine becomes gassy—with a thoroughly disagreeable aroma and taste resembling that of acescence—hazes, and loses its color. *Tourne* is caused by bacteria attacking tartaric acid and chemically shows a loss of tartrates, an increase of volatile acidity, and a decrease of fixed acidity and acid strength (as shown by a rise in pH value).

Graisse (fatty degeneration). The wine becomes turgid and viscous and flows like oil. There is a decrease in sugar, an increase both in total and volatile acidity, and a gummy deposit. The disease is often found in Champagne, where it affects the *rebêche* (the low-quality, last-run-of-the-wine press), which is vinified and given to the workers.

Amertume (bitterness). The wine throws a deposit and becomes bitter and very acid. It is caused by bacteria attacking glycerin and chemically shows a decrease in glycerin and an increase in total and volatile acidity.

These last three diseases are generally considered to be caused by either lactobacilli, leuconostoc, or bacilli.

Mannitic fermentation. When the temperature of the fermenting vat becomes excessive, the useful yeasts die and other bacteria take over, attacking the sugar. The resultant wine is cloudy and has a curious bittersweet, sometimes "mousy" taste. Instead of converting grape sugar to ethyl alcohol and carbon dioxide, these bacteria convert it to acetic acid, lactic acid, carbon dioxide, and mannite, a non-fermentable sugary substance. It is a particular menace in hot countries.

(2) *Chemical disorders (casses)*

There are four types of casse: oxidasic, protein, ferric, and cuprous.

Oxidasic casse. Caused by an enzyme (polyphenoloxidase), it makes wine cloud on exposure to air and change color—red wines turn brown and white wines yellow, and, after a time, form a deposit. It is often present in wines made from slightly overripe or moldy grapes. Wines containing a fairly high proportion of alcohol or acid, and especially of tannin, are best qualified to resist this breakdown. Preventive treatments for the condition are judicious use of sulfur dioxide; the addition of ascorbic acid (which in its natural state increases browning) at 100 to 200 milligrams per liter; heating of the musts (to 158° to 167°F., 70° to 75°C.) in a pasteurizer, by the addition of bentonite and yeast.

Protein casse. There is always a certain amount of protein matter in white wines and, if present in too great a degree, it reacts with the tannins to coagulate, first turning the wine hazy, later forming a precipitate. Once troublesome to makers of sweet white wines, protein casse has been reduced in importance by the practice of fining with bentonite, which removes protein matter, so that wines need no longer be aged until enough tannin has been absorbed to cause the reaction.

Ferric casse. In primitive times, nothing but bare feet and wood touched grapes. In installing labor-saving devices, wine-makers found that iron and copper often contaminated wines, imparting off-tastes and cloudiness. Ferric (iron) casse is caused by a high iron content (reacting with phosphates in the presence of air and causing blue or black clouding and precipitation) in a wine which may also be rich in tannin but of low acidity. Sometimes the casse is allowed to run its course, and then the wine is clarified. Many red wines, young and older, will become cloudy as a result of oxygen dissolving or exposure to the air. White wines also are subject to a form of phosphatoferric casse when they are rich in iron or phosphoric acid and are exposed to the air in the course of racking, bottling, or, especially, filtering. The deposit, which forms slowly, is grayish in color; the cloudiness will sometimes disappear when the wine is kept airtight and away from the light. One remedy is to add to the wine a solution of sodium bisulfite—not more than one gram per liter. In this case too, the best preventive measure is to keep the wine away from metal utensils. Ferric, like cuprous casse, can be prevented by "blue fining"—precipitating the metal with minute amounts of potassium ferrocyanide. Officially forbidden in many countries, including France, "blue fining" is, in some places such as Germany, allowed under rigid governmental control.

Two forms of iron compounds can form precipitates in wine. One, called white casse, is due to ferric phosphate and the other, called blue casse, is due to ferric tannate. The first forms if the pH of the wine is below 3.60 and sufficient iron (above five milligrams per liter) is present. If conditions are favorable then the compound will usually form, since there are sufficient phosphates present normally. The iron must be oxidized to the ferric state. The most obvious preventive measure is to have no iron in contact with the wines. However, this is not always a practical solution. Therefore, wines are either aerated and the casses allowed to form or, better, the metals are removed by the proper fining. This is accomplished by treating the wines with ferrocyanide, in countries where this is allowed, and with safer compounds (such as Cufex in the United States) if the use of ferrocyanide is forbidden. As a help against formation of these casses, citric acid can be added, and it will chelate the iron and prevent casse formation.

Cuprous (or copper) casse. Copper casse is usually considered as cupric sulfide. It will not form in the absence of protein but will quickly flocculate in its presence. Sulfur dioxide, or hydrogen sulfide, must be present and if one is not then a copper-protein precipitate will form slowly. Aeration will hinder formation of these compounds, as will organic acids to a small extent. Cold treatments, metal removal, filtration, and the usual methods of control will save the wine.

Cuprous casse may occur in white wines containing even a few tenths of a milligram per liter of protein and copper, when these wines have been kept for some time away from air and in a warm light place. The condition can be remedied by aerating the wine, by adding a few drops of hydrogen peroxide, or by clarification with bentonite to remove the protein matter. Since cuprous casse requires light to develop, vulnerable wines are often put into dark green bottles. Like ferric casse, this form of breakdown responds to "blue fining" with potassium ferrocyanide, in the few countries where its use is not forbidden.

Copper, exposed simultaneously to light and air, becomes oxidized—and so does the wine. Preventive measures can therefore be taken before introducing the wine into copper pipes or containers by washing them out with a solution of tartaric acid at a concentration of five grams per liter and then rinsing with clear water. Better still, the wine or the must should not be allowed to come in contact with copper at all.

3. *Accidents*

Most accidental off-tastes in wines are caused by carelessness on the part of the maker. Extraneous odors affect wines to a far greater extent than is generally realized, and wines may be spoiled by being stored in places where they come into contact with such strong-smelling things as gasoline, insecticides, tobacco, or even scent.

The odor caused by moldy barrels and unclean hoses or tools is dangerous because it may help to impart an off-taste to wine. The so-called romantic cellars shown with pride by their European owners all contribute to the creation of this problem.

Off-odors and -flavors can also be caused by the addition of excessive chemicals such as sorbic acid, sulfur dioxide, and diethylpyrocarbonate.

STEPS TO BE TAKEN AGAINST WINE DISORDERS

Sterilizing of utensils. Cobwebs clustering on the walls of the wine sheds harbor harmful bacteria. They must be cleared away, and the dirty walls sprayed with whitewash solution mixed with one per cent of copper sulfate. Moldy walls should be rubbed over with carbonate of soda—about 2 pounds to 10 liters (2.6 U.S. gallons, 2.2 imp.) of boiling water. After rinsing with clear water, the walls may be brushed over with a tepid solution of one per cent potassium permanganate. The floor, when it has been scrubbed, can be treated with calcium chloride (one per cent solution) and then rinsed with water.

Fermenting vats must, from time to time, be descaled; and wine presses and wooden vats (which should always be well scrubbed and rinsed) ought, when they accumulate a layer of gray mold, to be washed first in a 10 per cent solution of carbonate of soda, then with clear water.

WINE: THE SUM TOTAL

If in wine, as in geometry, the whole is the sum of its parts, it is at least theoretically possible to duplicate wine in the laboratory. The overwhelming complexity of such a job can be seen from the foregoing list of some of the ingredients and components of wine. At present, according to Professors Ribéreau-Gayon and Peynaud of Bordeaux, the scientist has successfully isolated and measured over one hundred different compounds, comprising about 97 to 98 per cent of the composition of wine. Of the nature of its all-important remaining two to three per cent, we have little or no idea, nor how many separate compounds they represent. More important still, if we take the known ingredients and mix them together in their proper proportions, we obtain nothing resembling wine. With this in mind, there can be no wonder that leading wine chemists admit that the final judgment of a wine must not be in the test tube but in the wineglass.

10 Spirit-Making

Potable spirits are beverages of high alcoholic content obtained by distillation—that is, the separation, by heating, of ethyl alcohol from wine or other spirituous liquids. Alcohol vaporizes at a lower temperature than water, and the process of distillation makes use of the differences in their volatility. Under normal atmospheric pressure, water boils at 212°F. (100°C.) and alcohol at 173.5°F. (78.4°C.). When heat is applied to a diluted mixture of water and alcohol between these temperatures, the alcohol will be converted to vapor; and if it is then drawn off through a tube and condensed by cooling, it will become separated from the original liquid—which may be wine or the fermented product (mash) of grain, from which whisky and many vodkas are made; or of molasses, the basis of rum; of potatoes, for some vodka; of apples, for applejack. These various liquids will evaporate at different temperatures, depending on the percentage of alcohol each contains—the smaller the amount of alcohol in the mixture, the greater proportionately will be the quantity of alcohol in the distillate.

APPARATUS

The apparatus in which the liquid is distilled is called a still, and the simplest form, known as a "pot still," consists of a pot where the mixture can be heated, a head, or alembic, through which the vapors pass, and a condenser in which the vapor is cooled and transformed into liquid again. The pot is heated either by direct firing or by steam, the heat being introduced by means of a heating jacket or a coil. To obtain a purer distillate, the mixture may undergo this process a second or third time, until spirit of the desired purity and strength is obtained (this is the disadvantage of the pot still; its advantage is that a finer flavor is preserved). In the first distillation, the wine or mash is brought to the boil and yields a spirit of some 25 per cent alcohol by volume or about 45° British proof or 50° U.S. proof. When it is distilled again, the first and last of the steam—the head and tail—are discarded and only the middle distillate, called the heart, is kept. This finishes at between 60 and 70 per cent alcohol by volume, 105° U.S. to 122° British proof.

The ancient pot still is used today in the distillation of Cognac and native Scotch and Irish malt whiskies; but most spirits are now made by a continuous process in patent stills derived from the one invented by Coffey, about 1830. Basically, this consists of two columns, long and rectilinear, and known as the rectifier and the analyzer. Each of these contains several compartments divided horizontally by perforated copper plates and communicating with each other by means of a drop-pipe—while the columns themselves are connected by two pipes, one of which carries vapor from the top of the analyzer to the bottom of the rectifier while the other, in reverse, takes the wash from the bottom of the rectifier to the top of the analyzer. Steam enters the still at the bottom of the analyzer (the left-hand column), and the cold wash comes in near the top of the rectifier (on the right), passes through a zigzag tube to the bottom of the column and up the connecting pipe to the top of the analyzer. As it enters this left-hand column, the now-heated wash meets the ascending vapors; and while it drips down step by step, onto the successive plates, the steam heats it and carries off its content of alcohol, so that in the final stage the spent wash falls as waste to the bottom of the analyzer and is drawn off—while the alcohol is carried up with the steam, which passes out of the column and is conducted by the vapor pipe to the bottom of the rectifier. Here again, the alcoholic vapor rises to the top, warming, as it goes, the zigzag pipe, which is introducing the new wash and, in consequence, growing cooler as the wash rises. Near the upper part of the rectifier, the vapors reach the "spirit plate" where they condense. This plate is fitted with a pipe which leads the alcohol to a cooler. Finally, it is collected in a spirits receiver. By means of strategically placed condensing coils, the alcohol is separated from certain aldehydes and volatile substances, particularly fusel oil.

Where a pot still can distill only one lot of wash at a time, the continuous still, which does not need to be emptied and recharged, is more economical and also enables the operator to exercise greater control over the product.

RAW MATERIALS

Wine is the foremost of the alcoholic liquids used to produce spirits, in the sense that it is itself already an alcoholic liquid; but sugary substances are also fermented into alcohol and then distilled, or the starch of cereals is converted into fermentable sugar, which in turn is fermented to obtain alcohol. (For a fuller description of the processes by which ingredients for different spirits are fermented and distilled see Gin; Rum; Cognac; Whisky, Scotch; etc.)

BY-PRODUCTS

The principal component of all spirits is ethyl alcohol, diluted with water and various secondary and tertiary ingredients to give the spirit its essential characteristics.

The raw material incorporates a quantity of substances which are carried throughout the fermentation and the distillation and enter into the ageing process. The various processes influence the conditions and the proportion of the secondary ingredients that will be present in the final alcoholic spirit. Such brandies as Cognac and Armagnac contain after fermentation substances coming from wine—mineral salts, fixed acids, tannin, and organic substances—which are not desirable in the distillation procedures. The distiller of brandies is concerned with the volatiles—alcohols (butyl, amyl, propyl, caproic, etc.), aldehydes, esters (for the bouquet of the finished product), and acids. These volatiles pass from fermentation into the distillation and distribute their value. Aldehydes, extremely volatile, pass into the distillate, and a proportion of them may combine with alcohol to form certain acetals. Acetification and esterification action, which develop in the later stages, contribute to the flavor and aroma of the brandy; but the complexity of the aldehydes, if not properly managed, may impart a certain bitterness to the brandy—and so an excess of aldehydes is undesirable.

The secondary substances of spirits can be classified as follows:

(1) *Higher alcohols*—fatty alcohols higher in acid than ethanol. The make-up of the higher alcohols depends on the raw material of the spirit. Pot-still whiskies produce a higher alcohol mixture composed of isoamyl and isobutyl ingredients as well as propyl alcohol. Patent-still whiskies, of higher proof and rectified, while containing a smaller amount of total higher alcohols than pot-still whisky, have a greater proportion of propyl and isobutyl and a low proportion of isoamyl ingredients. Neutral grain spirit for gin contains no appreciable amount of higher alcohols. Potato spirits produce isobutyl.

(2) *Esters.* These are formed during the fermentation period and are a result of the intermixture of alcohol and acids. Some of the esters arise from the fatty acids combining with a small amount of ethyl or amyl alcohols; e.g., ethyl acetate (the principal ester, known as acetic ester), ethyl valerate, butyrate, etc.

(3) *Acids.* Acetic acid forms the greater percentage, although acidity will vary according to the spirit. Butyric, tartaric, and succinic acids are among the best known.

(4) Aldehydes result from the oxidation of the ethyl alcohol. Furfural or pyromucic aldehyde is formed at the beginning of distillation and diminishes as the spirit develops in the casks.

(5) Other substances such as essential oils, terpenes, and minor volatile ingredients are called tertiary constituents and add to the character of the spirits.

AGEING

The time the spirit spends in the wood (the maturation stage) depends on its character. Brandy is all the better for fifteen or twenty years' ageing; gin, a highly refined spirit, need not be very much aged and would not benefit from maturation of more than one year. Generally, all the secondary ingredients—total acids, aldehydes, esters, etc.—tend to increase with age. Furfural increases in whiskies, but in some spirits it diminishes with ageing. The type of cask and the condition of storage are of major importance in this process. Limousin oak is the special wood used to heighten the quality of Cognac during the long time of maturation; charred white oak imparts flavoring and tannin substances to whiskies—especially American whiskeys. Water usually evaporates through the wood as time goes on, and the percentage of alcohol increases in proportion to the loss of liquid: after one year in barrel, an American whiskey will have an average proof of 116.5; after six years this will increase to 122.7, and at eight years, the whiskey will be 124.9 proof. The evaporation of liquid through the barrels will be greater in a dry cellar than a damp one; and the temperature of a cellar in which spirits are stored is generally constant.

See separate entries for Brandy, Cognac, Gin, Rum, Vodka, *and* Whiskey (Whisky).

Alphabetical Entries

Abboccato

Term for semi-dry or semi-sweet wine in Italy.

Abocado

Spanish term for wine which is of delicate bouquet and medium sweet.

Abricotine

French apricot liqueur made by steeping apricots in brandy. It is tawny in color and tastes of apricots, with a slight hint of almonds from the apricot stones.

Abruzzi (Abruzzo)

Red and white wines.
District: East-central Italy.

A mountainous agricultural region which makes a few agreeable wines. Montepulciano and Cerasuolo d'Abruzzo are light red wines, pleasant enough, particularly at lunchtime. The Montepulciano is named for the grape variety but is sometimes vinified with a little Sangiovese; the wine is ruby-red, with a slight froth and occasionally a sweetish aftertaste. It is grown around Canosa, Sannita, Casoli, and several other villages, and bears the D.O.C. (Denominazione di Origine Controllata). Cerasuolo is a clear cherry-red, and like the Montepulciano has about 12° of alcohol. The straw-colored Trebbiano d'Abruzzo is dry and well balanced; its name, too, comes from the grape variety, either Trebbiano d'Abruzzo or Trebbiano Toscano. The wine can come from anywhere in the region and still bear the D.O.C.
See Italy.

Absinthe

A light-green extremely potent liquor of spirits infused with herbs, chiefly anise and wormwood (*Artemisia absinthium*). Because of its potency and the harmful effect it is considered to have on the nerves, its sale has been banned in most Western countries. This is not so in Spain, where the dangers of absinthe are hotly denounced over full glasses of the cloudy liquid.

Absinthe was invented in Couvet, Switzerland, by Dr. Ordinaire, a Frenchman who sold the recipe to a M. Pernod in 1797. It enjoyed great popularity throughout Europe until it was banned, and many substitutes, similar in taste but without the dubious wormwood, have taken its place. Of these, anis and pastis (*qq.v.*) are the favorites, particularly in the south of France, and two of the best-known proprietary brands are Pernod and Ricard. The firm of Pernod used to manufacture absinthe in its Spanish distillery.

Acariose

A species of mite which feeds on the fruit and foliage of vines.
See Chapter Eight, p. 29.

Acariosis

A vine disorder resulting in stunted young shoots, its causes vary from country to country. Growth may be slowed or stopped either by the grape rust mite (*Calepitrimerus vitis, Phyllocoptes vitis*) or by the grape bud mite (a form of *Eriophyes vitis*).

Acescence

The formation in wine of an excessive quantity of acetic acid, often caused by prolonged exposure to air and apparent in the formation of a translucent gray film caused by the *Acetobacter* microbe. The result is a wine which is vinegary, or *piqué* (pricked).
See Chapter Nine, p. 38.

Acetic acid

An acid (CH_3COOH) always present in wine in very small quantities and the principal acid of vinegar. This is one of the volatile acids; if it is allowed to form freely, it will "acetify" the wine, turning it vinegary, or *piqué* (pricked).
See Chapter Nine, p. 38.

Acetification

See Acescence.

Achaea

A province of Greece on the Peloponnesus along the southern shore of the Gulf of Corinth. Especially around the town of Patras, the area produces a rather large quantity of red and white wine.
See Greece.

Acid

The generic term applies to substances which may exchange one or more hydrogen atoms for a metal or its basic radical. Acids, which give freshness and tang, are essential constituents of wine. An acid is known as monoacid, bi-acid, or tri-acid, according to whether it contains one, two, or three exchangeable hydrogen atoms.

Hydracids are combinations of hydrogen and certain metalloids. The term *hydro* or *hydric* appears in their names (e.g., hydrochloric acid, sulfhydric acid). Oxyacids derive from the action of an anhydride on water; generally speaking, their names end in -ic (e.g., nitric, sulfuric), but certain simple substances form different oxy-acids according to valencies. They can be distinguished in order of decreasing valency as follows:

per——ic	persulfuric acid	$H_2S_2O_8$
——ic	sulfuric acid	H_2SO_4
——ous	sulfurous acid	H_2SO_3
hypo——ous	hyposulfurous acid	$H_2S_2O_4$

(Yves Renouil and Paul de Traversay: *Dictionnaire du vin*.)

Acidity

Acids, which give freshness, tang, and protection from most bacterial spoilage, are essential constituents of wine. Without acidity, it would be insipid; with too much, sharp or vinegary. But when the proper balance is reached, the wine is flavorsome and fresh. Some acids are natural in grapes, some the result of fermentation; but the type and quantity in any wine will depend upon the grape variety, the soil of the vineyards, the climate during the growing season, the yeasts and other microorganisms, and the additions made to the wine during vinification.

Among the acids desirable in wine are tartaric and malic. The most undesirable is acetic. Citric acid is one of several found in very small quantities; and in sparkling wines some carbonic acid is present.

The expert recognizes three types of acidity: volatile, fixed, and total. Acetic is the predominant volatile acid, although the insignificant amounts of butyric, formic, and propionic acids which may be present are also in this category. Volatile acids in small quantities are indispensable to the stability and bouquet of wine, yet can be most unpleasant if they are present in excess, giving the wine a vinegary character. Of the fixed, or stable acids, the most important are tartaric, malic, and citric. Together, the two types make up total acidity.

See Chapter Nine, p. 38.

Aconcagua Valley

Red wines.
District: Central Chile.

One of the best vine regions of Chile, specializing in Cabernet and Malbec wines and producing wines which are strong in finesse, well-balanced, and long-lasting.
See Chile.

Acquavite

Italian spelling of *aqua vitae*, or brandy (*qq.v.*).

Acquit

More exactly *acquit-à-caution*; an official French document that accompanies all shipments of wines and spirits on which internal taxes have not been paid. (For tax-paid shipments, the *congé* is used.) The *acquit* is employed for exports—exempt from taxation—and for shipments made in bond. The color of the paper changes with the type of

wine or spirit to facilitate identification. *Papier bulle*, whitish-brown paper, is used for ordinary wines; green signifies table wines of controlled place of origin; yellow-gold is for Cognac and Armagnac; orange for sweet fortified wines of controlled place of origin; etc. If importing countries were to demand that these papers, which usually stop at the French border, accompany each shipment and be subject to strict controls, the amount of fraudulent wine now going out of France would be considerably curtailed.

A copy of the *acquit* must accompany the wines into the United States.

Adega

The Portuguese name for a *bodega* (*q.v.*).

Adom Atic

Leading red wine of Israel.
See Israel.

Advocaat

A beverage resembling egg nog, usually made of brandy and egg yolks, and bottled. In the Netherlands it has a rather low alcoholic content of 15% to 18% and is so thick that it is often taken with a spoon.

Agave

This, known also as the century plant, is the source of tequila, pulque, and mescal.
See Tequila.

Aglianico del Vulture

A deep-red sturdy warm wine from Aglianico grapes in the vineyards of Monte Vulture in southern Italy.
See Basilicata.

Agrafe (agraffe)

A clamp used to hold the cork prior to *dégorgement* and final corking of Champagne.

Aguardiente

The name for spirits in Spanish-speaking countries. Specifically, a spirit distilled from grapes in grape-growing countries and from molasses or sugar-cane in cane-growing countries.

Ahr

Red and white wines.
District: Northwest Germany.

The proportion of red Ahr wines to white is about three to one. The vineyards have some claim to be the oldest in Germany, and certainly they are among the oldest; definite records date from the third and seventh centuries A.D. Cultivation of red wine grapes began at the end of the seventeenth century, when the Pinot Noir plant was brought from Burgundy, and for nearly two-and-a-half centuries the Ahr wines were almost exclusively red. The descendant of the French plant is called Spätburgunder, and comprises 25% of all the vines in the Ahr Valley today. Ahr wines do not reach the outside world except in tiny amounts and as curiosities because they can in no sense be compared with better French red wines; in Germany, however, they are well known. Lately, more white wine varieties are being planted and the red wine seems to have fallen off. The Portugieser is the most widely planted red wine variety; of white wines, Riesling and Müller-Thurgau are most prevalent.

The most remarkable thing about Ahr wine is that it exists at all. The Ahr is north of the Mosel, and so the smaller vineland—about one-fifteenth of the acreage (800 hectares or 2,000 acres)—challenges the Mosel's claim to be the northernmost in the world. (In fact, one section of the Mittelrhein wins the contest.) Cold snaps, especially a deadly May frost, threaten the crop nearly every year, and the wine could not ripen if it were not for the steep narrow valleys which trap the sun's heat. Ahrweiler and Walporzheimer reds are the best-known growths; and a small quantity of quite good red wine is made at Bad Neuenahr.

For a complete list of the Ahr *Einzellagen* (individual vineyards) arranged by *Grosslage* (section of vineyards) and *Bereich* (sub-region—the Ahr is a sub-region unto itself), *see* Appendix B, p. 599.

Aiguebelle

French liqueur produced near Valence. It is said to be made according to an ancient formula discovered in a Trappist monastery, and its taste derives from a blend of some fifty herbs. There are two varieties—green and yellow—of which the green is the stronger.

Aiven

Tartar spirit made from fermented milk.

Aix-en-Provence

Red, white, and rosé wines.
District: South of France.

In and around Aix, the ancient capital of Provence, in vineyards that stretch from the rocky inland slopes down to the Riviera itself, some pleasant wines are made. They are usually heady and sturdy and are perfect to drink in their own district, slightly chilled, in the summer. Red, white, and rosé are made, but the rosés are generally the best.

See Provence; Coteaux d'Aix, Coteaux des Baux.

Akevit

See Aquavit.

Akvavit

Danish spelling for aquavit (*q.v.*).

Alambrado

The Spanish term for a bottle of wine enclosed in a light open wire netting called an *alambre*. Wines of better than average quality are often packaged this way.

Alasch

A variant spelling of allasch (*q.v.*).

Alavesa

One of the best types of Spanish Rioja wine, it is frequently identified on the label. It is somewhat like a Rhône wine.

See Rioja.

Alba Flora

A white wine of Majorca.

Albana di Romagna

The principal white wine of the Emilia–Romagna region of Italy. It may be dry or sweet, and in the good years it has a noticeably velvety quality.

See Italy.

Albariza

The typical chalky-white soil of the region around Jerez in the Spanish Sherry country, producing the best Finos and Manzanillas.

Alcamo

Red or white wine from Sicily (*q.v.*).

Alcohol

One of the principal components in wine. During fermentation the enzymes created by yeast cells convert the sugar in the grape juice into alcohol as well as into carbon dioxide gas. In fermented grape juice, alcohols combine with acids to produce esters. In general, alcohol (as defined by Yves Renouil and Paul de Traversay) is "the derivative resulting from the substitution of a hydroxyl radical for an atom of hydrogen in a hydrocarbon." Pure alcohol is colorless and will ignite at temperatures ranging between 10.4°F. (—12°C.) (absolute alcohol) and 51.8°F. (11°C.) (95% alcohol). It is antiseptic—admirably so in wine. A rectified alcohol is one which has been distilled.

See Chapters Nine *and* Ten *and* Rectification.

Alcoholic content (by volume)

The proportion of alcohol contained in a wine, or the alcohometric strength of that wine, is always expressed in France in terms of its volumetric alcohol content at 59°F. (15°C.), determined in accordance with the Gay-Lussac principle: pure alcohol has a strength equal to 100 degrees, and the alcohol content is equal to the number of liters of ethyl alcohol contained in 100 liters of wine, both these volumes being measured at a temperature of 59°F. (15°C.). One degree of alcohol then corresponds to 1 c.c. of pure alcohol contained in 100 c.c. of wine. The amount of alcohol can be expressed in grams per liter at 68°F. (20°C.). (Renouil and de Traversay: *Dictionnaire du vin.*)

The British evaluation is based on the "proof gallon" and on "proof spirit."

The proof gallon is a unit of volume and alcoholic content corresponding to 4.5459631 liters of standard proof spirit.

Proof spirit is a standard alcohol which weighs exactly, at a temperature of 51°F. (11°C.), twelve-thirteenths of an equal quantity by volume of distilled water. It is in fact a mixture of water and alcohol containing 49.28% by weight and 57.1% by volume of alcohol at 60°F. (15.6°C.).

For the calculation of alcoholic content, the graduation by Sikes degrees is used. Since "proof" corresponds to 57.1 degrees by Gay-Lussac, a higher alcoholic content is expressed in degrees Sikes O.P. (over proof) and 100 degrees Gay-Lussac is represented by 75.09 degrees Sikes O.P. Conversely, a lower alcoholic content is expressed in degrees Sikes U.P. (under proof) and in this case 100 degrees Sikes U.P. corresponds to 0 degrees Gay-Lussac. In the United States, alcoholic content of wine is expressed as per cent by volume at 60 degrees F.

See Appendix D, p. 634.

Aldehyde

A volatile fluid obtained by the oxidation of alcohol; a large class of compounds intermediate between alcohol and acids. These play an important part in wines, particularly in bouquet.

See Chapter Nine, p. 38.

Ale

A malt beverage.
See Beer.

Aleatico

A grape of the Muscat family which produces a sweet aromatic wine. Used in various parts of Italy for red wine.

Aleatico di Portoferraio

Sweet red dessert wine from Elba.
See Tuscany.

Aleatico di Puglia

Deep-colored, sweet, strong Italian dessert wine.
See Apulia.

Alella

Principally dry white wine produced north of Barcelona in the Catalonian village of that name. Some red is made.
See Spain.

Aleyor

A red wine of Majorca.
See Spain.

Algeria

Once among the leading wine-producers of the world, Algeria has cut production and begun a general reorganization of her wine and grape industries. While still a French *département* in 1961, Algeria made almost 16 million hectoliters of wine (413 million U.S. gallons, 344 million imp.) from nearly 360,000 hectares (900,000 acres) of vines. Though the production has dropped, Algeria's rank among the wine-making nations has changed little: it is now eighth, after many years of being sixth in total volume. Nearly all of the wine is red.

The indigenous population of the country consumed little of all this wine, since, although 35 to 40% of the working population is employed in wine-making, most Algerians are Moslems for whom the drinking of wines or any sort of alcoholic beverage is forbidden. The dark heady wine of Algeria had to find other outlets.

A great deal of it went abroad anonymously to be blended with the wines of France (particularly those of the Midi); and of the rest, millions of gallons went to France and other places abroad under its own labels as useful ordinary wine for washing down everyday meals. But with the declaration of Algerian independence in the summer of 1962, quality began to fall off: the Moslem workers missed the guidance of their French supervisors. There was also a large drop in imports into France; the growers of the Midi and other bulk-producing areas protested Algerian independence by putting pressure on the government to reduce the quantity.

As the quantity of wine sent to France and the other Common Market countries trickled to virtually nothing, the Algerian government began redirecting the wine industry and found a new customer for its exports. The 2.5 million hectoliters of Algerian wine (66 million U.S. gallons, 55 million imp.) which previously went each year to France now goes partially to the Soviet Union and Eastern Europe. With this change of trading partners have come steps to tear out old vine stocks and replace some of them with young table grape plants. The program aims to shift Algerian agriculture toward cereals, to improve the land under cultivation, and simply to plant healthy vines in the place of less fruitful ones. The area in wine grapes is being reduced to 225,000 hectares (563,000 acres) and production stabilized near the present level of 3 million hectoliters per year.

Not all Algerian wine was *vin ordinaire*: other wines of a very pleasant quality were made, most of them sold as V.D.Q.S. (Vin Délimité de Qualité Supérieure—Delimited Wine of Superior Quality), the French secondary classification, following their Appellation d'Origine Contrôlée. The greater quantity produced is bulk wine, however, and the growing is done strictly on an industrial basis. Throughout the vast domains modern machinery is found, and the grapes are brought to the enormous wine sheds where they are processed on a production-line basis into huge cement vats, where they ferment. So that the vats will be ready for the next batch of grapes coming in from the vineyards, selected yeasts are added to the grape must to ensure a quick and sound fermentation. When the fermentation is over, the wines are stored in other enormous vats and are later sold by the barrel, truckload, or tank car, the price depending on alcoholic content. Until recently, the vines planted have been the lesser varieties—Carignan, Cinsault (or Cinsaut), Grenache, Alicante-Bouschet, Aramon, Morrastel, and Mourvèdre for red wines; Clairette, Listan, Ugni Blanc, Faranan, Maccabéo, and Merseguéra for whites.

Algerian red wines, which make up 65% of the country's total production, are generally heavy, coarse, dark in color, and run in alcohol from 11% up. It is not unusual to find some which are naturally of 15% with very low acidity—an alcoholic content that would be extremely rare in cooler countries, where the summer sun is not sufficiently hot to generate so much sugar in the grapes. Since the wines of the French Midi may be light in acid and low in alcohol (sometimes no more than 9%), these Algerian wines were often used to "correct" them, adding color, body, and alcoholic content. The wines of Mascara were notorious as the base for many a shipper's "Burgundy."

Not only are the methods used in Algeria like those of southern and central California, the climate is often very similar too. The outlook is different, however, since Californians claim that in their sunny country every year is a vintage year, while the Algerian growers simply maintain that the vineyards are far enough to the south for vintage years to be unimportant. Both places also grow grapes of the same general type—the quantity-producing varieties and those which flourish in a hot climate. Most of these grapes reach maturity at the end of August or the beginning of September, whereas the temperate European varieties would mature too quickly and produce a wine so lacking in acidity that it would be flat and unpalatable. But the vines found in this North African country today are not those which have always been planted there.

WINE HISTORY

Grape-growing in Algeria started in ancient times, and the wines—or some of them—were known to have been transported to Rome for the delight of the rulers of the Mediterranean world. The arrival of the Moslem faith did not spell the end of all the vineyards, despite the interdiction of alcohol in any form, for table grapes and raisins have always been appreciated there. It is probable, as has been suggested, that the Muscat types exist solely because of the Moslem prohibition of alcohol and the resulting search for table grapes of quality, which could not keep many of the vineyards alive.

In about 1830 the French colonized Algeria, eventually making it a part of metropolitan France rather than a colony (until its independence in 1962), and under French rule viticulture revived. The first vineyards appeared in 1865. Later in the century, as the phylloxera, the devastating plant louse, took its toll of the French vineyards, various growers gave up their ruined fields and moved to Algeria; and in many cases the vines they planted were those they were accustomed to use at home. Colonists from Lyons imported the Gamay and Pinot vines; Burgundians leaned toward the same plants; Bordelais colonists put in Cabernets; ex-inhabitants of the Midi planted Aramon; and refugees from Alsace and Lorraine (some of them fleeing German occupation of their homeland as well as the phylloxera) nurtured Chasselas and Pinot Gris. Throughout, also, were found Mourvèdre, Morrastel, and Grenache. When the phylloxera finally hit Algeria too, many of these vines were abandoned and the vineyards were replanted mostly in Carignan, with some Cinsault and Alicante-Bouschet, all of them grafted onto American roots. Some Aramon remains in Algeria, but although the production of this vine is huge, it is losing ground with the growers because of its low alcoholic content and lack of color. In the case of white wines, the vines used are mostly Clairette, Merseguéra, Maccabéo, and Ugni Blanc.

VINE-GROWING REGIONS

The vineyards of Algeria are spread throughout the three regions of Oran, Constantine, and Alger. Most of these sections are planted along the plains and yield the great bulk of the nation's wines. But the departments of Oran and Alger have between them some 60,000 hectares (150,000 acres) of vines planted along the slopes which produce wines that had been granted A.O.G. (Appellation d'Origine Garantie) by the Algerian authorities. The better Algerian wines are often of extremely pleasant quality, softer and more alcoholic than those of the Midi, and with more fatness. These wines continue to be made mostly from the Cinsault, Carignan, Grenache, and Morrastel vines; some other varieties are allowed in certain cases. The whites come generally from Clairette and Muscat grapes. On the slopes, some vines of the Cabernet, Grenache, Mourvèdre, Pinot, and Syrah varieties are also cultivated. Red wine predominates and is customary throughout Algeria, but there is also a good deal of rosé (some of it very good when young) and some white—quite a large quantity is produced in Oran.

The following wines are those which were established by the Algerian authorities in 1970.

ALGERIA

Department of Alger

Aïn-Bessem-Bouïra: red and white wines—minimum 11.5% of alcohol.

Coteaux du Zaccar: red and white wines—minimum 12% of alcohol.

Haut-Dahra: red wines only—12.5% of alcohol.

Médéa: red and white wines—minimum 12% of alcohol.

Department of Oran

Coteaux de Mascara: perhaps the best of the Algerian wines, from the slopes around Mascara. (The word *Mascara* without the *coteaux* refers to wines grown lower down and without quite the same degree of quality.) These wines are red, white, and rosé and must have at least 12.5% of alcohol.

Coteaux de Tlemcen: red and white—minimum 12.5% of alcohol.

Monts du Tessalah: red, white, and rosé—minimum 12% of alcohol.

Mostaganem: red wines (minimum 12.5% of alcohol) and some white and rosé wines (minimum 12% of alcohol).

Mostaganem-Kenenda: red wines—minimum 12.5% of alcohol.

Oued-Imbert: red, white, and rosé wines—minimum 12.5% of alcohol.

Alicante

Red Spanish wine, known in Shakespeare's time as Tent.

See Spain.

Alicante-Bouschet

Extremely productive red-wine grape developed in the nineteenth century by the French hybridizers L. and M.

Bouschet. It is grown throughout the French Midi, Algeria, and California, but everywhere gives the same inferior characterless wine with low acidity and intense but quickly fading color.

Aligoté

Burgundian white grape which gives pleasant but unexceptional wines; these are at their best when young, as they tend to oxidize within three years.

Alkermes

A red cordial once made from the kermes insect of the Cochineal genus, long supposed (because invariably found on the tree) to be the berry of the Mediterranean kermes oak.

Allasch (alasch)

A type of kümmel favored in England, Poland, and Russia. The liqueur draws its name from Allasch near Riga (U.S.S.R.), a place famous for its caraway seeds, which are the essential flavoring agents of kümmel.

Aloxe-Corton

Burgundy red and white wines.
District: Côte de Beaune, France.

The commune is at the northern end of the Côte de Beaune, but its finest white wines rank with those from the unofficial "Côte de Meursault"—the great white wine-giving southern end of this famous slope—and its reds are the finest of the Côte de Beaune, among the finest of all Burgundy. But in order to get what you want, you must know what to ask for.

Some of the wines are sold as Aloxe-Corton. These are communal wines—pleasant and enjoyable, sometimes distinguished, seldom great. Others have, as well, the full communal name, such as Aloxe-Corton Les Maréchaudes, signifying that they come from one selected excellent vineyard and that the wine has attained higher than minimum standards. The most magnificent wines do *not* bear the name Aloxe; they are either Corton alone or Corton followed by some other, more specific designation. The three greatest names are:

Corton: more red wines than white, sometimes further defined to determine the exact portion of the vineyard from which they come (e.g., Corton-Bressandes, Corton-Renardes, etc.).

Corton-Charlemagne: the superb full-bodied white wine of Aloxe.

Charlemagne: applicable to certain outstanding white wines but rarely used, since these wines have equal right to the preferred Corton-Charlemagne.

See each under separate heading.

The vines grow on a prominent hill known as La Montagne, which stands back from the main road, its gentle slopes crowned with the Bois de Corton, a quiet peaceful woodland. The vineyard strip fronting these woods is Corton, but farther down are the even more outstanding sections of the same vineyard: Bressandes, Renardes, and the Clos du Roi. On a level with Corton is Charlemagne, and both Charlemagne and the upper portion of Corton are planted in Chardonnay. Local growers say that the upper sections are best for white wines, the middle and lower parts for red. The soil itself is the clue. At the top it is light and dry, with a whitish tinge from the chalky subsoil; farther down, it becomes ferruginous and reddish.

Aloxe is one of the oldest of the wine-growing communes along the ancient Slope of Beaune. Charlemagne, Henry II, and Charles the Bold (the Burgundian duke who lost both his life and his lands to Louis XI) have been growers, and Voltaire was one of the most celebrated admirers of the wines. In the famous letter to Monsieur Le Bault—who built the commune's Château Corton-Grancey—he said: "Your wine has become a necessity for me. I give a very good Beaujolais to my friends from Geneva but in secret I drink your Corton." Le Bault's reply was a note scribbled in the margin: "This man is a *villain*," implying Voltaire was at the very least a miser and a scoundrel. The château has been renovated a number of times since its construction in 1749, and today—thoroughly modernized—it is in the hands of the good shipping firm of Louis Latour.

Whether red wine or white comes first in Aloxe is a matter of choice, and most wine-lovers are willing to settle for both. The reds are powerful, full, and big, tending toward harshness when young but maturing beautifully and taking on a great balance. They have a magnificent aroma, with sometimes a hint of violets. Corton, of all Côte de Beaune wines, is the one to lay down, for it develops slowly and holds its majesty for years. The best Corton whites are sometimes in the same class as Montrachet—the wine from the south of the Côte de Beaune which many experts consider the greatest dry white wine in the world. These wines have a firmness that borders on a touch of steel and an almost overwhelming perfume of the grape, especially when young. Some connoisseurs maintain that they can also detect a scent of cinnamon in the bouquet; and the wines have exceptional breed and a lingering aftertaste with an enormous range of sensations.

The area on which the vines are grown is not large. The total for Aloxe-Corton is about 240 hectares (600 acres), and the best vineyards cover considerably less ground (some of these, entitled to the Appellation Contrôlée of Aloxe-Corton, are partly in the neighboring Pernand-Vergelesses and Ladoix-Serrigny). Production in an average year for quantity may amount to 5,250 hectoliters (139,125 U.S. gallons, 115,500 imp.) of red wine, and less than 25 hectoliters (662 U.S. gallons, 550 imp.) of white. These statistics do not include the production of the vineyards Corton and Corton-Charlemagne (*qq.v.*). Those vineyards which may produce wines that will carry both commune and vineyard name—the First Growths (*Premiers Crus*)—have only tentatively been established and the list is provisional—the acreage has not, at the time of writing, been fixed.

The minimum degree of alcohol allowed for these wines is: red, 11½%; white, 12%. Maximum production must not exceed 30 hectoliters per hectare (320.7 U.S. gallons, 267 imp. per acre). The *appellation* Charlemagne is seldom used, since most of the land is entitled also to the name Corton or Corton-Charlemagne.

Climats SOLD AS CORTON

In Aloxe-Corton: (red and white wine)

Le Corton	Voirosses
Clos du Roi	Les Fietres
Les Bressandes	Les Perrières
Les Renardes	La Vigne-au-Saint
Les Languettes (*in part*)	Les Grèves
Les Chaumes (*in part*)	Les Meix (*in part*)
Les Maréchaudes (*in part*)	Les Combes (*in part*)
En Pauland (*in part*)	Le Charlemagne (*in part*)
Les Meix-Lallemant (*in part*)	Les Pougets (*in part*)

In Ladoix-Serrigny: (red and white wine)

Les Vergennes	Le Rouget-Corton (*in part*)
Le Bois de Vergennes	Ladoix-Serrigny (red only)
Les Carrières	

In Pernand-Vergelesse: (red wine only)

Charlemagne (*in part*)

FIRST GROWTHS (*Premiers Crus*)

La Maréchaude	Les Fournières
La Coutière	Les Vercots
Les Petites-Lolières	Les Meix (*in part*)
La Toppe-au-Vert	Les Maréchaudes (*in part*)
Les Grandes-Lolières	En Pauland (*in part*)
Les Chaillots	Les Valozières (*in part*)
Les Guérets	

The following vineyards in Ladoix-Serrigny, bordering on Aloxe-Corton, are allowed the place-names of Corton and Corton-Charlemagne:

Les Vergennes-Corton
Le Rognet-Corton
Clos de Corton

Alsace

Rhine wines of France.
District: Northeast France.

Alsace makes the Rhine wines of France: dry and fresh, some spicy, some lively and light, with the faint prickle they call the *pointe de fraîcheur*. The vineyards are planted along the sheltered slopes of the Vosges; from high on the hills, one can look eastward over the wide river to Germany. The wine region, officially divided into Haut-Rhin and Bas-Rhin, is one of the most attractive in France. On the lower ground, orchards flourish as well as vines, providing some of the fruit for the superb white *eaux-de-vie*: kirsch, fraise, framboise, poire. Although pressing machines and the whole process of wine-making are extremely up to date, there is an unhurried rural atmosphere in the countryside where tractors rumble along to the *vendange*, and some of the villages, with their half-timbered houses, storks' nests, and flowery balconies, look like pictures from German fairy tales.

The vines stretch between the Rhine and the mountains for more than 75 miles (120 kilometers), from Thann in the south (Haut-Rhin) to Marlenheim in the north (Bas-Rhin), covering more than 12,000 hectares (30,000 acres) divided into many properties, often quite small, and worked by some ten thousand growers and their families. The wines are named from the grapes: only in Alsace is the Appellation d'Origine given for the vine-type instead of the place of origin. The wines which may be described as Vins d'Alsace come from the following grapes, which are classified as: *Standard Variety*—Chasselas; *Fine Variety*—Sylvaner and Pinot Blanc (or Clevner); *Noble Variety*—Riesling, Gewürztraminer, Muscat, and Tokay d'Alsace (or Pinot Gris). Vineyard names are not generally important here, although there are exceptions—such as Rangen at Thann, Sonnenglanz at Beblenheim, Les Sorcières at Riquewihr, and others attached to the towns listed below, under Famous Wine Towns, p. 66.

WINE HISTORY

From Roman times Alsace has made wine. Already in the eighth century the lower slopes of the Vosges were green with vines. In the Middle Ages, the Rhine as its waterway, Alsatian wine flowed downriver to Cologne, to be shipped to Scandinavia and England. Alsace was then called Aussay—spelled in various ways—and the wines of "Osoy" are mentioned by Shakespeare. But the Thirty Years' War caused terrible destruction in Alsace and much of the vineland was laid waste. It was the first of many crushing blows to the wine industry of the contested Rhineland. At that time (1635-48) France participated with Sweden in the final stages of the war—their common enemy being the troops of the Holy Roman Emperor and of southern Germany. Under the Treaty of Westphalia (1648) France received sovereignty over the landgraviate of Upper and Lower Alsace, and the government of ten imperial cities in Alsace.

In the eighteenth century, Alsatian wines were popular in Austria and Switzerland. Quality controls very much like the French wine laws of today, although in primitive form, had already been put into force, and shipments were rigorously inspected by the *magistrats de la vigne*, forerunners of I.N.A.O. (Institut National des Appellations d'Origine) inspectors and of our modern wine-brokers, still known in Alsace as *gourmets*. Place of origin of the wine and conditions of production were carefully inscribed on the invoices. Vine control laws also prohibited the planting of a larger proportion of quantity-producing vines than of quality producers.

The French Revolution brought drastic changes, breaking up all the large holdings and establishing the pattern of small ownership still in effect today. Yet by 1870 the vineyards were flourishing again and the wines, known as Vins d'Alsace du Rhin Français, were good.

But in that year war broke out between France and Germany and in 1871 Alsace became German. To protect their own Rhine wines the Germans forbade the Alsatians to call theirs Vins du Rhin; and so the name was cut down to Vins d'Alsace. The economics of German wine production also put Alsace into a position where every incentive was given to the producer of *vin courant*. This attempt to lower the quality of Alsatian wine remained in force until 1918, when France liberated Alsace.

With the return to France in 1918, there was a disheartening collapse of the market. It looked as if liberation carried a fatal sting for the Alsatian wine-growers. In Germany, where the wines produced along the Rhine and Moselle are fine but not plentiful, there had been an enormous demand for cheap table wines. But in France, the largest producer in the world of every kind and quality of wine, this need did not exist. Cheap Alsatian wines, produced on a mass scale, had nowhere to go.

The decision taken was courageous—and it proved to be right. In the 1920s, Alsace returned to making the best possible wines and is still doing so today. Success came from the fact that, many as her wines were, France had lacked native wines of the Rhine type. The light pleasant growths of Alsace, designed for drinking rather than sipping, filled a necessary need for the French.

Alsace experienced another tragedy in 1944-45, when the battle for the liberation of the province caused wide devastation. Yet travelers driving up now from Lorraine into the peaceful mountains would never guess how many of the towns were leveled and the vineyards destroyed; and Orbey, which lies waiting in the valley, is placid-looking and rich with good living—*foie gras* and trout, sausages and succulent ham, and piles of whipped cream. The people were quick to rebuild their towns, to reconstruct their cellars, and to replant their vines; and the wine business is more brisk than ever.

The wines have gained a world market. Annually, some 100,000 hectoliters (2.65 million U.S. gallons, 2.2 million imp.) are exported, the leading customers being (in this order): Germany, Belgium and Luxembourg, the United Kingdom, Switzerland, the United States, Canada, the Netherlands, Italy, Scandinavia, Mexico, and Africa; Common Market countries buy three-quarters of the wine shipped.

In spite of the checkered history of the vineyards there has been continuity of a kind in the history of the *vignerons*: among the well-known firms today are those of families who have been making wine in the same Alsatian villages for four hundred years—although now such firms will probably market not only wines from their own grapes but from small growers in the area. An Alsatian vineyard provides wines of different character and quality—Zwicker, perhaps, and one or more of Riesling, Gewürztraminer, Pinot, or Muscat. So the large grower-shippers, who not only produce *grands vins* but also store and blend the various wines to obtain a consistent character, play an important part in the Alsatian trade. In recent years a second branch of this trade has grown up: that of the cooperatives. After the last war some small proprietors decided that by pooling their resources they could more easily rehabilitate their vineyards and regain their sales. Now merged into the Union Vinicole pour la Diffusion des Vins d'Alsace, these cooperatives control 15% of the market. Trading on equal terms with such old-established family firms as Hugel, Dopff & Irion, Lorentz, and Willm, whose pre-eminence they do not challenge, they are instrumental in stabilizing prices and in supplying the chain-store trade.

In the cellars of the great family firms one is shown enormous wooden vats, carved with escutcheons, with mermaids and dolphins. Huge vats are still in use, although some of the wine is stored in glass-lined concrete containers. To preserve its freshness the wine is disturbed as little as possible, racked only once—in the January after the harvest—filtered, and bottled when it is from seven to twelve months old. The average Alsace wine should be drinkable at once, although it will improve for a few years in bottle. But some late-gathered (tardive) wines will mature to a greater age.

WINE LAWS AND LABELS

In all fine French wines except Alsatian, the place of origin is the thing to look for on the label. If the soil is worthy, it pays the grower to produce the best wines he can. The laws of Appellation Contrôlée, based on soil and location of vineyards, guarantee that the quality he achieves will be recognized.

Alsace used to be the only important still-wine zone in France which had no Appellation Contrôlée. If you asked the reason, you were told that control in this one French province was by grape variety and that the statute of November 2, 1945 served as a wine control.

(Statute of November 2, 1945 governing the wines of Alsace: *The designations* Grand Vin *and* Grand Cru, *indicating superior quality, may be used only for wines from noble grape varieties having at least 11% of alcohol. Such wines, if sold in bottle, may be sold only in the type of bottle designated* Alsatian Wine Bottle....)

Alsatian wine-makers considered the regulation concerning the type of bottle unfair, since it obliged them to use this bottle but did not protect them from the competition of other growers in other regions copying the shape; so they began a fight in the French wine jurisdiction, which ended in the winning of the decree of May 21, 1955. By this decree, the typical tall, slender, tapering bottle was limited almost entirely to Alsatian wines.

November of 1945 was also when the Comité Régional d'Experts des Vins d'Alsace was set up as guardian of quality wines. Its twenty-seven members, appointed by the minister of agriculture, must include eighteen growers and/or shippers and nine technical or administrative advisers. This body decides the limitation of vineyard acreage for wines allowed the Appellation d'Origine Vins d'Alsace and the grape varieties from which they may be made. It is largely due to the work of the Committee that the practice of late picking has been introduced for some grapes, resulting in fuller, more lasting wines; and that in 1962 the quality and purity of vine species used was recognized in the award of the A.O.C. (Appellation d'Origine Contrôlée) to the Vins d'Alsace. The A.O.C. laws are tighter than those passed in 1945. This form of control specifies that, in addition to other rules about maximum alcoholic content and minimum vineyard size, only wines from certain kinds of vines (already specified on page 64) may be called Alsatian Vins d'Origine. And in accordance with another law passed in 1972, all A.O.C. wines must be bottled in the region of production; that is, in the departments of Haut-Rhin or Bas-Rhin.

In 1963 the Comité Interprofessionel du Vin d'Alsace was founded as a semi-public body, in order to provide growers with technical and practical assistance, to act as liaison between growers and shippers, and to develop public relations with consumers. The committee is aided in its work by the oenological experiments of the Oberlin Wine Institute at Colmar, which has been in existence since 1893.

Another committee—or rather an ancient brotherhood invested with scarlet capes and black tricornes—exercises, through its voluntary ritual rules, a beneficial surveillance over the finest Alsatian wines. The Confrérie Saint-Étienne, founded in the fourteenth century at Ammerschwihr, was known originally as Herrenstubengesellschaft (Guild of Burgesses). The founder-members were local magistrates and their friends, who each year elected a grand master from among their number. It was he who arranged the tastings on which the new wines were judged, and the annual banquet on the Feast of Stephen (though the patron saint of the Society is St. Diacre). Having lapsed during the dark days of Alsatian viticulture, the Confrérie was revived in 1947 as a grand council for the whole wine region of Alsace. Its *raison d'être* is the organization of tastings, at which the fine wines of the last harvest are judged and graded. A dozen each of the best of the *grands crus* are laid down as collectors' items, setting a standard of quality for member-growers. Those with the highest qualifications may be granted the seal of the Confrérie, which is attached to each bottle with a gold ribbon. Every year at the Colmar Wine Fair the society selects (by examination and blind tastings) new candidates for admission to its ranks. Established members also entertain important visitors from abroad, who come to enjoy the fair and sample the wines on display in the different booths.

THE FAMOUS WINE TOWNS

The band of vineyard is one continuous strip stretching north-south along the eastern fringe of the Vosges Mountains, where the range touches the Rhine plain. The most important areas are the section between Riquewihr and Ribeauvillé, and the clusters around the villages of Barr to the north and Guebwiller to the south.

Most visitors to Alsace drive along the splendid Route du Vin. If they set out from Strasbourg they will see perhaps fifty of the more than one hundred communes allowed the *appellation* for the Vins d'Alsace. They might stop on the way at Colmar, a city which retains some of its old narrow streets, a few beautiful houses, and—in the museum which was once a convent—the extraordinary Isenheim Altarpiece painted by Matthias Grünewald in the early sixteenth century. It is at Colmar that the big Wine Fair is held every year. There is a special link between the town and the United States: Bartholdi, sculptor of Colmar's Lion de Belfort, created the Statue of Liberty. In the flatter agricultural land of this region lies the cabbage-growing center for sauerkraut, that most famous of Alsatian dishes, which goes much better with the local beer than with the wines.

Obernai

Sheltered by the Mont Sainte-Odile, this Bas-Rhin town, with its fountains and statues of the saint and its charming market square, prepares the traveler for the prettiness of the Route du Vin.

Barr

This, in the Bas-Rhin, is a thriving little place, with a fine town hall. Its wine is mostly Sylvaner, although some good Riesling is made. The town lies near the mouth of a valley descending from the highest peaks in that part of the Vosges.

Bergheim

Bergheim, just inside the Haut-Rhin, has a high reputation for its wines, especially the Gewürztraminers, and more especially those from the Kanzlerberg site. It is a charming walled village, approached through an archway on which the date, 1300, is carved. In some of the old streets the splashing gutters are so wide they have to be bridged. The center of the town is a shady square with a handsome town hall on one side and a parish church—which has a tower called La Tour des Sorciers, because here alleged witches of the sixteenth century were tried and condemned.

Ribeauvillé

Ribeauvillé is slightly less important than Riquewihr, farther along the route. Three castles look down from the mountains on this village, which preserves its historic tradition as the town where the pipers of France are protected. Each year the old winding streets of Ribeauvillé resound with the Festival of the Pipers (who themselves have long disappeared), and there is much wetting of whistles with Alsatian wines.

Riquewihr

Circled by its city walls and untouched by war, Riquewihr is lovelier than any wine town in France, except Saint-Émilion and perhaps Sancerre. The cobbled streets, lined with houses of the sixteenth and seventeenth centuries, bright with painted shop signs and flowering window boxes, are cooled by splashing fountains. A vine-trellised courtyard of one of the old inns is the best place in the world to taste the fresh Alsatian wines, green-gold in a green-stemmed glass.

Riesling, Gewürztraminer, Muscat, and Pinot all flourish here. The chalky mixture in the soil suits the Riesling, which develops a very fine bouquet. Sporen and Schoenenberg are the favored slopes.

Kaysersberg

Testing the wines in a cave such as that of Salzmann in Kaysersberg is a great experience. The courtyard is Gothic and unspoiled, a relic of the Middle Ages, overshadowed by the ruin of the old castle on a crag across the river. This charming village, with its reputation for fine wines, is the birthplace of Dr. Schweitzer.

Ammerschwihr

The ancient vineyards surrounding this village on the mountainward side are in some places scored by the ridges, moats, and battlements of vanished castles and fortresses. The town itself is utterly clean, modern, and completely new—for ancient Ammerschwihr disappeared almost to the last stick and stone in the bombardments of December and January 1944-45.

Reconstructed with the original stones, Ammerschwihr is as functional as a fine machine. M. Gaertner's Aux Armes de France is one of the best regional restaurants in France, proudly serving with *foie gras* or *choucroute* the wines from Ammerschwihr's great vineyards, of which the Kaefferkopf is perhaps the most famous. In this town, in the fourteenth century, the Confrérie Saint-Étienne was founded.

Turckheim

Slightly to the northeast of Colmar, Turckheim is a picturesque town with an old fortified wall pierced by three great gates. Its important vineyard is Brand.

Éguisheim

An ancient village, built in a circle. Visiting the Beyers, one of the family firms which, in a fashion not uncommon in Alsace, has descended from father to son since the sixteenth century, one might be entertained with Kougelhoff, the traditional Alsatian cake, accompanied by a fragrant Gewürztraminer, and a sip of the rosy Pinot Noir, a minor but agreeable local wine.

Guebwiller

Very good wines, mainly Rieslings, are produced with painstaking care at the terraced vineyards to the north and south of the town. Vines grow so high on slopes so steep that tractors work all year round to bring back the soil (which keeps sliding downhill), and masons follow to mend the walls. The best vineyard is Wannen.

THE GRAPE VARIETIES

Riesling and Gewürztraminer are the finest wines, the crown perhaps going to the Rieslings. There is much argument among non-Alsatian lovers of Alsace wine as to which of these ought to stand first, but no knowledgeable drinker would claim first place for any other than the Riesling. Alsatians themselves say firmly that the Riesling is the king of wines. The bulk of the common wines of the better type are Chasselas and Knipperlé.

Gewürztraminer

The confusion as to whether or not there is any actual difference between the Gewürztraminer (spicy Traminer) and the Traminer need no longer trouble the amateurs of wine, since it has been decided that only the term Gewürztraminer shall be used, and that the vine is a selected strain of the old species, Traminer. This wine (from a small reddish grape with a musky flavor) can be slightly sweetish in the biggest years but is generally fairly dry. It has a high alcoholic content for an Alsatian wine, reaching nearly 14% in the supreme year of 1976, with unresolved sugar remaining in the wine. It just lacks the breed, distinction, and steeliness of a really fine Riesling, and its pronounced taste and bouquet may be too unsubtle for some tastes. Gewürztraminer is the most individual-tasting white wine in France. It is the second most planted grape in Alsace and new plantings are forbidden by the I.N.A.O. A delicious fruity wine when good and an excellent accompaniment to such strong-tasting, spicy dishes as curry, it is also served with meat and with local cheeses.

Riesling

This grape, the oldest species in Alsace, produces the great German Rhines and Moselles. Alsatian Riesling can be a splendid wine with oysters, fish, and all seafood, and with meat. It has less body than the Alsatian Tokay, and it is less individual than a Gewürztraminer, but unquestionably it has more breed than either. Riesling is dry, fruity, and fresh, and can achieve great elegance. The vine thrives in a soil with a fair proportion of chalk; the great Riesling slopes are found near Riquewihr, Kellenberg, Ribeauvillé, and Dambach.

Tokay d'Alsace or Pinot Gris

Many people consider this next in quality after the Rieslings and Gewürztraminers. A very full-bodied golden wine, either dry or slightly sweet, it improves in bottle. There is a theory that it is called Tokay because the grape variety may have been imported three hundred years ago from the Tokaj district of Hungary. The wine has no other connection with the Hungarian Tokay, which comes from the Furmint, and there is some opposition to this misleading name; the *Dictionnaire du vin* simply states that the name Tokay is generally used for wines made from the Pinot Gris. It usually accompanies *foie gras* and meats.

Muscat d'Alsace

A very dry fruity Muscatel, often with a fine bouquet. This is another old species. A popular aperitif in Alsace.

Sylvaner

Intermediate in quality between the more common wines and the finer wines. A pleasant light luncheon wine, sometimes refreshingly prickling (with a *pointe de fraîcheur*) and comparable with Sylvaners of the same class from the German Palatinate. The wine has a pale green-gold color, fruitiness, and a discreet bouquet, and is the most popular of noble Alsatian wines. It should be drunk young. Sometimes qualifies as a *Grand Vin*.

Pinot Blanc

This has more body generally than the Sylvaner, which it resembles slightly, but is not among the most distinguished wines—though at its best it is well balanced, with a delicate bouquet. It may sometimes be slightly prickling. The wine may be served with *foie gras* or meat.

Chasselas

The largest producer of carafe wines, light and agreeable, with the alcoholic content of average Alsatian wines (about 9% to 10%). It is seldom bottled and so is rarely, if ever, exported. Much Chasselas forms the basis of many shippers' wines.

Müller-Thurgau

This crossing of Riesling and Sylvaner, gaining headway in Germany, is quite rare. At one time in Alsace it produced a wine somewhat like, but not as good as, the Chasselas.

Knipperlé

Another of the common wines of Alsace, not quite as good as the Chasselas. New plantings of Knipperlé are now forbidden by the I.N.A.O.

Zwicker

Not a grape variety but, on a bottle label, it indicates that the wine is a blend of both noble and common varieties. Most Alsatian wines bearing the invented name given by a shipper or grower are Zwickers.

Edelzwicker

A blend exclusively of noble grape varieties. *Edel* is the German word for "noble."

Vins Gris

Famous—except in Alsace—as the Alsatian *vin rosé* or pink wine, but more apt to be a blend of red and white wines than a true rosé. Important Alsatian wine authorities, such as René Kuehn of Ammerschwihr—a leading grower, ex-member of the French Chamber of Deputies, and former delegate to the United Nations—state that the best pink wine of Alsace is Rosé d'Alsace, which must come from the Pinot Noir grape and be made at the only two or three vineyards in each of the three or four communes throughout Alsace which produce true rosé. *Vins gris* are made on a considerable scale in Lorraine.

SPIRITS

The *eaux-de-vie* of Alsace are many and famous: these fruit brandies are called *alcools blancs* because they are aged not in wood but in crockery. Vineyards alternate with orchards along the east slope of the Vosges Mountains skirting the Rhine plain. The blue-plum trees producing quetsch fan out onto the plain; in the forest are the wild strawberries, raspberries, and holly.

Kirsch

The most important of all the *eaux-de-vie*, it is distilled from cherries, including their stones. Some 60 pounds of fruit render about eleven bottles at 50% of alcohol. The best section for the wild-cherry tree which produces kirsch is along the middle height of the Vosges slope between valley and summit, around Trois-Épis, Ammerschwihr, Haut-Koenigsbourg, and Sainte-Odile.

Fraise

Distilled from both wild and cultivated strawberries. The genuine *eau-de-vie* is very good and very expensive.

Framboise

Since a brandy distilled directly and exclusively from raspberries would be too concentrated to be palatable, *eau-de-vie de framboise* is made in a unique fashion by macerating the fruit in neutral spirits protected from exposure to oxygen. The liquid is then distilled to create the *eau-de-vie*. One liter of spirit with the desired percentage of alcohol is made from 8 or 9 pounds of fruit, as compared to the costly 60 pounds needed if the brandy were made in the usual way.

Mirabelle

Made from yellow plums of a size that can be enclosed in the hand. The finest mirabelle comes from neighboring Lorraine.
See Mirabelle de Lorraine.

Quetsch

This brandy comes from blue plums, of a tree more common and hardy than that of the mirabelle, producing successfully on the broad plain.

Houx or *Holly Spirit*

This extraordinary beverage distilled in the mountains above Ammerschwihr is one of the rarest and probably one of the most expensive in the world. Less than five hundred bottles of it are produced a year, by fermenting together holly berries and sugar, then distilling.

Enzian

This spirit is distilled from the astonishingly long roots of the yellow gentian.

Reine-Claude

This variety of plum (the greengage), named, in French, after the daughter of Louis XII, is infrequently distilled, but it gives a spirit with an almost overwhelming bouquet.

Other spirits are made from apricots, peaches, rowan or sorb-apples (*alises*), bilberries (*myrtilles*), and blackberries (*mûres*).

Altar wine

Wine used for sacramental purposes. It must be pure, unadulterated, natural wine.

Altise

A beetle that feeds on vine leaves.
See Chapter Eight, p. 29.

Amber dry

Name under which Clairette du Languedoc (*q.v.*) is often sold in Great Britain.

Ambonnay

Village of the Mountain of Reims district, producing a First Growth Champagne (*q.v.*).

Amelioration

Any treatment of, or addition (such as sulfur or sugar) to grape juice or new wine for the purpose of improving the quality.

Amer Picon

A proprietary French bitters used as an aperitif, made with a wine and brandy base to which has been added quinine (to impart a bitter taste), orange peel, and innumerable herbs. It is drunk with ice, diluted with water, and usually sweetened with grenadine or Cassis.

America

See United States.

Amertume

Bitterness in wine that has thrown a deposit and turned acid.
See Chapter Nine, p. 38.

Aminaean wine

One of the most lasting and famous of the Augustan Era, to which "even the royal Phanaean" paid homage. (Virgil: *Georgics II.*)
See Classical wines.

Ammerschwihr

Wine town in Alsace (*q.v.*).

Amontillado

A kind of Spanish Sherry, not so pale in color as the Finos and with more bouquet. It is naturally dry; but for the Anglo-Saxon trade sweeter wine, made from the Pedro Ximénez grape, is often added.
See Sherry.

Amoroso

Sweetened Oloroso Sherry prepared for the British market. Unknown in Spain.
See Sherry.

Ampelidaceae

Botanical family to which the grapevine belongs. Of the ten genera of the family only one, the genus *Vitis,* is important in wine-making, although others are capable of producing grapes. *Vitis* embraces two sub-genera, *Euvites* and *Muscadinia,* and numerous species. Of these, *vinifera* is the most important, for it yields the great wines of the world. Native to Europe, it has been transplanted to other continents.
See Chapter Eight, p. 29.

Ampelography

(1) The descriptive study, identification, and classification of vines.
(2) A book or document describing the structural characteristics of a vine. The written information is often accompanied by a detailed drawing or photograph of a leaf of each plant covered in the book.

Ampelotherapy

Treatment of human or animal ills with grapes which possess therapeutic properties.

Amphora

A two-handled vessel—pitcher or jar—used in ancient times for holding wine or oil.
See Classical Wines.

Angelica

(1) A sweet yellow liqueur, somewhat similar to Chartreuse, made in the Basque country.
(2) A very sweet Californian mixture of partially fermented grape juice and brandy.

Château l'Angélus

Bordeaux red wine.
District and Commune: Saint-Émilion, France.

One of the many Grands Crus, according to the 1955 Saint-Émilion Classification. The property has been owned by the Boüard family since 1924, and its wine is made by very up-to-date methods in a modern *chai.*
Vineyard area: 25 hectares (63 acres).
Average production: 150 *tonneaux* (13,000 cases).

Château Angludet

Bordeaux red wine.
District: Haut-Médoc, France.
Commune: Cantenac-Margaux.

Rated an Exceptional Growth (*Cru Exceptionnel*), just below Fifth Growth (*Cinquième Cru*), in 1855, the vineyard went through a bad period in the thirties and forties. In earlier times it had always been considered the equal of a Fourth Growth (*Quatrième Cru*). Formerly owned and run by the son-in-law of the owners of Château Coutet, the estate is now the property of Peter Sichel, the managing director of Sichel and Co.; he has done much to restore the vineyard, which deserves a higher classification. Ever since the turn of the century, the wine has been very popular in England.
Characteristics. A well-made wine from good soil. The vineyard certainly should be a classified one.
Vineyard area: 30 hectares (75 acres).
Average production: 120 *tonneaux* (11,000 cases).

Angola wine

Palm sap fermented in West Africa.

Angostura

Rum-based bitters made in Trinidad from a formula still the secret of the Siegert family, heirs of the inventor. Dr. Siegert was a German who became surgeon-general to Simón Bolívar during the liberation of South America. He developed his bitters from various herbs and plants to counteract the enervating effect of the tropical climate. The product proved so popular that in the early nineteenth century he founded the firm which still manufactures it.

Anis

Popular French and Spanish liqueur and aperitif. The dominant taste derives from the seeds of the star anise plant (an important ingredient of absinthe), whose pods resemble starfish. Anis was developed as a substitute for absinthe (q.v.) and, like absinthe, can be drunk diluted with water, turning cloudy with a pale greenish tinge when the water is added. A similar drink is pastis (q.v.). The difference between the two is that licorice replaces aniseed as the principal flavoring ingredient of pastis. One of the best-known brands of anis is that of the firm of Pernod, known as Pernod 45, although Ricard has now become the best-selling French aperitif of this type. The anis liqueur is the most popular of all the cordials in Spain.

Anisette

Liqueur of aniseed flavor. A well-known formula is said to have been confided by a West Indian traveler to Marie Brizard of Bordeaux.

Anjou-Saumur

White, rosé, and red wines.
District: Loire Valley, France.

There are over 12,000 wine-producers in the historic province of Anjou (now the department of Maine-et-Loire), which embraces a large vineyard area on the slopes west of Touraine and rising from the left bank of the Loire. Anjou and Touraine are alike in many ways: the hills around Saumur are made of the same chalky limestone deposit as those at Vouvray, and in both districts the wine is aged in caves dug deep into the hillside. In Anjou, west and south of Angers, however, the shallow soil covering a bed of hard rock resembles that of Brit-

tany. The château country proper is within Touraine, but in Anjou also the wide River Loire flows through a peaceful green countryside, past old manors and castles, relics of the days when the Plantagenet Kings of England were also Counts of Anjou. In the thirteenth century the wines were very popular in England. Later on, when the English were importing mainly Bordeaux, the people of the Netherlands were the biggest buyers, sailing up the river as far as Rochefort and Saumur to collect the barrels. In those days, the best wines were saved for the foreign trade and the lesser ones sent to Paris.

Today these wines are most popular in Belgium, Holland, Germany, and the United States. Like those from other parts of the Loire Valley, the Anjou wines are fresh and sprightly; even the lesser growths are often charming, though seldom seen outside their native region. Best known abroad now are the Muscadet and the Anjou rosés.

One-third of the 650,000 hectoliters (17.3 million U.S. gallons, 14.3 million imp.) of wine produced annually in Anjou is white, and rosé makes up most of the remaining quantity, although a small amount of relatively minor red wines is produced also. The best Angevin white wines are sweet, as were the vast majority at one time; but changes in taste have converted many growers to vinifying their wines at least comparatively dry, and this trend is healthy for Anjou. Those vineyards capable of producing natural sweet wines continue to do so; others—where doses of sugar once had to be added to impart the requisite sweetness—have turned to drier and better wines. A percentage of the annual output is made into sparkling wine, especially in and around Saumur, but the finest Angevin remains non-sparkling.

SOIL AND VINES

It has already been stated that the region divides into two basic types of soil: chalky clay around Saumur and along the slopes of the little Loir River; and elsewhere, a hard schist covered with a layer of flinty clay, so thin that growers are often forced to use dynamite to loosen the earth in which to plant their vines—or, if dynamite is not used, they must spend many weary hours with a pickaxe.

The only grape allowed for fine white wine is Chenin Blanc, a standard in Anjou since the ninth century. Red wines—made principally in Saumur in the communes of Souzay-Champigny, Chacé, Dampierre, and Varrains, as well as in Saint-Cyr-en-Bourg, Brézé, and Brain-sur-Allonnes—come from Cabernet Franc grapes with some Cabernet Sauvignon and ever-decreasing amounts of Pineau d'Aunis, which is giving way to the Cabernets. Two kinds of rosé are produced: Rosé d'Anjou from Groslot, Gamay, Cot, Noble, and Pineau d'Aunis grapes; and Rosé de Cabernet, entirely from Cabernet grapes. The latter is the better—fruitier, fresher, cleaner-tasting, and with a more appealing color. It also tends to be higher in alcohol, the legal minimum being 10%. Of the former, it should be noted that the Gamays from California are closer to Beaujolais and better. Some of the Anjou rosés are dry, others are sweet. There is a growing tendency for the ordinary consumer in the region to ask for a sweeter pink wine.

Only about a third of the wine is labeled Anjou. The rest (including the best) bears the name of one of the sub-districts with the Appellation Contrôlée, and these names are more likely to be found on bottles sent abroad.

ANJOU-SAUMUR SUB-DISTRICTS

Coteaux de la Loire

This area, on both banks of the river, is one of the best and most well-known in Anjou. In soils of varying consistency and quality, it grows Chenin Blanc grapes which give way, west of Montjean, to the Muscadet. The wines, therefore, also vary; sweet yet in general drier than those of the Layon district, they are lively and well made. A few, rather sharp when young, take some time to come around. Others will be mature after years in bottle.

Savennières. An attractive village and the best wine town on these slopes, Savennières has its own Appellation Contrôlée. The wines incline to dryness, are high in alcohol and slow to mature. The leading vineyards are La Coulée-de-Serrant, La Roche-aux-Moines (both of which make fine, very elegant wines), Château de Savennières, Château d'Epiré, Château de la Bizolière, and Clos du Papillon.

Other communes worth noting are Bouchemaine, La Possonnière, Saint-Georges-sur-Loire, Champtocé and Ingrandes, Montjean, La Pommeraye, and part of Chalonnes.

Coteaux du Layon

This is the other leading district of the region. Thirty miles of vineyard are scattered along the banks of the little stream, the Layon, which descends from the hills near Les Verchers to meander through a string of wine-growing villages until, just above Chalonnes, it enters the Loire. The wines are high in alcohol, and some of the best vineyards are picked only after the *pourriture noble* has set in. These sweet wines are probably the finest of all the sweet wines of Anjou, but dry white wines are also made in the area. The sweet whites are fuller in body and longer-lasting than any from the Coteaux de la Loire. In the seventeenth century they were very popular with the Dutch, but now are chiefly drunk in the north of France and Belgium.

Bonnezeaux. This Great Growth of the region has its own Appellation Contrôlée and ranks almost as a sub-district on its own. The vineyards, in the commune of Thouarcé, sprawl down the slopes toward the riverbank, and a solitary windmill stands guard above—once there were three. They produce a limited quantity of sweet white wine, soft and fruity.

Quarts de Chaume. Almost equally distinguished (indeed, some say it is really the best of the Layon slopes) is the sweet wine from this vineyard, near the village of Chaume in the commune of Rochefort. It resembles a sweet Vouvray and is more flowery than a Sauternes. In lightness and bouquet it is unique, and yet in most years its alcoholic content is between 13% and 16%. At one time the vineyard belonged to a single proprietor who rented it out in return for a quarter share of each vintage. He reserved the right to choose which section of the vineyard his quarter should come from, and so it came to be called Quarts de Chaume.

Six more communes in this area add their names to the Appellation Contrôlée of Coteaux du Layon. These are Beaulieu-sur-Layon, Faye d'Anjou, Rablay-sur-Layon, Rochefort-sur-Layon, Saint-Aubin-de-Luigné, and Saint-Lambert-du-Lattay.

From the middle reaches of the Layon comes a quite considerable quantity of white wine permitted the more general Appellation Anjou, although this is predominantly a district for *vin rosé*.

Coteaux de l'Aubance

The wines of this small district north of the Coteaux du Layon are better known in their own part of the country than elsewhere. Yet they are pleasant, typical Anjou wines. Most of them are white, but rosé is produced as well. The whites have not all the rich mellowness of a wine from the slopes of the Loire or the Layon but are often outstanding—especially the medium-dry, which have character and an agreeable bouquet. The leading communes are Brissac (making mainly good pink wines from Cabernet and Groslot grapes), Vauchrétien (good white wines), Saint-Jean-des-Mauvrets, Juigné-sur-Loire, Saint-Melaine, Soulaines, Mozé, Mûrs, and Denée, which is near Rochefort and makes very similar wines.

Coteaux du Loir

Now an Appelation Contrôlée in the department of the Sarthe, this former sub-district on a small tributary of the River Loire produces wines that are white and pleasant, red and indifferent, rosé and charming.

Saumur, Coteaux de Saumur, and Saumur-Champigny

The old town of Saumur is dominated by a rambling castle which has been turned into an equestrian museum—this is where the cavalry school of the French army is stationed. The riverside bluffs are tunneled with vast caves, perfect for ageing, and the sweeter white growths make a sparkling wine. A good deal of the wine, however, is dry or semi-dry, with 10% to 13% of alcohol, and sometimes it is slightly *crémeux*.

The sparkling Loire wines preserve their own flavor; they are different from Champagne, and Saumur is overpriced if it costs the same—the producers suffer from the fact that it is usually taxed as much. Made of two-thirds Chenin Blanc and one-third Cabernet, it is fuller and heavier than sparkling Vouvray.

Thirty-seven communes share the Appellation Saumur in the department of Vienne. They include Pouançay, Berrie, Saint-Leger-de-Montbrillais, Ternay, and Ranton.

The Coteaux de Saumur is still being defined by the I.N.A.O. In principle, the vineyards follow the slopes along the Loire. Dampierre is the leading commune, with a good production of two-thirds white wine, one-third red and rosé. Souzay-Champigny, Parnay, and Turquant make fresh fruity wines; the white wine of Montsoreau has a definite character. Located on the Thouel River, Varrains and Chacé are better known for their rosé and red wines than for their smaller harvest of white; Saint-Cyr-en-Bourg makes more white; Brézé, Epieds, and Saix do quite well with their red wines, but the white have the greater reputation.

Saumur-Champigny takes its name from Champigny, the wine village just south of Saumur, but wines with rights to the appellation are made in many of the surrounding villages, mentioned as part of the Coteaux de Saumur. Saumur-Champigny, as a Cabernet-Franc-based red wine, is, with the Borgueuils and Chinons, the best red wine of the Loire.

(See also under individual headings.)

Anthracnose

A vine disease of European origin.
See Chapter Eight, p. 29.

Aperitif

A broad term for nearly any drink taken before a meal to tease the palate and stimulate the appetite. Diverse flavored and fortified wines generally sold under some proprietary label such as Byrrh, Lillet, and Dubonnet are popular; so are stronger spirits and bitters usually served with soda or water. Among this second group are Campari, Amer Picon, and pastis. Perhaps the very best aperitif is either dry Champagne or Sherry.

Apoplexy

A spectacular vine malady.
See Chapter Eight, p. 29.

Appellation d'Origine

Guaranteed place-name for a French wine. Champagne, for example, is a name which can properly be applied only to the products of certain approved vineyards and wine-making processes inside that region; no other sparkling wine (even when made by the authentic champagne process) has a right to the name. In France this rule is enforced by the laws of Appellation d'Origine. For an account of the events and legislation which led to the formulation of these laws, and of further controls over the viticultural and vinicultural standards essential for the production of fine wines, *see* Appellation d'Origine Contrôlée, below.

Appellation d'Origine Contrôlée (control laws)

Literally "controlled place of origin"; on a bottle of French wine the guarantee not only of place of origin but of the quality standards traditionally associated with wines from that place. These control laws represent the most flexible, most enlightened, and most effective body of legislation existing at present for the protection of fine wines.

HOW THE LAWS WORK

Fine wines always bear the stamp of the place where the grapes were grown and—given the conditions necessary for producing fine wines—the more restricted the place, the better the wine. Recognizing this fact, the Frenchman drew his control laws as a series of large and small circles: the smaller the circle, the more elite the terrain and the stiffer the wine's minimum requirements. The result: the more specific the name or *appellation*, the higher the guarantee of quality.

A typical example is the large Bordeaux wine region in southwest France. Imagine a great circle drawn around the city of Bordeaux and the land surrounding it. Everything within this circle (excepting land obviously unfit for the purpose) has the right to grow grapes for Bordeaux. Just northwest of the city—but within the circle—is the district of the Haut-Médoc; to the southeast are Graves, Barsac, and Sauternes; to the east, Saint-Émilion and Pomerol. These are all districts represented by smaller circles within Bordeaux, and although their wines have the right to bear the more general name, they will always take the more restricted if they can qualify for it. Within these smaller circles, the terrain is finer, the requirements higher, and the wines better. The contraction of the circles does not end there. Within, for example, the Haut-Médoc, yet smaller circles represent specific towns or communes, the best of which are Margaux, Saint-Julien, Pauillac, and Saint-Estèphe. Again, growers always choose the most restricted name for which their vines qualify, and again the quality of the wines is raised and the characteristics more specifically determined. The system reaches its logical conclusion in Burgundy, where certain superb vineyards (one—La Romanée—a mere 2.1 acres) have special separate *appellations* and highly stringent requirements for their magnificent wines.

The system has the confidence of both grower and consumer, and thus prices for wines with specific names are higher than for those with general names, and the more specific, the higher. It is to the credit of the French lawmakers that such wines are almost invariably worth the increased price.

WHAT IS CONTROLLED

These laws control every factor that contributes to the wine, every process that may affect it—in fact, every detail literally from the ground up is regulated until the bottle of wine is sold to the consumer or leaves the boundaries of France. An easy and harmonious working relationship between the technical and administrative experts of the Institut National des Appellations d'Origine in Paris and technical experts in each wine region makes this complex and seemingly cumbersome system workable. The Institut National des Appellations d'Origine (it is usually referred to as the I.N.A.O.) sets down the broad outline of the controls, the local people contribute the specific points, the Minister of Agriculture makes it law, and the fraud inspectors see that the law is enforced. While each control law will be adapted to its specific area, all will contain the following broad general points:

(1) *Area of Production.* The geological composition of the soil deemed fit for the production of the wine in question is outlined. The land is then studied and marked out by experts in the region, and only vineyards within the delimited area are permitted to use the name. The boundaries are reflected on the property land maps or *cadastre* kept in each town hall of a village with Appellation Contrôlée vineyards.

(2) *Permissible Grapevine(s).* In different soils and under different skies, the same vine will produce grapes of different characteristics. Selection of varieties follows the best traditional practices of each area.

(3) *Minimum Alcoholic Content.* Alcohol helps to give wine its staying power—its ability to live long enough to develop into greatness. If vines are allowed to overproduce, the grapes may develop so little sugar that the wine will end up unbalanced, with too little alcohol to match its other characteristics. Stipulation of alcoholic content before enrichment of the wine is thus an assurance of quality.

(4) *Viticultural Practices.* Pruning, fertilizing, and the general handling of the vine show in the quality of the wine. Viticultural practices are closely regulated, hence the type of pruning is specified for each area, with special emphasis on outlawing methods which produce huge crops but mediocre fruit.

(5) *Permissible Harvest.* Since quality is inversely proportional to quantity, the amount of permissible harvest is specified. This is expressed in hectoliters/hectare (which may be converted into gallons/acre) and usually drops sharply as names get more specific.

(6) *Vinicultural Practices.* The traditional wine-making procedures of any region are largely responsible for the reputation of each of the great wines, instilling much of the wine's distinctive character. These have thus been codified into law. Tasting panels have become more frequent, especially in the Bordeaux region.

(7) *Distilling.* The I.N.A.O. also controls the *eaux-de-vie* of France. The traditional distillation procedures that made the fame of these spirits are also formalized into law.

THE EVOLUTION OF THE LAWS

The outlook for French wines at the turn of the century was bleak and unpromising. Phylloxera had invaded France in the middle of the nineteenth century, reducing vast areas of vineyard to rows of bare wooden stumps—resembling huge graveyards. Growers replanted prolific grape varieties in the southern plains once reserved for the cultivation of cereals, which, more often than not, yielded wine which was common and harsh and of inferior quality. A not uncommon practice, despite strict laws

forbidding it, was to add sugar and water to grape pomace, or pulp, let the concoction ferment, and then sell it as wine. Fine wines had been hit as badly as ordinary ones, and in many cases there was no connection between bottle contents and label. Into this chaos the French legislature stepped, with the law of August 1, 1905, creating statutes for eliminating fraud. This step saved the table wines from a major crisis. The laws were excellent; the pattern for all agricultural controls of place-names, they were often imitated abroad but never equaled. Where fine wines were concerned, the law was completed in 1908 in order to anticipate governmental restrictions and amendments. This is known as the administrative phase of appellation law.

The trouble was that the laws did not take into account that fine wines are produced not only by the place and the soil where they are grown, but also by the grapes planted and the manner in which they are cultivated. In controlling the geographical place of origin without either exacting certain traditional practices of cultivation or imposing tests of tasting or analysis, they opened the way to two abuses: (1) that wines of great name would be made without the care to which they owed their superlative characteristics, and (2) that some proprietors would take advantage of the geographical guarantee regardless of the grape variety, thus producing quantities of inferior wine which, under the letter of the law, were entitled to bear the label of a prestigious name.

The legislation of 1908 codified for wines the more general legislation of 1905. Thus were fixed the geographic zones of Bordeaux, Banyuls, Clairette de Die, Cognac, and Armagnac. But the government was unable to make any satisfactory decision regarding Champagne.

The region of Champagne extends over several French departments; growers in the Marne disputed the right to the great wine name "Champagne" with the growers of the Aube. The administration's delimitation was a compromise, intended to please both factions. Like so many decisions of the sort, it pleased neither. There was little outcry, however, before 1910. In that year severe frosts ushered in one of the most disastrous harvests in Champagne history and the growers erupted. They said that, had the limits of the region been more tightly drawn, and had the shippers respected the limits, the normal price of grapes would have been higher and the growers would have been able to save enough to tide them over a poor year. It should be pointed out that at this time the merchants in Champagne could produce simple sparkling wines without an A.O.C. but with an address in Champagne using grapes grown well outside the limits of Champagne. As it was, riots broke out in January 1911, and troops had to be sent to restore order. In June, the limits of the region were amended—and again there were riots. Thus, later in the year, the legislature declared the law unworkable and set it aside, without offering anything to replace it.

In 1911, a sensible modification of the previous laws was prepared and discussed in the Chamber. The opponents' argument, however, was: "Can you contest the right of a cultivator to make what use he pleases of the name of his property and the fruits of his soil?" The result was that no reforms were made. Trying again in 1914, Deputy Jenouvrier pointed out the collective character of the Appellation d'Origine: "The reputation attached to these products is the result of the sustained effort of successive generations; the fruit of their combined labor became famous, and the proprietorial right was thus established for the whole commune or region."

When, after the war, a new law was passed in 1919, M. Jenouvrier's modification was incorporated; but there was still no clause controlling varieties of grapevine, methods of cultivation, delimitation by soil type, and other guarantees of quality. The results of this law, therefore, were disastrous. Almost anyone who claimed that an Appellation d'Origine was contrary to his interests and rights or to customs *locaux, loyaux, et constants* (local, loyal, and constant) could go to law to demand an interdiction, causing a great deal of senseless litigation.

Called to clarify its understanding of the law of 1919, the court chose a strict geographical interpretation, thinking that such was the intention of the legislators. This precipitated a movement to create new and inferior vineyards in delimited areas. Deputy Capus, in his account of the long struggle to obtain the control law as we now know it, recalls the effect of the 1919 act on his native Barsac, a district of Bordeaux. The sweet, rich, justly famous white wines of Barsac traditionally stem from Sauvignon and Sémillon grapes grown on the hilly sections of the commune. In the valleys and along the *palus*—the moist lowland near the River Garonne—the traditional vines had been for red wine, none of it Barsac, all of it ordinary. In the litigation following the law, the courts authorized the producers who grew vines in the *palus* of Barsac to sell their wines under the label of the famous white wine, overlooking the fact that legal right could not endow the land with the proper geological conditions. A few growers balked, since the law of 1919 said nothing about vines, but most accepted the ruling and did the legal but improper thing. As Capus said: "Bad laws make bad citizens." The vines in the *palus* were rooted out, those for bulk production of white wine were planted or grafted with hybrids, and for the first time Barsac was grown in the *palus*. A further result was that the small-bearing noble vines of the slope could not match the productivity of the newcomers, and in some vineyards they were replaced by bulk varieties, often hybrids. So, great seas of wines ranging from mediocre to frightful went to market emblazoned with the famous name. Prices, of course, dropped. So did the reputation of Barsac, and the situation could have occurred elsewhere.

This state of things was bad for the grower as well as for the consumer; the honest man who spent money on his vineyard and worked hard to produce a small quantity of great wine was hit by less scrupulous competitors, turning out far more and far worse wine which bore the same label of authenticity. Soon the buyers from abroad began to complain that their customers were refusing to pay the prices asked for such inferior stuff; and when the agitators for a stronger law increased their activity, it became clear that public opinion was changing. Monsieur Cheron, the

Minister of Agriculture, had been shocked, when he paid a visit to the Gironde, by the number of vines in the Great Growths (*Grands Crus*) which were being uprooted to make room for the more prolific hybrids; and a commission was set up to inquire into the affair.

In all these years, the troubles in Champagne had never been settled, and now the two parties appealed to Monsieur Édouard Barthe, president of the Groupe Viticole, to mediate for them. He drew up a plan which both resolved satisfactorily the question of delimitation and established every necessary condition for the production of fine Champagne. This plan, since it had the approval of all the associations of viticulture concerned, was able to be incorporated intact into the new Law of 1927, which added to the regulations of 1919 amendments (1) restricting the place of origin to "the surface areas comprising communes or parts of communes for the production of wine of the *appellation*"; and (2) forbidding the right of *appellation* to wines produced from hybrids or from any vines other than those traditionally bearing the great wines. This was known as the Appellation Simple. The consequence was that the *palus* and other unsuitable lands dropped back to inferior status and the noble vines returned—in those regions which observed the Law. For one of the Law's weaknesses was that it was optional. Some districts did observe it—in the region of Châteauneuf-du-Pape, the Baron Le Roy, a proprietor himself, went further and persuaded the other growers to endorse guidelines related to quality. He then had these guidelines confirmed legally in court. Other regions followed this example and some one hundred appellations were created.

The Law of 1927, although a great improvement on its predecessors, was still imperfect—because, except in the separate clause dealing with Champagne, it ignored all guarantees of quality except those of soil and place-name: that is, it overlooked the extent of permissible harvest and the minimum alcoholic content of the wine, as well as the necessary standard of vine-tending and wine-making practices.

In spite of the imperfections of the Appellation Simple, it was significant that for the first time the French legislature admitted that the name of a wine embraced something other than geography. The way to the present stricter controls was not to be smooth; but from that point it had been marked out and paved. In 1935 these stricter controls began going into operation, and the fine French wines became the province of a committee, now the Institut National des Appellations d'Origine des Vins et Eaux-de-Vie (the National Institute of Place-names of Wines and Spirits), whose capable hands guide the fortunes of French wines both in France and in some instances abroad.

THE EFFECT OF THE LAWS

In the case of every Appellation Contrôlée that has gone into effect, the result has been an immediate and marked increase in quality. Passage of a control law cut out the lesser wines, and the grower—conscious that his efforts would be reimbursed—strove for high quality. The existence of an Appellation Contrôlée, is of itself immediate evidence that the wine is fine, and the gain is twofold: the grower gets more money for his wine, and the consumer gets better wine for his money. It is only unfortunate that other wine-producing countries have not followed the example more closely. It is as well to understand that it is the place-name which is controlled and not always the wine—i.e., Pommard Appellation Contrôlée means that geographical boundaries and minimum standards have been set up for Pommard. But the controlling of the wine in the bottle is much more difficult, with a limited "police-force." Therefore, there are still loopholes in the enforcement of authenticity of the wine.

Appellation Simple

"Simple name of origin"; a predecessor of the system of Appellation Contrôlée, which at present protects the quality and origin of fine French wines. Before the creation of the *Appellation d'Origine Contrôlée* in 1935, appellations were said to be *simple*. As pointed out, the creation of these laws went through administrative and judicial phases. These first laws of 1905, 1908, 1919, and 1927 were insufficient. They were repealed.

See Appellation d'Origine Contrôlée.

Apple brandy

Brandy made from apples; distilled cider. The best French apple brandy is Calvados; the American variety is applejack.

See Calvados; Applejack.

Applejack

Applejack, strictly speaking, is the American name for apple brandy. Americans do not always speak strictly about applejack, however, since the name applies both to apple brandy—which is a spirit made by the distillation of fermented apple juice—and to a rougher spirit made by a more primitive process. In the early days, both methods were used; but now the second method is confined to a few back-country areas, where the cider is still fermented completely and then frozen. Since water freezes at a higher temperature than alcohol, the ice which forms and is skimmed off is almost pure water, and the unfrozen liquid left behind is almost pure alcohol. This potent and slightly oily spirit is applejack.

Applejack was for a long time one of the most popular spirits in America—partly, perhaps, because at that time the common drink was cider. This was comparatively low in alcohol (about 6% by volume) and, if contemporary reports are to be believed, the early American liked his liquor as potent as it was plentiful.

Actually, neither cider nor applejack was popular, nor even available, when the first settlers came to America,

for the simple reason that there were no apple trees. The English and the Dutch brought beer with them; and the English set about planting hops and barley in New England—where they did not thrive. Then they planted fruit trees, which flourished exceedingly and began to bear fruit (so it was said) much sooner than they would have in England, where cider was already being drunk in the sixteenth century, and probably earlier. The word, spelled "sider" in earlier times, comes from the Hebrew *shekar*; at first it may have meant any strong drink, although by the sixteenth century it was specifically the strong drink made from apple juice.

Since New England had proved to be a poor place for the growing of hops, the taste for beer changed to a liking for cider, for rum—imported from the West Indies and later made in New England from West Indian molasses—and for applejack, which was soon being carried inland by travelers and Indians. As time went on, the Dutch and German settlers in Pennsylvania began brewing beer with great success, and the Scots and the Irish, who arrived early in the eighteenth century, started the whiskey industry; but for a long time after this, the common drink in rural areas was still applejack.

The economic factors which encouraged the Pennsylvania grain-growers to start making whiskey in quantity worked in the same way upon the New England apple-growers. Since roads were universally poor, it was risky to try to transport heavy or bulky cargoes, and so both grain and fruit were fermented or distilled. The lighter loads of liquor, much easier to carry, commanded better markets too. In the cider industry, New England, with Connecticut outstanding, led other producers. The ingenious Connecticut Yankee, in addition to making himself famous by selling wooden nutmegs, proved his adaptability in the field of spirituous beverages. By taking cider, coloring it with Indian corn, and letting it age for three months, he got fairly strong liquor quite like Madeira in color, and sold it as such to gullible Europeans. How much of this went on is not known, but the practice could not have been extensive, for cider was too much in demand at home to be wasted on others.

One of the strongest beliefs held by the American of Revolutionary times was that the drinking of strong spirits was necessary to health—and, with great gusto, he set about taking care of his health, not infrequently starting with cider or applejack for breakfast and then carrying the jug out to the fields with him. Social events of all kinds, from weddings to funerals, and from church suppers to political rallies, were well-supplied with rum, cider (or applejack), or some kind of strong punch—and sometimes with all three at once. At one church function in New England, thirty bowls of punch were drunk before the morning meeting by eighty Christians—and a great deal more of a formidable mixture of drinks that same evening. As stills became easier to buy, many farms set up their own, thus raising applejack to the level of a distilled spirit, although much of the primitive frozen type was made too. That the product was powerful is proved by the way it was referred to in the local taverns, where customers would ask for a "a slug of blue fish-hooks," "essence of lockjaw," or, after the center of the trade had moved to New Jersey, for "Jersey lightning."

For the making of applejack only the cider from sound, firm, well-matured apples is chosen. For commercial applejack the product is distilled. The kind of still used in the old days (and often, but not always, found today) was the pot still. In modern applejack-making, the fluid is distilled twice, the first time coming through at about 60° of proof, and the second time at anywhere from 110° to 130° of proof. (In America, a spirit that contains 50% alcohol by volume is said to be at 100° of proof.) Today, after distillation, the applejack is cut with water and grain neutral spirits to bring it down to 85° or 100° proof as the distiller desires—since apples are more expensive than grain, a pure applejack would cost the customer too much. In the more robust frontier days, applejack was often put on sale raw and fiery, straight from the still. It is placed in oak casks today and kept in bonded warehouses to age—anywhere from one to five years.

In other times, a rougher and inferior spirit was sometimes obtained by the slapdash method of distilling the pomace without pressing it first. Alternatively, the pomace from which all the juice had been pressed out was sometimes taken and soaked in water. The water was then fermented and became a weak spirit known as ciderkin which, in colonial days, was considered fit for children.

Among the terms for applejack are: apple brandy, cider brandy, cider spirits, cider whiskey, and sometimes just plain "apple." Although the name applejack is strictly an American one, apple brandy is made in various parts of the world, the most famous being that from the Calvados area in the province of Normandy in France.

See Calvados.

Apricot brandy

A dry unsweetened brandy made from the distilled juice of apricots. The original, and most famous, apricot brandy was Barack Pálinka, made in Hungary (*q.v.*).

Apricot liqueur

A beverage, not to be confused with apricot brandy, made of mashed apricots and sweetened brandy.

Apry

Tawny-colored liqueur made from apricots soaked in sweetened brandy. It is produced by the firm of Marie Brizard et Roger in Bordeaux, France.

Apulia (Puglia)

Red and white wines.
District: Southeast Italy.

Apulia, the largest wine-producing region in the country, juts down into the Mediterranean to form the "heel" of the Italian "boot." The sun-drenched, shadeless,

wheat-bearing plain changes farther south into a vast rolling sea of vines and gnarled olive trees, the two often rubbing branches in the same field. The soil is as heavy as the sun is hot, but the vine adapts itself so prolifically that Apulian grapes are crushed into 11 million hectoliters (291 million U.S. gallons, 242 million imp.) of wine annually—mostly red and mostly run from fermenting vat to tank or barrel to be sold throughout the country as the indispensable ordinary table wine. Some of it is used for blending—because of its rough body and high alcoholic content—and much floods into the vermouth plants or is concocted into the various wine-based aperitifs Latin countries consume in such abundance. As in the French Midi, one pretends that these bulk wines are fine. There are, nevertheless, some delightful exceptions.

Sansevero is a D.O.C. that applies to white, red, and rosé wines produced within the communes of San Severo and seven others in the province of Foggia. The white is a pale (straw-colored), dry, light, and eminently drinkable wine from the northern end of Apulia's *tavoliere,* the "chessboard" or plateau extending around Foggia. The wine is of medium strength and from Bombino grapes, and some experts consider it among the finest white wines of Italy. Other offerings from the "chessboard" are Locorontondo, Martinafranca, Castel del Monte, and Matino, all D.O.C.

Locorontondo and *Martinafranca* are both white wines produced from different proportions of Verdeca and Bianco di Alessano grapes grown in neighboring areas southeast of Bari. Both have a delicate bouquet, a dry taste, pale green color, and about 12° of alcohol.

Castel del Monte is the D.O.C. for white and red wines made respectively from Pampanuto and Uva di Troia in the area around Bari. White Castel del Monte is a dry fresh wine of good character, but not so good as the red, which improves quite well with ageing and may be given the cachet *riserva* after three years. It is excellent, with a good balance of tannin and acidity.

Matino comes from farther south, around the town of Lecce, famous for its baroque architecture; the wine takes its name from another small town called Matino. The reds and rosés bearing this name may contain up to 30% Malvasia and Sangiovese, and the Negro Amaro grape gives the wines their characteristic slightly burnt taste.

Moscato di Trani is a D.O.C. for the naturally sweet wines made from the Moscato Bianco grapes grown around Bari. The name is also given a *liquoroso* wine from the same area, but with a higher degree of alcohol.

Among other wines of note are *Aleatico di Puglia* and *Moscato del Salento*—but not for people who do not care for sweet wines. The former is a warm, orange-red, sweet, strong (15%) dessert wine with a special pungency that betrays its origins, the sun-dried Aleatico grape, which is something like a Black Muscat and leaves an unmistakable trace in the perfume of the wine it makes. Most Apulian Aleatico is grown around Bari, Brindisi, and Taranto. Muscat grapes grown along the Salento peninsula are both red and white and the wine also may be either. Both types are strong and sweet, but neither has quite the virtue of the Aleatico.

The lesser wines include Barletta and Squinzano. They derive their names from the towns near which they are made and are produced in enormous quantity. As a rule they are distinctly minor wines.

Aqua vitae

The early name for brandy, from the Latin, meaning "water of life." The Italians claim, however, that the original name was not *aqua vitae* but *aqua vite*, or *acqua di vite*, the Italian for "water of the vine," referring to the colorless fluid which has been distilled from wine. Later, they say, either because of the power of liquor to stimulate and revive, or through a simple mistake in spelling, the more familiar term came into use.

Aquavit (akvavit, akevit)

A spirit, found generally in the Scandinavian countries, distilled from grain or rectified potato spirit and flavored with certain aromatic seeds and spices—caraway seeds in particular. Aquavit is drunk chilled and traditionally accompanies Scandinavian smörgåsbord. The name, a contraction of the Latin *aqua vitae*, meaning "water of life," was coined during the thirteenth century in Italy to designate the first distilled liquor produced from wine.

Today, Sweden is generally considered the world's foremost producer of aquavit, or "snaps," as it is often called in that country. The first license to sell aquavit in Stockholm was granted in 1498. During the next century, the liquor was produced merely by distilling wine, and as the requisite grapes are not grown in Sweden, the wine had to be imported from abroad, which made aquavit so expensive that it was used mainly for medicinal purposes. Not until Swedish soldiers learned to produce the spirit from grain did it become more common. During bad harvest years, however, the authorities had to prohibit all distilling of aquavit, and so the search for substitutes continued. Experiments were made with roots and berries; but in the eighteenth century the potato was found to be so suitable for the purpose that it has been the main source of aquavit ever since.

Most of the potato distilleries in Sweden today are situated in the southern province of Skåne. The clean potatoes are first boiled in steam under pressure, and the resultant starch mass is then mixed with crushed malt (made from barley or mixed grains) to convert the starch into sugar. Yeast culture is added to the mash, and in the ensuing fermentation the sugar is converted into alcohol. The spirit is rectified again (to remove the taste of potato) before it is used as an ingredient in the finished product.

A high-quality aquavit cannot be obtained merely by diluting such alcohol with water, for it would have no flavor. For this reason the diluted spirit is allowed to come into contact with birch charcoal made active through the effect of steam at high temperature. This not only increases the aldehyde content of the alcohol but also forms small quantities of taste elements called esters. A few selected spices are generally accepted as especially suited to flavor aquavit, the most popular of which are caraway seed, aniseed, fennel seed, and bitter orange.

There is a general misconception that aquavit must be strictly an unsweetened spirit. In fact, the term aquavit has been adopted as a general term both for the spiced and sweetened liquor—specifically known in Sweden as aquavit—and for Brännvin, which is usually (but not always) unspiced and unsweetened.

At present there are some twenty aquavit brands in Sweden. The O. P. Anderson Aquavit is a leading export brand made with caraway seed, aniseed, and fennel seed. Another well-known brand is Ödakra Taffel Aquavit, which was brought into the market in 1899: it is lightly spiced and comparatively dry. Överste Brännvin has a stronger spice aroma than O. P. Anderson and contains somewhat more sugar; while Skåne Aquavit very much resembles the O. P. Anderson, although it is less spicy.

Second to Sweden in the production of aquavit is Denmark, where this beverage, usually known as schnapps, is looked on as the national drink—it accounts for 70% of Danish spirit consumption. Schnapps is generally a nonsweetened, colorless beverage.

The Danish Distilleries were founded in 1881, and up to 1914 aquavit could be purchased for about the equivalent of fifteen cents (sevenpence) a bottle. Today there is one distillery only, owned by Danish Distilleries, which since 1923 has enjoyed the sole right of producing alcohol and yeast in Denmark. The Danes sometimes use potatoes and grain. The latter is invariably used for export.

Aalborg Taffel Akvavit, which was first produced in 1846 and is the best-known brand in Denmark and abroad, is seasoned with caraway seeds and contains 43% alcohol by volume. Other brands worthy of mention are Brøndum Kummenaqvavit, a caraway seed aquavit with cinnamon; Aalborg Export Akvavit, which has a slight taste of Madeira; Harald Jensen Taffel Akvavit; and Perikum-Snaps.

Norway produces less of the spirit than either Sweden or Denmark, and its best-known brands are: Lysholm Aquavit, a light, elegant, and rather delicate type matured in newly-empty Sherry casks; Løiten Aquavit, a full-bodied, more robust type; and Linie Aquavit, a rather interesting type, the name of which refers to a "crossing of the Line" (i.e., the equator). This is in keeping with the old tradition that the liquor improves with a sea voyage—and today it is sent to Australia and back on the Wilhelmsen cargo liners.

Aramon

An enormously productive grape variety, giving ordinary wines, and cultivated principally in southern France and in California.

Arbois

White, red, and rosé wines.
District: Southeast France.

The best-known wine district of the Jura. White and red wines are made here, and rosés which are among the best in France.

See Jura.

Château d'Arche

Bordeaux white wine.
District and Commune: Sauternes, France.

Located on a hill near the village of Sauternes, this Second-classed Growth in the 1855 Classification makes a well-balanced wine. The property is one of the oldest in the district and is owned by M. Bastit-St. Martin.

Vineyard area: 42 hectares (105 acres).
Average production: 80 *tonneaux* (7,500 cases).

Ardine

Apricot brandy made by the French firm of Bardinet.

Areometer

Device for measuring specific gravity—a form of densimeter (*q.v.*) with arbitrary graduations. There are different versions of the instrument: the Oechsle, for one, and, of particular interest here, the Baumé.

This areometer (French: *mustimètre*) has always been used since the time of Chaptal (*see* Chapter Nine, p. 38) to check the density of the grape must, since luck would have it that the graduation so obtained represents approximately the proportion of alcohol which wine will contain after fermenting—so that 1° Baumé corresponds nearly enough to the density of 17.18 grams of sugar in a liter of water.

The instrument shows 0° in distilled water, 15° in a solution of 15 parts (by weight) sea salt in 85 parts water. *See* table *below*.

EQUIVALENCE TABLE OF THE DENSITY OF A WINE AND THE WEIGHT OF SUGAR IT CONTAINS

Specific Gravity of Dry Wine at Equal Strength	Sugar to be Added to Achieve Specific Gravity of 1,000 (in grams per liter)	Specific Gravity of the Same Wine *after* Adding Sugar per liter					
		9g	18g	27g	36g	45g	54g
990	25	994	998	0°1	0°6	1°1	1°6
991	22	995	998	0°3	0°8	1°3	1°8
992	20	996	1,000	0°4	0°9	1°4	1°9
993	17	997	0°2	0°6	1°1	1°6	2°1
994	15	998	0°2	0°7	1°2	1°7	2°2
995	12	999	0°4	0°9	1°4	1°9	2°4
996	10	1,000	0°5	1°0	1°5	2°0	2°5
997	7	0°1	0°6	1°1	1°6	2°1	2°6
998	5	0°2	0°8	1°3	1°8	2°3	2°8
999	2	0°4	0°9	1°4	1°9	2°4	2°9

EQUIVALENCE TABLE FOR BAUMÉ DEGREES, POTENTIAL ALCOHOL DEGREES AND SPECIFIC GRAVITY
(AT A TEMPERATURE OF 59°F. [15°C.])

Baumé Degrees	Alcohol Content Potential Coeff. 17	Corresponding Specific Gravity	Baumé Degrees	Alcohol Content Potential Coeff. 17	Corresponding Specific Gravity
6	5	1043	24	29.5	1199
7	6.2	1051	25	31	1209
8	7.4	1058	26	32.6	1219
9	8.6	1066	27	34.3	1230
10	9.9	1074	28	35.9	1240
11	11.1	1082	29	37.6	1251
12	12.4	1090	30	39.3	1262
13	13.7	1099	31	41.1	1273
14	15	1107	32	42.9	1284
15	16.4	1116	33	44.7	1296
16	17.7	1124	34	46.5	1308
17	19.1	1133	35	48.4	1320
18	20.5	1142	36	50.3	1332
19	22	1151	37	52.3	1344
20	23.4	1160	38	54.2	1357
21	24.9	1170	39	56.3	1370
22	26.4	1179	40	58.5	1383
23	27.9	1189			

EQUIVALENCE TABLE FOR BAUMÉ DEGREES, OECHSLE DEGREES AND SPECIFIC GRAVITIES
(AT TEMPERATURE OF 59°F. [15°C.])

Baumé Degrees	Oechsle Degrees	Corresponding Specific Gravity	Baumé Degrees	Oechsle Degrees	Corresponding Specific Gravity
0	0	1000.0	2.1	14.7	1014.7
0.1	0.7	1000.7	2.2	15.4	1015.4
0.2	1.4	1001.4	2.3	16.1	1016.1
0.3	2.1	1002.1	2.4	16.8	1016.8
0.4	2.8	1002.8	2.5	17.5	1017.5
0.5	3.5	1003.5	3.0	21.2	1021.2
0.6	4.2	1004.2	4.0	28.5	1028.5
0.7	4.9	1004.9	5	35.9	1035.9
0.8	5.6	1005.6	6	43.4	1043.5
0.9	6.3	1006.3	7	51.0	1051.0
1.0	7.0	1007.0	8	58.7	1058.7
1.1	7.7	1007.7	9	66.5	1066.5
1.2	8.4	1008.4	10	74.5	1074.5
1.3	9.1	1009.1	11	82.5	1082.5
1.4	9.8	1009.8	12	90.7	1090.7
1.5	10.5	1010.5	13	99.0	1099.0
1.6	11.2	1011.2	14	107.4	1107.4
1.7	11.9	1011.9	15	116.0	1116.0
1.8	12.6	1012.6	16	124.7	1124.7
1.9	13.3	1013.3	17	133.5	1133.5
2.0	14.0	1014.0	18	142.5	1142.5

Argentina

Argentina, with more than 300,000 hectares (750,000 acres) of wine-producing vines, makes more wine than any other country in South America; and in the entire world, only four countries produce greater quantities: Italy, France, Spain, and the Soviet Union. An average annual output of 30 million hectoliters (800 million U.S. gallons, 660 million imp.) ranks Argentina just ahead of the United States in wine production. Of this huge quantity, only a small amount reaches the world market, and a greater share cannot be expected if the quality of the wines does not improve. Argentina's exportation of wine was greatest at the end of the Second World War, when much was shipped to England; but now about 600,000 hectoliters leave the country each year. Among South American wines, the Chilean are better known, yet lack of exposure is not the reason that so little of the wine reaches world markets. While the quality of the wines could improve, quite simply, the Argentinian is a wine-drinking man: the population of 25 million consumes nearly 88 liters (23.2 U.S. gallons, 19.4 imp.) per capita every year, a very high average. Even so, certain sparkling wines and vermouths are occasionally found in the United States and in Europe. A tremendous quantity of vermouth is made, and sparkling wines are produced by all three methods: secondary fermentation in the bottle (the champagne method), bulk fermentation, and carbonation. About 70% of the country's wine is *vin ordinaire,* but a few *bodegas* (wineries) do make better-quality wines.

WINE HISTORY

The Jesuits brought wine to the land of the pampas from Mexico. In 1556 a Jesuit priest named Father Cedron planted the first vineyard in the Cuyo region. These very early plantings survive as the Criollas grape variety, the name given to the five closely related descendants of those vines brought to Argentina four hundred years ago. The Criollas Grande is still a leading producer of light red and rosé wines.

The modern story of Argentine wine is, however, a tale of Italians, not Spanish missionaries. A century ago, Italian immigrants began to sluice the snow waters from the Andes out over what was then the unpromising desert of Mendoza, a province which lies against the mile-high mountain boundary with Chile. The Andean waters worked the same miracle in Argentina that had been brought about by irrigation in Algeria and California: a new vineland was born.

VINE-GROWING REGIONS

Mendoza province, about 600 miles (1,000 kilometers) west of Buenos Aires, produces 75% of the wine of Argentina, and 40% of the entire cultivated acreage is devoted to the vine. Wine-making is the only important industry in the region. The total number of vine-growers is about 40,000, but as much as 20% of the output is produced by nine large firms, each of which maintains its own vineyards, bottling plants, and sales organizations throughout Argentina. Red wines represent 38% of total production, whites 15%, rosés 30%, and table grapes 17%. As might be expected in a new flat wine area under Italian influence, the methods are chiefly the modern ones of mass production. Yet, too, the land and climate encourage a tremendous quantity of reasonable wine.

Mendoza and the neighboring province of San Juan are gigantic flat platters of green vines stretching like an ocean, with island-like wineries containing some of the highest fermentation vats anywhere in the world. The positive and unsubtle qualities of the wines stem from the mass vinification methods. Wine fermented and matured in lots exceeding 10,000 hectoliters is not uncommon. In such conditions, individual care is impossible. One winery in the town of Mendoza processes a staggering total of one million hectoliters a year. Of course, not all of the two hundred *bodegas* in the town are so huge, but Mendoza is still a virtual honeycomb of cellars and storage sheds. Al-

together, 250,000 hectares (625,000 acres) are in vineyard in Mendoza province.

The northern zone of the province contains more than half of this total area. In the eastern section of north Mendoza, Criollas, Malbeck, and the incorrectly-named Pedro Ximénez varieties are irrigated with water from the Tunuyán and Mendoza rivers and with water from wells. In the saline soils of the northwestern part of the province, the same varieties predominate. The southwestern zone of northern Mendoza makes Argentina's very best wines. There the Malbeck is widely planted and produces a better wine than its more famous brother, the Cabernet Sauvignon. The wine is by no means fabulous, but is some of the best Argentina can offer.

The Uco River Valley is the central vineyard zone in Mendoza. Here the Malbeck, Tempranilla, and Sémillon are the most important varieties. In the southern sector of the province several stocks yield some quite good wines. These include the Criollas, again the Malbeck, Muscatel Rosé, and Chenin, all of which grow on land irrigated with water from the Atuel and Diamante rivers.

Directly north of Mendoza, in San Juan, also lying against the continental spine of the Andes, a heavier, richer wine is made. The vineyard area is about 60,000 hectares (150,000 acres). This is, of course, nearer the equator and the climate is therefore hotter, resulting in the heavier wine. San Juan produces 20% of Argentine wine, mostly in the Zonda, Ullun, and Tulun valleys. The grape varieties are generally the same as those grown in Mendoza. Since irrigation is essential in both San Juan and Mendoza, the familiar slope wines of European vineyards are unknown, and water coursing through the irrigation veins of the table-flat vineyards has brought death as well as life to the vines. While in most other countries the lethal vine louse phylloxera has traveled in the air or been transported on infected vine stalks, in Argentina the parasites may also have been flushed from one region to the next in the ducts of the irrigation system. Conversely, Argentinians use irrigation to fight phylloxera. Attacked areas are flooded or kept underwater for a short period so that the pest is drowned and the vineyards made phylloxera-free.

South of Mendoza, in Río Negro, about 5% of the country's total output is grown. Here in the southern hemisphere the pattern found in European countries is reversed and the lighter wines are found to the south, while pleasant dry white and sparkling white wines are produced in the colder, more rigorous climate. These are often considered some of the best Argentinian wines.

Along with Mendoza, San Juan, and Río Negro, the other important areas of wine-production in the republic of Argentina are Litoral (adjoining the provinces of Buenos Aires and Santa Fe), Córdoba, Occidente (La Rioja and Catamarca), Norte (Salta and Jujuy), and Entre Ríos.

Throughout the country the Malbeck grape produces two-thirds of the red wine, followed by other familiar European varieties, principally French and Italian. The

ARGENTINA
Zones of wine production

largest part of the white wine is made from Torrontes Sanjuanino and the Pedro Ximénez, followed by Sémillon, Sauvignon, Malvasia, Chenin Blanc, and Riesling. With the recent effort to upgrade the quality of Argentinian wine, the National Wine Institute has encouraged growers to buy good European stocks to expand and replant vineyards. Barbera, Bonarda, Carignan, Merlot, and Sangiavettoe are used for red wines; Chardonnay, Alexandrian Muscat, Sylvaner, and Listan for white.

About the only demand the average Argentinian makes of his wine is that the quantity be plentiful. Indeed, most of the extensive expansion of vineyards is geared to low-quality high-volume wines. But for the better wines of Argentina two real problems remain, especially with the coming of export trade. First, the taste in Argentina is for older wines. White wines in particular are poorly vinified in wood and then kept too long before drinking, so that the wine has lost its freshness and tastes of the cask. Many of the reds too are aged longer than they should be. In the United States red wines usually suffer by being consumed before their peaks are reached, but in Argentina the opposite is true. More serious than the taste for old wines is the problem of quality control. Other than fine wines, there are virtually no place-name laws or any statutes regulating vintage dates or the contents of varietal wines. Well-known European names such as Margaux, Chablis, "Borgona," Rioja, and Beaujolais are commonly used. All sparkling wines are called "champagne." A wine labeled "Riesling" may very well have been made from only Sémillon and Sauvignon Blanc. Only large investments in modern equipment that improves vinification and ageing, and laws that define wine-producing areas, exclude foreign place-names, and provide minimum standards can begin to make the quality of Argentinian wines as great as the quantity. Considering the technological progress of the past 20 years, this moment is in the not-too-distant future.

Arjan

Another name for koumiss or fermented sour mare's milk made by the Tartars.

Arkansas

Small wine-producing region of the United States. The vineyards are centered around the northern sector, in the Ozark Mountains.

See United States: Arkansas.

Armagnac

Brandy.
District: Southwest France.

Armagnac comes from the land of d'Artagnan, a land of vines, geese, and horses; of the bland cream-colored cattle of the Pyrenees and swarthy hot-blooded people, some of them descended from the Goths, Visigoths, and Basques who settled in the wide spaces of Gascony. They say that witches are still to be found in Armagnac, to

bring luck to their friends and put curses on their enemies; but here, in the country of Henry IV, there are many good Protestants, their farms marked by cypress trees as a sign of their faith. The landscape is blackened with short, knotty oak and pine; in winter, a cold wind howls down from the Pyrenees, and in summer the rolling plain, veined with streams, is burned brown by a searing sun. Armagnac brandy, matching the extreme climate in which it is nurtured and the determined character of the people who make it, is full-bodied, pungent, and strong. Much of it goes to market in a flat, fat, long-necked flagon, known as a *basquaise* and labeled, usually, Armagnac or Bas-Armagnac. Ténarèze and Haut-Armagnac also are permitted place-names but are seldom seen, since they are the lesser designations of the region. (This is the supreme example of the foolishness of assuming that *bas*—lower—must necessarily mean of lower quality than *haut*—higher; these words are used in France simply in the geographical sense.)

DELIMITATION

In 1909, in order to establish the name and capture a market after the example of Cognac, the region of Armagnac brandy was marked out. It is mostly in the department of Gers, although a little of the best corner juts into Les Landes, south of Bordeaux. The chief centers are Condom, for Ténarèze; Auch, for Haut-Armagnac; and Eauze, in Bas-Armagnac, scene of the Thursday market in Armagnacs, when the narrow streets bulge with men buying and selling the brandy, testing the quality by rubbing a drop between their hands and sniffing it.

Bas-Armagnac, to the west, flattening into the pine forest which extends to the dunes along the Atlantic, gives brandy of the greatest finesse, from a mainly sandy soil. This brandy, if it is to carry the choice name of Bas-Armagnac, must not only be 100% Bas-Armagnac but must also have been blended in a separate warehouse, apart from any other types which might be handled by the same shipper. The brandies from the south part of Ténarèze, where the soil is clay, are lighter and develop more quickly. Haut-Armagnac, to the east, is predominantly chalky—and although it is chalk content which determines the finest Cognacs, here the brandy is of a ruder type and never appears on the market, except as a basis for liqueurs, an important part of the Armagnac business.

VINTAGE

Armagnac age and vintage, though officially regulated, are still a matter of some dispute. The Armagnac producers and the Bureau National de Armagnac use the same system to date their brandies as is used in Cognac. In late September or October the wine is made and distilled almost immediately; its age is then designated as *compte* 00. On the thirtieth of April, all distillation must stop and all brandy be distilled; the harvest becomes *compte* 0. Every year on April 1, all of the brandies officially gain another year, although in fact they may be a number of months older. The minimum age at which Armagnac may be sold as Armagnac is *compte* 1; for Three-Star or its equivalent, *compte* 2; for V.S.O.P., *compte* 4; and for *Extra* or *Hors d'Age*, at least *compte* 5. Unlike Cognac, Armagnacs are still permitted to indicate specific vintage years and specific vintages (except when imported into the United States). Armagnac labeled as "ten years old" may be a blend of Armagnacs from different years, but the youngest Armagnac may be no younger than ten years old.

Since certain growers consider that vintage brandy is better than a blend (although, as in Port or Champagne, only in certain years), some firms produce an occasional vintage Armagnac, putting the other years into blends. Exceptionally, a producer will deal exclusively in vintage Armagnac. In the *chai* of one such grower, which is connected to his house beneath one long-sloped Basque roof in Bas-Armagnac, barrels of Armagnac are ranged on their scantlings into two tiers, each dated in chalk with the vintage. The proprietor, in sabots, Basque beret peaked forward over his eyes, will tell how the greater number of his customers come in person, from various parts of France and even from abroad, to taste the brandies of the different years and make their choice. A large shipper-grower a few miles away has the only glass-lined storage tanks in Armagnac. This might be thought a sad departure from tradition, an infiltration from the French Midi or Algeria—until the magic 1904, 1891, 1888, and other old vintage Armagnacs are drawn one by one with the little silver spigots and nosed and tasted. After about fifty years, Armagnac will no longer improve in the wood but will begin to go down; when in glass, like every other spirit, it does not change. That is why the Bas-Armagnac

shipper-grower has captured his old brandies at their height and put them into glass.

Nearly black from age in oak, smoldering with a fresh fire that seems to burn inside velvet, and with such an aroma that the perfume sometimes lingers for over a week in the emptied glass, these vintage Armagnacs are indeed supreme.

To bear a date on the label an Armagnac need not be from a single year; brandy blended down through the years will sometimes be dated, but in this case the date is required by law to be the year of the youngest brandy included.

AUTHORIZED VINES

For the white wines of the Gers from which Armagnac is made, Picpoule, Saint-Émilion, Jurançon, and Plant de Grèce (called Baco) are the chief vines. Blanquette, Mauzac, Clairette, and Meslier are also authorized but are seldom seen. Folle Blanche, which used to be the leading variety, is steadily giving way to the Saint-Émilion and other sturdier plants.

In recent years, the hybrid vine Baco 22A, a cross of the Folle Blanche and the American Noah, has been included among the authorized vines, but only in the sandy terrains of Bas-Armagnac. Its merits are hotly debated in Armagnac. A basic rule of French viticulture is that hybrid vines produce grapes inferior in quality, and in every vineyard with a controlled place-name for wine, they must be rooted out. In the sandy vineyards of Bas-Armagnac, the Baco seems, so far, to produce a wine which can be distilled into a brandy as fine as that from the Picpoule or Folle Blanche. It is early, however, to judge the ingredients of a product which must mature for forty years to reach its best.

COMPARISON WITH COGNAC

Armagnac differs basically from Cognac in several ways. The best of it comes from a sandy soil, while the fine Cognac is from the area richest in chalk. The climate is different, for in Cognac it is maritime, mellow, and misty; in a more primitive region, Armagnac is closer to its origins than Cognac, not so smoothed out by blending, a natural product to which no sugar need be added.

Many Frenchmen besides the Gascons prefer Armagnac, at its best, to Cognac—but unfortunately, it is not always at its best. Cheap Armagnacs are too prevalent, and some of the people who are in the habit of buying these are unacquainted with the finer types. In the United States no good was done to the name by false claims to great age; ninety-nine years was a frequent boast until the 1951 law stamped out this practice. Now, an Armagnac label may state (if true) that the brandy is "at least ten years old," but no greater claim can be made.

Different also in Armagnac and Cognac are the methods of ageing and distilling—a difference deliberately emphasized.

In the brandy cooperative at Réans, on the edge of

Eauze, new distillations of Bas-Armagnac wine, all from the same still and all 1952, were put into a row of barrels, half of which were of the native oak of Armagnac, and half of the Limousin oak in which Cognac is aged. The bung of every barrel was wax-sealed and officially taped. Tasted in 1956, the brandy in the Armagnac oak barrels was good, but the Limousin oak barrels contained something which was neither Armagnac nor Cognac. There was a practical reason for the experiment: Armagnac oak is slowly running out and is consequently soaring in price; yet again it had been proved that Armagnac must be made in Armagnac oak and nothing else.

Distillation of Armagnac in Cognac stills has often been tried. The result is indicated by the fact that since 1936 a law has decreed that Armagnac must be made in the native continuous still. Cognac is double-distilled, the final issue being around 70% of alcohol. Armagnac cannot exceed 63% and is usually 10% less. This means more non-alcoholic grape products in the brandy and more native taste. Originally, the Armagnac still resembled the one used in Cognac—but by the nineteenth century the present continuous still was becoming common. Fundamentally, it is a pot still in which the vapors are refined by the wine itself (see Chapter Ten, p. 52), and it is designed to distill wine of 9% to 10% of alcohol—a more highly alcoholic wine is not desirable, as the aim is to pass over as much as possible of the non-alcoholic taste and aroma-giving quality. The result is that Armagnac, retaining many of the original elements of flavor and scent, has an astonishing perfume, even when it is less than a year old and is too fiery to drink. This young brandy is often taken in coffee, to which it gives a heady burst of fragrance.

One hundred fifty or so of the smaller growers share the six perambulating stills. This alembic is one of the traditional sights of the countryside: like an ancient black locomotive drawn backward, it moves slowly across the Armagnac landscape. It halts in the night, its mouth gushing fire as the sticks of oak are thrust in, while everywhere else is silence and darkness. From peasant to peasant it goes—and thus the product of those without an alembic of their own is distilled. Now, however, the leading firms are studying a new type of alembic which will produce an equally pure eau-de-vie while eliminating certain ethers. This will cut short the period of ageing.

Some Armagnac was bad because of the lack of tradition among shippers; and Armagnac is still exported in smaller quantities than Cognac because the growers did not know how to advertise their brandy. These matters have now been taken in hand by some of the better shippers and the more important growers. At the head of these was the late Marquis de Montesquiou, Duc de Fézensac, a parliamentary deputy who worked his estate, the Château de Marsan, as a model farm and experimental station, and who made strenuous efforts to maintain the highest standards of Armagnac and to protect the small peasant grower from the sharp practice of certain shippers who would try to buy their brandy for the lowest price and then sell it at the highest. A visitor to the Château de Marsan would dine off the traditional Gascon dish, Henry IV's favorite, poule au pot, followed at the end of dinner by a fine old Armagnac. And in his bedroom, the visitor would find more Armagnac in a small decanter—another tradition in which the host believed.

Because this is the country of the famous companion of The Three Musketeers, most firms have their Réserve d'Artagnan: the one who is entitled to this splendid name is the Marquis de Montesquiou. He is a descendant of the hero, who really lived at the Château de Castelmore, near Lupiac, although his name was not d'Artagnan. The plaque over the gate of the neglected seventeenth-century building bears these words: Ici naquit vers 1615 d'Artagnan, de son vrai nom Charles de Batz (Here d'Artagnan was born, about 1615, under his real name, Charles de Batz).

Since 1951, Armagnac has had a brandy fraternity comparable with the wine orders of the Chevaliers du Tastevin in Burgundy and the Commanderie du Bontemps in the Médoc. These fraternities provide a good deal of dressing-up, oath-swearing, and other amusement for the members, and excellent means, also, of attracting attention to the brandy of the region. In Gascony, the Company of the Musketeers dress up in high boots, plumed hats, and magnificent mustaches; Cardinal Richelieu and the King of France appear, too. The hilltop city of Auch is crowned by a cathedral begun in the fourteenth century and finished by Louis XIV. It contains a choir-seat decorated with hundreds of wooden figures marvelously carved by a pupil of Michelangelo and approached by a fine flight of steps. Up these steps sweep the modern Musketeers; and at the top stands d'Artagnan, in stone—a surprisingly young and girlish figure, looking out over the land whose character he personifies.

Armillaria root-rot

A fungus disease of the vine.
See Chapter Eight, p. 29.

Aroma

The impression that a young wine makes on the nose—to be distinguished from bouquet. The aroma of a young wine relates directly to the smell of the fresh fruit from which it was made, and not to any esters which have a chance to develop when the wine is older. Aroma is most pronounced in those wines which, rather than being extremely dry, have retained some of the original grape sugar—as is the case with easily identifiable Gewürztraminers.

Arrack (arraki, arack, arak, raki, etc.)

The name derives from the Arabic for "juice" or "sweat" and generally designates "native spirits," so there are probably as many types of arrack as there are of native spirits in the Orient and in Eastern Europe. Arrack has been distilled in the East Indies from fermented palm sap and from rice, from grain spirits in Greece, and from dates in the Middle East and Egypt; and Batavia arrack is a highly aromatic rum distilled in Java. The number and type of herbs and spices which have been used as flavorings are probably as wide as the human imagination. In any case arrack is a coarse drink made for tough palates. A French proverb states that "He who has once tasted arrack never forgets the taste."

Arroba

Spanish wine measure of 11.5 kilograms (25.36 lbs.), approximately equal to one basket of grapes. Sixty *arrobas* theoretically give one butt of 516 liters (136.3 U.S. gallons, 113.5 imp.) of wine. The liquid *arroba* equals 16.0 to 16.5 liters (4.23 to 4.36 U.S. gallons, 3.52 to 3.63 imp.).

Artichoke brandy

Spirit distilled in France from the Jerusalem artichoke. In Italy there is an aperitif called Cynar which is made from artichokes.

Artisan (Cru Artisan)

The minor class of Bordeaux growths ranking below a Cru Bourgeois and above a Cru Paysan. These wines are the *vins ordinaires* of Bordeaux, usually blended and not château-bottled, and hardly ever showing a vineyard name. Yet in the present market, more and more of these wines are being bottled and sold under their proprietary labels.

Asali

An East African beverage fermented from honey.

Asciutto

Italian term for dry wine.

Assmannshausen

One of the two best red wines of the German Rhine. German red wines are never important, and are not to be compared with the great white wines; a considerable amount is seen in Germany, but it is of no significance in the export market.
See Rheingau.

Asti

Italian town celebrated for its sparkling white wine, Asti Spumante (which is sometimes dry, more often sweet, and always bubbly) and, to a lesser extent, for its Moscato d'Asti.
See Piedmont.

Astringency

With reference to wine, this means sharpness from acid content and tannin and sometimes indicates that the wine will be long-lived.

Asztali bor

Hungarian term for common wine. *Bor* means wine.

Athol Brose

Scottish drink based on whisky, mixed with honey and/or oatmeal.

Attemperators

Spiral-shaped metal coils which are immersed in fermenting vats, and through which hot or cold water is run to regulate the temperature of the fermenting must or grape juice.

Aubance

See Coteaux de l'Aubance; Anjou.

Aube

French department in the less important southern section of the Champagne region, with about 2,000 hectares (5,000 acres) of vines.
See Champagne.

Aude

Red and some white wines.
District: Southern France.

Quantitatively, one of the three most important wine-producing departments of France; the other two are Hérault and Gard. All three make up the bulk wine area known as the Midi. The Aude vineyards in the Roussillon region, near the Franco-Spanish border, produce very large quantities of undistinguished wines, mostly red; also a very limited quantity of fair white and rosé wines, more particularly those of Limoux, Corbières, and Minervois.

Aurum

A proprietary Italian liqueur, pale gold in color and with an orange flavor.

Auslese

A German term meaning wine made from selected bunches of grapes. Beerenauslese is the selection of individual grapes from the bunches, Trockenbeerenauslese the selection of overripe individual grapes.
See Germany.

Château Ausone

Bordeaux red wine.
District and Commune: Saint-Émilion, France.

Traditionally first among the wines of Saint-Émilion, Ausone is now sometimes thought to have fallen behind Cheval-Blanc—and is considered by some to be below

Figeac, although Ausone still commands fabulous prices. When Saint-Émilion wines were officially classified in 1955, however, Ausone and Cheval-Blanc were placed in their traditional position at the head of the First Great Growths (*Premiers Grands Crus*), the others following alphabetically, although they were not ranked in a class apart.

Ausone is believed by some to stand on the site of the villa of the fourth-century Roman poet Ausonius—and, if what Ausonius wrote is true, the wine was a favorite of Julius Caesar. In any case, the vineyard is magnificently placed on the western edge of the eleventh-century hilltop village of Saint-Émilion; the château looks over its terraced and sloped vines, all facing southeast. Because of its high situation, Ausone escaped the terrible frost of February 1956, in which so many other vineyards, including Cheval-Blanc, were frozen—they not only lost their 1956, 1957, and some later vintages, but were still feeling the effects into the sixties. The Ausone cellar is a deep rocky cane hewn centuries ago out of the soft stone upon which Saint-Émilion stands. Château Bel-Air wine (the vineyards adjoin) was, until 1974, aged in the Ausone cave. Both châteaux were owned by the late M. Dubois-Challon, who was the leading figure in the Saint-Émilion wine society—the Jurade. Madame Jean Dubois-Challon, his widow, and the family of Madame Cecile Vauthier, his sister, now own Château Ausone.

Characteristics. Less robust than many of the Saint-Émilions; nevertheless a full wine of considerable distinction.

Vineyard area: 7 hectares (17.5 acres).

Average production: 30 *tonneaux* (2,500 cases).

Australia

Australia is a land endowed by nature to produce abundantly all the fruits of the earth. This is especially true of "God's greatest gift to man"—the vine and wine. Not only does the vine flourish where it grows, but it is capable of limitless expansion in large tracts of land equally suitable to bear it. It is regrettable, however, that many vintners still parade their wines under European place-names instead of building up their own.

In 1801, Napoleon Bonaparte sent a delegation to spy on the land so recently discovered, and it was reported to him that because of Britain's great consumption of wine, Australia was destined to become the British vineyard. Years later, Hubert de Castella (original planter of the famous Lilydale vineyard of St. Hubert's) wrote a small book which he titled *John Bull's Vineyard*.

In Australia, as also in California, conditions are so congenial for vine-growing that almost every year is a vintage year and there is no necessity for that ceaseless control essential on the European continent. This evenness in climate does away with certain "lows" but does not necessarily increase the "highs."

The versatility of Australian soil has been amply demonstrated over the years by its ability to produce from, for example, Cabernet Sauvignon either a classical claret-style wine or a good Vintage port-type, and from Tokay either a dry white or a luscious dessert wine. Many other varieties are capable, in this country, of such a dual function. It is this adaptability that marks the difference between Australian and European wine practice. Years of experience have shown the Old World's vine-growers that their soil and climate are particularly adapted to certain varieties of grapes, and they concentrate on these to the exclusion of all others.

WINE HISTORY

The vine in Australia is as old as the settlement itself. When Captain Arthur Phillip set sail from the Thames with his fleet of eleven ships, he included in the cargo "plants for the settlement," among which were the first vines to enter Australia. He landed in Sydney on January 26, 1788 and planted the vines on the site where the Botanical Gardens now stand. It was soon found that this location was far from ideal for the propagation of the vine, since the humid conditions on the waterfront encouraged the development of a fungoid disease later identified as anthracnose—more familiarly known as "black spot." It was decided to replant in a more congenial area, and in 1791 three acres were planted by Governor Phillip twelve miles away from Sydney, on the Parramatta. At the same time, a settler named Schaffer planted an acre and thus can be given credit for being the first private *vigneron* in Australia. Unfortunately, however, his further activities appear to have been obscure.

The first man to make any serious attempt to produce wine on a commercial scale was Captain John McArthur, who was given a grant of land some 30 miles from Sydney. This he named Camden Park. Rootlings of all procurable varieties were obtained from the official collection, and afterward a certain number of seedlings were planted with a fair measure of success. Later, Captain McArthur was joined by his two sons—James, born in 1798, and William, born in 1800. The feud between McArthur and Governor Bligh is common knowledge, and it was even carried into the ordinary procedure of wine-making: when, in 1807, McArthur imported two stills for making brandy from some of his wine, Bligh had these confiscated, repacked, and returned to England. At the same time, he had McArthur tried in the criminal court, holding that the stills were illegally imported to produce rum—the currency of the N.S.W. Corps. The McArthur family nevertheless continued to thrive and to play an important part not only in Australian viticulture but in the public affairs of the state.

Another important individual in the early history of Australian wine was Gregory Blaxland, who was the first grower in Australia to export his wine to London. Certainly the quantity involved was not great, being only a quarter-pipe of red wine, but it can be cited as the forerunner of the subsequent very considerable trade in export "burgundy." Five years later, Blaxland exported from the same Parramatta vineyard three half-pipes of wine. He achieved further fame when, with Wentworth and Lawson, he crossed the formidable barrier of the Blue Mountains and explored the fertile plains beyond—a venture which was to mean much to the development of agriculture in New South Wales.

In 1824 a remarkable young man arrived in Sydney. His name was James Busby and he was then twenty-four years old. While still in Scotland, with only the viticultural background of a few months spent in the best wine districts of France, he was imbued with the belief that there was a great future for the vine in Australia. Shortly after his arrival he wrote his first book, *A Treatise on the Cultivation of the Vine and the Art of Making Wine.* On May 8, 1824 a grant of 2,000 acres of land in the Hunter River district was made to him. He named it Kirkton, afterward well known for its wine. After five years' experience in Australia, Busby wrote a second book, *A Manual of Plain Directions for Planting and Cultivating Vineyards and for Making Wine in New South Wales.*

At this time Busby arranged with McArthur, Blaxland, and others who had established vineyards, for their surplus cuttings to be distributed among intending planters. Busby's crowning work, however, was his voyage of viticultural research into southern European wine regions and the introduction into Australia of his great vine collection, which included nearly all the best varieties grown in France and southern Spain at that time. The vines reached Sydney in good condition, and Busby offered them to the government for the formation of an experimental garden there, "to prove their different qualities and propagate, for general distribution, those which may appear most suitable to the climate." The vines were planted in the Botanical Gardens, and of 678 varieties, 362 were successfully struck. This collection has been the basis of the vine population of Australian vineyards since 1833.

Right up until 1925, nearly all the wine exported from Australia was of the export burgundy-type. In 1854, consignments were only of a token nature, and it was not until 1872, when the firm of P. B. Burgoyne & Company started operations, that the wine trade showed any important development. It grew, was maintained at around 900,000 U.S. gallons (750,000 imp.), and was distributed throughout the United Kingdom by such firms as Burgoyne's, with Harvest and Tintara; as Gilbey's, with Rubicon; as Stephen Smith, with Keystone; and Pownall's, with Emu. Then, at the end of the First World War, it became the responsibility of the Bruce-Page government to absorb the returning soldiers into sound occupations. At that time, as established growers on the Murray were gathering crops of Gordo Blanco grapes at the rate of about 10 tons (11 short tons) to the acre, at A£12 per ton, grape-growing appeared to be the ideal occupation for the repatriated men. Despite warnings from the industry itself that only limited settlement was possible, the government went ahead with the greatest vigor, so that when the vines bore fruit, there was an inevitable glut of grapes, accompanied by an economic crisis of the worst kind. The government was impotent to solve this problem, which was flung back upon the industry itself. The Federal Viticultural Council advised that the only possible remedy was to establish new markets by the granting of an export bounty, which would have the effect of creating a de-

mand for fortifying spirit in this new market, and thus absorb the glut of Doradillo grapes—which were the distilling variety. Having no better plan, the government announced a bounty of 2s. 9d. a gallon and gave a drawback of excise on the fortifying spirit used, which was considered equivalent to 1s. 3d. a gallon, making a total remission of 4s. a gallon on all the sweet wine exported. Within a few years these measures had proved successful. The export of fortified wine sustained a great impetus, and in 1927 the total export of wines rose to 4,553,000 U.S. gallons (3,773,000 imp.).

At the present time, the export trade in Australian wine has considerably receded, to about 60,000 hectoliters (1.71 million U.S. gallons, 1.32 million imp.) per year.

In specialist shops abroad, such as the Australian Wine Centre in London, the old medicine-style tonic "burgundy" is a thing of the past. There is a considerable variety in the wines, many of them named for the grape and the estate—e.g., Tahbilk Estate Cabernet, or Orlando Barossa Riesling. In the regions of the world where the climate is reliably hot and sunny, red wine is by nature big and strong, sometimes—as in Australia—with a unique flavor of its native soil. Whites, full of character, tend to be low in the acidity which gives the wine zest. In this unfamiliar terrain Cabernet, Riesling, Shiraz, and Pinot have produced wines markedly different from the European types. But the present up-to-date methods of viniculture (such as the cold-temperature controlled fermentation of white grapes in sealed tanks) now make livelier, fresher whites and reds with a big bouquet, a rich color, and a good bracing of tannin—wines of all kinds, of a quality which the wine-makers of a hundred years ago would hardly recognize. Unless it is labeled Rhine Riesling, a "Riesling" wine may be made from the Sémillon grape.

The Australian wine industry is now embarking on a new program of vineyard establishment, largely conducted by firms which began in the 1800s. New vineyard areas best suited to the production of premium table wines are being sought out and planted with the best European varieties. Small wineries in both traditional and new viticultural regions are playing an increasingly significant role in the industry.

WINE REGIONS

New South Wales

The Hunter River Valley was significant in the early viticultural experiments of the Australian continent. Later growers of note there included the Lindeman family; in 1842, Dr. H. J. Lindeman planted Cawarra, famous for many years for its high-quality claret-type wines. In 1914 he acquired the vineyard of Kirkton from Catherine Busby, whose daughter later married Dr. Lindeman's son. This vineyard was to become the best known of the many plantations subsequently owned by the Lindemans—another is the Ben Ean Vineyard, planted by J. McDonald in 1870. In that year the acreage of the Hunter vineyards reached a high point of some 2,200

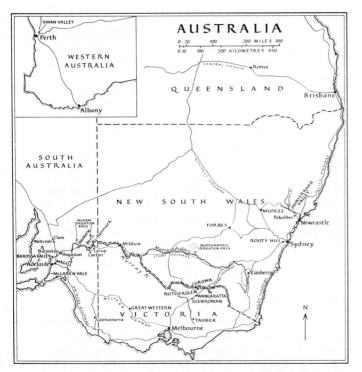

hectares (5,500 acres); but during the next seventy years, because of various adverse factors, the total fell, reaching 440 hectares (1,100 acres) in 1947.

Today, the Hunter Valley wine industry is soundly established and has a fine future, especially for white wines, above all Chardonnay and Sémillon; more than 3,400 hectares (8,500 acres) is planted in vines. The new breed of Hunter Valley wine-makers open their doors to the public, in California fashion, for tours and tastings. Some of the better-known places are Rothbury Estate, Wyndham Estate, Lake's Folly, Bellevue, Tulloch's, Drayton's, Elliot's, Tyrrell's, Lindeman's and McWilliams. Penfold's, Wybong Estate and Segenhoe Vineyards, owned by the Rosemount Company, are located in the Upper Hunter.

Another important district in New South Wales is the Murrumbidgee Irrigation Area, the principal centers of which are Griffith, Leeton, Beelbangera, and Mirroul. Large quantities of wine are produced there and help to make New South Wales the second largest wine-making state in Australia. A third major area is Corowa, which, though small, produces some of the best quality dessert wines in the country.

Other New South Wales districts are Mudgee, Forbes, and Rooty Hill. Mention can be made here of the Huntington Estate wines from the cooler area near Mudgee.

Victoria

The first record of a vineyard in Victoria was that planted at Yering in Lilydale in 1838 by William Ryrie, from vine cuttings obtained from Camden Park. In 1839 Charles La Trobe was appointed the first superintendent of Port Phillip—he afterward became first governor of the colony of Victoria. La Trobe married, in 1835, a Swiss lady (Mlle. de Montmollin), and there is no doubt that this union prompted the departure of a number of Swiss

vignerons for Australia, and more particularly Victoria. Eleven of these settled in Geelong, and very soon after their arrival they all possessed their own small vineyards. In 1848 Paul de Castella arrived in Victoria and took up land at Yering. George de Pury settled in Yeringberg, and in 1854 Hubert de Castella arrived and planted St. Hubert's. By 1886 Yering had 40 hectares (100 acres) of vines, Yeringberg 28 hectares (70 acres), and St. Hubert's 104 hectares (260 acres). The vines were mostly White Hermitage and Tokay, Red Hermitage and Cabernet.

Although vine culture in Victoria started later than in New South Wales and South Australia, the congenial conditions there attracted a number of settlers to the cultivation of the vine, so that by 1900 there were over 1,200 separate vineyards, in almost every part of the state. Victoria was by far the biggest wine-producer at that time, with 1889-90 production as follows:

	GALLONS	
	U.S.	*imp.*
South Australia	613,294	510,674
New South Wales	827,076	688,685
Victoria	1,895,808	1,578,590

Unfortunately for Victoria, the dread scourge of phylloxera began to appear, first in Geelong, then in Bendigo, and later in the vineyards of the northeast, with the ultimate result that the main areas devoted to viticulture were devastated. In many cases, the costly process of reconstitution with phylloxera-resistant vines from America proved too frightening and the land concerned was turned to more stable forms of agriculture. Another factor which reduced the number of growers, particularly of the lighter types of wine, was the lack of appreciation inside Australia of the quality of Australian wines, so that it often happened that a wine-maker was faced with the problem of storing the forthcoming vintage while his cellars were already filled to overflowing. The uncertainty, the comparatively poor prices, and the low yields per acre were also contributing factors to the loss in production.

The irrigated area of Mildura plays a dominant part today in the state's wine production, accounting for 85% of the total. Near Melbourne, the Château Tahbilk, Mitchelton, Balgownee, and Virgin Hills wineries produce quality wines, as do the Yarra Valley wineries of Yerinberg and Château Yering, and the Helen Vineyard to the north.

Farther north, near the Rutherglen area, lie the Wangaratta, Glenrowan, and Milawa districts, the latter known for its Brown Brothers wines. The Bailey, Chambers, and Morris family names have long been associated with the fortified wines made in this area. Westward, in the Great Western region, quantities of sparkling wines, including those of the Seppelts Co., are produced. The newly planted land near Avoca promises to yield some good red wines.

South Australia

Inferior in earlier years to Victoria, South Australia has shown steady progress because it escaped the vicissitudes of its neighboring state. From the first plantings in 1837, vines have suffered few setbacks, and eighteen family firms here have already celebrated their centenaries. Wine-making in South Australia ranks very high in popular esteem; it is classed with grazing as a most important rural industry. The Barossa Valley is probably the most successful of all from the point of view of quality. Here the soils are variable, ranging from heavy loams to light-backed sandy earth. Some excellent light table wines come from the vineyards located in the hilly country to the east. Penfold, Seppelts, Yalumba, Orlando, Tolley Scott & Tolley, Kaiser Stuhl (a Barossa cooperative), and Leo Buring are just a few of the wineries in the Barossa Valley. The area is planted with the best grape varieties for the production of dry Riesling, as well as Auslese-style wines.

It was in this district that the Barossa Wine Festival originated, to celebrate the harvest in the manner of the old festivals in Germany. Nothing could more adequately symbolize the spirit of the vine than the sight on a glorious day in early June of the red-gold sea of vines in their autumn colors spreading as far as the eye can reach.

Quite close to Adelaide fine wines of diverse types were successfully grown from European grape varieties, but as Adelaide expanded almost all of the vineyards gave way to housing. South of Adelaide, however, the McLaren Vale has gained a good reputation for its red wines, made by the firms of Thomas Hardy & Sons, Chateau Teynella, Tyecroft, Birramimma, Emu, Ingoldby, Arenberg, and the Southern Vales' Cooperative, to name a few.

Other small vine-growing districts in South Australia are Coonawarra, Clare, Watervale, and Langhorne Creek, of which the first two are the most important. In Coonawarra, the land is mostly flat, with red and black soils over limestone; a plentiful water supply close to the earth's surface promotes especially vigorous vine growth. Some of Australia's best table wines come from this district. The Redman, Wynn, Lindeman and Penfold companies have strong associations with the region. The Padthaway / Keppoch Valley, north of Coonawarra, also has some promising vineyards. The Clare and Watervale districts are known for good red and white table wines, Stanley Wine Co., Enterprise, Petaluma, and Taylors being the main producers. Langhorne Creek on the Bremer River has a very low average rainfall, but irrigation makes heavy crops possible. Although the soils here are generally alluvial, many of the dry red and dessert wines are good.

The Murray Irrigation Area, which includes Renmark, Lyrup, Berri, Waikerie, and Loxton, is more commonly known as the Murray River Valley. Until 1921, wines were made in these areas simply to be distilled into fortifying spirit; otherwise the main preoccupation of the growers was with drying varieties, such as sultanas, currants, and lexias. Since then, more attention has been paid to table wine and Sherry, and today 70% of the wines and brandies produced in South Australia come from the Murray River Valley.

When in 1921 Leo Buring—then an advisory expert—introduced the idea of producing commercially sweet wine of the same nature as that obtained from the dry non-irrigated districts, his efforts were not an unqualified success. But today, wines of quite exemplary quality are coming from this area. Most of the growers here are on a cooperative basis, the chief firms being Berri, Loxton, Renmark Growers, and Waikerie. Angove's Proprietary, Ltd., is an exception.

South Australia produces 50% of all Australian wine.

PRODUCTION FIGURES FOR A TYPICAL YEAR

	Hectoliters	U.S. Gallons	Imp. Gallons
South Australia	2,000,000	53,000,000	44,000,000
New South Wales	700,000	19,550,000	15,400,000
Victoria	350,000	9,775,000	7,700,000
West Australia	50,000	1,325,000	1,100,000
Queensland	1,500	39,750	33,000
	3,101,500	83,689,750	68,233,000

Western Australia

Not a great deal of wine is made in this state, but the principal *vignerons* are Valencia and Houghton's, both owned by Thomas Hardy & Sons. The other important winery is Sandalford. The Swan Valley near Perth is the center of production.

In the Busselton / Margaret River area, the wines from Vasse Felix, Leeuwin Vineyards, Cape Mentelle, Moss Wood, and Wilyabrup show considerable promise and fruit. Further south, the Franklin, Plantagenet, and Forestville vineyards are producing some fine table wines.

The Other States

Tasmania's cold climate has proven suitable to the production of European varietal wines; Heemskirk, Pipers Brook and Moorilla Estate wines are among the more successful producers.

With the total volume rarely exceeding 1,500 hectoliters, Queensland is the least significant of the wine-producing states. There is, however, a winery in Roma more than a century old.

Austria

Austrian wines are predominantly white and light—some crisp and tempting to gulp down, some fresh and fruity—with a few red. This small country, the heart of Europe (and, in the great days of the Habsburgs, the heart of the Holy Roman Empire), touches at its borders six others: Switzerland, Italy, Yugoslavia, Hungary, Czechoslovakia, and Western Germany—and its grapes are as diverse as the landscape. Vine-growing is older than the name Österreich, going back nearly a thousand years.

The word Austria conjures up pictures of Viennese cafés, zithers, and cream cakes, of baroque architecture, Strauss waltzes, and horses dancing—or else of a pastoral land of mountain lakes and wild flowers, of winter sports and haymaking farmers jolly in *Lederhosen*. Austria is all these things and more—although it is not true that the

Danube is blue. The vast ranges of the Alps tower over the land. In Carinthia, on the higher slopes of the Grossglockner, one of the highest mountains in Europe, is a remote glacial world where the snow never melts. But eastward, the steep massif declines toward the slopes outside Vienna, and the great plains of Burgenland and Lower Austria.

The spectacular western provinces of Tyrol and Vorarlberg produce little wine, all of it consumed locally. The 50,000 hectares (125,000 acres) planted in vine lie mainly, in order of size, in Lower Austria, Burgenland, Styria, and in the neighborhood of Vienna. The vineyards, where some 80,000 workers are employed, are mostly cut up into parcels of less than 20 hectares (50 acres), and the annual production of wine averages nearly 3 million hectoliters (79.5 million U.S. gallons, 66 million imp.)—89% white and 11% red. Most of the harvest is stored by the growers in their own vaults, but in abundant years some of it is taken over by the wine trade and the growers' associations. They combine voluntarily in these co-operatives, surrendering their crops for storage and sale on a trust basis. The societies have a reputation for good quality wines. Consumption of wine per capita is about 36 liters, a relatively small average for a European country—although this is more than Austria produces, so much of the wine (most of it red) is imported from Spain, Italy, France, and increasingly from Hungary, Yugoslavia, and the Balkan states. The annual importations are now around 225,000 hectoliters (5,850,000 U.S. gallons, 4,500,000 imp.).

Until a few years ago, the demand for wine meant that most of the native harvest was consumed at home. The situation has now changed and Austrian wines are seen abroad—from Schluck, perhaps made from Grüner Veltliner grapes, to luscious Spätlese and estate-bottled Auslese. The annual total is about 190,000 hectoliters (5 million U.S. gallons, 4 million imp.). Historically, the principal buyer has been Germany, but sales in other markets, particularly in Great Britain, are steadily increasing. A wine institute, established in 1968, has begun to regulate the export industry.

Wine labels state whether the wine is a natural one (*naturbelassen*) and, most important, if it is hand-picked (*gerebelt*). The labels carry either the name of the village or district of origin—or, less often, of the individual vineyard; or they may state the name of the grape variety, as in Alsace. Occasionally, both will be found. (For example, Wachauer 1974—i.e., wine of the 1974 vintage from the important Wachau region of Lower Austria; Grüner Veltliner 1974—i.e., wine of the 1974 vintage of the Grüner Veltliner grape; Steiner Veltliner 1974—i.e., wine of the 1974 vintage from Stein in the Wachau region and from the Grüner Veltliner grape.) Schluck is the light dry wine that asks to be swallowed. Among the better bottles, Riesling and Traminer will be found, and also some Spätlese wine from late-picked grapes; and ice-wines, such as the Nicholas wine from Krems. Among important place-names are Krems, Klosterneuburg, Gumpoldskirchen, Retz, Vöslau, Nussdorf, Grinzing, Oggau, and Rust—they will usually appear with the possessive.

WINE HISTORY

In A.D. 955 Otto I ordained the replanting of the Austrian vineyards for the first time since the departure of the Romans. Here, as elsewhere, the vines were to be tended principally by monks, in the monasteries of Bavaria and Salzburg. Those wines which were shipped up the Danube to Bavaria were known as Osterweine. The Austrian vineyards were most extensive in the sixteenth century, when Hungary came under Turkish rule and wine-making virtually ceased. Austria, free of her chief competitor, soon increased the size of her vineyards to ten times what they are today. Upper Austria, which now makes no wine, was then a leading producer.

About 1580, Johannes Rasch wrote the most important book on Austrian viticulture. In 1673 the *Landkompass* printed, by imperial patent, the classification of the vineyards, which had actually been graded in 1646; the classifications were good, fair, and ordinary. Over the years changes have occurred. The Wachau, now one of the best regions, was then in the third class, its wine, proverbially sour (*Sauer wie der Wachauer*—nothing could be sourer than Wachau wine). In 1780, the Empress Maria Theresa, setting out to simplify the administration of her dominions, revised the wine taxes (*Tranksteuer*). Under the new law, the aristocracy and the higher clergy were absolved from paying the taxes but as many as eight different taxes were levied on the rest of the population. Maria Theresa also approved some complicated regulations for the stocking and shipment of wines.

All producers were now allowed to sell their own wine (*Eigenbauwein*) free of tax. This law was extended to certain foods—and still causes trouble at the *Heurigen*, the popular Viennese wine-gardens based even now upon the laws of Maria Theresa.

When a grower wished to announce that stocks of his new wine were on sale, he hung up branches outside his house. The German verb "to hang out" is *aushängen;* hence, the name of these wines became *Hengelweine*—and the most prominent wine-selling family in Grinzing today bears the name Hengl. According to the dispensation of Maria Theresa, a man could sell only his own wine free of tax; therefore, a true *Heuriger,* when his barrels were dry, had to close his doors until next season.

No writing about Austrian viticulture is complete without some mention of Dr. Lenz-Moser; the importance of his work on *vinifera* hybrids and, above all, the revolutionary "high culture" method of growing vines that bears his name, are now recognized in all wine-growing countries. More than half of the vines in Austria are grown on the Lenz-Moser system.

WINE REGIONS

Lower Austria

This eastern province, with over 30,000 hectares (75,000 acres) of vineyard, watered by the Danube, is the granary of Austria—a country of cornfields, market gardens, and vines; a country, also, of churches, baroque monasteries, and romantic castles. It is the only district in

Austria: Wine Regions

Europe which actually produces oil in a vineyard region. The vineyards fall into the Danube area on both banks of the river—the hilly Weinviertel, and the Wienerwald-Steinfeld district. The principal varieties for white wines are Grüner Veltliner (a native vine that accounts for 23% of all Austrian production), Müller-Thurgau, Wälschriesling, Neuberger (another native vine), Rheinriesling, and Zierfander (Spätrot), which with Rotgipfler makes one of Austria's best-known wines—Gumpoldskirchner. The Muskat-Ottonel and the Pinot Blanc (called either Weisser Burgunder or Klevner) are also fairly important. For the very small production of red wines, the most common are Blau Portugieser and Blaufränkisch.

The Danube section begins west of Willendorf with the Wachau, a lovely stretch of country between there and Krems-Stein, where the vines climb up steep terraces of gneiss and mica schist. At Stein, the district of Krems begins. This belongs to the Wachau with its loess terraces, but the center is Krems itself, a historic wine town with big vaults for bulk storage, a school of viniculture, and a fascinating wine museum. Last harvesting in Strass bei Krems has been completed as late as December 10. In addition to those places already mentioned, Spitz, Dürnstein (lying picturesquely at the foot of a ruined castle), Weissenkirchen, and Loiben are worth noting. In both the Krems and the Wachau districts, the Riesling produces increasingly popular wines with a fine bouquet.

On the right bank of the Danube, the vineyards follow the river from Ober-Armsdorf to Traismauer. The Kamp Valley, on the left bank of the Danube, is an important wine-growing area in which the most important place is Langenlois. East of the Kamp Valley is the district known as Am Wagram, its vines planted along a terraced ridge of hills very like those at Krems. Downstream, on the right bank of the river, the valley widens into the fertile Tullnerfeld until, at Greifenstein, the mountains close in again, and the vines climb their slopes. Here the Klosterneuburg region begins. Klosterneuburg itself is a town celebrated for fine wines. It contains an experimental school of viticulture, a wine museum, and the enormous vault of the Chorherrenstift, three stories deep.

The principal place-names besides those cited above are Zöbing (distinguished for its excellent Riesling), Strass, and Schönberg; and, in the Klosterneuburg area, Kahlenberg.

Northward, on the left bank of the Danube, good wines grow on the slopes of the Bisamberg. Below Vienna, on the right bank, is the Hainburg and Bruck district.

The *Weinviertel* lies north of the Danube and consists of the countryside around Retz and south to the Eggenburg, Hollabrunn, and Ravelsbach districts. It includes also the "Brünnerstrasse" district, on both sides of the old main road between Vienna and Brünn, which is one of the most productive areas in the country. Light palatable wines come from this fertile country, although in the southwest the Veltliner produces spiced and fruity growths, and Matzen has some good red wines.

The principal place-names in the Weinviertel are Retz, Pulkau, Haugsdorf, and Mailberg; Eggenburg, Hollabrunn, and Ravelsbach; Poysdorf, Zistersdorf ("Steinberg"), Matzen, Wolkersdorf, and Falkenstein.

The Wienerwald-Steinfeld district. Some excellent vineyards are planted on the hill slopes of the Vienna Woods. Gumpoldskirchen, at the foot of the Anningen Mountain, is the best-known wine town. From Baden and Traiskirchen come fiery, spicy wines; and in Vöslau a red wine (Vöslauer Rotwein) is made from the Blauer Portugieser.

Burgenland

Until 1919, this southeastern province was part of Hungary, and even now some of the villages are entirely Magyar or Croat. The landscape here is different too; its dominant feature, set in the midst of *Puszta,* a kind of steppe, is the Neusiedlersee, a great lake rimmed with reeds—and exotic birds nesting on its marshy shores. The country, rich in orchards and vegetable gardens, also bears vines—nearly 15,000 hectares (37,500 acres) in four different areas, the Lake District, Eisenstadt and Mattersburg districts, and South Burgenland.

Here the main varieties are Muscat-Ottonel, Pinot Blanc, Wälschriesling, Neuberger, Grüner Veltliner, Traminer, Bouvier (a native vine), and Rheinriesling—all for white wines. Blaufränkisch (Gamay) and Blauburgunder (Pinot Noir) go into the red wines.

The lake district is the most important for wine, with vineyards bordering the Neusiedlersee on three sides. The vines are protected by the Leitha Mountains, and the glassy surface of the vast lake retains and reflects the warmth of the sun's rays. Excellent white wines are made here from Wälschriesling and Muscat-Ottonel, and some pleasant red ones from Blaufränkisch. At the end of a good summer there will be some fine Ruster Ausbruch from late-picked grapes, notably the Furmint. On the sandy soil of the Seewinkel the original vines escaped the phylloxera plague; this is one of the very few places in Europe where wine is still made from ungrafted vines. The principal place-names are Oggau, Mörbisch, St. Margarethen, and Rust.

The Eisenstadt district. The great center is Gols. Close to the lake, vines planted in sandy soil, immune from phylloxera, produce Sandweine. The principal place-names are Gross-Höflein, Klein-Höflein, St. Georgen, Podersdorf, Illmitz, and Apetlon.

The Mattersburg district. South of Eisenstadt, in the foothills of the Rosalien Mountains, the vineyards produce mainly red wines—one of them Blaufränkisch. The principal place-names are Pöttelsdorf, Trauersdorf, Neckenmarkt, Deutsch-Kreutz, and Lutzmannsburg.

South Burgenland. The wine-growing districts here center around Eisenberg and Rechnitz, where pleasant soft red wines are made from Blaufränkisch and Blau Portugieser.

Styria

Lying between the lovely lakes of the Salzkammergut (where St. Wolfgang and the White Horse Inn are to be found) and Yugoslavia, Styria is the green province, a country of meadows and woodlands, of fat cattle and plodding cart-horses, of rolling hills and rivers well stocked with fish. Its capital, Graz, is the second largest town in Austria. Once it was the peaceful resort of retired officers; now it is a busy industrial city. The *Steirerge-wand*—the gray loden suit with green facings—worn all over Austria, originated in Styria (Steiermark in German), where it is the national dress. The province has about 2,000 hectares (5,000 acres) of vineyard scattered over three districts: Sudsteiermark (Southern Styria), Weststeiermark (Western Styria), and Klöch-Oststeiermark (Klöch-Eastern Styria).

For white wines the important grape varieties are Wälschriesling, Ruländer (Pinot Gris), Pinot Blanc, Traminer, Muscat-Sylvaner hybrids, and Rheinriesling. Blauer Wildbacher (a native vine) goes into the West Styrian Schilcherwein; for the small red wine, the varieties are Blau Portugieser, Blaufränkisch and St. Laurent.

Western Styria. The wines of Weststeiermark are divided into two subdistricts: Schilcher and Sausal-Leibnitz. The Schilcher wines extend from Graz to Eibiswald on the southern frontier. In Stainz, a light red wine is made, and in Deutschlandsberg, a dark red one—fresh, spicy, digestible: this is the Schilcherwein. Other names to remember are Hitzendorf and Ligist.

The Sausal-Leibnitz district is a stretch of country lying east of the Schilcher district between two streams, the Lassnitz and the Sulm, the latter the home of the world's finest capons. Its highest point is Demmerkogel, where the vineyards are planted at nearly 1,920 feet (600 meters).

Southern Styria. Southern Styria's wine district is centered on the towns of Leutschach and Ehrenhausen. Extending to the northern slopes of the Windische Bühel, this is similar in soil and grape varieties (Wälschriesling, Sylvaner, Weissburgunder, and Traminer) to the Sausal-Leibnitz vineyards, but the wines are stronger and fuller.

Klöch-Eastern Styria. The vineyards of Klöch-Oststeiermark border Yugoslavia and are concentrated around the town of Klöch. These wines are of good quality, some of them sparkling, with a charming bouquet. They are particularly agreeable when young. The principal place-names are Radkersburg and Mureck.

The rest of eastern Styria is not greatly cultivated in vines. Wines are made, however, and the vineyards struggle up the slopes of hills as high as 2,000 feet (615 meters). The best-known places are Hartberg, Fürstenfeld, and Feldbach.

Vienna

The beautiful city is almost encircled by trees and meadows—the Vienna Woods, on the slopes of which the vines grow—nearly 800 hectares (2,000 acres) of them. From two of the hills, Kahlenberg and Leopoldsberg, the Turks were driven back from Western Europe—but their Oriental languor is said to persist in the leisurely café life. The wine villages of Grinzing, Sievering, and Nussdorf are now within the suburbs, and the stinging new *heurige* wine served in their wine-garden is, for the tourists who flock there, the essence of Viennese gaiety. Outside the little vine-covered houses, green boughs are hung out when the wine of the year is ready. Some may actually come from the proprietor's vine plot, but he will need more than he is likely to make to satisfy all the customers who come to the long wooden tables in his garden and sing to the music of zithers and guitars. There is a law permitting them only to sell wine which has been produced in their own vineyards, and to sell wine from other vineyards they must get a special permit.

Prevailing grape varieties: Grüner Veltliner, Neuberger, and some native vines.

Auxerrois

Grape grown in the Lorraine district for the light pink *vin gris.'*

Auxey-Duresses and Auxey-Duresses-Côte de Beaune

Burgundy red and white wines.
District: Côte de Beaune, France.

Auxey is one of the poor relations of the Côte de Beaune. Its wines are about 80% red and, while they are considered sound enough in body, fragrance, and color, they are rarely, if ever, distinguished otherwise. Yet, because of the difference in price between these and others from the famous slope, they are often good value.

The vineyards are set back in the hills, slightly too high to be first-rate. They cover about 170 hectares (420 acres)

and wines from grapes grown in about 100 hectares (250 acres) within this area may add the term Côte de Beaune to the commune name. Such wines may occasionally be slightly superior to the communal ones. In an average year Auxey produces 1,100 hectoliters (29,150 U.S. gallons, 24,200 imp.) of white and 3,200 hectoliters (84,800 U.S. gallons, 70,400 imp.) of red. Wines from the best vineyards may add vineyard name to commune name, and although the final list of these First Growths (*Premiers Crus*) has not yet been drawn up, the following vineyards are considered the best.

FIRST GROWTHS (*Premiers Crus*)

Vineyard	Acres	Hectares
Les Duresses	26.6	10.6
Les Bas-des-Duresses	5.9	2.39
Reugne	7.8	3.16
Les Grands-Champs	12.0	4.86
Climat-du-Val (or Clos du Val)	23.0	9.31
Les Écusseaux	15.9	6.43
Les Bretterins	5.0	2.02

N.B. Wines sold as La Chapelle come from grapes grown in a once separate vineyard now split between Reugne and Bretterins.

Ava-Ava

Another name for kava (*q.v.*).

Avelsbach

German commune in the triangle between the Mosel and Ruwer. The wines are classed sometimes with one group, sometimes with another. The best-known vineyards are: Altenberg, Dom Avelsbach, and Dom Herrenberg.

See Mosel-Saar-Ruwer.

Avize

Village in Champagne which produces one of the finest wines of the Côte des Blancs.

See Champagne.

Ay

Town in the Marne Valley near Épernay, whose cellars lie underneath the fine Champagne red-wine vineyards of that region.

See Champagne.

ℬ

Bacardi

A well-known brand of Cuban rum, now produced in Puerto Rico, Brazil, Mexico, and the Bahamas. Also a cocktail based on the rum.

See Rum, Puerto Rican.

Bacchus

(1) From the Greek *Bacchos*—an alternative name for their wine god, better known as Dionysos. The Romans adopted him as Bacchus, identifying him with their own wine deity, Liber.

(2) An American hybrid grape, small and black, which at best produces wines with body and of fair quality.

See Dionysos; Classical wines.

Baco

French hybridizer Maurice Baco, whose grapes are grown in France and America. Many Baco vines have become especially important in several parts of the United States. Baco 1 is widespread but produces better wine in New York State than in France; Baco 22A is legally allowed in the sandy soils of France's Bas-Armagnac to be used in making the region's fine brandy, but its merits are still disputed.

Bacterium (pl. bacteria)

Microscopic unicellular organism which lacks rigid cell walls and a well-defined nucleus.

Bad Dürkheim (Dürkheim)

See Dürkheim; Palatinate.

Bad Kreuznach

Wine town and region in the Nahe (*q.v.*).

Badacsonyi Kéknyelü

The best-known of the Badacsonyi wines—a dry greenish-white dessert wine. Both red and white wines are grown in this region.

For this and other Badacsonyi fine wines *see* Hungary.

Baden

White and red wines.
District: Southwest Germany.

The Baden vineyard, like an edging worked in vine and grape motif, borders the extreme southwest corner of Germany. It begins along the south shore of Lake Constance (or Bodensee, as it is called in German), skirts the thickly wooded slopes of the Black Forest on the fringes of Switzerland and France, and then marches parallel with Alsace on the other side of the Rhine, past Strasbourg on the Alsace side and Baden-Baden on the German side, until it reaches the Heidelberg region.

The wines are not among the most important in Germany and they are practically unknown abroad, but they are much better than they once were. In the 1860s, Baden was the largest German vineyard, but shortly afterward the phylloxera plague struck, reducing the plantation by almost half. A second catastrophe for local production—although good was expected to come out of it—was the law of 1938–40 which required the uprooting of hybrid vines. The Baden vine area then shrank another 20%; but the replanting with Ruländer, Sylvaner, Traminer, some Riesling, and Müller-Thurgau generally improved the wines as the vineyards aged. The Müller-Thurgau crossing of Riesling and Sylvaner has gained rapidly in this district, as it has elsewhere.

The region, now as large as the more famous Mosel area, has undergone much improvement with the coming of the great cooperatives. These giant organizations, which manage as much as 90% of the vineyard acreage in Baden, have shaped new vineyards suitable for modern machine cultivation by planing the old terraces with great earth-movers. With the improved quality of the local wine, prices are higher; Baden wines often fetch more than wines of the same quality from better-known regions. Most famous of the cooperative wineries is the Zentralkellerei Badischer Winzergenossenschaften at Breisach, the largest single winery in Europe.

Much of the good wine comes from the Müller-Thurgau grape; and better quality red wines are made from Spätburgunder, the variety brought originally from Burgundy, where it is called Pinot Noir—this is the standard grape for such good red wines as are found in Germany. In Baden, the Burgundy-import variety is known as the Blauer Spätburgunder; a wine called *Weissherbst* (white autumn, or white vintage) is made from the grapes, sometimes with the addition of a little Traminer or Riesling. It is really a rosé, very light in color and surprisingly heavy and full-bodied for a pink wine.

Gutedel, a grape variety brought from Vevey on Lake Geneva in 1780, produces the Markgräfler wines grown below Freiburg in the southwest corner of Germany. It is also found in considerable quantities over the Swiss border to the south and the French border to the west.

The Ruländer grape variety is actually the French Pinot Gris. Its German name derives from the fact that the grape was brought from France to Germany in 1711 by one Ruländ, a merchant of the town of Speyer. It gives a golden wine which can be very rich and fruity and in the big years quite full-bodied.

Riesling is becoming more common in Baden. There is

93

some on the south face of the Kaiserstuhl and in the Ortenau, the areas producing the best Baden wines. Riesling covers approximately 15 per cent of the 13,000 hectares (32,100 acres) in vines. The average annual harvest is 900,000 hectoliters (23,730,000 U.S. gallons, 19,791,000 imp.).

Important estates are those of Freiherr von Neveu, Graf Wolff Metternich, Schloss Staufenberg, and Max Markgraf von Baden.

VINE-GROWING SUB-REGIONS

The long hook-shape of Baden, following the Rhine from Lake Constance to Heidelberg, includes several distinct vineyard areas with their own characteristics of soil and climate, and therefore of wines. The main ones are Bodensee and the pleasant Seeweine (Lake Constance); and then, following the Rhine rather than any order of importance, Markgräfler, Kaiserstuhl, Ortenau, Kraichgau and Bergstrasse, and Badisches Frankenland. The Bergstrasse, above and slightly below Heidelberg, is in both Baden and Hessen and is considered separately. For a complete list of the Baden *Einzellagen* (individual vineyards) arranged by *Grosslage* (section of vineyards) and *Bereich* (sub-region), *see* Appendix B, p. 599.

Bereich Bodensee

The wines are known as the *Seeweine*, or Lake Wines. The name refers to the influence on them of the large lozenge-shaped lake along which they lie. Even more influential than the mild climate of the lake is the *Föhn*, a warm wind peculiar to the surrounding alpine area in Germany, Austria, and Switzerland. While it has such a disturbing effect on plants, men, and animals that it commonly causes insects to swarm and milk to turn sour, and has been taken into account by the Austrian penal laws covering crimes of violence, its hot breath brings the grapes quickly to ripeness. The better types are Spätburgunder, Ruländer, and Gewürztraminer. Each little lake port has its vineyard, but nearly all the wine of consequence grows around Meersburg, where acres are cultivated by the Baden State and are called Domäne Meersburg. None of the Bodensee wine escapes the tourists and you must go there if you want to taste it. You could hardly do better: the little lake steamer glides along from port to port, first in Switzerland and then in Germany; speedboats and sailboats cross from the Swiss shore, where snowy peaks tower in the distance. Meersburg itself is a medieval jewel set in vines; it has a castle which is thirteen hundred years old and still carefully preserved. In the lantern-hung outdoor restaurants on the shore of the lake, the wines accompanying the characteristic Bodensee blue trout taste better than they really are.

Bereich Markgräflerland

The name comes from Markgraf, a German title approximately equivalent to Count. Markgraf Karl Friedrich planted vines in this extreme southwest tip of Germany in the late eighteenth century. It was during this period that the Gutedel, the dominant variety, was brought from Vevey in Switzerland; but the best wines are the Sylvaners, Ruländers, and Traminers.

Bereich Kaisertstuhl-Tuniberg

Crossing the little bridge over the Rhine in the vicinity of Riquewihr in Alsace and going toward Freiburg, you see on your left a low cone-shaped hill ringed with vine. The Kaiserstuhl is of volcanic origin; and the mingled clay and volcanic soil gives rich red wines and darkish white wines with an amber tinge—all of which are likely to show the fieriness of their origin and to be definitely full-bodied, yet rather soft. Common vines, mostly Sonstige, grow on the north and the east faces. From the south and southwest slopes come the best Baden wines from the grape varieties Riesling, Sylvaner, Traminer, and Ruländer for white wines; and for red wines, the Blauer Spätburgunder. Among the best *Weinbauorte* (townships) are Achkarren, Ihringen, and Bickensohl. Wines are named both by the usual German method of village name followed by vineyard parcel name, and by the Alsatian method of naming the wine after the grape variety. Thus, two excellent white Kaiserstuhl wines are Ihringen Sylvaner and Achkarrer Schlossberg.

Bereich Breisgau

The small area just north of Kaiserstuhl and Markgräflerland produces wines that are undistinguished but just as pleasant as those from anywhere else in Baden. The town of Freiburg, with its great cathedral (the tower is among the highest stone structures in Europe), is at the southern end; Lahr is in the north. The *Weissherbst* from the Glotter Valley near Freiburg is one of the best Baden wines.

Bereich Ortenau

After the very circumscribed area of the Kaiserstuhl, the best Baden wines come from the region called the Ortenau. It stretches along the thin plantable zone from the Rhine to the forested mountains, from the town of Offenburg up to Baden-Baden. The soil is mainly crumbled granite. The best white wines are the Rieslings, the Traminers, the Ruländers; and in reds, the Blauer Spätburgunders. Red and white vineyards are intermingled, but among the best *Weinbauorte* for white wines are Durbach, Ortenberg, and Neuweier; and for red wines, Durbach. Here, near Offenburg, the Riesling is called Klingelberger, a name taken from a property of Markgraf Staufenberg. Another peculiarity is that the white wines around Neuweier are bottled in the Franconian flask, or Bocksbeutel (*q.v.*).

Bereich Bergstrasse-Kraichgau

This is the region lying between the Ortenau and the section just below Heidelberg where the Bergstrasse begins. Kraichgau is a zone where much of the vineyard had to be torn up when hybrids were outlawed in 1938-40. Where there has been post-war replanting, much of it has been in Ruländer and Blauer Spätburgunder.

Bereich Badisches Frankenland

The northernmost of the Baden *Bereiche* and somewhat separated from the main viticultural sections. Most of the vines grow around Tauberbischofsheim and in the valley of the River Jagst, a tributary of the Neckar.

Bagaceira

Portuguese spirit made from grape skins.

Balance

The degree of harmony achieved by the different parts of a wine when they are considered as a whole. Simply, a well-balanced wine has all of its aspects in control, with none too prominent and none obviously deficient. A well-balanced wine may not be great, but a great wine is always well-balanced.

Balaton, Lake

Center of one of the principal wine regions of Hungary.
See Hungary.

Château Balestard-la-Tonnelle

Bordeaux red wine.
District and Commune: Saint-Émilion, France.

Among the oldest growths in the district, the property is particularly famous due to a reference in a poem by François Villon (1431-1463): *ce divin nectar/Qui porte le nom de Balestard* (this divine nectar, which bears the name of Balestard). The energetic Capdemourlin family, some of the most dedicated promoters of Saint-Émilion wines, owns this *Grand Cru* of the 1955 Classification.
Vineyard area: 8 hectares (20 acres).
Average production: 40 *tonneaux* (3,700 cases).

Balling or Brix

A hydrometer scale used to measure the approximate sugar content of grape juice, sweet wines, and sugar solutions. The scale is calibrated to indicate percentage by weight of sucrose when it is immersed in sucrose solutions. The Brix hydrometer is usually calibrated at 17.5°C. or 20°C. and the Balling at 60°F.

Balthazar, balthasar

A bottle—notably in Champagne—more suitable for display purposes than for holding wine or spirits. It has a capacity of sixteen normal bottles.

Banadry

French banana liqueur made by Bardinet of Bordeaux.

Bandol

Controlled place-name for certain wines of Provence, France.
See Provence.

Banyuls

Sweet wine.
District: Roussillon.

Area on the Mediterranean border between France and Spain. Banyuls produces a sweet fortified wine known as *vin de liqueur,* of little interest in countries where Sherry and Port can be had. Banyuls is a sweet natural wine, often drunk before meals by those French who like sweet aperitifs; it is taken also as a dessert wine.
See Sweet fortified wines of France.

Barbados Rum

See Rum, West Indies.

Barbados Water

One of the earliest names for rum. From Barbados, a British island in the West Indies where rum originated.

Barbaresco

A red wine from Piedmont. One of the better red wines of Italy—big, strong, slow-ageing, with considerable depth and pungency.
See Piedmont.

Barbera

Italian red-wine grape, used especially in Piedmont (*q.v.*).

Barbera Amabile

Sweet, slightly sparkling red Italian wine from the Barbera grape, grown widely in north Italy.

Bardolino

Red wine grown in the vineyards between Verona and Lake Garda, Italy.
See Veneto.

Bärentrank

A beverage from East Prussia, distilled from potatoes and flavored with honey. The name in German means "bear's drink."

Barolo

A red wine from Piedmont. One of the best red wines of Italy—robust, heavy, and slow-maturing, with a pungent aftertaste.
See Piedmont.

Barossa Valley

Vine-growing district near Adelaide, South Australia.

Barr

Wine town in Alsace, France.
See Alsace.

Barrel

Standard container. In America, a barrel contains 31.5 U.S. gallons; in England, 36 gallons imp. For table of capacities of barrels, casks, and containers of various nations, *see* Appendix C, p. 630.

Barrica

Spanish for the Bordeaux *barrique,* or barrel, found in Spain.
See Barrique.

Barrique

French barrel or hogshead, especially the *barrique bordelaise,* or Bordeaux hogshead, containing 225 liters (59.4 U.S. gallons, 49.5 imp.). A *barrique* contains the equivalent of 288 bottles, or 24 cases of 12 bottles each. In Bordeaux, four *barriques* make up a *tonneau (q.v.).*
See Appendix C, p. 630.

Barriquot

Old French for small barrel or keg.

Barsac

Sweet white wine.
District: Bordeaux, France.

Even in the minds of people who are knowledgeable about wine, there is apt to be some confusion between Barsac and Sauternes—is Barsac a Sauternes or is it a place-name on its own? In fact, it is both.

The natural sweet white wine district of Barsac surrounds the town of that name in the northern stretch of the official Sauternes region, about 25 miles southeast of Bordeaux. Sauternes is composed of five communes, of which Barsac and Sauternes itself are two. (*See* map on p. 434.) All were once separate and known in their own right; but the production of the commune of Sauternes was small, and some considerable time ago it was decided to include in the *appellation* the similar wines grown in neighboring villages, in order to have a large enough production to make the wine known in the world market. But Barsac, although it was brought into the Sauternes communes, was considered too famous to give up its own name. Consequently, the French wine-law authorities decided that Barsac wines (grown in the vineyard region of Sauternes as now constituted and having all the characteristics of the wines of Sauternes, yet remaining in the

traditional district of Barsac) were entitled to both the place-names, Barsac and Sauternes. In practice, some are called Sauternes, some Barsac. Either is correct; the greatest are likely to keep the *appellation* Barsac.

Of the thirteen Second Growths (*Seconds Crus*) classified in Sauternes, eight are in Barsac which, however, possesses only two of the eleven First Growths (*Premiers Crus*). Château d'Yquem, the single First Great Growth (*Premier Grand Cru*), classed above all the others, is in the south of Sauternes. Yet Barsac can boast of Château Coutet and Château Climens, the two First Growths which deserve to be placed immediately after Château d'Yquem. The most aristocratic of the five Sauternes communes is Bommes, with one-third of its vineyards classified First Growths. In general, quality is spread quite evenly over the region of Sauternes, Barsac, and Preignac, where the soil is intermediate between that of the other two areas. The wines from the stonier, hillier southern section are slightly more unctuous and richer in sugar; the Barsacs tend to be lighter and more fruity and to develop more quickly. Differences, however, are very subtle, and grape varieties, methods of production, and general characteristics are identical.

The Barsac section is flat—in contrast to the rest of Sauternes, which is hilly—and its boundary is roughly parallel to a brook called the Ciron, which runs diagonally across the region and empties into the Garonne. It was tragic, in the summer of 1956, to drive along the Circuit du Sauternais, a road marked with golden directional arrows which winds among the greatest vineyards, and to pass one blighted vineyard of Barsac after another, the leafless stumps of vine like scorched arms. The February frost in that year was most devastating in the low-lying areas. On the slope vineyards of Sauternes, losses were not nearly as heavy as they were in Barsac, which lost most of its wine for the 1956 and 1957 vintages and was able to produce little during the recuperative replantation period which followed. The soil of Barsac is less stony and more chalky than that across the Ciron—hence the difference, slight though it is, between Sauternes and Barsac wine.

CLASSIFIED GROWTHS (1855 CLASSIFICATION) OF SAUTERNES SITUATED IN BARSAC

FIRST GROWTHS (*Premiers Crus*)

Château Coutet	Château Climens

SECOND GROWTHS (*Seconds Crus*)

Château de Myrat	Château Broustet
Château Doisy-Dubroca	Château Nairac
Château Doisy-Daëne	Château Caillou
Château Doisy-Védrines	Château Suau

See Château Climens; Château Coutet; Sauternes.

Bartzch

A spirit made from fermented hogweed in northern Asia. Hogweed is a general name covering various coarse plants such as ragweed and sow thistle.

Basi

A Philippine Islands spirit of fermented sugar-cane.

Basilicata

Red and white wines.
District: Southern Italy.

In this region, once known as Lucania, Aglianico del Vulture is the D.O.C. wine of note; a garnet-red, sturdy, warm wine from the vineyards of Monte Vulture, and one which is often very agreeable. Indeed, it is one of the very best red wines of southern Italy, capable of considerable improvement in the bottle. After three years of ageing, including two in wood, it may be called *vecchio* (old); after five years, *riserva* (special reserve). Southern Italian wines tend to pick up a tang from the volcanic soil, strange and rather unpleasant at first tasting; but the soil of Monte Vulture does not impart too strong a flavor and consequently its Aglianico is more immediately appreciated by outsiders.

Muscat and Malvasia vines abound here, as they do throughout Italy. Both are most at home in hot climates, and both lend themselves well to *passito* treatment—that is, letting the grapes dry before vinifying them, in order to obtain a stronger, sweeter wine. Both normal and *passito* styles are made in Basilicata and may be either red or white. Normal wines run to about 12% of alcohol, *passito* up to 15%, but neither is in the class of Aglianico.

Basler Kirschwasser

A Swiss kirsch.
See Kirsch.

Bas-Médoc

The northern end of the famous district of Bordeaux. Here the terrain is flatter and the rocky soil has less gravel and so is less good for vines than the soil of the Haut-Médoc (*q.v.*). There are no classified growths in the Bas-Médoc, and most of the wine originating here is sold simply as Médoc or under the names of any of the hundreds of châteaux in the area.

Bastardo

Important grape in the making of Port (*q.v.*).

Château Batailley

Bordeaux red wine.
District: Haut-Médoc, France.
Commune: Pauillac.

Situated a mile back from the River Gironde on high land just south of Pauillac, the vineyard overlooks Châteaux Pichon-Longueville and Latour. From 1942 until his death, the late M. Marcel Borie of the wine firm Borie-Manoux owned the estate. He was also proprietor of Château Trottevieille, the fine Saint-Émilion vineyard. A Fifth Growth (*Cinquième Cru*) of the Medoc, according to the 1855 Classification, Batailley is now owned by M. Borie's widow and other heirs. Château Grand-Saint-Julien is a secondary vineyard of the same property. The wine enjoys a limited reputation.

Characteristics: Fairly robust, but not one of the leaders.
Vineyard area: 50 hectares (125 acres).
Average production: 250 *tonneaux* (23,000 cases).

Bâtard-Montrachet

Burgundy white wine.
District: Côte de Beaune, France.
Commune: Puligny-Montrachet (and in part Chassagne-Montrachet).
Official Classification: Great Growth (Grand Cru).

This is one of the magnificent Montrachets which are the greatest of all white Burgundies and consequently among the most superb white wines in the world. Bâtard ranks next to Chevalier-Montrachet, which is second only to the great Montrachet itself. The vineyard, some 29 acres in size, is walled in from the road behind the village of Puligny. It is on the left, with Bienvenue-Bâtard-Montrachet beside it, and across the road, approached through stone archways, is Le Montrachet, backed by Chevalier and the vineyard once known as Les Demoiselles, now discreetly renamed Le Cailleret. Nearby is the remaining vineyard of the Bâtard trio—Criots-Bâtard-Montrachet, a small property of 1.6 hectares (3 to 4 acres) which falls entirely in the commune of Chassagne-Montrachet. Bienvenue-Bâtard, not a great deal larger with 3.6 hectares (9 acres), is, like Montrachet itself, partly in Puligny, partly in Chassagne. The average yield for Bâtard-Montrachet is about 325 hectoliters (8,581 U.S. gallons, 7,145 imp.), not a great deal for a delicious wine which is in demand all over the world; so it is not surprising that much spurious Montrachet is sold. This is why it is so important to get to know the names of shippers and of those growers who bottle their own good wines at the domaine. In its characteristics, Bâtard resembles the greater Le Montrachet: it is dry yet rounded, with great elegance and breed and a seductive bouquet. Often this wine is better made than Montrachet itself.

See Montrachet; Puligny-Montrachet.

Batavia arrack

See Arrack.

Batzi

A Swiss apple brandy. The French equivalent is known as Calvados, and the American as applejack.

Baumé

A hydrometer scale widely used for measuring the density of musts and sweet wines. One degree Baumé is approximately equal to 1.8 degrees Brix.

See Areometer; Balling.

Béarn

An old French province which is today most of the Basses-Pyrénées department. The best-known wine is the sweet white Jurançon (q.v.). A new place-name, Vin de Béarn, is for reds and rosés. All of the wines, however, must take second place to the gastronomic triumph of the province—shallots, vinegar, and tarragon-flavored *sauce béarnaise.*

Beaujolais

Red wine.
District: Southern Burgundy, France.

Beaujolais is now one of the most widely drunk red wines in the world. Like a blooming country girl whose freshness is her charm, it has been captivating the capitals of the world, and whether the quality of the wine will survive the inordinate demand remains to be seen.

Above all, Beaujolais is a wine to be taken young and to be drunk, not sipped. Nowadays it is fermented very quickly, depending on the maturity achieved on the vine in the particular summer, and this is why it is light, fruity, and flowery. Such a quintessential Beaujolais as Fleurie will be more characteristic than the bigger wines, the Morgon and Moulin-à-Vent. Tasters sometimes say they detect the taste or scent of peach, of apricot, or of rose in the wine: but whatever the individual may find, it will always be the flower and fruit and freshness that will give distinction and beauty. This is the reason for drinking Beaujolais young—although to some degree, exception may be made for the Morgon and Moulin-à-Vent. Obviously such a wine is in danger of being ruined by success, and both the *vin nouveau* which fills the carafes in Paris cafés, and the more consequential Beaujolais which goes abroad are increasingly apt to be stretched with the lesser wines of more prolific regions.

Beaujolais, lying in the Saône-Rhône Valley, which cuts France in two, has always been on a highway traveled by man. Plentiful relics remain from the Stone Age. Julius Caesar conquered the tribes of Beaujolais, and his name and vestiges of Roman occupation remain in ruined walls and chapels, especially in the north, on the border of the Mâconnais, and in the names of such regions and villages as Juliénas and Romanèche-Thorins. At the time of the Crusades, the River Saône was the eastern frontier of France, and even in very recent times it was still the habit of the river pilots on that broad stream to call out "Turn to the Kingdom!" if they wanted the helmsman to steer toward the Beaujolais side or "Turn to the Empire!" if they meant the other.

Yet the wine of Beaujolais is comparatively modern, and its wide success is quite new. In the eighteenth century, a certain amount of Beaujolais began to be carried over to the nearby Loire—the land route through Burgundy was then all but impassable—and ferried in boatloads down to Paris. Until lately, the young Beaujolais was strictly a child of Lyon, which lies just to the south. The saying is: "Three rivers flow into Lyon—the Rhône, the Saône, and the Beaujolais." Even today, a Lyonnais calls for his Beaujolais by the *pot,* not the bottle. A *pot* is now actually larger than a half-bottle, containing 50 centiliters or 17 fl. oz., but not long ago it was a gray mug with blue trimming. These mugs sat in rows in the cafés of Lyon, and down the throats of the men of Lyon was poured practically all the Beaujolais that existed.

Beaujolais stands on the parallel which divides the north of France from the Mediterranean south. Above this region roofs are pointed, below they tend to be flat. The accent changes, and the game of bowls (*boules*), becomes the rage. All Beaujolais takes the pitching and knocking together of the balls with deadly seriousness: there are clubs, leagues, and whole newspapers devoted solely to the sport. Every village café has its court of *boules,* its row of *pots,* and usually the "Fanny," an impudent figure of a young girl to be kissed by the losers.

Out of this country backwater existence, Beaujolais wine has come suddenly into the world. The people themselves show the change. Beaujolais was at least as peasant and country-mannered as any other wine area of France; but now the peasants have begun to be arrogant and difficult, because they are sought-after and successful. The wine shows the change: it is not called Burgundy any longer, which it may be, if it conforms to certain conditions—for instance, the wine must come from the Pinot grape instead of the now all but universal Gamay. But "*Beaujolais suis . . . ,*" they say—(Beaujolais I am).

A wine which is drunk very young and is sometimes very light in alcohol does not travel well. Ideally, a Chiroubles, for example, should be drunk from the barrel and only rarely bottled. Yet such wines may be exported to the far corners of the globe. Moreover, high alcoholic content is taken by too many people to indicate value. This has its effect in Beaujolais, where they shudder to hear their wine spoken of condescendingly as a "nice little wine." Many growers are trying, in fact, to make it "bigger"—that is, more alcoholic—and this means longer vatting, which is likely to ruin its freshness. Others begin to talk of the *goût parisien;* they are afraid that too much Beaujolais is going to conform to the Parisian taste, which seems to be for higher alcohol content at the expense of freshness.

In recent years something of a fad has developed in the United States and other countries abroad for drinking the very young wine, Beaujolais *nouveau.* Though touted as wine just as the Parisian and Burgundians are drinking around the end of the vintage year, Beaujolais *nouveau* as it is exported is far from that. To prepare the wine for bottling—for it is shipped in bottles, not casks—it must be racked and re-racked both to remove the sediment that would normally have time to settle out naturally and to prevent a malolactic fermentation. In the process of this premature preparation, the very heart of the wine is poured away.

RESTRICTIONS, PRODUCTION, AND GEOGRAPHICAL LIMITS

Most Beaujolais is red wine, but not all the wine made in the Beaujolais region is red. Some Pinot Chardonnay white wine growing on the boundary line of Beaujolais and Mâconnais is known as Mâcon or Saint-Véran—except for a small quantity known as Beaujolais Blanc. The latter, superior to the Mâcon, is of a quality equal to that of Pouilly-Fuissé but does not come from communes entitled to that name.

The red wines from the important place-name districts may be labeled Burgundy. They are Burgundies, but nowadays the tendency is to use the popular name of Beaujolais. The production is in Gamay grape, which makes a delightful wine here, although it produces a common wine further north on the Côte d'Or.

From the viticultural standpoint the region is divided into two sections: Haut-Beaujolais and Bas- (or sometimes Bâtard-) Beaujolais. The geographical division is the little stream of the Nizerand, which cuts across the region at Villefranche-sur-Saône; Haut-Beaujolais extends north to the border of Mâconnais, and Bas-Beaujolais stretches south. But the reason for the division is a distinct difference of soils. With the Gamay grape, the climate balanced between the sharp north and soft south, and the short fermentation period, the soil characteristic accounts for the nature of the wines. Since the soil of the lesser Beaujolais is more chalky, the best wines come from Haut-Beaujolais, where the soil is characteristically granitic, with a good deal of manganese in the subsoil—near Moulin-à-Vent and Fleurie is the site of a manganese mine which was worked from the time of the French Revolution until the First World War.

The Beaujolais vineyard begins about 5 miles south of the city of Mâcon and extends at a width of never more than 9 or 10 miles for a distance of about 45 miles to the outskirts of Lyon. The zone is very carefully marked out by the French wine authorities and technically is delimited by the Turdine on the south, by the natural termination of vineyards at an altitude of about 1,500 feet on the slopes of the Monts du Lyonnais to the west, by the national Paris-Riviera route and the Saône on the east, and by a boundary line with the Mâconnais to the north just above a stream called the Arlais. Except for a little bulge at Saint-Symphorien-d'Ancelles in front of Moulin-à-Vent, the vineyard never crosses the highway, for the good reason that the rest of the distance to the river is a flat plain which could never produce wine worthy of the name Beaujolais.

Within this expanse are four grades of wine: Beaujolais, Beaujolais Supérieur, Beaujolais-Villages, and the nine Growths (Crus)—Saint-Amour, Juliénas, Chénas, Moulin-à-Vent, Fleurie, Chiroubles, Morgon, Brouilly, and Côte de Brouilly.

Beaujolais, with less than 10% of alcohol (9° for red and rosé, 9.5° for white), is the wine of fifty-nine communes not entitled to a higher classification. Except for narrow strips on both the mountain and river sides of the greater areas in Haut-Beaujolais, the wine is almost entirely made in Bas-Beaujolais, and nearly all is bought in barrels by shippers for their blends. The product, if called Beaujolais, must be 85% Gamay. Beaujolais Supérieur is wine from the same communes which surpasses 10% of alcohol. The yield of Beaujolais may not exceed 50 hectoliters per hectare (535 U.S. gallons, 445 imp. per acre),

that of Beaujolais Supérieur 45 hectoliters per hectare (481 U.S. gallons, 400 imp. per acre). If it does, the wine must be called simply Vin Rouge.

The 17,200-odd hectares (43,000 acres) of vineyard making up all Beaujolais produce some 700,000 hectoliters (18.5 million U.S. gallons, 15.4 million imp.) yearly, a little more than half of which is Beaujolais. The nine Growths account for approximately two-thirds of the rest, with approximately 160,000 hectoliters (4.24 million U.S. gallons, 3.52 million imp.) a year; and there are also about 225,000 hectoliters (5.96 million U.S. gallons, 4.95 million imp.) of Beaujolais-Villages and Beaujolais Supérieur.

There are two ways of pruning the vine in Beaujolais. That method called Guyot is for the more ordinary wines, and the plant is trained on wires. The gobelet method calls for very close pruning, and the vines, not trained on wires, are most often hardly a foot high. The gobelet is the system for obtaining quality and is obligatory for wines entitled to be called either Beaujolais-Villages or listed among the nine Growths.

HAUT-BEAUJOLAIS

The wines of the nine Growths must not exceed 40 hectoliters per hectare (428 U.S. gallons, 356 imp. per acre) or they drop to the simple class of Beaujolais, although in certain great years the French wine authorities may allow the classification for wines surpassing the maximum if they are satisfactory in quality.

The nine select areas of the Growths lie islanded within the section of Beaujolais-Villages and Beaujolais Supérieur, all of which are in Haut-Beaujolais above Villefranche and comprise the heart and nearly the whole bulk of the zone. The wines not in the Growth area but entitled to the classification Beaujolais-Villages, an official place-name, may be called by their commune name, if the name Beaujolais is attached.

BAS-BEAUJOLAIS

The wines, not having the advantage of the granite soil, lack distinction and are generally less complete and lighter than Haut-Beaujolais wines. Although lighter, they are a little like the wines in the Mâconnais, as if the same general characteristics established themselves on both sides of the true Beaujolais area.

Topographically, the region is a vast bowl dotted with small farmhouses, and from certain points dozens of village steeples may be seen. The slopes are rolling rather than sheer, but the peasants consider their domain wild and rough. It must once have been so, in manners if not in landscape, if we are to believe the stories told in the town of Anse. There, if a girl tosses her head at men and looks hard to handle they say: "She's walked in front of the oven at Anse." Apparently, in Napoleon's day, the women of Anse ran the men like horses, and if the men balked they were tortured in front of the oven. When a village priest tried to stop the women, they popped him into the oven.

MÂCONNAIS
AND
BEAUJOLAIS

Cluny

SAÔNE-ET-LOIRE

Milly-Lamartine

Roche de
Vergisson

Vergisson

Roche de Solutré

Solutré-Pouilly

Chasselas

Chagny

St-Vérand

St-Amour

Jullié

Juliénas

Chénas

Fleurie

Chiroubles

Villié-Morgon

RHÔNE

St-Didier

Beaujeu

Laintignie

Morgon

Quincié

Cercié

Brouilly

St-Lager

Mont-Brouilly

Odenas

St-Étienne-
des-Ouillières

Vaux-
en-Beaujolais

Le Perréon

Denicé

Villefranche

à Lyon

D-981

Châlonnais

Azé

Verzé

la Roche-Vineuse

Prissé

D-980

N-79

Lugny

D-82

Viré

Clessé

Laizé

D-82

Macon

La Patte
d'Oie

Davayé

Pouilly

Fuissé

Leynes

Loché

Vinzelles

Chaintré

Chânes

Crèches-sur-Saône

Bellévue

La Chapelle-
de-Guinchay

Fontanevaux

Romanèche-Thorins

Lancié

Thoissey

St-Jean-d'Ardières

Belleville

St-Georges-
de-Reneins

A-6

N-6

D-103

D-933

Replonges

Vonnas,
Bourg-en-Bresse

N-79

A I N

Saône

D-95

D-9

D-17

N

D-43

D-333

D-936

KILOMETERS
0   5   10

MILES
0   5

D-18

D-37

Monts du Beaujolais

D-31

D-186

B E A U J O L A I S

D-20

BEAUJOLAIS-VILLAGES

The following communes are entitled to the official place-name or Appellation Contrôlée Beaujolais-Villages, or they may couple their names with Beaujolais:

Leynes, Pruzilly, Chânes, Saint-Amour-de-Bellevue, Saint-Véran (which also have white wine called Mâconnais Blanc), and

Arbuissonnaz	Odenas
Les Ardillats	Le Perréon
Beaujeu	Quincié
Blacé	Régnié
Cercié	Rivolet
La Chapelle-de-	Romanèche-Thorins
Guinchay	Saint-Étienne-des-Ouillières
Charentay	Saint-Étienne-la-Varenne
Denice	Saint-Julien-en-Montmélas
Durette	Saint-Lager
Emeringes	Saint-Symphorien-d'Ancelles
Jullié	Salles
Lancié	Vaux-en-Beaujolais
Lantigné	Vauxrenard
Marchampt	Villié-Morgon
Montmélas-Saint-	
Sorlin	

GROWTHS (Crus)

(Ranged from the fullest to the most delicate)

Moulin-à-Vent

Known as the king of Beaujolais wines, it is generally considered first among the noble growths—with the possible exception of Fleurie.

The bigness and fatness of a Moulin-à-Vent give it its character, but even this monarch of Beaujolais usually loses some of its fruitiness and freshness when it is bottled for more than two years.

The windmill itself, which has given its name to the wine and terrain, is a three-hundred-year-old stone cone standing up like a lighthouse in a rolling sea of vines. Far newer-looking is the stretch of the Paris–Riviera road passing a mile or so toward the Saône; neon signs flash on and off, several saying *Moulin-à-Vent;* yet it is the best place to taste the real Moulin-à-Vent.

Chénas is a place-name itself. Nevertheless, the best part of the commune of Chénas, about 475 hectares (1,200 acres), is within the zone of the place-name Moulin-à-Vent, and the wines are sold under this, the more famous name of the two. Three-quarters of the commune of Romanèche-Thorins, 600 hectares (1,500 acres) is in Moulin-à-Vent. Thorins and Moulin-à-Vent wines, always famous in the past, frequently compared for their very similar qualities and now joined as Moulin-à-Vent, grow on a very shallow soil of decomposed granite. The vine roots drive right down into the rock, so that it crumbles even more. The manganese, strong in the subsoil here, undoubtedly contributes to the breed of the wines.

Juliénas

The wines sometimes preserve the pleasant fruitiness of their youth into a lusty age—for these wines and the Morgons are the longest-lasting of the Beaujolais.

An average 22,000 hectoliters (583,000 U.S. gallons, 484,000 imp.) is made from some 445 hectares (1,100 acres). Château Juliénas is one of the best vineyards. Bessay and Château Les Capitans are well-known names.

Morgon

This, the hardest of Beaujolais wines and very full-bodied, is unlike the others in that it is not so delightful when young, but improves with some ageing; a "true Morgon" is not bottled until seven or nine months after the harvest and needs a year in the bottle. The heaviest of the Morgons stands on the dividing line of characteristics between a more typical Beaujolais and a Burgundy; and in fact a considerable amount of it is used by shippers for its strength in blending and never reaches the consumer in its true state. The area entitled to the name Morgon, with its 715 hectares (1,765 acres), is one of the largest of the Growths, but there really is no typical Morgon wine because the soil varies greatly. The part in Morgon is called "true Morgon," and that in Villié-Morgon produces a generally lighter wine. Not all Villié-Morgon can call itself Morgon, the remainder being Beaujolais-Villages. The best parcels of all lie on a ridge called the Côte de Py, where the brownish decomposed slate soil may be seen on the surface—the "rotted soil," as the peasants inelegantly put it, that gives the special *goût de terroir* often present in a Morgon. Until recently, these were robust, fat wines which repaid laying down. The tendency now, however, is to make lighter wines in Morgon. Their relative lightness or heaviness will still vary from vintage to vintage: in 1976, for instance, the wines were all harder and longer-lived than usual and will be an exception to the trend.

Chénas

Most of Chénas lies within Moulin-à-Vent. A small slice of the commune, however, caps Moulin-à-Vent on the north, and its wine is sold as Chénas. The production is not large and the wines are not quite as good as Moulin-à-Vent, yet often they closely approach it in character and they are likely to be excellent value.

Fleurie

If Moulin-à-Vent is the king of Beaujolais wines, Fleurie is the queen, best of all the fine Growths if the standard is the most typically Beaujolais. Before the strict place-name laws were drawn up—between the world wars—most of the wine was sold as Moulin-à-Vent, which adjoins Fleurie on the south side. The result is that the name is not nearly as well known as Moulin-à-Vent today. Fleurie is the only one of the best Growths entirely within one commune, that of Fleurie, but not quite all the wine is entitled to the place-name. A little produced to the west and south must be sold as Beaujolais.

The characteristic of the wine is its exceeding fruitiness, and while it is among the heavier Beaujolais, it does not seem as heavy as a Moulin-à-Vent, or, in their different ways, a Morgon or a Chénas.

Roughly 23,600 hectoliters (624,000 U.S. gallons, 520,000 imp.) are made each year on 688 hectares (1,700 acres), about a quarter of this coming from the Cave Coopérative, now well known and excellently run by Mme. Chabert. The best vineyards are Clos de la Roilette; Grand Cour; La Madone; Les Moriers; Augarant. There are approximately four hundred vineyard owners.

Saint-Amour

This is the farthest north of the Growths, nearly touching the domain of Pouilly-Fuissé in the Mâconnais. About 600 hectoliters (15,000 U.S. gallons, 12,500 imp.) of white wine are made, and 5,000 hectoliters (138,000 U.S. gallons, 115,000 imp.) of red. The white wine, sold as Saint-Véran, Mâcon Blanc or Beaujolais Blanc, bears a considerable likeness to the Pouilly-Fuissés and is definitely fruity and to be drunk young. This is equally true of the red, which carries the *cru* designation Saint-Amour and is one of the lightest of all fine-growth Beaujolais.

The wine grows on a granite and slate soil pebbled with stones sometimes as large as eggs. Most of the slopes face east and southeast on the mountain of Bessay, bordering Juliénas, and a smaller hill called l'Église.

Côte de Brouilly

The center of Brouilly. The wines from these 187 hectares (462 acres) have more character, longer life, and are more full-bodied than those simply labeled Brouilly.

In the exact middle, in vine only halfway to the summit, is the Mont de Brouilly. At the top of the hill, on the bush-covered crown, is Notre-Dame du Raisin (Our Lady of the Grape). Built a hundred years ago by penitents seeking to exorcise the vine plague of oïdium, it is the goal of a yearly pilgrimage on September 8, preceding the harvest. The friends of the wine wind up the long climb, acquiring a proper thirst. At the top there is a religious ceremony in which protection is asked for the coming crop. And then thirsts are whetted under the September sun, welcoming the Côte-de-Brouilly Beaujolais.

Brouilly

This, the southernmost of the Growths, gives the lightest wine. The 875 hectares (2,162 acres) are in the communes of Saint-Lager, Cercié, Odenas, Charentay, and a small segment of a little over 40 hectares (100 acres) in Quincié. The center and best part of Brouilly has the separate *appellation* Côte de Brouilly.

Château de la Chaize, built by the nephew of the confessor to Louis XIV, makes a fine Brouilly in its vast cellars. With its dignified, rather frigid rooms, preserved exactly in the style and spirit of the period, it is the tourist haven of the area.

Chiroubles

The wine is usually as elegant as a Fleurie and less hard than a Morgon. The vineyards adjoin both districts on the west.

This is a wine to be taken very young, and ideally it should never be drunk in bottle but only from the barrel. Although until recently it was the least known, it is now becoming the Growth best liked in France as a fast-maturing light Beaujolais.

The alcoholic content is actually fairly high but does not show in the wine, which is soft, light, exceedingly fruity, and, when very young, a fresh and typical Beaujolais. It can be drunk as early as two months after the harvest, and generally ought to be. Production averages 9,000 hectoliters (228,000 U.S. gallons, 190,000 imp.).

In the square of the village of Chiroubles itself, facing the church, is what must be one of the most appropriate statues in any wine town of France. Neither Napoleon nor Joan of Arc is commemorated here, but one Pulliat, the man who planted the first grafted vine in Beaujolais during the crisis of the phylloxera vine louse. The best wines from this area come from the Domaine de Raousset and from the growers Jean Desvigne and Marcel Dufoux.

Beaujolais-Villages

Name applied to the wines of thirty-six communes or townships in the French Beaujolais. After the fine-growth Beaujolais such as Fleurie, Moulin-à-Vent, Morgon, and others, the Beaujolais-Villages are the best of these pleasant fresh red wines now the rage in France and growing popular everywhere.

See Beaujolais.

Beaulieu-sur-Layon

Commune with the right to an Appellation Contrôlée in the Coteaux du Layon district of Anjou, France.

See Anjou: Coteaux du Layon.

Beaumes-de-Venise

Vin doux naturel and *vin de liqueur* are made in this area of Vaucluse, from the Muscat grape.

See Sweet fortified wines of France.

Beaune

Burgundy red and white wines.
District: Côte de Beaune, France.

The ancient city of the same name is the largest and most important of the Côte de Beaune and is called—not without reason—the "Capital of Burgundian Wines." It dates from the fifth century or earlier—there are grounds for believing that Beaune may have been the Bibracte mentioned by Caesar in his chronicles. Beaune's long history has been one of storm and terror, for many ambitious nobles converged there as they struggled for supremacy. Walls have been built and razed, castles constructed and toppled, and the city archives hold more stories of intrigue and violence than do those of many a Hollywood producer. Lying between the once-powerful strongholds of Autun and Besançon, Beaune is strategically placed, and its wines added to its desirability. Characteristic of the change that has come over the city is that the one remaining medieval fort is now the residence of the manager of the wine-shipping firm of Calvet et Cie., and the pillars—all that remain of the stout walls which once girdled Beaune—are used today to house wine instead of broad swords.

The great change in the life of the place occurred in the seventeenth century, when the citizens beat their swords into pruning knives and turned their attention to wine. Beaune's undisputed place as the center of the Burgundian wine trade and its aura of bustling commerce and prosperity date from that era. As a result of its energy and enterprise, the economy not only of the Côte de Beaune but of the entire Côte d'Or is based on the cellars of Beaune, and the city lives for its wines. Cellars tunnel and wind beneath the twisting streets, wine slogans adorn walls of buildings and restaurants, and billboards lure passing tourists and wine-buyers from all over the world into the storerooms of the great firms. Finding these firms is no trouble, but discovering the difference between them sometimes is. The Beaune telephone directory carries a couple of dozen under a single number; names of established and reliable firms are imitated by fly-by-nights to within an inch of a lawsuit, and merchants abound who will agree to sell any wine in any quantity, sometimes in excess of its production. Yet behind it all lies a genuine love of Burgundian wines, a conviction that there are no other in the world to rival them, and an enthusiasm unequaled in any region of the world.

There is more to Beaune than the winding streets, the clatter of great tank-trucks carrying wine, and the hum and buzz of conversations about vintages, comparative tastings, and prices. Outside the city, but still within the limits of the commune of Beaune, are more vineyards planted in fine vines than can be found in any other commune of the Côte d'Or, although both Pommard and Meursault generally make more wine each year. The wines from these vineyards—both red and white—are sold as Beaune or may have the vineyard name following that of the commune. Sometimes they are sold as Côte de Beaune, which means simply that they come from any vineyard allowed to use the name Beaune, and from several others as well. (When blended with wines from specified other communes of the slope they may also be sold as Côte de Beaune-Villages.)

The outstanding vineyards of Beaune today are substantially the same as those which received top rating when the vineyards of the Côte d'Or were classified in 1860. At that time, there were eight Outstanding Vineyards (*Têtes de Cuvées*) and all but one of them are still considered outstanding. The French authorities included all eight in their list of the thirty-four First Growths (*Premiers Crus*)—superior vineyards whose wines have the legal right to carry both commune and vineyard name on the label—established in 1936. The best Growth is generally considered that from the vineyard of Grèves and particularly from the section called L'Enfant Jésus. The name is said to have been bestowed by early monks and comes from the expression: "It goes down the throat as easily as the little Jesus in velvet trousers." Since the monks did not consider this irreverent, no one in Burgundy does either. Grèves is one of the fullest wines of Beaune and one of the suavest. Les Clos des Mouches is another wine noted for its body (considerable for a Beaune) and for its elegance. Slightly behind these is Fèves, a smaller vineyard and thus one with far less out-

FIRST GROWTHS (*Premiers Crus*)

Vineyard	Hectares	Acres
Les Marconnets	8.81	22.03
Les Fèves	4.40	11.00
Les Bressandes	21.80	54.50
Les Grèves	31.68	79.20
Les Clos des Mouches	25.13	62.83
Clos du Roi (*in part*)	8.44	21.10
Sur-les-Grèves	4.02	10.05
Aux (or Les Cras)	5.02	12.55
Le Clos de la Mousse	3.36	8.40
Les Teurons	21.52	53.80
Champimonts (or Champ Pimont)	18.07	45.18
Aux Coucherias (*in part*)	9.27	23.18
En l'Orme	2.02	5.05
En Genêt	4.32	10.80
Les Perrières	3.18	7.95
À l'Écu	5.00	12.50
Les Cent Vignes	23.50	58.75
Les Toussaints	6.43	16.08
Les Chouacheux	5.04	12.60
Les Boucherottes	8.60	21.50
Les Vignes Franches	8.56	21.40
Les Aigrots	22.00	55.00
Pertuisots	5.16	12.90
Tiélandry	1.98	4.95
Les Sizies	8.50	21.25
Les Avaux	13.40	33.50
Les Reversées	4.97	12.43
Le Bas des Teurons	7.32	18.30
Les Seurey	1.23	3.08
La Mignotte	2.41	6.03
Les Montrevenots (*in part*)	8.28	20.70
Les Blanches Fleurs (*in part*)	1.16	2.90
Les Epenottes (*in part*)	8.06	20.15
Les Tuvilains	8.73	21.83
Bélissaud	4.88	12.20

put, its wines noted for their fineness and delicate yet pronounced aroma. Beaune Bressandes—not to be confused with Corton-Bressandes in nearby Aloxe-Corton—and Marconnets, Champimonts, and Cras are also highly reputed, and the wines are light but firm with a distinctive bouquet. Finesse, delicacy, and an expressive and often remarkable bouquet are the characteristics which excel in all Beaune wines.

In the past, Beaunes were considered at their best immediately after harvest. During the seventeenth century, wines were generally drawn straight from the barrel instead of being bottled and were vinified to be very light, very fast-maturing, and for immediate drinking. Beaunes are still reasonably light and reasonably fast-maturing, but the drinking is nowhere near so immediate as it once was, and a couple of years in the bottle will aid the wines considerably. Some of the better wines will hold for a number of years, but they are the exception to the rule;

five years in glass will usually suffice. After this the wines tend to fade.

The great event in Beaune each year is the annual auction sale at the impressive Hospices de Beaune, the charity hospital which has been in continuous operation since the fifteenth century and which gains some of its revenue from the sale at auction of wines coming from vineyards donated by philanthropic Burgundians. The sale, usually held in mid-November, gathers swarms of buyers, mostly from France and Belgium, and the prices determine the value of the harvest throughout the Côte d'Or. The Hospices has holdings all over the Côte de Beaune; it vinifies its own wines and also distills a Marc de Bourgogne which is sold at the same time as the wine (*see also* Hospices de Beaune).

Within the limits of the commune there are 537 hectares (1,329 acres) of vineyard allowed for grapes going into Beaune, and this and twenty-two more for wines labeled Côte de Beaune. In an average-quantity year Beaune produces 8,700 hectoliters (230,000 U.S. gallons, 191,500 imp.) of red wine and about 200 hectoliters (5,300 U.S. gallons, 4,400 imp.) of white. The white is rarely in the class of the red, but some may be delicate and perfumed, and it is often excellent wine. Beaune is sold mostly in France, but large quantities go to the Low Countries and not only because of geographical proximity. The historical links forged when the Burgundian Ducal family held court in the Netherlands were strengthened by the Huguenot refugees from Beaune in the sixteenth century, many of whom settled in Belgium and Holland and retained, as do their descendants today, their traditional drinking preferences. England, Switzerland, the United States, and Austria are also big buyers.

See Côtes de Beaune.

Château Beauregard

Bordeaux red wine.
District and Commune: Pomerol, France.

This property owned by the Clauzel family faces south on the plateau of Pomerol and makes one of the soundest wines in the district.

Vineyard area: 13 hectares (32 acres).
Average production: 51 *tonneaux* (4,500 cases).

Château Beauséjour-Bécot

Bordeaux red wine.
District and Commune: Saint-Émilion, France.

Formerly owned by Dr. Jean Fagouët and now by M. Bécot. Impressive underground cellars hewn in rock.

Characteristics. Fine wine, with a fine bouquet in a good vintage year.

Vineyard area: 7.6 hectares (19 acres).
Average production: 30 *tonneaux* (2,900 cases).
See Château Beauséjour-Duffau-Lagarrosse, *below.*

Château Beauséjour-Duffau-Lagarrosse

Bordeaux red wine.
District and Commune: Saint-Émilion, France.

Placed on a little hill outside the walls of Saint-Émilion, with a view over the lazy curve of the Dordogne, the two Beauséjour vineyards were a single property until 1869, when they were divided between two branches of the Ducarpe family. Mademoiselle Ducarpe had become Madame Duffau-Lagarrosse by marriage, and it is in her line that the original château and the immediately surrounding part of the vineyard have descended. Both Beauséjour-Duffau-Lagarrosse and Beauséjour-Bécot, which adjoins it, were ranked First Great Growths (*Premiers Grands Crus*) of Saint-Émilion in the official Classification of 1955. Care must be taken not to confuse them, since in both cases the words Château Beauséjour will generally be found on the labels printed in large letters, with the proprietor's name in smaller print.

Characteristics. The vineyards are well placed between Canon and Fourtet, and they yield an agreeable wine, perfectly successful in the good years, although generally less fine than that of Beauséjour-Bécot.

Vineyard area: 6 hectares (17 acres).
Average production: 25 *tonneaux* (2,000 cases).

Beer

The origins of beer go almost as far back as those of wine; beer has been made by virtually all people in all stages of civilization. African tribes produce it from millet, the Japanese from rice; Europeans, Americans of both continents, Australians and countless others make theirs mainly from barley. It is consumed the world over—most of all in Belgium, whose citizens manage to down an impressive 134 liters (35.5 U.S. gallons, 29.5 imp.) per capita yearly.

Beer is the general term for all classes of beers—draft, bottled and canned, pale ales, lagers, and stouts. It is brewed from malt, sugar, hops, and water and is fermented with yeast. Beer quality is largely dependent on the suitability of these main raw materials for the type of beer being produced.

Malt begins its life as barley. Special types are grown and carefully ripened. In the malting, barley is dampened with water and allowed to germinate under controlled conditions in order to convert the insoluble starch to soluble sugar: it is then dried and cured, to a pale color for pale beers and to a richer color for dark beers.

Sugars used in brewing are manufactured from cane sugar which is treated in different ways to give various flavors and sweetness.

Hops are specially grown for brewing and give beer its bitter flavor. Only the flower, a cone of golden petals carrying resin and oils, is used.

The water used in brewing is usually specially treated with mineral salts for the particular type of beer being processed. Before the days of water analysis, famous brewing centers emerged because the local water was particularly suitable for the brewing of certain types of beer. For example, Pilsener, the famous beer of Pilsen in Czechoslovakia, is brewed with natural water and is recognized as one of the finest beers in the world.

Yeast, a living organism, is the agent which ferments the beer.

The brewing process is not very complicated. The malt passes through a mill and is crushed, after which it is mixed with water at a carefully controlled temperature. The sugar solution from the mixture is drawn off from the vessel. Rotating water sprinklers spray the grain to ensure that all the malt extract is used, leaving only husks, which are usually sold as cattle food.

The solution (wort) is pumped to the boiling coppers, where hops and sugar are added. The resultant mixture is boiled for an hour or two and in the process the aroma and distinct bitterness of hops combine with the sweetness and flavor derived from the wort and sugar. After boiling, the hops are removed by straining, and the wort is cooled and collected in a vessel where yeast is added, splitting the sugars into alcohol and carbon dioxide gas: the gas is usually collected for later use in carbonating bottled and canned beers.

Fermentation takes several days, at the end of which the bulk of the yeast, in lager, settles on the bottom of the fermenting vessel; in ale, it rises to the top of the beer; in both it is collected. The yeast produced during fermentation is several times the original quantity and is used for subsequent fermentations, the surplus forming a very valuable by-product, since it is a source of vitamins for humans or animals.

In most beer-consuming countries the beer is stored in large cold tanks near the freezing point to improve its stability and ensure long and satisfactory quality, after which it is filtered, carbonated, and filled into a cask, bottle, or can for dispatch to the consumer. Most beers are now pasteurized (heated to 140°F., 60°C.) to ensure that any minute quantities of yeast which may be left in the beer after filtration do not ferment and multiply and in so doing turn the beer cloudy.

Draft beer, which is drawn from a cask, now usually metal, is still very popular in most beer-drinking countries. All containers are washed and sterilized before being filled with beer. Bottles and cans are filled, labeled, and packaged on high-speed machines which can work at the rate of up to six hundred bottles a minute.

The quality of beers varies widely, depending upon the skill, plant, and management of the manufacturer. One of the most famous is the Tuborg plant in Copenhagen, which produces a product known throughout the beer-drinking world. Other countries and cities have become famous for their beers; Pilsen of Czechoslovakia, Carlsberg of Denmark, Heineken of Holland, the Munchener beer of Munich. England and Ireland are renowned for their heavier ales and stouts. The beers of Mexico, U.S.A., Australia, Cuba, and Canada are also very good.

MAJOR TYPES OF BEER

Lager

Light highly carbonated beer. The name comes from the German *lagern* (to store), and lager beer is one that is allowed to rest until all sediment of the fermentation has cleared and is then carbonated and bottled. Most American beers—unless the labels bear a statement to the contrary—are lager beers, although the term itself is seldom used.

Ale

A kind of beer, formerly made without hops and drunk fresh. Today there is little difference in Great Britain between this and other beers. In the U.S.A., ale is usually fermented at a higher temperature than beer and different yeast strains are used.

Stout

A dark heavy ale, often slightly sweet, with a pronounced taste of malt, usually heavily flavored with hops. Great Britain and Ireland are most famous for their stouts, which include the famous name of Guinness and Oyster Stout.

Porter

Similar to stout but not so strong, usually with a heavy creamy foam. The name is said to derive from the fact that it was the favorite drink of the London porters.

Bock

Special heavy beer made in the United States in the spring, purportedly from sediment taken out of the fermenting vats in their annual cleaning. The bock beer season usually lasts for about six weeks. In France, however, bock is the term for a mugful of light beer.

Beerenauslese

German wine term for the selection of individual grapes from bunches.
See Germany.

Beeswing

A light thin crust—resembling the transparent wing of a bee—which forms on some old bottled Ports.

Château Bel-Air

Bordeaux red wine.
District and Commune: Saint-Émilion, France.

Owned by Madame Jean Dubois-Challon—widow of the former leader of the Jurade (Saint-Émilion's wine society), and part owner of the neighboring Château Ausone—Bel-Air matured in the Ausone cellars until 1974. Many people feel that the distinction between Bel-Air wine and the much more famous Ausone is not very real. Others maintain that Bel-Air closely resembles Ausone but in most years is less generous and less fine. While Roman origins are often claimed for the vineyard, it is certain that in the fourteenth century it was the property of the Englishman Robert Knolles, when he was governor of Guyenne. Until 1916 the estate belonged to the French family Cannolle—French descendants of Knolles. Bel-Air was named a First Great Growth (*Premier Grand Cru*) in the Saint-Émilion Classification of 1955.

Characteristics. A subtle, very agreeable wine.
Vineyard area: 13 hectares (32 acres).
Average production: 50 *tonneaux* (4,000 cases).

Château Bel-Air-Marquis d'Aligre

Bordeaux red wine.
District: Haut-Médoc.
Commune: Soussans-Margaux.

One of the best wines of the tiny commune of Soussans, whose production is entitled to the place-name Margaux. A Cru Exceptionnel according to the 1855 Classification, many of its vines neighbor those of Château Margaux. The soil of the vineyard is gravelly and the subsoil flinty.

Vineyard area: 30 hectares (75 acres).
Average production: 110 *tonneaux* (10,000 cases).

Château Belgrave

Bordeaux red wine.
District: Haut-Médoc, France.
Commune: Saint-Laurent.
(Saint-Laurent is not a place-name and the wine has the place-name of Haut-Médoc.)

Classified a Fifth Growth (*Cinquieme Cru*) in 1855 and on the boundary line of Saint-Julien, the estate was known by varying names in the past. The name Belgrave, which it shares with a few other Bordeaux vineyards, is claimed to be the inspiration for the naming of Belgrave Square in London. This wine should not be confused with a lesser wine called Château Bellegrave.

Characteristics. Frequent changes in proprietors have made for a certain amount of variation in this wine, which is usually fairly full.

Vineyard area: 35 hectares (87 acres).
Average production: 100 *tonneaux* (8,000 cases).

Bellegarde

A commune on the great Languedoc plain of southern France in the confines of which Clairette grapes are planted for making a small white wine.
See Clairette de Bellegarde.

Bellet

Controlled place-name near Nice in the south of France. This is one of the best vineyard districts planted along the Riviera.
See Provence.

Ben Ean

Important vineyard in New South Wales.
See Australia.

Bench Grafting

For description of this method of grafting vines, *see* Chapter Eight, p. 29.

Benedictine D.O.M.

A famous and very popular liqueur supposed to have been first compounded about 1510 at the Benedictine monastery in Fécamp, France, by Dom Bernardo Vincelli, to fortify and restore the weary monks. The liqueur is said to have found royal favor in 1534, when Francis I passed through the region and tasted it; but at the time of the French Revolution the monastery was destroyed, the order dispersed, and manufacture of Benedictine halted. Some seventy years or so later, the formula came into the hands of M. Alexandre Le Grand, who established the present secular concern which produces the liqueur. It no longer has any connection with Benedictines or any other religious order. Every true bottle of Benedictine (numerous unsuccessful attempts have been made to counterfeit it) still carries the ecclesiastical inscription D.O.M., which means not "Dominican Order of Monks," as it has sometimes been construed, but *Deo Optimo Maximo* (To God, most good, most great).

The liqueur is greenish-yellow and flavored with a variety of herbs, plants, and peels on a base of brandy; and it is claimed that no more than three people at any given time know its exact formula. When the firm realized that great numbers of people were ordering their Benedictine mixed half-and-half with brandy in order to reduce sweetness slightly they put on the market an official "B & B" (Benedictine and Brandy).

Benicarlo

Muscular red wine from the region of Castellón de la Plana in Valencia, Spain.

Benin Wine

Nigerian palm "wine," or fermented palm sap.

Bentonite

A kind of clay, bentonite is an excellent clarifying agent for white wines, one which prevents protein precipitation and discoloration from copper. Its use is allowed by law.

The bentonite (a hydrated silicate of aluminum, composed mainly of montmorillonite) swells in water to form a gelatinous paste. After dilution, it should be stirred briskly into the wine to be treated. The most satisfactory dose is usually about 100 grams per hectoliter, diluted in at least two liters of water.
See Chapter Nine, p. 38, Fining.

Bercy

A section of Paris along the Seine known as the Quai de Bercy, where most of the city's everyday table wine is received and distributed.

Bereich

The German word for "district," especially sub-divisions of the eleven main German wine-producing areas.

Bergerac

Red and white wines.
District: Southwest France.

Bergerac's proximity (100 kilometers; 80 miles) to Bordeaux and the similarity of their wines, vines, and viticultural practices lead to widespread and—for Bergerac—unfortunate comparisons. For the most part the wines of Bergerac are simply not in the same class.

The city itself is dull and quiet—hardly worth visiting were it not for the castles and strongholds which guard the beautiful wide valley of the Dordogne above it. Many battles of the Hundred Years' War were fought along these hills, and it is easy to imagine the mounted knights emerging from the ancient fortresses in full battle array.

The vines are planted along the hills that girdle the city, especially on the right bank of the river, called the Côte Nord. The soil ranges from sandy gravel to flinty clay and ends in a chalky clay with traces of iron. Bordeaux varieties are the most common grapes: Cabernet Sauvignon, Cabernet Franc, Merlot, and Malbec for red wines; Semillon, Sauvignon, Muscadelle, Ondenc, and Chenin Blanc for whites. For red wines benefiting from the most general place-name—Bergerac—the Fer and Perigord vines are permitted.

PLACE-NAMES

Monbazillac

The most important. Sometimes known as the "poor man's Sauternes," it will, in good years, have much of the full sweet richness of Sauternes but generally fails in its full finesse, tending to be too obvious. In recent years the quality of Monbazillac has diminished as growers have abandoned the traditional methods of selective harvesting. It is grown in the parishes of Monbazillac, Pomport, Rouffignac, Colombier, and a part of Saint-Laurent-des-Vignes. The vineyards extend on the south side of the Dordogne and face north, an exception to the general rule that southerly facings are best for vines. The soil is the chalky clay, with occasional veins of gritty sandstone. As in Sauternes, the grapes stay on the vines until late in the autumn, when the noble rot mold *Botrytis cinerea* attacks them, drying up much of the water. The vineyards cover some 1,400 hectares (3,500 acres), and production averages slightly more than 75,000 hectoliters (2.1 million U.S. gallons, 1.65 million imp.).

Pécharmant

The best of the red Bergeracs. Light and vivacious, and sometimes bearing a resemblance to wines made in the lesser areas around Saint-Émilion—the closest of the Bordeaux districts—it is made in four communes to the north and east of Bergerac: Creysse, Mouleydier, Saint-Sauveur, and Lembras. The slopes closest to the city are thought to be the best. More than 2,500 hectoliters (66,000 U.S. gallons, 55,000 imp.) is seldom produced annually.

Rosette

Only applicable to white wines. Semi-sweet and rarely distinguished, the wine comes from six communes, three of which have title to the name Pécharmant for red wines. The small amount of 210 hectoliters (5,600 U.S. gallons, 4,400 imp.) is produced annually.

Montravel

Includes Haut-Montravel and the Côtes de Montravel. Grown in fifteen communes downstream—almost due west at this point—from the town of Bergerac, the vines are all on the north side of the river. Like Rosette, the wine is semi-sweet. Montravel makes about 30,000 hectoliters (795,000 U.S. gallons, 630,000 imp.) every year, while Haut-Montravel and the Côtes de Montravel annually produce approximately 15,000 hectoliters (390,000 U.S. gallons, 300,000 imp.) each.

Bergerac and the Côtes de Bergerac

Together, these two produce about 180,000 hectoliters (477,000 U.S. gallons, 378,000 imp.) of wine annually, two-thirds of which is white. They make up the most general place-names in the region, and thus the wine is less good than that carrying more specific names.

Bergheim

Beautiful old wine village in Alsace (*q.v.*).

Bergstrasse

White, and some red, wines.
District: Hesse, Germany.

The line of tumbled hills to the north and a little to the south of Heidelberg is known as the Bergstrasse. It divides into two sections: *Bereich* Starkenburg, the main part, and *Bereich* Umstadt, a little addition off to the northeast. There are but 350 hectares (under 875 acres) of vineyards.

The wines are seldom, if ever, seen abroad, because they are all consumed on the spot by the hordes of tourists who flock to the timbered inns and the open-air restaurants where students once fought their duels with sabers. It is said that those bottles of Bergstrasse which do not reach the tourists are snatched by the Heidelberg students. Most of the wines are bottled in the spring following the harvest, and few are left to see the summer. Some of these cheap wines used to be blended with such better-known Rhine wines as Liebfraumilch. But now there is a wine shortage in Hesse.

The wines vary surprisingly, considering the small size of the district. This is because, in an area where there has been much geological upheaval, the soil characteristics change almost from hill to hill. Certain Bergstrasse Rieslings grown on a shale soil will taste like lesser Mosels, while Sylvaner wines will have the fullness and body of some of the Rheinhessens. None of them is particularly distinguished, and too often they are likely to be over-sulfured. Red and white wines are both made, but the majority is white, especially in the Rheinhessen section.

Bensheim and Heppenheim are the two leading Hessen Bergstrasse wine towns. The Kirchberg vineyard is the most important on the Bergstrasse.

The State Domain owns about 20 hectares (50 acres) of vineyard in this district.

Other vineyards. Streichling and Paulus in Bensheim. In Heppenheim: Steinkopf, Eckweg, and Zentgericht. The vineyards of Auerbach just above Bensheim, once well known, are dying, perhaps on account of a strangling quantity of sand in the soil. A complete list of Bergstrasse vineyards is given in Appendix B, p. 604.

Bernkasteler Doctor (Doktor)

The most famous great Mosel wine. While not always first among Mosels, it is still a great wine. The market pressure from its fame causes it to be overpriced. The name Bernkasteler Doctor has been involved in a court dispute since 1971 when the new German Wine Laws greatly expanded the legal boundaries of the appellation, thus decreasing the significance it enjoyed as a guarantee of quality.

See Mosel-Saar-Ruwer.

Bernkasteler Graben

There is little to differentiate this magnificent wine from Bernkasteler Doctor. In fact, many men of the region say Graben is frequently the better of the two wines. At one time, the Graben was sold with the neighboring Doctors.

See Mosel-Saar-Ruwer.

Château Beychevelle

Bordeaux red wine.
District: Haut-Médoc, France.
Commune: Saint-Julien.

Owned today by M. Aymar Achille-Fould, former *deputé* of the Médoc, and by his sister, Mrs. Pray, Beychevelle is one of the largest vineyards in the district and commands a reputation, fame, and price considerably higher than one might expect from its official position as Fourth Growth (*Quatrième Cru*) of 1855.

The château, long and low, with a great wing, is one of the most beautiful and imposing in the Médoc. It stands on the site of earlier feudal fortresses and was reconstructed in its present style in 1757 by the Marquis de Brassier. An enormous belvedere, nearly 50 meters (28 feet) long, commands a vista of the lawns, which run down to the River Gironde for more than a kilometer. The prospect is not unlike some of those at Versailles, but on a smaller scale.

M. Armand Achille-Fould, former Minister of Agriculture and father of the present owner, tells the amusing story of how Beychevelle came into the family: his father went to the United States and married an American;

while on a tour of France, he was pleased to hear his wife say at Beychevelle, "This is where I would like best to live"—whereupon he bought the estate.

The name comes from *baissez les voiles* (strike sail), the salute once given by ships passing on the river to the Duke of Epernon, Grand Admiral of France, when he was lord of the domain in feudal times. The Grand Admiral also knew the secondary wine, Clos de l'Amiral, which is still produced.

Beychevelle is very well known in England and the United States and has been shipped there for more than a century.

Characteristics. Great finesse. This vineyard has a following, and some of its vintages are definitely remarkable; others may be rather disappointing.

Vineyard area: 61 hectares (152 acres).
Average production: 250 *tonneaux* (22,000 cases).

Bhang, Bang

A "wine" made in India from hemp leaves and twigs infused in water.

Bianchello del Metauro

Italian white wine from the Marches (*q.v.*).

Bianco

White. Italian term for white wine.

Bienvenue-Bâtard-Montrachet

Burgundy white wine.
District: Côte de Beaune, France.
Commune: Puligny-Montrachet (and in part Chassagne-Montrachet).
Official Classification: Great Growth (Grand Cru).

One of the memorable Montrachets, which are the greatest of the great white Burgundies. The vineyard, covering only about nine acres, is beside that of Bâtard-Montrachet. In character and quality the wines are similar. It is only in the past ten years that a distinction has been made between Bienvenue, Criots, and Bâtard. Before that, all three wines were sold under the last name. The average production of this wine is about 125 hectoliters (3,310 U.S. gallons, 2,750 imp.).

See Bâtard-Montrachet; Puligny-Montrachet.

Big

A wine that may be called big has more than the average amount of flavor, body, and alcohol. Not necessarily a term of distinction, since a wine that is too big tends to be coarse and heavy.

Bin

English term for the place in which bottles of wines are stored in a cellar—or cupboard, if it is in a flat. When a merchant sells wine "in bin" (or "ex-bin"), it means that the customer must pay the cost of packing and delivery.

Binger Rochusberg

An outstanding wine of Bingen on the German Rhine. It has great character and is from slate-quartz soil.
See Rheinhessen.

Bishop

Mulled Port. The Port wine is heated up with sugar, orange, and cloves and set alight before being poured. Some authors give Claret, not Port, as the wine in a Bishop, but others say that Claret is used in an Archbishop.

Bitters

Spirits of varying alcoholic content flavored with roots, barks, and herbs, having in common only their bitterness and their claims to medicinal powers. Originally they were elixirs, and some are still so called. Bitters are used either as flavoring for mixed drinks or may be taken as aperitifs, liqueurs, or digestives. Some of the better-known ones are: Amer Picon (France) (*q.v.*), Angostura (Trinidad, British West Indies) (*q.v.*), Boonekamp's (Holland), Campari (Italy) (*q.v.*), Abbot's Aged Bitters (U.S.A.), Fernet Branca (Italy) (*q.v.*), Law's Peach Bitters (England), Orange Bitters (England), Pommeranzen (Holland and Germany), Secrestat (France), Toni Kola (France), Unicum (Hungary), and Welling's (Holland).

Black Death

Popular name for the aquavit—and the national drink—of Iceland. This spirit is flavored with caraway seeds.
See Aquavit.

Black rot

A vine disease of American origin.
See Chapter Eight, p. 29.

Black Velvet

A mixture of stout and Champagne, popular in England in Edwardian days and still in existence. Usually associated with oysters.

Blackberry liqueur

A cordial made by steeping blackberries in sweetened brandy.

Blagny

The only Burgundian communal place-name that has no accompanying commune. Blagny is a hamlet, divided between Meursault and Puligny-Montrachet on the Côte de Beaune. Its wines are similar in almost all respects to those of Meursault. Meursault-Blagny denotes the wines from the best part of Blagny, adjoining Meursault.
See Meursault.

Blanc

White. French term for white wine.

Blanc de Blancs

Champagne made from the Pinot Blanc grape only. It is easily distinguishable by its light color from the golden wines made from red grapes. Blanc de Blancs is also becoming a widespread term for the white wines made from white grapes in many of France's lesser-known wine districts.
See Champagne.

Blanc Fumé de Pouilly

Dry white Loire Valley wine usually called Pouilly-Fumé.
See Pouilly-sur-Loire.

Blanc de Noirs

White wine from red grapes.
See Champagne.

Blanco

Spanish term for white wine.

Blanquette de Limoux and Vin de Blanquette

Sparkling, and some still, wines.
District: Southwest France.

Limoux, a small town near Carcassonne, makes two types of wine, both from the same grape. That called Blanquette de Limoux or Limoux Natur is a sparkling wine, and the Vin de Blanquette is the still variety. Made from grapes of the Mauzac (at least 90%) and Clairette Blanche (no more than 10%), the wines come from a delimited area of thirty-five communes of which Limoux is the center.

The sparkling Blanquette de Limoux has won some small renown. The wines contain at least 10% of alcohol and have been made sparkling by the Champagne process, that of secondary fermentation in the bottle. Recently, the efforts of trained oenologists have considerably improved the quality of this sparkling wine.

The amount of the wine that is not rendered sparkling is always a small proportion. It too must have at least 10% alcohol, and it usually has a slight sparkle to it. Together the wines are produced on some 202 hectares (500 acres) with an average yearly output of 1,900 hectoliters (50,000 U.S. gallons, 41,600 imp.).

Blauer Portugieser

A grapevine producing red wines and grown in the Vöslau region of Austria.

See Austria.

Blaufrankische

A red-wine grape cultivated in Austria, Hungary, and elsewhere.

Blaye, Premières Côtes de Blaye, Côtes de Blaye

Red and white wines.
District: Bordeaux, France.

White and red wines lacking distinction and produced in a large and ancient vineland on the Gironde in southwest France. The three distinct place-names or Appellations Contrôlées apply to the same area, circling the historic river-town of Blaye, and indicate gradations of quality. Blaye (or Blayais) and Côtes de Blaye both make white wines, neither of great distinction. Premières Côtes de Blaye, 15% white and the remainder red, alone merits consideration for certain bottles, and alone is restricted to noble grape varieties (except that, in red wine, Prolongeau, Cahors, and Béquignol are varieties permitted up to 10%).

The white wines are dry, or, if they are labeled sweet, will be found to be semi-sweet. The red wines are lighter than those from the adjoining region of Bourg, and if tasted together with red Bourgs in the Blaye-Bourg House of Wine opened in Blaye in 1955 they will be found to be less distinguished, if smoother and suppler.

Separated from the Médoc by the considerable width of the River Gironde, Blaye is a romantic-looking region of rolling hills, its chief landmark a huge starfish-shaped fortress, originally built in the eleventh and twelfth centuries, rebuilt by General Vauban, strategist of Louis XIV, and now largely in ruins. From thimble-topped watchtowers in the corners of its walls, the view over the Gironde includes Pauillac, in the distance on the opposite shore, and in the wide river a trio of large islands given over to vineyard. From the river in the vicinity of Blaye comes the only true caviar produced outside Russia, Rumania, or Iran.

Bleichert

German term for rosé wine.

Blending

The practice of mixing together or "marrying" wines or spirits to obtain uniform quality from year to year, or to obtain a product better than any one of the components taken individually. In some cases, blending is a practical way of increasing quantity—but not quality; for if the original wine or spirit has been a fine one, quality is lowered and all individuality or distinction lost.

All Sherry is blended, as is most Champagne, Cognac,

and whisky. In these instances the practice often enhances the product.

Blue Fining

Fining or clearing wines of copper casse with crystals of potassium ferrocyanide. This is effective in stabilizing white wines, but the results of an overdose are so dangerous that those countries which permit it do so only under very strict regulations. Blue fining is allowed in Germany but forbidden in France and the United States. In the United States a similar but safer commercial product called Cufex may be used to remove copper.

See Fining: Chapter Nine, p. 38.

Bõa Vista

One of the best known *quintas* of the Alto Douro in Portugal, for many years the property of the Forrester family.

Boal, Bual

A type of Madeira: full, sweet, rich in color, and with an extraordinary bouquet.

See Madeira.

Boca

Italian red wine from Piedmont (*q.v.*).

Bock

See Beer.

Bocksbeutel, Boxbeutel

The flat flask-shaped wine bottle of Franconia (Germany) and Styria (Austria), rarely used except for these wines—although Undurraga in Chile has a somewhat similar bottle for Riesling, and some Australian wines and some Portuguese rosés are now being marketed in flasks of this type. While a variety of Franconian wines appear in the Bocksbeutel inside Germany, it is principally the green-gold Steinwein which is found abroad.

The origin of the flask is accounted for in several ways. Obviously, it resembles the once common leather wineskin. A Bocksbeutel carryall favored by old-fashioned German women is also cited as a possible pattern—and so is an organ of the goat, which takes much the same shape. In any case, the Bocksbeutel has been in use for some time: in 1728, the Burgerspital wines of Würzburg began to be bottled in these flasks.

See Franconia.

Bocoy

Chestnut barrel used for shipping Spanish wines, holding usually 650 to 700 liters (172 to 185 U.S. gallons, 143 to 154 imp.). There is also a Media Bocoy, or half-bocoy, containing generally 350 liters (92 U.S. gallons, 77 imp.). The two measures are the same in content as the German Halbstück (half-"piece") and Viertelstück (quarter-"piece").

Bodega

In Spain a place for storing wine, not a cellar usually, but above ground; and, colloquially, a wine shop. The term is often used in England for a wine-bar.

Body

A wine with substance or body fills the mouth. Alcohol and tannin give the characteristic. Many great white wines, such as Moselles, can be light, lacking body, but all great red wines will have it. When young, a great wine often has excessive body. With age, if the wine succeeds, this modifies and becomes part of the full roundness. The French term is *corsé*.

Bois Ordinaires

See Cognac.

Bolivia

Not one of the more important of the South American wine-producing countries, Bolivia has about 5,000 acres planted in wine-producing vines. In addition there are about 4,000 more acres producing table grapes. The wine made amounts to a negligible 10,000 hectoliters (264,500 U.S. gallons, 220,000 imp.) or so a year; in addition there is an almost equal amount of brandy. Bolivian brandy is usually Pisco brandy, as in Peru and Chile.

See Pisco brandy.

Bombom Crema

A honey-flavored Cuban liqueur.

Bonarda

Grape used for dark red wine made principally around Asti in Italy. The wine is sometimes sparkling.

See Piedmont.

Bonde

French term for a barrel stopper, or bung (*q.v.*).

Bonded spirits or wines

Spirits or wines held in store by Customs and Excise until duty is paid by the purchaser. In the United States, a bonded whiskey must remain a minimum of four years in bond before it can be called Bonded Rye or Bourbon. Until 1958, these whiskeys could be aged for eight years only. After that, Internal Revenue taxes had to be paid.

Bonnes Mares

Burgundy red wine.
District: Côte de Nuits, France.
Communes: Chambolle-Musigny and Morey-Saint-Denis.
Official Classification: Great Growth (Grand Cru).

The origin of the name is obscure, but no one has seriously put forth the theory that it has anything to do with stagnant pools (the French word *mare*), good or otherwise.

A large vineyard by Burgundian standards, 11 hectares (37.8 acres), Bonnes Mares is split with 1.8 hectares (4.6 acres) in Morey-Saint-Denis and the rest in Chambolle. It borders Morey's Clos de Tart and the twisting vineyard road (on the uphill side). Although it lies in two communes, the name of neither will normally appear on bottle labels. Bonnes Mares is a Great Growth (*Grand Cru*), one of only thirty-one so designated among the hundreds of Burgundian vineyards, and is put on sale with no further indication of source than the vineyard name. The information on labels should include vineyard, year, grower, and/or shipper and his address—anything else is superfluous.

Like most Burgundian vineyards, Bonnes Mares is divided among a number of growers (one of whom is the author of this book) who all tend their own sections; but for some reason the very great wine they make is not very well known abroad. The peer of most red wines of the Côte de Nuits, and finer than most on the Côte de Beaune—with the exception of Corton—it is overshadowed nonetheless by many lesser but more widely recognized growths. Perhaps it has been eclipsed by the fabulous Musigny—on the opposite side of Chambolle—or bypassed by wine-lovers speeding north toward the fine wines of Gevrey-Chambertin.

As is true of all the great Côte d'Or reds, the grape used is the Pinot Noir. In the soil of Bonnes Mares, it produces wines which are generally softer than most of the great Moreys, with much of the elegance and delicacy of Musigny. Richer in tannins than most Burgundies, they have a firm strength which permits them to age and to round out beautifully, and they keep longer than many other red Burgundies.

No great quantity is made. In an average-quantity year, production is some 300 hectoliters (7,950 U.S. gallons, 6,600 imp.), or 3,100 cases.

Bonnezeaux

A small choice section of the Coteaux du Layon district of Anjou, France, with the right to an Appellation Contrôlée.

See Anjou.

Bons Bois

See Cognac.

Bor

Hungarian term for wine.

Bordeaux

Red, white, and rosé wines.
District: Southwest France.

Bordeaux is the most important wine region of France. More than half of the fine wines of the world come from France, and about half of these from Bordeaux, which has a long and troubled history.

When the Romans arrived in 56 B.C. to occupy what was then Burdigala, it was already a port (although not yet the most important of the Gironde) doing some trade with Britain and other northern ports; and it was connected by road and river with the earlier colony of Narbonne in the south. According to the Bordeaux writer Gaston Marchou, Roman rule was lenient in Burdigala and the native Bituriges were easily and happily Latinized. The city flourished and so did the surrounding vineyards—Pliny mentions the wines that were being made here in the first century A.D.; and in the fourth century, Ausonius was writing from his agreeable villa on an estate outside the town. This good life lasted through his time. Afterward, the Visigoths came and a dark age set in for the vineyards as well as for the city. Luckily Christianity had arrived first, and here, as elsewhere, it was the Church that preserved a vestige of the old learning and saved the culture of the vine—but with many setbacks, over several hundred years.

In 1152, Eleanor of Aquitaine married Henry Plantagenet, Count of Anjou and King of England, bringing Guyenne (Gascony) and Bordeaux as her dowry. At first the Bordelais resented their new rulers. Richard Coeur de Lion spent some time in the city and seems to have charmed them. Yet, in an edict of his successor, King John, on the French wines selling in England in about 1200, no mention was made of any from Bordeaux. Very soon, however, this same king was drinking the Gascon wines and granting favors to the Bordelais. By the end of the reign of Henry III (1216–72), the Bordeaux merchants had gained many privileges: their taxes were eased, and they were given the right to sell in English markets, to set up a council (the Jurade) in their own city, and to elect their mayor. Then, as at the present time, the products of Bourg and Blaye were also in demand. Although ships still sailed from Soulac and other harbors, the crescent-shaped port of Bordeaux (*le port de la lune*) was now first in importance, bristling with the masts of merchant ships. The wines of Graves became the fashion in England (as late as the sixteenth century, the Médoc was described as a savage district, and its wines were little known for another hundred years); the bourgeoisie began to build new houses. By the fourteenth century, the Jurade was very powerful. No one was allowed to sell his wines until the big burghers had made all the sales they wanted—even aristocratic families with estates outside the city were asking to be accepted as bourgeois. As for the wines of other towns (Libourne, Poitiers, and Gaillac), these could not be brought in for sale to foreign buyers until the very end of the autumn wine fair—in those days, wines were drunk from the wood in their first year, and the English ships had to be home with the new vintage

before Christmas, by which time the fragile wine would spoil. The underprivileged barrels were kept apart on the Quai des Chartrons, which was afterward to become the preserve of the great Bordeaux merchants themselves. When the Hundred Years' War (1337–1453) began, the Bordelais, quite happy under a rule so beneficial to them commercially, took the English side. In 1356, after the battle of Poitiers, the Black Prince held the French King John II prisoner and brought him into Bordeaux. "It cannot be recorded," said the chronicler Froissart, "the great feast and cheer that they of the city, with the clergy, made to the Prince." The French king also seems to have had a fair share of the good time before he was taken off to England. Next year came the Black Death, but as soon as the plague had died down the war revived. In his last years the Black Prince, spent, ill, and sadly changed from the magnificent conqueror of Poitiers, carried out senseless destructive raids in the country beyond Bordeaux, and what he did not destroy was ravaged afterward by the French armies in the struggle to recapture the whole of Gascony. For a long time, the Bordeaux vineyards remained untouched, and overseas trade went on. Even when the helpless Henry VI became king of England, Bordeaux and the famous Archbishop Pey Berland believed the English could defend them still. They asked for help. Little came. A small force under the eighty-year-old John Talbot, Earl of Shrewsbury, brave but outnumbered, was defeated at Castillon. Talbot was killed in 1453 (his name survives at Château Talbot in the Médoc) and Bordeaux was French again. At first the burghers were not pleased. The city lost its privileges, and the foreign trade on which, in those days of bad roads to Paris, they depended, was almost at a stop. But Louis XI, when he succeeded Charles VII of France, realized the value of a flourishing wine trade and restored many of the privileges, even at the expense of some of the upriver towns which had been loyal to the French kings. He allowed the Bordelais to elect their own parliament and the English to return for their wine.

In the next century, the troubles were religious. Calvinism spread in the district. There were religious persecutions, uprisings, and in 1572 Bordeaux had its own version of the Massacre of Saint Bartholomew. Henry IV, with his Edict of Nantes, recognized the Protestants (or Huguenots) and things began to look up again. By the seventeenth century, Bordeaux wine was known in Paris and at court. When Cardinal Richelieu planted a new vineyard in the Loire region, he sent for vines from Bordeaux. Mme de Sévigné said Bordeaux would soon go out of fashion "like coffee and Racine" but time has proved her wrong. Louis XIV is said to have washed down big helpings of meat with Saint-Émilion and Chambertin. But his rule was oppressive to the *grands bourgeois* of Bordeaux, who found all their power transferred to the king's intendant, while the king's wars were bad for trade. His unfriendly relations with England (and the change there to Dutch and German kings) led to the Methuen Treaty, which announced new customs duties, favorable to Iberian wines, taxing French ones almost out of the market. Yet the English upper classes wanted their Claret, and smugglers brought it in.

The middle of the eighteenth century was the *belle époque* in Bordeaux—in spite of the fact that at one time the intendant ordered growers to root up their vines and grow corn instead. Orders like that have never been universally obeyed, and one who defied this one was the writer and grower, Montesquieu. The wine trade was always first, but other industries (distilling, ship-building, glass-blowing, sugar refining) were started. Now Bordeaux had an important new customer in North America. The town grew rich, and elegant houses and public buildings appeared: the Place de la Bourse, the Allées de Tourny, and the splendid theater of Victor Louis—all these are still to be seen. When, in 1758, the Duke de Richelieu followed Tourny as intendant, he brought down troupes to act in the theater and invited actresses to supper. He was frivolous, to say the least, and quite unlike the rich bourgeoisie of Bordeaux, some of them Protestants, who lived well but rather austerely. During this period many of the foreigners whose names have become local in Bordeaux—Barton, Lawton, Johnston—first settled in; their descendants are there today.

The first Claret to be put down for ageing, in one of the first bottles sufficiently well rounded to be laid on its side, was the Château Lafite 1797. A dusty old bottle of that vintage is even now on show in the cellars of the château.

The Revolution and the Napoleonic Wars brought particularly bad times for Bordeaux. Cut off from English, American, and Colonial trade, some of the merchants were reduced to selling prunes instead of wine. By 1808, there was no life in the port. Napoleon paid a visit and promised a subsidy, but nothing came of it—except the warm support of Bordeaux for the Restoration. When the wars were over, trade naturally picked up. England lowered taxes in the eighteen-twenties and -thirties. In the fifties came the terrible mildew epidemic, but in spite of it the Classification of 1855, based on earlier classifications and on then current prices for the different wines, was drawn up so that the best wines of Bordeaux could be recognized when they were shown at the Paris Exhibition of that year. In 1860, Gladstone's government lowered the duties on wines coming into England and allowed grocers to sell them. The result was lower prices, bigger trade, and a boom in the import of Claret. The twenty pre-phylloxera years, from 1858 to 1878, produced some memorable vintages—ten good years, of which the greatest were 1858, 1864, 1865, 1870, and 1875. When this book was first published, connoisseurs then alive had tasted these wines and maintained that nothing like them would ever be seen again. Even if we do not agree that the great days are over, it must be allowed that today's fine wines are to some extent different, because they are produced from vines grafted onto American root-stocks, whereas the earlier vines were purely *Vitis vinifera*. Moreover, in those leisurely times, vatting and barrel-ageing lasted longer than is now economically possible. Nevertheless, 1893, 1899, and 1900 are agreed to have been excellent years in Bordeaux, as were 1904, 1906, and 1914. Wines from these years and even earlier often still appear at auction, principally in London. The post-First World War vintages of 1924, 1928, 1929, 1934, and 1937 are everywhere remembered. People who bought these wines to lay down before World War II were lucky: claret was unprecedentedly cheap in the nineteen-thirties. We know from Professor Saintsbury's *Notes on a Cellar-Book* that château-bottled wines were being sold for much the same figure in the 1860s, when money was worth more.

BORDEAUX PLACE-NAMES

In 1911, after long litigation and dispute, the boundaries of the zone of Bordeaux were fixed as those of the department of the Gironde—except for the strip of dune soil along the Atlantic coast, which is not accepted.

The Gironde, largest of the French departments, produces 2.5 million hectoliters (66 million U.S. gallons, 55 million imp.) of wine each year on the 240,000 hectares (600,000 acres) of vineyard which comprise one-eighth of its entire land surface. The name is derived from the French *hirondelle* (a swallow). The two rivers Dordogne and Garonne meet a little below Bordeaux and flow into the broad tidal Gironde, which descends another 50 miles into the Atlantic. The graceful confluence of the two tributaries sketches a swallow's tail; and around the *hirondelle* and the wider estuary, with Bordeaux at its center, the departmental boundaries of the Gironde are flung. The wines are mostly river wines—all the great ones, except the Saint-Émilions and the Pomerols, grow within sight of flowing water.

Within the region, at least three dozen place-names, or Appellations Contrôlées, designate different wines. All these are Bordeaux, although the wines carrying the looser designation Bordeaux are less distinguished than those with a more specific place-name. Yet, not all wine grown in the district is labeled Bordeaux, because, to be entitled to the *appellation*, minimum standards of viticulture and viniculture must be met (*see* Appellation d'Origine Contrôlée). The more restricted regional *appellations*—Haut-Médoc, Saint-Julien, etc.—will nearly always have been bought from different vineyards within the given region by a Bordeaux shipper and blended by him. His reputation will be the additional—and usually soundest—indication of the value of the wine. The Monopole Bordeaux of the various shipping houses are wines of this class, on which the shipper means to stake his name. Nearly all these regional wines are blends. If the vintage year appears on the bottle, it is a blend within the stated year; when the vintage date does not appear, the blend may be from different vineyards and different years. The best shippers blend with the intention of producing a consistently good wine, a "type" which can be reproduced year after year and which can therefore "follow itself"—a basic principle in the making of all the better blended wines and spirits. This means, nevertheless, that year-to-year conformity brings the standard down to a common denominator which can never be very high.

Bordeaux Rouge, Bordeaux Blanc, regional bottlings, and château bottlings are the types to be found on the market. The last are wines from individual vineyards or blends from several lesser vineyards or even from small châteaux, as Bordeaux vineyards are nearly always called—even when they do not possess a "castle" or big

BORDEAUX

ATLANTIC OCEAN

Pointe de Grave
le Verdon-sur-Mer
Soulac-sur-Mer
Gironde
Mortagne-sur-Gironde
N-137
D-2
MÉDOC
Montalivet
Lesparre
Vertheuil
St Estèphe
CÔTES DE
BLAYE
D-2E
Pauillac
St Julien-Beychevelle
Blaye
D-937
Lamarque
CÔTES DE BOURG
Listrac
Bourg
Dordogne
Moulis
Margaux
Macau
HAUT-MÉDOC
Castelnau
N-10
N
Lacanau
Océan
St André-de-Cubzac
Railroad
N-89
Lacanau
D-6
St Hélène
Salaunes
LALANDE-DE-
POMEROL
Montagne
CÔTES DE
CASTILLON
Saumos
Blanquefort
D-5
Libourne
POMEROL
St Georges
le Porge
Bordeaux
le Lac
St Émilion-Vars
ST-ÉMILION
St Médard-en-Jalles
PREMIÈRES
N-89
GRAVES-DE-
VAYRES
D-670A
Mérignac
N-89
D-936
Castillon-la-Bataille
Mérignac Airport
Bordeaux
CÔTES DE
D-936
Pessac
Gradignan
BORDEAUX
St Jean-de-Blaignac
STE-FOY
BORDEAUX
Léognan
ENTRE-DEUX-MERS
GRAVES
N-650
D-671
Sauveterre-de-Guyenne
Bassin
d'Arcachon
Cap Ferret
Arcachon
N-113
A-61
DUPIAC
Podensac
Cadillac
Loupiac
STE-CROIX-DU-MONT
la Réole
CÉRONS
CÔTES DE
Villats
Preignac
BORDEAUX
ST-MACAIRE
A-63
SAUTERNES
Sauternes
Langon
S
A-61
N-113
Limit of Appellation
D-106
D-10
Bazas
N-10
Casteljaloux

Bordeaux (inset)

Médoc-Le Lac
Esplanade des
Quinconces
Grand-Théâtre
Airport
Saint-André
Cathedral
Garonne
N
Gare
Saint-Jean
Graves
Sauternes

0   1   2   3 KM
0   1   2 MI

0   5   10   15 KILOMETERS
0   5   10 MILES

house; for, compared with the châteaux of the Loire, many of these are modest country houses, some of them merely villas. Château wine is never blended with wines from outside the limits of the château itself and is always marked with the vintage year—thus, it is the wine of one vineyard and one harvest. With weather and other viticultural conditions fluctuating as they do, these wines will never have the year-to-year consistency of regional bottlings; but they will touch the highest peaks in the finest years. They are bottled at the château itself and carry on the label the words *Mis en Bouteilles au Château*, or some slight variant of this phrase—the owner's guarantee that the wine is authentic, a guarantee that he could not make with assurance if it had left his premises unbottled.

About 200 of the more than 2,000 châteaux of Bordeaux have been officially classified at various times, beginning in the 16th century. Three of these lists—the Médoc and Sauternes Classification of 1855, the Graves Classifications of 1953 and 1959, and the Saint-Émilion Classification of 1955—are extant today (*see* Médoc, Sauternes, Graves, Saint-Émilion). All châteaux classified as outstanding are treated individually (*see* Château Lafite, Château Latour, Château d'Yquem, Château Cheval Blanc, *etc.*). The sub-regional and communal names or Appellations Contrôlées in Bordeaux wines are as follows:

APPELLATIONS CONTRÔLÉES OF BORDEAUX
(see all place-names as entered individually)
MOST IMPORTANT REGIONS

	Wine	Hectares	Acres
Sauternes	Sweet white	1,450	3,625
Barsac	Sweet white	500	1,250
Médoc	Red	2,700	6,750
Haut-Médoc	Red	7,300	18,250
Pomerol	Red	700	1,750
Saint-Émilion	Red	2,975	7,450
Saint-Émilion: The Satellites	Red	5,375	13,450
Graves	White	1,450	3,625
Graves	Red	1,525	3,800

CHARACTERISTICS

It is evident, from the multiplicity of names, that the range of Bordeaux wines is the greatest anywhere. Roughly, it may be said that red wines are made north of the city and white wines to the south, with the Graves district, in which the actual town is set, forming an intermediate zone where both white and red wines are grown, frequently in a single vineyard. The white wines, with some exceptions, change gradually from dry to sweet through the vineyards in Graves on the edge of Bordeaux to Sauternes at the southern extreme of the region.

Red Bordeaux is, in its own delicate yet firm, feminine style, the finest of its kind in the world; but its characteristic softness and subtlety come only with age. In a Bordeaux the tannin content—which, with alcohol, decides the "heaviness" or "lightness" of any wine—is actually higher than in an authentic and natural Burgundy. This might be said to disprove the theory that the wines of Bordeaux are light and those of Burgundy are heavy. This is not the case, but there are, in fact, a number of exceptions to the rule. The delicate characteristics of "light" Bordeaux are exemplified in the wines of Margaux, in the middle of the Haut-Médoc, which are definite in taste but mild in texture. Generally speaking, however, natural Bordeaux are sturdy when young, but they mature beautifully and attain softness with age; the greater the Bordeaux, the greater will be the recompense of patience, especially in the case of the wines grown around the village of Pauillac, and of the very sturdy wines of Saint-Estèphe, where the softening qualities of age are most necessary. Red Graves also is earthy and full when young and attains a magnificent splendor later on. In Burgundy, on the other hand, young wines tend to mature much faster; and some of those from the Beaujolais region of Burgundy are among the lightest red wines of France, if not of the world. A Côte de Nuits may well be more delicate than a Saint-Émilion, which usually has great fullness and is sometimes referred to as the "Burgundy" of Bordeaux.

Certain generic characteristics are shared by the great gamut of Bordeaux wine. Uniquely, for such volume, it is perfectly natural. White or red, dry or sweet, the châteaux wines never have anything added to them; and for this reason, and also because of their iron content, they are wonderfully health-giving. (Occasionally—1965 and 1968 are modern instances—the process of *chaptalisation*, or adding sugar before fermentation, a common practice elsewhere, is authorized in Bordeaux.) Bordeaux are characterized, too, by their longevity, tremendous for purely natural wines. Some of the greatest Médocs will live for a century in the bottle (the stubborn 1870 vintage did not fulfill its early promise until it was between fifty and seventy years old); and among the sweet white wines, Château d'Yquem also has been known to last a hundred years. In spite of the huge multiplicity and range, there is something peculiar to the scent of Bordeaux, especially the aged reds—a woodland freshness or an earthy smell of low-growing violets which is found in no other wine.

SOIL AND CLIMATE

Such a diversity of wines indicates an equal variety of vineyard soils. The most characteristic soil element, very widespread, is the presence on the surface and in the subsoil of pebbles, forming either the gravel or *graves* which gives the name to several of the finest vineyard areas, or the egg-sized and even fist-sized *cailloux* (pebbles) figuring proudly in the names of such vineyards as Château Beaucaillou in Saint-Julien and contributing largely to the character of, for example, Château Latour, Château Margaux, and Château Prieuré-Lichine. With only a few exceptions, the finest wines come from the vineyards planted on soil deposited in the Quaternary period. The extreme of this principle is that the most recent river soils are excluded as vineyards for wines accorded any of the Bordeaux Appellations Contrôlées. The late alluvial strips and marshy areas are called *palus*; an interesting sidelight on the changing tastes in wine is that a few hundred years ago these were the most sought-after areas in the four categories of land then established.

All Bordeaux wines—though not all to the same degree—are influenced by the mildness and humidity of the climate created by the rivers and the nearness of the sea, and by the pine forests which blanket the land toward the ocean. Summer heat rarely fails to generate a sudden thundershower, and long parched stretches are uncommon. Winters are very short and are seldom cold. The chief menace to the vines is hail, which in recent years has struck most often in the regions of Barsac-Sauternes, more than once destroying the crops of Château d'Yquem, Château de Rayne-Vigneau, and adjacent vineyards. Frosts are a danger, but are less frequent than in most fine vineland. For this very reason, the unprecedented freeze of February 1956 killed hundreds of acres of vineyard; vines unprepared to resist frost failed to withstand the coldest Bordeaux winter since 1709, and the crop was reduced by some 50% with a loss of about a million hectoliters (26.4 million U.S. gallons, 22 million imp.) of unmade wine.

GRAPE VARIETIES

Bordeaux red wine must be made from varieties of the Cabernet vine (Cabernet Sauvignon and Cabernet Franc), the Carménère, Merlot, Malbec, and Petit-Verdot. White wines are limited to the grapes of the Sémillon, Sauvignon, Muscadelle, and Merlot Blanc. Only very rare instances exist of a wine made from a single variety, and practically all are blends of the permitted grapes, varying somewhat in proportion according to the theories of the different growers, but tending to follow the rough formula which time has proved best suited to that particular section. Until 1953 a number of other, less noble vines were tolerated, up to a maximum of 10% of the wine; but in the decade beginning in March 1953 these all had to be systematically uprooted. The writings of Montesquieu indicate a very different situation in his time. In 1785, according to him, no less than twenty-seven varieties of red and twenty-two varieties of white vine contributed to the wines.

VINTAGES

Vintage is very much overemphasized in Bordeaux wines. From 1795 to 1870, 40% of the years were poor or mediocre and 60% were good or better. Since 1870, the proportion has been 80% good or excellent, and 20% mediocre: thus the number of poor years before 1870 was proportionately double the number today. Modern science has eliminated the conditions which gave rise to emphasis on vintage by helping to cut out the "lows."

This does not mean that vintages do not differ—they only fail to differ in commonplace wine zones—but it does mean that the terms used to describe vintages no longer conform to the real case, especially in the highly abbreviated and therefore misleading and sometimes biased vintage charts. On these lists, the opposite of a "great" year is always a "poor," or perhaps a "small" one. In fact,

small years occur in quantity, but never in terms of wine character or quality, and it is a distinct misnomer to refer to a light wine as "small." A "great" red Bordeaux is simply a Bordeaux which has been produced in a "big" year—when continuous sunshine has destined a wine to develop slowly and to last a long time. A "small" year is merely one when there is less sun, and the wines of this year will mature relatively quickly. Deluded by vintage charts, too many people suppose that they must buy the wines only of the big years, usually indicated by outsized ciphers on the vintage chart; in doing so, they are buying essentially what ought properly to be called long-lasting wine, and too often they drink it before it has come to its proper bottle-age. Had they chosen instead the wine of a lighter year, they would have paid less and had a better bottle *at the time they drank it.*

Yet it would not be correct to say that the big vintages are overvalued; properly laid down and waited for, they will finally achieve the highest peaks. It is true, however, that the lighter years are undervalued, for the wines of those years, ready to be drunk much earlier, are not always inferior but are merely going to develop more quickly and fade sooner.

HARVESTING

Bordeaux is usually harvested at the end of September, sometimes in early October, and very rarely in August or November. As a general rule, the hotter the summer, the earlier the harvest. In the last century and a half, the number of vintages starting in the effective month were as follows: August (1822 and 1893), 2; September, 122; October, 51; November (1816), 1. Red wines and most white wines are picked straight over the vineyard, but the extra-sweet Barsacs and Sauternes are selectively picked, bunch by bunch and almost grape by grape as the individual berries reach super-ripeness. Therefore, Barsac and Sauternes harvests take about twice as long as they do elsewhere, often ending in November. The following chart depicts the cycle of the vine in certain significant years.

RIPENING OF THE VINE AT CHÂTEAU MOUTON-ROTHSCHILD (GREAT VINTAGES ONLY)

Year	Flowering Beginning	End	Beginning of reddening of the grape	Start of harvest
1979	June 12	June 28	Aug. 6	Oct. 1
1978	June 10	June 26	Aug. 10	Oct. 10
1976	May 30	June 12	July 4	Sept. 15
1975	June 3	June 21	July 21	Sept. 23
1970	June 5	June 19	July 22	Sept. 28
1966	May 25	June 15	July 25	Sept. 26
1961	May 15	June 5	July 25	Oct. 2
1952	May 19	June 5	July 8	Sept. 18
1947	May 26	June 15	July 15	Sept. 17
1945	May 11	June 1	July 2	Sept. 7
1929	May 24	June 25	July 22	Sept. 21
1921	May 19	June 13	July 18	Sept. 10
1900	May 29	June 14	July 26	Sept. 25

MATURING

Wines of Bordeaux previously stored in jars, or amphorae, began to be kept in cask at the suggestion of Charlemagne. Centuries later—not long before the French Revolution—a greater integrity was established by the enforced use of the *barrique bordelaise*, the barrel which survives today and which was at that time forbidden to all other wines. It is an ideal size—225 liters—for maturing red Bordeaux, although in white Bordeaux some experiments are being made to see if a larger barrel, slowing the development of the wine and keeping it fresher and fruitier, will not better accord with the taste for ever younger white wines. The cost of the barrel itself, in Bordeaux as elsewhere, has risen sensationally and become a factor in the price of the wine. The hand-made oak barrels at the time of writing cost 1100 francs (approximately 275 dollars, or 110 pounds) per barrel. Oak used to be imported from Poland, Sweden, and the United States; but since the Second World War a great deal of it has come from Yugoslavia and the Limoges forest (where the wood is shared with makers of Cognac), and a certain amount of poorer-quality wood from Alsace is used to make up the deficit.

White wines are both fermented and matured in cask; red wines are matured in cask, but are fermented in large vats, generally oak, although at some vineyards they are now made of cement or stainless steel. Controversy rages between traditionalists and modernists in Bordeaux over the use of concrete vats, but no one has been able to prove that the modern method of fermenting in concrete is less efficient or entails loss of quality, and it is fast gaining adherents. There are a few vineyards which have begun cautious experiments maturing red Bordeaux in the oak vats in which it is fermented, an innovation which, if successful, will both reduce cost by eliminating expensive casks and produce a lighter wine which can be drunk sooner. The great red Bordeaux will never be made by this method, because part of the tannin which gives it longevity is absorbed from the new oak of the barrels, renewed for each vintage; but perhaps there will be room also for the lighter, younger wine. It is, however, understandable that since the Second World War there has been a widespread tendency in Bordeaux to hurry the bottling by additional rackings, which hastens the development of the wine. Thirty-five years ago, red Bordeaux was always kept for a minimum of three years in the wood. Nowadays, all the châteaux are bottling at anything from eighteen to thirty months; while most châteaux bottle their wines at the end of about two years.

BORDEAUX BOTTLES

The characteristic Bordeaux bottle has shoulders to retain the sediment and a neck very suited by its straight length to the long corks which distinguish and preserve the finest wines. Half-bottles, called in Bordeaux *fillettes* (little girls), are becoming common, especially for dry white wines, which ought to be drunk very young. A wine will mature more quickly in a half-bottle than in a bottle, because its ripening is partly caused by oxygen coming through the cork, relatively greater in proportion to the lesser quantity of wine in the small bottle. For this reason, a young wine may be good from the half-bottle, but old wines from the half-bottle will be "gone." The ideal bottle for great old Bordeaux is the magnum, with double the content of the standard bottle, in which the wine matures more slowly. The double magnum and the six-bottle jeroboam are rare; and the imperial, with the content of eight normal bottles, has not often been seen since the Second World War. Some experts contend that the old red Bordeaux are better in the sizes greater than the magnum, on the same law of ever lesser cork dimensions in relation to wine mass; while others believe the magnum is the optimum size. This is an argument limited almost entirely to the Bordelais and almost impossible to settle, since it concerns wines half a century old, bottled long ago and subject to dozens of subtly influential conditions.

EXPORT

Export in 1979 of Bordeaux-controlled place-name wines amounted to approximately 1.2 million hectoliters (32 million U.S. gallons, 26.5 million imp.). This figure represents a decrease of 5 percent from the amount exported in 1978. Of the total, Bordeaux exported 152,000 hectoliters (about 4 million U.S. gallons, 3.4 million imp.) to the United States alone.

BORDEAUX GROWTHS: CLASSIFICATION

In 1855 there was a great Exhibition in Paris; the organizers sent to Bordeaux for samples of its best wines, and this set off the local notables on a classification of their finest growths. Only two districts were dealt with—the Médoc and Sauternes. At that time Graves, which had once been the leading district, had fallen behind, and these two regions produced the recognized quality wines of Bordeaux, whose wine merchants discriminated (partly out of snobbery) against the merchants of Libourne and its adjoining vineyards in Saint-Émilion and Pomerol. Hence Château Pétrus of Pomerol, Château Cheval-Blanc and Château Ausone (celebrated as the oldest fine vineyard of the region) in Saint-Émilion were omitted from the 1855 Classification of the Wines of the Gironde and had to wait until 1955 to be officially rated. The grading was done by the Bordeaux brokers (or *courtiers*) who sell the product of the various vineyards to the shippers and are therefore considered to know the wines better than anybody else. The brokers based their judgments on soil, prestige, and prices.

That this was a sensible decision has been proved by the long life of the 1855 Classification. Climate, soil, and surface-exposure of vineyards do not change, and these elements have exercised the same beneficial influence since 1855 as they did before; but owners change, some tend their vines and make their wine better than others do—and there is no doubt that this century-old assessment is now, in some parts, obsolescent. There are few

THE APPELLATIONS CONTRÔLÉES OF THE BORDEAUX REGION

| | | Maximum Yield | | | Average Production | | | | | |
| | | HECTO-LITERS/ | GALLONS PER ACRE | | | WHITE | | | RED | |
Place-name	Date Established	HECTARES	U.S.	Imp.	Hectoliters	U.S. Gallons	Imp. Gallons	Hectoliters	U.S. Gallons	Imp. Gallons
Barsac	Sept. 11, 1936	25	267.25	222.5	13,000	397,500	330,000			
Blaye or Blayais	Sept. 11, 1936 white	45	481	400.5	35,000	910,000	700,000	500	13,250	11,000
	red	50	534.5	445						
Bordeaux	Nov. 14, 1936	50	534.5	445	650,000	17,225,000	14,300,000	300,000	7,800,000	6,000,000
Bordeaux Clairet or Rosé	Nov. 14, 1936	Figures not available.						7,500	198,750	165,000
Bordeaux Supérieur	Oct. 14, 1943	40	427.6	356	12,000	312,000	240,000	300,000	7,800,000	6,000,000
Bordeaux Mousseux (sparkling Bordeaux)	Mar. 16, 1943	Figures not available.								
Cadillac	Mar. 13, 1969	40	427.6	356	6,000	156,000	120,000			
Cérons	Sept. 11, 1936	40	427.6	356	12,000	312,000	240,000			
Côtes de Blaye	Sept. 11, 1936	42	448.9	373.8	6,000	156,000	120,000			
Côtes de Bordeaux Sainte-Macaire	July 31, 1937	42	448.9	373.8	8,000	208,000	160,000			
Côtes de Bourg, Bourg, or Bourgeais	May 14, 1941 white	50	534.5	445	5,000	132,500	110,000			
	Sept. 11, 1936 red	50	534.5	445				95,000	2,517,500	2,090,000
Côtes Canon Fronsac	July 1, 1949	42	448.9	373.8				10,000	265,000	220,000
Côtes de Fronsac	Mar. 14, 1938	42	448.9	373.8				25,000	662,500	550,000
Entre-Deux-Mers	July 31, 1937	50	534.5	445	70,000	1,820,000	1,400,000			
Graves	Mar. 4, 1937	40	427.6	356	8,500	225,250	187,000	40,000	1,040,000	800,000
Graves Supérieures	Mar. 4, 1937	40	427.6	356	30,000	795,000	660,000			
Graves de Vayres	July 31, 1937 white	42	448.9	373.8	17,000	450,500	374,000	7,000	185,500	154,000
	red	40	427.6	356						
Haut-Médoc	Nov. 14, 1936	43	459.6	382.7				70,000	1,820,500	1,400,000
Lalande de Pomerol and Néac	Dec. 8, 1936	40	427.6	356				25,000	650,500	500,000
Listrac	June 8, 1957	40	427.6	356				15,000	397,500	330,000
Loupiac	Sept. 11, 1936	40	427.6	356	10,000	260,000	200,000			
Lussac-Saint-Émilion	Nov. 14, 1936	42	448.9	373.8				35,000	910,000	700,000
Margaux	Aug. 10, 1954	40	427.6	356				30,000	780,500	600,000
Médoc	Nov. 14, 1936	45	481	400.5				90,000	2,340,000	1,800,000
Montagne-Saint-Émilion	Nov. 14, 1936	42	448.9	373.8				40,000	1,040,500	800,000
Moulis	May 14, 1938	40	427.6	356				10,000	265,000	220,000
Parsac-Saint-Émilion*	Nov. 14, 1936	42	448.9	373.8						
Pauillac	Nov. 14, 1936	40	427.6	356				31,000	821,500	682,000
Pomerol	Dec. 8, 1936	40	427.6	356				24,000	636,000	528,000
Premières Côtes de Blaye	Sept. 11, 1936 white	42	448.9	373.8	1,000	26,500	22,000	65,000	1,690,000	1,300,000
	red	50	534.5	445						
Premières Côtes de Bordeaux	July 31, 1937	40	427.6	356	45,000	1,170,000	900,000	30,000	795,000	660,000
Puisseguin-Saint-Émilion	Nov. 14, 1936	42	448.9	373.8				18,000	468,500	360,000
Sables-Saint-Émilion*	Mar. 4, 1937	42	448.9	373.8						
Sainte-Croix-du-Mont	Sept. 11, 1936	40	427.6	356	12,000	424,000	352,000			
Saint-Émilion	Nov. 14, 1936	42	448.9	373.8				190,000	5,035,000	4,180,000
Saint-Estèphe	Nov. 14, 1936	40	427.6	356				45,000	1,170,000	900,000
Sainte-Foy-Bordeaux	July 31, 1937	45	481	400.5	6,000	159,000	132,000	1,000	26,500	22,000
Saint-Georges-Saint-Émilion	Nov. 14, 1936	42	448.9	373.8				7,500	198,750	165,000
Saint-Julien	Nov. 14, 1936	40	427.6	356				25,000	662,500	550,000
Sauternes	Sept. 30, 1936	25	267.25	222.5	25,000	650,000	500,000			

* Now absorbed by the Appellation Contrôlée of Saint-Émilion.

important châteaux which have not changed their holdings. Patches of vineyard are continually being bought and sold. The classification is still, however, completely valid for the First Growths (*Premiers Crus*)—the three great Médoc châteaux, Lafite, Margaux, and Latour—and Haut-Brion, which has always been on the list. Although it is actually in Graves, Haut-Brion wine was too good to be left out and so, defying geography, was classed in with the Médocs. Château Mouton-Rothschild, which in 1973 was justifiably decreed a First Growth, was in the 1855 Classification listed as first among the Second Growths (*Seconds Crus*).

In considering the 1855 Classification, it should be emphasized that a Second, Third (*Troisième*), Fourth (*Quatrième*), or Fifth Growth (*Cinquième Cru*) is not a second-, third-, fourth-, or fifth-rate wine. Actually, only 62 among about 2,000 vineyards were considered worthy of being listed Great Growths (*Grands Crus*)—whether First or Fifth—and they are the absolute cream of the vineyards which, as a group, are probably the world's finest in red wine. To be second after only Lafite, Latour, Margaux, and Haut-Brion is very far from being second-rate. Moreover, it is only on average that the first are the best; in certain years, others equal and even surpass them. Anyone can be sure of a superb bottle when he buys the best years of the famous vineyards (at a price); but there is adventure—and economy—in seeking out other years and other vineyards from the splendid list of Bordeaux wines.

Exceptional Growths (*Crus Exceptionnels*) are *not* classed higher than the Great Growths, but are those classified in 1855 after the 62 great vineyards—and were themselves followed by the Bourgeois and Artisan classes (*Crus Bourgeois* and *Crus Artisans*). Among these are some fine wines which now deserve to be elevated to greater recognition.

In fact, the old classification no longer tells the whole truth; and opinions expressed in the press and elsewhere have proved that even in Bordeaux uneasiness has, in certain quarters, been steadily increasing—although the general view was that, while the ruling of 1855 had its faults, it was impossible to improve upon it. And this in spite of the fact that some of the vineyards then listed are no longer in existence.

In 1959, a committee was formed to decide what was to be done about reclassifying the work of 1855. Two alternatives were discussed: should the 1855 Classification be amended to reflect the changes of today; or should the Classification of 1855 remain untouched and a new one be drawn up? The author, feeling that many alterations are needed, was a member of one of the original committees, which consisted of leading Bordeaux growers, shippers, and brokers, and he published in 1959 a private classification of all the red wines of Bordeaux, on the lines of the recent official ratings for Saint-Émilion and Graves—Pomerol has not even yet been classified. Revised several times, the most recent classification was prepared in 1973. Each expert was interviewed privately and "off the record," therefore, no one person's views are quoted: but it was soon evident that on certain points

there was no difference of opinion. Investigation of land records in the various communes revealed that some of the châteaux no longer occupied the same terrain they did in 1855; in many cases changes were insignificant, but in others important transfers of parcels of land had been made—and therefore even the essential qualification of first-rate soil cannot, in these instances, go unchallenged. Other classified châteaux, including some Second and Third Growths, no longer make any wine; the names stand for Great Growths of 1855 as a Roman ruin may persist as a reminder of a vanished monument of classical times. This absurdity does harm to the Bordeaux wine trade; and the reverse case, of a vineyard classed as a Fifth or even a Bourgeois Growth, when it deserves to be sold as a Second or Third Growth, deprives both grower and customer of a satisfactory transaction.

It was generally agreed that if the 1855 standards were applied today, they would have to rate as a First Growth Château Pétrus—still unclassified in the as yet unclassified district of Pomerol; would have to advance Château Mouton-Rothschild from Second to First Growth and elevate Cheval-Blanc from a First of Saint-Émilion to a Bordeaux Great Growth. Indeed, so many vineyards of Saint-Émilion, Graves, and Pomerol clamored for their rightful place that it became obvious that any workable classification should include all Bordeaux wines. In fact, the system of 1855 should not now be used, for if a guide is no longer completely reliable, the public loses confidence. This is now happening.

As to the form a new classification should take, opinions were almost unanimous that the error of grading vineyards First, Second, and so on must not be repeated. In an age of publicity and competitive salesmanship, any wine listed as a Second, Third, or Fourth would be unfairly handicapped; the newer classifications for Saint-Émilion and Graves do not follow this pattern, and grade their wines First Growths, Great Growths, and Other Principal Growths (*see* Appendix A). In his suggested revision of the Classification, the author has adapted and expanded these as follows: Outstanding Growths (*Crus Hors Classe*), Exceptional Growths (*Crus Exceptionnels*), Great Growths (*Grands Crus*), Superior Growths (*Crus Supérieurs*), and Good Growths (*Bons Crus*).

Finally, most of the experts consulted were of the opinion that, in assessing the position of the vineyards, price would still be (as it was in 1855) the most reliable indicator; and it was on this basis, of the prices the individual wines command in today's market, that the following classification was prepared. The fact that a great soil, given proper management, will produce great wines was taken into account: certain vineyards have not been downgraded as much as their present management warrants, because the soil is intact and, under new management, these vineyards may rise again.

A classification should not be planned for a shorter span than 25 to 50 years. The present condition of the 1855 list proves that no such ruling can remain valid indefinitely; but, conversely, too frequent change would cause confusion and loss of confidence among buyers.

Bordeaux Growths: Classification

In 1960, after the committee had made a formal request for a revision of the 1855 Classification, the Institut National des Appellations d'Origine was called in to arbitrate. Two years later, however, it was decided in Bordeaux that the jurisdiction of this body was too limited for it to resolve a matter so complex and so controversial. The Bordeaux Chamber of Commerce and the Académie des Vins de Bordeaux then took up the question of the proposed reforms. At the time of writing, there is insufficient courage and leadership in Bordeaux to push through the necessary changes in the obsolete 1855 Classification.

More and more the problems of the 1855 Classification are recognized. In 1973 Mouton-Rothschild was named a First Growth by decree of the Minister of Agriculture. The 1855 ranking is the exclusive property of the Comité des Grands Crus Classés and can never be officially altered. The following, revised as of September 1978, is the only classification that "dares" combine the best red wines of the four important Bordeaux regions.

CLASSIFICATION DES GRANDS CRUS ROUGES DE BORDEAUX

Crus Hors Classe (Outstanding Growths)

HAUT-MÉDOC

Château Lafite-Rothschild (*Pauillac*)
Château Latour (*Pauillac*)
Château Margaux (*Margaux*)
Château Mouton-Rothschild (*Pauillac*)

GRAVES

Château Haut-Brion (*Pessac, Graves*)

SAINT-ÉMILION

Château Ausone
Château Cheval-Blanc

POMEROL

Château Pétrus

Crus Exceptionnels (Exceptional Growths)

HAUT-MÉDOC

Château Beychevelle (*Saint-Julien*)
Château Brane-Cantenac (*Cantenac-Margaux*)
Château Calon-Ségur (*Saint-Estèphe*)
Château Cos d'Estournel (*Saint-Estèphe*)
Château Ducru-Beaucaillou (*Saint-Julien*)
Château Gruaud-Larose (*Saint-Julien*)
Château Lascombes (*Margaux*)
Château Léoville-Barton (*Saint-Julien*)
Château Léoville-Las-Cases (*Saint-Julien*)
Château Léoville Poyferré (*Saint-Julien*)
Château Montrose (*Saint-Estèphe*)
Château Palmer (*Cantenac-Margaux*)
Château Pichon-Lalande (*Pauillac*)
Château Pichon-Longueville (Baron) (*Pauillac*)

GRAVES

*Domaine de Chevalier (*Léognan*)

120

*Château La Mission-Haut-Brion (*Pessac*)
*Château Pape-Clément (*Pessac*)

SAINT-ÉMILION

*Château Figeac
Château Magdelaine
Château Magdelaine

POMEROL

Château La Conseillante
Château l'Évangile
Château Lafleur
Château La Fleur-Pétrus
Château Trotanoy

Grands Crus (Great Growths)

HAUT-MÉDOC

Château Branaire (*Saint-Julien*)
Château Cantemerle (*Haut-Médoc*)
Château Cantenac-Brown (*Cantenac-Margaux*)
Château Duhart-Milon-Rothschild (*Pauillac*)
Château Durfort (*Cantenac-Margaux*)
*Château Giscours (*Labarde-Margaux*)
Château d'Issan (*Cantenac-Margaux*)
Château La Lagune (*Haut-Médoc*)
*Château Lynch-Bages (*Pauillac*)
Château Malescot-Saint-Exupéry (*Margaux*)
Château Mouton-Baronne-Philippe (*Pauillac*)
Château Pontet-Canet (*Pauillac*)
*Château Prieuré-Lichine (*Cantenac-Margaux*)
Château Rausan-Ségla (*Margaux*)
Château Rauzan-Gassies (*Margaux*)
Château Talbot (*Saint-Julien*)

GRAVES

*Château Carbonnieux (*Léognan*)
*Château Haut-Bailly (*Léognan*)

SAINT-ÉMILION

Château Beauséjour-Bécot
*Château Bel-Air
*Château Canon
Clos Fourtet
Château La Gaffelière
Château Pavie
Château Trottevieille

POMEROL

Château Gazin
Château Latour-Pomerol
Château Petit-Village
Vieux-Château-Certan

Crus Supérieurs (Superior Growths)

HAUT-MÉDOC

Château Batailley (*Pauillac*)
Château Boyd-Cantenac (*Cantenac-Margaux*)
Château Chasse-Spleen (*Moulis*)
Château Clerc-Milon-Rothschild (*Pauillac*)
Château Gloria (*Saint-Julien*)
Château Grand-Puy-Lacoste (*Pauillac*)
Château Haut-Batailley (*Pauillac*)
Château Kirwan (*Cantenac-Margaux*)
Château Lagrange (*Saint-Julien*)
Château Langoa (*Saint-Julien*)
Château Marquis d'Alesme-Becker (*Margaux*)
Château La Tour-Carnet (*Haut-Médoc*)

These wines are considered better than their peers in this classification.

GRAVES

Château Bouscaut (*Cadaujac*)

Château de Fieuzal (*Léognan*)

*Château Malartic-Lagravière (*Léognan*)

Château Smith Haut-Lafitte (*Martillac*)

SAINT ÉMILION

Château l'Angélus

*Château Balestard-la-Tonnelle

Château Beauséjour-Duffau-Lagarrosse

Château Cadet-Piola

Château Canon-la-Gaffelière

Château La Clotte

Château Croque-Michotte

Château Curé-Bon-la-Madeleine

Château La Dominique

Château Larcis-Ducasse

Château Larmande

Château Soutard

Château Troplong-Mondot

Château Villemaurine

POMEROL

Château Beauregard

Château Certan-Giraud

Château Certan-de-May

Clos l'Église

Château l'Église-Clinet

Château Le Gay

Château Lagrange

Château Nénin

Château La Pointe

Bons Crus (Good Growths)

HAUT-MÉDOC

Château Angludet (*Cantenac-Margaux*)

Château Beau-Site (*Saint-Estèphe*)

Château Beau-Site Haut-Vignoble (*Saint-Estèphe*)

Château Bel-Air-Marquis d'Aligre (*Soussans-Margaux*)

Château Bel-Orme (*Haut-Médoc*)

Château Belgrave (*Saint-Laurent*)

*Château de Camensac (*Haut-Médoc*)

Château Citran (*Haut-Médoc*)

Château Cos-Labory (*Saint-Estèphe*)

*Château Croizet-Bages (*Pauillac*)

Château Dauzac (*Labarde*)

Château Ferrière (*Margaux*)

Château Fourcas-Dupré (*Listrac*)

Château Fourcas-Hosten (*Listrac*)

Château Grand-Puy-Ducasse

Château Gressier-Grand-Poujeaux (*Moulis*)

Château Hanteillan (*Haut-Médoc*)

Château Haut-Bages-Libéral (*Pauillac*)

Château Haut-Marbuzet (*Saint-Estèphe*)

Château Labégorce (*Margaux*)

Château Labégorce-Zedé (*Margaux*)

Château Lafon-Rochet (*Saint-Estèphe*)

Château Lamarque (*Haut-Médoc*)

Château Lanessan (*Haut-Médoc*)

Château Lynch-Moussas (*Pauillac*)

Château Marquis-de-Terme (*Margaux*)

Château Maucaillou (*Moulis*)

Château Les Ormes-de-Pez (*Saint-Estèphe*)

Château Pédesclaux (*Pauillac*)

*Château de Pez (*Saint-Estèphe*)

Château Phélan-Ségur (*Saint-Estèphe*)

Château Pouget (*Cantenac-Margaux*)

Château Poujeaux (*Moulis*)

*Château Saint-Pierre (*Saint-Julien*)

Château Siran (*Labarde-Margaux*)

Château du Tertre (*Arsac-Margaux*)

Château La Tour-de-Mons (*Soussans-Margaux*)

GRAVES

Château Larrivet-Haut-Brion (*Pessac*)

Château La Louvière (*Léognan*)

Château La Tour-Haut-Brion (*Talence*)

Château La Tour-Martillac (*Martillac*)

SAINT ÉMILION

Château l'Arrosée

Château Bellevue

Château Cap-de-Mourlin

Domaine du Châtelet

Clos des Jacobins

Château Corbin (*Giraud*)

Château Corbin (*Manuel*)

Château Corbin-Michotte

Château Coutet

Château Dassault

Couvent-des-Jacobins

Château La Fleur-Pourret

Château Franc-Mayne

Château Grâce-Dieux

Château Grand-Barrail-Lamarzelle-Figeac

Château Grand-Corbin

Château Grand-Corbin-Despagne

Château Grand-Mayne

Château Grand Pontet

Château Guadet-St. Julien

Château Laroque

Château Moulin-du-Cadet

Château Pavie-Decesse

Château Pavie-Macquin

Château Saint-Georges-Côte-Pavie

Château Tertre-Daugay

Château La Tour-Figeac

Château La Tour-du-Pin-Figeac

Château Trimoulet

Château Yon-Figeac

POMEROL

Château Bourgneuf-Vayron

Château La Cabanne

Château Le Caillou

Clos du Clocher

Château La Croix

Château La Croix-de-Gay

Domaine de l'Église

Château l'Enclos

Château Gombaude-Guillot

Château Guillot

Château Moulinet

Château Rouget

*Clos René

Château de Sales

Château Tailhas

Château Taillefer

Château Vraye-Croix-de-Gay

*These wines are considered better than their peers in this classification.

Note: All Saint-Émilion and Pomerol châteaux classified above bear the strict commune designations of Saint-Émilion and Pomerol respectively.

Bordeaux: Mousseux, Supérieur

Mildly sparkling wines with Appellations Contrôlées in the Bordeaux region.
See Bordeaux.

Bordeaux mixture

A mixture of copper sulfate and slaked lime used as a fungicide spray in many parts of Europe. Applied in the summer months to fight mildew and oïdium, the spray gives French and German vineyards a characteristic blue-green tinge.
See Chapter Eight.

Borderies

Lesser region of Cognac, producing brandies with considerable body and usually lacking in finesse.
See Cognac.

Bosa

Malvasia di Bosa is a richly-colored red wine of Sardinia (*q.v.*).

Bota

(1) Wine bag; the modern conventional Spanish wine bag is of untanned goatskin, holding about a liter. It has a bone or wooden nozzle out of which the wine may be squirted by squeezing the bag. It is thus possible for several different persons in turn to drink from the *bota* without touching the nozzle with their lips.
(2) Spanish wine barrel of 500 liters (132 U.S. gallons, 110 imp.) widely used for storing and ageing wines. A Sherry butt. There is also a *media bota*, or half-*bota*, with a capacity of 250 liters (66 U.S. gallons, 55 imp.).

Botrytis cinerea

A parasitic fungus or mold that attacks grapes; in certain climates the grapes then develop gray rot and spoil, while in others the *Botrytis cinerea* produces some of the greatest sweet white wines of the world. Called *pourriture noble* by the French (literally, noble rot), it is carefully cultivated in Sauternes, Monbazillac, Anjou, and Touraine—as well as in Germany, where it is known as *Edelfäule* and is responsible for the Auslese, Beerenauslese, and Trockenbeerenauslese wines of the Rhine and Mosel. It also produces Tokay in Hungary. In no other area has it so far proved possible to make those late-gathered sweet wines from overripe grapes, since the climate must be exactly right for them. (The proper weather conditions have reportedly been found in the New York State Finger Lakes district and in California, but few wines have been made.)

The fungus penetrates the skin of the fruit without breaking it, and thus without exposing the pulp to air. If all is in order, the grape begins to wither and become desiccated, and there is a corresponding concentration of the juice. In the shrinking of the fruit, loss of acidity is greater than loss of sugar. Consequently the percentage of soluble solids becomes greater, sugar and glycerin mounting faster than acidity. When vinified, the wines become smooth and almost oily in texture, very sweet and high in alcohol. The climatic conditions must be such that as the grapes mature moisture must be present in the air to allow the fungus to grow, alternating with periods of dry weather to cause the water in the grapes to evaporate and so keep the mold from growing too fast. Yet if the temperature rises too high, the fungus will be killed. At the end of this uncertain and difficult culture, the juice that remains in the grape makes only a small amount of wine, which is thus extremely expensive.
See Chapter Nine, p. 38.

Bottle sickness

A temporary indisposition to which wine is sometimes subject when it is first bottled.

Botticino

An Italian red wine, good to drink young.
See Lombardy.

Bouché

French term for a wine-bottle stoppered with a cork; not to be confused with *bouchonné* (spoiled by the cork).

Bouchet

One of the grape varieties of the Saint-Émilion and Pomerol districts of Bordeaux; synonymous with Cabernet Franc and Cabernet Sauvignon.

Bouchon

French term for cork.

Bouchonné

A bottle of wine spoiled by a bad cork. Corky.

Bouquet

Volatile acidity is responsible for the bouquet of a wine. It should be clean, with no trace of moldiness. The scent is produced by the vaporization of esters and ethers, those elusive chemical components which the wine contains. When a wine is cold or when a bottle is first opened, the bouquet is faint and hard to identify. (The first perfume is the bouquet; the later, more lingering odor, is the aroma.)

Bourbon

A type of American whiskey.
See Whiskey, Bourbon.

Bourg, Bourgeais, Côtes de Bourg

Red and white wines.
District: Bordeaux, France.

Official French wine place-names, all applying to the red and white wines made in nearly equal quantity on the hills of Bourg fringing the River Garonne and the River Dordogne as they enter the Gironde, and all but enclosed within the larger Blaye wine region. The two ancient fortified towns of Bourg and Blaye are less than half a dozen miles apart, and the wines can be considered together. Red Bourg is fuller-bodied than red Blaye, and, all in all, is superior. Some of the white Premières Côtes de Blaye are the best white wines of the linked regions.

Bourgogne: Aligoté, Mousseux, Passe-tous-Grains

Wines with Appellations Contrôlées in Burgundy (*q.v.*).

Bourgueil and Saint-Nicolas-de-Bourgueil

Loire Valley red and rosé wines.
District: Touraine, France.

These growing areas are separate and distinct but are adjacent; and the wines are so alike that they are invariably classed together. They have also in common the fact that they are the only Loire vineyards where the place-name is restricted to red and rosé wines; white can be called only Touraine.

The wines are light, soft, and delicate, with a pronounced fruitiness and a strong bouquet which calls to mind raspberries, or perhaps violets. Wine labeled Saint-Nicolas-de-Bourgueil comes from grapes grown only there and is generally better than Bourgueil, for which the grapes may be grown in seven parishes. Soil throughout is a gravelly sand enriched with limestone and clay, and the only permissible grape is Cabernet Franc. Wines must have a minimum alcoholic content of 9.5%. About 45,000 hectoliters (1,188,000 U.S. gallons, 990,000 imp.) are made annually.

Château Bouscaut

Bordeaux red and white wines.
District: Graves, France.
Commune: Cadaujac.

Classed in 1953 among the five top Graves vineyards making white wine and the eleven top Graves vineyards making red wine, Château Bouscaut is the first important estate on the Graves-Sauternes road leading to Toulouse. The rebuilt house is a handsome mixture of medieval and modern, with its tapestries, swimming pool, and huge walled park. The *chais* divide in two—for the making of red wines (which are fermented in huge oak vats) and white wines, which are crushed in electric presses, contained in a reservoir the first day, and are then tapped off directly into barrels in the *chai*, where both red and white ferment and age. Once in barrel, red and white wines age side by side.

In October 1968 a small group of American wine-lovers led by Charles Wohlstetter, chairman of the board of Continental Telephone, and Howard Sloane purchased the vineyard. Lucien Lurton, proprietor of Château Brane-Cantenac and Château Durfort, as well as Château Climens in Barsac, bought the property in 1979.

The red wine is made from 40% Merlot, 25% Cabernet Sauvignon, 25% Cabernet Franc, and 10% Malbec. The white is 60% Sémillon and 40% Sauvignon Blanc.

Characteristics. Strong and full. In 1970 a better wine was made than before. The vineyard bears watching for great improvement.

Vineyard area: Red—39 hectares (97 acres); white—5 hectares (12.5 acres).

Average production: Red—120 *tonneaux* (10,000 cases): white—18 *tonneaux* (1,500 cases).

Bouzy

Village of the Mountain of Reims district, producing red grapes for a First Growth Champagne, and a red still wine.
See Champagne.

Boxbeutel

A flat flask-shaped wine bottle.
See Bocksbeutel.

Château Boyd-Cantenac

Bordeaux red wine.
District: Haut-Médoc, France.
Commune: Cantenac-Margaux.

There is no château, but the vineyard itself, owned by M. P. Guillemet, is a Third Growth (*Troisième Cru*) of the Médoc, according to the 1855 Classification. The wine is made at Guillemet's Château Pouget. Until 1961 the vineyard did not deserve its high classification but it has improved considerably and is again making wine worthy of the 1855 rank, thanks to the enormous efforts of M. Guillemet. The breakdown of vines planted in this now well-tended vineyard is 70% Cabernet Sauvignon, 20% Merlot, 6% Cabernet Franc, and 4% Petit Verdot. The vinification is supervised by Dr. Peynaud, professor of oenology at the University of Bordeaux.

Characteristics. Light, round, and elegant.
Vineyard area: 18 hectares (45 acres).
Average production: 60 *tonneaux* (5,000 cases).

Brachetto

Red wine grape of Italy, which produces a wine of strong color and agreeable flavor.
See Piedmont.

Brachetto d'Acqui

A semi-sparkling red wine from the Italian Piedmont
(q.v.).

Château Branaire

Bordeaux red wine.
District: Haut-Médoc, France.
Commune: Saint-Julien.

Facing Château Beychevelle across the vineyard road
as it winds north into Saint-Julien, Château Branaire,
Fourth Growth (*Quatrième Cru*) by the 1855 Classification,
is now owned by M. Tapie, the son of an enterprising
Algerian wine-grower who in the early fifties acquired the
vineyard. In 1969, M. Tapie Père simplified the name of
the vineyard by removing the surname of a former owner,
a M. Ducru, from the title. The vineyard is well placed
on the flattish top of rising ground, and there is an excellent large *chai* for old wines sunk two-thirds underground
to achieve a beneficial dampness. Mme Tari, wife of the
owner of Château Giscours, and her able son also have a
share in the vineyard.

Characteristics. Sturdy, big wines, sometimes quite hard
at the outset; but among the best of Saint-Julien.

Vineyard area: 49 hectares (123 acres).

Average production: 200 *tonneaux* (19,000 cases).

Brandy

The word alone means distilled wine. It has been appropriated to refer to distillates from other fruits—apples,
pears, cherries, etc.—but in such cases will always be
qualified by the source. Brandy, when it stands alone, is a
product of the grape and is distilled throughout the
world.

The best brandies are the French Cognac and Armagnac. A fact too often overlooked is that Cognac is not
brandy, but *a* brandy. It is perhaps, at its best, the world's
most exquisite example of spirits of this type; Armagnac
can be almost as perfect. Brandies are made in most wine-
growing countries, sometimes of extraordinarily good
quality, sometimes not. The secret of a fine brandy is
partly in the wine distilled, partly in the distilling process
(the best is made in pot stills), but also in the age and the
wood in which it is aged. Cognac, for instance, matures
best in Limousin oak. It should be remembered that once
brandy is bottled, it ceases to improve and may even deteriorate after a certain time. Such labels as "Napoleon
Brandy" thus become meaningless or worse, as any
brandy kept in barrel since the days of Napoleon would
have evaporated, and any kept in bottle would be the
same, or perhaps not so good as when it was placed in
glass. In any case, there would be none left.

Fruit brandy is made from all kinds of fruit.

Other leading brandies of the world are:

Calvados: the apple brandy of France.
Marc: distilled from grape pomace.
Grappa: another name for marc.
Applejack: American apple brandy.
See under separate headings.

Château Brane-Cantenac

Bordeaux red wine.
District: Haut-Médoc, France.
Commune: Cantenac-Margaux.

Once famous as Château Gorce, this, the largest vineyard with the largest production of any Classified Growth
in the Haut-Médoc, was acquired early in the nineteenth
century by the "Napoleon of the Vines," Baron de Brane.
In 1820 he gave it his name, a bold gesture for the day.
"Gorce is widely known," he wrote to the press, "but I
have faith in the name of Brane." Acquiring a vineyard
in Pauillac named Château Pouyallet, he named it
Brane-Mouton—now famous as Mouton-Rothschild. In
those days, Brane-Cantenac was considered the superior
vineyard, and the Baron disposed of the present Mouton-
Rothschild in order to devote all of his attention to it.
Lucien Lurton is now the owner of this huge Second
Growth (*Second Cru*) as well as Durfort-Vivens in Margaux, Château Climens in Barsac, and Château Bouscaut
in Graves.

Brane long lingered in a twilight zone of quality. Some
rather mediocre wines were made in this very great vineyard which disappointed many Médoc admirers. Several
recent vintages have definitely re-established its waning
reputation. To hold the huge production, Lurton has
built large storage tanks resembling the silo-like vats one
finds in California.

Characteristics. The wine has the delicacy and suppleness
of a typical Margaux, and a particularly delightful perfume.

Vineyard area: 115 hectares (288 acres).

Average production: 375 *tonneaux* (35,000 cases).

Brännvin

An alternate name for aquavit (*q.v.*).

Brauneberger Falkenberg

One of the two best elegant wines of Brauneberg on the
German Mosel.

See Mosel-Saar-Ruwer.

Brauneberger Juffer

The more famous of the two best wines in the Brauneberg vineyard section, one of the top quality regions of the
German Mosel. Flowery, elegant wines.

See Mosel-Saar-Ruwer.

Brazil

Brazil's 3,287,203 square miles make it the largest of
the South American countries. Roughly 68,000 hectares
(170,000 acres) of the country are cultivated in vines. Of
late years there has been considerable development in
wine production, and a greater demand for wine inside
the country. Growers have introduced modern fertilizers
and more efficient methods of processing and purifying,
and so quality has been improving.

Brazil was colonized by wine-drinking Portuguese, yet
vine-tending was not one of their early occupations. Few

vines were brought into the country until the turn of this century, and most of them were planted after the First World War by settlers from Italy.

The principal wine region is the southern state of Rio Grande do Sul, which produces approximately 180,000 hectoliters (4,752,000 U.S. gallons, 3,960,000 imp.) of wine per year. It lies in the southern temperate zone and is the part of the country where the climate is most favorable to the wine. Other centers are São Paulo, and the states of Rio de Janeiro, and Minas Gerais, at an altitude of between 2,300 and 6,000 feet. Santa Catarina, also, is expanding its vineyards and shipping the harvest to São Paulo to be fermented into wine.

Eighty per cent of the vines planted in Brazil are hybrids of the variety *Vitis labrusca* and only twenty per cent, unfortunately, are *Vitis vinifera*. The *labrusca* bears the hot damp climate better than does *Vitis vinifera*. Other grapes are: Duchesse (also known as Riesling de Caldas), Niagara, Folha de Figo (Fig Leaf), Black July, Seibel, Two 10096, 6905, several of the Couderc types, Delaware, Jacques Gaillard, and different kinds of Bertille-Seyve. In Santa Catarina, Concord, Cintiana, Herbemont, Gothe, Trebbiano, Poverella, and several of the Moscatelle type are planted too. For quality wines, some distinguished European stocks are cultivated.

The leading types of Brazilian wine are:

Cheaper Table Wines. Reds of the "burgundy" and "claret" types, rosés, and white wines—dry, semi-dry, sweet, and sparkling.

Good Table Wines. Reds from the Barbera, Bonarda, Cabernet, Merlot, and other fine vines. White wines from Trebbiano, Poverella, Malvasia, Riesling, and others.

Expensive Wines. Espumante (fermented in bottle and in vat) Moscatels, Malvasias.

Brazil's best wine is made by the firm which is also the largest producer, turning out some 275,000 hectoliters (7,287,500 U.S. gallons, 6,050,000 imp.) a year. This firm—with the somewhat staggering name of Indústria, Comércio e Navegação, Sociedade Vinícola Rio Grandense, Ltda.—distributes its wines under the label Granja União. These are both red and white. Some of the reds come from Merlot and Cabernet (or Caberat) grapes; the white are Trebbiano (Trebiano) and Riesling. Trebbiano is the Italian name for the Ugni Blanc and shows the Italian influence. Much of the recent development of the Brazilian wine industry can also be attributed to the Central Vinícola do Sul (VINOSUL S/A).

Special Wines. Vermouths, medicinal wines, and others.

Distilled Liqueurs. Conhaques, and liqueurs of various types.

Most Brazilian wines are sold inside Brazil. São Paulo and Rio de Janeiro are the heaviest consumers, but the rest of the country absorbs most of what is left over. Wines are imported, also: from Europe, and from South American neighbors, particularly Chile. Among the sixty-odd wine firms in Brazil, the most important, after the ones already cited, are: Luiz Antunes & Cia., Luiz Michelon S.A., Sociedade Vinhos Unico, Ltda., Carlos Dreher Neto, E. Mosele S.A., Sociedade Brasileira de Vinhos, Ltda, and Almadén Vineyards.

Breathing

A wine breathes or oxidizes when it comes in contact with air. In general, red wines need more airing than whites, and young red, with high tannin content, requires most of all. To enjoy the bouquet of a wine at its best, uncork the bottle and let the wine breathe for an hour or two—the best way of letting it show to its best advantage.

See Chapter Four, p. 12.

Château de la Brède

Bordeaux white wine.
District: Graves, France.
Commune: La Brède.

La Brède, the home of Montesquieu at the end of the seventeenth and the beginning of the eighteenth centuries, was the estate not only of a great writer, but also of a great wine-grower. Montesquieu's vineyard was much larger than the La Brède of today, spreading over miles of Graves and including many of the vineyards now famous under other names. The great author plied his vines as actively as his pen and pushed the sale of his wines with energy both in France and England. Today La Brède is only of historical interest, although the château remains Bordeaux's most beautiful castle. The small quantity of wine made is undistinguished; the quality of the wine does not match the beauty of the château. The vineyard was not included in the 1959 Graves Classification.

Vineyard area: 6 hectares (15 acres).
Average production: 10 *tonneaux* (900 cases).

Breed

Delicacy and discretion are the attributes of breed in wine. This undisputed superiority comes from the soil (*terroir*). The French words for it are *race* and *finesse*.

Breganze

Italian red or white wines.
See Veneto.

Brenner

A fungus disease of vines found notably in Germany.
See Chapter Eight, p. 29.

Breton

The Cabernet Franc grape is so called in the Touraine region of France.
See Cabernet.

Bristol Cream

Sweetened old Oloroso Sherry bottled in Bristol, England.

Bristol Milk

Sweetened Oloroso Sherry, less rich than the "Cream," bottled in Bristol, England.

British Compounds

British excise term for redistilled, rectified, or flavored spirits.

Brizard

Firm of Marie Brizard & Roger, liqueur-makers in Bordeaux, France.

Brolio

An excellent classical chianti; the best is sold, not in the popular *fiasco*, but in bottle.
See Tuscany.

Brouilly

See Beaujolais; Côte de Brouilly.

Château Broustet

Bordeaux white wine.
District: Sauternes, France.
Commune: Barsac.

The property makes a typically sweet wine, classed among the Second Growths of Sauternes in 1855.
Vineyard area: 16 hectares (40 acres).
Average production: 30 *tonneaux* (2,700 cases).

Brown Sherry

Sweet, dark Oloroso Sherry.
See Sherry.

Brunello di Montalcino

One of the best, longest-lived red wines of Italy.
See Tuscany.

Brunissure (browning)

Vine disease. Brown skins appear on the leaf, which drops off—the result of overproduction and insufficient pruning of the vine.
See Chapter Eight, p. 29.

Brut

This word on the label of a bottle of Champagne indicates that the wine is very dry, and is, in fact, drier than that labeled Extra Sec—or Extra Dry.
See Champagne.

Bual, Boal

A full, sweet Madeira wine.

Bucelas

A golden Portuguese wine, once world-famous but now little seen abroad.
See Portugal.

Buchu

A South African liqueur virtually unknown elsewhere. The reason for this may be inferred from C. de Boscari's account of buchu in his *Wines of the Cape*, where he describes it as: "The herb with which savage Africa cured all its ills, from stomach-ache to snake-bite, from housemaid's knee to witch-doctor's spell, for centuries before the White Man appeared. Grafted on to the European pharmacopoeia, buchu is today cultivated as a farm crop round Paarl: its extract is used externally as an embrocation and internally, mixed with brandy, for disorders of the digestive tract. It is credited with miraculous powers of healing, and it certainly tastes noxious enough to possess them."

Bulgaria

Few countries can claim older traditions of wine-making than Bulgaria: the commercial organization of viticulture and the marketing of wine are believed to have started in ancient Thrace, part of which is now within her borders.

As with all the Balkan lands, frontiers have advanced and receded over the centuries, and today the country is bounded to the north by the Danube, her Rumanian frontier; to the east, there are 150 kilometers (94 miles) of coastline on the Black Sea and to the south and west, frontiers with Turkey, Greece, and the Yugoslavian states of Serbia and Macedonia. Nearly half the land surface is mountain range: the Balkan Mountains to the west, and the Rhodope Mountains to the south; but the fertile lands of the Danube and Meritza valleys endow Bulgaria well for the agriculture which is the basis of the economy. A geographical location on about the same latitude as northern Spain and the Tuscan and Umbrian regions of Italy means that the land is well situated for growing grapes and making wine.

HISTORY

Bulgarian viticulture was brought almost to a standstill under five centuries of Turkish Moslem rule, yet it survived here as elsewhere in the Ottoman Empire. The country did not become completely independent of Turkish influence until the end of the First World War; but from that time the area of vineyards and the annual total of wine production increased until, in 1940, it reached about 2 million hectoliters (53 million U.S. gallons, 44 million imp.), of which about 300,000 hectoliters were exported, mainly to Germany. The Second World War and the disturbed times that followed caused the virtual collapse of Bulgarian viticulture. In 1948, the "Vinprom" State Enterprise was formed to revive and take charge of all wine production and marketing, and today Bulgaria is perhaps the most interesting and successful example of modern commercial production methods applied to a basis of ancient traditions of peasant cultivation—the common pattern now in all Balkan states. The 450,000 peasant growers already had a well-established experience of cooperatives, which gave a foundation for the "collectivization" of existing production. In addition, vast new vineyards have been established by "Vinprom," and Bulgaria's annual production of wine is now well over 5 million hectoliters (132 million U.S. gallons, 110 million imp.). Plans to treble this figure over the next ten years or so may seem ambitious, but Bulgaria is successful as an exporter of wine, mainly to Russia—where there is an apparently insatiable demand—and to West Germany, her oldest export customer, but also, and increasingly, to wine-importing countries all over the world. The Bulgarians claim now that 70% of their production is exported, and half of this goes to the Soviet Union. They also claim to be the world's biggest exporters of bottled wine—surprising, but difficult to disprove. Experts from the West, mainly Germany, were called in to advise in the vast post-war reorganization, and the nationwide network of wineries and cellars is equipped with the latest German, French, and Italian machinery.

Bulgaria makes no fine wines, and never has, but she now has the capacity to produce enormous quantities of good wines to supply an ever-increasing world demand. Because of its geographical situation, the vineland is an eminent producer, and certainly the best are red; but the vintners have always also made the deep-flavored sweetish whites that are typical of the southern Balkan States. Such wines are not liked in general by Western Europeans, but under the new organization—and undoubtedly as a result of German expertise—Bulgaria is now also making surprisingly good, light, acidic white wines to meet the ever-growing demand for drier wines. The Bulgarians drink 22 liters of wine per capita annually (not a big total for this part of Europe), but they also like beer, and, of course, the plum brandy which is distilled in all parts of southeastern Europe.

GRAPE VARIETIES AND TYPES OF WINE

White Wines. The most widely grown native vine is Dimiat, used both for wine-making and as a table grape. It also gives the wine from which the good Bulgarian brandy (*koniac*) is distilled. Dimiat is the same as the Serbian Smederevka and is probably closely related to Chasselas. The wine made from it is of no distinction. A much more interesting wine comes from the red Misket, one of the big Muscat family, with the distinctive flavor and aroma of that grape. It flourishes in the region of Karlovo in central Bulgaria in the Sangulare Valley near the Black Sea, and in the northern part of the country generally. Although there are more than twenty vine-growing

districts of varying importance in most parts of the country, place-names are of minor importance in considering Bulgarian wines, which are increasingly described by grape names only, especially those for export. The huge wineries, where most wine is made, draw from wide areas. This is particularly true of the wines produced from vines planted in the big state vineyards: Rhine and Wälschriesling, Sylvaner and Chardonnay from Western Europe, Furmint from Hungary, and the Georgian Rczaziteli from the Soviet Union. They have some well-established brand names, however: "Hemus," a sweet Misket from Karlovo; "Rosenthaler Riesling," from a blend of both types of Riesling, grown near the Valley of the Roses, again in the Karlovo district; "Euxinograd," a blend of Dimiat, Misket, and Wälschriesling; and "Sonnenküste," a Dimiat. The last two are made in the Black Sea area near Varna. Wines made from Chardonnay and Sylvaner imported into Great Britain are pleasant, dryish, surprisingly light wines. The Bulgarians also have a large and old-established production of sparkling wine (*champanski*) sold under the brand name "Iskra." Production is centered on the town of Ljaskovec in the north of the country, and both the Champagne and Russian tank methods of manufacture are employed, as much as 15% of the total still being made by the *méthode champenoise.*

Red Wines. Many Bulgarian red wines are good, Gamza—a vine similar to the Balkan Kadarka—being the most widely grown, making wine that is best drunk when young, like a Beaujolais. The best native vine is Mavrud (meaning "black"), which gives a wine deep in color and flavor, needing time to become drinkable, and improving with age. The best of it is made in Asenovgrad near Plovdiv, Bulgaria's second largest city. In the south, they grow Pamid (the same as the Serbian Plovdina grape, which is used to make a *Siller* wine for local consumption) and also the Russian Saperavi. But again, as with the white wines, the Bulgarians have been very successful with new plantings of Western European vines, notably Cabernet Franc and Cabernet Sauvignon, from which they make wine with more than a touch of Bordeaux quality.

SPIRITS

Good brandy is distilled at Preslav in the Balkan Mountains from Dimiat wine, the best being bottled mainly for export under the trade name of "Pliska." As in all Balkan countries, a strong spirit is made from the blue plum, Slivova. They also produce a version of the Greek Mastika, something like the French pastis. A Bulgarian specialty is Rosa, a sweet liqueur from the petals of the damascene rose, from which they have made attar of roses for centuries.

Bulk gallon

A gallon (128 U.S. fl. oz., 160 imp.) of wine or spirits irrespective of proof or alcoholic strength; a wine gallon. *See* Proof gallon.

Bumper

A cup or glass filled to the brim. To "drink a bumper" is an old English expression specially used for a toast.

Bung

The cork for a wine cask. It may be made of wood, earthenware, or glass. The last two types are generally used as light stoppers for barrels of new wine, in which secondary fermentation may occur. Some contain a device to facilitate the escape of carbonic gas. In the second year of ageing, the racked wine is sealed into its barrel with a wooden cork, often bound in linen; or with a patent unbroachable stopper, such as the *Bonde Bordelaise de Sûreté*. The barrel is then set on its side, or *couché*.

See Chapter Nine.

Burdin

A French hybridizer who has developed a red-wine grape, Burdin 4503, out of a white-wine grape, comparable with the Sylvaner, and known as Burdin 5201.

Burgenland

White and red wines.
District: Southeast Austria.

Wine region of Austria. The principal vineyard towns are Rust, Oggau, Saint-Margarethen, and Mörbisch. Burgenland touches the Hungarian border, and one of the principal grape varieties is the Furmint, which also goes into Tokay.

See Austria.

Burgunder

The Pinot grape of Burgundy transplanted to German-speaking countries, where vines of this variety are known as Spätburgunder, Frühburgunder, Weissburgunder (white), or Grauerburgunder (gray). The more usual name for the Pinot Gris, however, is Ruländer.

Burgundy

Red and white wines.
District: Central Eastern France.

The ancient realm of the Dukes of Burgundy is neither the largest nor the financially most important wine region in the world, but it is one of the very greatest. Nowhere else is wine so much a part of daily life and conversation, and nowhere is there such honest love of wine and such pride in its perfection, except in Bordeaux.

For more than two thousand years Burgundians have been making and drinking magnificent wines and shipping them all over the world. From father to son the tradition has been passed, from nobleman to priest to peasant. Over the centuries, the finest vineyard sites have been carefully tended, the best vines for the soil planted.

However, the criticism of this great wine region today is that between pruning for greater quantity and planting new vines, Burgundy has lost considerably in quality. Unfortunately, in the late 1960s as well as in the 1970s production has tended to be inconsistent.

It is true, unfortunately, that one man's Burgundy is another man's *ordinaire*, for no other name is so persistently misapplied. In large areas of the world "Burgundy" has become almost synonymous with a heavy, dark red wine, sometimes too rough, sometimes oversweetened; and the buyer (if not the seller) is often unaware that many Burgundies are light, subtle wines—and that some of the greatest Burgundies are white.

The red wines of the Burgundian district of the Beaujolais, for example, are at their best light and fresh and fruity; and the red wines of the Côte d'Or vineyards of the communes of Volnay, Pommard, and Beaune can be exquisitely fine and delicate. The misconception is encouraged by sellers the world over who do not hesitate to put the name Burgundy on red wines, no matter where they originated. In fact, the only wines with any historical, geographical, moral, or (in France at least) legal right to the name, are those from certain clearly defined sections of the French departments of the Côte d'Or, Yonne, Saône-et-Loire, and the *arrondissement* of Villefranche-sur-Saône in the department of the Rhône. As is the case with all French wines of Appellation Contrôlée, the permissible vines are legally controlled, the amount of harvest is legally controlled, and the methods of pruning, growing, and fertilizing, as well as of vinifying and ageing, are all legally controlled—and if the resultant wine does not meet the minimum standards it is not Burgundy. (These controls are applied not in Burgundy alone, but to all French wines of Appellation Contrôlée.) This means that bottles labeled California burgundy, South African burgundy, or Chilean burgundy may all have their merits but will *not* be Burgundy (*see* Appellation d'Origine Contrôlée). Burgundian vineyards cover only 30,000 hectares (75,000 acres).

HISTORY

It is not known who first introduced the vine into Burgundy. The Romans found vines when they made their conquest, and under their influence the vineyards certainly increased and prospered. It is probable that the barbarians who followed destroyed the plantations, and the Burgondes began to reconstitute them at the end of the fourth century. In the fifth century A.D. Pliny told of Gauls drinking wine at Auxerre.

In the year 581, Gontran, King of Burgundy, gave the vineyards of Dijon to the Abbey of Saint Bénigne, a move that was to have far-reaching consequences. The monks were happy to receive the gift, which assured a steady source of pure wine for their religious services. In the centuries that followed, Burgundy changed from a kingdom to a duchy and various nobles, following Gontran's example, gave to different religious orders such vineyards as those of Aloxe, Fixey, Fixin, Santenay, Auxey, Comblanchien, Chassagne, Savigny, Pommard, and Meursault.

To the medieval world wine was wealth, and, overwhelmed by the sudden influx, some of the clergy began to forget the strict monastic rules and live too well. By the twelfth century the great reformer, Saint Bernard of Clairvaux, was denouncing this luxuriousness and greed. He came, in 1112, to the Cistercian monastery at Cîteaux and transformed it. With the Benedictine monastery of Cluny, Saint Bernard was at complete odds. Cluny had been the most powerful arm of the Church in France and its vineyard holdings were substantial. Adopting the motto *Cruce et Aratro* (By Cross and Plough) the Cistercians began cultivating sections of the desolate countryside. In Burgundy, nothing else thrives so well as the vine, and viticulture became one of the main occupations of the order. Their greatest accomplishment was the founding of the Clos de Vougeot, built up slowly from grants given by land-owners who were impressed by the sanctity and industry of the monks. Their sister order founded the Clos des Dames de Tart, later shortened to the Clos de Tart.

As the Middle Ages wore on, the vines flourished and increased—too much in variety if not in quantity. In 1395, Philip the Bold, Duke of Burgundy, banned from Burgundian vineyards the grape he refers to as the "disloyal Gaamez," which gives wine in abundance but wine full of "very great and horrible harshness." The introduction into fine wine regions of inferior grapes which produce quantity rather than quality is a recurrent evil. The Gamay vine mentioned by the Duke is not unknown in Burgundy today; one of its varieties is responsible for the excellent wines of Beaujolais, but on the Côte d'Or it gives a wine similar to that described by Duke Philip more than five centuries ago. Another ducal edict of the Middle Ages attempted to ban the storage of wines coming from any other district.

The wines of Burgundy, of Beaune especially, appealed to the kings of France. Philip Augustus, faced by the Imperial army, is said to have called for a barrel of Beaune; during the coronation of Philip VI, at Reims, the wine flowed from the nostrils of a bronze stag set up outside the cathedral. Louis XI was extremely fond of Volnay, and he had the happiness in his reign of adding the rebellious Dukedom of Burgundy to the French crown.

At peace at last from ducal wars, Burgundy was to be trampled in the wars of religion—and again in the Thirty Years' War (1618-48). Here, as in Bordeaux, there were sporadic orders to root up vines and plant more corn, but this does not seem to have seriously prevented the sale of wine. As late as the seventeenth and early eighteenth centuries, Burgundy came back into favor. A gigantic peasant named Brosse trundled some casks of his Macon safely over the bad roads to Paris, attracted the attention of Louis XIV by his great stature, and successfully sold his wine. Fagon, the king's physician, now credited with killing off most of the heirs to the throne, did a better thing when he recommended to his master the good wine of Burgundy. It was not yet the wine we know: it was very much lighter, and sometimes white grapes were mixed with the red to produce the pinkish, partridge-eye color then preferred. Foreign customers—particularly Germans and Dutch—are said to have wanted a heavier drink and for them, before the days of *chaptalisation*, sugar was some-

times introduced when the vintage was not big enough. Stories about Napoleon and various wines of Burgundy have been too often told to be repeated here—it seems certain that a heavy luggage of casks followed some of his marshals around the battlefields of Europe. Chambertin was the growth of which Talleyrand is quoted as saying: "Sir, when one is served such a wine, one takes the glass respectfully, looks at it, inhales it, then, having put it down, one discusses it." And of the same wine Dumas said: "Nothing inspires such a rosy view of the future."

When the French Revolution erupted, a great part of the Burgundy vineyard was in the hands of the Church. So the established pattern of Burgundian viticulture was completely disrupted by the wave of anti-clericalism that swept France in the 1790s and through the First Empire. The vineyards were seized by the state, and afterward sold to the people. The most important consequence was the setting up of the pattern of small ownership that still prevails in this region: the system has been maintained as a primitive kind of insurance. A grower who has all his grapes in one vineyard might be ruined if hail should hit that vineyard; whereas, if he owns only part of that one and part of another some miles away, he is likely to salvage something from the storm. The result was—and is—that the great vineyards continue to exist as entities, but each one is divided between a number of owners, each with his own parcel of land. Thus, two bottles of wine coming from the same vineyard, in the same year, may be quite different from each other, their characteristics depending to some extent upon the wine-maker's industry and talent. The Bordeaux system of large estates—unified under one ownership—is today practically unknown in Burgundy; with a very few exceptions, there are no Burgundian châteaux in the Bordeaux sense of the word, and a domain may include bits and pieces of a number of widely scattered vineyards unified only in the ownership of one man. In Burgundy, there are more than a hundred separate place-names; at first glance the system appears complicated and confusing. Actually it is neither.

BURGUNDIAN PLACE-NAMES

There is a large number of different controlled place-names in Burgundy simply because there is an equivalent number of separate and distinct wines. The names run from the general to the particular, and—as is true with all French wines of Appellation Contrôlée—the more specific the name, the better the wine. The vineyard of Chambertin provides an example of how the system works.

Chambertin is one of the greatest of Burgundian vineyards and its wines, when well made and from a good year, are unsurpassed. The 13-hectare (32-acre) vineyard is legally rated a Great Growth (*Grand Cru*)—one of only thirty-one of the hundreds of Burgundian vineyards to receive this distinction. Its wine can take the name Chambertin, the commune name of Gevrey-Chambertin, the district name of Côte de Nuits, or the general name of Burgundy (Bourgogne); yet it will always be labeled with the famous name of Chambertin if the wine meets the high minimum standards demanded. The name is more

Chablis inset map

Joigny — Paris — N-77 — Ligny-le-Châtel — N N-91 — Serein — Auxerre — CHABLIS — Chablis appellation contrôlée — Chablis — Tonnere — D-965 — D-944 — Sérigny — A-6

0 10 20 KM
0 10 MI

Main map

Dijon — Longvic — N-5 — CÔTE D'OR — CÔTE DE NUITS — Pouilly-en-Auxois — Marsannay — Fixin — Brochon — Gevrey-Chambertin — Morey-St-Denis — Chambolle-Musigny — Vougeot — Vosne-Romanée — Flagey-Échézeaux — Nuits-St-Georges — Prémeaux — N-74 — Comblanchien — Pernand-Vergelesses — Aloxe-Corton — Savigny-les-Beaune — Corgoloin — Pommard — Volnay — Savigny — Beaune — D-973 — Monthélie — Auxey-Duresses — La Rochepot — Meursault — Autun — Puligny-Montrachet — Santenay — Chassagne-Montrachet — Chagny — Rully — D-978 — N-83B — Mercurey — CHALONNAIS — Chalon-sur-Saône — Givry — D-978 — Montagny — Buxy — A-37 — N-6 — Saône — Sennecey-le-Grand — N-78 — N

SAÔNE-ET-LOIRE

D-980 — D-980 — N-6 — Tournus — D-971 — D-56 — CHAROLLAIS — Chardonnay — MÂCONNAIS — D-981 — Lugny — A-6 — Viré — D-975 — Paray-le-Monial — Charolles — Cluny — Clessé — D-103 — N-79 — POUILLY-FUISSÉ — Solutré — Mâcon — Fuissé — Loché — A I N — St-Véran — Vinzelles — Chaintré — N-79 — RHÔNE — Juliénas — St-Amour — Chénas — Fleurie — Romanèche-Thorins — Chiroubles — Thoissey — Bourg-en-Bresse — Villié-Morgon — D-979 — Lantignié — Morgon — Belleville — Brouilly — Châtillon-sur-Chalaronne — Odenas — N-83 — B R E S S E — Vaux-en-Beaujolais — Monts du Beaujolais — BEAUJOLAIS — D-936 — N-75 — Villefranche-sur-Saône — D-933 — Lyon 25 km — Mionnay

BURGUNDY

0 10 20 30 KILOMETERS
0 10 20 MILES

specific, the minimum standards are higher, the wine is finer, and the system is strong enough to guarantee the grower a higher price for the better wine as reflected by the name. Vineyard name—commune name—district name—regional name. Chambertin—Gevrey-Chambertin—Côte de Nuits—Burgundy. The formula is repeated over and over again in each commune along the famous Côte d'Or (Slope of Gold), and through the other sections of Burgundy (although here and there may be minor exceptions to the rule).

The fact that there will be a number of growers in even so small a vineyard as Chambertin has given rise to a special way of handling the wines and putting them on sale—a method that was worked out to decrease the inherent confusion. Under this system, the shipper (*négociant*) buys wines from various growers in, for example, Chambertin, blends them together and sells them labeled as Chambertin from his own particular firm. The wines will be blended so that they will be reasonably the same year after year. The system has this advantage: that a number of growers will not be putting out different wines under the same name, and the customer can learn the name of the wine and the firm he prefers and feel comfortably sure that he can buy the wine year after year and it will always be very similar. The disadvantages are that, in spite of the shipper's care, the wine will not be identical, and that when wine from a talented wine-maker is blended with that from an inept one, the quality of the finer wine is inevitably dragged down.

Burgundy is not large and the 1 million hectoliters (40 million U.S. gallons, 33 million imp.) of wine—80% red, 20% white—made each year do not, for example, compare with the annual 2.5 million hectoliters (66 million U.S. gallons, 55 million imp.) that come out of Bordeaux. Furthermore, authentic Burgundy is not cheap, nor can it be. The weather is too often unfavorable for growers to count on a good harvest every year, and the proceeds from good years must tide them over the others. When quantity is lowest the revenue to the grower is correspondingly small—although he must still eat, and the vines must receive the usual expensive care, to keep them healthy. This does nothing to reduce prices. Since these prices are rather high, and variations in the wines considerable, it is more important to know what you are buying from Burgundy than from any other fine wine region, for get-rich-quick shippers have for centuries found it expedient to buy wines other (and cheaper) than the great Burgundies and use them to stretch the supply when it runs low, so that they can sell more wine at lower prices and make a higher profit on each sale. The great epoch of fraud occurred shortly after the First World War and was flourishing in the 1930s when some enlightened Frenchmen banded together to amend and perfect the laws of Appellation d'Origine, which gave wide powers to the inspectors of fraud. The laws have not completely done away with deceit, but they have made it much more difficult. And some of the growers themselves are adopting a system (modeled on the château-bottling of Bordeaux) which makes fraud practically impossible. This is known as estate or domain bottling. An estate-bottled wine is simply a wine that has been grown, made, and bottled by the same man, usually a small peasant grower with anything from two to ten acres of vines. In such a case, the label will tell the name of the wine, the year, the name of the grower, and the fact that the wine is *Mis au Domaine* (bottled at the domain). Alternative phrases are *Mise du Domaine* or *Mis en Bouteilles par le Propriétaire,* or else *Mis en Bouteilles à la Propriété.*

The greatest wines come from the golden slopes of the Côte d'Or, a low range of hills topped by brush and scrub and rolling along the western edge of the Burgundian plain. Geographically, it begins at Dijon (in days gone by, there was a Côte de Dijon, too, and an effort has been made to bring it back into currency, particularly with the rosés of Marsannay) and ends just south of Santenay. It is divided into two sections: the Côte de Nuits, to the north, making the regal reds, Chambertin, Musigny, Romanée—the first great vineyard the motorist sees is Clos de Vougeot; and, to the south, the Côte de Beaune with its more delicate red wines (Beaune, Pommard, Volnay) and the magnificent whites of Meursault and Montrachet.

Of the great number of Burgundian place-names there are several that will seldom or never appear on bottles outside Burgundy. These most general names are applied to wines which often make very pleasant drinking if caught young and near the place where they were made, but which neither age nor travel well. Among them may be such names as listed on page 132.

BURGUNDIAN VINES

Vines for Red Wines

Pinot Noir. The noblest vine of them all. Head of a distinguished family (although the other members do not generally come up to the excellence of the Noiren, as it is sometimes called), it adapts itself in the varying soils of the Côte d'Or to produce grapes giving some of the world's most magnificent wines. Oddly enough, in the granite of the Beaujolais it can give no better than flat and undistinguished wine and is replaced by the Gamay.

Gamay. Except in the Beaujolais—where it gives a fruity, light, and eminently delightful wine—Burgundian Gamay wine tends to be common, acid, and harsh. Much was once planted on the Côte d'Or, but this practice is passing and most of the Gamay today is maintained by the workers for their own consumption. However, a very small amount of Passe-Tous-Grains (a vatting together of Gamay and Pinot Noir) is still put on the market.

Pinot Liebault. Indistinguishable, to all intents and purposes, from the Pinot Noir, except to a specialist.

Pinot Gris. No wine is made exclusively from the Pinot Gris in Burgundy, as it is, for example, in Alsace. Some plants may be found, however, and growers claim that the addition of some of this to Pinot Noir results in a wine with more elegance, finesse, and delicacy.

César. Only allowed in the Yonne for wines taking the most general of place-names.

Tressot. Only allowed in the Yonne for wines taking the most general of place-names.

Place-name	Date Established	Maximum Yield HECTOLITERS/ HECTARE	GALLONS PER ACRE U.S.	Imp.	Average Production WHITE Hectoliters	U.S. Gallons	Imp. Gallons	RED Hectoliters	U.S. Gallons	Imp. Gallons
Bourgogne Vin Fins des Hautes Côtes	July 31, 1937	50	534.5	445	10,000	265,000	220,000	100,000	3,180,000	2,640,000

The most general name of all. It is allowed to any wine coming from the specified area of Burgundy—red wines to be made from the Pinot Noir grape (with allowances for the Pinot Liebault and Pinot Beurot, for the César and Tressot in the Yonne, for Gamay in certain parts of southern Burgundy); white wines from the Chardonnay. The wines must have a minimum alcoholic content of 10% if red, 10.5% if white.

Place-name	Date Established	HECTO-LITERS/HECTARE	GAL U.S.	Imp.	White Hectoliters	U.S. Gallons	Imp. Gallons	Red Hectoliters	U.S. Gallons	Imp. Gallons
Bourgogne-Passe-Tous-Grains	July 31, 1937	50	534.5	445				42,500	1,126,250	935,000

Once made in enormous quantity, this is a mixing or vatting together of grapes of Pinot Noir and Gamay—at least one-third Pinot. The wine must have an alcoholic content of 9.5% and can often be pleasant on the spot but does not travel or keep well.

Bourgogne Aligoté	July 31, 1937	50	534.5	445	50,000	1,537,000	1,276,000			

White wines exclusively, from the Aligoté grape. Chardonnay may also be used, but in practice it is not. Alcoholic content of 9.5%.

Bourgogne Ordinaire	July 31, 1937									
Bourgogne Grand Ordinaire	July 31, 1937	50	534.5	445	8,000	212,000	176,000	15,000	662,500	550,000

Only in France could a wine be "great" and "ordinary" at the same time. These two place-names cover red, white, and rosé made from Pinot and Gamay grapes (and Tressot in the Yonne) and white from Pinot Blanc, Chardonnay, Aligoté, Melon de Bourgogne, and, in the Yonne, Sacy. At least 9% of alcohol for red and rosé, 9.5% for white.

Crémant de Bourgogne or **Sparkling Burgundy**	March 16, 1943	Figures not available.								

Sparkling Burgundy may often be pleasant enough, but too often is mediocre or worse. It is vinified from any red or white wine that has the right to a general Burgundy *appellation* but rarely from those with any merit or distinction. Since taxes are as high in Great Britain and the United States on this as on Champagne, the latter is almost inevitably much better value.

Listed below are the districts of Burgundy, followed by the place-names of the Appellations Contrôlées, making wines more distinguished than the foregoing:

Côte d'Or	red and white wines	Mâconnais	red and white wines
Chablis	white wine	Chalonnais	red and white wines
Beaujolais	red (and very few white) wines		

See under individual headings.

THE APPELLATIONS CONTRÔLÉES OF THE BURGUNDY REGION

Vineyards benefiting from special, controlled place-names are indented under pertinent commune.

Place-name	Date Established	HECTO-LITERS/HECTARE	GALLONS PER ACRE U.S.	Imp.	Hectoliters	WHITE U.S. Gallons	Imp. Gallons	Hectoliters	RED U.S. Gallons	Imp. Gallons
I—CÔTE D'OR—*best communes marked with an asterisk* (*).										
*Aloxe-Corton	March 11, 1938	35	374.1	311.5	25	662	550	5,250	139,125	115,500
Corton	July 31, 1937	30	320.7	267	25	662	550	3,250	86,125	71,500
Corton-Charlemagne	July 31, 1937	30	320.7	267	1,100	29,150	24,200			
Auxey-Duresses	July 31, 1937	35	374.1	311.5	1,150	30,475	25,300	3,200	84,800	70,400
*Beaune	Sept. 11, 1936	35	374.1	311.5	600	15,900	13,200	15,000	397,500	330,000
Blagny	July 31, 1937	35	374.1	311.5				225	5,960	4,950
*Chambolle-Musigny	Sept. 11, 1936	35	374.1	311.5				6,500	172,250	143,000
Bonnes Mares	Dec. 8, 1936	30	320.7	267				500	13,250	11,000
Musigny	Sept. 11, 1936	30	320.7	267	10	265	220	300	7,950	6,600
*Chassagne-Montrachet	July 31, 1937	35	374.1	311.5	3,750	99,375	82,500	6,200	164,300	136,400
Bâtard-Montrachet	July 31, 1937	30	320.7	267	450	11,925	9,900			
Chevalier-Montrachet	July 31, 1937	30	320.7	267	160	4,240	3,520			
Criots-Bâtard-Montrachet	June 13, 1939	30	320.7	267	50	1,325	1,100			
Montrachet	July 31, 1937	30	320.7	267	275	7,285	6,050			
Cheilly-les-Maranges	July 31, 1937	35	374.1	311.5				400	10,600	8,800
Chorey-les-Beaune	July 31, 1937	35	374.1	311.5	7	185	154	4,000	106,000	88,000
Côte de Beaune	July 31, 1937	35	374.1	311.5	15	395	330	450	11,925	9,900
Côte de Beaune-Villages	July 31, 1937	35	374.1	311.5				6,800	180,200	149,600
Côtes de Nuits-Villages	Aug. 20, 1964	35	374.1	311.5	5	130	110	6,500	172,250	143,000
Dezize-les-Maranges	July 31, 1937	35	374.1	311.5						
*Fixin	Dec. 8, 1936	35	374.1	311.5				1,000	23,850	19,800
*Gevrey-Chambertin	Sept. 11, 1936	35	374.1	311.5				15,500	410,750	341,000
Chambertin	July 31, 1937	30	320.7	267				500	13,250	11,000
Chambertin-Clos de Bèze	July 31, 1937	30	320.7	267				500	13,250	11,000
Chapelle-Chambertin	July 31, 1937	32	342	284.8				210	5,565	4,620
Charmes-Chambertin	July 31, 1937	32	342	284.8				1,000	26,500	22,000
Griotte-Chambertin	July 31, 1937	32	342	284.8				85	2,250	1,870
Latricières-Chambertin	July 31, 1937	32	342	284.8				250	6,625	5,500
Mazis-Chambertin	July 31, 1937	32	342	284.8				350	9,275	7,700
Mazoyères-Chambertin	(same as Charmes-Chambertin)									
Ruchottes-Chambertin	July 31, 1937	32	342	284.8				130	3,445	2,860
Bourgogne Hautes-Côtes-de-Beaune	Aug. 4, 1961	50	534.5	445	150	3,975	3,300	8,500	225,250	187,000
Bourgogne Hautes-Côtes-de-Nuits	Aug. 4, 1961	50	534.5	445	150	3,975	3,300	1,750	46,375	38,500
Ladoix	July 31, 1937	35	374.1	311.5	125	3,310	2,750	2,200	58,300	48,400
Bourgogne Marsannay-la-Côte	June 3, 1965	50	534.5	445				1,500	39,750	33,000
*Meursault	July 31, 1937	35	374.1	311.5	12,500	331,000	275,000	800	21,200	17,600
Monthélie	July 31, 1937	35	374.1	311.5	50	1,325	1,100	3,000	79,500	66,000
*Morey-Saint-Denis	Dec. 8, 1936	35	374.1	311.5	40	1,060	880	2,600	68,900	57,200
Bonnes Mares	(see under Chambolle-Musigny)									
Clos de la Roche	July 3, 1944	30	320.7	267				500	13,250	11,000
Clos Saint-Denis	July 3, 1944	30	320.7	267				200	5,300	4,400
Clos de Tart	Jan. 4, 1939	30	320.7	267				275	7,285	6,050
*Nuits-Saint-Georges	Sept. 11, 1936	35	374.1	311.5	50	1,325	1,100	12,500	331,000	275,000
Pernand-Vergelesses	Dec. 8, 1936	35	374.1	311.5	400	10,600	8,800	2,600	68,900	57,200
*Pommard	Sept. 11, 1936	35	374.1	311.5				13,250	351,125	291,500
*Puligny-Montrachet	July 31, 1937	35	374.1	311.5	7,000	185,500	154,000	300	7,950	6,600
Bâtard-Montrachet	(see Chassagne-Montrachet)									
Bienvenue-Bâtard-Montrachet	June 13, 1939	30	320.7	267	125	3,310	2,750			
Montrachet	(see Chassagne-Montrachet)									

THE APPELLATIONS CONTRÔLÉES OF THE BURGUNDY REGION
(continued)
Vineyards benefiting from special, controlled place-names are indented under pertinent commune.

| | | Maximum Yield | | | | Average Production | | | | |
| | | HECTO-
LITERS/ | GALLONS PER
ACRE | | | WHITE | | | RED | |
Place-name	Date Established	HECTARE	U.S.	Imp.	Hectoliters	U.S. Gallons	Imp. Gallons	Hectoliters	U.S. Gallons	Imp. Gallons
Saint-Aubin	July 31, 1937	35	374.1	311.5	800	21,200	17,600	2,000	53,000	44,000
Saint-Romain	Oct. 14, 1947	35	374.1	311.5	1,100	29,150	24,200	750	19,875	16,500
Sampigny-les-Maranges	July 31, 1937	35	374.1	311.5	150	3,975	3,300	100	2,650	2,200
Santenay	Dec. 8, 1936	35	374.1	311.5				10,000	265,000	220,000
Savigny-les-Beaune	Dec. 8, 1936	35	374.1	311.5	400	10,600	8,800	11,000	291,500	242,000
*Volnay	Sept. 9, 1937	35	374.1	311.5				9,000	238,500	198,000
*Vosne-Romanée	Sept. 11, 1936	35	374.1	311.5				6,500	172,250	143,000
Échezeaux	July 31, 1937	30	320.7	267				1,100	29,150	24,200
Grands-Échezeaux	July 31, 1937	30	320.7	267				350	9,275	7,700
La Tâche	Sept. 11, 1936	30	320.7	267				250	6,625	5,500
Richebourg	Sept. 11, 1936	30	320.7	267				300	7,950	6,600
Romanée-Saint-Vivant	Sept. 11, 1936	30	320.7	267				300	7,950	6,600
Romanée-Conti	Sept. 11, 1936	30	320.7	267				75	1,985	1,650
La Romanée	Sept. 11, 1936	30	320.7	267				35	925	770
*Vougeot	Dec. 8, 1936	35	374.1	311.5	75	1,985	1,650	650	17,225	14,300
Clos de Vougeot	July 31, 1937	30	320.7	267				2,100	55,650	46,200
II—CHABLIS										
Chablis	Jan. 13, 1938	40	427.6	356	30,000	530,000	440,000			
Chablis Grand Cru	Jan. 13, 1938	35	374.1	311.5	4,000	66,250	55,000			
Petit Chablis	Jan. 5, 1944	40	427.6	356	6,000	159,000	132,000			
Chablis Premier Cru	Jan. 13, 1938	40	427.6	356	15,000	331,000	275,000			
III—BEAUJOLAIS										
Beaujolais	Sept. 12, 1937	50	534.5	445	5,000	132,500	110,000	500,000	9,937,500	8,250,000
Beaujolais-Supérieur	Sept. 12, 1937	45	448.9	373.8				20,000	662,500	550,000
Beaujolais-Villages	Sept. 12, 1937	45	448.9	373.8	300	7,950	6,600	320,000	5,300,000	4,400,000
Brouilly	Oct. 19, 1938	40	427.6	356				50,000	728,750	605,000
Chénas	Sept. 11, 1936	40	427.6	356				10,000	265,000	220,000
Chiroubles	Sept. 11, 1936	40	427.6	356				15,000	291,500	242,000
Côte de Brouilly	Oct. 19, 1938	40	427.6	356				15,000	397,500	330,000
Fleurie	Sept. 11, 1936	40	427.6	356				35,000	728,750	605,000
Juliénas	March 11, 1938	40	427.6	356				25,000	583,000	484,000
Morgon	Sept. 11, 1936	40	427.6	356				45,000	927,500	770,000
Moulin-à-Vent	Sept. 11, 1936	40	427.6	356				30,000	795,000	660,000
Saint-Amour	Feb. 8, 1946	40	427.6	356				15,000	397,500	330,000
IV—MÂCONNAIS										
Mâcon	July 31, 1937	50	534.5	445	15,000	79,500	66,000	2,500	66,250	55,000
Mâcon-Supérieur	July 31, 1937	50	534.5	445	35,000	2,120,000	1,760,000	47,000	1,590,000	1,320,000
Mâcon-Villages	July 31, 1937	50	534.5	445	60,000	662,500	550,000			
Pouilly-Fuissé	Sept. 11, 1936	45	448.9	373.8	40,000	954,000	792,000			
Pouilly-Loché	April 27, 1940	45	448.9	373.8	1,500	39,750	33,000			
Pouilly-Vinzelles	April 27, 1940	45	448.9	373.8	2,200	58,300	48,400			
Saint-Véran	June 1, 1971	45	448.9	373.8	12,000	318,000	264,000			
V—CHALONNAIS										
Givry	Feb. 8, 1946	40	427.6	356	350	9,275	7,700	3,500	92,750	77,000
Mercurey	Sept. 11, 1936	35	374.1	311.5	1,000	26,500	22,000	20,000	530,000	440,000
Montagny	Sept. 11, 1936	40	427.6	356	3,000	66,250	55,000			
Rully	June 13, 1939	40	427.6	356	1,500	52,000	44,000	1,500	58,300	48,400

Vines for White Wines

Chardonnay (also called Aubaine, Beaunois). Once erroneously thought to be a member of the Pinot family (and called Pinot Chardonnay), this vine is responsible for all the great white wines of Burgundy. In chalky soil—as on the Côte d'Or, Chablis, and the Mâconnais—it gives wines that vary with local conditions, but tend at their best to be rather full yet delicate, imbued with the scent of the grape, beautifully balanced and with enormous finesse.

Pinot Blanc. The white grape of the Pinot family. It is added to the Chardonnay in the making of the better white wines.

Aligoté. The grape that makes the common secondary white wine of Burgundy. The wine rarely has much breed and does not travel well, but when young and drunk on the spot it can be extremely pleasant; it is sometimes made to be slightly sparkling (*pétillant*).

Sacy. Only allowed in the Yonne for wines taking the most general of place-names.

Melon de Bourgogne. Allowed throughout Burgundy, but only for wines taking the most general of place-names.

BURGUNDIAN VINICULTURE

After the harvest—which starts in the middle of September in good years, but not until the first weeks of October in bad—Burgundian red wines are not long-vatted. Here, as elsewhere, they are fermented in their skins, while the white are pressed from their skins and fermented apart; but in Burgundy, red wines only stay in contact with the skins for from five to eight days—the optimum is about six. This contrasts markedly with Bordeaux—where wines are vatted for ten to fifteen days—and the results are apparent.

Long-vatted Bordeaux reds pick up more tannin—from the skins, seeds, and stems—than do Burgundies. This makes them harder at the outset and allows them to reach a greater "high" with longevity; only with age do the great reds of Bordeaux achieve their full glory. Red Burgundies, not having so much tannin, will be ready to drink far sooner, often from two to five years after harvest. Furthermore, the Cabernet Sauvignon grape of Bordeaux produces wines that are bigger and fuller than those produced by the Pinot Noir of Burgundy. Thus, a natural Burgundy may, by its lightness, confound the traditional notion that all Burgundies are full-bodied and all Bordeaux light.

Apart from the duration of vatting time, wine-making in Burgundy does not differ significantly from standard practice as outlined in Chapter Nine (*q.v.*). The only major modification is the widespread use of *chaptalisation* (adding sugar to sugar-deficient musts), for in most years the Burgundian summer sun does not generate enough sugar in the grapes to make a perfectly balanced wine. The additional sugar—added under strict control by the government—ferments with the natural grape sugar and results in a wine with a higher alcoholic content than it would otherwise have had, and sometimes with more force and body as well. Yet the present regrettable tendency is to overchaptalise fine wines.

Burgundian wines are aged, from eighteen to twenty-four months, in containers of varying sizes. Wines for current consumption are kept in large vats, but finer wines need smaller cooperage. The standard barrel size is the *pièce*, holding 228 liters (60 U.S. gallons, 50 imp.). Very occasionally reference is made to the old measure *queue*, which is simply two *pièces*; there is no actual barrel of this size. Half-barrels are called *feuillettes* and quarter-barrels *quartauts*, and they each hold exactly what one would expect. In Chablis, however, there is another *feuillette* holding 132 liters (34.9 U.S. gallons, 29 imp.); the traditional *pièce* of the Mâconnais holds 215 liters (56.8 U.S. gallons, 47.3 imp.); and that of the Beaujolais 216 liters (57.1 U.S. gallons, 47.5 imp.). Fortunately these odd sizes are rapidly being replaced by the more standard Burgundian *pièce*.

White wines in Burgundy are given less ageing than was once customary: twelve to twenty months is now standard practice. This results in a cleaner, fresher, fruitier wine, and experts feel that the change is thoroughly justified. When bottled, Burgundian wines are always put in the typical, squat, slope-shouldered Burgundian bottle.

Although many a Burgundy will be ready to drink any time from a few months to a few years after being put into bottle, others will sometimes hold their excellence as long as a half-century or perhaps more. Unfortunately these old bottles are becoming exceedingly rare. Burgundies are not made in the same way as they used to be. Before the First World War the wine was long-vatted and the extra tannin it picked up naturally from the contact with the skins and the wood gave it longevity. Tannin occasionally added to young wine by some shippers does not have the same effect but serves instead to deform the taste of the wine. Another deformation suffered by a great deal of the Burgundy in the cellars of shippers (*négociants*) is caused by the practice of giving the wine a so-called Burgundy character by blending it with heavy wines from other regions. The past hundred years have seen the supply of honest Burgundy running so far short of the demand that cheap heavy wine from the Rhône valley or Roussillon has been brought in to stretch the precious supply. As the contents of Burgundian bottles grew further and further away from the characteristics of real Burgundy wine, a market was built up among inexperienced wine-drinkers who were taught to believe that if a wine did *not* have the thick or oversugared consistency they had come to associate with Burgundy, it lacked the true characteristics. This puts them in the paradoxical position, when they manage to obtain a bottle of estate-bottled wine or one put out by an honest shipper, of finding fault with it, because it is utterly different from any "Burgundy" they have ever drunk. To those who judge wine by taste rather than by labels, it is often a revelation.

See Côte de Beaune; Côte de Nuits; Côte d'Or.

Butt

Standard British cask. A butt of ale, Sherry, or Málaga

Buza

contains 491 liters (129.6 U.S. gallons, 108 imp.); of any other wine, 573 liters (151.3 U.S. gallons, 126 imp.). In general use, a synonym for a cask or barrel to hold wine, beer, or rainwater.

Buza

Alcoholic beverage of Egypt distilled from fermented dates.
See Egypt.

Buzz

British university term for a glass of Port from the bottom of the decanter.

Bybline

A sweet Phoenician wine mentioned in classical writings. Native to Byblos, it was probably grown afterwards in Thrace also.
See Chapter One, p.1; Classical wines.

Byrrh

Very popular French proprietary aperitif based on wine, flavored with quinine, and fortified with brandy. It is made at Thuir on the Mediterranean coast near the Spanish border.

C

Cabernet

The outstanding grape variety used for the finest clarets of the Médoc district of Bordeaux, for superior wines in California, Chile, Australia, and elsewhere. The finest and most widespread is Cabernet Sauvignon; Cabernet Franc is grown in the Médoc, in Graves, in Saint-Émilion, and the Loire Valley and is spreading slowly; Ruby Cabernet is an American hybrid that combines Cabernet Sauvignon and Carignane.

Cabinet wine, Kabinettwein

A term, applying chiefly to German Rhine wines, which originally was used to identify the special reserve of the vineyard owner. It may have originated at Kloster Eberbach on the Rhine, where the finest Steinbergers were kept in a special small cellar called Das Kabinett, which may be seen today. The importance of Cabinet wines was and is based on the fact that fine German wines are not only harvested and barreled individually from the different parts of the vineyard, but also on different days of the harvest. The barrels therefore vary greatly in quality. In most vineyards today the designation Cabinet may be applied to a wine and put on the label if the barrel has surpassed a certain price when sold. This price level varies at different vineyards but always marks off the small, very superior upper portion of the vintage.

Cachiri

Guiana liqueur from the cassava plant, from which tapioca is also obtained.

Cadillac

Bordeaux white wine.
District: Southwest France.

On the right bank of the River Garonne, facing Graves and Sauternes, the vineyards of this recent Appellation Contrôlée are planted with Sémillon and Sauvignon Blanc. The wines are similar to those of neighboring Sainte-Croix-du-Mont.

Cahors

(1) Red grape, not a noble variety, permitted in limited quantities in, for example, the district of Bordeaux. Known also as Malbec and Cot.

(2) *Red wine.*

District: Southwest France.

As it flows to meet the Garonne, the River Lot cuts through the great Causse plateau, a limestone highland which produces more truffles than Périgord. On either side of the Lot for 50 kilometers (30 miles), between Cahors and Soturac, lie the vineyards of the Cahors Appellation Contrôlée. The delimited region of nearly 40,000 hectares (100,000 acres) is 160 kilometers (100 miles) east of Bordeaux and 100 kilometers north of Toulouse. Most of this acreage does not produce wine. The annual production of 25,000 hectoliters (630,000 U.S. gallons, 583,000 imp.) comes from small plots scattered along the riverbank which total only 550 hectares (1,325 acres). The best vineyards face south and southeast.

The Cahors grape is the Malbec or Cot, known locally as the Auxerrois. Alone it makes a rather inky-looking, dark, hard wine, so Merlot and Jurançon as well as some Tannat and Syrah are also planted. The wines, however, are still 70% Cot. The vines grow in the old alluvial soils which have formed terraces and little hills inside the steeply banked bends of the River Lot. About one-third of the grapes are cultivated along the edge of the Causse plateau, where the soil consists primarily of Kimmeridge clay, the well-known limestone of Chablis. Throughout Cahors limestone pebbles cover the fine red earth, so that the vines in many places seem to grow only in broken stones. What little soil exists is very shallow, but the fissured subsoil allows for very deep roots; thus, vigorous stems and vines with an almost unlimited life span.

The wines of Cahors have often been described as "black." Here the Malbec makes a very heavy and dark wine, one that was commonly used in centuries past to color and flavor lighter Bordeaux wines. Since the devastation of the vineyards by phylloxera, the wines have not been so terribly high in alcohol or tannin but still require long ageing in the barrel and in the bottle. When the wine is properly matured, it can be soft-scented and smooth, and it is always dark in color. In recognition of the wine's quality, the district was granted an Appellation d'Origine Contrôlée in 1971.

At Parnac, near the center of the delimited area, the large cooperative Les Caves d'Olt handles almost half of the region's production. Tesseydre and Jouffreau are two good growers who estate-bottle their own wine.

Château Caillou

Bordeaux white wine.
District: Sauternes, France.
Commune: Barsac.

Château Caillou, classified a Second Growth (*Second Cru*) in 1855, adjoins the two Barsac First Growths (*Premiers Crus*), Château Climens and Château Coutet. *Caillou* is French for "pebble," and pebbles are thick in the vineyard soil which gives so much to the quality of the Bordeaux wines. M. Bravo, the proprietor, also owns the Barsac vineyards, Château Baulac and Château Petit-Mayne.

Characteristics. Small and pleasant, yet high in alcohol.
Vineyard area: 17 hectares (42.5 acres).
Average production: 40 *tonneaux* (3,700 cases).

Cairanne

One of the best communes of the Côtes-du-Rhône, producing red, white, and rosé wines.
See Rhône.

Cajuada

A West African beverage made from fermented cashew nuts.

Calabria

White and red wines.
District: Southern Italy.

Calabria is the "toe" of the Italian "boot." The land is hot, mountainous, and poverty-stricken, except for a strip along the coast cooled by the sea and fruitful with orange and lemon trees. The soil is for the most part volcanic, and vines do as well as anything here, where they have been grown since the time of the Greek settlers. Most Calabrian wines, however, are not of the first order.

Cirò is a D.O.C. applicable to red, white, and rosé wines from Cirò, Cirò Marina, and parts of the communes of Crucoli and Melissa, due east of Cosenza. The white is made of Greco Bianco with some Trebbiano Toscano, the red and rosé of Gaglioppo and a bit of Greco and Trebbiano. White Cirò is straw-colored with pleasant enough taste and bouquet; the red and rosé are full-bodied and warm.

Greco di Gerace is a sweet yellow wine very high in alcohol and famous for its flowery bouquet. It is produced in small quantities around Gerace in the Calabrian Apennines and apparently was held in high esteem in classical Rome.

Savuto is a frequently encountered red wine. In spite of the dissimilarity of the grapes used, it shares certain characteristics with Cirò *rosso*, notably pungent strength and headiness. It comes from Arvino, Pecorello, Greco, and some Malvasia. Lacrima di Castrovillari and Moscato di Cosenza (sometimes Moscato di Calabria) complete the list of the better-known wines. The first is a red table wine obviously from around Castrovillari; the second, the inevitable Muscat, is sometimes made from dried grapes and is not one of Italy's more distinguished examples of that wine.

Caldaro

An almond-flavored red wine from North Italy.
See Trentino-Alto Adige.

Caledon

Wine-growing district of the Cape province, South Africa.
See South Africa.

California

See United States: California.

Calisaya

A Spanish liqueur with the bitter taste of quinine.

Château Calon-Ségur

Bordeaux red wine.
District: Haut-Médoc, France.
Commune: Saint-Estèphe.

The vineyard is a classified Great Growth. Here, as at Château Latour, the vines are allowed to achieve their maximum age and are not uprooted by sections; individually removed and replaced, some live for ninety years and more. Quality at the expense of quantity is the consequence of this method: the vine produces better and better wine all its life, but there is less and less of it after the twelfth or fifteenth year. Yet, since the vineyards are large, there is no shortage of the wine.

In early times, Calon-Ségur was one of only three vineyards in Saint-Estèphe. It is ironical to consider that while in 1855 Calon-Ségur was classed a Third Growth (*Troisième Cru*) and Château Montrose a Second Growth (*Second Cru*), in 1825 Montrose had been a forestland parcel of the Calon-Ségur estate. Today Calon-Ségur could be classed as a Second Growth. It is the best of all the Thirds and better than many Seconds.

The name Calon comes from a little river skiff used in the Middle Ages to ferry timber across the Gironde; eventually the name spread to the whole district of Saint-Estèphe, which was known as the Calones or Saint-Estèphe-de-Calon, until the eighteenth century. At that time the property had passed, by marriage, into the hands of the Président de Ségur—Marquis de Ségur-Calon. He was the proprietor at the same time of the great Châteaux Lafite and Latour, but Calon was his favorite, apparently, for he said: "I make wine at Lafite and Latour, but my heart is at Calon"—and this motto is still inscribed on an archway in the courtyard. This charming legend has been disclaimed, but there are those who say that the word "calon" in Welsh means "heart"; hence the presence of the heart on the label.

The soil is of three types: sandy gravel, giving finesse and nose to the wines; fatty gravel, or a limy and heavy soil, which, if it were not blended with the other, would give common but full-bodied wines; thinnish gravel, which alone could produce wines with breed but with considerable harshness. The late proprietor, Édouard Gasqueton, played the scale of these soils to produce his outstanding wine. Since his death in 1962, the vineyard has been owned by his widow and heirs.

Characteristics. Body is the foremost characteristic, although this robustness is held in the traces of a certain suppleness. The wines of Saint-Estèphe are the heaviest and most masculine of the Médocs, and generally Calon-Ségur produces one of the most powerful and longest-lived wines of the Saint-Estèphes.

Vineyard area: 55 hectares (137.5 acres).
Average production: 280 *tonneaux* (26,000 cases).

Caluso

A sweet white wine of different types made near Turin. *See* Piedmont.

Calvados

Apple brandy, the finest in the world. It is distilled from cider, in Normandy: the name is taken from the department of Calvados, and the best comes from the Vallée d'Auge, its greatest cider-making district. When old, Calvados can be a magnificent brandy, but fine ones can rarely be found outside the cellars of Normandy. While cider is being produced, a distillation is made from the residue of apple pressings, and this is usually called Eau-de-vie de Marc de Cidre.

Château Camensac

Bordeaux red wine.
District: Haut-Médoc, France.
Commune: Saint-Laurent.

(*Saint-Laurent is not a place-name and the wine has the* appellation *Haut-Médoc.*)

A little-known and almost-forgotten Fifth Growth (*Cinquième Cru*) as classified in 1855. In recent years new plantings have increased the size of the vineyard, which yields a relatively small production.

Characteristics. A marked improvement in quality.
Vineyard area: 59 hectares (148 acres).
Average production: 260 *tonneaux* (25,000 cases).

Campania

Red and white wines.
District: Southwest Italy.

Campanian wines are the very essences of the sunny province which produces them. Nowhere else is life so exuberant and carefree as it is in Naples, Campania's capital, but without its wines even Naples might lose some of its gaiety. The city is surrounded by beaches and islands—Sorrento, Capri, Ischia—of such legendary beauty that ever since classical times they have been resorts of pleasure.

The entire coast of the Bay of Naples might be Paradise on earth—and this, according to Neapolitan mythology, is precisely the case.

MAJOR WINES

Lacrima (or *Lacryma*) *Christi*. The "tear of Christ" is a dryish pale golden wine, made from grapes grown along the southern slope of Mount Vesuvius. The story they tell about it may well have been established to rival that of Latium's Est! Est!! Est!!!, but the Neapolitans swear that it is true. They say that when Lucifer fell from grace, he and his retinue landed with such a crash that the land beneath them collapsed, to form the Bay of Naples. Lucifer soon realized that he was in the place nearest to his lost Paradise, and so he populated Naples and its surrounding areas with his demons—with the result that Naples soon became a citadel of wickedness. The Savior, looking down one day, grieved to see the terrestrial paradise so steeped in sin and He wept, His tear falling on Mount Vesuvius. From the tear a vine sprang up, and it multiplied into a vineyard, and every year the tear is reproduced in the wine vat as a reminder of the glory which awaits the honest wine-maker. This all happened, of course, a very long time ago, and Greco and Fiano have been planted to replace the original vines, but the story still lives on, retold with each glass. The wine, incidentally, has nothing in common with Spanish Lágrima Christi (*see* Málaga) except that Italian and Spaniard each claim the original inspiration for the name.

Falerno is another wine with a long history. In Roman times it was known as Falernum and seems to have been considered almost as one of the wonders of the ancient world, but unfortunately we do not know from what grapes it was made and have only an imperfect idea of how it tasted. Modern Falerno is made in Campi Flegrei, Capua, Sessa Aurunca, and Mondragone and the wine today, from Falanghino grapes, is generally golden-yellow, semi-dry, and of medium strength. Much of it is exported. Red Falerno is made also, mainly from Aglianico grapes, and is pleasant enough provided that the price is reasonable.

Capri. These white wines are more typical of Campania than the more famous Lacrima Christi and Falerno. The better of the two is Capri, from Greco and Fiano grapes grown on the island, and vinified into a heady, sprightly, dry (or sometimes semi-sweet) white wine which is perfect with seafood fresh from the Bay, with a sandwich or a meal, or as an aperitif sipped on a vine-shaded terrace. This is a delightful wine and one almost never found outside Capri, for it is made in such small quantities that it could never satisfy the thirst even of Capri itself—and so rather similar wines are imported to masquerade under Capri labels. (The same is true of the comparable wine of the neighboring island of Ischia—some of which is sold as Arturi.) Some red and rosé Capris are also made, but there is even less of them than there is of the white.

Ischia. Now a Controlled Denomination of Origin for white (Ischia Bianco) and red (Ischia Rosso) wines produced entirely on the island. White Ischia is from Forastera and Biancolella grapes; it has a straw color, inclining to gold, with a delicate bouquet and a pleasant enough taste. Some of the white grown in one of the better sections of the island may be called Ischia Bianco Superiore. The red wine of Ischia may come from anywhere on the island and is produced from Guarnaccia, Piedirosso, and Barbera grapes. The taste is dry and slightly tannic.

Greco di Tufo. A D.O.C. white wine from the area about the town of Avellino. Greco di Tufo and Coda di Volpe grapes go into the wine, which is dry and has a good golden yellow color. The name may also be rightfully given the sparkling wine made in the same region.

Taurasi. Vigorous and strong red wine made from Aglianico grapes, together with some Piedirosso, Barbera, and Sangiovese. Since the wine is often too harsh when young, it can be sold only after three years of ageing.

LESSER WINES

Conca. Made from Sangiovese, Canaiolo, Malvasia, and Aglianico grapes grown on slopes overlooking the Bay of Sorrento.

The wine is red, sometimes slightly coarse, generally high in alcohol. It is typically Italian and like so many Italian wines is excellent with pasta and other Italian dishes, but usually disappointing with more subtle fare.

Fiano di Avellino. Light, white, slightly flowery wine grown from Fiano grapes about 30 miles east of Naples.

Gragnano. The least of the Campanian red wines, made inland from Amalfi on the peninsula which juts out between Naples and Sorrento. It has a rich, deep hue but a light texture, and its outstanding charms are its freshness and a bouquet recalling violets or fresh strawberries. These, of course, are characteristics of young wines, and it follows that Gragnano should be taken fairly young. Jaculillo, Piede di Palumbo, and Aglianico grapes are the traditional components, and the wine is now and again brought out *frizzante,* or slightly sparkling, but whether by accident or design it is difficult to say.

Ravello. Red, white, and rosé wines are made in (and named for) this flower-filled resort; the rosé, or Rosato, is the most appealing. Greco and Fiano grapes produce the white, the others are from Aglianico.

Solopaca. Red and white wines from the small city in northern Campania from which they take their name. The white is made from Trebbiano and Malvasia grapes, the red from Sangiovese and Piedirosso.

Vesuvio. Red wine from Aglianico and also white from other grapes grown along the slopes of Mount Vesuvius. Not very distinguished, but it can be agreeable if the price is reasonable. It is said that Vesuvio is used to augment the production of red Capri, at a distinct mark-up in price.

Campari

Reddish-brown Italian bitters flavored with herbs and orange peel, made by Fratelli Campari of Milan. It is used in the Americano and Negroni cocktails or drunk straight with a twist of lemon peel and a dash of soda as an aperitif.

Campbeltown

One of the two chief centers for West Highland malt whisky: the other is the nearby island of Islay. Campbeltown is on the sea-girt peninsula of Kintyre, which extends southward down the Firth of Clyde. Until two centuries ago Kintyre was always considered a detached island of the Inner Hebrides.

See Whisky, Scotch.

Canada

The vineyards of Canada are mainly in the Niagara peninsula of southern Ontario (by far the more important region) and in the Okanagan Valley of British Columbia.

WINE HISTORY

It is told in the Norse sagas that Leif Ericson first discovered North America and named the country Vineland because of the profusion of wild vines there, which in reality were probably blueberries. The first wines were probably made by French missionaries for sacramental purposes, for in Le Jeune's *Relation of the Jesuits for 1636* it is stated: "In some places there are many wild vines loaded with grapes. Some have made wine of them through curiosity. I tasted it, and it seemed to me very good." While this is the first record of wine-making in Canada, it was not until much later that viticulture assumed commercial importance, and then it was due to German, not to French, influence. In 1811, John Schiller, an ex-corporal of the German army, settled in Cooksville near Toronto, Ontario, and established a vineyard and a small winery. Canadians accept this date as the beginning of their wine industry. By the year 1890, grape-growing had become established principally in the Niagara peninsula with about 2,000 hectares (5,000 acres) planted. These have increased through the years to approximately 10,000 hectares (25,000 acres). Another 1,000 hectares of vineyards lie in the region near the west coast of British Columbia, where vines were planted in the 1920s by a Hungarian wine-maker named Eugene Rittich. The western wineries prospered not with their local grapes, but with fruit trucked in from California. Until the 1960s, nearly all of British Columbia's "Canadian" wine was made from California grapes. At that time quotas were established to specify the percentage of Okanagan grapes that must be present in wines carrying the local label. The quota is now 65%. Wine production of the two major regions is 728,000 hectoliters (19 million U.S. gallons, 16 million imp.), but several more thousand gallons are made from grape juice concentrates by wineries in the eastern Atlantic provinces, although this practice is declining.

A major portion of the vineyards are planted with North American varieties. These are still the backbone of the industry but are gradually being augmented with European hybrids and certain varieties of *Vitis vinifera*. At first, it was thought that *Vitis vinifera* could not be grown in Canada, but research and experimentation indicate that it is possible. Vineyards of this variety are not yet extensive, but they are being expanded. The focal point of Canadian viticultural research is the Ontario Department of Agriculture Experimental Station at Vineland, Ontario, where more than three hundred varieties of vines have been under test for wine-making qualities. One of the successes of the station's work is the "Veeport" vine, which produces the popular "port" wine. While most of the wine produced in Canada is of this sweet dessert fortified type, demand for table wines has been growing, with production of them now about 40% of the total. With the exception of the table varieties, most of the wines are blends of different years and different vineyards. They are aged in wood. Contrary to European practice, the wines must be marketed by the winery producing them. In all provinces, except Ontario, wineries may sell only to the Alcohol Control Boards, which sell retail through their stores to consumers and to hotel and restaurant establishments. In Ontario, wineries sell to the Alcohol Control Board, which operates 600 retail stores, and to consumers through a limited number of winery-operated retail stores.

Eight of the Dominion's provinces voted for prohibition of alcoholic beverages in 1916, but in Ontario, which did not ban liquor, wineries flourished. Quebec province held out against prohibition until 1919 and even then only banned spirits. During the prohibition, repealed for the most part in 1927, each of Ontario's then fifty-one wineries had a license to sell wine, and that number of licenses has remained constant even today, although now some of the larger concerns own several of the licenses apiece. Wine in the government liquor stores tends to be over-priced, since duties on imported European wines are high, so at least as much wine is made in Canadian homes as in the country's wineries. Many Canadians make their home-wine from local or Californian grapes or from the juice concentrates favored by the several east coast producers.

VINE-GROWING REGIONS

About 90% of the grapes grown in Canada come from the fertile alluvial soils of the Niagara peninsula, bordered by Lake Ontario, Lake Erie, and the Niagara River. The principal vineyard area is west of Niagara Falls and across Lake Ontario from Toronto. Most of the wines are planted below the 100-meter (350-foot) Niagara escarpment, but recently many vineyards have been moved to the top of the cliff as land grows scarce. Although the climate of the country is generally supposed to be cold and harsh, the Niagara region has an average growing season of 173 days. Because it is near these large bodies of water, the district actually has more frost-free days than do many areas 200 to 300 miles south. The winters are mild, and the average temperature during the dormant season is about 25° to 30°F. ($-4°$ to $-1°$C.). Adequate rainfall, hot summers, and long autumns provide good conditions for growth and harvesting.

Nearly three-fourths of the nation's wine is produced on the peninsula by eight of the twenty-five wineries in Canada. Niagara peninsula grape production is second only to apples as Canada's largest fruit crop. Labrusca grapes such as Concord, Niagara, Elvira, Agawam, Catawba, and Fredonia with their foxy taste predominate, but a few French Seibel hybrids are also cultivated. One of these, De Chaunac, is fast becoming the second most important variety in the area. Outside of the city of Niagara Falls, at T. G. Bright and Co., Canada's largest winemaker, the case for *Vitis vinifera* and hybrid vines was made after the Second World War by a French chemist

named Adhemar de Chaunac (hence the grape variety of the same name) who imported such plants to eastern North America. Bright's vineyard includes Pinot Noir and Pinot Chardonnay from which a sparkling white wine has been made since the late 1950s. The firm has also had good success with a Gewürztraminer. Other important wineries on the peninsula are Château-Gai at Niagara Falls, which buys its grapes from local producers, and the Andres firm in Winona. Also of interest is the Jordan Winery and its adjoining wine museum at Twenty Mile Creek. Although the vineyards are concentrated on the Niagara peninsula, some grapes are grown south of Toronto, where Château Cartier and Turner make wines, and as far west as Windsor, across the river from Detroit.

Twenty-five hundred kilometers (more than fifteen hundred miles) west of the Ontario vineyards lies the Okanagan Valley grape-growing region of British Columbia. Situated between the Trepanier Plateau and the Monashee Mountains east of Vancouver, the 100-kilometer-long (over 150-mile) valley extends south from the head of Okanagan Lake. As in the east, the lake waters moderate the climate, and the growing season is as long as 185 days. Irrigation with water from the lake and the upland streams supplements the meager rainfall of 20 to 30 centimeters (8 to 12 inches) per year. Unfortunately, the wineries specialize in a semi-sweet port-type wine with an alcoholic strength of 15%, a fourth more than standard table wines. The sweetness of this wine is supposedly balanced by sufficient acid and tannin to make it quite drinkable. Okanagan growers are encouraged to plant French hybrids and Labrusca-type vines. *Vitis vinifera* may also prove successful, especially if the vines are not forced to produce high yields per hectare.

Canada's wine industry has reached the point where it can turn away from making so much sweet fortified dessert wine and begin to concentrate on higher quality table wines. Production of the sweet wines now equals the demand for them. But with demand for table wines now rising, as it is in the United States, the future of the industry will come with answering the call for sound wine made from good grape varieties.
See also Whisky, Canadian.

Canadian whisky

See Whisky, Canadian.

Canaiolo

One of the red grapes used in making Chianti.
See Tuscany.

Canary

See Spain.

Candia

Crete. This name is sometimes found on the labels of Cretan wines.
See Greece.

Cane

A mature shoot of the vine.

Cannelle

Cinnamon-flavored liqueur.

Cannonau di Sardegna

Red or rosé wine from Sardinia (*q.v.*).

Château Canon

Bordeaux red wine.
District and Commune: Saint-Émilion, France.

Classed a First Great Growth (*Premier Grand Cru*) in 1955, the vineyard is planted right over some of the ancient quarries out of which the building stone of the medieval town of Saint-Émilion was dredged. The "château" is an unprepossessing farmhouse. The 1929 is outstanding even among the great bottles of that year. Canon has always been one of the top Saint-Émilions, its recognition antedating by generations the recent official classification.

Characteristics. A supple, generous wine with considerable finesse.

Vineyard area: 20 hectares (50 acres).

Average production: 90 *tonneaux* (7,500 cases).

Canteiro

A rather rare type of Madeira: the designation means that the wine was matured in the heat of the sun.

Château Cantemerle

Bordeaux red wine.
District: Haut-Médoc, France.
Commune: Macau.

(*Macau is not a place-name and the wine has the* appellation *Haut-Médoc.*)

Classified a Fifth Growth (*Cinquième Cru*) in 1855, Cantemerle is now universally considered to be very much superior to its official classification. Actually it deserves to be reclassed as a Second or Third Growth (*Second or Troisième Cru*). The second great Médoc vineyard north of Bordeaux (the first is La Lagune), Cantemerle lies about two miles south of the first cluster of famous growths within the grouped communes entitled to the place-name Margaux. The château is surrounded by one of the largest and most beautiful parks in Médoc, and the vines planted at either side of the woodland produce an excellent wine.

Cantemerle existed long before many of today's famous vineyards were established. In the Middle Ages it was the site of a fortress called Sauves, and it played its part in the turbulent history of that time as a portion of the Barony of Cantemerle. Acquired in 1579 by the family of Jehan de Villeneuve, it remained in their hands until 1892,

when it was bought by the father of the late M. Pierre J. Dubos; after Pierre Dubos' passing, the vineyard was run by his son-in-law, the highly regarded Henri Binaud. The property was sold to an insurance group in October 1980.

The present high reputation of the wines was achieved largely through the efforts of old M. Dubos, a twinkling little man with his sturdy legs wrapped in field puttees, still remembering the English he learned to speak in England decades ago, and revered as one of the most dedicated wine men of Médoc. His Vintage Book is a legend in Bordeaux, recording unfailingly every morning, afternoon, and evening, for more than sixty-five years, wind direction, temperature, and barometer readings, with, alongside, the behavior of the vine, its flowering, ripening, etc. His dictum ("You must harvest ninety-five days to 105 days after the flowering regardless of the weather through the summer") is an opinion considered unorthodox in the Médoc. When the vintage arrived, each day was graphed by M. Dubos—section harvested, yielding how many tubs, put to ferment in which vat, day's weather, condition of the grapes at picking. All other processes throughout the life of the wine were charted just as carefully. This tremendous care has borne splendid fruit in the fine wines of Cantemerle.

Château La Tour de Mons in Soussans-Margaux, in his wife's family for three centuries, came to M. Dubos by marriage and is one of the highest-rated of the non-classified vineyards.

Characteristics. Beautiful, fine, supple, fast-maturing wines with remarkable finesse. Another example of how obsolete the 1855 Classification is, since Cantemerle, a Fifth Growth, has come up with many a superb bottle.

Vineyard area: 21 hectares (53 acres).

Average production: 90 *tonneaux* (8,000 cases).

Cantenac

Sometimes Cantenac-Margaux. A village of the Haut-Médoc district of the Bordeaux wine region in southwest France. The wines are sold under the controlled place-name of the adjoining commune, Margaux. There is no appreciable difference in quality or style between the wines of the two communes. Eight vineyards of Cantenac were classified in 1855: Château Brane-Cantenac, a Second Growth (*Second Cru*); Château Kirwan, d'Issan, Palmer, Boyd-Cantenac, and Cantenac-Brown, all Third Growths (*Troisièmes Crus*); and Châteaux Prieuré-Lichine and Pouget, Fourth Growths (*Quatrièmes Crus*).

See under individual headings.

Château Cantenac-Brown

Bordeaux red wine.
District: Haut-Médoc, France.
Commune: Cantenac-Margaux.

Accorded the right in 1955 to the place-name Margaux with the other vineyards of Cantenac, Brown faces the village of Margaux from a distance of about half a mile (one kilometer). The huge red brick château with its many chimneys looks like an English boarding school.

The vineyard, a Third Growth (*Troisième Cru*), as classified in 1855, was established by a M. John Lewis Brown, a Bordeaux merchant, who sold it in 1860 to the owner of Léoville-Poyferré, M. Armand Lalande. At that time the vineyard was more than double its present size. The Vicomte Bertrand du Vivier, who formerly headed the de Luze shipping firm in Bordeaux, bought the property in 1969 from Jean Lawton, the jovial chief of another shipper, Lalande. A few years after acquiring the vineyard, M. du Vivier purchased the château itself from M. André de Wilde. With its beautiful park, well-decorated *chai*, and scrupulously tended vines, Cantenac-Brown is truly a showplace and a credit to M. du Vivier, who lives at Château Malleret, another of the most elegant houses in the Haut-Médoc.

Characteristics. Big full wines, made from the typical Médoc varieties: Cabernet Sauvignon, Merlot, Cabernet Franc, and Petit Verdot. Rather heavier than the wines of the neighboring châteaux. The new owner has vastly improved both the quality and reputation of the wine.

Vineyard area: 32 hectares (80 acres).

Average production: 150 *tonneaux* (13,000 cases).

Cap Corse

French wine-based aperitif made with the heady wines of the Cap Corse (northernmost) peninsula of Corsica and flavored with quinine and herbs.

Château Capbern

Bordeaux red wine.
District: Haut-Médoc, France.
Commune: Saint-Estèphe.

The property of 150 acres, approximately half of it in vine, is set on high gravelly land at the edge of the village of Saint-Estèphe and overlooking the River Gironde. Directly across the town is Château Calon-Ségur, which nowadays produces one of the finest red Bordeaux; both châteaux are owned and worked by the Gasqueton family. Capbern wines are as well cared for by these expert vinicultors as the famous Calon-Ségur and deserve elevation to classification among the Great Growths (*Grands Crus*). Various parts of the production are sold as Château Capbern, Château Grand-Village-Capbern, and Château La-Rose-Capbern.

Characteristics. A full-bodied, round wine combining a certain amount of hardness and finesse. Better made than many Classified Growths.

Vineyard area: 36 hectares (90 acres).

Average production: 100 *tonneaux* (9,000 cases).

Cape Smoke

South Africa's cheapest and worst brandy. A wise policy of favorable taxes on high-quality brandy and high taxes on the poorer examples is causing it to disappear.

Cape wines

See South Africa.

Caperitif

South African aperitif, deep gold in color, based on wine, blended with spirit, and flavored with herbs. It is bitter but reminiscent of vermouth.

Capri

Mainly a dry white wine from the island of Capri. Some of this is made in Capri itself, some in Ischia and other neighboring places. A small quantity of red and rosé wine is also made.

See Campania.

Carafe

In French, a decanter or glass bottle for serving wines. In French restaurants the ordinary wine is usually drawn straight from a cask and brought to the table either in a carafe or a *carafon*, a small carafe.

Caramel

Burnt sugar added to spirits as coloring matter. All spirits emerge pale and colorless from the still, and unless color is absorbed from the wooden barrels during ageing, caramel—tasteless and practically odorless—must be used.

Carbon dioxide

CO_2, produced in approximately equal weight with alcohol when sugar is fermented by the action of yeast. Normally it escapes, but it is trapped in the fluid in the production of sparkling wine, beer, and cider. In French, *gaz carbonique*.

Carbonated wines

Wines in which an unnatural sparkle has been induced by gasifying with carbon dioxide.

See Sparkling wines.

Château Carbonnieux

Bordeaux red and white wines.
District: Graves, France.
Commune: Léognan.

With the charming wine goes a charming story. To sell their wines in Turkey (which meant getting round the Islamic interdiction on wine) the fathers of the Abbey of Sainte-Croix of Bordeaux, then owners of the vineyard, sent off bottles of Carbonnieux labeled as mineral water. The sultan tasted it and said: "If the French mineral water is so good, why do they take the trouble to make wine?"

Set in the ancient vineyard, the beautiful château dates from the fourteenth century. In 1959 both red and white Carbonnieux wines were classified as among the leading Graves growths. The Perrin family makes a very good, full-bodied red wine but, excellent and consistent as this is, it is the dry, brilliant white wine that has made the vineyard famous.

Characteristics. A wine with both vigor and finesse. The preponderance of Sauvignon Blanc grapes, especially in the white, gives it a particularly agreeable flavor. The white is dry, clean, and well known.

Vineyard area: red—17 hectares (42 acres); white—28 hectares (70 acres).

Average production: red—90 *tonneaux* (8,000 cases); white—150 *tonneaux* (14,000 cases).

Carboy

A large bottle of glass, or occasionally earthenware, with a wicker or wooden frame. The name is derived from the Persian *garabana* (large flagon); a demijohn.

Carema

A fresh wine of Nebbiolo grapes from the area of Turin. *See* Piedmont.

Carignan

Grape grown mostly in southern France and similar hot climates for robust, heady table wines and dessert wines. It has also been transplanted to America, where it is spelled Carignane.

Cariñena

Best-known wines of Aragón, both red and white. *See* Spain.

Carmel

Some of the wines of Israel bear this name, followed by a grape variety or wine type—e.g., Carmel muscat, Carmel port. *See* Israel.

Carpano

The oldest maker of Italian vermouth, now producing in Turin two kinds, the regular and a special bittersweet one called Punt e Mes.

Carta Blanca (White Label)

A light-bodied Puerto Rican or Cuban rum, a little lighter, paler, and less sweet than Carta Oro. *See* Rum: Cuban, Puerto Rican.

Carta Oro (Gold Label)

A light-bodied Puerto Rican or Cuban rum which, owing to the addition of caramel coloring, is slightly darker than Carta Blanca. It is usually a little heavier and sweeter, too. *See* Rum: Cuban, Puerto Rican.

Case

A case of wine contains twelve 24- to 26-oz. bottles or twenty-four such half-bottles; or forty-eight splits, six magnums, or three jeroboams of Champagne. The cases used to be made only of wood, but today so many wines are being shipped in cardboard cartons that these are also called cases.

Casein

This useful protein is employed in the ageing of white wines, both as a clarifier and as a remedy against maderization. The substance, which contains phosphorus, is generally extracted from milk, where it is present as a calcic salt. When it has been washed, dried, ground and sieved, it can be used, in doses of from 5 to 20 grams per hectoliter, for clearing wines; or from 25 to 30 grams per hectoliter as a preventive and curative treatment for oxidation, or maderization.

Cask

A wine barrel, usually of wood and bound with hoops. Sizes and capacity vary widely, following traditional customs of particular localities (for standard casks and containers, *see* Appendix C, p. 630). Casks are used for maturing, storing, and transporting wines, spirits, and beers. In Europe ordinary wine is always sold in cask, the wine being drawn off as needed.

Casse

Clouding and precipitation, with an off-taste, caused in wine by the presence of too much air, protein, iron, or copper. *See* Chapter Nine, p. 38.

Cassis

(1) Controlled place-name in the wines of Provence, France. The vineyards are planted on the hillsides behind the picturesque fishing village of Cassis, some 20-odd kilometers (32 miles) east of Marseille. *See* Provence.

(2) Sweet, dark red liqueur made from blackcurrants. The most notable Cassis is that of Dijon, in northeast France, although it is also made elsewhere. Around Dijon, Cassis is used as a popular aperitif: a little is put in a glass that is then filled with a fairly neutral dry white wine. The local and somewhat inelegant name for this is *rince cochon* (pig rinse). Also called kir.

Castel del Monte

Fresh Italian red and white wines from Apulia (*q.v.*).

Castelli di Jesi

See Verdicchio dei Castelli di Jesi.

Castelli Romani

Inexpensive wines very popular in the restaurants of Rome.
See Latium.

Catalonia

The northern provinces of Spain where Catalan is spoken—Barcelona, Gerona, Lérida, and Tarragona—produce a wide variety of usually inexpensive wines, ranging from heavy and sweet Priorato to light and pale Panadés—a sparkling wine made by the champagne process. Many sound but never great table wines come from the region as well.
See Spain.

Catawba

Pink American grape of uncertain origin, said to draw its name from the River Catawba in western North Carolina. Its juice is white, dry, and heavy-flavored, and was widely used in the nineteenth century, particularly for sparkling wine. "Sparkling Catawba," the most famous of which was made by the Longworth Vineyards of Cincinnati, Ohio, was extremely popular.

Caudle

Spiced and sweetened hot wine or ale, with an egg yolk beaten in.

Cave

French term for cellar.

Cavistes

French term for cellarmen.

Cellar

Place for storing wine.
See Chapter Six, p. 22.

Centerbe

Italian liqueur said to be made from a hundred different herbs, with mint outstanding. It is also called Silvestro, from the reputed originator, Fra San Silvestro, an Italian monk.

Central Valley

Californian wine region. The major district is Escalon-Modesto, in San Joaquin County. The area comprises also part of Stanislaus and Merced counties.
See United States: California.

Cépage

French term for grape variety—e.g., Pinot Chardonnay, Pinot Noir, Cabernet Sauvignon, or Riesling.

Cerasella

Dark, red, sweet Italian liqueur made from and flavored with cherries, although the taste is enriched by the addition of a number of herbs.

Cerasuolo d'Abruzzo

Italian light red wine.
See Abruzzo.

Ceres

Wine-growing district of Cape Province, South Africa.
See South Africa.

Cerise d'Alsace

White *eau-de-vie* made with cherries.
See Alsace.

Cérons

White wines.
District: Bordeaux, France.

The vineyard road goes down the left bank of the River Garonne, past the great châteaux of Graves, and eventually in among the hills of Sauternes, winding through a flat country of neatly kept vines as solid as a carpet. The highway is beaded with gaudy stands, some in the shape of wine bottles or clapboard castles, into which the public is urged to step and taste the wines. The district is Cérons, and while it is a continuation of Graves, its wines are neither as dry as the white Graves nor as sweet as Sauternes. They are produced by impeccable wine-making methods from the same grapes as Sauternes—Sémillon, Sauvignon, and some Muscadelle—and according to the Sauternes system of letting the grapes achieve a sugar-rich overripeness, in which condition they are selectively picked. Finally, as indicated by the many stands along the road, Cérons white wine is far more popular in France than might be imagined from its small fame abroad.

(In Bordeaux it is assumed that Cérons has failed to make a definite impression in the world market, where there are so many names to choose from, because it is an in-between style, neither sweet nor dry.)

A considerable amount of dry Cérons is being made now, however, in response to present market conditions. But the typical Cérons is a little less sweet than a Barsac, which region it touches and of which it once was a part, just as a Barsac will be a little less sweet than a Sauternes. Cérons makes about 12,000 hectoliters (312,000 U.S. gallons, 240,000 imp.), as compared with 15,000 hectoliters from neighboring Barsac and 27,500 hectoliters from Sauternes.

Château Certan-de-May

Bordeaux red wine.
District and Commune: Pomerol, France.

Once a part of the Barreau family property that also included Vieux-Château-Certan, the château makes a typical Pomerol wine, but one that has failed to show in recent vintages some of its earlier success.

Vineyard area: 4 hectares (10 acres).
Average production: 18 *tonneaux* (1,500 cases).

Certosa

Red Italian liqueur resembling Chartreuse.

Cesanese

Grape variety found in Italy.

Cesanese del Piglio

The outstanding red wine of Latium, made from Cesanese grapes.
See Latium.

Chablis

White wine.
District: Burgundy, near Auxerre, Central France.

Chablis is one of the most famous wine names in the world but, used correctly, it refers to one of the world's rarest great wines—to the steadily decreasing quantity of magnificent flinty-dry white wines which are made from grapes grown on hilly acres in and around the Burgundian town of Chablis, about 183 kilometers (114 miles) southeast of Paris.

The village lies in a small valley in the department of the Yonne, surrounded by gently rolling hills on which the vines are grown—but not in any great numbers. The bare hills overlooking the town are astonishingly empty, and it is sometimes said that if present trends continue the wines of Chablis may cease to exist within a few generations.

The soil is hard and hard to work. Easily exhausted, the vineyards must rest as much as twenty years at a time, and at present about half of the land is resting. The topsoil is thin and in many spots the white, marly, calcium-rich subsoil (a formation known as Kimmeridge clay) shows through. The thin top layer is easily washed down the slopes by the rains and must be carried up again on the backs of the workers, for only at mid-slope can the greatest wines be produced.

A further hazard is the inclemency of the climate, for Chablis is more to the north than any other fine-wine district of France except Champagne and Alsace. When the vine is planted that far north it must expend a great part of its vigor simply struggling to survive the hard winters, the uncertain summers, and the often disastrous frosts—the month of May is by far the most critical, for a May frost can ruin the prospects for the entire year.

The Burgundian *vigneron* is passionately attached not only to his land but to his wine. For the older growers no sacrifice is too great if the result may, in very favorable years, be great wine. The younger men, however, are not inspired with this ideal of perfection, and many are leaving to find occupation elsewhere. In regions as unrewarding as Chablis, the exodus is greater than in more favored spots. Thus the amount of land in cultivation and the quantity of wine being made is slowly but steadily dropping. In the past century the vineyards have dwindled by more than half, and the Yonne, once the most productive department of Burgundy, now makes a negligible amount of wine.

The greatest Chablis vineyards are on one hill visible from the main square of the town; they cover a mere 100 hectares (247 acres) of which only half is usually in production, and are generally sold with the name of the vineyard or the words *Grand Cru* (*see* Grands Crus *below in this entry*). Another 700 hectares (1,750 acres), half of which are in production, are divided into vineyards designated First Growth (*Premier Cru*), and these form the second-rank vineyards, producing excellent wines which only occasionally reach the high level of the Great Growths. Chablis and Petit Chablis are the minor wines—but minor only in comparison with their splendid cellarmates. The I.N.A.O. has authorized doubling the vineyard size by 1978.

All of the vineyards now encompass an oblong area of only 1,500 hectares (3,750 acres). They fall in the communes of Chablis, Chichée, Chemilly-sur-Serein, Poilly-sur-Serein, Préhy, Fyé, Rameau, Courgis, Beines, Poinchy, Maligny, Milly, Béru, La Chapelle-Vaupelteigne, Villy, Lignorelles, Ligny-le-Châtel, Fontenay, and Viviers, but the name of the town will rarely be found on the labels. The single permissible grape is Chardonnay, known in the district as Beaunois, Burgundy's only noble white-wine vine. At one time Sacy, Melon, and Aligoté vines were fairly prevalent, but these have been rooted out and their grapes forbidden. The present vines are grown low to the ground—to allow the brown and white chalky soil to deflect the sun's rays onto them and so hasten the maturing of the fruit—and they are severely pruned, with the result that the amount of fruit they give is small, even in the finest years.

Chablis growers normally have a number of small and often widely separated vineyard plots, the total acreage of each grower amounting to anything between 1 and 8 hectares (2 and 20 acres). Though small, each of the famous vineyards is divided into as many as half a dozen sections, each section owned and worked by a different man; for this reason, the wine shippers adopted the general Burgundian practice of blending wine from different growers in any given vineyard and selling it under the firm's label. Many growers, however, have started estate-bottling their wines—harvesting the grapes, making the wine, caring for it themselves, and bottling it under their own labels.

CHABLIS

The low-lying vines are planted in rows running up and down the slopes—in contrast to the planting of earlier days, when they followed the ridge lines. Both cultivation and drainage are enhanced by this method.

Harvest time in Chablis generally falls in the first two weeks of October and the weather is often chilly. As soon as the grapes are ripe they are picked and taken, the same day, to be pressed. If they were left overnight, fermentation might start by itself, bringing trouble for the vintner.

The great heaps of grapes are brought and taken off the stems to prevent the bitter tannin in the stems from imparting harshness to the eventual wine. The grapes are then crushed lightly in presses and the juice run off into barrels: the Chablis barrel is traditionally the *feuillette*, containing 132 liters or about 35 U.S. gallons (29 imp.). Many growers are abandoning this slightly odd-sized container and adopting the more widespread Burgundian *pièce* of 228 liters (60 U.S. gallons, 50 imp.) or the larger *fûts* of 400 liters (105.7 U.S. gallons, 88 imp.). Once the juice is in the barrel, fermentation begins.

In all the cellars and *chais* of Chablis, just after harvest

time, there is a pungent sweetness mixed with the unpleasant smell of gases rising from the fermenting grapes. During the first tumultuous days of fermentation winemakers are careful not to remain too long in the cellars, for the gas is powerful and could overcome them. Cellars are small and dark, usually with rows of barrels stacked two or three high down both sides and sometimes with another row down the center. In one corner is a small stove, for the weather gets cold quickly and unheated cellars might become too cold for the yeast to work and the wine to ferment.

In most years the summer sun does not instill enough sugar into the grapes to produce the amount of alcohol essential for great wine, so the vintner has to resort to *chaptalisation*, the addition of sugar. In many years this is necessary; in some years it is advised; occasionally it is unnecessary. *Chaptalisation* has the full sanction of the French law and is carried out under government control.

When the grape must has fermented, the wine is ready for its first clearing or racking—normally done in the February after the harvest. The slow, careful pumping from one barrel to another—leaving behind the deposit and a small amount of wine, which together form the lees—both airs the wine and clarifies it. Some of the very minor wines (such as Petit Chablis) are bottled in the summer following the harvest, but the great ones are left to sleep longer in wood. Bottling for them will not usually occur until fourteen to twenty months after the harvest. The smallest wines are never bottled at all but are sold to restaurants and served directly from the barrel.

WINE HISTORY

The fame of Chablis goes back to ancient times. It is one wine which has kept its reputation and renown while others once equally well known have been forgotten. The department of the Yonne once produced two-thirds of all Burgundies, but now Chablis is the only significant area remaining. (Minor red wines are still grown in the villages of Irancy, Saint-Bris-le-Vineux, Chitry and Joigny, but production is small and the wines command neither great acclaim nor high prices.)

No one knows when the first vines were planted in Chablis. It is certain that, whether or not Julius Caesar found vines in the region when he arrived in Gaul, they were there when the Romans departed. The decline of the Roman Empire was accompanied by a decline of the vineyards, but in the twelfth century they revived under the care of the monks. The Cistercian Abbey at Pontigny, ten miles from Chablis, had extensive holdings throughout the vineyards and it is thought that the Chardonnay vine was introduced then. Most of the monks came from the Côte d'Or, where the Chardonnay rules the slope for white wines, and the Chablis word *beaunois* (plant of Beaune), for the Chardonnay, supports the theory. Other orders had portions of the Chablis vineyards too: the Church of Saint Martin at Tours, for example, whose vineyards were donated to one of the abbots by his brother, Charles the Bald, in the ninth century. The association between Tours and Chablis lasted until 1790, when the revolutionary state confiscated all church property.

One factor in the decline of Chablis is the lack of adequate compensation for the amount of labor required, another was the onset of phylloxera.

This lethal vine louse came to Chablis about 1893. Previously discovered in other French vineyard regions, it had caused little trouble in Chablis until an extremely hot summer gave it the conditions in which it thrived. By this time, the French growers had discovered that grafting French *vinifera* vines onto hybrids or American rootstock was an effective way of combating the scourge, and many Chablis vineyards were quickly reconstituted in vines grafted onto roots with such numerical tags as 161-49, 3.309, 41-B, and B.31. But, because of the expense of reconstitution, some growers took this opportunity to find different employment.

In the 1930s, Chablis was again in production, but again in trouble. Fame had brought the wines into great demand and much wine was supplied which was white and dry but otherwise had nothing in common with Chablis. The French control laws, beginning in 1936, have taken the matter in hand, and today the amount of fraudulent Chablis found on the market is nothing compared to what it was.

GREAT GROWTHS (Grands Crus)

Seven vineyards, totaling 100 hectares (250 acres), comprise the Great Growths of Chablis. They are adjoining vineyards halfway up the southwesterly slope and with one exception (Blanchots, in neighboring Fyé) are all within the limits of the town of Chablis. The wines are almost always sold with vineyard names on the labels: Blanchots, Les Clos, Valmur, Grenouilles, Vaudésir, Les Preuses, and Bourgros.

Another vineyard which might have been included is La Moutonne, but it has never received official recognition, although such action was considered. Its somewhat hazy status began with the French Revolution, when the vineyard was taken over by the state and sold to a local grower. The document accompanying the sale seems to have been extremely vague and the location of the vineyard not well established, although people in Chablis can point it out with no trouble. (It takes in about five acres between Vaudésir and Les Preuses.) In 1951, the French wine authorities recommended to the Minister of Agriculture that the vineyard be recognized as a Great Growth of Chablis but, as the quality was disappointing, the request was never followed up and the edict died a quiet bureaucratic death.

Just what makes these vineyards clearly superior to the others—and even to those close by—is impossible to define. The interplay of soil, sunlight, and whatever other mysterious elements combine to produce just exactly the right grapes for making a specific wine is too complex for analysis. The differences between them will, however, be abundantly clear in the wines themselves.

Wines from these Great Growth vineyards are Chablis, but they are Chablis with a difference. All Chablis has a certain green-tinged yellow-gold color, an impeccable dryness, and a delicate light perfume. The greater the wine, the more varied and richer it will be, and the more it will have that indescribable quality known as elegance or breed. Since the wines from these specific vineyards are consistently superior, they alone are rated Great Growths. In addition to their source in a Great Growth vineyard, these wines must have a minimum of 11% alcohol. Wines of a good year may be expected to hold their greatness as long as ten years—a considerable life span for a dry white wine. In most cases, however, the rewards for keeping them more than five are not great enough, since only about 4,000 hectoliters (104,000 U.S. gallons, 80,000 imp.) are made annually—the equivalent of some 20,000 cases—and the greater part is exported to the United States.

FIRST GROWTHS (Premiers Crus)

Thirty-odd vineyards in various towns around Chablis on both sides of the River Serein have the right to the name. The wines stand just below the Great Growths but are often so similar that even the most accomplished wine-taster finds it difficult to differentiate between them. They are usually sold with the name Chablis and that of the vineyard (e.g., Chablis-Montée de Tonnerre).

Wine must have an alcoholic content of 10.5% or forfeit the right to the designation. An average 15,000 hectoliters (390,000 U.S. gallons, 300,000 imp.)—about 120,000 cases—are made each year.

The vineyards, and the towns from which they come, are as follows:

RIGHT BANK OF THE SEREIN

Vineyard	Commune
Chapelot	Fyé
Côte de Fontenay	Fontenay
Vaupulent	Fontenay (part), La Chapelle-Vaupelteigne (part)
Fourchaume	La Chapelle-Vaupelteigne
Mont de Milieu	Fyé and Fleys
Montée de Tonnerre	Fyé
Pied d'Aloup	Fyé
Vaucoupin	Chichée
Vaulorent	Poinchy

LEFT BANK OF THE SEREIN

Vineyard	Commune
Beauroy	Poinchy
Beugnon	Chablis
Butteaux	Chablis
Châtain	Chablis
Côte de Léchet	Milly
Les Forêts or Forests	Chablis
Les Lys	Chablis
Mélinots	Chablis
Montmain	Chablis
Séchet	Chablis
Troesme	Beines
Vaillon and Côte de Vaillon	Chablis
Vosgros or Vogiras	Chichée

CHABLIS

On a wine label, Chablis, without any further qualification, means a wine from one of the slopes in the district, but not one of the outstanding ones. About 25,000 hectoliters (650,000 U.S. gallons, 500,000 imp.) of this wine, which must contain at least 9.5% of alcohol, are made annually. Much of it is sold in barrel, but some is bottled.

PETIT CHABLIS

The least of the wines made mostly from grapes grown in the Chablisian hinterlands. The towns in which the vineyards lie are Lignorelles, Ligny-le-Châtel, and any allowed the place-name Chablis. The wines are mainly sold in barrel, mostly in France or the Low Countries.

However, much of the better wines are shipped in bottle to the U.S. Annual output averages about 2,500 hectoliters (65,000 U.S. gallons, 50,000 imp.).

Chai

A wine shed, or place above ground where wine is stored in cask. In Bordeaux wine properties, where virtually all wine is kept in such sheds, there is one *chai* for *vin nouveau* (wine of the year) and another for *vin vieux* (wine of the previous year not yet bottled).

Chalonnais

Red and white wines.
District: South Burgundy, France.

The slope is almost an extension of the Côte de Beaune and there is a distinct resemblance between the wines of the two districts. The Chalonnais are lesser wines, indeed, only rarely attaining the same level of excellence, but they are well known, produced in considerable quantity, relatively inexpensive, and often very good.

The name derives from Chalon-sur-Saône, a small quiet town about five miles west of the vineyards. Vines are grown between these vineyards and the city, but the output is not, oddly enough, Chalonnais. To benefit from the name the grapes must be grown along specified hillsides in the four communes of Givry, Mercurey, Montagny, and Rully. Anything else in the vicinity cannot hope for a place-name more specific than Burgundy.

The favored slopes generally face east, although some look southeast and a very few face directly south. The soil is virtually the same as that of the Côte de Beaune but more fertile.

The standards ordained for these wines do not differ markedly from those in other sections of Burgundy. Red wines must be made from Pinot Noir (with allowance for the almost identical Pinot Liebault and Pinot Beurot) grapes, and the white are restricted to Pinot Blanc and Chardonnay; the permissible amount of harvest is 35 hectoliters per hectare (374.1 U.S. gallons, 311.5 imp. per acre) for Mercurey, and 40 hectoliters per hectare (427.6 U.S. gallons, 356 imp. per acre) for the other three communes (all subject to modification in abnormal years). Red wines must have a minimum alcoholic content of 10.5%, white of 11%; no rosé is made.

Chalonnais red wines are usually lighter than Côte d'Or Burgundies, often have considerable perfume, and do not hold for any length of time. A bottle which is more than five to eight years old could conceivably be excellent, but the odds are against it. White wines are pleasant enough as a rule, but only a few are worth exporting. As for sparkling Burgundy—vast quantities of which are made in the Chalonnais—this is a drink which has its followers, but it is not to be taken seriously.

PLACE-NAMES

Rully

Most of the output is sparkling. Rully, northernmost of

the Chalonnais wine communes, has been a center for sparkling Burgundy since 1830 and for a considerable period it supported itself almost entirely on the sales of these wines, which are not made from top Burgundies.

At the end of the First World War, once-prosperous wine-growers of France found themselves in serious difficulty. No provision had been made to protect the names of fine wines, and in the chaotic aftermath of the war many members of the trade found more incentive in fast profits, so the market was flooded with cheap bulk wine sold under famous names. Simultaneously, agitation for workable controls was gaining strength. The growers of Rully found themselves in trouble. The wines were—and are—above the average; but Rully had been selling them under the name of neighboring Mercurey, whose growers were not entirely pleased with this practice. When they drew up their controls, they excluded the wines of Rully from the place-name Mercurey.

Three courses were open to the vintners of Rully: to press Mercurey to readmit their wines; to establish a control of their own; or to sell their wines simply as Burgundy, at a considerable reduction in price. Rather than try to establish Rully as a name in its own right—which might have taken a considerable time—the growers chose the first course; but, fortunately for them, the town had its sparkling Burgundy trade to support it, for the French wine authorities proved as stubborn as the Mercurey growers. In 1939 the fight was given up and Rully, benefiting from its own controls, has become a producer of still as well as sparkling wines. Rully produces 1,500 hectoliters (39,700 U.S. gallons, 33,000 imp.) annually, 50% of which is white, 50% red.

Though the red is not so good as Mercurey, the white shows more quality—and in fact is considered one of the better offerings of southern Burgundy, just below the whites of the Mâconnais. Rully's still white is marked by a pronounced bouquet and a winy flavor described as "vinosity," but, like most dry white wines, it should be consumed young. Wine stemming from the better vineyards is elevated to the rank of First Growth (*Premier Cru*)—assuming that it attains a half-degree of alcohol more than the normal minimum. These vineyards, some of which produce red as well as white wines, are:

Vauvry	Raboursay
Mont-Palais	Ecloseaux
Meix-Caillet	Marisson
Les Pierres	La Fosse
La Bressande	Chapître
Champ-Clou	Préau
La Renarde	Moulesne
Pillot	Margoty
Cloux	Grésigny
Raclot	

Mercurey

The best-known and the best wines of the Chalonnais. The grapes are grown in the communes of Mercurey, Saint-Martin-sous-Montaigus and Bourgneuf-Val d'Or

and, although the law permits growing grapes for both red and white wines, those of Mercurey are about 95% red.

The wines are often very like those of the Côte de Beaune, light but sometimes surprisingly rich, and while not generally as fine, they come astonishingly close in good years. These are definitely wines to be consumed when young—from two to five years old. They are sound and pleasant but rarely stamped with greatness. One of the best organizations of the commune is the Cave Coopérative, run in a more than usually enlightened manner, respectful of the wines of each one of its members, and used as a source of supply rather than as a blending mill. Each member has his own wines, his own tools, and his own equipment, and the great advantage is that he can procure his supplies more cheaply since the organization buys in bulk and at wholesale prices.

The fame of Mercurey is so widespread that it is one of the few communes which did not go through the periods of recession after the two world wars. The renown of the wines, coupled with the fact that they are generally less expensive than comparable wines from the Côte de Beaune, was the dominant contributing factor to Mercurey's continued prosperity. The grapes are mostly Pinot Noir and the amount of wine grown is about 20,000 hectoliters (520,500 U.S. gallons, 400,000 imp.) per year.

Here, as elsewhere, certain vineyards have the right (if their wines attain half a degree of alcohol higher than the standard minimum limit) to add the words First Growth to the label, or to be sold as Mercurey, followed by the name of the vineyard. These vineyards are:

Clos-du-Roi	Clos-des-Fourneaux
Les Voyens	Clos-des-Montaigus
Clos Marcilly	

Givry

The wines are predominantly red, although some white is grown. Tradition claims that Givry was one of the favorites of Henry IV of France, a monarch who seems to have had a colossal thirst and a penchant for almost every wine in France. The red wines of Givry are slightly lighter and generally coarser than those of Mercurey, although very often wines of the finer vineyards (Clos-Saint-Pierre, Clos-Saint-Paul, Cellier-aux-Moines, and Clos-Salomon) stand on a fairly equal footing with them. One of the more important owners is Baron Thénard, who has holdings in numerous vineyards, including Givry's Cellier-aux-Moines and the famous Montrachet on the Côte de Beaune. His cellars in Givry house wines from all his holdings. They consist of caves dug deep below the town—huge ornate chambers which look like the set for a Hollywood costume-piece.

About 4,000 hectoliters (104,000 U.S. gallons, 80,000 imp.) of wine are made each year, most of which is sold as Givry and 80% of which is red. Provision has been left in the decree of 1954 for certain vineyards to be designated First Growths, but the French authorities have not yet drawn up a definite list of those that may add vineyard name to that of the commune.

Montagny

The only name of the Côte Chalonnaise which applies to white wines exclusively. The vineyards are in the towns of Montagny, Buxy, Saint-Vallerin, and Jully-les-Buxy, but only in those portions selected by experts as fit and proper for growing Montagny wines. The permitted area totals just over 300 hectares (750 acres).

After Mercurey, Montagny is the largest producer of the district but little of the wine is of first quality. *Pleasant* is the word most frequently used to describe it and is particularly apt if the wines are caught young. The dominant grape is the Chardonnay, and about 3,000 hectoliters (79,500 U.S. gallons, 66,000 imp.) of wine are made annually.

A surprising number of vineyards have been selected as superior, their wines allowed to be sold with the designation First Growth, the vineyard name following that of the commune. Although bottles carrying these indications are rare, the vineyards are:

Sous-les-Roches	Les Bouchots
Les Combes	Les Vignes-sur-le-Clou
Les Saint-Catages	Les Vignes-Couland
Les Vignes-Saint-Pierre	Les Trouffières
Les Charmelottes	Les Vignes-du-Soleil
Les Champs-Toizeau	Les Marais
(or Chantoiseau)	Les Perrières
Les Garchères	Le Pallye
Les Chacolets	Le Varignus
Les Clouseaux	Les Thilles
Les Carlins	La Vigne-Devant
Le Breuil	La Corvée
Les Champs-de-Coignée	Les Vignes-Dessous
Les Burnins	Les Marcques
Les Montcuchots	La Thi
Les Crets	Les Mâles
Les Beaux-Champs	La Condemine
Les Pandars	Les Vignes-Longues
Les Jardins	Les Vignes-Blanches
Les Saint-Morille	Cornevent
Le Clou	Le Mont-Laurent
Les Vignes-Derrière	Les Bonnevaux
Les Resses	Les Bassets
Le Perthuis	La Mouillère
Les Gouresses	Les Pasquiers
Les Bordes	Les Coères
Les Las	Les Thillonnés
Clos-Chaudron	Les Chandits
La Grande Pièce	Les Chazelles
Les Pidans	Le Vieux-Château
	Les Vignes-du-Puits

Chambertin

Burgundy red wine.
District: Côte de Nuits, France.
Commune: Gevrey-Chambertin.
Official classification: Great Growth (Grand Cru).

Chambertin is the *Grand Seigneur* of Burgundy, partly because of the unquestionable magnificence and nobility of the wine, and partly in deference to Napoleon, who preferred it to all others. It is not suprising that the commune of Gevrey chose to add this name to its own, becoming Gevrey-Chambertin—although this does tend to confuse inexperienced buyers.

When buying Chambertin, make sure the label says simply Chambertin. If it says Gevrey-Chambertin, the wine is regional, could come from any vineyard in the commune, and will be a lesser wine (albeit lesser only in respect to its great neighbor). It hardly needs to be pointed out that a bottle of Chambertin should always carry the vintage year.

The vineyard lies on the gently sloping midsection of the hill to the south of the village, next to the Route des Grands Crus (Route of the Great Growths), which leads to Morey-Saint-Denis. It directly adjoins the vineyard Clos de Bèze—the only other which has the right to produce wines to be called Chambertin. Since the Clos de Bèze is less well known—but no less outstanding—than its neighbor, this right was inserted as a clause in the law. In practice, some of its wine is sold as Chambertin-Clos de Bèze and the rest simply as Chambertin. But Chambertin has no right to the name Clos de Bèze.

Together, the two vineyards comprise some 28 hectares (70 acres)—13 as Chambertin and 15 as Clos de Bèze. Within this area are more than two dozen growers. Each tends his own vines, harvests his own grapes, makes his own wines, and sells to whom he pleases and, for this reason, there is always a certain amount of variation between bottles. The scrupulous care of one grower contrasted with the more casual methods of another creates shades of difference even in wines from the same small vineyard and the same year. Yet there will also be a strong family resemblance between Chambertins from different growers in the same year, and between wines from Chambertin and from the Clos de Bèze. Some local experts maintain that the wines from the two vineyards are so similar that it is impossible to tell them apart.

At its finest, Chambertin is big and sturdy with a deep, strong color—the color or *robe* is one of the wine's most distinctive characteristics—and a pronounced, lingering, and glorious aftertaste. It is a wine with a tremendous "nose" (for the wine-taster often transfers the perceptive organ to the wine itself). The nose is so outspoken that bouquet—the usual term—fades into insignificance beside it. In a well-made and distinctive Chambertin of a good year, all the characteristics are welded together into a balanced unity, and the wine improves with age, developing the wonderful austere masculinity which causes experts to exclaim "Chambertin," and novices, "Great wine!"

The quantity made is not great, yet it is perhaps greater than might be expected from the size of the vineyard because of the amount of Clos de Bèze which assumes the name; but in an average year for quantity only 490 hectoliters (12,985 U.S. gallons, 10,780 imp.) were made. This is the equivalent of about 5,000 cases and obviously not enough to satisfy the clamorous demand for Chambertin all over the world.

Chambertin-Clos de Bèze

Burgundy red wine.
District: Côte de Nuits, France.
Commune: Gevrey-Chambertin.
Official Classification: Great Growth (Grand Cru).

In A.D. 630, Almagaire, Duke of Lower Burgundy, founded the Abbey of Bèze near Dijon, endowing it with nearby lands and fields from which to draw support. One such holding was a wooded lot of 15 hectares (37 acres) in what is today the commune of Gevrey-Chambertin. The monks cleared the land, planted vines, and established the vineyard of Clos de Bèze. They tended it until the thirteenth century, when it passed into the hands of another order; but the vineyard did not really become exceptional until the eighteenth century, when a man named Jobert—secretary to the king's legal representative and reputedly a very clever businessman—took over both Chambertin and the Clos de Bèze and proceeded to make them famous. The vineyard was so good that its reputation lasted, and when the French wine authorities classified Burgundian vineyards in 1937, it was recognized as a Great Growth (*Grand Cru*)—one of only thirty-one outstandingly great vineyards of Burgundy.

The Clos de Bèze stands just to the south of Gevrey-Chambertin on the twisting, winding vineyard road. On the side away from the village, and adjoining it, is Chambertin, and the two vineyards are the commune's finest, although there are others near them. Wines from both may legally be sold as Chambertin; and although the Clos de Bèze is considered slightly the superior of the two, many growers take advantage of this rule, feeling that the shorter and simpler name is the better known and the easier to sell.

The official name—that which will be found on bottle labels—is Chambertin-Clos de Bèze, and not very much is made in any year. The figure in an average year for quantity amounts to a little more than 510 hectoliters (13,515 U.S. gallons, 11,220 imp.) or the equivalent of about 6,000 cases, not including the amount sold as Chambertin. The characteristics of the two wines are virtually the same and are discussed under Chambertin (*q.v.*).

Chambéry

An old city of Savoy in France, famous for the extra-dry vermouths produced there.

Chambolle-Musigny

Burgundy red and some white wines.
District: Côte de Nuits, France.
Commune: Chambolle.

The red wines are delicate, elegant, entrancingly perfumed, and have the fragile yet resolute charm of "feminine" wines. The whites—made in very small quanti-

ties—share this same charm but tend to lack some of the finesse of their great counterparts.

The wines have been famous for centuries and they succeeded for a long time in overshadowing those of neighboring Morey-Saint-Denis, with which in fact they have little in common. Morey's wines tend to be big, hard, assertive—the reverse in every way of the Chambolles. Yet much of the production of Morey once went to market under Chambolle place-names until the laws of Appellation d'Origine outlawed the practice and established Morey as a place-name in its own right. One outstanding vineyard—Bonnes Mares—is shared by the two communes; the wines are more like the Chambolles than the Moreys.

Bonnes Mares and Musigny (*qq.v.*), lying on opposite sides of the town, are Chambolle's greatest vineyards. Both are legally rated Great Growths (*Grands Crus*) and the wines are labeled only with the name of the vineyard, signifying outstanding excellence. Other superb wines are included among the First Growths (*Premiers Crus*)—wines that have stature and breeding but generally fall just below the topmost two, and this status is signified by labels bearing both communal and vineyard name. The best is Les Amoureuses, directly below the vineyard of Musigny and lying on the imaginary dividing line which separates Chambolle-Musigny and Vougeot. "Women in Love" is the meaning of the name, and Burgundians consider it highly appropriate. The wines are slightly less distinctive than those of Musigny, and in a good year are delicate and feminine, with a warming bouquet.

Nineteen other vineyards are considered in the same category as Les Amoureuses, and while their output seldom attains the same extraordinary quality, they too may often be perfectly made and beautiful wines. The wines which do not stem from one of these, or from other vineyards classified but not tested here (and do not otherwise meet the elevated minimum standards demanded for these ratings), are sold as Chambolle-Musigny and have many of the same characteristics.

Chambolle-Musigny has about 175 hectares (437 acres) of vines and annually produces some 6,500 hectoliters (172,250 U.S. gallons, 143,000 imp.) of red wine.

GREAT GROWTHS (*Grands Crus*)

Vineyard	Hectares	Acres
Les Musigny	10.7	26.5
Les Bonnes Mares (*in part*)	13.7	33.9

(*See* under individual headings.)

FIRST GROWTHS (*Premiers Crus*)

Vineyard	Hectares	Acres
Les Amoureuses	5.25	13
Les Charmes	5.8	14.4
Les Cras	4.5	10.4
Les Borniques	1.5	3.6
Les Baudes	3.5	8.8
Les Plantes	2.6	6.3
Les Hauts-Doix	1.75	4.3

FIRST GROWTHS (*Premiers Crus*) (continued)

Vineyard	Hectares	Acres
La Combe d'Orveau	5	12.5
Les Chatelots	2.6	6.3
Les Gruenchers	3	7.3
Les Groseilles	1.5	3.7
Les Fuées	6.2	15.3
Les Lavrottes	1	2.5
Derrière-la-Grange	0.73	1.8
Les Noirots	2.9	7.1
Les Sentiers	4.8	12.2
Les Fousselottes	4	10
Aux Beaux-Bruns	2.4	6
Les Combottes	0.65	1.6
Aux Combottes	2.27	5.6
Les Carrières	0.7	1.7
Les Chabriots	1.5	3.6
Combe d'Orveau (*in part*)	2.3	5.7
Aux Échanges	1.0	2.5
Les Grands Murs	0.9	2.3

Chambrer

French term for bringing a red wine slowly to the temperature of a room (*chambre*), the best temperature for most red wines. Warming the wine by plunging the bottle in hot water or putting it before a fire is not to be recommended: such sudden shocks are apt to change the chemical equilibrium of a wine with the result that its excellence is impaired or destroyed. A wine that is too cold can be warmed by the heat of the hands on the glass, but one that has been heated too quickly is ruined.

Champagne

*Principally white sparkling wine; some still white wine and
a small quantity of red and rosé.*
District: Northeast France.

The deliciously sparkling wines of Champagne are the most famous in the world. There are indeed some people who feel that Champagne should be reserved for launching ships and debutantes, and others who would like to drink it with meals, before meals, after meals, in the middle of the morning, or in the middle of the night. But most everyone experiences a thrill of pleasure as the cork slowly pops out of the bottle, the whiff of smoke curls up into the air, and the pale-gold wine foams into the tall glasses. Champagne is unique—a fact which, outside France, is too often ignored.

The only wine with any right to the name Champagne is that made from certain legally specified grapes grown in limited and well-defined sections of the province of France called Champagne—vines tended and vinified according to a body of strict local rules. Soil, climate, vines, labor, and tradition all make Champagne what it is. Sparkling wines produced in other parts of the world may be good, but none will ever be Champagne—although some of them masquerade under the name. What is not universally known is that several wines of Champagne are not sparkling. Still wines are also made in the province

and gaining in popularity despite high prices. For the sale of the still Champagne, which has grown steadily for the last five years, the name Côteaux Champennois is now required, replacing the name "vin Natur de Champagne."

The region of Champagne begins some 55 kilometers (90 miles) to the east and slightly to the north of Paris, is a vast chalky plain, carefully cultivated, broken only now and again by an occasional river and dominated by the Mountain of Reims. Between the city of Épernay, on the Marne, and Reims on the Vesle, a deformed hunch rises from the sturdy back of Champagne; an outcropping of chalk which, when viewed from above, resembles a huge question mark superimposed on the plain. This Mountain of Reims could only be a mountain in a flat country, since its average height is 200 meters (600 feet), with a maximum of about 300 meters (900 feet) in a few places. The stem of the question mark extends beyond Reims, moving north to the section known as the Petite Montagne—the "little Mountain"—and the arc curls round toward Épernay to the south, terminating in the section known as the Côte de Bouzy, after the principal town. At Épernay, the region of the Great Growths splits, one part following the Marne toward Château-Thierry, and the other heading due south to form the famous Côte des Blancs, where the Pinot Noir gives way to the white-grape Chardonnay vines. These sections are not all of Champagne, but they are the best. All are in the department of the Marne, but the limits of Champagne extend slightly beyond these borders. Four-fifths of Champagne comes from the Marne, the rest from the adjoining departments of Aube, Aisne, and Seine-et-Marne.

From these three lesser departments flow many of the cheap Champagnes which are sold throughout the world.

HISTORY

The vines in Champagne are among the oldest in Europe; there is adequate fossil evidence that vines were there during the Tertiary era, which geologists set at from 1 to 60 million years ago. The use of the vine for the making of wine may have been established before the Romans, although there are no records, but the Romans increased the planting of the vine throughout Champagne, as they did throughout France. The wines were originally still, however, and provided strong competition for Burgundy. A bitter rivalry broke out between these two districts, eventually coming to a head over the question of which was better for the health. The point was finally decided when the court physicians of Louis XIV cast their votes in favor of Burgundy.

Sparkling wines did not make any headway in Champagne until the seventeenth century, when, it is said, the discoveries of a Benedictine monk, Dom Pérignon, drastically changed the methods of wine-making. Sparkling wines had certainly been known over the centuries. All the growers of the world must have noticed that certain wines refermented in the spring and, if enclosed, became sparkling, usually breaking the container in which they were kept. Such wines were often referred to as *saute bouchon* (cork popper) or as *vin diable* (devil wine). Dom Pérignon (or some of his contemporaries) realized that the pressure built up was due to carbon dioxide and recommended that stronger bottles be used. Until this time, stoppers had not usually been made of cork but of cotton wadding soaked in oil. Now they began to make thicker ones and tied them down with a string. Dom Pérignon is also credited with being one of the pioneers in blending the wines of Champagne—most of which need the additional qualities only blending can give. He was cellarmaster at the Benedictine Abbey of Hautvillers for forty-seven years until his death in 1715, and his name is still honored in Champagne. Once each year there is a wine festival in Hautvillers celebrating the achievements attributed to him.

Alongside the work of Dom Pérignon, that of another seventeenth-century Champagne monk should be noted. Frère Jean Oudart ran the cellars at the Abbey of Pierry and did much to improve the techniques of bottling the sparkling wine. Frère Jean was among the first to use stoppers made of Spanish cork rather than the old ones of wood and oakum. It is conceivable that the two monks knew one another and compared their wine experiments.

CLASSIFICATION AND RATING

The small towns of Champagne and the vineyards lying within them are classified according to a complicated percentage scale, and the rating given the town will determine the price for the grapes in any given year. Each autumn the growers meet with the shippers who will be buying their harvests and haggle over the prices to be paid. Seldom do the growers in Champagne vinify their own grapes, and price must be decided in advance: once the harvest is started, there can be no delay if the grapes are not to suffer. The price decided on is for the very best growths, officially rated at 100%; that for the produce of other places will be proportionate to the town's percentage rating. In lesser districts, premiums may also be paid for certain types of grapes, encouraging the growers to plant the vines which give better fruit but less of it. Since 1966, the base price of grapes per kilogram has been augmented by various premiums paid to the growers. In 1973, for example, the base price was 6.37 francs, plus .45 franc for white Chardonnay grapes, plus 1 franc for grapes from a 100%-rated commune. On top of this total of 7.82 francs an 8% premium is paid to those growers willing to sign a supply contract for several years, making the grand total 8.45 francs (about $2) per kilo (about 2¼ pounds) for Pinot Chardonnay grapes from the best vineyards. The premium paid for the Pinot Chardonnay reflects the demand for lighter Champagne.

The Mountain of Reims boasts five growths rated at 100%: Beaumont-sur-Vesle, Mailly, Sillery (at one time the most renowned wine-name in England), Puisieulx, and Verzenay. Moving south toward the Marne Valley, off the Mountain and into the Côte de Bouzy, the best growths are Ambonnay, Ay-Champagne, Bouzy, Louvois, and Tours-sur-Marne, and, on the Côte des Blancs, Avize and Cramant. In towns where there are both red and white grapes grown, the percentage will be different for

each, and except in the Côte des Blancs, the higher rating nearly always goes to the red, plants giving white grapes being more or less curiosities in other sections.

GROWTHS (Crus)
ARRONDISSEMENT DE REIMS

Canton d'Ay	%
Ambonnay	100
Avenay	93
Ay-Champagne	100
Bisseuil	93
Bouzy	100
Champillon	93
Cormoyeux	85
Cumières	90
Dizy	95
Hautvillers	90
Louvois	100
Mareuil-sur-Ay	98
Mutigny	93
Romery	85
Tauxières	99
Tours-sur-Marne red	100
Tours-sur-Marne white	90
Canton de Beine	
Berru	84
Cernay-les-Reims	85
Nogent-l'Abbesse	85
Canton de Bourgogne	
Brimont	83
Cauroy-les-Hermonville	83
Cormicy	83
Merfy	84
Pouillon	84
Saint-Thierry—basses vignes	87
Thil	84
Villers-Franqueux	84
Canton de Reims	
Ormes	82
Reims (lot Brisset)	88
Taissy	94
Trois-Puits	94
Canton de Verzy	
Beaumont-sur-Vesle	100
Chamery	88
Chigny-les-Roses	94
Ludes	94
Mailly-Champagne	100
Montbré	94
Puisieulx	100
Rilly-la-Montagne	94
Sermiers	88
Sillery	100
Trépail	95
Verzenay	100
Verzy	99
Villers-Allerand	90
Villers-Marmery	95

The Vineyards
of
CHAMPAGNE

Heaviest concentrations of
vineyards .... ⟋

GROWTHS (Crus) (continued)

Canton de Châtillon-sur-Marne	%
Baslieux	83
Belval-sous-Châtillon	83
Binson-Orquigny	85
Champlat-Boujacourt	83
Châtillon-sur-Marne	84
Courtagnon	82
Cuchery	83
Cuisles	84
Jonquery	84
Montigny-sous-Châtillon	85
La Neuville-aux-Larris	83
Olizy-Violaine	84
Passy-Grigny	84
Pourcy	84

	%
Reuil	85
Sainte-Gemme	84
Vandières	84
Villers-sous-Châtillon	85
Canton de Fismes	
Châlons-sur-Vesle	84
Chenay	84
Crugny	86
Hermonville	84
Hourges	86
Pévy	83
Prouilly	84
Trigny	84
Unchair	86
Vandeuil	86

Champagne: Classification and Rating

Canton de Ville-en-Tardenois

Bligny	83
Bouilly	86
Bouleuse	82
Branscourt	86
Brouillet	86
Chambrecy	83
Chaumuzy	83
Coulommes-la-Montagne	89
Courcelles-Sapicourt	82
Courmas	87
Écueil	90
Faverolles	86
Germigny	85
Gueux	85
Janvry	85
Jouy-les-Reims	89
Lagery	86
Les Mesneux	90
Marfaux	82
Paigny-les-Reims	89
Poilly	83
Rosnay	83
Sacy	90
Sainte-Euphraise	86
Sarcy	81
Savigny-sur-Ardre	86
Serzy-et-Prin	86
Tramery	86
Treslon	86
Villedommange	90
Ville-en-Tardenois	81
Vrigny	89

ARRONDISSEMENT D'ÉPERNAY

Canton d'Avize

Avize		100
Brugny-Vaudancourt		86
Chavot-Courcourt	red	87
	white	88
Cramant		100
Cuis	red	90
	white	95
Grauves	red	90
	white	95
Le Mesnil-sur-Oger		99
Mancy	red	86
	white	88
Monthelon		88
Morangis		84
Moslins		84
Oger		99
Oiry		99

Canton de Dormans

Boursault	83
Champvoisy	84
Comblizy	83
Courthiézy	83
Dormans (Try, Vassy, Vassieux, Chavenay)	83

Festigny	83
Le Breuil	83
Le Mesnil-le-Hutier	84
Leuvrigny	84
Mareuil-le-Port	84
Nesle-le-Repons	83
Oeuilly	83
Port à Binson	84
Soilly	83
Troissy-Bouquigny	83
Verneuil	84
Vincelles	85

Canton d'Épernay

Chouilly	red	90
	white	95
Damery		86
Épernay		88
Fleury-la-Rivière		86
Mardeuil		84
Moussy		88
Pierry		90
Saint-Martin-d'Ablois		86
Vauciennes		83
Venteuil		87
Vinay		86

Canton d'Esternay

Bethon	red	84
	white	85
Chantemerle	red	84
	white	85

Canton de Montmort

Baye	85
Beaunay	85
Broyes	85
Coizard-Joches	85
Congy	85
Courjeonnet	85
Étoges	85
Fèrebrianges	85
Oyes	85
Talus-Saint-Prix	85
Villevenard	85

Canton de Sézanne

Barbonne Fayel	red	84
	white	85
Fontaine Denis Nuisy	red	84
	white	85
Saudoy	red	84
	white	85
Sézanne	red	84
	white	85
Vinedey	red	84
	white	85

ARRONDISSEMENT DE CHÂLONS

Canton de Vertus

Bergères-les-Vertus	red	90
	white	93

ARRONDISSEMENT DE CHÂLONS (continued)   %

Coligny		85
Etrechy	red	87
	white	90
Givry-les-Loisy		85
Loisy-en-Brie		85
Soulières		85
Toulon-la-Montagne		85
Vert-la-Gravelle		85
Vertus		93
Villeneuve-Renneville		93

Canton de Suippes

Billy-le-Grand	95
Marne (crus non côtés)	80
Vaudemanges	95

ARRONDISSEMENT DE SOISSONS

Canton de Braine

Cerseuil	84

ARRONDISSEMENT DE CHÂTEAU THIERRY

Canton de Condé-en-Brie

Barzy-sur-Marne	84
Baulne-en-Brie	83
Passy-sur-Marne	84
Trelou-sur-Marne	84
Aisne (less the communes of the Canton de Condé-en-Brie listed above)	80

Canton de l'Aube

Balnot-sur-Laignes	80
Buxeuil	80
Courteron	80
Gye-sur-Seine	80
Les Riceys	80
Montgueux	80
Neuville-sur-Seine	80
Polisy	80
Other Growths of Aube	75

Most of the sparkling wines of Champagne are made from a blend of red and white grapes. Some are Blancs de Noirs, or white wines made from black grapes; and a few are Blancs de Blancs, or white wines made from white grapes—the latter are almost entirely confined to the Côte des Blancs south of Épernay. (Most Champagnes do not carry any designations, although it is fairly common practice to use them on labels for still Vin Nature de la Champagne.) Some Champagne makers say that white grapes tend to improve the final blend. The present vogue is toward the Blancs de Blancs. Thus, whether for blending with red grapes or not, the increased demand for Chardonnay has made them more expensive than the Pinot Noirs. A certain small amount of pink, or rosé, Champagne is also made, as well as various still wines known correctly as Vin Nature de la Champagne, or commonly as Champagne Nature, Bouzy Rouge, and Rosé de Riceys. But the name Champagne, with no other qualification, always refers to the sparkling variety.

The total area of Champagne planted in fine vines amounts to about 21,000 hectares (52,500 acres). Of this, 17,000 hectares (42,000 acres) are in the Marne, with the remaining vineyards divided among the Aube, Aisne, and Seine-et-Marne. Rather more than half a century ago, the area planted came to about 15,000 hectares (40,000 acres), but the rapacity of the vine louse phylloxera, which arrived in Champagne about 1890, and the ravages of the First World War (throughout the war, from 1914 until 1918, the countryside was cut up with trenches) combined to decrease the vineyard area. However, each year over 500,000 hectoliters (10 million U.S. gallons, 8 million imp.) of wine are taken to the cellars to be made sparkling. The amount of still wine varies considerably. No matter how abundant the crop, the grapes for sparkling wine cannot be harvested in excess of 7,500 kilograms per hectare (about 7.5 tons per acre), and everything else must be vinified into Vin Nature de la Champagne. In some years there may be as little as 2,000 hectoliters (100,000 U.S. gallons, 83,000 imp.) and in others as much as 75,000 hectoliters (2,000,000 U.S. gallons, 1,700,000 imp.). The still Bouzy Rouge (red Bouzy) hardly ever exceeds 1,000 hectoliters (24,000 U.S. gallons, 20,000 imp.); and Rosé de Riceys is made virtually every year but in negligible amounts.

Almost all Champagne is made sparkling in the cellars of the big shipping firms, most of which are in Reims and Épernay. Deep below the cities the chalk subsoil has been cut out into vast caves and cellars. One firm has 11 miles of underground cellars so deep that the visitor must descend 116 steps to reach them. Most of these cellars are laid out in broad alleyways, named after the principal cities of the world where Champagne is sold. Statues carved into the chalk walls give them a certain resemblance to art galleries. These cellars were used during the war as underground shelters, but they provide a better home for wine than for refugees. Holding their temperature of about 50°F. (10°C.) the year round, they are fresh and clean and require no attention to keep them fit for the storage of wine.

Épernay and Reims, in whose splendid cathedral the kings of France were once crowned, are the two main headquarters for the shipping firms, many of which maintain offices in both. Some of the more important firms with their main headquarters in Reims are: Veuve Clicquot-Ponsardin, Heidsieck Monopole, Charles Heidsieck, Mumm, Piper-Heidsieck, Pommery and Greno, Louis Roederer, Ruinart, and Taittinger. Those with their main offices in Épernay include Mercier, Moët et Chandon, Perrier-Jouët, Castellane, and Pol Roger. In addition to these, there are a few firms in the small city of Ay overlooking the Marne, among them Ayala, Besserat de Bellefon, and Bollinger.

CLIMATE, SOIL, AND VINES

The vineyards of Champagne are the farthest north of any producing French wines of Appellation Contrôlée. When a vineyard is so critically close to the northern limit, every care must be taken to protect the vine from the unfavorable climatic conditions—not only because of the natural hazards which afflict it, but also because the vitality of a plant is lowered while struggling for existence, and such a plant is less fitted than one grown in more favorable climates to combat the dangers of frost and disease. Yet it is this northerly climate which is responsible for the exquisite delicacy of Champagnes. The situation and exposure of the vineyards is important, and most of the vines look to the south and southeast. The exceptions are those of the Côte des Blancs, which look east, and of the town of Verzenay (rated 100%), which actually faces the north. Southern exposure means that the hills will provide a shield against harsh winter winds and the vines will get the full benefit of the summer sun. The frosts and cold waves of the winter have a tendency to settle in the valleys and depressions and therefore the vines are mostly planted along the midsection of the hills, where they are relatively unaffected, although disastrous frosts have been known. Humidity is not excessive—an important factor, since most fungus diseases which attack vines thrive on moisture. The important Chardonnay vine is also subject to the *pourriture grise,* a type of rot which is at its worst in humid climates.

Climate is only one factor which contributes to making Champagne what it is. Another is the exceptional soil from which the vines draw their nourishment and whose qualities are reflected in the grapes and in the wines. Chalk is the major element, but there are others. Silicon and clay give the soil a workable consistency, and various trace elements add to the mixture. Most of the chalk in Champagne is Kimmeridge clay and is the same formation found in the soil of Chablis (*q.v.*) and in the village of Kimmeridge in southern England, where it was first studied and identified. The coarse-grained composition of this soil throws off excess moisture but holds at the same time enough to nourish the vine. The white pebbles absorb the heat of the sunshine, reflecting and radiating it evenly onto the ripening fruit and holding it well after the sun has disappeared below the horizon. Without this extra source of heat, the grapes, in some years, would never ripen at all.

The vines which may be planted in Champagne are closely controlled; predominating is the Pinot Noir, a vine which gives red grapes for making wines of the purest gold. Pinot Noir is by far the major vine, but also important are Pinot Meunier and Chardonnay (sometimes called Pinot Chardonnay, although modern research has established that it is not a member of the Pinot family); and a very little of Meslier and Arbanne is also planted. In the department of Aube there were still some plantations of Gamay after the war, and the result was not particularly happy. Originally, all the Gamay vines were to have been rooted out by 1942, but because of the war the date was postponed until 1962. The firms which buy the grapes generally pay a slight premium over the fixed price to any grower who brings in grapes from the permissible vines, but not for Gamay, which lately has gone only into the cheapest Champagnes.

The vines are generally planted in rows some three feet apart, the plants about 30 inches from each other and trained along wires which run the length of the rows.

There are generally two or three rows of wires along which the vine tendrils grow, bending their bunches of fruit toward the ground. Pruning is controlled by law, and the only permissible methods are Chablis, Royat Cordon, guyot, and gobelet—all measures to ensure that the vines will give a moderate production of high quality grapes year after year.

The grapes are usually small and quite acid. The comparatively cold climate of Champagne matures them slowly and in some years incompletely. Acidity drops as the summer wears on and the sugar content rises, but never gets so high as it does in warmer regions. Yet in some years these acid-high grapes are capable of producing 12% of alcohol; in exceptionally hot years the wine-maker may even be forced to add acid; and in most years the grapes are vinified into a delicate sparkling wine with the subtlest combinations of color, aroma, and taste.

Champagnes, like all great wines, are dependent on the weather, and like all great wines they will, in some years, be superb. Some of the better years for Champagne have been: *1928,* 1929, 1934, 1937, 1945, *1947,* 1949, *1952, 1953,* 1955, *1959,* 1961, 1962, *1964, 1966,* 1967, 1969, *1970,* 1973, 1975, 1976, and 1979 (greatest years in italics).

WINE-MAKING IN CHAMPAGNE

As is the case with any wine, the making of Champagne begins in the vineyards at the harvest. In ancient times the date of the harvest was set by law, and anyone who started too early was brought before the regional officials for punishment. The Ban de Vendange, the official proclamation, still exists, although now as a formality rather than a legal requirement. The deciding factor today is the grape, which must be ripe but not overripe. Harvests are fairly late in the autumn, usually beginning during the second and third weeks in October; the minimum amount of sugar in the grapes and the minimum alcoholic content to be formed by this sugar in fermentation are decided each year by the Comité Interprofessionel du Vin de Champagne (Interprofessional Committee for the Wine of Champagne)—the semi-official body in Épernay which governs all Champagne activity, including promotion.

When the harvest starts, the women and children go out into the vineyards, their heads protected by characteristic faded blue sunbonnets, and cut the heavy ripe bunches of grapes. The younger men patrol the rows with cone-shaped baskets on their backs and carry the grapes to the ends of the rows, where they are inspected. The overripe or defective ones are discarded and the others placed in *caques* or *mannequins*—deep wide baskets holding about 60 to 80 kilograms (150 to 175 pounds) of grapes. The baskets are loaded onto carts and are then taken to the *vendangeoir,* or press-house.

Only in a few isolated cases does the grower in Champagne vinify his own grapes—they are nearly always sold to one of the shipping firms, sometimes before the harvest has started, and the firm makes the wine and carries it through the extensive series of operations which will result in Champagne. Most of these shipping firms have their own holdings in the vineyards to ensure at least a part of each year's harvest, and an estimated 3,000 to 3,400 of the 22,000 hectares (7,500 to 8,500 of the 55,000 acres) are owned by them. They maintain *vendangeoirs* in all the important towns, and the grapes are pressed on the spot. Here and there, however, cooperative cellars can be found where the growers themselves make the wine. Such is the case in the 100%-rated town of Mailly. During the depression, the big wine firms refused to buy grapes from the growers, who banded together and built a cooperative in their spare time, starting with no capital and doing all the work themselves after they had finished in the fields. Today, the cooperative has some seventy members; it makes both pink and white vintage Champagnes and ships them all over the world.

Throughout the harvest, the roads are packed with the laden carts on their way to the press-houses, and pressing starts as soon as they arrive. Most of the grapes in Champagne are red, and if the juice is left in contact with the color-imparting skins, an undesirable tinge may discolor the wines. This tinge can be removed by passing the juice through charcoal, but the wine-makers prefer to press their grapes immediately, before the color has had time to form. Pink (or rosé) Champagne is sometimes made by adding some red wine to the white, a practice held in the lowest esteem except in Champagne alone, where the results seem to justify the practice. However, the usual way is by short-vatting red grapes, ensuring only a small amount of coloration. Either way, Champagne makers consider the pink variety something of an oddity and not in the same class as the rest.

The oak presses are round and wide and built close to the ground with a trough around them to collect the juice as it runs out. The size and shape of the presses are such that they take exactly four tons of grapes, evenly distributed in a thin layer. The first pressings, called first, second, and third *serre*, give the high quality wine, and the last (*rebêche*) produces common wine to be given to the workers. The first *serre* gives the top quality wine, the *vin de cuvée*, amounting to 2,000 liters (528 U.S. gallons, 440 imp.) or the equivalent of ten *pièces*, or barrels. The second gives from one and a half to two barrels of wine, called *première taille*, and the third, another one and a half of *deuxième taille*, both of which go into the secondary wine of the makers. Between each *serre* the mass of grapes is spaded over with wooden spades (in none of the fine-wine districts does metal ever touch the grapes) to ensure that the pressure, which is greatest in the middle of the press, is equally applied to all the grapes. Before the marc, or pomace, is pressed for the *rebêche*, it is moistened slightly and again spaded over.

The wine which flows from the presses usually goes into huge vats and then into barrels, to be sent to the cellars of the firms in Ay, Épernay, and Reims. The pressing takes place in the vineyards, but everything else is done by the firms, and the newly extracted juice is usually given a light dose of sulfur to stop fermentation before the wine-maker is prepared for it. Once in the cellars, it is tested to determine its consistency. In Champagne, in many years, sugar must be added, a practice known as *chaptalisation*, which is widespread in Burgundy and is even found in a very few vintage years as far south as Bordeaux. The aim in Champagne is to make a wine which will have from 10% to 12% of alcohol and a moderate acidity. Depending on the year, the wine-maker may add sugar, or he may de-acidify his must, or unfermented grape juice. Sometimes citric or tartaric acid has to be added. Apart from sugar, which is added fairly frequently, these measures are exceptional and undesirable except in difficult years.

After the additions are made, the wine begins to ferment. For eight to ten days, it boils ferociously in the barrels, sounding like a hive of angry bees. After this preliminary action, it calms down considerably and for another ten to twenty days bubbles serenely and quietly. During this fermentation, the sugar is converted by the action of yeasts into alcohol and carbon dioxide gas, and the gas is allowed to pass off into the air through the bung-hole of the barrel. When the fermentation is finished, the wine is allowed to rest and clarify.

By the December after the harvest, the wine will have settled and all the grape particles left from the pressing as well as the spent yeasts will have fallen to the bottom of the barrel. The wine is ready for its first racking, in which it is carefully drawn off from the barrels, and the lees (or impurities) are left behind. After the first racking, the *assemblage* of wines from different vineyards, which have fermented separately in the same cellar, takes place. This is the blending of wines from a single town, and when it has been completed, all those from Ay or from Sillery or Verzenay will be uniform and consistent throughout. After a second racking at the end of January and a third just before the wine is bottled, the wines are ready for the second fermentation, which will make them full-blown Champagnes. Those which are to remain non-sparkling undergo the racking, but their development stops there and they are sold as Vin Nature de la Champagne.

THE CHAMPAGNE PROCESS

The Champagne process is the name for the traditional method of making a wine sparkle by allowing it to ferment a second time in the bottle. The preparations for it usually start after the second (January) racking, when the *assemblage*, or blending, is done. Some firms specialize in *vins de cru*, or wines which come from one town only, but most Champagnes are blends. The wines from a single town are almost certain to be from one of the Côte des Blancs, usually Cramant or Avize. Most of the rest are blended, and the top quality wine of any firm is referred to as the *vin de cuvée*. Sometimes only wines from 100%-rated towns are used and may be sold as Champagne Grand Cru.

The delicate blending process starts with samples taken from the various wine barrels in the firm's cellars. These samples are taken up to special tasting rooms—spotlessly clean, airy, and hygienic, free from any extraneous odors or anything which might divert the taster's attention from the wine. These measures are of great importance, since the man is working with raw wines and must be able to detect any flaws or possible impurities before they develop. The desired result is a Champagne which will resemble the product the firm has put out in the past. When the proportions have been decided, the chosen wines are blended together and the lesser ones kept aside to be bottled under another label as the second quality of the firm.

After the wine has been made and racked and blended, it is ready to be bottled and to undergo the secondary fermentation which will impart the sparkle. Bottling usually starts about April and lasts until July. The first step is the addition of the *liqueur de tirage,* usually a solution of cane sugar dissolved in wine, very occasionally with a little citric acid added. (The acid speeds up the splitting of cane sugar into the fermentable grape sugars.) The amount of sugar added is usually calculated at 20 to 26 grams per liter of wine to be treated (equivalent to about one and a half pounds for each ten gallons). Sometimes less liqueur is added, and the result is a Champagne which is *crémant,* or only lightly sparkling. The word *crémant* (literally, "creaming") should not be confused with the town of Cramant, one of the leading or 100%-rated towns of the Côte des Blancs.

The sugar added as *liqueur de tirage* ferments to make the wines sparkling. It ferments under the action of yeasts which may already be present in the wine or which may be added from special strains. The fermentation is the exact replica of the first, forming alcohol (the alcoholic content of the wine will be raised by about 1%) and carbon dioxide gas. This time, however, the wine is not lying free in an open barrel, but is confined in a stout bottle and capped with an extra-heavy cork wired in place.

In the spring, as the sap begins to rise in the vines, the wine mysteriously starts its second fermentation, as though there were some mystic bond between the two. The cellars are cool and prevent temperature from speeding the action of the yeasts, since experience has shown that a better wine will result if the fermentation is allowed to proceed slowly. The bottled wine is laid in great stacks in the cellars, and every six months or so the stacks are moved and the bottles are given a hearty shake to free any sediment which may have formed. Marks painted on the bottoms of the bottles indicate which way they were lying, and they are always put back in the same position. As they are restacked, those which were in the middle of the pile are placed on the outside and vice versa, since the warmth generated in the middle will be greater than at the sides.

As fermentation continues, the carbon dioxide generated builds up pressure. Eventually, this pressure will amount to some five to six times that of the atmosphere, and it is for this reason that the bottles and corks are of such heavy construction. Occasionally during this process a bottle will break, because the mounting pressure exceeds it in strength, and each time the bottles are moved from place to place these broken ones must be abstracted. The fermentation itself will only take about three months, but the wines are left in these cellars for a period of years to "ripen," during which time the bottles are shaken occasionally to keep the sediment from forming permanently. At the end of this ripening period, the wines are ready for the *remuage* and *dégorgement,* the long series of operations to remove the sediment from the bottle.

Remuage means "shaking," and bottles of Champagne must be shaken in a particular manner. The first step is the gradual *mise sur pointe,* turning them upside down. This is done in special racks or *pupitres*—hinged, sloping boards, much like artists' easels. Holes are cut on both sides of the *pupitre* in such a way that they will hold a bottle firmly when it is inserted neck first in any position between the horizontal and the vertical. The bottles are put in at a very slight angle—usually about thirty degrees—and over a period of time are slowly changed until they are literally upside down. Each day a trained man, a *remueur,* goes through and carefully shakes each bottle, putting it back at a slightly more elevated angle, and turning it about a quarter turn each time. This slightly shakes the sediment, and slowly, as the bottle is raised, it slides down to the neck, where it rests against the cork. The *remueur* is a highly expert man, one who works at top speed, using both hands; and he is capable of turning 32,000 bottles a day. To ensure that the bottles are absolutely sound, he is given a bonus for any defective ones he finds. When he has finished, the bottles are standing on their heads in the racks, the sediment is next to the cork, and the wine is ready for the next step—the *dégorgement* which will shoot out the sediment.

Dégorgement is another ticklish procedure, particularly if it is done in the old traditional manner. The bottles are taken, the cork slowly pried off, and the sediment is allowed to shoot out, propelled by the pressure in the bottle. The trick is to lose as little wine as possible but not to leave any sediment. The high degree of skill and practice necessary for this job has been modified by the more modern method of freezing the necks of the bottles. The sediment and a small amount of the wine become frozen, and again the pressure that has been built up shoots it out in a solid lump. The wine is then brought back to its original level with a little of the same wine from another bottle and is ready for *dosage* and the final cork.

The *dosage* of a Champagne depends on the potential clientele. Sophisticated customers usually prefer their Champagne *brut*—that is, as dry as possible, except when it is to be served with sweets or fruit, when a Champagne of one of the varying degrees of sweetness should be chosen. The wine is sweetened by the addition of sugar dissolved in some *vin de reserve.* Generally only the best quality wines are used for *brut* Champagne, since any defects, which in the others will be masked by the added sugar, will here be apparent.

The sweetening is referred to as *liqueur d'expédition* and consists of a small amount of sugar mixed up with a little of the same Champagne to be dosed and a little brandy. The amounts generally added are:

French Name	Percentage	English Name
Brut	0 to 1½	Brut
Extra-Sec	1 to 2	Extra Dry
Sec	2 to 4	Dry
Demi-Sec	4 to 6	Semi-dry
Doux	8 to 10	Sweet

After the *liqueur d'expédition*, the bottles are ready for their final corking. Although the cork changes, the wine remains in the same bottle throughout its development, except when it is to be transferred into larger bottles. Champagne is always re-fermented in the regular Champagne bottle of 26 ounces, in magnums of 52 ounces, or in half-bottles of 13 ounces. As 2% to 3% of the bottles break each year, it is too risky to use the larger sizes, into which the wine is poured only at the time of *dégorgement*. The corks, however, change. The best come from Spain or Portugal, from special cork trees from twelve to fifteen years old. However, many firms are now using plastic corks until the final bottling, and some Champagnes are retailed with plastic stoppers.

All corks used finally, according to French law, must have the word *Champagne* printed on them. If the word does not appear, the wine is not Champagne. These corks are soaked in water to soften them and are driven into bottles which are then returned to the cellars for another period of checking and ageing. Watched fairly closely, to ensure that the *liqueur d'expédition* has mixed well into the wine, and to see that no unwanted third fermentation will start, they remain there sometimes for as much as two years. In total, the finer Champagnes may be six to seven years developing before they are ready for the consumer, and a bottle may be handled from 150 to 200 times before it leaves the cellar.

Name	Metric		fl. oz.
Split (*quart*)	18.7	centiliters	6
Pint (*demi-bouteille*)	37.5	"	12.7
Quart (*bouteille*)	75	"	25.4
Magnum (*2 bouteilles*)	1.5	liters	50.7
Jeroboam (*double magnum*)	3.2	"	104
Rehoboam (*6 bouteilles*)	4.8	"	156
Methuselah (*8 bouteilles*) (Methusalem)	6.4	"	208
Salmanasar (*12 bouteilles*)	9.6	"	312
Balthazar (*16 bouteilles*)	12.8	"	416
Nebuchadnezzar (*20 bouteilles*)	16	"	520

SERVING CHAMPAGNE

It is usually considered that Champagne is at its best served chilled—not iced. The makers generally take a slightly more tolerant view about opening the bottle than do some drinkers, suggesting that the cork should come out in your hand rather than being encouraged to careen across the room to the accompaniment of popping noises and spilled Champagne. Letting the cork come out too fast, they say, allows too much pressure to escape, and with it some of the bubbles which have been so carefully developed over the years. Swirling Champagne with swizzle-sticks has the same effect. That and dropping ice cubes into the wine are looked upon with horror by connoisseurs.

Some Champagne growers also suggest that tall flute-shaped glasses be used rather than the wide shallow ones; an eight-ounce tulip-shaped glass is even better. The bubbles disappear too quickly in the open-bowled glasses;

and it is the bubbles which make Champagne. As the columnist Art Buchwald put it: "I like Champagne, because it always tastes as though my foot's asleep."

Chantepleure

In Vouvray, a *pipette* or tube for removing wine from a cask or other bulk container.

Chapeau

A "hat" or thick layer of solids, consisting of pulp and skins, which forms on the must in the vats during fermentation.
See Chapter Nine, p. 38.

Chapelle-Chambertin

Burgundy red wine.
District: Côte de Nuits, France.
Commune: Gevrey-Chambertin.
Official Classification: Great Growth (Grand Cru).

Chapelle is one of the more delicate of the wines of this northerly commune of the Côte de Nuits. Generally, the wines of Gevrey are full-bodied and robust, assertive and strictly masculine; and while those from Chapelle share these qualities, they have a lightness, a fruitiness sometimes, and a certain finesse which tends to set them apart.

All of the nine vineyards which make up the family of Chambertin are clustered around the nucleus of Le Chambertin and Chambertin-Clos de Bèze and either adjoin or are visible from the little road which runs through the vineyard joining Gevrey and Morey-Saint-Denis. Leaving Gevrey by this road, Chapelle is the first of the important vineyards on the left, though there is little chance that the newcomer will notice it unless a local inhabitant points it out. Throughout these renowned wine communes there is little to distinguish one great vineyard from another, the significant differences becoming apparent only in the wines themselves.

The vineyard of Chapelle has been rated as Great Growth (*Grand Cru*) and covers some 5.37 hectares (13.3 acres). The amount of wine made by the several growers who own sections of it comes to 150 hectoliters (3,975 U.S. gallons, 3,300 imp.) in an average year for quantity. This is the equivalent of about 1,800 cases.

Chaptalisation

The addition of sugar to the fermenting wine must, in order to build up the alcoholic content.
See Chapter Nine, p. 38.

Charbono

A wine grape which probably came from Italy but which is now cultivated extensively in California, especially in the Napa Valley, where it produces a full-bodied, pleasant, but somewhat rough red wine.

Chardonnay

Excellent white grape grown, notably, in Burgundy. It resembles the Pinot Noir but is not a true Pinot, although it was once thought to have been a white variant of that grape and therefore is now often called Pinot Chardonnay. Other local names include Arnoison, Aubaine, Beaunois, Melon Blanc. It yields rich well-balanced wine with a distinctive aroma and a superb, lingering aftertaste. It has been particularly successful in California.

Charente wines

Principally, the light, thin, tart white wines which are distilled into Cognac brandy, although this district also produces some red wine (from which Cognac is never made) and some white wine which is not made into Cognac.

See Cognac.

Charlemagne

Burgundy white wine.
District: Côte de Beaune.
Commune: Aloxe-Corton.
Official Classification: Great Growth (Grand Cru).

The vineyard area is about 35 hectares (88 acres), and the white wines are excellent; but the name Charlemagne is rarely used alone, since growers are entitled to the preferred Corton-Charlemagne. The Emperor Charlemagne once owned the vineyards that bear his name and which he afterward gave to the Church, in the person of the Abbot of Saulieu. In the sixteenth century the lands were leased to an innkeeper of Beaune, appropriately named Charles; by the seventeenth century the holdings had been carved up, and some of them became the property of the Hospices de Beaune (*q.v.*).

Charmat

In 1910 the French wine-scientist Eugene Charmat developed a process for making sparkling wines in bulk which is still, with modifications, used today.

The original Charmat process required four tanks—three for wine and the other for yeasts. Still wine is run into the first tank and artificially aged by being heated for twelve to sixteen hours, then cooled. Pumped into the next tank, it has yeast and sugar added and ferments for ten to fifteen days; then it is pumped into the third tank, where it is clarified by refrigeration; and finally it is filtered and sent to the bottling machine. The entire process is interconnected, and the wine never loses the pressure built up during fermentation.

Although no replacement for the Champagne process of second fermentation in the bottle, the Charmat system allows the wine-maker to produce a continuous flow of sparkling wine of sound but uninspiring quality.

Charmes-Chambertin

Burgundy red wine.
District: Côte de Nuits, France.
Commune: Gevrey-Chambertin.
Official Classification: Great Growth (Grand Cru).

Charmes-Chambertin and Mazoyères-Chambertin form a partnership with Mazoyères—the silent senior partner. The ruling is that wine from either Charmes or Mazoyères may be sold as Charmes but that Charmes may not be sold as Mazoyères. In practice it is all Charmes.

The two vineyards form an unbroken expanse to the left of the vineyard road as you move south toward Morey-Saint-Denis, with the smaller Charmes coming up first, directly opposite Le Chambertin, and Mazoyères following, opposite Latricières-Chambertin. Together they compose some 31.61 hectares (79.02 acres). The wines are considered by local growers to be almost identical; Charmes has slightly more body and Mazoyères more finesse. Mazoyères, they say, would be the superior growth except that it is sold as Charmes, with the result that there is no way of telling between them.

Whichever vineyard it comes from, wine sold as Charmes is remarkably light and delicate for this commune where the emphasis generally is on austere masculinity. Classified in 1937 as a Great Growth (*Grand Cru*), the highest rating given to Burgundian wines by the Institut National des Appellations d'Origine des Vins et Eaux-de-Vie (National Institute of Place-Names of Wines and Spirits), the wines must live up to the rigid standards demanded by both law and tradition (for standards, *see* Côte de Nuits). The vineyard is reasonably divided up among several growers. The average amount of wine grown in the two vineyards comes to about 1,000 hectoliters (26,400 U.S. gallons, 22,000 imp.), a fairly representative figure, which is roughly the equivalent of 11,500 cases.

Charnu

French term for full in body; literally, "fleshy."

Chartreuse

The famous liqueur made in Tarragona, Spain, and Voiron, France, by monks of the Carthusian (Charterhouse) order. The Spanish distillery was established in 1903 when the order was expelled from France for the second time (the first was from the Revolution until 1815), and they have continued to operate it since their return in 1932. In the early part of the present century there was considerable confusion because the goods of the order were seized and sold at the time of their expulsion; the trademark went, but not the formula. The "Chartreuse" thus sold in France was no more than a pallid imitation of the real liqueur, and the monks were forbidden to use the name and resorted to the inscription *Liqueur fabriquée à Tarragone par les Pères Chartreux*. This has, of course, been changed since the return, and the name now belongs exclusively to the rightful owners.

Chartreuse is made on a base of brandy, with extracts of a considerable number of herbs and plants to provide the flavoring. The still-secret formula is said to have been given to the order in 1605 and perfected some time thereafter by Father Jérôme Maubec; but it was not sent outside the monastic walls until 1848, when a group of French army officers tasted it and were so impressed that they undertook to make it known everywhere. The original liqueur was the Elixir, white and stronger than it is now, but its manufacture has been discontinued. Chartreuse is either green or yellow, the green the stronger and the yellow less alcoholic and sweeter.

Chassagne-Montrachet and Chassagne-Montrachet-Côte de Beaune

Burgundy red and white wines.
District: Côte de Beaune, France.
Commune: Chassagne.

At the southern end of the Côte de Beaune is the Côte des Blancs, where the finest white wines of the Côte d'Or are produced. The greatest by far is wine from the vineyard of Montrachet—shared in almost equal parts by Chassagne-Montrachet and Puligny-Montrachet—but those just a shade below it are still magnificent. Chassagne also makes some very good red wines which, because they are little known and are slightly eclipsed by the celebrated whites, are often comparatively inexpensive and sometimes exceptional value. This has not always been the case.

During the eighteenth century Chassagne was famous for red wines. It is reported that red wine from the vineyard of Morgeot was so highly thought of that the rate of exchange was two bottles of Montrachet for one of Morgeot. The tables are so far turned today that Morgeot no longer makes red but, although they do not merit the ancient exchange rate, its whites are among the finest in the commune.

Chassagne, whose wines are often exceptional, is the last of the important communes of the Côte de Beaune. To the south is Santenay, where the wines are often good, seldom extraordinary; and after Santenay the slope tails off eventually to merge with the Côte Chalonnaise.

The leading vineyard is, of course, the incomparable Montrachet, but Bâtard-Montrachet and Criots-Bâtard-Montrachet are others of topmost rank (*see each under individual heading*). These are all Great Growths (*Grands Crus*) as rated by the French government and are thus on a level with the handful of the finest wines of Burgundy. Slightly behind them in the legal hierarchy—but often their equal in quality—are such vineyards as Morgeot, Ruchottes, and Caillerets. Chassagne's whites share many of the characteristics of Puligny—the dry, firm but never hard, full, flowery richness and lingering aftertaste. Montrachet itself has astonishing stamina for a dry white wine, but the others tend to maderize reasonably quickly. Ten years will usually kill them, and they are generally at their best when from two to five years old.

The reds of Chassagne are generally finer than those of Puligny and often finer than the better-known Santenays. They are hardish well-rounded wines, with a *goût de terroir* which is characteristic, and they form a transition between the other reds of the Côte d'Or and those of the southern Burgundian wine districts. Boudriottes is the most masculine at the outset, but it matures into a mellow and not over-assertive richness; while Clos Saint-Jean reaches its peak rather faster, has more finesse, and develops its bouquet considerably earlier. In general, the red wines of Chassagne are at their peak after about five years.

Chassagne has about 348 hectares (860 acres) planted in vines. The wine—when it meets the legal minimum standards—is allowed to use the commune name. It may add the designation Côte de Beaune if it comes from a 332-hectare (820-acre) section of this greater whole.

The better vineyards are the First Growths (*Premiers Crus*), which are entitled to be labeled with vineyard name and commune name, and the finest are the Great Growths, which carry the vineyard name only. Average production in Chassagne is about 6,200 hectoliters (164,300 U.S. gallons, 136,400 imp.) of red wine, 3,750 hectoliters (99,375 U.S. gallons, 82,500 imp.) of white.

GREAT GROWTHS (*Grands Crus*)
WHITE WINES

Vineyard	Hectares	Acres
Montrachet (*in part*)	3.56	8.8
Bâtard-Montrachet (*in part*)	5.82	14.4
Criots-Bâtard-Montrachet	1.42	3.5

(*See* Puligny-Montrachet.)

FIRST GROWTHS (*Premiers Crus*)
WHITE AND RED WINES

Vineyard	Hectares	Acres
Les Grandes Ruchottes (*white wines only*)	0.64	1.59
Les Ruchottes (*white wines only*)	1.73	4.26
Morgeot	3.94	9.75
Les Caillerets	5.49	13.6
Clos Saint-Jean	14.36	35.5
Clos de la Boudriotte	2.02	5
Les Boudriottes	17.81	44.3
La Maltroie	8.9	22.8
Champgain	28.35	70.7
La Romanée	3.16	7.86
Les Brussanes	17.72	43.8
Les Chaumées	10.12	25.1
Les Vergers	9.54	23.6
Les Macherelles	8.01	19.8
L'Abbaye de Morgeot	10.92	26.99
La Grande Montagne	8.18	20.22
Les Champs-Cain	4.24	10.48
Bois de Chassagne	8.79	21.73

Chasselas

This is one of the best European table grapes, but it is used only for small light wines: although these have a delicate bouquet, they are low in acid and do not keep well. Varieties of this family are the Gutedel (Germany), the Fendant (Switzerland), and the Chasselas Doré (California).

Château Chasse-Spleen

Bordeaux red wine.
District: Haut-Médoc, France.
Commune: Moulis.

Moulis is an official place-name in its own right, and the commune lies a little to the north and to the west of Margaux. Its best wine is Chasse-Spleen, classified Exceptional Growth (*Cru Exceptionnel*) in 1855. A reclassification of Médoc wines today would find this vineyard rated higher, among the great Classified Growths. Served frequently in recent years at banquets of the Médoc wine fraternity, the Commanderie du Bontemps, it has held its own among Médocs of high classification and worldwide reputation.

Characteristics. One of the best of its class, round and full. Very good breed.

Vineyard area: 23 hectares (57 acres).

Average production: 60 *tonneaux* (5,000 cases).

Château

In the wine world this means not a great castle, like a château of the Loire, but a wine estate (especially in the region of Bordeaux) where vineyards and wine sheds are controlled as a rule from the country house which is the center of the estate. This may look like a small castle; it may just as well be an average villa. The wine made and bottled on the estate is the fine château-bottled wine always more prized than regional wines, which may be blends.

For the names of the wine châteaux of Bordeaux (e.g., Château Haut-Brion, Château Lascombes) *see* under individual names.

Château-bottled

Wine bottled at the château where it was grown and made: a guarantee that it is untampered with and authentic. At most leading vineyards the legend *Mis en Bouteilles au Château* is also a guarantee of quality. If the vintage of any year does not come up to standard it will be disposed of to shippers and sold as regional wine.

Château-Chalon

A *vin jaune* of the French Jura. Yellow-colored, this wine is akin to Sherry and can last up to sixty or seventy years.
See Jura.

Châteauneuf-du-Pape

Rhône Valley red, and some white, wines.
District: Rhône Valley, France.

Midway between Avignon and Orange, on the left bank of the Rhône, Châteauneuf has about 3,000 hectares (7,500 acres) of vines, producing one of the Côtes du Rhône's finest red wines, and boasts the most stringent wine controls in the world. Were it not for Châteauneuf and its most distinguished grower—the Baron Le Roy de Boiseaumarié—there would probably be fewer controls in France today, for in 1936 the authorities followed the rules which had already been established by the Baron and others in Châteauneuf since 1923 and applied them to other fine French wines. Today, Philippe Dufaye, who abandoned medicine for viticulture, is a moving spirit in the commune.

Legislation in Châteauneuf came about through necessity, for after the First World War a bottle was apt to contain something quite other than its label claimed, and anything but good wine. Since 1923, however, the picture has changed drastically, and fraud, while not completely rooted out, has been given an almost mortal blow.

Most Côtes du Rhône wines are the product of one grape, but in Châteauneuf there are thirteen varieties. Because of this there will be differences between wines coming from different growers, all of whom maintain that each type of grape adds certain characteristics and that only by playing the scale of the varieties can a Châteauneuf-du-Pape be achieved.

Grenache gives mellowness and alcohol; Mourvèdre, Syrah, Muscardin, and Vaccarese add body, color, and firmness; Counoise, Picpoule, and Cinsault give vinosity, bouquet, and freshness; Clairette and Bourboulenc, finesse and warmth. Terret Noir, Picardan, and Roussanne are also allowed. The vines grow far apart, with often as much as 1.5 meters (5 feet) between rows, in soil covered with flattish stones the size of small coconuts. The bunches of grapes mature, caught between the scorching heat of the sun and the reflected heat from the stones. As a result of this roasting and of new, shorter vatting methods, the wines usually surpass the required 12.5% of alcohol (a legal minimum matched by few French wines and exceeded by none) and often reach 13% or even 14%. The wine is characteristically deep in color and full-bodied, but softer than either a Hermitage or a Côte Rôtie, and is much quicker to mature than are most Côtes du Rhônes. It is often ready after three or four years. The wine has a good bouquet (through not so intense as in the Côte Rôtie) and a special winy taste termed "vinosity."

Some very pleasant white wines are made and, while conserving the same distinctive taste, they are less well known—almost curiosities compared with the reds.

The name Châteauneuf-du-Pape comes from the crumbling ruins of an old castle built in the time known as the Babylonian Captivity (1305–1377), when successive popes were French, and Avignon, not Rome, was the seat of the Papacy. The "New Castle" was to be their summer headquarters and was started by Clément V, a lover of wine and former Bishop of Bordeaux—in which region Château Pape-Clément still stands in tribute to him. The building of the castle was finished by Pope Clément VI, although the vines were probably established by an intervening pontiff, John XXII. The holdings were attacked during the religious wars and the castle burned in 1552. Most of the remaining donjon was destroyed in the Second World War.

It is probable that wine from the district was not called Châteauneuf-du-Pape much before the nineteenth century; in earlier times it was known as "Wine of Avignon." Today a varying amount is made each year, for in areas as dry as this the grapes sometimes remain small from lack of water; but in a good year there will be about 100,000 hectoliters (2.65 million U.S. gallons, 2.2 million imp.), nearly all of it red.

The word Châteauneuf, with its associations with châteaux and Bordeaux, is attractive to the public. In the last year or two, some of these wines have been bottled within twelve months of the harvest and are thus lighter than the traditional Châteauneuf-du-Pape, and comparable with the best growths of Beaujolais.

Some important Châteauneuf-du-Pape vineyards are:

Vineyards	Hectares	Acres
Domaine des Fines Roches	47.35	117
Domaine de la Nerthe	46.54	115
Clos Saint-Jean	44.49	109.9
Domaine de Nalys	46.54	115
Château de Vaudieu	29.70	73.04
(about 40% of this is actually in production, although the whole rates an Appellation Contrôlée)		
La Gardine	24.44	60.5
Château Fortia	25.86	63.9
Domaine des Sénéchaux	23.59	58.3
Clos-des-Papes	13.51	33.4
Domaine de Saint-Préfert	14.16	35

Châtillon-en-Diois

French red, white, or rosé wine from the Drôme department.
See V.D.Q.S.

Chauché Gris

This grape is grown in the Livermore and Santa Cruz regions of California. The wine it makes is sold as "Gray Riesling" or "Rhine Wine" (although the grape is not a Riesling) or even as a "Chablis."

Chaume

See Quarts de Chaume.

Chautauqua

Wine-growing district in New York State.
See United States: New York.

Cheilly-les-Maranges and Cheilly-les-Maranges-Côte de Beaune

Burgundy red and white wines.
District: Côte de Beaune, France.

Cheilly and its neighbors (Sampigny and Dezize)—all of which have added the name of the vineyard they jointly share to their own—make up the southernmost communes of the Côte de Beaune. Cheilly's wines are usually blended with those from other communes along this famous slope and sold as Côte de Beaune-Villages, but may occasionally be found over some 125 hectares (310 acres), and grapes grown on 43 hectares (106 acres) enclosed within the larger area may be made into wine that has the right to add Côte de Beaune to the communal name. The vineyards Les Maranges, Plantes-de-Maranges, and La Boutière are the commune's best, and wines from these three may—although they almost never do—carry both commune name and vineyard name on the bottle label.

Chénas

Wines of Beaujolais, France, grown in small quantity, generally inside the famous district of Moulin-à-Vent; not quite of that excellence, they are nevertheless first-rate and, being much cheaper, are outstanding value.
See Beaujolais.

Chenin Blanc

The dominant white grape of the lower Loire Valley, going into Vouvray and other wines of the Touraine, and into most of the white wines of Anjou. Sometimes known as Pineau de la Loire, Blanc d'Anjou, etc. It is also used in California.
See Anjou; Touraine; California.

Cherry brandy

Technically a brandy distilled from fermented cherry juice, but in practice a liqueur derived from it, containing a proportion of crushed cherry stones to impart a bitter-almond taste.

Cherry Heering

This cherry liqueur made by the firm of Peter Heering of Copenhagen has made its name throughout the world. Having a true cherry flavor and made according to Heering's special formula, it is not over-sweet, on account of the proportion of cherry stones used in the distillation. This is one of the most popular cordials sold in the United States.

Cherry liqueur

Cherry cordial made by steeping cherries in sweetened brandy. Cherry Rocher is famous in France. An English variety is produced by Thomas Grant & Sons.
See Cherry Heering; Maraschino.

Château Cheval-Blanc

Bordeaux red wine.
District and Commune: Saint-Émilion, France.

Generally considered the best Saint-Émilion wine today, Cheval-Blanc is one of the twelve vineyards officially classified First Great Growth (*Premier Grand Cru*) of Saint-Émilion in 1955 and is privileged to stand with Château Ausone at the head of the list, the others following alphabetically. The vineyard is predominantly gravelly, although it covers various soils, and lies on flat land on the northeast borders of Saint-Émilion, on the edge of Pomerol. As a building the château is not distinguished.

The geographical position, otherwise excellent, proved disastrous in the freeze of February 1956. The Pomerol area was the hardest hit; and since the frost lay on the lower, flatter land and spared the hills, of all the great Saint-Émilion vineyards Cheval-Blanc suffered most. The late owner, M. Fourcaud-Laussac, in whose family the property has been for a little more than a hundred years (and whose heirs still own it), afterward made an average of about eight barrels of wine in each of the vintages of 1956, 1957, and 1958 (his usual yield is 600 barrels), because the cold killed the productive shoots and branches, which cannot be renewed under three or four years. Approximately a quarter of the plantation was actually destroyed, so that the vineyard was unable to return to normal production until the early 1960s.

Characteristics. Undoubtedly one of the greatest red vineyards of Bordeaux, on a par with the First Growths of the Médoc. Its reputation has grown tremendously in recent years, and three qualities may be said to have contributed to its success. The wine is one-third Pomerol, for the vineyard touches the Pomerol boundary, it is one-third Graves, since the soil is gravelly, and the remaining one-third is a typical Saint-Émilion. The result is a strong, supple, excellent wine.

Vineyard area: 35 hectares (87 acres).

Average production: 160 *tonneaux* (14,000 cases).

Domaine de Chevalier

Bordeaux red and white wines.
District: Graves, France.
Commune: Léognan.

One of the few Bordeaux estates to be called a *domaine* instead of a château. The vineyard was placed among the top eleven red-wine vineyards of Graves in 1959 and among the top five white-wine vineyards for its lesser quantity of white wine. This is to the credit of the Ricard family, who has owned this excellent estate for nearly a century. The red is not quite what it was at the turn of the century, but Chevalier is still an outstanding Graves, with quality often compared to that of La Mission Haut-Brion. The white is something of a connoisseur's favorite.

Characteristics. A very fine wine with great vigor, even in the lesser years. Among the best of the red Graves. The white is excellent.

Vineyard area: red—17 hectares (42.5 acres); white—3 hectares (7.5 acres).

Average production: red—40 *tonneaux* (3,800 cases); white—10 *tonneaux* (950 cases).

Chevalier-Montrachet

Burgundy white wines.
District: Côte de Beaune, France.

Commune: Puligny-Montrachet.
Official Classification: Great Growth (Grand Cru).

These wines are the closest to the great Montrachet itself. They have the same enveloping richness with no trace of sweetness, and the same overwhelming perfume and magnificence. This is not really surprising, since the vineyards are contiguous. Chevalier is lighter and not as powerful a wine as Montrachet, but, depending upon the skill of the grower, it can sometimes be as great or even greater. Superb finesse is the attractive characteristic of this beautiful white wine.

The Chevalier is directly above Montrachet in the commune of Puligny-Montrachet. On one side of it is Cailleret—good, but not in the same class as the other two—and on the other two sides no vineyards at all.

Chevalier, not much more than 5 hectares (12 acres), is split among several owners. Mme Boillereault de Chauvigné is one; and much of the rest is in the hands of Bouchard Père et Fils, Jadot and Latour (joint ownership), and Chartron. The average production of the vineyard is 160 hectoliters (4,240 U.S. gallons, 3,520 imp.).

Cheverny

Facing Blois across the Loire in the heart of Touraine is the village of Cour-Cheverny with its fine château. In the surrounding district lie the vineyards of the V.D.Q.S. wines called Cheverny. White wines are made mostly from the Chenin Blanc and Pineau de la Loire grapes, reds from the Gamay Noir and Cabernet Franc; some rosé is produced from the same grapes used for red. The V.D.Q.S. name—which was recently shortened from Mont-près-Chambord-Cour-Cheverny—also applies to the *vin blanc mousseux* of the region.

Chian wine

A Greek wine famous in antiquity.
See Classical wines.

Chianti

Chianti is one of the most abused names in the world of wines. Almost every wine-growing country has taken the name and applied it to almost any red wine as long as it is sold in straw-covered flasks. Real Chianti is made in a small district in the region of Tuscany in central Italy, and it may come in a flask (*fiasco*) or in a bottle. In either case, Chianti Classico will have on the neck of the bottle or flask a seal depicting a black cockerel on a gold background; and other permissible Chianti from a wider area in Tuscany will show a white cherub on the seal. The nine Chianti associations, called consorzios, each have their own seal.
See Tuscany: Chianti.

Chiaretto

An Italian rosé from Lake Garda.
See Italy.

Chica

South American drink, brewed from maize by the Indians.

Chicken

General name covering various types of native American grapes, some of which can be used by the wine-maker.

Chile

Chile makes the best wines in South America, and in quantity produced is counted fourteenth among the wine-producing countries of the world. Soil and climate helped by irrigation are favorable to viticulture; the French *vignerons* who planted the better vineyards have left behind them a high tradition of wine-making—although the Spaniards have been growing vines in Chile ever since they conquered it; and finally, the Chilean government takes a progressive and enlightened interest in wine and the vine.

From its roughly 116,000 hectares of vineyards (290,000 acres) Chile makes annually about 6 million hectoliters (158,500,000 U.S. gallons, 132,000,000 imp.) of wine. Only about 100,000 hectoliters, 2% of the total, is exported, mainly to other South American countries, a few European ones, and the United States. Before the 1973 coup, much wine went to Cuba. It is everywhere appreciated, for although not great wine, it is good—and usually a very good buy for the price. The amount of wine consumed each year inside Chile has been limited to 60 liters (15.9 U.S. gallons, 13.2 imp.) per inhabitant, and average consumption is well below the limit. The restriction was placed some years ago as the government attempted to control alcoholism. Two percent of all arable land in the country is planted in vines, and about 50,000 workers are constantly employed in the wine industry, about four times the number working the big copper mines.

Three types are produced: fortified wines in the north, good table wines in central Chile, and ordinary table wines in the south. Those of the central section often bear a close resemblance to the lesser Bordeaux wines. This is not really surprising, for the soil and climate in the two regions are very similar and the vines and viticultural practices are direct imports. Chilean wines might not, of course, match a château-bottled Claret of a good year, but they often equal or surpass some of the regional bottlings—and they have the advantage of being much cheaper. In addition to the wines of the Bordeaux-type from Cabernet grapes, there are some Burgundy types from Pinot Noir, but the former is by far the more successful. Though the wines can be good values, not all Chilean wine-makers have the skill to produce sound, clean wines.

One of the best Chilean white wines is the Riesling, but its production is reduced, not because of the quality of the wines but because the growers find the results too expensive. Chilean white wines are now made from the Pinot Blanc, Sauvignon, and Sémillon vines, for the most part.

The red *vin ordinaire* grown in the southern section of the country comes both from grapes of French stock and from the País, a vine of Spanish origin which has been in Chile long enough to be considered a native. The País is very much like the prolific Mission variety common in California. In Chile it accounts for 70% of all vines.

TERRAIN AND CLIMATE

Chile is so fortunately situated that the country has so far escaped the devastation of mildew—the most crippling fungus disease of the vine—and of phylloxera, although this vine louse has taken its toll in the vineyards of Argentina to the east and Peru to the north. Chileans say that the Andes, which lie between Chile and Argentina, have prevented the influx of the pest from that side; that the desolate Atacama Desert has obstructed its entry from Peru; and that the prevailing winds blowing in from the sea guarantee that it will not make its entrance by air. The result is that in Chile even the most tender of European vine-types need not be grafted onto American roots; yet experiments have been made, and this could be done with a minimum of confusion should phylloxera ever get into the country, though precautions taken at Chilean border stations make this improbable.

As there are three types of wine, so there are three zones of grape-production. The northern zone, from the Atacama Desert to the River Choapa, consists of vineyards planted mostly in Muscat and produces the country's best table grapes. Irrigation is a vital necessity since as a rule the rainfall is negligible; what there is, however, is closely connected with the cold Humboldt Current off the coast and when—as sometimes happens—this current is displaced by warmer water, catastrophic rains result, ruining the vineyards and everything else in the region. The vines are mostly cultivated in the transversal valleys, and irrigation is based on the occasional rivers which flow down from the mountains. The wines are strong and high in alcohol, and some are fortified to resemble Sherry, Port, or Madeira.

From a quality standpoint, the most important vine-growing region is the central portion which runs from the Aconcagua River to the River Maule. Here the influence is almost entirely Bordelais, both in viticultural practices and in vine planting. The most important vines are Cabernet Franc, Cabernet Sauvignon, Merlot, Malbec (here spelled Malbeck), and Petit Verdot for red wines, and Sémillon and Sauvignon for whites. All these come from the Bordeaux area. Other important vines are Pinot Noir, Pinot Blanc, and, of lesser importance, Riesling and País. The vines are tended and cared for according to traditional Bordeaux methods, with the single important exception that they are virtually all irrigated and therefore give more output than those which are watered naturally. This factor is not prejudicial to the quality of the wine. Since all the best vineyards of Chile are irrigated, it cannot at this point be decided whether or not the wine would improve under different conditions. In irrigated vineyards, the Cabernet Sauvignon may yield as much as 200 hectoliters per hectare, or nearly 12 tons to the acre.

Atacama Desert

ATACAMA

NORTHERN ZONE

CENTRAL ZONE

R.Maipo

O'HIGGINS

COLCHAGUA

CURICO

TALCA

R.Maule

MAULE

LINARES

Coquimbo

R.Elqui

COQUIMBO

NUBLE

Concepción

CONCEPCIÓN

R.Limari

BÍO-BÍO

R.Bío-Bío

R.Choapa

ARAUCO

MALLECO

ACONCAGUA

R.Aconcagua

VALPARAISO

CAUTIN

Valparaiso

VALPARAISO

SANTIAGO

Santiago

VALDIVIA

R.Maipo

CENTRAL ZONE

SOUTHERN ZONE

The Andes

ARGENTINA

N

CHILE

| 0 | 25 | 50 | MILES | 100 |
| 0 | 40 | 80 | KILOMETRES | 160 |

The most important grape for white wine, the Sémillon, will produce almost as much in similar situations.

The two best sections of the central region (and thus the best of Chile) are the Aconcagua Valley and the valley of the River Maipo. Both specialize to a large extent in Cabernet vines, and the wines are strong in finesse, are well balanced, and tend to hold their excellence longer than most other Chilean growths. The Maipo Valley, in the section southeast of the Chilean capital city of Santiago, is the top vineyard district. The soil has more limestone than elsewhere (there is generally a higher percentage of sand and slate), and the Cabernet Franc and Cabernet Sauvignon produce wines which are strong and stable, deep in color and rich in perfume. There is a good yield per acre in this district, although this claim can be attributed partly to irrigation.

The southern section of Chile is the area between the rivers Maule and Bio-Bio. With a few exceptions in the extreme north, the vineyards are not irrigated. The subsoil is hard and the topsoil is made up of slate and mud, sometimes rich in iron, with occasional outcroppings of lime. These wines are distinctly less interesting than those farther to the north, and while there are some vines of French origin (Cabernet, Malbec, Sémillon) and a little Riesling, much of the area is in the bulk-giving País. A certain amount of blending is done with these wines and the rest make up the everyday wine of the Chilean. Though the product is perhaps inferior to wines made farther north, viticulture is important in this part of Chile as the livelihood of some 13,000 small vineyard owners. South of the Bio-Bio River, the climate becomes too harsh for the successful cultivation of wine grapes.

WINE HISTORY

Despite the fact that they were conquered and settled by wine-drinking Latin people, most of the countries of South America had to await the influx of Italians after the First World War before they had substantial vineyards of their own. But both Chile and Peru have had vines for just about as long as they have had Spaniards.

Vines were brought into these countries by the missionaries who followed the Conquistadores and were established as a source for altar wine. It is thought that the first vines were carried into Chile by either Francisco de Carabantes or Bartoloméo de Terrazas—two missionaries who were instrumental in planting vines in neighboring Peru. One of these two—it is not known definitely which—took part in the expedition into Chile of Diego de Almagro, somewhere between 1535 and 1537. The vine they brought with them is recorded as giving grapes which were small and red and extremely tasty.

Culture of the vine received its first impetus about 1556, in the neighborhood of Santiago, whence it spread to what is today Argentina. The important vines of this era were Muscats, in particular the Muscat of Alexandria. Another useful variety was one that Chileans, for lack of a better name, call the País; it is known to have come from Spain, but otherwise its origins are shrouded in mystery. The wines were mostly altar wines or were modeled on Spanish types, and the real upsurge in the industry had to wait until the middle of the nineteenth century.

In 1851, the "Father of Chilean viticulture," Silvestre Ochagavia, realized that the country had the potential of becoming one of the best vineyard regions of the American continent. Acting on his conviction, he imported from France a number of viticultural experts. In addition, he imported a variety of cuttings from the better French vines, which were mostly planted in the central valley of Chile, where the better vineyards are still to be found. As his experiment became an almost unqualified success, the Chilean government stepped in and had more French vines imported, and the new industry was well launched.

Today, the typical vineyard of Chile is a small one indeed. Of the 32,000-odd vineyards, more than 26,000 are of 5 hectares (12.5 acres) or less. This raises various problems of cultivation; problems which have a direct bearing on the quality of the wine. A small Chilean grower who has neither the capital nor the proper equipment cannot hope to produce a really fine wine and stay in business. But the Chilean government has established a fund to provide loans for the building of cooperative cellars. This eliminates the necessity for each grower to buy all the expensive machinery he would otherwise need and provides a central place for a technical expert to advise growers on the latest and best methods. There are now only about a dozen cooperatives, making some 15% of all Chilean wine.

The Maipo River Valley, as an area with some of the best vineyards, is the location of some of the best wineries in Chile. Concha y Toro owns 500 hectares (1,250 acres) of vines in Pirque, Torconal, Maipo, Cachapoal, and San Juan de Peteroa; its two wineries are in San Miguel and Pirque. There, good wine is made, especially from Cabernet Sauvignon, Sauvignon Blanc, Sémillon, and Riesling grapes. Bulk process "champagne" is produced at the Pirque winery from a blend of Pinot Blanc, Pinot Chardonnay, Pinot Gris, and Riesling.

The Canepa winery at Valparaiso makes wine from grapes grown in the Maipo Basin southwest of the capital. Most of the vineyards, planted with Cabernet Sauvignon and Riesling, are along the sand and gravel banks of the Puangue River where the geography is not unlike that of Bordeaux.

West of Santiago in Santa Ana is Viña Undurraga, whose founder, in 1912, was the first to export Chilean wines to the United States, and whose vines now thrive in a moderate climate on land irrigated with river water. Most of the good *Vitis vinifera* varieties common in Chile are grown, along with the Pinot Noir, and sparkling wine is produced.

Also south of Santiago in the Llano del Maipo—the Maipo Basin—is Viña Santa Rita, and farther to the east, Viña Cusiño-Macul. At Cusiño-Macul, as in other good Chilean vineyards, vine cuttings were brought from the great vineyards of France, in this case from Pauillac in the Haut-Médoc and Martillac in Graves. More than half of the 260 hectares (650 acres) produce grapes for red wine, mostly Cabernet Sauvignon. Sémillon accounts for most of the white wine. Here, and at Undurraga, among other *viñas*, the better wines age in American oak barrels.

Two other important wineries lie south of the Maipo district. In Talca Province at Molina is Viña San Pedro, founded in 1865, with vineyards dating from the first years of the eighteenth century. Two-thirds of the 300 hectares (750 acres) yield red-wine grapes, especially Cabernet Sauvignon and Merlot. Riesling is the most prevalent grape for good white wine. And in Colchagua Province are the 150 hectares (375 acres) of Viña Santa Teresa, where Pinot Chardonnay, Cot, Cabernet Sauvignon, and Sémillon have grown since 1920. Santa Teresa wine is made in Santiago.

GOVERNMENT CONTROLS

The Chilean wine industry is one of the best regulated in the world. Perhaps the main reason for this is the effort to control alcoholism; but the outcome is that the wine which is encouraged is of high quality.

Chilean growers have a production figure they may not exceed—and if by any chance they do exceed it, they must get rid of their surplus, the two most popular methods being the attempt to export and distillation to industrial alcohol. In any year, each grower must declare to the government how much wine he has made. If the total comes to more than the legal maximum for the country, he must dispose of a certain amount, depending on the national total and the percentage of the wine he has made in proportion to his acreage. He must also declare to the government how much wine he eventually disposes of, and the way in which he has done it. The dumping of poor wine on the export market is prevented by restrictions imposed by the National Council of External Commerce. These rules decree that, for export, white wines must have at least 12% of alcohol, red wines 11.5%; and that the wines must be clear, healthy, and at least one year old.

The final control placed on Chilean wines by the government refers to age. There are four classes of export wines: Courant refers to wines one year old, Special to two-year-olds, Reserve to four-year-olds, and Gran Vino applies to wines six years old or more. In many cases the Reserve wines may be Chile's best.

SPIRITS

Much of the production of fine Muscat wine made in the northern zone is used for the distillation of fine brandy native to Chile and to some other South American countries.

See Pisco Brandy.

China

From very early times, wines have been made sporadically—but seldom in any significant quantity—in China. Today, returning travelers have told of wild vines still growing in the south, of experimental stations for viticulture, and of a small number of cooperative vineyards,

part of the agricultural plan of the state. Some European grapes (such as Pinot and Riesling) appear to have been introduced, and visitors have seen American-type vines, descended from *Vitis labrusca*, as well as native Asian stock. Some of the vines are cultivated in irrigated land, on a curious system by which the plants are supported on a fan-shaped trellis-work of wires; in other, non-irrigated vineyards, the pergola method of training was seen.

Wine is, however, apparently a drink for special occasions; lemonade or beer seems to be the common accompaniment for everyday meals. But wine has a place in the plans for the future. Wineries have been rebuilt and more are planned. Officials of the government confirm that grape, fruit, and rice wines, plus a variety of distilled beverages are now produced, and that the total output of the "wines" from 1949-1972 has increased more than four times.

WINE HISTORY

Chinese history has it that wine-making started as early as 2500 B.C., when the wine was called Li or Chang, instead of Chiu, its present name. According to legends and written history, the originator of sweet wines was one I Ti (who was perhaps a woman), a contemporary of the Emperor Yu (2205-2197 B.C.). The product did not find imperial favor, and a prohibition of alcoholic drink seems to have followed. Chinese spirits—often called "wine"— may have been invented soon after the unfortunate debut of fermented wine. Shao K'ang is credited with distilling Kaoliang from sorghum, and variations of his original formula are still made today, with alcoholic strengths ranging from 50-100 proof.

None of these earliest concoctions were wines by the Western definition of wine as a drink fermented from grapes, for grapes did not arrive in China until the late second century B.C. The first vines came from the Arabs in Turkestan, and even today many of the best Chinese grapes come from around Turfan in the section of old Turkestan along the main route to Central Asia. Having introduced the Chinese to vines, the Arabs might also have taught them the art of making wine from grapes.

Even though vines—and probably wine, too—had for years traveled to China from the Mediterranean and Persia on the long, slow relays of caravans which brought silk westward, it was not until the seventh century A.D.— when the Chinese dominated all of Central Asia—that viniculture spread more widely. By the time of the Sung Dynasty (1066) it had made considerable progress. It was not a drink for the masses, but poets and mandarins loved it. In the resplendent period of the T'ang Dynasty art and poetry flourished, and the drink of the courtiers and the artists was wine. The famous poet Li Po, a sort of innocent Villon who wandered from tavern to tavern writing and reciting his poems and always praising wine, was most poetically drowned: being drunk, and wanting to clasp the reflection of the moon in his arms, he plunged into the river.

In 1322, the emperor ordered the vines in his territory to be uprooted to make way for cereals: in the town of

Chang-Si, wine was offered to one Hong Wu "for the last time." But such edicts did not occur everywhere. Marco Polo was to find wine plentiful in Taiyuan. In the late seventeenth century, the Emperor K'ang-hsi was introducing new vines from Turkestan.

Today, red and white wines, dry, sweet, and sparkling—and some which could be called rosé—are being made from grapes. The Chinese name for grape wine is *p'u t'ao chiu.* Vines are grown north of the Yangtze and south of the Great Wall and the River Liao. Production is especially heavy along the Yellow River in parts of Shantung, Honan, Kiangsu, Hopeh, and Shansi. Peking, too, is a center. Most of the grape wines have between 12% and 16% of alcohol. Those likely to be encountered outside of the mainland are the sweet red and white Chefoo, dry Tsingtao red and white, and the sparkling wine called Ta-hsiang-pin-chiu. The red Chefoo is rather like a light Port, the white is strong and aromatic. The Tsingtao wines are closer to the Western conception of table wine. Some wine may even be seen from the famous Lung Yen vineyard at Peking, where wine popular with the Ming Emperors was grown.

RICE WINE

This traditional Chinese drink is made by sweetening and fermenting glutinous rice or millet. Called Shaohsing, the name of the town in Chekiang Province where the wine was first made during the period of the Warring States (403-221 B.C.), the wines are a golden color, with a distinctive bouquet. Alcoholic content ranges from 15° to 19°, and the sugar content may be as high as 20%. Though rice wine is consumed throughout China, it seems to be especially popular in the provinces along the Yangtze. The best-known brands are Yen Hung, Shan Niang, Chia Fan, Hsiang Hsueh, and Hua Tiao. Other rice wines are Fukien Loh Chiu and Mi Lao Chiu, made from yellow rice in Shantung Province.

SPIRITS

Brandy is made from wine, some of which is seen abroad, but it is not the most typical distilled Chinese drink. Spirits made from grains are the most popular alcoholic products in China. Called *pai chiu,* these gained great attention during the Yuan Dynasty (1280-1368); they are made from cereals which have undergone various processes of yeasting, sweetening, and fermenting. By far the most famous is the fiery Mao-t'ai, from the town of that name in Kweichow Province in southwest China. It is distilled from fine millet and wheat and is generally aged for a considerable time before being consumed. A drink for special occasions, Mao-t'ai has an alcoholic content of 53 proof or more.

The other famous *pai chiu* is Fen Chiu, from a place called Sing Hua Village in the Shansi Province town of Fen. Distilled from millet, wheat, and beans, it is quite fragrant, with a clear, crisp taste.

Ta Chu from Szechwan, Si Fen from Shensi, and Wu Liang Yu, also from Szechuan, are other well-known Chinese spirits.

Chinchon

Spanish anis-flavored spirit diluted with water and drunk in a tall glass.

Chinon

Loire Valley red, white, and rosé wines; still, semi-sparkling, and sparkling.
District: Touraine, France.

The ruined medieval fortress of Chinon rising above the quiet River Vienne stands on the top of a steep hill, to the slopes of which cling the picturesque buildings of the old town. Chinon, a wine center for a considerable period, claims as its most exuberant admirer the writer Rabelais, who once tended a nearby vineyard—La Devinière—and made there what he described as "taffeta wines," soft and velvety. The description has lived on in Chinon and is still apt.

Red, rosé, and white wines are made, the red being the most interesting. White Chinon is almost invariably overshadowed by Vouvray or Montlouis and the rosé by Anjou; but the reds are apt to be soft, flowery, and have a bouquet often compared with raspberries. To be good, Chinon requires great vintage years, and such vintages only fall about twice in a decade. Red and rosé—a fresh and clean-tasting if unexceptional wine—are made from Cabernet Franc grapes grown in flinty clay soil, white from Chenin Blanc grapes grown in chalky soil. All wines must have at least 9.5% of alcohol. About 30,000 hectoliters (795,000 U.S. gallons, 660,000 imp.) are made each year, nearly all of which is red.

Chiroubles

A village in the Beaujolais producing an excellent light red wine now becoming the most popular of all red Beaujolais wines in Paris and throughout France.
See Beaujolais.

Chlorosis

A vine disease caused by an excess of calcium in the soil which prevents the vine from assimilating iron. It is treated by adding iron to the soil, by injecting iron into the vine, or replanting with vines grafted onto calcium-resistant root-stock.
See Chapter Eight, p. 29.

Chopine

French pint.

Chorey-les-Beaune

Burgundy red and white wines.
District: Côte de Beaune, France.

A Burgundian wine village where there is more village than wine. Like so many of her sister communes, Chorey has the option of selling her wines either as Chorey or, after blending with those from other specified communes, as Côte de Beaune-Villages (*q.v.*). The result is that one year may see 750 hectoliters (20,000 U.S. gallons, 16,500 imp.) and another 4,000 (106,000 U.S. gallons, 88,000 imp.).

Chorey is on the right side of the railway but the wrong side of the road. Throughout the Côte d'Or the hills descend gently to a plain, the start of which is marked by Route Nationale (National Highway) No. 74. As you drive south, you will see vines on both sides of the road; but only on the hilly right are the vineyards really good. To the left, on the plain which extends to the railway, they are distinctly minor—and most of Chorey is on the left. A small pocket, amounting to 167 hectares (412 acres), crosses the road but does not climb far enough up the hill to make a great deal of difference; and none of the vineyards is classified First Growth (*Premier Cru*). Both red and white wines could be made, but in practice all are red.

Chromatography

A process of analysis by selective absorption of a mixture of substances on a porous material. In wine-making, paper is generally used. Chromatography has been found to be effective in assessment of certain organic acids as well as in the differentiation between *Vitis vinifera* and hybrids.

Chusclan

One of the best communes of the Côtes du Rhône, producing rosé wines.
See Rhône.

Cider

Fermented juice of sweet apples, commonly made in England, France, and other parts of Europe. English settlers introduced it into North America.

The apples were first reduced to a pulp known as "pomace." At first this was done by beating the apples in a stone or wooden trough with wooden paddles; but the earlier practice was supplanted by the cider "mill," consisting of a large wheel that revolved on its side in a circular trough filled with apples and reduced the fruit to a jelly. (The modern method is to place the apples between two cylinders equipped with sharp knives which, when revolved at high speed, perform the same operation much more quickly.) The pomace was then made into a "cheese" to be pressed. This "cheese" was produced by putting on a bed of straw enough of the pomace to make a pile several inches high, followed by another layer of straw at a different angle from the first, and then more pomace. Care was taken that the straw was not only on the top and bottom of the "cheese" but could fold over the sides as well to keep it in shape and act as a filter during pressing. When the "cheese" was about three feet high, it was taken to a press and then squeezed until all the juice had been taken out of it. Today, the substitution

of collapsible forms which mold the "cheese" and are removed before pressing, using cloths instead of straw, brings the procedure up to date without changing any of the essentials. Now, however, the dry pomace is no longer fed to the pigs, as it often was in earlier times. Once the juice of the pomace has been expressed, it is put into vats or barrels to ferment until it is quite dry.

On some of the Somerset and Normandy farms, it will then be aged for a year or more and will be unexpectedly strong. Commercially manufactured cider will sometimes have cultivated yeasts added to the natural fermentation. Sweet cider is filtered before all the sugar has fermented out; the champagne type continues to ferment in the bottle; the cheaper sparkling ciders are carbonated.

Cinqueterre

White Italian wine made from Vernaccia grapes. *See* Liguria.

Cinsault (or Cinsaut)

Grape used in the wines of southwest France, the Midi, the Rhône Valley, and Algeria. It is known also as Picardan Noir, Espagne, Malaga, and by other local names. In combination with Grenache, this grape produces warmth and fullness in the wine.

Cirò di Calabria

One of the best-known red wines of Calabria (*q.v.*), Italy.

Citric Acid

Though abundant in citrus fruits and at least present in most others, this acid is found only in very small amounts in grapes, and hence very little of it is found in wine. $COOH \cdot CH_2 \cdot C(OH)(COOH) \cdot CH_2 \cdot COOH$.

Clairet

In French, formerly a light blend of red and white wine or sometimes simply a very light red one. From the word was derived the English claret, applied to the red wines of Bordeaux.

Nowadays, a Clairet is not a rosé but a light red wine, supple and fruity but lacking in tannin—one that can be drunk cool and young. A good Clairet is the product of grape varieties which tend to give a delicate wine of this nature, and which, because of low acidity, have been allowed to achieve full maturity. The skins of the fruit are not left in the fermenting vat for more than a day or two. So that malolactic fermentation may not be hindered, the wine is lightly treated with sulfur. Once alcohol and malolactic fermentation have been fully achieved, the wine is stabilized by fining or by treatment with sulfur.

Clairette de Bellegarde

White wine.
District: Southern France.

The commune of Bellegarde, about ten miles from Nîmes, southern France, makes a small, light, yellow wine from the Clairette grape variety. Grown on a mass of pebbles washed down by an arm of the River Rhône, it is one of the few white wines of the Languedoc area enjoying an Appellation Contrôlée, or legal place-name. Subject to the usual restrictions of geographical area and pruning, and required to attain 11.5% of alcohol, the wine must also—and this is not universal under French wine law—submit to a committee of tasters and receive their seal of approval, which will go on the bottle. Otherwise, it cannot be called Clairette de Bellegarde. The commune produces an average of 6,000 hectoliters (159,000 U.S. gallons, 132,000 imp.) of Clairette each year.

See Languedoc.

Clairette de Die

White wine.
District: Southern France.

A semi-sparkling, yellowish-gold wine and a still wine made in 25 parishes around the village of Die on the River Drôme—a tributary of the Rhône—in southeast France. Produced from grapes of the Clairette and Muscat de Frontignan, Clairette de Die dates back to Roman times, when it was the wine of Dea Augusta.

In making the wine, the growers must use a minimum of 50% Clairette and may vinify by either one of two methods. The modern way is the Champagne process of secondary fermentation in the bottle. The other is the more traditional "rural" way. Following this method, the maker allows his wine to ferment slowly, filtering frequently and adding sulfur in small quantities to slow down the yeasts. The sulfur has a cleansing effect, killing all the harmful bacteria. When the wine has finished its first fermentation, the vintner closes it up tightly in the barrel and allows any unresolved sugar to re-ferment. He puts it through a pressure filter and effectively stops all action, purifying his wine but allowing the carbon dioxide gas which has been generated to remain in it. This is the more usual process at present.

The result is a more or less sparkling wine with a pronounced flavor of Muscat and an alcoholic content of at least 10.5%. The average yearly output is 40,000 hectoliters (1,060,000 U.S. gallons, 880,000 imp.), most of which is produced by the Cave Cooperative de Die. Appreciation of this wine is an acquired taste.

Clairette du Languedoc

White wines.
District: Southern France.

The great plain of Languedoc in southern France stretches from Arles, near the River Rhône, toward the Spanish border and produces almost half of the wines of France. Very few of these, however, are more than the most ordinary of *vins ordinaires*. Scattered here and there are small holdings of vineyards whose product has been considered good enough to be controlled by French law as wines of Appellation d'Origine Contrôlée. Clairette du Languedoc is one example.

The wine is grown principally in the seven communes of Adissan, Aspiran, Paulhan, Fontès, Cabrières, Péret, and Ceyras, somewhat to the west of Montpellier in the department of Hérault. Two types of wine are made along the sun-scorched slopes, both coming only from grapes of the Clairette vine, with some Picpoule and Terret. The first is that wine carrying on its label simply Clairette de Languedoc, with or without the name of the commune of origin. This is a dry, heavy, white wine of at least 13% of alcohol. The other has the qualification *rancio (q.v.)* added to it. To earn the name of *rancio*, this unpleasant wine must come from grapes which have been left on the vine until well after they are ripe. The wine must have an alcoholic content of at least 14%, must be allowed to maderize and age for at least three years before it is put on sale, and must have the taste characteristics associated with a rancio.

The vineyards growing the Clairette du Languedoc comprise about 1,130 hectares (2,800 acres) and average production is less than 11,200 hectoliters (297,000 U.S. gallons, 265,000 imp.).

See Languedoc.

Claret

In Great Britain, and frequently in the United States, red Bordeaux is known as claret.

From the first days of the wine trade with the Bordelais (which began to flourish early in the thirteenth century), the pinkish light wine became a favorite in England and has remained so. The French called it Clairet; the blunter English tongue clubbed it into claret—but the wine was not claret as we know it now. At the time of the Roman occupation, wines were aged; but not again, until almost modern times, was Bordeaux anything but "wine of the year," drunk sometimes as early as two weeks after its harvesting—or the time it took the fleet of wine ships to return to England. It was a wine very briefly fermented. The practice was for a listener to stand posted with ear to the vat, and soon after the boiling of fermentation was heard, the wine was run off.

Today, too, some wine is made after a short fermentation of less than four days. With the new taste for young light wine, Clairet is again being produced in Bordeaux, and it is so called to distinguish it from claret, now the term for the old red wine of Bordeaux. It is also called rosé; and recently this rosé from Bordeaux has become very popular and many excellent examples are made.

Bordeaux Clairet—or rosé—is not red and white wine blended together, though in the past the light claret sometimes was *vinum claratum* (clarified wine), often confused with *vinum clarum* (wine light and clear by its nature). Clarified wine was common white wine added traditionally to red wines which were too murky; but the mingling of red and white wines to make Clairet or rosé is forbidden by law throughout France today.

See Bordeaux.

Clarete

A Spanish term used mostly in the Rioja district for any red wine with a light body and color.

Classical wines

A great deal is known about wine and the vine in ancient Greece and Rome. In viticulture, in particular, methods have not changed radically since about 700 B.C., when Hesiod wrote of the planting and pruning of the vines on his Boeotian farm. What we cannot learn from books is exactly how the wines tasted, and so modern specialists in the subject pursue their own fancies. One says that the liquors would have been disgusting to us, boiled down to a muddy sediment, smoked, cloyed with honey, ruined with resin or salt water. Another maintains that those Greek wines kept to a ripe age actually were what the primitive heroes believed them to be—the most divine drink ever enjoyed by man. A few shipwrecked amphorae dredged up from the bottom of the Mediterranean are still in existence and still sealed. The date and the name of shipper or grower are decipherable; but if the jars were opened, the tantalizing liquid inside—brackish and half-evaporated—would not taste like wine. It was the opinion of the nineteenth-century wine historian Cyrus Redding that the better growths probably tasted like Malvasia, or the sweet wines of Cyprus, which (in his day as sometimes in ours) were made by the traditional methods.

GREECE

Vines grew from earliest times in Greece and the Greek islands, and the inhabitants were naturally wine-drinking people. In the adventures of Odysseus wine played an important part. Nausicaa, when she found Odysseus by the stream, revived him with food and the wine she had brought in a goatskin bottle. Later on, in the king's palace, he ate and drank with Alcinous and the chieftains; and afterward the king said: " 'Mix the bowl and serve out the wine to all in the hall, that we may pour forth before Zeus' . . . and Pontonius mixed the honey-hearted wine and served it out to all when he had poured for libation into each cup in turn." (A custom that might be compared with the loyal toast.)

Sweet Wines. Generally, the wine seems to have been sweet. That with which Odysseus made the Cyclops drunk was given to him by Maron—"sweet wine, unmingled, a draught for the Gods." When Maron broached this best vintage (he kept it hidden from his servants)—"that red wine, honey sweet"—he would mix it in the silver bowl with twenty parts to one of water, "and a marvellous sweet smell went up from the mixing-bowl." Hesiod's wine would have been sweet too—he spread the grapes in the sun for ten days after they were

picked. Just so, Mago of Carthage, about 550 B.C., and Columella, repeating six hundred years later his instructions for making *passum optimum* (the best luscious wine), said that the sun-dried grapes should be laid out on a raised frame and covered with reeds until they were sufficiently shriveled—after which they would be kept in a jar of good must for six days, before pressing. The practice is near enough to that followed in the making of straw wines today. Sweet wines have never lost their appeal for the people of southern Italy, of Cyprus and the Aegean. It is not surprising that the ancient Greeks liked them and that they preferred old wine to new—even now, the rich Commandaria of Cyprus may live to a great age. The best wines are said to have been made from a blend of red and white grapes; and the famous Pramnian must have been an essence like Tokay.

Mixing of Wines. Not all Greek wines, however, were pure and unmingled. Sometimes honey was put in the wine jars. Pliny was later to describe the Greek habit of invigorating wine with potter's earth, powdered marble, and salt water. And, although the use of resin in ancient Greece is not unanimously accepted, it is improbable that the pitch-pine so common in early Roman viniculture and surviving in the peasant wine-making of modern Greece was really avoided in classical Greece. The mixing of sea water in the must was not quite as crude as it sounds. The water (taken from the sea when it was calm) was boiled down to one-third of its original volume (with spices for flavoring), strained, and kept for several years before use. One wine would be improved by blending with another; great growths which had been kept until they were sticky and thick as honey were often fit for nothing else, and many of the well-matured sweet vintages had to be strained before drinking. These would be mixed with water—indeed, the Greeks usually drank their wine well diluted. Sometimes, as a finishing touch, they would add perfumes.

Wine-jars and Pots. At an Athenian dinner-party, while the guests (all men usually) reclined on sofas, slaves would mix wine and water in bowls, take the mixture around in jugs, and pour it into each cup. First a libation would be offered; then the host or leader of the feast would decide how much wine was to be taken, and how strong it should be. In summer, the wine would be cooled with snow brought down from the mountains. Many of the pots and jars for the keeping and serving of wine have been preserved. *Pithoi* (Latin: *dolia*) were the fermenting jars. For the better conservation of lighter wines, these would be smeared with pitch and sunk in the ground. Amphorae were the tall two-handled jars in which the wine was aged and brought from the storeroom; the squatter *hydria* was the covered water pot which was taken out to be filled at the fountain; the *krater* was a wide bowl for mixing wine and water; the *kantharos* a ladling cup with two handles; the *kylix* a shallow goblet, somewhat like a Champagne glass—when the wine was drained, a surprising picture would sometimes be discovered at the bottom. In classical Greece, where there was no paper and little papyrus, talented artists and topical illustrators used wine jars as their canvases. On these we can see the Greeks at their banquets, and expensive flute-players and dancing-girls who sometimes came to entertain them, or the young men aiming their heel-taps into a raised saucer in the game of *kottabos,* said to have been invented in Sicily. As he flung the dregs, a youth would often invoke a girl's name.

Women and Wine. Women, apart from *hetairai* and flute-girls, seldom came to these parties, but some of the courtesans had strong heads, and from Nausicaa onward, Greek women generally drank wine—which is only to be expected in a country where it is the normal drink. A lot has been written by old writers about almost legendary times in Greece and the austere early days in Rome, when women drank nothing but innocuous *sapa* (unfermented wine); but the women of a more sophisticated Rome drank with the men and sometimes got very drunk. As for the Greek rites of Dionysos, a fever which broke out originally in Thrace, women were the more numerous of the worshippers and the more violent—and even when the worship of the wine god had sobered down to a ritual without Maenad dances and destruction, women, as Mr. Charles Seltman has pointed out, still made Bacchic pilgrimages to Delphi.

ROME

Wild vines flourished in the temperate zones that border the Mediterranean, and no doubt the primitive people who lived there made a weak kind of wine. But the Greeks, the Phoenicians—wine-makers also—and ultimately the Romans, taught the natives to prune their vines and make a wine that would keep. The Greeks were early and adventurous navigators, and their first Italian settlement is believed to have been made by Euboeans at Cumae, on the coast of Campania, probably in the eighth century B.C. By the end of the seventh century B.C. there were Greek cities along the east coast of Sicily and around the Tarantine Gulf, as well as on the mainland. Whether or not it is true that the Greeks found the Etruscans already making good wine from cultivated vines, it is accepted as fact that these people were fond of luxury and feasts, in which the women took part and drank their share. In general, it is assumed the Romans learned viticulture and viniculture from the Greeks and passed on the knowledge to most of the people they conquered. The first true wine was precious and used sparingly: a victorious general vowed only a single cup to Jupiter. At a time when small cultivators were being persuaded to take vine-tending seriously, Numa Pompilius (715–673 B.C.) is said to have forbidden the people to make libations with wine from unpruned vines.

Roman Viticulture. The earliest first-hand account in Latin of Roman vines and wines comes down to us from Cato the Censor (234–149 B.C.). From *De Agri Cultura,* his book on farming (referred to with admiration by Pliny two hundred years later), from Pliny the Elder himself, and from Columella (roughly contemporary with him), we get the most connected account of vine-growing—how to plant and graft, when to prune—and of wine-making in the first century A.D. and earlier. Pliny relates that even

in his day some of the vines, particularly in Campania, were allowed to grow as tall as houses and to twine around treetops, so that a man hired to prune them had to ask for danger money. But "here our vines are kept short by pruning," he wrote, "in order that their strength may be concentrated in the shoots." Grape varieties in Greece he believed to be uncountable, and in Italy he knew of eighty sound wines, the best of which were from the Aminean grape (dividing into five varieties), the Nomentane vines with red-tinged stalks, and the Muscatel, which flourished greatly in Tuscany. All these were indigenous. Among others transplanted from Greece and the islands, he picked out the Graecula (rivaling the Aminean), and the Eugenia, successfully imported from Taormina to the Alban district. The Rhaetian and the pine-flavored Allobrogian from Gaul would not produce quality wines on Italian soil, but they made up for it in quantity.

How the Wine Was Made. The natural flavor of pitch (or resin) in the Allobrogian grape was considered desirable, since the Romans smeared the insides as well as the outsides of their wine jars with this piny gum. In the twelfth book of his *Res Rustica,* in which he outlines the innumerable duties of a steward's wife, Columella gives clear instructions for doing this. Then he describes various ways of preserving the must: with liquid resin mixed with vine-ash, with salt water and sweet herbs and spices. So that they might age more quickly, the wine jars were kept in a loft above the *fumarium,* or smoke-room, where wood was seasoned. In the city, those not in need of smoking would be kept in public cellars (or in private ones) and treated much as wines are today. Even the apparently superstitious rule that wine should never be racked except in a north wind becomes reasonable when one realizes that the opposing wind in parts of Italy is apt to be the sirocco, maddening men and turning milk sour. Pliny considered that, within reason, smoking improved the flavor of wine; but he had hard things to say of the forced ageing by smoke of wines imported from Narbonne, some of which might also be adulterated with obnoxious herbs and drugs. The only Gallic wine he seems to have found passable was that from Marseille. The Spanish he liked better, rating the growths of Tarragona, Lauron, and the Balearics as high as the best Italian.

The Prized Wines. Imported Greek wines, of course, were held in high esteem, although not so rich and rare in Pliny's lifetime as they had been two generations earlier, when guests at a dinner party would not be offered more than one glass. In the first century A.D., the Greek was rivaled by the Falernian. The Greek islands (Lesbos, Chios, Thasos) which shipped the favorite wines knew the value of publicity: they had their coinage stamped with clusters of grapes or with the head of Dionysos. All these expensive growths, Greek and Italian, must have gone untasted by the common people, who no doubt washed down their meals with drafts as new and as ordinary as our *vin ordinaire.*

The Romans made black (very dark red) wines, clear red, amber, and white ones; those they laid down for ageing were as concentrated as the old vintages of Greece.

In the *Satyricon* of Petronius, the newly rich tycoon Trimalchio produces at his supper party (overloaded, pretentious, but not well conducted) a little glass amphora labeled *Opimian Muscadine, a Century old*. "Alas," he said, "that wine should live longer than man. We'll try if it has held good ever since the consulship of Lucius Opimius." This wine of a vintage year (121 B.C.), as celebrated as the Comet Year of 1811, was one of the longest lived in history. When Pliny tasted it, it was so dried and thick that it had to be scraped off the sides of the amphora and mixed with a younger wine. Trimalchio also offered his guests a *vino cotto* "boiled off a third part and kept underground to preserve its strength." Before the meal, there had been *antepasti*—a honey-sweet aperitif and the olives and hot sausages that would appear at a cocktail party today, and dormice covered with honey and poppy-seed, which would not.

SOME LITERARY SOURCES OF CLASSICAL WINE LORE

Greek

Homer. From references throughout the *Iliad* and the *Odyssey*, a few of which have been quoted above, we know that the heroes of epic times—and their women—habitually drank wine. We know they liked it sweet and diluted with water; and how they served it and poured libations, in princely gatherings, between the eleventh and the eighth centuries B.C.

Hesiod. The first plain if limited account of viticulture in Europe is to be found in Hesiod's *Works and Days*. The Boeotian farmer-poet, writing in about 700 B.C., reckoned his calendar by the stars, but he pruned and planted his vines much as small-holders do to this day. It is clear that he had to work hard on his land, and he complained of the oppressions of the local princes.

Alcaeus. The lyric poet of Mytilene, who flourished a hundred years after Hesiod, was himself one of the nobles of Lesbos. Island tyrants rose and fell and his love-songs and verses in praise of wine ("Hurry, my boy, and pour me out a cup of luscious Lesbian wine") were interspersed with patriotic odes. His "Let us drink and dance, since Myrsilus is dead" is the model for Horace's ode on the death of Cleopatra, which begins *Nunc est bibendum*. Alcaeus was banished for his political behavior, and Sappho may have been exiled at the same time.

Anacreon. A generation or so later, Anacreon of Teos came to Athens. He was another lyric poet and boon companion, singing of wine and garlands. He referred to the game of *kottabos*—"heel-taps flying from the Teian cup."

Plato, Xenophon, Aristophanes. In the great classical age of Athens, they described the drinking customs of their time: Aristophanes by topical references in his comedies; Plato and Xenophon each by a *Symposium* in which Socrates took part, giving a valuable account of a Greek supper party.

Dioscorides. For sixteen hundred years from the time when it was written (in the first century A.D.), his *Materia Medica* remained the authority on every vegetable substance used in medicine and on natural, medicinal, and doctored wines, both Greek and Roman.

Galen. This great physician, born in Asia Minor, court doctor to Marcus Aurelius, was also a connoisseur of wines. Searching in the Palatine cellars for the best Falernian for his master, he would only consider that which had reached twenty years of age. Athenaeus referred to his surpassing output in philosophical and medical writings, and to his *Treatise on Wines*—but these were lost.

Athenaeus. The author of the long-winded *Deipnosophists* (learned, indeed pedantic, banqueters) is an unrivaled source of gossip and information, accurate or not. In long dialogues and discussions on fish, riddles, wine-making, cheesecakes, and the use of words he inserts quotations from almost every author of his day (c. A.D. 230) and earlier. His accounts of different kinds of wine are valuable; his preservation of fragments of lost writings even more so. Athenaeus himself was born at Naucratis in Egypt. As his work proves, he was a great reader and amasser of encyclopedic knowledge. The *Deipnosophists* is a description of a banquet at the house of Laurentinus, a Roman noble. Galen was one of the guests.

Latin

Cato. The first practical account, written in Latin, of Roman wine-growing appeared in *De Agri Cultura* by Cato the Censor, a hard-headed old Roman born on a farm in 234 B.C. Pliny, writing two hundred years later, quoted some of his precepts with approval.

Marcus Varro. This "learned historian," who lived in the time of Julius Caesar and Augustus Caesar, wrote a handbook on farming, *De Re Rustica*, always considered one of the best of its kind and not begun until his eightieth year. He gives lucid instructions on vine-tending and wine-making, and cites in his work the maxims of earlier Greek writers—and of Mago of Carthage.

Virgil. Because of his supremacy as a poet, Virgil's second *Georgic* is one of the (if not *the*) best-known works on the vine. Yet he was not an experienced cultivator (although his father was a farmer), and Varro was said to be his authority. Pliny remarked that, gracious poet though he was, Virgil only mentioned fifteen varieties of grape.

Pliny the Elder (A.D. 23–79). Book XIV of his *Naturalis Historia* is devoted to vines and different kinds of wines with recipes for making them. He referred in his work to most of the important wine writing then extant. Always keen in pursuit of scientific knowledge, he died investigating an eruption of Vesuvius.

Horace. He knew wine (and grew it), and famous vintages are mentioned in the *Odes* and *Satires*—Chian, Lesbian, Caecuban, and Falernian. The Lesbian, he said, was harmless, leaving no headache. Calenian, produced near the Falernian vineyards, was one of the wines he liked, and he offered it to his patron Maecenas in place of the Falernian he could not afford.

Juvenal and *Martial.* Both were writers of satire, flourishing about A.D. 100. Each wrote of wines and of customs fashionable at the time. Martial especially has a lot to tell—of old wives' tales about wine, about faked wines from Marseille, etc.

Petronius. Very little is known about him. He may have been the same Titus Petronius who was known as a lazy, dissipated fellow, who yet managed to be a consul. His account of Trimalchio's feast in the *Satyricon* has already been mentioned.

Columella. Of this writer, also, little is known. From internal evidence he seems to have been born about the beginning of the first century at Cadiz. He had an uncle, also Columella, a farmer in Spain, whom he sometimes quoted. He wrote a book about trees and twelve books of *Res Rustica,* a remarkably clear and complete treatise on Roman farming and viniculture. In Books III and IV are detailed directions for planting and dressing a vineyard; in Book XII (the responsibilities of the steward's wife) instructions on preparing the vintage, making wine, correcting the must, and so on.

Ausonius. The Bordeaux professor who became tutor to the future Emperor Gratian (son of Valentinian), and afterward governor of the province of Gaul and a consul, retired in old age to his villa and his vineyards—he had one at Pauillac, another small property on the Dordogne, and later, a property in the Charente district. It is by no means certain that he ever lived on the site of Château Ausone. During his travels with the Emperor Valentinian he visited the Mosel Valley, which delighted him because it reminded him of the Bordeaux vineyards. In his writings, however, he had more to say about food than about wine.

SOME ANCIENT WINES

Descriptions of the following wines whose names have not been forgotten are collected from the writers listed above, who sometimes contradicted each other. Some of them would grow lyrical about rose and violet in the bouquet of a wine, as writers on wine do now.

Greek

Maronean. This, already referred to as the wine that Odysseus gave to Polyphemus, was described by Pliny as the most ancient of all—grown near the Thracian shore, dark in color, and generally mixed with eight parts of water to one of wine. According to Pliny, the Maronean retained in his day all its strength and vigor.

Pramnian. This most glorious wine of antiquity was said by Homer to be Nestor's favorite, and the wine—"very strong and nutritious"—which he gave to the wounded Machaon with relishes of goat cheese and raw onions. It was the base of Circe's magic potion and still known in Athens when Aristophanes was writing—he did not care for it. It was the opinion of Dioscorides that the grapes pressed out the must by their own weight (thus producing a rich essence); but Athenaeus reported that it was neither a sweet nor a thick wine, but dry and hard and extraordinarily strong.

Chian. According to more than one writer this was the best of Greek wines, "faultless, never causing a headache," and the island's first growths appear to have been Phanean and the wine of Arisium. Horace got in amphorae of Chian for a party and gave orders that half of it

should be mixed for the temperate guests, nine cups of water to three of wine; the rest for the hard drinkers, nine cups of wine to three of water. The Chians, who were great gourmets, had a legend that the son of Dionysos first taught them to make the dark red wine. Evidently it was sweet and rather thick.

Lesbian. This was a sweet wine. "How sweet the Pramnian Lesbian wine," said one of the characters quoted by Athenaeus (thus, Pramnian must have been a type, not a place-name). Some declared it the nicest of all but, in the opinion of Athenaeus, it was less astringent, more diuretic than the Chian, and not so pleasant. No sea water was mixed with it, he said.

Thasian. A "rich and rosy" wine, said to have been a noble growth when mellowed by age. Theophrastus told that it was "wonderfully delicious and well flavored; they knead dough with honey and put that in the jars, so that the wine receives sweetness from the honey and fragrance from itself." It was a wine that had to be strained.

Coan. The wine of the island of Cos, where Hippocrates wrote his famous treatise on medicine, was heavily mixed with sea water and white in color. Cato gives a recipe for faking it with Italian wine and salt. It has been described as headachy.

Bybline. Originally the famous wine of ancient Byblos in northern Syria. Vines were probably transplanted to Thrace afterward. It must have been sweet and fragrant. Hesiod wrote, "In weary summer, when the goats are fattest and the wine is at its best, then let me have the shadow of a rock and some Bybline wine."

Helbon, or *Chalybon.* A celebrated sweet wine of Syria, made near Damascus and mentioned in the Bible. It was a favorite of the Persian kings.

Roman

Falernian. The most famous of all the Roman wines was often praised by Horace, although Pliny classified it among the second growths, while admitting that it ranked high at that time. He added that it was the only wine which would take fire when lighted, and that it came in three styles: light and dry, yellow, sweet and dark. Trimalchio's Opimian wine was a Falernian. Galen's view was that the wine (of other years than the Opimian, presumably) was not fit to drink until it was ten years old, at its best between fifteen and twenty, and liable to give one a headache after that. Redding, describing the Falernian that grew in volcanic Campania near Naples, where Massic was also produced—rough, dark, and strong until it grew mellow—guessed that it would have resembled Lacrima Christi.

Setine. The favorite of Augustus Caesar, diplomatically placed in the first class by Pliny. Athenaeus also recorded that it was first-class, "like Falernian," but lighter and not so apt to make one drunk. It was produced at Setia on the Appian Way.

Caecuban. Another of Pliny's "firsts." Athenaeus said it was a wine of breed, generous and heady, not reaching its peak for many years. Horace knew it; but the vineyards disappeared when Nero started to make a canal from Lake Baiae to Ostia.

Alban. The wine of Alba, referred to by various writers, seems to have been of two kinds, sweet and dry. Pliny classified it a "third," and it was said to be good for the stomach.

Sorrentine. Opinions differed about this. Galen considered it was no good until it was twenty-five years old. Doctors recommended it for the health, but Tiberius called it "generous vinegar." Pliny said it was made from Aminean grapes, grown low on props.

Mamertine. The wine was produced near Messina, in Calabria. Galen found it light, well balanced, and pleasing. Julius Caesar brought it into fashion when, to celebrate his third Consulship in 46 B.C., he dispensed not two wines but four: Falernian, Chian, Lesbian, and Mamertine. A wine of that name, pale in color, high in alcohol, is still made in the same district.

Classification of 1855

See Bordeaux.

Clean

A clean wine is one that is refreshing and agreeable, without any definite off-taste.

Château Clerc-Milon

Bordeaux red wine.
District: Haut-Médoc, France.
Commune: Pauillac.

Adjoining Châteaux Lafite and Mouton-Rothschild, the vineyard is a Fifth Growth (*Cinquième Cru*) of the Médoc as classified in 1855. The property was purchased by Baron Philippe de Rothschild in 1970, joining his other two Pauillac growths, Mouton-Rothschild and Baron-Philippe.

Characteristics. Well-made wines with typical Pauillac traits: hard at the outset, full-bodied, and quite rich.

Vineyard area: 25 hectares (62.5 acres).
Average production: 100 *tonneaux* (9,000 cases).

Climat

Burgundian term for a vineyard, equivalent of Growth (*Cru*) in Bordeaux.

Château Climens

Bordeaux white wine.
District: Sauternes, France.
Commune: Barsac.

One of the two best vineyards in Barsac—the other is Château Coutet, an eighth of a mile away—Climens stands in a winding country lane running between old stone walls and marked at turnings with golden arrows to direct visitors along the Route de Sauternes. Entitled to either of the place-names, Barsac or Sauternes, the wine often uses Barsac-Sauternes. (In the past Barsac was a celebrated district; but since 1936 the wines of the com-

mune have been allowed to take the name of Sauternes, which has become more famous. Barsac wines are legitimate Sauternes, slightly lighter and drier.)

In 1855, the year Climens was classified a First Growth (*Premier Cru*) of Sauternes, M. Henri Gounouilhou acquired the property, and his heirs sold it in 1971 to Lucien Lurton of Brane-Cantenac and Durfort in Margaux, and Bouscaut in Graves. The unpretentious low wooden château is not lived in by the proprietors; but the *chais* across the gravel courtyard from it are large and impressive. The vineyard is four-fifths in Sémillon vine and one-fifth in Sauvignon and Muscadelle, and in the summer after the February 1956 freeze it presented a tragic picture. Most of the vines were blackened stubs, with hardly a sprout of green, and Climens vintages of 1956 and 1957 were non-existent. Afterward, the vines began to bear again, except in those patches so badly struck they had to be replanted. All the flat-lying Sauternes vineyards were in the same plight.

Characteristics. A wine which is much better when young. It reaches the height of finesse in great years. For sheer delicacy in sweetness, the beautiful 1929s, 1947s, 1949s, and 1971s were classics. In such years, Climens possibly excels Château d'Yquem—it is lighter, with less vinosity and body, yet miraculously subtle.

Vineyard area: 30 hectares (75 acres).
Average production: 65 *tonneaux* (6,000 cases).

Château Clinet

Bordeaux red wine.
District and Commune: Pomerol, France.

Traditionally one of the best growths of Pomerol, the château is now owned by Georges Audy and makes a sound but unremarkable wine.

Vineyard area: 6 hectares (15 acres).
Average production: 35 *tonneaux* (3,400 cases).

Clinton

Productive American vine giving small, black, spicy grapes yielding wines suitable for blending but little else. The vine is mostly cultivated for root-stock for other vines rather than for its fruit.

Clone

A group of individual plants propagated asexually from one single source.

Clos

A walled vineyard—or a vineyard which was once enclosed by a wall. These occur mainly in Burgundy. Some of their wines are sufficiently important to be entered under individual headings. Other well-known vineyards are as follows: Le Clos (Pouilly-Fuissé); Les Clos (Chablis); Les Clos (Côte Rôtie); Clos des Arlots (Nuits-Saint-Georges-Prémeaux); Clos Blanc (Pommard); Clos de la Boudriotte (Chassagne); Clos du Chapitre (Fixin); Clos de la Commaraine (Pommard); Clos des Corvées (Nuits-Saint-Georges-Prémeaux); Clos des Ducs (Volnay); Clos des Forêts-Saint-Georges (Nuits-Saint-Georges-Prémeaux); Clos des Lambrays (Morey); Clos de la Maréchale (Nuits-Saint-Georges-Prémeaux); Clos des Mouches (Beaune); Clos du Papillon (Savennières-Loire); Clos des Perrières (Meursault); Clos des Porrets-Saint-Georges (Nuits); Clos des Réas (Vosne); Clos du Roi (Aloxe-Corton); Clos du Roi (Beaune); Clos Saint-Jacques (Gevrey); Clos Saint-Jean (Chassagne); Clos Saint-Paul (Givry); Clos Saint-Pierre (Givry).

Clos de Bèze

See Chambertin-Clos de Bèze.

Clos Fourtet

See Fourtet, Clos.

Clos Haut-Peyraguey

See Haut-Peyraguey.

Cloudy

Cloudiness in wine is caused by tiny particles in suspension and often clears spontaneously. This condition is sometimes brought on by a rapid and excessive change in temperature.

Coarse

Cheap California "burgundies" or most French, Italian, and Spanish *vins ordinaires* are basically coarse wines. They both have plenty of body but are completely without character or finesse.

Cobblers

In America, long iced drinks concocted with fruit juice, wine, or spirits and decorated with pieces of fruit or berries.

Cochineal

Grubs of various sorts which attack the vines (*see* Chapter Eight, p. 29).

Cochylis moth

The Cochylis pest, attacking by laying eggs on the grapes and eventually smothering them in cocoons, was formerly one of the most dangerous enemies of the vine. It was fought ineffectively by nicotine and arsenic. Now, however, the Swiss chemicals Nirosan and Gesarol, sprayed individually or used in combination with Bordeaux mixture (copper-sulfate and chalk solution), are successful in eradicating the pest.
See Chapter Eight, p. 29.

Cocktail

A mixed aperitif, containing spirits and served iced in small glasses. The best-known examples are the Manhattan (two parts rye whiskey to one of Italian vermouth, and a dash of bitters) and the Dry Martini (four parts gin and one part French vermouth—which in the United States is sometimes sprinkled in with an atomizer).

Cocuy

Venezuelan liquor from the desert plant sabila.

Coffey still

The Coffey (or patent) still, developed by the Irish inspector-general of excise whose name it bears, made possible the rapid and therefore large-scale production of grain whisky. Other patent stills, such as the Barbet and Ilye, are now also in use.

Cognac

Brandy.
District: Western France.

In 1860 a French geologist named Coquand made a trip to the Charente district of France on the Bay of Biscay, an often misty seaboard region irradiated with a strange quality of ultraviolet light. With him he took an odd companion for a scientific excursion—a professional taster of brandies and wines. From farm to farm the pair went, from one brandy warehouse to another, each pursuing his own science. Coquand, the geologist, went into the vineyard and analyzed the soil; the taster merely stayed inside and sniffed and sipped the brandy. At the end of the trip the two compared notes on the qualities and characteristics of each of the Cognac brandies—one as he had deduced them from the soil, the other as he discovered them in the grape. And their notes tallied in every single case.

Coquand had proved his theory on the relationship of the soil and the Cognac, and this changing relationship accounts completely for the division of the region into six zones—Grande Champagne, Petite Champagne, Borderies, Fins Bois, Bons Bois, and Bois Ordinaires—but it does not quite account for Cognac.

It is interesting to speculate upon the unique excellence of Cognac and its causes. To begin with, there is the chalk in the soil—the exact degree decreasing from Grande Champagne down the range of officially marked-out areas to Bois Ordinaires, the value and the quality of the brandy decreasing with it. But chalk does not create a fine wine beverage in Cognac only—it produces Champagne and Sherry too. Chalk-lime is a mother-bed for exceptional vines.

Cognac wine (or, correctly, Charente wine—the name of the town had not then overspread the district) was always sourish, it seems; but in early days it was not distilled, and the acidity had not become a virtue. English and Norse seamen used to come to the Charente not for the wine but for the salt in the region; but once they were there they bought wine as well. In the centuries that followed the vineyards were encouraged to overproduce. The next significant development was that the wines were boiled down—to save space in the ships which carried them away, to strengthen them before the North Sea voyage, and finally to avoid taxation which was then on bulk. The idea was to reduce them and later on to restore them with water. Nobody could have imagined what a miraculous essence would be distilled from the hard Charente wines.

When Cognac was first distilled, sometime after 1600, other brandies were already being made in France: but where Charente wine gave a drinkable natural brandy, all other spirits—until the invention of multiple distillation a century later—had to be doctored by herb and fruit flavors to hide the bad taste. The final contributing factor to the unique perfection of Cognac was the barrel in which it was aged.

Immediately to the east above Charente, in the first rises of the Massif Central, where the River Charente has its source, is a forested district around Limoges, the land of Limousin oak.

When the distillation of Cognac was an art almost two hundred years old, the makers began to age the brandy in barrels of the Limousin oak which happened to be at hand. The result was Cognac as we know it now. Prices these days are high, and the oak forests of the world have been combed for another wood that would do for the brandy what the Limousin oak does. But there is no substitute. "It's hard to say which is more important, the wood or the wine," they tell you in Cognac. In one hectoliter (26.4 U.S. gallons, 22 imp.) of the brandy aged twenty-five years in the oak there will be one pound of wood extract, an immense factor in the bouquet and taste of old Cognac. The oak from the forest of Tronçais in the Allier was used extensively because of its fine grain. It gave excellent results though a little more slowly than the Limousin oak. It is used less and less, since its prices are extremely high.

Until 1860 Charente brandy was not shipped in bottle, and it probably was not called Cognac. Old-timers in the industry opposed shipping in bottle, saying that since brandy ages only in wood it should travel in the barrel. True though this was, bottling the brandy for the first time gave the makers control over what would be in the bottle when it reached the consumer. This is an example of a fundamental law in wine: the surest bottle is the one that passes through the hands of middlemen with its cork in. Moreover, the name on the label of the place the brandy came from became famous, until finally the brandy was known as Cognac.

Today there may be Coñacs and Koniaks (a Greek imitation now suppressed)—but there is only one Cognac by law in France, and in many other countries. It is specifically a brandy distilled from the wine of certain varieties of grapes grown in delimited areas of the Charente and Charente-Maritime departments of France (and to a very small extent in two others) and which has been twice distilled in a pot still—never in the more common continuous still—and has then been aged.

Roughly a century ago the whole vineyard was wiped out by the vine pest phylloxera, and the industry had to be restarted. The makers, while they were doing this, realized that the many neutral spirits then being developed by multiple distillation were competing in their own market; and since, because of the growing tendency to vend in bottle, the spirit could no longer be aged abroad, the Cognac firms themselves undertook the ageing of the brandies. The financial load may be assessed when it is considered that the sale of Cognac now touches 400 million new francs (or nearly 100 million dollars) a year, and that a man selling five-year-old Cognac must, of course, have the full supplies for five different years in stock. If his sales were exclusively of forty-year Cognac he ought theoretically to have forty years' worth in stock—which would demand an astronomical capital sum and warehouses of a size to cover half the Charente. With proportionately smaller stocks of older brandy, two firms today each hold about 52,000 barrels of old and new Cognac.

TYPES OF COGNAC

Nowadays most firms concentrate on three types of Cognac. The youngest, still rather raw, is best drunk with soda. The second is Three-Star, which amounts to about 65% of the Cognac sold. Various legends account for the star device; it began to be used about a century ago, when the blending of Cognacs to type was coming into fashion—it is said in Cognac that the first Three-Star was made and shipped for the Australian market. It is important to know that this sign does not mean that the brandy is three years old. It does, however, indicate a Cognac usually older than those designed for mixing with soda, and one always younger than a V.S.O.P. Generally, with many important firms, the Three-Star has about five years of barrel-age (spirits do not age in glass as wine does, so that an 1860 Cognac bottled in 1900 and a 1900 Cognac bottled in 1940 are exactly the same age).

The third type is V.S.O.P.: the letters stand for Very Superior Old Pale—somewhat contradictorily, because the longer a Cognac is left in the barrel to age the more of the darkening tannin it absorbs from the oak. It begins as a colorless liquid; tannin tans it. Very Superior Old Dark would be a more logical name.

As with Three-Star, V.S.O.P. is really a style of brandy, not a brandy of any specified age. It is the oldest of the three types described here; but many firms put out a Reserve, Extra, X.O., Cordon Bleu, or in rare cases even a straight vintage brandy, all in relatively small quantities.

In fact, a V.S.O.P. put out by one of the better houses may approach twenty years of barrel-age. It is essential to understand, however, that "twenty years old" refers to a type; Cognac, except in the "straight Cognacs," which are seldom made commercially now, is always a blend of brandies from different areas and different years. Each firm establishes its V.S.O.P.—the process is exactly the same for its Three-Star—and continues by skillful blending to copy the original model and so to repeat the same bottle over and over again. Master samples are kept, and with great care and art—by "sniffers," so called because they smell the Cognacs rather than taste them—diverse brandies are mixed to reproduce the sample, always from year to year in differing proportions to equalize the differences of the years. A "twenty-year-old" brandy is likely to contain Cognacs both older and younger than twenty years.

V.S.O.P. describes what the brandy is: i.e., a particular firm's interpretation of V.S.O.P. style. V.S.E.P. (E for Extra) is also seen sometimes on the U.S. market.

It is worth mentioning that the buyer gets greater value for his V.S.O.P. or the other older Cognacs than for Three-Star. Duty, casing, bottling, etc. are the same, and the extra cost for a much finer Cognac is often comparatively little, whereas enjoyment will be doubled.

VINTAGE AND AGE

Age is considered the great virtue in Cognac, and at present there are four age indications for the British-American market based on facts that can be checked. They are:

(1) In England, Cognac must be at least three years old by British law.
(2) In the United States, Cognac must be at least two years old by American law.
(3) V.S.O.P., by French law, must be at least four years old to be exported from France.
(4) British Bonded—Cognac shipped in cask to England and matured in the warehouses of London docks—is aged in bond, and a record of the years is kept. This record is generally authentic, and at the present time a British Bonded may be seen not only in England but also in the United States, because it bears the only age indication beyond the American legal minimum, and the Cognac can be sold at a premium which makes transshipment worth the trouble. In the trade, British Bonded is also known as "Old Landed" because it is landed before it is bottled. The style, matured in the London climate, very different from that of Cognac, has a somewhat clean, melted taste (which some people like and some do not); and it may be expected to have lost strength, as brandies do when they age in damp places. Yet some of the greatest Cognacs available today are London bottlings which have never been blended but are straight vintage brandies. Delicate with age, they often become the prototypes of great Cognac. Since the Second World War, shipment in cask to England has dwindled greatly.

In Cognac itself, the age of brandy is not controlled beyond five years. Six official categories exist after the new brandy: (1) one year old; (2) two years old; (3) three years old; (4) four years old; (5) five years old; (6) six years old and any number of years beyond. Like every other regulation in Cognac, these controls are rigid and reliable.

There is sound sense in limiting age control at a five-year maximum. Cognac is aged by shippers, by farmers, and by cooperatives. There are some 175 Cognac firms, numerous cooperative distillers, and, of the approximately 50,000 peasants and others who grow wine to make Cognac, a little over 20,000 distill and age some or all of their own product. Many firms sell under more than one name. In addition to this multiplicity of individuals, the great Cognac stores of the principal firms are spread in series of warehouses over the towns of Cognac and Jarnac and into the countryside. This is done to prevent a fire from destroying the stock; although indemnified by insurance, a firm wiped out by fire would need years to build up old brandies in order to re-establish its brands and by that time would have lost its customers. Faced with so many owners and so many small collections of casks, Cognac authorities know that a realistic control of very old brandies is impossible. "Most of all we value public confidence and we prefer not to certify anything we can't be absolutely sure of," they rightly say.

Except for an occasional British Bonded, no Cognac can be positively identified as more than five years of age. (The V.S.O.P. and older brands of all reputable houses of course *are* older, and the rare straight vintage Cognac from a fine firm will be exactly what it claims to be and perhaps very old—the point is that it can't be proved.) Less and less, Cognac makers themselves like to talk about age. "We go to the impractical, enormous cost of producing a twenty-year-old Cognac," they say, "and our reward is that the public thinks it is too young because it did not travel to and from Russia with Napoleon." The brandies would be no older than the day they were bottled if they *had* been on that march to Russia; and in fact, no brandy from that time is on the commercial market. Undoubtedly, the worst deception in Cognac brandies is the fraud and fakery connected with alleged "Napoleon" brandy—but a distinction must be made between brandies pretending to derive from Napoleon's time and the Napoleon-style. The latter is an indication akin to V.S.O.P., and the Cognac will be at least six years old.

Beyond an optimum of about forty years—it depends both on the Cognac and how it is housed—barrel-ageing itself ceases to be a good thing. Cognac from 1815 to 1850, which may still be tasted in the *paradises*—inner sanctums of the oldest casks—of firms in Jarnac and Cognac, are only echoes, although they are still useful in blends of very old Cognacs because they keep their bouquet after they have lost everything else.

The opinion in Cognac seems to be that within a dozen years V.S.O.P. brandies will not be more than ten years old and that Three-Star will dominate the output. Interest rates, duties, and taxes which double and triple the price of Cognac in most countries have made the price of a bottle so high that the makers cannot add the real cost of ageing old brandy; to do so would be to price it out of the market. Twenty-year-old V.S.O.P. is already considered by many firms to be a losing proposition. The debatable question is whether small firms selling very old Cognacs to a select clientele will be able to survive. It is regrettable that Three-Star Cognacs of the smaller houses are being driven out of business as the advertising campaigns of the biggest brands gather cumulative force. Some makers believe that in a generation there will be only a half-dozen or so mammoth firms; others, while admitting that the monopolies are likely to corner Three-Star and perhaps V.S.O.P., contend that there will always be sufficient demand for brandies too old ever to be produced on a big scale, and small de luxe houses will thus be kept alive.

Vintage in Cognac brandy is a debatable point. A "straight" Cognac is the brandy of one area and one year. Blending—the nearly universal practice in Cognac—clips off the peaks to fill up the valleys. But if this were always true, all blend Cognac would be a mere compromise, a concession to marketing conditions and the demand for a stable product. But most houses in Cognac contend that no region, and seldom any year, produces by itself a fully balanced, complete, and harmonious Cognac. Granting that Grande Champagne is the best region, finest in bouquet, finesse, elegance, and charm, they point out that the Borderies sector produces Cognacs with more body—a touch of heartiness often needed in a too-princely Grande Champagne.

GRANDE CHAMPAGNE, PETITE CHAMPAGNE, FINE CHAMPAGNE, FINE MAISON, BORDERIES, AND BOIS

Vineyards as such play no role in Cognac and do not appear on labels, but the following districts are important to know and are often indicated on labels of bottles in the higher categories. The vineland of Cognac—within the boundaries of which all wine that is to become Cognac must grow—is geographically proportioned as follows:

	%
Grande Champagne	14.65
Petite Champagne	15.98
Borderies	4.53
Fins Bois	37.82
Bons Bois	22.19
Bois Ordinaires	4.83

The order of quality, downward from Grande Champagne to Bois Ordinaires, is also a rough indication of the geographical order, Grande Champagne being the heart and the other zones circling it. All the districts produce some red wine (from which Cognac is never made) and some white wine which is not made into Cognac; the poorer the district the greater the proportion of these non-Cognac wines. Altogether, Cognac accounts for about half of the crude wine.

Grande Champagne

The best and the most expensive. But the difference in price is nothing like that between the wines of great vineyards and lesser ones in other famous areas. Grand Champagne has great finesse, bouquet, and elegance. But it is hard to the taste when young and must age fifteen years or longer; it has less body than Borderies but more body than Petite Champagne. It is also called Grande Fine Champagne.

Petite Champagne

Similar to Grande Champagne except that its characteristics appear in slightly lesser degree and it matures rather more quickly. The difference is due to a somewhat smaller proportion of chalk in the soil. In France, Champagne indicates a region of chalky soil.

Fine Champagne and Fine Maison

The old blend of brandies exclusively from the Grande and Petite Champagne district. The so-called house specialty of a restaurant in France is called Fine Maison and will vary in quality, from fair to excellent, depending on the desire and ability of the restaurant to give something special.

Borderies

The district does not, as is frequently supposed, "border" the regions of Petite and Grande Champagne. It faces them—and the town of Cognac—from across the River Charente on the north. It gives the Cognacs with the greatest body.

Fins Bois, Bons Bois, Bois Ordinaires

The lesser zones, much larger in area but less thickly planted in vine. All but a patch of the Bois Ordinaires lies along the shore, and the sea air has a tangible effect on the brandy.

OFFICIAL REGIONS OF COGNAC: COMMUNES ENTITLED TO THE MOST IMPORTANT NAMES

The zone within which Cognac may be produced is divided into six regions, of which Grande Champagne, Petite Champagne, and Borderies are the most important.

Grande Champagne (Grande Fine Champagne)

Communes: Ambleville, Angeac-Champagne, Bonneuil, Bourg-Charente (right bank of River Charente), Bouteville, Château-Bernard, Cognac (left bank of Charente), Critéuil-la-Magdeleine, Éraville, Gensac-la-Pallue, Genté, Gimeux, Gondeville, Juillac-le-Coq, Lignières-Sonneville, Mainxe, Malaville, Merpins, Salles-d'Angles, Saint-Brice (left bank of Charente), Saint-Fort-sur-le-Né, Saint-Même, Saint-Preuil, Segonzac, Touzac, Verrières, Viville.

Petite Champagne

Communes in the department of Charente: Angeac-Charente, Ars, Barbezieux, Barret, Birac, Bourg-Charente, Châteauneuf, Graves, Guimps, Jurignac, Lachaise, Ladiville, Lagarde-sur-le-Né, Montchaude, Mosnac, Nonaville, Saint-Amant-de-Graves, Saint-Bonnet, Saint-Hilaire-de-Barbezieux, Saint-Médard-de-Barbezieux, Saint-Palais-du-Né, Salles-de-Barbezieux, Vignolles.

Communes in the department of Charente-Maritime: Allas-Champagne, Archiac, Arthenac, Biron, Bougneau, Brie-sous-Archiac, Brives-sur-Charente, Celles, Chadenac, Champagnac, Cierzac, Coulonges, Clam, Échebrune, Germignac, Jarnac-Champagne, Jonzac, Lonzac, Meux, Moings, Montils, Neuillac, Neulles, Pérignac-de-Pons, Peaux, Rouffiac, Saint-Ciers-Champagne, Saint-Eugène, Saint-Germain-de-Lusignan, Saint-Germain-de-Vibrac, Saint-Martial-de-Coculet, Saint-Martial-de-Vitaterne, Saint-Maurice-de-Tavernolles, Saint-Lheurine, Saint-Seurin-de-Palenne, Saint-Sever, Salignac-de-Pons.

Borderies

Communes: Burie, Chérac, Cherves, Cognac (right bank of River Charente), Javrezac, Louzac, Saint-André, Saint-Laurent-de-Cognac, Saint-Sulpice, Richemont.

THE VINE AND THE WINE

The vine used to be largely Saint-Émilion. By law, sub-regional Cognac—that is, entitled to one of the district names of Grande Champagne, etc.—may be distilled from wine of only the Folle Blanche, Colombard, and Saint-Émilion vines. No other grape variety is authorized by the law. The law is very exact, and since 1955 any grower planting any part of his vineyards in unauthorized vine has his total crop refused.

Colombard and Folle Blanche together now account for less than 6% of the total yield, nearly all of which is Saint-Émilion, a variety of Ugni Blanc. In Cognac perhaps alone, the quantity of yield does not affect quality—and enormous quantity is achieved from the Saint-Émilion—whereas in all fine wine areas yield is strictly limited by law to protect quality.

This is one indication of the peculiar relationship between the wine and the brandy. It is a local axiom that the best Cognac comes from the worst wine. Rightly understood, this is true. The wine is tart, fit only to be drunk with shellfish—or not at all, if anything better is handy. On the other hand, it must be *sound*. Distillation removes neither perfections nor imperfections—it emphasizes them; if there is a taint in the wine, the Cognac distilled from it will be undrinkable. But the virtues in wine for drinking and in wine for making Cognac are not the same. Technically the Saint-Émilion is a third-epoch vine. It is the grape called the Trebbiano in Italy and the Ugni Blanc in Algeria, in the extreme south of France, and in California. In those hotter regions—in what viticulturalists, marking off growing zones for the vine, call the Third Epoch—it is quite at home. But in Cognac, much farther north, it is not: it seldom ripens properly and gives a sourish, highly acid wine low in alcohol—which happens to be the perfect basis for the world's best brandy.

LIFE-CYCLE OF A COGNAC

The countryside, rolling and misty, infused with that special clarity of actinic sunlight said to account in part for the taste of Cognac, possesses a few great stone châteaux, but the feeling of the landscape is much more primitive and simple than is that of the Loire Valley. The living unit in Cognac is not the castle but the close, a Saracen heritage. A wall encloses house, courtyard, sheds, and hen coops; it is broken only by two arched portals, which may be closed by great wooden doors.

Inside one of these domestic forts that dot the vineland, time may well seem to have stood still since the Saracens—and in a way it has. No peasant is more individual and independent than the Cognac grower. After all, he makes it his business to keep a supply of something far more stable than the fluctuating franc in his sheds.

The grapes are brought in from the vines, and the wine-making is much the same as in other regions. With distillation, the difference—and the Cognac—begins.

The wine is heated in a massive fixed copper kettle sitting in its bed—a square brick furnace—and after a time the furious brandy elements pass up as steam into the gracefully curved "swan-throat." Condensed by cooling, the steam becomes the *brouillis*—a milky liquid with an alcoholic strength of from 27% to 28%. The process is repeated, and this time the "head," which comes over first, and the "tail," which comes last, are eliminated—and only the "heart" of the distillate is used. This is the infant Cognac, raw and unsophisticated, a white brandy of 70% alcohol.

In spite of the seeming timelessness of the walled houses and the way of life, there have been changes here as everywhere else. All through the winter patient men and women must sit beside the pot stills—and the older generation was more willing to do this than the young people are. More and more shippers are finding that they must do their own distilling because the farmers' sons and daughters won't stay beside the stills.

Once distilled, Cognac goes into a Limousin oak barrel—not too full, so that the liquid may be in contact with oxygen, and in a spot which is to some extent affected by outside temperatures. In theory, the Cognac goes into a new barrel for a year, at which time it is transferred to one that still has some tannin left. This move leads to a certain amount of additional evaporation. In practice, to overcome this loss, about half of the Cognac is put into new barrels and the other half straight into used barrels. In this way the brandy absorbs enough tannin from the new oak but does not stay in contact with it too long. Ideally, the cask should be made from a tree eighty to a hundred years old, which in turn has been aged for five or six years in open air to lose its harshest tannin. Only Limousin oak and that from the Tronçais forest in the Allier department may be used—and it must be weathered four or five years out-of-doors beforehand. The price for a single stave has now climbed so high that peasant-growers tend to put their brandies into old barrels to save buying new ones, and a paler Cognac is the result. (The ability to meet the high cost of old casks is one more advantage Cognac shippers have over the growers.)

During the ageing period, various changes occur: a decrease in the volume of the brandy, a change in degree of alcohol, dissolution of tannins. At the same time there are less evident chemical changes: hydrolysis, acetylization, and the development of the rancid taste.

Blending is always done in the establishments of the shippers—some as large and grim as prisons, others converted medieval castles. Barrels of different Cognacs are opened over gutters in the floor above the blending vats. The liquid streams into the vat below, where great paddles moved by machinery slowly turn and agitate it. Blending is done a stage at a time, with long halts between to let the brandies rest. Slowly they "marry."

In about half a century evaporation will reduce a new Cognac of 70% to the proper drinking and shipping strength of 40%. Because it is not economically possible to wait for this natural process, Cognac must be "reduced" before bottling. This is done by adding distilled water either directly or indirectly. Since the draft of water tends to shock the brandy, a few of the better firms reduce indirectly by means of *faible*, or weak brandy—Cognac which has been brought down by distilled water to about 27% and then given a long rest. Fit again, it is used to reduce other Cognacs—even then reduction is only 8% or 9% at a time. (The brandy is filtered and allowed to rest after each operation.) The more elaborate process and the addition of the *faible* increase loss by evaporation. This is the costly element in Cognac-making: the special porousness of the Limousin oak which allows the brandy to ripen also lets in air—and so it lets out the brandy. The loss by evaporation into the sky above Charente is almost precisely the yearly figure of consumption in France and one-fifth of that throughout the world.

The Cognacs age in low, above-ground storehouses called *chais*, easily distinguishable by the blackening on the walls, which looks like soot but is a wine fungus. The casks or *tierçons* hold from 350 to 450 liters (90 to 120 U.S. gallons, 75 to 100 imp.). Some makers contend that ageing in the bigger barrel is better, others dispute it. At the end of each row of barrels is the *chanteau*—usually marked *CH*—the partly empty barrel used to replenish the others. Evaporation is encouraged, expensive as it is, for without it there would be no ageing, and the sheds are airy.

When it is ready, the brandy is put into a bottle which has been rinsed with Cognac, and a cork which has been dipped in Cognac is flogged home. It is ready to go out to the world.

EXPORT

Roughly 80% of Cognac is exported. England remains the largest customer, with the United States second. Cognac brings in the largest revenue of any French agricultural product exported.

Sales are going up in both Britain and the U.S.—annual import has passed 500,000 cases in the U.S. and is approaching 1 million cases in England.

All wines and spirits in France must have a tax certificate (*acquit*), even if they are moving only from one warehouse to another. By this means, every movement can be traced. An adaptation of the domestic French *congé* is the *Acquit Jaune d'Or* which now accompanies every Cognac shipment exported. Though originally devised to expedite processes of export, the yellow-gold certificate in effect guarantees the important specifications of the brandy.

Cointreau

A famous proprietary liqueur of the Curaçao type made in Angers, France, and in the United States by the Cointreau family. Although the bottle and label are always identical, the alcoholic content varies from country to country. The original name for it was Triple Sec White Curaçao, but so many makers started using the name Triple Sec that it was changed to Cointreau.

See Curaçao.

Colares, Collares

Port wine apart, this is the most distinctive wine of Portugal. Grown on sandy vineyards overlooking the Atlantic, a forty-minute drive from Lisbon, the wine achieved prominence during the invasion of the vine pest phylloxera, which devastated world viticulture about twenty years before the end of the last century. Sand-grown wines were immune and thus sold at an enormous premium during the phylloxera wine drought. A liking for the wine itself (which is often matured in Angola mahogany or American redwood for as long as a decade and a half) is an acquired habit, for it has an individual taste.

See Portugal.

Collage

The fining process to which wine must be subjected before it is ready to be bottled.

See Chapter Nine, p. 38; Fining.

Collar

Label on bottle neck. The French term is *collerette*.

Colli Albani

White, sometimes sparkling wines from Latium (*q.v.*).

Colli Euganei

Light red or white wines from Italy.
See Veneto.

Colli Orientali del Friuli

Wine from North Italy.
See Friuli-Venezia-Giulia.

Collio

A dry, white, slightly sparkling wine from the north of Italy.
See Friuli-Venezia-Giulia.

Collioure

Red wine.
District: Roussillon.

The Appellation Contrôlée of Collioure is given to the "natural" red table wines of the Banyuls region, just north of the Spanish border on the Mediterranean coast. The sweet fortified aperitif or dessert wine from the same area has its own place-name—Banyuls (*q.v.*). Grenache Noir and Carignane grapes are grown on 600 hectares (1,500 acres), which gives the wine the additional place-name of Collioure de Grenache. The average annual production is 2,000 hectoliters (53,000 U.S. gallons, 44,000 imp.).

Colmar

Wine town in Alsace.
See Alsace.

Colombard

White wine grape grown in the Dauphiné region, where it is also known as Bon Blanc; in Charente as Pied-Tendre; and in Tarn-et-Garonne as Blanquette.

Colombia

There are an estimated 200 hectares (500 acres) of vineyard in Colombia, producing some 100 hectoliters (2,600 U.S. gallons, 2,200 imp.) of wine, almost entirely sweet and fortified with brandy. These are generally called vermouth and Muscatel or mis-called "manzanilla" and "port." Some light table wines are made too, but these also are distinctly sweet.

Native fruits, such as bananas, oranges, and blackberries, provide the source for most of the alcoholic beverages, and the making of spirits is a monopoly of the provincial governments. Aguardiente, rum, and types of whisky and gin are produced in various parts of the country; but the more popular drinks are whisky, among the more influential classes, and Guarapo and Anisado among the others. Anisado is a species of brandy flavored with aniseed, while Guarapo is made from fermented sugar and water. Guarapo is not commercially sold and it generally constitutes a home-made beverage for the peasants in certain regions of the country; when fresh, it has some resemblance to new apple cider.

Color in spirits

Spirits and liqueurs are by nature colorless, and the color is added after they leave the still. They may darken somewhat in the barrel, but most tawny spirits take their color from a dose of caramel; and the green color of crème-de-menthe is likewise added.

Comète, Vin de la (comet wine)

It sometimes happens that a good vintage year is glorified by the appearance of a comet. One such year was

1630, but 1811, more famous (and not so long ago), is the vintage usually referred to as the "comet year."

Commandaria

The great wine of Cyprus and one of the longest-lasting wines in the world.
See Cyprus.

Commanderie du Bontemps de Médoc et de Graves

The local wine society and promotional organization of the Médoc now includes Graves and is composed of growers, shippers, and various dignitaries interested in wine. Dressed up in medieval caps and long robes, the members hold meetings, inauguration ceremonies, and luncheons.

Common clean

The light style of Jamaican rum.
See Rum, Jamaican.

Commonwealth wines

Wines from British Commonwealth countries, notably Australia, Canada, and New Zealand (*qq.v.*). Not of the same quality as European fine wines, they are not in the same price class either and may prove extremely enjoyable—if unexceptional—and inexpensive drinking.

Commune

In France, a parish or township. In the fine wine areas, the wines of a district clustered around one or more parishes are likely to take the name of the commune as an official place-name or Appellation Contrôlée—meaning they are legally recognized to have a certain similarity and certain standards of quality. For example, Margaux, Saint-Julien, Saint-Émilion are important commune names in Bordeaux red wine.

Coñac

Designation improperly used for Spanish brandy.
See Spain.

Concord

The most important blue-black grape of the American East Coast, hardy and productive, adaptable to an astonishing variety of soils and climates, but yielding incredibly mediocre wine—which is, however, widely sold throughout the United States, either blended with others or as kosher wine—sweet, strong, and utterly undistinguished. Concord wine is known for its pronounced foxy taste and aroma.

Condrieu

Rhône Valley white wine.
District: Rhône Valley, France.

The wines are heavily perfumed, with a distinctive taste—or *goût de terroir*—picked up from the granitic soil of the vineyards, and are practically unknown outside the district. Indeed, the output is tiny—less than two thousand cases per year. Modern methods of vinification and early bottling are doubtless responsible for the latter development; and the rising reputation of the wines is due to the patronage of the widow Point, owner of the great Michelin three-star restaurant, the Pyramide, at Vienne, south of Lyon.

Confrérie

French term for wine society.
See Wine societies.

Congé

Official French document which accompanies shipments of wines and spirits and indicates that internal taxes have been paid. It is used when wines or spirits are sent to a wholesaler, retailer, or to the consumer, inside the country—but not for export. There are about six different types of *congé*, distinguished by different initials and colors for various types of wine—e.g., the green ARB for wines of Appellation d'Origine; the gold 4B for Cognac and Armagnac. For shipments on which taxes have not been paid, the *acquit* (*q.v.*) is used.

Congenerics, congeners

Distilling term for the characteristics of taste and aroma retained by distilled spirits coming from the material distilled. When distillation is done at a very high proof the spirit will carry over less congenerics and will be more "neutral" than if distilled at a low proof.

Connétablie de Guyenne

Society devoted to the promotion of white sweet wines in the Bordeaux region. The members are descendants of the *connétables* (constables) of Bordeaux who, in the Middle Ages, judged the wines passing on the river and decreed whether or not they could go to market.
See Premières Côtes de Bordeaux.

Consorzio

Italian term for a group of wine growers and shippers who have banded together to introduce some control on the use of place-name in Italian wines. Voluntary organizations are formed in which members are bound to respect the geographical limits imposed on the wine in question and to observe certain minimum standards of quality. For this they get a seal—which differs with each *consorzio*—to put on the neck of every bottle. The seals have a distinctive design and are consecutively numbered. A brief discussion of *consorzi* can be found in the section on Italian wines, and a discussion of the workings of a typical *consorzio* appears under Tuscany.
See Italy; Tuscany.

Constantia

Celebrated Cape wines which were already being exported from South Africa by the beginning of the nineteenth century.
See South Africa.

Consumo

Portuguese term for ordinary wine.

Cooper

(1) A craftsman who makes casks.
(2) A merchant occupied with the sampling and bottling of wine.
(3) An English drink made from a mixture of stout and porter.

To Cooper

(1) To make or repair casks.
(2) To stow away in casks.

Cooperage

General term for casks or the manufacture and repair of casks or barrels; the fee charged for the work done by a cooper.
See Appendix C, p. 631.

Cooperative

A jointly owned and operated winery or cellar common in Europe and the rest of the world. These arrangements usually begin as a small operation for a few producers who need expensive equipment for wine-making and marketing networks. Some always remain modest in size, but other cooperatives are among the largest wineries in the world.

Copper Sulfate

A copper salt also called blue stone used in fungicidal sprays. $CuSO_4 5H_2O$.

Corbières

The Corbières is the last vineyard region in the Languedoc Province before the beginning of the Roussillon vineyards. In the north, its 33,000 hectares (82,500 acres) of vines stretch from Narbonne nearly to the fortified *cité* of Carcassonne, and in the south to the northern border of the Roussillon. In 1980 the Corbières was the largest expanse of V.D.Q.S. (*vins délimités de qualité supérieure*) in France, accounting for 40% of all French V.D.Q.S. wine; about 900,000 hectoliters (23,760,000 U.S. gallons, 19,800,000 imp.) are produced annually.

Ninety-five percent of the wine is red, 4% is rosé, and 1% white.

Recent developments in the Corbières region, such as *maceration carbonique*, vineyard parceling, and better vatroom techniques, have greatly improved the quality of the wines produced there.
See Appendix G.

Cordial

A beverage compounded from spirits with fruit or aromatic substances added by a variety of methods such as maceration, steeping, or simply by mixing. They are always sweetened. The word has come to be almost synonymous with liqueur.

Cordon

Method of training vines. Usually, the trunk of the plant is bent sideways to run parallel with the ground, and is supported by a wire or style. The number of canes that grow up and down from this trunk, as well as the number of buds on each cane, may be regulated.
See Chapter Eight, p. 29.

Corkage

A fee charged for opening and serving a customer's own bottle in a restaurant or hotel, or sometimes an additional charge made on any bottle that is opened and consumed on the premises.

Corkscrew

Any device used for extracting corks; in its most traditional and simplest form, only a wire spiral affixed to some sort of handle. The variations on this idea are seemingly endless, as are the modern substitutes.

More important than any of the attendant gadgetry is the screw itself. For fine wines whose bottles usually have longer than average corks, it is essential that the metal spiral be between 2¼ and 2¾ inches in length, long enough to get a good grip through all of the cork. The metal should be thin and tapered into an open spiral, without a sharp cutting edge, which could shred the cork when it is removed. The tip is best rather sharp and fashioned so that it is not centered in the spiral.

Screws with levers and double-screw arrangements can be helpful as long as the spiral itself is well designed. Recent use of a needle to pierce the cork, injecting gas underneath it, and thus pushing the stopper out, does work if the needle is long enough to get all the way through the cork. These inventions may be a bit far-fetched, but they can bring out a friable cork in one piece.

Corky or corked wine

Spoiled by a bad cork. The defect originates in the cork; it can happen to any wine if a faulty cork is used. The French term for corky is *bouchonné*.

Cornas

Rhône Valley red wine.
District: Rhône Valley, France.

The wine is never great, often good, and seldom expensive. It is red, comes from Syrah grapes, and contains the characteristics generally expected of the Rhône Valley (*see* Rhône), although not to the same exalted degree as some of its neighbors. It is usually good value, however.

As is the case throughout the Côtes du Rhône, the vines grow on terraced plots carefully built into slopes so steep they must be cultivated by hand. There are some hundred acres of vineyard, and annual production averages some 1,300 hectoliters (34,000 U.S. gallons, 28,300 imp.).

Coronata

Thin, light, white Italian wine.
See Liguria.

Corowa

Vineyard region in New South Wales.
See Australia.

Corsé

French term used of a robust full-bodied wine.

Corsica

The island of Corsica lies to the south of France and to the west of Italy in the Mediterranean Sea, and the climate is almost ideal for growing vines. Climate is not the only vital factor in agriculture, however; and of the island's 850,000 hectares (2,125,000 acres), only 26,000 hectares (65,000 acres) are in vines.

The wines produced are not of any high degree of quality, with the exception of a very few grown around the principal city of Ajaccio and a few more around Sartène. Most Corsican wines are rough and common, haphazardly vinified, and improperly cared for. The 12,000 growers on the island live a generally poor and wretched existence and have neither the money nor the time to improve their product, and perhaps for this reason the wines are rarely, if ever, found outside the island. Corsica does not generally make enough for its own consumption; and in many years wines must be imported, the major sources being Algeria, the mainland of France, and Tunisia. Much of this wine is drunk by the tourists who flood the island for about two and a half months each year, most of them more interested in the island's savage beauty than in the wines it can offer.

Among the better wines of Corsica are those grown on the Cap Corse, the peninsula which points like a finger at the French Côte d'Azur. The best are the whites and rosés, and these, the Corsicans say, were the preferred wines of the island's most spectacular son, Napoleon Bonaparte. The peninsula is also noted for the only considerable wine export of Corsica—the fortified, wine-based

aperitif Cap Corse, about 3,400 hectoliters (90,000 U.S. gallons, 75,000 imp.) of which are sent to the mainland of France each year. Other wines (mostly white) are grown around Bastia, around Corte in the center of the island (red and white), Ajaccio and Cauro (white and rosé), and the southern towns of Sartène, Santa-Lucia-di-Tallano, and Bonifacio (red and white). The best wine of Corsica, and the only one deserving of attention abroad, is Patrimonio Rosé, grown near Bastia. Patrimonio wines are given the A.O.C., and another new Appellation Contrôlée includes the other good Corsican wines. All these wines have a distinct flavor and are higher in alcohol than the inexperienced drinker expects. Corsican wines are often compared to those of the Côtes du Rhône and the Côtes de Provence, although not as good. All supplies and equipment needed to care for vineyards and for wines must be brought in from France, and it is one of the problems of Corsica that it has little to export in return.

Most of the vines cultivated on the island are of Italian rather than French origin; they include Moscata, Aleatico, Vermentino (a variety of the Malvasia or Malvoisie), Genovesella, Sciaccarello, Biancone, Nielluco, Grenache, and Biancolella. The amount of Corsican wine made each year is almost impossible to estimate—so much of it is drunk on the spot—but it is something like 1,500,000 hectoliters (39 million U.S. gallons, 30 million imp.).

Cortaillod

The best red wine of Neuchâtel—its well-known vineyard is Cru de la Vigne du Diable.
See Switzerland.

Cortese

White-wine grape of Italy, which produces a dry light wine.
See Piedmont.

Corton

Burgundy red and white wines.
District: Côte de Beaune, France.
Commune: Aloxe-Corton.
Official Classification: Great Growth (Grand Cru).

From the little town of Aloxe (pronounced Alosse), the vineyard road meanders down to Beaune. This small district produces the finest red wines of the Côte de Beaune, and the best of the Corton vineyards are Le Corton, Corton-Bressandes, and Corton-Clos du Roi. There is some white wine also, more vigorous and perfumed than the neighboring Meursault, but elegant and delicate; and Corton-Charlemagne is one of the great white growths of the Côte de Beaune. Corton, like most vineyards in Burgundy, is cut up into parcels, and some of the largest slices are owned by the excellent shipper Louis Latour and by the Prince de Mérode. Wine from five parcels in Aloxe is auctioned in the Hospices de Beaune sale as Cuvée Dr. Peste and as Charlotte Dumay, after the benefactors who gave the land to the Hospices. On the label, the great name of Corton precedes that of any other fine vineyard, such as Corton-Bressandes, Corton-Clos du Roi and Corton-Charlemagne. Great wines take the name of the famous vineyard rather than that of the commune. Le Corton covers some 78 hectares (193 acres). About 30% of the production is in white wine.

Corton-Charlemagne

Burgundy white wine.
District: Côte de Beaune, France.
Commune: Aloxe-Corton.
Official Classification: Great Growth (Grand Cru).

This is one of the great white Burgundies—at its best it is in the class of the illustrious Montrachet. Since production is small, in comparison with the world-wide demand (24.7 hectares—61.5 acres), this is a rare wine, rich, with great breed, not as soft as the white Meursaults, and more steely. Corton-Charlemagne, made exclusively from the noble Chardonnay grape (at one time, the lesser sections could be planted in the coarser Aligoté, but this is no longer allowed), is big and of a golden color. The vineyard is divided into three parts: two of the principal owners are the estimable shippers Louis Latour and Louis Jadot; the rest belongs to half a dozen or so very fine growers, the most considerable of whom produces about 200 cases, the smallest only 14 cases. This splendid wine, unfortunately, is slowly shrinking in quantity, mainly because the vines planted on the steep slopes must be tended by hand, and after heavy rains the workers have to haul back the soil on their own backs, since horses and oxen cannot climb here. This is a form of hard labor which does not appeal to the younger generation of *vignerons*.

See Aloxe-Corton.

Château Cos d'Estournel

Bordeaux red wine.
District: Haut-Médoc, France.
Commune: Saint-Estèphe.

Owned by the Prats family since 1970, and before them by Pierre Ginestet, proprietor of Château Margaux, the estate is directly across the vineyard road—which is the commune boundary between Saint-Estèphe and Pauillac—from Château Lafite. Classified a Second Growth (*Second Cru*) in 1855, Cos d'Estournel is certainly one of the greatest of the great Seconds. Typical of Saint-Estèphe, it is a big, hard wine which, under the able direction of the Ginestets and now of Bruno Prats (grandson of M. Fernand Ginestet), is one of the most popular Classified Growths in the Médoc. According to the Ginestets, the name Cos was given to the vineyard by the Templar Knights returning from the Crusades, which had taken them to Rhodes and its neighboring island, Cos. M. Prats thinks the name is a phonetic distortion of "Caux," as the name appears on an eighteenth-century map. The vineyards rise comparatively high above Pauillac, and the château itself, a charming Chinese gothic fantasy unique

in the Médoc, dominates the landscape. During the Second World War, the little pagodas which decorate the vineyard walls served the Germans as anti-aircraft batteries. They were destroyed but have since been restored. The present owners have compounded the exotic appearance of the château by adding to the main entrance a carved door once owned by the Sultan of Zanzibar.

Characteristics. The wines reflect the position of the vineyard—halfway between Pauillac and Saint-Estèphe. They are lighter and more supple than the other important Saint-Estèphes but are still full and rich, with a tendency to fatness, or *gras*.

Vineyard area: 60 hectares (150 acres).
Average production: 275 *tonneaux* (25,000 cases).

Château Cos-Labory

Bordeaux red wine.
District: Haut-Médoc, France.
Commune: Saint-Estèphe.

The only Fifth Growth (*Cinquième Cru*) in Saint-Estèphe as the great vineyards were classified in 1855, Cos-Labory is beautifully situated on the high-rising roll of hills on the boundary line of Pauillac and Saint-Estèphe. Its two neighbors are Château Lafite, just over the line in Pauillac, and Château Cos-d'Estournel. With the latter vineyard, it was once the common property of a London owner, Mr. Martyn; but it belongs now to M. François Audey.

Characteristics. The wines are big and well rounded. A well-made, typical Saint-Estèphe.

Vineyard area: 27 hectares (67 acres).
Average production: 100 *tonneaux* (8,000 cases).

Cosecha

Spanish for harvest; indicates vintage year on Spanish wines—i.e., *cosecha* 1971, *cosecha* 1972.

Costières-du-Gard

Red, white, and rosé wines from the fantastically productive Hérault area of southern France. Though entitled to the V.D.Q.S. seal, the wines may be made from any or all of eighteen different grape varieties and are at best just a little better than a good *vin ordinaire*.

Cot

Another name for the Malbec grapevine; also known as Pied-Rouge, Cahors, etc.

Côte

French term for a slope with vineyards. When used to designate a wine—as Côtes du Rhône, Côte de Nuits, etc.—it will usually mean a wine of lesser quality than a Clos, Château, or other wine indicated by a specific vineyard name.

Côte de Beaune

Burgundy red and dry white wines.
District: Côte d'Or, France.

Although 80% of the 70,000 hectoliters (1,855,000 U.S. gallons, 1,540,000 imp.) annually produced is red, the slope is chiefly famous for its dry white wines, the greatest of which come from the southern end, the unofficial Côte de Meursault or Côte des Blancs. In fact, however, both red and white are made throughout, and either may be superb.

The slope, the southern or lower half of the Côte d'Or, begins at Ladoix, a long stone's throw from the end of the Côte de Nuits, and runs some fifteen miles, to just below Santenay. The name derives from its major city, ancient Beaune, the "Capital of Burgundian Wines," which stands in the same relationship to wine-shippers as Chicago does to meat-packers. Beaune is simple even for the most stubbornly non-Gallic tongue, whereas many of the other Burgundian place-names look quite formidable. One apocryphal story is that a well-known London wine-merchant habitually introduced his apprentices to Burgundies with this terse advice: "There are two kinds of Burgundy: Beaune and the rest. We sell Beaune." Massive though its output may be, however, all that is Côte de Beaune is not necessarily Beaune.

The slope is composed of nineteen separate communes, whose wines, ranging in quality from indifferent to incomparable, are sold under a variety of names. Some bottles have only the name of a single exceptional vineyard, signifying that the wine is from grapes grown only in that vineyard, that the vineyard is one which the French authorities consider among the very greatest of Burgundy (there are eight on the Côte de Beaune), and that the wine has attained the quality commensurate with the name. Slightly lower in the legal hierarchy is wine sold with the name of a commune followed by that of a vineyard. The minimum standards are rather lower than those for the greatest wines, but the difference is often impossible to detect—in many cases these wines equal or even better their more renowned cellar-mates. The lesser wines of the Côte are sold with the name of the commune of origin and nothing more. This is the skeleton of the slope's system of nomenclature, but there are always a few variations and exceptions.

Bottles will sometimes be found bearing the word Cuvée followed by someone's name, signifying that it is wine from Beaune's Hospices or Charity Hospital and comes from a vineyard donated by the person indicated (*see* Hospices de Beaune). By the time this wine gets to the consumer, it is usually higher in price than any of its peers—usually too high—in spite of the fact that the annual November auction sale of wines at the Hospices de Beaune traditionally sets the price standards for the entire Côte d'Or. To console him for the price he has paid, the buyer has the double pleasure of getting a good wine, provided it has not been falsified, and contributing to a worthy charity at the same time.

Another name sometimes found on bottle labels is Côte de Beaune-Villages, used to indicate a blend of wines from two or more communes along the slope. Very occasionally, labels will have the name of a commune followed by Côte de Beaune. The appendage has little real significance and the wine may be considered the same as any other bearing simply the name of the commune concerned.

As is particularly true throughout Burgundy, it is difficult to generalize about the wines. Most red wine is reasonably light and fast-maturing, delicate, and full of perfume, but exception must be made for red Corton from the commune of Aloxe-Corton, a wine which is noble and full, of a resplendent deep-red color, and one of the longest lasting in Burgundy. White wines from the Côte de Beaune are always dry, but there is a world of difference between the great whites of Aloxe-Corton, on the northern end of the slope, and those from the Côte de Meursault to the south. Even within the Côte de Meursault, wines from Meursault itself will differ markedly from those of Puligny-Montrachet and Chassagne-Montrachet next door, the former tending to be delicate and feminine, the latter more austere. Yet all come from the same grape variety and all are vinified in much the same way, perhaps proving that if there is any justification for the abundance of wine names in Burgundy, it is simply in this very obvious truism: that two vines of the same family may be planted within less than half a mile of each other and the fruit each gives will not resemble that given by the other. If any general summary of the wines of the Côte de Beaune were to be made, it would be that, at their best, the white wines are without peer in the entire world; the reds cede top honors to their counterparts of the Côte de Nuits.

CÔTE DE BEAUNE SOIL

Geologically, the slope is composed of three types of soil, dating from different periods of the Jurassic age; but of these only two are important to the wines. Bathonian-era soil, consisting of a base of hard rock topped with a thin layer of earth and sometimes with a whitish marl, is found to some extent in the vineyards of Beaune and Pommard. The whitish marl assumes more importance in the Côte de Meursault, where it forms the best soil for grapes grown for white wines. Soil from the Oxfordian era tends to leave an iron-rich oolite at the base of the slopes, and grapes grown in it give light red wines with a pronounced bouquet. As this soil climbs the slopes, it turns grayish, its clay content increases, and the resulting grapes ferment into red wines with enormous finesse and elegance, but full and rich and beautifully balanced. Corton is the prime example. But even where this soil is at its grayest, it nevertheless preserves the iron-imparted tinge of red, with the result that the difference between vineyards giving grapes for fine red wines and those producing white is immediately apparent: the soil color is the exact indication. Perhaps nowhere else in the world is this difference so marked or so dramatic.

LEGAL WINE STANDARDS

Côte de Beaune wine must—as is the case with all French wines of Appellation Contrôlée—attain certain minimum standards before it is granted the right to any legal place-name. These standards vary according to the vineyard where the grapes were grown. Six of them have the right to carry only vineyard name and the words Great Growth (*Grand Cru*) if the wines meet the high standards required; these are asterisked on the list on this page. The other wines are communal First Growths (*Premiers Crus*) if they stem from the better vineyards, or simple communal wines. Any wine not meeting the standards for the name for which it is theoretically qualified is declassified into the highest rank for which it can qualify, but there is no advancement; no First Growth may ever be sold as a Great Growth no matter how good the wine. The standards are:

RED WINES

Great Growths (Grands Crus)

(1) Wine must be made exclusively from Pinot Noir, Pinot Liebault, and Pinot Beurot grapes. A maximum of 15% Pinot Blanc or Chardonnay grapes may be used at the discretion of the wine-maker.

(2) Production must not exceed 30 hectoliters per hectare (320.7 U.S. gallons, 267 imp. per acre) of vines.

(3) Wine must contain at least 11.5% of alcohol by volume.

First Growths (Premiers Crus)

(1) Same grape varieties as for Great Growths.

(2) Production must not exceed 35 hectoliters per hectare (374.1 U.S. gallons, 311.5 imp. per acre).

(3) Wine must have at least 11% of alcohol.

Communal Wines

(1) Same grape varieties as for other *appellations*.

(2) Production must not exceed 35 hectoliters per hectare (374.1 U.S. gallons, 311.5 imp. per acre).

(3) Wine must contain at least 10.5% of alcohol.

WHITE WINES

Great Growths (Grands Crus)

(1) Only Chardonnay (also called Beaunois and Aubaine) grapes may be used.

(2) Production must not exceed 30 hectoliters per hectare (320.7 U.S. gallons, 267 imp. per acre).

(3) Wine must have at least 12% alcohol, 11.5% for wine from the vineyards of Bâtard-Montrachet, Bienvenue-Bâtard-Montrachet, and Criots-Bâtard-Montrachet.

First Growths (Premiers Crus)

(1) Only the Chardonnay vine may be used.

(2) Production must not exceed 35 hectoliters per hectare (374.1 U.S. gallons, 311.5 imp. per acre).

(3) Wine must contain at least 11.5% alcohol.

Communal Wines

(1) Only Chardonnay grapes may be used.

(2) Production must not exceed 35 hectoliters per hectare (374.1 U.S. gallons, 311.5 imp. per acre).

(3) Wine must contain 11% of alcohol.

OUTSTANDING VINEYARDS—RED WINES

Vineyard	Commune
*Le Corton	Aloxe-Corton
Le Clos du Roi	Aloxe-Corton
Les Renardes	Aloxe-Corton
Les Chaumes	Aloxe-Corton
Les Bressandes	Aloxe-Corton
Clos Saint-Jean	Chassagne-Montrachet
Clos de la Boudriotte	Chassagne-Montrachet
Clos Morgeot	Chassagne-Montrachet
Les Vergelesses	Savigny-les-Beaune
Les Marconnets	Savigny-les-Beaune
Les Santenots	Meursault
Les Fèves	Beaune
Les Grèves	Beaune
Les Marconnets	Beaune
Les Bressandes	Beaune
Les Clos des Mouches	Beaune
Aux Cras	Beaune
Les Champimonts	Beaune
Les Épenots	Pommard
Les Rugiens	Pommard
Les Jarollières	Pommard
Le Clos Blanc	Pommard
Les Pézerolles	Pommard
Clos-de-la-Commaraine	Pommard
Les Caillerets	Volnay
Les Champans	Volnay
Les Fremiets	Volnay
Les Angles	Volnay

OUTSTANDING VINEYARDS —WHITE WINES

Vineyard	Commune
*Le Montrachet (*in part*)	Puligny-Montrachet
*Le Montrachet (*in part*)	Chassagne-Montrachet
*Chevalier-Montrachet	Puligny-Montrachet
*Bâtard-Montrachet (*in part*)	Puligny-Montrachet
*Bâtard-Montrachet (*in part*)	Chassagne-Montrachet
*Bienvenue-Bâtard-Montrachet	Puligny-Montrachet
*Criots-Bâtard-Montrachet	Chassagne-Montrachet
Les Combettes	Puligny-Montrachet
Les Pucelles	Puligny-Montrachet
Les Chalumeaux	Puligny-Montrachet
Blagny-Blanc	Puligny-Montrachet
Les Ruchottes	Chassagne-Montrachet
Clos des Perrières	Meursault
Les Perrières	Meursault
Les Charmes	Meursault
Les Genevrières	Meursault
*Corton-Charlemagne	Aloxe-Corton
*Le Corton	Aloxe-Corton

See separately under the respective communes: Aloxe-Corton, Savigny-Les-Beaune, Beaune, Pommard, Volnay, Chassagne-Montrachet, Puligny-Montrachet, Meursault. *See also these Côte-de-Beaune communes:* Pernand-Vergelesses, Ladoix-Serrigny, Chorey-les-Beaune, Saint-Romain, Monthélie, Auxey-Duresses, Saint-Aubin, Santenay, Dezize-les-Maranges, Sampigny-les-Maranges, Cheilly-les-Maranges.

Côte de Beaune-Villages

A very general name for Burgundian wines. To gain the use of it, wines must be a blend of two or more red wines of at least 10.5% of alcohol and must have the title to one of the place-names listed below. There will be enormous variation in the amount made in any year, following the decisions and speculations of the wine-shippers who do the blending and the amount of wine to stem from the various communes concerned. This can be anything between 5,000 and 7,000 hectoliters (132,500 to 185,000 U.S. gallons, 110,000 to 154,000 imp.). The place-names which have the right to be used for this minor Côte de Beaune wine are:

Auxey-Duresses	Meursault Blagny
Chassagne-Montrachet	Monthélie
Cheilly-les-Maranges	Pernand-Vergelesses
Chorey-les-Beaune	Puligny-Montrachet
Côte de Beaune	Saint-Aubin
Dezize-les-Maranges	Sampigny-les-Maranges
Ladoix-Serrigny	Santenay
Meursault	Savigny-les-Beaune

Côte des Blancs

A ridge of the Champagne district planted in white Pinot and Chardonnay grapes. The principal towns are Avize, Cramant, and Mesnil.
See Champagne.

Côte de Brouilly

Côte de Brouilly red wines are from the heart or best section of Brouilly in Beaujolais, Burgundy.
See Beaujolais.

Côte de Nuits

Burgundy red and dry white wines.
District: Côte d'Or, France.

The Côte de Nuits stretches for about 19 kilometers (12 miles) along the Côte d'Or, south of Fixin and ending on the verge of a stone quarry just below Nuits-Saint-Georges, the principal town, from which it takes its name. Some of the vineyards planted on the slope are, within carefully defined limits, among the best in the world.

The natural hazards which can make wine production as uncertain as any other form of crop farming are particularly troublesome in this small area—the only district in which the Pinot Noir grape will, in favorable circumstances, give its best. Farther north, it would yield a thinner, harder wine; farther south, one which would be softer and less robust. Even in the Côte de Nuits this delicate grape is not easy to raise; and only certain sections of the slope have the soil which favors the vine. That is why the great vineyards of this region are so small, and why one will produce a fine wine while the growth from its near neighbor will be mediocre. And so the vineyards of the whole Côte d'Or are called *climats*—each "climate" varying, for better or worse, according to its exposure, soil, and drainage.

On the Côte de Nuits, all the *climats* face southeast, where the rising sun strikes the vineyards, drawing the moisture up through the vines. Farther south, the sun would be too hot and the vines would wither; farther north, it would not be hot enough. In such a region, where it takes so little to spoil a vintage, wine-making is a difficult and exacting art; and each *vigneron* adds something to the character of his own wine. So, tasting one against another, anyone accustomed to wine-drinking will perceive the difference between a Côte de Nuits and a Côte de Beaune, or even between a Charmes-Chambertin and the contiguous Clos de Bèze.

The soil of the Côte de Nuits is a reddish clay full of small chalky pebbles, with varying amounts of lava, fuller's earth (a type of clay rich in the silicates of calcium and magnesium), salts of lime, potassium, and phosphorus. The subsoil, which dates from the Jurassic age, is a flinty clay with iron and chalk; but the "trenching," or deep-plowing that vineyards go through, turns it up and mixes it all together.

The 1,400 hectares (3,500 acres) of vines are mostly Pinot Noir, but there are some Chardonnay, and a few sections are planted in Gamay, Melon, and Aligoté for

wine reserved almost entirely for the workers and their families. Most of the wine is red, although a little white is grown, principally in the communes of Vougeot and Chambolle-Musigny, and the informing grape is the noble Pinot Noir. (Two other varieties may be used in wines bearing great names—Pinot Liebault and Pinot Beurot; but these vines, offshoots of the Pinot Noir they closely resemble, are planted only in small quantities.)

The wines vary in quality from the magnificent Great Growths to those bearing the names of their communes—third-grade in a classification of three. The first is Great Growth (*Grand Cru*), the intermediate First Growth (*Premier Cru*). The standards demanded by law for the wines of the Côte de Nuits are:

Great Growths (Grands Crus)

(1) The harvest must not exceed 30 hectoliters per hectare (321 U.S. gallons, 267 imp. per acre), except in the vineyards of Latricières-Chambertin, Charmes-Chambertin, Mazoyères-Chambertin, Mazis-Chambertin, Ruchottes-Chambertin, Chapelle-Chambertin, and Griotte-Chambertin in the commune of Gevrey-Chambertin, where the maximum is 32 hectoliters per hectare (342 U.S. gallons, 285 imp. per acre).

(2) Red wines must contain 11.5% alcohol, white wines 12%.

(3) The only permissible grape varieties are Pinot Noir, Pinot Liebault, and Pinot Beurot for red wines and Chardonnay for white. Red wines may, at the discretion of the grower, include up to 15% Pinot Blanc or Chardonnay.

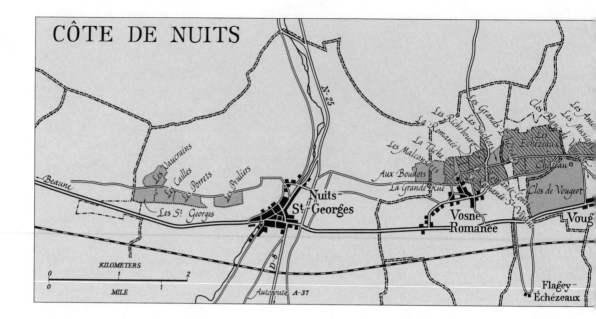

CÔTE DE NUITS

KILOMETERS
0   1   2
0   1
MILE

First Growths (Premiers Crus)

(1) The harvest must not exceed 35 hectoliters per hectare (374 U.S. gallons, 312 imp. per acre).

(2) Red wines must contain at least 11% alcohol, white wines 11.5%.

(3) The grape varieties are required to be the same as for Great Growths, listed above.

(4) These wines may be sold under the name of the commune and of the vineyard, or with the commune name followed by the words First Growth. If they fail to meet the necessary requirements, they are downgraded to the communal wines.

Communal Wines

(1) The harvest must not exceed 35 hectoliters per hectare (374 U.S. gallons, 312 imp. per acre).

(2) Red wines must contain at least 10.5% alcohol, white wines 11%.

(3) The grape varieties are required to be the same as for Great Growths.

(4) Wines that fall below these standards are declassed and sold with those of more general *appellations,* such as Bourgogne.

These regulations cover all the good wines of the slope, except those named Vins Fins de la Côte de Nuits (*q.v.*). These last are superior to the more general Burgundian *appellations,* yet do not rank among the distinguished and truly fine wines of the Côte de Nuits.

OUTSTANDING VINEYARDS—RED WINES

Vineyard	Commune
Clos de la Perrière	Fixin
Clos du Chapitre	Fixin
Le Chambertin	Gevrey-Chambertin
Le Clos de Bèze	Gevrey-Chambertin
Latricières	Gevrey-Chambertin
Mazys (or Mazis)	Gevrey-Chambertin
Mazoyères	Gevrey-Chambertin
Charmes	Gevrey-Chambertin
Ruchottes	Gevrey-Chambertin
Griotte	Gevrey-Chambertin
Chapelle	Gevrey-Chambertin
Clos Saint-Jacques	Gevrey-Chambertin
Varoilles	Gevrey-Chambertin
Clos de Tart	Morey-Saint-Denis
Les Bonnes Mares	Morey-Saint-Denis
Clos de la Roche	Morey-Saint-Denis
Clos Saint-Denis	Morey-Saint-Denis
Clos des Lambrays	Morey-Saint-Denis

(Clos des Lambrays is a great vineyard in Morey-Saint-Denis, but it is not an Appellation Contrôlée because the owners have been bickering with the Institut National des Appellations d'Origine for a number of years.)

Les Musigny	Chambolle-Musigny
Les Bonnes Mares	Chambolle-Musigny
Les Amoureuses	Chambolle-Musigny
Clos de Vougeot	Vougeot
Les Grands-Échezeaux	Flagey-Échezeaux
Les Échezeaux	Flagey-Échezeaux
La Romanée-Conti	Vosne-Romanée

Vineyard	Commune
La Romanée	Vosne-Romanée
La Tâche	Vosne-Romanée
Les Gaudichots	Vosne-Romanée
Les Richebourg	Vosne-Romanée
La Romanée-Saint-Vivant	Vosne-Romanée
Les Malconsorts	Vosne-Romanée
Clos des Réas	Vosne-Romanée
Les Suchots	Vosne-Romanée
Les Beaux-Monts (also Les Beaumonts)	Vosne-Romanée
La Grande Rue	Vosne-Romanée
Les Saint-Georges	Nuits-Saint-Georges
Aux Boudots	Nuits-Saint-Georges
Les Cailles	Nuits-Saint-Georges
Les Porrets	Nuits-Saint-Georges
Les Pruliers	Nuits-Saint-Georges
Les Vaucrains	Nuits-Saint-Georges
Clos de la Maréchale	Prémeaux
Les Didiers	Prémeaux
Clos des Forêts	Prémeaux
Clos des Corvées	Prémeaux
Aux Perdrix	Prémeaux

OUTSTANDING VINEYARDS—WHITE WINES

Vineyard	Commune
Musigny Blanc	Chambolle-Musigny
Clos Blanc de Vougeot	Vougeot

See separately under the respective communes: Fixin, Gevrey-Chambertin, Morey-Saint-Denis, Chambolle-Musigny, Vougeot, Flagey-Échezeaux, Vosne-Romanée, Nuits-Saint-Georges, Nuits-Saint-Georges-Prémeaux.

Côte d'Or

Red and dry white wines.
District: Burgundy, France.

The Côte d'Or is variously referred to as the "backbone" and as the "heart" of Burgundy, proving perhaps that the Burgundian knows his wine-making better than his anatomy. Whatever its relation to the other sections of this great region, it produces some of the most magnificent Burgundies. Some of its reds are peerless and at least one white, Montrachet, is considered by many experts to be the most perfect of all dry white wines. In good years even the secondary Côte d'Or wines are equaled only by a handful of wines the world over. Unquestionably, the "Slope of Gold" is well named.

The slope is composed of a series of bleak, disorderly, low-lying hills stretching some 65 kilometers (40 miles) between Dijon and Santenay, and taking in twenty-four communes and one hamlet. All the vineyards are remarkable, but only those in the favored tenderloin strip—averaging 300 meters (under 1,000 feet) in width—are truly great by Burgundian standards; they alone can produce the superlative Burgundies—but in incredibly small quantities and often at fairly elevated prices. An authentic Côte d'Or Burgundy can never be cheap. Few are completely authentic, since the 6,000 hectares (15,000 acres) produce scarcely 200,000 hectoliters (5.3 million U.S. gallons, 4.4 million imp.) per year. The average holding is less than 2 hectares (5 acres).

These wines stem from two types of grapes—Pinot Noir for red and Chardonnay for white. Neither vine produces abundantly. Several close relatives of these grapes are allowed as well, but they are planted in insignificant amounts; other vines may be found on the slope, but their wines are not properly Côte d'Or, and if permitted a place-name will revert to the more general Burgundy (q.v.). In addition to the relatively low yields of the noble vines, the hazards of their cultivation are considerable in so northerly a climate, where inclement weather is frequent and punishing. It is just this northerly climate, however, which is responsible for the fineness of the wines in years when they do succeed, since it exacts the maximum effort from the vine simply to bring its fruit to maturity and ensures that the hard-won grapes will be of superb quality. Not every year, of course, turns out to be an unqualified success—although here again the importance of vintage charts has been largely overestimated. Admittedly there will be more difference between the vintage years in the wines of Burgundy than there will be in those of comparatively sunny Bordeaux; yet a bottle of a Côte d'Or wine from a lesser year—if the wine is authentic and appropriately priced—may well provide a delightful experience. Often, an excellent wine is made even in the most "disastrous" of years—which proves that wine refuses to obey the rules laid down by the statisticians and chart-makers. This shows that a well-selected wine is a greater quality factor than the claim of a vintage year.

The important wines of the Côte d'Or fall into three categories: wines labeled with the name of a commune; those with the name of the commune followed by that of a vineyard—for instance, Nuits-Saint-Georges Les Porrets; and those with only a vineyard name (e.g., Chambertin). Wines with communal place-names only (e.g., Gevrey-Chambertin) may come from virtually any vineyard in that commune, and the standards they must attain are the lowest exacted along the slope. Such wines are often excellent, sometimes distinguished, but never great. The second group embraces wines from grapes grown only in the specific vineyard indicated, and the minimum standards are rather higher. The wines include some of the most splendid Burgundies. The third group dispenses with everything but the name of the single outstanding vineyard where the grapes are grown and makes up the class of the Great Growths (Grands Crus), of which there are only thirty-one on the Côte d'Or. The wines may generally be expected to be peerless, although some others which carry both vineyard and commune name equal and very occasionally better them. What is important for the buyer is an ability to distinguish commune from vineyard on the label. This is not always so simple as it seems.

Many a beginner has inadvertently bought a bottle of Gevrey-Chambertin for Chambertin, or Chambolle-Mu-

signy for Musigny. The mistake is an honest one made possible by the peculiar Burgundian custom of adding to the name of a commune that of its most famous vineyard. The practice is by no means standard—Pommard, Volnay, and Beaune, for example, consider their names far more valuable than those of any vineyard the commune might possess—and to complicate matters further, several vineyards themselves have hyphenated names. Thus Gevrey-Chambertin is a commune but Chambertin, Latricières-Chambertin, Charmes-Chambertin, and several others are vineyards, and outstanding ones at that. Fortunately there are only twenty-four communes on the Côte d'Or, of which about thirteen are of real importance. (A list of these communes with their leading vineyards follows at the end of this entry; and they are listed with average production under the heading Côte d'Or in the entry on Burgundy—q.v.)

The slope of the Côte d'Or itself falls neatly into two parts: the Côte de Nuits to the north and the Côte de Beaune to the south. In general it might be said that the former is responsible for the greatest red Burgundies, the latter for the whites, but there are exceptions. In bygone times there was a Côte de Dijon extending to the north of the Côte de Nuits, but the expansion of the city of Dijon and the lesser quality of the wines it produced have combined to reduce its importance almost to nothing, despite the fact that the slope was once held in considerable esteem. In the commune of Chenôve—even today the source of a few minor wines—there stands what is said to be the biggest wine press in the world. "The Duke's Wine Press" is the official name, but to the natives it is "Big Maggie," affectionately named for Marguérite, a lusty fifteenth-century Duchess who purportedly bestowed her favors on those pickers and wine-makers who did the fastest and the best jobs. Chenôve, Marsannay, and Couchey still produce wines in a minor way, but Fixin, at the beginning of the Côte de Nuits, is the first commune of any real importance.

The midsection of the hills between Fixin and Santenay has become the great vineyard region of the Côte d'Or. Determining factors are the vine, the angle of the hill and the way it is struck by the sun, the amount of rainfall, and the drainage of excess water; but perhaps most important of all is the soil—the most critical element in the production of any fine wine. The Burgundian hills date from the same time (and are part of the same formation) as the easterly Jura Mountains which give their name to the period in which they were formed, the Jurassic age, some 130 to 155 million years ago. In the intervening 129-or-so million years between their formation and the first stumbling appearance of man, the hills were alternately baked by the sun and covered with ice, drenched with water and whipped by savage winds, and the net result is the iron-rich oolitic rubble and chalky clay at present composing the soil. The Burgundian is firmly convinced that the entire scheme was preordained, that the precise combination of factors found on his hills was planned expressly for his vines and nothing else. What else could possibly grow on the Côte d'Or? And where else can you possibly equal wines such as these?

While the Côte d'Or Burgundies are among the world's handful of great wines, there are obviously some which are better than others. A classification is an ephemeral thing at best, for the men concerned have much to do with the quality of the individual wines, and men are subject to change. It is nevertheless possible to make an overall classification of the wines. The order of the following list represents a personal opinion based on the author's years of testing Burgundies and comparing them one against the other, and no wholesale agreement is anticipated. In order to give a true estimate of the quality of these vineyards, the wines should reflect the character of the soil and be estate-bottled, or *Mis en Bouteilles à la Propriété*.

RED WINES

Vineyard	Commune
La Romanée-Conti	Vosne-Romanée
Chambertin-Clos de Bèze and Chambertin	Gevrey-Chambertin
La Tâche	Vosne-Romanée
Les Richebourg	Vosne-Romanée
Musigny	Chambolle-Musigny
Clos de Vougeot	Vougeot
Les Bonnes Mares	Chambolle-Musigny
Grands-Échezeaux	Flagey-Échezeaux
La Romanée-Saint-Vivant	Vosne-Romanée
Corton-Clos du Roi	Aloxe-Corton
Les Saint-Georges	Nuits-Saint-Georges
Latricières-Chambertin	Gevrey-Chambertin
Le Corton	Aloxe-Corton
Les Bressandes	Aloxe-Corton
Cuvée Nicolas Rolin	Beaune (Hospices de Beaune)
La Grande Rue	Vosne-Romanée
Les Renardes	Aloxe-Corton
Cuvée Dr. Peste	Aloxe-Corton (Hospices de Beaune)
Clos des Porrets-Saint-Georges	Nuits-Saint-Georges
Mazis-Chambertin	Gevrey-Chambertin
Les Amoureuses	Chambolle-Musigny
Clos de Tart	Morey-Saint-Denis
Les Pruliers	Nuits-Saint-Georges
Les Cailles	Nuits-Saint-Georges
Les Caillerets	Volnay
Clos de la Perrière	Fixin
Clos Saint-Jacques	Gevrey-Chambertin
Les Varoilles	Gevrey-Chambertin
Les Échezeaux	Flagey-Échezeaux
Les Beaux-Monts (also Beaumonts)	Vosne-Romanée
Les Malconsorts	Vosne-Romanée
Clos de la Roche	Morey-Saint-Denis
Les Fremiets	Volnay
Les Champans	Volnay
Les Suchots	Vosne-Romanée
Clos des Réas	Vosne-Romanée
Chapelle-Chambertin	Gevrey-Chambertin
Charmes-Chambertin	Gevrey-Chambertin
Griotte-Chambertin	Gevrey-Chambertin
Clos du Chapitre	Fixin
Clos des Lambrays	Morey-Saint-Denis
Les Rugiens	Pommard
Les Épenots	Pommard
Les Jarollières	Pommard
Clos de la Maréchale	Nuits-Prémeaux
Didiers-Saint-Georges	Nuits-Prémeaux
Clos des Corvées	Nuits-Prémeaux
Les Vaucrains	Nuits-Saint-Georges
Les Santenots	Meursault
Les Fèves	Beaune
Les Grèves	Beaune
Clos des Mouches	Beaune
Clos de la Boudriotte	Chassagne-Montrachet
Clos Saint-Jean	Chassagne-Montrachet
Clos Morgeot	Chassagne-Montrachet
Clos de la Commaraine	Pommard
Les Angles	Volnay
Le Clos Blanc	Pommard
Les Pézerolles	Pommard
Clos Saint-Denis	Morey-Saint-Denis

WHITE WINES

Vineyard	Commune
Le Montrachet	Chassagne and Puligny-Montrachet
Chevalier-Montrachet	Puligny-Montrachet
Clos des Perrières	Meursault
Bâtard-Montrachet	Chassagne and Puligny-Montrachet
Corton-Charlemagne	Aloxe-Corton
Les Perrières	Meursault
Les Ruchottes	Chassagne-Montrachet
Musigny Blanc	Chambolle-Musigny
Les Charmes	Meursault
Les Combottes	Puligny-Montrachet
Clos Blanc de Vougeot	Vougeot

See also Côte de Nuits; Côte de Beaune; Burgundy.

Côte Rôtie

Red wine.

District: Rhône Valley, France.

The second most celebrated of the Rhône wines, coming after Châteauneuf-du-Pape, is the red Côte Rôtie, generous, rich in color and tasting of truffles or raspberries. The "roasted slope" is on a hillside, barely two miles long and terraced steeply with old stone walls. Here, in the exiguous parcels of vineyard, the grapes sun themselves on the vines all the summer long. The Côte lies on the right bank of the River Rhône at the northern end of the Côtes du Rhône region. The vineyards are split between the communes of Ampuis and Tupin-et-Semons and face south-southeast. The wines are high in alcohol and have a concentrated astringent characteristic.

The slope is in two parts: the Côte Brune and the Côte Blonde. The difference can be seen in the soil and tasted in the wines. In the Côte Brune, the land is brownish, rich in clay, containing large amounts of iron oxide; the Côte Blonde's soil, lighter in color, is dominated by chalk and clay. The wines of the Côte Brune are the milder at the outset but become strong and vigorous with age, while their blond counterparts are sprightly and gay when young but fade considerably faster. Legend has it that the real reason for the difference between the two is that Maugiron—an early lord of Ampuis—presented these vineyards to his two daughters, one blond, the other brunette, and the slopes assumed the characteristics of their respective mistresses and have retained them ever since.

The wines of both slopes are red. Full to a point of concentrated warmth and long-lived, they have an assertive bouquet, and a suave satiny finish. To avoid an excess of vigor, the *vigneron* adds to his fermenting wine a small amount—never more than 20% of the total—of white grapes. This addition rounds it out and adds a measure of finesse. Syrah is the red grape used, Viognier the white, and the two grow side by side on the plunging cliffs.

In recent years the vineyards have been shrinking because of the steepness of the slopes where they are set out. Mechanization is impossible, and all the labor must be done by hand. Paradoxically enough, the wines have been gaining in reputation as the vineyards have been shrinking, and the obvious temptation to "stretch" the wines has not, unfortunately, always been resisted. Present official figures reveal about 65 hectares (162 acres) of vines in the Côte Rôtie, and about 2,000 hectoliters (53,000 U.S. gallons, 44,000 imp.) of wine annually.

Coteau

French for hillside (plural: *coteaux*). The word occurs in the names of certain wine districts—e.g., Coteaux de la Loire.

Coteaux d'Aix, Coteaux des Baux

Red, white, and rosé wines.
District: Provence, France.

Provençal wines harvested in and around the city of Aix-en-Provence in certain delimited areas. The wines have the right to the qualification Vins Délimités de Qualité Supérieure, the secondary classification of French wines. They may be red, white, or rosé, the minimum alcoholic content of the reds and rosés being 11% and the whites 11.5%. Permissible vines are the Grenache, Carignan, Clairette, Cinsault, Ugni Blanc, Mourvèdre, Cournoise, and the Muscat vine-types.

The name Coteaux des Baux cannot stand alone but must always be Coteaux d'Aix, Coteaux des Baux. The area in which it is harvested takes in six communes, none of which may be included among the twenty-eight which may grow wines simply labeled Coteaux d'Aix. In both cases they are minor Provençal wines.

Coteaux de l'Aubance

White and some rosé wines.
District: Anjou, France.

The small lazy River Aubance flows northward into the Loire, joining it about 48 kilometers (30 miles) downstream from Saumur, running through gently sloping hillsides which support vineyards of a quality only slightly below those of Anjou's Coteaux de la Loire and Coteaux du Layon. The white wines made in Aubance are generally sweet, sometimes semi-sweet, and are among those Angevin wines most frequently encountered abroad. The rosés do not differ appreciably from any others made in the region. Chenin Blanc grapes only are allowed for white wines—the sweetest of which are allowed to attain the noble rot (*q.v.*) before they are picked—and Cabernet Franc is dominant for rosé. Some 12,000 hectoliters (318,000 U.S. gallons, 264,000 imp.) are produced annually.

See Anjou.

Coteaux du Languedoc

Red, white, and rosé wines.
District: Languedoc, France.
(Vins du Midi.)

Although the Hérault department—midway between Marseille and Toulouse in southern France—produces the pleasant Appellation Contrôlée wines of Muscat de Frontignan and Clairette du Languedoc, its real reputation comes from the V.D.Q.S. wines of the Coteaux du Languedoc, which are produced in far greater quantities. The Coteaux du Languedoc *appellation* was created in 1963 as a generic name under which a dozen smaller local *appellation* V.D.Q.S. wines could be sold. Only red and rosé wines are eligible to qualify for the Coteaux du Languedoc label. Once they qualify, they may be sold with or without the commune name. Total area is about 10,000 hectares. The total amount of wine sold as Coteaux du Languedoc depends on how much is *labelisé*, varying from 100,000 to 200,000 hectoliters (265,000 to 530,000 U.S. gallons, 220,000 to 440,000 imp.) per year. The eligible wines are:

> Pic-Saint-Loup
> Cabrières
> Coteaux de la Méjanelle
> Coteaux de Saint-Christol
> Coteaux de Vérargues
> Faugères
> Saint-Chinian
> Saint-Saturnin
> Montpeyroux
> Saint-Drézéry
> Saint-Georges-d'Orques
> La Clape and Quatourze

In cases where the production is both red (or rosé) and white, only the red and rosé are eligible for the Coteaux du Languedoc label. The name Cabrières applies only to rosé wine. The reds and rosés are made mostly from a blend of Carignan, Cinsault, Grenache Noir, and Aramon. Since the soil, climate, and style of vinification are nearly the same for each of these wines, it is the blend of grapes which distinguishes one from another.

La Clape, Côtes de Cabardès et de l'Orbiel, and Quatourze lie in the neighboring Aude *département* but are considered part of the Coteaux du Languedoc.

The maximum legal yield for all the wines is 50 hectoliters per hectare, or about three tons to the acre. In this most productive of French vineyards, where the vines are those varieties which can give huge crops, the permissible yield is far below the level harvested in the "premium" wine districts of California. If the French can take steps to control the quality of some of their least-known wines, certainly the growers and legislators in the United States could do the same for the most famous American ones.

See Appendix G.

Coteaux du Layon

Loire Valley white wine.
District: Anjou, France.

Principally, the sweetest, richest, and most mellow of all the Angevin white wines, and, when successful, the best. Although less flowery than a Sauternes, they have an inimitable bouquet and a lightness that belies their alcoholic content, often as high as 15%. They are slow to mature but long-lived. Some dry white wines, also, are made in the district.

See Anjou.

Coteaux du Loir

Loire Valley red, white, and rosé wines.
District: Department of the Sarthe, France.

A small wine district north of the Loire producing red, rosé, and white wines and easily confused with the Coteaux de la Loire. The River Loir is actually a tributary of the main stream.

As is true throughout the Loire, white wines tend to be better than reds. They come from Chenin Blanc grapes, must contain a minimum of 10% alcohol, and are dry wines, except when an exceptionally hot summer generates enough sugar in the grape for the making of sweet and semi-sweet wines. These, in contrast to the fast-maturing dry wines, sometimes require a certain amount of bottle-age before they are ready to drink.

Red and rosé wines come from Pineau d'Aunis (rapidly being replaced by Cabernets), from Cabernet Franc, Gamay, and Cot grapes, and Groslot (up to 25% of grapes used) is allowed for rosé. The vines are planted in soil ranging from chalky clay (which in general supports grapevines for white wines) to a mixture of clay and flint; and the wines are occasionally semi-sparkling or crackling (*pétillant* in French). Annual production is about 200 hectoliters (5,300 U.S. gallons, 4,400 imp.).

See Anjou.

Coteaux de la Loire

Loire Valley white wines.
District: Anjou, France.

Slightly harder and not quite as sweet as growths from the Coteaux du Layon across the river, these are nevertheless very agreeable dessert wines. The better ones among them have up to 12% or 13% of alcohol, and preserve a certain amount of extra sugar. The rich sweetness is achieved in the same manner as in the Sauternes region of Bordeaux—by leaving the grapes on the vine in the autumn until the noble rot (*q.v.*) sets in.

The finest vineyard plot in this area is Savennières, to which the French wine authority awarded a special Appellation Contrôlée in 1953.

Not all the wines grown on these slopes are sweet. The area extends into part of the Muscadet region, near Nantes, and here the wines, though the more robust of their kind, are light, pale, and dry.

See Anjou.

Coteaux de Saumur

See Saumur; Anjou.

Coteaux de Touraine and Coteaux de Touraine-Mousseux

See Touraine.

Coteaux du Tricastin

Rhône Valley red, white, and rosé wines.
District: Rhône Valley, France.

Motorists driving on the Paris-Riviera superhighway pass by the vineyards of this recent Appellation Contrôlée some 50 kilometers (about 31 miles) south of Valence in the department of the Drôme. The grapes grow on the slopes to the left of the road. Tricastin adjoins the much larger Côtes du Rhône region, and accordingly the grape varieties in the two districts are similar; Grenache, Mourvèdre, and Cinsaut are used to make both wines. Most of the annual 50,000 hectoliters produced (1,325,000 U.S. gallons, 1,100,000 imp.) is red wine.

Côtes d'Agly

Sweet fortified wines.
District: Roussillon, France.

Not far from the Spanish border in the eastern Pyrenees the Appellation Contrôlée of Côtes d'Agly produces on the average about 100,000 hectoliters (2.65 million U.S. gallons, 2.2 million imp.) of strong, sweet white wine every year. A small quantity of red is also made, but it is generally inferior to the wine from nearby Corbières and seldom leaves the area.

See Sweet fortified wines of France.

Côtes de Bergerac

See Bergerac.

Côtes de Blaye

See Blaye.

Côtes de Bordeaux

See Premières Côtes de Bordeaux.

Côtes de Bordeaux Saint-Macaire

White wine district of Bordeaux making good secondary wines.

Côtes de Bourg

See Bourg.

Côtes de Buzet

Red and white wines.
District: Southwest France.

Between the great Bordeaux and Armagnac regions in Aquitaine lies an important fruit orchard area whose products are known throughout France. In the heart of this district on the left bank of the River Garonne is the Buzet Appellation Contrôlée. All of the wine—about 10,000 hectoliters (265,000 U.S. gallons, 220,000 imp.) every year—is made by the cooperative run by a former manager of Château Lafite. The red wines are better than the white wines, and fortunately more red is produced.

Côtes Canon Fronsac, Côtes de Fronsac

Red wines.
District: Bordeaux, France.

The medieval town of Fronsac, near which Charlemagne once had a castle, set in the fork of the rivers Isle and Dordogne, 24 kilometers (15 miles) east of Bordeaux, has two of the Appellations Contrôlées or official place-names in Bordeaux wines. Some white wine is made, but only red is entitled to an *appellation*. Côtes de Fronsac encloses the smaller zone of Côtes Canon Fronsac, which produces the finer wines, although some of the first vineyards in the larger area are almost equally good. Côtes Canon Fronsac lies on the high rim of the Canon Hills, a great green bluff overlooking the Dordogne. The small region is proud of its name and boasts two separate Châteaux Canon, as well as eight other vineyards which include Canon in their name. These are not to be confused with *the* Château Canon of Saint-Émilion.

The wines are heavy for Bordeaux, and a delicacy formerly found only in a few of the best growths is very slowly making its way downward among the wines, which in the past have not been as well made as they should. The heavy, hearty red wines find their main following in the countries bordering the English Channel and North Sea. In 1956, led by an industrialist from the north of France who has retired to his Fronsac vineyard with his American wife, the first organized attempt was made to bring the region up to date and into competition with famous neighboring places such as Saint-Émilion, Pomerol, and Médoc.

In the February 1956 freeze which destroyed or damaged one-third of the Bordeaux vineyards, Fronsac was least touched of all, because of its elevated position on high bluffs which escaped the cold; and with this fresh start the growers of the region decided both to improve their wine-making and to make the wine better known abroad. Convincing an essentially peasant and parochial-minded populace of the necessity of this has been the most difficult part of the project.

Côtes de Fronsac produces about 25,000 hectoliters (6,625,000 U.S. gallons, 5,500,000 imp.) of wine each year, much of it big and fruity. Canon Fronsac makes approximately half that quantity.

Côtes de Castillon

Red wines.
District: Bordeaux, France.

Pleasant secondary wines of Bordeaux (*q.v.*). Many excellent values can be found among the well-selected vineyards of this district which neighbors Saint-Émilion.

Côtes de Duras

Red and white wines grown in fifteen communes around the town of Duras about 112 kilometers (70 miles) to the southeast of the city of Bordeaux, in France. The white wines are made from the Sémillon, Sauvignon, Muscadelle, and Mauzet grape varieties, and the red from the Cabernet, Merlot, and Malbec vines. The wines must have a minimum alcoholic content of 10% for red wines and 10.5% for white.

Most of the wines produced on the 1,000 hectares (2,500 acres) of vineyards are white and the total varies from about 10,000 to 50,000 hectoliters per year (265,000 to 1,325,000 U.S. gallons, 220,000 to 1,100,000 imp.).

Côtes du Jura or Côtes du Jura-Mousseux

See Jura.

Côtes-du-Marmandais

V.D.Q.S. wines made in a small district centered around the town of Marmande, just southeast of the Bordeaux region on the River Garonne. The red and white wines are only of local interest.

Côtes de Montravel

See Bergerac.

Côtes de Provence

Designation for wines of secondary guaranteed quality (V.D.Q.S.) in Provence, France.
See Provence.

Côtes du Rhône

The name of a vineyard region (and its wines) bordering the River Rhône in southeast France.
See Rhône.

Côtes du Roussillon

Wedged between the Pyréneés and the Mediterranean, the Roussillon vineyards produce dry red, rosé, and white wine as well as a large assortment of fortified sweet aperitif wines—*vins doux naturels.*
See Grand Roussillon.

Côtes de Toul

One of the two controlled place-names in the Lorraine area of France. The qualities are classed Vins Délimités de Qualité Supérieure (delimited wines of superior quality) and most of them are *vins gris,* the traditional light pink of Lorraine (*q.v.*).

Côtes du Ventoux

Rhône Valley red and rosé wines.
District: Southern France.

Between Provence and the Rhône Valley the dry and wind-swept Vaucluse plateau rises 40 kilometers (25 miles) east of Avignon. The Côtes du Ventoux vineyards which extend over 10,000 hectares (25,000 acres) of this plateau lie directly east of Carpentras, a town famous for its melons, and just south of Mont Ventoux.

The Grenache Noir grape, the basic variety for all the regions of the southern Côtes-du-Rhône, is grown along with Cinsaut, Syrah, Mourvèdre, and Carignan. Each of these grapes does well in the poor, red Mediterranean soil, which is here a mixture of the hard limestone of the Ventoux massif itself, talus, and drift boulders. The forty-six communes included in the Appellation Contrôlée, created in 1971, make about 100,000 hectoliters (2.65 million U.S. gallons, 2.2 million imp.) of predominantly red wine each year. One-fourth of the wine made is solid, fruity, and tannic red, while over half of the Côtes du Ventoux production is so-called *café* or "one night's" wine. Lighter in character and in alcoholic content than the other reds, these *café* wines are de-vatted and pressed before the end of fermentation. They are by far the most popular wines of this Appellation Contrôlée.

Couderc, Georges

A French hybridizer who has developed vines suitable for sound but unspectacular wines both in France and elsewhere.

Château Couhins

Bordeaux white wine.
District: Graves, France.
Commune: Villenave-d'Ornon.

Adjoining Château Carbonnieux and Château Bouscaut, Couhins and the former Château Pont de Langon (now one vineyard), until 1969 belonged to the proprietors of Château Calon-Ségur in the Médoc. Past owners of parts of the property have been a Spanish ambassador to France and a bishop of Algiers.

The estate was purchased in 1969 by the French government for use as a center for wine experiments. André Lurton, the brother of Lucien Lurton of Château Brane-Cantenac in the Médoc, leases Couhins and makes good wine from 50% Sauvignon, 25% Muscadelle, and 25% Sémillon grapes. The wine was ranked as one of the best white Graves in 1959.

Characteristics. Light but full of character, with a charming flavor. A very well-made dry wine.
Vineyard area: 10 hectares (25 acres).
Average production: 30 *tonneaux* (2,500 cases).

Coulant

A wine-taster's term for wines low in tannin and alcoholic content, light, fresh, and very easy to drink. In French it means "running," as applied to a stream or brook.

Coulure

Vine disease: dropping of flower-clusters or berries during the initial period of development—or simply a failure to develop.
See Chapter Eight, p. 29.

Court noué

Another name for infectious degeneration of vines. Also called fanleaf.
See Chapter Eight, p. 29.

Courtier

French term for a wine-broker—who is known in Alsace as a *gourmet.*

Château Coutet

Bordeaux white wine.
District: Sauternes, France.
Commune: Barsac.

Château Coutet is entitled to use either of the legal French place-names Sauternes or Barsac. Barsac, an Appellation Contrôlée in its own right, is one of the five communes included in the Sauternes district. In 1855, when the wines were officially classified, Coutet, situated a mile below the town of Barsac, was made a First Growth (*Premier Cru*) of Sauternes.

A web of connections links the vineyard with Château d'Yquem. The architecture of the oldest parts of both châteaux—dating from the thirteenth century—is identical; the well in the courtyard of Coutet has its exact duplicate in the courtyard of d'Yquem, half a dozen miles away; Château Coutet belonged until 1923 to the Lur-Saluces family, which has for two centuries owned d'Yquem.

The present proprietor is M. Marcel Baly of Strasbourg, who purchased the estate from M. and Mme Edmond Rolland a few years ago. Mme Rolland's father had bought Coutet in 1925 from the syndicate which acquired it from the great-uncle of the present Count de Lur-Saluces.

The *chais* stand across the courtyard from the château. Grapes are brought in at vintage when they have achieved the sugar-rich state of overripeness standard in Sauternes and are pressed in one of the big electric Guy et Mital presses before being pitchforked into a suction funnel which carries them into a huge rolling tube. This carries away the stems, and then the pulp is pressed twice again, the juice dripping and gushing down through trapdoors into the vat below the floor. The juice must be run off every night into barrels, where it ferments and then remains for three years achieving maturity.

Believed by many to be the best of the Barsacs, the wine is the result of the most careful viniculture. When the proprietor feels that it does not come up to his standard, he sells it as anonymous Barsac, refusing to give it the name of the château.

Like all other flat-lying vineyards in Sauternes, Coutet was badly hit by the February 1956 freeze. The present label is the same as that of Château Filhot, which belongs to the Lur-Saluces family.

Characteristics. The wine is more *nerveux,* or more piercing, than its Sauternes counterparts, and it is this particular quality which is said to have given the château its name. (Coutet comes from the French word *couteau,* or knife; and the wine takes its characteristics from its rocky, calcareous subsoil.) Although Barsacs have the same degree of sweetness, or *liqueur,* as the nearby Sauternes, usually varying from 3% to 6% Baumé, they are drier to the taste because of this piercing quality. This wine has great breed and holds its fruit for a long time.

Vineyard area: 32 hectares (80 acres).

Average production: 75 *tonneaux* (6,500 cases).

Cradle

A wicker or wire basket designed to hold a wine bottle in a position slightly above the horizontal and theoretically to ensure that the sediment will be stirred up as little as possible when the wine is served.

If the wine is carefully transported from cellar to table in a cradle and all of it is poured into glasses in one smooth action—which obviously requires a number of glasses—the cradle may be of some service. Otherwise the rocking back and forth of the wine in the cradle stirs up the sediment, and it is preferable to decant.

Cramant

Village in the Épernay district of Champagne which makes one of the greatest wines of the Côte des Blancs. *See* Champagne.

Cream Sherry

Heavily sweetened Oloroso Sherry. Unknown in Spain, launched in England, the style is now highly popular in the United States. *See* Sherry.

Crémant

A white wine made of red and white grapes and only partly sparkling. This wine is found in Champagne, but the word is not to be confused with Cramant, a wine-making village of Champagne.

Crémant de Bourgogne

Formerly known as Sparkling Burgundy (*q.v.*), Crémant de Bourgogne is the sparkling wine made from any of a number of Burgundian grape varieties (Pinot Chardonnay, Pinot Noir, Gamay, César, Tressot) according to the Champagne method. In the past, the sparkling wines were red, rosé, and white; at present, however, the term "Crémant de Bourgogne" is reserved for whites and rosés alone. Annual production averages around 5,000 hectoliters (13,250 U.S. gallons, 11,000 imp.).

Crème

Literally "cream"; on a liqueur-label, the word once designated a drink that had been sweetened, to differentiate it from a dry spirit such as a brandy. In contemporary usage it still generally means a sweet liqueur. Some of the better known Crèmes are:

Ananas (pineapple)	Mandarine (tangerine)
Banane (banana)	Menthe (peppermint)
Cacao (cocoa)	Moka (coffee)
Café (coffee)	Noyau (almond)
Cassis (blackcurrant)	Prunelle (sloe)
Chocolat (chocolate)	Roses (rose)
Cumin (caraway seeds)	Thé (tea)
Fraise (strawberry)	Vanille (vanilla)
Framboise (raspberry)	Violette (violet)

Crème Yvette

Very sweet American liqueur flavored with the Parma violet and named for Yvette Guilbert, the incomparable French diseuse who had a memorable success in the 1890s.

Crépy

Crépy is a light white wine of at least 9.5% of alcohol from the chalky slopes on the southern side of Lake Geneva in the French department of Haute-Savoie. The wines are grown on a scant 60 hectares (150 acres) and are dry and aromatic. Some of them are naturally *pétillant*, the semi-sparkling condition usually translated as "crackling." Some 4,000 hectoliters (106,000 U.S. gallons, 88,000 imp.) are made yearly from the Chasselas grape, and they are rarely, if ever, shipped.

Crescenz

Common misspelling of Kreszenz (*q.v.*), one of the German words indicating the grower.

Criollas

A *Vitis vinifera* variety descended from the vines brought by the Spanish Conquistadores to Mexico, from where it was spread by the Jesuits to Argentina. In the early eighteenth century the grape was planted in California, where it is known as Mission. Though still a leading producer, the Criollas lacks acidity and color and as a result makes only fair quality white and rosé wines.

Criots-Bâtard-Montrachet

Burgundy white wine.
District: Côte de Beaune, France.
Commune: Chassagne-Montrachet.
Official Classification: Great Growth (Grand Cru).

Yet another of the splendid Montrachets, coming from a vineyard of about 1.4 hectares (3.5 acres). The wines of Chassagne have an unmistakable flavor: dry but not hard, inclined to be flowery, but with no sweetness in the aftertaste. The average production is about 50 hectoliters (1,325 U.S. gallons, 1,100 imp.).
See Bâtard-Montrachet; Chassagne-Montrachet.

Château Croizet-Bages

Bordeaux red wine.
District: Haut-Médoc, France.
Commune: Pauillac.

One of the several Fifth Growths (*Cinquièmes Crus*) in the 1855 Classification of great vineyards, the vineyards are planted on what was the old domain of Bages, in the hamlet now with the same name on hilly land near Pauillac. The estate is sometimes known as Château Calvé-Croizet-Bages. The proprietors, the widow and son of the late M. Paul Quié, also own the Second Growth (*Deuxième Cru*) vineyard Rauzan-Gassies in Margaux and Château Bel-Orme-Tronquoy-de-Lalande, a Bourgeois Supérieur growth near Saint-Estèphe.
Characteristics. Good but not outstanding.
Vineyard area: 25 hectares (62.5 acres).
Average production: 100 *tonneaux* (9,000 cases).

Crozes-Hermitage

French red and white wines.
See Hermitage; Rhône.

Cru

French for growth. In French usage the word denotes a vineyard of high quality, usually considered worthy of independent recognition under the laws of classification. An officially classified vineyard is *Cru Classé*.

Crushing

The process of mashing the grapes in a mill or pounding them with a rammer to extract the juice. The French term is *broyage*.

Crust

The deposit in old Port. It is so called because it forms a crust around a bottle.

Crusted Port

Bigger and fuller-bodied than most Tawny Ports or Ruby Ports, the style is like that of Vintage Ports and improves in bottle. Seldom from a single vintage year and never from a great year (because in such a case a Port vintage would have been declared), it will not have quite the magnificence of a vintage-year Port. Decanting is required.
See Port.

Cruzan Rum

Of St. Croix, Virgin Islands.
See Rum, Virgin Islands.

Cryptogams

A genus of fungi, some of which cause a disease that affects vines.
See Chapter Eight, p. 29.

Culaton

This is the Piedmontese word for the bottom of the bottle, or dregs. In Piedmont, northern Italy, there is an old superstition that the dregs should be saved until the day after the bottle is opened and then given to friends. Considering the heaviness of the deposit formed by Piedmontese wines this seems an odd, unfriendly gift.

Cumin Liquidum Optimum Castelli

Generally referred to as C.L.O.C. This is a Danish liqueur, white and flavored with caraway seed. The name means "The best caraway liqueur in the castle." A form of kümmel.

Cup

A summer drink served in glass jugs and made of iced wine diluted with soda-water, with an addition of spirit or liqueur, decorated with pieces of fruit, and iced.

Curaçao

Originally a Dutch liqueur made from the skins of oranges which grow on the Dutch island of Curaçao off the coast of Venezuela. It became so popular that many distillers sell it, under different names. Cointreau and Grand Marnier are examples of proprietary types; while Triple Sec is made by many firms.

Cut

To adulterate liquor with water, or one wine with another—for example, ordinary red wines of France may be cut with Algerian.

Cuve

French term for wine vat.

Cuvée

French term for contents of wine vat; hence a vatting. The term now usually means all the wine of a vat, or all the wine made at one time and under similar conditions. In France it also means a vineyard parcel or lot. In Champagne, there are two further meanings. Vin de Cuvée is the wine of the first pressing. A *cuvée* is also a blend of Champagnes, or a special lot of wine.

Cyprus

The island of Cyprus, edged by jagged beaches, lies in the eastern-most part of the Mediterranean, about 96 kilometers (60 miles) from the Lebanon coast. Its plains are sun-baked, but snow lies on the mountain peaks from January until April, and most of the wine comes from the slopes. Viticulture is important in the island. Out of a farming population of some 64,000 families, about 30,000 are dependent to a certain extent on vine cultivation and the wine industry—which has expanded considerably in the past twenty years. The island's vineyards now cover more than 50,000 hectares (125,000 acres)—about 10% of the arable land.

These vineyards, which look so romantic to tourists, are to be found mainly in the volcanic soil of the southern foothills of the Troödos Mountains, in the districts of Limassol, Paphos, and to a lesser extent in Nicosia and the region of the Makheras Mountains. Driving from Limassol to Paphos, one sees vines planted in orderly rows—sweet table grapes twined round arches and arbors interspersed with wine grapes; young vines set out sparsely in the ash-gray soil; mature plants, tall and bushy. At harvest-time, when loads of grapes are being rushed to the big wineries in trucks, the road is slippery with red juice. On the zigzag mountain roads, the view is spectacular: a vast patchwork of vines spread over the mountain slopes, dwindling higher up into small plots around the old villages. Peasant farmers make wine for themselves—sometimes the thick, strongly concentrated dark wines of tradition—but most of the grapes are sold to the big shipping firms.

With an average harvest of over 100,000 tons (112,000 short tons) of grapes, production per head of the population is relatively higher than that of various important wine-making countries in Europe. About 1 million hectoliters of wine (26.5 million U.S. gallons, 22 million imp.) is made annually.

WINE HISTORY

Cyprus, island of Aphrodite, who was worshipped in the temple at Paphos, is known to have been inhabited since the Mycenean Age, and to have traded with other Aegean peoples. Both Greeks and Phoenicians founded colonies there. In the Cyprus Museum there is a beautiful amphora believed to date from about 900 B.C. Recent excavations of mosaics and other remains bear witness to the fact that wine-making flourished in ancient Cyprus; and it is known that the wines were drunk in ancient Egypt, as well as in classical Greece and Rome. Many of the local legends are connected with the cult of Aphrodite, in whose honor great feasts were held, especially on the occasion of the annual pilgrimage to her temple at Palaipaphos. Hesiod described how the Cypriot Nama was made from the sun-dried grapes. This sweet wine was renamed Commandaria by the Knights Templar, to whom, in 1191, Richard I gave the island. Because of its superb quality, the Commanders monopolized its sales, and their Commandaria has been made in Cyprus ever since. Today's Commandaria has the oldest tradition of any individually named wine. In the chronicle of Richard Coeur de Lion's journeys during the Crusades, it is recorded that on his first arrival on the island, there was a banquet at which were offered "the very best wines from the vineyards of Cyprus, which, it is reported, are unlike those of any other country." Centuries later, in 1743, Richard Pococke wrote in London of "The rich Cyprus wine which is so much esteemed in all parts of the world and is very dear and produced only about Limassol. In some places indeed they make good red wine." Cyprus wine was imported into Britain in the times of the Plantagenets. Commandaria was drunk at a great banquet given in London in 1352 by Henry Richard, Master of the Vintners' Company, in honor of King Peter I of Cyprus. There were five monarchs at the dinner: Edward III of England, David of Scotland, John of France, and Waldemar of Denmark, besides Peter I of Cyprus—and so the party came to be known as "The Feast of the Five Kings." More than two hundred years later, Queen Elizabeth I granted a profitable monopoly to Sir Walter Raleigh for the importation of Cyprus wines through Southampton, where a small colony of Cypriot merchants flourished.

There is a story that a taste for the local wine decided the Turkish Sultan Selim II to capture Cyprus in 1571. Selim, renowned for his indulgence in wine (he was nicknamed The Sot), summoned his commander-in-chief and ordered him to take the island, with the words: "Within the island there is a treasure which only the King of Kings is worthy of possessing."

Viticulture was not abolished under Turkish rule;

wines were made in large quantities, but the quality was no longer that which had been eulogized by writers at the beginning of the century. It was not until 1878, when the English began to administer the island, that new life came to the vineyards. By some miracle, the phylloxera plague did not reach Cyprus, and the old vines have continued growing on their own roots.

Cyprus vines have played their part in the creation of some famous wines abroad. They were introduced into Madeira in the fifteenth century, for the famous Madeira wine. A similar origin has been attributed to Marsala and Hungarian Tokay. In the past twenty years there has been a marked improvement in the Cyprus wine trade. The foundations of the island's success in the foreign market were laid by Mr. F. Rossi of London. In 1956, he drew up a report on the Cypriot wine industry, recommending improvements and experiments. As a result, cuttings of new varieties were sent to Cyprus—where the government has since been vigorous in following up Mr. Rossi's recommendations. A wine council, representing all sides of the industry, was formed. Other investigations were carried out by such specialists as Professor J. Branas, professor of viticulture at the University of Montpelier. Consequently, the Cypriot wineries were modernized and the latest production equipment installed—including controlled fermentation units. Systematic checks and studies on viticulture, site selection, soils, and diseases were undertaken by the government agencies, and technical assistance was provided for those who needed it. Because Cyprus had never had the phylloxera, the new varieties had at first to be most carefully isolated and so were planted at a quarantine station at Ayia Irini. Gradually, these have been coming into commercial production, making an important contribution to the quality of Cyprus "sherry" and beverage wines.

The European vines have been useful in offsetting a natural tendency for white wines grown in hot climates to be a bit flat, lacking in acidity and freshness.

GRAPE VARIETIES

About 80% to 85% of the wine-making grapes are red (Mavron), 10% to 15% white (Xynisteri), and about 2% to 3% Muscat.

The local Mavron wine is grown in most of the vineyards of Cyprus—the finest of the variety on the slopes of a hill named Afames, near the village of Platres. Some of the best red wines are made from grapes from this area.

The white Xynisteri vine is cultivated in many districts. Pitsilia and the vineyards of the Paphos area in the west are noted for this variety, which forms 90% of the production of the Famagusta and Larnaca vineyards.

TYPES OF WINE

Red Wines

These are made mainly from the local red grapes, but other species are introduced to give acidity, color, and a more balanced must; notably an oval grape named Oph-

thalma and the Maratheftika, so called because it was grown originally in the Marathassa area.

The Mavron grape also is used in the production of the rosé known on the island and in Greece as Kokkineli. It is deep in color for a rosé, fresh to the palate, and usually quite dry. When iced, it can be drunk with almost any food. Among the better-known red wines are Afames and Othello, both dry. It is important to remember, however, that much of the wine is made to appeal to the local taste which, in reds, is for a very full, deep-colored wine with a high tannin content. This goes well with the strongly flavored spicy foods of Cyprus.

White Wines

The finished white wines are full-bodied with a flavor entirely their own. Most of them are fairly dry: people like them so, and the local yeasts are capable of fermentation (if any free sugar is also present) in the presence of even the usual high degree of alcohol found in Cypriot wines. Among the better-known white wines are Aphrodite and Arsinoë, both dry.

Commandaria

This luscious dessert wine, the one for which Cyprus is famous, has been made for hundreds of years in the mountain villages—and especially in Kalokhorio, Zoopiyi, and Yerassa. The informing grape varieties are Mavron and Xynisteri. Now, as in ancient Greece, the growers blend white grapes with red, and some of them still mature their wine as it was aged in Homeric days, in huge earthenware jars, but most of it is now matured in modern cement tanks, although the grapes are first spread out in the sun as they were in Hesiod's day. Traditionally, Commandaria was developed by the Mana system, in which the oldest jar is never empty but is filled up with younger wines, as in the Sherry *solera*. The basic wines change from village to village, according to the method used and the proportion of red grapes to white. Nowadays, all the processes in the blending and maturing of commercial Commandaria are carried out by the big companies which buy the wines from the farmers; and the sweet brown product has little in common with the concentrate—so thick it can be scraped from the sides of the container with a knife—which still, sometimes, is found in the villages. Quality varies: the role of the blender is all-important. Guests of the shippers may be lucky enough to taste Commandaria a century old: dark, velvety, mellow, with the rich, toasted sweetness of the sun-baked grapes.

Sherry-types

A large range of "sherries" is made in Cyprus for the home and export markets. They vary considerably in style. Britain, the principal market abroad, has received some wines of the same alcoholic strength as Spanish Sherry, clarified and bottled in England; wines of differing alcoholic content to be blended by the importer; and a sweet wine, lower in alcohol, and least expensive of all these moderately priced sherry-types. Lately, however, the Cypriots have been concentrating on high-strength sherries, and Flor Fino. The very dry style is now exported, though not as widely as the popular sweet type. In the Keo *bodega*, the "cream sherries" are left out in their casks to mature in the sun for two or three years before they are moved into the cellars for further ageing in the wood. In making Fino, butts of American oak are almost entirely filled with a specially selected white wine, and the *flor* yeast, carefully cultivated, is placed onto the surface, converting a part of the alcohol present in the wine. Each year, about half the contents are drawn from the cask and replaced with younger wine, while the more mature is transferred to the next store for further ageing in wood.

EXPORT

Limassol, the busy port of the wine-shippers, has been described by the Cypriots as "the Bordeaux of Cyprus." It possesses spacious wineries, equipped with up-to-date installations for pressing, cooling, filtering, and testing wine. Casks are piled high in warehouses beside the sea, and in the sheds outside. At Keo, bottles are shipped in containers each holding 850 cartons, which saves freight charges. The three largest firms are KEO, SODAP, and UC (the oldest), now combined with ETKO.

In 1972, about one-third of a million hectoliters (8,833,000 U.S. gallons, 7,333,000 imp.) of table wine and sherry were exported, with the United Kingdom taking more than half. Cyprus is, increasingly, a source of inexpensive table wines. As a result of changes in the industry, these have been improving, and more and more is being exported, especially for restaurant carafe wines.

Until Britain joined the Common Market, Cyprus enjoyed a preferential Commonwealth tariff from this largest outlet of her market. Special arrangements were made to protect the Cypriot interests, at least in the early stages of the changeover. Naturally, it is hoped on the island that even as a member of the E.E.C., Britain will continue to be a major customer in the Cyprus vineyards. In fact, an agreement between Cyprus and the European Economic Community was signed and came into effect in February 1973, whereby the island was allowed to ship 200,000 hectoliters (5.3 million U.S. gallons, 4.4 million imp.) of "sherry" a year free of countervailing charges to Britain and Ireland. This annual quota continued until January 1, 1975, and was extended to include the marketing of the 1974 vintage. The government of Cyprus, for its part, undertook to adopt regulations over vines and their products corresponding to those applied inside the Community, and to bring those regulations into force from January 1, 1975.

SPIRITS

The island produces about 75,000 hectoliters (1,987,500 U.S. gallons, 1,650,000 imp.) a year of brandy, about a twelfth part of which is exported. In proportion to the sale of wines abroad, the figure for spirits has fallen of late years. Inside Cyprus, people often drink the brandy as a long iced drink or "sour." "V.S.O.P." is made by the cognac method.

Production of brandy and other spirits on a large scale

dates only from the beginning of the British administration. Filfar, rather like Curaçao, and KEO Spécialité, which resembles Cointreau, are two of the liqueurs now being made. The government generally buys up all the grape alcohol, or Zivania, of the island. Flavored with gum mastic and aniseed, it becomes Cypriot spirit in the forms of Masticha and Ouzo.

Czechoslovakia

Czechoslovakia produces wine but is mainly a wine-importing country. While all three regions—Bohemia, Moravia, and Slovakia—make wine, the total harvest does not meet the national demand. In these conditions, little of the product is seen abroad.

Viticulture is an ancient craft among the Czechs but has had a more than usually turbulent history. Wine was certainly grown in Bohemia by the ninth century. In the second part of the fourteenth century, at the direction of Emperor Charles IV, Burgundian vines were imported and planted systematically. Cultivation, especially around Prague in Bohemia, was prolific in the sixteenth century and at the beginning of the seventeenth century before the devastations of the Thirty Years' War. A revival of viticulture was wiped out anew in both the eighteenth and nineteenth centuries, so that Czech wine-growing as it exists today dates only from the 1920s, when the whole natural viticulture was reconstructed.

Production each year is around 1,300,000 hectoliters (34.3 million U.S. gallons, 28 million imp.), nearly all of it white wine. All of the wine is consumed in Czechoslovakia except for a very small quantity of the local "Tokay" sent to foreign markets. And in fact, the Czechs must import 500,000 hectoliters—about one-half of the volume they make—to meet the growing demand. Each person drinks 12 liters per year (3.18 U.S. gallons, 2.64 imp.). More than 40,000 hectares (1 million acres) is in vineyard. The province of Slovakia produces about two-thirds of the total and Moravia makes most of the rest; little is made in Bohemia. The wine-grape growers sell most of their fruit to the state for vinification; only one-fourth of Czechoslovak wine is made by the growers themselves.

Bohemian wines inevitably have an affinity with German wines. Prague is at the same latitude as the Rheingau and the Palatinate, and the principal vines are the same: Rhine Riesling, Traminer, and Sylvaner for the white wines; and Blauer Burgunder, Portugieser, and Saint-Laurent for red wines. The best quality zone is that of the three towns, Litoměřice, Roudnice, and Mělník on the Elbe River not far north of Prague, and also at Brezanky and Velké Zernoseky.

The majority of Moravian wine comes from the southern central area of Czechoslovakia below Brno and just across the border from the Krems-Vienna wine sector in Austria. Here again are affinities which cross national frontiers. The Czech area is bounded by Znojmo in the west, Mikulov on the Czech-Austrian border, and by Hustopeče to the northeast. The Veltliner grape, producing excellent white wine along the Danube in Austria, is used in this region for two types of Riesling, Rhine Riesling and Italian Riesling, the latter accounting for one-third of all vineyard acreage. Important also are Sylvaner, Traminer, Weiss Burgunder, and a variety the Czechs call Rulany, which may be the Ruländer. The wines around Mikulov are exclusively white and are light and aromatic with rather high acidity.

At the eastern end of Czechoslovakia, lying to the north of Hungarian Tokaj, a "Tokay" is made from the Furmint, Lipovina, and Muscatel grapes. The Furmint is widely used in Hungary. The best-known place-name in Czechoslovakia is Malá Trňa. Throughout the rest of the Slovakian region on the borders of the Tatra and Carpathian mountain ranges much wine is made. In the west of the region is the largest vineyard area of Czechoslovakia, about 20,000 hectares (50,000 acres). The chief vines are Veltliner, Italian Riesling, Neuberger Sylvaner, and Muscatel. The largest wine area is north of Bratislava, the most concentrated production at Modra and Pezinok.

D

Dalwood

Important vineyard in New South Wales.
See Australia.

Dame-Jeanne

French term for a large glass bottle containing anything from one to ten gallons, usually covered with wicker and used for storing and transporting wines and spirits; the English equivalent is a demijohn. In Bordeaux, the name is also used for a bottle containing more than a magnum but less than a double magnum; the equivalent of 2½ liters.

Dampierre

Commune producing rosé and red wines in the Coteaux de Saumur district of Anjou (*q.v.*).

Damson gin

A British gin flavored with damsons—small, dark plums.

Danziger Goldwasser

White aniseed and caraway-flavored liqueur, originally plain, later with the addition of gold flakes floating in the bottle. A Silverwasser was also made in which flakes of silver replaced the gold. Both were originally made in the old port of Danzig. A number of firms put out similar liqueurs, of which the Liqueur d'Or made in France is probably the best-known.

Dão

Portuguese red wines, and some white, from the vineyards south of the Douro.
See Portugal.

Château Dauzac

Bordeaux red wine.
District: Haut-Médoc, France.
Commune: Labarde-Margaux.

The vineyard, a Fifth Growth (*Cinquième Cru*), lies on flat gravelly soil in Labarde and is allowed the place-name Margaux. Formerly owned by the Bordeaux wine firm of Nathaniel Johnston, then the property of H. Bernet. Previous owners, the Lynch family, emigrated from Ireland in the eighteenth century. They left their imprint on several châteaux in the Médoc and are an example of the great influence of the Irish in the area.

Mr. A. Miailhe, owner of the adjoining Château Siran, bought Dauzac in 1966. In the early seventies he planted considerable acreage, more than doubling original production; he sold the property in 1977 to Felix Chatellier, who has grown fruit trees in Morocco for many years.
Characteristics. Excellent improvement. It is to be hoped that the new proprietor will continue the progress.
Vineyard area: 40 hectares (100 acres).
Average production: 160 *tonneaux* (14,000 cases).

Debrői Hárslevelű

One of the better dry white wines of Hungary. Wine made from the grape variety Hárslevelű, which also goes into Tokay.
See Hungary.

Decant

To pour wine from its bottle to another container, from which it will be served, in order to separate the wine from its deposit or to oxidate or aerate it.

Decanter

Glass vessel or container usually of attractive design used for serving old wines which have been decanted to separate them from their deposit. It is much too often used also for holding Sherries, Ports, and other wines which do deteriorate, although not rapidly, once the cork is pulled. The best decanters are made of clear crystal, to show off the color of the wine to its best advantage. When the decanter is brought to the table it is customary also to bring the cork from the wine bottle for the inspection and approval of the master of the house.

Deidesheimer Grainhübel

Best wine of Deidesheim in the German Palatinate, or Pfalz.
See Palatinate.

Dégorgement

French term for the removal of the deposit from bottles of Champagne and other sparkling wines.
See Champagne.

Deidesheimer Herrgottsacker

Best-known wine of Deidesheim in the German Palatinate.
See Palatinate.

Deidesheimer Leinhöhle

An outstanding wine of Deidesheim in the German Palatinate.
See Palatinate.

Delaware

One of eastern America's better white-wine grapes, found particularly in Ohio and the New York Finger Lakes district. It yields clean, fresh, spicy but "foxy" wine, much of which is made sparkling.

Délicat, Delikat

French and German terms for the subtle taste of a wine of low alcoholic content—less than 12% of alcohol by volume and sometimes, as in the case of many fine German wines, as low as 8% of alcohol by volume.

Delicatessen

Unexceptional red hybrid grape developed by T. V. Manson of Texas; said to have taken its name from the large number of different grape varieties that went into it.

Demi

Literally "half," meaning half a liter, the term to use when asking for a large glass of draft beer in France. *Demie* (the French feminine) refers to a half-bottle.

Demie-queue

Half a *queue*. Since a *queue* is an ancient Burgundian term for two *pièces* or barrels, a *demie-queue* would be one *pièce*. It holds 228 liters (60.2 U.S. gallons, 50.1 imp.). The term is rarely used.

Demijohn

A large glass bottle with a wicker wrapping, holding anything from one to ten gallons. It is commonly used for storing and transporting wines. The name is a corruption of the French Dame-Jeanne (literally "Lady Jane") and attempts to trace it back to Arabic or Persian have been largely discounted on the evidence that the Arabs seem to have developed their word from the Italian.

Demi-Sec

French for semi-dry. These words appearing on the label of a bottle of Champagne do not, in fact, indicate a dryish wine, but rather one which is sweetish.
See Champagne.

Denaturant

A substance added to alcohol to make it unfit for drinking, thus legally avoiding the heavy excise duty on potable alcohol. Denatured spirits are spirits so treated.

Denmark

Wine is not produced in Denmark, because of the cold climate.

There is considerable trade in "fruit wines," and most popular are the Danish berry wines such as blackcurrant, blackberry, and cherry. In addition, liqueurs are made. The best-known is probably Cherry Heering (*q.v.*), and most of the cherries for this come from the beautiful little Danish island of Sealand. Another popular liqueur is Cloc Brun, a spicy drink with a slight taste of caraway seed, and which is 38.5% alcohol by volume.

SPIRITS

For many years the Danes have been experimenting with the production of whisky. In 1952, Cloc Whisky, the first to be distilled in Denmark, was put on the market. The manufacturers use malt barley which has been dried over a peat fire. The whisky is distilled in pot stills and seasoned in oak barrels.

The most important of the potable spirits industries in Denmark is the making of aquavit (spelled akvavit in Danish).
See Aquavit.

Denominación de Origen

Guarantee of validity on Spanish wine labels.
See Chapter Five, p. 14; Spain.

Denominazione di Origine Controllata

The new system of Italian controlled place-names, usually abbreviated D.O.C.
See Italy.

Densimeter, Densimetry

The densimeter, used for reading the density of grape must, consists of a hollow cylindrical float with a weighted ball beneath and a graduated rod above. The instrument is based on the Archimedean law that a body displaces a quantity of water equal to its own bulk.
See Mustimeter.

Deposit

The sediment that is commonly precipitated from many red wines and some white ones during the normal course of their development in the bottle. In white wines the sediment is usually a tasteless, harmless, and colorless bit of tartaric acid crystal, but in red wines it generally contains bitter tannin and pigment and so should be left in the bottle. Fine old red wines sometimes with a considerable amount of deposit are decanted to separate the wine from the layer in the bottom of the bottle. Bottles for good red wines, such as Bordeaux or Burgundies, have indentations called punts which help hold the sediment apart from the rest of the wine.

Deroldego

Widespread grapevine in Trentino, Italy, producing red wines, especially in the districts of Mezzolombardo and Mezzocorona.

Château Desmirail

Bordeaux red wine.
District: Haut-Médoc, France.
Commune: Margaux.

The vineyard, classed a Third Growth (*Troisième Cru*) in the Gironde Classification of 1855, has been absorbed by Château Palmer. The building, in the village of Margaux, belongs to M. Zuger, the owner of Château Malescot-Saint-Exupéry, and no vineyards are connected with it. The *chais* are in a complete state of disrepair; and the fact that this non-existent vineyard is still included in the lists of the 1855 Classification is further proof of the obsolescence of this classification.

Dessert wine

Full or fortified sweet wine suitable for drinking with or after dessert. In the United States, any wine fortified with brandy or spirits. The table wines in this category are Barsac, Sauternes, sweet Vouvrays or Loire, as well as Beerenauslesen and Trockenbeerenauslesen of the Rhine and Mosel.

Dézaley

Well-known white wine of Lavaux in the canton of Vaud.
See Switzerland.

Dezize-les-Maranges and Dezize-les-Maranges-Côte de Beaune

Burgundy red and white wines.
District: Côte de Beaune, France.

A minor wine-growing commune at the southern end of the Côte de Beaune. The wines are very light, fast-maturing, and sometimes they have a good deal of fruitiness. They are usually blended with wines from certain other communes of the slope and sold as Côte de Beaune-Villages but may occasionally be bottled under their own names. The difference is one of geography and quality. Dezize-les-Maranges alone refers to wine which has been grown on the 60 hectares (150 acres) within the legally approved communal limits. If Côte de Beaune is added, it must come from the 30.4 hectares (75.8 acres) comprising only the best part of the larger area.

Dhroner Hofberg

Outstanding wine of Dhron on the Mosel.
See Mosel-Saar-Ruwer.

Diamond (Moore's Diamond)

An American hybrid grape—developed by Jacob Moore—once widely used as a source for white wine but better adapted to producing table grapes.

Diana

Early American hybrid grape, an attempt to improve the famous Catawba grape. It is still fairly widespread in Ohio and New York State for white wines but is not ideal, since it tends to vary considerably in quality from year to year.

Diastase

A ferment which has the power to convert starch into dextrine, and then into sugar.

Die

See Clairette de Die.

Dimyat

White-wine grape grown on the Black Sea coast of Bulgaria.
See Bulgaria.

Dionysos

Greek god of wine. Originally a nature deity of fruitfulness and wine, he probably came from Thrace. According to Greek mythology, he was the son of Zeus and Semele, a divinity with prophetic gifts, who traveled over the then known world, spreading the knowledge of vine cultivation. He also spread worship of himself, with the frenetic Bacchic rites which (according to the *Bacchae* of Euripides) destroyed Pentheus, King of Thebes, who opposed them. Bacchos, another name for the wine god, was afterward adopted by the Romans as Bacchus (*q.v.*).

Dipping rod

Graduated measure for ascertaining contents of casks.

Distillation

The art or science of distilling. It is based on the fact that alcohol, being lighter than water, vaporizes at a lower temperature, with the result that when a slightly alcoholic liquid is heated to a temperature between the two boiling points, the vapors that rise can be caught and condensed back to form a liquid with a higher alcoholic content. Distilling is done either in single-shot pot stills or continuous patent stills, the quality and characteristics desired dictating the method.

Distillation is defined by J. H. Perry in the third edition of *The Engineers' Handbook* as "the separation of the constituents of a liquid mixture by partial vaporisation of the mixture and separate recovery of vapour and residue. The more volatile constituents of the original mixture are obtained in increased concentration in the vapour; the less volatile in greater concentration in the liquid residue. The completeness of separation depends upon certain properties of the components involved and upon the arrangements of the distillation process.

"In general, *distillation* is the term applied to vaporisation processes in which the vapour evolved is recovered, usually by condensation. *Evaporation* commonly refers to the removal of water from aqueous solution of non-volatile substances by vaporisation. The vapour evolved, *i.e.* the water, is discarded.

"The majority of the applications of distillation are found in the separation of one or more of the components from mixtures of organic compounds."
See Chapter Two, p. 6.

Dizy

Commune near Ay, in the Marne Valley, producing a First Growth Champagne.
See Champagne.

D.O.C.

See Denominazione di Origine Controllata; Italy.

Château Doisy-Daëne

Bordeaux white wine.
District: Sauternes, France.
Commune: Barsac.

The château, classed Second in 1855, makes a sweet wine typical of the district and also a small amount of dry white wine, made in part from Riesling grapes, but not under the château name.
Vineyard area: 11 hectares (28 acres).
Average production: 20 *tonneaux* (1,900 cases).

Château Doisy-Védrines

Bordeaux white wine.
District: Sauternes, France.
Commune: Barsac.

A Second Growth of the 1855 Classification, the property is situated between Châteaux Coutet and Climens, both First Growths according to that ranking. The wine is rich and full. Pierre Casteja—brother of Emile Casteja, vineyard owner in the Médoc—owns the property.
Vineyard area: 25 hectares (62 acres).
Average production: 60 *tonneaux* (5,700 cases).

Dolceacqua (or Rossese)

Red wine of Rossese grapes from along the Italian Riviera.
See Liguria.

Dolcetto

Italian grape producing red wine.
See Piedmont.

Dôle

Good red wine of the Valais from the Dôle or Gamay grape.
See Switzerland.

Dom

The German word for cathedral, several of which have vineyards as part of their endowment. Most notable among these is the Cathedral of Trier on the Mosel, which owns vineyards at Avelsbach south of the town and at Wiltingen on the Saar.

Dom Pérignon

According to legend, the father of Champagne as we know it.
See Champagne.

Domaine, Domäne

French and German terms for wine estate: *Mis en Bouteilles au Domaine* means bottled at the domain or vineyard; the former is the French term for estate-bottling.

Donnaz

Red wine from the Valle d'Aosta in North Italy.
See Piedmont.

Dop brandy

The South African equivalent of marc, or the distillation of grape husks after the wine is pressed out. Dop is of dubious quality, and incredibly high taxes were put on it to make its production economically impossible, with the result that it is now seldom seen.

Dosage

French term for the addition of sugar syrup to sparkling wine before final corking and shipment.
See Champagne.

Doubling

Redistilling spirits to improve strength and flavor.

Douro

One of Portugal's three important rivers.
See Port.

Dousico

Heady Greek drink flavored with aniseed.

Doux

French for sweet, as applied to wines—e.g., Sauternes, Barsac. On the label of a bottle of Champagne this word indicates a very sweet wine which is seldom sold in Great Britain or the United States.

Douzico

A Turkish spirit rather like kümmel (*q.v.*).

Downy mildew

Also called false mildew in America and mildew in Europe, to differentiate it from powdery mildew; the most crippling fungus disease of the vine.
See Chapter Eight, p. 29.

Draff

In whisky-making, the residual solid matter after fermentation of the grain.

Draft

Beverage, notably beer, drawn from bulk, or supplied and taken directly from barrels or casks.

Drambuie

A liqueur compounded from Scotch whisky, heather honey, and herbs by a secret formula belonging to the Mackinnon family near Edinburgh. The formula is said to have been given to an early Mackinnon by Bonnie Prince Charlie, as a reward for helping him to escape to France. The derivation of the name is a corruption of the Gaelic *An Dram Buidheach*, meaning "the drink that satisfies." One of the three most popular liqueurs in the United States.

Dreimännerwein

"Three men wine," as the wine of Reutlingen in Germany is jokingly referred to. It is so called because it is said to be so bad that to make one man drink it, a second is needed to hold him fast, and a third to pour the wine into his mouth.

Dry

Opposed to sweet. A wine is dry when all the sugar in the grapes has been completely fermented into alcohol. White Burgundy, most Alsatian wines, certain Graves and Champagnes, many Mosel and Rhine wines, are dry. So also are such aperitif wines as Fino and Amontillado Sherries. In American wine parlance, the term "dry wines" is mistakenly given to wines under 14% or table wines as opposed to "sweet wines," which are synonymous with fortified wines. The acid content of a wine also determines the sense of dryness, unless the latter is covered up by excessive sugar.

Dubonnet

A dark red proprietary French aperitif made of a sweetened wine base with bitter bark and quinine added to impart the characteristic taste. It is also manufactured in the United States, where a white variety, seen also in England, may be found.

Château Ducru-Beaucaillou

Bordeaux red wine.
District: Haut-Médoc, France.
Commune: Saint-Julien.

The vineyard forms an unbroken carpet with that of Château Beychevelle. The name, given by the former owner, M. Ducru, means literally "beautiful pebbles," and is very appropriate. The chief feature of the vineyard is its richness in the pebbles, or *cailloux*, which contribute to the greatness of so many of the wines of the Médoc, especially Château Latour. At Beaucaillou the gravelly soil is very deep.

The large, beautiful château itself is set away from the road on the lip of the slope over the River Gironde.

This vineyard has become one of the showplaces of the Médoc, and unquestionably produces one of its best wines. It was revived in the fifties by the efforts of its owner, Jean-Eugène Borie, and is now not only one of the best Saint-Julien vineyards but one of the best Second Growths (*Seconds Crus*) of the 1855 classification.

Characteristics. Supple yet full-bodied, a typically fine Saint-Julien. One that is definitely to be counted on for year-in year-out quality.

Vineyard area: 45 hectares (113 acres).
Average production: 170 *tonneaux* (15,000 cases).

Château Duhart-Milon-Rothschild

Bordeaux red wine.
District: Haut-Médoc.
Commune: Pauillac.

Some of the vineyard lies alongside that of Château Lafite. Duhart-Milon-Rothschild is the only Fourth Growth (*Quatrième Cru*) of the Classification of 1855 found in Pauillac. M. Leroux, who lived in Madagascar, sold the vineyard to the Rothschilds of Château Lafite.

Characteristics. Has characteristics in common with the other Pauillac wines, but the quality has not been all that it might be. The Rothschilds have already improved the wine, and its reputation is growing fast.

Vineyard area: 46 hectares (115 acres).
Average production: 173 *tonneaux* (17,000 cases).

Dulce

Spanish for sweet, especially in terms of wine; the sweet wines added to dry Sherry to make it more appealing abroad.

Dumb

Wine slang, describing wines of quality which stubbornly remain hard for many years before reaching their peak. Usually these wines have a great deal of tannin; 1937 produced such wines.

Dunder

Sugar-cane lees used to promote fermentation of rum.

Dur

French for hard; used of wine.
See Dumb.

Duras

See Côtes de Duras.

Château Durfort

Bordeaux red wine.
District: Haut-Médoc, France.
Commune: Margaux.

The vineyard, rated as a Second Growth (*Second Cru*) in the Gironde Classification of 1855, was owned by M. Pierre Ginestet. Originally the property of M. Durfort de Duras, the château was given its present name when purchased by M. de Vivens in 1924. The estate is situated at the entrance to the village of Margaux near Châteaux Margaux, Palmer, Rausan-Ségla, and Rauzan-Gassies. In 1963 the vineyard and *chai* were purchased by M. Lucien Lurton, who became president of the Comité des Grands Crus Classés in 1971. A most dedicated viticulturalist, who also owns Brane-Cantenac, M. Lurton has increased the vineyard area threefold from its original 10 hectares (25 acres). The château itself is now owned by Bernard Ginestet, who lives there instead of at Château Margaux, also the property of his family.

Vineyard area: 35 hectares (87.5 acres).
Average production: 90 *tonneaux* (8,000 cases).

Duriff

Californian grape—another name for the Petite-Sirah (*q.v.*).

Dürkheim (Bad Dürkheim)

The *Wurstmarkt* held here in September is Germany's greatest wine festival. Dürkheim produces the best-known red wine of the Palatinate and a great deal of white.
See Palatinate.

Dutchess

American hybrid grape developed in Dutchess County, New York, during the mid-nineteenth century. It gives light dry white wines and is still cultivated to some extent in New York State.

ℰ

East India

In the days when sailing ships went round by the Cape of Good Hope, casks of Sherry and Madeira were often put aboard as ballast: the long, rocking voyage to India and back improved and aged the wines. Some merchants still use this name for their good dessert blends, and an Amoroso (sweetened Oloroso) may be so called.

Eau-de-vie

Generic French term for brandy or spirits.

Eau-de-Vie d'Andaye

A Basque spirit from the Pyrenees near Hendaye.

Eau-de-Vie de Cidre

Calvados or apple brandy.
See Calvados; Applejack.

Eau-de-Vie de Danzig

French equivalent of Danziger Goldwasser (*q.v.*); also called Liqueur d'Or.

Eau-de-Vie de Lie

Spirit distilled from lees (wine deposit) in wine casks.

Eau-de-Vie de Marc

See Marc.

Eau-de-Vie de Vin

Spirit made from wine; brandy.

Ebullioscope

Apparatus for determining the alcoholic content of wine and spirits. It is based on the fact that at 760 millimeters of atmospheric pressure, water boils at 212°F. (100°C.), while alcohol boils at 172°F. (78°C.). The boiling point of the tested liquid will indicate its proportion of alcohol and water by its position between 172° and 212°F. (78° and 100°C.).

Échezeaux

Burgundy red wine.
District: Côte de Nuits, France.
Commune: Flagey-Échezeaux.
Official Classification: Great Growth (Grand Cru).

Échezeaux is a place-name, not a vineyard—a situation which could only happen in Burgundy. It is a place-name which takes in all or parts of eleven different vineyards (including one called Upper Échezeaux, but none

called Échezeaux) and has been granted the rating Great Growth (*Grand Cru*), the highest Burgundian rating.

As though they were not satisfied with having cast their net and called everything within it Échezeaux, the French wine authorities took another step and situated their place-name in a town which has no other important vineyards (with the exception of Great Growth Grands Échezeaux). Flagey-Échezeaux is on the wrong—or east—side of the main road, between Dijon and Lyon, on the plain where no wines of note grow, and has only a small foothold on the sloping west side of the road. If wines from the vineyards of Échezeaux do not meet the high minimum standards, they are sold as Vosne-Romanée.

In fact, little wine is sold as Échezeaux, most of it going to market as Vosne-Romanée—which is next door. Another reason why little Échezeaux is sold under that name is that few people know about it and fewer have any confidence in their ability to pronounce it.

The size and diversity of the assembled vineyards means that an Échezeaux—when found under its own name—will be subject to considerable variation. Some will be beautifully rounded-out, stepping-stone wines, bridging the gap between the full, sturdy Vougeots and the light, delicate Vosne-Romanées; others will have less distinction than they should. Their lack of worldly fame, however, makes them wines of value, for there is relatively little demand for them, and they sell for lower prices than wines of similar quality but greater repute.

The vineyards from which these wines come are:

Vineyard	Hectares	Acres
Les Grands Échezeaux	9.2	22.8
Les Échezeaux	30	74.2
En Orveaux	9.7	24
Les Treux	4.9	12
Clos Saint-Denis	1.8	4.5
Les Cruots (or Vignes-Blanches)	3.3	8.1
Les Rouges-du-Bas	4	9.9
Champs-Traversins	3.6	8.8
Les Poulaillières	4.2	10.4
Les Loachausses	3.8	9.3
Les Quartiers de Nuits	2.6	6.4
Les Échezeaux-de-Dessus	3.6	8.8

Production in an average year comes to 1,100 hectoliters (29,150 U.S. gallons, 24,200 imp.), or the equivalent of 12,000 cases.

Echt

A Russian or Polish kümmel of the crystallized type.
See Kümmel.

Edelfäule

German term for *Botrytis cinerea* (*q.v.*) or noble rot.

Edelweiss

Proprietary Italian Fior d'Alpi, or liqueur flavored with extracts from alpine flowers.

Edelzwicker

On an Alsatian bottle label, Edelzwicker indicates a wine that is a blend of noble grape varieties.

Eelworm

Parasite harmful to vines.
See Chapter Eight, p. 29.

Egg nog

Hot or cold drink of egg beaten up in rum or brandy, sweetened and flavored with nutmeg.

An egg flip is a similar drink, made with hot spirits, ale, or wine.

Égrappage

French term for the separation of stalks from grapes before they are pressed or placed in the fermenting vats. This is necessary because the stalks contain oils and tannins that would render the wine bitter and harsh. The machine used is known as an *égrappoir*, or stemmer.
See Stemming.

Egri Bikavér

Probably the best-known wine of Hungary, apart from Tokay. The wine is red and the name means "Bull's Blood of Eger."
See Hungary.

Egypt

From time to time a tomb is opened and jars are found with dried traces of what, perhaps fifty centuries ago, was wine. From the remains found of ancient Egypt we know how the grapes were picked and pressed and how wine was buried in the tombs. Except for one man, that might be all. The twentieth-century adventure of the Egyptian Nestor Gianaclis is in some ways one of the most fascinating of our time. With every modern scientific help, it has been a struggle to go forward to a past lost for two thousand years.

It was well known in classical times that the wines of Egypt were very fine. Cleopatra served to Caesar Mareotic wine, which was said to come from ancient Meröe, near the fourth cataract of the Upper Nile. There were other Egyptian wines in great vogue throughout the Mediterranean world.

At the beginning of this century, Egyptian wine, so far as it existed at all, was undeniably bad. Nestor Gianaclis set out to search for the soil on which good wine could be grown. At the same time he tried to find out how good the wine of his ancestors had really been. Would not tastes have changed greatly in two thousand years? From evidence in the works of Virgil, Horace, Pliny, and others who wrote of wines in ancient Greece and Rome he came to the conclusion that if they had liked Egyptian wines, then we would like them too.

Under the sand which buried it, on the brink of the desert, he found a soil that was utterly different from the alluvial soils which came down with the river and were deposited in the delta and the valley of the Nile. Chemical analysis confirmed that the soil, chalky and free of salts, was almost identical with that of Champagne in France. This was a more than promising beginning, and the first vines were planted in 1903.

Most of the difficulty lay ahead. The ancient vine plants were barely a memory in the most weighty books on wine, hardly more than a scratch or two here and there on a pyramid or tomb. It would have been as easy to locate an ancient Egyptian as a grape of ancient Egypt.

Seventy-three known grape varieties were tried over the years, in cooperation with experts from France, Italy, Hungary, and other wine-growing countries; and twenty new types developed by Gianaclis were subjected to laboratory analysis. Great wine required the sun, the soil, the proper vine, all the right combinations. Gianaclis had to do in a few years what in other lands had taken centuries of trial and error: to match the right technique and the right vine to the climate and soil.

In 1931, after more than a quarter of a century of effort, it looked as if the battle were won. In that year, wines from the Mariout vineyard west of the Nile delta presented by Nestor Gianaclis before the Chambre Syndicale des Courtiers Gourmets of Paris were optimistically judged as worthy of being classed with the wines of the Rhine and such white Burgundies as Montrachet and Meursault. Two years later, it was being said in France that the wine of the Pharaohs had been resurrected and that the world could drink again the nectar which had been praised by Virgil. Needless to say, the quality left something to be desired.

Today, some of the wines fulfill part of their promise and are drinkable. Quantity, though increasing, is relatively small. But a serious effort is being made to bring these wines from what might be called a super-Californian or super-Algerian climate into the world market. Samples have been sent to world fairs and, with production expanding (some 50,000 hectoliters or 1,325,000 U.S. gallons, 1,100,000 imp.) a year from about 15,000 hectares (37,500 acres), exports have increased, especially to Eastern Europe.

SPIRITS

The difference in price between domestic and foreign spirits in Egypt is not great. Imported Cognac and whisky give strong competition to the domestic rum, arak, and brandy, which are taxed at 30%. The rum, distilled from the molasses of Egyptian sugar-cane, is of good quality. Tafia, however, a cruder spirit also from the residue of sugar-making, is produced in about twice the volume of rum and is stronger in alcohol, usually over 100° proof. Rum and tafia together, combined with a tafia-and-30%-brandy mixture made in about one-tenth the quantity of rum, account for an average 15,000 hectoliters (397,500 U.S. gallons, 330,000 imp.) annually. Brandy is made (from imported raisins or fresh grapes) in about half the volume of rum, and arak and ouzo are produced in fairly substantial amounts. A popular alcoholic beverage of Egypt is buza, distilled from fermented dates. The distillation process is usually haphazard and poorly conducted, and the dates are often half-rotten. This contributes, however, to the popularity of the beverage, which is usually the only one the fellahin, who make up most of its market, can afford.

Einzellage

The German term for individual vineyard, especially in the context of the 1971 vineyard land consolidation programs.

Eitelsbacher Karthäuserhofberg

Outstanding vineyard of Eitelsbach in western Germany.
See Mosel-Saar-Ruwer.

Elbling

Grape grown in Luxembourg, Lorraine, and Germany—where it is also known as Kleinberger.

Elefantenwein (Elephant wine)

Reference to a wine from Tübingen, Germany, which is said to have been made from grapes so hard that no men could have trodden them, but only elephants. The same comment is made of the Reutlinger wine of the Neckar region.

Élixir d'Anvers

Belgian liqueur made in Antwerp by F. X. de Beukelaer. It is compounded of herbs and plants on a base of brandy, is golden in color, moderately sweet, and very fragrant.

Elixir Longae Vitae

Another name for Pommeranzen bitters.
See Bitters.

Elongated wine

British term for wine "lengthened" by addition of water to reduce strength for purposes of excise duty.

Eltviller Sonnenberg

Most elegant of the Eltville wines. The other outstanding vineyard here is Eltviller Langenstück.
See Rheingau.

Elvira

American hybrid grape developed in the late nineteenth century in Missouri and still used for white wines, usually sparkling.

Emilia-Romagna

Red and white wines.
Central Italy.

South of the River Po, running from the Apennines to the Adriatic, stretches one of the great productive plains which recur throughout the Italian peninsula. Here a mountain soars up from the flat, with the operetta republic of San Marino perched on top and vines clinging to its steep sides; but most of Emilia-Romagna is level, even ground, where the dominant activity is agriculture. Wheat and maize are cultivated and vines are not neglected, although they used to be. Solid chunks of vineyards were rare, but everywhere vines could be seen; they ran rampant over the countryside, twining around any available support, apparently without benefit of cultivation or bite of the pruning knife. This haphazard growth lent a curious charm to the scenery, but today the vineyards are neat and orderly, the vines diligently trained.

Sangiovese di Romagna

Lambrusco and Albana produce the honored fruit of Emilia-Romagna, but Sangiovese is the widespread vine. The wine it gives is variable in the extreme, sometimes slightly bitter and hard, sometimes mellow and warming. It is always, however, available, and always red and always dry—this last characteristic is enough to endear it to many visitors to the region; but in this case the D.O.C. has been granted solely through Italian enthusiasm. Sangiovese accounts for the bulk of the 1.5 million hectoliters (39 million U.S. gallons, 30 million imp.) the area produces annually.

Lambrusco

This has no connection with *Vitis labrusca*, a native North American vine species. It is perhaps the best-known example of the region's viticulture, the wine-name deriving from the grapevine. It is a red, dry or sweetish semi-sparkling wine with a disconcerting bright ruby foam.

There are four D.O.C.'s for Lambrusco: Lambrusco di Sorbara, Lambrusco Grasparossa di Castevetro, Lambrusco Salamino di Ste. Croce, and Lambrusco Reggiano. The first three are made near Modena, the fourth near Reggio-Emilia. Though none of the wines is especially good, particularly when too sweet and sparkling, Lambrusco is the single largest-selling wine in the United States.

Albana di Romagna

A golden-yellow wine of controlled denomination of origin—which may be semi-sweet or dry (although the dry type usually retains a slight trace of sugar). Perhaps its outstanding characteristic is an almost voluptuous velvetiness, when the wine is well made. Galla Placidia, Regent of the Western Roman Empire (A.D. 435), is said to have been an early devotee of Albana. Traveling through the region, she stopped at a small town to quench her thirst at the local inn and was served with the wine, but in a coarse mug. Her reaction to the Albana was: "I must drink you in gold." And Bertinoro ("Drink-you-in-gold") has been the name of the town ever since.

Gutturnio dei Colli Piacentini

A controlled Denomination of Origin applicable to a red wine of some character produced in Ziano and six other communes in the province of Piacenza from Barbera and Bonarda grapes. It is dry, faintly sweet.

Trebbiano di Romagna

A D.O.C. wine produced from Trebbiano di Romagna grapes in a vast area that is part of the provinces of Bologna, Forli, and Ravenna. It is a straw color, with a pleasant bouquet and a dry taste. A sparkling wine is also made and is either dry, semi-sweet, or sweet.

Bianco di Scandiano

Made in the foothills of Reggio-Emilia, this is a sweetish white wine, low in alcohol, often crackling.

Colli Bolognesi Monte San Pietro

From the vineyards in the hills between Modena and Bologna, this wine is not yet a D.O.C., but it is thought to be promoted soon. As a regional wine, it is above average and is made from Pinot Blanc, Sauvignon Blanc, and Barbera, which are sold as varietals of Monte San Pietro.

Entre-Deux-Mers

Red and white wines
District: Bordeaux, France

Light, clean, fruity red and white wines, tending in the last few years to be vinified dry. Traditionally, the white wines are mellow, soft, and sometimes sweet. The red wine made in the district is sold as Bordeaux and is not entitled to the place-name. There are no outstanding growths or vineyards. Much of the wine is made by the fifteen admirable modern cooperatives, with a combined capacity of 410,000 hectoliters (11 million U.S. gallons, 9 million imp.).

Deriving its name from its location, the region lies between the two rivers—"seas"—the Garonne and the Dordogne; and lies, also, between Bordeaux and Libourne in the zones of Pomerol and Saint-Émilion wines. The range of hills along the River Garonne facing the Graves, Barsac, and Sauternes wine districts and a small enclave of gravel soil on the Dordogne near Libourne are the best parts, but they have been given separate place-names.

Loupiac, Sainte-Croix-du-Mont, Cadillac, and Premières Côtes de Bordeaux on the Garonne and Graves de Vayres from the small gravel enclave on the Dordogne are wines of higher quality made within the limits of Entre-Deux-Mers.

Enveloppe

French term for the straw sheaf, now rarely used, which is put around bottles to protect them. Cardboard is used for wines entering the United States, because American laws forbid straw as a possible carrier of disease, pestilential insects, and parasites.

Enzian

Spirit distilled in the alpine and adjoining countries from the yard-long roots of the yellow mountain gentian. It makes one of the most aristocratic forms of schnapps.

Enzymes

Large proteins produced by organisms to catalyze chemical reactions. Enzymes may be recovered and purified, then added to a solution to produce a chemical change. The enzyme pectinase is occasionally added to freshly crushed white grapes to break down the slimy pectins and thereby facilitate pressing. At present, it cannot be used to produce very good wines.
See Chapter Nine, p. 38.

Épernay

An important center of the Champagne trade.
See Champagne.

Épesses

White wine of Lavaux in the canton of Vaud, Switzerland.
See Switzerland.

Erbacher Markobrunn

See Markobrunn; Rheingau.

Erdener Treppchen

Best-known wine of Erden on the German Mosel, an outstanding dry wine.
See Mosel-Saar-Ruwer.

Erinose

A disease caused by a very small mite.
See Chapter Eight, p. 29.

Ermitage

See Hermitage.

Erzeugerabfüllung

A German term for estate-bottling.

Espalier

Method of training vines. The trunk terminates in one or two arms and several canes, all in the same plane and supported by a trellis or wire. There are several variations on this method, including the decorative trellis-trained vine; and the practical guyot pattern of a trunk and one arm.
See Chapter Eight, p. 29.

Espumoso

Spanish term for sparkling.

Est! Est!! Est!!!

The dry wine of Montefiascone, Italy.
See Latium.

Estate-bottling

The all-important practice in which individual vineyard owners bottle the unadulterated product of their own vines. The term printed on a label should always be a guarantee of authenticity and, to some extent, of superior quality. Statements that the wine is estate-bottled and comes from someone who definitely is the vineyard owner, and a clear indication that the wine was bottled by the person who made it (or at least on his premises), should appear on the main label. In France estate-bottling is virtually the same thing as château-bottling (indicated as *Mis en Bouteilles au Château*) and is most often noted with one of the following terms: *Mise du Domaine, Mise au Domaine, Mis en Bouteilles au Domaine, Mise du Propriétaire, Mis en Bouteilles par le Propriétaire*, or *Mise à la Propriété*. In Germany the phrase used to be *Original-Abfüllung*, but it has been replaced by *Auseigenem Lesegut* or *Erzeugerabfüllung*. In the United States the term can be used only on the labels of wines made from grapes grown solely by the producer himself.

Esters

Slow reaction between the acids of the wine and the alcohols forms esters, which have a sweet, fruity smell.
See Chapter Nine, p. 38.

Estufades

Huge heating chambers in which wines of Madeira are "cooked."
See Madeira.

Étampé

French term for branded.

Ethers

Chemical compounds, important components of wines and spirits imparting bouquet or aroma.

Ethiopia

Though several African nations produce much wine, Ethiopia is not among them. Compared to the quantities from Algeria, South Africa, Morocco, Tunisia, and Egypt, the average annual total of some 50,000 hectoliters (1,325,000 U.S. gallons, 1,100,000 imp.) is indeed small. The three principal regions for both wine and table grapes are Abadir-Dukem, Guder, and Eritre in the north of the country. Sultana and Black Muscat predominate in the less than 500 hectares (1,250 acres) of vineyards, but a large portion of the wine is made from concentrates. Some of the wineries include the Elaberet Estate, Makanissa, Altavilla, and Alexandrakis, and most of their wines still show the strong influence dating from Mussolini's occupation.

Étiquette

French term for bottle label.

Etna

Red, white, or rosé wines from Sicily (*q.v.*).

Étoile

One of the best white wines of the French Jura comes from this southernmost area of the region.
See Jura.

Eudemis

One of the distinctive grape-moths.
See Chapter Eight, p. 29.

Eumelan

Red-wine-giving grape of the eastern United States. It is a poor producer and not outstanding for the wine-maker.

Château l'Evangile

Bordeaux red wine.
District and Commune: Pomerol, France.

Excellent wine is made by this property, a neighbor of Château Cheval-Blanc in Saint-Émilion. It is owned by the Ducasse family.
Vineyard area: 13 hectares (32 acres).
Average production: 36 *tonneaux* (3,400 cases).

Excise

Tax on home product as compared with customs.

Excoriose

A rare vine malady.
See Chapter Eight, p. 29.

Exportation of wine

Figures change, inevitably, from year to year, influenced by the season's harvest and by industrial and political fluctuations. The exports from the two largest producers, Italy and France, have been steadily increasing, but those from Algeria—which used to be the largest exporter—have been declining. Although Argentina, the United States, and the Soviet Union produce a great deal of wine, none of these three countries exports very much. The figures below are averages from the past several years, corrected to project the trends of the next few years. In some cases, notably Great Britain and the Netherlands, statistics include wines re-exported.

WORLD WINE EXPORTS

Exporting Country	Hectoliters	U.S. Gallons	Imp. Gallons
Italy	12,000,000	317,400,000	264,000,000
France	7,000,000	185,500,000	154,000,000
Spain	4,000,000	106,000,000	88,000,000
Algeria	3,000,000	79,500,000	66,000,000
Bulgaria	2,300,000	60,835,000	50,600,000
Hungary	1,700,000	44,965,000	37,400,000
Portugal	1,500,000	39,700,000	33,000,000
Greece	1,000,000	26,500,000	22,000,000
Rumania	1,000,000	26,500,000	22,000,000
West Germany	1,000,000	26,500,000	22,000,000
Yugoslavia	700,000	18,550,000	15,400,000
U.S.S.R.	700,000	18,550,000	15,400,000
Argentina	600,000	15,870,000	13,200,000
Tunisia	500,000	13,225,000	11,000,000
Morocco	440,000	11,660,000	9,680,000
Cyprus	300,000	7,950,000	6,600,000
Austria	210,000	5,565,000	4,620,000
Great Britain	150,000	3,967,000	3,300,000
South Africa	125,000	3,312,000	2,750,000
Albania	115,000	3,041,750	2,530,000
Belgium	100,000	2,650,000	2,200,000
Chile	100,000	2,650,000	2,200,000
United States	90,000	2,383,000	1,980,000
Australia	80,000	2,120,000	1,760,000
Luxembourg	70,000	1,855,000	1,540,000
Israel	40,000	1,058,000	880,000
Turkey	40,000	1,058,000	880,000
Malta	35,000	925,750	770,000
Egypt	25,000	662,000	550,000
Czechoslovakia	20,000	529,000	440,000
Netherlands	20,000	529,000	440,000
Switzerland	10,000	264,500	220,000
Total	38,970,000	1,031,575,000	857,340,000

Extra Sec

French for Extra Dry. These words appearing on the label of a bottle of Champagne do not, in fact, indicate an extra-dry wine, but only one which is fairly dry. A really dry Champagne will be labeled Brut.

Ezerjó

White-wine variety grown in Hungary. Also the full gold-colored wine of Mór, near Budapest.

F

Factory House

A club and club building in Oporto where the finest Ports in the world are drunk. Nowadays it is correctly called the British Association, but everyone refers to it as the Feitoria Inglesa or English Factory House. In early days the Factory system was one of British extra-territorial rights in foreign countries, which is why out of courtesy to Portugal the name of the Club has been changed. Even today, however, British Port companies have rights in Portugal accorded no other nation.

Members of the Factory House comprise the most exclusive British Port circle, every one being a partner in a British Port firm in Oporto.

Even so, no British partner may join the Factory House if there is a Portuguese partner in his firm.

Falerno

The vineyards where the modern Falerno is grown are on the slopes of Monte Massico (about halfway between Rome and Naples), and the wine is generally white, semi-dry, and moderately strong.

Falernian was the most famous of all the ancient Roman wines, and it too came from the vineyards of Monte Massico; but we do not now know what grapes went into it, and we have only a very imperfect idea of how it tasted.

See Campania; Classical wines.

Falernum

A flavoring syrup, not very strong (6% alcohol by volume), made in Bermuda and the West Indies of syrup, lime, almonds, ginger, and spices. It is a popular flavoring for rum drinks.

Fan leaf

Another name for infectious degeneration of vines. *See* Chapter Eight, p. 29.

Fara

Red wine from the Italian Piedmont (*q.v.*).

Fass

German for cask.

Fassle

A German drinking vessel rather similar in principle to the *porrón* of Spain, in that the liquid is spurted from a tube into the drinker's mouth. The *Fassle*, or little barrel, is a five-liter wooden cask into whose bung-hole cork a tube, the *Spitzle*, has been inserted. As with the *porrón*, the trick of drinking from the vessel entails a steady hand and

a quick flick of the wrist for the drinker to avoid being doused in the stream of liquid.

Fat

A big, soft wine without the hardness to give it body and containing much natural glycerin. Typical examples are the Bordeaux Pomerols and some Saint-Émilions.

Faye d'Anjou

Commune with the right to an Appellation Contrôlée in the Coteaux du Layon district of Anjou, France. *See* Anjou.

Federweisser

New wine, milky or "feather white," found in German inns after the vintage.

Fehér Bor

Hungarian term for white wine. *Bor* means wine.

Feints

Leavings of second distillation of Scotch malt whisky.

Fendant

Best white wines of Valais, Switzerland, made from the Fendant (or Chasselas) grape. *See* Switzerland.

Ferme

Firm or stubborn. Usually a wine of quality; but as long as it is in this condition, it is hard and tannic and not ready to drink.

Fermentation

The decomposition of sugar chiefly into ethyl alcohol and carbon dioxide. The classic equation is given by Gay-Lussac:

$$C_6H_{12}O_6 \rightarrow 2C_2H_6O + 2CO_2$$
$$\text{(180 grams)} \quad \text{(92 grams)} \quad \text{(88 grams)}$$

Unfortunately, this is not quite accurate, careful measurement proving that whereas the alcoholic content should be the equivalent of 51% of the sugar, in reality 47% is normal and the odd 4% forms a number of side-products including higher alcohols, nitrogenous compounds, and glycerin. Fermentation is carried out by yeasts as their primary source of energy for growth. It can take place only when the amount of oxygen is limited, for in the presence of oxygen, the sugar would be converted completely to CO_2 and water.

Stainless steel or concrete fermentation vats are much preferable to the traditional oak ones because they effectively keep oxygen from the fermenting musts. Although the old wooden vats are picturesque, their disappearance from Bordeaux and Burgundy will improve the quality of the wine. So that fermentation should proceed satisfactorily, temperature and aeration must be properly regulated.

See Chapter Nine.

Fernet Branca

The best-known Italian bitters. It is used as an aperitif and generally recommended to settle upset stomachs and hangovers.

See Bitters.

Château Ferrière

Bordeaux red wine.
District: Haut-Médoc, France.
Commune: Margaux.

This excellent vineyard, in the very heart of the village of Margaux, classed a Third Growth (*Troisième Cru*) of the Médoc in the Classification of 1855, is at present leased to Château Lascombes. Each year a limited quantity of Ferrière is made by the owners of Château Lascombes.

Fiano

The grape which makes the light, white, slightly tart wines of Avellino, near Naples.

Fiasco

Italian straw-covered glass flask holding about two liters of wine. It is associated particularly with Chianti.

Field-grafting

For a description of this method of grafting vines, see Chapter Eight, p. 29.

Château de Fieuzal

Bordeaux red and white wines.
District: Graves, France.
Commune: Léognan.

The vineyard, which once belonged to the La Rochefoucauld family, is planted on good gravelly slopes, and is very well managed by the present owner, M. Negrevergne, a Bordeaux pharmaceutical manufacturer. The vineyard was made a Classified Growth (*Cru Classé*) in 1959.

Characteristics. In quality, the wines can hold their own with almost any of the Graves. The red is generous and velvety, with a charming bouquet; the white, dry and *racé*.

Vineyard area: red—15 hectares (37 acres); white—1 hectare (2.5 acres).

Average production: red—60 *tonneaux* (5,500 cases); white—4 *tonneaux* (400 cases).

Château Figeac

Bordeaux red wine.
District and Commune: Saint-Émilion, France.

Long one of the best-known Saint-Émilions, and in 1955 classed among the First Great Growths (*Premiers Grands Crus*), Figeac must not be confused with other Saint-Émilion vineyards employing the word in various combinations of the name. Six other of these Figeac vineyards surround Château Figeac (Charles de Figeac was a nobleman of Saint-Émilion), but the unmodified name belongs to the best of the growths, one of the largest important vineyards in Saint-Émilion. Touching Cheval-Blanc, and near the Pomerol boundary, the vineyard surrounds a château and wine *chai* widely separated by the length of a broad avenue which bisects a splendid park. The young owner, Thierry de Manoncourt, is an ardent and progressive wine-maker and has recently built a very fine new *chai*.

Characteristics. The wine has made a dramatic comeback over the past few years. It is a characteristic Saint-Émilion, robust and well-rounded, and one of the best wines of the district.

Vineyard area: 34 hectares (85 acres).
Average production: 180 *tonneaux* (17,000 cases).

Château Filhot

Bordeaux white wine.
District and Commune: Sauternes, France.

Owned by the Comte Durieu de Lacarelle, the vineyard produces somewhat drier wines than Yquem and is generally considered to have been unjustly classed a Second Growth (*Second Cru*) of Sauternes in 1855. If the wines were now re-rated it might be made a First. The château, a beautiful eighteenth-century country house set in smooth lawns, looks more English than French; and as it happens, Filhot wines have always had a large following in England.

Characteristics. Was high in alcohol; one of the driest of Sauternes, but is now being made sweeter and is no longer the exception it once was.

Vineyard area: 60 hectares (150 acres).
Average production: 100 *tonneaux* (9,500 cases).

Fillette

French slang term for a half-bottle in certain parts of France, as for instance, in Anjou. Literally, "a little girl."

Film yeast

Another name for *flor*.
See Sherry.

Filtering

The clarification of wine by passing it through special devices—or simply through a layer of filter paper—with the object of ridding it of any suspended particles. In many fine wine districts the older method of fining (*q.v.*) is used. Filtering, for all its ease and practicality, can rob a fine wine of some of its quality. This is also true of the much-used Seitz Filter, which has layers of asbestos. Too many layers or slipshod handling can filter out all distinction, leaving the wine insipid and without character.

Fine Champagne

Not a Champagne but a Cognac brandy, properly a blend from the districts of Grande Champagne and Petite Champagne.

Une fine (pronounced feen) is the popular way of calling for a Cognac in France—any Cognac—but correctly it is liqueur Cognac of the Champagne (chalky and best) Cognac district.

See Cognac.

Finesse

French term for exceptional elegance or breed (*q.v.*).

Finger Lakes

Wine-growing region in New York State. This is the most important district in the eastern states, and some of the finest sparkling wine in America is produced here. The best vineyards are beside Lake Keuka and Lake Canadaigua; and there are others around Lake Seneca and Lake Cayuga. Some of the leading firms are established in the Pleasant Valley–Hammondsport district, and some excellent sparkling wines, as well as other types, are made here.

See United States: New York.

Fining

Fining, or *collage*, is the process by which wine is clarified of any suspended particles. This can be done either with an organic agent such as blood, casein, protein, or gelatine, which will coagulate and carry down with it the clouding particles, or with a clarifier which has a mechanical action—such as bentonite, cellulose, infusorial earth.

See Chapter Nine, p. 38.

Finish

Lingering aftertaste.

Fino

The driest type of Sherry (*q.v.*).

Fins Bois

One of the lesser districts in the Cognac region of France.

See Cognac.

Fior d'Alpi

Literally, alpine flowers. It is a sweet Italian liqueur, yellow in color and usually containing a branch of rock-sugar crystals inside the characteristic tall narrow bottle.

Firkin

English beer barrel with a capacity of 41 liters (10.8 U.S. gallons, 9 imp.).

Fitou

Red wine.
District: Southern France.

A French wine-growing area of more historical than contemporary importance. Fitou, which adjoins Roussillon, near the Spanish border, is made up of nine communes: Fitou, Leucate, Caves-de-Treilles, Lapalme, Tuchan, Paziols, Cascastel, Villeneuve-les-Corbières, and Treilles. The hot Mediterranean sun beats down brutally on the scarcely fertile slopes, 240 hectares (600 acres) of which are given over to vines.

The vine-types are mostly Carignan and Grenache, which must—singly or together—make up 75% of any wine carrying the name of Fitou. The other 25% may be made up of one or several of the following: Cinsault, Terret Noir, Malvoisie, Maccabéo, Muscat, or Picpoule. The maximum that the French authorities allow is 30 hectoliters per hectare (312 U.S. gallons, 260 imp. per acre), except in certain extraordinary years.

Fitou is one of the best wines of the Midi. It is a dark, pungent, heavy red wine, high in alcoholic content, making a good, rather common, but sound table wine. To gain the name it must be aged in the barrel for at least nine months (until 1953 the ageing period was two years in the barrel) before it is sold. The average yearly production of Fitou is less than 5,000 hectoliters (132,500 U.S. gallons, 110,000 imp.), and for this reason it is not often found outside its native area.

Fixed acidity

The presence of natural and desirable acids (principally tartaric), which are the cause of an agreeable tartness in wine. Fixed acids cannot be removed by steam distillation.

See Chapter Nine, p. 38.

Fixin

Burgundy red wine.
District: Côte de Nuits, France.

Fixin is the northernmost of the wine communes of the Côte de Nuits, the upper arm of Burgundy's famous Côte d'Or. Present-day Fixin includes the area that was, before 1850, that of its neighbor, Fixey. In spite of the augmentation of property, the town did not gain a great deal as far as vineyards were concerned.

Most of the wines of the town are not sold under the commune name at all but are included in the Vins Fins de la Côte de Nuits. However, rather more than 40 hectares (100 acres) within the town are allowed to be sold as Fixin, the best of which comes from the 4.8-hectare (12-acre) vineyard, Clos de la Perrière. According to the now obsolete classification of the Côte d'Or vineyards made in 1860, this vineyard was considered as an Outstanding Growth (*Tête de Cuvée*) and was the only one so honored in Fixin. The more recent classification made by the Institut National des Appellations d'Origine des Vins et Eaux-de-Vie (the National Institute of Place-names of Wines and Spirits) has, more realistically, demoted it to First Growth (*Premier Cru*) of Fixin, a status which it shares with five other vineyards. The wines from the Clos de la Perrière are generally deep, alcoholic, and slow to mature, and while they bear a strong resemblance to those from the neighboring commune of Gevrey-Chambertin, they have less breed and magnificence than do Gevrey's greatest wines. In some years, however, they can be better than many from the secondary vineyards which rank just behind the great Chambertin.

Within the confines of Fixin there are some 202 hectares (500 acres) growing wines allowed to go to market only as Vins Fins de la Côte de Nuits and about 43 hectares (105 acres) whose wines are sold as Fixin. These 43 hectares include the following Classified Growths, all of which may be sold as Fixin Premier Cru, or with the town name followed by the name of the vineyard.

FIRST GROWTHS (*Premiers Crus*)

Vineyard	Hectares	Acres
Clos de la Perrière	6.53	16.3
Clos du Chapitre	4.79	11.9
Les Hervelets	3.83	9.5
Les Meix-Bas	1.88	4.7
Aux Cheusots (Clos Napoléon)	1.75	4.55
Les Arvelets	3.36	7.8

Flagey-Échezeaux

Flagey-Échezeaux in Burgundy is a town but not a place-name—in the vinous sense of the word—although the two great vineyards within its confines are place-names in their own right. The town stands to the left of the main road which runs through the Côte de Nuits, and its boundaries are so staked out that they force a small passage between Vougeot and Vosne-Romanée and fan out into a beachhead on the great slope.

The two vineyards within the town are Échezeaux and Grands-Échezeaux (*qq.v.*). Both are Great Growths (*Grands Crus*)—the highest official rating given to Burgundian vineyards—and in the years when the wine does not meet the rigorous minimum standards, they are declassed either into First Growths (*Premiers Crus*)—slightly less than Great Growth—of neighboring Vosne-Romanée, or into the more general Vosne-Romanée with no other indication of origin.

Flagon

A large bottle usually of flattened globular shape, its capacity entirely dependent upon the wishes of its user; a squat bottle similar to the Bocksbeutel (*q.v.*) of German Franconia used for Commonwealth (and especially Australian) "burgundies."

Flat

A Champagne or other sparkling wine that has lost the sparkle—i.e., its bubbles. In the case of still wines, one that is dull, unattractive, and too low in acidity.

Fleurie

Only in recent years sold consistently under the communal name of Fleurie, these wines are not as well known as some other Beaujolais, but they are among the most typically Beaujolais of all, perfectly expressing the fresh fruity charm of this French red wine.
See Beaujolais.

Fliers

Tiny tasteless particles sometimes appearing in wine. They are caused usually by cold and disappear if the wine is warmed to normal room temperature.

Flip

A mixed drink made with wine, brandy, or both, along with shaved ice, sugar, bitters, nutmeg, and an egg.

Flohpeter

Waggish reference to a German wine so sour that any *Flöhe*, or fleas, which bit the drinker would be instantly killed by the acid in his bloodstream.

Flor

The white skin or layer which appears uniquely on some Sherries and on certain wines of the Jura in France. When *flor* develops on Sherry, the wine becomes Fino; when it does not, the wine is Oloroso.
See Sherry; Chapter Nine, p. 38.

Floraison

French term for flowering of the vines, at the end of which very small green berries will have formed.
See Chapter Eight, p. 29.

Flowery

Taste reminiscent of flowers, found in young wines; the younger the wine the more flowery it is apt to be. Few great wines have this quality.

Fluid ounce

In the United States, one-sixteenth of a standard U.S. pint. In Great Britain, the volume of one standard ounce weight of pure water measured at a temperature of 62°F. (17°C.) and a barometric pressure of 30 inches. The equivalents under the metric system are 2.957 centiliters to an American ounce and 2.841 centiliters to a British fluid ounce. The American is about 4% greater than the British.

Flûte

In France, the tall and thin bottle similar to that used for Alsatian and Rhine wines but made of clear glass. Many rosé wines are now shipped in flûtes. Also, the traditional and most successful glass used for sparkling wines, especially Champagne. Its slender V shape helps conserve the precious bubbles.

Folle Blanche

Once the principal grape for the thin white Charente wines which are distilled into Cognac, this has now been largely displaced by the Saint-Émilion vine, although a small percentage is still used. The Folle Blanche is now grown primarily in the area surrounding Nantes, to produce Gros Plant, the V.D.Q.S. of the Muscadet.

Forbidden Fruit

An American liqueur perhaps better known abroad than at home. It is made from the shaddock—a citrus fruit somewhat like a large grapefruit—infused in brandy. It is reddish-brown in color and is sold in a round bottle the size of a grapefruit.

Foreshots

The first crude spirit to emerge from the still in whisky-making.

Forster Jesuitengarten

Best known of the outstanding Forster wines in the German Palatinate, or Pfalz.
See Palatinate.

Forster Kirchenstück

Best of the outstanding Forster wines in the German Palatinate, or Pfalz.
See Palatinate.

Fortified wine

Wine to which brandy has been added sometimes to stop fermentation and to increase alcoholic content. Some examples are Port, Sherry, Málaga, and Madeira. In America use of the term is illegal and such wines are usually called dessert wines.
See Port; Sherry; Madeira; Málaga; Sweet fortified wines of France.

Forzato

Italian term for wine made from overripe grapes.

Foudre

French term for large cask for maturing, storing, and transporting wine. Used to some extent in Alsace, where the word was adopted from the German *Fuder*, and for ordinary or bulk wine.

Château Fourcas-Hosten

Bordeaux red wine.
District: Haut-Médoc, France.
Commune: Listrac.

The hill of Fourcas—really not so much a hill as the culmination of the Listrac Plateau—on the north edge of the commune is shared by Fourcas-Hosten and the less well known, but pleasantly countrified, Fourcas-Dupré, just to the north. Château Fourcas-Hosten, classified *Bourgeois Supérieur* in 1855, is perhaps rated below its true worth and might be considered a Great Growth (*Grand Cru*) of the Médoc. For many years before 1951, there were two Fourcas-Hostens, each belonged to one of two cousins; the vineyard is now united under one ownership. In 1971, under the management of Arnaud de Trabuc and Bertrand de Rivoyre, the property was syndicated to a group of American wine-lovers. A sizable program of replanting and improvements has begun. In 1973, 10 hectares (25 acres) of Cabernet Sauvignon, Cabernet Franc, and Merlot were planted. In 1974-75, the planting of another 10 hectares was completed. A renovation program of the *chai* and the *cuvier* has been completed, using the most modern techniques. M. Peynaud, dean of the Oenological Institute of Bordeaux, now oversees the vinification of the wine. Château Fourcas-Hosten (pronounced foor-cass) is on the way to establishing an excellent name for itself.

Characteristics. A full, slightly hard, and yet distinguished wine.
Vineyard area: 44 hectares (110 acres).
Average production: 180 *tonneaux* (15,000 cases).

Fourtet (Clos)

Bordeaux red wine.
District and Commune: Saint-Émilion, France.

One of the twelve First Great Growths (*Premiers Grands Crus*) of Saint-Émilion, as officially classified in 1955. The vineyard is planted along the wall of the eleventh-century village, one of the most picturesque in France. The cellars, cut in solid rock under the vines, are among the sights of the town. The estate is the property of the Lurton heirs.

Characteristics. Saint-Émilion is typified in this full-bodied fine wine. Recently, however, it has been criticized as having somewhat declined in quality.

Vineyard area: 20 hectares (50 acres).

Average production: 80 *tonneaux* (7,500 cases).

Fox-Grape

Popular name for grapes of *Vitis labrusca*, which runs wild in northeast and north-central America. It can be used for wines which have a very pronounced taste and aroma. Termed "foxy," although it has nothing in common with the scent of a fox, it is a strongly flavored grape.

Foxy

The special taste quality of the American wines—i.e., wines made from native grapes in eastern America. It is a particular characteristic of wines made from grapes of the species *Vitis labrusca*, of which type Concord is probably the best-known example.

Fraise

French *eau-de-vie*, or white alcohol, a brandy distilled from strawberries.

Framboise

French *eau-de-vie*, or white alcohol, a brandy distilled from raspberries.

Franc-de-goût

French term for clean-tasting.

France

Enjoyment of fine wines is one of the most civilized of pleasures; and the greatest wines in the world come from France, center of modern civilization, not in the fine arts only, but in the minor delightful arts of eating and drinking. Wine is a source of inspiration for her artists and the delectation of her workmen; a symbol of French *savoir-vivre* and a major French industry. The mysteries of wine-making cannot be reduced to statistics, any more than a picture can be analyzed by the size of its canvas or the time it took to paint; yet statistics are striking and important.

There are some 1.2 million hectares (2.9 million acres) of vines in France, most of which exist solely for wine—although a few produce table grapes—and their output is some 75 million hectoliters (1.98 billion U.S. gallons 1.64 billion imp.) per year. Of this, by far the greatest proportion is *ordinaire* for everyday drinking, but about 10 mil-

lion hectoliters (265 million U.S. gallons, 220 million imp.) are classed as Appellation Contrôlée—the fine wines of France. The vineyard area is now stabilized after having diminished by nearly 100,000 hectares (250,000 acres), in consequence of a subsidized uprooting of vines for common wine as a measure against overproduction. Some 6 million of the 40-odd million Frenchmen owe their livelihood directly to wine, including growers (about 1.5 million of them), wholesalers and shippers, regularly employed vineyard workers, manufacturers of wine-making equipment and machinery, laboratory technicians, and a host of civil servants, part of whose task is keeping track of statistics such as these. Then, carriers transport wine, among other loads; shops sell it, among other commodities; and many other Frenchmen would be living far less well than they do were it not for wine.

France exports about 4 million hectoliters (106 million U.S. gallons, 88 million imp.) and imports about twice that much, mainly from Mediterranean countries. West Germany is the largest export customer, followed by England, the Benelux countries, and the United States, generally in that order. The average French family spends from 8% to 13% of its food budget on wine, and consumption is among the highest per capita in the world—110 liters (26.4 U.S. gallons, 22 imp.). But this amount only includes wine that has been taxed; considerably more is consumed on large and small vineyards without the interference of tax collector or official statistician. Wine is a huge industry, an incalculable economic asset, an invaluable source of foreign currency, and the means by which innumerable Frenchmen earn all or part of their living. But it is more than just this. It is almost a way of life.

WINE HISTORY

Wine was made in Gaul before the Roman occupation, mainly, no doubt, around the Greek colony of Massilia (Marseille). The Romans spread the knowledge of wine further and taught the natives to prune and tend their vines. There were two great trade routes by river and road from the early settlement of Narbonne: from Béziers to the Garonne (whence there was already a sea route to Britain); and by the Rhône and Saône to the Moselle and Loire valleys. Goods went by water to the inland port of Chalon-sur-Saône, and from there by wagon. The Gauls made barrels, and as early as Roman times these were in use. Centuries later the saintly King Louis IX liked to make casks in his spare time and as he made his visits from monastery to monastery he would stay to taste the wine the monks had made.

Gradually, as new and hardier grape varieties were discovered, the vineyards pushed farther north: to Gaillac and the Côtes du Rhône; then as far as the Loire, Brittany, and the Île-de-France. In the early Middle Ages, before the trade with Gascony had become important, Rhine wines were coming into London, along with *Vins de France*, the French wines from the districts near Paris which were greatly esteemed. As the demand increased, more supplies of wine came in from La Rochelle, Angers, and Saumur. Rouen was then a very busy port. Argen-

FRANCE
WINE AND BRANDY DISTRICTS

ENGLISH CHANNEL

Cherbourg

Le Havre

Rouen

Caen

N-13

Seine

CALVADOS

NORMANDY

Pa[ris]

St Malo

Versaill

N-10

N-12

BRITTANY

Chartres

Brest

N-12

A-11

N-10

N-165

Rennes

N-157

Le Mans

N-157

Maine

Or

N-152

LOIRE

Loir

Angers

Tours

Blois

Nantes

ANJOU

TOURAINE

R

Saumur

Loire

Cher

QUINCY

REUILLY

MUSCADET

Sèvre Nantaise

A-10

Châtelleräult

Château

Indre

Poitiers

Île de Ré

Vienne

N-20

La Rochelle

Gue

ATLANTIC OCEAN

N-10

COGNAC

Limoges

Cognac

Angoulême

MAS

MASS

HAUT MÉDOC

Andre de

N-89

Dordogne

Libourne

POMEROL

Cubzac

St. Émilion

Bergerac

BORDEAUX

Bordeaux

MONBAZILLAC

Lot

CAHORS

GRAVES

Langon

Cahors

Barsac

N-113

SAUTERNES

A-61

Agen

N

Garonne

BAY OF BISCAY

D-932

ARMAGNAC

GAILLAC

Albi

D-935

Gaillac

San Sebastian

Bayonne

Auch

N-21

Toulouse

Biarrit

PAYS BASQUE

N-117

JURANÇON

Pau

N-125

A-61

N

Bilbao

Tarbes

Carcasso

CORB

PYRÉNÉES

ROUS

Lourdes

SPAIN

ANDORRA

| 0 | 50 | 100 | 150 | 200 | 250 KILOMETERS |

| 0 | | 50 | | 100 | 150 MILES |

BELGIUM LUXEMBOURG
Luxembourg
ussels,
gne
Saarbrücken
Reims
Verdun
Metz
GERMANY
Épernay
Châlons-sur-Marne
Nancy
Strasbourg
Baden-Baden
Obernai
Sélestat
CHAMPAGNE
VOSGES
ALSACE
Colmar
nebleau
Mulhouse
CHABLIS
Chablis
Belfort
Basel
Auxerre
LIECHTENSTEIN
AUSTRIA
erre
cerre
Dijon
Besançon
AUSTRIA
Pouilly-
sur-Loire
CÔTE
DE NUITS
Beaune
Berne
SWITZERLAND
Nevers
CÔTE
DE BEAUNE
JURA
Neuchâtel
Chagny
Chalon
Fribourg
Loire
BURGUNDY
CÔTE D'OR
Moulins
Tournus
Lausanne
çon
CHAROLLAIS
Mâcon
BRESSE
Montreux
Vichy
Geneva
Rhône
Roanne
BEAUJOLAIS
VINS DE
Chamonix
Mont
Blanc
Milan
ermont-
rrand
Lyon
SAVOIE
Annecy
TRAL
St Étienne
Vienne
Chambéry
ITALY
Grenoble
Turin
Valence
ALPS
Gap
CÔTES DU RHÔNE
Genoa
Rhône
Orange
Châteauneuf-du-Pape
Menton
Ventimiglia
Avignon
MONACO
MonteCarlo
Nîmes
Arles
PROVENCE
BELLET
Nice
LANGUEDOC
Aix-en-Provence
Draguignan
CÔTE D'AZUR
Montpellier
PALETTE
Cannes
Béziers
Marseille
BANDOL
St Tropez
Narbonne
GULF OF LIONS
Cassis
Toulon
Rivesaltes
Perpignan
MEDITERRANEAN SEA
celona

Bastia
Calvi
Corte
Ajaccio
CORSICA
Propriano
Sartène
Porto-Vecchio
Bonifacio

0   50 KM
0   25 MI

teuil, celebrated in the nineteenth century in the paintings of the Impressionists, was famous more than six hundred years earlier, when its wines appeared on the table of King Philip Augustus. Before Champagne began to sparkle, its wines probably went in with those of the Seine; toward the end of the seventeenth century, the growths of Reims, Ay, and Épernay were praised by Saint-Evremond and others.

Nor were any of the wines as strong in alcohol or as lasting as those we are accustomed to. The light red Clairet of Gascony, as it arrived in England in the fourteenth century, was drawn fresh from the cask and drunk within a year of the harvest. In 1352 this edict was issued in London: "mixing of old Bordeaux wine with young Bordeaux and passing off the blend for young Bordeaux is forbidden as an offence against the king and the people." Since the wine was kept in porous casks at the time, there was no way of ageing it, and an old wine would no doubt have been *passé* and unpleasant.

In those days, many of the vineyards of France belonged to the Church—the monks took almost as much pains to spread the vine as they did to spread the Word, and their wines became an important source of revenue. In Burgundy, the Dukes as well as the Fathers cultivated vines, and they were good publicists for their own wines. For many years Burgundy was consumed principally in France and in Flanders (the Burgundian nobles also held court at Brussels); but when, in 1685, the Edict of Nantes was revoked, fleeing Huguenots introduced it abroad, especially in Switzerland, Holland, and Germany. About 1750, the first commercial houses and travelers in wine were set up.

In Bordeaux, the wine-making *bourgeoisie* became rich and powerful. Throughout the Hundred Years' War and afterward, England remained the chief customer, with Holland later gaining second place for white wines. In Tudor times the English took to drinking more of both beer and Sack, and French wine did not flow so freely or so cheaply as before. But it continued to come in, even when most of it had to be smuggled, at the time of Marlborough's wars and the heavy duties imposed by the Methuen Treaty.

Wars on French soil constantly damaged French vineyards, which were patiently reconstituted. The fortunes of the vine-grower wavered over the centuries. In spite of bitter struggles and the passage of armies, monk and peasant (and noble as well) continued to care for the vines and to make wine, adapting their customs to local conditions. Vines were pruned short in Bordeaux, long in the Rhône Valley; grapes were left to rot on the vines in Sauternes; Dom Pérignon (they say) discovered the cork as a bottle fastener and how to make sparkling wines; growers in Château-Chalon put their grapes on straw mats and left them to dry in the autumn sun. Other growers in other parts of the world have developed parallel systems, but in no other country have these techniques been so devotedly applied; nor has any other country been so richly endowed with variations of soil and climate. It is not surprising that France produces the greatest variety of great wines in the world.

Building the tradition of quality in French wines has not been without its setbacks. The attempt by the Duke of Burgundy to ban the "disloyal gaamez"—the productive grapevine Gamay which did no honor to the wines of the Côte d'Or—is one chapter in this struggle. The continual fight against fraud is another. The strict and enlightened laws of Appellation Contrôlée should provide the happy ending to the story; but the number of convictions for fraud that occur each year in France demonstrates that not all the community is motivated by the desire to strive only for the finest quality. Nevertheless, in the great wine regions the majority of growers strain all their resources to make the best possible wine year after year, though the cards in the modern era are perhaps more heavily stacked against them than ever before.

The present cry is for more of everything, turned out faster and more cheaply. If there is anything that does not respond to this call, it is wine. It can be made inexpensively, but it will not then be fine wine; it can be made in bulk, but cannot thus be great wine. The best wines have always been those from comparatively non-productive grapevines—from vines that are deliberately pruned short in order to reduce output and channel the plant's energy into the production of superior fruit, but little of it. The grower cannot obtain quantity and quality at the same time.

Another trend working against the contemporary grower is that toward a standard product. Wines will be different in different years; they can be standardized by blending, but no blending vat in the world is capable of turning out a standard wine of the highest quality. Ordinary wine from southern France, southern Italy, or Algeria can be pleasant enough with a meal; but cut with finer wines they do no justice to themselves or to the consumer.

The question is: will fine wines survive this trend? The French growers think they can continue in the traditional way; and the admirably stringent laws of Appellation d'Origine support their conviction. Many wine-drinkers, in France and abroad, support their efforts to maintain the old high standards by taking an interest such as has never before been manifested in fine wines. Others, more pessimistic, quote the rising cost of labor and equipment, which may cause the making of fine wine to become an economic impossibility, especially since even a comparatively short stretch of unfavorable weather can devastate the greatest vineyards. Fortunately for France, the high quality of her wines—admirably maintained by the laws of Appellation Contrôlée—is so firmly established throughout the world that she can charge the extra premium necessary for the protection of such standards. The extraordinarily high prices paid for the best French wines seem testimony enough that they are far from dying away in a mechanized age.

VINE-GROWING REGIONS

France is divided into ninety departments, and about two-thirds of these have commercial vineyards. Each wine is the result of the specific climate and soil from which it comes, the grape varieties from which it is made, and of the men and traditions behind it—factors which will differ with each wine. The history of Burgundy would not have been the same without the Cistercians and the French Revolution; the wine trade of Bordeaux was a development of her close ties with England; Champagne is inextricably linked with the discovery—whether by Dom Pérignon or another—of the champagne process; the wines of the Rhône Valley owe much of their present success to one extraordinary man—the Baron Le Roy de Boiseaumarié. But although the wines of France are numerous, the great regions are comparatively few. These are the most important (*see also under separate headings*):

Alsace

More than most other districts, Alsace is perfecting her wines. The best of them, superior to many of Germany's lesser wines, have not yet achieved the quality of rivals from the better domains in the Rheingau, the Palatinate, and the Mosel; yet some of the Alsatian wines are quite excellent.

Bordeaux

The largest of the great wine regions of France and the most productive. The reds—or clarets—of the Haut-Médoc, Graves, Saint-Émilion, and Pomerol, the sweet, rich whites of Sauternes and Barsac, and the drier whites of Graves have been imitated the world over—but rarely very successfully.

Burgundy

The wines vary so much that it is absurd to use the name to describe a single "type" of wine. Reds may be austere and aristocratic, as are Corton and Chambertin, or light and delicate as any fine wine from Chambolle should be. The whites are always dry; but the enormous variation between Chablis, Montrachet, and Meursault, for example, can only be appreciated by tasting.

Champagne

The name is so famous that many people don't know precisely what it is, but erroneously suppose it to be any "bubbly" white wine. Yet Champagne is rigidly controlled and strictly defined in France, and the name, far from applying to all sparkling wine, is only legal when applied to one that is unique and made, uniquely, in the district for which it is named.

Loire Valley

The white wines may be dry, semi-sweet, or sweet and are usually better than the reds. All are beguiling; but many are better buys at home than abroad, because they do not always travel well.

Rhône Valley

The reds are sturdy, big, perfumed, and often magnificent. The whites also have a distinctive vigor of their own. The rosé from Tavel is probably the best known of all rosé wines.

See also Anjou; Aude; Bergerac; Corsica; Fitou; Gaillac; Gard; Grand Roussillon; Hérault; Jura; Jurançon; Languedoc; Lorraine; Midi; Provence; Southwest France; Sweet fortified wines of France; Touraine; V.D.Q.S.; etc.

SPIRITS

As the greatest wines in the world come from France, so do the finest spirits: no brandy can compare with French Cognac, Armagnac, and Calvados; and in addition to these peerless brandies, the fertile French mind has developed countless cordials, liqueurs, and aperitifs, many strictly for the French palate, others equally appreciated outside France. The important ones, which will be found under their own headings in this book, are:

Armagnac

Wine brandy from the Gascon country, home of the boisterous musketeer d'Artagnan.

Calvados

Apple brandy from the old province of Normandy. When well made and properly aged it can be fabulous.

Cognac

Not any brandy, but a specific brandy. It is, perhaps, the most celebrated wine brandy in the world, and the one whose name is most commonly misused. True Cognac is made only in the Charente district.

Marc

Brandy from the pomace rather than the juice of the grape. Much of it too harsh and rough for consideration among fine spirits, but some, particularly an old marc of Burgundy, can be remarkable.

Brandies, or *eaux-de-vie*, are made from fruit as well as from wine; and many are called *alcools blancs* because of their white color. Quetsch is distilled from purple plums, mirabelle from yellow plums, framboise from raspberries, fraise from strawberries, and kirsch from cherry-stones. These white spirits are matured slowly in crocks and are very dry and high in alcohol. A great many of them come from Alsace and Lorraine; the Dordogne makes prune, another plum spirit.

All over France, liqueurs are made—a dazzling variety: Chartreuse (green and yellow), Benedictine, Cointreau, Crèmes (de menthe, etc.), anisette (*qq.v.*), and aperitifs both spirituous and sickly. Among the best known of these are the dry French vermouth, Dubonnet, Amer Picon, Suze, Saint-Raphaël, Pernod, and Ricard (*qq.v.*).

Franciacorta

A pleasant red or white wine from Bresica.
See Lombardy.

Franconia, Franken

White and red wines.
Central Germany.

The *gebiet*, or region, is officially divided into three *Bereiche*, or sub-regions: Mainviereck, in the west, with the Tauber Valley; Maindreieck, in the center, including the area around Würzburg and Karlstadt; and Steigerwald in the east.

The wines vary considerably, but they can be divided roughly into four groups, corresponding to four different prevailing soil conditions. Franconian (or Franken) wines are mostly white, and the best of them grow in the eastern part of the W-shaped zigzag of the River Main, east of the Rheingau. Iphofen, Rödelsee, Castell, and Abtswind are neighboring communities which lie east of the last bend of the Main in Franconia, giving their names to white wines grown on what is the most reliable soil in the region. Loamy and thick, it holds the moisture; and if this is not the ideal ground for noble wines, it has the advantage of providing a fairly consistent crop in a part of Germany where wine-growing is even more precarious than elsewhere. Sylvaner was almost the exclusive grape variety in this strip, and the wines tended to be full, round, and rather soft. Sylvaner and Müller-Thurgau now cover about the same amount of acreage, and most of the wines are solid and not too sweet.

The famous Stein wines are the only ones known widely abroad, although all Franconian wines tend to attract attention wherever they are exported, because of the unusual shape of their flattish flask or Bocksbeutel (*q.v.*) in which they are bottled.

Steinwein, or the "stone wine," is properly—and in Germany legally—the wine only of the Würzburger Stein, a steep slope above the town of Würzburg, with a southern aspect and a soil which is predominantly lime. So famous have the wines of this slope become that abroad all Franconian wines in the characteristic bottle are apt to be called Stein wines. The true Steinweine are green-gold, with an uncompromising quality that destines them for connoisseurs.

Würzburg, along with Escherndorf and Randersacker, the other two most important towns, lies in the second of the four distinct soil areas, moving westward from the Abtswind-Castell-Iphofen region. The soil is primarily chalky. Riesling, Müller-Thurgau (the crossing of Riesling and Sylvaner), and Traminer wines are grown, as well as Sylvaner, the principal type throughout Franconia. The wines of this section often have a distinct *goût de terroir*, a taste contributed by (but not a taste of) the soil. Like the Hospices de Beaune in Burgundy, two asylums for the ailing and poor support themselves here, largely by the sale of wines, and incidentally provide a consistently high standard of bottles. They are the Juliusspital and the Burgerspital of Würzburg. Both have dealt in wines for more than three centuries. The Juliusspital cellars are vast, and it is the boast of their owners that only natural wines have ever been made there. The former Royal Cellars, now part of the State Domain and also in Würzburg, are particularly fine.

Due west of Würzburg, in the other deep bend of the Main, a sandy soil characterizes the third geological division of Franconia. Here the wines, both red and white, are interspersed in the vineyards. The most important wines come from Klingenberg. The red wines are made chiefly from the Spätburgunder variety, which came originally from Burgundy.

The fourth district is the most westerly one, nearest the Rheingau; and perhaps for this reason, the wines are reminiscent of Rheingaus. Hörstein is the best *Weinbauort*, or wine-producing town.

That the Franconian wine-culture is the most marginal in Germany can be strikingly shown with figures. Before the Thirty Years' War (1618-48) the vineyard extended over 40,000 hectares (100,000 acres); in 1870 it was 9,000-odd hectares (about 24,000 acres); in 1900, 7,000 hectares (17,500 acres); and today about 3,100 hectares (7,750 acres). This shrinkage has been caused by war; the Thirty Years' War destroyed the whole plantation, and the Second World War was devastating, especially around Würzburg. The climate has been just as disastrous; Franconia has cold winters and hot summers, with severe frost often striking in the critical blossoming time in spring or at harvest time in October. Such conditions have driven viticulture up onto the steepest slopes where nothing else will grow, and the lower, more fertile areas have been turned over to other crops. On the credit side, in this century, and intensively since 1950, experiment has developed by both chemical and botanical methods a much-improved vine, more capable of resisting frost, disease, and rot. X-ray, hot and cold shock, and chemical treatment have been used to force beneficial mutations in Sylvaner, Riesling, and Müller-Thurgau vines. Moreover, the mere retreat of the vine to the higher, more difficult slopes has undoubtedly caused an improvement in the quality, along with the lessening in quantity, of Franconian wines. The grape is always best where the vine must struggle for life.

For a complete list of the Franken *Einzellagen* (individual vineyards) arranged by *Grosslage* (section of vineyards) and *Bereich* (sub-region), see Appendix B, p. 605.

THE BEST VINEYARDS

Town or Village (Weinbauort)	Vineyard (Einzellage)
Würzburg	Abtsleite, Innere Leiste, Kirchberg, Pfaffenberg, Schlossberg, Stein, Stein-Harfe
Castell	Schlossberg
Escherndorf	Lump, Berg, Fürstenberg
Randersacker	Marsberg, Pfülben, Teufelskeller
Iphofen	Julius Echter Berg, Kronsberg, Kalb
Rödelsee	Küchenmeister, Schwanleite
Abstwind	Altenberg
Hörstein	Abtsberg
Homburg	Kallmuth
Sommerach	Katzenkopf

Frappé

French term for a drink, chilled or iced—or with shaved ice, as in the case of Crème de menthe frappée.

Frascati

Dry white wine of the Castelli Romani, Italy.
See Latium.

Frecciarossa

A good light wine made in Lombardy (*q.v.*).

Fredonia

Prolific American red grape used for red wine, especially in New Jersey.

Free-run

Wine running freely from the residue after fermentation, or from pressed wine at the first light pressing. It is the best, and in many regions it is bottled separately.

Freisa

Grape used for a sprightly red Italian wine with a delightful bouquet.

French West Indies

See Rum, French.

Fresh

The engaging, bright charm of all rosés, most white, and some red wines exhibited only in their youth. Most of the white and all of the rosé wine made today is best drunk young, before this early pertness, one of their finest assets, is lost.

Friuli-Venezia-Giulia

Red and white wines.
District: Northeast Italy.

This rather small and mountainous region in the extreme northeast corner of Italy which borders Austria and Yugoslavia is perhaps more well known for its ham and dairy products than for its wine. But a great deal of wine is produced each year: about 1 million hectoliters (26.5 million U.S. gallons, 22 million imp.).

Collio (*D.O.C.*), also known as Collio Goriziano, is a dry white wine with a slight sparkle made from Ribolla Gialla, Malvasia, and some Tocai in a small area called Collio near Yugoslavia. If the denomination is followed by the name of a grape variety, that grape is the predominant one found in the wine.

Colli Orientali del Friuli (*D.O.C.*) is the official name given all wines from the eastern hills of Friuli in the province of Udine, once the major city of a Roman colony founded in the second century B.C. As with Collio, the name may be

followed with the grape variety mostly used to produce the wine. Most interesting of these is Colli Orientali del Friuli Picolit, a golden dessert wine some consider among the best wines of its type found anywhere in Italy.

Grave del Friuli (*D.O.C.*) is the name for seven sound wines from the part of Udine and Pordenone known as Grave.

Frizzante

Italian term for semi-sparkling wine.

Fronsac

See Côtes Canon Fronsac.

Frontignan-Muscat

A Mediterranean district of southern France producing Muscat wines (Muscat de Frontignan). Frontignan is a term often used in France for a 75-centiliter bottle.
See Sweet fortified wines of France.

Fronton

Simple, pleasant red and rosé wines made just north of Toulouse in southwestern France. They are entitled to the V.D.Q.S. seal.

Fruity

The springlike first expression of many wines, innocent and fresh, most pronounced to the nose. The characteristic is caused by a high volatility of the esters (flavor and perfume essences) and is likely to disappear quickly in wines not rich in sugar. The fruity dry or semi-dry wine should be drunk young, before it begins to fade. A fruity red wine will not have been fermented on the lees for a long time. It will lack tannin and will have been bottled young. Beaujolais is an example of a fruity red wine. The Mosel is known for its fruity white wines.

Fuder

German term for large cask holding 1,000 liters (264 U.S. gallons, 220 imp.) of wine.
See Foudre.

Fumarium

Roman hot room for "improving" wine by exposing it to smoke.

Fumé de Pouilly

A white French wine, also known as Pouilly-Fumé.
See Pouilly-sur-Loire.

Fumigation

Burning of a wick of sulfur in a vat or barrel of wine to destroy bacteria or unwanted yeasts—to a considerable extent the destruction is achieved by replacing the air in the container and by bringing the wine into contact with sulfuric acid gas. Too much sulfur will spoil the taste of the wine. In Bordeaux, a quarter of a wick of sulfur to a *barrique* holding 225 liters (59.4 U.S. gallons, 49.5 imp.) is generally effective. The French term for the process is *méchage*, from *mèche*, meaning wick.

In California, wherever oak has grown, soils must be fumigated before vines are planted.

See Sulfur dioxide; Chapter Nine.

Funchal

The port and principal town of Madeira where much of the wine is stored and aged and whence all of it is shipped.

Furfural

An aldehyde present in minute quantity in wines and spirits. An oxidation product of glucose, furfural is an important flavor component of sweet wines produced by heating, such as Marsala and Madeira.

Furmint

The fine white grape from which Hungarian Tokay is made. It also goes into some of the German wines.

Fusel oil

Term generally designating the volatile, nauseous higher alcohols removed by the rectification of spirituous liquors.

Fût

One of the French terms for a cask or barrel.

G

Gaillac

Still and sparkling white wines.
District: Southwest France.

Southeast of Bordeaux is the French department of the Tarn and the River Tarn—not a big river but one of the most beautiful in France, a sparkling trout stream cutting through rocky passes. In the hills near the city of Gaillac, the slopes are planted in vines which give the wines called Premières Côtes de Gaillac or Gaillac Mousseux.

The wine produced by the Gaillac vineyards in the Middle Ages seems to have been better than the sweetish and uninteresting whites, reds and rosés yielded now. (Tastes have changed too.) The Plantagenet kings of England were devoted to Gaillac, as was Henry VII. In his *Mémoires de Languedoc* (1633), Catel wrote that this wine, much prized by foreign princes, left a taste of roses in the mouth.

The right conditions for the making of Gaillac wine are laid down in a series of decrees beginning in 1938. There are six grapes which may be used for white wines: Mauzac, l'En de l'El, Ondenc, Sémillon, Sauvignon, and Muscadelle. Mauzac usually accounts for 80% to 100%, varying with the vineyards. Red and rosé wines are vinified from Ouras, Gaillac, Syrah, and Negrette grapes. To qualify for the place-names under French wine law, the vines must attain 12% of alcohol for Premières Côtes de Gaillac and 10.5% for wines designated simply Gaillac. The sparkling wines must be made according to the champagne method of secondary fermentation in the bottle, or by the Gaillac method—a slight variation of this—in which the wines are bottled while they still hold unresolved sugar, causing imprisoned fermentation and often a fairly heavy bottle-sediment as well.

Galgenwein (Gallows Wine)

Humorous reference to a German wine so harsh and strong that after it has been drunk the gallows is unnecessary: the *Galgenwein* trickling down the throat can choke the drinker so effectively that no gallows rope is needed.

Gallization

Another term, used in Germany, for *chaptalisation* (*q.v.*).
See Chapter Nine, p. 38.

Gallon, British imperial

The volume of ten standard pounds of distilled water weighed in air at a temperature of 62°F. (17°C.) and a barometric pressure of 30 inches; 277.274 cubic inches. It is the equivalent of 1.20095 U.S. gallons or 4.54596 liters.

Gallon, U.S.

The former British "wine gallon" of 231 cubic inches which was replaced in Great Britain in 1826 by the standard imperial gallon. It is the equivalent of approximately five-sixths of the volume of the imperial gallon (.83267), or 3.78531 liters.

Gamay

A red grape from which red wine is made. Undistinguished in the rest of Burgundy, it yields admirable wine in Beaujolais. It is equally temperamental in California, where it does excellently in the mountainous vineyards of Santa Cruz but makes very ordinary wine in the Napa Valley.

Gambellara

A light white wine similar to Soave.
See Veneto.

Gamza

One of the principal grape varieties in Bulgaria, producing red and some white wines.
See Bulgaria.

Gard

Quantitatively, one of the three most important wine-producing departments of France. (The other two are Aude and Hérault.) From Gard in the south of France comes a great deal of ordinary wine, as well as the robust red Costières (*see* V.D.Q.S.) and the white Clairette de Bellegarde (*q.v.*).

Garda

Name of groups of Italian wines (Chiaretto-del-Garda, Moniga-del-Garda, and Riviera-del-Garda) grown near Lake Garda.
See Lombardy.

Garrafeira

Term on Portuguese wine labels indicating that the wine has been matured for some years in bottle before being offered for sale. It could perhaps be equated with Reserve or Special Reserve.

Gattinara

A popular full-bodied red wine of Piedmont (*q.v.*).

Gay-Lussac

French chemist who produced the classic chemical formula for the process of fermentation (*q.v.*). His work on the alcoholometer and sulfuric acid were great contributions to wine-making.

Gazéifié

French term for sparkling wine in which the sparkle comes from artificial carbonation.

Chateau Gazin

Bordeaux red wine.
District and Commune: Pomerol, France.

Owned by M. de Baillencourt and among the largest properties in the district, the château makes a wine that sometimes does not live up to its high reputation.

Vineyard area: 25 hectares (62 acres).
Average production: 80 *tonneaux* (7,500 cases).

Gean whisky, Geen whisky

A liqueur made in Scotland of whisky and black cherries.

Gebiet

The German term for region, specifically one of the eleven producing areas now defined by West German law.

Geisenheim

In this Rheingau town is the most important viticultural school in Germany. Its vineyards produce some good wines, notably Morschberg and Rothenberg.
See Rheingau.

Gemarkung

German town or village name of a wine. Comparable to commune name in France. Now replaced by the term "weinbauort" according to the new West German wine laws.

Generous

A wine is generous when it has warmth and is rich in alcohol and vitality.

Geneva

The English spelling for Jenever (*q.v.*), the name used in Holland for Dutch gin.
See Gin.

Gentiane

French and Swiss liqueur distilled from the root of the gentian plant. The most popular French aperitif of this style is Suze.
See Enzian.

Gentil

Alsatian synonym for Riesling grape (*q.v.*).

Gerk

See Grk.

Germany

"The breed of the fine German wines is the result of the struggle for life at the northernmost climate in which the vine can grow. Costs are higher, cultivation is more intensive, the fight against insects and disease sterner, fertilizing more essential."

This statement by the late Professor Steinberg, director of Germany's most important viticultural school at Geisenheim on the Rhine, sums up the story of German wines. While various German vineyard areas claim to be the farthest north in the world, the fact is that more of the German wine-belt lies in a colder and less friendly climate than any other important zone. The vine accepts the challenge and, especially if it is the Riesling, produces wines of pure gold. It demands in return to be treated like a prima donna.

Viticulture is carefully controlled. A plot may only be planted in vine if it is going to produce wine of a certain quality. All owners are obliged to declare their vineyards and their stocks. Less than 1% of the agricultural land is in vine, but in the south and southwest of the country, where the vineyards are located, the culture is economically important. Plantings are gradually being extended, and the total area of the vineyards is now more than 100,000 hectares (250,000 acres). Eighty-five per cent of the grapes produce white wines. About 300,000 people are regularly employed in viticulture—over 500,000 at harvest time—but, directly or indirectly, some 1 million live off the wine industry. As wages have risen, so has the domestic consumption of wine: now more than 20 liters a head (5.3 U.S. gallons, 4.4 imp.). Out of a total production exceeding 8.6 million hectoliters (227 million U.S. gallons, 189 million imp.), 1,000,000 hectoliters (26,450,-000 U.S. gallons, 22,000,000 imp.) are exported each year; and both figures are continually rising. In East Germany, only some 50,000 hectoliters (1.32 million U.S. gallons, 1.1 million imp.) of rather average wine is made annually.

WINE HISTORY

The long and tangled story of German wines, woven deeply though it is into the gothic tapestry of history along the Rhine, may be sketched fairly briefly.

It is probable that wine was being made in what is now Germany at about the beginning of the Christian era. The Romans came and left their imprint on the people, the towns, the wines, the history and customs of the Mosel and the Rhine. Most significant, perhaps, in viticulture has been the influence of the Roman inheritance law, which decreed that estates were not to be passed on intact to a single heir, but were to be handed down to descendants in equal shares. In Germany, the snipping of vineyards into postage-stamp parcels, each with its individual owner and vinous method, has created a maze of vineyard names and wines. This confusion has been recognized as detrimental, and the West German wine laws of 1971 were directed toward simplification of nomenclature and consolidation.

After the Roman period and a later phase, in which vineyards were bandied about by medieval kings and knights, wine became the domain of the Church. The consequences are apparent to anyone who visits the Mosel, the Palatinate, or the Rhine. The great estates retain the shape given them by the monasteries; and some of the monastic wine sheds themselves may still be seen, out of use now, their giant beam presses recalling the days when cowled men were making the wines. A little anecdote told at Kloster Eberbach catches the spirit of the time. The cellar-master of this cloister above the Rhine, sampling a cask one day, detected the taste of iron. Dismayed, he ran to the cook, who, tasting in his turn, discovered not iron but a taint of leather. Both together hurried to the prior. He tasted too, to decide between them, but found them both wrong: in his opinion, the wine tasted slightly of wood. When the cask was emptied, after much sturdy drinking and disputing, a key was found at the bottom, fastened to a bit of wood by a leather strap—or so they say.

In 1803, Napoleon secularized the German vineyards. A few great holdings remained intact, and today most of these are run by the state. But for the Gall process, small growers would probably have perished altogether: Gallization of wine is the addition of sugar, now regulated by the laws of the European Economic Community. "Sugar may be added to grape must or wines . . . provided this is done for the purpose of supplementing a natural lack of sugar or alcohol, or of counteracting a natural excess of acid, to an extent sufficient to produce in the said wines a composition equal to that of wines derived in a good year from grapes of the same kind and origin . . . and provided also that the sugar is added to the must before fermentation." This treatment, generally known by the French name, *chaptalisation*, carried small growers over the bad years, which they might not otherwise have survived. It is important to note, however, that no quality wines (*Qualitätswein mit Prädikat*) may be *angereichert* (chaptalized) except within the limits closely specified by the recent laws. The word *natur* has been eliminated from all wine labels in West Germany, since nearly all wine made there must be slightly sugared or otherwise stabilized, and thus the designation "natural" is plainly untrue.

In spite of this, there was, in the first years after the Second World War, a pronounced trend toward sweeter wines—the result of wartime sugar-starvation in Germany. This trend has continued and the Germans have not reverted to the drier wines. Years which give great vintages in France do not usually produce the wines most to the German taste; but the 1959s, for some, would now be considered too sweet.

The peak of German vineyards was reached before the Thirty Years' War (1618-48), but a much greater quantity of wine is being made now than at any other time—even though war, vine plague, and other devastations have all had their way. Moreover, vines grown in low ground (not conducive to high-quality wines) had to give way to other crops. Yet the figure has risen substantially in recent years.

Like the Gall process in its time, Spätlesen wines saved the German growers at the end of the eighteenth century. The exact origin of these left-on-the-vine wines is disputed, but the Bishop of Fulda may have been the originator. One year his messenger, bearing the permission necessary to harvest the Bishop's Johannisberg estate, was captured by robbers and held for several weeks. When he finally arrived and the picking began, the grapes were nearly rotten and were thrown to the peasantry—for whom they produced a glorious elixir. This technique of letting the grapes reach noble rot (*q.v.*) late in the autumn produces the great Sauternes and the German Spätlesen and Trockenbeerenauslesen wines today, but the enormous risk of early frosts and the additional cost of labor in the individual picking of the berries are gradually forcing prices too high for the market on both Rhine and Mosel.

Changing public taste has also played its inevitable role. The real wine-taster prefers the older wines, the Edelfirne, in which the oils have been transformed by a beneficial maderization. "One bottle of the young wine may have the effect of three bottles of the old—the next morning," they say; this is because the older wine has achieved balance. The public taste, however, is inclining more and more toward the younger vintages; but through better vinification, these now have lower sulfur acidity.

THE WINE DISTRICTS

The designated quality wine-producing areas, or *bestimmten Anbaugebiete*, such as the Rheingau, the Mosel, the Palatinate, and Rheinhessen, are treated separately under their own headings. But something can be said about them comparatively and as a group.

The Palatinate, or Pfalz, is the largest producer of the major districts and the Rheingau the smallest. The Palatinate makes about nine to ten times as much wine yearly as the Rheingau in about seven times the vineyard space. Approaching the Palatinate in size is Rheinhessen, followed by the Mosel-Saar-Ruwer area, always lumped into one by the Germans; then Baden, Württemberg, Franconia (Franken), and Rheingau. Ahr is the smallest *Gebiet* (region).

RED WINES

Some red wine is grown in the Rheingau, in the Palatinate, in Rheinhessen, Franconia, Baden, and Württemberg (although there is more white here); but the only red wines at all well known abroad are Assmannshauser from

WEST GERMANY

0   10   20   50 MILES
0 10 20   50 KILOMETRES

HOLLAND

Cologne

BELGIUM

Bonn

Dresden   Leipzig 150 m.

AHR

R. Ahr

R. Rhine

MIDDLE-RHINE (MITTELRHEIN)

N 51

Koblenz

R. Lahn

AUTOBAHN

AUTOBAHN

N 40

MOSELLE (MOSEL)

R. Moselle

N 49

Rüdesheim

Wiesbaden

Frankfurt

RHEINGAU

Eltville

Wehlen

Bingen

Hattenheim

Mainz

FRANCONIA

Bernkastel

Piesport

RHEINHESSEN

Darmstadt

LUXEMBOURG

NAHE

Nierstein

R. Main

Wurzburg

Trier

Eitelsbach

Oppenheim

R. RUWER

R. Nahe

N 50

R. Ruwer

N 48

Wiltingen

Worms

Saarburg

Ockfen

BERGSTRASSE

SAAR

R. Saar

N 53b

Bad Dürkheim

Deidesheim

PALATINATE
(RHEINPFALZ)
N 9

Heidelberg

N 53

N 40

Paris
170 m.

Nuremberg 65 m.

R. Moselle

AUTOBAHN

N 61

WÜRTTEMBERG

Karlsruhe

B A D E N

AUTOBAHN

N 68

Baden-Baden

Stuttgart

BAS RHIN

N 3

N 4

Strasbourg

R. Neckar

Munich 80 m.

Black Forest

N 28

F R A N C E

N

HAUT-RHIN

N 422

Freiburg

BODENSEE

Basle

R. Rhine

Constance

L. Constance

N 34

SWITZERLAND

236

the Rheingau, Ahrweiler and Walporzheimer from the Ahr, Ingelheimer from Rheinhessen, Kaiserstuhl from Baden, one or two wines from around Bad Dürkheim in the Palatinate, and some from Württemberg. No German red wine is, or deserves to be, internationally important.

WHITE WINES

Mosel (with Saar and Ruwer)

The most delicate of them all. Light and elegant. The most important characteristic is that derived from the slate soil.

Nahe

Something between a Saar and a Rheinhessen, and in the lower reaches of the river very similar to Rheingau wines.

Rheinhessen

The easiest to understand and place. Less acid, and therefore flatter than the Rheingaus. Mild, fruity, and elegant.

Palatinate (or Pfalz)

The common wines are the lightest of the Rhine—mellow, soft, without much alcohol, and for drinking in quantity. Yet some of the best wines can be very full, alcoholic, and sweet, having that typical and special perfume the Germans call "the Pfalz wine character." In recent years the average quality is much improved.

Rheingau

Producing the finest characteristics of German wines and with the greatest amount of fruit acidity. More style, firmer, heavier, greater fruitiness, and more noble taste than Rheinhessens or Palatinates.

Middle Rhine

Small and quite insignificant. Lighter than Rheingaus but in many ways similar; some of the best have a flinty taste imparted by the slate soil.

Franconia (Franken)

Stronger than Rhine Valley wines and quite pleasant when young. These are likely to be similar in taste to Baden and Württemberg wines when the same grape varieties have been used.

Baden and Württemberg

Baden wines often resemble those from Alsace, across the Rhine, which have more alcohol, however. Wines of both districts are inclined to be heavy and pungent when they come from the Ruländer grape, a descendant of the Pinot Gris, which is in wide use.

Ahr

Small wines. They used to be mostly red, but more white is being made now.

Bergstrasse

Inferior. Small, light, pleasant wines to be drunk on the spot.

STATE DOMAIN

The State Domain is the largest vineyard owner in all Germany. Holdings in the Rheingau and along the Bergstrasse near Heidelberg total about 200 hectares (500 acres), producing between 1,500 and 2,000 *Halbstücke* (102,000 to 136,000 cases) each year. Made up for the most part of former Church holdings secularized in 1803 by Napoleon, the State Domain was the domain of the Dukedom of Nassau until 1866, then of the Hessian State (often miscalled the Prussian State Domain) from 1866 to 1945, and of the Hessian State Domain since that date. There are seven estates, two wine-making centers, and a major nursery. From the point of view of quality, the State Domain holdings in the Rheingau are ranked as follows by many experts: first, those in Rauenthal; second, Markobrunn and Hattenheim; third, Steinberg; fourth, those in Rüdesheim; fifth, those of Hochheim. The true determination of quality, however, is the vintage year.

GRAPE VARIETIES

The grape used is of paramount importance in German wines.

Riesling. This is the best German white-wine grape. If the grape-variety is not named on the label of a high-quality wine, it may generally be presumed to be Riesling—for many wines made from Riesling do not carry the grape-name on the label. All great Spätlesen, Auslesen, and Trockenbeerenauslesen wines are Rieslings, although they may be made from other varieties; all the best Rheingau vineyards, and practically the whole of the Mosel, are planted in Riesling. A steely aristocracy is the outstanding characteristic of a Riesling wine, particularly when it has been grown in the slate soil of the Mosel. The grape is small and the yield not high, but the character and staying-power and the incomparable bouquet which seems to be composed of mingled fruit scents more than compensate for the lack of quantity. The vine ripens late and is resistant to cold. Once taken away from its habitat along the Rhine and Mosel (and in nearby Alsace) and planted abroad, something happens to it, and it is Riesling in name only. This vine produces more than 55 hectoliters per hectare (600 U.S. gallons, 500 imp. to the acre).

Sylvaner. Softer and milder, the biggest producer. In some parts of Germany it is called Franken Riesling and in others Österreicher (from Austria—Österreich—whence it came). The Sylvaner yields double the output of the Riesling and is usually prominent in an average wine which carries no grape-name. The German spelling is Silvaner.

Müller-Thurgau. The crossing of the Riesling and Sylvaner plants, named for the man who created it, produces a wine milder than the Riesling and with a taste that has

237

something of Muscatel. This variety is now the most widely-planted vine. The yield is up to 190 hectoliters per hectare (2,000 U.S. gallons, 1,700 imp. per acre).

Gewürztraminer or Traminer. It gives a special spicy wine which is unmistakable; but despite its fineness, the vine has had an up-and-down fate because it is hard to grow. It produces about the same quantity as the Riesling.

Muskateller. Rare; this southern type does not like the northerly climate and generally remains too acid.

Gutedel. Produces the light, sweet table wines of the Markgräfler, below Freiburg in Baden.

Ruländer. The Pinot Gris—also called Grauerburgunder or Tokaier. It gives a full, heavy, and sometimes fiery wine.

Elbling. Mediocre. Grown especially for the German sparkling wines known as Sekt.

Red wines come from the following plants: Spätburgunder (all of the best); Frühburgunder; Portugieser (light and of less distinction); Trollinger in Württemberg (the same vine is called Blauer Malvasier in the Palatinate); and Müller-Schwarzriesling.

WINE LAWS

Eighty-five per cent of West German wines—and all the important ones—are white. The cost of producing them is twice that of wine-production in France, four times as great as in Spain. France has twenty times as much vineyard as West Germany; but the yield per acre in West Germany is very much higher than that in such fine regions of France as Burgundy and Bordeaux. The leading customer for exported West German wines, which are short on quantity but long on quality, is the United States, followed by Great Britain; until recently, this order was reversed for many years.

Fortification of wine by the addition of alcohol is not allowed in West Germany. Rhine wines grow on wires, trained to two—sometimes three—parallel strands, except in the Mosel vineyards, which are so steep that stakes are used instead. Bowed out at either side of these stakes, the Mosel vines look rather like lorgnettes.

Almost all the best vineyards face south, to get the maximum sun—or, if not south, then west, because sunshine is stronger in the afternoon than in the morning. The surfaces are carefully leveled so that one section of vine will not overshadow another—an apparently slight disadvantage which might make all the difference in such a marginal area.

The West German wines are classed in two groups—those for the everyday table (*Tafelwein*—the English translation is not to be confused with the term meaning any non-fortified, non-sparkling wine) and those of special quality (*Qualitätswein*). The two groups of wines come from nearly the same ground, but the *Tafelwein* districts include many vineyards not good enough to produce a "quality wine." The *Tafelwein* area called Mosel corresponds to the quality-wine *Gebiet* (region) of Mosel-Saar-Ruwer. The Rhein *Tafelwein* district covers the quality *Gebiete* of Ahr, Mittelrhein, Rheingau, Nahe, Rheinpfalz, Rheinhessen, and Bergstrasse. Main is the *Tafelwein* name

for the Franken vineyards. Likewise, Neckar covers the Württemberg quality *Gebiet*. The *Tafelwein* district Oberrhein, with two parts, corresponds to the *Qualitätsgebiet* of Baden.

The system of double names is meant to help, not hinder, the consumer. A West German wine from 1971 or some later vintage labeled Rhein can only be a lowergrade blend or bottling from anywhere in that extensive district and cannot be mistaken for a better wine from the Rheingau, Rheinpfalz, Rheinhessen, or Mittelrhein.

Since little *Tafelwein* is exported, more *Qualitätswein* is apt to be found in markets outside Germany, and it is of some importance to understand the system by which the eleven designated quality-wine producing regions (the *bestimmten Anbaugebiete*) are subdivided. Each region is composed of one or more sub-regions called a *Bereich*. For Mosel-Saar-Ruwer these sub-regions are Bernkastel, Obermosel, Saar-Ruwer, and Zell. Immediately it is apparent where the names originated: in some cases (Saar-Ruwer) the logical geography-related name was kept for the sub-region; in others (Bernkastel) a famous town name was given an entire sub-region, with the simple bonus of adding luster and appeal to a purely regional wine label. A wine labeled Bereich Bernkastel can come from anywhere in that sizable area, but one called Bernkasteler must come from the vineyards associated with that famous town. Though the names obviously will be different, the situation is much the same in the other parts of Germany.

Each *Bereich* is divided into one or more *Grosslagen*. The German word means "large site," but it is best to think of a *Grosslage* as a section of similar vineyards. The process for choosing names for the *Grosslagen* was not unlike that for naming the *Bereiche*. In the Bereich Bernkastel, for example, one of the *Grosslagen* is called Badstube, a name which used to belong to one of the best vineyards of the town. A wine labeled Bernkasteler Badstube (from 1971 on) is a regional blended wine, though admittedly from a good part of the larger *Bereich*. Wines with a *Grosslage* name should be of higher quality than those with only the *Bereich* name. They will ideally have some of the same taste and characteristics of the wines from the specific vineyards within the *Grosslage* (see below) and will be less expensive.

Each *Grosslage* is composed of individual vineyards called *Einzellagen*. It was the great and confusing number (about 30,000) of these sites throughout West Germany that was one of the major reasons for passing the 1971 wine law. For a vineyard to retain its own name, it must now be a minimum size—between 5 and 10 hectares (12 and 25 acres) depending on the terrain. Those plots smaller than the legal minimum either were absorbed or grouped together in tracts large enough to bear an individual name. The move reduced the number to about 3,000, but at the same time eradicated more than a few well-respected wine names. Quality too may have suffered with this streamlining. The wine from a great vineyard may not be as fine once less good neighboring vines are appended to the original plot.

The *Einzellagen* are still associated with towns, now

called in wine terminology *Weinbauorte* (wine-growing places). A town and its surrounding vineyards may fall into more than one *Grosslage*. Thus Bernkastel Kardinalsberg is part of the *Grosslage* Kurfürstlay, while Bernkastel Doctor lies in *Grosslage* Badstube. The town name will always appear on the label of a quality wine from a single vineyard.

Wines bottled since the revised laws were passed in 1971 appear under labels rather easier to read than the previous ones. Those likely to be seen abroad come under the following three categories:

(1) Table Wine (*Deutscher Tafelwein*). These pleasant and uncomplicated wines must be made from approved grape varieties (those listed above are nearly all of the permissible vines) in any one of the five districts: Mosel, Rhein, Main, Neckar, or Oberrhein. This last is divided into Oberrhein Burgengau and Oberrhein Römertor. The name of the region and of the bottler (*Abfüller*) appear on the label. Brand names are permitted. The name of a grape variety may be given if 85% of the wine in the bottle was made from the specified plant. A vintage date is similarly optional and may be given if 85% of the wine is from the vintage year named.

(2) Quality Wine (*Qualitätswein bestimmten Anbaugebiet*). These finer, fuller wines must show the typical character of the region and the grape, as determined by a government test and local testing panel. The wines must have a minimum degree of alcohol (which varies from region to region) and must come from one of the eleven quality wine regions (*bestimmten Anbaugebiete*): Baden, Rheinpfalz, Württemberg, Franken, Rheinhessen, Hessiche Bergstrasse, Rheingau, Nahe, Mittelrhein, Mosel-Saar-Ruwer, or Ahr. (See above for a comparison of these regions to the *Tafelwein* districts.) If a wine meets these requirements, the tasting authorities record it and assign it a control number (*amtliche Prüfungsnummer*) which is printed on the label, together with the names of the region, subregion, town, section of vineyards, or single vineyard—as long as 85% of the wine was made in the smallest named area. The other 15% must come from anywhere in the same sub-region, or *Bereich*. The name of the bottler or grower will also appear. As with the *Tafelweine*, the grape name may be given if 85% of the wine was made from the variety indicated.

(3) Quality Wine with Special Attributes (*Qualitätswein mit Prädikat*). This is the highest class of German wines, produced from fully matured grapes of an approved variety in a specified *Bereich*. These wines must attain 10% of natural alcohol with no sugar added. Government officials control the grapes in the vineyard and the must in the cellar. The harvest date is set and registered by the state. Like the simple quality wines, those in this category are scrutinized and tasted by various panels and finally given a control number if worthy of its name. The *Prädikat*, or special attributes, are Kabinett, Spätlese, Auslese, Beerenauslese, and Trockenbeerenauslese (see definitions on the following pages)—as well as Eiswein, a rarity made from grapes harvested and crushed while still frozen. Estate-bottled wines, formerly *Original abfüllung*, are now known as *Erzeugerabfüllung* (producer's bottling) or *aus*

eigenem Lesegut (from producer's own harvest). But no wine, not even one from a famous vineyard, will be allowed a *Prädikat* if it does not exhibit the fine qualities associated with its name. This rating of the actual wine, not the vineyard, is one of the great triumphs of the new law.

After a law has been passed and its regulations seem cut and dried, comes the period of application—and, inevitably, of modification. When local officials are faced with details, they will certainly raise questions to which no one as yet has answers. The many test cases will take time to decide and some will surely prove the exceptions to the rule.

A WINE-LABEL BAEDEKER

A German wine label is one of the hardest things to find your way around. The following tips may be of some help in reading those pre-1971 labels which are still on sale. If a term is still legally found on post-1971 labels, it is so noted. (For a general description of recent labeling, see above.)

Apart from special designations, the old-style basic wine label will read: district . . . vintage year . . . town or village . . . vineyard . . . grape variety (*e.g.*, Rheinpfalz . . . 1967er . . . Forster . . . Ziegler . . . Riesling). The grape type was optional and did not always appear.

A Fass number on unsugared Rhine wines and a Fuder number on unsugared Mosels are seen on some older wine labels; these were cask numbers indicating the actual barrel from which the bottle was drawn. Unlike most others in the world, West German vineyards seldom vat or equalize wines. Each wine is made alone in its own cask. These numbers do not appear on recent labels.

Wachstum, Kreszenz, Naturwein, Korkbrand, Rein, Naturrein, Echt, Ungezuckert, Originalabfüllung, Originalabzug, Kellerabfüllung, Kellerabzug, Schlossabzug, Originalwein, and Eigenegewächs were all terms denoting in one way or another that the wine was a pure and natural product and had not been sugared.

Kabinett (Cabinet). This was originally a Rheingau nomenclature for specially reserved wines kept locked up in the cellar; but the term was gradually stretched to include any fine growth to which a proprietor chose to give his stamp of approval, although it had a more specific meaning in some of the Rheingau vineyards. As defined by the 1971 law, a Kabinett wine (Kabinett must now only be spelled with a *k*) is made from fully matured grapes, without added sugar and from the harvest of a limited area.

The words Spätlese, Auslese, Beerenauslese, and Trokkenbeerenauslese on a bottle label all indicate some degree of special selection. Spätlese (late-picked) and Auslese (selected) are determined in the vineyard at the time of picking. Beerenauslese and Trockenbeerenauslese (berry-selected) are determined in the vat-room. (At harvesttime the better and riper grapes are brought in and spread out on a big trough-like table, and experienced vintners select the berries individually—the ripe dry ones for Beerenauslese and Trockenbeerenauslese, in ascending order of dry ripeness.)

After selection, these fine sweet grapes are processed for the crushing, which often takes place in huge, cylindrical, galvanized metal vats with a blown-up sausage-like inner tube called a Willmespresse. The wines are almost as rich as liqueurs in the autumn; a mold or noble rot called *Botrytis cinerea*, or *Edelfäule*, covers the ripest grapes, improving and concentrating them. Nearly always this extra ripeness comes late, after the vineyard has been gone over once, in which case the special grapes are called Spätlese, or late-picked. When the picking is by individual berry among bunches, some of which are overripe and some not, the wine is a Beerenauslese (berry-selected). When the berries have been left to shrivel on the vine almost to the condition of raisins and are then individually selected, the wine is the peak achievement of German viniculture, a dried-berry-selected Trockenbeerenauslese.

A Spätlese is not always sweet, however; in lesser years when there is no excess sugar, late-picking does not imply extra sweetness—and in such years it is impossible to make an Auslese. West German law now forbids the selling of a late-picked wine as Spätlese unless it has all the characteristic ripeness and fullness. Trockenbeerenauslesen wines cost up to twenty times the price of the ordinary wines from the same vineyard. Nevertheless, they are now generally sold at a loss. The quantity of juice lost from the drying of the berries is about ten times the normal loss; and when the grapes are left so late on the vine the grower risks the destruction of his entire crop through frost—which happens in the best Mosel vineyards, for example, on an average of two years in three. Hardly any vineyard makes more than a quarter of a *Stück* (400 bottles) of such wine even in the most favorable years.

BARREL SIZES AND UNITS OF SALE

West German wines are sold either at auction or in the cellars directly to the purchasers through commission brokers; the latter is called *Freihand* sale. Cask dimensions are not uniform, although there is an increasing trend toward a change to the hectoliter measure, which is the standard in international usage.

Rheingau wines are sold in the *Halbstück* (half-cask), whether *Freihand* or at auction; a *Halbstück* contains 600 liters or 828 bottles. If an entire *Stück* (an oval cask of 1,200 liters) is sold, the price is nevertheless reckoned in terms of *Halbstücke*. Most wine is shipped in bottles. The finest wines are also both auctioned and sold *Freihand* in bottle.

Mosel wines are sold in the large, long barrel called the *Fuder*. It was formerly supposed to contain 960 liters, but in the last quarter of a century this has been standardized at 1,000 liters or 1,370 bottles. The finest are also sold in bottle.

Rheinhessen wines are generally sold in the *Stück* of 1,200 liters (equal to 1,656 bottles), although sometimes, and usually with the finest, the unit is 600 liters. Peak wines are also sold in bottles.

WINE COOPERATIVES

With the motto "We've got plenty of wine but no bread or money," the cooperative movement in wine-making began from necessity 120 years ago in Württemberg. Today there are 466 cooperatives, fairly evenly distributed. Certain wine-towns had two, one for the Catholics and the other for the Protestants. The approximately 37,000 growers affiliated with cooperatives have small or medium holdings; the average is about an acre apiece. Wines are cellared in common, and vineyard machinery is provided which would be beyond the means of the individual small proprietor.

Probably most important in raising the general level of the wines has been the combined effort to fight vine disease in the always critical marginal wine area; also, the cooperatives offer their members credit, saving them from the necessity of selling their wines when unfit or not ready simply to maintain vineyard and homestead.

In recent years, the cooperatives have begun to play an even more important part in German viniculture. New wineries with large capacities (from 10 to 80 million liters), modern equipment, and well-trained personnel have been built across the country. But these organizations are especially important in the southern German vineyards. Cooperatives in some parts of Baden control up to 90% of the vineyard acreage. And the Centralkellerei Badischerwinzergenossenschaft, or main winery of the Baden wine cooperative, is the largest single winery in all Europe. The membership of the cooperatives in the more northern regions, such as the Rheingau or the Palatinate, numbers about 20% to 30% of the growers; throughout West Germany some 60,000 wine producers vinify their grapes at the central wineries. Not all of the cooperative movement has been for giant wineries and increased production. The organizations have continually fought for improving the quality of their wines so that they could better compete with the offerings of the more famous individual estates.

Geropiga, jeropiga

Grape syrup used in Portugal for sweetening Port.

Gers

A department in southwest France whose wine is mostly unexceptional and often used for blending with other white wine. Some is distilled into Armagnac.

Gevrey-Chambertin

Burgundy red wine.
District: Côte de Nuits, France.

Gevrey-Chambertin is one of the communes of Burgundy's Côte d'Or, and more specifically of the Côte de Nuits, the northern section of the Côte d'Or. Working from north to south, it is the first of the important Côte de Nuits communes. Like almost all of the other villages along the famous strip of hills, this one has capitalized on its most famous and best vineyard and has added that name to the name of the place. Until 1847, the *appellation* was legally Gevrey, but since that time it has been Gevrey-Chambertin. The town fathers were not the only ones to be impressed by the name of their celebrated growth. At one time, practically every vineyard tried to tack Chambertin onto its own name, perhaps in hopes that some of the qualities of the wine would rub off with it. In 1936 the French authorities stepped in and decided who had the right to the name and who had not, and the matter was settled.

About 630, the Duke of Burgundy endowed the Abbey of Bèze with some land in Gevrey. The monks turned the land into a vineyard and found that they could produce an extraordinary wine. According to the stories that have come down from these ancient times, the field next to the abbey was later owned by a peasant named Bertin and was called the Champs de Bertin, or "Bertin's field." Thanks to the success of the abbey vineyards, Bertin also planted vines on his field and the name was soon shortened to Chambertin. But it was not Bertin, nor even the monks of the Abbey of Bèze, who expanded the fame of the vineyard; that was left to a man named Jobert, who owned not only Chambertin but the Clos de Bèze as well, and he made the vineyards famous. At some time, he changed his own name to Jobert-Chambertin. The vineyards are no longer united, as they were under Jobert, and are divided up into plots belonging to more than two dozen growers.

Chambertin has a great history and a great reputation, and there can be no wonder that the other vineyards of the town have wished to capitalize on it. Under the present law, the only ones which are allowed to use the name Chambertin with their own are several immediately adjoining it. Since the Clos de Bèze is considered on a par with Chambertin—and indeed can sell its wines as Chambertin if it so desires—it is allowed to place the magic name before its own, while the others must add it on after. Chambertin-Clos de Bèze is the full and proper name, and the vineyard is included in the special decree which covers Chambertin. The others fall under a different decree, the major difference being that the maximum permissible yield is raised from 30 hectoliters (780 U.S. gallons, 600 imp.) of wine per hectare to 32 hectoliters (832 U.S. gallons, 640 imp.) per hectare. The vineyards are the following: Latricières-Chambertin, Mazoyères-Chambertin, Charmes-Chambertin, Mazis- (or Mazys-) Chambertin, Ruchottes-Chambertin, Griotte-Chambertin, and Chapelle-Chambertin. Altogether, they comprise the Great Growths (*Grands Crus*) of the commune, and each one is treated under its own heading.

The vineyards, most of which lie between Gevrey-Chambertin and the next town to the south, Morey-Saint-Denis, are along the midsection of the hill and they can be seen from Route Nationale (National Highway) No. 74, which runs along the plain at the foot of the slope. A repaved, winding vineyard road halfway up the slope provides a better vantage point, however. If you leave Gevrey-Chambertin by this road, the first important vine-

yards to come into sight will be those of Mazis (the second half of the name is usually left out in any discussion of the vineyards but should always be included on the labels) with Ruchottes just above it on the slope. Both of these are on the right, and they adjoin the Clos de Bèze with Griotte and Chapelle on the left, directly across the road from it. A small toolhouse stands in the Clos de Bèze bearing the name of Pierre Damoy, one of the better growers and the largest single owner in the place, but aside from that there is nothing to distinguish one vineyard from another. After passing the Clos de Bèze, there is a large but simple sign informing the passer-by: "Here starts the vineyard of Chambertin." Almost before he has had time to digest this information, there is another sign to tell him: "Here ends the vineyard of Chambertin." The length—and it is roughly twice as long as it is wide—is barely more than 490 meters (1,500 feet). Aside from these landmarks, there is no sign in the earth or in the vines that here the soil is such that the resulting wine will be a greater or a slightly lesser one. There is no way for the newcomer to identify the various vineyards at all. For that it is necessary to go to the wines.

Like most of the villages of the Côte d'Or, Gevrey-Chambertin sits in a small defile, called a *combe*, between two hills in the range that makes up the Côte d'Or. All the Chambertins are on the slope on the southern side of the village, but there are other excellent vineyards on the north side as well. In the classification made in 1860 of the vines of the Côte d'Or, only Chambertin and the Clos de Bèze were classed as Outstanding Vineyards (*Têtes de Cuvée*), and all the others, including those which have been elevated to the modern ranks of the Great Growths (*Grands Crus*), were classed below them as First Growths (*Premiers Crus*). With these vineyards, in 1860, were several others, such as the Clos Saint-Jacques, Varoilles, Fouchère, Étournelles, and Cazetiers. Today, most of these are included among the official First Growths and are allowed to add the vineyard name to the name of the commune (selling, for example, as Gevrey-Chambertin Clos Saint-Jacques) or may add the words *Premier Cru* to the name of the commune. Many experts consider it unfortunate that the vineyards of Varoilles and Clos Saint-Jacques were not included with the finest vineyards of the commune and given Great Growth status. In many years, the excellent wines from these two vineyards compare very favorably with the others, except possibly for the wines of Chambertin and the Clos de Bèze.

The communal wines of the village, those that go to market with the words Gevrey-Chambertin and no other indication of origin, are the least of the wines of the commune, although some of them may certainly be very pleasant. Most of them are grown in Gevrey-Chambertin, but some may come from the better vineyards in the neighboring town of Brochon. The amount of wine sold as Gevrey-Chambertin or as Gevrey-Chambertin Premier Cru comes to very slightly over 15,000 hectoliters (397,500 U.S. gallons, 330,000 imp.) in an average year. The total vineyard area for Gevrey is 205 hectares (506.5 acres). The vineyards of note in the commune are listed below. (*See also* Great Growths *under separate headings.*)

Gewächs

GREAT GROWTHS (*Grands Crus*)

Vineyard	Hectares	Acres
Chambertin (Outstanding Vineyard)	17.7	44
Chambertin-Clos de Bèze (Outstanding Vineyard)	15.7	39
Latricières-Chambertin	6.23	15.51
Mazoyères-Chambertin	19.18	47.75
Charmes-Chambertin	12.42	30.92
Mazys- or Mazis-Chambertin	9.47	23.58
Ruchottes-Chambertin	8.45	21.04
Griotte-Chambertin	3.18	7.91
Chapelle-Chambertin	4.06	10.10

FIRST GROWTHS (*Premiers Crus*)

Vineyard	Hectares	Acres
Varoilles	5.94	14.7
Clos Saint-Jacques	6.92	17.1
Aux Combottes	4.9	12.4
Bel-Air	3.72	9.2
Les Cazetiers	9.11	22.5
Combe-au-Moine	4.78	11.8
Étournelles	2	5
Lavaut	9.43	23.3
Poissenot	2.19	5.4
Champeaux	6.76	16.7
Les Goulots	1.82	4.5
Issarts (or Plantigone)	1.82	4.5
Les Corbeaux	3.12	7.7
Cherbaudes	2.19	5.4
La Perrière	2.47	6.1
Clos-Prieur (upper section only)	1.98	4.9
Le Fonteny	3.80	9.4
Champonnet	3.32	8.2
Au Closeau	.5	1.3
Craipillot	2.75	6.8
Champitennois (also called Petite Chapelle)	3.97	9.8
En Ergot	1.17	2.9
Clos du Chapitre	.97	2.4

Gewächs

German term meaning "growth of." Same as Kreszenz (*q.v.*).

Gewürztraminer

A type of Traminer vine, and therefore Traminer wine, said to be even more spicy than this spiciest of grape varieties in forming many Alsatian and German wines. Actually, in usage, the two names are practically interchangeable and any real difference in meaning has been lost.

For description of Traminer and Gewürztraminer wines *see* Alsace; Germany.

Ghemme

A dry red wine from the Italian Piedmont (*q.v.*).

Gigondas

One of the best communes of the Côtes du Rhône, producing red, white, and rosé wines.
See Rhône.

Gill

Quartern, or a quarter of a British pint.

Gin

Gin is a juniper-flavored spirit obtained by the distillation and rectification of the grain spirits of malted barley and rye—or sometimes of corn or maize. Yet the definition of gin as a grain spirit is not entirely correct. Theoretically, it can be made from any rectified spirit. During the last war, gins were, in fact, distilled in England from raw molasses spirit; and some London Dry gins for domestic consumption are still based on this, although the majority of gins are now based on grain, both for home and export markets. The price of gin in the home market is the same for practically all varieties based on grain.

The two principal types of gin are British (the gin produced in the United States is made in a similar manner) and Dutch. The latter is known in the Netherlands as Jenever and in England as Hollands, or else as Schiedam, after one of the towns where it is manufactured. The English words *gin* and *geneva* are corruptions of the French *jenever* and *genièvre*, both meaning juniper—nothing to do with the Swiss city. *Genièvre* is a word seldom heard in France now: *gin* (pronounced jeen) is one of the anglicisms which have crept in since the war, and which, purists complain, are ruining the French language.

Both the Dutch and the English claim, and sometimes disclaim, the invention of gin. It is certain that in the seventeenth century gin was being made from barley, hops, and juniper berries in England; Hogarth's famous picture "Gin Lane" shows the consequences. In 1736 the Gin Act banned gin. Like most prohibitions, it did not work, and repeal followed in 1742, because illegal gin was worse than the legal kind.

Since the discovery of redistillation, or rectification, it has been possible to remove the harmful characteristics from any raw spirit, leaving practically pure alcohol. In the making of Dutch gins (as of rums and the heavier whiskies) preliminary rectification is not part of the process, which thus preserves some of the taste of the barley, malt, and grain.

Hollands is often sold in stone jars or crocks, and the Dutch usually drink it neat, out of narrow tall glasses. It is made by infusing a mash of malted barley and rye, or, occasionally, maize. When it has cooled, it is set to ferment with yeast; in two or three days, fermentation is complete and the alcoholic liquid is then distilled. The distillation is redistilled with flavoring—juniper berries and various other ingredients, according to the recipe of the maker. (In some cases, the juniper berries are mashed in with the malt.) If the process of redistillation over flavoring is repeated, the result is what is known as Double

Gin. Hollands is distilled at a lower proof than British gin; and it is generally aged in bond. By law, it must contain 35% of alcohol by volume.

In the making of British or American gins, a highly rectified—or neutral—spirit, by now colorless and tasteless, is redistilled with the juniper berries and coriander or other flavorings. If this process is repeated, the product is a gin of the London Dry variety. Dry gin is so easy to make that it may fairly be classed as an art of the kitchen: since it is merely flavored neutral spirit, it must be a natural temptation to the home distiller. Some makers buy their spirit already distilled. (Inferior gins are made by adding essential oils to plain spirit and omitting distillation altogether.) Dry gins, being so highly distilled (or rectified) contain no fusel oil, and need not, therefore, be aged to remove this harmful taint. In fact, they gain nothing by ageing and are ready to drink at once.

Gins take their character from the flavoring recipe which is the secret of each maker. After the base spirit has been rectified, flavoring matter is added by one means or another. Sometimes alcohol, juniper berries, and such other ingredients as may be used are simply steeped together. Another technique is that of passing the spirit over into a flavor still, a box-like small still in which the vapors contact volatile juniper, angelica, coriander, etc. The flavors used by the various distillers, while always including juniper, are diverse. Some of the others are fennel, licorice, orange peel, anise, caraway, calamus, orris, and almond.

In addition to the variations between the different brands, there are two other distinct types of gin. Old Tom Gin is one which has been sweetened by adding sugar to the dry variety. Plymouth Gin is made in Plymouth, England, by a single firm (Coates) and is intermediate in style between the ordinary English gin and Dutch gin. (Sloe Gin [q.v.] utilizes gin but is not properly a gin.)

In the United States, London Dry gins may be of three kinds: gin imported from England; gin made in the U.S. under license or grant from the original British distiller; or any dry gin made in America and simply given the name as a type-name. In all cases, the general principles of preparation are the same.

Golden gin is gin which has been barrel-aged, taking its golden hue from the wood, but it is quite uncommon. The great preference in the United States is for neutral gins, because they are generally used as bases for cocktails and should harmonize with a wide range of flavors—although most gin is drunk in Dry Martinis, in Collinses, or with tonic water.

Lemon gin, orange gin, and so on are usually artificially flavored gins, but they can be produced from the named ingredient.

Gin Fizz

A long, cool, effervescent drink composed of gin, lemon juice, a little sugar, ice, and soda-water. There are several other fizzes, variations on this recipe and based on either gin or brandy.

Ginger

Ginger Ale

A favorite English or American mineral drink, frothy and of a ginger color; it is often added to gin or whisky to make a long drink comparable with gin and tonic. The ale is carbonated water to which coloring matter has been added, drops of capsicum extract or essence of ginger, and some glucose or sugar. "Froth heading" may also be added to make the drink more foamy.

Ginger Beer

A pale frothy bottled drink popular in England. It is made by the fermentation of sugar, ginger, cream of tartar, and yeast with water, and is bottled before it has finished fermenting. The carbonic acid thus generated produces an aerated drink.

Ginger Wine

A homely English beverage—but made commercially. The ingredients: ginger, yeast, sugar, lemon rind, raisins, and water. It is often fortified with spirits and a little capsicum.

Ginger brandy

Tawny-colored, ginger-flavored spirit made in Great Britain.

Girò di Cagliari

A Port-like wine from Sardinia (q.v.).

Girò di Sardegna

Sweet red dessert wine of Sardinia (q.v.).

Gironde

The department of Bordeaux. Also, the wide tidal estuary formed by the Dordogne and Garonne rivers, which meet north of the city.

Château Giscours

Bordeaux red wine.
District: Haut-Médoc, France.
Commune: Labarde-Margaux.

Château Giscours had fallen completely from its traditional place as one of the best of the Third Growths (*Troisièmes Crus*) of the 1855 Médoc Classification, when the present owner, M. Tari—a major wine-maker in Oran, Algeria—took it over in 1954. A formerly fine growth had been debased by plantings of hybrid vines. By 1955-56, these were all ripped out by M. Tari, and the vineyard was entirely reconstituted through grafting with first-class vines. Subsequent vintages have shown a great improvement, and in the hands of the present owner and his dedicated son future wines can be expected to continue to do so.

The records of Giscours go back to 1552, when a Seigneur de la Bastide sold it to Pierre de l'Horme. During the Revolution, the property was confiscated from the Saint-Simon family by the state and was then sold to a M. Jacob on behalf of two Americans, John Gray and Jonathan Davis of Boston.

The present château was built by Count Pescatore, a banker in the time of Napoleon III. Eventually, in 1852, it was purchased by Édouard Cruse, in whose family it remained until 1913. The building, with its two great wings, stands at the head of one of the most magnificent parks in Bordeaux, with a lake, lily-choked canals, and at least one giant California sequoia.

The British I.D.V. group, owners of Gilbey's, became exclusive world distributor of the wine in 1973.

Characteristics. Light and delicate, highly perfumed, and often elegant. The quality has lately made great strides, and the wine deserves its growing reputation.

Vineyard area: 78 hectares (195 acres).
Average production: 350 *tonneaux* (33,000 cases).

Givry

Commune of the Côte Chalonnaise producing mainly red wines.
See also Chalonnais.

Glen Elgin

Important vineyard in New South Wales producing red table wines and some white. The principal grape varieties are Syrah and "Riesling" (actually Sémillon).
See also Australia.

Glenloth

Vineyard in the Reynella district of South Australia.
See Australia.

Glögg

A hot wine drink spiced with brandy or aquavit, almonds and raisins, traditionally served in Sweden during cold weather.

Château Gloria

Bordeaux red wine.
District: Haut-Médoc, France.
Commune: Saint-Julien.

The vineyard contains parcels from Château Léoville-Poyferré and Château Gruaud-Larose (Second Growths—*Seconds Crus*), and from Château Saint-Pierre and Château Duhart-Milon (Fourth Growths—*Quatrièmes Crus*). The *chais* were originally those of Château Saint-Pierre. The owner and manager of the vineyard is M. Henri Martin, mayor of Saint-Julien and one of the leading figures both in Médoc and Bordeaux wines; in 1956 he became president of the Interprofessional Committee

of Bordeaux Wines. Qualities of terrain and intelligent, energetic management have raised the wine far above its official rating. At present ranked as a Bourgeois Growth (*Bourgeois Cru*) of Médoc, it amply justifies elevation to the status of a Classified Growth.

Characteristics. Round and subtle with, at the same time, some of the best characteristics of Saint-Julien—fullness with delicacy. Usually a well-made wine.

Vineyard area: 44 hectares (110 acres).
Average production: 200 *tonneaux* (18,000 cases).

Gluco-oenometer

An instrument to test the sugar content of new musts; used in making Port.

Glycerin

A tri-hydritic alcohol formed from sugar during the fermentation of grape juice to wine. An abundance of glycerin gives wine a characteristic "fatness" and softness (a lack of body). $CH_2OH \cdot CHOH \cdot CH_2OH$.

Gobelet

Method of training vines: a single trunk terminates in several arms rising in the shape of a vase or goblet.
See Chapter Eight, p. 29.

Goblet

A drinking cup or glass with foot and stem.

Goldwasser

See Danziger Goldwasser.

Gourmet

Alsatian term for a winebroker—who is known in the Bordeaux district as a *courtier*.

Goût américain

To the American taste. The term is a misnomer, for it refers to sweet Champagne, although this is not, in fact, shipped to the United States now.

Goût anglais

To the English taste. The term refers to dry Champagne for the English market.

Goût de pierre à fusil

French term for the gunflint taste of a very dry white wine, such as Chablis.

244

Goût de terroir

In French this means, literally, earthy taste; it denotes a peculiar flavor imparted by certain soils, and not the taste of the soil itself.

Graacher Himmelreich

Best-known of the Graach wines inside Germany, and usually best of the wines of Graach on the German Mosel. Josephshof, second in quality to Himmelreich, is the better-known wine abroad.

See Mosel-Saar-Ruwer.

Gragnano

Leading red wine of Campania, Italy.

See Campania.

Graisse

A disorder of wine; fatty degeneration, by which the wine becomes viscous and turgid.

See Chapter Nine, p. 38.

Grand Cru

French term for a great vineyard.

Grand Cru Classé

A special designation for the very best of the some 2,000 wine châteaux of the Gironde. Médoc, Sauternes, and Barsac were classified in 1855, Graves in 1953 and 1959, and Saint-Émilion in 1955. In 1965, this designation was reserved by law exclusively for Bordeaux.

Château Grand-La-Lagune

See Château La Lagune.

Grand Marnier

An orange-flavored, brandy-based, very sweet proprietary French liqueur of the Curaçao type made by the Établissements Marnier-Lapostolle in Neauphle-le-Château and Château de Bourg, in France. It is made in two types, yellow and red, of which the red is stronger and the yellow sweeter.

See Curaçao.

Château Grand-Pontet

Bordeaux red wine.
District and Commune: Saint-Émilion, France.

The château is situated on the plateau in the midst of the great vineyards of Saint-Émilion and makes one of the most reliable wines in the district. The property was owned until 1979 by Barton & Guestier, a subsidiary of Seagrams.

Vineyard area: 14 hectares (35 acres).
Average production: 60 *tonneaux* (5,500 cases).

Château Grand-Puy-Ducasse

Bordeaux red wine.
District: Haut-Médoc, France.
Commune: Pauillac.

A third of the vineyard is the portion of the old Château Grand Puy, the remainder of that vineyard now being Château Grand-Puy-Lacoste; another third lies near Château Batailley south of Pauillac; and a third to the north near Châteaux Pontet-Canet and Mouton-Rothschild.

Grand-Puy-Ducasse is rated Fifth Growth (*Cinquième Cru*) in the Classification of 1855, and the château itself is on the wide street bordering the river docks of Pauillac, where it now houses a wine museum and the headquarters of the Médoc and Graves wine fraternity, the Commanderie du Bontemps.

Characteristics. Lighter, with good breed, but less well-constructed than those of Grand-Puy-Lacoste (*q.v.*).

Vineyard area: 26 hectares (65 acres).
Average production: 125 *tonneaux* (10,000 cases).

Château Grand-Puy-Lacoste

Bordeaux red wine.
District: Haut-Médoc, France.
Commune: Pauillac.

The wine is mostly exported to England, Germany and the United States. A Fifth Growth (*Cinquième Cru*) of Médoc, the vineyard lies on one of the highest parts of Pauillac. In Old French the word *puy* meant "high point," and the eminence on which the vines are planted is conserved in the name. Grand Puy, dating from at least the fifteenth century, was acquired after the French Revolution by a M. Lacoste, who tacked on his own name. Like Château Calon-Ségur and a few others, it is one of the rare Médoc vineyards to be entirely in one section and undivided, and intact since the Classification of 1855.

Characteristics. Excellent, full-bodied wines; they mature into sturdy and extremely pleasant wines of great breed. The gastronomically minded M. Dupin, the owner during the postwar period, did much to give them the good reputation they have acquired. Today, Grand-Puy-Lacoste belongs to Jean-Eugène Borie (owner of Ducru-Beaucaillou) and deserves a better classification than the 1855 Fifth rating. Since the 1978 vintage, M. Borie's Ducru-Beaucaillou touch has even further improved the quality of these very fine wines.

Vineyard area: 40 hectares (100 acres).
Average production: 160 *tonneaux* (14,000 cases).

Grand Roussillon (Côtes du Roussillon)

Red, white, and rosé wines.
District: Southern France.

Grand Roussillon is the former name for the wine district which has now become the Appellation d'Origine Contrôlée Côtes du Roussillon. The region in southern France encompasses the districts of Banyuls, Côtes d'Agly, Côtes du Roussillon, Maury, and Rivesaltes in the departments of Pyrénées-Orientales and Aude, bordering Spain and the Mediterranean. The Roussillon vineyards produce dry red, rosé, and white wines from Carignan, Cinsault, Grenache, and Mourvèdre. Within Grand Roussillon, Côtes du Roussillon is an Appellation d'Origine Contrôlée limited to dry reds, whites, and rosés. The classification Côtes du Roussillon Villages is further limited to reds and rosés made in the best villages, most located in the slate-rich hills above the Agly River. Among the best are Planèzes, Estagel, Montner, Latour-de-France, Rasiguères, Vingrau, and Caramany. Côtes du Roussillon plus the Villages produce about 270,000 hectoliters or 3 million cases per year.

The Roussillon also produces several *vins doux naturels* (V.D.N.): Rivesaltes, rosé and white wines from Muscat, Grenache, and Maccabéo; Muscat de Rivesaltes, made from Muscat only; Banyuls and Maury, made from Grenache Noir. Banyuls also produces a heavy, dry red wine, Collioure de Grenache. Production of V.D.N. averages 600,000 hectoliters per year.

See Appendix G.

Grand Vin

French for "great wine"; a freely used term on labels and one that is not a legally defined indication of superior quality.

Grande (Fine) Champagne

Best district of the Cognac vineyards and consequently the mark, on a Cognac label, of the finest brandy from the point of view of vineyard quality. Some say that a certain percentage of brandy derived from wine of the Borderies across the River Charente is needed to combine heartiness with the splendid finesse of Grande Champagne. Its distinction comes from the chalk in the soil; the word *champagne* in French indicates chalky soil. Similarity of sort is the only thing Grande Champagne Cognac has in common with Champagne wines.

See Cognac.

Grands-Échezeaux

Burgundy red wine.
District: Côte de Nuits, France.
Commune: Flagey-Échezeaux.
Official Classification: Great Growth (Grand Cru).

(*Flagey-Échezeaux is not an appellation, and when the wines do not meet the required minimum standards they are declassed into communal wine of Vosne-Romanée.*)

The widely prevalent myth that all Bordeaux is light and all Burgundy heavy can easily be scotched by placing a bottle of Grands-Échezeaux next to a fine Saint-Émilion. Grands-Échezeaux lies between Vougeot and Vosne-Romanée, and the wines provide the logical half-step between the sturdy fullness of the former and the easy aris-

tocratic elegance of the latter; they balance the body necessary for a well-rounded wine with a delicacy and a finesse which prompts the Burgundian to characterize them as *en dentelle* (like lace). Despite the fact that they are little known, they are unquestionably among the greatest of all red Burgundies.

The vineyard embraces 9.15 hectares (22.6 acres) up the hill and across a road from the Clos de Vougeot—on the southern side of the vineyard—and the entire Clos is visible from it. A number of growers own sections, including the Domaine Civile de la Romanée-Conti and such able and excellent wine-makers as René Engel and the sons of Louis Gros. Average production of the entire vineyard is about 350 hectoliters (9,275 U.S. gallons, 7,700 imp.).

Granja União

Brand name for some of the best wines of Brazil. Both red and white are sold by this company.

See Brazil.

Granjo

A natural sweet white wine of Portugal made by letting noble rot form on late-picked grapes, as is the method in Sauternes and with the Spätlese German wines.

Grape

Fruit of the vine. Wine is made from the fermented juice of the grape, of which there are many varieties.

See Chapter Eight, p. 29.

Grappa

The Italian word for marc, or spirit distilled from grape husks. The term is also used in California and in Spanish-speaking countries. Most grappa is harsh, coarse, young, and fairly mediocre.

Graves

Red and white wines.
District: Bordeaux, France.

Because they have met only with mediocre blended wines of the district, Graves, to many people outside France, is simply a sweetish white wine. In fact, the better white wines of Graves are dry, the greatest wines red. This large region—40 miles long and at some points 12 miles wide—stretching from the fringe of the Médoc to the edge of Sauternes and containing a variety of sites and soils, naturally produces wines of different types.

Graves encloses the city of Bordeaux and, as the suburbs spread, the vineyard is thrust back. Only such great estates as those of Haut-Brion and La Mission-Haut-Brion are too valuable to be given up to building, and these are now islands surrounded by houses and shops and touched by the main road. In the Middle Ages, however, when the bourgeois growers of Bordeaux used to hurry back at nightfall to the sheltering walls of the city, its closeness was a great advantage, and Graves was in both senses of the word the first district of Bordeaux. Indeed, in England, where most of the wine went, the names were synonymous. This was still the case in the seventeenth century, when Pepys wrote of the good wine of Haut-Brion; but during the next hundred years the wines of the Médoc came into fashion. For some time after the Napoleonic wars even the great vineyard of Haut-Brion sank, through mismanagement, into mediocrity. The oïdium epidemic of the early 1850s struck hard

in Graves, and the growers were slower than those of other districts to reconstitute their vines. Whether for this reason or because of local politics, Graves was not included in the 1855 Classification of the Gironde wines. Yet Haut-Brion, restored to its former glory, could not be left out: so, ignoring geography, the classifiers added it to the First Growths (*Premiers Crus*) of the great vineyards of the Médoc. In fact, all the big red wines of Graves—vigorous, full-bodied, and lasting—always had their partisans. The growers pulled themselves together, and in the splendid pre-phylloxera years of 1864-65 the shippers were again doing keen business with them.

The name Graves comes from the gravelly soil in which the red grapes (Cabernet Sauvignon, Cabernet Franc, Merlot, Malbec, and Petit Verdot) flourish. The same soil occurs elsewhere, in Pomerol, Saint-Émilion, and the Médoc. The vines, also, are Médoc vines, and there is a family resemblance between the red wines of these adjoining areas. If the Médocs (especially the Margaux) are more feminine and delicate, the Graves have more body, a distinct character, and a pleasing frankness.

The white Graves actually outnumber the red. In the southern part of the district toward Sauternes, and in a soil which contains a proportion of sand, white wine grapes (Sémillon, Sauvignon, and a very little Muscadelle) predominate. The same vines grow in Sauternes. These white wines are mainly dry, especially in the north of Graves (the best of all is the small production of Haut-Brion Blanc); but some, near Sauternes, are suave, soft, and *moelleux*. Down here, the land is well-wooded and crossed with little streams, the country of the most romantic Bordeaux châteaux: Olivier, mirrored in the still waters of its moat, once the hunting lodge of the Black Prince; and the Château de la Brède, moated too, and even more beautiful. Montesquieu lived here and cultivated his vineyard. It is more famous now for its library than its wines.

In 1953, the best vineyards of Graves were classified in both red and white wines. This rating was much criticized, and was revised in 1959. Only two vineyards were added in red wines, three in white, and the revision brought little satisfaction. In each, Château Haut-Brion is classified a red wine of Graves, while remaining a First Growth of the Médoc. A glaring error in the original Graves Classification was its failure to include among the whites Château Haut-Brion Blanc, one of the finest dry white wines in the world. This error was rectified in 1960.

GRAVES 1959 OFFICIAL CLASSIFICATION

(For the individual Classified Growths, see under separate headings, and for the list of all Graves Growths, see Appendix A, p. 511.)

CLASSIFIED VINEYARDS MAKING BOTH RED AND WHITE WINES

Vineyard	*Commune*
Château Bouscaut	Cadaujac
Château Carbonnieux	Léognan
Domaine de Chevalier	Léognan
Château Haut-Brion	Pessac
Château La Tour-Martillac	Martillac
Château Malartic-Lagravière	Léognan
Château Olivier	Léognan

CLASSIFIED VINEYARDS MAKING RED WINE

Vineyard	*Commune*
Château de Fieuzal	Léognan
Château Haut-Bailly	Léognan
Château Haut-Brion	Pessac
Château La Mission-Haut-Brion	Pessac
Château La Tour-Haut-Brion	Talence
Château Pape-Clément	Pessac
Château Smith-Haut-Lafitte	Martillac

CLASSIFIED VINEYARDS MAKING WHITE WINE

Vineyard	*Commune*
Château Couhins	Villenave-d'Ornan
Château Laville-Haut-Brion	Talence

See Bordeaux.

Graves de Vayres

White and red wines.
District: Bordeaux, France.

Facing Libourne on the River Dordogne in southwest France, an enclave of gravel soil juts into the predominantly clay soil of the large wine region of Entre-Deux-Mers (carafe white wine). The quality on the gravel terrain is definitely superior and merits the individual wine *appellation*, Graves de Vayres. Vayres is the chief village, and *graves* is the regional term for the type of gravel. This place-name is famous beyond all reason in Germany, where the cheap Graves de Vayres are sold as the wines of Graves, although the resemblance is remote.

The red wines mature quickly and are very attractive and supple, standing comparison with all but the best of the Pomerols and Saint-Émilions from across the Dordogne, but the quantity in an average year (7,000 hectoliters) is tiny. The white wines (17,000 hectoliters; 442,000 U.S. gallons, 340,000 imp.) are suave and mellow, distinguished by their quantity of natural fatness.

Graves Supérieures

White wines.
District: Bordeaux, France.

An official French wine designation which means a white wine of the delimited Graves district surrounding Bordeaux in southwest France which has obtained 12% or more of alcohol by natural fermentation. While Graves produces both red and white wines, only white are eligible for this designation. It is often correctly pointed out that, in French, Supérieures does not indicate a better Graves but merely one higher in alcohol; yet it is true that most of the classified and best-known and best Graves white wines are Graves Supérieures.

See also Graves.

Gray Riesling, Gray Dutchess

A white Californian grape which is not, in fact, a Riesling at all but a descendant of the French Chauché Gris.

Gray rot

Ignoble rot, a disease of the grape. When this rot forms, it causes stains on the leaves and alterations within the fruit.

See Chapter Eight, p. 29.

Greco

The grape used in Greco di Gerace, in some of the wines of Calabria and elsewhere in Italy.

Greco di Gerace

One of the best wines of Calabria, sweet and golden, with a flowery bouquet.
See Calabria.

Greco di Tufo

Dry white Italian wine from the Campania (*q.v.*).

Greece

The cultivation of the vine ranks among the first products of Greek agriculture. A grower of wine from ancient times (there are many references to it in the *Iliad* and the *Odyssey*), Greece was destined to be so by her soil and climate. The chalky soils of the Greek mainland, Crete, and other islands, and the volcanic soils of important vine-growing islands such as Santorin, are favorable to viticulture. Of the 212,000 hectares (530,000 acres) planted in vines, 200,000 hectares (500,000 acres) are devoted to wine grapes. Because the climate is so dry, the grapes grow sweet and the wines have a characteristic fresh flavor—best of all are the luscious sweet varieties. Those destined for export are made by up-to-date methods at the plants of big manufacturers. For their own use, the peasants are apt to go about their wine-making as their ancestors did in the old days when Dionysos was still worshipped.

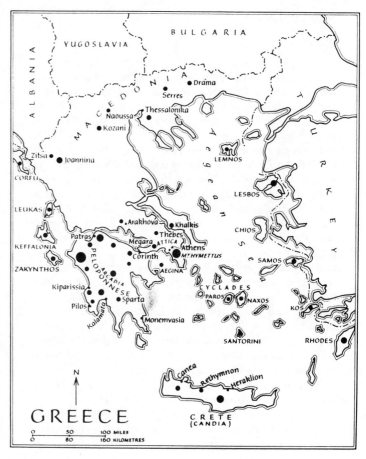

After the First World War, refugees coming in from wine-growing regions in Asia Minor increased the vineyard area of Greece, and a great deal of wine was exported, particularly between 1926 and 1929. In the years after the Second World War, general conditions, allied to outbreaks of phylloxera and mildew, did a great deal of harm. Anti-phylloxera measures were introduced and vineyards reconstituted, so that the area in vine is now equal to the pre-war vineyards, and export figures have surpassed their pre-war status. Ranking ninth in European wine production, and thirteenth in world production, Greece now takes a comparable place in the world market. The average annual harvest is some 5,600,000 hectoliters (148,120,000 U.S. gallons, 123,200,000 imp.), of which about 1 million hectoliters (26.5 million U.S. gallons, 22 million imp.) are exported each year. Her principal customers are West Germany, Switzerland, Sweden, the Benelux countries and the United States.

Even lately, there have been few attempts to control quality or enforce the laws of appellation, and the easygoing Greek consumer has made no demand upon the producer, with the result that vineyards have not maintained an even character. In general, wine is taken for granted as something plentiful and often cheap, most of which is not even bottled but is aged in huge vats. This has meant that there has been no luxury trade to speak of, with the minimum of estate-bottling among small growers. However, legislation was set up to bring in certain controls, which were made law in 1963, and have gradually become effective. The government began control of wine prices in 1970. Since 1976, new legislation designed to conform with the laws of the Common Market and to meet the demands of current wine-making has been in effect. Twenty-six regions of production have been defined and recognized as place-names. The Wine Institute, a branch of the Ministry of Agriculture, is responsible for maintaining quality standards. Unfortunately, a lack of trained oenologists makes this difficult.

As it is now, the Greek wine business can be divided into three main groups: (1) the cooperatives; (2) large private producers; and (3) the smaller individual producers. There are 70 cooperatives, which account for 40% of the total production, and 250 private companies. Four of the most important concerns are the Societé Hellenique des Vins et Spiritueux; A. Cambas, S.A.; Caviros; and Achaia-Clauss—which supplies nearly 80% of all the domestic wine consumed in Greece, some 15 million bottles, and a good deal more in bulk. Per capita consumption is about 40 liters a year; and a great deal of this wine is unquestionably made by the peasant farmers themselves for almost immediate consumption.

During the last ten years, great investments have been made by the wine merchant and shipping firms in order to modernize their plants and their centers of vinification. In addition, there is a growing trend toward wine in bottles (rather than bulk).

WINE REGIONS

The Peloponnese

The peninsula is the largest wine-growing district in Greece, producing about 30% of the total quantity; and one of the most important firms is the cooperative of Patras in the extreme north, across the straits from Missolonghi where Byron died of fever—since those days, the place has been cleared of mosquitoes. The town of Patras, reached by the lovely coast road along the shores of the Corinthian Gulf, or by the railway which runs parallel with it, nestles at the foot of a steep mountain. The vineyards, five miles wide, cover the beautiful slopes. Several wine shipping and merchant houses such as Achaia-Clauss S.A., Beso S.A., and Transetcom S.A. are located near Patras, an important maritime center. The principal grape varieties are Mavrodaphne, Muscat, Aghiorghitico and Phileri. There are few neat rows of trimmed vines—they grow everywhere, like bushes, basking in the full heat of the sun. Some of the best Greek wines come from this district—a few red, but mainly dry white, like the clean-tasting Santa Laura, and Santa Helena. But a sweet white Muscat is made here, too, and more important, the luscious Mavrodaphne (grown also on the island of Cephalonia); Mavrodaphne is one of the few dessert wines which seem to express themselves best when served at room temperature rather than chilled. It is an expensive, heavy, sweet red wine with 14% to 16% of alcohol by volume. Other wines of the region are the light pinkish Tegea; the supple Mantinea; and Nemea, dry but very dark, almost black, in color.

Attica

Attica is the second most productive region, accounting for about 15% of the wine. In this country, south of Athens, bordered by splendid beaches and a well-paved coast road, the vineyards yield a great deal of the ordinary wine for domestic consumption. The white Savatiano grape, used for the best retsina, appears here; Mandilaria and Mavroudi for red wines, and some Rhoditis for rosé. Here also the dry Hymettus is made, near Mount Hymettus, a wine that should be drunk when it is two to four years old; and Marco. The best white wine of Greece is from a small estate called Pallini.

Macedonia

The west and central parts of this region are particularly favorable to viticulture and have become an important red-wine production center. On the southern slopes of Mount Vilia a sweet wine is made from the red Muscat. In the 1960s, the Greek shipbuilding Carras family planted an entire vineyard near their tourist resort. The wine, called Porto Carras, is supervised by Émile Peynaud, the eminent oenologist from Bordeaux. On the east coast, in Chalkidiki, new vines are being planted.

Island of Rhodes

This island, already civilized in Mycenean times, once famous for its Colossus, then as the stronghold of the Hospitallers, has been making wine for many centuries. The principal company is the cooperative C.A.I.R. The best-known wine, the dry white Lindos, is grown around the city of that name, where the ruins of the Parthenon stand. The red wine of Rhodes, the "Knight of Rhodes," has been granted a new appellation of origin.

Island of Samos

The island, divided from Turkey by a narrow strip of the Aegean Sea, was denuded of vines when it was conquered by the Turks at the time of the fall of Constantinople (1453). Yet, when the Greeks regained it in 1912, they found the vines replanted and the wines as good as ever. Laws were passed in the following twenty-five years which made Samos one of the very few guaranteed place-names in Greece. No wine not grown on the island may take the name; nor may the Samos wine be blended with any other—most Greek wines are allowed an admixture of up to 30%. In order to enforce this rule, wines from other parts of Greece are forbidden in Samos. The sweet Muscat of Samos is one of two Greek wines most often seen abroad and most liked (the other is Mavrodaphne). The white Muscat grape, resembling the Muscat de Frontignan, produces the bulk of Samos wines. The island is mountainous, and the steep slopes, often terraced, are well suited to the vine. The yellow-gold grapes flourish in the mild climate, but there is considerable variation in the times of ripening in different parts of the island: on the plain, harvesting starts in August, but it does not begin until October in the high mountain vineyards.

In addition to the natural sweet wine, dry and fortified sweet wines are made on Samos, and nearly all have the distinct, heavy flavor and bouquet of the Muscat.

Island of Santorin

Both dry and sweet wines are made from a variety of vines which flourish in the volcanic soil, and sometimes they are very pleasant. A good dry wine will always be labeled Santorin; the sweet may be either Santorin or Vino Santo. On the sun-parched hills of this beautiful island the grapes achieve such a high degree of sugar that the wines often run 15% of alcohol per volume.

Island of Crete

This large island is an important center of Greek viniculture. The hilly country gets a great deal of sun, and production is fairly prolific. Among the vines planted are Romeiko, Kotisphalo, Mandilari and Liatico; and the resulting table wines are big and fleshy, rich in alcohol, developing in finesse as they mature. Here, as on Samos, a serious effort is made to protect the appellation of the wines. Some of these may be labeled Candia—or Archanes. The big cooperative is Chania. A small area of the vineyard is owned by A. Cambas, S.A. and Achaia-Clauss, but little of what they sell comes from their own land.

Epirus

Mountainous region to the northwest of the country. The viticultural region of Zitsa near the city of Ioannina produces lively country wines. The main grape variety is the Debina.

Other regions

The island of Cephalonia produces a white wine from Robola. Around the town of Rapsani in the center of the country, good reds from Mavroudi are made.

OTHER GREEK WINES

Retsina

This is the most popular name in Greek wines, yet it is not an individual type but a generic one. It is simply any wine which has been flavored with pine resin—and that means about 50% of the wine made in Greece. White and rosé wines may be treated in this way, but red are not. In the southern and central parts of the country, almost everyone—especially among the peasants—prefers his wine with this piny, resinous taste. More than 80% of the Savatiano wines of Attica are treated with resin.

There are many stories of how the use of resin came about. One theory is that the ancient Greeks preserved the wine with the pine gum and, incidentally, liked to add a flavor they had soon grown accustomed to. Another suggestion is that it happened accidentally, when a shortage of oak forced growers to store their wine in barrels made of pine—this is unlikely, since discoveries in Egyptian tombs have proved that, before the days of classical Greece, the bottoms of wine jars were smeared with resin and bitumen to preserve the wine. It was considered even then that the resin improved the flavor. The ancient Romans also added pitch and other ingredients to their wine, but the use has not, in Italy, persisted into modern times. Retsina should be drunk cool. The Greeks say that the best of it comes from around Athens. The peasants who make it for their own consumption do so in the old-fashioned way and often drink it quite soon after fermentation. The usual alcoholic content of Retsina is 12.5% to 13% by volume. Unlike most wines, it does not improve with age.

Monemvasia or Malmsey

Nowadays, the name Monemvasia merely refers to wines that are more or less characteristic of the Malmsey type produced in any part of Greece. In the old days, however, Monemvasia, lying on a deep harbor in the south of Greece, was a busy port, from which this wine was exported and which gave its name to a type of wine it shipped but did not grow; the wine was produced on Naxos and others of the smaller Cyclades—and also on the island of Crete, or Candia. Monemvasia spread through the Mediterranean world, appearing in Spain under the name Malvagia, in Italy as Malvasia, in France as Malvoisie—while in the English-speaking countries to which it was imported, it was known as Malmsey. It was famous in England in Shakespeare's day and earlier—everyone remembers that the Duke of Clarence was drowned in a butt of Malmsey. Some confusion has been caused by a general failure to realize that

Malmsey has long denoted not a place-name but a style of wine, or a wine from the Malvoisie grape variety, and that it is not restricted to Spain, Madeira, or Crete.

Other Greek wines occasionally seen abroad include Mantineia, a pinkish dry wine from the uplands of Arcadia, at its best at around five years of age and well cooled; and Mavro Naoussis, a deeply-colored dry red wine from the Naoussa district in central Macedonia.

SPIRITS

Brandy

The better Greek brandies are made from the Savatiano and other white and red grape varieties generally grown on the mainland or on the island of Samos. They are now being produced in three styles: the youngest, five years old; the Five Star, about twenty-five years; the Seven Star, over forty. The color and aroma are the natural results of ageing in cask. Other brandies may be sweetened and flavored for use as aperitifs or liqueurs. Metaxa, Botrys, Cambas, and Lizas are the popular dry, light-colored brandies.

Ouzo and Mastika (or Masticha)

These are the principal aperitifs. Ouzo, an anise-flavored liquid, is usually taken cold, with water or on the rocks. It turns cloudy when water is added, and thus resembles absinthe or French pastis or Pernod. Mastika, which has a brandy base to which gum mastic is added, is made on the island of Chios, but both drinks originated on the mainland of Greece.

Raki

This is an arrack-type spirit, usually made on the east coast, from a neutral wine base with a maceration of figs and other fruits. It is clear white in color, strong and fiery in character, and usually consumed without any significant ageing period. It is a rustic drink, not one for export.

Green

A term for any wine that is too acid, raw, and harsh, thus lacking softness and maturity. The condition is not necessarily a matter of age, although young wines are more frequently green than older ones. The word is also used for the wines which come from the area of Portugal that is north of Oporto. There the grapes are prematurely picked, thus causing the wine to have that trait of acidity which is referred to as green.

Grenache

A sweet grape which gives wines high in alcohol and distinctive in bouquet. It is used for the sweet Grenache dessert wine of Banyuls in the Roussillon region and is planted elsewhere in France, where it is known as Alicante, Carignane Rousse, Tinto, etc. In Spain it appears as Alicantina or Garnacha. It is grown also in northern California, where it makes excellent rosés.

Grenadine

Sweet red syrup, usually non-alcoholic but sometimes with a very slight alcohol content, used as a sweetening agent. Originally made from pomegranates.

Grignolino

An Italian grape which in Piedmont produces a red wine—dry and rather heady or semi-sweet and *pétillant*. Cultivation of the vine is, unfortunately, on the decline in Italy. Transplanted to California, it is yielding some pleasant wine.

Château Grillet

Rhône Valley white wine.
District: Rhône Valley, France.

The estate, perched above the River Rhône, covers about 2.7 hectares (6.75 acres) of the communes of Verin and Saint-Michel-sous-Condrieu and produces some 200 to 700 cases of wine annually. The wine is dry, white, heady, well-balanced, and full, and sometimes has a slight aroma of Muscat grapes, although it is made entirely from Viognier. In good years it can be wonderful, among the best of the Rhône Valley's white wines, surpassing or ranking with white Hermitage, but its production is so small that it is rarely seen outside the district. Much of it is sold at the Restaurant de la Pyramide, in nearby Vienne, where wines must meet rigorous standards before they are admitted to the cellars. Nevertheless, the wine is renowned more for its scarcity than for its quality.

Grinzing

Wine-making slopes and suburb of Vienna. Here new *heurige* wine is drunk.
See Austria.

Griotte-Chambertin

Burgundy red wine.
District: Côte de Nuits, France.
Commune: Gevrey-Chambertin.
Official Classification: Great Growth (Grand Cru).

A full wine which can produce splendid bottles, but few of them appear under their proper names. The number of growers in the vineyard is small—for Burgundy—and the wines are generally sold to various shipping houses, some of which engage in the practice of stretching the wines of better-known place-names. Despite this regrettable habit, production of Griotte's 5.5 hectares (13.5 acres) amounts to 85 hectoliters (2,250 U.S. gallons, 1,870 imp.) of wine, or the equivalent of about 1,000 cases.

Grk, Gerk

White Dalmatian wine, dry, pale yellow in color, with an individual aftertaste.
See Yugoslavia.

Grog

Originally a diluted rum, said to be called after the nickname (Old Grog) of Admiral Vernon, who first ordered the dilution of the British navy's rum. The name is sometimes used for undiluted rum and for spirits in general, but is usually applied to hot rum, with or without lemon and spices.

Grolleau (Groslot)

Grape used in France, notably in the rosé wine of Anjou. It is also known as Pineau de Saumur.

Grombalia

Region which produces 90% of Tunisian wines.

Château Gruaud-Larose

Bordeaux red wine.
District: Haut-Médoc, France.
Commune: Saint-Julien.

M. Gruaud purchased the estate, Fond-Bedeau, in 1757, and changed the name. Thirty years later, M. Larose married Gruaud's daughter and bought the lands, adding his name to that of his late father-in-law. Before 1934, labels will show Gruaud-Larose-Faure or Gruaud-Larose-Sarget. The one original vineyard was divided over one hundred years ago when the Sarget heirs, sole owners, sold the larger part to a M. Faure. In 1925, Désiré Cordier acquired the Sarget vineyard. His son Georges, the father of Jean, the present owner, reunited Gruaud-Larose-Sarget and Gruaud-Larose-Faure in 1934. (The Cordier family, who owned one of the most successful shipping firms in Bordeaux, also has Chateau Talbot, another classified growth of Saint-Julien nearby.) Gruaud-Larose has made consistently good wines since then. M. Cordier is also to be congratulated on the way he keeps his cellars. Unfortunately, however, in June 1965 the *chais* containing half the 1964 vintage were burnt down. Gruaud-Larose is a Second Growth (*Second Cru*) of Médoc by the Classification of 1855.

Characteristics. Big, fruity, and fast maturing, typical of the best Saint-Juliens, with considerable finesse and a light perfume.

Vineyard area: 76 hectares (190 acres).
Average production: 320 *tonneaux* (30,000 cases).

Grumello

Red wine of Valtellina, Italy, made from the Nebbiolo grape.
See Lombardy.

Grünberg

A small isolated German wine district in Silesia, surrounding the town of Grünberg, in East Germany.

Grüner Veltliner

Chief grape variety of Lower Austria.

Guebwiller

Alsatian wine town near Colmar.

Guignolet

Black cherry liqueur brandy found mostly in France in the Anjou and Touraine districts and the department of the Vendée.

Château Guiraud

Bordeaux white wine.
District and Commune: Sauternes, France.

Château Guiraud and Château d'Yquem are the only First-classified Sauternes (Official Classification of 1855) actually in Sauternes. This is because the commune of Sauternes was considered too small to provide enough wine to earn worldwide reputation, and the designation was extended to four adjoining communes, in which all the twelve best vineyards are situated except those of d'Yquem and Guiraud. In early days, the Guiraud vineyard was known as Château Bayle. The characteristic French pepperpot turret, capped with a black conical roof, is attached not to the château but to the wine *chai*; the château is a box-like nineteenth-century-style dwelling in a nest of trees, in front of which the long, low, L-shaped *chai*, with its unexpected turret at one end, extends along the rim of a beautifully kept vineyard.

Characteristics. Rather sweet, without great breed; some remarkable vintages.

Vineyard area: 52 hectares (130 acres).

Average production: 120 *tonneaux* (11,000 cases).

Gumpoldskirchner

A delicate white wine, one of the best in Austria, made in the vineyards of Gumpoldskirchen.
See Austria.

Gunflint taste

A special taste in white wines from chalky subsoils. Chablis is the prime example of a wine with this quality.

Gutedel

German variant of the Chasselas family of grapes, found also in California.

Gutsname

German term for wine estate. The same as château or clos in Bordeaux and Burgundy.

Gutturnio dei Colli Piacentini

A good dry red wine from Italy.
See Emilia-Romagna.

Guyenne, Connétablie de

See Connétablie de Guyenne; Premières Côtes de Bordeaux.

Guyot

A variation of the espalier method of training vines. This consists of a trunk and one arm and is largely used in such fine-wine regions as the Médoc.
See Chapter Eight, p. 29.

Gyöngyös

The white sparkling wines of Gyöngyös are among the best in Hungary. Red wines are grown in this district too and in greater quantity.
See Hungary.

H

Halbrot

Swiss term for rosé wine.

Halbstück

The cask used for ageing and storing Rheingau wines, containing 660 liters or about 68 cases of finished wine.

Half-bottle

A bottle holding about half the contents of a standard bottle. The American half-bottle holds roughly 12.5 U.S. fluid ounces; the British, 12 British fluid ounces; 35 centiliters.

Half-on-half

Tawny-colored Dutch liqueur, half Curaçao and half orange bitters.

Hallgartner Schönhell

Outstanding vineyard of Hallgarten, producing one of the best Rheingau wines. Another important Hallgarten vineyard is Jungfer.
See Rheingau.

Hard

Excessive tannin in a wine gives hardness which may disappear with age. A drawback at first, it later becomes an asset, for it preserves the wine and changes with age to firmness. Usually hardness is a sign of youth and quality, but 1945 Bordeaux red wines were hard until the middle sixties.

Haro

A tiny city on the upper Ebro River in Spain which is the center of the Rioja wine trade.
See Rioja.

Harriague

Grape grown in Uruguay and elsewhere.
See Tannat.

Harsh

Hardness pushed to the most unpleasant extreme.

Hárslevelŭ

A Hungarian variety of grape used in making Tokay and other wines.

Hattenheimer Nussbrunnen

One of the greatest Rheingau wines.
See Rheingau.

Hattenheimer Wisselbrunnen

With Hattenheimer Nussbrunnen and with Steinberg, one of the great Rheingaus, and in the triumvirate of the greatest Hattenheimers.
See Rheingau.

Haut

French for "high"; in the feminine, *haute*. This word affixed to a regional name on a wine label is erroneously believed to imply "higher in quality." What it actually means is "higher" in the geographical sense—more northerly, upriver, etc. Example: Haut-Médoc, so named because it is above Médoc on the River Gironde. That it makes better wine is mere coincidence. As for the designation Haut-Sauternes, geographically there is no Haut-Sauternes, and from the point of view of quality, the term is meaningless.

Château Haut-Bages-Libéral

Bordeaux red wine.
District: Haut-Médoc, France.
Commune: Pauillac.

Divided into two parts, one adjoining Pontet-Canet and the other close to Château Latour, the vineyard was classed a Fifth Growth (*Cinquième Cru*) of the Médoc in 1855. The name derives from the high slopes of Bages, where it is situated, and from an early owner, a M. Libéral. The Cruse family bought the property in 1960 and incorporated part of the vineyard with its neighbor, Pontet-Canet. That move, which was entirely legal, left a small portion whose wine continues to be sold as Haut-Bages-Libéral.

Characteristics. Fairly full-bodied, but sometimes on the common side, the wines seem to have improved.

Vineyard area: 19 hectares (57 acres).

Average production: 80 *tonneaux* (7,000 cases).

Château Haut-Bailly

Bordeaux red wine.
District: Graves, France.
Commune: Léognan.

Unlike most of the great Graves vineyards, Haut-Bailly makes no white wine; but the red wine is among the eleven Classified Growths (1953 and 1959) of the district.

Replanted after the devastation by the vine louse phylloxera almost a century ago by Bellot des Minières, whose fame at the time caused him to be called King of Vine Growers, the vineyard was excellent for a period but then fell on bad times. The successor of Minières, a little too eager to rival his predecessor, carried "improvements" in wine-making so far that the wine was being bottled only eight months after vintage, instead of the former four years, and was pasteurized. Having abandoned such "progressive" practices, Haut-Bailly has recovered its early prestige and the wines are balanced and full, distinct among Graves red wines, and rather resembling certain Médocs. The plantings at present are 70% Cabernet Sauvignon, 20% Merlot, and 10% Malbec.

Characteristics. A full, well-rounded wine with great finesse.

Vineyard area: 15 hectares (37 acres).

Average production: 55 *tonneaux* (5,000 cases).

Château Haut-Batailley

Bordeaux red wine.
District: Haut-Médoc, France.
Commune: Pauillac.

A part of Château Batailley until 1924, the vineyard shares with that estate a position of Fifth Growth (*Cinquième Cru*) of the Médoc as classified in 1855. It is now owned by Mme des Brest-Borie, the sister of Jean-Eugène Borie, who has done so much to bring Château Ducru-Beaucaillou to its present high quality. It is M. Borie who directs the vinification of this very fine vineyard.

Characteristics. Better than Château Batailley, with a certain robust strength.

Vineyard area: 22 hectares (55 acres).

Average production: 60 *tonneaux* (5,800 cases).

Château Haut-Brion

Bordeaux red and white wines.
District: Graves, France.
Commune: Pessac.

A château with a history dating back almost five hundred years, Haut-Brion is today unquestionably one of the greatest red-wine producing vineyards in the world. It is now owned by Douglas Dillon, former Secretary of the Treasury of the United States and former United States ambassador to France, and his family. More than any other vineyard, Haut-Brion has been regarded as the quality symbol of Bordeaux and as the producer of the most traditional of all Bordeaux wines.

The spelling of the château has undergone several changes over the centuries; in the records it is given variously as d'Obrion, Daubrion, and Hault-Brion. We know that in 1509 the property was bought by Jean de Ségur and that in 1525 it passed into the possession of the Admiral Philippe de Chabot, who was with King François I when he was taken prisoner at Pavia. But Chabot did not retain the château for long. Before the end of the sixteenth century Haut-Brion went to the Pontac family as part of the dowry of Jeanne de Bellon, and remained with

the Pontacs for two hundred years, until, in the eighteenth century, it became the property of the Fumel family, at one time the owners of Château Margaux.

The Pontacs had another vineyard at Blanquefort, producing white wines, but the "Pontack" wines famous in England in the seventeenth century were the red wines of Haut-Brion. In 1666 François-Auguste de Pontac acquired an interest in a London tavern known as Pontac's Head, fashionable with the nobility, where Haut-Brion was dispensed in large quantities. This, it is said, marked the first time a Bordeaux wine was referred to by name abroad, instead of being sold simply as "claret."

There was another tavern, on Lombard Street, in which a member of the Pontac family was said to have an interest, the Royal Oak, where Samuel Pepys went to drink "a sort of French wine called Ho Bryen that hath a good and most particular taste." In 1683 John Evelyn noted in his diary that he had had a talk with M. Pontac, son of the famous president of Bordeaux, owner of the excellent vineyard of Haut-Brion, whence came the greatest of the Bordeaux wines. Dryden, Swift, and Defoe also dined at the same place in their turn, and Swift found the wine dear at seven shillings a flagon. In 1677, John Locke, who had visited Haut-Brion, remarked that prices had risen "thanks to the rich English who sent orders that it was to be got for them at any price."

It was during the prosperous years of the eighteenth century that the wines of the Médoc gained in popularity on those of Graves. But Haut-Brion was never outshone. In 1770, the Comte de Fumel divided the estate in half. He kept the château and part of the vineyard; the rest, known as Chai Neuf, he sold to the Marquis de Latresne. At the time of the Revolution, the owner of the château was his fifth son, Joseph, who was the mayor of Bordeaux. In 1794, Joseph was guillotined; part of the château property was seized by the government, part remained with the family, who afterward bought back the state's share—and in 1801 sold it to Talleyrand, who kept it only until 1804.

There is no record of Talleyrand having lived there, but no doubt he found a use for the wines. His success in diplomacy depended not only on his quick wit, the charm of his conversation, and the talents of his famous chef, Câreme, but also on the excellence of his wines. At the Congress of Vienna he got the better of everyone, and one of the ways in which he influenced people was by inviting them to his splendid dinner parties.

After 1804 Haut-Brion saw one of its least glorious periods under a succession of businessmen until, in 1836, M. J. E. Larrieu bought the château. Four years later he was able to buy back the "Chai Neuf," too, and so restored the property to its true state. Before long he had done the same for the wine; and when in 1855, the Classification of the Great Growths of the Gironde was made, although other leading wines of Graves were omitted, Haut-Brion was rated a First Growth (*Premier Cru*) with the three great Médocs, Lafite, Latour, and Margaux.

When the rest of the Graves were at last classified, in 1953 and again in 1959, the great red wine of Haut-Brion was, of course, listed at the head of the classification, and is now a First Classified Growth of both Graves and Médoc. The white wine is one of the most prestigious of France and certainly one of the best dry white wines of Bordeaux.

Whereas all the other First Growths have increased in production or in size, Haut-Brion has remained restricted to approximately 13,000 cases per year, its growth limited by the boundaries of the surrounding suburbs. The vineyard is situated on the outskirts of Bordeaux and is enlaced with the buildings of this city and those of the sizable township of Pessac.

Haut-Brion was the first among the great châteaus of Bordeaux to initiate fermentation vats of stainless steel, which are now preferred by all modern oenologists (from the standpoint of fermentation and temperature controls as well as cleanliness) to the old wooden vats found in the *chais* of some other Great Growths. This ambitious conversion was made in the early 1950s under the direction of Seymour Weller, who was president of Haut-Brion for nearly forty years. The château and its grounds today present a superbly dignified and well-tended picture. In the late 1960s the majestic stone entrance to Haut-Brion was restored, and a beautiful large underground cellar was built in 1973. As recently as 1974 Haut-Brion was magnificently redecorated, and its outer walls brightened to show the beauty of the original stone, by Douglas Dillon's daughter Joan, the Duchess of Mouchy, who is now the president of the corporation. She and her husband, who live in France, are regularly at Haut-Brion and run the vineyard together. Since the 1974 restoration, the château has been lived in and is not open to the public.

The soil where the white wines grow is inclined to be clayey, while the vines for the red wine flourish in the famous soil of deep *graves*—the regional word for gravel. This gravel, which has given the Graves district its name, is nowhere so prevalent as at Haut-Brion, where in places it is 50 and 60 feet deep. The porous soil, with its pebbles which reflect the sun and retain the heat, is said to be the factor that causes Haut-Brion to be good even in lesser years. The excess water drains away quickly, giving the vine the semi-aridity it likes.

Characteristics. The red wine is great and often very full, with a special taste imparted by the gravelly soil of its native Graves. It achieves great elegance, and even in the lesser years it is apt to succeed better than others of the district because, owing to its situation, the grapes mature a little earlier at Haut-Brion than in most of the other quality vineyards. Also, the recruiting of harvest workers is easier in the suburbs of Bordeaux, where large crews are available and can easily be suspended during rain. The dry white wine is one of the very best of Bordeaux.

Unlike Châteaux Lafite, Latour, Margaux, and Mouton, Haut-Brion cannot expand its vineyard acreage; and so as the other First Growths have greatly increased production in the past few years, the quantity of Haut-Brion has remained relatively small.

Vineyard area: red—40 hectares (100 acres); white—3 hectares (7.5 acres).

Average production: red—130 *tonneaux* (12,000 cases); white—8 *tonneaux* (700 cases).

Haut-Médoc

Red wine.
District: Bordeaux, France.

The finest part of the Médoc red wine region, near Bordeaux in southwest France, and an official wine place-name, or Appellation Contrôlée. The name designates the upper Médoc, in the sense that it is up-river. The famous districts of Margaux, Pauillac, Saint-Julien, and Saint-Estèphe, and all the famous Médoc châteaux, are in Haut-Médoc.

See Médoc.

Haut-Montravel

See Montravel.

Haut-Peyraguey (Clos)

Bordeaux white wine.
District: Sauternes, France.
Commune: Bommes.

The sloping vineyard surrounds a "château" that looks like a white farmhouse. The vines grow in a clayey and gravel soil. The wine was classed a First Growth (*Premier Cru*) of Sauternes in the Official Classification of 1855.

Characteristics. Carefully made, sweet, rich wine of breed and distinction.

Vineyard area: 11 hectares (27 acres).
Average production: 25 *tonneaux* (2,400 cases).

Heavy

Very full-bodied, but without much distinction or finesse. Certainly a less pejorative term than "coarse."

Hectare

Metric measure of area containing 10,000 square meters (2.471 acres).

See Appendix E, p. 637.

Hectoliter

French unit of measure equaling 100 liters (26.4179 U.S. gallons, 21.9976 imp.). All ordinary French wines are sold by the hectoliter. Abbreviation: hl, or colloquially, hecto.

Heidelberg Tun

A barrel in Heidelberg Castle constructed in 1751 by the cellarmaster Jakob Engler the Younger for the Elector Karl Theodor. It holds 220,000 liters (58,100 U.S. gallons, 48,400 imp.—about 300,000 bottles) but has only been filled three times and long ago sprang a leak. The pump by which wine used to be drawn out of the cask may be seen in the Königsaal, or Great Hall, of the castle.

Hérault

Quantitatively, one of the three most important wine-producing departments of France. (The other two are Aude and Gard.) The area produces 20% of all French wine. From Hérault, in the Montpellier-Béziers district of southern France, comes a great deal of ordinary wine, as well as the superior dry wine Clairette du Languedoc (*q.v.*) and the sweet Muscat de Lunel (*see* Sweet fortified wines of France; Corbières; Minervois).

Hermitage, Ermitage

Rhône Valley red and white wines.
District: Rhône Valley, France.

The big, long-lived Hermitage wines are grown on the slopes above Tain, a little town by the Rhône, 80 kilometers (50 miles) south of Lyon and 19 kilometers (12 miles) north of Valence. Small terraced vineyards, divided by stone walls into parcels known locally as *mas*, climb the hill which rises abruptly behind the town. At the summit, a local landmark is the ruined chapel of Saint-Christophe, built on the site of a Roman temple of Mercury. According to some stories, Saint Patrick planted vines here during his first sojourn in Gaul. On this hillside lived the hermit from whom the wines take their name: the knight Gaspard de Stérimberg, who turned penitent after the Crusade of 1224 against the Albigensian heretics and chose to spend in this beautiful spot the rest of a life which was to be divided between religious meditation and the cultivation of his vineyard. To the many visitors who came to see him he offered wine—all he had—and so the fame of Hermitage was spread.

The soil is meager—a thin layer of chalky limestone on a hard granite subsoil—and the whole extent of the vineyards is 152 hectares (375 acres), yielding some 40 hectoliters to the hectare (428 U.S. gallons, 356 imp. to the acre). When they are bearing, the vines are susceptible to *coulure* (*q.v.*). It is not surprising, therefore, that genuine Hermitage is a comparatively rare and expensive wine.

The red-wine grape is the Syrah, variously reported to be the Shiraz of Persia, brought home by Crusaders (some say by Stérimberg himself), or to have been introduced by the Romans. In any case, the vineyards here are said to be among the oldest in France. The white-wine grapes, cultivated in the center of the slope, are Marsanne and, to a small extent, Roussanne. Less than 30,000 cases is the average yield of this distinctive white wine—full, with a flinty flavor and a character so definite that it can hold its own with such highly seasoned foods as curry. This is among the longest-lasting of all dry white wines and will sometimes be good after twenty years. But it maderizes eventually and is usually at its best at somewhere between six and fifteen years old.

Both white and red wines incline, in youth, to harshness. The red may be rough at first, but in maturity it is soft and velvety, big and generous, forming a heavy sediment. In age, it develops a rich aroma and aftertaste, a bouquet redolent of raspberries and wallflowers, and a glowing *robe* which shifts in color from deep purple to the brownish cast known as *pelure d'oignon*. In nineteenth-century England, Hermitage was much esteemed, and Professor Saintsbury described it as "the manliest of wines."

Twice as much red wine is made as white. In addition to the predominant Syrah, other grape varieties are per-

mitted in small quantities, and these add their own qualities to the wine. The best vineyards for red are: Les Bessards, Le Méal, L'Hermitage, La Varogne, Les Diognières, Les Greffieux, and La Pierelle.

Chante-Alouette is the most celebrated of the white Hermitages, which are dry and delicate yet have body as well as bouquet. This is the name of a vineyard and also the trademark of the firm of Chapoutier, and the wine is usually a blend from the better vineyards, such as Beaumes, Les Murets, Les Rocoules, La Chapelle, Maison-Blanche—and, of course, Chante-Alouette itself. Some of the growers, aware of the value of publicity, have painted their names in whitewash on the dividing walls between the *mas*—Chapoutier, Paul Jaboulet Aîné, and Jaboulet-Vercherre—these three are shippers as well as important growers. Production is around 3,000 hectoliters (79,000 U.S. gallons, 66,000 imp.) a year.

L'Hermitage is just below that group of vineyards which produce wines that are sold as Crozes-Hermitages: agreeable wines, but not to be compared with those permitted the distinguished name Hermitage.

Hessia

See Rheinhessen.

Heurige

New light wine served, and sometimes made, in the vine-covered houses of Grinzing on the outskirts of Vienna. The literal translation is "wine of this year" but it is more generally known as May wine.

Highball

A long, iced drink, usually whisky and soda.

Hippocras

An aromatized wine, popular in the Middle Ages. It was made, probably, from sour wine sweetened and spiced and then filtered through wool, the filter being known as Hippocrates' Sleeve.

Hochheimer-Domdechaney

This big, fruity wine is probably the best of the Hochheimers from the River Main beyond Wiesbaden, but owing to great similarity in quality, it is always classed with the Rheingau wines nearby on the Rhine. This Hochheimer contributed the name Hock used in England for Rheingaus and loosely for all Rhine wines.
See Rheingau.

Hock

British term which applies accurately to the wines from the Rheingau section of Germany and loosely to all wines of the Rhine type. The word derives from Hochheim, a town in the Rheingau.
See Rheingau.

Hogshead

A cask of varying capacity; the most commonly used container for shipping wines and spirits in bulk. The name is said to be a corruption of the Scandinavian *ox-hoft*, which itself varies from 67 to 70 U.S. gallons (56 to 58 imp.). Some of the more widely used hogshead capacities are:

		GALLONS	
	LITERS	*U.S.*	*Imp.*
Burgundy and Bordeaux	225 to 228	59.4	49.5
Beer and cider	246	64.8	54
Sherry	246	64.8	54
Whisky	250	66	55
Port	259	68.4	57
Brandy	273	72	60

See Barrique.

Holland

See Netherlands.

Hollands

The style of gin usually seen in Holland, where it is called Jenever, and distinguished by the stone jar or crock in which it is frequently sold. It differs from London Dry gin, the basic British and American type, by being less thoroughly distilled. In common with Scotch whisky, Cognac, and Jamaican-style rum, it is distilled lightly enough to permit the original taste-factors to pass over into the final product. (London Dry gins are made colorless and tasteless in distillation and flavored afterward.) Hollands is not a neutral cocktail ingredient like London Dry types, but a spirit which the Dutch take neat.
See Gin.

Homeburn

In Norway, spirit distilled at home; "home-brew."

Honey brandy

A distilled mead.
See Mead.

Hops

A climbing perennial with rough lobed leaves like those of the vine. The ripened cones of the female plant are used in brewing to give flavor to the beer. Cultivated in Europe, Central Asia, and America.

Hospices de Beaune

The ancient façade of the Charity Hospital rises in the center of Beaune; and the sale of its wines each year sets the prices for those of the entire Côte d'Or, dictates the value of the harvest which is the life-blood of Beaune, and ushers in the Trois Glorieuses—the three lavish banquets at which Burgundians congregate to glorify and drink their favorite wines.

The Hospices were founded in 1443 by Nicolas Rolin, chancellor to the Duke of Burgundy, and his wife, Guigone de Salins. Beaune at that time seems to have been entirely populated by beggars (only twenty-four of its families were considered solvent), and so it was undoubtedly a wise choice as a site for the charity hospital. There were those who said that Rolin—who was, among other things, a collector of taxes—could well afford to build a hospital for the poor he had helped to grind down; but his charity has been perpetuated, and grants, often in the form of vineyards, have been coming in through the centuries.

In the high outer wall of the Hospices is an arched doorway leading into a cobbled court dotted with groups of visitors and crossed now and again by members of the Dames Hospitalières, the lay organization which, from the start, has cared for the sick. Since the Dames were members of a lay organization, the Hospices did not fall into the hands of the state during the French Revolution, when anti-clerical feeling was high and Church property confiscated. Inside the court the architecture is medieval, with peaked, wood-carved dormers rising from the superb roof of multicolored tiles. Pillars hold up a balcony which runs around the court, in the middle of which is a massive stone well. There are other courts behind this one, rarely seen by visitors, and off one of the last of these the wine is made.

The auction sale of the wines of the Hospices de Beaune is one of the biggest events of the Burgundian year, and the wine merchants who come to take part are mainly French and Belgian, but others come from all over the world. The city begins to get crowded a few days before the sale—usually the third Sunday in November—and the day before, they all troop into the *chais* to taste the wine. At the end of the day, the first banquet of the Trois Glorieuses is held in the ornate hall of the Clos de Vougeot.

The actual auction of the wines takes place in one of the outer courts, or in one of the halls leading off it, and is always presided over by some public figure. Prince Bernhardt of the Netherlands and the British and American ambassadors to France have been among recent presidents. All bidding is done in true medieval manner "by the candle": three small tapers are placed in a holder, and as the auction starts one of them is lit; when it dies, the second is lit and then the third, and the last bid heard before the third has snuffed itself out takes the dubious prize. Competition is keen, because ownership of even a small amount of Hospices de Beaune wine carries considerable prestige, both for wine merchants and restaurateurs, and prices frequently soar far above value. (However, the buyer always has the consolation that he is contributing to a worthy cause.) A slight defect in the system is that all wines are carted off in barrel within a month of the sale, and buyers do not always take proper care of it. With prices so high and demand so great, the temptation to stretch these wines is strong.

The vineyards owned by the hospital are scattered throughout the Côte de Beaune, and all wines are sold under the name not of a vineyard but of the original donor. Cuvée Dr. Peste, for example, is made from grapes grown in the vineyard of Corton, in the section of Aloxe-Corton called Maréchaude; but since this parcel of land was donated by Dr. Peste, the wine is always sold under his name. The Hospices have a total of some 55 hectares (137 acres) of vines and make about 1,400 hectoliters (37,100 U.S. gallons, 30,800 imp.) of wine annually, more than three-fourths of it red.

In addition, they distill a Marc de Bourgogne, and when the wines are auctioned off, the marc of the previous year is sold with them. About 300 hectoliters (8,000 U.S. gallons, 6,650 imp.) of marc is average for any year and, as is the case with the wines, prices run slightly higher than for comparable spirits distilled elsewhere in Burgundy. At the conclusion of the auction, the second of the Trois Glorieuses—a dinner held in the cellars of the Hospices—begins. The following day the trinity is brought to a close with La Paulée, a banquet in the village of Meursault, where growers are supposed to bring a bottle of their best and rarest wine and pass it around the table. At the end of this, everyone goes home to recover.

The results of the 1973 sale follow. (A *pièce* is the equivalent of a barrel of 228 liters, or 24 cases of 12 bottles each.)

(1) Pommard—Dames de la Charité, 31 *pièces*; (2) Savigny-les-Beaune—Arthur Girard, 22 *pièces*; (3) Beaune—Maurice Drouhin, 55 *pièces*; (4) Beaune—Dames Hospitalières, 44 *pièces*; (5) Volnay-Santenots—Gauvain, 28 *pièces*; (6) Pernand-Vergelesses, 13 *pièces*; (7) Beaune—Nicolas Rolin, 40 *pièces*; (8) Savigny-les-Beaune—Borneret, 37 *pièces*; (9) Beaune—Clos des Avaux, 54 *pièces*; (10) Volnay-Santenots—Jehan-de-Massol, 25 *pièces*; (11) Corton—Docteur Peste, 33 *pièces*; (12) Monthélie—Lebelin, 14 *pièces*; (13) Beaune—Brunet, 29 *pièces*; (14) Volnay—Général Muteau, 33 *pièces*; (15) Meursault-Genevrières—Baudot, 33 *pièces*; (16) Meursault—Humblot, 6 *pièces*; (17) Meursault-Charmes—de Bahèzre de Lanlay, 20 *pièces*; (18) Beaune—Guigone de Salins, 43 *pièces*; (19) Savigny-les-Beaune—Fouquerand, 38 *pièces*; (20) Auxey-Duresses—Boillot, 13 *pièces*; (21) Beaune—Rousseau-Deslandes, 45 *pièces*; (22) Pommard—Billardet, 39 *pièces*; (23) Beaune—Hugues et Louis Bétault, 55 *pièces*; (24) Volnay—Blondeau, 34 *pièces*; (25) Corton—Charlotte Dumay, 39 *pièces*; (26) Corton-Charlemagne—François de Salins, 4 *pièces*; (27) Meursault-Charmes—Albert Grivault, 11 *pièces*; (28) Meursault—Goureau, 11 *pièces*; (29) Meursault—Loppin, 11 *pièces*; (30) Meursault-Genevrières—Philippe-le-Bon, 11 *pièces*.

Hotte

French term for a longish back-basket for carrying grapes.

Houghton

Outstanding vineyard in Western Australia, owned by the Emu Wine Company.
See Australia.

Houx

Alsatian holly spirit.
See Alsace: Spirits.

Hudson River Valley

A wine-producing region on the west bank of the Hudson, between Newburgh and Kingston, in New York State. Principal vineyards are Benmarl, High Tor, and those of the Hudson Valley Wine Company. American vines are grown, of which the favorites are the Catawba and the Delaware. Red, white, and rosé wines are produced.
See United States: New York.

Huelva

Province of Spain which produces strong heavy wines.
See Spain.

Hungary

The most famous Hungarian wine, the wine of kings and emperors, is Tokay (*q.v.*), and other wines of Hungary suffer the fate of younger brothers. Yet, eclipsed though they may be in fame, some of them are excellent. Hungarian wine-making standards are claimed to be among the highest of all; strict controls have been the rule, and Hungary was one of the pioneers of place-name and grape-variety regulations.

Wine has always been made in Hungary. Though three-quarters of the vines were wiped out by the vine louse phylloxera in 1875 and by the vine fungus pernospora in 1891, the industry was rebuilt on grafted American root-stocks and with the most modern methods. Over 100,000 hectares (nearly 250,000 acres) of "sand" vineyard were created, the sandy soil being practically immune to phylloxera. Production now averages about 5 million hectoliters (132.5 million U.S. gallons, 110 million imp.) per year; of this about 70% is white wine and the balance red and "Siller" wines. Hungary makes several high quality red wines.

WINE REGIONS

Hungary falls naturally into four regions, defined by

259

the following geographical features: The Great Plain (Alföld), Northern Transdanubia, Southern Transdanubia, and Northern Hungary.

The Great Plain (Alföld) covers nearly half the land surface east of the Danube to the Rumanian border. Transdanubia, the Roman Pannonia, is between the Danube and Drava rivers, and Lake Balaton divides the region into the Northern and Southern sections. Northern Hungary, in the Carpathian foothills east of Budapest along the Slovakian border, is very mountainous.

Between 1948 and 1956, all Hungarian vineyards were registered and classified. About 170,000 hectares (425,000 acres) are planted in vines. The land is broken down into fifteen wine-making regions.

The Great Plain

1. Alföld	79,400 hectares	198,500 acres

Northern Transdanubia

2. Aszar-Neszmely	1,800 hectares	4,500 acres
3. Badacsony	2,400 hectares	6,000 acres
4. Balatonfüred-Csopak	2,000 hectares	5,000 acres
5. Balatonmellek	2,200 hectares	5,500 acres
6. Mór	1,000 hectares	2,500 acres
7. Somló	400 hectares	1,000 acres
8. Sopron	1,100 hectares	2,500 acres

Southern Transdanubia

9. Mecsekalja	1,500 hectares	3,750 acres
10. Szekszárd	1,800 hectares	4,500 acres
11. Villány-Siklós	2,000 hectares	5,000 acres

Northern Hungary

12. Bükkalja	4,000 hectares	10,000 acres
13. Eger	3,400 hectares	8,500 acres
14. Mátraalja	9,000 hectares	22,500 acres
15. Tokajhegyalja	6,500 hectares	16,250 acres

According to production and quality, the vine-growing regions can be grouped as follows:

Districts Producing White Wines of "Outstanding Quality":

Tokajhegyalja, Badacsony, Balatonfüred-Csopak, Somló.

Districts Producing Mainly White Wine of "Excellent Quality":

Aszar-Neszemely, Balatonmellek, Bükkalja, Mátraalja, Mecsekalja, Mór.

Districts Producing Mainly Red Wine of "Excellent Quality":

Eger, Sopron, Szekszárd, Villány-Siklós.

The Great Plain produces the bulk of Hungary's commercial wine.

GRAPE VARIETIES

Hungary has several indigenous grape varieties, from some of which the finest wines are made.

For white wines, the most important of these are Fur-

mint, the main ingredient of Tokay (Tokaj); Hársleveü (which means "lime leaf," the characteristic shape of the leaves), the second ingredient of Tokay; Kéknyelü (meaning "blue stalk," a characteristic of the vine); and Szürkebarát ("Gray Friar"), a type of Pinot Gris. Other indigenous vines include Ezerjó ("a thousand boons"); Leányka ("young girl"); Mézesfehér ("honey white"); Juhfark ("lamb's tail"); Budai; and Piros Cirfandli. Varieties grown in other European wine districts include Olaszrizling (Wälschriesling, or Italian Riesling), now the most widely grown white vine in Hungary; some Rheinriesling; Sylvaner (Szilváni); Traminer; Pinot Blanc (Fehérburgundi); Sauvignon; the Austrian Grüner Veltliner, Müller-Thurgau, and Bouvier; and two Muscats, Ottonel and Sárgamuskotály ("Yellow" Muscat)—a little of the latter is used in making Tokay.

For red wines, Hungary grows mainly the Balkan Kadarka, and, from Western Europe, Pinot Noir, Kékfrankos, Médoc Noir (Merlot), Cabernet Franc, and Cabernet Sauvignon, as well as some of the Austrian Blau Portugieser.

Tokay, Hungary's greatest wine—indeed one of the greatest wines in the world—is described in detail in a separate entry.

Badacsony, Balatonfüred-Csopak, and Balatonmellek, the districts numbered 3, 4, and 5 above, cover all the hill vineyards facing southeast on the northern shores of Lake Balaton. Vines have been cultivated here and wine made for over 2,000 years; in the time of the Roman occupation, the fine Balaton wines were transported to the emperors in Rome. The soil of the Badacsony district is one of heat-absorbing basaltic rock with loess topsoils; this, combined with the aspect and the Balaton micro-climate of the district, makes it a perfect site, with terraced vineyards on the hillsides producing white wines of the highest quality from Szürkebarát and Kéknyelü—and, since the replanting following the phylloxera devastation, Olaszrizling, which here makes wine of the highest quality. Hungarian wines are invariably labeled with the place-name and the possessive -i added, followed by the grape variety—e.g., Badacsonyi Kéknyelü. The adjoining hills of Balatonfüred-Csopak are of a different geological structure (crystalline slate with a red sandstone topsoil), and they enjoy a particularly warm climate. The wines, softer and richer than those of Badacsony, are made chiefly from Sylvaner, but also from Traminer, Muscat, and Olaszrizling. They are of the highest quality, individual in style and, in their fashion, bear comparison with the finest white wines of France and Germany. The rest of the Balaton district makes good, very pleasant, light white wines, popular in style, from Olaszrizling, Sylvaner, and the Magyar Mézesfehér and Ezerjó.

Somló is a small, vine-covered volcanic mountain, prominent in the Transdanubian plain. It has made wines of the very highest quality since the days of St. Stephen (Hungary's first king, in the 11th century), wines which are considered, next to Tokay, to be the country's finest. The production is small, the best in big dessert wines made from Furmint with some Olaszrizling, Riesling and Traminer, and, on the vineyards with less favored aspects, from indigenous vines. The wines of Somló have the reputation of possessing philoprogenitive qualities; for this reason, they were much favored by the Habsburg princes—and, perhaps not for the same reason, by Queen Victoria. Like Tokay, they need time to make and mature; the production is small, and they are always relatively expensive.

The Aszar-Neszmely and Mór districts, nos. 2 and 6 above, are, by Hungarian standards, quite recent wine-lands, the oldest part having been planted by Bavarian settlers in the mid-eighteenth century on cleared woodlands. They are of interest mainly for the Ezerjó wine (Móri Ezerjó) grown on the quartz and mica sandy soil of the Mór district. Because phylloxera cannot survive on soil of this nature, the vines are grown on their own roots. Ezerjó, producing wine of no great distinction in other parts of southeastern Europe, makes, in these conditions, a dry wine of excellent quality with fine bouquet and flavor.

The Mecsekalja district, no. 9, is part of a pre-Roman wine complex in southern Transdanubia, formerly known as Pécs-Villány. The Mecsek hills form a white wine district around the town of Pécs and five hill villages, producing mainly excellent white wines from Olaszrizling, Furmint, and Cirfandli, pleasant, well-balanced wines, largely exported in bulk, particularly to Great Britain, where they are popular.

The large area of Mátraalja, or Mátravidék, no. 14, is, after the Great Plain, the biggest vine-growing area in Hungary. In the foothills of the Mátra mountains, it was formerly two areas, Gyöngyös-Visonta and Debrő, and it adjoins the district of Eger, no. 13. Most of Hungary's table grapes are grown here from Chasselas hybrids, and much good wine, white and red, is made from Olaszrizling, Leányka, Traminer, Ottonel Muscat, and Kadarka; but Mátraalja is famous mainly for a very good sweetish, aromatic green-white wine, Debrői Hárslevelű, made from the lime-leaf Tokay vine of that name.

THE BEST RED WINE AREAS

The most famous of Hungary's good red wines is Egri Bikavér—"Bull's Blood of Eger"—grown in the country around the beautiful old baroque town of that name, on a topsoil of clay on volcanic rock—good red wine land. Of course, the wine has nothing to do with bulls or blood and is now made from Kadarka, Kékfrankos, Médoc Noir, Oporto or Cabernet Franc grapes. At its best, it is a full, smooth, deep-colored wine, benefiting enormously from bottle-age, which it rarely gets. The legend of the name comes from a story of the sixteenth century, when strong Turkish forces attacked the town and were repulsed by the local troops, encouraged by liberal quantities of Egri Bikavér served to them by their women. Egri Kadarka can be excellent too and equally improves from long maturing in bottle. Many good white and Siller wines are also made in this district, rich dessert wines from the Magyar vines Leányka and Mézesfehér, drier table wines from Olaszrizling and Ezerjó, and Siller wines from Kadarka.

Probably the best Hungarian red wine is the Kékfran-

kos grown in Villány and known as Villányi-Burgundi. It has many of the qualities of the Burgundy grape and, like most other Magyar red wines, develops qualities of greatness when matured for a few years in bottle. Excellent red wines are also made in the Villány-Siklós district from Kadarka, and rather coarse wines from the Blau Portugieser. This is clearly a good red wine district. Szekszárd, a little to the northwest, also makes a good full-bodied wine from Kadarka, more in the Bordeaux style. Cabernet-Franc and Kékfrankos vines are also grown here. These areas are old winelands, many of them dating back to pre-Roman times, before the Emperor Probus, who came from Pannonia and was famous for his encouragement of viticulture.

Sopron, fourth of the Hungarian red wine districts, is in the extreme northwest, in the Hungarian Burgenland, adjoining Austria. Its wine-making dates back to the pre-Roman Celts, and it was the produce of Sopron centuries ago that first spread the fame of Hungarian wines to Western Europe. Wines of many styles, red and white, are made here, but the district's fame rests on one made from a grape closely related to the Burgundian Gamay— Soproni Kékfrankos, which is of the style of Beaujolais, and to be drunk young and fresh.

THE SANDLANDS

The Great Plain is, in general, the land of huge State Farms, on the sandlands that, over the centuries, the Magyars have tamed and made into arable land. It was, and is, an epic struggle, but vines, with their long-ranging root systems, can flourish there. This became of great importance at the time of the phylloxera scourge, since the phylloxera aphid cannot survive in soil of this nature. Most of the wine made in the Alföld is not of high quality but is useful for the large export demand (from Germany, for example), for the making of Sekt, for distillation, and to form the basis for vermouth. But there are some ancient oases in the Alföld, mainly between the Danube and the Tisza: notably at Kecskemét, an ancient vine and fruit-growing area; at Jászberény, Csengőd, and Szeged in the extreme south. Kadarka, Olaszrizling, Ezerjó, Leányka, Cirfandli, and Veltliner are the principal varieties grown, particularly in the huge new plantations, although most of the indigenous vines are found in the ancient vine areas, where some wines of high quality are made. A remarkable cabernet is also produced at Hajós.

BOTTLE TYPES AND MARKINGS

Tokay Aszú and Tokay Szamorodni are marketed in special white half-liter bottles (for a description of the labeling by grades, see Tokay). Most other Hungarian bottled wine, including the other styles of Tokay, is sold in the tall slender bottles usually identified with German wines. Egri Bikavér and other red wines are in the short-shouldered Bordeaux bottles.

These wines carry the guarantee of authenticity—the words *Magyar Állami Export Pincegazdaság* forming a circle which encloses the word *Budafok*. Anyone who finds this emblem stamped on the bottle label knows he has the real thing. Monimpex, Budapest is the only agency entitled to export wines from Hungary. Large quantities are exported in bulk for bottling by the importing country.

SPIRITS

Hungary produces a wide range of liqueurs and brandies. The most famous is Barack Pálinka (apricot brandy), an unsweetened spirit distilled from fresh apricots which come from the orchards of Kecskemét. This is sold in the standard 70 cl. and 35 cl. bottles and in the traditional *fütyülős* (flask) of 50 cl., which has a very long neck. From the same area comes Kecskeméti Barack liqueur, a mellow apricot, rich with the fragrance of the fruit.

The best of the rest of the fruit liqueurs are the cherry brandy and the golden pear liqueur (Császárkörte in Hungarian). Another interesting liqueur is Hubertus, based on herbs and slightly more bitter in taste.

Of the other unsweetened spirits, the most renowned are Szilva Pálinka or Szilvorium (plum brandy), vodka, Kirsch of Eger, and Casino rum. All of these are more or less known in Great Britain, Canada, the United States, and South America. The best of Szilva Pálinka comes from Szatmár County and is made from three varieties of plums.

Hunter River Valley

Wine district of New South Wales, Australia. The vineyards here are the oldest in the country and among the few that produce almost entirely table wines. They center around Pokolbin and Cessnock.
See Australia.

Hybrid

A cross between two different vine varieties, usually one of *Vitis vinifera* stock and one from an American species. The ultimate aim of the experimental hybridizer is to develop a vine with the hardiness and resistance to disease of American vines but bearing fruit of *Vitis vinifera* quality. A number of sound hybrids exist, and a few are

very good for certain localities; but the field is still uncrowded. Hybridization is carried on in the United States (in New York, Maryland, and California), in Canada, and in European countries, notably Germany and France. The vines developed by French hybridizers usually bear the name of the hybridizer and a number. Some of the better-known names are Baco, Couderc, Seibel, and Seyve-Villard. Philip Wagner in Baltimore is contributing greatly through his hybrids to the improvement of eastern American vineyards. Having found many hybrids that are indigenous to the climate and soil of the eastern states, he is beginning to reduce the "foxy" taste in the vines of this region.
See Chapter Eight, p. 29.

Hydromel

See Mead.

Hydrometer

An instrument used to measure the sugar content of musts, consisting of a weighted bulb with a stem containing a scale calibrated in grams of sugar per 100 grams of solution. The must is poured into a chemist's calibrated cylinder, then the hydrometer is inserted and allowed to sink to an equilibrium level, depending on the density of the solution. Since sugar accounts for most of the increase in density of the must above the density of water, the instrument can be calibrated to read the percentage of sugar directly on the stem at a specified temperature.

Hydrometer, Sikes

In Great Britain, the hydrometer is legally recognized for measuring the strength of alcoholic beverages.
For comparison with French and American measures, *see* Appendix C, p. 630.

Hymettus

Light wines, both red and white, produced near Mount Hymettus in Attica.
See Greece.

I

Illinois

Wine-growing region of very little importance, in the United States.

Immiscible liquids

Liquids which do not mix: the classic example, oil and wine. For this reason, wine was sealed by a thin film of olive oil before corks came into use.

Imperial (impériale)

An outsized bottle used for fine French Bordeaux wines put down for long keeping. The capacity of the imperial is approximately eight ordinary Bordeaux bottles or six liters.

Importation of wine

Few generalities can be made from the amount of wine a country imports. Some of the large producers import large quantities, others do not. Some relatively wineless countries seem to require much wine, and, even more obviously, others do not. Of note is the fact that the Soviet Union—long only an importer of average quantity—has risen to near the top of the list. Most of the wine bought by the U.S.S.R comes from Algeria.

The figures opposite are averages over the past few years, adjusted to show the patterns which may be expected in the near future.

Incrustation

The formation of a crust in wines, specifically Ports.

India

The history of wine in India is sporadic, but it is known to have been made there two thousand years ago and was still enjoyed in the era of the Moguls—Kashmir was then a wine region. In 1628, the monarch Jahangir was pictured on a coin with a goblet of wine in his hand. There were vineyards, then, at Golconda, Kandahar, and Surat. A century ago, the wines which had survived were those of Kashmir—some were shown at the Calcutta Exhibition of 1888. But the vines, which had been imported from Bordeaux, were attacked by phylloxera and had to be grafted onto American root-stocks.

Today, there are a few vineyards near Madras. Started by French missionaries, about 1889, they have been en-

WORLD IMPORTS OF WINES

Importing Country	Hectoliters	U.S. Gallons	Imp. Gallons
France	7,500,000	198,750,000	165,000,000
West Germany	7,250,000	192,125,000	159,500,000
U.S.S.R.	6,500,000	172,250,000	143,000,000
United States	3,500,000	92,750,000	77,000,000
Great Britain	3,300,000	87,285,000	72,600,000
Switzerland	1,950,000	51,675,000	42,800,000
Belgium	1,900,000	50,350,000	41,800,000
Netherlands	1,400,000	37,030,000	30,800,000
East Germany	1,400,000	37,030,000	30,800,000
Canada	1,000,000	26,500,000	22,000,000
Sweden	690,000	18,250,000	15,180,000
Denmark	645,000	17,060,000	14,190,000
Poland	480,000	12,696,000	10,560,000
Czechoslovakia	343,000	9,072,000	7,546,000
Austria	300,000	7,950,000	6,600,000
Hungary	297,000	7,855,000	6,534,000
Italy	216,000	5,713,000	4,752,000
Japan	195,000	5,157,000	4,290,000
Bulgaria	186,000	4,919,000	4,092,000
Finland	129,000	3,412,000	2,838,000
Australia	80,000	2,120,000	1,760,000
South Africa	72,000	1,904,000	1,584,000
Luxembourg	70,000	1,855,000	1,540,000
Ireland	66,000	1,745,000	1,452,000
Brazil	50,000	1,325,000	1,100,000
Spain	35,000	927,500	770,000
New Zealand	32,000	846,000	704,000
Mexico	20,000	529,000	440,000
Rumania	1,000	26,500	22,000
Total	39,607,000	1,049,107,000	871,254,000

larged in recent years around Kodaikanal, Dharmapuri, and Penukanda. Even so, this growing of vines is more of a hobby than a serious business, and the Madras market absorbs the harvest. At the other end of the sub-continent, in Kashmir, the surviving vines, which now show some of the characteristics of American species and grow half-wild, are used for table grapes. Vineyards besides those around Madras are located in the states of Maharashtra and Mysore, near the southern tip of the country. Vineyards near Delhi, in the north Indian state of Haryana, also produce wine grapes.

While there is little demand for wine among a people who do not much care for alcoholic drinks, or are forbidden by their religion to taste them, spirits, nevertheless, are manufactured—not only fermented palm and rice drinks, but brandy, gin, rum, and whisky. In 1972 the following quantities were made:

	Hectoliters	U.S.	Imp.
		GALLONS	
Brandy	46,000	1,219,000	912,000
Gin	40,000	1,060,000	880,000
Whisky	115,000	3,047,500	2,530,000
Rum and bitter	75,000	1,987,500	1,650,000

Infectious degeneration

A virus, or virus-like vine disease, also known as fan leaf and *court noué*.
See Chapter Eight, p. 29.

Inferno

Red wine of Valtellina, in Italy, made from the Nebbiolo grape.
See Lombardy.

Ingelheimer

With Assmannshauser, this is one of the best—perhaps the best—of German red wines, but certainly not among the world leaders. For even at their best, German red wines are mediocre by world standards.
See Rheinhessen.

Inspissated wine

Boiled-down must, or unfermented grape juice, used in flavoring or coloring certain wines.

Institut National des Appellations d'Origine

Commonly known as I.N.A.O.
See Appellation d'Origine Contrôlée.

Iona

Native American hybrid grape, developed in New York, where it is cultivated today mostly for sparkling white wine. The fruit is sweet and dark red, and it ferments into a clean distinctive dry wine—one of several examples of white wine made from red grapes. The name comes from Iona Island, in the Hudson River near Peekskill.

Iran

The fame of Iran as a wine-making country is in the past, when it was one of the earliest lands to practice viniculture. According to one legend, wine was discovered accidentally by a shah of Persia, and Herodotus says the Persians were deep drinkers. There are many other refer-

ences to the wines and to the size and prodigality of the vines in classical literature. And even after the Moslem interdiction Omar Khayyam continued to sing the praises of his native wine. Shiraz was the celebrated wine, and there was a theory that the Syrah grape, grown now in the Rhône Valley and other places, was originally brought to Western Europe from Shiraz by returning Crusaders. Ancient vines, stout as trees, still grow there. Other famous wines (according to Mr. L. W. Marrison) were Khorasan and Mazandaran.

Today vines grow on about 135,000 hectares (337,500 acres), mainly in the foothills of the mountains and especially in the provinces of East Azerbaijan, West Azerbaijan, Khorasan, Teheran, Farse, Hamedan, Lorestan, and Zanjan. Annual production is about 4,000 hectoliters (105,800 U.S. gallons, 88,000 imp.), nearly all of which is drunk in the country. The average Iranian drinks less than half a liter of wine a year, however. One of the most widely planted grapes is the Thompson Seedless; it is good for fresh table grapes and raisins but makes poor wine. Among those cities with wineries are the capital, Tehran; Shiraz (*q.v.*); Hamedan, 320 kilometers (200 miles) west of the capital; Malayer, near Hamedan, Shiravan in the northeast; Shahrooh in the north and Abadeh, about 160 kilometers (100 miles) north of Shiraz.

SPIRITS

Arak is the principal spirit, and some 80,000 hectoliters (2.12 million U.S. gallons, 1.76 million imp.) are made each year. Beer is also much more popular than wine, which is sometimes reinforced with raki and sugar.

Irancy

Rather ordinary red and rosé wines produced in the department of Yonne, some 16 kilometers (10 miles) south of Chablis in northern Burgundy.

Irouléguy

Red, white, and rosé wines.
District: Southwest France.

In the extreme southwest corner of France amid the dramatic valleys of the Pyrenees are the towns of St. Jean-Pied-de-Port and St. Étienne-de-Baïgorry. Neither is far from Biarritz, famous as a resort, or from Bayonne, famous for its hams. The two villages lie in the center of the area which makes the Appellation Contrôlée wine called Irouléguy. The white wines are similar to the naturally sweet ones produced in nearby Jurançon. But better than these are the reds, which are rather light in color but with good flavor nonetheless.

Isabella

A prolific American grape, once highly thought of but now used almost exclusively for blending in the production of sparkling wine in New York State. The grape is blue, but it gives a pale, slightly "foxy" wine with no pronounced characteristics. It can also be found under the name Americano in southern Switzerland.

Ischia

Pleasant red and white wines from the island off the coast of Naples.
See Campania.

Isinglass

A whitish semi-transparent gelatinous substance obtained from the bladders of certain freshwater fishes, especially the sturgeon, and used for fining or clarifying wines and beers.
See Chapter Nine, p. 38.

Israel

Wine of almost every type is made in Israel: red and white table wine; medicinal wine; and sparkling wine for every palate—*brut,* extra-dry, semi-dry, sweet—made by the champagne method of secondary fermentation in bottle. All those designed for export are prepared under religious supervision, since for Jewish communities abroad they may be sacramental as well as beverage wines. Aperitifs are also produced, as are brandy and liqueurs.

The mainstays of Israel's production were, until recently, full-bodied, sweet red wines, golden Muscatels, and a sweet wine of the Tokay type. Now, however, dry and semi-dry table wines, both red and white, are gaining in popularity. In 1974, about 60% of the production was in table wine. In the past, appellations were often borrowed from other countries, and bottles might be labeled Carmel Málaga or Carmel Port. This practice is gradually being abandoned, and most of the wines have new Hebrew names. Some of the most important are:

Sweet Dessert Wines

Muscatel; Partom and Vered (formerly Port); Topaz, Tokeah, Tivon, and Savion (formerly Tokay); Almog, Gilon, and Nalagenia (formerly "Málaga"); Sharir ("Sherry"); Yakeneth ("Alicante"); Yashan Noshan; Yenon; Moriah; Atzmauth.

Dry and Semi-dry Table Wines

Red. Adom Atic; Primor (formerly Pommard); Vin Rouge Supérieur; Château Windsor; Carmelith; Atzmon; Mont Rouge.

White. Carmel Hock; Mont Blem; Massadah; Château Montagne; Levanan; Doron.

Red and white. Avdad; Ashkalon; Ben-Ami.

Sparkling Wines

President.

Aperitifs

Vermouth (red, white, dry).

WINE REGIONS

Zikhron-Yaacov

As the country's largest vine-growing region, 40% of Israel's vines grow on the slopes of Mount Carmel, where they have been cultivated since the late 19th century. The specialty of the region is a rosé wine.

Sydoon-Gezer

In the center of the country, and second in size to the Zikhron-Yaacov region, the grapes grown here have also been cultivated since the late 1800s, and produce white and especially good red wines.

Galilee

Located in the mountainous northern part of the country, this new grape area with its relatively good climate has turned out some good red and white wines.

Jerusalem environs

New vineyards, planted in the last twenty years in this relatively small area, produce some good red and white wines.

Negev

The hot and dry climate of this southern region, recently planted with vines, has succeeded in producing some good white wines.

WINE HISTORY

Canaan must have been among the earliest countries to enjoy wine. It is generally assumed that the first known vineyards were those of Anatolia, Persia, Mesopotamia, and Egypt, all of them growing vines over three thousand years ago. At an early date there was communication between Palestine and Egypt. A letter written about 1800 B.C. reported that Palestine was blessed with figs and with vineyards producing wine in greater quantity than water—in fact, "the children of Israel sit each beneath his vine and his fig." Another correspondent wrote that all the gardens of Canaan were full of fruit-giving vines, and the wine flowed from her cellars like waterfalls—this was about 1500 B.C.

The many references to wine in the Bible need not be repeated here. One of the first things Noah did, when the flood was over, was to begin "to be a husbandman, and he planted a vineyard and he drank of the wine." According to one theory, there actually was a flood and the approximate date was 2800 B.C. During the 18th Dynasty (1580–1450 B.C.) the Egyptians conquered Palestine, and again, about 925 B.C., Jerusalem was taken. When the Egyptian soldiers destroyed Israelite cities, they tore up the vineyards, but these were replanted and soon flourished again. As for Canaan, the land flowing with milk and honey flowed also with wine. In the book of Numbers, Chapter xiii, the story is told of how the two men Moses sent to spy out the land came back with a great cluster of grapes which they tied to a staff and carried between them. The place where they cut it down was the brook named Eshcol.

The vintners of biblical times were knowledgeable about wine-making (as was Mago of Carthage) and many of their customs are still known and respected today. In a country where there was sometimes more wine than water, the wine was used for all kinds of things in addition to drinking and as a medicine: houses were washed out with it, clothes were dyed in it—it has been estimated that the population used as much as 3 to 4 liters a head every day.

Vines grew all over the country—on the hills, in the valleys, on the plain, even on the shores of the Dead Sea. Grapes were carefully selected for picking—the whole process was not unlike that in use in parts of Cyprus (q.v.). There were many different types: white; red or "pretty" wine; dark-colored "negro" wine; sultana wine; milk wine (a posset, perhaps); and asparagus wine, boiled with the vegetable. Various mixtures were prepared, also— honey and peppers with sweet wines, herbs and peppers with sharp wines. There was wine to be drunk at one year of age, at three years, or after long storage in cellars. Before big festivals, the wine was racked three times, and at the Feast of the Tabernacles the booths were decorated with wine jars. Wines from Lebanon were highly thought of; and famous Helbon, to be bought in Damascus (Ezekiel, Chapter xxvii), was a cooked white wine. It is probable that there were more white wines than red.

Wine production was at its peak in Palestine in the time of the Second Temple—destroyed in A.D. 70 in the war with the Romans. Many famous vineyards were then torn up. Some were reconstituted, but although the Jewish people continued for some time to cultivate the vine in a desultory way, production did not flourish again until modern times. Yet in the first four centuries of this era, Roman writers described various Palestine wines—Shechem, Lydda, Caesarea, Ashkelon, and Gaza—which were highly esteemed and exported to Syria, to Egypt, and even to England. After the Arab conquest (A.D. 600–1000) most of the vineyards were uprooted; so strict was the Moslem prohibition that even table grapes were destroyed in case they should be pressed for wine.

In the Middle Ages, however, Crusaders found a few vineyards near the Mount Carmel Range, near Bethlehem and Nazareth, and some of them stayed long enough to cultivate vines for themselves. In 1280 it was reported that "Near Bethlehem there are still magnificent vines. The Moslems do not tend them, but the Christians make very good wine." The Christians had to pay heavy taxes for the privilege, and Moslems living near the Christian settlements made wine to sell to their neighbors.

WINE OF MODERN ISRAEL

Modern wine history in Palestine began in 1870, with the foundation of the first agricultural school. This started with a vineyard at Mikveh, bearing a few eating grapes, but mainly wine grapes, all of *Vitis vinifera*: Alicante, Bor-

deleau, Carignan, Petit Bouchet, and others. There were at this time some Christian monastic holdings, also planted in *Vitis vinifera*, but these were small. In 1880 the German Templars planted sizable areas in the Carmel district, bringing their vines from the Rhine Valley.

In 1882, at the time when the earliest Zionists were arriving in Israel, the first vineyards, under the patronage of Baron Edmond de Rothschild, were planted, again with *Vitis vinifera*. Soon there were large cellars in use, and vineyards at Shomron and in different parts of Galilee. In 1890 the area under Jewish cultivation was 2,800 hectares (7,000 acres), there was beginning to be a surplus of wine, and growers were considering problems of marketing and export when the phylloxera plague arrived, destroying many plants and putting an end to the surplus for some time. Rothschild advised the growers to replant with vines grafted onto American root-stocks.

By 1906 the industry was able to stand on its own, and Rothschild handed over to the growers the cellars at Richon-le-Zion, near Tel-Aviv, and at Zikhron-Yaacov, south of Haifa. These are still the main centers. The name given to the cooperative which was then formed was Société Coopérative Vigneronne des Grandes Caves Richon-le-Zion et Zikhron-Yaacov. It still functions today, producing 75% of the wine of Israel. The viticultural methods were French, introduced by Baron de Rothschild.

At first, Israel's wine industry was run at a loss. Once the Jewish state was established (in 1948), with thousands of immigrants arriving, many from wine-growing countries, cultivation began to flourish. In the first five years, acreage doubled, and approximately 2,000 hectares (5,000 acres) have since been added. Today, domestic consumption of wine is some 150,000 hectoliters (4 million U.S. gallons, 3.3 million imp.), and there is a surplus of about 1 million U.S. gallons for export.

With so much of the land in new vine, the quality of the wine has not yet declared itself. Certain wines produced from European grape varieties grown in different regions of Israel are showing themselves to be pleasant and satisfactory; and a few of the Israeli wines have lately won prizes at international competitions and exhibitions. They will undoubtedly continue to improve with the technical help and good equipment prevalent, thus making Israel a good wine-producer with regard to both quality and quantity. In 1957, the Israeli Wine Institute was established at Rehovot for the purpose of scientific and market research and/or the testing, for quality, of all wines for export.

RECENT PRODUCTION

For the past ten years average annual production of wine in Israel has stabilized near 430,000 hectoliters (11,373,000 U.S. gallons, 9,460,000 imp.). About 70% of this figure was made by the Cooperative Society of Wine Growers, Richon-le-Zion, and Zikhron-Yaacov. Other important wineries are Hamartef, Eliaz, Friedman-Tnuvah, and Carmel Zion. About five hundred growers are today members of the Cooperative Society, which is responsible for some 90% of the export trade in wine. In 1952 the society established in the U.S. a company called Carmel Wine Co., Inc., New York, and this is their representative for wines exported anywhere in the United States or Canada. There is also a branch in Great Britain, The Carmel Wine Company, which is almost as old as modern viticulture in Israel, for it was founded in 1897, only fifteen years after the revival of the Palestine vineyards. Wines and spirits are imported partly in bottle, and partly in bulk for London bottling. Great Britain and America are Israel's principal customers, but wine is exported in smaller quantities to twenty-six other countries.

Today most wines are made from the Carignan, Alicante, Grenache, Sémillon, Bourboulenc, and a local variety called Dabuki. In hopes of improving the quality of their wines, growers are limiting the plantations of the ubiquitous, mediocre Carignan in favor of such better grapes as the Cabernet Sauvignon, French Colombard, and Sauvignon Blanc. In addition, Ruby Cabernet, Emerald Riesling, and other hybrids developed in California have been planted as the Israelis continue to work toward reasonable table wines for consumption at home and export abroad.

Château d'Issan

Bordeaux red wine.
District: Haut-Médoc, France.
Commune: Cantenac-Margaux.

Before the fall of the Austro-Hungarian Empire during the First World War, Château d'Issan was the favorite wine of the Royal Court at Vienna. It is said that Emperor Franz Josef would drink no other, and everyone else followed his lead.

"For the Table of Kings and the Altar of God" is the proud motto of the vineyard and may be seen carved in the stone of the gate. The beautiful fourteenth-century château, a replacement of a fortress-castle from the thirteenth century, was near collapse when restoration was begun in 1952.

Lying across the road from Château Prieuré-Lichine on the north side of Cantenac, the château is owned by Mme M. E. Cruse, the widow of the late Emmanuel Cruse, and her son Lionel, who heads the shipping firm of Cruse et Fils, Frères. The property is entitled to the place-name Margaux. Château d'Issan lies near Château Palmer, both Third Growths (*Troisièmes Crus*) in the Classification of 1855.

Characteristics. While the delicacy and the typical taste of a Margaux are present, the wines have a body and fleshiness slightly reminiscent of those made farther north in the Médoc—the Pauillacs, for example. Contrary to past practices, the wine is now château-bottled and has somewhat regained throughout the world the reputation lost in the thirties and forties.

Vineyard area: 35 hectares (87 acres).

Average production: 130 *tonneaux* (11,000 cases).

Italy

Of all the large wine-producing countries in the world, Italy along with the United States has made the most revolutionary strides, from backward mediocrity to oenological highs. Since the latter part of the 1960s, the human factor, one of the four main contributors to quality, has manifested itself in region after region and traditional methods, often bad, have given way to the modern science of wine-making. This is especially true for white wines. New grape varieties, controlled fermentation, and estate-bottling have resulted in fresh, attractive wines in place of wines previously subject to oxidation.

The Italian likes his wines heady, red, and, above all, plentiful. He is the most natural wine-drinker in the world, downing his annual 110 liters (29 U.S. gallons, 24 imp.) a head of wine—good, bad, or indifferent—with the greatest satisfaction. The ordinary wine may be rough, incompletely fermented, thick, lacking in finesse; but it will always be a welcome accompaniment to the meal.

Italy has been described as one vast vineyard—and the description is apt. Vines spill out everywhere, climb trees and drape their branches, run along roads and hang festooned from fences, flourish in glorious disorder beside olive trees and in fields of grain. The vine grows easily, flowering into great bunches of grapes. One does not see nearly so many of the serried ranks of disciplined, close-trimmed vineyards here as in France and Germany. And Italian viniculture is sometimes as easygoing as its viticulture. Indeed, in some vineyards it seems that the vintner's main concern is with getting wine from fermenting vat to mouth in the shortest possible time. Wines splash constantly from one end of the country to the other.

Italy is the largest producer and exporter of wine in the world. The average annual production is about 65 million hectoliters (1.71 billion U.S. gallons, 1.43 billion imp.), of which 12 million hectoliters (nearly 20% of the total) is shipped out of the country. Italy imports wine too—some 204,000 hectoliters (5.4 million U.S. gallons, 4.4 million imp.) each year.

In fewer and fewer plots do vines still grow among other crops. Today about 700,000 hectares (1.75 million acres) are in mixed cultivation as compared with more than 2 million hectares (5 million acres) in 1964. Land devoted exclusively to intensive viticulture covers 1,406,000 hectares (3,515,000 acres). The young men who tended the many hectares under mixed cultivation have continued to leave the land for the cities, where the tremendous growth of Italian industry has made factory jobs plentiful. Still, there are about two million vineyard workers registered in Italy, and peasant owners of small parcels might bring this number up to three million.

Some of the wines are excellent—among the best of them, the Barolos and Barbarescos of Piedmont, the Valpolicellas and Soaves of Veneto, and Tuscany's celebrated Chianti—and, indeed, the traveler may discover an exceptional bottle almost anywhere along the road. But, unfortunately, these fine wines are not always to be found. Many of the best wines of Italy are made, for their own consumption, by the smaller growers who sell what surplus they have to old-established customers, often inherited along with the vineyard—and the casual tourist is unlikely to meet with such a cultivator or his wine. What he will normally drink will be the output of the large companies—standardized wine, its quality depending entirely upon the firm which makes it.

WINE CONTROLS

Italian wines have suffered not only from the haphazard methods of viniculture but also from an easygoing attitude to nomenclature which before the advent of the D.O.C. laws made it possible for wines which did not even deserve the name Tuscan to be sold under the label of Chianti. The root of the trouble was the government's failure to safeguard the place-names of the fine-wine regions.

The French government, afraid of having its market flooded with cheap Italian wines as the tariff barriers were constantly lowered to comply with the Common Market Agreements, urged the Italian government to set up control laws, somewhat along the lines of the Appellations d'Origine Contrôlée.

Denominazioni di Origine

At last, in July 1963, regulations for controlling place-names, or denomination of origin, were made law. There are three different denominations, graded as follows:

(a) Simple
  e.g., Rosso Toscano, a red wine from anywhere inside Tuscany.
(b) "Country wine," a half step between Simple and Controlled.
(c) Controlled
  e.g., Barolo, a fine wine of Piedmont, produced only in Barolo, Castiglione Faletto, Serralunga d'Alba, and parts of Monforte d'Alba, La Morra, Verduno, Monchiero, and Diano d'Alba.
(d) Controlled and guaranteed
  e.g., a true Barolo sealed and labeled with the official governmental seal.

Simple denomination (Denominazione di Origine Semplice) is allowed to ordinary wines made from grapes traditionally cultivated in an area—the zones are determined by decree of the Ministry of Agriculture and Forestry. But such wines carry no official guarantee of quality; no provision is made for special control, and only in doubtful cases of territorial complication does the law demand that the zone of production be defined by ministerial decree.

"Country wine," or vini tipici a denominazione geografica, is restricted to a general region. But the guidelines for the cultivation and vinification are more lax than for the controlled wines.

Controlled denomination (Denominazione di Origine Controllata, usually abbreviated D.O.C.) is an appellation reserved for wines which have achieved the stipulated standards for quality. Vineyards producing such wines are inscribed in an official register.

Controlled and guaranteed denomination (Denomina-

zione di Origine Controllata e Garantita) is awarded only to fine wines attaining qualities and prices established after the recommendation of the Ministry of Agriculture and Forestry. Such wines must be sold in containers not exceeding 5 liters (1.3 U.S. gallons, 1.1 imp.). The labels must state that the origin of the wine is controlled and guaranteed and list the net content of the bottle, the name of the grower and bottler, the place of bottling, and also the alcoholic strength. Growers who wish to have their wine classified in this top category must send in a request to the Ministry of Agriculture and Forestry for a government inspector, who will have the wine analyzed. Such applications must be backed by copious documentation as to region, average annual production, details of vine variety, characteristics of wines, etc. For wines of controlled and guaranteed origin the application can only be put forward if it has the support of a fair percentage of the growers concerned. The recognition of these two higher denominations is finally effected by the president of the republic on the advice of the ministries concerned. From that time forth, the wine-makers must adhere strictly to the following rules:

(1) Inscription of the vineyards in the appropriate register, with compulsory declaration of production and stocks.
(2) Correct labeling of bottles and flasks.
(3) Inspection by control agents appointed by the Ministry of Agriculture.
(4) Cooperation in preventive steps taken to repress fraud and assert the controls of the denomination of origin.
(5) Paying of penalties for infraction of the regulations.

The National Institute for the Protection of Denomination of Origin (Istituzione del Comitato Nazionale per la Tutela delle Denominazioni di Origine) is nominated by the Ministry of Agriculture and Forestry in association with the Ministry of Industry and Commerce. It is composed of a president and twenty-eight members, including one from the Italian Institute for Foreign Trade (I.C.E.). The function of this committee is to promote and watch over the controlled and guaranteed Italian wines and to initiate studies for their improvement. Although membership of this class of denomination is voluntary, it is considered that all the better producers are anxious to win the certificate of guarantee for export and are very ready to submit their wines for inspection and analysis.

Because membership is voluntary, not all wine for export is so controlled—it is up to the customer to read the label before he buys a bottle of Italian wine.

Following what was undoubtedly a regrettable lack of controls, these new laws are certainly to be commended. If the laws are indeed to work, everyone concerned in the Italian wine trade will have to be persuaded that quantity of production is worth sacrificing to quality. The law of July 12, 1963, amending and replacing earlier regulations which had become out of date and ineffective, requires the government to issue a decree controlling the production of musts, wines, and vinegars, and establish regulations to prevent fraud in the preparation and sale of these products.

BEST-KNOWN WINES

Aglianico del Vulture ——— 1
Albana ——————— 2
Aleatico di Portoferraio — 3
Asti Spumante ———— 4
Barbera ——————— 5
Barbaresco ————— 6
Bardolino ————— 7
Barolo ——————— 8
Capri ——————— 9
Castelli Romani ——— 10
Chianti —————— 11
Cinque Terre ———— 12
Cirò ——————— 13
Est! Est!! Est!!! ——— 14
Frascati —————— 15
Gattinara ————— 16
Gragnano ————— 17
Lacrima Christi ——— 18
Lago di Caldaro ——— 19
Lambrusco ————— 20
Marsala —————— 21
Moscato di Pantelleria _ 22
Orvieto —————— 23
Sangiovese ————— 24
S. Maddalena ———— 25
Soave —————— 26
Valpantena ————— 27
Valpolicella ————— 28
Verdicchio ————— 29

ITALY

THE CONSORZI

Inside Italy, any of the local *consorzi* may, if they wish, check up on the control of their wines and help to safeguard the regulations. Before the introduction of the Denomination of Origin laws, the only wine which carried any guarantee of quality was that wearing the seal of a local wine society, or *consorzio*. The system is voluntary. Some regions have a *consorzio*, others do not; and where one exists, some firms and growers may be members, others may not. Both members and non-members, unfortunately, had equal right to the local appellation, although members alone could receive the *consorzio* seal. One consequence of this vague arrangement (in the years before the regulations of 1963) was the predicament of Chianti. Some of the wine came from Tuscany and bore some resemblance to the real thing. Much more was concocted from Chianti or other Tuscan wine, stretched and blended with inferior growths from elsewhere. It is hoped that the Denominazioni de Origine laws will succeed in protecting these fine wines and controlling the sales.

As for the *consorzi*, the standards for each are drawn up by its members and are thus subject to wide variation. Sometimes they are so high that their wines will always be excellent; sometimes they settle for a fairly low average. They generally dictate the permitted grape varieties, the limits of the district, the minimum alcoholic content, and whether or not wines may be imported from outside the area. A universal rule is that all wine must be tasted by a select committee and approved before the seal is given—and affixed in such a way that the bottle cannot be opened without the seal's being broken. Each *consorzio* has its own apparatus for enforcing rules, and in cases of gross or repeated violation the penalty may be expulsion. A degree of collaboration between the *consorzi* and the Institute for the Protection of Denomination of Origin could result in a great improvement in the overall standard of Italian wines.

WINE REGIONS

The Italian peninsula is characterized by its ever-changing landscape. The Alps give way to the Apennines, and plains and mountains alternate all the way down to the rugged hills of the "arch" and "toe" of the Italian "boot." In general the finest wines are made in the north, but the south has several that are entrancing, particularly when drunk on the spot. The Italians have divided their nation into regions, or administrative sub-sections, and it is convenient to discuss the wines under these categories. The regions and their wines (*see the principal districts also under separate headings*) include:

Abruzzi

This region on the Adriatic seaboard gives way to central Italy. It produces some unpretentious and often pleasant wines. Red Montepulciano di Abruzzo and Cerasuolo di Abruzzo, and white Trebbiano di Abruzzo are all names for the dominant contributing grape variety; all are agreeable at home but would almost certainly lose some of this charm were they to be shipped.

Apulia (Puglia)

The great southern bulk-producing plain of Italy. The output is generally used for making vermouth, for blending, or for ordinary wines.

Basilicata (Lucania)

This southern region, once known as Lucania, is a jumble of forbidding mountains and inaccessible valleys. Some wine is made. The best-known is Aglianico del Vulture; the first part of the name is that of the vine, the second of the mountain on which it is cultivated. Fairly large amounts of Muscat and Malvasia vines are also grown.

Calabria

The extreme southern tip of Italy. Sweet white Greco di Gerace (from grapes of the same name) and deep red Cirò di Calabria (mainly from Gaglioppo grapes grown in Cirò) are the best-known wines; lovers of Muscats may also find the region to their liking.

Campania

The most popular wines in this region around Naples are the red and dry white Falerno, red Vesuvio (mainly from the Aglianico grape and grown on the volcanic foothills of Mount Vesuvius), and the red and white Ravello grown near the charming village of that name on the Amalfi coast. Also from this region comes Lacrima Christi, generally a soft and fairly dry white wine, though a little red is also produced. Close to Amalfi is made the red Gragnano, which is so delicious to drink on a flower-laden terrace over the Bay of Naples; and from the islands of Capri and Ischia come the gay light wines known by those names.

Emilia-Romagna

A vast agricultural area in central Italy, not outstanding for wines. Red, usually slightly sweet and sparkling, Lambrusco is often recommended to newcomers, and Albana accommodates those who like their wines white and not too dry. Large amounts of Sangiovese (red) and Trebbiano are also made on the hills of Romagna.

Latium (Lazio)

The wines of the Castelli Romani (Castles of Rome), among the country's best, are generally dry and white and are almost invariably captivating on their native ground—the best-known is Frascati. Many withstand the rigors of ocean travel. Est! Est!! Est!!! from Montefiascone is the white, dry, and semi-sweet wine with the best wine legend of Italy.

Liguria

The Italian extension of the French Riviera is not famous for wine. Dry and slightly sweet white Cinqueterre is about the best known, although there are others, such as Dolceacqua (red).

Lombardy

The Valtellina reds—Sassella, Grumello, Valgella, Fracia, and Inferno—are highly prized; and the wines from the banks of Lake Garda are often delightful; they come in all three colors, but the rosés are probably the best, especially the Chiaretto.

The Marches

No wines of great distinction are made in this area between the Apennines and the Adriatic. The principal red wine is Rosso Piceno; and Verdicchio dei Castelli di Jesi is white, usually well made, often found abroad.

Piedmont

The home of Italy's two finest red wines, Barolo and Barbaresco, and also of the sweet sparkling Asti Spumanti. Other good still wines are Freisa, Barbera, Gattinara, Gignolino d'Asti, Nebbiolo d'Alba, Dolcetto, and Ghemme. The city of Turin is also the center of the manufacturing of Vermouth, from Moscato and herbal extracts.

Sardinia

The wines from this beautiful rugged island, whether drunk on the Aga Khan's Costa Smeralda or on the mainland, are very pleasant, dry whites; less attractive reds. These table wines are a welcome change from the fortified sweet wines which were the island's traditional wines.

Sicily

One was inclined to associate Sicily with sweet fortified wines. Today, modern oenology and cooperative winemaking have transformed Sicilian wine production, and many good, popular table wines are being produced instead of Marsala, which was the island's most famous wine. Indeed, Sicily is now in the enviable position of accounting for 25% of Italian wine exports. Notable wines are white Marmertino, red Faro, the red and white wines of Etna, and especially the dry whites and full reds of Corvo. Sicilian Marsala can be fine although it has become difficult to find.

Trentino-Alto Adige

Although politically bound, the regions of Trentino and Alto Adige (South Tyrol) are quite distinct in culture and language. Red wines from the area, including Cabernet, Merlot, Pinot Noir, and Santa Magdalener, go largely to Germany and Austria. White wines, including Riesling, Traminer, Pinot Grigio, and Pinot Bianco, are enjoyed both at home and abroad. Cooperative winemaking has resulted in generally high quality.

Tuscany

The best—and most famous—wine is Chianti. There are a number of different Chiantis, but the growers of the Chianti Classico district maintain that only they have a real right to the appellation. Under different names, some of the others would be wonderful wines, but they are not always true Chiantis. Some claim that the best wine is Brunello di Montalcino, a powerful wine which ages for half a century.

Umbria

This section north of Rome is the home of Orvieto. Traditionally sweet, this beguiling wine is now being made dry as well, and conservative drinkers are not wholeheartedly in favor of the trend. The dry is becoming the rule rather than the exception.

Umbria also produces the less known Torgiano wines. The red is rich and full and made much like Chianti. The white, made mostly from Trebbiano, is sharp and strong.

Valle d'Aosta

Usually considered part of the Piedmont, the French-speaking Valle d'Aosta produces two quality wines, called Donnaz and Enfer d'Arvier. Both are red, the former from Nebbiolo, the latter from Petit Rouge.

Veneto

The wines of the Verona district are the best of this region and include dry red Valpolicella, Valpantena, and Bardolino, and dry white Soave.

Friuli-Venezia Giulia, Valle d'Aosta, and Molise

The three remaining regions of Italy are not very important as far as wine production is concerned.

Ives

Native American variety of grapes, hardy and vigorous but inconsistent. The red coarse-skinned grape yields a strong "foxy" red wine.

Izarra

A Basque attempt to reproduce Chartreuse, made in Bayonne in southwest France. Like its more famous prototype, it is fabricated in two styles, yellow and green, of which the green is the more highly alcoholic.

J

James

American Muscadine grape sometimes used in the south for making a strongly flavored, not very agreeable wine.

Japan

From Kyushu in the south to northernmost Hokkaido, the Japanese islands count some 30,000 hectares (75,000 acres) of vines producing both table and wine grapes. Production of all wines made from grapes is over 270,000 hectoliters (7.14 million U.S. gallons, 5.94 million imp.) per year, yet for every Japanese who picks up a glass of wine, one hundred reach for saké or beer. Consumption of saké (fermented from rice), beer, and other local grain beverages has reached such enormous proportions that the public has been warned consumption must be reduced to conserve the dwindling grain supply. Wine is being represented as a possible alternative, but alcoholic beverages imported into the country have become very popular among the well-to-do.

The wine-growing regions of Japan are the Yamanashi and Osaka districts, and to a lesser extent those of Yamagata, Okayama, and Nagano—equally large but yielding still more mediocre wines. All are on the principal island of Honshu, and their acreage accounts for more than half of the lands planted in vines. The combination of high humidity and acid soil makes grape-growing difficult, and the vines selected must be early ripeners to mature before the torrential September rains destroy the labor of an entire growing season. Vines are planted in rows about 5 meters apart with about 2,500 to the hectare (150 feet); they grow on trellises or among vegetables.

Japan is one of the few countries in the world where the three families of vine—European, American, and Asian—are able to flourish. Yet in Japanese soil none produces fruit for making truly good wine. Varieties of the American *Vitis labrusca* and some of the hybrid vines are about the only ones which yield adequate and occasionally agreeable wines. Delaware and Campbell's Early are more widespread than any other vines, covering more than half of all the vineyards. European Sémillon, Chardonnay, and Riesling are used increasingly for white wines, and Cabernet Sauvignon, along with Merlot, accounts for 75% of the red wines produced. But in general, *Vitis vinifera* vines are particularly susceptible to such fungus diseases as mildew and oïdium, both of which run rampant in the humid climate of Japan.

Although the history of the Japanese vine goes back to the twelfth century, and vines have always been used as decoration and grapes for medicinal purposes, the story of Japanese wine is as recent as the nineteenth century, which saw the influx of Europeans and Americans. The agriculturally inquisitive Japanese, who had been recording their success with the Konshu *vinifera* variety since 1186, responded quickly to the new idea and sent people to France and to California to study the wine industry. The twentieth century has seen this industry grow and prosper in Japan, but it has yet to come into its own. The phenomenal growth of nearly every other sector of the Japanese economy since the Second World War has not been achieved in the wine industry.

Too many of the vineyards are small, hindered by inexperienced personnel and poor handling. Harvesting is all done by hand and no modern methods of frost control are in use. There are many cooperatives, but these are generally no better equipped or managed than the vineyards of individual producers. Four giant companies—Sunraku Ocean, Mans Wine, Godo Shusei, and Suntory—control over 80% of the entire market. Most of these firms have plantations in the best wine district, the Kofu Valley in the Yamanashi prefecture 120 kilometers (75 miles) west of Tokyo. There the humidity and rainfall are less than in most other areas, and the warm days and cool nights help to produce better-than-average grapes. The very best wines made in the valley come from Cabernet Sauvignon, Merlot, and Sémillon, with a few pleasant ones made of the native Konshu variety. Many of these wines resemble those from the Hunter River Valley of Australia, where the temperatures, rainfall, and gravelly soil are not unlike those of the Kofu region. The best wines are light and dry; they are nearly all consumed in Kofu, so few are available in the tourist centers of Tokyo and Kyoto, and hardly any are exported.

Japan imports annually about 195,000 hectoliters (5.1 million U.S. gallons, 4.2 million imp.) of wine. The Japanese have recently taken a greater interest in importing good wine in addition to other aspects of Western culture. Optimists look to Japan as a vast new market for the future.

A commentary on the quality of at least one Japanese wine has been given by a Japanese scientist writing on Japanese "port." According to Isama Yokosuka in the *American Journal of Oenology:* "Natural production of Port wine by fermentation is not performed. Instead Port wine is made by blending 1–15% wine with ethyl alcohol, tap water, dye, perfume, sugar, and organic acids, and the resulting product is of unduly poor quality."

Japanese beetle

A parasite which attacks American vines.
See Chapter Eight, p. 29.

Jasnières

Loire Valley white wines.
District: Anjou, France.

A tiny Loire vineyard district in the Coteaux du Loir,

north of the main stream. The wines are white and *moelleux,* or semi-sweet, and come from Chenin Blanc grapes grown in predominantly chalky soil. The vineyards are in the twin parishes of Lhomme and Ruillé-sur-Loir, and their output is not high.

Jenever

The name used in Holland for Dutch gin, which in English-speaking countries is usually called Hollands. Jenever is a combination of the French and Dutch words for juniper, on which the gin taste is based, and has no connection with the Swiss city.

Jerez de la Frontera

Andalusian town which is the center of the Sherry trade.
See Sherry.

Jeriñac

A registered name (also occasionally spelled Xereñac and Cherinac) for the brandy of Jerez de la Frontera, Spain. A little-used and unsuccessful substitute for the improper designation Coñac for Spanish brandy (because Cognac, however spelled, may correctly only be the brandy of Cognac in France).
See Spain.

Jeroboam

An outsized bottle, the capacity of which is open to variation. In Champagne it holds the equivalent of four bottles, in Bordeaux five. In England it is normally (but not necessarily) six.

Jeropiga

See Geropiga.

Jigger

American term for shot-glass, or small measure of spirits. It equals 1.5 fluid ounces.

Johannisberg

(1) Great Growth of the Rheingau. The best-known of these wines is Schloss Johannisberger.
See Rheingau.
(2) Swiss wine from the Sylvaner grape which probably owes its renown to the fact that it shares the name of the great German Johannisberger.
See Switzerland.

Johannisberg Riesling

The name used in California for the true Riesling grape.

Johanniswein

From as early as *Minnesinger* records of the thirteenth century, St. John—who sat next to Christ at the Last Supper, and to whom legend ascribes the drinking of a goblet of poisoned wine without harm, after he had made the sign of the Cross over it—has been connected in a special way with the blessing of wine in Germany. In Deidesheim, on St. John's day, December 27, the folk of the community take an especially fine bottle from their vineyards to Mass for blessing. This St. John's Wine, as it is called, is considered not only to benefit health and fertility but to bring peace as well, and it is often drunk as a loving-cup. Johanniswein is also much in demand as a wedding drink, and in many parts of Germany farewell drinks of "one for the road" are often served of St. John's Wine. It is known that Martin Luther himself served these.

Jordan

Although in the distant past vineyards flourished in this part of the world and wine was regarded as a good familiar thing, some 18,000 hectares (45,000 acres) of land now planted in vine are devoted almost entirely to table grapes.

The inhabitants of Jordan are not wine-drinking people; here, as elsewhere in the area, more arrack is made than wine.

Josephshof

Throughout the world (except in Germany, where Himmelreich is more famous) this is the best-known vineyard of the Graach district of the German Mosel. Inclined, like the other Graach wines, to be long-lasting and mouth-filling, for a Mosel, this is almost the only one known by the vineyard name alone. It is called simply Josephshof; the township name of Graach does not appear.
See Mosel-Saar-Ruwer.

Journal

An old Burgundian measure of area, about one-third of a hectare or five-sixths of an acre.

Julep

A long cold drink made with spirits, sugar, mint, and crushed ice.

Juliénas

Widely known wines of the French Beaujolais. They tend to be obvious and seldom come quite up to the reputation of the other more famous villages, Fleurie, Brouilly, or the wine of Moulin-à-Vent.
See Beaujolais.

Jura

Red, white, and rosé wines.
District: Jura Mountains, France.

From the slopes of the Jura Mountains, lying midway between the Côte d'Or of Burgundy and the Swiss border to the east, come a number of wines which make up in variety what they lack in quantity. Still and sparkling wines, red, white, and rosé wines, *vins de paille* or "straw wines," and the curious *vins jaunes,* or yellow wines, are all made under the inclusive *appellation* Côtes-du-Jura or Côtes-du-Jura Mousseux. Arbois, Château-Chalon, and L'Étoile are more specific: L'Étoile wines may only be white or *jaune;* the best white wines of the region are made at Arbois.

A landscape of sunny plains and steep cliffs, the Jura region has a wide variety of soil. Ranging from the almost pure clay of the lowlands, through the pebbly marl which has eroded the base of the cliffs, to the limestone-rich silt at the top, these slopes were once producers of wine in great quantity. The advent of phylloxera caused the vineyards to shrink drastically, and they have never been reconstituted. From about 18,400 hectares (46,000 acres) planted in 1836, the figure has dropped so far that today there are less than 1,000 hectares (2,500 acres) devoted to fine vines in the whole Jura area.

Perhaps the most characteristic wine of the Jura is the *vin jaune.* Coming exclusively from the grape variety known as the Savagnin, thought to be the Alsatian Traminer, this wine is one of the longest-lived—drinkable bottles aged fifty years or more are by no means rare. To obtain *vin jaune,* the grapes are harvested late and pressed in the same manner as for white wine. The juice is then sealed up in barrels and remains there for a length of time which varies from six to ten years—six years is the legal minimum. Shortly after the wine is put into the barrels, a film forms on the top, effectively sealing it off from the air. This film, which is made up of microorganisms, lives on oxygen from the air and contributes the peculiar yellow color and nutty fragrance that mark *vin jaune.* The film, or "flower," is the same as is found in the making of Sherry, where it is called *flor.* It is related to a disease of wine caused by the vinegar microbe, which combines oxygen and alcohol to make vinegar. The difference is that the vinegar microbe spoils the wine completely, whereas the microbe which appears on the wine of the Jura changes it slightly, with beneficial effect, and remains the same white color as long as it is allowed to stand.

Another type of wine made in the Jura is the *vin de paille.* It derives its name from the time-honored process of allowing the grapes to dry out on beds of straw before pressing, as well as from the straw color of the wine. Actually, *vin de paille* is usually made today by hanging the grapes up in well-ventilated rooms. The long drying process, which by law must be at least two months, provides a wine of richness and longevity. Because of the difficulties of making this wine, and particularly because of the high price at which it has to be sold, the growers of the Jura are turning away from it, and there is some reason to fear that *vin de paille* may disappear from the area.

Very few of the wines of the Côtes-du-Jura are exported or shipped. Some is sold to Alsace and Switzerland, both in the vicinity of the Jura, but for the most part it is drunk in the area where it is made. One reason for this is that the wine is much appreciated by those who make it; and another is that, distinctive and unusual though they may be, the wines of the Jura are generally considered among *vins de pays,* excellent when drunk on native ground, but unable to stand comparison with the great wines of France. The wine of lesser quality, sold under the inclusive *appellation* Côtes-du-Jura, accounts for less than 7,500 hectoliters (198,750 U.S. gallons, 165,000 imp.) a year, and the balance is sold under the more exclusive names Arbois, Château-Chalon, and L'Étoile.

Arbois

Perhaps the best-known of the wines of the Jura. Made in thirteen towns in the lower foothills of the Jura Mountains, centering around the charming town of Arbois, it includes all the types described above.

The Savagnin grape variety, in addition to making *vin jaune,* also goes into the white wine to augment the Melon d'Arbois (as the Chardonnay variety is called in that area) and the Pinot Blanc *vrai.* The Poulsard, the Trousseau, and the Gros Noiren (the Pinot Noir of Burgundy) are the varieties that go into the red and rosé wines. Some of the white wines can be extremely pleasant. The red wines are not considered distinctive, but many Frenchmen, particularly around the Arbois area, maintain that the Rosé d'Arbois is on a par with Tavel. Expert opinion, however, ranks it lower than this famous rosé wine of the Rhône.

The town of Arbois, besides being famous for its wines, is also known as the birthplace of Louis Pasteur, and as the place where he performed his famous experiments on wine. These experiments were made when the growers became concerned about the way their wines were spoiling on ocean voyages. The work had worldwide repercussions.

Château-Chalon

To the south and slightly to the west of the Arbois area is the small town of Château-Chalon, which gives its name to the wine grown there and in three adjoining towns. Under the Appellation d'Origine laws, only *vin jaune* is allowed to be sold under the name. This wine remains in the barrel for as long as six years; an excessive period for a white wine. At the end of this period the wine must—by law—be bottled. Less than 1,000 hectoliters (26,000 U.S. gallons, 20,000 imp.) is made each year.

The name is derived from an old castle which overlooks that area but which has nothing to do with the vineyards. (Note, therefore, that this is *not* a château wine.) Always bottled in wide, rather square bottles called *clavelins,* the only wine allowed to be put into such bottles, the *vin jaune* of Château-Chalon is considered to be the best example of this unique wine.

L'Étoile

Some of the best white wines of the Jura come from the

southernmost area, that of L'Étoile, which comprises a small region of three communes. With an average production of less than 1,000 hectoliters (26,500 U.S. gallons, 22,000 imp.), L'Étoile produces within its small area all the white wine types allowed in the Jura—white, yellow, *vin de paille,* and sparkling wines.

Jurançon

White wine.
District: Southwest France.

The vines are grown on the extremely steep hillsides in the foothills of the French Pyrenees—hillsides which are, for the most part, too steep to be cultivated by anything except the hand of man, although in some places animal and tractor power may be used. A limited amount of wine is grown along these slopes and among the foothills, the best toward the Atlantic—in the Jurançon region, near the city of Pau. The deep golden-white wines are usually sweet and have a flowery perfume uniquely their own. Only white wines are made.

At one time the vineyards of Jurançon were vast and important, but since the scourge of the phylloxera, they have never reached their former productiveness. Some of the local growers are said to have shown a strong prejudice against grafting their vines onto American rootstocks—the only effective way of restoring the vineyards.

The spring frosts have a deadly effect upon the young shoots—and to combat this the vines are grown very tall. Stakes with cross-arms, making them look like fields of crosses—the unusual aspect of the region—support the vines, which are anywhere from 4 to 6 feet high. The productive parts of the vines are those trained on wires running from 3 to 4 feet from the ground, along which the vine shoots are trailed after the danger of frosts has passed.

The noble vines of the Jurançon area are the Gros Manseng, Petit Manseng, and Courbu, all of them old and all peculiar to the region. The wine made must be 85% from these vines and no more than 15% from the Carmaralet and Lauzet, the permissible secondary varieties. The vines are trimmed to carry from one to four long shoots, cut to yield from nine to fifteen cluster-producing buds or eyes. Short pruning (leaving only two or three eyes) is forbidden, and if a vine overproduces at the expense of its growth, it is regulated by leaving less shoots the next year. The fourth year after planting, the vines can produce grapes which may be included in the making of Jurançon wine. The maximum legal yield is 40 hectoliters per hectare (428 U.S. gallons, 356 imp. per acre).

The harvest in the Jurançon region is an extremely late one, the growers usually waiting for the *pourriture noble,* or noble rot, to form on their overripe grapes—this dries the liquid from them and leaves only a small amount of honey syrup. Sometimes the grapes are left on the vines until after Halloween. The rich, sweet wine is kept for four years in the barrel before it is bottled—and would probably be much better if it were bottled younger. Rather poor dry wine is produced—which has given this district a bad name. Less than 2,000 hectoliters is made each year—and much of it is consumed in the region of the Pyrenees, although the wine can be bought in Paris and elsewhere. About 15,000 hectoliters (400,000 U.S. gallons, 330,000 imp.) of the sweet wine is made annually.

K

Kabinettwein

German term for Cabinet wine, or a special reserve, denoting wines from the better selected barrels. This is more than just a term and can be considered a reliable line of quality demarcation, based mainly on price.
See Germany.

Kadarka

The leading red variety of grape in Hungary, known also in Rumania as Codarcă.

Kaefferkopf

Important vineyard in Ammerschwihr, Alsace.
See Alsace.

Kafir, kefir

A Caucasian alcoholic beverage made from fermented cows' milk (*see* Koumiss). Kefir grain is added.

Kaiserstuhl

Best vineyard area in German Baden (*q.v.*).

Kallstadt

Wine town in the district of Bad Dürkheim.
See Palatinate.

Kamptal, Kamp Valley

Wine region of the River Kamp in Lower Austria. Some of the best slopes for vineyards are those of the Heiligenstein and the Gnisberg.
See Austria.

Kanyak

Turkish brandy whose name, to the suspicious, seems remarkably close to Cognac.

Karthäuserhofberg

Outstanding vineyard in the German town of Eitelsbach.
See Mosel-Saar-Ruwer.

Kasel

Most important village of German Ruwer wines. The best vineyard is Kaseler Nies'chen.
See Mosel-Saar-Ruwer.

Kava, ava-ava

A native wine of the South Sea Islands prepared from the root of the Polynesian kava shrub.

"The liquor which they make from the plant called the ava-ava is expressed from the root. The manner of preparing this liquor is as simple as it is disgusting to a European. It is thus: several people take some of the root, and chew it until it is soft and pulpy: then they spit it out into a platter or other vessel, every one into the same: when a sufficient quantity is chewed more or less, water is put to it according as it is to be strong or weak: the juice thus diluted is strained through some fibrous stuff like fine shavings: after which it is fit for drinking, and this is always done immediately. It has a pepperish taste, drinks flat, and rather insipid."—Captain Cook 1774, at Tahiti.

Nowadays kava is usually made in a screw-type press.

Kaysersberg

Wine town in Alsace (*q.v.*).

Keg

Small wood or metal cask usually of less than 12 U.S. gallons (10 imp.) capacity.

Kéknyelü

A white wine, best-known of the Badacsony growths in Hungary (*q.v.*).

Kellerabfüllung, Kellerabzug

German term for bottled at the estate where the wine was grown. Literally, "bottled in the cellar."

Kintyre

A peninsula on the west coast of Scotland which, with the island of Islay, produces all West Highland malt whisky. Well into the eighteenth century, Kintyre was still considered a main island of the Inner Hebrides.
See Whisky, malt.

Kir

A popular aperitif usually made with a light white Burgundy wine and a bit of Cassis. The drink is named for the leader of French resistance in Lyon and former mayor of Dijon, Canon Félix Kir.

Kirsch, Kirschwasser

Brandy distilled from cherries complete with stones. After distillation, it is matured in paraffin-lined casks or earthenware, to prevent it taking on the color that wood would impart; true kirsch is always pure white.

Kirsch is made notably in Alsace, Germany, and Switzerland; the German kirsch often goes under the name Schwarzwalder. Much Swiss kirsch is made in the vicinity of Basle and carries the name Basler Kirschwasser.

Château Kirwan

Bordeaux red wine.
District: Haut-Médoc, France.
Commune: Cantenac-Margaux.

The vineyard lies on slightly rolling land behind Cantenac, one of the first important villages encountered on the Médoc wine road. Kirwan is between Château Brane-Cantenac, a Second Growth (*Second Cru*) vineyard, and Château Prieuré-Lichine, a Fourth Growth (*Quatrième Cru*).

Since 1956, all Cantenac vineyards have had the right to the place-name Margaux, the famous wine town a mile away which produces a very similar wine.

Kirwan was rated a Third Growth (*Troisième Cru*) in the Classification of 1855. It was then owned by a M. Godard, Mayor of Bordeaux, who left it to the city of Bordeaux upon his death. The city sold it to Daniel and Georges Guestier. Daniel's daughter married Alfred Schyler, and in 1924 his firm, Schröder & Schyler, purchased the property and has owned it ever since.

In the 1950s and early 1960s the wine was not château-bottled. A few years ago the vineyard was in very poor condition and production dropped significantly. Schyler, the present head of Schröder & Schyler, owns the handsome château and has gone into partnership with M. Jean-Marie Moueix, cousin of Jean-Pierre Moueix, the Saint-Émilion grower and shipper. They did an exemplary feat of revitalizing the vineyard with earthmovers in 1972 and planting in 1973. Such expense would have been unthinkable had not the Classified Growths reached prices in 1970, which justified the tremendous cost.

Characteristics. Fruity and distinguished, Kirwan is one of the most elegant, feminine wines of Margaux. It has become much more reliable since château-bottling began in 1967.

Vineyard area: 23 hectares (58 acres).
Average production: 100 *tonneaux* (9,000 cases).

Kislav

A Russian spirit made from watermelons.

Kloster Eberbach

Once a Cistercian monastery, now owned by the state. The vineyard, near Hattenheim, produces the fine Steinberg wine.
See Rheingau.

Knipperlé

A white-wine grape used in Alsace. Among other local names for it are Kipperlé, Kleinergelber, and Kleiner Rauschling.

Königsbacher

One of the outstanding wines in the Mittelhaardt region of the Palatinate.
See Palatinate.

Konsumwein

German term for ordinary wine.

Kontuszowka

A Polish liqueur with the flavor of oil of lavender.

Kornbranntwein

A liquor made in Germany and Holland from fermented cereal grains. Since rye is the usual ingredient, it is almost a continental equivalent of rye whiskey.

Kornschnapps

A European liquor made of fermented corn.

Kosher wine

In its strictest sense, wine made according to Rabbinical law for use during Jewish religious services. The term also covers what is essentially Passover wine, which was for some time, by a considerable margin, the largest-selling wine in the United States.

Jewish ritual calls for wine at the Friday evening service, on the eve of a festival, on Holy Days, and during the Passover season. The wine must be pure, natural, unmixed, and sound, and must be made according to rigid standards of purity under the supervision of a rabbi, but otherwise it is not different from wine for domestic consumption. Kosher wine can serve both purposes. Passover wine—once homemade for the most part—differs in that it is thicker and sweeter than is usual, and it has become synonymous with Kosher wine in most of America.

It comes almost entirely from Concord grapes grown in the vineyards of New York State—where Concord used to command such a good price that it pushed out finer grape varieties.

American Kosher wine centers are New York City and Chicago, neither of which is noted for vines. As a general rule, grapes grown in upper New York are bought by fruit-packers who freeze them and ship them as needed to the wineries, where they are thawed, allowed to ferment, dosed with cane sugar (partly to increase sweetness, partly to counteract the otherwise unpleasantly high acidity of the Concord grape), and doctored with sulfur to prevent fermentation after bottling. Wine-making is thus a year-round occupation, no longer dependent upon such old-fashioned matters as time of harvest.

Koumiss, kumiss

A Siberian or Caucasian beverage of fermented mare's, cow's, or sometimes camel's milk.

Krajina

Yugoslav wines, mainly red but some white, grown on the borders of Rumania and Bulgaria. Krajina means "borderland."
See Yugoslavia.

Krampen

A section of wineland around Cochem on the lower River Mosel in Germany, so called because of the sharp bend or cramp taken by the Mosel to accommodate itself to the increasing hardness of the slate cliffs. The wines are not among the best of the Mosel because the soil is too hard.
See Mosel-Saar-Ruwer.

Kreszenz

One of the German words indicating the grower of a wine. Kreszenz Hans Muller on a label would mean wine from the vineyard, or parcel, of Hans Muller. This is important in Germany, where each barrel may be harvested individually and most vineyards have many owners, often handling their wines differently and getting widely different results.

Kriska

West African palm wine.

Kümmel

Both Germany and Holland claim to have invented the liqueur, but Russia, Poland, and the Baltic countries have always been among its staunchest admirers. It is distilled from grain alcohol and is flavored with caraway seeds; it is sweet and pure-white. Sugar is sometimes allowed to crystallize in the bottle, in which case it is known as Kümmel Crystallize. One of the most famous types of kümmel is Allasch Kümmel, made in Allasch near Riga, now in the U.S.S.R.
See Liqueurs.

Kvass

A refreshing Russian beer home-brewed from rye, barley, and malt and flavored with mint or cranberries.

L

La Brède (Château de la Brède)

See Château de la Brède.

Château La Conseillante

Bordeaux red wine.
District and Commune: Pomerol, France.

The vineyards of this top Pomerol château are separated from those of Château Cheval-Blanc in Saint-Émilion by only the width of a cart-path. Owned by the Nicolas family since 1871, the vineyard was destroyed in the 1956 frost but is regaining the high reputation of its past.

Vineyard area: 12 hectares (30 acres).
Average production: 40 *tonneaux* (3,500 cases).

Château La Gaffelière

Bordeaux red wine.
District and Commune: Saint-Émilion, France.

Considered by some experts to have reached second place among Saint-Émilions in recent vintages, led only by Château Cheval-Blanc, the property is beautifully situated on the sharply curving short road which cuts from the main Bordeaux-Bergerac road up to the hillcrest town of Saint-Émilion. It is the property of Comte Malet-Roquefort, and was classed a First Great Growth (*Premier Grand Cru*) in 1955. The name has been shortened since 1963 by dropping Naudes and calling it simply Château La Gaffelière.

Characteristics. Good wines, yet variable. In good years, among the very best of Saint-Émilions.

Vineyard area: 20 hectares (50 acres).
Average production: 110 *tonneaux* (10,000 cases).

Château La Lagune

Bordeaux red wine.
District: Haut-Médoc, France.
Commune: Ludon.

(*Ludon is not a place-name and the wine has the place-name of Haut-Médoc.*)

A Third Growth (*Troisième Cru*) as classified in 1855, La Lagune is the first of the classified vineyards reached on the wine road of the Médoc going north from Bordeaux. The wines were both great and famous at the turn of the century. At that time, in order to distinguish the vineyard from others known as La Lagune, the name was changed to Grand-La-Lagune, but in the late sixties, the name reverted to La Lagune. The quality of the wine fell from its former high standard in the thirties and forties; when the severe 1956 frosts cut production to only 15 *tonneaux*, considerable replanting was necessary. The vineyard was until recently the property of the Société Civile Agricole du Château Grand-La-Lagune. After the 1956 frost they embarked on the boldest planting program in the Médoc:

a scheme which called for enlarging and improving the vineyard, modernizing the wine-making installations, and restoring the château to what it was when built during the reigns of Louis XIII and Louis XIV. It is now owned by the heirs of M. Chayoux of Champagne fame.

Characteristics. A wine of great quality, as a result of the efforts now being made, it has regained and surpassed its former high position. The wine is full, with a depth of flavor, and has much of the breed found in Margaux to the north and some of the character associated with Graves to the south.

Vineyard area: 60 hectares (150 acres).
Average production: 220 *tonneaux* (20,000 cases).

Château La Magdelaine

Bordeaux red wine.
District and Commune: Saint-Émilion, France.

Particularly well known in England and Belgium, the wine was classified as a First Growth (*Premier Cru*) of Saint-Émilion in 1955. The vineyard lies alongside those of Ausone and Bel-Air on the heights of Saint-Émilion village. The vineyard is owned by Jean-Pierre Moueix.

Characteristics. The well-tended vineyards produce a pleasant wine which is full and velvety with distinctive aftertaste.

Vineyard area: 11 hectares (27 acres).
Average production: 40 *tonneaux* (3,500 cases).

Château La Mission-Haut-Brion

Bordeaux red wine.
District: Graves, France.
Commune: Pessac.

The château, placed behind symmetrical vines and directly across the main road from Haut-Brion, is less than a mile out of Bordeaux on the road to the seaside resort of Arcachon. The red-wine vines surround the château and border the tracks of the Bordeaux-to-Spain railway, running in a cutting a hundred paces from the *chais*. The red wine was classified in 1953 and in 1959 among the eleven best in Graves.

The vineyard was founded in the seventeenth century by the priests of the Mission of Saint Vincent de Paul. A gem of monastic art remains to commemorate the founders, a tiny peaked chapel, on the inner roof of which the years of the great vintages used to be lettered in gold—until the gold was given to the government during the war.

When the grapes are brought in, they are pitched into a sixteenth-century wooden trough; but the wines ferment in immaculate modern glass-lined vats which give the *chai* something of the look of a prosperous confectioner's kitchen. The Woltner family, the owners, sell wines at a high price—often justified since the vineyard produces some remarkable bottles. They are also the owners of Château La Tour-Haut-Brion and Château Laville-Haut-Brion, which produce a good red and a fine white wine respectively.

Characteristics. A superb red wine. Many knowledgeable brokers classify the wine as having the same character as Château Haut-Brion across the road. It achieves full big roundness with considerable breed.

Vineyard area: 18.5 hectares (46 acres).

Average production: 70 *tonneaux* (6,000 cases).

Château La Pointe

Bordeaux red wine.

District and Commune: Pomerol, France.

Owned by M. d'Arfeuille, wine merchant of Libourne, this flavorful wine is, as is the estate, one of the biggest in Pomerol.

Vineyard area: 20 hectares (50 acres).

Average production: 80 *tonneaux* (7,500 cases).

La Rioja

Wine-producing province of Argentina (*q.v.*).

La Romanée

Burgundy red wine.

District: Côte de Nuits, France.

Commune: Vosne-Romanée.

Official Classification: Great Growth (Grand Cru).

La Romanée is the smallest (less than a hectare or about 2.1 acres) of the great vineyards of Vosne. It stands directly above La Romanée-Conti, from which it is divided by a footpath, and despite their proximity and the similarity between the names and the wines, the two are separate and distinct.

It is generally conceded in Vosne that the wines which come from this plot often lack some of the elegance and finesse of those from La Romanée-Conti; but the two are difficult to tell apart, even by the most expert tasters. La Romanée is perhaps the more robust of the two, gaining in fullness and body what it cedes in finesse.

The vineyard is now owned by the Domaine de la Romanée-Conti and annually makes but 30 hectoliters (795 U.S. gallons, 660 imp.) of wine, or the equivalent of a mere 350 cases. But as the sale and distribution of the wine are now entrusted to a shipper, the wine is never estate bottled, and this is regrettable.

See Vosne-Romanée.

La Romanée-Conti

Burgundy red wine.

District: Côte de Nuits, France.

Commune: Vosne-Romanée.

Official Classification: Great Growth (Grand Cru).

The vineyard of the Romanée-Conti, one of the most famous in the world, is contained in a scant four and a half acres. The fabulous prices paid for the wine that

trickles out are as high as any and the wine-drinker who manages to get a bottle considers himself lucky indeed. If the wine has become over-priced it is largely the fault of the wine snobs who order it to impress and so send up prices.

Contrary to usual Burgundian practice, *all* wine from the Romanée-Conti is estate bottled, and every bottle carries on label and cork the seal of the Société Civile de La Romanée-Conti, owners of this vineyard and the renowned La Tâche, as well as of parts of others. The property has been in the same family since 1869, when it was bought by Monsieur Duvaut-Blochet, and that was only the ninth time it had changed hands since the thirteenth century. The vineyard has been passed down within the family and is owned today by Monsieur de Villaine, a bank manager in Moulins. Among previous owners have been the Government of France, which seized the vineyard during the French Revolution; and the Prince de Conti, from whom it was seized. The Prince acquired it in 1760, in spite of the protests of Madame de Pompadour who wanted it for herself.

Because the wine is estate bottled, the only significant collection of older vintages of Romanée-Conti is at the Domaine, and a visit to its cellars is a mouth-watering experience. These cellars are primitive and modest, but stacked with bottles the contents of which have been described by P. Morton Shand as "a mingling of velvet and satin."

Actually, the wines fall into two distinct categories: the pre-1945 vintages, and those thereafter. Until that year the owners of the vineyard kept it planted in French vines, rather than graft their French plants on to American root-stocks as did the other growers when phylloxera first hit France. The vines had been allowed to reproduce by *provignage*—burying the old vine in the ground with only one shoot emerging to become a new one—and thus were direct descendants of the vines planted by the monks more than twelve centuries earlier. But phylloxera, the devastating vine louse, is a constant menace and the vines had to be treated with enormous care and expensive chemicals. The latter were, of course, non-existent during the war years, manpower was desperately short, and the vines deteriorated until they were giving a meager fifty cases a year. In 1945 the owners gave up the old ways and tore up their vineyards, replanting with vines grafted on to phylloxera-resistant American root-stocks.

The result is that the quantity of Romanée-Conti has risen sharply since 1945, but the quality is at present below that of the nectar once made.

At their best, the wines of the Romanée-Conti have perfect, rich balance combined with extraordinary breed and finesse, and local experts maintain they are the most "virile" of the wines of Vosne—meaning, perhaps, that there is an iron hand beneath the velvet glove. The wines have an aftertaste that stays in the mouth an amazingly long time. While quantity is definitely higher than it was once, it is still not considerable. An average harvest may come to only 60 hectoliters (1,590 U.S. gallons, 1,320 imp.) or 700 cases.

See Vosne-Romanée.

La Romanée-Saint-Vivant

Burgundy red wine.
District: Côte de Nuits, France.
Commune: Vosne-Romanée.
Official Classification: Great Growth (Grand Cru).

The vineyard is a Great Growth (*Grand Cru*), one of the thirty-one outstanding great vineyards of the Côte d'Or, five of which are in Vosne. Occupying 9.5 hectares or 23.6 acres, it is the largest of the Great Growths of Vosne and takes its name from the long-since-destroyed Abbey of Saint-Vivant, its owner for a considerable period.

Romanée-Saint-Vivant is just down the hill from Romanée-Conti and Richebourg, above the village of Vosne, and despite its large size there are only four growers who share it. The wines have the qualities and characteristics of the other Great Growths of Vosne: the same velvety grace, and the expansive perfume. However, if the vines were not pruned so as to produce maximum quantity, the wines could be even better. It is also unfortunate that some unworthy vintages were bottled under the La Romanée-Saint-Vivant place-name, a practice which only harms the name. Today, the wines are vinified and managed by Domaine de la Romanée Conti. They are undoubtedly among the great wines of Burgundy. Some 300 hectoliters (7,950 U.S. gallons, 6,600 imp.) are made each year.

La Senancole

Herb-based liqueur named after the River Senancole resembling yellow Chartreuse, made originally by Cistercian monks of the Abbey of Senanque, in Provence. It is now made by a commercial distiller, but under the supervision of the monks.

La Tâche

Burgundy red wine.
District: Côte de Nuits, Vosne-Romanée, France.
Official Classification: Great Growth (Grand Cru).

La Tâche means "the task" and is associated with the concept of piecework. It is not known, however, whether the early workers in this vineyard were paid by work accomplished rather than by the hour, or whether the name is a corruption of some other, unknown word.

The legal place-name actually embraces more than just the vineyard of La Tâche. This comprises some three and a half acres, but the name has been extended to take in 6 hectares (14.9 acres) by giving the franchise to adjoining plots such as Les Gaudichots and La Grande Rue, which stand between La Tâche and the twin Romanée and Romanée-Conti. This enlargement took place in 1936, when the laws covering Burgundy were drawn up.

La Tâche, like Romanée-Conti, is a vineyard that has but one owner: the Société Civile de la Romanée-Conti. The wines resemble those of the society's more famous growth, but are more delicate, yet they are full-bodied, with an amazing depth of flavor. In recent years, La Tâche has frequently come forth with better wines than those of Romanée-Conti, although neither is largely made. Production is the equivalent of about 1,700 cases.

Château La Tour-Blanche

Bordeaux white wine.
District: Sauternes, France.
Commune: Bommes.

The estate has slipped from the quality that caused it to be placed high among the Sauternes First Growths (*Premiers Crus*), second only to Château d'Yquem in the Classification of 1855. On the other hand, the wine now being made, definitely lighter and less sweet than its neighbors in the Bommes-Sauternes district, has its followers. M. Daniel Osiris gave the château and vineyards to France in 1910 on the condition that it be used as a viticultural school. The Ministry of Agriculture has operated the vineyard since 1955.

Characteristics. Light and less sweet for a Sauternes, tending very slightly to be dry, and with a typical vigor.

Vineyard area: 27 hectares (68 acres).

Average production: 60 *tonneaux* (5,500 cases).

Château La Tour-Carnet

Bordeaux red wine.
District: Haut-Médoc, France.
Commune: Saint-Laurent.

(*Saint-Laurent is not a place-name and the wine carries the* appellation *Haut-Médoc.*)

Classified a Fourth Growth (*Quatrième Cru*) of the Médoc in 1855. The square tower—the donjon of a thirteenth-century castle—that gives the wine its name overlooks one of the most beautiful properties of the Médoc, and the vineyard was famous and commanded leading prices as far back as 1354. Until recently very little wine was made, and cow pastures seem to have been more important to the former owner than the vines. But since the mid-sixties, through the considerable time and effort of its present owner, M. Lipschitz, the vineyards, *chai*, and château have been vastly improved. The estate is a good example of the marginal property which has been able to regain its standing in the 1855 Classification through the very high prices paid for it in Bordeaux today.

Characteristics. Improved in recent years. Good and sound wine.

Vineyard area: 30 hectares (75 acres).

Average production: 120 *tonneaux* (11,000 cases).

Château La Tour-Haut-Brion

Bordeaux red wine.
District: Graves, France.
Commune: Talence.

La Tour-Haut-Brion is one of the three Haut-Brion suffix wine châteaux on the outskirts of Bordeaux—the others are La Mission-Haut-Brion and Laville-Haut-Brion. Like La Mission-Haut-Brion, La Tour-Haut-Brion was classed as a First Growth (*Premier Cru*) of Graves in 1953 and 1959. Both belong to the Woltner family. These châteaux should not be confused with Château Haut-Brion, in Pessac, the great First Growth (*Premier Cru*) belonging to the Dillon family.

Characteristics. Full, rather hard wines, similar to those of La Mission-Haut-Brion but less fine.

Vineyard area: 7 hectares (17.5 acres).

Average production: 30 *tonneaux* (2,500 cases).

Château La Tour-Martillac (Kressmann-La Tour)

Bordeaux red and white wine.
District: Graves, France.
Commune: Martillac.

In front of the low, long farmhouse-like château on the slope of Martillac, south of Bordeaux, is the tower which gives the wine its name. It is all that remains of a château built in the twelfth century and probably destroyed in the French Revolution.

Red and white wines are made. For many years, the white wine has been aged in big barrels the size of the German Rhine and Mosel *Halbstück,* instead of the usual Bordeaux barrel of 225 liters, to see if fruitier wines might not be obtained from the greater mass of liquid in proportion to the wood surface through which the wine breathes. A slightly larger barrel means less oxidation, so that the wine should stay young longer. This experiment has had ample time to prove itself, and the owners believe that they have improved the quality of their wine, classified with the other best whites of Graves in 1955. The red wines, too, were classified, both in 1953 and 1959.

Since 1928 La Tour-Martillac has belonged to the Kressmann family of Bordeaux. The Kressmanns, well-known shippers of good wine, bought it outright when the last owner died and they were threatened with the loss of a wine which had been a favorite of their clientele for several generations.

Characteristics. Both the red and white wines are pleasant and clean, and happily now château-bottled.

Vineyard area: red—17 hectares (42 acres); white—4 hectares (10 acres).

Average production: red—50 *tonneaux* (4,500 cases); white—6 *tonneaux* (500 cases).

Château La Tour-de-Mons

Bordeaux red wine.
District: Haut-Médoc, France.
Commune: Soussans-Margaux.

Owned by the proprietor of Château Cantemerle, La Tour-de-Mons has for years had the benefit of the careful viticultural treatment which has raised Cantemerle far above its position as a Fifth Growth (*Cinquième Cru*). Château La Tour-de-Mons, ranked a Bourgeois Growth (*Cru Bourgeois*) in the 1855 Médoc Classification, also justifies a higher rating. The vineyard is today managed by M. Bertrand Clauzel, former mayor of Soussans. The estate has an old ruined tower tangled in vine and was founded in

1289 by Jehan Colomb of Bordeaux, one of whose Italian relatives was to discover America two centuries later. Subsidiary vineyards are Château Terrefort and Château Richeterre.

Characteristics. A very fine round wine with all the delicacy of Margaux. Although a Bourgeois Growth, it is one of the best in this old-fashioned category. It deserves a better rating, since it produces wines finer than many Classified Growths. Its excellent ownership guarantees that the wine will be well made.

Vineyard area: 30 hectares (75 acres).

Average production: 120 *tonneaux* (10,000 cases).

Labrusca

A species of grapevine (*Vitis labrusca*) found in North America.

See Chapter Eight, p. 29.

Lacrima (or Lacryma) Christi

A soft and fairly dry white wine made from grapes grown along the southern slopes of Mount Vesuvius—not to be confused with the Lágrima of Málaga. A red wine is also produced.

See Campania.

Ladoix-Serrigny

Burgundy red and white wines.
District: Côte de Beaune, France.

Little wine is sold under the place-name Ladoix-Serrigny. Wines are made, but the bulk may be sold as Côte de Beaune-Villages, and the best with those of next-door Aloxe-Corton. Because of the option, the amount of Ladoix-Serrigny varies; about 2,000 hectoliters (53,000 U.S. gallons, 44,000 imp.) is average for red wine, but only 100 hectoliters of white is generally produced.

The town is the northernmost of the Côte de Beaune and is bisected by the Route Nationale (National Highway) No. 74, which runs from Dijon south to Lyon and on to the Côte d'Azur. The name comes from the Celtic *doix* (fountain), for besides being a source of wine, the town has a spring. Serrigny, the other half of the commune, is an ancient hamlet which sits on the east—and, viticulturally speaking, the wrong—side of the National Highway. Throughout the Côte d'Or, vines growing on the slopes west of the highway have the right to the great place-names, while those to the east can do no better than the general name Burgundy.

The vineyards Les Vergennes and Le Rognet, bordering on Aloxe-Corton, are officially allowed the place-names of Corton and Corton-Charlemagne, and those immediately adjoining are Aloxe-Corton (for list *see* Aloxe-Corton). These wines tend to resemble their neighbors in all respects, and the lesser wines of the town are light-bodied and fast-maturing, often with an entrancing bouquet. The grapes are grown on about 136 hectares (335 acres).

Château Lafaurie-Peyraguey

Bordeaux white wine.
District: Sauternes, France.
Commune: Bommes.

Placed on a slightly lower hilltop opposite that of Château d'Yquem, the Moorish-looking walled castle, built in the thirteenth century, looks out through its fortified gates over the sloping sea of its vines. The *chai* is inside the courtyard, and there one of the most full-bodied of the Sauternes may be tasted, excellent when very young from the barrel, as fine Sauternes always are. The vineyard was classified a First Growth (*Premier Cru*) in 1855.

Characteristics. If the 1855 Classification were to be revised, these wines might be downgraded. Not as rich as many of the better Sauternes, yet distinguished wines.

Vineyard area: 18 hectares (45 acres).

Average production: 60 *tonneaux* (4,500 cases).

Château Lafite

Bordeaux red wine.
District: Haut-Médoc, France.
Commune: Pauillac.

Château Lafite, one of the best red wines of Bordeaux—which is to say, one of the most elegant wines in the world—has eight centuries of history behind it. In 1234 it was the property of Gombaud de Lafite; and a hundred years later the wines were already famous. In the eighteenth century, Mme de Pompadour served them; and Mme Dubarry said that since Bordeaux was the king's favorite, she would drink nothing else. Lafite claims to have been in each case the chosen wine, and it may very well have been so.

The vineyard was at one time owned by the Marquis Alexandre de Ségur, proprietor also of Château Latour and Château Calon-Ségur. It became public property in 1794, after the owner (the president of the parliament of Guyenne) had been guillotined in the Revolution; and afterward it was bought, first by a Dutch syndicate (in whose time the first bottles of vintage wine were laid down) and in 1821 by the English banker Sir Samuel Scott. The Rothschild family acquired Lafite when it was put up for auction in 1868. The bidding was so extraordinarily high that it was said only a Rothschild could triumph; and, indeed, the château went to Baron James de Rothschild for what, today, would be slightly more than $3,000,000 dollars (£1,200,000). By an odd coincidence—or perhaps it was the association that whetted his interest—the Rothschild bank in Paris is in the rue Laffitte.

Lafite will be found on early labels spelled with two *t*'s or two *f*'s or both; and the name itself is said to derive from the old Médoc word *lahite*, which was a corruption of *la hauteur* (the height). Lafite is the highest knoll of the Pauillac area, which merges into the adjoining commune of Saint-Estèphe. The château sits high above the marshland bordering the Gironde. Great ocean-bound vessels can be seen from the windows, throwing up feathers of smoke into a clear sky, or can be heard hooting their way through the mist.

One of the present owners of Lafite, Élie de Rothschild, is the cousin of Philippe de Rothschild of Château Mouton-Rothschild, and between their wines—the vineyards actually touch—a kind of competition has developed. Lafite is made from the grape varieties Cabernet Sauvignon and Franc, Petit Verdot, and much Merlot, which imparts the softness for which this wine is famous. Mouton, however, having very little Merlot, is 70% Cabernet Sauvignon, and so is harder.

Lafite is proud of its great name, and no wine which is not of the first quality (the wine from young vines, for instance) is allowed to bear it. Such wine is sold instead as Moulin des Carruades. Other properties of this Rothschild branch of the family include the Château Duhart-Milon in Pauillac (*qv*), Clark-Malmaison in Saint-Estèphe, recently bought and autonomously run by Eric de Rothschild, and La Cardonne in the Bas-Médoc.

The estate now run by Eric de Rothschild consists of some 120 hectares (300 acres), three-quarters of them devoted to viticulture. There, as in other vineyards of the Médoc, the vines are planted about a meter apart and are carefully trained along two or three rows of thin sticks to keep them from damage by contact with the earth, with the plow, or even with a brisk wind. Here, as everywhere in the Médoc, the trellises are 35 centimeters from the ground and each vine runs horizontally along a wire. The owners of Lafite say that the north-south exposure of the vineyard is conducive to early ripening and that the misty atmosphere gives the grapes their thin skins, which, when they ripen, become glassily transparent. From this time nobody is allowed in the vineyard, in case the grapes should be bruised.

The *chais* cluster round the château; and in the great *cuverie*, or vat-house, are twenty-four Bosnian oak vats, each holding 12,500 liters (3,300 U.S. gallons, 2,750 imp.). The château itself, set on a handsome eighteenth-century terrace, is shown on the labels. Vines grow right up to the garden walls; the house is built of pale stone, throwing into relief the green of two magnolias and an ancient cedar tree.

The cellars of the château are heavily vaulted, their four long galleries lit by wrought-iron chandeliers, each holding six electric candles. Here is the most impressive sight in Lafite: a rank of bins, each with its wooden vintage plaque. The walls are black with mold and the bottles seem to be covered with fur. The earliest is 1797; others still have their labels 1801, 1805, and 1811, the year of the comet, said to be the best vintage of the early nineteenth century. 1870 was a famous year in the history of Lafite. Other great classical vintages were 1893, 1895, 1900, 1906, 1923, and 1926. Fine years were 1874, 1875, 1878, 1899, 1904, 1911, 1916. In 1905 the wine was light but had an exquisite flavor; in 1934 it was full-bodied and mellow. Although slow-maturing, 1945 is a classic of all time; 1949 and 1952 are excellent; while 1953 was one of the greatest of recent decades, exemplifying Lafite at its very best. Since then, the superb 1955 has been overshadowed by the fabulous 1959, 1961, 1966, 1970, and especially 1978, which reached ridiculously high prices but will nevertheless be regarded as classics.

Since wine ages more slowly in large bottles, there are many magnums and double magnums stocked in the Lafite cellars, as well as imperials, which hold eight bottles; the stone staircases leading to the cellars are lined with jeroboams (five bottles). The bottles are recorked every twenty-five years. When the cork deteriorates, so that the wine begins to evaporate, the bottle is "leaky"—*bouteille couleuse*—and is then filled up again; at Lafite this happens to about 5,000 bottles every year.

Characteristics. In great years, when Lafite is successful, it can be supreme. It has great finesse and a particular softness imparted by the Merlot grape. The wine tends to be firm yet delicate and supple, with an eventual lightness developed in age. Lesser vintages are still excellent wines, lighter than those of great years, but always showing breed, fragrance, and depth of flavor.

Vineyard area: 95 hectares (238 acres).

Average production: 250 *tonneaux* (22,000 cases).

Château Lafleur

Bordeaux red wine.
District and Commune: Pomerol, France.

On a very gravelly soil, producing a very flavorful wine, this superb small vineyard has for many years been owned by the Robin sisters, who also own Château Le Gay in Pomerol.

Vineyard area: 4 hectares (10 acres).

Average production: 14 *tonneaux* (1,200 cases).

Château Lafleur-Pétrus

Bordeaux red wine.
District and Commune: Pomerol, France.

Adjoining the very famous Château Pétrus, this reliable vineyard lives up to the connotations of its name. It is owned and excellently managed by J.-P. Moueix, the largest shipper of Saint-Émilion wines.

Vineyard area: 9 hectares (22 acres).

Average production: 35 *tonneaux* (3,000 cases).

Château Lafon-Rochet

Bordeaux red wine.
District: Haut-Médoc, France.
Commune: Saint-Estèphe.

The only Fourth Growth (*Quatrième Cru*) Classification of 1855 in Saint-Estèphe, Lafon-Rochet is owned by Guy Tesseron, who has recently increased the size of the vineyard and improved the wine.

Rebuilt in 1973, a good-looking château is located in the midst of the large plateau overlooking the vineyards; at the same time, considerably new cellarage was built under the château.

Characteristics. The wine has improved in the past decade. Recent vintages have achieved encouraging results.

Vineyard area: 45 hectares (113 acres).

Average production: 130 *tonneaux* (10,500 cases).

Lager

See Beer.

Château Lagrange

Bordeaux red wine.
District: Haut-Médoc, France.
Commune: Saint-Julien.

The large estate spread over the high slopes a mile back from the Gironde looks down over vineyards, among them Château Beychevelle and the Léovilles. Improved and developed by the wealthy wife of the French minister who held it just before 1855, it was classed a Third Growth (*Troisième Cru*) of Médoc in that year. Later in the nineteenth century the vineyard was the largest Classified Growth in the entire region, with nearly 300 hectares (750 acres) of vines.

Characteristics. The vineyard, though encompassing soils most appropriate to great quality, until the middle 1960s made poor wines which simply did not deserve the high classification of Third Growth. Within the past few years Lagrange has improved dramatically and is now making good wines, although some critics consider them common.

Vineyard area: 55 hectares (137 acres).

Average production: 220 *tonneaux* (20,000 cases).

Château Lagrange

Bordeaux red wine.
District and Commune: Pomerol, France.

A good wine characteristic of the district is made by this château situated on the Pomerol plateau in the midst of the best vineyards. Sometimes referred to as Lagrange-Pomerol to distinguish it from Château Lagrange in St.-Julien.

Vineyard area: 8 hectares (20 acres).

Average production: 30 *tonneaux* (2,500 cases).

Lágrima

A sweet, fortified Málaga wine, not to be confused with the Lacrima Christi grown near Naples, although both wines are golden in color and Lágrima and Lacrima both mean "tear."

See Málaga.

Lake Erie

Important wine district in the eastern United States. Vineyards are established on the mainland, centering around Sandusky but also on the islands Kelley, North Bass, South Bass, and Middle Bass. Good American grape varieties are used, of which the favorites are the Catawba and the Delaware. Both red and white wines are produced and some interesting sparkling wines.

See United States: Ohio.

Lalande de Pomerol

Bordeaux red wine.
District: Bordeaux, France.

The commune, which now includes Néac, adjoins the famous region of Pomerol in southwest France, but the wines, although similar to Pomerols, have a distinct taste. Several of them compare well with all but the finest Pomerols. Château Bel-Air, just across the line from Pomerol, is outstanding.

See Pomerol.

Lambrusco

(1) A sweetish semi-sparkling red wine of little virtue, made in the Emilia-Romagna region of Italy. It has no connection with *Vitis labrusca* of America.

(2) Grape grown in Italy for red wine, especially in Emilia and Alto Adige.

Château Lamothe

Bordeaux white wine.
District and Commune: Sauternes, France.

Second-classed Growth in the 1855 Classification, this wine is not well known outside of France.

Vineyard area: 10 hectares (25 acres).
Average production: 25 *tonneaux* (2,000 cases).

Château Lanessan

Bordeaux red wine.
District: Haut-Médoc, France.
Commune: Cussac.

(*Cussac is not a place-name and the wine carries the place-name Haut-Médoc.*).

Ranked a Bourgeois Growth (*Cru Bourgeois*) of the Médoc in 1855, the vineyard produces wine which sells well above its class and ought to be elevated to a higher position. The museum of horse-trappings, coaches, carriages, and carts draws numbers of visitors.

Characteristics. The very good wines are carefully made by the owner of Château Pichon-Longueville-Baron, M. Bouteiller. The wine is full and round, with a pleasant amount of finesse, and at the same time a delicacy which has astounded the Bordeaux merchants whenever they have tasted old bottles of this fine vineyard. Severe spring frosts in 1956 and 1957 have curtailed production.

Vineyard area: 30 hectares (75 acres).
Average production: 125 *tonneaux* (11,000 cases).

Château Langoa-Barton

Bordeaux red wine.
District: Haut-Médoc, France.
Commune: Saint-Julien.

Glimpsed between gates a little back from the vineyard road as it prepares to wind steeply through the town of Saint-Julien, Langoa houses not only the cellars and *chais* of its own Third-Growth (*Troisième Cru*) vintages but also those of the Second-Growth (*Second Cru*) Château Léoville-Barton. The two estates adjoin. Ronald Barton, the great-great-grandson of the Hugh Barton who bought Langoa in 1821 and a third of the great Léoville vineyard in 1826, lives in Château Langoa, and makes both wines.

Characteristics. Lighter than, but very similar to neighboring Léoville-Barton, yet not attaining quite the same degree of excellence. The wine was not bottled at the château before 1969 but in the cellars of the well-known Barton & Guestier shipping firm. All of the 1969 was château-bottled.

Vineyard area: 17 hectares (42 acres).
Average production: 60 *tonneaux* (5,000 cases).

Languedoc

A vast plain in southern France embracing the departments of Gard, Hérault, and Aude, where quantities of wines are made, mostly mediocre. However, recent efforts have demonstrated that pleasing, attractive wines can be made from the hillside vineyards. The better table wines are Clairette du Languedoc, Minervois, Fitou, and Corbières (*qq.v.*).

See Appendix G.

Château Lascombes

Bordeaux red and rosé wines.
District: Haut-Médoc, France.
Commune: Margaux.

A feudal holding of the Dukes of Duras, Lascombes may have acquired its name from the Chevalier de Lascombes who owned it early in the eighteenth century, or he may have taken his title from the estate. The local people say that the derivation was *La Côte—Lascote—Lascombes*, a corruption over the centuries of the original designation, meaning the hill, knoll, or slope. In any case, the vineyard spreads over the knoll of Margaux, the highest elevation of the commune. This outstanding situation caused the wines to be ranked equal with those of the adjoining vineyard of Château Margaux on many occasions in the past; and in 1855 the estate was classified a Second Growth (*Second Cru*) of Médoc.

By unwise selling of parcels, the vineyard had dwindled to nearly 16 hectares (40 acres) and become a patchwork when the Ginestets, former owners of Château Margaux, acquired it in the early twenties. The reconstruction and improvement of the vineyard begun then have been continued by the author and a group of American friends who bought Château Lascombes in 1952; today the vineyard has been reunited in an expanse of over 100 hectares (250 acres) northeast of Margaux.

In 1971 the author and his associates sold Lascombes to Bass-Charrington, a British wines, spirits, and brewery group that had already acquired the author's shipping firm in Bordeaux several years before.

The gray stone château, on the edge of the village and the chief landmark in the village itself, was built by a nineteenth-century owner, M. Chaix d'Est-Ange, who was at the time president of the French Bar—and famous for having won the case of the Suez Canal for France against Egypt. The Sèvres coffee service given him in gratitude by Napoleon III may still be seen in Margaux, profusely decorated with portraits of the mistresses of Louis XIV.

In 1953 the American owners enlarged and improved the château and *chai*, and in 1973 the present British proprietors built a completely new *chai* and vat-rooms; hence Lascombes is considered something of a Médoc showplace. Many visitors used to come from all parts of the world to see the exhibition of paintings on the theme of Vine and Wine which was organized in 1961 by the author but discontinued ten years later.

Characteristics. Excels in finesse and has an indefinable light Margaux bouquet epitomizing the "feminine" qualities of the Médoc—a bouquet many have found reminiscent of violets. The wine matures fairly rapidly and has great staying power, so that it may be enjoyed young or old.

Vineyard area: 105 hectares (263 acres).
Average production: 375 *tonneaux* (40,000 cases).

Latium (Lazio)

White and red wines.
District: around Rome.

If the Castelli Romani wines ever lose their place among the eternal wonders of Rome, there is no justice in Heaven. These bright dry or semi-sweet white wines from the Alban hills just south of the city provide the finest single means of diverting the mind from aching feet after a touristic morning in Rome and, judging by the amount sold, the Roman loves them as much as the visitor. The sources are the towns of Frascati, Colonna, Castel Gandolfo, Grottaferrata, Montecompatri, and Marino, although Velletri, Colli Albani, and Colli Lanuvini are names which may also be found—but the wise visitor seldom bothers to specify his wine. Every self-respecting *trattoria* keeper has his own supplier, and whether you ask for Frascati, Colonna, or *vino bianco*, the chances are that the waiter will agree and then bring you whatever he happens to have. In any case, it is almost certain to be eminently drinkable. (The best is probably Frascati, which tends to be sturdier and longer-lasting than the others. Its light texture should be viewed with suspicion, however, as it has an alcoholic content that makes it extremely insidious.)

Colli Albani is a D.O.C. wine produced from Malvasia Rossa, Trebbiano Toscano, Malvasia del Lazio, and Bonvino grapes in the communes of Albano and Aricca and also in parts of four other villages in the immediate vicinity of Rome. The wine is straw-colored, with a pleasant, delicate bouquet and a semi-sweet taste; when it contains 12.5% of alcohol, Colli Albani may be called *superiore*. This Denomination of Origin is also given a white sparkling wine made from the same grapes. Quite similar is another D.O.C. white wine called Colli Lanuvini from the communes of Genzano and Lanuvio between Lake Nemi and Aprilia.

Cesanese di Affile, often called simply Affile, comes from grapes of the same name grown around the tiny commune called Affile, near Rome. It is red but may be dry, semi-sweet, or plainly sweet; the wine ages moderately well and is not unlike two other D.O.C. wines—Cesanese di Piglio and Cesanese di Olevano Romano.

Frascati is made from Malvasia, Greco, and Trebbiano cultivated on ground especially rich in potassium and phosphorus but deficient in nitrogen and calcium, which helps to give this wine its distinctive character. There are three types: dry, semi-sweet, and sweet—the last is known as *canellino*.

Marino is a delightful city and is rather well known for its wines: thus wrote Bacci, the physician of Pope Sixtus V, in the year 1500. Marino wines are still produced in the area between Albano Lake and Rome; they are all usually white, delicate, and fruity.

The D.O.C. Velletri covers the red wines made from Sangiovese, Montepulciano, and Cesanese and the white wines made from Trebbiano and Malvasia. White Velletri is better known and more appreciated, though the red too is likable enough.

Zagarolo, another D.O.C. white wine from Latium, takes its name from the town southeast of Rome. Typically, it is made of Malvasia and Trebbiano, is either dry or a bit sweet, and may be labeled *superiore* should the wine have at least 12.5% of alcohol.

The Castelli Romani wines come mainly from Malvasia and Trebbiano grapes; they run from about 11% to 13% of alcohol, have a yellowish tinge, and are dry, sweet, or semi-sweet. Much wine is made annually and most of this is gulped down in Rome, although a certain amount is shipped abroad. Red wines also are produced in this Roman province.

Perhaps even more famous than these Roman offerings is Est! Est!! Est!!! (*q.v.*), the D.O.C. white wine of Montefiascone near Lake Bolsena. Labels sometimes appear without exclamation points, sometimes with one following each "Est," and sometimes as given above, and there seems to be no approved formula. The name is credited to the German Bishop Fugger, who made a trip to Rome in A.D. 1111. The Bishop was a drinker of discrimination, and since he did not wish to risk inferior wines on his long journey, he sent a trusted servant ahead with instructions to taste those along the route and to mark on the wall of each inn and tavern *Est* (It is) where the wine was good and *Non Est* (It is not) on the others. All went normally until the servant reached Montefiascone, where he tasted the wines, then rushed forth to scrawl the triple epithet on the wall before returning to settle comfortably into the wine cellar. According to the legends, both master and man passed the rest of their lives there, drinking themselves contentedly to death.

The wine itself is sometimes dry, more often slightly sweet. It is small and tinged with yellow, a darkness in shade which actually offers little to the cultivated palate but is certainly worth trying at its source if only in deference to the Bishop, remembering that the story is better than the wine.

Finally, from the north of Latium comes a little-known but excellent wine, Aleatico di Gradoli (D.O.C.). The Aleatico grape, semi-dried, produces a sweet, rich, red dessert wine of great strength and flavor. It is usually served cold and goes especially well with fruit.

Among lesser wines are Muscats and Malvasia, a sweet white wine sometimes sold fresh out of the fermenting vat (the best comes from Grottaferrata—which also makes a dryish, fairly light wine). Terracina, a city some 120 kilometers (75 miles) south of Rome on the fabled Appian Way, is known for a Muscat which tends to be slightly lower both in alcohol and sugar content than is normally expected. It is often recommended to accompany the exquisite Roman pastries—and with good reason.

Château Latour

Bordeaux red wine.
District: Haut-Médoc, France.
Commune: Pauillac.

Château Latour, already famous, was discussed in the *Essays* by Montaigne, himself a vine-grower in Bordeaux in the sixteenth century. It was near the end of the seventeenth century that the estate passed by marriage from de Chavanas, counselor-secretary to King Louis XIV, to the Ségur family, ancestors of the recent proprietors. The second Ségur to own it was known as the Vine Prince, celebrated as the possessor at the same time of Château Lafite, Château Latour, and Château Calon-Ségur. In the French Revolution the property was divided, and it was not until 1841 that the family succeeded in regaining the lost half. In 1842, the Société Civile de Château Latour was formed, at that time unique but since widely copied: only members of the family could belong. In 1963, the de Beaumont family sold 75% of their interest to the Pearson group of London. The firm of Harveys then bought one-

fifth of this. M. Henri Martin, the mayor of Saint-Julien, who was also the president of the Bordeaux Wine Association, and Jean Gardère, administer the estate.

The tower—La Tour—stands alone at the edge of the vineyard. It was once part of a wall raised against pirates by the Médoc people of the Middle Ages. The actual stones stand as they were placed in a reconstruction, ordered by Louis XIII, from the debris of a leveled fortress. The fort itself, which stood where the *chais* are now placed, was razed during the Hundred Years' War. It is said that a great quantity of gold pieces was thrown into the moat, thus starting the legend of buried gold at Château Latour. In fact, the story may not be altogether a myth, since a map found not long ago in the Tower of London affirms the presence of the gold, and corporations have been formed in England—so far unsuccessfully—to recover it.

The principal contribution to the quality of Château Latour wine is made by the soil, half of which is composed of egg-sized stones. Strain two pounds of it and a pound of stones will remain in your sieve. The plows of Latour have to be sharpened twice a day, and the soil itself has so much body that in the early sixties, before tractors were used, two oxen were required to draw a plow through it. A former Marquis de Ségur stunned the Court of Versailles with his glittering waistcoat, and King Louis XV announced: "Messieurs, here is the richest man in my kingdom. His soil produces nectar and diamonds." The gleaming stones sewn on to the Marquis de Ségur's silk waistcoat were cut and polished quartz from the vineyard of Latour. A few such stones can still be seen today in the entrance hall at Latour and in the wine museum of the Maison du Vin in Pauillac.

Latour still partly employs the method of vine replacement called *jardinage.* Every vine is allowed to live to its maximum age and is then torn out and replaced individually, although in most vineyards plants are now uprooted in sections at a set retirement age—usually thirty-five or forty years. The result is that, until recently, Latour had one of the oldest average plantations, and consequently greater body, higher alcoholic content, and extra fullness in the wine. In very old vines, quality increases but quantity decreases. Latour makes about 100 cases per acre, whereas 125 to 130 is normal for some of the lesser vineyards. Seven-tenths of Latour's 59 hectares (130 acres) are in Cabernet Sauvignon grapes, the remainder in Merlot, Cabernet Franc, and Petit-Verdot.

The grape must, or fermenting juice, of Château Latour is left in the new gleaming stainless steel vats from fifteen to twenty days, depending on the characteristics of the vintage; this is almost twice the time allowed in most of the other Médoc vineyards. This method creates a harder, slower-maturing wine, which will finally achieve great heights but which must be waited for. Only the grower of an aristocratic wine commanding a very high price can afford this expensive process. Château Latour is classed a First Growth (*Premier Cru*) with Château Lafite, Château Margaux, and Château Haut-Brion.

Characteristics. Full-bodied and hard when young, Latour develops into something firm, rich, and noble. Needing long ageing to reach its peak, it is well worth waiting for. The vineyard often succeeds in years when the others are inclined to falter.

Vineyard area: 70 hectares (175 acres).
Average production: 250 *tonneaux* (22,000 cases).

Château Latour-Pomerol

Bordeaux red wine.
District and Commune: Pomerol, France.

This beautiful and velvety wine has been made for some time by Jean-Pierre Moueix on the estate owned by Mme Lacoste, co-owner of Château Pétrus.

Vineyard area: 9 hectares (22 acres).
Average production: 40 *tonneaux* (3,500 cases).

Latricières-Chambertin

Burgundy red wine.
District: Côte de Nuits, France.
Commune: Gevrey-Chambertin.
Official Classification: Great Growth (Grand Cru).

Latricières is officially rated a Great Growth (*Grand Cru*) of the Côte d'Or (for the significance of this and the standards demanded *see* Côte de Nuits). It is in all respects the closest vineyard to Le Chambertin.

Chambertin and Latricières lie to the right of the vineyard road as you move south from Gevrey-Chambertin to Morey-Saint-Denis and only a tiny rutted track divides them. At the top of the vineyard, a tumbledown stone wall separates it from the matted and tangled undergrowth and the woodland which extend to the top of the hill, and below this stone wall is a small section of which the author is part-owner. As is true of most great Burgundian vineyards, a number of growers own sections of Latricières.

After Chambertin and the Clos de Bèze, Latricières produces the best wines in the commune. While not generally having all the fullness and nobility of the two top Growths (*Crus*), it will share much of the same strength, the deep and virile color, and especially the breed; for its main attribute is that it excels in finesse, often to a greater degree than Chambertin and Chambertin-Clos de Bèze. The area of the vineyard is 7 hectares (17 acres), and the grapes which are grown in it are made into just over 2,000 cases of wine.

Laudun

One of the best communes of the Côtes du Rhône, producing red, white, and rosé wines.
See Rhône.

Lavaux

Terraced vineyards in the canton of Vaud, which produces one-third of the wines of Switzerland. The white wines of Lavaux come from the Chasselas grape.
See Switzerland.

Château Laville-Haut-Brion

Bordeaux white wine.
District: Graves, France.
Commune: Talence.

This is one of three Graves vineyards bearing the suffix Haut-Brion. It makes only white wine and is among the five First Growths (*Premiers Crus*) for Graves white wines. Like Châteaux La Mission-Haut-Brion and La Tour-Haut-Brion, it belongs to the Woltner family.

Characteristics. A typical pleasant dry Graves.
Vineyard area: 4 hectares (10 acres).
Average production: 20 *tonneaux* (1,800 cases).

Layon

See Coteaux du Layon; Anjou.

Lazio

Italian spelling of the region of Latium (*q.v.*).

Leaf reddening (rougeau)

See Rougeau; Chapter Eight, p. 29.

Leaker

A bottle with wine oozing from the cork, indicating that air is reaching the wine, which is likely to spoil due to premature oxidation.

Lebanon

See Syria and Lebanon.

Lees

The sediments or dregs, consisting of tartrates, left at the bottom of a wine cask. These are left after racking a wine from one barrel to another.

Château Léoville-Barton

Bordeaux red wine.
District: Haut-Médoc, France.
Commune: Saint-Julien.

Léoville-Barton, with the other two Léoville vineyards, is a Second Growth (*Second Cru*) in the Classification of 1855 and forms one-fourth of the original Léoville estate, now divided into three. There is neither château, *chai*, nor cellars on the property. The owner, Ronald Barton, previously of the wine firm of Barton and Guestier in Bordeaux, lives at the nearby Langoa-Barton estate and makes both Langoa and Léoville-Barton there. His nephew Anthony Barton shares the direction of this beautiful vineyard. Langoa-Barton was bought by the present owner's great-great-grandfather in 1821 and Léoville-Barton five years later. The vineyard has recently been producing one of the best Saint-Juliens of all.

Characteristics. One of the best wines in the area, with excellent body and breed.

Vineyard area: 38 hectares (98 acres).

Average production: 125 *tonneaux* (11,000 cases).

Château Léoville-Las-Cases

Bordeaux red wine.
District: Haut-Médoc, France.
Commune: Saint-Julien.

Léoville-Las-Cases comprises roughly half the old estate of Léoville, the other half being divided between Châteaux Léoville-Barton and Léoville-Poyferré. It extends from the edge of the town of Saint-Julien to the borders of Château Latour, and in the past the combined Léoville vineyard stretched from Château Beychevelle to Château Latour. One of the most notable landmarks along the Médoc vineyard road is the Las-Cases gateway just past Saint-Julien, which appears on the wine label.

Las-Cases, with the other Léovilles, is a Second Growth (*Second Cru*) in the 1855 Classification, but one which had a temporary setback in quality during the early fifties. In 1959, 1961, and 1964, however, it was repeatedly one of the best Médoc wines. The vineyard is now run by M. Delon, but until 1900 it belonged to the Marquis de Las Cases, from which comes both the name of the principal Growth and also a secondary bottling under the label of Clos du Marquis, about one-fifth of the production.

Characteristics. At one time the wines were too light and slightly thin. There has been a marked improvement lately—the 1959 was superb, the 1961 was a classic, the 1970 and 1978 excelled. This is an example of a vineyard in which the quality of wine was improved by replanting. The young vines produced light acidic wines, but in 1959 the comparative maturity of the vines was combined with a change in the methods of vinification—brought about by Dr. E. Peynaud, professor of oenology at the University of Bordeaux—to create a metamorphosis in this wine.

Vineyard area: 60 hectares (150 acres).

Average production: 250 *tonneaux* (22,000 cases).

Château Léoville-Poyferré

Bordeaux red wine.
District: Haut-Médoc, France.
Commune: St.-Julien.

A Second Growth (*Deuxième Cru*) of the Médoc as classified in 1855, Poyferré once formed a single vineyard with the two other Léoville Growths, Barton and Las-Cases. Started in the seventeenth century, it was bought and renamed by a president of the parliament of Bordeaux, a M. Léoville, who died in 1769. During the Revolution the entire Léoville property was sequestered, but eventually, in 1830, one-fourth of the vineyard was purchased by Baron Poyferré. The Cuvelier family now owns the estate.

The wine can be the best of the Léovilles, and the 1929 in particular was considered one of the finest bottles of this century in the Médoc, though it is now little more than a memory. Poyferré is now perhaps the least good of the Léovilles. A secondary mark, Château Moulin Riche-Poyferré is popular in England.

Characteristics. Not so good as neighboring Léoville-Las-Cases, the wine is more supple and lacks the breed of the other two Léovilles. The wine has slipped sadly from what it once was, losing distinction partly because of the youth of the vines.

Vineyard area: 55 hectares (125 acres).

Average production: 200 *tonneaux* (18,000 cases).

L'Étoile

See Étoile; Jura.

Levure

French term for yeast.

Liebfrauenstift

The wine of the Liebfrauenkirche vineyards near Worms, in the Rheinhessen. In the days before the name became almost meaningless these wines could have been labeled Liebfraumilch, and were considered as the best of what is now a vague place-name.

Liebfraumilch

One of the most misleading names in wine. It may mean anything—and therefore nothing. Today, by West German law, Liebfraumilch, originally the wine of Liebfrauenkirche and Worms, may be applied to any wine of Rheinhessen. Rheinhessen wines, distinctive in their own right, are so named; the remainder call themselves Liebfraumilch. The nomenclature and regulations seem in a constant state of flux.

See Rheinhessen.

Liechtenstein

The wine of the "postage-stamp" principality on the Swiss-Austrian border is light-red—almost rosé—and two-thirds of it comes from around Vaduz, the capital.

See Vaduzer.

Light

In red wines this will mean a small inconsequential wine, low in alcoholic content and in tannin, though it may be very pleasant. But a light white wine such as a Mosel can be great.

Liguria

Red and white wines.
District: Italian Riviera.

Liguria forms a slim half-moon along the Mediterranean, a block of mountains rimmed with beach, its flanks formed by the Alps to the west, the Apennines to the east, with Genoa in the center. It is an extension of the French Riviera, and in keeping with the atmosphere of this lovely region, wine-making is romantic. The grapes have to be lowered down forbidding cliffs from practically inaccessible vineyards, to be carried to the press in skiffs. But however much he may enjoy watching the harvest here, the wise visitor will generally drink wines from somewhere else. Liguria makes 400,000 hectoliters (10.6 million U.S. gallons, 8.8 million imp.) annually, but most of it is quite ordinary wine.

Dolceacqua (Rossese di Dolceacqua)

This red wine with the Controlled Denomination of Origin comes from western Liguria where flower-laden hills slope upward behind Ventimiglia and Bordighera. Most of the wine is made in the vineyards of Dolceacqua, so it has taken on that name, or that name preceded by the grape variety—Rossese. Although the Italian means "sweet water," Dolceacqua usually has enough acidity to make it an adequate table wine; it is not low in alcohol (12% to 14%). Apparently the wine was something of a favorite with Napoleon.

Cinqueterre, Cinqueterre Sciacchetra

These famous white wines are often highly praised. The name means "five lands" and the wine comes from the five towns of Vernazza, Campiglia, Riomaggiore, Monterosso, and Biassa. It is usually semi-sweet, less frequently fully sweet, is made from Vernaccia grapes, and is a sound but not inspiring wine. Nevertheless, this is by far the best-known wine of the region. The type made from dried grapes is called Sciacchetra and has a minimum alcoholic content of 17%, a slightly aromatic deep bouquet, and an almost amber color.

Vermentino Ligure, Coronata, and Polcevera

Thin, light wines, similar in taste and bouquet, since each is mainly made from the Vermentino grape (although Bosco and Brachetto vines are grown too, particularly in the Coronata district). The wines should not be expensive. Vermentino Ligure may sometimes sparkle slightly.

Likörwein

German term for dessert wine.

Lillet

Semi-dry French aperitif made of white wine and brandy. It is pale in color and slightly resembles vermouth, but leaves a sweetish aftertaste.

Limoux

A small town near Carcassonne in southwest France, which makes a little-known still wine (Vin de Blanquette) and a slightly better-known, rather good, sparkling wine (Blanquette de Limoux).
See Blanquette de Limoux.

Liqueur d'expédition

French term, used in Champagne for a solution of sugar, wine, and sometimes brandy added to sparkling wine after extracting the cork just before shipment.
See Champagne.

Liqueur Jaune

Name often given to imitations of yellow Chartreuse.
See Chartreuse.

Liqueur d'Or

Pale yellow French herb liqueur with gold flakes floating in the bottle; a variation of Danziger Goldwasser.

Liqueur de tirage

French term for the solution of sugar and old wine added to Champagne and other sparkling wine to ensure a second fermentation.
See Champagne.

Liqueur Verte

Name often given to imitations of green Chartreuse.
See Chartreuse.

Liqueurs

These sweet, usually strongly alcoholic drinks which are served in very small glasses after dinner are made of sugar, syrup and spirits, flavored with plants, fruit or herbs, and are often an aid to digestion. The white fruit-brandies or *eaux-de-vie* produced in Alsace and elsewhere—framboise, quetsch, kirsch, slivovitz, etc.—sometimes referred to as liqueurs, do not really come into this category; nor do the excellent old dry Cognacs and Armagnacs, which are drunk undiluted after meals although these are commonly known as "liqueur" brandies.

HISTORY

Although the distillation of water and aromatic liquids was known in earlier times and mentioned by Hippocrates, Galen, and Pliny, alcoholic spirits were not distilled until probably about A.D. 900 by the Arabs—unless, indeed, they were made from cereals in northern Europe somewhat earlier. Liqueurs, a still later invention, began with the mollification of crude spirits by sweet syrups and continued with the addition of sweet herbs to enhance the flavor—and also to improve the health of the drinkers. In the Middle Ages, as we know, wine (and later spirits) was the principal antiseptic for dressing wounds, while plants, roots, and herbs provided the remedies for most diseases. The monks grew these in their monastery gardens and experimented with their use; the alchemists carried their researches further. Arnáu de Vilanova, Catalan physician and chemist, born *c.* 1240, was "the inventor of modern tinctures in which the virtues of herbs are extracted by alcohol." He and his pupil, Raimundo Lulio, were the first to write about alcohol and to make known their recipes for healing liqueurs. Beginning with sweetened spirit, they were soon introducing lemon, rose, and orange-flower. Afterward, they might add particles of gold, then considered to be a universal panacea. Arnáu, whose advanced ideas brought him into trouble with the Inquisition, was protected by the Pope, whose life he had saved with potions of wine mixed with herbs and gold. When the Black Death came to Europe, liqueurs mixed with vegetable balms and tonics were treasured medicines.

By the fifteenth century the Italians had become the leading liqueur-makers, and Catherine de' Medici took some of their recipes to France with her. Montpellier was a famous center of manufacture; a liqueur that Louis XIV liked very much is said to have contained amber, aniseed, cinnamon, and musk. Other spirit bases besides wine-brandy were brought into use, including rum from the new colonies. Housewives often concocted their own liqueurs and then, as now, they were used as flavoring in the kitchen. But during the last century the industry made such progress in most of the countries of Europe and such a variety was put on sale that homemade ratafias and liqueurs began to disappear.

MANUFACTURE

One system—a simple mixing of spirits, sugar-syrup, and bottled essence of peppermint or some other flavor—would be comparatively easy to carry out in the kitchen. In a rather more complicated form, this method is sometimes used commercially. The result, in either case, is a crude liqueur.

The finest are generally those that have been distilled; but some fruits and delicate herbs which cannot be submitted to distillation will merge very satisfactorily with the spirit through the processes of maceration or infusion. The purpose of distilling liqueurs is the opposite of that achieved in the distillation of pure alcohol. There, the vegetable matter constitutes the impurity which must be separated from the spirit; whereas in the liqueur the flavoring substances must be extracted and blended with the spirit base. Of the fruit rinds, kernels, seeds, flowers, leaves, and roots which are used in the mysterious blends, a large number can be distilled. The usual process is to steep the materials in alcohol for varying lengths of time and then, when the spirit is well impregnated with the flavor, to distill it. Afterward comes the sweetening with sugar-syrup. The distilled liquid is normally colorless. Some liqueurs, such as kümmel and Cointreau, will remain so; but since many brands of liqueur are traditionally green, amber, red, or yellow, harmless coloring matter will then be added to the majority. All liqueurs, whether colored or clear, are filtered to ensure perfect clarity. In the varying intervals before bottling they repose in modern stainless steel or brass-lined vats.

Of the alternative methods, infusion is suitable for substances which are soluble in water and not very volatile. The slower cold infusion, or maceration, is resorted to when the ingredient is easily soluble in water and would be injured by heat; in such a case, the fruit or plant is steeped in spirit until this is thoroughly permeated with the taste and perfume. After maceration, the liquid may well be thick and in need of preliminary straining; and, although fruity liqueurs made without distillation often retain their natural color, the maceration of more than one substance may produce a muddy color which must be corrected. As a rule, an innocuous dye, tasteless and without scent, is added in an alcohol solution before filtration. A fine crimson, for instance, can be produced with cochineal, powdered alum, cream of tartar, water, and alcohol.

When sugar is added, the mixture gains in suavity and body as well as in sweetness. Sometimes the sweetener is simple sugar-syrup, sometimes a blend of sugar and glucose or, occasionally, honey. When one of the ingredients is the juice of a sweet fruit, the dose of sugar is, of course, proportionately smaller.

It is on the choice of flavoring substances that will blend harmoniously and easily, and on the balance of sugar and alcohol, that the success of the finished liqueur depends. Every manufacturer guards the secrets of his recipes. In some cases, the prevailing ingredients are known. Cointreau, for example, is made with orange-peel steeped in wine-brandy—but there are other unnamed components. Aniseed, clearly, is the principal flavoring in the anis liqueurs, caraway in kümmel, peppermint in crème de menthe. The Italian mentuccia is known also as centerbe, after the hundred herbs that go into its making. The famous Benedictine, of Normandy, on the other hand, is made to a secret formula. Among the flowers, fruits, spices, and plants which have their savor extracted for liqueurs are lavender, rose, orange, lemon, juniper, vanilla, angelica, thyme, fennel, mint, orris-root, camomile, cinnamon, almonds, curaçao bark, and cloves.

See also under individual headings: Benedictine, Grand Marnier, etc.

Liquor

The most widely employed word for spirit or alcoholic spirit in America; in some isolated instances, the word still retains its original meaning, "liquid."

Liquoreux

French term meaning "rich and sweet."

Lirac

Rhône Valley rosé, and some white, wines.
District: Rhône Valley, France.

Lirac lies near Tavel, and its vineyards resemble the more famous growths of its neighbor. The difference is that white wines—albeit in small quantity—are made in Lirac, only rosé in Tavel. Lirac has sandier soil than Tavel, with the result that its rosé is less full, less distinctive, but often a good value compared to the higher-priced Tavels. The white wine is enjoyable but not extraordinary.

See Rhône.

Lisbon port

A port-type wine from the Lisbon area which sought to capture some of the export market for legitimate Port before this was made illegal by Portuguese wine laws early in the century.

Listofka

A Russian aperitif flavored with blackcurrants.

Listrac

Bordeaux red, and some white, wines.
District: Haut-Médoc, France.

Listrac is a commune of Haut-Médoc, important in wine production although none of the classified châteaux stands within its boundaries. The 302 hectares (755 acres) of vineyard, planted on a good stretch of gravelly soil, rising into hummocks with a favorable exposure, yield full-bodied wines—a good deal of respectable *vins fins,* and some good red classed as Bourgeois Supérieurs and Crus Bourgeois. Among the Supérieurs are Château Fonréaud, Château Fourcas-Dupré, and Château Fourcas-Hosten. There is also a cooperative cellar. The annual harvest is some 15,000 hectoliters (397,500 U.S. gallons, 330,000 imp.).
See Bordeaux.

Liter

Standard metric liquid measure; the volume of one kilogram of pure water measured at a temperature of 40°F. (4°C.) and an atmospheric pressure of 760 millimeters. It is equal to 1.0567 U.S. quarts, 1.9531 British pints, 33.8146 U.S. fluid ounces (35.1961 British), and 100 centiliters.

Livermore Valley

California wine region producing, notably, very good white wines in Alameda County.
See United States: California.

Ljutomer

Yugoslavian spelling of that country's best-known wine. On labels destined for English-language countries, the *j* is customarily omitted. Lutomer white wines are of several styles identified by the grape variety and also indicated on the wine label.
See Yugoslavia.

Lobe

The division of a leaf. A typical vine leaf has five.

Locorotondo

Dry white wines from Apulia (*q.v.*).

Lodge

The word *loja* in Portuguese refers to a warehouse above the ground. However, it is the English who have made Port, in respect of its wealth, its renown, and even the wine itself, and the English tongue is notoriously unwilling to bend itself around words in other languages. *Loja* was transformed into "lodge," and the warehouses of Port wine along the River Douro in Portugal, those in Vila Nova de Gaia for example, are referred to as lodges.

Logroño

Important wine town and district in Rioja-Alta, the best table-wine region of Spain.
See Rioja.

Loir

A tiny French river, a tributary of the Loire, on the banks of which several pleasant wines are grown.
See Loire; Coteaux du Loir; Jasnières.

Loire, the

Red, white, and rosé wines.
District: Loire Valley, France.

The title in itself is almost a misnomer. No wine—excepting a small quantity of Muscadet de Coteaux de la Loire and Anjou, Coteaux de la Loire—is actually sold under the label Loire, and in fact a number of the vineyard areas along the river—Vouvray, Anjou, Sancerre, Pouilly, Muscadet, and Saumur—are far better known.

Yet, the wines are almost invariably considered as a group and as Loire wines. This nomenclature is justified by the fact that all of them share certain characteristics—all have a stamp that indelibly marks them Loire.

They can best be defined as "charming." If they lack some of the magnificent breed of the great Bordeaux and Burgundies, they have nevertheless a special style, a grace and gaiety which makes them wonderfully refreshing. All manner of wines are made—dry red and sweet white, rosé and dry white, sparkling, *pétillants,* and still, and the better ones are found abroad in fair quantity. It is usually best to drink them fairly young—red as well as white—since they tend to decline after three to five years in bottle, especially after a voyage. This does not apply to the sweet whites, for the extra increment of sugar and increased alcoholic content helps to preserve the wine and allows it to age gracefully and withstand shocks which might be fatal to one of less robust constitution. Here, more than in almost any other district of France, good vintage years are of paramount importance, for if there has not been enough sun, there will be excessive acidity, throwing the wines out of balance.

The Loire comes down from the Massif Central in south-central France, flows due north, turns through a right angle, and then flows west to Nantes, where it empties into the Atlantic to finish a journey of some 1,070 kilometers (668 miles). Almost half this journey is completed before the first vineyards with controlled place-names—those of Pouilly-sur-Loire and Sancerre—spring up on the gently sloping banks; but from this point on, vine and vineyards abound. Quincy and Reuilly are skirted (they are drained by a tributary, the Cher), but near Tours the twin districts of Anjou and Touraine stand back to back, with the Coteaux du Loir and tiny Jasnières close by on the small River Loir (*le* Loir, not to be confused with the greater *la* Loire, of which it is a tributary), and vines continue all the way to the Muscadet district, around Nantes.

WINE HISTORY

It is not clearly established whether vines existed before the Roman invasion, or whether they were introduced by Caesar's wine-drinking legions. Certainly the Romans developed and extended the vineyards of Gaul. What is well established is that the early Church was instrumental in advancing viticulture and viniculture in the Loire as elsewhere, and that the Church of St. Martin at Tours had considerable vineyard holdings at various periods, some as far afield as Burgundy, but considerably more along the banks of the Loire. The local growers, in fact, declare that the art of pruning was discovered by that saint's donkey.

The story goes that in A.D. 345 St. Martin was making one of his periodic vineyard tours: he was an early wine enthusiast, aiding growers throughout the valley and bringing them up to date with what viticultors elsewhere were doing. Early one morning he came riding into Anjou, heading for a vineyard which belonged to the Church. When he got there, he tethered his mount at the end of a row of vines. The inspection was a thorough one, St. Martin stopping here and there to ask questions or advise the monks who were tending the vines—and perhaps he went into the cellars to taste the last year's vin-

tage. When, some time later, he returned, he was horrified to discover that his donkey had been munching the leaves, and that some of the tender young shoots had been nibbled right down to the trunk of the vine. But the next year those same shoots were the ones which grew back the most abundantly and produced the best fruit. The lesson was not lost on the monks, who quickly developed a more efficient method of pruning than donkey-tethering.

During the turbulent Middle Ages the vineyards of Touraine and Anjou assumed a considerable importance in Anglo-French trade, for the English Plantagenet kings were also Counts of Anjou; but before England lost all her French possessions, English taste veered toward the wines of Bordeaux. Ships from the Netherlands still sailed up the Loire to buy stocks of wine; but this trade too was curtailed when France and Holland went to war in 1672—a war in which the famous song *Auprès de ma Blonde* was first sung. Having lost two of their best markets, the Loire growers were forced to start building up a trade inside France—much more difficult than shipping wines down to the coast in those days of poor roads, high tolls, and constant danger from thieves and highwaymen. Yet they succeeded. And now, as then, France and Belgium remain the most important customers for Loire wines, although recent advances in viniculture have made it possible to send them overseas without damage, and they can be found in fair quantities in England, the United States, and elsewhere.

TYPES OF WINE

All the important types of still table wines are made along the Loire, as well as a substantial amount of sparkling and some semi-sparkling, or *pétillant*—a word that has become all but synonymous with Vouvray. The sparkle was introduced in the nineteenth century, when Champagne and other bubbly wines became the fashion.

Most Loire sparkling wines are white and most come from Saumur and its environs, but there are others as well.

The best of the Loire wines are the still whites, both sweet and dry. The dry varieties should be consumed fairly young—nine months to five years old as a general rule—while the sweet may sometimes take as many as fifteen years to please the exacting palate of the local *vignerons*. These sweet wines are best bought young (although they must be stored until they are ready to drink), because for them, as for all good wines, the price is considerably lower when they are newly bottled. Rosé wine is something of a Loire specialty, and there are two types: a light rosé, and another fuller in color and character and sweeter, made entirely from Cabernet grapes. This Rosé de Cabernet, somewhat sweet, is the better wine of the two. Red wines are generally dry, fairly soft, fruity, and quick to mature, and when drunk young can be perfectly delightful.

VINE VARIETIES

Loire Valley wines do not always carry the name of the grape variety from which they come, as do those from Alsace, for example; but the names do guarantee that they were made from specific types of grapes. Those used are:

Cabernet Franc. The dominant grape (called Breton in Touraine) for makers of red wine, who also employ it in making vin rosé. This vine is said to have been brought to the Loire in the twelfth century. In the seventeenth the Abbé Breton planted a new vineyard for Cardinal Richelieu; hence the local pseudonym Breton for the grape. The vines came originally from the Gironde, where the grape is grown for the red wines of Bordeaux. Other local names for the grape are Véron, Bouchy, Bouchet, etc.

Cabernet Sauvignon. Some Sauvignon is found, mostly in Anjou, where plantings have increased of late years. Most of the grapes are pressed for pink wine.

Chasselas. A grapevine used for about three-quarters of the production of dry white Pouilly-sur-Loire, the minor wine of the district of the same name. The best wines of Pouilly are Blanc Fumé de Pouilly, or Pouilly-Fumé, and are made with the Sauvignon Blanc, also known as Blanc Fumé.

Chenin Blanc. Despite its restriction to the districts of Anjou, Touraine, and Jasnières, this is the most widely-planted grapevine for white wines along the banks of the Loire. It is called Pineau de la Loire in Touraine. The vine is known to have grown in Anjou from very early times. It is no doubt a selection of once-wild plants. The fruit is used both for sweet and for dry white wines, the main factor being in many cases the weather—hot summers give sweet wines, chill rainy ones give dry wines. The other factor is the method of fermentation used at will by the wine-grower. Dry wines can be made in hot

summers if all the sugar is allowed to be converted into alcohol.

Cot. A minor vine cultivated in the valley of the Cher in Touraine. The red wines it produces are uninteresting. Other names for this grape are Pied-Rouge, Malbec or Malbeck, Cahors.

Gamay. The vine of Burgundy's Beaujolais district is planted to a slight extent in the Coteaux de la Loire and in the Touraine. It is used for rosé wines rather than red, except in the Ancenis district.

Groslot. This grape is used for rosé wine in Anjou.

Gros Plant du Pays Nantais. Planted around the Muscadet district, it produces fresh white wines. Sometimes on the acid side, these wines are only consumed locally along the Atlantic coast.

Muscadet. Actually Melon de Bourgogne, but when transplanted in 1639 from its native Burgundy to the vineyards at the mouth of the Loire, the vine took on a new name. The dry white wines made from its grapes are light, fresh, slightly hard and acid, and excellent with seafood.

Noble. This is used in small quantities for red wine in the Touraine and is synonymous with Pinot.

Pineau d'Aunis. Once the important grapevine for red wines but now almost entirely replaced by Cabernet Franc. It is still found in limited amounts in Anjou, where it has been growing since the twelfth century.

Pinot Noir. This grape variety was cultivated in abundance in Sancerre up to the beginning of the twentieth century. Since then, little by little, it has been replaced by the Sauvignon. Recently, there has been a strong tendency to replant certain vineyards of Sancerre in Pinot Noir, since in good vintages it produces very good rosés. The red wines, because of their quality, are acquiring a noteworthy following.

Sauvignon Blanc. The white grape of Bordeaux does exceptionally well in the upper Loire, where it is used exclusively for the dry white wines of Sancerre, Quincy, Reuilly and the best wine of Pouilly-sur-Loire, the Blanc Fumé.

LOIRE WINE DISTRICTS

There are nine major districts of the Loire of which three—Anjou, Muscadet, and Touraine—are huge and contain a number of sub-districts, while the rest are small and of lesser importance. These districts are:

Anjou

Makes red and white wines (the latter both sweet and dry, of which the sweet are the better) and dry and semi-sweet rosé. It includes the sub-districts of Anjou-Coteaux de la Loire, Savennières, Bonnezeaux, Coteaux de l'Aubance, Coteaux du Layon, Quarts de Chaume, Saumur, and Coteaux de Saumur.

Coteaux du Loir

A minor and very small district taking its name from the tiny River Loir and producing red, white, and rosé wines. The white are sweet, the rosé quite charming, the red sometimes not very good. It must be repeated that the Loir, a tributary of the Loire, is not to be confused with the greater river.

Jasnières

A small district making up the heart of the Coteaux du Loir and producing the superior wine. The wines are entirely white and are usually described as *moelleux*—slightly sweet, velvety and rich in texture.

Muscadet

The vineyards at the mouth of the Loire produce a fresh and delightful dry white wine which once served the dubious purpose of stretching the limited supply of Burgundy's Chablis. Now sold under its own name, the wine is building a substantial reputation for itself both in France and abroad. Muscadet is divided into three placenames. The most famous is Muscadet de Sèvre et Maine, some 16 kilometers (10 miles) south of Nantes, deriving its name from two small rivers running through the vineyard area. The second is Muscadet Coteaux de la Loire; and the third is referred to simply as Muscadet.

Pouilly-sur-Loire

A district of the upper Loire where Sauvignon Blanc grapes are pressed to make the excellent dry white Pouilly-Fumé, otherwise known as Blanc Fumé de Pouilly, and Chasselas grapes to make the similar but less distinctive Pouilly-sur-Loire.

Quincy

Although Quincy is 48 kilometers (30 miles) from the Loire and adjoins a tributary, its output is always considered as Loire wine. Dry and white, it is much like Sancerre, Pouilly-Fumé, and Reuilly, with a slightly distinctive *goût de terroir*.

Reuilly

Dry white wine—often thin, harsh and acid—from Reuilly on the Arnon, a tributary of the Cher. It resembles the wine from nearby Quincy.

Sancerre

One of the best-known growing districts of the upper Loire, famous for its dry white wine made entirely from Sauvignon grapes. There is also a very good dry rosé and occasionally a red wine—both made from Pinot Noir.

Touraine

The second of the two largest districts of the Loire. The wines may be red, white, or rosé and the whites may either be sweet or dry. The sub-districts of the Touraine include Bourgueil and Saint-Nicolas-de-Bourgueil, Chinon, Montlouis, Touraine-Amboise, Touraine-Azay-le-Rideau, Touraine-Mesland, and the world-renowned Vouvray.

See also under separate headings.

Lombardy

Red, white, and rosé wines.
District: Northern Italy.

From the towering Alps along its northern boundary to the pleasure resorts of Lake Garda and almost to the city limits of Milan, Lombardy is a region of wines and vines. There are stretches, of course, where no vine is seen: northern reaches where the land is too forbiddingly mountainous, or central lowlands where the soggy valleys are given over to the culture of rice. In general, however, the vine is found throughout. It does best in the Valtellina section, an Alpine corner near the Swiss border, some 30 kilometers (20 miles) due south of Saint Moritz, but the wine from grapes grown near Lake Garda is also popular with the Italians. In addition, Lombardy can boast of the well-known vineyard Frecciarossa, dealing in something quite rare in Italy—estate-bottled wines.

Valtellina

In this valley centered around the town of Sondrio, the four almost identical red wines are Fracia, Sassella, Grumello, and Inferno—all from Nebbiolo grapes grown on the less steep Alpine slopes. Almost the whole production of Fracia comes from one grower, the house of Negri, based in Chivro. A similar but lesser growth is the red Valgella.

Perhaps the mountaineer is a different type from the plainsman, but wine, and even life, in the Valtellina does not seem to have changed for centuries. The peasant who pours you a glass of wine and warns you not to stay out too late (werewolves inhabiting the upper slopes are still dangerous at night) might well be from another age entirely, and it is difficult to conceive that he would change his wine-making techniques. Mechanization is rare and even animals often find the slopes too steep, leaving man to struggle alone to till the land. For this reason, and because the Nebbiolo is always a shy bearer, the amount of wine made is small—less than 27,000 hectoliters (700,000 U.S. gallons, 580,000 imp.) a year for the combined five wines. Once made, they seem to epitomize not only the virtues but the faults of Italy's wines. All are lighter in alcohol (11% to 12%) than the Nebbiolo wines of Piedmont. All fit neatly into an Italian meal with its amazing ability to reduce the pungent harshness so often found in the wines and bring out unsuspected characteristics. But these virtuous characteristics may be developed to a fault, as the wines become rough, coarse, sometimes common; yet at their best they have an agreeable freshness, and occasionally, as is true throughout the country, they have a light sparkle, as unexpected to the wine-maker as to the drinker. When these wines succeed, they are hearty and good. They are made from a minimum of 95% of Nebbiolo grapes, known locally as Chiavennasca, and grown on steep terraces, facing south, in those areas called Fracia, Sassella, Inferno, Grumello, and Valgella. The wines are in fact *Valtellina Superiore*, and bear on the label their own geographical specification added to the D.O.C. Valtellina. One of the best of these wines is Sfursat, made from partly dried grapes so that the alcoholic content reaches 14.5% or more. When aged four years, this wine may be called *riserva* and becomes a fine table wine of great character.

Lugana

This, Lombardy's leading white wine, is made from Trebbiano grapes with some Vernaccia not infrequently added. For all the fuss made about it, this is a small D.O.C. wine, generally yellowish in color, running to about 11% to 12.5% of alcohol. It is regrettable that Italian wine-makers—contrary to their general practice—usually age their white wines too long; if it were brought young out of the barrel, Lugana would probably be delightful.

Frecciarossa

The district is in the province of Pavia, bordering on Piedmont. The carefully made wines come strictly from a 28-hectare (70-acre) vineyard on a castle-topped hill near Casteggio and are of four types: Bianco (dry, white), Ambrato (semi-sweet, white), Rosso (dry, red), and Saint George (dry, rosé). The white wines are made from Riesling and Pinot Noir grapes, the others from Pinot Noir, Bonarda di Gattinara, Barbera, and Croattina. Something under 2,000 hectoliters (50,000 U.S. gallons, 41,500 imp.) are made annually, split into almost equal parts among the four, and the wines are distributed widely throughout the world. Estate-bottled wines are to be found here—something very rare in Italy. Other wines of the region are the red Barbacarlo and Buttafuoco.

Lombardy also makes a Muscat and a sparkling Muscat in commercially important (but fortunately not significantly large) quantities, selling them as Moscato di Casteggio and Moscato di Casteggio Spumante. The former is a typically sweet Muscat wine, the latter something like Asti Spumante (*see* Piedmont).

Several other less well-known wines of Lombardy deserve mention here. From the southwestern shore of Lake Garda come Rivera del Garda Chiaretto and Rosso, both wines of Controlled Denomination of Origin. Both are made from Groppello and Sangiovese grapes and share something of the same marked, bitter aftertaste. The Rosso is a very deep ruby color, while the Chiaretto is a rather dark rosé.

A good D.O.C. red wine from the province of Brescia is Botticino, whose name comes from a small commune near Lake Garda. Barbera, Schiava, Gentile, Marzemino, and Sangiovese make up the wine which is best drunk young.

Oltrepò Pavese is the Controlled Denomination of Origin for six wines from part of the province of Pavia, south of the River Po. The name is generally followed by the name of the principal grape variety used to make the wine—Barbera, Bonarda, Riesling, Cortese, Moscato, etc.—but when the name appears alone, the wine will contain mostly Croattina and Barbera.

Finally, Lombardy gives two pleasant D.O.C. wines called Franciacorta Rosso and Franciacorta Pinot made throughout twenty-one communes in the province of Brescia. The *rosso*, or red, contains Cabernet, Barbera, Nebbiolo and Merlot; it is dry and even robust. The white wine named Pinot, after the principal grape used, is sometimes sparkling and always best consumed young.

London Dry gin

One of the two basic styles of gin—the other is Hollands. This is the gin of both the United States and England. The base spirit is distilled until neutral, and flavoring, from a number of different herbs but chiefly juniper, is added afterward. Less totally distilled, Hollands (or Dutch gin) retains flavor characteristics from the original spirit.

See Gin.

Lorraine

Red, white, and rosé wines.
District: Northeast France.

Since 1951 the wines of Lorraine, which had practically ceased to exist, have been making a small comeback. This northeastern province of France had at one time been well known for its *vin gris* (a type of rosé made from Gamay) and for its sparkling wines. Three wars, phylloxera, and the passing of rigid control laws in Champagne all but wiped Lorraine off the wine map. Two controlled place-names exist today, both established in 1951 and both of them having the right to the name of Vins Délimités de Qualité Supérieure, the secondary French classification of wines. They are the Côtes de Toul and Vins de la Moselle.

Lorraine has always been one of the more troubled parts of France. After the war of 1870 the province was split in two, half going to France and half to Germany. During this period, the wines of Lorraine probably enjoyed as much renown as they have ever had. Those grown on the German side were made into Sekt, or German sparkling wine; and those on the French side became either *vins gris* or were made sparkling and sold as Champagne; the Champagne shippers did this with Lorraine wine, until in 1908 Champagne had a disastrous year and virtually all the wine had to be brought in from Lorraine. The Champagne growers objected so violently that riots and havoc broke out in the region and a rigid delimitation law was passed in 1908, strengthened further in 1911; Lorraine wines therefore had to find another outlet.

Before the growers could get back on their feet, the First World War came. Such vineyards as survived in the battleground area fell victim to phylloxera. Hybrid vines were planted for the making of very ordinary wine to be drunk in Lorraine by the inhabitants. Only after the Second World War did the growers of Lorraine start replanting their finer vine types with any consistency.

The better wines of Lorraine are today much what one would expect from a vineyard area so cold and so far north. Low in alcohol and high in acid, the grapes are harvested late—the end of October. The red wines which result are far less pleasant than the white and rosé. High acidity in red wines is a definite defect.

Côtes de Toul

Most of the wines are *vins gris*, the traditional light rosé wine of Lorraine. They come from parts of the communes of Lucey, Bruley, Pagney-derrière-Barine, Écouvres, Dongermain, Mont-le-Vignoble, Charmes-la-Côte, Blénod-les-Toul, and Bulligny. The permitted vines are the Gamay de Toul, Gamay de Liverdun, Pinot Noir, and Pinot Meunier (all of these either separately or together must comprise at least 80% of the wine); and Aubin Blanc, Blanc d'Euvézin, and Aligoté (these three comprise up to a maximum of 20%). The vines are allowed to yield no more than 16 hectoliters per hectare (416 U.S. gallons, 346 imp. per acre).

The alcoholic content of the Côtes de Toul will only run about 8.5% in an average year, but may go as high as 10% or even 11% in years that are particularly hot and acidity is markedly high. Only about 3,000 hectoliters (79,500 U.S. gallons, 66,000 imp.) are made each year. The vineyards of the Côtes de Toul are in the process of being expanded, and this figure may rise.

Vins de la Moselle

The Vins de la Moselle are made in three separate areas and each of the wines has its own characteristics. The wines from around the city of Metz are mostly light rosé wines often found under the name of Clairet de Moselle. Those which come from around Sierk are generally white. The traditional *vin gris* is made principally around Vic-sur-Seille. All must derive from the same vines, which are the Gamay (30%), Auxerrois Blanc, Auxerrois Gris, Meunier Blanc, Meunier Gris, Pinot Noir, Pinot Blanc, Sylvaner (30% maximum), Riesling, and Gewürztraminer. Like the wines of the Côtes de Toul, these tend to be extremely acidic but are often pleasantly fruity when young.

Spirits

Among the colorless *eaux-de-vie* that are made from fruits here, as elsewhere, the Mirabelle de Lorraine is the best known. It is made from small yellow plums.

Loupiac

White wine.
District: Bordeaux, France.

This is the continuation northward of Sainte-Croix-du-Mont on the right bank of the River Garonne, and facing Sauternes across the river. It produces approximately the same quantity as Sainte-Croix-du-Mont and under identical conditions, the sole difference being that these vineyards are in the commune of Loupiac. The wines may be considered with those of Sainte-Croix-du-Mont, as there are no important differences.
See Sainte-Croix-du-Mont.

Low wines

Whisky after first distillation and before redistillation.

Lugana

Principal white wine of Lombardy, made from Trebbiano grapes, sometimes with an addition of Vernaccia.
See Lombardy.

Lunel, Muscat de

See Sweet fortified wines of France.

Lussac-Saint-Émilion

Commune with an Appellation Contrôlée, making red wines, in the region of Bordeaux (*q.v.*).

Lutomer

English spelling of Yugoslavia's best-known white wine. There are different styles identified as Lutomer Riesling, Lutomer Sylvaner, etc.
See Yugoslavia; Ljutomer.

Luttenberger

The German name for the wines of Ljutomer in Yugoslavian Slovenia during the Austrian occupation before the First World War. The white wines became famous under this name, by which they are still occasionally called. They are now correctly Ljutomer wines, or Lutomer on English-language labels.
See Yugoslavia; Ljutomer; Lutomer.

Luxembourg

The white wines grown on the rolling, pretty Luxembourg bank of the Moselle are very similar to those of Alsace. Light and fruity, they are stay-at-home wines for the most part, since few of them are ever seen outside the Benelux Union.

Each year the 1,200-hectare (3,000-acre) strip produces a rough average of 160,000 hectoliters (4.24 million U.S. gallons, 3.52 million imp.).

Of the wines, 75% are consumed in the Grand Duchy itself, amounting to two bottles in three of all the wine the Luxembourgers drink, the odd bottle being made up by importation, mainly from France and Italy. The per capita consumption is twenty-seven or twenty-eight bottles per year, far down the list for a European nation. Most of the wine not used at home goes to Belgium. Holland and Germany receive a token quantity, and the amount exported to the rest of the world is a statistical drop in the

Trier 9 m.
Grevenmacher
Luxembourg 8 m.
Machtum
Ahn
R. Moselle
Wormeldange
Ehnen
Saarburg
Greival-dange
GERMANY
Lux. 8 m.
Stadtbredimus
Remich
Wellenstein
Schwebsingen
Wintrange
Remerschen
Schengen
N
LUXEMBOURG
0 1 2 3 4 5 MILES
0 1 2 3 4 5 KILOMETRES
Metz 23 m.

When this practice was ended by the First World War and severance from Germany, Luxembourg had no sale for the characterless bulk wine that was being produced. A long crisis extended from 1914 to 1925. Then the government Viticultural Station was founded at Remich on the Moselle. Premiums were paid for uprooting second-class vineyards. Luxembourg viticulture had accepted the principle, in force to this day, that wine is a quality—not a quantity—product. The Viticultural Station is the teacher and policeman of this movement. There is a department of analysis, free instruction and help for growers, a scientific campaign against vine disease, and supervision of the laws governing place-names on bottle labels.

Vines have grown here from the time of the Romans. Luxembourg vintage records extend as far back as 809 (when the wine was a failure). In 1866 the wine was so sour that, as a joke topical at the time, the people named it Bismarck. One of the worst setbacks occurred in 1944, when the Moselle was caught in the von Rundstedt counteroffensive, finishing with the Battle of the Bulge; but the following year the vineyards were flourishing again.

WHAT THE WINES ARE CALLED

The Luxembourg vineland faces east, across the Moselle to the German bank. Wine is grown nowhere else in the tiny country. The advantage of catching the early sun on the east-facing slope is augmented by the forest protection crowning the hills, cutting off a wind which usually blows from the west all the year round. The whole gentle length of the Moselle is an alternating patchwork of vineyard and orchard. The cherry and plum trees provide the fruit for the kirsch, quetsch, and mirabelle distilled in the Duchy.

Luxembourg wine labels carry, according to law, name designations of the following four types:

Vin de la Moselle Luxembourgeoise. Seldom used and limited to wine exported in cask and to the ordinary wine, known as *grâchen.*

Vin de la Moselle Luxembourgeoise, used in combination with the grape variety. This is what appears on most common wines—e.g., Vin de la Moselle Luxembourgeoise Riesling.

Locality name, with or without vineyard site, and grape variety—e.g., Wormeldange Riesling, Riesling from the Elterberg vineyard near Wormeldange.

Appellation Complète, sometimes also called Appellation Contrôlée, and corresponding to the French designation of that name. This is the category of fine wines. Labels must indicate vintage year, locality, vineyard site, grape variety, name of grower, and his domicile. Wines of one of the first three types may or may not be vintage-dated, but those of the fourth must be. There are also strict regulations governing treatment and the type of vine, and wines must pass official tasting tests of the Commission of the Marque Nationale.

bucket. To taste Luxembourg wine you must go to Luxembourg itself, or at least to Belgium.

WINE HISTORY

At the time of the French Revolution Luxembourg was a part of France, and the Revolution drove the monks from the vineyards they had tended. The vineland was broken up into small parcels, a condition which has survived to this day, when there are 1,670 vineyards. The size of the average plot is just under one hectare, only a few being much larger. This extreme tendency to division is counteracted by the cooperatives, one existing in each main town of the wine belt; between them they account for 65% of total production.

At the turn of the century Luxembourg wine went almost entirely into blends called vaguely Moselblümchen—mixtures of low-quality German Palatinate and Lower Moselle wines with the Luxembourg product.

Since its establishment by the government in 1935, the Marque Nationale has begun to appear on more and more Luxembourg wine. A small label prominently lettered Marque Nationale and indicating that the wine is from Luxembourg is affixed to the neck of the certified bottles. Marque Nationale wines are bottled under government observation and control, subjected to blind tasting tests.

GRAPE VARIETIES: BEST WINES

The best vineyards are found on the chalky marl soil of Remich and the stony chalk-and-clay soil of Grevenmacher. A chalky soil with scattered stones and a marly subsoil is considered good Riesling soil, while the peculiar clay soil varying in hue from green to red is the soil for the Pinot varieties.

The grape varieties of Luxembourg are Riesling, Traminer, Ruländer, Pinot Blanc, Auxerrois, Sylvaner, Riesling × Sylvaner, Elbling, and Muscat Ottonel. From these, the best wines are the following:

Riesling × Sylvaner. A light table wine with a slight Muscat taste. Best locality: entire Moselle. The grape is better known as the Müller-Thurgau.

Pinots. Auxerrois, Pinot Blanc and Ruländer (or Pinot Gris). Fuller, more generous and with more body than the Riesling × Sylvaner, though often with less bouquet. Best localities: Wellenstein, Remerschen, Schengen.

Riesling. Elegant and full of distinction, tending to be acidic in the wet years. Best localities: Wormeldange, Stadtbredimus, Wintrange, Schengen, Remich, Grevenmacher, Ehnen.

Traminer. Velvety, big, and with the typical spicy perfume and taste. Best localities: Ahn, Wellenstein, Schwebsingen, Schengen, Machtum.

SPIRITS

Kirsch, quetsch, and mirabelle are produced from the cherry and plum orchards. The number of distilleries in operation varies but is usually around 950.

Château Lynch-Bages

Bordeaux red wine.
District: Haut-Médoc, France.
Commune: Pauillac.

Classified a Fifth Growth (*Cinquième Cru*) of Médoc in 1855, Lynch-Bages actually commands prices equal to those of some Second Growths (*Seconds Crus*). It is located at Bages, hardly a quarter of a mile south of Pauillac, and is plainly seen on the left of the wine road approaching Pauillac. Originally the property of an Irishman, Mr. Lynch—who was mayor of Bordeaux—the vineyard has been, since 1933, in the Cazes family, and in recent years in the hands of the bright and energetic mayor of Pauillac, André Cazes, and his son Jean-Michel. With this capable management the growth has come rapidly into its own. In both 1955 and 1956, at blind tastings held at Château Prieuré-Lichine in Cantenac-Margaux, with leading vineyard owners, wine brokers, and Bordeaux shippers participating, Lynch-Bages took first place among the leading Médoc Classified Growths. That this fine vineyard is still classed a Fifth Growth indicates the obsolescence of the 1855 Classification.

Characteristics. Can produce rich, full, round wines. It is flattering to the taste in its youth, but in ageing it does often show a lack of breed and distinction.

Vineyard area: 65 hectares (163 acres).
Average production: 250 tonneaux (24,000 cases).

Château Lynch-Moussas

Bordeaux red wine.
District: Haut-Médoc, France.
Commune: Pauillac.

The output of this small vineyard, which was classified a Fifth Growth (*Cinquième Cru*) of the Médoc in 1855, is principally sold in Holland and Belgium. In common with its large neighbor, Château Lynch-Bages, the estate was once the property of Mr. Lynch, an Irish mayor of Bordeaux. The present owner, Jean Casteja, has replanted much of the vineyard.

Characteristics. Still to be drunk young, but the wine is improving.

Vineyard area: 35 hectares (88 acres).
Average production: 175 tonneaux (17,000 cases).

M

Macadam, vin de

An old Parisian term for a sweet white wine brought right out of the fermenting vat and rushed to the boulevards of Paris. Much of this wine was drunk in the open-air cafés, overlooking the macadam-paved streets and squares. The most famous of these wines came from the area around Bergerac (*q.v.*).

Mâché

French term for a wine which tastes tired, either from racking or from travel; tastes as though it had been mashed up by chewing.

Mâcon

Market town and wine center for Lower Burgundy. *See* Mâconnais.

Mâcon Supérieur

An Appellation Contrôlée of the Mâconnais region (*q.v.*).

Mâconnais

White wine, some red and rosé.
District: Southern Burgundy, France.

The southern Burgundy section of the Mâconnais adjoins that of the Beaujolais. It occupies one corner of the department of Saône-et-Loire, and its southeast corner overlaps the wine district of the Beaujolais, specifically the commune of la Chapelle-de-Guinchay. The wines made in this corner are usually sold as Beaujolais if they are red and as Mâconnais if they are white—one of the rare cases where the vintner can make the best of both worlds.

The best and the most famous of the Mâconnais is the dry white Pouilly-Fuissé, a wine which has commanded a place on many good tables over the years and is still growing in popularity. It is not, however, the only Pouilly to be made. Nearby are the vineyards of Pouilly-Loché and Pouilly-Vinzelles, and in the valley of the Loire there is another dry white wine made in the town of Pouilly-sur-Loire. The Pouilly-Fumé (*q.v.*) from this last town is similar in color and in name, but the grapes used are different—Sauvignon Blanc—and so are the wines.

Pouilly-Fuissé is to the white wines of southern Burgundy what the Beaujolais is to the red. Neither of them is ever a very great wine, either may often be an excellent wine, both are usually extremely pleasant wines. The public affection for Pouilly-Fuissé and the wines of the Mâconnais is far older than for those of Beaujolais, which has only gained its wide circle of admirers during comparatively recent times.

The Mâconnais has been sending its wines to clamoring markets since the seventeenth century, thanks, so they say, to an imaginative grower named Claude Brosse. About 1660, Brosse decided that it was high time that someone outside the region knew about the excellence of the Mâconnais wines. A man of enormous stature, and evidently fearless as well, he loaded his cart with two barrels of his finest wine and started off for Paris. Trips to Paris were rare in those days, for there were some 400 kilometers (250 miles) of muddy and nearly impassable roads, and highwaymen in waiting. But Brosse managed to arrive safely with his wine in Paris—it took him thirty-odd days. His imposing stature caught the attention of Louis XIV, who wanted to know what he was doing so far from home, and since the business was wine, he wanted to taste it. When the King had sipped the wine, Brosse got an immediate order for the royal cellars. What the King happened to like was also exactly what the court had always wanted, and Brosse and the wines of the Mâconnais were launched.

The present Mâconnais growers produce more than white wines. A large amount of red is also made, and the makers could add rosé, although there is comparatively little of this at present. Being next to the Beaujolais, where the noble vine is the Gamay, the growers of the Mâconnais tend to plant the same vine, but the results are less happy. The traditional red-wine vine has always been the Gamay à Jus Coloré (Gamay with colored juice), sometimes called Gamay-Teinturier. It produces large grapes in vast quantities and these, unlike those of most vines, give a dark juice. This particular vine, of all the varieties of Gamay, has come in for an enormous amount of abuse and it has been condemned and forbidden in Burgundy over and over again. Since 1970, in fact, all Mâconnais red and rosé wine may only include 15% Gamay-Teinturier. The major part of these wines is made from Pinot Noir, with some Gamay Noir à Jus Blanc. Any replanting for these wines is done with Pinot Noir.

The reason why the Gamay vine does so much better in the neighboring Beaujolais than in the Mâconnais is the soil. Nowhere in the Mâconnais does one find the granite soil which gives Beaujolais its special appeal. By the same token, the chalky hills of the Mâconnais permit the Chardonnay vine, Burgundy's only noble white-wine vine, to produce, with delightful results. Actually there are three areas of soil, the best that of Pouilly-Fuissé, slightly to the southwest of Mâcon. Here there is a series of dips and rises where the soil is limestone mixed with slate, dating back to the Jurassic age some 150 million years ago. To the northwest of Mâcon there is a slightly different formation, this time a long valley where the disintegration of the chalky oolite has allowed enough topsoil for the planting of vines. Both of these sections are excellent for growing grapes for white wines. Toward the northern end of the district the terrain gets more varied and confused. At one point there is a preponderance of chalk, and at another of slate, and the wines tend to follow the lead given by the soil. Some are good, some not so good, the characteristics depending upon the particular soil in which they were grown.

The soil of certain parts of the Mâconnais has always had a fascination for geologists and diggers in the earth. Not only are there several layers of rock formation underlying the district, each one dating from a different period, but the area has proved a good place for digging up relics of the distant past. Fossils dating back 6,000 years have been excavated from the vicinity of Solutré—one of the communes making Pouilly-Fuissé—and there is hardly a plowman in the region who has not at one time or another turned up some ancient bit of equipment, often dating back to Roman days. But the history of the Mâconnais is written not only in the soil. The great medieval monastery of Cluny was built at the town of that name, some 16 kilometers (10 miles) northwest of Mâcon. Its monks did a great deal to keep learning alive during the Dark Ages, and Cluny was once the most powerful arm of the Church in France. The monks also helped to forward the knowledge and practice of vine-growing and wine-making and to inspire the local peasants to increase their vineyards and care for them properly. It is not recorded whether the monks inspired the wine or whether the wine inspired the monks, but it is certain that Burgundian viniculture virtually owes its existence to the industry of the inhabitants of Cluny.

In this corner of southern Burgundy growers have their own methods of viniculture. The sun is warmer than it is farther north, on the Côte d'Or, and the warm seasons are slightly longer. The Chardonnay vine, in particular, is allowed to grow much higher here than elsewhere in Burgundy. The growers say that because of the stronger sunshine, the grapes need not be pruned close to the ground where the stony soil will reflect heat on to them. Furthermore, in the Mâconnais they can often afford to wait as much as two weeks longer than in the Côte d'Or for the grapes to ripen.

Most of the wine sold is Mâcon Supérieur, or Mâcon, followed by the name of the commune where the wine was grown. A slightly lesser amount will be sold simply as Mâcon with no other indication of source, while the best, of course, is sold under one of the three Pouilly *appellations*. As is usual with French wines, the names include more than simply place of origin.

PLACE-NAMES OF THE MÂCONNAIS

Pouilly-Fuissé

Pouilly-Fuissé is the king of the Mâconnais white wines, and the very finest rank high among white Burgundies. In general, these wines are fairly light and very dry. The better ones have a forthright round fullness that distinguishes them from the lesser light wines which are lacking in character and are over-acidic. They are less hard than the Chablis and not so fruity, with a slight *goût de terroir*, the taste imparted by the soil in which they are grown. They tend to have a very light, fine bouquet, and at their youthful best are of a pale golden color with over-

tones of green. They are definitely wines to be drunk when they are young, reaching their peak after about six months in bottle and holding it for from three to five years. Some of them have enough alcoholic content to last longer than that, but there will be no improvement and therefore little point in keeping them.

To be a real Pouilly-Fuissé, the wine must have been grown in one of the communes of Solutré-Pouilly, Fuissé, Chaintré, or Vergisson. It must be made only from the Chardonnay vine, the amount harvested not to exceed 45 hectoliters per hectare (481 U.S. gallons, 400 imp. per acre). The content in the must—or unfermented grape juice—should amount to 187 grams (6.5 ounces) of natural sugar per liter, and the finished wine must have a minimum alcoholic strength of 11%. The sugar is always stated to be natural, since the growers here, as elsewhere in Burgundy, are allowed to add a certain amount of extra sugar to the wine, a process known as *chaptalisation*. The purpose of this practice is to raise the sugar content in years when the sun has been too weak to instill enough natural grape-sugar into the fruit, and what is added gets converted into alcohol with the grape-sugar. *Chaptalisation* is a tricky business, for when it is practiced to excess it tends to diminish the finesse and elegance of the wine, making it fuller, heavier, and sometimes very much coarser than it should be.

Within the area of the four towns allowed the use of the name of Pouilly-Fuissé, there are about 600 hectares (1,500 acres) of vines. From these come an average of about 36,000 hectoliters (954,000 U.S. gallons, 792,000 imp.) of wine each year. The best is sold as Pouilly-Fuissé with the name of the vineyard added, and to qualify for this the sugar content of the must is elevated to a minimum of 204 grams (7.25 ounces), and the alcoholic content must be 12%. The better vineyards, and those apt to be found on a bottle label, are: (in the town of Solutré-Pouilly) Les Chailloux, Les Boutières, Les Chanrue, Les Prâs, Les Peloux, Les Rinces; (in the town of Fuissé) Château Fuissé, Le Clos, Clos de Varambond, Clos de la Chapelle, Menetrières, Versarmières, Les Vignes-Blanches, Les Châtenets, Les Perrières, Les Brûlets.

In general, the wines from Solutré-Pouilly tend to be more feminine and delicate than those from the other communes, while those from Fuissé are apt to be the strongest. The cooperative at Chaintré produces some of the best Pouilly-Fuissé, superior to that of Vergisson.

Pouilly-Loché, Pouilly-Vinzelles, and Saint-Véran

The first two are the two lesser Pouillys of the Mâconnais. Although the legal restrictions—exclusive of growing area—are identical with those of Pouilly-Fuissé, they never attain quite the same degree of excellence. As a rule, they are lighter, with less breed than the Pouilly-Fuissé, although they often have more fruitiness.

The geographical distinction is simply that Pouilly-Loché must be harvested within the town of Loché, nearest to Fuissé, and Pouilly-Vinzelles comes from Vinzelles, directly south of Loché. Together they account for about 4,000 hectoliters (106,000 U.S. gallons, 88,000 imp.) of wine per year.

Saint-Véran is a new place-name now gaining favor due to the rising prices of Pouilly-Fuissé. It does not, however, reach the quality of the better Pouilly-Fuissés.

Mâcon Supérieur or Mâcon

This *appellation*, followed by the name of the commune, could include red, white, and rosé wines, but in practice slightly more than half are white, and most of the rest red. The red wines are small, generally not of outstanding quality, and even in the headquarters for the area, the town of Mâcon, the red wines drunk are often from the neighboring district of the Beaujolais. The whites are perhaps less distinctive than those of Pouilly-Fuissé, but every now and then one of the better growers will come up with one which will be their equal or even better than some of the lesser Pouillys.

The wine must be grown in the delimited area that lies within the *arrondissement* of Mâcon, or within the communes of Boyer, Bresse-sur-Grosne, Champagny-sous-Uxelles, Champlieu, Etrigny, Jugy, Laives, Mancey, Montceaux-Ragny, Nanton, Sennecey-le-Grand, or Vers. It must be made from a certain selection of grapes. For red wines, only the Gamay Noir à Jus Blanc, Pinot Noir, and Pinot Gris are allowed, with up to 15% Gamay Noir à Jus Coloré and also up to 15% of Pinot Blanc or Chardonnay, the allowable vines for white wines. The normal production of any wine may not exceed 45 hectoliters per hectare (481 U.S. gallons, 400 imp. per acre). In the red there must be a minimum of 180 grams of sugar per liter and 10% of alcohol when that sugar has fermented; and for white wines there must be at least 187 grams (6.5 ounces) of sugar per liter fermenting into 11% of alcohol.

The white wines could be sold as Burgundy, if so desired, and if the reds came only from the Pinot plants, they too could be sold as Burgundy; but there is small incentive for this to be done. As it now stands, about 150,000 hectoliters (3,975,000 U.S. gallons, 3,300,000 imp.) per year are sold as Mâcon Supérieur, a little more than half of it white.

Mâcon; Pinot-Chardonnay-Mâcon

At the bottom of the Mâconnais scale are those wines which are sold simply as Mâcon-Rouge, Mâcon-Blanc, or Pinot-Chardonnay-Mâcon (something of a misnomer, since the wines can be made from the Pinot Blanc as well as the Chardonnay, the same as the less cumbersome Mâcon-Blanc). All told, the *appellation* covers the lesser red and white wines, but mostly the red.

To earn this place-name, these wines must be harvested in a quantity not exceeding 50 hectoliters per hectare (535 U.S. gallons, 446 imp. per acre), as opposed to the 481 U.S. gallons (400 imp.) figure for the other wines of the district. It is always important to remember that quantity and quality seldom if ever coincide in wines. The same growing area is prescribed as for Mâcon Supérieur; but in the wines themselves, the differences are that red wines for this *appellation* need only have a sugar content in the grape of 162 grams (5.75 ounces) of sugar per liter, giving 9% of alcohol, and the white wines must have 170 grams (6 ounces) of sugar, giving 10% of alcohol. Less wine is made today under this *appellation* than before, just over 5,000 hectoliters (132,500 U.S. gallons, 110,000 imp.), about half of it red, half white.

Madagascar

This island lying off the coast of Africa makes a certain amount of rum.

See Rum, French.

Madeira

Until the middle of the eighteenth century, Madeira—like its cousins Port and Sherry—was exported as an unfortified beverage wine. It is known that brandy was distilled from surplus grapes on the island of Madeira as early as 1704. However, it is not until 1753 that we have the first indication that some of the wine was being roughly fortified; at that time one Francis Newton complained that his deceitful competitors were "putting a bucket or two of brandy with every pipe." Some twenty years later, the practice was general for export wines. In those days too the custom developed of sending casks of the brandied wine on a voyage to the East Indies and back in order to mature it. Madeira then possessed its present character, a distinctive wine with its own unique excellence. It was about this time also that the wine became most popular in the United Kingdom and the American Colonies—where the trade flourished until, in 1852, the vineyards were blighted by oïdium.

Some great Madeiras were, and still are, made, but the markets built up during the days of sailing ships and exploration have shrunk. Madeira is no longer primarily produced for Britain and the United States (although these are still good markets) but is now also sold largely in Scandinavia, France, Germany, Belgium, Holland, and Canada. Since the shippers united to form the Madeira Wine Association, in order to promote the wine, sales have improved.

WINE HISTORY

The history of the island is almost the history of its wines. Madeira is politically an integral part of Portugal and geographically an island in the Atlantic 575 kilometers (360 miles) from the coast of Morocco and 850 kilometers (530 miles) from Lisbon. It is 57 kilometers (36 miles) long and 23 kilometers (14.5 miles) wide, a holiday-maker's paradise of steeply sloping, intricately terraced hillside vineyards and shady flower-filled valleys.

Madeira and its tiny volcanic neighbors, Porto-Santo and the Desertas, were islands known to the ancient Phoenician, Genoese, and Portuguese as the "Enchanted Isles." But none was so audacious as to penetrate the thick woods and see what was there until Prince Henry the Navigator sent the intrepid Captain João Gonçalves (known as Zarco) to claim them for Portugal in 1419.

Zarco apparently landed near where modern Funchal stands but found it impossible to move further. Madeira, "Isle of Trees," was aptly named. Trees intertwined and woven together claimed the entire island and defeated all attempts to hack through them. Zarco solved the problem. He set the island on fire and sat back to wait.

According to legend he waited a long time. It is said that the fire raged for seven years . . . and when it had finally gutted itself out the trees were gone and the centuries-old humus and leaf-mold volcanic soil had been enriched into the most fertile in the world.

Settlers arrived from Portugal, Spain, Holland, and Italy; sugar-cane and the Malvoisie vines were planted. The rich soil and sub-tropical climate made Madeira a lush garden in the midst of the Atlantic. Mariners called in at Funchal in search of fresh water, fresh food, and to replenish wine casks. Treaties between Portugal and Britain helped Madeira as well as Port wines. Englishmen who departed to establish colonies in America took their tastes with them, and Madeira began to be shipped to the New World as well as the old. As the American colonists moved toward rupture with England, Madeira became more and more the wine of America and its consumption almost a patriotic duty. In drinking Madeira, the rebellious colonist could feel he was thumbing his nose at a tyrannical king and parliament who had established a ruling that European goods going to the American Colonies could only be carried in British ships. Naturally, British shipmasters were not above charging a premium price for the exercise of this monopoly; but, geographically, Madeira is in Africa, and under the terms of the law its wines could arrive on ships bearing any flag. The idea was quickly grasped by the Americans, and Madeira was a common sight on American sideboards. In *The House of the Seven Gables*, Nathaniel Hawthorne described the glories of an old, golden Madeira. The popularity of the wine along the Eastern Seaboard lasted for the period of the clipper ships.

The English writer Captain Frederick Marryat remarked in his *Diary in America*: "Claret and other French wines do very well in America, but where the Americans beat us out of the field is in their Madeira, which certainly is of a quality which we cannot procure in England. This is owing to the extreme heat and cold of the climate, which ripens this wine; indeed, I may almost say that I never tasted good Madeira until I arrived in the United States. The price of wines, generally speaking, is very high, considering what a trifling duty is paid, but the price of good Madeira is surprising. There are certain brands which if exposed to public auction, will be certain to fetch from twelve to twenty, and I have been told, even forty dollars per bottle."

During the eighteenth and early nineteenth centuries, the fortunes of Madeira were probably at their peak. The Napoleonic Wars had cut into French wine exports, but Madeira was untouched and business boomed. Fortification had put strength into the wines, and the long sea voyage aged and ripened them. Shipments to England and America were heavy, with the ports of the southern states—Savannah and New Orleans, Charleston and Baltimore—handling the bulk of the trade.

Disaster fell on Madeira in 1852, when oïdium struck the vines. They were just recovering from the attack of this fungus blight when they were again attacked, by phylloxera in 1872. This time, weakened by the ravages of the oïdium, they succumbed to the *Phylloxera vastatrix*, which attacked their roots and killed the vines. Many of the old-established British shippers left the island, and it is to the courage, endurance, and persistence of a handful who remained that we owe the present Madeira wine. They imported American root-stocks which had become immune to the disease (phylloxera having originally spread from America to Europe). It was many years before these American vines were in full production, and when there was enough wine to ship, this was found to be coarse, although plentiful, since the American plants are prolific. The vines had to be cut down and grafted with the pre-phylloxera European vine.

WINE-MAKING

The vintage is probably as picturesque in Madeira as anywhere in the world and is certainly the longest. Starting at sea level in mid-August it continues as the grapes ripen on the slopes until October. The crushing of the grapes is still done in *lagares*, or large wooden troughs, by barefooted men, although no doubt the old custom will soon be superseded by mechanical pressing. The "dance" of the grapes is followed by a more rigorous pressing, after which the grape juice (*mosto*) is carried in goatskins to the wine sheds to be tipped into wooden casks and then carried by truck to the shippers' lodges in Funchal.

The *mosto* ferments and turns itself into wine or *vinho claro*, which is put into an *estufa* to go through a process, peculiar to Madeira, known as *estufagem* (bringing the wine up to a warm temperature either in glass jars laid out in the sun or in a sort of heating chamber). This process is a relic of the old days of the East India voyages. The rolling of the ship and the heat of the tropics obviously hastened the maturing of the wine, but during the Napoleonic Wars, when freights were difficult to obtain, the process of *estufagem* was invented.

The *estufa* today is a large store with central heating in which casks of wine are placed for six months. The temperature of the wine is gradually brought up to 104° to 114°F. (40° to 46°C.) and then allowed to drop to normal in the sixth month, thus producing much the same effect as would a voyage around the world.

The sweeter Madeiras are fortified with brandy before they go into the heating chamber; but the dry styles are allowed to ferment out, and the brandy is added after they have been in the *estufa*.

Wine which has never been *estufado* is known as *canteiro*. When the wine comes out of the *estufa*, it goes through an *estágio*, which is an eighteen-month rest to recover from the treatment. Then it is matured in a *solera* system, as used for Sherry (*q.v.*), and some wines are afterward blended before shipping.

303

There are no vintage Madeiras now and—since the wines were blended—the dates of old vintages serve to tell the age of the wine rather than celebrate a special year.

Madeira lives longer than any other wine; there are still some priceless old pre-phylloxera vintages in existence. Tasting them is not only a pleasure but an exciting and memorable experience.

WINE TYPES

There are four distinct types of Madeira, named after the grapes from which they are produced, ranging from dry to full-rich, with intermediate steps between. These are:

Sercial. The best of the dry Madeiras, generally taken slightly cooled, as an aperitif. Sometimes pale, sometimes golden, often slight in body, but always dry with an overwhelming nose. André Simon, the famous writer on wines, has described one of them as "a soul with a nose."

Verdelho. Sweeter and softer than a Sercial; leaves a dry, clean taste in the mouth; excellent with soup, and is the proverbial companion to turtle soups. In Victorian days, mid-morning callers were frequently entertained with a slice of cake and a glass of this Madeira.

Bual (Boal). Fuller and sweeter than either of the preceding, russet to dark in color with a distinctive bouquet. A dessert wine.

Malmsey. From the Malvoisie grape. A rich, luscious, generous wine with considerable body, balance, and bouquet. This type of Madeira is excellent after dinner.

Other names to be found on bottles of Madeira are:

Rainwater. A blend. Originally a trademark, it has now become almost a generic name. The wine may be dry or medium-rich but is always pale and light, as the name implies.

Southside. Another blend found principally in America. Not so dry as Rainwater.

Dated Soleras. Many dated *soleras* are offered for sale; the word *solera* before or after the date denotes that these wines are not only of that date but have from time to time been topped up with specially chosen younger wines of equal quality and similar characteristics. The average age of a *solera* is estimated to be some eighty years. These are always particularly fine wines.

Leading shippers in the Madeira Wine Association are Blandy's Madeiras Lda., Leacock & Co. (Wine) Lda. (whose founder arrived in Madeira in 1741), Rutherford & Miles Ltd., Cossart Gordon & Co. Ltd., T.T.C. Lomedino Lda. (a firm with a remarkable reserve of old wines), Shortridge Lawton & Co. Ltd., F.F. Ferraz Lda., Luis Gomes (Vinhos) Lda., and Freitas Martins Caldeira Lda.

Others, outside the Association, are Henriques & Henriques, H.M. Borges, Vinhos Barbeito, Marcel Gomes & Cia Lda., and Veiga Franca & Co. Ltd.

In his most explicit book, *Portuguese Wine,* Raymond Postgate also mentions Avery of Bristol who, although a merchant and not a shipper, "has a selection of Madeiras approached by no other, and taken from many sources. . . .The oldest is a Verdelho of about 1846."

Maderization

Owing to age or poor storage, white wines may lose their freshness and fruitiness and acquire a brown tinge. This browning or oxidation has been named maderization, from the Madeira taste, which is connected with the presence in the wine of ethylic aldehyde—the result either of oxidation of alcohol, or of the dissociation of aldehyde-sulfurous acid through progressive oxidation of sulfurous acid. Maderization also results from leaving white wines in the barrel too long before bottling. In the Madeiras, Marsalas, Sherry and the Château-Chalons of the French Jura, maderization adds to the greatness of the wines, producing a taste called *rancio.* In other white wines it is a flaw. It is particularly unpleasant in the Montrachets and Meursaults of the Côte de Beaune and is more unpleasant in Graves than in Sauternes (whose sweetness hides the flat, musty, brownish taste).

By combining the action of sulfur dioxide with that of casein, it is possible to protect wines against maderization, and the flat taste can be corrected with sulfurous acid.

Madiran

Red wine from the Hautes-Pyrénées district of southwest France. The wine, full in body and of a pronounced bouquet, is made from Tannat (30% to 70%), Cabernet Sauvignon, Bouchy, Cabernet Franc, and Pinenc grapes and attains 11% of alcohol. The white wine made in this area in the valley of the Adour is Pacherenc du Vic Bilh (*q.v.*). Annual production averages 18,000 hectoliters.

Magnum

A bottle twice the normal capacity. Since some red wines age more successfully in larger quantities, Bordeaux and Burgundies of fine years are sometimes bottled in this larger size for laying down.

Mailly

Village near Reims producing a first-quality Champagne (*q.v.*).

Maipo Valley

One of the best wine regions in Chile (the other is the Aconcagua Valley), specializing in Cabernet and Malbec grapes and making long-lasting wines of finesse and balance.

See Chile.

Maître de chai

French term for the man in charge of vinification and ageing of all the wine made on an estate in Bordeaux. The name, which may be shortened to *maître,* is used especially in Bordeaux, of the head cellarman at the château or at the shipper's *chais.* He is of necessity an experienced wine-maker and a good taster. In other districts, the *maître de chai* will be called a *caviste.*

Málaga

Spanish dessert wines.
District: East Andalusia.

This hottest, once sleepiest, corner of the Spanish coast, where sun-ripened grapes oozed sweetness and where the soft climate may well have induced a certain lethargy in the inhabitants, has been modernized, its capital urbanized, and its way of life transformed by the *tourismo* of Torremolinos, Marbella, and the rest of the Costa del Sol. In the past, Málaga was famous for its sweet wines, which had a great success abroad. There are many references in English literature to "Mountain" and to Málaga "Sack"; but little is seen of them in Anglo-Saxon countries today. Yet Málaga is made—some of it, produced by traditional methods, is as good as ever—and it is still exported. Germany heads the list of customers, followed by Switzerland, Scandinavia, and France. In 1975, 5,000 hectares (12,500 acres) of vineland granted the Denominación de Origen produced 55,000 hectoliters (1,457,500 U.S. gallons, 1,210,000 imp.) of wine.

The vineyards, hardly visible from the coast, are planted up the mountain slopes, with the finest plots around Archidona, Antequera, and Velez-Málaga. The Pedro-Ximénez grape, here coming into its own, is used in a ration of 60% for blending with about 20% Lairen, 15% Moscatel, and 5% other grapes of the area, all combining to make this strong, rich, dark wine. The region has a long history. The great variety of grapes, both for wine and for eating, have been praised by ancient Greek, Roman, and Renaissance writers. The Moorish conquerors, whether or not they drank the forbidden wine, enjoyed the luscious table grapes—which are still grown, many of them to be dried into the succulent raisins of the region. Presents of wine are said to have been sent to Tamerlane the Great and Catherine the Great; the History of the Pedro Ximénez was traced in *Cosmografía de Merula*, published in Amsterdam in 1636. Columella who, in the first century, discussed the wines in his *Re Rustica*, was himself of Andalusian descent.

Málaga, unlike the dark Sherries, is a natural wine with about 16% of alcohol. It is not fortified with brandy. Formerly, the celebrated Lágrima Christi (not to be confused with the Italian Lacrima Christi, which is quite different) was made by allowing the grapes to shed their sweetness drop by drop without pressing. Such wines are not now made commercially; the name is usually given to a rather average, sweetish brown wine. From a multitude of small vineyards (some of which will produce, for the growers' own use, excellent pure "Mountains") come red wines and others; but the characteristic Málaga, the quality wine protected by the Denominación de Origen, is made by traditional methods in the big *bodegas* of the town, from wine, must, or grapes supplied by small farmers. The best are matured by the *solera* system described under Sherry (*q.v.*).

Before pressing, the grapes are spread on straw mats to grow overripe and sugary in the sun. They ferment in large oak vats (in big *bodegas*, some of these have an enormous capacity); then the new wine is piped into oak butts to mature for two or three years, when it will either be sold to the wine shops or will take its place in the *solera* of the *bodega*'s fine wines. These, in all their nuances of sweetness and color, develop in different styles, as follows:

Málaga dulce color	Very sweet; very dark (blackish brown).
Málaga blanco dulce	Very sweet; golden yellow to topaz.
Málaga semi-dulce	Fairly sweet; both golden yellow and red.
Málaga Lágrima and *Lágrima Christi*	Very sweet; old gold or dark; undistinguished.
Málaga blanco seco	Only fairly dry; pale gold; agreeable aftertaste.
Málaga Moscatel	Amber color; distinct flavor of the grape.
Pedro Ximénez	Luscious-sweet; very dark with reddish glint.
Málaga Rome	Strong wines, vinified both red and golden white.
Málaga Pajarete	Strong (15% to 20%); pale and dark amber.
Tintillo de Málaga	15% to 16% alcohol; red color.

In maturity, a well-made Málaga may be a wine of considerable distinction. Describing such a one, tasted in the *bodega* Scholtz Hermanos, Mr. H. W. Yoxall wrote: "Just as a touch of something cold leaves you uncertain whether it has frozen or burnt you, so in the taste of great Málagas, the sugar is sublimated and becomes almost astringent"—adding that, in England, few Málagas are seen now, and none of the best.

Here, as elsewhere, common, cloying wines are made; others, such as Rome and Pajarete, and some of the semi-sweet types, are often mixed with *vino tinto*. The wines listed above range between 14% and 23% of alcohol.

The principal producers and exporters in Málaga are: Hijos de A. Barceló, S.A.; Luis Barceló, S.A.; Flores Hermanos, S.A.; Felix García Gómez; José Garijo Ruiz; Carlos J. Krauel; Larios, S.A.; López Hermanos, S.A.; Compañia Mata, S.A.; Juan Mory & Cía., S.A.; Pérez Texeira, S.A.; Guillermo Rein Segura; Casa Romero, S.L.; Scholtz Hermanos, S.A.; Hijos de José Suárez Villalba; Vinícola Andalucía, S.A.; and Manuel Pacheco Morón.

Château Malartic-Lagravière

Bordeaux red and white wines.
District: Graves, France.
Commune: Léognan.

The red wine has had a good reputation for many years; it was included among the eleven best red wines of Graves in the 1953 and 1959 Classifications. The white wine was classified in 1959 and is less well known than the red.

Characteristics. The red is a big, mouth-filling wine with a distinctive taste, probably arising from the high proportion—75%—of Cabernet Sauvignon grapes. Merlot makes up the remaining 25%. The white wine is exclusively Sauvignon Blanc.

Vineyard area: red—11 hectares (27.5 acres); white—1.5 hectares (nearly 4 acres).

Malbec

Average production: red—45 *tonneaux* (4,000 cases); white—6 *tonneaux* (550 cases).

Malbec

One of the lesser grapes contributing to the red wines of Bordeaux, prolific and light in character. It is grown in other places too, and is sometimes known as Cot.

Château Malescot-Saint-Exupéry

Bordeaux red wine.
District: Haut-Médoc, France.
Commune: Margaux.

The vineyard name derives from the Counts of Saint-Exupéry, who purchased the vineyard in 1827, and the château itself, a substantial gray-stone manor-house, is right in the town of Margaux. The building, nothing but a shell after being gutted by the Germans, was repaired in 1964 by the son of the present owner.

In recent years, until 1955, the estate belonged to Seager Evans, British distillers, who sold it in that year to Paul Zuger—up to that time their administrator in the vineyard and one who has always been an able wine-maker. Zuger is the president of the association of the official wine place-names of Margaux, which came into being in 1956.

The vineyard was classified Third Growth (*Troisième Cru*) in the Médoc Classification of 1855.

Characteristics. Quite full for a Margaux wine, very elegant and sometimes slightly hard at the outset. The wines reflect the high proportion—80%—of Cabernet Sauvignon grapes used.

Vineyard area: 32 hectares (80 acres).
Average production: 140 *tonneaux* (12,000 cases).

Malic acid

One of the most abundant acids in unripe grapes, but one that is partially destroyed as the fruit matures; $COOH \cdot CH_2 \cdot CHOH \cdot COOH$.

Château de Malle

Bordeaux white wine.
District: Sauternes, France.
Commune: Preignac.

The wine is light, fresh, and clean—every bit as pleasant as the château, beautifully maintained by the owner, Comte Pierre de Bournazel. The vineyard was placed among the Second Growths in the 1855 Classification.

Vineyard area: 20 hectares (50 acres).
Average production: 40 *tonneaux* (3,700 cases).

Malmesbury

Wine region in the coastal belt of the Cape province. *See* South Africa.

Malmsey

English corruption of the name of a vine which started out as Monemvasia in Greece, became Malvasia in Italy, Malvoisie in France, and Malvagia in Spain. Malmsey is also used to refer to the wines from this vine, the most famous of which—during the present day—come from the island of Madeira (*q.v.*), a Portuguese possession in the Atlantic.

Malmsey was famous in the England of Shakespeare's day, and the references to it are numerous. Perhaps the best-known fact about Malmsey is that the Duke of Clarence was drowned in a butt of it. It is likely that the wine in which the unfortunate Duke found his end came from the island of Crete rather than from Madeira.

Malolactic fermentation

Secondary fermentation, caused by the conversion of malic acid into lactic acid and carbon dioxide. When this occurs while the wine is in barrel, the result is simply a reduction in acid strength; but in bottle, the malolactic fermentation causes the wine to become turgid and gassy. This happens much more frequently in Burgundy than it does in Bordeaux and may be the result of premature bottling.

The fermentation is caused by certain acid-tolerant species of *Lactobacillus* and *Leuconostoc* bacteria. The distinctiveness of different species of these malolactic bacteria endogenous to specific wineries may be an important factor in establishing the individual character of the wines produced.

See Chapter Nine, page 38.

Malta

Vines are grown mostly along the southern coastal strip of the island, but since the climate changes from torrential early rains to scorching heat, the resulting wine is generally harsh and rough; an ordinary wine, either red or white. An attempt is being made to produce sweet, rich dessert wine from Muscat grapes, principally for exportation to England. About 2,000 hectares (5,000 acres) are vineyard, especially around Burmarrad, Rabat, and Siggiewi. Gellewza, Gannaru, Nigruwa, and Dun Tumas grapes are among the better-known varieties. Production is probably about 30,000 hectoliters (795,000 U.S. gallons, 660,000 imp.) annually.

Malvasia

Originally Monemvasia in its native Greece, the grape Malvasia has spread throughout the viticultural world, sometimes with modifications in name. In France it is Malvoisie, in Spain Malvagia, and the sweet, heavy wines it gives became famous long ago in England as Malmsey.

Mandarine

Sweet, gold-colored liqueur with the flavor of tangerines.

Manganese

This is present in almost all wines, in quantities never large but varying with the different vineyard soils. More of the mineral is found in Beaujolais than in Bordeaux, more in red wine than in white. Most of the manganese in a grape is contained in the pips.

Mannitic fermentation

When the temperature of the fermenting vat rises above 95°F. (35°C.) and when the wines are lacking in acidity, then the good yeasts die and other bacteria take over. The wine then throws a deposit and becomes cloudy, with a bitter-sweet, "mousy" taste.
See Chapter Nine, page 38.

Manzanilla

The dry fine wine, fortified and unfortified, of Sanlúcar de Barrameda, Spain, sold as a type of Sherry.
See Sherry; Montilla.

Maraschino

A liqueur made from the sour cherry Marasca, which only grew in Dalmatia. Before the Italian enclave in Dalmatia was incorporated in Yugoslavia, maraschino was not made anywhere except in Zadar (sometimes known by its former name, Zara). Maraschino, 50% proof, is sold in wicker half-liter bottles. Luxardo is the largest distiller. After the war the company moved from Trieste to Padua; to ensure their supply they planted 80 hectares (200 acres) of Marasca cherries. Drioli, a lesser firm, is the other well-known Italian maraschino distiller.

Marc, eau-de-vie de marc

Spirit distilled from the pomace which remains when the grapes have been pressed and the juice run off. It is usually distilled at a high strength and has a distinctive taste—grapey, almost leathery—when it is well aged. Most districts have their own marcs; those from Burgundy are the best-known, and excellent marcs come from Romanée-Conti, Musigny, Chambertin, Nuits-Saint-Georges, Meursault, and Montrachet. Marcs from the white-wine Burgundy districts are lighter and have a little more finesse than those from the red-wine areas. The most expensive is the Marc des Hospices de Beaune; one of the lightest, and one with great finesse, comes from Champagne. Another of repute is the Marc d'Auvergne.
In Italy and California, this spirit is known as grappa.

The Marches

Red and white wines.
District: East-Central Italy.

Like the rest of the peninsula, this Italian state is steeped in history—even the name is said to date from the days when the area was a frontier province in the empire of Charlemagne. Here as elsewhere in Italy, the countryside is strewn with vines, both well-tended and ragged, which yield as much as 2 million hectoliters (53 million U.S. gallons, 44 million imp.) of wine annually—most of it fit solely for local drinking.

Exception might be made for the Verdicchio dei Castelli di Jesi, a good light D.O.C. wine, either dry or semisweet, with a pale gold or straw color. Sometimes it can be surprisingly high in alcohol—up to 14%. The wine is from Verdicchio grapes grown at Cupramontana, Monteroberto, and Castelbellino in the province of Ancona and is one of the few lesser wines of Italy which travels. The classico is a better wine from the old area, or zona antica. Verdicchio di Matelica is another D.O.C. wine similar to Verdicchio di Jesi but made a bit further inland from the Adriatic coast. The annual production is about 25,000 hectoliters (662,500 U.S. gallons, 550,000 imp.), only one-fourth of the volume of di Jesi.

Rosso Conero (D.O.C.) derives its name from the word the Greeks gave to the marine cherry tree that still grows on the slopes of the Conero mountain. Red, dry, fairly acid, yet fruity, this is just a pleasant local wine made near Ancona from Montepulciano and Sangiovese grapes.

Bianchello del Metauro is a D.O.C. white wine made of Bianchello and some Malvasia grown on the picturesque hills of Metauro, where one of the greatest battles of antiquity was fought when the Romans defeated the Carthaginians. The wine is understandably light and dry, and the large production goes well with local fish cookery.

The Marches, too, yield a sweet red sparkling wine called Vernaccia di Serrapetrona. Made from the Vernaccia grape grown in Macerata, it has been given the right to Controlled Denomination of Origin (D.O.C.).

Marcottage or layering

Traditional method of propagating vines.
See Chapter Eight, p. 29.

Mareotic wine

A fine wine of Ancient Egypt, very well known in classical times. Cleopatra is said to have served it to Caesar.
See Egypt.

Mareuil-sur-Ay

A village in the department of the Marne and the commune of the Champagne district, near Épernay, producing very fine wines.
See Champagne.

Margaux

Bordeaux red wines.
District: Haut-Médoc, France.

Margaux wines form a royal family. The Great Growths (Grands Crus) and the least among the modest vineyards all share the same characteristics. No other commune of Bordeaux and the Médoc contains such a distinct gradation of similar vineyards.

It is the summer of great sun that brings Margaux to its prime. In the best years, the greater Growths of the fine districts a little to the north, in Saint-Estèphe and Pauillac, may overreach themselves; in any case, it will be a long time before they are ready to drink. But in Margaux, the strong sun will have awakened the subtle hidden virtues which lie in the vines. In these best years, Margaux vineyards are likely to surpass all others in the Médoc. The wines they give are the most feminine, the most delicate, the most elegant; and it is the bolder Saint-Estèphe or, characteristically, a Pauillac which will sometimes excel in the lighter years.

The name Margaux is said to derive from Marojallia, so called by Ausonius, the fourth-century Latin poet after whom the Château Ausone, in Saint-Émilion, was also named.

The village of Margaux itself lies some 30 kilometers (20 miles) north of Bordeaux, and it is a sleepy place. In the season of fermentation the smell of the wine is everywhere in the air, as thick as the smoke from burning leaves. Tall châteaux with steep roofs stand right in the village, and plots of vine encroach on the dwellings and shops. Beyond, everything is vine—a calm ocean, brown in winter and green in summer, but always ruffled by a breeze. An occasional château rises in the distance, with its park around it like a froth of waves.

Five villages, not one, have the right to the place-name of Margaux. A quarter of a century ago, the wine of all five was considered as one—Margaux itself, Arsac, Soussans, Cantenac, and Labarde produced similar wines and shared the same light gravelly Margaux soil. Then, the mayor of Margaux, a wine man himself, brought a suit against a certain proprietor in Soussans. This grower had a strip of land along the riverbank where the soil, a muddy alluvial deposit, is not the true soil of Margaux, and its wine had no right, therefore, to the place-name. The legal process was fought and won, but the result was hardly what had been intended. The court ruled that neither the wine from this one vineyard nor any other made in Soussans could be called Margaux.

Within a few years, similar rulings denied the Margaux name to Arsac, Labarde, and Cantenac. There was consternation, for only a single important Margaux vineyard had all its vines in Margaux, and every other overlapping into the outcast communes by even an acre now had no right to the name, since some of its wine did not come from within the permitted circle. Margaux was almost in a state of civil war—because certain rather undistinguished growers safely within the commune now had a vested interest in resisting change.

For twenty years nothing could be done. Even when the Appellation Contrôlée, or officially controlled place-name, was established, the authorities were obliged to respect the earlier rulings of the courts. Then in 1953 someone had a bright idea. If Margaux could not mean what it ought to, why have any Margaux at all? At last action could be taken; and the place-name Margaux, which could not be extended back to its rightful limits, was totally suppressed: not even Margaux wine could now call itself Margaux. Again there was consternation, and this

time the sit-tight Margaux growers found that they could not sell their wines, could not get the proper documents, could not export. They demanded a decision, and the Appellation Contrôlée authorities suggested that perhaps the whole problem ought to be reconsidered.

As a result, new regulations were laid down defining Margaux wines as those from the communes of Margaux, Soussans, Arsac, Cantenac, and Labarde. The regulations also stated that the wines must be grown from soils ascertained by the experts of the Appellation Contrôlée to be typically Margaux, and that they may not yield more than 40 hectoliters to the hectare (424 U.S. gallons, 352 imp. to the acre); and in type of noble grape variety, in methods of pruning, cultivation, and wine-making, they must come up to high quality standards and must satisfactorily pass an anonymous taste test. Some 1,000 hectares now have the right to the *appellation*—or less than 2,500 acres, producing some 4,000,000 bottles per year.

The first of the tastings for the Appellation Contrôlée Margaux took place in 1956, and the subsequent banquet and festivities were held in the great salon of Château Lascombes.

It is rare that the leading vineyard of an area epitomizes and brings to the highest perfection the district characteristics, rather than stands out for excellences more peculiarly its own, but this is the case with Château Margaux. The Margaux vineyards rated as Classified Growths (*Crus*) in the 1855 Classification are:

FIRST GROWTH (*Premier Cru*)
Château Margaux

SECOND GROWTHS (*Seconds Crus*)

Château Rausan-Ségla	Château Durfort-Vivens
Château Rauzan-Gassies	Château Brane-Cantenac
Château Lascombes	

THIRD GROWTHS (*Troisièmes Crus*)

Château Kirwan	Château Cantenac-Brown
Château d'Issan	Château Palmer
Château Giscours	Château Desmirail
Château Malescot-Saint-Exupéry	Château Ferrière
	Château Marquis d'Alesme
Château Boyd-Cantenac	

FOURTH GROWTHS (*Quatrièmes Crus*)

Château Prieuré-Lichine	Château Marquis-de-Terme
Château Pouget	

FIFTH GROWTHS (*Cinquièmes Crus*)

Château Dauzac	Château du Tertre

(*For the individual Classified Growths, see individual châteaux names.*)

Château Margaux

Bordeaux red wine, some dry white.
District: Haut-Médoc, France.
Commune: Margaux.

Château Margaux, with its colonnaded portico and an interior which is pure Empire, stands in a large park beside a magnificent magnolia tree. In the fifteenth century the wine, under such names as Margou and Margous, was already known, and the site was occupied by a forti-fied castle known as Lamothe. It is interesting to note that one of the owners of Lamothe was the Seigneur de Dur-fort, whereas, until recently, the proprietor of Margaux owned the nearby Château Durfort.

The vineyard was greatly improved by M. de Fumel, also owner of Château Haut-Brion, with replantings in 1750. The present château was built at the beginning of the nineteenth century—by a pupil of Victor Louis, ar-chitect of the Bordeaux opera house. In 1836 a banker, the Vicomte d'Aguado, bought the property. His son sold it in 1879 to the Comte Pillet-Will, who introduced var-ious vinicultural improvements. By 1925 the château had come into the possession of the Duc de la Trémoïlle, from whom a corporation (including Fernand Ginestet, then owner of the adjacent Château Lascombes) acquired it. Between the years 1935 and 1949 Ginestet bought out his partners, and became principal owner. Bernard and Pierre Ginestet owned and managed Château Margaux until 1977, when they sold it to Laura and the late André Mentzelopoulos, owners of the Felix Potin grocery-store chain in France. The vineyards and the château have been entirely renovated with great care, all to the credit of the new owners.

With Château Lafite, Latour, and Haut-Brion, Mar-gaux has been ranked first among Médoc wines since 1855. There is also a small amount of dry white wine, a rarity in Médoc, known as Pavillon Blanc de Château Margaux.

No other commune of Bordeaux has a château of the same name—there is no Château Sauternes or Château Pauillac. All the wine of Château Margaux is château-bottled.

Characteristics. At its best, the most elegant and deli-cately feminine of the region. Perfectly balanced and quick to develop, for a Médoc. Finesse is synonymous with its name. In 1965, Pierre Ginestet instituted the con-troversial policy of affixing a vintage only to great vin-tages; the lesser years were sold as non-vintage wines as is done in Champagne. This practice was discontinued in 1969. Since the Mentzelopoulos takeover, the wine has once again become great.

Vineyard area: 66 hectares (165 acres).
Average production: Red—175 *tonneaux* (16,000 cases). Some 4,000 cases of white.

Marino

Usually white wines from Latium (*q.v.*).

Markobrunn, Marcobrunn

From Erbach on the German Rhine, Markobrunn is occasionally labeled Erbacher Markobrunn—but it is one of the few German wines so great in its own right as to eliminate the town or village or district name in most cases. Not perhaps the greatest of the Rheingau, although easily the best of the Erbachers, it is certainly one of the liveliest, heartiest, spiciest, and deservedly best-known Rhine wines.

See Rheingau.

Marl

The crumbly combination of calcium carbonate and clay which is often added to soils lacking lime.

Château Marquis d'Alesme

Bordeaux red wine.
District: Haut-Médoc, France.
Commune: Margaux.

Originally planted in 1616, the estate was acquired in 1803 by a M. Becker, which accounts for some confusion about the name of the wine. For a long time Becker at-tached his name to that of Marquis d'Alesme, and Becker being the simpler name, the wine began to be called sim-ply Becker in Bordeaux. Bottles labeled until a few years ago are likely to carry the name Marquis d'Alesme-Becker; but Becker has now been dropped.

The small vineyard occupies one of the finest positions in Margaux, the knoll of Margaux, or La Combe, which it shares with the Second Growth (*Second Cru*) vineyard Château Lascombes. Thirty-five years ago, Château Marquis d'Alesme was bought by Comte Chaix-d'Est-Ange, then owner of Château Lascombes, who meant to combine the two vineyards. This plan was not carried out, and today Marquis d'Alesme is run jointly with Châ-teau Malescot-Saint-Exupéry by Paul Zuger and his son.

This Third Growth (*Troisième Cru*), according to the 1855 Classification of Médoc wines, has two secondary vineyards: Cru La Fleur-Margaux, place-name Mar-gaux; Domaine du Balardin, place-name Bordeaux Su-périeur.

Characteristics. A minor and not well-known wine with the typical finesse of Margaux.

Vineyard area: 15 hectares (38 acres).
Average production: 75 *tonneaux* (7,200 cases).

Château Marquis-de-Terme

Bordeaux red wine.
District: Haut-Médoc, France.
Commune: Margaux.

This Fourth Growth (*Quatrième Cru*) of Médoc, Classifi-cation of 1855, is in the opinion of many one of the best-kept vineyards in the Médoc. If the wine fails to come quite up to the expectation of the marvelously handled vines, it is perhaps because, through forcing, the plants are made to produce too great a quantity, losing propor-tionately in essential elements such as the tannin and glycerin needed for the finest wine. The vinification has not been so well cared for as the vineyard. The Séné-clauze family are the present owners.

Characteristics. Relatively full for a Margaux, and al-though not among the top wines of this commune, despite its large production it sometimes attains finesse and per-fume.

Vineyard area: 42 hectares (104 acres).
Average production: 170 *tonneaux* (16,000 cases).

Marsala

The principal dessert wine of Italy is made in northwest Sicily, where the town of that name is situated. In the late eighteenth century it was introduced into England by Mr. John Woodhouse, whose family soon built up a flourishing trade. The dark wine, which has a taste of burnt sugar, is a blend of an aromatic white wine, of *passito* made from grapes dried and fortified, and of grape-juice syrup. It is matured in cask for from two to five years.

Marsala all'uovo, or Marsaluovo, is a smooth, warming winter drink of Marsala combined with egg yolk and spirit—a development, perhaps, of zabaglione, the frothy sweet made from egg and Marsala.

See Sicily.

Marsannay, Marsannay-la-Côte

A town on the very northern part of the Côte de Nuits, just south of Dijon. Some pleasant white called Chardonnay de Marsannay and a small quantity of agreeable red labeled Pinot Noir de Marsannay is made, but the best wine of the town is its Rosé de Marsannay. Also made from the Pinot Noir, it is one of the most delightful and refreshing *vins rosés* in all France. The official name of the *appellation* is Bourgogne Marsannay-la-Côte.

Marsanne

White wine grape planted in Provence, Algeria, Savoy, and elsewhere.

Martina

Italian white wines from near Bari.
See Apulia.

Mascara

Important Algerian wine region, near Oran. Red, white, and rosé wines are grown here. This dark red wine was often used as a base for many of the better-known wines of France, especially in Burgundy, where it was a favorite part of a "shipper's blend."
See Algeria.

Mash

In whisky-making, grain which has been steeped in hot water. During the mashing process, the starch in the grain is converted to fermentable sugar.

Mastika (Masticha)

A favorite Greek aperitif, made on the island of Chios from a brandy base with gum mastic added.
See Greece.

Maury

Small area of Grand-Roussillon producing fortified sweet wines.
See Sweet fortified wines of France.

Mavrodaphne

This heavy, sweet, red dessert wine is one of the two best-known wines of Greece (*q.v.*).

Mavroud

One of the grapes widely used in Bulgaria. It produces wines of about the same acidity and alcoholic strength as those made from the Gamza, but this wine has a dark ruby color.
See Bulgaria.

Maximin Grünhäuser Herrenberg

One of the best wines of the Ruwer. Herrenberg is the top vineyard of Mertesdorf-Grünhaus.
See Mosel-Saar-Ruwer.

May wine

Traditional preparation of a light Rhine wine into which the aromatic leaves of the herb Waldmeister (woodruff) have been infused. May wine is served chilled and ladled from a bowl, usually with strawberries or other fruit floating in it. A gay and refreshing drink, it can actually be prepared almost anywhere with either a Rhine wine or any light, dry, white wine.

Mazis-Chambertin

Burgundy red wine.
District: Côte de Nuits, France.
Commune: Gevrey-Chambertin.
Official Classification: Great Growth (Grand Cru).

Mazis (sometimes Mazys) is only slightly below Latricières-Chambertin in the hierarchy of wines which add Chambertin to their names, and to achieve this place is no mean accomplishment. The two giants of the commune of Gevrey-Chambertin are Le Chambertin and Chambertin-Clos de Bèze. Latricières is generally conceded to come next.

The vineyard adjoins the Clos de Bèze on the south side of Gevrey-Chambertin and its wines often have much in common with those from the ancient Clos, although they are generally lighter and with enormous finesse, perhaps lacking some of the austere strength of the Clos wines. There are 12.6 hectares (31.5 acres) planted exclusively in Pinot Noir grapevines and production in an average year for quantity is the equivalent of some 2,500 cases.

Mazoyères-Chambertin

Burgundy red wine.
District: Côte de Nuits, France.
Commune: Gevrey-Chambertin.
Official Classification: Great Growth (Grand Cru).

Mazoyères is a vineyard listed as a Great Growth (*Grand Cru*) in the official classification of the wines of the Côte d'Or of Burgundy. The ruling reads Mazoyères or Charmes, and in practice it means that Mazoyères may be sold as Charmes although Charmes may not be sold as Mazoyères. Most of the growers take advantage of this ruling, feeling that Charmes is both easier to say and better known than Mazoyères.

See Charmes-Chambertin.

Mead

The drink of ancient Gauls and Anglo-Saxons, made from fermented honey. It is a clear, pale, golden liquid tasting of honey, with usually about 8% alcohol by volume. Hydromel (honey-water) was the Roman equivalent and metheglin (from the Welsh) is a spiced mead. When mead has been distilled it is called honey brandy.

Mealie beer

A native grain beverage drunk in southern Africa.

Meal-moth

The meal-moth, or *Pyralis*, feeds on the foliage and fruit of the vine.

See Chapter Eight, p. 29.

Medford rum

Name given to virtually all rum made in colonial America.

See Rum, New England.

Medicated and medicinal wines

Wines enriched with spices and/or drugs have long been used by physicians in treating diseases. Dioscorides, Galen, and others through the ages have given various recipes. Medical use of wine is mentioned in all medieval regimes for health. In modern times, cheap, red, fortified wines often have meat extract or extract of malt and other substances added, purportedly to render them more health-giving. In some instances, wines are treated with ipecacuanha or pepsin, in which case they cease to be wines and become medicines.

Médoc (Haut-Médoc)

Red wine.
District: Bordeaux, France.

The Haut-Médoc, first in importance of the great Bordeaux districts, is rated by many experts as the greatest in the world for fine red wines. Considering the bulk of good wine produced, and the incomparable vintages of some of the châteaux, this is probably a fair assessment.

A Médoc is a typical claret, possessed of a subtle bouquet in age which suggests the scent of rose or violet, or an indefinable smell of woods in springtime and clean earthiness. The wines are distinctive and delicate, compared with the fuller, heartier clarets of Saint-Émilion; they have often been described as the greatest of the world's red wines. Médocs have tremendous finesse, when properly aged; even the lesser Growths (*Crus*) respond to some ageing, and the greatest can be drunk when they have been sixty (or even more) years in bottle and still be found full of life, mellow, and magnificent.

With a few exceptions, only red wines are made in this region, and no white wine has the right to be called Médoc. The wines from the Margaux vineyards, nearest Bordeaux, are most feminine of all: heartiness increases on a gradually rising scale to the other end of the zone at Saint-Estèphe, a village about 65 kilometers (40 miles) north of Bordeaux. This is the range of Haut-Médoc (the best part of the region), a place-name in its own right which will appear on labels. Médoc is the name given, in this sense, to the wines north of the Saint-Estèphe, the point of the peninsula gradually narrowing to Soulac, where the Gironde flows into the sea. The region beyond Saint-Estèphe produces high-quality table wines, and there are many cooperatives—one of them at Bégadan, 25 kilometers (16 miles) north of Pauillac, with a capacity of nearly 30,000 hectoliters (750,000 U.S. gallons, 625,000 imp.)—but all the famous wines are in Haut-Médoc. In addition to the two place-names, or Appellations Contrôlées, Haut-Médoc and Médoc, which will appear on labels, six communes within Haut-Médoc have official place-names of their own: Margaux, Saint-Julien, Saint-Estèphe, Pauillac, Moulis, and Listrac, of which the first four are the best known (*see under individual headings*). The more precise the designation, the more distinguished the wine—a Margaux will generally be more individual and will have submitted to higher wine-making requirements than the wines of a broader designation, such as Haut-Médoc. All but five of the sixty-two classified vineyards are within the four communes.

This district has the advantage over all others in that vintage years, although important, mean less here than elsewhere in France because, although the wines sometimes reach great peaks, they never sink much below their normal standard—even in the lesser years a well-made Médoc will be an agreeable wine, because the great châteaux always make good wines. The vintages of the best years will be slow in maturing; the others will be ready to drink much sooner.

The Médoc takes its name, a corruption of the Latin *in medio aquae*, from its geographical position, almost in the middle of the water, for the 130-kilometer (80-mile) strip of peninsula, with its gravelly, sandy soil is seldom more than 25 kilometers (15 miles) in width as it stretches between the Atlantic and the Gironde. The vineyard strip is far narrower. Only lands on the Gironde side, a belt hardly 3 kilometers (2 miles) wide, produce the great

HAUT-MÉDOC

St Yzans 5.5 km

St Seurin-de-Cadourne

Château Calon-Ségur

St Estephe

Château Les Ormes-de-Pez

Château Philan-Ségur

Château de Pez

ST-ESTÈPHE

Château Montrose

N

Château Lafon-Rochet

Château Cos d'Estournel

Château Cos Labory

Château Lafite-Rothschild

Château Duhart-Milon

Raffinerie de Pérrole

Château Clerc-Milon

Château Mouton-Rothschild

Le Pouyalet

Ch. Mouton-Baronne-Philippe

Château Pontet-Canet

PAUILLAC

Pauillac

Château Grand-Puy-Ducasse

Ch. Grand Puy-Lacoste

Château Lynch-Moussas

Château Croizet-Bages

Ch. Haut-Bages-Libéral

Château Lynch-Bages

Château Batailley

Château Haut-Batailley

Château Pichon-Lalande

Château Latour

Château Pichon-Longueville

Ruisseau de Juillac

Château Larose-Trintaudon

Château Léoville-Las-Cases

D-1E

St Julien-Beychevelle

Château Talbot

Château Léoville-Poyferré

St Laurent-et-Benon

Château Belgrave

ST-JULIEN

Château Léoville-Barton

Château La Tour-Carnet

Château Langoa-Barton

Château Ducru-Beaucaillou

Château Camensac

Château Lagrange

Beychevelle

Château Gloria

Château Branaire

Château Gruaud-Larose

Château Beychevelle

Château Lanessan

La Gironde

Royan 52 km

MÉDOC HAUT-MÉDOC

Lesparre, Le Verdon, Montalivet, St Germain-d'Esteuil

Vertheuil

Railroad

D-2E

D-1

D-2

Bordeaux 42 km

0   1   2   3 KILOMETERS
0   1   2 MILES

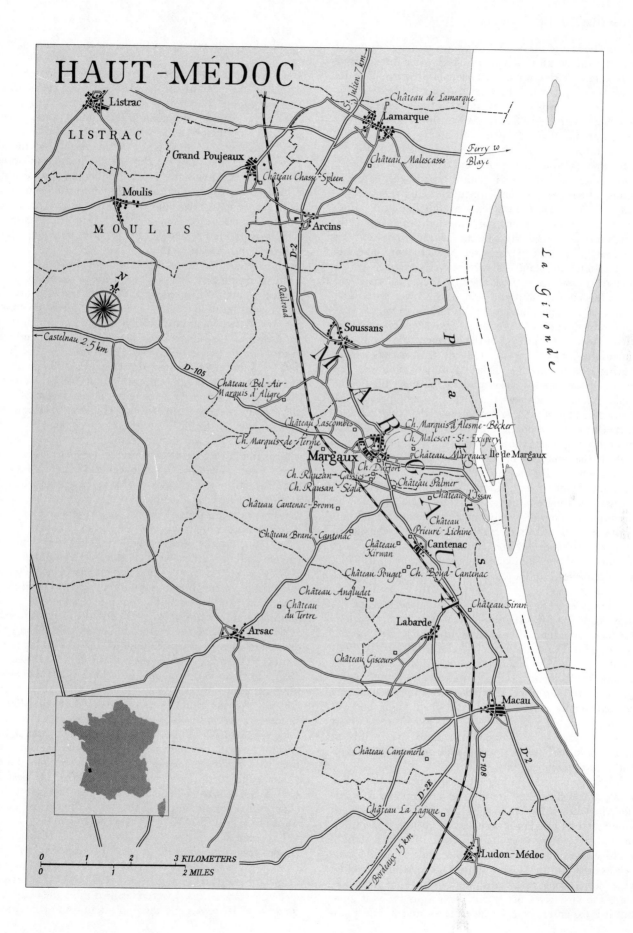

HAUT-MÉDOC

Listrac

LISTRAC

Grand Poujeaux

Château Chasse-Spleen

Moulis

MOULIS

Arcins

St. Julien 7 km.

Château de Lamarque

Lamarque

Château Malescasse

Ferry to Blaye

D-2

Railroad

Castelnau 2.5 km.

N

D-105

Soussans

M A R

Château Bel-Air-Marquis d'Aligre

Château Lascombes

Ch. Marquis de Terme

Ch. Marquis d'Alesme-Becker

Ch. Malescot-St.-Exupéry

Château Margaux Ile de Margaux

Margaux

Ch. Dufort

Ch. Rauzan-Gassies

Ch. Rausan-Ségla

Château Palmer

Château d'Issan

Château Cantenac-Brown

Château Brane-Cantenac

Château Prieuré-Lichine

Château Kirwan

Cantenac

Château Pouget

Ch. Boyd-Cantenac

Château Angludet

Château du Tertre

Château Siran

Arsac

Labarde

Château Giscours

Macau

Château Cantemerle

D-108

D-2

D-2E

Château La Lagune

Bordeaux 15 km.

Ludon-Médoc

La Gironde

P a l u s

0   1   2   3 KILOMETERS
0   1   2 MILES

wines. The rest of the Médoc westward to the giant dunes rimming the ocean is a region of pinewoods interspersed with a few fields and an occasional vineyard, and its wines are simply called Bordeaux. Along the best strip of land, the vineyards are in clusters. In the wine center in Pauillac, a map thirty feet by six feet shows in microcosm the panorama of the Médoc, with all the classified châteaux and a few others superimposed; and a glance reveals how the vineyards group thickly around Margaux, Saint-Julien, Pauillac, and Saint-Estèphe, with gaps between. The reason for this is plain: the land rises moderately at Margaux, most steeply at Pauillac and Saint-Estèphe. The moist lower land, through which the little creeks furrow to the river, is unfit for fine wine. Study of the geological chart explains the phenomenon. The ancient Quaternary land—a very gravelly, pebbly soil in modern times—appears islanded by the newer river soil which has eddied in around it in all the lower parts. The newest of all, the alluvial soil, is forbidden any of the important Médoc place-names. The Médoc's previous gravel dates from the end of the Tertiary and the beginning of the Quaternary eras. It is said that glaciers, slowly moving down from the distant Pyrenees, followed the course of the nearby river, pushing back its high right bank. When the glaciers thawed, the small pebbles remained in the soil. These pebbles give the Médoc gravel its special virtue of holding the sun's heat during the day and reflecting it back to the low-pruned grapes at night.

With the qualities of the soil—the *cailloux*, or small stones, which give *race* to the wine—the elements of weather, of vine variety, viticulture, and wine-making are necessary to the formation of a characteristic Médoc. The Atlantic climate is distinctly softer and damper here than in the other Bordeaux districts. The Médoc is the closest wine zone to the sea, and the Gironde, formed by the confluence of the Dordogne and the Garonne, is as wide, when it passes Pauillac and Saint-Estèphe, as the great Mississippi.

The Cabernet Sauvignon is the characteristic grape variety, contributing different proportions to the various Médocs, but generally making up about 60% of the grapes used. Cabernet Franc, Merlot, Malbec, and Petit Verdot are used in smaller amounts, and Carménère is included infrequently and contributes a fraction. No other grapes are permitted. The wines with the most Cabernet Sauvignon will be the hardest when young but will last very long. Merlot is generally included, up to about 25%, to give a suppler balance, and these wines will be at their best in the sunnier years, the harder ones holding up better in the lighter years.

Vines are generally allowed to achieve about thirty-five years, after which they are torn up and replanted. A few fine vineyards still cling to the old method of letting each vine reach its maximum age and die before replacing it individually. Most vineyards, however, use the system of rotative planting—tearing up and replanting smaller parcels at different times. Most owners try to keep their older vines for as long as possible, thus improving the wine, since the vine gives better and better quality as it ages; but it is expensive both in added labor and in lost quantity, the latter dropping sharply in the older years of the vine.

Harvesting usually starts in the last days of September; or, about one year in six, in October; and one year in fifty, in August. The hotter the summer, the earlier the harvest. Separation of the stalk from the grapes, juice, and pips is obligatory and is done by either of two methods. The new device is a revolving perforated metal sleeve: grapes and juice fall through the holes, and stems are carried off down the cone. Smaller and more old-fashioned vineyards separate by hand-scrubbing over a grid; grapes and juice fall through it, stems remain on top. In the course of great discussions, no one has ever demonstrated that either method is better than the other in producing wine of quality.

After separation from the stalks, the hulls and juice ferment together in vats, and the wine acquires its color (the pigment lies just inside the skins) and the tannin which contributes longevity. At most vineyards the wines are now vatted from ten to twelve days, after which they are drawn off the skins into barrels, where they spend the twenty-two to twenty-eight months before they are bottled. A handful of aristocratic vineyards still vat from three weeks to a month, the traditional Médoc method, by which they achieve a wine with the maximum of tannin. Some of these same famous châteaux continue to ferment their wines in the traditional wooden vats. This practice may be good public relations, but in fact better wine is made in cement or stainless steel fermenters—of which shining examples may be seen at Châteaux Latour and Haut-Brion. Big wines of this style demand longer ageing, which they will finally repay in extra long life; the slower process is possible only for growers able to command the prices their wines will eventually cost.

In 1855, for the World's Fair in Paris, the wines of Médoc (and Sauternes) were classified by a commission of Bordeaux brokers basing their judgments principally on the verdict of the previous hundred years. The listing, from First to Fifth Growths, requires considerable overhauling, but is completely valid for the First Growths (*Premiers Crus*). The three great First Growths of the Médoc are Château Lafite, Château Margaux, and Château Latour. To these, Château Haut-Brion was added in 1855, rightly from the standpoint of wine, if not of geography; because although geographically it is situated in Graves, its wine ranks with the great three of Médoc. Because of its quality and the high prices at which it is sold, Château Mouton-Rothschild, classified first of the Second Growths (*Seconds Crus*) in 1855, really belongs with the First Growths, too. And, incidentally, a Second, Third (*Troisième*), Fourth (*Quatrième*), or Fifth Growth (*Cinquième Cru*) is not a second-, third-, fourth-, or fifth-*rate* wine. (For a fuller treatment of this subject, *see* Bordeaux: Classification.)

Exceptional Growths (*Crus Exceptionnels*)—it is easy for Anglo-Saxons to make the mistake of supposing these to be *better* than the Great Growths (*Grands Crus*), *which they are not*—Bourgeois Growths (*Crus Bourgeois*), and Artisan Growths (*Crus Artisans*) were classified after the sixty-two greatest in 1855. Among these are many fine wines, and some which deserve elevation to the greater Growths. The Classification of 1855 will be found in Appendix A (p. 549). A suggested reassessment of the Bordeaux Growths, as graded by the author in 1958, 1966, and 1973 follows the general entry on the Bordeaux Growths Classification. From this it will be seen that classification of Growths no longer represents the truth in a number of cases. For the individual Classified Growths, *see* Château Lafite, Château Latour, Château Margaux, etc.

Today these wines have become the most expensive and sought-after red wines in the world. In the late 1960s prices started to climb, and soon many of the greatest Médocs were selling at five times their mid-1960s prices, reaching a peak with the 1970 vintage. A combination of factors obviously was responsible: general affluence and prosperity mingled with inflation and speculation, the tremendous growth of the American market, expanded demand from the Common Market countries, increased interest on the part of the French for their finest wines, and—in the case of the top five Growths—the discovery by the Japanese of the Western style of luxury. Most important was the fact that in times of inflation the prices had remained stable—until 1969. Fortunately, the abundant 1973 harvest has begun to return prices to a reasonable level, thus making the greatest red wines of the world a bit more accessible.

CLASSIFIED GIRONDE WINES
Classification of 1855

FIRST GROWTHS (*Premiers Crus*)

	Commune
Château Lafite	Pauillac
Château Margaux	Margaux
Château Latour	Pauillac
Château Haut-Brion	Pessac (Graves)

SECOND GROWTHS (*Deuxièmes Crus*)

*Château Mouton-Rothschild	Pauillac
Château Rausan-Ségla	Margaux
Château Rauzan-Gassies	Margaux
Château Léoville-Las-Cases	Margaux
Château Léoville-Poyferré	St.-Julien
Château Léoville-Barton	St.-Julien
Château Durfort	St.-Julien
Château Lascombes	Margaux
Château Gruaud-Larose	St.-Julien
Château Brane-Cantenac	Cantenac-Margaux
Château Pichon-Longueville	Pauillac
Château Pichon-Longueville, Comtesse de Lalande	Pauillac
Château Ducru-Beaucaillou	St.-Julien
Château Cos-d'Estournel	St.-Estèphe
Château Montrose	St.-Estèphe

THIRD GROWTHS (*Troisièmes Crus*)

Château Giscours	Labarde-Margaux
Château Kirwan	Cantenac-Margaux
Château d'Issan	Cantenac-Margaux
Château Lagrange	St.-Julien

*Declared a First Growth in 1973.

	Commune
Château Langoa	St.-Julien
Château Malescot-Saint-Exupéry	Margaux
Château Cantenac-Brown	Cantenac-Margaux
Château Palmer	Cantenac-Margaux
Château La Lagune	Ludon (Haut-Médoc)
Château Desmirail	Margaux
Château Ferrière	Margaux
Château Calon-Ségur	St.-Estèphe
Château Marquis d'Alesme	Margaux
Château Boyd-Cantenac	Margaux

FOURTH GROWTHS (*Quatrièmes Crus*)

Château Saint-Pierre-Bontemps	St.-Julien
Château Saint-Pierre-Sevaistre	St.-Julien
Château Branaire	St.-Julien
Château Talbot	St.-Julien
Château Duhart-Milon-Rothschild	Pauillac
Château Pouget	Cantenac-Margaux
Château La Tour-Carnet	St.-Laurent (Haut-Médoc)
Château Lafon-Rochet	St.-Estèphe
Château Beychevelle	St.-Julien
Château Prieuré-Lichine	Cantenac-Margaux
Château Marquis-de-Terme	Margaux

FIFTH GROWTHS (*Cinquièmes Crus*)

Château Pontet-Canet	Pauillac
Château Batailley	Pauillac
Château Grand-Puy-Lacoste	Pauillac
Château Grand-Puy-Ducasse	Pauillac
Château Haut-Batailley	Pauillac
Château Lynch-Bages	Pauillac
Château Lynch-Moussas	Pauillac
Château Dauzac-Lynch	Labarde-Margaux
Château Mouton-d'Armailhacq (now called Mouton-Baronne-Philippe)	Pauillac
Château du Tertre	Arsac-Margaux
Château Haut-Bages-Libéral	Pauillac
Château Pédesclaux	Pauillac
Château Belgrave	St.-Laurent (Haut-Médoc)
Château Camensac	St.-Laurent (Haut-Médoc)
Château Cos Labory	St.-Estèphe
Château Clerc-Milon	Pauillac
Château Croizet-Bages	Pauillac
Château Cantemerle	Macau (Haut-Médoc)

EXCEPTIONAL GROWTHS (*Crus Exceptionnels*)

Château Villegeorge	Avensan
Château Angludet	Cantenac-Margaux
Château Chasse-Spleen	Moulis (Haut-Médoc)
Château Poujeaux-Theil	Moulis (Haut-Médoc)
Château la Couronne	Pauillac
Château Moulin-Riche	St.-Julien
Château Bel-Air-Marquis-d'Aligre	Soussans-Margaux

Meleto

A good Chianti Classico of the firm of Ricasoli.
See Tuscany.

Mendoza

Province of Argentina producing 75% of the wine of that country.
See Argentina.

Mentuccia

In Italian, "small piece of mint"; a liqueur of the centerbe type made by the Aurum Distillery.
See Centerbe.

Meranese

Wine from Trentino-Alto Adige (*q.v.*).

Mercurey

Burgundy red and white wines.
District: Chalonnais, France.

One of the four leading wines of the district. The Chalonnais wines bear a resemblance to those of the Côte de Beaune, perhaps because the Pinot Noir is the grape used. The best wines of the slope are the reds of Mercurey.
See Chalonnais.

Merlot

The blue-black, thick-skinned grape which imparts softness and roundness to the red wines of the Médoc district in Bordeaux. This grape is grown also in Italy, Switzerland, Chile, a little in California, and elsewhere.

Mersin

White liqueur flavored with oranges and herbs; the Turkish Curaçao.

Mescal, mezcal

One of the names for the Mexican cactus plant from which pulque and tequila are made. Also another name for tequila (*q.v.*).

Mesnil

Village in Champagne which produces one of the best wines of the Côte des Blancs.

Metaxa

A slightly sweet deep-colored brandy made in Greece (*q.v.*).

Metheglin

A word meaning "spiced drink," derived from the Welsh; it was generally used for mead.

Methuselah, methusalem

A giant bottle used—if at all—in Champagne. It has the capacity of eight standard bottles.

Meursault

Burgundy white, and a very little red, wine.
District: Côte de Beaune, France.

Meursault is the Capital of the Slope of the Great White Wines, and although the "Côte de Meursault" does not exist in official terminology, it does in popular fancy, which is, in a large measure, justified. This section of the Côte de Beaune includes the communes of Meursault and Puligny-Montrachet, and the hamlet of Blagny, ranged along a cluster of hills distinct from the rest of the slope. On the north, a defile cuts it off from Auxey-Duresses and Monthélie; to the south, another separates it from Saint-Aubin; the west side terminates at the top of the slopes; and the east is set by the main road from Beaune to Chagny, which marks the beginning of the Burgundian plain and the end of the fine vineyards. A further unifying factor on the Meursault slope is the chalky, coarse-grained subsoil which predominates and provides the perfect base for the Chardonnay grapevine. Some of the Meursault vineyards fall on the wrong side of the northern divide and grow, mainly, Pinot Noir grapes; and the resulting red wines borrow the name of adjoining Volnay (*q.v.*) or are sold as Volnay-Santenots.

Meursault means "mouse-jump," and it is said the vineyards for red wines and those for white were once only a mouse-jump apart. Today it would take a pretty herculean mouse to bridge the gap in most places, although throughout the vineyards Pinot Noir vines can still be found, and the wine-makers of Meursault annually produce anywhere from 500 to 600 hectoliters (13,200 to 15,900 U.S. gallons, 11,000 to 13,200 imp.) of red.

As Côte d'Or places go, Meursault is fairly large, qualifying either as an overgrown village or a stunted town. The hills roll gently around it, rising to the hamlet of Blagny—set off in the southwest corner—where wines are sold as Blagny, Meursault-Blagny, or occasionally as Blagny-Côte de Beaune. They are both red and white; and wines having the right to the last-mentioned place-name are sometimes blended with those from certain other communes of the Côte de Beaune and sold as Côte de Beaune-Villages. Meursault itself is prosperous and has several interesting monuments. The delicate spire which rises from the rather squat church reminds Burgundians of a "beaver hat on a peasant"; and nearby is a grim, gray edifice which served as a leper colony during the Middle Ages. The Hospices de Beaune have been given several vineyards in Meursault; and as is customary with the Hospices, the wines are sold under the name of the donors: Loppin, Jehan Humblot, Baudot, Goureau, Albert Grivault, and Behèzre de Lanlay. Meursault also has a smaller Hospice of its own, older than its neighbor of Beaune, whose gate adjoins the main road leading up to the village.

Most Meursault is white, and the wines are soft, round, and feminine in texture, with a bouquet that eludes description, bordering now on the scent of violets, now on the aroma of almonds. Dry, but not so dry as the steely Chablis, they have a quiet luxuriousness and a lasting and marvelous aftertaste. They reach their peak fairly quickly, and only the best respond to ageing at all happily—the lesser ones tending to maderize fairly quickly. The finest of the Meursault whites is Perrières and those from the heart of the vineyard—the Clos des Perrières—are superb wines, often fit to challenge the incomparable Montrachet. After Perrières come Charmes and Genevrières and La Goutte d'Or, the appropriately named "drop of gold," all of which incorporate the same seductive grace and elegance but are apt to have a shade less finesse. Meursault reds are sturdy and require a certain ageing before they open up and reveal a fiery strength and excellent bouquet, but they do not quite come up to the qualities of the reds of the Côte de Nuits.

In slight contrast to the white wines of Meursault, those of tiny Blagny are long-lasting, becoming ready to drink after about two years in the bottle and holding for as long as twenty. Blagny white is, understandably enough, very close to Meursault in taste characteristics, but will be, if anything, a little firmer and slightly more assertive. The reds are much the same, and Blagny red is apt to be slightly better than Meursault red.

If you include the hamlet of Blagny, Meursault has more surface area devoted to vines than any other commune of the Côte d'Or, and it ties with Pommard and Beaune each year for first place in amount of production. The official figures for Meursault are 480 hectares (1,188 acres) of vines (wines from two hundred of which may add Côte de Beaune to the communal name), and production for an average-quantity year is 12,500 hectoliters (331,000 U.S. gallons, 275,000 imp.) in white. The best vineyards of the commune are given the designation First Growth (Premier Cru) and the right to produce wines that will carry both commune name and vineyard name on the label. These vineyards are:

In Meursault

FIRST GROWTHS (Premiers Crus)

Vineyard	Hectares	Acres
Clos des Perrières and Les Perrières	17.8	42.2
Les Charmes-dessus	15.5	38.3
Les Charmes-dessous	12.5	30.8
Les Genevrières-dessus	7.7	19.3
Les Genevrières-dessous	5.25	13.0
La Goutte d'Or	5.3	13.8
Le Porusot-Dessus	1.8	4.4
Le Porusot	1.6	4.0
Les Bouchères	4.25	10.5
Les Santenots-Blancs	2.95	7.3
Les Santenots du Milieu	7.7	19.8
Les Caillerets	1.3	3.3

In Meursault

FIRST GROWTHS (Premiers Crus)

Vineyard	Hectares	Acres
Les Petures	11.0	27.0
Les Cras	4.8	11.7

In Blagny

La Jennelotte	4.5	11.9
La Pièce-sous-le-Bois	11.2	27.8
Sous le Dos d'Âne	5.6	13.3

Mexico

Wine is made, mainly in the north of the country, in vineyard areas extending altogether over some 40,000 hectares (100,000 acres); a tenth of the vine-growing zones produce wines, the rest are devoted to spirits production. The zones are: northern Baja California, the Laguna district at the border of Coahuila and Durango, Parras and Saltillo in Coahuila, Aguascalientes, the San Juan del Río region in Querétaro, Delicías in Chihuahua, and the Hermosillo district in Sonora. Grapes are also grown in San Luis Potosi, Zacatecas, Tlaxcala, and Hidalgo.

WINE HISTORY

As governor from 1521 to 1527, Hernando Cortez ordered Spanish grapevines planted on the farms of New Spain. Before the new wines bore fruit, the conquistadores made wine from wild grapes. The first vineyard was planted at Parras by a Spanish captain, Francisco de Urdiñola. His vineyard was one of the earliest cultivated in the Americas, although wild vines had been growing freely on the hillsides and in the gullies of the region. The name Parras means vine-trellises, and Parras is still a center of viticulture, with the plantation of Don Francisco, between Monterrey and Torreón, always in vine.

As the Romans had become jealous of the wine of Gaul 1,500 years before, the Spanish became envious of the viticulture in sixteenth-century Mexico. As, in A.D. 89, Domitian had ordered Burgundian vines ripped up, so in 1595 Philip II issued an edict forbidding new planting or replacement of vines in Mexico. Viceroys continued the crown's command over the following centuries, and wine remained a Spanish monopoly. In spite of the prohibition, wine-making spread from Mexico to Chile, Peru, and Argentina in the sixteenth century and to what is now the western United States in the eighteenth.

When Miguel Hidalgo began the revolution against Spain in 1810, one of his goals was to end the Spanish wine monopoly and to renew viticulture in Mexico. However, with the eventual success of the uprising, the Mexican wine industry did not immediately prosper. The Mission, or Criolla, grape brought by the conquistadores from Spain over three hundred years earlier still dominated most of Mexico's vineyards. Though a Vitis vinifera, Mission lacks acidity and color and yields mediocre wine. By the end of the nineteenth century the first large-scale experiments with good European vine stocks had been made. James Concannon—an Irish-American grower from Livermore, California—sent thousands of cuttings from his better French varieties throughout northern Mexico. Six years after Concannon completed his project and returned to California came the Revolution of 1910. Though a few vineyards were temporarily protected by the bandit leader and Mexican general Pancho Villa, most were neglected or destroyed during the long war. Vineyard area and wine production have expanded since the start of this century, but consumption is still very low—about a third of a pint per capita, one-fiftieth of the rate of the United States. Mexican wines cannot fully develop until their audience becomes more critical. Wine is a new product for most Mexicans, who drink instead much pulque (q.v.), beer, and soft drinks. What wine is consumed is bought by the wealthy on special occasions, for which they choose the heavily taxed wines imported from France and Spain. In order to promote wine consumption, the Vine-Growers' Association and the big marketing firms launched a campaign that resulted in improved quality and increased consumption, about 15% a year. Approximately 150,000 hectoliters (4 million U.S. gallons, 3.3 million imp.) of inexpensive table wines are produced annually. A large quantity of wine spirit, or *aguardiente*, is also produced.

It is to be regretted that Mexico is one of a number of countries which appropriate for some of their wines the place-names properly applicable only to specific geographical areas of the world.

VINE-GROWING REGIONS

The vineyards of Baja California are situated in the fertile valleys in the northwest corner of that forbidding, barren peninsula. Within 160 kilometers (100 miles) of the border with the United States are the five important regions: Santo Tomás, 40 kilometers (30 miles) south of Ensenada; Rancho Viejo, inland from Ensenada; Guadalupe, 80 kilometers (50 miles) south of the California border; and the districts of Valle Redondo and Tañama near the town of Tecate, just across the U.S. border. Since the rainfall ranges from only 5 to 18 inches per year, the plantings are limited by the underground water supply. Since the coast of southern California in the United States is tempered by the Pacific, these valleys are cooled by breezes and fog from the ocean.

The largest vineyard in Baja California, with an annual production of 250,000 cases, is the Bodegas de Santo Tomás, now at Ensenada. Founded by an Italian goldminer and once owned by the president of Mexico, the *bodegas* is now the property of the Elias Pando wine-importing company in Mexico City. The technical director of the vineyard, Dmitri Tchelistcheff (taught by his father, of the Beaulieu Vineyards in California's Napa Valley), has dramatically increased the quality of the wines. Tomás wines are now some of the best and best-known wines in Mexico. Half of the vineyards are in such standard vines as Mission, Rosa de Perú, and Palomino; Valdepeñas, Grenache, Carignan, and French Colombard are also grown, along with Cabernet Sauvignon, Pinot

Noir, Johannisberg Riesling, Sémillon, and Chenin Blanc. Tchelistcheff has introduced sound vinicultural techniques: cold fermentation of white wines, bottle-ageing of red ones, and bottle-fermentation of sparkling wines. Many of the grapes for these wines come from private growers. Though its winery is in Ensenada, the Santo Tomás vineyards are in the valley of that name south of town and in the Guadalupe region to the northeast. Two modern wineries are also in the Guadalupe area: the Productos Vinícola makes "Terrasola" wines, and a large production-vinification facility built especially for quality wines is part of the Mexican division of Pedro Domecq, the Sherry producers from Spain. In this region, Domecq, as well as the Luis Cetto Vineyards, cultivates noble European grape varieties according to the most modern methods; their efforts have produced the best-known wines of Mexico today, the Los Reyes and Calafia.

At Saltillo, 200 kilometers (130 miles) southwest of Laredo, Texas, are the headquarters for the interests of Nazario Ortiz Garza, the most important wine- and brandy-maker in Mexico. His vineyard in Saltillo itself has been reduced to half its original size of 180 hectares (450 acres), since the expanding town must now use the land he once used for reservoirs for irrigation. Don Nazario's most important vineyard is in the state of Aguascalientes, 300 kilometers (200 miles) northwest of Mexico City. His Viñedos San Marcos covers 3,200 hectares (8,000 acres) and straddles the Inter-American Highway (CN 45) which runs between El Paso, Texas, and the capital. Other wineries include the Bodegas de San Ygnacio, owned by Filemon Alonzo; Bodegas de Monte Casino, by Victor Manuel Castelazo; Productos de Uva Aguascalientes of the Cetto family; and the Industrias de la Fermentación, owned by David Alonzo.

Fifty kilometers (30 miles) west of Saltillo is Parras de la Fuente, where Spanish vines first grew alongside the native grapes in 1593. The original winery of Mexico, the Vinícola del Marqués de Aguayo, now concentrates on good still and sparkling table wines. All that remains of the first structure built by Franciso de Urdiñola is an adobe wall in one of the modern offices. Not far from the oldest vineyard in Mexico is the second oldest, the huge Bodegas de San Lorenzo of Casa Madero, owned by cousins of the late president Madero. The family has constantly upgraded their holdings since first purchasing the Parras vineyards in 1870. Late in the nineteenth century Evaristo Madero Elonzindo brought fine grapevines and distillation equipment from Europe, and his wines won honors at the international expositions around the turn of the century. The family has replanted the vineyards after the ravages of phylloxera and the Revolution, and since 1962 has made Casa Madero one of the handsomest wineries in the world. Parras has a climate similar to that of Lodi, California, but because of its high altitude (1,600 meters—5,000 feet) the vines are often exposed to crippling frosts. Other Parras firms are the Bodegas del Delfín, owned by Aguirre Benavides; Bodegas del Rosario, by Señor Antonio Benavides and Señor Elías T. Tejada; Bodegas de Perote, the property of Señor Arturo Perez de

Yarto; and Bodegas del Vesubio, which belongs to Señor Nicolás Milonás. West of Parras, at Torreón, the Mexican government established its first vineyard to supply growers with healthy stock varieties from the Oenological Department of the University of California at Davis. In this same district, but across the border in Durango, is the Vinícola del Vergel at Gómez Palacio. Vergel, built in 1943, is a combination of old European vaulted marble cellars and modern American outdoor stainless steel tanks. Although much of the Vergel vineyard is given over to table grapes and inferior vines, such fairly good stock vines as Ugni Blanc, Ruby Cabernet, and Colombard have recently been added.

One hundred and fifty kilometers (95 miles) north of Mexico City is the southernmost vineyard area in Mexico, the valley of Río de San Juan. The valley is also the very highest vine-growing region in the country, with an altitude of nearly 2,000 meters (6,100 feet). In this high valley the Cavas de San Juan grow Cabernet Sauvignon, Pinot Noir, Gamay, and Pinot Gris, as well as lesser grapes, to make their "Hidalgo" wines. North of San Juan del Río at Tequisquiapan, the Martell Cognac company of France produces table wine and brandy.

SPIRITS

The characteristic Mexican spirits are tequila, pulque, and mezcal (qq.v.) made from the juice of the century plant. Others are obtained from sugar-cane. Among other spirits produced in Mexico are ron (rum), anis, and brandy. Brandy has replaced tequila and rum as the most popular distilled liquor in Mexico. The spirit's success is in part due to semantics. The Spanish word for aged brandy is coñac, but after the Second World War the Mexican government rightly reserved it for use only on brandies imported from the Cognac district of France. Mexican distillers then adopted the English name, even though the word "brandy" does not exist in the Spanish language. The appeal has been tremendous, and now almost 90% of the grapes grown in Mexico are made into brandy.

Michigan

Wine-growing district in the United States. The principal vineyards are situated in the southern part of the state. Sweet and sparkling wines are made there, but unfortunately they are of poor quality.
See United States.

Midi

The vast stretch of land west of the mouth of the Rhône in southern France, which supplies the greatest quantity of ordinary wine in France. The Midi includes the departments of Aude, Hérault, and Gard (qq.v.).
See Grand Roussillon; Languedoc; Corbières.

Mildew

The European name for downy mildew, a vine disease of American origin.
See Chapter Eight, p. 29.

Millefiori

Pale gold Italian liqueur said to have been made from the extracts of a thousand Alpine flowers. The bottles usually contain a small twig, around which sugar has crystallized. Made by Vigevanese.

Millerandage or shot berries

Vine disease; clusters with grapes of varying sizes. An aftermath of coulure, following unsatisfactory flowering or insemination.
See Chapter Eight, p. 29.

Millésime

French term for vintage year.

Minervois

Red wine.
District: Languedoc, France.

Minervois, just north of the Corbières wine district, is 100 kilometers (about 62 miles) southeast of Toulouse. The grapes grow on 22,000 hectares (55,000 acres) in the departments of the Aude and Hérault, northeast of Narbonne and northwest of Carcassonne, the medieval fortress-town. The land is wild and rugged, a series of giant steps where veins of shale alternate with lignite or gneiss. Most of the vineyards are on alluvial soil rich in minerals and heavy with pebbles, which improve the drainage.

The name Minervois comes from Minerve, one of the strongholds built when Rome controlled the south of France. Both Minervois and Corbières were popular in Roman days: the Tenth Legion camped in and around Narbonne, drinking much of the local wine and even importing it to Italy when they returned. Pliny the Younger and Cicero apparently liked the wine. And today some of the loyal residents are convinced that Minervois and Corbières are the wines found in the sunken wrecks of ancient galleys in the western Mediterranean.

The seacoast is only 30 kilometers (18 miles) from the heart of the vineyards; it has recently become a widely developed resort. The wine-making center is, however, still inland at the small town of Olonzac. There, Minervois is made from a blend of 60% Carignan, 20% Grenache Noir, and 20% Cinsault. It is strong and full-bodied and improves with a few years in the bottle. The average annual volume is 300,000 hectoliters (7.8 million U.S. gallons, 6 million imp.). Nearly all of the wine is made in forty-four cooperatives, since the small wine-maker working alone cannot make a living in this part of France from everyday inexpensive wine.
See Languedoc, Appendix G.

Mirabelle de Lorraine

The *eau-de-vie* or spirit distilled from the mirabelle (yellow plum) is made in both Lorraine and Alsace in the east of France, but only spirit from the plums of the region of Nancy and of Metz have the right to the place-name of Mirabelle de Lorraine. This is an official Appellation d'Origine, or controlled place-name, under French law.

Of the two, Metz plums are the better. Mirabelle Fine du Val de Metz is the designation to look for. The plums are picked in dry weather, fermented by specially selected yeasts, kept in the wood for approximately two months and then double-distilled in exactly the manner of Cognac. The liquor is afterward aged in casks.

See also Alsace.

Mis en Bouteilles au Château

French term for château-bottled. This description on the label means that the wine has been bottled at the vineyard where it was grown and made. It guarantees the authenticity of the wine. The term is general in Bordeaux wines.

Mis en Bouteilles au Domaine

French term for estate-bottled. Same as *Mis en Bouteilles au Château*. The term is generally used in Bordeaux; but the practice is much less general in Burgundy, where many of the vineyards are split up into small parcels, than it is in Bordeaux. *Mis en Bouteilles à la Propriété* is another term for estate-bottled. It guarantees the authenticity of the wine.

Mission

The first variety of European *Vitis vinifera* planted in California.

See Criollas.

Mistelle

A fortified "wine" made by adding spirit to grape juice before it ferments. The excess of alcohol prevents fermentation, and all the natural sugar is retained in the juice. It is used mainly as a base for vermouth and other wine aperitifs. Huge amounts of mistelle were made in, and shipped from, Algeria every year.

Mittelhaardt

Part of the Palatinate district in Germany, where the best of these wines are made.

See Palatinate.

Mittelrhein

White wine.
District: German Rhineland.

With craggy shores, crumbling castles, the racing Rhine, and its legend of the siren Lorelei, the section of the river from below Bingen down to Coblenz and beyond is the most interesting to travel by steamer, but not, unfortunately, by palate. The wines are ordinary, as varied as the quartz, clay, and lime soils in which they grow, and are hardly ever exported. Some of the best Rieslings can be suggestive of Mosel; Sylvaner and Müller-Thurgau vines also produce the copious white wines. Red wine was once fairly common here, but now what little remains is for local consumption only. Nearly all of the local wines are drunk on the spot, and in fact there is something of a shortage.

Wine grows not only on the slopes along the Rhine, but also in the side valleys branching into the hills, where conditions are particularly unfavorable. The cold winds coming down from the Hunsrück Mountains meet the warm air rising from the Rhine and cause sudden frosts in late spring and early autumn. On the other hand, the Mittelrhein below St. Goarshausen is one of the few sections of the world's vineyards where phylloxera has not yet struck.

The *Gebiet Mittelrhein* (as it is called in West Germany) is the northernmost vineyard land in Europe. The 1971 West German wine law divided it into two *Bereiche*, or sub-regions: Rheinburgengau in the north and Bacharach in the southern end. None of the wine is great and little will be encountered abroad. In the entire long, narrow region there are about 1,000 hectares (just under 2,500 acres) of vineyards.

Among the better vineyards are those in Boppard, where the best face south in a great bend of the river; Wolfshöhle in Bacharach *Weinbauort* (village) is good; St. Jost and Schloss Strahlberg in Bacharach-Steeg; Langgarten and Mönchwingert in Manubach; Fürstenberg and Bischofshub in Oberdiebach; and the Sieben Jungfrauen and Goldemund in Oberwessel.

For a complete list of the Middle Rhine *Einzellagen* (individual vineyards) arranged by *Grosslage* (section of vineyards) and *Bereich* (sub-region), see Appendix B, p. 606.

Moelleux

Literally "marrowy." A French term used of soft, sweet, fruity white wines, especially in Sauternes.

Mohammedan Prohibition

The tenet of Mohammed denying the use of alcoholic drink to his followers in Islam. With the decrees of early emperors in China, it is the only prohibition which has had a lasting effect. The consequence has been the almost total death of viniculture throughout the Islamic world, though isolated vineyards have held out among non-believers enclosed within Islam and among Mohammedans for table grapes. In modern times, Europeans, notably the French in North Africa, have restored wine-making in Mohammedan lands.

Monbazillac

A sweet white dessert wine from the Bergerac region in southwest France.
See Bergerac.

Monemvasia

Original Greek name for the style of wine anglicized as Malmsey (*q.v.*).

Monica di Sardegna

Sweet fortified wine of Sardinia (*q.v.*).

Monimpex

The Hungarian State Export Agency for wines and spirits.

Monopole

This designation, frequently found on wine labels, literally means "an exclusive." Blank Monopole would be the proprietary brand of the wine-shipper whose name would occupy the blank. The wines are blends and are seldom if ever sold by the vintage year. The shipper attempts to produce a uniform wine year after year, sacrificing the high points which individual growths or years might achieve in order to be able to provide a consistent reliable wine.

Montagne-Saint-Émilion

A large commune in which lie some respectable vineyards of Saint-Émilion (*q.v.*) in the Bordeaux region of southwest France.

Montagny

A commune of the Chalon slope in Burgundy which is allowed the Appellation Contrôlée.
See Chalonnais.

Montagu

Wine region in the Little Karoo district.
See South Africa.

Montefiascone

White wine grown in the foothills of the Volsini Mountains, Italy. It is concerning this wine that the story about Est! Est!! Est!!! is told.
See Latium.

Montepulciano

Known as Vino Nobile di Montepulciano. This light red wine achieved some literary fame in the eighteenth century.
See Tuscany.

Montepulciano di Abruzzo

Light, red Italian wine.
See Abruzzi.

Monthélie and Monthélie-Côte de Beaune

Burgundy red and white wines.
District: Côte de Beaune, France.

Monthélie is the *frère bâtard* of Volnay. It is one of the most picturesque wine communes of Burgundy, with steep streets and tiny houses, venerable with age. The best *premiers crus* of Monthélie, those from Champs Fulliot, Le Rougeot, La Taupine, and Le Clos Gautey, are equal to some of the best Volnay reds.

Red, white, and some sparkling wines are made, although the balance is heavily weighted toward still reds. The grapes are Pinots, as they are throughout the Côte d'Or, and are grown in soil so poor that Burgundians claim: "A chicken, in Monthélie, would starve during the harvest." Within the ancient commune—the remains of a Gallic cemetery testify to its age—are about 100 hectares (250 acres) of vines, and production in an average-quantity year is 3,000 hectoliters (79,500 U.S. gallons, 66,000 imp.), nearly all of it red. Wines may be sold indiscriminately as Monthélie or as Monthélie-Côte de Beaune-Villages. A standard, and generally accurate, rule of thumb is that Monthélie should cost about three-quarters the price of a Volnay of the same year. The best vineyards are given the rating First Growth (*Premier Cru*) and may add vineyard name to commune name on labels. Although these vineyards have not yet been finally established, interim right is granted to the following:

FIRST GROWTHS (*Premiers Crus*)

Vineyard	Hectares	Acres
Sur la Velle	6.1	15.2
Les Vignes Rondes	2.7	6.7
Le Meix-Bataille	2.4	5.9
Les Riottes	.7	1.8
La Taupine	4.3	10.7
Le Clos-Gauthey	1.4	3.5
Le Château-Gaillard	.9	2.3
Les Champs-Fulliot	8.74	21.6
Le Cas-Rougeot	.4	1.4
Duresse	10.3	25.6

Montilla-Moriles

Aperitif and table wines.
District: Southern Spain.

The important wines of Montilla-Moriles (generally known as Montilla) resemble Sherries; but they have their own character and climate and their separate Denominación de Origen. They are the products of the province of Córdoba and are grown in the great carpet of vineyard, stitched with olive and almond trees, which stretches around the ancient city of Córdoba, 400 kilometers (250 miles) northwest of Jerez and about 200 kilometers (125 miles) from Seville. Most of the region north of Córdoba is a great plain, with the best of the region situated in the southern part of the province, its heart a countryside of hills and plateaus rising from the olive groves and the ocher-colored soils of southern Andalusia. Plenty of good ordinary wines (*vinos corrientes*) are made, but fine *solera* wines are also produced on the slopes of the Sierra de Montilla and Moriles Alto. These are the fruit of the chalky *albariza* soil which, around Jerez, also nurtures the Sherry grapes. The Montilla Finos are glinting gold, with a slightly tart undercurrent; the smooth Amontillados have a faint scent of apple peel; the natural Olorosos are deep, nutty but still dry. There exists also a dark, piercing-sweet wine of the region, bottled under many names, which might be compared to a Cream Sherry.

This ancient Córdoban province, which has a long history of occupation and conquest by Phoenicians, Romans, Moors, and the Spanish kings, has been described as the frying pan of Spain. Continental in climate, it has, on the Sierras, cold winters and blazing summers. The vines are pruned low and dug deep into the wrinkled white soil, well-mulched to hold the winter rain which will moisten the roots through the scorching months to come. The principal grape planted here is the Pedro Ximénez (plus about 10% of Lairen, Baladí, and Moscatel). P.X., as it is called in Jerez, there makes only sweet wine; but in Montilla-Moriles, where the grapes ripen quickly and are harvested early, their high sugar content is fermented right out into alcohol, with the result that the wine is strong and bone-dry. With 16% to 16½% of alcohol in the Finos, and up to 19% to 21% in the Olorosos, there is no necessity to fortify further with brandy before the wine for export is shipped abroad. Only for the sweet P.X. wine of the area is fermentation arrested while the sugar content of the must is still high.

Towns and villages important in the production of Montilla are Córdoba, Montilla, Los Moriles, Aguilar de la Frontera, Lucena, Cabra, Doña Mencia, and Puente Genil. The wine is made in much the same way as in Jerez, but there are differences: the grapes are not laid out to dry in the sun before pressing; their long fermentation takes place not in casks but in *tinajas*—"Ali Baba" jars like those of Valdepeñas, except that these are even larger and made of concrete instead of clay. In these jars the new wine is fined with egg-white and a local clay called lebrija. When it is clear and bright, it is pumped out to start its slow maturation in oak butts inside the spacious high *bodegas*. By this time, the Montilla will have shown its inclination either to be an Oloroso, or to develop the yeasty scum known as *flor* and become a Fino. The *flor* forms in the spring, disappears, and returns in a mysterious way at harvest time. At the end of the first year, much of the young wine will be sold for local drinking, in bars or at the table. The best of it will remain in the nursery (*criadera*) casks of the *bodegas* until, at six years of age, it is ready to go into the *solera* system (*see* Sherry). A few of the *soleras* contain barrels so old that the age is reckoned in centuries rather than years, their precious liquid dropped very sparingly into the next butt in the *solera* line-up. Going back further into history, amphorae from Munda (Roman name for Córdoba) have lately been unearthed in Italy—the wines were praised by Columella in his *Re Rustica*.

At one time, before the restricting laws of Denominación de Origen were established, much of the Montilla wine went down to Jerez to reappear as Sherry—perhaps some still trickles through. But now, as always, the wine is relished for its own character, especially in Córdoba; the Finos and Amontillados are drunk as aperitifs, with prawns and tasty *tapas*, and even with the first course of a meal. The Amontillado is, of course, the amber wine into which some Finos deepen with age. The use of the term Amontillado in Jerez has sometimes been questioned by Montilla as a trespass on its name; in fact Amontillado is the style—perhaps first known in perfection in Jerez—for which the Amontillados of that district are named.

A very palatable red wine comes from Doña Mencia, a few miles east of Montilla; and at the larger village of Rute, the making of Montilla is combined with a considerable industry in *aguardientes* and *anisados*.

Montillas are quite well distributed in England; in particular, those from the big *bodega* of Alvear are easily found.

Latest figures for the controlled wines of Montilla-Moriles are as follows: 600,000 hectoliters (15.9 million U.S. gallons, 13.2 million imp.) from 16,000 hectares (40,000 acres) of vineyard. A list of export companies follows: Alvear, S.A. (Montilla); Aragón y Cía., S.A. (Lucena); Carbonell y Cía., S.A. (Córdoba); J.J. Cobos, S.A. (Montilla); Cía. Vinícola del Sur, S.A. (Montilla); Rafael Cruz Conde, S.A. (Córdoba); Gracia Hermanos, S.A. (Montilla); Montialbero, S.A. (Montilla); Montisol, S.A. (Montilla); Montulia, S.A. (Montilla); Moreno, S.A. (Córdoba); Bodegas Navarro, S.A. (Montilla); Luis Ortiz Ruiz (Montilla); Pérez Barquero, S.A. (Córdoba); Miguel Velasco Chacón, S.A. (Montilla); and Vinsol, S.A. (Montilla).

Montilla Sierra

Like Sherry Fino. One of the two best Montillas, from Spain.

See Montilla-Moriles.

Montlouis

Loire Valley white wine; still and sparkling.
District: Touraine, France.

This is known as the unsophisticated younger brother of Vouvray, because of its resemblance to the district which faces it across the Loire and because the wines are so similar that sometimes even experts cannot distinguish between them. But while the finest Montlouis can often be classed with fine Vouvray, the bulk cannot compete. Most of the annual 18,900 hectoliters (500,000 U.S. gallons, 416,000 imp.) of Montlouis is not up to Vouvray standards.

The wine is entirely white, from Chenin Blanc grapes grown in Montlouis, Lussault, and Saint-Martin-le-Beau, and it usually remains in the twilight zone where wines are never really sweet nor really dry. A certain amount is made sparkling; but the still and semi-sparkling—or *pétillant*—are best and the most beguiling. Still wines must have 10% of alcohol; sparkling, only 9.5%.

Montrachet

Burgundy white wine.
District: Côte de Beaune, France.
Communes: Puligny-Montrachet and Chassagne-Montrachet.
Official Classification: Great Growth (Grand Cru).

Little-known as late as the seventeenth century, these wines began to achieve renown in the mid- and late eighteenth century and are now considered by many connoisseurs to be the greatest of all dry white wines. "Divine," "magnificent," "formidable," "to be drunk on one's knees with head bared," "gorgeous with martial pageantry"—this and much more has been said about Montrachet, with only Professor Saintsbury demurring slightly with his "very great, but the best makes the veins swell like whipcord." It is a wine of exceptional elegance and breed, quite dry, yet it has depth and a seductive bouquet.

The vineyard stands at mid-slope, straddling the line dividing Puligny-Montrachet from Chassagne-Montrachet. At this point, nothing is to be seen but seedy wild grass and outcroppings of the meager, chalky subsoil, in direct contrast to the dense underbrush and foliage which crown the slopes in other parts of the Côte d'Or. Around it are such other famous Growths as Chevalier-Montrachet and Bâtard-Montrachet and the vineyard once called Les Demoiselles, now Caillerets. All produce exceptional wines; all are rightfully placed among the greatest of the world's dry white wines.

The vineyard of Montrachet produces a wine that is as rare as it is magnificent. The average yearly production is variable, usually under 250 hectoliters (6,625 U.S. gallons, 5,500 imp.). In the past, the harvest was often reserved for years in advance and prices were so high as to be almost meaningless. A bottle of authentic Montrachet is still a great rarity and will always be so. In 1962 the French government paid $1,201,000 (£429,000) to preserve the 7.7 hectares (19 acres) of Montrachet—the cost of diverting the new Paris-Lyon motor road, which would otherwise have passed by Puligny and affected the vineyards.

The sad fact is that infectious degeneration (sometimes called *court noué*) has been detected in the vineyard. So little is known of this lethal disease that it is referred to as a virus or virus-like malady, of which even the cause is obscure. What is certain is that it kills vines. It also lives in the soil, and the life span of vines planted consecutively in the same spot becomes progressively shorter. Unfortunately, no cure has yet been discovered and, unless one is forthcoming (the foremost vine pathologists in many countries are working together to overcome the menace), the world's finest and most famous dry white wine may become only a memory.

Little is known of the early history of the vineyard, and nothing of the geniuses who first started making the white wines and later perfected them. Montrachet was for many years largely in the hands of the Marquis de Laguiche, and the present Marquis still has nearly a quarter of the vineyard, making about eight *pièces,* or barrels, a year. The family of the late Baron Thénard is another relatively large owner, with slightly less than the Marquis de Laguiche; and although they have other important holdings, both in vines and in outside interests, they are proudest of their slices of Montrachet.

The best section of Montrachet is that lying in the commune of Puligny-Montrachet, comprising 3.9 hectares (9.8 acres), just over half the vineyard. Perhaps it is the fact that the slope faces more to the east than in the south-exposed section which falls into Chassagne, or perhaps it is some subtle combination of imponderables that makes the wines what they are, but they have always had the finer reputation. Yet, today, a few of the well-made wines from the surrounding vineyards sometimes rival the Montrachet.

See Chassagne-Montrachet; Puligny-Montrachet.

Montravel

Dry and semi-sweet wine of Bergerac, France.
See Bergerac.

Château Montrose

Bordeaux red wine.
District: Haut-Médoc, France.
Commune: Saint-Estèphe.

Buried in the vineyard and far from the main roads, Montrose is a pleasant villa with an unusual galleried annex that looks rather like a Swiss châlet. The grounds run down to the river, past rows of small numbered houses tenanted by the workers. A peculiar touch is given by the "street names" here: rue d'Alsace, rue Mulhouse, and so on, commemorating the homesickness of a former Alsatian owner. The vineyard, classified Second Growth (*Second Cru*) in the Classification of 1855, is divided into square plantations, separated by alleys, and it is owned and worked by Mme Charmolue and her son.

Characteristics. Hard, slow-maturing, with a bigness and fullness that characterizes so many of the wines of Saint-Estèphe—although it is with Latour in neighboring Pauillac that it is sometimes compared. Its deep fullness gives Montrose its distinctive character. In some of the recent vintages the wine has seemed lighter and less hard, but a very even quality is maintained over the years. This full-bodied wine is very popular in England.

Vineyard area: 49 hectares (120 acres).
Average production: 230 *tonneaux* (21,000 cases).

Morey-Saint-Denis

Burgundy red, and some white, wines.
District: Côte de Nuits, France.

The wines of Morey-Saint-Denis vary slightly more than those from most Côte d'Or communes. Some reflect the position of the vineyards, providing a half-step between the austere majesty of Gevrey-Chambertin and the delicate elegance of Chambolle-Musigny; others, excelling in sturdy masculine strength, are acknowledged as the most *corsés* wines of the slope. Either way, one thing is certain: the wines are little known.

In bygone days hardly any wine was sold as Morey,

although a considerable quantity was made. The output of the commune was usually blended with that of its neighbors or sold outright as Gevrey-Chambertin or Chambolle-Musigny. As a result, Morey never became famous, and even today relatively few wine-lovers are familiar with the commune or its wines—which are thus seldom demanded and often exceptional value.

The village has little to offer in the way of attractions, and few visitors see more than the dusty main square through which the sloping vineyard road winds and the vineyards of both sides. Beside the square—enclosed in a great wall—is the domain of the Clos des Lambrays (one of Morey's outstanding vineyards), and next to it is the Clos de Tart. The other top vineyards are on the outskirts.

In 1860, and again in 1936, the best vineyards of Burgundy were rated. By the earlier Classification, the finest wines of Morey were considered to be Clos de Tart, Clos des Lambrays, and Bonnes Mares—although Bonnes Mares has but a small foothold in Morey, most of it falling into Chambolle-Musigny. This has been altered slightly and the new official list counts the commune's finest wines as: Clos de Tart; Clos de la Roche; Clos Saint-Denis; Bonnes Mares (see under individual headings).

The Clos des Lambrays is omitted from this list and has been given a slightly lesser status, and many critics feel that this was a grave mistake, for the wines that come from Lambrays are always impeccably made and in good years are among the very greatest of the slope. At the time the Classification was drawn up, however, the owner of Lambrays did not prove herself so adept at advancing the claims of her property as did some others, and the prestige of the wines has suffered accordingly.

Lambrays and the Clos de Tart are the sturdiest of the commune's wines, followed generally by the Clos de la Roche. Bonnes Mares often verges on the delicacy of the Chambolle, yet maintains a firm strength and considerable stamina, and the Clos Saint-Denis is the lightest and most fragile. In addition to these wines are others sold each year as Morey-Saint-Denis or as that followed by the name of the vineyard. The latter come from the First Growth (Premier Cru) vineyards of the commune—specially selected for the superior quality of the wines they produce—and are usually excellent wines, although without the magnificence of the greatest Growths, which are identified on labels only by vineyard name. Apart from the four top-rated Growths, there are 102 hectares (251 acres) of vineyard in the commune, producing annually some 2,500 hectoliters (62,250 U.S. gallons, 55,000 imp.) of red wine and a bit of white.

GREAT GROWTHS (Grands Crus)

Vineyard	Hectares	Acres
Bonnes Mares	1.8	4.6
(see also Chambolle-Musigny)		
Clos de la Roche	16	40
Clos Saint-Denis	6.6	16.5
Clos de Tart	7.5	18.75

FIRST GROWTHS (Premiers Crus)

Vineyard	Hectares	Acres
Clos des Lambrays	6	14.8
Les Ruchots	2.6	6.5
Les Sorbet	3	7.3
Clos Sorbet	3.3	8.2
Les Millandes	4.3	10.6
Le Clos des Ormes (in part)	4.8	12
Meix-Rentiers	1.2	2.9
Monts-Luisants	3.2	7.7
Les Bouchots	2	5
Clos Bussière	3.1	7.4
Aux Charmes	1.2	3.1
Les Charnières	2.4	6
Côte Rôtie	.4	1.3
Calouères	1.3	3.3
Maison Brûlée	1.8	4.6
Chabiots	2.2	5.4
Les Fremières	2.4	5.8
Les Genevrières	.9	2.2
Les Chaffots	1.25	3
Les Chénevery (in part)	3.25	8
Aux Cheseaux	2.42	6
La Riotte	2.47	6.1
Clos Baulet	.8	2.1
Les Gruenchers	.6	1.5
Les Faconnières	1.7	4.3
Les Blanchards	1.8	4.5

Morgon

Heartiest of the good French Beaujolais red wines, sometimes so much so that it resembles the Burgundies grown a few miles to the north.

See Beaujolais.

Móri Ezerjó

Wine of the Ezerjó grape, made in the village of Mór.
See Hungary.

Moriles

A section of the Montilla vineyard near Córdoba in the south of Spain. The wine produced is a dry Fino.
See Montilla-Moriles.

Morocco

The wine industry of the not very long established state of Morocco is at once very young and very old. Indigenous vines were grown in Morocco in classical times and some of them were sent to Rome. But wine-making died out under the Moslems, with their strict prohibition of alcoholic beverages, and cultivation of wine-grapes, as distinct from dessert-grapes, was only re-established after the French took control of the region in 1912, and the real expansion of Moroccan viticulture was fostered by the

French settlers between 1929 and 1935, an expansion that has largely resulted in the present 55,000 hectares (137,500 acres) planted in vines.

There are no very important place-names. A few will be found on Moroccan wines as indications of superiority, but they are not to be classed with the French system of Appellation d'Origine Contrôlée. Wines, with or without these place-names, do account for one-quarter of the agricultural revenue of the country, however. Most of these are red or rosé. A smaller quantity of white wines is made too, in spite of the fact that in the hot climate these tend to maderize, or oxidize, too quickly; the makers have somewhat the same trouble with the rosés, although in this case they are more successful. *Vin gris* is produced south of Casablanca and east of Marrakech; sweet dessert wines of a deep ruby color are made and exported; and sparkling wines are produced by the champagne method.

With independence in 1956, the Moroccan ministry of agriculture inaugurated controls of vineyards, of quality of vines as well as wines; and regulation of the wine market. All wine must be sound, healthy, and saleable, and must contain at least 11% of alcohol (not very difficult in this semi-tropical country) or Moroccan law, initiated by the French, will not permit it to be exported. Most of the controls of wine were formerly in the hands of French nationals, and Moslems had very little to do with the industry beyond providing most of the manual labor. In 1973, the Moroccan government nationalized all foreign-owned vineyards, most of which were French. Today, the marketing of Moroccan wines is handled by the Office of Commerce and Exports in Casablanca. Some 50% of the annual production of 900,000 hectoliters (23.5 million U.S. gallons, 19 million imp.) is consumed in the country. The rest of the wine is exported, especially to the Common Market countries of Europe, where Moroccan wine has filled some of the gap left when Algeria ceased sending wine to the Continent. The future of the industry in Morocco lies in supplying Europe with cheap red wine for blending.

The wines are, on the whole, rough, heady reds, much like those of Algeria and Tunisia. Just under half of them are grown in the region around Meknes, although some also come from Rabat-Rharb, Casablanca, Fez, Oujda, and Marrakech. The vines used are mostly the bulk-giving types, such as Cinsault, Carignan, Grenache, and Alicante-Bouschet, for red. The first two are the best, and also give a rosé which can be very pleasant when young and which is probably the most popular type inside Morocco. The principal white wine grapes are Clairette, Maccabeo, Ximénez, Plant X, and Grenache. Native grapes, still grown in the traditional vineyards, are mainly for the table, although the Rafsai white grape of the Rif mountain region is now being used in wine-making. These vines are not resistant to phylloxera, which has been ravaging the vineyards of the north.

The other ancient vineyards bearing table grapes are situated on the northern (Zerhoun) and southern (Atlas) mountain slopes. The existence of all these old vineyards, divided into small parcels and peasant-owned, is menaced by the phylloxera louse. The modern vineyards, planted in imported vines, are to be found in the flat regions of Meknes-Fez, Oujda-Taza, and Rabat-Casablanca. Cultivation is intensive here, and mechanization has largely replaced animal-drawn plows. From the northeast come the best rosés, comparable with those of west Algeria, and the muscats of Berkane. Taza, in the center, produces a red wine good for blending; red and rosé, as well as a straw-colored white, are made around Fez; one of the most important red-wine products of Morocco, a growth with color, body, and a distinctive flavor, is found at Meknes, southwest of Fez. South of the capital Rabat is Sidi Larbi, the other important red wine district, where a fat, soft wine is made. Red wine comes also from the Daiet or Roumi slope vineyards east of Rabat; while to the north of these, around Sidi Slimane, richly colored Dar Bel Hamri is the principal wine. The wines of the Casablanca region are not, regrettably, allowed to come to full maturity, so quickly are they consumed; and the rosés from here resemble in color the *pelure d'oignon* (q.v.). South of Casablanca, in the old vineyards of El Jadida and Demnate, are made the dry, fruity *vins gris* which are considered very special in Morocco. At best, Moroccan wines leave something to be desired.

Moscatel de Setúbal

Fortified wine made near Lisbon.
See Portugal.

Moscato

The Italian name for the Muscat grape.

Mosel-Saar-Ruwer

West German white wines.

One of the eleven quality wine producing regions of West Germany—the *bestimmten Anbaugebiete*—Mosel-Saar-Ruwer covers nearly 11,000 hectares (27,500 acres) of charming river valleys in western Germany. The area is now divided into four *Bereiche,* or sub-regions, which roughly correspond to the subdivisions common before the promulgation of the 1971 West German wine law. Bereich Obermosel (Upper Mosel) is perhaps the least important but does include the vineyards around Nittel, Wellen, Igel, and Wincheringen; Bereich Saar-Ruwer understandably covers the Saar and Ruwer river valleys as well as the vineyards on the southeast bank of the Mosel around Trier; Bereich Bernkastel has taken its name from the famous wine town and roughly corresponds to the section of great vineyards known before as Middle Mosel; Bereich Zell lies between the Bernkastel region and Koblenz—where the Mosel joins the Rhine—and includes the Lower Mosel Valley.

The main river itself is called Mosel in Germany and Moselle in France, where it is born. The French spelling is most generally used in English, though the German spelling is used here to be consistent with the 1971 West German wine laws.

THE MOSEL BEREICHE

The secret of Mosels can be told in two words: slate and Riesling. Like the linked syllables of a sorcerer's spell, they produce the variety that makes each wine different even from its nearest neighbor and the light delicate quality, full of incomparable bouquet, which proclaims it inimitably Mosel.

In prehistoric times, the Devonian Sea covered the area where today the deep cleft of the Mosel runs from the French Vosges Mountains down to meet the Rhine. The sea sank away, and the sea-life and the sea-flowers fossilized and became a kind of slate or shale the Germans call *Schiefer*.

Caught between the walls of slate, the River Mosel cut deeper and deeper. When the Romans arrived, bringing vines (though vines may or may not have been planted by the people who were there before them), the river canyon was already deep enough to be below the wind. The river twists like a snake, and the countless bends screen it from the wind. The wide river in the narrow valley tempers the air and reflects and intensifies the sun. The canalizing of the river, damming it between eleven locks, has broadened the water surface and strengthened the reflected rays of the sun. The slate itself has given way slowly to the water and elements until the banks are worn and steep; where the vines are rooted the slate holds moisture and heat and reflects this heat upward when the sun is shining. These elements of the secret of the Mosel explain why for two thousand years wine has been made without interruption in the northernmost of the important vineyards of the world. The Mosel lies on a parallel a little north of Newfoundland, but frosts do not reach the protected valley until late November. Long before this, the winter has numbed the crowns of the hills and the surrounding country.

The people who work single-mindedly in their remote, precipitous vineyards are of mixed stock, and even today distinct types can be recognized, such as pure Celts, or Roman heads which might have been cut on ancient coins. In their isolation, they have remained conservative, religious, and hard-working, dedicated throughout the centuries to the terrific task of bringing the fruit down from the nearly perpendicular cliffs of vineyard, where the sticks which support each vine shine like steel ranks of bayonets high above the bend of the river. Mosel growers tell how no machine or animal can labor on these sheer slopes—only a man, carrying everything up and down on his back. Fortunately, a certain amount of mechanization is now developing year by year: washed-down earth, fertilizer, cylinders of spray, and even cutting plow-blades can be hauled slowly to the top by cables wound onto the drums of engines, and often suspended cable cars carry the workers up like mountaineers. Helicopters are now commonly used for much of the spraying and hauling.

Slate is half the key to the Mosel. The vineyard names frequently end in *-lay* (or *-ley*): this means simply that the soil is slaty. The Bereich Bernkastel (Middle Mosel), roughly between Longuich and Zell, is the best section. The clue again is slate, which crumbles here at just the right rate to renew the soil, keeping it constantly virgin. Below Zell, the slate is harder: too hard for the vine to develop fully. In the Obermosel (Upper Mosel) the soil is not slaty but chalky, and an inferior wine results. "The slate is the *race* of the wine," they say on the Mosel. They mean that the breed of the wine comes from the peculiar and beneficial working of the Riesling vine with the slate. The grape is the other half of the secret.

Riesling was not always grown on the Mosel. The Romans planted *Vitis elvenea*, a vine like the Elbling, which still produces common wines on the Upper Mosel today. The Riesling probably began as a grape for red wine (growth of red-wine types is prohibited by law on the Mosel now), and even today the Riesling variety occasionally reverts and produces dark grapes. White Burgundy grapes were prevalent in the fifteenth and sixteenth centuries; in the seventeenth century, Riesling began to appear. In 1787 Prince-Bishop Clemens Wenzeslaus of Trier made the planting of Riesling obligatory.

It is not Riesling, however, which makes it possible to track down the special characteristics and worth of almost every individual vineyard parcel. Except in the Upper Mosel, Riesling is universal in this region. The third largest German vineyard area (after the Palatinate and Rheinhessen), the Mosel is the most extensive Riesling vineyard of all. A few small plots test out various early-ripening varieties, and there is some Müller-Thurgau (the crossing of Riesling and Sylvaner) which is gaining in most German sections but does not seem very suited to the steep slate slopes, dry and full of stones; the rest is all Riesling, with some Elbling. What does vary is the slate.

The infinity of differences among the wines, one of the things which makes the drinking of Mosels so delightful, comes from the exposure of the slope to the sun and the side of the river on which it is found. Since the character of the slate has made the character of the river, in the long run everything can be traced back to that one single factor.

They explain this very interestingly in the half-timbered wine taverns along the banks of the river, when they bring out a map of the Mosel and chart the individual curves. Wherever the river has encountered the hardest shale, it has had to bend; and at the same time it has silted the facing shore. The result is that the inside of the bend is steep, hardish shale or slate, and the outside is always a low promontory of heavier earth deposited by the eddy of the river. The noblest wines, with the great breed, fight for life on the sheer shale slopes. Directly opposite, a lazier, fuller wine will grow on the alluvial soil. Piesport, Bernkastel, Graach, Wehlen (the village itself is on the other shore facing the vineyards), Zeltingen, Ürzig—they are all on the inner bends of the river. By happy chance the excellent sections face a few points either east or west of south—Piesport southeast, the strip from Graach to Zeltingen southwest, and Ürzig southeast; so they get the maximum sun exposure too. The single exception to this would seem to be Bernkastel, the most famous of all. The town lies in the mouth of a small valley running back between two hills and forking out

around the base of a third. The Doktorberg, on the downriver side above the town, curves in from the Mosel edge in such a way that Bernkasteler Doctor grows on a slope turned only a little west of south. This is the most costly piece of vineyard in Germany, and perhaps in the world, although its real value is not quite up to its fame.

The great events in Mosel wines have been well spaced out—the founding of the vineyards at about the beginning of the Christian era: the spreading of vine and wine by the Cistercian monks who cultivated huge areas after their arrival on the Mosel in 1134; the establishment of Riesling as the universal variety by the end of the eighteenth century; and finally the great and significant increase of production, particularly in the last fifty years. Yield per acre varies so much that no average figure can be struck that would not be deceptive. Nevertheless, the amount of Mosel produced each year is much greater than it used to be. Improvement in growing methods and the use of commercial fertilizer, along with the pressure of increasing demand, accounts for this. Today about 9,000 hectares (22,500 acres) are in vine, most of which is free of disease; the battle against vine diseases and the grape louse phylloxera was intensive, but the neighboring Bereich Saar-Ruwer was the most heavily attacked.

The precarious struggle accounts for the high price of good Mosel wines: the grower must make up in his best years for all the other years when the northerly climate prevents him from making any great quantity. The approximately 20,000 vineyards of Mosel are divided into 180 wine-growing communities (*Weinbauorte*); nearly all the growers have less than one hectare (2.5 acres) and fewer than 1% have more than 5 hectares (12.5 acres). Nearly all of the wine cooperatives are now banded together into a central association. Many have been grouped together into such giant wineries as those at Bernkastel, Wiltingen, Cochem, and Zell. The Mosel wine cask is called the *Fuder* and originally held 960 liters (254 U.S. gallons, 211 imp.), although today for purposes of reckoning it is almost always considered a lot of 1,000 liters (264 U.S. gallons, 220 imp.).

In this most dramatic of all wine areas—in the timbered medieval inns of Bernkastel, or in over-exploited Cochem—where the towers are like a toy-maker's fantasy—one of the most spectacular German vinicultural achievements is probably beginning to die out. This is the amazing golden, mouth-filling, Trockenbeerenauslesen wine. This incomparably rich concentrate of all that is the Mosel's truest gift to the drinker is gradually becoming too costly. It can only be obtained by the repeated picking over of the sheer slopes to select each individual berry on the very point of maximum overripeness. In a country where the rising cost of labor is the most significant factor in the economy this is becoming impossible. Manfred Prüm of Wehlen still sells his Mosel under the name of his grandfather, Johann Josef Prüm, and he has what may well be the finest private cellar in existence for the range and quality of wines grown within the family. His father before him said that Trockenbeerenauslesen Mosels, at today's prices, are losing propositions for the grower and are produced only as a matter of pride in the art and tradition of wine-making (though in recent years the high prices for these great wines have kept the tradition alive and profitable).

BEREICH BERNKASTEL

The middle section of the Mosel begins below the confluence with the Ruwer and ends just before the great bend at Zell, downstream from Reil. The wine boundaries can be more exactly defined. No wine of any importance, and few with a widely known name, grows either above or below the section of the Middle Mosel between Piesport and Erden. The greatest wines, going downriver, are the Piesporters, Braunebergers, Bernkastelers, Graachers, Wehleners, Zeltingers, Ürzigers, and Erdeners. The best parts of the Middle Mosel are so valuable that parcels are valued at sixty to seventy, and in rare cases two hundred, times the price of similar parcels in the Obermosel (Upper Mosel). The *Grosslagen* (sections of vineyard names) for the Bernkastel Bereich are Badstube, Beerenlay, Kurfürstlay, Michelsberg, Münzlay, Nacktarsch, Probstberg, Sankt Michel, Schwarzlay, and Vom heissen Stein.

VINEYARDS AND PLACE-NAMES

Bernkastel-Kues

Numbering 8,000 inhabitants today, Bernkastel was founded as a city in 1291, receiving city rights from Barbarossa. Nestled down between the Doktorberg and the Schlossberg, crowned by the ruin of Landshut Castle, the town, with its medieval square, half-timbered houses and wrought-iron signs, is almost too neat and new-painted, like a film set; yet it is an authentic, if carefully preserved, old town, kept spick and span for the thousands of tourists—the greatest concentration arrives for the vintage festival on the first weekend in September, when the baroque fountains actually flow with wine. The mixed soil of earth and shale gives the wines their special character. In some ways, the earthy terrain imparts something of the roundness and mouth-fillingness of a typical Pfalz wine, but with this, and outweighing it, is the characteristic Mosel nuttiness and spicy flavor imparted by the slate. The Bernkastel slate is harder than any other—this has been proved by the oaks of Bernkastel. Oak is used for tanning shoe-leather: the Bernkastel oak for the tanning of sole-leather, the oak of Wehlen and other neighboring zones for the rest. This same influence declares itself in the *race* of the wines. Some Bernkastelers, and especially Bernkasteler Doctor, have a slight smoky undertaste, like the wines of Bingen on the Rhine. This may come from the soil; or the smoke of the town rising up over the Doktorberg when the wind is from the west, may have something to do with it. Bernkastel vineyards make up the entire Grosslage of Badstube and part of Grosslage Kurfürstlay. The best plots are in Badstube.

Area: Nearly 200 hectares (500 acres) in white wine.

Bernkastel Vineyards

Bernkasteler Doctor. The most famous Mosel wine, unquestionably first-rate, but ridiculously over-priced today. In the fourteenth century Prince-Bishop Boemund II of Trier is said to have been cured of illness by the wine: hence the name, and countless jokes, rhymes, and poems. The slope faces south and a little west above the town, and the wines are said to profit by the sun's heat reflected from the roofs as well as from the broad surface of the river. Bernkasteler Doctor Feinste Auslese was chosen by the late Dr. Adenauer for his state gift to the late President Eisenhower—fifty bottles of what he considered to be Germany's greatest. The owners are the widow of Dr. Hugo Thanisch, Lauerburg, and Deinhard and Co., Thanisch and Deinhard having nearly all of it. When the Deinhard share was purchased in 1902 from Herr Kunst, the mayor of Bernkastel, payment was in gold, the highest price ever paid for a vineyard up to that date.

Graben. Thanisch is the principal owner, and the vineyard is beside the town: there is little difference in quality between Graben and Doctor and many people prefer the former.

The other principal vineyards are Lay, Rosenberg, and Bratenhöfchen.

The lesser vineyards in Bernkastel are Matheisboldchen, Schlossberg, Johannisbrünnchen, and Stephanus Rosengärtchen.

Kues Vineyards in Bernkastel

Kues, across the river, became part of Bernkastel in 1905. The famous sight, where the broad bridge from Bernkastel touches shore, is the St. Nikolaus Hospital, founded in 1448. Thirty-three old, poor men were to be taken in and cared for, never more nor less; and it has been done from that time to this. Kues is not as charming as Bernkastel, and the wines grown on the outer bend of the river, and therefore on a heavier soil deposited by the river eddy, are less distinguished.

Weissenstein is generally the best of these, having the same south exposure as Bernkasteler Doctor, although across the river; but it is a fuller wine, with less breed because it grows on the heavier soil of the promontory shore. Other vineyards are Kardinalsberg and Rosenberg.

Brauneberg

The great wines are elegant, feminine, and exceedingly flowery. In 1806, when Mosel vineyards were classified, Brauneberg was placed first. For centuries the slope, the Braune Berg, facing the village of Brauneberg across the river, was known as Dusemond, deriving from the Roman term for sweet mountain. It is the largest unbroken stretch in the heart of the Mosel (about 3 kilometers or 2 miles) and averages approximately 275 meters (900 feet) in height. Brauneberg vineyards are part of the Grosslage Kurfürstlay. Recently the Filzen vineyards have been added to those of Brauneberg.

Area: About 260 hectares (650 acres) of outstanding white wine.

Vineyards: Juffer and Klostergarten are the best, and of the two, Juffer is by far the more famous. Hasenläufer; Kammer—part of the Bergweiler estate—produces very good wines; also Juffer-Sonnenuhr and Mandelgarten.

Erden

The Erden slope is called Mosel's Gold Mountain, and the tribute is justified. After the Doktorberg, this gives the best returns of any Mosel area. The wines are particularly fruity and have great breed, coming from slate harder than usual, as is the case at Bernkastel. Along the Mosel they have a saying that the wines of Wehlen are more *Mädel* (girl) and the wines of Erden are more *Bube* (boy). They are certainly fuller than the delicate Wehleners. The vineyards are part of the Schwarzlay Grosslage.

Area: 65 hectares (160 acres) of white wine.

Vineyards: Prälat is perhaps one of the best of these excellent vineyards; it is almost exclusively held by the heirs of the Beeres family. Treppchen (little staircase) accurately describes the high terraced vineyard, the best-known of Erden, producing an outstanding, dry Mosel. Busslay, Herrenberg.

Graach

The wines are long-lasting and strong, and they fill the mouth. Even so, grown on slaty soil, they have the characteristic breed or steely *race*. When there is no rain in September and October, Graach makes wonderful wines; in general they are at their best in the dry years. Practically all the vineyard once belonged to the Church; today, Prüm, Thanisch, Deinhard, and Kesselstatt are the main owners, and they, not the Graach vintners, have the best parts.

Graacher vineyards are part of the Grosslage Münzlay.

Area: About 100 hectares (250 acres) for white wine.

Vineyards: Himmelreich, lying very high up and on pure slate soil, is first in quality and the best-known Graacher within Germany. Josephshöfer is perhaps the best-known abroad. It was one of the few Mosels to be sold without the town name. Originally called St. Martinshof after the St. Martin Monastery, it was renamed for Joseph Hain, who acquired it after the secularization of the church property; he sold it to Count Kesselstatt in 1858, and it is entirely owned by the Kesselstatt Domain today. The other vineyards are Domprobst and Abtsberg. Some of the best vineyards belong to the Friedrich Wilhelm Gymnasium, or secondary school.

Kesten

The vines are grown on a small plain, in mixed cultivation with fruit orchards.

Area: 70 hectares (175 acres) of white wine of lesser importance.

Vineyards: Paulinsberg and Herrenberg.

Lieser

Located between Braune Berg and Kues. Some of the wines are quite sprightly, though most are only average.

Area: Nearly 120 hectares (300 acres) of white wine.

Vineyards: Schlossberg, Niederberg-Helden.

Maring-Noviand

Neighbor to Lieser in the Middle Mosel. Smaller and less well-known wines.

Area: 105 hectares (263 acres) of good wines, but much less famous than some of their neighbors.

Vineyards: Sonnenuhr, Honigberg, Kirchberg, Klosterberg, and Römerpfad.

Mülheim

The best-known vineyard, Sonnenlay, lies inland on the alluvial side of the river.

Area: 60 hectares (150 acres) of white wine, most of it rather unimportant.

Vineyards: Sonnenlay, Elisenberg, Helenenkloster, and Amtsgarten.

Osann-Monzel

Area: 76 hectares (196 acres) of good but not outstanding white wines. The wines of this and other less well-known *Weinbauorte* can be reasonable values.

Vineyards: Paulinsberg, Kirchlay, and Kätzchen.

Piesport

The wines are round, with great breed and spiciness. They tend to be long-lived and are especially distinguished by their fruitiness and a particular piquancy. They show at their very best in dry years, while in wet years they may be poor. The Mosel makes a sharp bend at Piesport and the sun is caught in a land-locked amphitheater facing southeast. The slope is about 53 meters (1,500 feet) high, and above the vineyard are rocks and oak forest. In a wet summer, the forest holds too much moisture and the vineyard cannot dry out.

Area: 60 hectares (150 acres) of white wine.

Vineyards: Goldtröpfchen (1st quality), Schubertslay (2nd quality, holding of the city of Trier), Falkenberg, and Günterslay. Other vineyards are Domherr, Gärtchen, and Treppchen. Michelsberg is the *Grosslage* regional name, and thus a blended wine from any of the lesser vineyards.

Ürzig

The vines, growing on a very sheltered (and in some places incredibly steep) southern exposure, have a soil structure different from that in any other part of the Mosel—a deep-strata volcanic soil of mixed slate and croppings of colored sandstone, giving a special taste. The wines, as male as any, are spicier than others and have great fruitiness; in the opinion of some experts, their overall quality is better than that of Bernkastelers. In hot years these wines are magnificent. Schwarzlay is the *Grosslage* name for the section of vineyards that includes those of Ürzig and so will appear on common blended wines from the area.

Area: About 66 hectares (165 acres) of white wine.

Vineyards: the famous Würzgarten (*Würz* means "spice" in German) and Ürziger Goldwingert.

Veldenz

An extremely picturesque village with a ruin-crowned

little mountain, but well inland from the Mosel.

Area: 68 hectares (170 acres) of white wine of lesser importance.

Vineyards: Carlsberg, Elisenberg, Kirchberg, Mühlberg, and Grafschafter Sonnenberg.

Wehlen

An unassuming village compared to some of its neighbors, Wehlen nevertheless looks across the Mosel to what, in Germany, is commonly considered the best Mosel vineyard. Wehlener Sonnenuhr does not quite reach the fabulous prices commanded by Bernkasteler Doctor, but Germans say it is the better wine. The distinguishing character of the Wehleners is their extreme elegance and finesse, unsurpassed in any other wine. Like Graach, part of the Münzlay Grosslage.

Area: 100 hectares (250 acres) of white wine.

Vineyards: Wehlener Sonnenuhr, a wine of enormous elegance and bouquet. The best parts are held by the Prüms of Wehlen, Sebastian Alois Prüm and Peter Prüm, and the best sections of all—the wine estate Johann Josef Prüm—is now owned and run by the great-nephew of Sebastian and Peter, Manfred Prüm, the great-grandson of Johann Josef. Nonnenberg and Klosterberg.

Wintrich

Area: Just less than 100 hectares (250 acres) of white wine.

Vineyards: Ohligsberg, Grosser Herrgott, Sonnenseite, and Stefanslay.

Wittlich

More significant historically than for the present-day vines. It was from here that the Cistercian monks, arriving from an establishment in nearby Himmerode in 1134, spread viticulture over much of the Mosel and Ruwer.

Area: 38 hectares (94 acres) of white wines of lesser importance.

Vineyards: Klosterweg, Kupp, Lay, Bottchen, Portnersberg, Felsentreppchen, and Rosenberg.

Zeltingen-Rachtig

These outstanding wines have the widest range of any Mosel village, and this is not always to their advantage. In a good year, Zeltingen will produce about 2.5 million bottles of wine. No other Mosel area approaches this. As a result, many ordinary bottles of Zeltinger are seen, obscuring the fact that some splendid ones are also made. It is hard to pin down Zeltinger as to type, for there is a considerable range, from light, flowery wines to others with as much body as is likely to be found in a Mosel. The very finest have a charming feminine quality.

Area: About 215 hectares (550 acres) of white wine.

Vineyards: Sonnenuhr (best sections owned by the Johann Josef Prüm estate, marked by and named for one of the many sundials set in the rocks above the Mosel vines); Schlossberg (perhaps nearly as much body as Sonnenuhr); Himmelreich; Deutschherrenberg; Schlossberg.

LESS IMPORTANT VINEYARDS

No wine (except Schwarze Katz) outside the heart of the Middle Mosel has been really well known. The greatest names are great because the vineyards are held in part or in entirety by the big owners; most active in the wine auctions, these men have made their wines famous. Few renowned wines are found outside the region between Piesport and Erden; but, simply because they are less famous and therefore cost less, certain wines from outside the area are excellent value. Cooperatives have done much to improve the quality of these wines, which are usually bought directly from the vineyards by tourists from Köln or Düsseldorf. While space forbids discussion of the following villages and vineyards, those where the wines have been found to be of really high quality, though relatively unknown and low-priced, are designated by the capitalized word VALUE. Town or village (*Weinbauort*) names are italicized; better vineyards within each *Weinbauort* are named within parentheses.

Cröv or *Kröv:* the quaint famous name Nacktarsch is now given to the *Grosslage,* which is identical with Kröv and its vineyards. (Paradeis); Burglay, Herrenberg, Kirchlay, Letterlay, Steffensberg.

Detzem: (Maximiner Klosterlay, Würzgarten).

Enkirch: very large production, up to 1.75 million bottles in the best years, from about 180 hectares (450 acres). (Edelberg, Herrenberg, Steffensberg, Weinkammer); Batterieberg, Ellergrub, Monteneubel, Zeppwingert.

Kinheim: (Rosenberg); Hubertslay.

Klüsserath: (Brüderschaft, Königsberg).

Leiwen: (Klostergarten); Laurentiusberg.

Lösnich: (Försterlay); Burgberg.

Longuich: (Maximiner Herrenberg); Hirschlay.

Neumagen-Dhron: probably the oldest wine community in Germany. Much of the ancient viticultural equipment displayed in the famous Trier wine museum was excavated here. (Rosengärtchen VALUE, with Dhronhofberg VALUE the best from the town; Laudamusberg VALUE); Engelgrube, Pichter, Roterd, Grosser Hengelberg.

Reil: (Kalklay, Goldlay, Sorentberg).

Thörnich: (Ritsch VALUE, Engass).

Traben-Trarbach: linked villages across the Mosel, wine-trade center with a restaurant surprisingly set in the ancient portal of the bridge; wines are strong, do not always last long, and have the quality the Germans call "steel." (Königsberg, Kräuterhaus, Würzgarten, Burgberg, Hühnerberg, Schlossberg, Ungsberg); Gaispfad, Kreuzberg, Taubenhaus, Zolltum. In *Wolf,* now a section of the *Weinbauort,* (Goldgrube, Herrenberg, Sonnenlay).

Trittenheim: (Altärchen and Apotheke VALUES, two excellent but scarcely known wines, but also hard to find); Felsenkopf, Leiterchen.

BEREICH ZELL-MOSEL

The sub-region is divided into the following *Grosslagen:* Goldbäumchen, Grafschaft, Rosenhang, Weinhex, and Schwarze Katz. The Schwarze Katz section includes the town and vineyards of Zell. Since only bottles containing at least 85% of the *Grosslagen* wine can bear the once-infamous name, perhaps fewer of them will now appear. The Schwarze Katz bottled before the 1971 West German wine law was a poor indication of the quality possible in the best Mosel wines, and the wines dating from the 1971 vintage are hardly any better.

Except for a small amount of Müller-Thurgau in the section called Krampen, the vine is the same as that of the great wines of the Middle Mosel Riesling. But the slate soil structure below Eller is too hard to crumble. This restricts the area in which the vine can grow; nor is the earth constantly refreshed by the decay of the shale as it is in Middle Mosel. This makes all the difference, and the wines incline to be ordinary.

The chart below shows the principal wine towns and villages (*Weinbauorte*) and their better-known vineyards (*Einzellagen*). For a complete list of the *Einzellagen* of Zell-Mosel, arranged by *Grosslage*, see Appendix B, p. 608.

BEREICH OBERMOSEL

The vineyards of the Mosel across the river and above Trier belong to the Upper Mosel but they are really linked in name only, since they lack the essential elements which go to make up true Mosel wines: slate soil and Riesling. Most of the vine on the Upper Mosel is Elbling, related closely to the variety brought to the Mosel by the Romans 2,000 years ago; there is a little Müller-Thurgau (a crossing of Riesling and Sylvaner), and recently some Ruländer has been planted. The soil is

of chalk substance, not slate. Yet Upper Mosel wines often have a particular charm of their own, and, taken on average, they are probably better than the Lower Mosels, although neither can challenge the wines of the middle strip. Many Upper Mosels, good wines in their own right, are sound value, being little known and therefore not driven up in price.

The *Bereich* consist of two *Grosslagen*: Gipfel (formerly the name of a fine plot in Nittel) and Königsberg. Nittel is the biggest and the best-known of the *Weinbauorte*. Other towns of some importance are Wellen and Wincheringen.

The best vineyards lie opposite Luxembourg, where the river runs between the two countries just before joining the Saar and plunging toward Trier. The *Einzellagen* of Bereich Obermosel are listed in Appendix B p. 608.

BEREICH SAAR-RUWER

The *Bereich* is composed of three areas brought together by the recent West German wine law: the Saar River Valley, the Ruwer Valley, and a large section of vineyards around the town of Trier, between the bends where the Saar and the Ruwer join the main stream. There are nearly 1,000 hectares (2,500 acres) of vines. (For a complete list of the *Einzellagen* arranged by *Grosslage* and *Weinbauort*, see Appendix B p. 608.)

The Saars can outclass the Mosels in the best years. A hot, dry summer brings great wines along this tributary that leads into the Mosel—light, spicy, unique in flavor, with a special taste like that of blackcurrants, and a bou-

Town or Village (Weinbauort)	Hectares	Acres	Vineyards (Lagen)
Aldegund	68	170	Klosterkammer, Palmberg
Alf	60	150	Herrenberg, Kapellenberg, Kronenberg
Beilstein (Krampen)	18	45	Schlossberg
(Krampen, German for "cramp," refers to the tremendous contortion of the Mosel from Eller to Cochem)			
Bremm	72	180	Abtei
(Probably the steepest vineyard in Europe, parcels terraced, no cable lift, and everything carried upward on shoulders)			
Briedern (Krampen)	36	89	Servatiusberg
Bruttig (Krampen)	53	131	Rathausberg
Cochem (Krampen)	150	375	Nikolausberg
(As pretty as a Swiss clock, but spoiled by tourists, being on the main route from Bonn)			
Ediger (Krampen)	106	266	Feuerberg, Osterlämmchen, Pfaffenberg
Ellenz-Poltersdorf (Krampen)	40	100	Woogberg
Eller (Krampen)	50	125	Bienenlay, Calmont
Klotten	110	275	Rosenberg
Kobern-Gondorf	40	100	Pfarrberg, Uhlen, Weissenberg
Moselkern	33	82	Übereltzer
(Below Burg Eltz, one of the most amazing castles on the Mosel and property of Count Eltz, one of the best proprietors in the Rheingau)			
Pommern (Krampen)	57	142	Goldberg, Rosenberg
Senheim (Krampen)	74	185	Bienengarten, Rosenberg
Treis-Karden	80	200	Kapellenberg
Valwig (Krampen)	72	180	Herrenberg, Schwarzenberg
Winningen	180	450	Hamm, Uhlen

quet resembling Muscatel. The wines are generally longer-lasting and slower to age than the Mosels. The vine is entirely Riesling and the soil characteristics in the lower Saar are the same as on the Mosel—a slate which crumbles slowly and replenishes the earth. Above Saarburg there is less of this slate characteristic. From Serrig to Konz-Karthaus, where the River Saar enters the River Mosel, the banks are almost solid vineyard. Saar wines, which in the great years are in some respects almost super-Mosel in their development of the characteristic elements of *race* and steely elegance, are always classed with the Mosels.

Ockfen probably has the highest average of good wines, but the general opinion is that the best individual vineyard is the famous Scharzhofberg, lying a little farther down the river behind the village of Wiltingen.

The Ruwer wines, at their best, are the lightest of Germany—lighter than those of the Saar or of the Mosel. In the best years they have a bouquet suggesting cinnamon, but in poorer years they may be too acidic for most tastes. In general, the nearer to the Mosel the wine grows, the better it is likely to be. Ruwer (and Saar) wines are always classed with the Mosel, and the German wine label simply lumps them as Mosel-Saar-Ruwer. While the Saar is a substantial river, the surprising thing about the Ruwer is that it is a stream almost narrow enough to jump across. It boils down out of a narrow valley through the little town of Ruwer on the Mosel edge and enters the broad river not far below Trier. Upstream the valley widens. It is there, and in a small side valley devoted to the Avelsbach vineyards, that the Riesling vine grows and the wines are made.

BEST VINEYARDS

Ayl

The quality of the wines closely rivals the Ockfeners. Ayler Herrenberg, Ayler Kupp (a connoisseur's wine, exquisite in a hot year, from a perpendicular vineyard mainly owned by the Bischöfliches Priesterseminar, Trier), Ayler Scheiderberg.

Filzen

Neuberg, Pulchen, Urbelt.

Kanzem

Very delicious wines, heavier, fuller, and rounder than most Saars, less *race* but charming when drunk young. Altenberg (probably best), Unterberg, Berg, Kelterberg, Sonnenberg, Wolfsberg.

Kasel

This is the most important Ruwer *Weinbauort*, producing more wine than any other on that river. It has about double the vineyard of its peers; and the only Ruwer town equaling it in quantity—Waldrach further up the valley—makes only small wines. Probably the best is Kaseler Nies'chen, a splendidly soft, light wine in good years. Other vineyards are Kehrnagel, Hitzlay, Dominikanerberg, Kohlenberg, and Paulinsberg.

Konz

Kelterberg, Zuckerberg, and Falkenstein.

Mertesdorf

Maximin Grünhaus will be a very good Ruwer wine in a dry year. It is the outstanding growth of the Weinbauort Mertesdorf and derives its name from the fact that before the secularization of Church property in Germany by Napoleon, it belonged to the St. Maximin Abbey of Trier. It is now owned by von Schubert. Another good vineyard is Mäuerchen.

Niedermennig

Euchariusberg, Herrenberg, and Sonnenberg.

Oberemmel

Fine wines. Altenberg, Agritiusberg, Hütte, Karlsberg, Raul, and Rosenberg.

Ockfen

The best wines of the Saar. Bockstein is the best vineyard and rivals Scharzhofberger from Wiltingen as the finest Saar wine; it is fuller than Scharzhofberger but less elegant, and in certain years it may be the better wine. Geisberg, Herrenberg, and Heppenstein.

Saarburg

Antoniusbrunnen, Klosterberg, and Schlossberg.

Serrig

Good wines. Kupp, Vogelsang, Würzberg, and Antoniusberg.

Trier

The largest town on the Mosel, important as a wine-trading center and for its fine museum of wine and viticultural objects. *Weinbauort* Trier includes many *Einzellagen*, perhaps more than any other subdivision in all of West Germany. Unfortunately, the vineyards of Eitelsbach and Avelsbach—two of the best Ruwer towns—were included in this large lump. In Eitelsbach, Karthäuserhofberg is the remaining outstanding Ruwer vineyard. A property of about 13.5 hectares (34 acres), it is probably the largest single vineyard in the whole of the Mosel area. It was given to the Carthusians by the ecclesiastic Baldwin in the middle of the fourteenth century and passed intact into the hands of the Rautenstrauch family at the time of the secularization of Church lands in 1802. Werner Tyrell, president of the German Wine Grower's Association, is the owner today. The vineyard is in the town of Eitelsbach and the wine is called Eitelsbacher Karthäuserhofberg. Marienholz, Rothenberg, and Sonnenberg.

The Avelsbach vineyards lie in the jagged triangle between the Mosel and the Ruwer, sometimes classed with one group, sometimes with the other. Convict labor cut away the forests about ninety years ago; consequently the soil is new, the slate not as matured as in vineyards where vine may have grown as long as 2,000 years, and the wines have a rougher taste, which some do not like. In very hot summers they may have quality, but in general they lack breed. Altenberg, Avelsbach and Herrenberg (both owned by Cathedral of Trier), Hammerstein (State Domain), Herrenberg, and Tielslay.

Waldrach

Although this *Weinbauort* only has about 72 hectares (180 acres) in small wines, it still produces good Ruwers. The vineyards are Ehrenberg, Jesuitengarten, Krone, and Meisenberg.

Wawern

Goldberg, Herrenberg, and Ritterpfad.

Wiltingen

Scharzhofberg is the finest vineyard, and in most years finest on the Saar. The wines have a superb elegance. The vineyard faces south and west on a large hill behind Wiltingen, and the story of its ownership is a curious one. It was planted 200 years ago by the monastery of St. Maria of Trier. At the beginning of the nineteenth century when Napoleon was secularizing Church property, a priest named Müller enrolled the vineyard under his name to protect it. Napoleon came and went; Müller held on to the vineyard, married a young woman, and founded a family. His descendant, affable Egon Müller, with Koch probably the best grower on the Saar, has the main part of the vineyard today. Some Scharzhofberger is from the portion of the vineyard belonging to the Dom (Cathedral) of Trier. Braune Kupp, Gottesfuss, Braunfels, Johannislay, Klosterberg, Kupp, Rosenberg, Schlangengraben, Schlossberg.

PRINCIPAL MOSEL-SAAR-RUWER ESTATES

Zach. Bergweiler-Prüm Erben

Wehlen/Mosel. Property consists of 44 hectares (110 acres) distributed among the towns of Wehlen, Graach, Bernkastel, and Brauneberg. Holdings comprise the principal parts of many of these vineyards, including Brauneberger Kammer, but are divided among five heirs.

Geschwister Beeres, Christoffel Beeres

Ürzig/Mosel. Domain of slightly more than 1.32 hectares (3.5 acres), which includes the Würzgarten vineyard in Ürzig.

C. H. Beeres Erben (Peter Nicolay)

Ürzig/Mosel. About 14 hectares (35 acres), mainly Ürziger Würzgarten, Ürziger Goldwingert, Erdener Treppchen, and Erdener Herrenberg.

Richard Josef Beeres (Joh. Beeres Jr. Erben)

Ürzig/Mosel. Holdings comprise about 4 hectares (10 acres) and include sections of Würzgarten and Treppchen.

Hohe Domkirche

Trier/Mosel. Domain composed of approximately 13 hectares (33 acres) in the two Saar *Weinbauorte* of Avelsbach and Wiltingen. Hohe Domkirche parcels are Altenberg and Herrenberg, plus Dom Scharzhofberg, Dom Wiltinger Braunfels, and Dom Wiltinger Rosenberg. The Hohe Domkirche, Bischofliches Konvikt, and the Bischofliches Priesterseminar now form one vineyard holding, although the labels will continue to bear the names of the three original domains.

Le Gallais

Kanzem/Saar. Approximately 2.4 hectares (6 acres) distributed between the *Weinbauorte* of Wiltingen and Wawern. Properties in Wiltingen include Kupp and Braune Kupp; and in Wawern, Le Gallais owns Goldberg. Managed by Egon Müller.

Gebert

Ockfen/Saar. The total domain of 7.5 hectares (18 acres) comprises portions of the vineyards Bockstein, Herrenberg, and Geisberg in Ockfen.

Forstmeister Geltz (Bes. Krick-Geltz)

Saarburg/Saar. Holdings of 3.5 hectares (9 acres) in the *Weinbauorte* of Saarburg and Ockfen. Saarburg properties include parcels in Antoniusbrunnen, and Ockfen holdings include sections of Bockstein and Geisberg.

Forstmeister Geltz (Bes. Zilliken-Haring)

Saarburg-Beurig/Saar. Proprietor of sections in Rausch, Antoniusbrunnen, and Mühlberg in Saarburg; and Bockstein and Geisberg in Ockfen. Approximately 3.2 hectares (8 acres) in all.

Graf zu Hönsbröch

Rauhof, Wiltingen/Saar. Property of 2.4 hectares (6 acres) composed of shares in the vineyards of Kupp and Braunfels in Wiltingen.

Von Hövel (Friedrich von Kunow)

Oberemmel/Saar. Total holdings of approximately

11.3 hectares (28 acres) spread between the two *Weinbauorte* of Oberemmel and Wiltingen. Oberemmel sections include parts of Rosenberg, Agritiusberg, Hütte, and Altenberg. Wiltingen properties are some of the best vineyards.

Max Keller

Saarburg/Saar. Domain consists of nearly 3.5 hectares (13 acres) and is composed of parcels in Bockstein, Neuwies, and Geisberg in Ockfen and the Stirn vineyard in Saarburg.

Dr. Fischer

Ockfen/Saar. Proprietor of 15 hectares (37.5 acres) in Wawern. Principal holding is Herrenberg.

Egon Müller

Scharzhof, Wiltingen/Saar. Holdings comprise 8.5 hectares (21 acres) and include the largest portions of the Scharzhofberg vineyard.

Bischöfliches Konvikt

Trier. The preparatory school for the Catholic seminary in Trier, whose entire domain consists of some 22 hectares (54 acres) in eight towns and villages on the Mosel, Saar, and Ruwer. Mosel properties include parcels of the Piesporter vineyards, Falkenberg, Goldtröpfchen, Pichter, and Lay, as well as parcels of the following lesser vineyards often sold as Piesporter growths: Niederemmel, Piesporter Schubertslay, Taubengarten, and Güntherslay; Minheim: Piesporter Lay; Dhron: Piesporter Grafenberg. Saar properties include Ayler Herrenberg. Ruwer properties are in Eitelsbach-Trier, part of Marienholz, and in Kasel Niesgen and Kernagel. Holdings now joined with the Domkirche and Priesterseminar.

Bischöfliches Priesterseminar

Trier. The Catholic seminary in Trier. Aggregate holdings comprise 30 hectares (75 acres) in eight towns and villages on the Mosel, Saar, and Ruwer. Mosel properties include portions of the Erdener vineyards of Treppchen; portions of the Ürziger vineyard Würzgarten; sections of the Trittenheimer vineyards; and a part of the Dhron vineyard Dhronhofberger. In the Ruwer at Kasel they have part of Hitzlay, Kernagel, Niesgen, and Herrenberg. In the Saar: Ayler Kupp, Wiltinger Kupp, and Altenberg in Kanzem. Together with the Domkirche Bischöfliches Konvikt these vineyards form one holding.

Dr. Weins Erben (Vorm. S. A. Prüm Erben)

Wehlen/Mosel. A member of the Prüm family, whose domain of approximately 4.5 hectares (11 acres) takes in sections of the choicest of vineyards of Sonnenuhr, Nonnenberg, and Klosterberg in the towns and villages of Wehlen, and of Himmelreich, Domprobst, Abtsberg, in the town of Graach. Willi Weins and Hubert Selbach-Weins have divided the estate.

Ferdinand Haag (Vorm. Conrad Fehres Erben)

Brauneberg/Mosel. Holdings comprise slightly more than 2.5 hectares (6 acres) and include excellent shares in the vineyards Hasenläufer, Juffer, and Juffer-Sonnenuhr in the town of Brauneberg. Often makes superb wines. Fritz and Willi Haag have divided the estate.

Kesselstatt Domain

Mosel. The Counts von Kesselstatt came to the Mosel from Austria two hundred years ago. Sine 1858 the domain has owned the Josephshof vineyard in Graach in its entirety and has augmented its holdings with choice parcels in Piesport since 1847. Also Kasel properties in the Ruwer and the Saar. This company was recently bought by the R. E. H. shipping firm.

Josef Milz, Jr.

Trittenheim/Mosel. Property consists of nearly 5.2 hectares (14 acres) in the town of Trittenheim and includes sections of Altärchen, Apotheke, and Leiterchen.

Fritz Pathiger Erben

Kasel/Ruwer. Proprietor of 5 hectares (12 acres) in Kasel, with parts of Kernagel, Niesgen, and Herrenberg.

Johann Josef Prüm (Wachstum)

Wehlen/Mosel. Probably first among all Mosel estates for stupendous range of wines all of superb quality. Total domain comprises 14 hectares (35 acres) in Zeltingen, Wehlen, Graach, and Bernkastel, producing 1,100 hectoliters (29,150 U.S. gallons, 24,200 imp.). Manfred Prüm, heir of his father, Sebastian, owns and manages the estate; cellars under the house and wine sheds on the bank of the Mosel stream with moisture like a cave under a waterfall. Inside these dripping walls he keeps what must be one of the finest collections of Auslesen and Trockenbeerenauslesen wines in the world. J. J. Prüm holdings include: almost exclusive ownership of Zeltinger Sonnenuhr and sections of Zeltinger Schlossberg; the choicest parcel of Wehlener Sonnenuhr as well as portions of the other Wehlener vineyards, Nonnenberg and Klosterberg; major sections of the Graacher vineyards of Himmelreich, Abtsberg, and Domprobst; and parcels of Lay, Bratenhöfchen, Rosenberg, Matheisbildchen, and Pfalzgraben in Bernkastel.

Peter Prüm (S. A. Prüm Erben)

Wehlen/Mosel. Wines definitely challenge those of the J. J. Prüm estate but the quantity is less, Peter Prüm's holdings comprising about 4 hectares (10 acres). Peter Prüm, great-uncle of Manfred Prüm (owner of the J. J. Prüm estate), inherited his properties from his father and now owns choice parcels in Wehlener Sonnenuhr, Klosterberg, and Nonnenberg; and, in addition, he holds substantial portions of the Graacher vineyards of Himmelreich and Domprobst. Dr. Engelberting Prüm and Stefan Studert-Prüm each have part of the estate.

Sebastian Alois Prüm (S. A. Prüm Erben)

Wehlen/Mosel. Brother of Peter Prüm and the other great-uncle of Manfred, the present owner of the J. J. Prüm estate, Sebastian Alois likewise inherited an excellent domain from his father. Consisting of nearly 3.5 hectares (8 acres), it includes a very select part of Wehlener

Sonnenuhr as well as other choice Wehlener morsels in Nonnenberg and Klosterberg. Sebastian A. Prüm's Graacher holdings are composed of superior parcels in Himmelreich, Domprobst, and Abtsberg.

Werner Tyrell

Property composed of approximately 18 hectares (45 acres) within the *Weinbauort* of Trier. Holdings include the entire vineyard of Eitelsbacher Karthäuserhofberg, as well as portions of the vineyards Orthsberg, Kronenberg, Stirn, Sang, and Burgberg.

Von Schubert

Mertesdorf/Ruwer. Sole owner of Maximin Grünhaus, a vineyard of major importance in Mertesdorf. The holdings total 20 hectares (50 acres).

Adolf Rheinhart

Saarburg/Saar. Total domain consists of 14 hectares (34 acres). Rheinhart properties include sections of Bockstein, Herrenberg, and Geisberg in Ockfen; and a parcel of Feils in Schoden.

Freiherr von Schorlemer

Lieser/Mosel. A noble domain which includes some of the best Zeltingen and Brauneberg growths: Zeltinger Rotlay and Brauneberger Juffer; as well as other properties in the towns of Graach, Wintrich, and Lieser.

Dr. Hugo Thanisch Ww.

Bernkastel-Kues/Mosel. The present owners are the Thanisch and Müller-Burggraeff families, descendants of Dr. Thanisch, whose most famous vineyard was Bernkasteler Doctor. The estate, now managed by Fräulein Mechthild Thanisch, consists of over 12 hectares (30 acres) distributed between the towns of Bernkastel, Brauneberg, Lieser, and Graach. Bernkasteler properties include outstanding portions of Doctor, Graben, and Lay. Graacher holdings comprise major sections of Domprobst and Himmelreich.

Oscar Tobias

Müstert/Niederemmel-Piesport/Mosel. A principal owner in the town of Niederemmel-Piesport with nearly 1.5 hectares (4 acres), Tobias's properties include sizable parcels in Goldtröpfchen and Güntherslay.

Otto van Volxem

Oberemmel/Saar. Proprietor of approximately 6 hectares (15 acres) distributed between the two *Weinbauorte* of Wiltingen and Oberemmel. Wiltingen holdings include Klosterberg, Braunfels, and Scharzhofberger. Oberemmel holdings include parcels in Altenberg.

Maximilian von Othegraven

Kanzem/Saar. Holdings consist of 4.9 hectares (12 acres) of good parcels.

Vereinigte Hospitien

Trier. A public hospital in Trier with total holdings of over 48 hectares (123 acres) in five towns and villages on the Mosel and Saar. In addition to parcels in the Augenscheiner, Thiergärtner, and Maximiner Pichter vineyards of Trier, the hospital owns the largest share of the well-known vineyard Piesporter Schubertslay as well as sections in the other Piesporter vineyards of Goldtröpfchen and Treppchen. The Saar sections of the domain include Kanzemer Altenberg, Wiltinger Kupp, and Serriger Schloss Saarfelser Schlossberg.

Moselblümchen

"Little Flower of the Mosel." The wine name, akin to Liebfraumilch from the German Rheinhessen, refers to a common, enormously overrated wine, upon which the additional sin of adding sugar is usually wreaked. When you see this wine you can be certain that the individual vineyard growth sold under this generalized invented name had nothing to recommend it in its own right.
See Mosel-Saar-Ruwer.

Moselle

See Mosel-Saar-Ruwer.

Mother wine

Wine concentrated by boiling, used to strengthen young wines. A mural in the tomb of Menopth in Egypt shows that this process is at least 4,000 years old.

Mou

French term for flabby.

Mouillage

French term for reduction by addition of water.

Moulin-à-Vent

Fullest in body and in some markets the best-known of the red Beaujolais wines, France.
See Beaujolais.

Moulis

Bordeaux red wine.
District: Haut-Médoc, France.

A commune of Haut-Médoc which has its own Appellation Contrôlée.

Mountain

Od English name for Málaga wine (*q.v.*).

Mourisco

Important grape in the making of Port (*q.v.*).

Mourvèdre

Red-wine grape grown in the Midi and elsewhere in France, in Algeria and in Spain. Among its many synonyms are Négron, Espar, Mataro, Catalan, Beni Carlo, and Tinto.

See Provence.

Mousseux

This designation found on a French label means that the wine is sparkling. In France it is the term used for all sparkling wines except those grown in the geographical district of Champagne. (Only sparkling wine of that area may be called Champagne.)

Château Mouton-Baronne-Philippe

Bordeaux red wine.
District: Haut-Médoc, France.
Commune: Pauillac.

Until about two hundred years ago, Château Mouton-d'Armailhacq and the present Château Mouton-Rothschild formed one estate. In 1855 Mouton-Rothschild was classified first among the Second Growths (*Seconds Crus*) of Médoc, a position it would undoubtedly surpass if the vineyards were reclassified today; and Mouton-d'Armailhacq was classified a Fifth Growth (*Cinquième Cru*) and is today better-known than some Third (*Troisièmes*) and Fourth Growths (*Quatrièmes Crus*). Mouton-Baronne-Philippe, as it is now known, lies between the famous vineyards of Mouton-Rothschild and Pontet-Canet to the north of Pauillac. The wines are excellent, and much of the credit must be given to Baron Philippe de Rothschild, owner of Mouton-Rothschild, who since 1930 has also been making Mouton-Baronne-Philippe and in 1951 gave this vineyard his first name—calling it Château Mouton-Baron-Philippe. He later changed the name a second time, to Château Mouton-Baronne-Philippe, to honor his late wife Pauline. The two vineyards join but the wines are made separately.

Characteristics. A very good Pauillac, lighter than Mouton-Rothschild, but with a fine characteristic bouquet.

Vineyard area: 50 hectares (125 acres).

Average production: 170 *tonneaux* (15,000 cases).

Château Mouton-Rothschild

Bordeaux red wine.
District: Haut-Médoc, France.
Commune: Pauillac.

There are several explanations of why the vineyard is called Mouton. One suggested by the owner, Baron Philippe de Rothschild, is that in Old French the hilly land was called Mothon, meaning "mound." Moreover, the series of little rises and hills comprising the vineyard suggests the backs of a flock of sheep. The Rothschilds' predecessor, Baron de Brane, who bought Mouton in 1853, also owned prominent members of the Parliament

of Bordeaux. Until 1730, Mouton was all part of Château Lafite, belonging to the Prince de Ségur, and prior to that was owned by the Duke of Gloucester (1430), Jean Dunois, and Gaston de Foix. For four generations now, and more than one hundred years, the vineyard has been held by Barons de Rothschild—Nathaniel, James, Henri, and today the great-grandson, Philippe—and the quality and reputation of the wine have been constantly improving. Mouton was already highly rated in 1855 when Médoc wines were classified, and since at that time it was neither selling quite with the First Growths (*Premiers Crus*) nor with the Second Growths (*Seconds Crus*) it was placed first of the Seconds. This compromise did not please Mouton and the famous motto of the vineyard originated: *Premier ne puis, Second ne daigne, Mouton suis.* Translated as "First I cannot be, Second I do not deign to be, I am Mouton," the motto has been made into a practical reality by the Rothschilds. And in a new Classification by the Ministry of Agriculture in 1973, Mouton deservedly became a First Classified Growth—perhaps the first of many necessary amendments to an outmoded ranking.

This eminent position is due to the high quality of the wine itself and to the brilliant publicity and promotion given the name, especially since, in 1926, Philippe de Rothschild took over the administration and later the ownership. He was assisted in the running of the estate by the able late M. Marjary and now by directors Philippe Cottin, Raphael Heras, and Lucien Sionneau. A production of an average 600 barrels is mostly in Cabernet Sauvignon grapes and is long-vatted. Pierre and Raoul Blondin, cellarmasters at Mouton, insist that great wine cannot be made except by long-vatting. The practice of leaving the grape juice in contact with the hulls and residue of the grapes in the fermentation vats for only nine to fifteen days is now almost universal throughout the Médoc. But at Mouton, juice and grape residue macerate together for a full month; that is, for twenty days or more after fermentation has ceased. This, and the high percentage (75%) of Cabernet Sauvignon used, is designed to produce a big, hard wine, which requires long bottle-ageing but matures finally into a splendid, very-long-lasting wine. The demand for old vintages of Mouton justifies this practice, and the price commanded makes it possible.

The great *chai* of new wines at Mouton-Rothschild is the most spectacular in Bordeaux. Double doors are thrown open at the side of the room where the baron gives his banquets, and neatly aligned barrels stretch away for a hundred yards in five or six rows. The *chai* is at ground level; but down below, in moss-blackened cellars, tunnels store more than 100,000 bottles of Mouton at a constant temperature of 52°F. (11.1°C.). Here, too, is the fabulous wine "library" of which the showpieces are cobweb-covered bottles a hundred and more years old. Along the rear wall there is a bin of bottles made up from every vintage since the Rothschild ownership began. The sense of good taste is not restricted to the estate. Bottle labels carry each year an original illustration by a different celebrated artist—Salvador Dali, Henry Moore, Jean Cocteau, Marc Chagall, Picasso. For years Baron Philippe, expertly aided by his late wife, has been collecting paintings, goblets, tapestries, vases, and any other objects connected with wine. These were assembled in a superbly lit museum, which was opened in 1962, and form a collection for which every wine-lover should be grateful. The museum is but one achievement for which Baron Philippe de Rothschild shall always be remembered. His dedication to quality and to the artistic expression of wine are without equal.

Characteristics. Always heavy, full, and almost fleshy, with a special taste that natives of Bordeaux refer to as a *goût de capsule* or "taste of the capsule" from its distinctive, hard, and almost metallic flavor. The high percentages of Cabernet Sauvignon grapes used make it very slow to mature and very full-bodied.

Vineyard area: 70 hectares (175 acres).
Average production: 250 *tonneaux* (22,000 cases).

Mulled wine

Diluted red wine, brought to the boil, spiced and sweetened, and served very hot. It has an extraordinary ability to discourage a cold in the early stages.

Müller-Thurgau

The grape and the wine derived from the crossing of the Riesling and Sylvaner vine varieties and rapidly increasing in popularity in Germany. There is also a small amount of it in Alsace. The name is not likely to appear on bottle labels.

See Germany; Alsace.

Munson, Thomas V.

American hybridizer who developed several hybrid vines, notably Delicatessen. Munson set up his experimental vineyards in Denison, Texas, and all but revolutionized hybridization by his zealous efforts to bring in new families of grapes as "blood lines." His own work, however, is of somewhat limited importance to the winemaker, since it was oriented toward table grapes rather than wine.

Münster-bei-Bingerbruck

Better wine district of the two Münsters of the Nahe Valley, West Germany.

See Nahe.

Murray River

Vineyards on the boundary between Victoria and South Australia. They produce fortified wines and brandy and also grow Palomino and Pedro Ximénez grapes for sherry-type wines.

See Australia.

Murrumbidgee

Irrigated vineyard region on the Murrumbidgee River, New South Wales, producing mainly fortified wines.

See Australia.

Muscadel

Another name for sweet, usually fortified wine from the Muscat grape (*q.v.*). It should not be confused with Muscadet (*q.v.*).

Muscadelle

A white-wine grape grown in the Bordeaux region, where it contributes to both sweet Sauternes and dry Graves.

In the last century, an excellent Muscadelle was grown in South Africa, where it produced the good Cape wine called Constantia.

Muscadet

White wines.
District: Brittany, France.

The Muscadet vineyards, the only ones in Brittany to be classified, lie far down the River Loire, south of the city of Nantes. Brought to the Muscadet region by monks in the seventeenth century, the grape is the Melon de Bourgogne rechristened, though it is no longer to be found in Burgundy itself. The light, fresh wine, with a trace of musk in the bouquet, is a perfect accompaniment to seafood, and within the last few years has achieved great popularity throughout France and abroad. Muscadets should be drunk when young, the harvests there being the earliest in France, beginning September 10–20 each year. If the grapes are allowed to overripen (a problem that occurred in the area in 1974, and in some instances in 1975), the wines will lose their characteristic freshness and acidity.

Good Muscadets are bottled directly from the vats where they are fermented, and the district has the only subterranean system of underground vats carved into the cool rocky earth beneath the cellar floors. A certain amount of carbon dioxide gas is in these wines (Muscadets, if racked, will oxidize and flatten) which makes them slightly crackling or *pétillant.* The term "*sur lie*" means that the wines have been drawn off the lees for bottling to retain this natural sparkle. Many of the cheaper Muscadets, however, have the sparkle added artificially and may also contain a trace of unfermented sugar, which covers the natural acid taste of the wine.

A newly discovered region, the Muscadet district has only recently begun to produce fine wines. There are in this area about 6,000 sharecroppers, some working vineyards as small as two hectares (five acres). The growers, for the most part, have remained unorganized, while the shippers are strong, controlling fully one-third of Muscadet's production of 9,000 hectares (22,500 acres).

The entire region produces some 400,000 hectoliters (10.5 million U.S. gallons, 8.8 million imp.) of wine each year, of which 80% comes from the Sèvres-et-Maine, the hilly rise between the banks of these two rivers, and 10% from the rocky shores of the Coteaux de la Loire. An additional 10% is called simply "Muscadet." The problem for the enthusiast who wants to find the best-made wine of the region is that Muscadet does not classify the production of its separate communes; the individual qualities of Saint-Fiacre, La Haie-Fouassière, and Le Pallet are not distinguished in the same way, for example, that Beaujolais differentiates between the place-name of Beaujolais and Beaujolais Villages, and among the production of the better villages of Fleurie, Brouilly, and Morgon.

In Muscadet the best wines come from Sèvres-et-Maine, and a further discrimination of the nose and palate notes that the southern part of this district is superior to the northern. Noteworthy names are Vallet (unofficial capital of Muscadet), Mouzillon, Le Pallet, Saint-Fiacre, La Haie-Fouassière, Vertou, Monnières, and Gorges.

The V.D.Q.S. (Vins Délimités de Qualité Supérieure, a category of wines of less distinction than the Appellation Contrôlée) is Gros Plant, which tastes slightly more acid than the Muscadet from Sèvres-et-Maine and is made from the Folle Blanche, a vine formerly grown in the region of Cognac, north of Bordeaux. Abandoned as a favorite producer of Cognac brandy, the Folle Blanche now exists only in the area surrounding Nantes. Gros Plant is a larger, more common wine than Muscadet, fine for local drinking, but not considered an export wine.

Muscadine

Vines native to southern sections of North America, the best-known example of which is the Scuppernong—the others are the James and the Mish.

The grape is not popular with the wine-maker, partly because of its low sugar content and high acidity, and partly because of its very pronounced and unattractive aroma when vinified.

See Chapter Eight, p. 29.

Muscat

(1) A sweet grape, usually white, subdivided into many varieties. The wines tend to be heavy, strong in scent and flavor, and to produce sweet dessert wines or are eaten as table grapes. In California, the Muscat d'Alexandrie is extensively cultivated for wine, but this is not a grape of good quality.

(2) Muscat de Beaumes-de-Venise, Muscat de Frontignan, Muscat de Lunel, Muscat de Saint-Jean-de-Minervois.

See Sweet fortified wines of France.

Muscat d'Alsace

A dry, fruity Muscatel of Alsace.
See Alsace.

Muscat of Samos

See Samos; Greece.

Muscatel

Wine made from Muscat grapes. These may be red or white, dessert or sparkling wines. Two of the better-known are Muscat de Frontignan and Muscat de Samos.

In California a regrettable quantity of fortified wine known as "Muscatel" is sold as a substitute for spirits.

Muselage

In French, literally "muzzling"; the wiring which clamps the corks on to Champagne bottles.

Les Musigny

Burgundy red and white wines.
District: Côte de Nuits, France.
Commune: Chambolle-Musigny.
Official Classification: Great Growth (Grand Cru).

The remark "If our slope were not the richest in the world it would be the poorest" was prompted by a view of Musigny. The vineyard lies along a small dirt road, and across it is nothing but underbrush and rubble. On one side, the land is virtually worthless. On the other, it has been known to bring up to approximately $30,000 (£10,700) per acre.

The vineyard is in three parts: Les Musigny, Les Petits Musigny, and La Combe d'Orveau. The three stretch out along the slope, with Les Petits Musigny between the other two, and on a plateau below stands the château of the Clos de Vougeot surrounded by its vineyards. Pinot Noir is the dominant vine, but there is also some Pinot Blanc and Chardonnay, not all for making white wine.

In general, the vintners who own parts of Musigny make red wine. White is produced sporadically, and rarely if ever exceeds about 7 hectoliters (200 U.S. gallons, 165 imp.). The reds, however, are noted for their delicacy, their elegance and, above all, their finesse. Burgundians claim that a slight addition of Pinot Blanc or Chardonnay grapes to the must heightens these qualities considerably. The law allows 15% of the vines to be of white variety, but the growers usually feel that 10% is sufficient.

In a good year the wines, in addition to their matchless feminine delicacy, have an incomparable bouquet reminiscent of violets or raspberries. They become ready to drink after two years or so, but a fine estate-bottled Musigny can be expected to develop for years and to profit enormously from imprisonment in the bottle.

The vineyard covers 6.5 hectares (16 acres). The amount of wine made in an average year for quantity is 300 hectoliters (7,950 U.S. gallons, 6,600 imp.) or the equivalent of less than 3,600 cases.

Must

Grape before it ferments completely and becomes wine. The French word is *moût*.

Mustimeter or saccharometer

The mustimeter, or saccharometer, is defined in the *Dictionnaire du vin* as a densimeter brought into popular use by Salleron and bearing the Gay-Lussac centesimal scale; it shows the weight in grams of a liter of the liquid into which it is immersed. This instrument of paramount importance in wine-making is used in almost every vineyard in France.

The division in the center of the scale and marked

I. EQUIVALENT DENSITY TABLE FOR WINES AND ABNORMAL AND NORMAL GRAPE-MUSTS OF LESS THAN 10% PROSPECTIVE ALCOHOL

with their sugar and probable alcohol content and the weight of sugar which must
be added to raise them to 10% (according to Salleron)

Mustimeter density or degree	Areometer degree Baumé	Grams of sugar per liter of must	Alcoholic content of the wine to be made	Weight of crystallized sugar to be added to 1 liter of must to get a wine of 10% alcoholic strength in volume (in grams)
1,000	0			
1,001	0.1			
1,002	0.3			
1,003	0.4			
1,004	0.6			
1,005	0.7			
1,006	0.9			
1,007	1.0			
1,008	1.1			
1,009	1.3			
1,010	1.4			
1,011	1.6			
1,012	1.7	2	0.1	168
1,013	1.8	5	0.2	166
1,014	2.0	7	0.4	163
1,015	2.1	11	0.6	159
1,016	2.3	13	0.7	157
1,017	2.4	15	0.9	154
1,018	2.6	18	1.1	151
1,019	2.7	21	1.2	149
1,020	2.8	23	1.4	148
1,021	2.9	26	1.5	146
1,022	3.1	29	1.7	142
1,023	3.2	31	1.8	139
1,024	3.4	34	1.9	137
1,025	3.5	37	2.1	134
1,026	3.7	39	2.3	130
1,027	3.8	42	2.4	127
1,028	3.9	45	2.6	124
1,029	4.1	47	2.8	122
1,030	4.2	50	3.0	120
1,031	4.3	53	3.1	119
1,032	4.5	55	3.2	115
1,033	4.6	58	3.4	112
1,034	4.7	61	3.5	110
1,035	4.9	63	3.7	107
1,036	5.0	66	3.9	104
1,037	5.2	69	4.0	102
1,038	5.3	72	4.2	99
1,039	5.4	74	4.4	95
1,040	5.5	76	4.5	93
1,041	5.7	80	4.7	90
1,042	5.8	82	4.8	88
1,043	6.0	84	5.0	85
1,044	6.1	87	5.1	83
1,045	6.2	90	5.3	80
1,046	6.3	92	5.4	78
1,047	6.5	95	5.6	75
1,048	6.6	98	5.7	73
1,049	6.7	100	5.9	70
1,050	6.9	103	6.0	68
1,051	7.0	106	6.2	65
1,052	7.1	108	6.3	63

(Chart continues overleaf)

Mustimeter density or degree	Areometer degree Baumé	Grams of sugar per liter of must	Alcoholic content of the wine to be made	Weight of crystallized sugar to be added to 1 liter of must to get a wine of 10% alcoholic strength in volume (in grams)
1,053	7.3	111	6.5	59
1,054	7.4	114	6.7	56
1,055	7.5	116	6.8	54
1,056	7.7	119	7.0	51
1,057	7.8	122	7.2	48
1,058	7.9	124	7.3	46
1,059	8.0	127	7.5	42
1,060	8.2	130	7.6	41
1,061	8.3	132	7.8	37
1,062	8.4	135	7.9	36
1,063	8.6	138	8.1	32
1,064	8.7	140	8.2	31
1,065	8.8	143	8.4	27
1,066	8.9	146	8.6	24
1,067	9.0	148	8.7	22
1,068	9.2	151	8.9	19
1,069	9.3	154	9.0	17
1,070	9.4	156	9.2	13
1,071	9.6	159	9.3	12
1,072	9.7	162	9.5	8
1,073	9.8	164	9.6	7
1,074	9.9	167	9.8	3
1,075	10.0	170	10.0	

2. EQUIVALENT DENSITY TABLE FOR GRAPE MUSTS OF MORE THAN 10%
with their sugar and probable alcholic content and the volume of water that must be added to reduce them to 10% (according to Salleron)

Mustimeter density or degree	Areometer degree Baumé	Grams of sugar per liter of must	Alcoholic content of the wine to be made	Volume of water which must be added to 1 liter of must to bring it to a density in liters of 1,075
1,076	10.2	172	10.1	0.01
1,077	10.3	175	10.3	0.02
1,078	10.4	178	10.5	0.04
1,079	10.6	180	10.6	0.05
1,080	10.7	183	10.8	0.06
1,081	10.8	186	10.9	0.08
1,082	10.9	188	11.0	0.09
1,083	11.1	191	11.2	0.10
1,084	11.2	194	11.4	0.12
1,085	11.3	196	11.5	0.13
1,086	11.4	199	11.7	0.14
1,087	11.6	202	11.9	0.16
1,088	11.7	204	12.0	0.17
1,089	11.8	207	12.2	0.18
1,090	11.9	210	12.3	0.20
1,091	12.0	212	12.5	0.21
1,092	12.2	215	12.6	0.22
1,093	12.3	218	12.8	0.24
1,094	12.4	220	12.9	0.25
1,095	12.5	223	13.1	0.26
1,096	12.6	226	13.3	0.28
1,097	12.7	228	13.4	0.29
1,098	12.9	231	13.6	0.30
1,099	13.0	234	13.8	0.31
1,100	13.1	236	13.9	0.33
1,101	13.2	239	14.0	0.34
1,102	13.3	242	14.2	0.36
1,103	13.5	244	14.4	0.37
1,104	13.6	247	14.5	0.38
1,105	13.7	250	14.7	0.40

1000 represents the weight of distilled water (1,000 grams per liter); the divisions above measure lower densities and those below measure higher densities—i.e., the weight in grams of a liter of the must or liquid being tested.

To determine the density of a must, a few bunches of grapes are crushed into a container, the juice being filtered through a cloth into a test tube. The mustimeter and a thermometer are immersed one after the other in this juice and the readings are taken—e.g., 1065 on the mustimeter scale and 18°C. on the thermometer. Reference is made to the Correction Table below to see what adjustment is necessary to the mustimeter reading to arrive at what it would be if the must temperature were 15°C.

CORRECTION TABLE

Temperature °C.	Correction	Temperature °C.	Correction
10°	−0.6	21°	+1.1
11°	−0.5	22°	+1.3
12°	−0.4	23°	+1.6
13°	−0.3	24°	+1.8
14°	−0.2	25°	+2.0
15°	0	26°	+2.3
16°	+0.1	27°	+2.6
17°	+0.3	28°	+2.8
18°	+0.5	29°	+3.1
19°	+0.7	30°	+3.4
20°	+0.9		

For example:

The must is tested at a temperature of 18°C.; the mustimeter shows 1065; the Correction Table shows that 0.5 must be added to the mustimeter reading, so that the weight of the must at the normal temperature of +15°C. is 1065.5. If the temperature were 12°C. instead of 18°C., the correction—0.4—would have to be deducted from 1065, the reading then being 1064.6.

Taking the corrected density of 1065.5 we refer to Table I (page 340) to see what is the weight of sugar contained in a liter of the must and what will be the alcohol content which the wine will have after fermentation.

In California a similar instrument is used. Called a Brix or Balling hydrometer (q.v.), it is calibrated in terms of grams of sugar per 100 grams of solution.

The first column of the table (pages 339-340) shows the density of the must—i.e., the mustimeter reading. The second column shows the corresponding values for the Baumé areometer (or gluco-oenometer) and of the Gay-Lussac densimeter or saccharometer. The third column gives the weight of grape sugar contained in a liter of the must. The fourth corresponds to the probable alcohol richness which the wine will have after fermentation, presuming all the sugar is fermented—which does not always occur, particularly beyond 14% to 15%. The fifth column indicates the weight of pure crystallized sugar which must be added to a liter of must for the wine to contain 10% of

alcohol after fermenting. By pure crystallized sugar is meant white sugar standardized at 100°. When using less pure sugars, white or brown, the table figures would be too low; they would have to be raised proportionately to the degree of impurity of the sugar used. In Table 2 there will be found, conversely, the amount of water which each liter of must exceeding 10% will have to have added to bring it down to the normal density of 1075.

If we refer to the example given earlier we find:

(1) That a must of 1065 density corresponds to 8.8° Baumé.

(2) That it contains 143 grams of grape sugar per liter.

(3) That, after fermentation, this sugar will give 8.4% of alcohol, which means that the wine will contain 8.4 liters of alcohol per hectoliter.

(4) That 27 grams of crystallized sugar per liter must be added in order to bring the alcohol content up to 10%.

Mutage

French term for artificial interruption of fermentation. Often this is achieved by the addition of sulfur dioxide, leaving unfermented sugar in the wine; and it used to be done in the Entre-Deux-Mers district of Bordeaux, producing a white wine with a very sweet finish.

Muté

Partially fermented or completely unfermented wine whose fermentation has been stopped, usually by the addition of a high-proof brandy. *Vins mutés* are often used in the production of aperitifs and in the blending of wines that need both sweetness and body.

Mycodermi aceti

Bacterium which forms vinegar, or vinegary wines. Today usually called *Acetobacter*.

Mycodermi vini

The yeast commonly believed to be responsible for the formation of a film on certain wines.
See Flor; Sherry.

Château de Myrat

Bordeaux white wine.
District: Sauternes, France.
Commune: Barsac.

The property, belonging to the Poutac family, was included in the Second Growths of the 1855 Classification. In the early 1970s, this vineyard was ripped up as a losing proposition. The Château no longer makes wine.

N

Nackenheimer Rothenberg

Best of the Nackenheimers in the German Rheinhessen (*q.v.*).

Nahe

White, and some red wines.
District: Northwest Germany.

The wines of the valley of the River Nahe, a tributary of the Rhine, have been showing a distinct improvement since the local method of mixed cultivation (in which different grape varieties grew more or less side by side) has been almost entirely eradicated. Some 4,400 hectares (11,000 acres) are in vine. Today, the less-favored sites are planted in Sylvaner vines, accounting for about 32% of the total; and of the best sites producing the *Spitzenweine* (peak wines), most of these are in Riesling, which accounts for 25% of the total. And 30% of the Nahe vines are Müller-Thurgau, the crossing of Riesling and Sylvaner that gives spicy, tasty wines. About 10% of the wines are red.

The best wines come from the section of the valley between Bad Kreuznach and Schloss Böckelheim. These two towns should not be confused with the two *Bereiche* (sub-regions) called Kreuznach and Schloss Böckelheim, which comprise the entire Nahe *Gebiet,* or district. As two of the most well-known Nahe names, they were given to the large subdivisions with the passage of the 1971 West German wine law. Farther upstream the wines are extremely light, usually Riesling, and rather suggestive of the Saar wines (although they never attain the same finesse). This is not surprising, as a glance at the map will show. Saar and Nahe are close to each other in this section, and in earlier times it used to be customary to lump the Saar wines with those of the Upper Nahe, instead of with the Mosels as they are classed now.

The Nahe empties into the Rhine at Bingen opposite Rüdesheim. For the same reason that the wines of the Upper Nahe are Saar-like, these wines downriver from Bad Kreuznach are like Rheingaus. They come into the same climatic belt. These divisions are not to be taken as hard and fast, however; in anything as capricious and various as wine that would be impossible. In a recent tasting in the Nahe, some of the Roxheimers and Gutenbergers were lighter than Mosels.

The Nahe district includes two smaller river valleys. These are the Alsenz and the Glan, neither producing especially interesting wines.

Modernization of wine-growing methods all along the Nahe is the consequence of vine disease which destroyed whole areas. The government came to the aid of the ruined growers—otherwise viticulture on the Nahe might have ceased. Today, methods are much improved, but this has turned out to be a mixed blessing. The cost of wine-making has risen in proportion to the gain, one re-

sult of which is that only the State Domain and a relatively small number of fairly large owners can afford the risks implicit in making wine of quality. May frosts, common enough in the Nahe, may wipe out the entire crop of the year. The problem has been solved in part by the wine cooperatives, now making about one-fifth of the total annual production of nearly 250,000 hectoliters (6,625,000 U.S. gallons, 5,500,000 imp.).

VINEYARDS

The best wines come from Schloss Böckelheim, Bad Kreuznach, and Niederhausen, followed by Norheim, Rüdesheim, and Roxheim (Rüdesheim-Nahe must not be confused with the Rüdesheim in the Rheingau). For a complete list of the Nahe *Einzellagen* (individual vineyards) arranged by *Grosslage* (section of vineyards) and *Bereich* (sub-region), see Appendix B, p. 613.

Schloss Böckelheim and Niederhausen

Schloss Böckelheimer Kupfergrube and Niederhauser Hermannshöhle (the latter growing on a slate soil rare in this part of the Nahe) are the best and the best-known Nahe wines, the former perhaps a little better. Hermannshöhle, however, can have great elegance and breed. Both vineyards are on the terraced Kupferberg, or Copper Mountain, and both are owned chiefly by the State Domain, which, by use of convict labor, has cleared and planted the slopes within the past fifty years. One of the most familiar sights here during the First World War was Hindenburg sitting at a table on one of the terraces, sipping his favorite wines and brooding over the Western Front.

Schloss Böckelheim and Niederhausen vineyards are part of the Grosslage Burgweg in the Schloss Böckelheim Bereich. A Grosslage Burgweg wine will have little wine from either of these famous towns. Most of it will be from a less well-known *Weinbauort*, such as Duchroth or Traisen.

Schloss Böckelheimer Kupfergrube, Felsenberg, Mühlberg, and Konigsfels are among the most important Nahe wines.

The best Niederhausen vineyards are Hermannshöhle, Rosenheck, Rosenberg, Klamm, Kerz, and Steinwingert.

Bad Kreuznach

The principal vineyards are Narrenkappe (one of the outstanding Nahes), Krötenpfuhl (very good), Kahlenberg, Brückes, Hinkelstein, Mönchberg, and St. Martin. The von Plettenberg and Anheuser estates make very good wines.

Rüdesheim-Nahe

One of the old, famous Rüdesheim vineyards was Rosengarten, often used unofficially as a regional wine name. This practice was made legal with the 1971 wine law: the Rosengarten vineyard was absorbed into the Goldgrube and Weisberg plots, and the name was given to the *Grosslage* (and thus to the regional wine) of the section including Rüdesheim and nine other *Weinbauorte*.

Norheim

The vineyards are Kafels, Kirscheck, Dellchen, Götzenfels, Klosterberg, and Oberberg.

Roxheim

Wines are usually sold under other names and therefore are not well known. The main vineyards are Birkenberg, Höllenpfad, Berg, and Hüttenberg.

Other Vineyards

Laubenheim (well known and of fair quality, resembling Rheingaus): Krone, Vogelsang, Karthäuser.
Altenberg (Alsenz wines, not very interesting).
Bad Münster or *Bad Münster a. St. Ehernberg* (the better-known of the two Münsters of the Nahe, but the other has better wines): Felseneck, Höll, Rotenfels.
Dorsheim: Goldloch, Honigberg, Burgberg.
Langenlohnsheim (second largest area after Bad Kreuznach, but the Rheingau-like wines are not outstanding): Rothenberg, Steinchen.
Münster-Sarmsheim (better wines of the two Nahe Münsters): Kapellenberg, Pittersberg, Trollberg, Dautenpflänzer.
Waldböckelheim: Kronenfels.
Among the many other communities, those with occasionally interesting wines are Bretzenheim, Sponheim, Gutenberg, Meddersheim (light wines), Merxheim (light wines), and Windesheim.

Château Nairac

Bordeaux white wine.
District: Sauternes, France.
Commune: Barsac.

After many years of neglect, this small property near the entrance to Barsac has been revived by its new owners, Thomas Heeter, an American, and his wife, Nicole Tari, the daughter of the owner of Château Giscours. The vineyards have been replanted and the beautiful eighteenth-century house has been restored. The wine is classified a Second Growth but it is typical of Sauternes.
Vineyard area: 14 hectares (35 acres).
Average production: 25 *tonneaux* (2,000 cases).

Napa Valley

California wine region producing some of the finest red and white table wines.
See: United States: California.

Nasco di Cagliari

A dessert wine from Sardinia (*q.v.*).

Natural wine

Wine to which nothing has been added which can influence the taste or strength.

Nature

In France *vin nature* is natural unsweetened wine. A special meaning applies in Champagne, where it denotes still wine.

Néac

Bordeaux red wine.
District: Southwest France.
Previously a very small district adjoining Pomerol, Néac ceased to exist in 1954 when it was joined to that of Lalande de Pomerol. The move was a wise one, for it did away with a place-name that served no purpose, since the two wines are similar in every respect.
See Lalande de Pomerol.

Nebbiolo

A grape used in Italian red wines; e.g., in Lombardy for Sassella, Inferno, etc.

Nebuchadnezzar

An oversized bottle containing the equivalent of twenty ordinary bottles.

Nectar

The drink of the ancient Greek gods. The name was later used for wines of special quality, and even today bottles of nectar may be found in Greece.

Negus

An old-fashioned hot drink made with Port, sugar, lemon, and spice.

Nerveux

French definition of an assertive, rigorous wine not complicated by any subtle overtones.

Netherlands spirits

In the Netherlands, the making of spirits is generally referred to as the "old national industry" and dates back to about 1500. Originally alcohol was distilled from wine, but in the second half of the sixteenth century the processing from cereals was started. It was not until the government imposed a high import duty on German brandy in 1670 and prohibited the importation of French brandy that the Netherlands distilling industry could reach its full development. In the eighteenth century, distilleries flourished, the greatest advances being made on the River Meuse, particularly at Rotterdam, Delfshaven, and

Neuberger

Schiedam. At least forty of the 140 distilleries in the Netherlands today are established in Schiedam.

Jenever

This is the original distillation of the Netherlands. It is often supposed to be identical with gin, but in fact there are considerable differences in the taste as well as the ingredients of the two products.

The original Jenever type is made by distilling malt-wine, or a mixture of malt-wine and spirit, over juniper berries, and possibly over other aromatic vegetable ingredients, with or without the addition of sugar. Jenever is traditionally drunk neat, slightly cooled, and sipped rather than swallowed, though young Dutchmen often take it in long drinks.

Brandewijn

One of the oldest forms of brandy, it is popular in some districts of the country. The essential factors in its preparation are ripening on charcoal and the addition of certain flavors. The brandewijn is also used as the raw base for advocaat, and for putting various fruits in—cherries, plums, and the characteristic brandewijn raisins and apricots.

Bessenjenever or Blackcurrant Gin

This is another typically Dutch product, processed on a neutral alcohol base and flavored with an extract of blackcurrants.

Advocaat

This drink, so thick that it has to be taken with a spoon, is made of brandewijn, eggs, sugar, and vanilla, and it has an alcoholic content of 15% to 18%. A somewhat thinner type of advocaat is exported to England.

Raisins in Brandewijn

Sugar candy and cinnamon are added to the raisins and the spirit. The alcohol content is approximately 15%.

Liqueurs

The favorite Dutch distillations are anisette, apricot brandy, cherry brandy, Curaçao, crème de cacao, kümmel, maraschino, and persico (this last is distilled from peach stones).

Whisky

Holland manufactures a certain amount of whisky. The barley, maize, and rye are dried on peat fires, for the sake of the smoky flavor.

Elixirs (Bitters)

These are made by the infusion of herbs, seeds, and peels in alcohol, sometimes to be distilled, sometimes not. There is usually a good deal of coloring matter and very little sweetening. Elixirs are not as much in favor as they were forty or fifty years ago; the best liked are red and green Pommeranz, which have a higher alcoholic content than most—particularly important for red Pommeranz when it is used in cafés for Schilletje or Voorburg of their

own making. Other elixirs or bitters are Longae Vitae, Catz bitters, Angostura, Boonekamp, and so on.
See Advocaat; Gin.

Neuberger

Grape cultivated for Austrian wines.

Neuchâtel

Swiss canton which produces dry, light, sprightly wines, mostly white.
See Switzerland.

Neutral brandy

Brandy distilled at a very high proof. Completely neutral brandy would be distilled 200° proof, or 100% alcohol, and would lack any distinctive characteristics save those of pure alcohol. In practice, anything over 170° proof is considered neutral. The same applies to neutral spirit used as a blending agent in whiskies.

New Jersey

Wine-producing region in the United States, with Egg Harbor as its center, where the Renault Wine Company owns 72 hectares (180 acres) of native grape varieties.

New Zealand

New Zealand owes the birth and growth of its wine industry to some remarkable men—Samuel Marsden, Anglican missionary and chief chaplain to the New South Wales government, who pioneered European agricultural methods; James Busby, first British resident in New Zealand; and Bishop Pompallier, Catholic missionary from France. These were the men who introduced the early wine cuttings. Later, Romeo Bragata, first New Zealand government viticulturist, a graduate of Italy's school of oenology at Comegliano, was to put the infant industry on a proper footing and demonstrate to the settlers how good wine should be made.

The earliest written record of vine planting is contained in Samuel Marsden's journal on September 25, 1819: "I planted [at Kerikeri] about 100 grape vines of different kinds brought from Port Jackson [Sydney]. New Zealand promises to be very favourable to the vine as far as I can judge at present of the nature of the soil and climate."

The earliest written record of wine made in New Zealand is contained in the journal of the famous French explorer Dumont d'Urville of the Astrolabe, who revisited the Bay of Islands in 1840. He was offered at Busby's home at Waitangi "a light white wine very sparkling and delicious to taste. Judging from this sample I have no doubt that vines will be grown extensively all over the sandy hills of these islands."

Bishop Pompallier brought vines from France in 1838

as did French settlers at Akaroa in 1840 and Germans at Nelson in 1843.

By 1894 vines were planted in many places on the North and South Island. All the vines introduced were of the *Vitis vinifera* variety. But two cruel diseases, phylloxera and the rise of prohibition, inhibited the new industry. Phylloxera was to have a great effect, for many farmers went out of production altogether while others, after uprooting their *vinifera* vines, cultivated the American type of hybrid grapes which, though phylloxera-resistant, did not produce wine as good as the original *vinifera* strains. Unfortunately, too, these strains derived from *Vitis labrusca* proved prolific bearers in the humid conditions of the North and were marketable as either table or wine grapes.

By 1906 there were 220 hectares (550 acres) under vines; by 1909, when Bragata resigned from the Department of Agriculture, there were 268 hectares (668 acres). The acreage dwindled to 179 in 1923. Government apathy, the rise of prohibition, the hard work necessary to combat the diseases of phylloxera, oïdium, and bunch rot caused many settlers to give up vine cultivation and return the land to other uses. Growers narrowed to three main classes: Yugoslav immigrants and some others in the Auckland province; the occupiers of the land originally planted by the gentlemen farmers of Hawke's Bay; and the religious descendants of Bishop Pompallier, the Marist Fathers, who finally established their permanent vineyard at Greenmeadows in Hawke's Bay.

During the First World War the industry languished. Labor was not available, the prohibitionist element was strong, and more dry districts (as no-liquor-license areas were known) were established, thus depriving winemakers of their outlets.

A new government in 1935 proved of considerable benefit. It cut the imports of wines 50% by import licensing and increased the duty on imported wines by 50%. But the greatest fillip of all was the outbreak of war in 1939. Overseas supplies were greatly reduced and New Zealand had to rely more on its own resources.

Grape acreage approximately doubled during the war, and increased gradually in the years following. By 1973 there were some 2,000 hectares (5,000 acres), producing at least 300,000 hectoliters (7.95 million U.S. gallons, 6.6 million imp.) a year. One company has planted nearly 500 hectares (1,250 acres) of *vinifera* vines in Blenheim, in association with an American concern. This and other new vineyards will bring the total of land in vines to more than 3,500 hectares (8,715 acres) in 1974.

In the early days, Northland was the main center. By the end of the century Hawke's Bay became the most important. Later, Henderson/Auckland came into its own, and now Gisborne and Waikato have become prominent wine-growing areas. But in 1973 Blenheim in the South Island created interest by the planting of 1,200 acres and in time, because of favorable climatic conditions, this area may have as great an acreage as the rest of New Zealand put together.

For many years, almost from the turn of the century till the present, the New Zealand wine industry has suffered from a form of schizophrenia. Public demand has been for fortified wines—ports, sherries, madeira, and the like.

Experts from the beginning have testified that New Zealand's temperate climate cannot produce a natural dessert wine. "The climate is not sufficiently warm to produce grapes of a sufficiently high sugar content," said the Royal Commission on Licencing in 1946. It noted that cane sugar is added to make up the deficiency and that some sweet wines contain as much as 30% by weight of added sugar.

And this has been the wine-grower's dilemma. His climate is suited to the production of light table wines; and the demand has been for fortified wines. Under the circumstances he has coped very well, but now with a more educated interest, he is able to turn to producing table wines for which the climate and soil is most suitable. Hawke's Bay is very similar in climate to parts of Burgundy and Bordeaux. Blenheim tops the sunshine record in New Zealand and has a very low rainfall, particularly at vintage time, though it is susceptible to ground frosts at times. Contrary to some people's belief, the vine-growing areas of New Zealand do not have a cool climate similar to Germany and Switzerland. Heat summation and yearly sunshine figures are much higher.

The most consistent wine at annual competitions has been a Cabernet Sauvignon from Hawke's Bay. It is one of the very few wines which is accepted overseas as being up to international standards and is available as yet in small quantities; but other growers, noting its success, are busy planting vines as they are released from quarantine by the department of agriculture. Good Cabernet Sauvignon wine was made in New Zealand nearly seventy years ago. Other red wine grapes which have done well in the past are Pinot Noir, Pinot Meunier, and Hermitage (Shiraz).

In the white wines, Pinot Chardonnay is creating interest, as is Traminer. As yet these are available in very limited quantities, but the growers have plenty of Riesling-Sylvaner (Müller-Thurgau), which is producing some of New Zealand's most popular white wines and is readily available under the name of "Riesling." The true Riesling grape used to be planted in the early pre-phylloxera days and should do as well here as it does in Australia.

In some areas New Zealand has the soil and climate to produce superb table wines in quantity. But more European varieties of grapes must be grown instead of the American hybrid types and other kinds commonly planted—which are prolific bearers but not suited for producing quality wine in the temperate climate. The last grape acreage census taken in 1970 showed that the most commonly planted variety was Palomino, followed by Baco 22A and Riesling-Sylvaner (Müller-Thurgau). It is believed that the planting of *vinifera* table wine varieties, both white and red, has increased since then.

In July 1972, there were 138 holders of wine-maker's licenses, of which 122 were active. Of these, 112 had up to 20 hectares (50 acres) of vines, four 20 to 40 hectares (51 to 100 acres), and six 40 hectares (101 acres) and over.

Present wine consumption, both local and overseas

wines, has been estimated by the Viticultural Association as being 8 liters (2.1 U.S. gallons, 1.7 imp.) per person, whereas beer consumption is thought to be 132 liters (29 U.S. gallons, 24 imp.) per person. While up-to-date statistics are not available from government sources, the three leading wine-makers (Montana, McWilliams, and Corbans) stated that in 1973 their production was 25% in sparkling wines, 29% in table wines, and 46% in fortified wines. Thus table wines now represent 54% of the total.

Niagara

(1) Wine-growing region in Canada and New York State. The important vineyard is Chateau Gay and its best wine is an unblended sparkling Delaware.

(2) One of the older American hybrid grapes, yielding white wine of pronounced "foxiness."

See United States: New York.

Niederhäuser Hermannshöhle

One of the best-known wines of the Nahe Valley in Germany.

See Nahe.

Niersteiner

Best Rheinhessen wines, with great nose and elegance. All the finest are Rieslings.

See Rheinhessen.

Nip

British term for a quarter-bottle; reputed to be half a pint.

Noah

Green-colored grape giving white wine; an American hybrid first recorded in Illinois. After the phylloxera disaster in Europe in the late nineteenth century, Noah was taken to France but was soon discarded by French growers because of the "foxiness" of its wine. It may still be found here and there, however.

Noble

A word usually applied to any grape variety, vineyard, or wine that shows inherent, lasting superiority when compared to other examples of its type. A noble grape will give outstanding wine in the proper setting and much better than average wine in a poor one. A noble vineyard shows at least a part of its greatness even in the worst of vintages. And a noble wine will impress even the rank beginner as remarkable.

Noble rot

A grape fungus which in sweet white-wine grapes becomes a virtue.

See Botrytis cinerea.

Noblejas

Wines of Toledo, usually sturdy reds somewhat comparable with those of the lesser Côtes du Rhône in France. *See* Spain.

Noggin

A gill or a quarter of a British pint.

Norheim

Wine district of the Nahe Valley, Germany. *See* Nahe.

Norton

Perhaps the best of the native American vines for red wine. It yields wines that are full, well balanced, agreeable, and not "foxy."

Norway

In the old days, lasting through the Middle Ages almost into the seventeenth century, the popular alcoholic beverages in Norway were beer and mead. Although they were, at an early stage, in contact with wine-drinking people, the Norwegians did not take much to wine until centuries later. The revolution in drinking habits came with the introduction of spirits. This was a comparatively late innovation, for not until the seventeenth century could spirits be bought on a commercial scale. Then they came very much into use. Except in the years between 1756 and 1816, every householder was allowed to make his own liquor—aquavit being favorite. In 1830 about 11,000 stills were active.

In 1845 the change came. By then the potato had emerged as the foremost raw material for the production of spirituous drinks; and potatoes are awkward for amateur distillers to handle. In this year (1845) a law was passed to prohibit the use of stills with capacities of less than 200 liters (52.8 U.S. gallons, 44 imp.). These two factors combined to diminish the attractions of spirit-making as a home industry.

Gradually most of the trade came into the hands of the two large firms of distillers: Jørgen B. Lysholm, Trondheim; and Løiten Braenderis Destillation, Kristiania. In 1927, however, the wine monopoly A/S Vinmonopolet took over the distilleries and still controls the sale of all potable spirits in Norway. The board of this institution and its managing directors are appointed by the king. The object of the monopoly is to control sales and thus control alcoholism. A/S Vinmonopolet is responsible for the rectification of locally produced alcohol, for the importation of wines and spirits and for their wholesale as well as retail sale. Even alcohol destined for medical and industrial use is controlled. The wholesale importation of beer is similarly controlled, although this is allowed to be sold in certain licensed shops. The total amount of wine sold in 1976 was more than 100,000 hectoliters (2.65 million U.S. gallons, 2.2 million imp.). There is no duty on wines and spirits, but fiscal taxes are fairly high.

In 1976 sales of spirits were more than 150,000 hectoliters (3,975,000 U.S. gallons, 3,300,000 imp.), made up as follows:

Foreign bottled spirits
A/S Vinmonopolet bottling of imported spirits
Imported spirits mixed with Norwegian alcohol
Norwegian-produced alcohol

According to the official statistics, every adult over fifteen years of age in the country consumed 5.1 liters (1.35 U.S. gallons, 1.12 imp.) of pure alcohol in that year.

The Løiten and Lysholm varieties of Norwegian aquavit are exported on a large scale to most markets in the world.

Norway also produces "Linie Aquavit," which is a unique "crossed" specialty. "Linie Aquavit" is aquavit that has crossed the Line—i.e., the Equator. To uphold an ancient tradition, aquavit that has already been aged in oak is sent to Australia and then back to Norway on the Wilhelmsen cargo liners, thus crossing the line twice. During this journey the aquavit undergoes an extra maturation process influenced by the movement of the ship. The salt sea air and the changes in temperature also assist this maturation. The A/S Vinmonopolet guarantees on the label that the trip was made, when, and aboard which ship. "Linie Aquavit" is excellent with hors d'oeuvres and spicy foods.

Nose

The neutral term for the bouquet of a wine.

Noyau

Colorless or slightly pink sweetened liqueur with the flavor of oil of almonds, or of peach or cherry kernels.

Nu

In France, the price of wine given *nu* is the price without the cost of cask or bottle.

Nuits, Côte de

See Côte de Nuits.

Nuits-Saint-Georges

Burgundy red, and some white, wines.
District: Côte de Nuits, France.

The ancient town of Nuits, which in 1892 incorporated the name of its most cherished vineyard to become Nuits-Saint-Georges, lies close to the southern end of the slope to which it gives its name. Unlike most others of the Côte de Nuits, the official place-name covers vineyards in Nuits and in nearby Prémeaux, a little to the south, these two making up the last of the important communes before the soil changes to emerge as the Côte de Beaune. Actu-

ally the Côte de Nuits extends slightly farther to the south, through the towns of Comblanchien and Corgoloin, but neither of these two is outstanding and their wines benefit only from the name Vins Fins de la Côte de Nuits (*q.v.*).

No vineyard in Nuits was included among the thirty-one Great Growths (*Grands Crus*)—the top-rated vineyards of the Côte d'Or, as classified by the I.N.A.O. (Institut National des Appellations d'Origine); nevertheless some very great vineyards are to be found there. Entering the town from the north, one sees the first of them on the right of the old vineyard road and on the lower slope descending from Vosne-Romanée. This slope drops gently to the River Meuzin—only a dried-up trickle most of the year—and another begins on the other side, rising steeply in a great rock-strewn bluff topped with trees and underbrush. Only the lower third of this slope is planted in vines, but along it are the best of the vineyards of Nuits: Les Pruliers, Les Porrets, Les Cailles, Les Saint-Georges, and slightly above Saint-Georges, Les Vaucrains. Les Saint-Georges lies along the town line and to its south are Didiers, Clos des Forêts, and the Clos de la Maréchale, the best growths of Prémeaux.

Nuits, largest town on the slope named after it, is nevertheless not very big. The population is slightly less than 5,000 and virtually every man, woman, and child is engaged in the wine business in one way or another, although Nuits is also famous for its Marc de Bourgogne (*see* Marc), its cassis, a sweet blackcurrant liqueur (*q.v.*), its grape juice, and its sparkling Burgundy. Despite all these extras, the true fame of Nuits will always rest where it belongs, on its natural wines. The I.N.A.O. may not have considered any of the vineyards of the commune to be worthy of the highest rank among Burgundian vineyards, but the earlier 1860 Classification recognized no fewer than nine as Outstanding Vineyards (*Têtes de Cuvées*), the top rung of the ladder. Les Saint-Georges, Aux Boudots, Les Cailles, Aux Cras, Aux Murgers, Les Porrets, Les Pruliers, Aux Thorey, and Les Vaucrains were the nine; all of them are now officially First Growths (*Premiers Crus*) of the commune, and all produce superb wines.

(Throughout Burgundy, First Growths are labeled with both name of vineyard and town name—e.g., Nuits-Saint-Georges Les Porrets, while the Great Growths carry *only* vineyard name—e.g., Chambertin.)

The outstanding distinction of the wines of Nuits is their firmness. Fuller in body than most Burgundies, they are apt to take years to mature. The firmest is generally Vaucrains, one of the finest of the commune and indeed of the whole Côte de Nuits; it is a wine to be laid down rather than drunk young. Bouquet is also a Nuits characteristic, and the wines are sometimes quite pungent. Les Saint-Georges will, because of its finesse, in most years take the honors in this field and in addition will be deeper in color and more "winey" than the others. Les Pruliers often starts out with a slightly metallic taste, but this passes and the wine ages wonderfully. Les Porrets, and the Clos des Porrets in particular, are the fruitiest. Clos des Porrets is a small section of the larger vineyard, and is the best part. It is owned entirely by Henri Gouges, one of the staunchest advocates of authentic Burgundian wines, and one of Burgundy's most respected growers. Gouges also makes a good white wine but only in small quantities, and most of it is sold in Paris. Boudots is another good vineyard, and Cailles combines the Nuits characteristics with a special velvety quality all its own.

The vineyards of Nuits-Saint-Georges total about 215 hectares (536 acres). In an average quantity year, they produce some 10,000 hectoliters (265,000 U.S. gallons, 220,000 imp.) of red wine and a very small amount of white.

In Nuits-Saint-Georges

FIRST GROWTHS (*Premiers Crus*)

Vineyard	Hectares	Acres
Les Saint-Georges	7.5	18.6
Les Vaucrains	6	15
Les Cailles	3.8	9.4
Les Porrets or Porets	7	17.5
Les Pruliers	7	17.5
Aux Boudots	6.4	15.8
Les Haut-Pruliers	4.5	11.2
Aux Murgers	5	12.4
La Richemone	2.2	5.5
Les Chaboeufs	3	7.2
La Perrière	4	10
La Roncière	2.1	5.3
Les Procès	1.9	4.7
Rue-de-Chaux	3	7.7
Aux Cras	3	7.7
Aux Chaignots	5.6	13.8
Aux Thorey	6.2	15.3

Vineyard	Hectares	Acres
Aux Vignerondes	3.4	8.4
Aux Bousselots	4.5	11.2
Les Poulettes	2.4	5.8
and portions of the following vineyards		
Aux Crots	8.9	21.2
Les Vallerots	9.7	24.25
Aux Champs-Perdrix	2.1	5.3
En La Perrière-Noblet	2.2	5.5
Aux Damodes	13.1	32.75
Les Argillats		
En La Chaine-Carteau	2.6	6.6
Aux Argillats	2.5	6.2

In Prémeaux

FIRST GROWTHS (*Premiers Crus*)

Vineyard	Hectares	Acres
Clos de la Maréchale	9.5	23.6
Clos des Arlots	4	10
Clos des Corvées	5.1	12.8
Clos des Forêts	6.7	16.6
Les Didiers	2.8	7
Aux Perdrix	3.4	8.3
Les Corvées-Paget	1.6	3.9
Les Clos Saint-Marc	.9	2.2
Clos des Argillières	4.2	10.4
Clos des Grandes-Vignes (*in part*)	2.1	5.3

O

Oak

The only wood from which the very best barrels and casks for ageing wine are made. In a sound oak cask, new wine lacking tannin and character is sure to improve, but if left too long it may become withered (*seché*). The most famous oak used for cooperage comes from Limousin and Nevers in France or from Yugoslavia. Tennessee white oak is most common in the United States, but some of the European species are imported for ageing fine red wines in California.

Oast house

A building containing a kiln for drying hops.

Oberemmeler

Fine wines of the Saar, in Germany. Karlsberg, Raul, Rosenberg, Hütte, and Scharzberg are well-known vineyards.
See Mosel-Saar-Ruwer.

Obscuration

In brandy, the difference between actual alcoholic strength and that shown by measuring its specific gravity. The difference comes from the addition of coloring matter, changing specific gravity but not strength; its amount will sometimes, but very rarely, be noted on labels.

Ockfener Bockstein

Always one of the best, and in certain years *the* best, of the wines of the German Saar. Big and full-bodied for one of the Saar wines, which tend to be light.
See Mosel-Saar-Ruwer.

Octave

Small cask of one-eighth of the capacity of a pipe. As the pipe varies considerably in capacity, so does the octave, which may range from 54.5 to 81.8 hectoliters (14 to 21 U.S. gallons, 12 to 18 imp.), but is usually given as 63.6 hectoliters (17 U.S. gallons, 14 imp.).

Oechsle

The Grad Oechsle is the German equivalent of the American Balling scale (*q.v.*), expressing the quantity of sugar in grape juice before fermentation.

Oeil de perdrix

French for "partridge eye." A term derived from the pinkish tint in a partridge's eye and applied to a pinkish tinge in white wines. It is found in some of the white Burgundies and in Champagnes. This term has been dying out since *vin rosé* began to be popular.

Oenology

The science of wine. In their *Traité d'Oenologie,* J. Ribéreau-Gayon and E. Peynaud define it also as the science which deals with the preparation and preservation of wine and its elements by the application of the rules of chemistry. The authors of the treatise have also stated that the function of oenology is to prevent wine sickness and, in general, to aid the production of the best possible wines with the minimum of waste and of unnecessary expense. There is no question of making a good wine out of a bad one: quality is governed by the soil, the weather, and the grape variety. Wine should be a natural product. But the best of wines, left to mature on its own and according to the whims of nature, would be spoiled. Man must intervene to arrange for the developing wine the conditions in which its natural characteristics and bouquet can come to perfection.

An oenologist is a technician who has gained his diploma in the science of vinification.

Oesterreicher

The Sylvaner or Franken Riesling grape.

Off-license

In England, a license permitting sale of wine, beer, and spirits to be consumed off the premises, and by extension, the shop department of the public house itself, usually referred to as an "off-license." There is a corresponding term "on-license" in the trade for public houses and wine shops, and the permit they require is an on-license. The American term is off-premises.

Oggau

Wine town in Burgenland. This is one of the important place-names in Austria (*q.v.*).

Ohio

See: United States: Ohio.

Oïdium

Powdery mildew; a fungus disease of the vine.
See Chapter Eight, p. 29.

Okolehao (oke)

Hawaiian beverage distilled from a mixture of molasses, rice lees, and juice of baked ti-root (the root of the taro or kalo plant). It is dark and smoky, and usually bottled at 80° proof.

Old Tom gin

Gin which has been sweetened with sugar.

Oldest bottled wine in existence

The Wine Museum in Speyer, German Palatinate, boasts of the oldest bottled wine in existence. It is estimated to be approximately 1,600 years old and is tightly sealed by the hardened oil used in Roman times to provide a protective film which floats upon the wine surface. Sealed amphorae dating from Roman days have also been found in the Mediterranean.

Oleron's disease

Vine malady found to some extent in South Africa, rarely elsewhere.
See Chapter Eight, p. 29.

Château Olivier

Bordeaux red and white wines.
District: Graves, France.
Commune: Léognan.

Although both the red and white wine are rated among the top Graves Growths as classified in 1959, the dry white wine is generally the favorite. The thirteenth-century château itself, turreted and buttressed, and enclosed by a moat, is no longer concerned with wine; but *chais* and vineyard have for many years been controlled by the firm of Eschenauer in Bordeaux. The castle was the hunting lodge of the Black Prince in the fourteenth century.

Characteristics. Not château-bottled, but pleasant; wine of character; and there are some good bottles.

Vineyard area: red—2.5 hectares (6.5 acres); white—20 hectares (50 acres).

Average production: red—10 *tonneaux* (900 cases); white—80 *tonneaux* (7,000 cases).

Oloroso

A nutty, pungent Sherry, richer than Fino. For comparison and discussion of Oloroso and Fino, *see* Sherry.

Oltrepò Pavese

Italian red or white wine from Pavia.
See Lombardy.

Opimian wine

One of the half-dozen great wine names of antiquity

and unlike all the others—Pramnian, Falernian, etc.—not the name of the geographical place from which the wine came, but the name of a vintage. During the consulship of Opimius in the year 121 B.C., the Roman summer was one of such splendor that great wines were made—chiefly Falernian and others, which were said (probably with some exaggeration) to have retained their full quality for a hundred years.

Oporto

A city at the mouth of the River Douro in northern Portugal. According to Portuguese law, any fortified wines that are to be labeled Port must be shipped from Oporto.
See Port.

Oppenheimer

In certain hot, dry years this will surpass Niersteiner as the best German Rheinhessen wine.
See Rheinhessen.

Orange

(1) Orange Bitters. Popular in England as an addition to mixed drinks. The flavoring ingredient is the peel of sharp Seville oranges. *See* Bitters.

(2) Orange Brandy. Made from brandy and oranges. The recipe, according to André Simon, is 1 gallon best brandy; the rinds of 8 Seville oranges and 2 lemons, cut very thin; 2 lbs. loaf sugar. Put it into a stone jar and cork down. Shake the bottle for a few minutes every day for twenty-one days. Strain it, bottle, and cork.

(3) Orange Wine. Made in Brazil from fermented orange juice.

Ordinaire

French term for the common wine the people drink every day.

Oregon

Wine-producing region of the United States, one of the few where *Vitis vinifera* will grow.
See United States: Oregon.

Orgeat

Flavoring syrup originally made from barley, but now made from an emulsion of almonds.

Originalabfüllung

Formerly, a German term used for estate-bottled. *Erzeugerabfüllung* is now the legally accepted phrase. For full description of this and other terms of the same meaning, *see* Germany.

Originalabzug

A German term formerly used for estate-bottled. For full description of this and other terms of the same meaning, *see* Germany.

Orvieto

One of the most consistently delightful white wines of Italy.
See Umbria.

Osaka

One of the main vine-growing districts of Japan (*q.v.*).

Ouillage

The topping up of wine barrels to compensate for evaporation. This is done repeatedly during the initial period of ageing.
See Chapter Nine, p. 38.

Ouvrée

An old Burgundian land measure, about one twenty-fourth of a hectare, or one-tenth of an acre.

Ouzo

A spirit popular in Greece, sometimes seen in the United States, England, and elsewhere. Ouzo is a close cousin to pastis, absinthe and French Pernod. It is drunk cold with water, in which, like pastis, Pernod, and absinthe, it turns milky.
See Greece: Spirits.

Oxhoft

Scandinavian liquid measure, 254 to 264 liters (67-69 U.S. gallons, 56-58 imp.).

Oxidation

Term most generally used as a synonym for maderization—i.e., a flaw in white wine which turns it brownish in color and flat in taste, usually after too long a time in cask or bottle.

A substance is oxidized when it fixes oxygen or when it gives up hydrogen or, more basically, when it accepts electrons from another source—e.g., the oxidation of sulfurous into sulfuric acid; or of sulfuretted hydrogen, where sulfur is freed. Wine embodies such oxidizable substances as tannins, coloring matter, iron, or sulfurous acid added during ageing.
See Maderization; Chapter Nine, p. 38.

P

Paarl

River valley in Cape Province, South Africa; a region of light table wines.

See South Africa.

Pacherenc du Vic Bilh

White wine of the French Pyrenees which is made in virtually the same general area as red Madiran (*q.v.*)—that is, the valley of the Adour. The principal grapes used are Ruffiat, Mansenc, Courbu, Sémillon, and Sauvignon.

País

A grape and wine of Spanish origin which has been in Chile long enough to be considered a native.

Palatinate (Pfalz, Rheinpfalz)

German white and red wines.
District: Southern Germany.

The Palatinate, or Pfalz, is one of the more charming provinces of Germany, and the sunniest. The picture-book villages, bright with painted shop signs and flowery window boxes, are set among orchards and the "wine garden," as the people call it here. The winters are so mild and the summers so hot that figs and lemons flourish; the fruit-trees are heavy with cherries, apricots, and peaches, and the grapes ripen early to produce soft, full-bodied wines. Lying west of the Rhine and north of the French frontier and Alsace, the Pfalz is covered with great woods, rising with the fringe of the Haardt Mountains at the edge of the plain of the Rhine. The province derives its name from the Latin *palatium* (palace), in German, *Palast* or *Pfalz*. The first palace of the emperors was on the Roman Palatine Hill; but afterward, every royal residence was called a "palace," and the officer in charge became the *comes palatinus* or *Pfalzgraf*—a title which was later to be handed down from one ruler of the Palatinate to another.

The beautiful bouquet and characteristic taste of the Pfalz wines come as much from the soil, which is a mixture of chalk, lime, and basalt, as from the climate. In fact, most of the wine is pleasant rather than distinguished; but, since the autumns here are long and mild, there is a great deal of rich, sweet dessert wine—Spätlesen and Trockenbeerenauslesen made from specially selected, late-gathered grapes. The Palatinate is the largest wine district of Germany, contributing about one-fifth of the national total; but the greater part of this is kept for domestic consumption.

There used to be more than 3,500 individual vineyard place-names in the Pfalz, and some 2,500 vineyard parcels, nearly all of them 1 hectare (2.5 acres) or less.

Though the 1971 West German Wine Law has reduced the number of legal vineyard names to about 300, the confusion of nomenclature is still rather tangled. Only the middle section of a strip of vineyard 100 kilometers (about 62 miles) long and 4 kilometers wide produces wines worthy of export to the world market.

Most of the vines grow along the Weinstrasse, a wine road beginning on the French border at the Weintor—a high stone-roofed gate topped with a gigantic figure of the German eagle—and reaching north to the edge of Rheinhessen. The countryside is lightly broken, flattish, and sunny, with the hills of the Haardt on the one hand and the Rhine sometimes visible at a distance on the other; the old villages are very South German, with twisting, narrow, cobbled streets and half-timbered houses, often decorated with vine motifs worked into stone—the whole Weinstrasse lives almost solely by wine and great is the rejoicing in a good year, great the sorrow in a bad one.

Eighty-four per cent of Palatinate wine is white. Of the remaining red wines some of those from Bad Dürkheim are best; but they do not equal the quality of Bad Dürkheim white wines.

England and the United States are the chief importers of high-quality Palatinate wines, followed by Belgium, Holland, Switzerland, and Scandinavia. The great wines, coming from the Mittelhaardt section of fifteen or eighteen communities out of a Palatinate total of more than 250, are from the Riesling grape variety, and this will nearly always be indicated on the label if 75% of the wine in the bottle is made from that variety. The Rieslings, with their fine bouquet and great breed, sometimes produce the fine, rich Spätlesen, Auslesen, Beerenauslesen, and Trockenbeerenauslesen wines but comprise only about 15% of the Palatinate total of white wine. Thirty-three per cent is from the Sylvaner grape, which generally goes into commoner wine. Excellent wines, spicy and with great bouquet, but in small quantity, are made from the Gewürztraminer. In the south, there is some Muskateller, white Burgunder, and Tokayer, the Palatinate name for the Ruländer or Grauer Burgunder grape. Thirty per cent Müller-Thurgau, the crossing of Riesling and Sylvaner, is grown; and around the village of Maikammer a light wine, drunk very young, is made. Practically all the red wine comes from the Blauer Portugieser variety, and only the Dürkheimers are of any interest. Generally, the Palatinate wines, owing to the milder climate, have more body than any others in Germany; and a larger proportion of unchaptalized wine is produced, since there is less temptation to use sugar here than there is in the colder areas. Much of the common wine, because it provided a soft base, was used by shippers for blending with Rheingaus and Mosels.

Of the three areas into which the Palatinate is divided—Upper Haardt, Middle Haardt, and Lower Haardt—only the Middle Haardt produces interesting

1.7 million hectoliters (46 million U.S. gallons, 37.4 million imp.).

The Pfalz is officially divided into two *Bereiche* or subregions: Südliche Weinstrasse, and Mittelhaardt-Deutsche Weinstrasse. The *Grosslagen* (sections of vineyards) in the Südliche Weinstrasse are Bischofsberg, Guttenberg, Kloster Liebfrauenberg, Königsgarten, Mandelhöhe, Ordensgut, Herrlich, Schloss Ludwigshöhe, and Trappenberg. The Mittelhaardt is composed of the *Grosslagen* Feuerberg, Grafenstück, Hochmess, Höllenpfad, Hofstück, Honigsäckel, Kobnert, Mariengarten, Meerspinne, Pfaffengrund, Rebstöckel, Rosenbühl, Saumagen, Schenkenböhl, Schnepfenflug vom Zellertal, Schnepfenflug an der Weinstrasse, and Schwarzerde. The division of these larger vineyard areas into the separate vineyards (*Einzellagen*) is often confusing, because some of the *Einzellagen* overlap *Weinbauort* (commune) boundaries. (For a complete list of the Pfalz *Einzellagen* arranged by *Bereich* and *Grosslage*, see Appendix B, p. 622.)

The strip of the Weinstrasse producing what the Germans call *spitzen* (peak) wines begins at the resort town of Neustadt and extends northward, like the broadening course of a river of vine, to the area around Herxheim, Dackenheim, and Freinsheim. A little more than half of the thirty-two villages are important, and the *Weinbauorte* of Deidesheim, Forst, Königsbach, Ruppertsberg, and Wachenheim, producing the Deidesheimer, Forster, Königsbacher, Ruppertsberger, and Wachenheimer wines, are outstanding.

Forty per cent of the wine is made in cooperatives, of which there were often two in each village, one for the Catholics and one for the Protestants—or, occasionally, the division was Conservative-Liberal. The cooperatives generally undersell the big estates; they make estate-bottled and occasionally Auslesen wines, but the Beerenauslesen and Trockenbeerenauslesen wines come mostly from the big estates. Important cooperative wineries are at Weintor, Pallenberg, Reitberg, and Mussbach.

Rain is held off by the east-lying Haardt hills, and the zone has less rain and more sun than any other part of Germany.

THE IMPORTANT MITTELHAARDT VINEYARDS

Forst

A hill of volcanic basalt called the Pechstein or Basaltsteinbruch, lying to the west of the village, provides a special soil which holds the sun's heat and releases it upward onto the vines during the night. The equalization of temperature permits the grapes to ripen more completely than anywhere else in Germany, and many late-gathered wines are produced. The best sites are in the vicinity of the Basalt Mountain, often dressed with the rubble from the quarries, and one of these, Forster Kirchenstück, has been valued under the West German Valuation Law at more than DM 30,000 per hectare (about $5,000 per acre), the highest rating given to any site. The sale price, however, is considerably higher than the price it is valued at—many say more than a dozen times greater.

wines. The soil of the other two sections is heavier. The Upper Haardt, in the south, is a vast sea of vineyard. An occasional superior wine is produced, such as some Maikammerer and the very sweet Edenkobener, but the emphasis is on quantity. The yield frequently reaches 160 hectoliters per hectare (1,500 U.S. gallons, 1,250 imp. per acre) as against 51 hectoliters or so (about 550 U.S., 450 imp. per acre) in the great vineyards, and quality and quantity do not go together. The average total harvest is

Vineyard area: 206 hectares (510 acres)—white; a trace of red.

Grape varieties: Riesling 70%, Sylvaner 25%, Traminer 5%.

Important vineyards: Kirchenstück. Jesuitengarten, perhaps the best-known, now covers nearly 6 hectares (15 acres). Important owners are Bassermann-Jordan, Bürklin-Wolf, Spindler, and Buhl. Two hundred years ago, owing to the demand for Jesuitengarten wine, the mayor of Forst allowed the four vineyards surrounding the famous plot to use the name; Bassermann-Jordan sued the village of Forst, but lost after a very long legal process. Freundstück. Ungeheuer.

Other vineyards: Elster, Musenhang, Pechstein.

Deidesheim

The competition between the Forster and Deidesheimer wines is very close, but the two communities certainly lead all others in the Pfalz in most years. Deidesheim itself is an old, attractive place; and Gasthaus zur Kanne, founded in 1160, is well worth a visit. Each May, in a famous wine festival, a prize goat is auctioned at the baroque town hall. The custom has been in force for nearly six hundred years; the little village of St. Lambrecht has had to pay this forfeit for grazing its goats on Deidesheim land ever since the fifteenth century. The Bassermann-Jordan estate, with holdings in many towns and villages, is located in Deidesheim, as is Reichsrat von Buhl, and the two estates together have the largest Deidesheim holdings.

Vineyard area: white—352 hectares (870 acres); red—15 hectares (37 acres).

Grape varieties: Riesling 60%, Sylvaner 30%, Gewürztraminer 5%, Portugieser 5%.

Important vineyards: Generally first in quality, although less well-known than Herrgottsacker, and on a steep south-facing slope, is Hohenmorgen. Herrgottsacker is first-class but in most years not quite up to Hohenmorgen. Leinhöhle, a deservedly very famous vineyard. Kalkofen. Kieselberg. Mäushöhle. Grainhübel.

Other vineyards: Langenmorgen, Paradiesgarten, Nonnenstück, Letten.

Ruppertsberg

Strong fruity wines with a great deal of breed come from the best vineyards of this ancient wine town, founded before the birth of Christ, and an important junction in Roman days. It lies on the south border of Deidesheim and shares two vineyards with that village.

Vineyard area: white—109 hectares (270 acres); red—42 hectares (107 acres).

Grape varieties: Riesling 20%, Sylvaner 50%, Portugieser 30%.

Vineyards: Hoheburg (first in quality), Linsenbusch, Nussbien, Gaisböhl, Reiterpfad, Spiess.

Königsbach

Königsbach is famous in its province for having contributed the stone from which the Reichstag in Berlin was built. The vineyards lie quite high up against the pine-crowned hills, and the best wines are white. Red wines, however, are of considerable local interest. Sold generally as Königsbacher Rotwein, and made from the Spätburgunder and Frühburgunder variety (Pinot Noir), they share with some Bad Dürkheimers the name of the best Palatinate red wine.

Vineyard area: white—69 hectares (170 acres); red—18 hectares (44 acres).

Grape varieties: Equal amounts of Riesling and Sylvaner; some Gewürztraminer; best red wines from Spätburgunder and Frühburgunder; bulk of red wines from Portugieser.

Vineyards: Idig, Jesuitengarten, Ölberg, Reiterpfad.

Wachenheim

The tale they tell in Wachenheim is that generations ago the mayor of the town challenged the Abbot of Limburg to a drinking bout to the finish. Both had strong heads; but it was the mayor who was still under full sail when the abbot, overcome by good Wachenheim wine, slipped under the table. As a mark of his esteem, he freed Wachenheim from paying the tithe of one-tenth of its wealth to Kloster Limburg. For the last seventy years Wachenheim has concentrated entirely on high-quality wine, some of it from Dr. Bürklin-Wolf, the vice-president of the German Wine Growers' Association and the owner of one of the three leading estates of the Pfalz. Schloss Wachenheim makes quantities of Sekt (sparkling wine) from Riesling and Burgunder vines.

Vineyard area: white—300 hectares (750 acres); red—60 hectares (150 acres).

Grape varieties: Riesling 25%, Sylvaner 50%, Portugieser 20%, Traminer 5%.

Important vineyards: Gerümpel (some very fine wine is made by Bürklin-Wolf); Altenberg, Rechbächel, Luginsland, Goldbächel.

Other vineyards: Böhlig, Belz, Bischofsgarten.

OTHER MITTELHAARDT TOWNS

Bad Dürkheim

Dürkheim Feuerberg is the best-known Pfalz red wine; but about three times as much white is made as red. The Dürkheim Wurstmarkt (Sausage Market) in the second and third weeks of September has been held for more than 500 years and is Germany's greatest wine festival, just as Dürkheim, with 800 hectares (2,000 acres) is one of the biggest wine towns in Germany; the wine barrel on the northern outskirts of the town (it is now a restaurant) is said to be the largest in the world, holding 2 million bottles.

Vineyard area: white—600 hectares (1,500 acres); red—200 hectares (500 acres).

Grape varieties: Riesling 15%, Sylvaner 35%, Müller-Thurgau 15%, Portugieser 25%, Gewürztraminer and others 10%.

Vineyards: Michelsberg, Fronhof, Fuchsmantel, Hochbenn, Nonnengarten, Steinberg, Abtsfronhof, Herrenmorgen.

Dackenheim

Some good wines from chalk and lime soil on the border of the Middle Haardt and the Lower Haardt; the best of them incline to be long-lasting.

Vineyard area: white—53 hectares (132 acres); red—27 hectares (66 acres).

Grape varieties: Riesling 20%, Sylvaner 20%, Portugieser 40%, Müller-Thurgau 20%.

Vineyards: Liebesbrunnen, Kapellengarten, Mandelröth.

Freinsheim

A very great range of wines, from ordinary to excellent, both red and white. The village has a Gothic church, a baroque town hall, and is quite lovely, especially at cherry-blossom time, when visitors crowd to see the "sea of blooms."

Vineyard area: white—100 hectares (250 acres); red—80 hectares (200 acres).

Grape varieties: Riesling 10%, Sylvaner 30%, Portugieser 35%, Traminer 5%, Müller-Thurgau 20%.

Vineyards: Musikantenbuckel (most important); Oschelskopf, Schwarzes Kreuz.

Gimmeldingen

On two rolling hills at the foot of the Haardt range; white wines are mostly Sylvaner and are rather soft, full and sweet.

Vineyard area: white—130 hectares (320 acres); red—25 hectares (67 acres).

Grape varieties: Riesling 20%, Sylvaner 65%, Portugieser 15%.

Vineyards: Bienengarten, Kapellenberg, Schlössel, Mandelgarten.

Haardt

Since 1971 the Haardt vineyards have been included in the Grosslage Meerspinne—whose name came from one of the old important plots in neighboring Gimmeldingen. The Herzog *Einzellage* has produced some quite elegant wines in good years; Bürgergarten has developed full-bodied and very sweet wines. These and other individual vineyard names (Herrenletten, Mandelring) will in most cases be found only on better bottles, while more and more Haardtherzchen will be encountered.

Vineyard area: 148 hectares (370 acres), nearly all white.

Grape varieties: About one-half Riesling and one-half Sylvaner.

Herxheim (Herxheim am Berg)

Wines here are familiarly known as Herxheimer Oil. Some have the hardness and character the Germans call "steel."

Vineyard area: white—120 hectares (300 acres); red—69 hectares (170 acres).

Grape varieties: In white, Sylvaner 75%, Riesling 25%; reds, Portugieser.

Vineyards: Honigsack (most important); Himmelreich, Kirchenstück.

Kallstadt

The wines are usually rather full-bodied and heavy, grown on a peculiar chalk hill, the soil of which is classed as "hot"; and for some reason they are particularly popular in England. The small village, with the vines sloping away below, is very peaceful, and a beautifully simple war memorial embossed with grapes and leaves marks its center. Two of the previously well-known local vineyard names were given in 1971 to two of the *Grosslagen* in which the Kallstadt *Einzellagen* lie: Saumagen and Kobnert. The other Kallstadt plots are in the *Grosslage* of Feuerberg.

Vineyard area: white—243 hectares (600 acres); red—81 hectares (200 acres).

Grape varieties: Riesling 40%, Sylvaner 35%, Portugieser 20%, Gewürztraminer 5%.

Vineyards: Nill, Steinacker, Horn, Kirchenstück, Kronenberg, Annaberg, Kreidkeller.

Leistadt

Rather interesting wines, half white and half red. All the whites are Sylvaner; all reds Portugieser. Annaberg is quite good.

Vineyards: Kalkofen, Kirchenstück, Herzfeld.

Mussbach

Red and white wines.

Grape varieties: Sylvaner; small amount of Riesling and Portugieser.

Vineyards: Eselhaut, a newer planting, which has become the best. Bischofsweg, Glockenzehnt, Johannitergarten, Kurfürst, Spiegel.

Neustadt an der Weinstrasse

Middle point on the wine road, the southern boundary of the Mittelhaardt, and the largest town in the Pfalz wine country, Neustadt is more renowned as a wine market and resort than for the usually unexciting products of its vines. The town has more vineyards than any other in the Pfalz.

Vineyard area: white—2,000 hectares (5,000 acres); red—200 hectares (500 acres).

Grape varieties: Riesling 40%, Sylvaner 30%, Portugieser 25%, Traminer 5%.

Vineyards: Grain, Erkenbrecht, Mönchgarten.

Ungstein

"Ungsteiner awakens the dead" is the motto of Ungsteiner wine. Whether it does or not, the quite heavy white wines from the south- and east-facing slopes tend to be fiery.

Vineyard area: 210 hectares (525 acres), about equally divided between red and white wine.

Grape varieties: Riesling 20%, Sylvaner 40%, Portugieser 40%.

Vineyards: Weilberg, Herrenberg, part of Michelsberg, Osterberg, Bettelhaus, Nussriegel.

Estate	Headquarters	Hectares	Acres	Location of Holdings
Bassermann-Jordan	Deidesheim	40	100	Forst: Forster Kirchenstück, Forster Jesuitengarten, Pechstein, Ungeheuer, etc. Deidesheim: Deidesheim Hohenmorgen Grainhübel, Geheu, Kalkofen, Leinhöhle, etc. Ruppertsberg: Ruppertsberg Reiterpfad, Nussbien, Spiess, Hoheburg, etc. Bad Dürkheim Ungstein

Some of the vineyards date from before 1360; the present-day estate has been built up by the Bassermann-Jordan family since it came into their hands at the end of the eighteenth century. In the half a mile of low, black-walled cellars under Deidesheim are some of the most wonderful Pfalz wines. The historic estate, its guest book signed by celebrities—from Mendelssohn to Max Schmeling—belonged to the grand old man of Pfalz wines, the late Dr. Friedrich von Bassermann-Jordan, once president of the German wine growers. His gigantic book in three volumes is the authority in the language of the history of wine. His son, Dr. Ludwig von Bassermann-Jordan, now manages the estate.

Estate	Headquarters	Hectares	Acres	Location of Holdings
Josef Biffar	Deidesheim	11	27.5	Deidesheim; Ruppertsberg
Reichsrat von Buhl	Deidesheim	100	250	Deidesheim: Deidesheimer Leinhöhle, Kieselberg, etc. Forst: Forster Freundstück, Kirchenstück, Pechstein, Ungeheuer, etc. Wachenheim: Wachenheimer, Luginsland, etc. Ruppertsberg: Ruppertsberger Hoheburg, Reiterpfad, etc. Königsbach: Königsbacher Rolandsberg, Idig, etc.
Dr. Albert Bürklin-Wolf	Wachenheim	105	262	Wachenheim: Wachenheimer Gerümpel, Goldbächel, Odinstal, Böhlig, Rechbächel (exclusive), Luginsland, etc. Forst: Forster Kirchenstück, Jesuitengarten, Pechstein, Ungeheuer, etc. Deidesheim: Deidesheimer Hohenmorgen, Kalkofen, etc. Ruppertsberg: Ruppertsberger Hoheburg, Gaisböhl (exclusive), Reiterpfad, Nussbien, etc. Bad Dürkheim

Bürklin-Wolf properties have been in the same family since 1790. A tall, oval, carved cask of even earlier vintage stands at the bottom of steep stairs down into one of the two great cellars in Wachenheim. Within are more contemporary touches in the moist, dripping dankness; each cask is named with its vineyard parcel, and a cartoon in white paint also depicts the wine's origin; a cemented-up bomb hole gapes in one wall, and Dr. Bürklin-Wolf tells how his cellars served as shelters in the war. The single direct hit killed no one but exploded a lot of Pfalz wine. Dr. Bürklin-Wolf is one of Germany's most energetic wine defenders and promoters. In 1951 he became the vice-president of the German Wine Growers' Association. His name is synonymous with the quality that he demands and produces.

Estate	Headquarters	Hectares	Acres	Location of Holdings
Dr. Deinhard	Deidesheim	37	92.5	Deidesheim: Deidesheimer Leinhöhle, Kalkofen, Kieselberg, Grainhübel, Herrgottsacker, etc. Forst: Forster Kirchenstück, Ungeheuer, etc. Ruppertsberg: Ruppertsberger Hofstück, Spiess, Nussbien, etc.
Herbert Giessen	Deidesheim	7	17.5	Ruppertsberg; Deidesheim; Forst
Ferdinand Kimich	Deidesheim	9	22	Deidesheim; Forst; Ruppertsberg
Dr. Kern	Deidesheim	5	13	Deidesheim; Ruppertsberg
Köhler Ruprecht	Kallstadt	8	20	Kallstadt
Lehmann-Hilgard	Freinsheim	11	27.5	Freinsheim; Herxheim
Josef Mehling	Deidesheim	6	15	Deidesheim; Ruppertsberg
Jos. Reinhardt II	Deidesheim	9	22	Deidesheim; Ruppertsberg; Forst
Friedrich Ruprecht Erben	Kallstadt	7	17.5	Kallstadt
Georg Siben (heir of)	Deidesheim	12	30	Deidesheim; Forst; Ruppertsberg
Wilhelm Spindler	Forst	15	37.5	Forst; Deidesheim; Ruppertsberg; Wachenheim
Stumpf-Fitz	Annaberg near Bad Dürkheim	6	15	Kallstadt; Bad Dürkheim

WINE ESTATES

Palatinate wines are sold either at the vineyard (*Freihand* sale) in 1,000-liter lots, at auction in 100-liter lots, or in bottle.

The three most important estates are known in the Pfalz as the Three B's (Bassermann, Buhl, and Bürklin), and there is little to choose between them; one or the other may be slightly in the lead, depending on the year. Dr. Deinhard, Fitz-Ritter, Stumpf-Fitz of Annaberg, and Georg Siben Erben are also very important.

Practically all the best growers in Germany belong to the Verband Deutscher Prädikatswein-Versteigerer (German Natural Wine Association), identified on bottle labels by the emblem of a black eagle with grapes on its breast. The membership of the V.D.P.V. in the Palatinate is found on page 356.

Palette

Controlled place-name in the wines of Provence (*q.v.*).

Palm wine

Spirit obtained by fermenting palm sap.

Palma

An export term for a very clean, delicate Sherry Fino. *See* Sherry.

Château Palmer

Bordeaux red wine.
District: Haut-Médoc, France.
Commune: Cantenac-Margaux.

Lying between the vineyard road and Château Margaux, and directly across the road from Château Rausan-Ségla and Château Rauzan-Gassies, Palmer is one of the two or three best-known and most sought-after Third Growths (*Troisièmes Crus*) as classified in 1855. Its name, taken from General Palmer, the English general who owned it early in the nineteenth century, may contribute, by its easy pronunciation, to its fame in English-speaking countries, but the reputation is deserved. Then known as Château de Gasq, the vineyard, along with Château Lafite, was popular at the court of Versailles in the time of Louis XV.

The owners are international: French, Dutch, and British. Sixty per cent is owned by the Bordeaux firm of Mähler-Besse. Mr. Mähler-Besse has for many years been the Dutch consul in Bordeaux. Sichel and Co., headed by the Englishman Peter Sichel, who lives at nearby Château Angludet, owns 30%. Ten percent belongs to the family of M. Alain Miailhe, who also own Pichon-Lalande and Siran, and at one time, Dauzac. The three owners combine to sell the wine on the markets in which they are strong; hence Palmer fetches deservedly high prices. Before the Second World War, the owners of Palmer bought Château Desmirail, another Third Classi-

fied Growth in Margaux, and did away with the name. The Palmer vineyard is planted 40% in Cabernet Sauvignon, 40% Merlot, and 10% each of Cabernet Franc and Petit Verdot.

Characteristics. Full and big, often resembling the wines of adjoining Château Rausan-Ségla, though in recent years Palmer is apt to be finer and harder. In the past two decades, because of its excellent qualities, it has become one of the most popular château-bottlings of the Médoc, and with Calon-Ségur one of the two most popular Third Growths.

Vineyard area: 40 hectares (100 acres).
Average production: 140 *tonneaux* (12,000 cases).

Palo Cortado

Rare Sherry wine combining the characteristics of an Oloroso and a Fino.
See Sherry.

Palomino

The dominating white grape in the making of Sherry at Jerez, Spain; used also for lesser wines in other parts of Spain. It has been planted in California, where it is used both for dry table wines and for the best of the sherry-types; it is known there as the Golden Chasselas.

Palus

Vineyard land adjacent to the rivers Dordogne, Garonne, and Gironde in the Bordeaux region of France; also the islands in the Gironde. The land is too heavy and moist for grapes to produce fine wine, but considerable quantities of *vin ordinaire* are made there, part of which becomes the everyday wine of the Bordeaux vineyard worker.

Pamid

An ancient and prolific grape variety grown in Bulgaria and used for the ordinary red wine.

Château Pape-Clément

Bordeaux red wine.
District: Graves, France.
Commune: Pessac.

Founded in 1306 by Bertrand de Goth, Archbishop of Bordeaux, the vineyard acquired its name when he became Pope Clement V. The vineyard was not ranked when the Graves Growths were classified in 1953, but the dedicated owners upgraded their vineyards and vinification techniques, so that Pape-Clément was included in the 1959 Classification. The wines have continued to improve and are now among the best red wines of Graves; they often unjustifiably fetch prices equal to those paid for the top Second Growths of the Médoc.

Characteristics. A very good wine, with the best qualities of a typical Graves. Some bottles from great vintages are superb.

Vineyard area: 27 hectares (68 acres).
Average production: 120 *tonneaux* (11,500 cases).

Parfait Amour

A very sweet spiced liqueur, either red or violet, from France and Holland.

Paris

Paris once counted her own wines among her attractions. Vineyards existed in numerous quarters of the city, the most famous in Montmartre, where there is still a street named rue de la Goutte d'Or, or "street of the drop of gold," in memory of the reputed excellence of Montmartre white. In the Passy section, warm springs once provided cures for disordered city-dwellers, and the route led to the rue des Vignes (street of the vines) for a sip of wine afterward. The heyday of Parisian viticulture was the thirteenth century, but most of the vines were afterward destroyed. Those that were not have been swallowed up by the city—with the exception of a few in Montmartre, kept for the sake of tradition. Their wines are auctioned off each year at foolishly high prices.

Parras

Center of Mexican viticulture, site of the Bodegas del Marqués de Aguayo, among others.
See Mexico.

Parsac-Saint-Émilion

Bordeaux red wine.
District: Saint-Émilion.

Commune whose vineyards, planted on chalky slopes, produce full-bodied wines of rich color. This place-name has not existed since 1975 when it was incorporated into the Montagne-Saint-Émilion place-name.
See Saint-Émilion.

Passes

French for the strip, or small label, affixed to bottles, giving subsidiary information not covered on the neck or on the main label.

Passe-Tout-Grains

Decent red Burgundy wines made from a blend of Pinot with Gamay or other lesser grapes.
See Burgundy.

Passion fruit liqueur

Deep golden, very sweet Australian liqueur from the passion fruit.

Passito

Italian wine made from dried grapes. Usually it is a dessert wine, although such grapes are sometimes added to dry wines.

Passover wine

The wine of the great Jewish festival.
See Kosher wine.

Pasteur, Louis

The great French chemist of the Jura, eastern France, discovered pasteurization while experimenting with the local wines. Before his time (1822-95), wine-making methods were mainly practical, owing little to scientific theory. Pasteur isolated the microorganisms which make grape juice ferment; but surprisingly, the practice of centuries has been little changed by this discovery. Quantity production of wine has definitely been influenced by Pasteur; quality production only very slightly.

Pasteurization

The process, named after Louis Pasteur, of sterilizing wine (or other liquids) by heat.

Stabilization of wine, milk, or other liquid by heating it briefly and rapidly to a temperature usually 140° to 150°F. (60° to 66°C.), thus ridding it of most microorganisms. It is sometimes effective in the case of ordinary wines but is not recommended for fine wines. Not only are the bacteria destroyed but the wine also becomes dead to evolution. The process may be carried out before or after bottling.
See Chapter Nine, p. 38.

Pastis

The aperitif of Marseille. Pastis is made on an alcohol base with herb flavorings, notably licorice. It bears a strong resemblance to anis but is slightly less distinctive in taste; and when diluted with water, it clouds and turns milky, with none of the green tinge of anis. Both pastis and anis have certain characteristics in common with absinthe. They are lower in alcohol, however, and wormwood, the ingredient which caused absinthe to be banned in most civilized countries, is omitted. Three of the better-known brands of pastis are those produced by Pernod, Ricard, and Berger in France; and a certain amount is illicitly homemade in southern France and Corsica.

Patent still

Continuous distilling apparatus. It is more economical than the older pot still in that the latter is basically a copper pot which has continually to be opened and refilled. The patent still is sometimes called the coffey still, because it is based on a patent taken out by Aeneas Coffey in 1832. Coffey's patent was an improvement on one by Robert Stein of Scotland, who patented the first design for a still of this type in 1826. Most of the finest rums and whiskies are always pot-distilled, this method allowing more of the taste and aroma to pass over with the distillate. Except for those favoring light-style liquors, pot-distilled remains synonymous with highest quality in most brandies and spirits.

Patras

Region of Greece producing good, mainly white wines. The town of Patras contains many of the large wine companies and cooperatives.

See Greece.

Patrimonio Rosé

Wine produced between Bastia and Île Rousse. This is the best of the Corsican wines.

See Corsica.

Patron saints of wine in Germany

The Germans have borrowed a French saint: Urban, the Bishop of Autun (between the Saône and the Loire), is one of their most honored patrons of the grape. His day, May 25, is fêted in many of the German wine districts, and a vast number of chapels and statues of St. Urban are to be found in the wine-growing areas of the country.

St. Kilian, the Frankish saint, is the patron of the vintners and their product in the wine districts of Franconia. And the vineyards bordering the Lake of Constance boast of Otmar, abbot of the monastery of St. Gallen, to whom legend ascribes a barrel which replenished its store of miraculously healing wine as quickly as its contents were drunk. Common sense should have told the vintners of Lake Constance that the potential threat of this neverending source would in time have made their product and themselves unnecessary, yet they have chosen to commemorate the abbot as their patron.

Other saints and holy figures connected with wine in Germany include St. Cyriakus in the Palatinate, St. Genoveva and St. Magdalena, St. Walter, St. Werner, the holy Elizabeth, and even the saintly Mary—as well as St. Peter, connected with the grape through many stories and legends.

See also Saint Martin; Saint Vincent.

Pauillac

Bordeaux red wine.
District: Haut-Médoc, France.

Most important of the four great wine communes—Margaux, Saint-Julien, Pauillac, and Saint-Estèphe—of the Médoc peninsula jutting out from the mouth of the Gironde, Pauillac is paradoxically the least known. This is because the fame of the individual vineyards overshadows that of the town. Château Lafite, Château Latour, Château Mouton-Rothschild, and others are known as

themselves, not as Pauillac wines, though all are in the commune. Consequently, with so much château-bottling, there is little regional wine to be sold as Pauillac.

Vineyard grading in this district is curiously uneven. Pauillac now has three First Growths (*Premiers Crus*); a single Second Growth (*Second Cru*), divided into two Pichon-Longueville vineyards; no Third Growths (*Troisièmes Crus*) at all; a little-known Fourth Growth (*Quatrième Cru*), Château Duhart-Milon-Rothschild; and then, suddenly, twelve Fifth Growths (*Cinquièmes Crus*)—out of the eighteen in the entire list of *crus classés* of the Médoc. The absence of Pauillac Seconds, Thirds, and Fourths illustrates the present considerable inaccuracy of the 1855 Official Classification, since several of the Fifths would be placed higher on any realistic scale drawn up now.

The wines do not possess much generic similarity, tending rather to be individual, except that all share the characteristic of being fairly full-bodied for Médocs. They are bigger than the more delicate Margaux, and, with one or two exceptions, less hearty than the Saint-Estèphes. On the other hand, no very accurate generalization can be made about wines as different as, for example, Lafite and Mouton-Rothschild, where special selection of grape variety gives the former an added finesse and the latter an advantage of stamina.

Beginning in the south at Château Latour, which touches Saint-Julien, the land is gently rolling, with vineyards placed along the soft ridge which slopes down into inferior marshy land beside the Gironde. At the old enclave of Bages, just before the town of Pauillac, there is a more pronounced rise; after Pauillac, the highest land holds Pontet-Canet, Mouton du Baron Philippe, and Mouton-Rothschild, side by side on a plateau; and then Lafite, bordering Saint-Estèphe on the most sloping vineyard land of Pauillac. This is the only part of the first-class land in the Médoc which is almost hilly.

For centuries Pauillac itself was an important port. Even today there is a customs post, and a few ships arrive from America and Africa. But with the coming of steam and the shortening of the distance up to Bordeaux, Pauillac went to sleep. But in the middle 1960s, the town became a bustling little city—not very pretty, but perhaps the most prosperous in the whole Haut-Médoc. An unfortunate oil refinery mars the river scenery and certainly does nothing to improve the quality of the air or the wines. Few remember that it was from Pauillac that La Fayette set sail for the American Revolution. Recently, however, the Pauillac waterfront has been renovated; the cafés that look out onto the yacht-filled harbor have been spruced up.

The Commanderie du Bontemps de Médoc et de Graves, the local selling organization composed of growers, shippers, and various dignitaries interested in wine, has its headquarters in the river port, and today ceremonies of the wine society are the most vivid events in the place where once river pirates met with a hot reception, and engagements of the Hundred Years' War were fought.

The Pauillac vineyards rated as Classified Growths (*Crus*) in the 1855 Classification of Médoc wines are:

FIRST GROWTHS (*Premiers Crus*)
Château Lafite-Rothschild
Château Latour

SECOND GROWTHS (*Seconds Crus*)
*Château Mouton-Rothschild
Château Pichon-Longueville Baron
Château Pichon Lalande

FOURTH GROWTH (*Quatrième Cru*)
Château Duhart-Milon-Rothschild

FIFTH GROWTHS (*Cinquièmes Crus*)
Château Batailley
Château Haut-Batailley
Château Croizet-Bages
Château Clerc-Milon
Château Grand-Puy-Ducasse
Château Grand-Puy-Lacoste
Château Haut-Bages-Libéral
Château Lynch-Bages
Château Lynch-Moussas
Château Mouton-Baronne-Philippe
Château Pédesclaux
Château Pontet-Canet

*Declared a First Growth by the Minister of Agriculture in 1973.

See also under separate headings.

Château Pavie

Bordeaux red wine.
District and Commune: Saint-Émilion, France.

Considerably subdivided in recent years, Château Pavie is still the largest of the outstanding Saint-Émilion vineyards. It is beautifully situated on the completely vine-covered flank of hill which faces, from the south, the other flank on which Ausone and the village of Saint-Émilion stand. All the vines are south-exposed. It may be the frequent change of ownership which caused the Pavie wines to fall off for a time, but for the last decade or so they have been back in form, and in 1955 Château Pavie was classified one of the twelve First Great Growths (*Premiers Grands Crus*), while the split-off vineyards, Château Pavie-Decesse and Château Pavie-Macquin, in the lower category, were classed Great Growths (*Grands Crus*) of Saint-Émilion.

Characteristics. A big production and a good, typical Saint-Émilion—generous wine with a big nose.
Vineyard area: 35 hectares (88 acres).
Average production: 190 *tonneaux* (17,000 cases).

Pays, vins de

See Vins de pays.

Peach brandy

Properly, brandy distilled from peaches, but often used for peach liqueur, obtained by steeping peaches in sweetened brandy.

Pécharmant

The best of the red wines of Bergerac, in southwest France, bearing a resemblance to the lesser wines of Saint-Émilion.
See Bergerac.

Pecsenyebor

Quality category for Hungarian wine.

Château Pédesclaux

Bordeaux red wine.
District: Haut-Médoc, France.
Commune: Pauillac.

Classified a Fifth Growth (*Cinquième Cru*) in 1855, the small estate now belongs to M. Lucien Jugla.
Characteristics. A small uneven wine. The vinification is not always what it might be.
Vineyard area: 15 hectares (38 acres).
Average production: 62 *tonneaux* (7,000 cases).

Pedro Ximénez

A very sweet grape grown in Andalusia and elsewhere in Spain. It is used mainly in the making of sweet wines, or as a sweetener for sherries.

Pelin

Iced Rumanian wine drink with an infusion of herbs.

Pelure d'oignon

"Onion-skin." The term applies to the brownish tinge which marks some old wines. It was once used, also, for many pink wines before *rosé* became the popular term, and it is still sometimes so used.

Perlada

Just north of Figueras on the Spanish side of the Pyrenees is this tiny wine-producing town dominated by an impressive castle. Its rosé is quite popular and a good deal better than the red and white wine made there. But best-known of Perlada's wines is a "Spanish champagne" sent to London, where its name was struck down by the British courts in a suit by the French Insitut des Appellations d'Origine, thus confirming in Britain the exclusive right of French Champagne producers to the name Champagne.

Perlant

French term for mildly sparkling wine.
See Pétillant.

Perlwein

A sparkling wine popular in Germany, made by artificial carbonation.

Pernand-Vergelesses and Pernand-Vergelesses-Côte de Beaune

Burgundy red and white wines.
District: Côte de Beaune, France.

The village of Pernand-Vergelesses is one of the most ancient and certainly the most primitive of all the wine communes of Burgundy. It lies on the back slope of the "mountain"—the high hill that rises behind Aloxe-Corton—and is skirted by Ladoix-Serrigny and Savigny-les-Beaune. A small rutted dirt-track leads up to the tiny jumbled-together houses, and in these buildings live many of the growers of Corton-Charlemagne, one of Burgundy's greatest white-wine vineyards. Few of these growers own more than a handkerchief-sized portion of the vineyard, and their annual production varies from upward of a dozen down to three or four barrels, or even less.

There are no great or famous vineyards entirely within the communal limits. Portions of vineyards allowed the place-names Corton, Corton-Charlemagne, and Charlemagne (*qq.v.*) fall within the commune, but this is an accident of geography and the wines are rightly considered with those of Aloxe-Corton. Wines sold under the commune name are predominantly red and are minor Côte de Beaunes. They are light, sometimes have considerable bouquet, and are often very fruity. Some Burgundians say they are wines that burn with a hot and intense flame but burn out reasonably quickly. The whites are simultaneously soft and heavy, without the breed of the great whites of Aloxe.

About 400 hectoliters (10,600 U.S. gallons, 8,800 imp.) of white wine are made annually; the amount of red varies but 2,500 hectoliters (62,500 U.S. gallons, 55,000 imp.) per year is average, even though it may be sold as Pernand-Vergelesses, Pernand-Vergelesses-Côte de Beaune (there is no difference in the wines of these two names), or, after blending with others from specified communes of the slope, as Côte de Beaune-Villages. There are about 60 hectares (150 acres) of First Growth vineyards.

The French authorities have not yet finished the task of selecting the First Growth (*Premier Cru*) vineyards—those that may (if the wine meets slightly higher than normal qualifications) be sold with both commune name and vineyard name on bottle labels. While this work is in progress, the following vineyards have been given this rating provisionally.

FIRST GROWTHS (*Premiers Crus*)

Vineyard	Hectares	Acres
Île des Vergelesses	9.3	23.1
Les Basses Vergelesses	17.5	43.3
Creux de la Net	5	12.4
Les Fichots	11	27.5
En Caradeux	20	49.8

Pernod

A popular anis-flavored aperitif made by the firm of Pernod Fils in France. Like others of this family it becomes cloudy when water is added.
See Pastis.

Perry

A kind of pear cider, either still or sparkling.

Persia.

See Iran.

Peru

Peru is one of the oldest South American wine-producing countries, but is not one of the largest or most important. Vines have been grown in Peru at least since 1566, when Francesco de Carabantes planted some in the vicinity of Ica, an oasis south of the capital city of Lima.

The terrain and climate of Peru are such that it supports vines only in its suitably irrigated coastal regions. The snow-capped Andes are generally too cold and too rugged, and the northern part of the country is suitable for other types of cultivation, mining, and the rearing of livestock—especially the llama. Most of the vines are of European stock and many wines are natural, both red and white, although some are fortified and modeled on Sherry, Port, and Madeira. One of the best grape varieties is Malbec. The table wines somewhat resemble the warm, vinous wines of Spain. Only about 80,000 hectoliters (2.12 million U.S. gallons, 1.76 million imp.) of wine are made and the 14,000 hectares (35,000 acres) of vineyard are found around Ica, where the famous Facama Vineyard is located, around Lima itself, and around the ancient Inca cities of Cuzco and Arequipa. In the south, the vineyards of Moquega are also fairly important.

While the Spanish population habitually drinks wine, the Indians prefer *chicha*, brewed from corn and molasses, or one of the alcohols distilled in the country. The best of the Peruvian alcohols is the Pisco brandy (*q.v.*) which they distill from partially fermented Muscat wine. This brandy is the base of the Pisco sour, which is made with the white of an egg and Angostura bitters.

Pessac

Fine wine commune of the Graves district of Bordeaux. This is the village of Châteaux Haut-Brion and Pape-Clément.

See Graves.

Pétillant

French term for wine which is slightly sparkling or crackling; an alternative term is *perlant*. *Pétillant* is used only of wines which owe their sparkle simply and naturally to unfermented sugar still present in the wine when it is bottled. The maximum pressure admitted in France for *pétillant* types is 2 atmospheres at 68°F. (20°C.).

Petit-Chablis

Pleasant but lesser wines of Chablis produced in Lignorelles, Ligny-le-Châtel, and other places allowed the *appellation* Chablis.

See Chablis.

Petit Verdot

Grape grown in the Bordeaux region.

See Verdot.

Château Petit-Village

Bordeaux red wine.
District and Commune: Pomerol, France.

This expensive wine made by the Prats family contains much more Cabernet Sauvignon than the average Pomerol wine. The Prats brothers also own Cos d'Estournel at Saint-Estèphe in the Haut-Médoc.

Vineyard area: 9 hectares (23 acres).
Average production: 42 *tonneaux* (4,030 cases).

Petite Champagne

Not a Champagne, but the second best of the regions producing Cognac, which will bear its name or be called Fine Champagne.

See Cognac.

Petite-Sirah (Syrah)

A grape planted in California, yielding a fairly good red wine. It is also known as the Duriff. Though some authorities say that this grape descends from the Syrah from which French Hermitage is made, others maintain that it does not.

Château Pétrus

Bordeaux red wine.
District and Commune: Pomerol, France.

The outstanding wine of Pomerol and one of the top eight Bordeaux red wines, Pétrus commands prices comparable with those of the First Growths (*Premiers Crus*) of the Médoc. On gravelly soil mixed with clay, covering a smooth rise of land higher than the surroundings but not steep enough to be called a hill, the vineyard lies about a mile from Libourne and two miles or so from Saint-Émilion on the road linking those historic vinous villages. The attractive small house in which the *chai* is to be found is decorated with the symbols and keys of St. Peter (Pétrus), and he is also the venerable gentleman carved in wood who guards the portals. Until her death in 1962, the owner was Mme Loubat, a lady of great energy and character, in her eighties and still a car driver and active *vigneronne*. Tasting the wine in the *chai* with her was a double delight; her old-fashioned French courtesy was as charming as the wine she made. The vineyard, very well run by Christian Moueix, is now the property of M. J. P. Moueix and Mme Lacoste, the niece of Mme Loubat. Along with Château Lafite, Pétrus is one of the most expensive wines of Bordeaux.

Characteristics. Superb, well-rounded and fruity—sometimes velvety; it can be drunk before it is very old.

Vineyard area: 12 hectares (30 acres).
Average production: 40 *tonneaux* (3,800 cases).

Château de Pez

Bordeaux red wine.
District: Haut-Médoc, France.
Commune: Saint-Estèphe.

Traditionally one of the leading Bourgeois Supérieur wines of the Médoc, but actually deserving a higher classification. The vineyard is directly across the road from Château Calon-Ségur in the village of Saint-Estèphe.

Characteristics. Less full than many of its neighbors, it has the characteristic hardness and slow-maturing qualities of Saint-Estèphe. It is one of the lesser vineyards of the Médoc consistently producing good wines which could be a good value when they were inexpensive.

Vineyard area: 40 hectares (100 acres).
Average production: 150 *tonneaux* (14,000 cases).

Pfalz

Alternative name for the Palatinate (*q.v.*) in Germany.

Phylloxera

A parasitic disease of the vine. The *Phylloxera vastatrix* is a burrowing plant louse of the Aphididae family, probably indigenous to the native vines of eastern America and certainly less harmful to them than to any other vines. In the second half of the last century, phylloxera caused considerable damage in Californian vineyards. Then, on vines sent from the United States, it was brought to Europe, where it devastated the vineyards of most of the wine-making countries. It was extremely destructive in France, where it was active in the 1870s, and elderly connoisseurs of wine are still debating the respective merits of pre-phylloxera and post-phylloxera clarets. The remedy for the disease is the grafting of *Vitis vinifera* varieties onto the native American root-stocks, which are naturally resistant to this root-eating grub. The grafting does not change the nature of the *Vitis vinifera* grape, but it does affect its longevity.

Vines no longer live as long as they once did. Old vines give quality but few grapes. Young vines give more grapes but less quality. Another consequence, not yet proven, but graver if it is a fact, is this: only since phylloxera has the vine disease fan leaf, or infectious degeneration, been found. Leading scientists have come to the conclusion that phylloxera may spread the disease.

See Chapter Eight, p. 29.

Pichet

French term for a pitcher, sometimes of wood or earthenware, for wine or cider.

Château Pichon-Lalande

Bordeaux red wine.
District: Haut-Médoc, France.
Commune: Pauillac.

The vineyard comprises about three-fifths of the old estate of Pichon-Longueville, separated a little more than 140 years ago, and is entirely enclosed within the semicircle of the Châteaux Latour and Pichon-Baron vineyards behind it. The wine from some parts of the estate has a character very similar to that made at Château Latour. A Second Growth (*Second Cru*) of the 1855 Classification, the wine was previously labeled Pichon-Longueville-Lalande, or Pichon-Longueville, Comtesse de Lalande. Pichon-Longueville found with no qualification will mean the wine is Pichon-Longueville, Baron de Pichon (*q.v.*). The heirs of M. Miailhe are the owners of Château Pichon-Lalande, as this *Cru* is commonly referred to today in Bordeaux and the Médoc.

Characteristics. More supple than Pichon-Longueville-Baron, the wine seems in recent years to have gained an edge in popularity over Pichon-Baron, which in its turn was perhaps more popular twenty years ago. The quality of 1970 Pichon-Lalande is so good that it should still further increase in demand.

Vineyard area: 49 hectares (123 acres).
Average production: 220 *tonneaux* (20,000 cases).

Château Pichon-Longueville, Baron de Pichon

Bordeaux red wine.
District: Haut-Médoc, France.
Commune: Pauillac.

More than a century ago, the two Pichon-Longueville vineyards, now facing each other across the vineyard road, were one. The Pichon-Longueville (Baron) bottle will sometimes be found labeled simply Pichon-Longueville; the wine of the Comtesse de Lalande portion has always been labeled Pichon-Longueville-Lalande, or Pichon-Longueville, Comtesse de Lalande, and recently Pichon-Lalande. Jacques Pichon, Baron de Longueville,

was the first president of the *parlement* of Bordeaux in the seventeenth century.

The château of Pichon-Longueville-Baron, built in the nineteenth century, is probably the most striking of its period in Bordeaux, with its "renaissance" turrets soaring up like spires. The outline of the château is perfect for a label, but unfortunately it is not used for this purpose. The vineyard is a Second Growth (*Second Cru*) of Médoc, and is most expertly managed by M. Bouteiller, the present owner.

Characteristics. This good wine is full-bodied and rich, although inconsistently so.

Vineyard area: 27 hectares (87 acres).
Average production: 98 *tonneaux* (8,000 cases).

Picpoule (Picpoul)

A white-wine grape grown extensively in southern France. It produces a rather thin white wine and is used also for vermouth. Catalonians call it Avillo.

Piedmont

Red and white wines.
District: Northwest Italy.

Piedmont, "foot of the mountain," is the extreme northwest corner of Italy. Its capital is the prosperous city of Turin, center of the vermouth industry, and the region produces two of Italy's finest red wines: Barolo and Barbaresco. White, and sometimes sickly sweet, sparkling Asti Spumante and the rather less popular Moscato d'Asti are also products of the province. They all have controlling organizations—or *consorzi*—to define and administrate their quality and authenticity.

Piedmont is a vast plain spreading out from the sinuous valley of the upper Po and surrounded by Alps to the north and west, Apennines to the east and southeast, and the Monferrato Hills to the south. In spite of the precipitous slopes of some of its mountains and the unsuitability of part of its plain, Piedmont is fifth—after Apulia, Sicily, Emilia-Romagna and Veneto—in wine production in Italy, making more than 5 million hectoliters (132.5 million U.S. gallons, 110 million imp.) annually, 80% of it from the southern section of the tumbled-together Monferrato Hills. These are fairly low, but often incredibly steep, resembling somewhat the hills of the Beaujolais district in France, but far less orderly. Yet in this region the tall vines used to be everywhere, sometimes sharing their plots with olive trees and wheat or other crops. Today, as a consequence of the 1963 wine law, intensive viticulture has for the most part replaced the haphazard planting. Vines also extend into the rest of Piedmont, but the wines—while sometimes pleasant—are inferior to those from the Monferrato district. Piedmont's chief grapevine is Nebbiolo, but there are also significant numbers of Muscats and of Barbera, Bonarda, Freisa, Brachetto, Cortese, Dolcetto, Erbaluce, and Grignolino grapevines scattered from the low river valley to the austere heights of the Valle d'Aosta—the mountainous corner which climbs to the Swiss border.

BAROLO AND BARBARESCO

Both are big, strong, enormously robust wines with powerful depth and a heavy pungency. Barolo, which is slower to mature, reaches the greater heights of the two, but because of its pungency and uncompromisingly masculine aftertaste (so strong that it is often characterized as "the aftertaste of tar") it is not always so well liked as the lighter Barbaresco. The color of both is deep red—in a fine Barolo, almost black—fading slightly with age and assuming the brownish "onion-skin" hue around the edge when poured into a glass.

Both wines are offspring of the Nebbiolo grapevine, whose temperament is ideally suited to the climate of Piedmont and its steep, rocky slopes. Both are fermented for fifteen to eighteen days before the juice is drawn off the must, to be run into huge oak vats to age—Barolo for four to seven years, Barbaresco not so long. These vats range in size from fairly small to enormous and the best are made from time-blackened Slovenian oak from the forests of Czechoslovakia. During the long ageing process, the wines settle, rid themselves of much of their heavy deposit, and lose their harshness. Bottle-age is necessary—particularly for the finest wines—to soften them; but even after considerable ageing they will still be heavy wines

which go best with red meat, pasta, or game. At best they lack the finesse and breed of better French wines.

The growing areas for the wines are almost adjacent in the depths of the Monferrato Hills—Barolo covering some 10,000 hectares (25,000 acres) in the towns of Barolo, Castiglione, Monforte d'Alba, Verduno, and Diano d'Alba; the smaller Barbaresco area slightly to the northeast in Barbaresco and three other communes in the province of Cuneo. Some bottles will bear the seal of the local *consorzio* which approved the wine, and the seal bears the name of the organization (Consorzio per la Difesa dei Vini Tipici Barolo e Barbaresco): in the case of Barolo, the seal is a golden lion in a field of blue; in Barbaresco, the imprint of an ancient tower which stands in the town.

GATTINARA

A full-bodied dry red wine of garnet color from Nebbiolo grapes (known locally as Spauna) and grown around the town of Gattinara, to the north of Turin. With Barolo and Barbaresco, this is one of the best wines of the Piedmont, rich in tannin and with a bouquet of roses. During a lull in the Crimean War, a group of Italian officers was disputing with some French colleagues the values of the wines from their respective countries. Some British officers were brought in to assess the qualities of the wine in question, and Gattinara was chosen among the many outstanding wines of Piedmont and Burgundy as the best!

ASTI SPUMANTE AND MOSCATO D'ASTI

The bottle is tilted at the proper angle, the white towel wrapped around the neck, the cork eased, but suddenly it comes out of the bottle with a vigorous "pop" and the opener will be told to "go back to Asti," no matter what the sparkling wine, nor where it is opened. For there is no doubt that Asti Spumante makes a small explosion when the cork is pulled.

When Charles Gancia brought the secrets of its manufacture back to his firm in Canelli in the late 1850s the wine was sold as Asti champagne, Muscat champagne, or Italian champagne; but the reaction of the French combined with national pride to advocate a more original name, and Asti Spumante was finally chosen. Curiously enough, this name is now sometimes taken by growers in distant parts of the world when they wish to differentiate their sweet sparkling wine from one which is nearer to Champagne or sparkling Burgundy.

Asti Spumante is a sweet, slightly flowery, sparkling Muscat. With its very low degree of alcohol (9% to 10%), large content of sugar, and its gay bubbles, it is the perfect wine for unsophisticated festivity, and is a particular favorite in its own country. For one thing, it is cheap inside Italy—compared with sparkling wines in other parts of the world—but once import duties are added, in other countries, it jumps out of its price class. Moscato d'Asti is a similar wine, but slightly lower in alcohol and made by the bulk process rather than the regular champagne process employed by the better houses for their good wines. (*See* Champagne, *and particularly* champagne process *within it.*) The wines are made in forty-four communes near the small city of Asti in the Monferrato Hills, entirely from Muscat grapes.

In spite of its fame Asti Spumante is not selling as it once did. Popular taste is turning from sweet wines, and vintners are slowly overtaking the trend with dry variations on their traditional themes. In Asti, almost all the large houses are now diverting a part of their production to dry sparkling wines, mostly from Riesling and Pinot grapes but seldom from those grown in the immediate vicinity. The better firms have special vineyards where their grapes are grown and vinification is accomplished as soon after picking as possible. Some other houses are apt to import grapes from anywhere, depending on where they happen to be able to buy them in that particular year. Asti's dry sparkling wines do not usually carry the name of the city—that is reserved for the more famous sweet ones—but are usually sold as Pinot, Pinot Spumante, Gran Spumante, or some similar name; and a few are sent abroad as "Lacrima Christi"—an appellation which belongs to Campania. These dry wines are generally thin, usually undistinguished, but in Italy their low cost makes them fairly good buys.

Of the sparkling wines, only Asti Spumante and Moscato d'Asti enjoy *consorzio* protection. Bottles guaranteed by the *consorzio* as being worthy of the name they bear will carry a seal portraying San Secondo, the patron saint of Asti, on horseback, and the name of the organization: Consorzio per la Difesa dei Vini Tipici Moscato d'Asti e Asti Spumante.

MINOR WINES

Most of the minor wines of Piedmont are named for the grape variety from which they are made. As a rule these wines can be considered variable in the extreme, depending largely on where they come from and the skill of the wine-maker. They have, however, certain more or less typical characteristics. Wines named after grapevines are marked with an asterisk.

Barbera*

Heavy, deep, very often harsh red wine made in quantity throughout the region and indeed all Italy, but principally in the provinces of Asti, Alessandria, and Cuneo. There are four D.O.C.s for good Barbera: Barbera del Monferrato, d'Alba, d'Asti, and dei Colli Tortonesi.

Bonarda*

Dark red wine mostly from around Asti; it is sometimes rendered sparkling.

Brachetto*

Undistinctive, almost invariably sparkling red wine, and rather sweet.

Caluso Passito (D.O.C.) and Caluso Passito Liquoroso (D.O.C.)

A *passito*—a wine from dried grapes—made from Erbaluce vines grown in Caluso, not too far from Turin. The wine is sweet and white and made only in very small quantities. The *liquoroso* is a fortified wine.

Carema (D.O.C.)

Light and fresh red wine from Nebbiolo grapes grown in the commune of Carema, along the banks of the Dora Baltea in the province of Turin.

Cortese di Gavi* (D.O.C.)

Still and unexceptional dry white wine, sometimes made sparkling. It should be taken very young.

Dolcetto*

In Piedmont the wine from this grape is not sweet, as its name suggests. It is dark red in color, rather light in body. The wine has the following Denominations of Origin: Dolcetto d'Acqui, di Ovada, di Diano d'Alba, delle Langhe Monregalesi, d'Asti, and Dogliani.

Freisa d'Asti and Freisa di Chieri* (D.O.C.)

Sprightly red wine with a charming fruitiness and a delightful bouquet. The best is from around Chieri (near Turin) or the Monferrato Hills. Perhaps the finest of the lesser wines of Piedmont. Some Freisas are sold as *frizzante* (with a slight sparkle), which the French would call *pétillant.*

Grignolino d'Asti* (D.O.C.)

Dry, slightly bitter, pinkish-red wine lacking some of the depth and density usually found in most Piedmontese reds.

Erbaluce di Caluso* (D.O.C.)

Made in the province of Torino and part of Vercelli, this is a dry white wine with a straw color and a rather delicate, simple bouquet.

Boca (D.O.C.)

A red wine mainly from Nebbiolo, with some Vespolina and Bonarda. It is produced in Boca and four other villages in Novara. With a bouquet of violets and a bright ruby color, this wine is dry and even suggests pomegranates.

Brachetto d'Acqui* (D.O.C.)

From Acqui and several other communes in the provinces of Alessandria and Asti, this pale ruby-colored wine is delicately sweet and *frizzante*, or semi-sparkling.

Ghemme (D.O.C.)

A red wine, garnet in color, with a pleasant enough bouquet reminiscent of violets. Dry and slightly bitter, the wine ages well; it is made from Nebbiolo and a bit of Vespolina and Bonarda at Ghemme and Romagnano Sesia.

Rubino di Cantavenna (D.O.C.)

From Barbera, Grignolino, and Freisa grapes grown at Cantavenna and three other villages in Alessandria. The wine is pale-red, dry, but full in the mouth.

Sizzano (D.O.C.)

Also dry and ruby red, made at Sizzano in the province of Novara from Nebbiolo, Vespolina, and Bonarda. This wine needs to mature at least three years, two of them in cask, before it is sold.

Fara (D.O.C.)

Quite like Sizzano, except that it is made at Fara and Briona and has a finer bouquet.

Nebbiolo d'Alba* (D.O.C.)

The noble vine of Piedmont gives a light red wine with a scent of violets; the taste may range from dry to slightly sweet.

VALLE D'AOSTA

In this autonomous region high above Piedmont, there are two wines worthy of mention.

Donnaz is the Controlled Denomination of Origin for a red wine made of Nebbiolo grapes (known locally as the Picoutener) in parts of Donnaz, Perloz, Bard, and Pont St. Martin. It is produced on both sides of the River Dora Baltea, just above the commune of Carema, after which another red wine is named. Donnaz is soft, with a bouquet which suggests almonds; the nut scent is most apparent when the wine has attained some degree of maturity. The color is pale garnet.

Enfer d'Arvier (D.O.C.) is made around the commune of Arvier from Petit-Rouge grapes, plus some Vien du Nus, Neyret, and Dolcetto. Like Donnaz, the wine is garnet-colored and has a pleasing bitter aftertaste. Enfer d'Arvier is aged for a minimum period of one year in wooden casks holding not more than 3 hectoliters (about 80 U.S. gallons, 66 imp.). The grapes are grown on steep terraces, which make viniculture something of a challenge.

Pierce's disease

A disease that afflicts vines in California.
See Chapter Eight, p. 29.

Piesporter Goldtröpfchen

Usually the best of the very great wines of Piesport, German Mosel. The Piesporter are incomparable when produced in a dry summer.
See Mosel-Saar-Ruwer.

Pimm's Cup

There are four Pimm's Cups, and it is said that they were originated by a bartender at Pimm's Restaurant in London and so delighted the customers that the staff was continually being asked to put some up for people to take home. As a result, they began to be made commercially.

When bottled, each resembles a heavy cordial; but once mixed with fruit juice, cooled, garnished with borage and cucumber rind, and served in tall glasses, they become refreshing summer drinks. The four types are:

Pimm's No. 1	Gin-based
Pimm's No. 2	Whisky-based
Pimm's No. 3	Rum-based
Pimm's No. 4	Brandy-based

Pinard

French slang for wine, usually cheap and red.

Pineau d'Aunis

A grape used in rosé wines of Anjou, and in red wines of the Loire Valley, where it is gradually being replaced by Cabernet Franc.

Pineau des Charentes

Fortified wine of Cognac region, drunk as an aperitif. *See* Sweet fortified wines of France.

Pineau (Pinot) de la Loire

Another name for the grape Chenin Blanc (*q.v.*).

Pinot (Pineau)

One of the most distinguished families of wine grapes, responsible alone or in part for the greatest Burgundies and Champagnes and for many other fine wines. Pinot is a temperamental vine, however, and is not well adapted to areas outside northern France. The outstanding member of the family is Pinot Noir or Noirien, the red-wine vine of Burgundy. Pinot Liebault and Pinot Meslier contribute to Burgundian wines, but are, for all practical purposes, identical with the Noirien. Pinot Gris and Pinot Blanc, eminently noble vines, contribute to white Burgundies. All Pinots abound also in the finer Champagne vineyards. Pinot Chardonnay is actually a misnomer, for it is not a Pinot. Current usage is simply to call it Chardonnay.

Pinot Blanc

The white grape of the famous Pinot vine, used in making the fine white wines of Burgundy; and, mixed with Pinot Noir, it goes into Champagne. In Germany, it is known as Klevner and sometimes as Weissburgunder.

Pinot Chardonnay

See Chardonnay.

Pinot Gris

A grape of the Pinot family which yields good wine in Alsace, where it is also known as Tokay d'Alsace. In other parts of France, it appears as Pinot Beurot; Fauvet; Malvoisie; and Auxerrois Gris. In Germany, it is called Ruländer.

Pinot Meunier

An inferior strain of the Pinot Noir, the grape is no longer legal in Burgundy but is used for some pleasant Loire Valley rosés. Since its leaves on the underside are powdery white, as if covered with flour, the vine was given the name *meunier,* which in French means "miller."

Pinot Noir

The Pinot Noir is one of the greatest of fine-wine grapes. It makes the fabulous red wines of Burgundy, and it is largely responsible for Champagne. The vine is difficult, only moderately prolific, but in the right soil and the right climate it produces with splendor. The Pinot Noir is planted, to a lesser extent, in other parts of Europe and in California. Here it is sometimes confused with the Pinot Meunier, and with the Pinot St. Georges, which is not a real Pinot grape. In Germany, under the name of Spätburgunder, it produces the best of that country's red wines. Synonyms: Pineau; Savagnin; Klevner (Alsace); Clevener (east Switzerland).

Pint

Standard liquid measure, one-eighth of a gallon. The American pint contains 28.875 cubic inches, equal to 0.473 liter, or 16 U.S. fluid ounces; the British pint, 34.677 cubic inches or the equivalent of 0.568 liter or 20 British fluid ounces.

Pipe

A large cask with tapered ends and of varying capacity, used especially for Port. Some of the more widely used are:

		Gallons	
	Liters	*U.S.*	*Imp.*
Madeira	418	110.5	92
Marsala	423	111.7	93
Wine	477	126.1	105
Port and Tarragona	523	138.1	115
Lisbon	532	140.5	117

Piquant

French term, entirely derogatory, for wine which is sharp, acid, and biting on the palate.

Piqué

French term for vinegary wine.

Piquette

French term for wine made by adding water to the husks and skins of grapes, the juice of which has already been pressed out. This is low in alcohol, tart, and fresh, and has made up the wine ration of the European vineyard worker since Roman times at least. By extension, the term is used in a derogatory sense for any poor or mediocre wine.

Piqûre (acescence)

A disorder of wine which produces a gray film. *See* Chapter Nine.

Pisco brandy

Brandy distilled from Muscat wine in Peru, Chile, Argentina, and Bolivia. Originally Peruvian, the best comes from the Ica Valley, one of Peru's better wine districts, near the port of Pisco. After distillation, the brandy is placed in clay containers and is usually drunk young. This fiery brandy is still the preferred drink of Peruvian natives and has not gained popularity outside its country of origin, as Mexican tequila has in the United States.

Plastering

Addition of plaster of Paris (gypsum or calcium sulfate) to low-acid musts to induce the necessary degree of acidity. In all but a very few instances the practice is not conducive to high wine quality, but it is an accepted step in the process of Sherry-making.

Plavac

Native Yugoslavian species of grape used extensively in red Dalmatian wines. *See* Yugoslavia.

Plum brandy

A white *eau-de-vie* made from plums. *See* Quetsch; Mirabelle de Lorraine; Slivovitz.

Plummer

A medium-bodied type of Jamaican rum. *See* Rum, Jamaican.

Plymouth gin

Made in Plymouth, England, the style is intermediate between Dutch gin or Hollands, and London Dry gin, the type seen almost universally in Britain and the United States. *See* Gin.

Poiré

French for perry or fermented pear juice. *Eau-de-vie de poire,* made in Switzerland and some parts of France, is pear brandy, which can be superb.

Poland

Vodka, the drink associated with Poland, has been made there for hundreds of years. Indeed, the people say that vodka was originally Polish, not Russian. In the Middle Ages, the Poles made the spirit, first as a medicine, then as a drink, in monasteries and small manors all over the country. As it became popular, the word *woda* (water) achieved the affectionate diminutive and the spirit its name, wodka, or vodka. Different makers had, naturally, various recipes handed down as family secrets; and some of these formulas are still in use as bases for modern processes of manufacture.

Vodka is now seldom made from potatoes, although there is a Wodka Luksusowa, or luxury vodka, which is still obtained from potato spirits, doubly rectified and purified. Generally, the spirit comes from grain—often rye. This is filtered repeatedly, stored for a considerable time in tall steel vats, and afterward pumped out into mixing machines, diluted with a special soft distilled water, then refined by filtering. A finished product, such as the well-known Vyborova, or Wyborowa, should be neutral, mild, and crystal clear. The Polish vodka, unlike the Russian, is all bottled at home. In the last decade or so, export figures have risen by about 800%. For Western countries, there is a system of labeling according to alcoholic strength: blue for 79% British (90% U.S.) Vyborova; red label for 66% British (75.5% U.S.). Polish vodka, probably because it is expensive, is considered to be a very chic drink in France. The recommended way to drink it is freezing cold: a Pole will probably take the bottle from the ice compartment of his refrigerator and have it brought to the table in an ice bucket; and he may serve it not only at the beginning of a meal, but throughout. (For this purpose, Krakus, a high-quality vodka made according to traditional recipes, is held to be the best.)

Several types of vodka are manufactured in Poland, some of them flavored with fruit, flowers, or herbs. Among these are Żytnia, a pale spirit which retains the taste of the rye; Soplica, a dry brandy vodka to which wine distillates and matured apple spirit have imparted the aroma; Jarzębiak, rowan vodka, its rather tart sorb apple flavor sometimes mellowed with a little sugar and softened by distillates of wine; Tarniówka, a sloe spirit. Especially characteristic of Poland and much liked abroad is the Żubrówka vodka with the bison on the label. This, when it is the genuine high-quality spirit, is flavored with the wild "holy" grass which the *żubra*, or Polish bison, love to eat in the forests of eastern Poland. This vodka, pale olive green in color, has an odd, subtle taste and scent; and in each bottle there is a blade of grass. A glass of Żubrówka is traditionally offered to returning hunters in the region of the Białowieża Forest. The state has now taken over the monopoly of distilling all the well-known vodkas exported or drunk locally.

Liqueur Vodkas and Brandies

Starka, a very old type of vodka, is made from rye, distilled at lower proof than the Vyborova, aged in oak wine casks, and afterward blended with wine. The resulting drink is dry with a characteristic flavor and a pale brown color. Poland also produces its own brand of Śliwowica (slivovitz or plum brandy); and a Winiak Luksusowy, or brandy, from pure rectified spirit and imported wines.

Other Liqueurs and Cordials

Wiśniówka, a cordial made from black cherries, is the most popular abroad. Poland exports other fruit cordials: cherry liqueur and honey cherry brandy; a goldwasser, or Złota Woda; a strong herbal liqueur called Likier Ziołowy; and—a specialty—old Krupnik Honey Liqueur, made from rectified spirit, honey, and spices. This drink, handed down from the Middle Ages, has the peculiarity of being served hot. The legend goes that Giedymin, a Lithuanian prince of the fourteenth century, was saved from freezing to death by one of his knights who, just in time, brought him a cup of the hot liqueur.

Polcevera

Thin, light, white Italian wine.
See Liguria.

Polychrosis

One of the grape-moths.
See Chapter Eight, p. 29.

Pomace

Crushed or pulped grapes or fruit after the juice has been extracted. In French, *marc*. The spirit distilled from it is also known as *marc (q.v.)*.

Pomace brandy

California "*grappa*" from pulp of grapes.

Pombo (pombe)

A beverage of the Bantu people of Africa made from millet or sorghum.

Pomerol

Red wines.
District: Bordeaux, France.

The red wines are like sturdier Médocs or Saint-Émilions with the finesse and subtlety of Médocs added. For this reason, they are often said in Bordeaux to be intermediate between the two other great red-wine types of that region. Pomerol, situated next to Saint-Émilion, uses the grape varieties which produce the Médocs, and this is sufficient to account for the transitional wines. It is true that the Pomerols on gravel soil, bordering on the Saint-Émilion vineyards on gravel soil (of which the greatest is Cheval-Blanc), greatly resemble their neighbors. Pomerol wines, however, are distinct and individual, having a velvety fatness, or *gras*, among the red Bordeaux. To liken

POMEROL & ST-ÉMILION

N

R. L'Isle

N 89

LUSSAC-
ST. ÉMILION

LALANDE DE POMEROL
(NÉAC)

R. Barbanne

P O M E R O L

Pomerol
Ch.Lafleur
Ch.Lafleur-Pétrus
Néac
• Ch.Gazin
Ch.Trotanoy• • Ch.Pétrus
Vieux-Château-Certan• • Ch.Évangile
Ch.Nénin• ○ Ch.La Conseillante
Ch.Cheval-Blanc
Ch.Petit-Village • Ch.Ripeau

MONTAGNE-
ST-ÉMILION

ST. GEORGES-
ST. ÉMILION

PUISSEGUIN-
ST-ÉMILION

N 89

D 17

SABLES-ST-ÉMILION

• Ch. Figeac

ST.-ÉMILION

PARSAC-
ST.-ÉMILION

R. Barbanne

Libourne

Bordeaux
15 m.

N 670A

D 17

Clos Fourtet

ST.CHRISTOPHE-
DES-BARDES

• Ch.Trottevieille

Ch.Beauséjour-Duffau-Lagarrosse
Ch.Beauséjour-Bécot
Ch.Canon•
Ch.La Magdelaine
Ch.Ausone •
Ch.La Gaffeliere

St.Émilion
Ch.Bel-Air
• Ch.Pavie
•Ch.Larcis-Ducasse

ST.ÉTIENNE-
DE-LISSE

• Ch.Monbousquet

ST-LAURENT-
DES-COMBES

ST.
HIPPOLYTE

ST.SULPICE-
DE-
FALEYRANS

FRANCE

ST.PEY-D'ARMENS

N 136

Castillon

VIGNONET

R. Dordogne

| 0 | | 1 | | 2 | | 3 MILES |
| 0 | 1 | | 2 | | 3 KILOMETRES |

them either to Médocs or to Saint-Émilions is to give a false impression. Intermediate in fullness of body between the other two, they nevertheless derive a special taste from the iron in the subsoil of the small Pomerol district, with the result that the wine is one of the most characteristic of the red Bordeaux.

The district of 700 hectares (1,750 acres), nearly all of it in the commune of Pomerol but a fraction in the com-

mune of Libourne, is situated on a plateau above and behind the river town of Libourne. Like Saint-Émilion, not half a dozen miles away, the region was important, a junction in Roman times, when most travel and transport was along the waterways.

The vine flourished in Pomerol in those days, as it did in Saint-Émilion. Templars had come to Pomerol in the twelfth century to carry forward and enlarge the viticul-

Pommard

ture of the Romans. The fighting in the Hundred Years'
War destroyed some of the vineyards, but these were afterward re-established. Thereafter, the growers of Pomerol did their wines no permanent good by parading them
as Saint-Émilions; and not until the nineteenth century
did these begin to be known abroad. Today, however,
more and more connoisseurs are discovering the virtues of
Pomerol.

The ground varies from vineyard to vineyard, and with
it the wines. Soils are gravelly, clayey or sandy, sometimes
all three in a single vineyard; a little clay in a gravelly soil
seems to produce wines of the greatest suppleness, while
those from predominantly gravel soil may be less fine.
The best-known vineyards are not found in the sandy
terrains.

In comparison with the manorial Médoc and such regions as Sauternes, where medieval fortresses still stand,
Pomerol is almost homely. Its "châteaux" are often villas,
their gardens necessarily small in a region where space is
at a premium, since the great vines demand every inch.
After the February 1956 freeze, which struck hardest of
all in Pomerol, the area took on a blighted look, and the
following summer thousands of dead vines could be seen
lying in the churned soil from which they had been uprooted. It was like a battlefield.

No Pomerol 1956 and little 1957 and 1958 were seen.
Where the vine was blighted but not killed, wine was
made again in 1958 and 1959 vintages.

Pomerol vineyards are not classified. The best of them,
and one of the eight best red Bordeaux, is Château Pétrus
(q.v.). Similar in type are Château La Conseillante, Château Vieux-Château-Certan, and Château Trotanoy.
Château Petit-Village (belonging to the owner of Château Cos d'Estournel in the Médoc) is on an entirely
gravel soil and produces very full-bodied wines with a
splendid nose and the gleaming dark ruby color typical of
Pomerols.

While not classified, the outstanding Pomerol vineyards are considered to be the following:

OUTSTANDING GREAT GROWTH

Château Pétrus

FIRST GREAT GROWTHS

Château l'Évangile
Château Gazin
Château La Conseillante
Château Lafleur
Château Lafleur-Pétrus

Château Latour-Pomerol
Château Petit-Village
Château Trotanoy
Vieux-Château-Certan

Pommard

Burgundy red wine.
District: Côte de Beaune, France.

Pommard ranks second among Côte de Beaune wine
communes, producing something over 10,000 hectoliters
(265,000 U.S. gallons, 220,000 imp.) annually. Before the
laws of Appellation d'Origine brought a measure of control into the wine business, a Burgundian writer estimated
that the amount of Pommard sold throughout the world
each week was more than the commune could make in

ten years. Its amazing popularity still makes it one of the
most abused place-names, and experts are slightly at a
loss to explain it. Pommard, they maintain, even when it
comes from Pommard, is almost always an extraordinarily pleasant wine, but hardly ever among the greatest
Burgundies.

Just south of Beaune the main highway forks, one road
heading for Chagny, the other swinging into the hills past
Pommard, Volnay, and Monthélie, and on to Autun.
The road curves sharply, skirting the town, with vineyards on both sides of it, many of them enclosed in walls
bearing the names of various shippers. If you take this
road, the vineyard of Les Petits Épenots starts on your
right at the fork, followed by Les Grands Épenots, Le Clos
Blanc, and finally the town itself. Pommard is sleepy and
small with a curious belfry standing in the main square,
and a sluggish stream divides the town approximately in
half. Almost before you have entered it, you are out again
in the midst of a sea of vineyards, this time leading up the
hill to Volnay.

There is less difference between wines of different vineyards in Pommard than is usual in Burgundy, although
Les Épenots is generally extremely soft and round with a
good bouquet, Les Rugiens the firmest, and Les Argilli-
ères the lightest. Another outstanding vineyard is Les
Chaponnières. All the wines share the characteristics of
firmness, fairly deep color, and bouquet. Sturdier than
those of Beaune, they fill the mouth, leaving a pleasant
aftertaste; but when set aside, most of the red wines of the
Côte de Nuits show themselves much fuller both in body
and in texture. *Chaptalisation,* or the addition of sugar to
the fermenting must, will raise both body and alcoholic
content; unfortunately, some shippers tend to overdo a
good thing, producing a sturdier but coarser wine.

Pommard emerged better from the first of the important Côte d'Or vineyard classifications than the second.
In 1860 three of the village's vineyards were ranked
among the finest of the Côte d'Or, but the official list
drawn up in 1936 has set them back, giving them a right
only to the designation First Growth (*Premier Cru*). In
practice, this means that all the wines of Pommard will
carry the town name, and the better bottles are sold with
both the name of the town and the vineyard, such as
Pommard-les-Épenots, or Pommard-Rugiens.

One reason why Pommard has become so well known
is that the vineyards are huge and production high.
There are 300 hectares (750 acres) of vines in Pommard
for fine wines, considerable areas of which are owned by
the large shipping houses who have kept the name well
before the public.

The First Growths of Pommard have not yet been officially established. Until they are, the following vineyards
have interim right to the designation:

FIRST GROWTHS (*Premiers Crus*)

Vineyard	Hectares	Acres
Les Rugiens-Bas	5.8	14.5
Les Rugiens-Hauts	7.6	18.8
Les Épenots	11	25.6
Clos des Épenots	3.64	9.1

FIRST GROWTHS (*Premiers Crus*)

Vineyard	Hectares	Acres
Les Petits-Épenots	20.2	50.1
Clos de la Commaraine	4	9.8
Le Clos Blanc	4.3	10.6
Les Arvelets	8.5	20.9
Les Charmots	3.6	8.9
Les Argillières	3.64	9.0
Les Pézerolles	7.3	15.6
Les Boucherottes	1.7	4.1
Les Saussiles	3.8	9.4
Les Croix-Noires	1.2	3.1
Les Chaponnières	3.3	8.2
Les Fremiers	4.9	12.2
Les Bertins	3.7	9.1
Les Jarollières	3.2	7.9
Les Poutures	4.2	10.9
Le Clos Micot	3.9	9.8
La Refène	2.5	6.1
Clos du Verger	2.55	6.2
Derrière Saint-Jean	1.2	3.0
La Platière	5.8	14.3
Les Chanlins-Bas	7.1	17.7
Les Combes-Dessus	2.8	6.9
La Chanière	10	24.7

Pommeranzen bitters

Bitters that derive their flavor from the fruit of the pommerans (a type of orange) tree. Sometimes called *Elixir Longae Vitae* (Elixir of Long Life).

Ponsigue

Venezuelan cordial flavored with the Ponsigue cherry on a base of rum.

Château Pontet-Canet

Bordeaux red wine.
District: Haut-Médoc, France.
Commune: Pauillac.

Classified a Fifth Growth (*Cinquième Cru*) in 1855, and traditionally at the head of its class, Pontet-Canet actually sells with the Seconds and Thirds. It is one of the best-known and largest of the Médoc vineyards. The wine is made principally from Cabernet Sauvignon (75%) and Merlot grapes. The huge plantation, next to the entrance of Château Mouton-Rothschild, slopes down rolling hills towards the port of Pauillac. Early in the nineteenth century, the estate was created by a M. Pontet on lands known as Canet. Many years later, in 1865, M. Pontet's heirs sold the vineyard to Hermann Cruse, head of the Bordeaux shipping firm of Cruse et Fils Frères. The property is now owned by Guy Tesseron. Up to 1972 the wine was aged for nine months in the impressive underground cellars at Pauillac and then transported to the Cruse *chai* at 124 Quai des Chartrons in Bordeaux, where it was bottled.

The underground cellars at Pontet-Canet can hold 2 million bottles. Châteaux Mouton-Rothschild, Lafite, and Beychevelle are among the few others with deep cellars, rare in the Médoc. The Pontet-Canet *chai* for first-year wines has a high roof and is uniquely airy, since the owners believe that variations in temperature during the first winter of ageing is beneficial for the wine. Guy Tesseron—owner of Château Lafon-Rochet in Saint-Estephe and, since 1979, of Château Malescasse in Lamarque—bought Pontet-Canet from the Cruses in 1974. Alfred Tesseron, his son, is in charge at Pontet-Canet.

Characteristics. In the past sometimes very distinguished and slow to mature; some years are very common.

Vineyard area: 76 hectares (190 acres).

Average production: In previous years it was impossible to determine, since the wine was not château-bottled; but with château-bottling, as of 1972, the production is 400 *tonneaux* (40,000 cases).

Pony

Spirit measure of one fluid ounce; a small glass containing about four fluid ounces, used for brandy.

Porrón

A spouted glass drinking vessel used in Spain and derived from the leather *bota,* or Spanish wine-skin. One of the sights of Spain is the skill and good humor of the expert *porrón* drinker as he shoots a thin stream of wine through the air from spigot to mouth. This is not to be recommended to the wine-taster, however, because the wine must be gulped down to keep up with the arching stream. In Spain, the method is believed to multiply the effect of the wine.

Port

Portuguese fortified wine.

By Portuguese law, Port is the wine of the Upper Douro (Alto Couro, Alto Corgo, and Baixo Corgo), fortified by the addition of Portuguese grape brandy, and shipped from Oporto, the city at the mouth of the Douro which has given Port its name. By British law, Port proper is exactly the same thing. This law permits, however, the use of the designation *port-style* for Australian port, South African port and even British port, manufactured from imported musts.

In the United States, port-type wines are allowed the name if they carry the modification of the name of their place of origin, which generally means Californian port. Actual Port from Oporto is recognized by American laws under the name "Porto," which is the Portuguese designation of the wine, and is not referred to as "port wine," which is considered a generic category. Whatever they may be, the ports made in South Africa, Australia, California, and in North and South America are neither Port nor Porto.

What is meant when Port *tout court* is discussed, is, or ought to be, Port from Portugal, and generally red. A certain type of rock called schist is probably the factor which, in conjunction with the climate and with methods of treatment worked out carefully over a long time, gives the wine its character. The Upper Douro has only half the rainfall of Oporto, and the lowest rainfall in northern Portugal.

There are few great wine districts in the world that are as export-oriented as Oporto is: it is still easier to get vintage Port in England than it is in a good Lisbon restaurant—notwithstanding the decline in the Port tradition among the English.

Originally, Port was not fortified but was harsh and raw and did not travel well. Douro wines were imported into seventeenth-century England for reasons of government policy, but were not liked (see Portugal). Then Port began to be treated with brandy, probably to help it travel, possibly to make it more competitive with gin. By the middle of the eighteenth century, the Port shippers were learning to make the matured and balanced fortified wine we know now. The brandy arrested the fermentation of the sugar into alcohol, retaining some of the sweetness. It is interesting to know that Port is fortified up to 20% alcohol by volume, so that today 20% of a bottle of Port is brandy.

The history of the actual development of the Port region shows what a role the schist plays. Like the slate of the Mosel, it contributes breed, and the wine would not be the same without it. Two hundred years ago the area of the Douro was first marked out, a much smaller plot than it is today. It was gradually enlarged until it came to include the present officially delimited zone of Port wine—the region of Upper Douro, stretching about 96 kilometers (60 miles) along the river from Régua toward the Spanish frontier. This is the terrain of the schist, a soft kind of crystalline rock which easily splits and crumbles and which is set down in the midst of a tumbled, wild country otherwise almost entirely granite. These granite soils produce wine, for instance the table wines of the Lower Douro or neighboring Dão, but not Port.

Port is also a consequence of British enterprise and climate, and of the British palate too. English merchants played a leading part in the development of Port, and their wine lodges hold nearly half of the maturing wine at the mouth of the Douro today. They also own some of the biggest *quintas* (wine estates), some of which are very large. Before the Second World War, Britain bought half of all the Port produced. The post-war decline in the British market for Port, mainly due to the rise in cheaper, alternative fortified wines (but apparently also indicating a real change in taste), has by now lost the traditional Port-drinking nation its first place, a position which has gone to France. The United Kingdom is still second, and although cheap red Port has ceased to be a popular drink in pubs, Vintage is again in demand, and there has been some recovery in the market since the early 1960s. Inside Portugal itself there is a growing interest in Port-drinking—including the dry white aperitif-style unique to the home market, rather than the dessert wine—and figures show that sales to the Portuguese are third highest, following France and Britain.

About 550,000 hectoliters are made in an average year (14,575,000 U.S. gallons, 12,100,000 imp.) from about 30,000 hectares (75,000 acres) of vineyards.

THE MAKING OF PORT

The vines grow on stepped or terraced levels on the sometimes very steep cliffs of the Douro. If it were not for the terracing, built up laboriously over generations, nearly the whole of the vineyard would wash into the river during the violent rains falling between October and May. The climate is hard-blazing in summer and iron-cold in winter.

The vines are planted, often by blasting, so that the roots can find their way deep enough to secure moisture during the dry summers. Before the scourge of the phylloxera the wine was made from any number of grape varieties derived from the Pinot Noir family. To a considerable extent, this is still the case. Today all vines are grafted on phylloxera-resistant American root-stocks, and while the types are not quite so various, the chief grapes still number over a dozen. It is a truly tragic sight to see the "mortuaries," as they are called—the terraces left abandoned since the phylloxera and crumbling to ruin along much of the Douro, after they were created with such enormous human effort. Often it has been considered easier to begin new terraces than to try to salvage the old ones—and the tendency is to avoid the old south-facing slopes and plant on north-facing ones to escape the heat, too extreme for men to work in.

Every Port is, at least to some extent, a blend, for it is universally considered that certain plants do better in some weather conditions, some in others, and that different types contribute different qualities, no one vine being able to produce the best wine. Touriga (similar to the French Cabernet Franc), Bastardo, and Mourisca are very important, and four or five dark-red types are considered to give deep color. These are Sousão and the Tintas. Important among these are Tinta Cão and Tinta Francisca, the latter probably very close to the French Pinot Noir. White Ports are produced from the Verdelho, Malvasia, Rabigato, and others.

Traditionally, the bunches of grapes were cut and heaped by the picker into a tall wicker basket which he balanced at the back of his neck on a roll slung from a forehead band. In this manner the grapes were carried to the treading-troughs by a single file of men; or, if the distance was long, they were tumbled from the tipped baskets into tubs on tractors. At some *quintas*, the old custom survives. The troughs, called *lagares*, are usually made of large granite slabs. In them the fun—and the wine—begins. Barefooted men jump in, grasp one another by the arms, in a chain, to keep upright on the slippery mass, and begin to tread the grapes. While they do this, a few instruments give them a tune, and they chant in a lament which sounds Arabian. In four-hour shifts, they trample out all the juice, which has already begun to ferment from the heat and the action. Today, however, this sight is rare, and most of the work is done by mechanized crushers. But, there is still music and dancing at the *vindima*.

At the moment when the overseer considers that fermentation has reached the proper point, and his saccharometer tells him that just the desired amount of sugar remains unconverted into alcohol, the juice, now raw wine, is let off into large containers called *toneis*. Brandy is waiting, to be introduced simultaneously in proportion of about one part to five parts of the wine. Since wine cannot ferment at over 16.5% of alcohol, fermentation stops. The sugar, which would have fermented out, remains in the wine—that is why most Ports are sweet. The degree of sweetness is determined by the point at which fermentation is checked and, of course, by the later marryings and blendings.

In the early spring of the year following the vintage, the blended wine and brandy, a young crude Port, is put into Port pipes (casks of 600 liters—159 U.S. gallons, 132 imp.) and either sent to Oporto by rail or loaded onto a truck; the *rabelo*, a single-sailed boat like a longish scow, guided by a giant sweep, is hardly ever used now. When it used to go by *rabelo*, the wine had a dizzy trip down to the mouth of the Douro; in the spring, the river is high and swift-flowing after the rains and boils over the rapids.

It is not actually in Oporto but at Vila Nova de Gaia, just across the river, that the wine finds a home. This is where the wine lodges are.

VINTAGE PORT

If it has been a great year, the maker will set the best of his wines aside to make Vintage Port. A vintage is often declared by agreement among most of the shippers, but not always. For one thing, the non-vintage Ports are blends of the wines of the various vintages; and if a shipper has a heavy demand for excellent Ports from the wood, he will be reluctant to divert his wines into a Vintage. On an average, a Vintage is declared roughly three or four times in a decade. The greatest year among Vintage Ports now obtainable is usually considered to be 1927, and it has practically disappeared. Typical of great years since are 1934, 1935, 1942, 1945, 1947, 1948, 1950, 1955, 1958, 1960, 1963, 1966, 1967, 1970, and 1972. Years still talked about over a glass of Port, but rarely a Port of the year in question, are 1878, 1896, 1908, and 1912. Of all the great vintages, 1945 was generally considered the greatest, and of the recent years, 1963 and 1970 are the best. All these can, in fact, still occasionally be found—even, with great difficulty, the 1878s and 1896s.

A wine selected for Vintage Port was shipped, almost invariably to England, two years, or sometimes a little longer, after its vintage, and almost immediately bottled; but since 1974, all Vintage Port must be bottled in Portugal. Vintage Port is aged in glass, the rest is aged in wood.

During the war, Vintage Ports were bottled in Portugal, but generally they were bottled at their destination and were then laid down. Port always throws a heavy deposit as it matures; when thrown in the bottle, the deposit is called the "crust." If the deposit, or crust, is disturbed, it will take some time to settle down again, and the wine will be spoiled. Thus, shipping in bottle is not advisable.

Vintage Ports require from ten to fifteen years to mature, and in some cases longer. Their true prime, in the great wines, lies years further on, for they improve in the bottle for a long time.

Port should be served at room temperature, which it should achieve gradually by being brought to the room several hours before use. A bottle of Vintage Port (which should be drunk after dinner) will suffer if it is open to the air very long, though a Ruby Port or Tawny will survive better. (Some people in Vila Nova de Gaia maintain that they will keep ten days, providing the decanter is full or nearly so.) When the lighter Ports are drunk as aperitif wines they may be served slightly chilled.

The small "Port glasses" do not give the wine a chance, and this is especially true of Vintage Port, which has a much bigger bouquet than any other and must have room within the glass to realize it. There is, in fact, no reason not to use the tulip-shaped clear wineglass which serves so well for most other wines, and there are good reasons for doing so. In the chimney of the tulip glass, the nose of the wine will develop fully and not be dispersed, and the color will be seen at its best through the crystal.

Vintage Port must be carefully decanted in order to bring the clear wine safely off the crust, which will have formed on the inner underside of the bottle. It is not too difficult to pour the wine without disturbing it. For some vintages, for instance 1935 as bottled by Sandeman, a granite-shotted bottle is used, because granite chips roughen the inside and anchor the deposit.

CRUSTED PORT

A wine which is not necessarily that of a single vintage, but which is handled in the same way as Vintage Port and develops in the same way, is called Crusted Port— because of the sediment which forms in the bottle. A blend of a few fine wines, it is generally bottled at about four years old and allowed to mature in bottle for some six to eight years before drinking. It has something of the quality of Vintage Port, at a lower price.

It can be excellent and will be more full-bodied and, in particular, have more nose than one of the Ports aged in wood; but it will not reach the heights of Vintage Port, simply because it will have been made from a slightly lesser wine.

TAWNY PORT

In the *amazens* (wine lodges) of Vila Nova de Gaia, wine from different years is blended and matured in oak. However, this is not done with those wines selected to be bottled or Vintage Ports. Each shipper tries to achieve a uniform wine year after year and does this by blending the vintages of various years together, and by blending differing wines to reach an orchestration he considers right. This is why the Ports of this style differ from trademark to trademark but run true to type. The term often used in Vila Nova de Gaia—and suggestive of the care and art used—is "bred": they breed the wines, not blend them, they say.

As the wine ages, it turns in color from purple to ruby, and then, gradually, brown-golden, the shade called tawny. The Tawny Port takes a long time to age in the wood; years elapse before it can be bottled and sold, and therefore it is not cheap. It should be drunk soon after it has been bottled, when, if it is an old Tawny, it will have acquired a great elegance. An after-dinner drink, it will never have the majestic power of a grand Vintage Port but can have extreme finesse. A great Vintage Port is more suited to a cold climate; a splendid, but lighter, old Tawny to a warmer climate. Unfortunately, there is another method of producing Tawny Port which results in a wine which may be good but certainly will not have the refinement of an old Tawny: Ruby and White Ports are sometimes blended together to make "Tawny." With the exception of Vintage Ports, all wood Ports are shipped ready to drink and do not improve in the bottle.

Tawny Port is never cheap, and if you are in one of the big *armazens* in Vila Nova de Gaia you will see why it cannot be. More than 2% of the wine evaporates each year. You glance along the three-tiered rows of casks and may see a thousand of them. Shudder then, because, from those 1,000 pipes, 15,000 bottles of good Port will vanish into the Portuguese air before you can return to the same spot a year later.

RUBY PORT

A young wood Port; rich in color, fruity, and sweet. It is a blend of the wines of several years and does not improve much in bottle. This is the wine which was used for the Port-and-lemon drink once a favorite in English pubs.

WHITE PORT

A sweet, topaz-colored fortified wine made from white grapes—it was as popular as an aperitif in France as was Ruby Port in England and is still enjoyed by some French people. In the 1950s, an effort was made to revive a flagging market by exporting a dry White Port—already doing well as an aperitif inside Portugal—made by fermenting out all the sugar before fortification. It did not, however, have much success abroad.

LATE-BOTTLED VINTAGE PORT

The wine of a good year which has been kept longer in the wood than the classic Vintage Port, usually five years or more, will by that time have deposited its crust in the cask and its ruby color will have begun to fade but not yet turn tawny. Once bottled, it will be clear and soon ready to drink. It is a lighter wine than Vintage Port.

THE FUTURE OF PORT

The post-war drop in sales to Great Britain caused an experimental swing to dry Port. Since the amount of sweetness in any Port is determined by the residue of unfermented sugar left at whatever point fermentation is arrested, it is perfectly possible to make it dry. It is only necessary to let the sugar ferment out. The resultant wines are completely natural. The only question is, whether or not they are fully realized Ports; in any case, the new trend did not catch on in Britain. The Portuguese themselves enjoy the wine as an aperitif, as do the French, Oporto's biggest customer.

For the present, the long-term effort to produce the finest possible wines by rigid quality controls is being intensified. Port was the first strictly delimited wine area in the world—the original zone was marked out by the Marquês de Pombal in 1756. With a climate ideal for the ageing of wines, Vila Nova de Gaia—originally selected because the empty sheds already there have been used for centuries to store Douro wines—has always been a tightly guarded *entreposto*. Until very recently, watchmen patrolled with guns under orders to shoot on sight if anyone was found in the restricted area out of hours. The Port Wine Institute—the Instituto, as everyone refers to it in Oporto—conducts blind tastings in what must be one of the finest tasting rooms in the world. Running water effectively blots out all smells; tasters may not answer the telephone during sessions, so there can be neither disturbance nor briefing. All Ports are tasted "blind" by experts who must pass examinations and then serve as assistant tasters for four full years before acquiring a vote. Only about one-third of the approximately 250,000 pipes produced annually win the right to be called Port wine. (Most of the remainder becomes brandy for fortifying Port or table wine; some is drunk in Oporto and the district, but not as Port.)

The improvement in sales of Port has been significant over the past few decades; sales have surpassed the prewar figure. Where the wine as wine is concerned, market considerations aside, the answer probably lies in the summary of what gives Port wine its special character, expressed by the late José Joaquim da Costa Lima, the vigorous and optimistic ex-director of the Instituto. He said Port must strive to be more "Port" than ever. It needs brandy, he said, because the greatest Port wines have the greatest body and the greatest *dis*equilibrium. Were it not for this, the wine could not assimilate 20% of brandy and would go out of balance; but a wine in *dis*equilibrium like a great Port accepts the brandy and is put *into* balance. Dry Ports have their place but could never equal these unique and sumptuous wines.

As Raymond Postgate said, in his instructive book *Portuguese Wines,* each shipper determines the character and quality of his Port. The history of the old companies founded in the eighteenth and early nineteenth centuries is fascinating and well documented. (A useful resumé can be found in *The Englishman's Wine* by Sarah Bradford.) Some of the firms have now been taken over by larger interests, but most are allowed to keep their own characteristics, and a sufficient number have retained their independence. The following is a list of the principal names in the Port trade:

Sandeman; Croft (including Delaforce, which was bought up not long ago); Warre; Calem; Ferreira; Tuke Holdsworth; Offley; Taylor (including Guimaraens, shipper of Fonseca's, taken over in 1949); Silva & Cosens (which merged with Dow's in 1877 and still ships to England under the Dow label); Cockburn & Martinez; Gonzalez Byass; Kopke; Barros Almeida; Real Companhia Velha; Quinta da Noval; and Ramos Pinto. Symington's now owns Warre (founded in 1680), Silva & Cosens, Graham's, and Quarles Harris.

Porter

A very dark brown British beer with a bitter taste. It is brewed from malt which has dried at such a high temperature that it has become browned or charred. This is the drink to which Elizabeth Barrett Browning had such an objection.

See Beer.

Portland

A moderately productive American hybrid vine yielding both table grapes and those for wine-making. The grapes are green, the wines white.

Portugal

The wines of Portugal divide naturally into three groups: the famous fortified Port and Madeira; the table wines of Denominação de Origem from certain delimited areas, grown and produced under strict legal controls; and the ordinary wine of the country (*consumo*).

HISTORY

It is probable that wine grapes were grown in the country before the arrival of the Romans; and the making of wine must have continued almost uninterrupted in the north, where Moorish rule did not last very long. As early as the twelfth century, Monção wine was being imported and enjoyed in England, produced evidently from the Minho area in the northwest and shipped from the port of Viana do Castelo. Edward III, in the mid-fourteenth century, encouraged the two-way trade—wool for wine—with commercial treaties and fishing rights for the Portuguese. Monção was still popular, as were the wines of Algarve and Douro, although Charneca—believed to have come from the region near Lisbon—was perhaps more in favor when, in 1580, Philip of Spain annexed Portugal and its Far Eastern possessions and interrupted the trade with England. In *Henry VI*, Part II, Shakespeare's rebels cheer each other with toasts in Sack, Charneca, and beer.

Spanish rule continued until 1640. In the interval, Dutch and British ships had been fighting the Portuguese on the high seas and interfering with Portugal's trade monopolies in India and Asia. The famous alliance between England and Portugal was restored with the marriage of Charles II and Catherine of Braganza—but not, for some time, the popularity of Portuguese wines. Compared with the French, they now appeared rather primitive—coarse and ill-made. The fairly ineffective ban on French wines made when, in the reign of William of Orange, England and Holland went to war with France, imposed on the English a rising quantity of imports from Portugal; but very unflattering remarks were made about them. Yet the government persisted with the ban, and the Methuen Treaty of 1703 maintained the supply of cloth to Portugal and wine to Britain.

For a century at least there had been a "Factory" (factor's club) in Oporto, where English and other foreigners were establishing themselves in the trade, although Port wine as we know it was not to be perfected until the second half of the eighteenth century—at much the same time as Madeira developed its present character. It soon became a great success not only in Great Britain but in the newly liberated country of the United States. With the rise of these fortified wines, the table wines of Portugal lost ground and were not, outside their own country, to come to the forefront again until the wine-making industry was reorganized and new laws were passed in the 1930s and 1960s.

Portugal ranks with Italy, France, Spain, and West Germany as one of the great wine countries of Western Europe. The total production of table wine annually averages about 10 million hectoliters (267 million U.S. gallons, 222 million imp.). Only one-fourth of this quantity is wine with a Denomination of Origin. There is more red than white, and a great deal of rosé. Much less of the fine fortified wine is produced: 500,000 hectoliters (13,250,000 U.S. gallons, 11,000,000 imp.) of Port each year and only one-tenth that amount of Madeira. In the entire country 360,000 hectares (about 900,000 acres) are in vineyard. Three thousand of these hectares are on the island of Madeira. In Portugal itself there are more than 300,000 plots, so the average holding is just larger than 1 hectare. Well over 235,000 people (20% of the active agricultural population) make a living from wine. Local consumption is very high—an average of 85 liters per head per year, more than twelve times the U.S. rate.

Although the volume has greatly decreased in recent years, more wine (700,000 hectoliters—about 18.5 million U.S. gallons, 15.4 million imp.) was exported to the Portuguese colonies than to any other single nation. The United States is the next best customer, importing 300,000 hectoliters (8 million U.S. gallons, 6.6 imp.) each year. France, Great Britain, and Denmark each buy about half that quantity.

WINE LAWS

All Portuguese wines carry certificates of origin and are produced under controlled conditions in officially demarcated areas. Of these, Port is by far the most important. Port and Madeira apart, the principal wines of Denominação de Origem are Vinhos Verdes, Dão, Colares, Bucelas, Carcavelos, and Moscatel de Setubal. The last two are sweet dessert wines seldom, if ever, seen abroad. (*For Port and Madeira, see separate entries.*)

As written into the laws, controls in Portugal are now extremely thorough. It is hoped that in the future they will be more respected in practice than they are now. The whole wine trade comes under one of two associations, The Instituto do Vinho do Porto, in Oporto, is obviously concerned with Port; the Junta Nacional do Vinho in Lisbon, with the remaining wines. Under their aegis, supervision of wine-making is carried out by local committees of growers at every stage from vineyard to labeling and shipping. A certificate is issued to each farmer, establishing his production and stocks of wine; another document will show that wine has reached the standard for

R. Minho

Monção

R. Lima

Viana do Castelo

Braga

ENTRE-DOURO
-E-MINHO

Amarante

Oporto   Penafiel   Régua   UPPER
DOURO

R. Douro

DÃO

Viseu

R. Mondego   Guarda

Coimbra

ESTREMADURA

Alcobaça

R. Tagus

Cartaxo   Almeirim

Torres
Vedras

Bucelas

Colares

Lisbon

Carcavelos

Setúbal

S P A I N

N

PORTUGAL

0   25   50   75 MILES

0   25   50   75 KILOMETRES

Denomination of Origin, its quality judged by expert tasters. A later certificate of *estágio* (wine in the making) is a permit for the capsule seals of the bottles—the precise number for the exact quantity of wine contained in the vats of each grower. When the wine is taken to a warehouse, new records are made by both the local committee and the government organization; before shipment abroad, there will be a final inspection of quality and issue of the permit for export under the name of the wine's place of origin.

WINES WITH CERTIFICATES OF ORIGIN

Vinhos Verdes

The region, in northwest Portugal, lies between the rivers Minho and Douro, forming the area Entre-Douro-e-Minho, a name which the wines occasionally carry. The land presents a smiling face but a wrinkled one. In shape it is a huge bowl rising gradually away from the Atlantic. The bowl form, buttressed by higher ranges, holds the wet on-shore winds, and Minho is both warm and rainy. It is cut and furrowed by many rivers. As a result, the terrain is divided into numerous zones, five of which were declared distinct enough to be declared official sub-regions: Lima, Basto, Braga, Amarante, and Monção. Rather similar, but not the same, is Lafões, south of the Douro. There are 30,000 hectares (75,000 acres) of vines.

The greenness of the wines is in their youthfulness, not their color: pressed from grapes picked early and not always ripe, and drunk at about one year old, they are light, lively wines, rather tart, with a foamy sparkle as they are poured into the glasses and a refreshing prickle when the foam has subsided. This evanescent *pétillant* character is caused by a slight secondary fermentation in the bottle. The Minho country is delightfully green and wooded, the winters cold, the summers often wet and sometimes extremely hot. In a highly populated oasis in a largely arid country, full use must be made of the fertile land; fruit-trees, vegetables, and other crops are planted and then encircled by vines which grow freely, away from scorched or waterlogged soil, climbing around trees and hedges, sometimes so high that they have to be picked from a cart. Thus sheltered from extremes of heat and moisture, the grapes produce thinner wines, with less alcohol than one would expect so far south. The whites are the most attractive: well chilled and drunk as aperitifs or with fish, they are thirst-quenching summer wines. The reds are unusual: dark in color, strong in tannin. Though interesting, they are not as easy to know as the whites. The rosés are not important, outside their own district— the famous Mateus Rosé (one of the most widely sold wines in the world) comes from outside the delimited area, although the proprietors also make the white Aveleda. Principal Verde wines are Azal Branco, Loupeiro, Trajadura, Pederna, and Alvarinho for white wines; Bastardo, Alvarelhão, Azal Tinto, Espadeiro Tinto, Boaraçal, Vinhão, and Verdelho Tinto for red.

With their charm depending on freshness and youth, the Vinhos Verdes are among the wines which once did not travel. Under the improved conditions of shipping today, they can be enjoyed abroad—although in the United States, where the faintest sparkle is highly taxed, they arrive with their *pétillement* already stilled.

Among the best of the demarcated Vinhos Verdes are the following:

Agulha. Dry, with a faint prickle; a wine of the true character, presented in a stone bottle.

Alvarinho de Monção, Cepa Velha. Particularly good in its style; slightly stronger and with more flavor than most; a little longer-lived; in a slim brown glass bottle; from Monção.

Casa da Calçada. Very dry, not much spark, a bit tart; distinct Verde taste; from Amarante.

Casa da Seara. This white wine comes in two styles: the drier (*meio seco*), with more savor and *pétillement*, comes in a slim green bottle; from Louro.

Casa de Vilacetinho. This has a distinct Verde flavor and comes in a slim brown bottle.

Aveleda. Made near Penafiel, this pleasant, *pétillant* white wine is now widely exported; it is perhaps the most popular of the Vinhos Verdes abroad.

Casal Mendes. A lively, agreeable white with the true Verde character; from Aliança.

Casal Miranda. A typical wine of the region, from Louro.

Casalinho. A very light wine, not entirely dry, from Felgueiras.

Gamba. A distinct sparkle, and flavor of Verde; comes in a flask.

Gatão. A typical Vinho Verde.

Lagosta. Well-known and successful export wine, really *pétillant* and full-flavored.

Meireles. A good example of the type, refreshing, with a delicate sparkle.

Mirita. Another, and slightly sweeter, wine from Aliança.

Moura Basto. A fair crackle, but less flavor than some of the others; from the Azal grape; Amarante or Basto.

Souto Vedro. Not for beginners; very tart and dry *pétillant* Verde; from Amarante.

Tãmega. A strong flavor, but less acid than Souto Vedro.

Tres Marias. Sweetish and not very brisk; from Vizela.

Quinta de Curvos. The special domain-bottled wine of Esposende.

Dão

The Dão wines (pronounced downg) come from the north-central area of the country, where the climate is cold and wet in winter and very hot in summer. The landscape is wild, wooded, and mountainous, and much of the vineyard is terraced—as on the Upper Douro, where Port is made. In parts of the region, granite crops to the surface and cultivation of any kind is impossible. The best vineyards lie in forest clearings in the valleys where the soil is composed of weather-crumbled granite and schist. Wine has been made around the city of Viseu for at least seven centuries; but only in this century has the Dão region been officially marked out in a triangle, the points of which are Viseu, Guarda, and Coimbra.

Several hundred times as much red wine is produced as

white, and many of the white grapes suffer the fate of being thrown in with the red to make a bright, ruby wine. The leading red wine grapes are the Bastardo, Alvarelhão, Tourigo, Tinta Carvalha, and Preto Mortágua. A variety in wide use is called Tinta Pinheira, probably a strain of the French Pinot. The most important white varieties are the Dona Branca, Cerceal, Fernão Pires, and the Arinto, the last supposedly close in origin to the German Riesling. Most of the vineyard plots owned by the peasants are quite small, producing perhaps 50 hectoliters (1,325 U.S. gallons, 1,100 imp.) in an average year. In the more prosperous vineyards, Dão vines are pruned fairly low, with space between the rows; but elsewhere they grow more freely, up stakes or around bow-shaped saplings. Cultivation is very difficult, and the planting often involves blasting. The rugged nature of the countryside has enforced a continuance of primitive life. Gathered grapes are still carried to the vats in baskets on women's heads, but except in rare cases the wine is no longer trodden out by the barefoot *trabalhadores*.

The chief characteristic of red Dão wines, taken as a whole, is their smoothness and suavity, a quality which shows up in chemical analysis as an unusually rich glycerin content. Yet in the coarser growths there may be a distinct *goût de terroir*. And unlike the neighboring Vinhos Verdes, these are as strong as the French Rhône wines, with an average of about 12% of alcohol. There is frequently a hint of yeast in the nose, for in this region yeasts are customarily forced. Some of the darker reds may be reminiscent of wine made from the Pinot Noir. The whites, clean on the palate, dry, and inclining to hardness, have a good distinctive taste and can be very pleasant. Though they may last up to three or four years in bottle, youth and freshness become these wines. The red wines, on the other hand, should be still good at ten years but of course do not attain the ripe age of old clarets.

The delimited area of Dão contains some sixteen communes, among which Nelas, Penalva do Castelo, Mortágua, and El do Hospital are worth remembering. But, although there may be a marked difference in the wines of these villages, they tend to be evened out by blending, though some blends naturally will be better than others. There is virtually no domain-bottling. Both local firms and big shippers are patrolled by the Federation of Dão Wine-Growers, which has been very successful in setting up cooperatives in the region; the number of such peasant combines is increasing. Each makes its own wine but leaves the selling of it to the Union of Cooperatives, which has effective regulations for checking the quality of the wine both by tasting and by chemical analysis. But its power does not, unfortunately, extend to any real control of planting in the peasant vine plots: certain grape varieties may be recommended, but there is no guarantee that the growers will accept the recommendation. Already the district produces some of the best table wines exported from Portugal; with a little extra care and control, these might be raised to the class of fine wines.

Local firms making wine inside the area are Vinícola do Vale do Dão (Viseu), Sociedade Vinícola do Dão (Viseu), J. P. Ferreira dos Santos (Povolide, Viseu), J. M.

Fonseca, União Comercial da Beira (Oliveirinha), and Vinícola de Nelas (Nelas).

Reliable shippers of Dão wine who have no cellars inside the demarcated district include Sociedade dos Vinhos do Porto Constantino, S.A.R.L.; Caves Aliança-Vinícola de Sangalhos, S.A.R.L.; Real Companhia Vinícola do Norte de Portugal, S.A.R.L.; Caves Solar das Francesas, S.A.R.L.; Imperial Vinícola, Limitada; Sociedade dos Vinhos Vice-Rei, S.A.R.L.; Sociedade dos Vinhos Borges & Irmão; Caves do Casalinho, Limitada; and João T. Barbosa, Limitada.

Colares

The true wine of Colares profited by the scourge of phylloxera. When, toward the end of the last century, the vine pest was imported into Europe on American vines, it devastated practically all the plants in Continental vineyards. Behind this region, terraced on the foothills of the mountains, are inferior vineyards on firm soil (*chão rijo*). Here the phylloxera took the same course as everywhere else, and today all vines are grafted on phylloxera-resistant American root-stocks. But the Colares vineyards are planted in sand with a subsoil of clay, and, though such soil is harder to work, the phylloxera grub does not live in sand.

The result is one of the most unusual vineyards in Europe. Thirty-two kilometers (about twenty miles) from Lisbon, across the thick neck of a headland which rises to its apex in the mountain of Sintra with its woods and splashing streams, is the *chão de areia*. In this dune and seacoast vineyard, divided and sheltered by screens of reed woven together with willow and briar, the work of wine-planting is appallingly hard. A trench more than man-high must be dredged with the mattock right down to the clay, and the vine-shoot is planted deep in the hole so the root can grip in firm soil. The stem is buttressed with shoveled-back sand, but the vine roots themselves will not thrive in it. Because the sandy walls might cave in while the wide pit is being dug, the work is dangerous as well as back-breaking. In the years before phylloxera there was little incentive to endure this hard labor, and the area was mostly a ridge of sand and scrub pine; when the plague sliced Europe's wine production by half, it became profitable to work the arid Colares terrain. Afterward the loamy vineyards were restored with plants grafted onto American root-stocks; but the higher prices brought by the wines could not sustain prosperity in the wild region for long. Much of the true Colares is now consumed locally and only this wine is by law entitled to the Marca de Origem; some consider them the best table wines of Portugal, while others rate the red Dão more highly. As more land is given over to beach resort development, the wines grow very scarce.

These special Colares dune wines come from the Ramisco grape, a variety believed to have originally come from Bordeaux. To ease the work of planting, the vines are encouraged to propagate horizontally; as the shoot tips are buried they begin to grow new roots. The Ramisco produces a wine slow to develop, one that is sometimes left in the large casks of Angola mahogany or American redwood for as many as fourteen years. This practice is unfortunately very irregular, which accounts for the fact that a range of Colares shows great inconsistency. A successful wine should be dark red, with a big nose; but, though robust, it is unlikely to be as strong as the Rhônes, with which it might otherwise be compared. A white Colares is made, but is of little interest.

Of all the various companies vatting in the Adega Regional de Colares, only one produces a vintage wine in the true sense. Bottles of other firms will be found to carry the designation Vindima or Coheita, followed by the year; but the wines are blends, containing only some wine of that year. It is supposed to be the informing or predominating year, but this is very dubious and vague.

Peculiar also to Portuguese wines generally, and to Colares wines in particular, is the term and usage Garrafeira, or Reserva. A bottle carrying the designation Garrafeira on the label is one which has been kept a certain number of years before sale. Vintage year is indicated on these wines. A Vindima will generally have been sold as soon as bottled, unless otherwise indicated.

Carcavelos

The dry and sweet wines from old-established vineyards planted near the mouth of the Tagos on the Costa do Sol suffer, as do the wines of Bucelas, from the proximity of the vineyards to the suburbs of Lisbon and the seaside resort of Estoril, both steadily encroaching on their acreage. Carcavelos achieved great fame in the eighteenth century when the Marquês de Pombal, having reformed various departments in the state, turned his attention to the vineyards of his own district. In model wineries, his methods were ahead of their time, and control of quality was strict. But with the growing reputation of Carcavelos, the name was borrowed for lesser growths, and gradually the wine fell out of fashion.

In 1908, local authorities took the affair in hand, delimited the area, and introduced renewed controls for the wine. The districts allowed the name are S. Domingos de Rana, Carcavelos, parts of Oeiras and Estoril. Both red and white wines are made, but the whites (from the grape Galego Dourado, with some Arinto and Boal) are by far the more important. The sweet, amber wines, fortified to about 19% of alcohol, have a nutty aroma; they improve with age up to about four or five years, when they develop in bouquet and finesse. They are used in Portugal as aperitifs and also, as a Sauternes is used in France, as dessert wines, or to take with a biscuit at the end of the afternoon.

Bucelas

The wine from Bucelas, from immediately north of Lisbon, used to be very well known and a century ago was widely exported, but today little of it is seen abroad. Inevitably, with the growth of the city, vineyards near Lisbon are shrinking and their output diminishing. The Bucelas wine enjoyed by the troops in the Napoleonic wars, and afterward popular in England for some time, was sweet and fortified. Yet it was sometimes known as Portuguese Hock. The addition of sugar and brandy was for-

bidden by law in 1911, and the wine of today is dry, with acidity, rather light and fugitive, sometimes with a certain *goût de terroir*, but very pleasant, at its best with shellfish. The name Bucelas (guaranteed on the seal of the bottle) is allowed to eleven villages, among them Charneca and Bucelas itself; the principal vineyards are in the Trancão Valley; the leading grape is the Arinto, which may be related to the Riesling.

Moscatel de Setúbal

A sweet golden dessert wine grown on untrained irregular vines which rise like black twisted arms from the earth and which are seldom planted in rows. It is produced in very small quantities in a region across the bridge from Lisbon, where the vineyards rise to the slopes of the lovely Serra da Arrábida, near two villages—Palmela and Azeitão—inland from the port of Setúbal, which gives the district its name. The wine is fortified and very sweet, with a strong scent and flavor of the Muscat grapes from which it is made; fruity when young, it grows darker and softer as it improves with age. A common red wine is also grown in the area but does not bear the regional name as yet.

The Portuguese government has, for some few years now, paid serious attention to increasing its exports of wine, and the Export Promotion Board has been promoting competition among the big firms to produce new brands. At the same time, the delimitation of new areas of Denominação de Origem is being considered. The districts from which the choice is likely to be made are as follows:

Lafões. Close to the Dão region, its vines grow on granitic soil more or less in Vinhos Verdes country, where the grapes are trained along trellises and harvested before they are quite ripe. Leading white grapes are Arinto and Sercial; for reds, Amaral and Tourigo. Some pleasant light reds or *claretes* come from here. Among the better-known wine names are Evelita, Allegro, and Grandjo.

Águeda. The vineyards are in the north-central part of the country, near the rivers Vouga and Águeda. Here vines grow on the edges of tilled fields, sometimes pruned low, sometimes twined high on trellises. Some wines are light, rather in the style of the Vinhos Verdes, but fuller and not so lively; others are more inclined to resemble the Dãos.

Bairrada and Lamego. Situated south of Águeda and between the coast and the mountains of Caramulo and Buçaco, this is an area of big production, centered in Anadia. Some good table wines are made here—quite pleasant whites, but mostly full-bodied reds. There are rosés also, some of them carbonated for the British market; the Portuguese and the Americans take them as still wines. The good sparkling white wines of Portugal also come from this region; clean and crackly, with a flavor of their own—quite unlike that of Champagne—they are made by the *méthode champenoise*. Here, as in France, only the wine labeled Bruito is really dry.

Alcobaça. This region in central Portugal, situated near the coast, to the west of the mountain range which separates it from the Tagus basin, produces wines from a variety of soils and a variable climate. The wines, known since the twelfth century, are both red and white: the reds, bright in color, have a distinctive scent. The best of the whites come from around the beautiful walled town of Obidos.

Torres Vedras. The chief producer of ordinary wines lies to the south of Alcobaça and north of Colares. Most of the harvest is in robust, full reds, rich in tannin; among the whites, those worth noting are from Alenquer and Cadaval—strong and aromatic and flavory. Some sweet dessert wines are made also.

Ribatejo. East of Torres Vedras, the vineyards of this big production area are centered around Almeirim and Cartaxo and yield mainly full-bodied reds, strong in color and alcohol.

Lagoa. From the vineyards of the Algarve, basking in the southern sun, come more robust everyday wines, both red and white.

Rosados. The rosés of Portugal do not come under the Denominação de Origem, but one of them, Mateus Rosé, in its popular flagon with the pretty label, is one of the world's best-selling wines, followed fairly closely by Lagosta, and prepared for the Anglo-Saxon taste with added sweetness. Other pleasant pink wines are the estate-bottled Barros from the Upper Douro; Faisca, which has more sparkle than most and is a favorite in Portugal; and Casa de Cerca. All these wines are crackling, or *pétillant.* Escudo Rosé is a still wine, drier and paler than the others, and rather strong.

SPIRITS

Portuguese brandies (known in their own country as *aguardentes*) have been distilled for centuries, ever since the time of the Moorish rule. They have a characteristic flavor and smell, with little resemblance to Cognac—but neither are they sweetened and scented with caramel and vanilla as many brandies are.

Pot

(1) An attractive and much-needed small wine bottle in southern Burgundy, notably the Beaujolais, of about a half-liter capacity (approximately 17 ounces) into which wine is run from the cask to be served in restaurants and cafés. Larger than a half-bottle, smaller than a whole one, the *pot* Beaujolais has become very popular in France; as a result of the author's efforts it has been taken up in the United States also and is likewise to be found in England.

(2) A French wine measure, now obsolete.

Pot still

Old and simplest form of still, used in the distillation of Cognac, etc.
See Chapter Ten, p. 52.

Poteen (potheen)

Illegal Irish whiskey.

Pottle

An obsolete English wine measure equivalent to a half-gallon.

Château Pouget

Bordeaux red wine.
District: Haut-Médoc, France.
Commune: Cantenac-Margaux.

A Fourth Growth (*Quatrième Cru*) as classified in 1855, the vineyard before the Revolution belonged to the monks at Le Prieuré, a château now owned by the author. The vineyard is now worked cooperatively with Château Boyd-Cantenac, a Third Growth (*Troisième Cru*), by M. Guillemet, who owns the two estates. Both wines are made at Château Pouget and have made considerable progress since 1961.

Characteristics. Generally full and round for a Margaux.
Vineyard area: 7 hectares (17.5 acres).
Average production: 30 *tonneaux* (2,200 cases).

Pouilly-Fuissé

The finest dry white wine of southern Burgundy and one that has for some years received the renown which it deserves in England and the United States. Pouilly-Fuissé has made great inroads into the market once controlled by Chablis. It is made from Chardonnay grapes grown in four communes of the Mâcon slope.
See Mâconnais.

Pouilly-Fumé

Excellent dry, white, Loire Valley wine.
See Pouilly-sur-Loire.

Pouilly-Loché

A minor dry white wine from southern Burgundy's Mâcon slope bearing a considerable resemblance to the more famous and better Pouilly-Fuissé.
See Mâconnais.

Pouilly-sur-Loire

Loire Valley white wines.
District: Loire Valley, France.

At Pouilly, below Nevers in the Loire Valley, the land rises gently, almost imperceptibly, from the often sluggish river, but sufficiently for vines to grow—they are always happier on hillsides than on plains. Two types of grapevines are grown and two types of wine made, both white, both dry, but otherwise entirely different.

Pouilly-Fumé is the better wine. It comes from Sauvignon grapes and is light yet round, crisp, and eminently pleasing and refreshing. Similarities in both style and name cause it to be confused with Pouilly-Fuissé from the Mâcon district, but in truth the two are entirely different. The Loire's slightly lesser offering is marked by what is usually called a "gunflint" dryness and an indescribable flavor often compared to truffles. But although the flavor can be delightful, the wines usually lack breed.

The lesser wine is Pouilly-sur-Loire from Chasselas grapes, which are mostly grown in clay soil. The wine is almost as dry as its more impressive neighbor but has far less staying power and tends toward commonness; a respectable carafe wine in its native habitat, but of little interest elsewhere.

Some 800 hectares (2,000 acres) are devoted to Pouilly's vineyards, on which there is more Chasselas planted than Sauvignon. The yearly output is close to 15,000 hectoliters (397,500 U.S. gallons, 330,000 imp.) of Pouilly-Fumé, and only about one-third that much of Pouilly-sur-Loire.

Pouilly-Vinzelles

Dry white wines from the Mâcon district which, in very good years, resembles, though it never quite equals, the wine of Pouilly-Fuissé, near which it is made.
See Mâconnais.

Pourriture noble

French for "noble rot" caused by the fungus or mold *Botrytis cinerea* under favorable conditions.
See Botrytis cinerea.

Powdery mildew

Also called true mildew and oïdium—a widespread and damaging disease of the vine.
See Chapter Eight, p. 29.

Pramnian wine

Famous Greek wine of antiquity.
See Classical wines.

Precipitation

A deposit of bitartrate of potassium (cream of tartar) may appear in the form of small crystals in young wine, either red or white, which has been subjected to the cold. The remedy is to warm the wine bottles and turn them about until all the crystals have dissolved and the germ is destroyed. In Europe (for cheap wines) and in California, wines are subjected to temperatures below 0°C. for three days to four weeks in order to precipitate the potassium bitartrate before bottling.

Premières Côtes de Blaye

A district of Bordeaux producing white and red wines. The white wines are the best of the Blayais.
See Blaye.

Premières Côtes de Bordeaux

White and red wines.
District: Southwest France.

The official place-name or Appellation Contrôlée accorded red and white wines from a district on the Garonne opposite Graves, Barsac, and Sauternes. Beginning just above the city of Bordeaux and running southward up the river for almost 50 kilometers (30 miles), the zone is never more than a mile or two wide. In its southern part, it encloses the good, sweet, white-wine communes of Loupiac and Sainte-Croix-du-Mont.

White wine surpasses the red in volume by six or seven times and is finer in quality. While it is not an absolute rule, red wine generally grows in the downriver half of the region nearer Bordeaux, and white wine upriver. Specified vines for red wine are the same as for Médoc: Cabernet, Merlot, Malbec, Petit Verdot, and Carménère—and for white wine are the same as those used in Sauternes and in Loupiac and Sainte-Croix-du-Mont: Sémillon, Sauvignon, and Muscadelle. White wines range from dry through semi-sweet to sweet. They do not quite come up to those of Loupiac and Sainte-Croix-du-Mont, but it must be remembered these compare well with all but the finest Sauternes.

The right side of the river, if a little less important in wine production, is unquestionably the prettier. The slope is steep, whereas on the Graves-Barsac-Sauternes side the land is flat. Frequent cuttings into the bluff reveal the white chalk and clay soils which contribute to the character of the Premières Côtes de Bordeaux wines. The exposure is generally south.

Cadillac, in the white-wine part of the region, houses one of Bordeaux's great wine fraternities, the Connétablie de Guyenne, devoted to the promotion of white, sweet wines. Descended from the Connétables or constables of Bordeaux who in the Middle Ages judged the wines passing on the river and decreed whether or not they could go to market, the society is housed in Cadillac's gigantic medieval château of the Dukes of Épernon.

Preuve

A small glass vessel like a test tube lowered on a chain into Cognac barrels to obtain some of the liquor, to taste or "prove" it. Called, in the local slang, a *taupette.*

Pricked wine

Sour wine with an excess of volatile acidity.

Château Prieuré-Lichine

Bordeaux red wine.
District: Haut-Médoc, France.
Commune: Cantenac-Margaux.

Originally the priory of Benedictine monks, who early spread the gospel of the vine in Bordeaux, the vineyard was bought by the author in 1951. The château is just behind the church of Cantenac, which was built partly in the seventeenth century and burned down during the Revolution, but whose façade was reconstructed in 1802. The monks were under the supervision of the Abbaye de Vertheuil, higher up in the Médoc. Over the past 27 years the property has been grouped and reconstituted on the best slightly rising ground in Cantenac, Arsac and Margaux. Some of the recent vineyard acquisitions included the lands known as La Bourgade, which were owned by the La Chapelle family from the fifteenth century to 1867. In 1667 Guy de la Chapelle presented wines from his vineyard to Louis XIV. They were placed in competition with Burgundies recommended by Fagon, the king's doctor. Nevertheless, the wines from La Bourgade remained among the favorites of the Sun King for many years. Since 1952, by exchanging two meters of land for one and sacrificing quantity for quality, the poorer, lower, and sandier plots have been bartered for higher, gravelly, and better-drained land. These exchanges brought into the Prieuré-Lichine vineyard portions of Châteaux Palmer, Ferrière, Kirwan, Giscours, d'Issan, and Boyd-Cantenac, Third Growths *(Troisièmes Crus)*; and of Brane-Cantenac, Second Growth *(Second Cru)*. The property was classified a Fourth Growth *(Quatrième Cru)* in the Médoc Classification of 1855, and it is the hope of the owner that by the acquisition of these excellent plots, and by extensive replanting and improvements in vinicultural methods and equipment, he is creating a wine well above its classification. A subsidiary vineyard is Château Clairefont, a Cru Bourgeois in the village of Margaux.

Since the change in ownership, the wine has become very popular in America, and the château itself (which contains many mementos from the world's wine countries acquired by the author during the preparation of this book) was for a time, when the author founded and managed Alexis Lichine & Co. in Margaux and Bordeaux, a kind of Anglo-American club in southwest France. As they drive along the vineyard road to Margaux, visitors are welcomed to the château by elegantly lettered signs. As a vineyard situated in Cantenac, Château Prieuré-Lichine is now entitled to the place-name Margaux, a privilege accorded to Cantenac wines in 1955, because of the proximity of the famous commune of Margaux and the great similarity between wines of the two places. The vineyard was known as Château Cantenac-Prieuré until 1953, when the new name was officially recognized by the Marquis of Lur-Saluces.

Characteristics. Soft, fast-maturing, relatively full-bodied, yet with all the delicacy for which the wines of the commune of Margaux are so justly renowned.

Vineyard area: 55 hectares (137 acres).

Average production: 260 *tonneaux* (25,000 cases).

Production of wine

It is safe to say that half of the total production of wine in the world is supplied by Italy, France, and the Soviet Union, although quantities vary from country to country and season to season as a result of climate changes and diseases affecting the vine—and this in spite of the mod-

ern scientific discoveries which have solved many of the old problems both of viticulture and viniculture. Wine, a natural phenomenon, is always unpredictable, so it is difficult to strike the proper figures for national productions, especially in these times of rapid expansion of vineyards in many parts of the world. The statistics below are averages for the past several years, in many cases revised upward to reflect the major plantings which will come into full production in the near future.

WORLD WINE PRODUCTION

Producing Country	Hectoliters	U.S. Gallons	Imp. Gallons
France	73,000,000	1,930,850,000	1,606,000,000
Italy	65,800,000	1,740,410,000	1,447,600,000
U.S.S.R.	32,000,000	846,400,000	704,000,000
Spain	28,000,000	740,600,000	616,000,000
Argentina	28,000,000	740,600,000	616,000,000
United States	17,000,000	450,500,000	374,000,000
Portugal	10,100,000	267,650,000	222,200,000
West Germany	8,600,000	227,470,000	189,200,000
Rumania	8,000,000	212,000,000	176,000,000
Yugoslavia	6,300,000	166,635,000	138,600,000
Chile	6,000,000	159,000,000	132,000,000
South Africa	6,000,000	159,000,000	132,000,000
Greece	5,600,000	148,120,000	123,200,000
Algeria	5,000,000	132,250,000	110,000,000
Hungary	4,700,000	124,550,000	103,400,000
Australia	3,700,000	97,865,000	81,400,000
Bulgaria	3,000,000	79,500,000	66,000,000
Austria	2,900,000	76,705,000	63,000,000
Brazil	1,970,000	52,106,000	43,440,000
Mexico	1,556,000	41,156,000	34,232,000
Czechoslovakia	1,388,000	36,712,000	30,536,000
Switzerland	1,194,000	31,581,000	26,268,000
Cyprus	1,100,000	29,150,000	24,200,000
Uruguay	1,010,000	26,714,000	22,220,000
Morocco	764,000	20,207,000	16,808,000
Tunisia	700,000	18,550,000	15,400,000
Canada	500,000	13,225,000	11,000,000
Israel	430,000	11,373,000	9,460,000
Turkey	332,000	8,781,000	7,304,000
Japan	270,000	7,141,000	5,940,000
New Zealand	265,000	7,009,000	5,830,000
Albania	170,000	4,496,000	3,740,000
Luxembourg	128,000	3,385,000	2,816,000
Peru	80,000	2,120,000	1,760,000
Egypt	70,000	1,855,000	1,540,000
Lebanon	40,000	1,060,000	880,000
Libya	30,000	795,000	660,000
Malta	20,000	530,000	440,000
Madagascar	20,000	530,000	440,000
Jordan	15,000	397,000	330,000
Netherlands	10,000	265,000	220,000
Syria	7,000	185,000	154,000
Belgium	4,000	105,000	88,000
Bolivia	4,000	105,000	88,000
Iran	4,000	105,000	88,000
Total	325,781,000	8,619,743,000	7,166,482,000

Prohibition

Prohibition of wines, spirits, and other alcoholic beverages has been tried at various times by various groups and nations. With the sole exceptions of a period in ancient China and of the successful edict prohibiting alcohol to the Moslem, no attempt has been in the slightest way a success. Probably the most spectacular one was that of the United States government between the years 1920 and 1933 with the 18th Amendment to the Constitution.

The 18th Amendment to the Constitution read, in part, that "the manufacture, sale or transportation of intoxicating liquors within, the importation thereof into or the exportation thereof from the United States and all territory subject to the jurisdiction thereof for beverages purposes is hereby prohibited." It was eventually ratified by forty-six states and it went into effect on November 16, 1920. It had been preceded slightly by the Volstead Act (October 1919) which had been passed over the veto of President Wilson and which had prohibited the manufacture, sale, or transportation of any beverage over 1% of alcohol by volume. The general result was chaos.

Throughout the nearly fourteen years of Prohibition speakeasies flourished, "bathtub gin" became the national drink (although the name was more colorful than accurate), bootleggers made fortunes, and products were sold under labels advising the purchaser that he should under no conditions add so much water to the contents or leave the solution at such and such a temperature for a certain length of time, or an illegal alcoholic beverage might result. The cellars of the country resounded with the explosions of bottles of homemade beer, and many a solid and otherwise law-abiding citizen considered it a duty to smuggle some sort of spirit home with him when he went abroad. The supreme act of illogicality was the opening in New York of a speakeasy operated by the Federal government on the theory that by breaking the laws they might better catch the lawbreakers.

The matter was resolved on December 5, 1933 when the 21st Amendment to the Constitution declared the whole dismal experiment a failure and repealed the 18th Amendment. Since that time the system of local option has prevailed whereby states are allowed to choose for themselves (Mississippi was the last dry state to vote wet in 1961), and counties, townships, and villages within states often decide for themselves. The consequences of a town remaining "dry" often recall the phrase of George Bernard Shaw referring to a dry town in Ireland: "The inhabitants neither swear nor get drunk, and look as though they would very much like to do both."

Prokupac

The "national vine of Serbia," an important producer in Yugoslav wines.

Proof gallon

A gallon of spirit at proof strength; the basis for most customs and excise charges.
See Wine gallon.

Proof spirit

"I must explain for the information of Mr. Snowden that when we speak of these degrees, what we mean is degrees of proof spirit; and when we speak of degrees of proof spirit, what we mean is degrees." This was Sir Winston Churchill's clarification when asked in the House of Commons what proof spirit was. The confusion was justified. When Clark invented the hydrometer late in the eighteenth century, he knew that if he dropped his weighted float into spirituous liquor, he could determine its density and calculate the amount of alcohol by the depth to which the float sank. A certain concentration he arbitrarily named proof; anything over the mark was O.P., over proof; anything under was U.P., under proof. Thirty years later a hydrometer was developed (by Bartholomew Sikes—sometimes spelled Sykes) which has remained in use from 1816 to the present day. By Sikes's measurement, proof, in the United States, is 50% of alcohol by volume at 60°F. (16°C.). In England, proof is 49.28% of pure alcohol by weight or 52.10% by volume, at 60°F. (16°C.). Each 0.5% of alcohol over or under proof is reckoned as one degree O.P. or U.P. Alcoholic content in a spirit is usually stated as so many degrees proof: 70° proof (or, correctly, *of* proof, though it is seldom so stated) means the same as 30° under proof, in either case seventy parts of proof being present and thirty lacking. It must always be remembered that 100% pure alcohol is not at proof, but 75.35° O.P.

Provence (Côtes de Provence)

Rosé, red, and white wines.
District: South of France.

Provence is the old province of the troubadours and the Courts of Love in southeast France, and traditionally the land of gaiety and sunshine. It faces the Mediterranean Sea, and from Marseille, which secures its western corner, it moves east through the great naval seaport of Toulon and on to Cannes and Nice. The vine grows, not far away from sun-bathing crowds, in meager soil that is rich in sand, limestone, or slate—and little else.

The first vines brought into France are said to have been planted in Provence by Phocaeans, plying their routes from Italy, Greece, and Asia Minor. Caesar is recorded to have chosen these wines to give to his returning legions as they made their way back to Rome laden with spoils of the Gallic Wars. One village, still growing vines, is reputed to have been named by Caesar himself: this is La Gaude, which stands just above Cannes; and Caesar, tasting the local wine, is said to have smacked his lips together and proclaimed: *Gaudeamus!* (Let us rejoice!)

Officially, Provence no longer exists but is divided into the French departments of Bouches-du-Rhône, Var, Vaucluse, Basses-Alpes, and Alpes-Maritimes. To the tradition-loving French, however, and everyone else as well, it will always be Provence. With its clear, blue sea, its sun and its Mistral—the dread wind that blows from the north always for three, six, or nine days—Provence will never change its character. And an essential part of its character is the Provençal wines.

The region produces annually almost 6 million hectoliters (159 million U.S. gallons, 132 million imp.) of wines, all of which maintain a certain Provençal character. They are wines to be taken in gulps rather than sips. While they often have a certain roughness, they manage to combine with it considerable liveliness and gaiety, and their alcoholic content is such that the drinker is apt soon to take on the same characteristics.

The greatest quantity of wine made in Provence is rosé, but white and red are produced here too—the reds sometimes resembling the wines of Italy. The rosés are among the finest of France—and the perfect accompaniment to the regional specialties, most of which are sea foods fresh from the Mediterranean. These wines should be drunk when fairly young. Some of the better red wines can be aged for a few years but rarely is any Provençal wine at its best after more than five years.

On a quantity basis, red and rosé wines outrun the whites. These white wines, rarely found outside France, have a strength which has prompted one grower to describe them as "tarpaulin edged with lace." The rosés are fresh, clean, and heady, and the best of them (now that they are better made than once they were) have no orange cast.

PLACE-NAMES

Bandol

Some 32 kilometers (20 miles) to the east of Marseille, along the Mediterranean coast, an area of about 120 hectares (300 acres) has been marked off and given the right to grow wines bearing the place-name Bandol. The area falls into the communes of Bandol, Sanary, La Cadière

d'Azur, Le Castellet, and several portions of the communes of Ollioules, Evenos, Saint-Cyr-sur-Mer, and Beausset, in soil that is predominantly a flinty limestone.

One of the more confusing aspects of Provence is the large number of vine-types allowed to be used for the various wines. In Bandol, there are sixteen different grapes, seven for white wines and nine for red and rosé. To complicate matters further, red and rosé are permitted to include up to 20% of their volume of grapes allowed for white wines, providing they are all vinified together. The result is then a lighter wine but not an inferior one.

Clairette and Ugni Blanc are the primary vines allowed for the whites, of which at least 50% must be Clairette; Grenache, Cinsault, Mourvèdre, and Mourvaison are the principal grapes for red and rosé. (Accessory vines are Columbeau, Frontignan, Malvoisie, Doucillon, and Sauvignon for white wines; and Carignan, Pécoui-Touar, Tibouren, Syrah, and Pinot for the others.)

For the place-name Bandol, the wine must have an alcoholic content of at least 11%. Here in the sunny south of France the limits are usually higher than the legal minimum. Wine can be sold as Bandol after an ageing period in the barrel amounting to eight months for white and rosé and a minimum of eighteen months for the red.

The name on a wine label may be Bandol or Vin de Bandol, either one meaning the same thing. Production is just about 14,000 hectoliters (3.7 million U.S. gallons, 3 million imp.) of wine annually, of which more than three-quarters is red and rosé and the remainder white. Although some export is beginning, most of the wine is sold in Provence or in the restaurants of Paris.

Bellet

Bellet, with Bandol and Cassis, is grown along the Riviera. What there is of it is usually drunk on the spot. The wine is made in a number of localities standing behind and slightly to the east of Nice, and in Nice itself.

The soil for the wines of Bellet is made up of pudding-stone, a curious formation composed of innumerable small pebbles which have been rounded and worn down by the action of wind and water. They are rich in flint, and perhaps it is this that causes the wines to be among the very best in southern France. The pudding-stone soil which falls in the communes of Les Séoules, Le Pilon, Le Grand-Bois, Golfan, Cappan, Saint-Romain-de-Bellet, La Tour, Candau, Saquier, Saint-Sauveur, Gros-Pin, Serre-Long, Crémat, Mont-Bellet, Puncia, and Lingesteria has been delimited as the growing area. Here, as in the rest of Provence, a fairly large number of vines are allowed, divided into primary and accessory types.

Folle (or Fuella) and Braquet are primary for red and rosé Bellet, and the whites come from Rolle, Rousanne, Clairette, and Chardonnay. These must make up at least 60% of the grapes going into the wines. (Accessory vines are Cinsault, Carignan, Bourboulenc, and Grenache for red and rosé, and Sauvignon, Moscatelle, Sémillon, Listan, and Pignerol for whites.)

Although there are about 350 hectares (875 acres) within the Bellet appellation, only 60 hectares (150 acres) are planted. Production over the past five years has averaged around 800 hectoliters (21,000 U.S. gallons, 17,600 imp.), equally divided between the red, white, and rosé.

Cassis

One of the best of the Provençal rosés is that of Cassis, a little seaport town about 24 kilometers (15 miles) to the east of Marseille and one of the main supply points for the fish sent into that city. Fish and wine, in Cassis, are a perfect combination—for the sturdy dry rosé, or the full, heady white make magnificent companions for *bouillabaisse*, the succulent rock-fish and lobster stew which most Frenchmen rightly maintain can only properly be made in Marseille.

The vineyards growing grapes for Cassis are all in the single commune. The growers maintain that the gentle breezes from the Mediterranean are so constant that the temperature rarely changes. This, they say, explains the annual harvest, which also varies very little from year to year, amounting to some 5,000 hectoliters (132,500 U.S. gallons, 110,000 imp.). In Cassis white wines predominate over red, a situation which is not typical of Provence. The principal vines are Ugni Blanc, Sauvignon, Doucillon, Clairette, Marsanne, and Pascal Blanc for white wines; and Grenache, Carignan, Mourvèdre, Cinsault, and Barbaroux for red and rosé.

Wine must have a minimum alcoholic content of 11%. This applies equally to all Cassis wines, regardless of color.

They are often served too cold, even in Cassis—a practice that ruins their flavor—but are wonderful wines. The whites and rosés are the best. They are strong, fine, heady, and robust.

Palette

Near the ancient city of Aix-en-Provence, the hills start rising in a steep rocky cliff leading up to the growing area of Palette. This is the only superior wine area in Provence that is not along the coastal strip. It lies in the communes of Meyreuil, Tholonet, and Aix-en-Provence. The white wines made here are among the best in Provence; the red wines are good and keep well.

Palette wines have only come under strict controls lately, and some of the practices from earlier and more haphazard days continued into the 1960s. Vine growers who had olive trees in their vineyards were ordered to uproot them by 1963. The new laws decree, however, that Palette has more permissible vine-types than are usually found even in Provence, the total coming to twenty-five or more. For white wines, the growers are allowed to use Clairette, which must comprise at least 55% of the final mixture, and in addition any combination of the following: Grenache Blanc, White Muscats (most types), Terret-Bourret (limited to less than 20% of the total), Picpoule, Pascal, Araignan, Colombaud, and Ugni Blanc or Ugni Rosé. Red and rosé wines must be made from more than 50% of a combination of Grenache, Mourvèdre, Cinsault, and Plant d'Arles, though Mourvèdre is now particularly favored.

The Palette vineyard area used to be far greater than its present 20 hectares (100 acres), but the expansion of nearby Aix has pushed the vines back. Presently there are only two properties dividing the land, the more substantial by far being the Château de Simone. Total annual production amounts to around 500 hectoliters (13,250 U.S. gallons, 11,000 imp.). Very enjoyable when drunk in the old city of Aix-en-Provence, Palette loses most of its sprightly charm and gaiety when shipped.

Côtes de Provence

In 1977 the I.N.A.O. and the French Ministry of Agriculture upgraded Côtes de Provence from V.D.Q.S. (Vins Délimités de Qualité Supérieure) to A.O.C. The vineyards of the Côtes de Provence are split into five different areas extending from Marseille inland to the city of Draguignan and on to the River Var just above Nice. Grenache, Cinsault, Carignan, Mourvèdre, Tibouren, Clairette, Ugni Blanc, and Rolle are the principal grape varieties. The resulting wines are not always of the caliber of the four Provençal wines already discussed, but they are often extraordinarily pleasant. Some of the better villages are Les Arcs, Lorgues, Pierrefeu, Cuers, and Puget-Ville. The total annual production has increased in the last decade and now averages around 700,000 hectoliters (185 million U.S. gallons, 154 million imp.).

Côtes de Provence wines are becoming known on the markets of the world, thanks to a group of growers who have formed the Syndicat de Défense des Vins des Côtes

Provignage

de Provence (Syndicate for the Protection of the Wines of the Côtes de Provence). One of the many ideas the group is promoting is the use of special bottles designed to catch the eye of the Riviera tourist; now most of the companies connected with the organization are beginning to sell their wines in shapely bottles that mark a departure from tradition. This group of growers owes much of its energy to its president, the Comte de Rohan-Chabot, himself the owner of one of the better classic Growths, the Château de Saint-Martin.

Provignage

Method of propagating vines.
See Chapter Eight, p. 29.

Prunelle

A green French liqueur made from the kernels of sloes. It is produced by the firm of Garnier.

Prunellia

A green liqueur made from the kernels of sloes by the French firm of Cusenier.

Pruning

The centuries-old viticultural art of cutting back and trimming vines to effect their life span, quality, or production. Certainly the yield from the vine is one of the most obvious factors in which pruning plays an important part: a vine's production can be multiplied by two to five times depending on the method of trimming. Since high yield does not hurt the quality of the grapes from most of the vines in the world, these plants are generally cut back for maximum production. But for the dozen or so varieties whose quality suffers with quantity, the proper pruning style is crucial for maintaining the high standards of the wine. In the great vineyards of France and Germany, the method of pruning is specified by law.

Puglia

See Apulia; Italy.

Puisseguin-Saint-Émilion

A commune of Saint-Émilion producing full-bodied red wines.
See Saint-Émilion.

Puligny-Montrachet and Puligny-Montrachet-Côte de Beaune

Burgundy red and white wines.
District: Côte de Beaune, France.

Puligny is near the southern end of the Côte de Beaune, in the unofficial sub-district locally called the Côte de Meursault—the slope that takes its name from the nearby commune of Meursault and lays claim to the greatest white wines of the world. The claim is not without justification. The wines which come from the vineyards of Puligny-Montrachet and Chassagne-Montrachet are certainly among the very greatest of the dry white wines of France, and that from one vineyard (the fabulous Montrachet) is considered by many experts as undeniably the world's greatest dry white wine.

In Puligny, everyone makes wine. The mayor himself—a powerful, heavily-set man—is a leading grower and he maintains a cordial but deep-rooted rivalry with his genial counterpart in Chassagne. The village priest is another respected grower, and between Masses he is apt to be out in the vineyard, supervising work or just inspecting his vines. At harvest time, the entire village may be found in the vineyards on the slope behind the town. This slope has a slightly different appearance from the rest of the Côte de Beaune. In Puligny and Chassagne, the rolling hills are bare of trees; areas not planted in vine are covered not in the tangled underbrush found elsewhere along the slopes but in close-cropped, sickly-looking grass punctuated with rock and slabs of calcareous outcropping. The low-lying vines, however, share none of this unprepossessing appearance.

The vineyard of Montrachet is so outstanding that it is a case completely apart from the other wines of Burgundy and is treated separately under its own heading. In addition to Montrachet, Puligny shares another Great Growth with Chassagne—Bâtard-Montrachet—and has other incomparable vineyards that it owns outright. Chevalier-Montrachet and Bienvenues-Bâtard-Montrachet are two of the greatest, and all these vineyards are ranked by the French authorities as Great Growths (*Grands Crus*). In theory, this means that the authorities consider the wines among the thirty-one most magnificent of the Côte d'Or of Burgundy, and in practice, that the wines—when they meet the high minimum requirements—will be labeled simply with the name of the vineyard instead of (as is the case otherwise) with commune name and vineyard name or simply with commune name. (*See all Great Growths as individually entered.*)

Although the Great Growths are generally accepted as the finest, some of the others are also superb and in the hands of a talented wine-maker may turn out equal to the topmost. One of them is Pucelles, just north of Bienvenues-Bâtard-Montrachet; and above Pucelles is Le Cailleret, adjoining the Chevalier. Cailleret was once called Les Demoiselles, but its position next to the Chevalier was responsible for the change in name—the jokes were too frequent and too bad. On the opposite side of town—bordering the Meursault—is the excellent Les Combettes divided by the road that forms the town line from Charmes in Meursault. Higher up the slope, toward the tiny hamlet of Blagny—which spills over from the upper corner of Meursault to the upper corner of Puligny—is Les Chalumeaux, another exceptional vineyard.

All of Puligny's white wines share approximately the same characteristics. They are eminently dry, not so soft or so luxurious as Meursaults, and are apt to have a full, rich, flowery, or sometimes fruity, bouquet. The green-gold color takes on different highlights and hues, and the wine has a strength and a masculinity rare in white wines. It leaves the mouth fresh and full of varying sensations and the better the wine is, the more lingering will be the aftertaste.

In addition to white wines, a small amount of red is made—but not generally from grapes grown in the highest ranking vineyards—and it is seldom the equal of the reds made in neighboring Chassagne, although it often has good body and a distinctive and expressive bouquet.

Throughout the commune there are about 234 hectares (580 acres) devoted to vines. Wines that stem from 140 hectares (345 acres) within this larger area have the right to add the designation Côte de Beaune to the commune name and are often of superior quality. The best wines, of course, are those which carry simply vineyard name (Great Growths) or vineyard name and commune name (First Growths or *Premiers Crus*). The amount of wine produced in Puligny in each year is about 7,000 hectoliters (185,000 U.S. gallons, 154,000 imp.), only a few hundred hectoliters of it red.

GREAT GROWTHS (*Grands Crus*)

Vineyard	Hectares	Acres
Montrachet (*in part*)	4	9.9
Bâtard-Montrachet (*in part*)	6	14.9
Chevalier-Montrachet	7.1	17.7
Bienvenues-Bâtard-Montrachet	2.3	5.8

FIRST GROWTHS (*Premiers Crus*)

Vineyard	Hectares	Acres
Les Combettes	6.7	16.6
Les Pucelles	6.8	16.8
Les Chalumeaux	7	17.3
Le Cailleret	5.4	13.4
Les Folatières	3.4	8.5
Clovaillon	5.5	13.7
Le Champ-Canet	4.6	11.4
Le Refert	13.2	32.6
Sous le Puits	6.9	17.1
Garenne	.4	0.9
Hameau de Blagny	4	9.9

Pulque

A Mexican brew known to the ancient Aztecs, obtained from the milky juice of the cactus variously called the agave, century plant, American aloe, maguery, and mezcal. Pulque is a fermented beverage of 4% to 6% alcohol, usually drunk when it is freshly made, and very popular among the Mexicans. Millions of gallons are sold annually on country farms and at *pulquerías* in the cities.

Punch

(1) A hot, strong winter drink made with spirits, fruit and spices and traditionally served in a bowl.

(2) Norwegian Punch: a sweetened after-dinner liqueur based on Batavia arrack and running about 26% to 27% alcohol by volume. It is made by the Norwegian state-controlled wine and spirit company, A/S Vinmonopolet.

Puncheon

A large cask of varying capacity, formerly 264 liters (70 U.S. gallons, 58 imp.), but now usually about 378 liters (100 U.S. gallons, 83 imp.). Used in the West Indies for rum.

Punsch (punch), Swedish

Swedish liquor on a base of rum. It dates from the eighteenth century, when Swedish merchants began trading with the East Indies, importing, among other things, the rice and sugar-cane spirit which is the foundation. Originally the punch was served hot, but since the nineteenth century it has generally been taken cold.

Punt (kick)

Indentation in bottle bottoms, originally to reinforce them and to hold the sediment, thus preventing it from spreading throughout the bottle.

Pupitre

French term for a hinged rack for holding sparkling wines neck down while they are prepared for the *dégorgement* or ejection of the deposit accumulated during the second fermentation.
See Champagne.

Puttonyos

Hungarian buckets used for measuring quantity of specially selected grapes used in Tokay wine. Thus the collar label on every bottle of Tokaji Aszú will state: 3 Puttonos, 4 Puttonos, etc.—the export agency simplifies the spelling by removing the *y*.
See Tokay.

Pyralis

Meal-moth which feeds on the vine.
See Chapter Eight, p. 29.

Q

Quart

A quarter of a gallon, whether U.S. or imperial. An American quart equals 94.6 centiliters, a British quart 1.136 liters. (In France the term *quart* is used in restaurants and cafés for a small carafe, reputedly a quarter of a liter; also in Champagne for a small bottle used in bars for Champagne cocktails or for one glass.) The standard American quart equals 32 U.S. fluid ounces; the British quart, 40 British fluid ounces.

Quarter-cask

Originally a cask of one-fourth the capacity of a pipe (*q.v.*). In practice, quarter-casks vary from 113 to 160 liters (30 to 42 U.S. gallons, 25 to 35 imp.).

Quarts de Chaume

Section of Coteaux du Layon, in Anjou.
See Anjou.

Quetsch

Blue plum spirit made in Alsace and in Lorraine.
See Alsace: Spirits.

Quincy

Loire Valley white wines.
District: Loire Valley, France.

Minor dry white-wine district classed with those of the Loire, although Quincy is drained by the River Cher some 48 kilometers (30 miles) away. The vineyards are in the communes of Quincy and Brinay. They are planted in a chalky soil, and the wines resemble those of neighboring Reuilly, of Sancerre and Pouilly-sur-Loire, and, like the output of these towns, come only from Sauvignon grapes. About 223 hectares (550 acres) are devoted to vines; output averages an annual 4,000 hectoliters (106,000 U.S. gallons, 88,000 imp.).

Quinquina

A French aperitif with a base of fortified wine and quinine added to impart a slightly bitter taste.

Quinta

The word means, literally, "agricultural estate" in Portuguese, and, by extension, has come to mean vineyard.

R

Château Rabaud-Promis

Bordeaux white wine.
District: Sauternes, France.
Commune: Bommes.

Originally the single estate of Rabaud, one of the oldest Sauternes properties; known to have been an enormously productive vineyard of more than 80 hectares (200 acres) by 1660. The present château, owned by M. Lanneluc, the mayor of Bommes, was built by Victor Louis. The holding, having come into the hands of M. de Sigalas in 1864, was sold in part to M. Promis in 1903. In the thirties, the vineyards of Rabaud-Promis and Sigalas-Rabaud were reunited, only to divide again in 1952. Since then, Sigalas-Rabaud has become the superior wine and is considered one of the best Sauternes after Yquem. When they were constituted as the single vineyard of Rabaud in 1855 the wine was classified a First Growth (*Premier Cru*) of Sauternes, and this classification extends to both Rabaud-Promis and Sigalas-Rabaud.

Characteristics. Not one of the greatest. Sweet, and a certain lack of breed.

Vineyard area: 30 hectares (75 acres).
Average production: 65 *tonneaux* (7,000 cases).

Rabigato

A grape variety used in White Ports.

Rablay-sur-Layon

Wine commune with the right to an Appellation Contrôlée in the Coteaux du Layon district of Anjou.
See Anjou; Coteaux du Layon.

Race

French word for distinction and breeding in a wine.

Racking

The draining or pumping of wine off its lees from the barrel in which it has been maturing into a new, clean one. This process is repeated several times during the ageing of wine.
See Chapter Nine, p. 38.

Rainwater

Originally a trademark, now a type denoting a light dry Madeira.

Ramisco

A grape variety which makes the dune wines of Colares in Portugal.

Rancio

This term is applied in Spain to the nutty flavor in Sherry. In California it applies to the taste brought about by cooking in sweet dessert wines. In somewhat the same sense it is used to describe a pungent taste in Madeiras, Marsalas, Málagas, and others. In France the adjective is applied particularly to the characteristic taste of the sweet dessert wines of Banyuls when they are well-aged, and also to the wine of Château-Chalon.

Raspail

French herb liqueur, yellow in color, said to be made from a formula devised by François Vincent Raspail in 1847.

Ratafia

It is claimed that the name was applied to any liqueur drunk at the ratification of a treaty or agreement. It now applies to sweetened aperitifs made from wines, such as Ratafia de Bourgogne and Ratafia de Champagne.

Rauchbier

In Germany, literally "smoke beer"—a beer made there from smoked malt.

Rauenthaler

The different Rauenthalers such as Langenstück and others taken together are probably the greatest of the German Rheingaus and certainly, with the exception of Schloss Johannisberg, command the highest prices. Practically no inferior wine is made in this district, which is not always true of the other great Rhine sections.
See Rheingau.

Château Rausan-Ségla

Bordeaux red wine.
District: Haut-Médoc, France.
Commune: Margaux.

Adjoining Rauzan-Gassies, with which it originally formed a single vineyard, Rausan-Ségla lies across the Médoc vineyard road from Château Margaux and Château Palmer, on the south side of the village of Margaux. It is classed a Second Growth (*Second Cru*) in the Classification of 1855.

Acquired by Pierre des Mesures de Rausan in 1661, it

remained in the Rausan family for two hundred years. Thomas Jefferson wrote: ". . . Rozan-Margau, which is made by Madame de Rozan . . . this is what I import for myself . . . ." In addition to the vineyard carrying their name, the Rausans—or Rozans—for a time leased Château Margaux and Château Latour, also making those wines. In 1866, Rausan-Ségla was sold to the maternal grandfather of the Cruse family, Bordeaux wine merchants, who sold it again in 1956 to M. de Mesnon, who in 1962 resold it to British Holt group, the owners of Eschenauer, the Bordeaux wine shippers.

Characteristics. Very fine, perfumed, and perhaps slightly fuller than the other Margaux wines. The best of them usually require a good deal of ageing. If the wines have a fault, it is that they are not as consistent as they might be. As recently as 1959 the production was only some 35 *tonneaux,* but the new plantings have been most auspicious both for quality and quantity.

Vineyard area: 40 hectares (100 acres).
Average production: 175 *tonneaux* (15,000 cases).

Château Rauzan-Gassies

Bordeaux red wine.
District: Haut-Médoc, France.
Commune: Margaux.

Once a single vineyard with Rausan-Ségla, now adjoining it on the south of Margaux, Rauzan-Gassies was already well known in 1530. Of the many proprietors over more than four centuries, none could have been more eccentric than a Chevalier de Rauzan who, when he could not get the price he expected for his wines, put them aboard ship and sailed to London. Proclaiming that he was going to sell his wines himself from the deck of the boat, he awaited customers. Still not getting his price, he announced that he would pour one barrel into the Thames each day until he got a better offer—or had no more wine. The story goes that by the third day all London was crowding to watch this unheard-of performance; and the fame of it spread so that he was soon offered a high price for every barrel left aboard.

The vineyard is now owned by a M. Quié, owner also of Château Croizet-Bages. Rauzan-Gassies is a Second Growth (*Second Cru*) in the Classification of 1855. Today critics feel that the character of the wine is not equal to the quality of the vineyard as it is at present being cultivated. Hence prices paid on the Bordeaux market make Rauzan-Gassies one of the cheapest Second Growths (*Seconds Crus*), and its reputation has fallen accordingly.

Characteristics. In the fifties and early sixties, many Bordeaux critics remarked that Rauzan-Gassies had slipped considerably in quality. Some vintages from the 1940s and 1950s were marked by an excess of volatile acidity. Since 1973 there has been progress in the vinification, as it has been overseen by Émile Peynaud, Bordeaux's dean of oenology.

Vineyard area: 27 hectares (68 acres).
Average production: 100 *tonneaux* (8,000 cases).

Ravat

A French hybridizer whose greatest achievement was probably the vine Ravat 262, giving, in the United States, a light red wine akin to a Beaujolais. Ravat 6 is his best white-wine grape, but is of questionable value in the United States because of its susceptibility to cold winters.

Ravello

An especially beautiful little village not far from Naples and Amalfi in southern Italy which produces a moderate quantity of white and rosé wine not however as memorable as the town itself.

Château de Rayne-Vigneau

Bordeaux white wine.
District: Sauternes, France.
Commune: Bommes.

Classified a First Growth (*Premier Cru*) of Sauternes in 1855. The vines grow in a large vineyard sloping away from the dark turreted château. The wine is not the only treasure produced by the soil. For some reason which experts have never solved, in this patch of earth alone in the whole region, precious and semi-precious stones appear. Sapphires, opals, jasper, onyx, and topaz have been found and are collected in the museums of France and many other countries. The principal owner is a M. Dumas, who produces cheap sparkling wines; the other owner is a shipping firm now partly owned by Pepsico.

Characteristics. This potentially great vineyard is capable of improvement.

Vineyard area: 62 hectares (155 acres).
Average production: 150 *tonneaux* (11,000 cases).

Rebate brandy

South African trade term for brandy made under fairly rigid conditions imposed by the government and aged at least three years in wood. The measure was initiated to encourage distillers to increase brandy quality, the government giving a tax rebate on any brandy which contains at least 25% of "rebate." Lesser and harsher spirits, on the other hand, are very heavily taxed.

Recioto di Soave

A sometimes sweeter version of the famous Italian white wine.
See Veneto.

Recioto della Valpolicella

A fuller, interesting sort of the fine wine of Veneto (*q.v.*).

Récolte

French for wine harvest. It may be either the harvesting or the crop, but generally *récolte* is used to refer to the crop, and *vendange* to the harvest.

Rectification (rectifying) of spirits

In distillation (the object of which is to separate or purify substances, making use of the differences in their volatility), the components of a mixture are vaporized in order of their boiling points, so that one part can be drawn off from another. If the substance is already purified or of constant composition (i.e., all components with equal boiling points), then the operation is rectification. A rectified spirit is one which has undergone purification by distillation at a licensed rectifier's premises.

The definition of rectification given by J. H. Perry in *The Engineers' Handbook* (3rd ed.) is as follows:

Rectification is a distillation carried out in such a way that the vapour rising from a still comes in contact with a condensed portion of vapour previously evolved from the same still. A transfer of material and an interchange of heat result from this contact, thereby securing a greater enrichment of the vapour in the more volatile components than could be secured with a single distillation operation using the same amount of heat. The condensed vapours, returned to accomplish this object, are termed *reflux*.

The generally used devices, in which vapours from a still on their way to a condenser can flow counter-currently to a portion of the condensate returned as reflux, are called *rectifying columns* or *towers*.

See Chapter Ten, p. 52; Gin.

Regional

Any wine whose name comes from a district or region and not from a specific vineyard. Such wines are usually inexpensive blends. Bordeaux, Provence, California, and Rioja are examples of regional names.

Rehoboam

An outsized bottle sometimes used for Champagne. It holds the equivalent of six normal bottles.

Reims

This ancient French cathedral city is also one of the principal centers of the Champagne trade—the other is Épernay.

See Champagne.

Remuage

Remuage (moving around) is a term used in the process of making Champagne. Bottles placed in specially built racks are turned or shaken a little every day for about four months before they are shipped, so that the sediment may move down toward the cork. Finally, sediment and cork will be removed in one skillful movement in the process of *dégorgement*.

See Champagne.

Repeal

To Americans, Repeal refers to December 5, 1933, when the 21st Amendment to the Constitution of the United States was passed, repealing the 18th (Prohibition) Amendment and allowing alcoholic beverages once again to be sold legally in the United States.

See United States; Prohibition.

Reputed pint

British half-bottle; there are twelve to the imperial gallon (1.2009 U.S.).

Reputed quart

British regular bottle for wines and spirits; about 75 centiliters; three-quarters of a U.S. quart; one-sixth of an imperial gallon.

Reserva

Indication on Rioja (Spain) wine labels that the wine has been aged; sometimes indicates quality, sometimes enfeeblement.

See Rioja.

Retsina

Greek wine, ordinary white and rosé, which has been treated with pine resin. This means a considerable quantity of the wine consumed in Greece. In the southern and central parts of the country almost everyone—especially among the peasants—prefers his wine with this piny, resinous taste.

See Greece: Other Greek Wines.

Reuilly

White, rosé, and red wines.
District: Loire Valley, France.

Small little-known Loire wine district lying along the Arnon, a tributary of the River Cher, producing a small quantity of dry white wine from Sauvignon grapes. Some vines giving grapes for red and rosé wines are also grown, but their output does not receive an Appellation Contrôlée. About 100 hectares (250 acres) of Sauvignon produce about 1,000 hectoliters (26,500 U.S. gallons, 22,000 imp.) of Reuilly annually, the wine resembling that of Sancerre and Pouilly-sur-Loire—although it is usually more acid and lighter.

Réunion Island

Rum-making island in the Indian Ocean, formerly a French colony.

See Rum, French.

Rhein

German spelling of Rhine.
See Palatinate; Rheingau; Rheinhessen; Mittelrhein.

Rheingau

Mostly white and a few red wines.
District: German Rhineland.

The Rheingau wines are, if a choice must be made, the best in Germany when they are at their finest. As such they become, with their peers of the Mosel and the great white Burgundies, the finest white wines in the world for their variety in taste characteristics.

In an average or poor year, the lower Rheingau wines from around Rüdesheim and Hochheim in the upper part of the district will be better than the wines from the greater areas, which will be too light; but in the big years, the famous Spätlese and Trockenbeerenauslese Riesling wines from the strip of the Rhine front between Eltville and Winkel will be incomparable. Wonderful as the loveliest Mosels may be, they will never quite touch the character and breed of the greatest Rheingaus. A few white Burgundies have the character and strength to challenge the dry Rheingaus, and it can be argued that in one sense such a wine as Château d'Yquem in Sauternes is their superior in sweet wines, for, owing to the milder climate in the Bordeaux district, the productivity, comparable in quality, is infinitely greater in quantity. Yet the long-lived, late-gathered Rheingau great growths are true kings in the royalty of wines. Rich and with exquisite breed after a sunny summer and a hazy autumn, blessed with the river mist the Rheingau peasants call the "Wine-Maker," they will last for thirty or forty years.

Wine is the only important product from Eltville to Rüdesheim and Assmannshausen, the town of red wines a little farther around the river bend where the water races. Because of this, everyone is dependent on the weather as it bears on the grape, and the area has its crises. Manuring was once standard procedure in German vineyards, and a further problem of the Rheingau was that, unlike most German growers, these had too little domestic husbandry to provide their own dung, which had therefore to be bought—an expensive matter. Artificial fertilizers now have eliminated this difficult process. The slopes facing due south are guarded from the north wind by the heavily-treed ridge of the Taunus Hills, and further protected because the river bends enough to cut off most of the wind from east or west. The vineyards are broken and steep, rolling in green waves parallel to the river. "If the plow can go there, the vine should not," is a Mosel proverb, and in a rough way it is true for the Rheingau too. The steepness, the southern exposure, and the sheltered slopes make possible the production of the late-gathered wines, the grapes sometimes being left on the vines until the noble rot of the *Botrytis* has set in, sometimes as late as December. The Rhine itself, at its widest at the Rheingau (about one kilometer, or two-thirds of a mile) serves to warm the vines by reflecting back the sunrays during the day, thus doubling their effectiveness; and by holding the

day's warmth in the night, causing a greater equality of day and night temperature, very beneficial to the vine. In the early spring, and particularly in the late autumn when the grape must hang long on the vine through the critical days of falling temperature, the soft Rhine mist keeps off the frost.

The Rheingau extends along the north bank of the river from a little below Wiesbaden to Lorchhausen, a short distance downriver from Assmannshausen. Viticulturally, it also includes Hochheim, on the other side of Wiesbaden and on the River Main, where the wines are of the same type. It is Hochheim which gives the name Hock, used properly in England for all Rheingau wines and loosely for all wines of the Rhine area.

The total planted area is a little less than 3,100 hectares (7,750 acres), a very small piece of the vineyard area of the world considering its reputation. A little red wine is grown at Niederwalluf, Hattenheim, and much more at Assmannshausen, only the latter of which merits any attention; but the Rheingau is a kingdom of white wines—and a kingdom of the Riesling grape, also. In other Rhine districts, the Riesling grows only in the finest plots, always outstripped numerically by the Sylvaner variety; but in the Rheingau, 78% of all the vine is Riesling, 20% is Müller-Thurgau, which is a crossing of the Sylvaner and Riesling, and 2% is of new grape varieties; while the red wines of Assmannshausen come from the Spätburgunder Pinot Noir variety, brought a long time ago from France. The Riesling grape of the Rheingau has a very small, very aromatic, late-ripening berry with a tough hide. It is this tough skin which makes the Riesling chief of all Rheingau varieties in resistance to the late-autumn cold; and it is the final penetration of the thick skin by the noble rot *Botrytis* which causes the intense sugaring and mysterious chemical changes of the great peak wines.

Of nearly three thousand Rheingau growers, more than a thousand own less than half a hectare (about 1.2 acres); another thousand own between one-half and two hectares (1.2 to 5 acres); only two hundred–odd growers own more than two hectares. These figures, however, are deceptive if taken to mean that there are no large estates in the Rheingau. There are. The great owners, few though they may be, hold a fair proportion of the whole acreage, and a very much higher proportion of the best parts. These large holdings are today suffering severely from labor shortage. The big Opel automobile plant, the chemical industries in Ludwigshafen, Frankfurt, and Mainz (the Rhine-Main triangle), and the jobs in Wiesbaden siphon off the Rheingau working force; and in Germany, as elsewhere, the higher the standard of living rises, the fewer land-workers there are. In spite of the difficulties of large ownership, since about 1935 the tendency has been to concentrate holdings by exchanges. Areas parceled up and divided by inheritance and by the practice of holding small bits of vineyard in various sections as a protection against losses from frost or hail (which may be extremely localized) are gradually being consolidated.

This amalgamation has taken another form with the passage of the 1971 West German Wine Law. In the

Rheingau and the ten other quality wine-producing regions of Germany—the *bestimmten Anbaugebiete*—the minimum size of a specific vineyard entitled to the use of its name on a wine bottle label was set variously between 5 and 10 hectares (about 12 to 25 acres), depending on the terrain. Vineyards too small to retain their old and sometimes very famous designations were for the most part assigned to the name of a large adjoining plot whose wine was of a similar character.

At the great vineyard of Schloss Johannisberg above the village of Geisenheim, it is the custom to shoot off a gun at the completion of the harvesting of each 100 barrels. In days past a single shot would be heard in the crisp autumn, but today there will be two or three; the production has been doubled. Taking an average across the whole Rheingau, production has been 100% to 150% more per vineyard acre since the turn of the century. A few areas yield as many as 100 hectoliters per hectare (1,070 U.S. gallons, 890 imp. to the acre). Total production averages 300,000 hectoliters (8 million U.S. gallons, 6 million imp.) for the entire Rheingau. This striking gain, achieved by improved methods of fertilizing and spraying, by greater knowledge of vine selection and fighting of vine disease, has been a necessary means of combating the rising cost of labor and the generally uncertain conditions of a single-crop area so entirely dependent on the weather. Another factor is that the growers transplant grafts of Riesling and unite them with phylloxera-resistant vines. Yet the quantity and quality of the grapes are higher.

Has the quality of the wine been hurt? Experiments conducted by Professor Birk of the Viticultural School and Research Station in Geisenheim, the finest wine school in Germany, have established that certain strains of the Riesling can be made to yield three to four times more in quantity without loss of quality. (This is a new development, going counter to the age-old rule that in viticulture quantity can only be obtained at the expense of quality.) However, experience in the Rheingau seems to prove that close-pruning of the vine—the method of ensuring high quality in, for example, the Bordeaux region of France—causes the Riesling to cast off its flower (the eventual grape cluster) in order to give all its strength to the development of the leaf. When it is allowed to grow taller, the vine flowers fully and develops well. Despite the general German practice of growing the vine tall, and the highly-developed methods at Geisenheim in the Rheingau by the State Domain and by other leaders, some connoisseurs maintain that Rheingau wines are falling off as a result of the stepping up of quantity. Perhaps the real truth is that this must be done if the Rheingau wines are to survive at all economically. In fact, in the last decade or so, a move has been made to plant the rows wider apart, following the method of Lenz Moser of Austria, to permit machine cultivation and so to reduce labor. The vines must then be trained even higher if the level of quantity production is to be maintained.

All of the Rheingau is included in one *Bereich*, or subregion, called Johannisberg. The *Grosslagen* (sections of vineyards) into which the region is divided are Burgweg,

Steil, Erntebringer, Gottesthal, Mehrhölzchen, Honigberg, Deutelsberg, Heiligenstock, Steinmächer, and Daubhaus. These *Grosslagen* are in turn divided into some 120 single vineyards, or *Einzellagen*. (A complete description of the terms *Bereich, Grosslage,* and *Einzellage,* as well as what these names mean on wine labels is found under Germany: Wine Laws, p. 238. A listing of *Einzellagen* by *Grosslage* and *Bereich* for each of the eleven official German wine regions is given in Appendix B, p. 599.)

Grosslage Burgweg includes the vineyards around the towns (*Weinbauorte*) of Lorchhausen, Lorch, Rüdesheim, and parts of the vineyards of Assmannshausen-Aulhausen and Geisenheim.

Grosslage Steil includes Assmannshausen and the remaining vineyards of Assmannshausen-Aulhausen.

Grosslage Erntebringer contains the plantings around the town of Johannisberg itself, the Schloss Johannisberg, the other Geisenheim vineyards, plus some of the vineyards of Mittelheim and Winkel.

Grosslage Daubhaus covers the vineyards around Hochheim and some plantings further afield.

Grosslage Gottesthal consists of most of the Östrich vineyards and the large estate or Ortsteil of Schloss Reichartshauen.

Grosslage Mehrhölzchen includes another section of Mittelheim and Östrich and the famous vineyards of Hallgarten.

Grosslage Honigberg takes in the remaining Mittelheim vineyards, those of Winkel, and the Schloss Vollrads.

Grosslage Deutelsberg is made up of the Erbach and Hattenheim plantings plus the great Steinberg estate.

Grosslage Heiligenstock consists of the vineyards around Kiedrich and part of the Sandgrub *Einzellage* in Eltville.

Grosslage Steinmächer is the remaining Eltville properties and those of Dotzheim, Frauenstein, Martinsthal, Niederwalluf, Oberwalluf, Rauenthal, and Schierstein.

THE IMPORTANT RHEINGAU TOWNS AND VINEYARDS

There are a little over two dozen Rheingau wine *Gemeinden* or *Weinbauorte* (towns and villages), of which a scant dozen are in the top class. Many experts feel the best towns and villages, in terms of quality in the great years, run from east to west and are: *first,* best vineyards of Rauenthal; *second,* best vineyards of Erbach-Hattenheim-Hallgarten; *third,* best vineyards of Johannisberg, with Schloss Vollrads and Winkler Hasensprung, in Winkel; *fourth,* best vineyards of Rüdesheim. The latter rise in medium years to the top of the list in relation to the other vineyards. In dry years, the vineyards nearest the moisture-retaining forests will make the best wine.

Assmannshausen

Assmannshausen is often said to produce the best red wine in Germany, although others favor Ingelheimer, from farther upstream on the other side of the Rhine. No red wine of Germany is outstanding, particularly if measured against German white wine or French red wine.

The Rhine is extremely swift at Assmannshausen, and as you stand in the steep vineyards you see the river steamers form in line, cabled together, for the stubby tug to pull them around the bend to Rüdesheim. When a stiff wind blows upriver through the narrows, all the flags fly forward from the sterns as if the boats were backing up. The red-wine vine growing in the characteristic bluish-red shale is the Spätburgunder, so called because it was brought from Burgundy by the Cistercian monks in the twelfth century. The wine it makes is mild and velvety, with a slight undertaste of almonds—something like a middling Burgundy but without any of its powerful characteristic aroma. The same vine, called Pinot Noir in France, produces the red Burgundies today. During the centuries, the Spätburgunder has grown poorer in quality in its transplanted home and the Assmannshausen vineyards had shrunk considerably by the time of the First World War. Since then, the State Domain, now holder of 80% of the total acreage, has developed the vineyards intensively and they are again improving.

In the years when the wines do not come up to standard, the State Domain sells them to be made into Sekt (sparkling wine). Assmannshausen is unique in being a wine at once sweet and red and nearly great—but in the last respect, it never quite succeeds.

Vineyard area: 150 hectares (375 acres): red—110 hectares (275 acres); white—40 hectares (100 acres).

Grape varieties: Spätburgunder, Sylvaner, and Riesling.

Important vineyard: Höllenberg, in the adjoining town of Assmannshausen-Aulhausen (very early records show this vineyard was already in cultivation by 1108).

Other vineyard: Frankenthal.

Eltville

The Eltville wines tend to be better in years when the more important sections fall off. In 1953, for example, these were among the best in the Rheingau, because the finer vineyards had too much sun, causing a loss of freshness. The name of the village on the Rhine bank is of Roman origin: *alta villa*. Until the end of the fifteenth century it was the summer seat of the Prince-Electors of Mainz, and ruins and palaces of the period still stand. Nearby on the riverbank are the major wine estates of Landgraf von Hessen and Frh. Langwerth von Simmern.

Vineyard area: 220 hectares (550 acres) white.

Grape varieties: Riesling, Sylvaner, and Müller-Thurgau.

Important vineyards: Sonnenberg (lively and elegant); Langenstück (generally more full-bodied than Sonnenberg, grown on heavy loam); and Taubenberg.

Other vineyards: Rheinberg and Sandgrub (on the border with Kiedrich; the better parts are in Kiedrich and Langenstück).

Erbach

Generally full-bodied wines of masculine character, of which the best and the most famous is Markobrunn.

Markobrunn. Sometimes written Marcobrunn, sometimes Markobrunn, the wine is one of the greatest and best-known Rheingaus. It does not reach the superb elegance of a top Rauenthaler but it has more body and is characterized by a spicy, lively quality. It was preferred to all other Rheingaus by Thomas Jefferson on his Rhine journey in 1788. The name derives from an ancient spring (*Brunnen* means "spring" or "well") which may still be seen, with a neglected wall bearing the name Markobrunnen, the spring of Saint Mark. The fact that this well and the famous vineyard lie on the boundary line of Erbach and Hattenheim has given rise to a story legendary along the Rhine. For generations the two villages contested the right to claim the site as theirs. Finally, ancient records were unearthed which proved that the well was on the Erbach side of the communal boundary. Great was the rejoicing among the Erbachers. But on the fourth or fifth morning they fell silent and became very glum. During the night some wit from Hattenheim had gone to the well and scrawled in huge letters:

> So ist es recht und
> So soll es sein,
> Nach Erbach das Wasser,
> Nach Hattenheim den Wein.
>
> (All is right, all is fine,
> Now Erbach has the water,
> But Hattenheim has the wine.)

Perhaps the best Markobrunn is made by Graf von Schönborn (Graf von Schönborn-Wiesentheid'sches Rentamt), and by Frh. Langwerth von Simmern, who between them own the heart of the vineyard, which is first both in quality and quantity. Other owners of excellent parcels are Schloss Reinhartshausen, State Domain, Frh. von Oetinger, and Frh. Kryphausen.

Vineyard area: 260 hectares (650 acres) white.

Grape variety: Riesling.

Important vineyards: Markobrunn (see above); Hohenrain (mainly owned by Schloss Reinhartshausen—heavy, full-bodied wines); Siegelsberg, situated just above Markobrunn (these wines, usually quite full, are owned primarily by the State Domain and the Schloss Reicharthausen); and Steinmorgen (a good section but divided up among numerous owners).

Other vineyards: Honigberg (lies just below Kloster Eberbach and is the highest-lying site in Erbach); Michelmark (good, medium-class wines); Schlossberg; and Rheinhell.

Geisenheim

The *Weinbauort* or *Gemeinde* lying between Rüdesheim and Johannisberg is not as well known as its wines deserve. There are some famous domain holdings besides that of Graf von Schönborn—the estates of Frh. von Zwierlein Erben, of Erbslöh'sches Weingut, of Staatl. Lehr- und Forschungsanstalt, and some smaller growers, such as Philipp Graf and A. Vollmer. It is these estates which by concerted promotion have made the vineyard names now famous throughout the Rheingau. The castle of one of the most important wine growers, Graf von Schönborn, stands in the town and has a considerable historical importance of its own. Inside it, in 1648, an ancestor of the present count drafted the treaty which ended the Thirty Years' War. Opening out of a small back street in the town are the spacious grounds of the Geisenheim Viticultural School, founded in 1872 and the highest-ranking viticultural and vinicultural institute in Germany. In the ugly red brick buildings in the parklike grounds, in the greenhouses, vineyards, experimental nur-

series, laboratories, and classrooms, techniques have been worked out which fundamentally influence vine-growing and wine-making in Germany. The Rheingau growers send in samples for study, analysis, and suggestions as to how to improve the vines; and the school adjudicates court trials based on wine fraud. Students must have had four years of practical experience before they can enter the school. One of the post-war Geisenheim projects was the attempt to stamp out fraudulent sugaring of wine, now further controlled by the new law but always the main problem in northern vineyards. Radioactive sugar was put into wine and then traced with a Geiger counter. By this method it was possible to see how the added sugar acts in contrast to the natural sugar—which ferments first, which remains longer, and so on.

Vineyard area: 400 hectares (1,000 acres), of which less than half is presently planted.

Grape varieties: Riesling, Sylvaner, and Müller-Thurgau.

Important vineyards: Kilzberg, Klaus, and Klauserweg.

Other vineyards: Schlossgarten, Fuchsberg, Münchspferd, and Mauerschen.

Hallgarten

Some important wines and many small wines. The plantations are high-lying, just opposite the great Steinberg vineyard. At the time of the Boer War three cooperative associations were formed. The most flourishing was nicknamed "The English"; the poorer group called itself "The Boers." Later on a third was added, with the name of "The Germans"; and finally, a fourth cooperative, "The Boxers," was installed at the time of the Boxer Rebellion. Two cooperatives remain today: Die Engländer ("The English") and the Winzergenossenschaft (simply "winegrowers' cooperative"), which incorporated "The English" and "The Boers" in 1970. The names of the two present cooperatives may well appear on wine labels, since in effect each group is an *Abfüller* (bottler) as well as producer. The best and largest growers are Fürst von Löwenstein and Karl Franz Engelmann. The famous vineyard of Deutelsberg has been absorbed into another *Einzellage* and the name given to the *Grosslage* which includes the neighboring village of Hattenheim.

Vineyard area: 200 hectares (500 acres) white.

Grape varieties: Riesling and Müller-Thurgau.

Important vineyards: Schönhell (in big years this is among the best in the Rheingau) and Hendelberg (full-bodied wine, very sweet in great vintages).

Other vineyards: Jungfer and Würzgarten.

Hattenheim

The home of great wines—Steinberger, Hattenheimer Nussbrunnen, Hattenheimer Wisselbrunnen, and Hattenheimer Mannberg, owned mainly by Frh. Langwerth von Simmern and in part by the State Domain. The wines are very similar to the Markobrunner. The twisted gothic village lies a little back from the Rhine, with the vineyards above. In the old-world *Weinstuben* or on a hotel terrace on a sparkling day, the wonderful wines taste better than they do anywhere else. The biggest of them are typically great Rheingaus.

Vineyard area: 190 hectares (475 acres), not including the Steinberg property, for white wine.

Grape varieties: Riesling and Müller-Thurgau.

Kloster Eberbach and Steinberg

Steinberg, a few miles out of Hattenheim, is associated with that town but does not bear its name. Steinberger is among the best Rheingau wines, in a great year. The variation in quality from year to year is enormous, and the high prices vary accordingly. The wine has become so sought-after that it is no longer sold at auction by *Halb-stück* (equivalent to 68 cases), but by bottle. The 1969 Steinberger Riesling Kabinett brought DM 3.70 (about $1.50 per bottle without taxes) while the great 1971 Kabinett fetched nearly DM 7.00 (almost $3.00 a bottle). The Riesling Trockenbeerenauslese from that same year has been sold to the local Rheingau wine firms at prices ranging between DM 94 and 250 for each bottle (roughly $37 to $98).

The vineyard, a long narrow strip extending up a steepish rise, lies 60 or 70 yards west of Kloster Eberbach, where all Steinberger is vintaged and stored (there is no Kloster Eberbach wine as such). The monastery, nearly a thousand years old, was first established by Augustinian monks; with the changeover to the Cistercians, the first of this order in Germany, the real success began. By 1135 they were planting vines in the tract which is today the Steinberg. With their motto "By Cross and Plough," with the aim of opening up areas to farming and viticulture, and with their knowledge of wine from Burgundy, it is not surprising that they cut away the forest, put in vines, and prospered. By the thirteenth century, their wine fleets were sailing the Rhine to Cologne, and in its greatest day Kloster Eberbach held 10,000 hectares (25,000 acres) in the Rheingau and Rheinhessen. Today, the vast church built between 1150 and 1200 is a huge empty shell, the rows of medieval screw wine presses gather dust, and interest has shifted to the ultramodern wine-making plant, one of the finest in Germany. (The fourteen giant wooden wine presses of the fourteenth, sixteenth, seventeenth, and eighteenth centuries, in the chamber of the Lay Brothers, were in use until 1925.) At different times a lunatic asylum, a prison, and (during the First World War) a military hospital, Kloster Eberbach is now state-owned, making not only Steinberger but also State Domain wines such as Erbacher, Markobrunn and the State Domain Hattenheimers. The Steinberg vineyard itself is completely state-owned. In 1803 the property was secularized by Napoleon; in 1806 it fell into the hands of the Duke of Nassau; in 1866 it was taken over by the Prussian State, and in 1945 by the Hessian State. The private cellar of the Duke of Nassau may still be seen. It was this special "Kabinett" of his that originated the term Kabinettwein.

Vineyard area: The total area of the Steinberg vineyard is 28 hectares (70 acres). It produces about 20,000 to 22,000 cases in an average year, of which 25% is sold direct and 75% auctioned, always at Kloster Eberbach.

Grape variety: Riesling.

Vineyards: Steinberg (see above); Mannberg (owned by Langwerth von Simmern); Nussbrunnen (a typically great Rheingau); Wisselbrunnen (another great wine); Engelmannsberg (big, powerful, masculine wines, mostly owned by the State Domain); Hassel (rather soft compared to its neighbors); Pfaffenberg (excellent and extremely dry): Schützenhaus (among the better Hattenheimers, *spritzig* or fresh, medium-bodied); and Heiligenberg (good, medium quality).

Hochheim

The wines are fruity, mellow, well balanced, with a characteristic taste derived from the soil that varies almost from parcel to parcel. In some of the vineyards there is an unmistakable smoky characteristic reminiscent of certain Mosels. While the Hochheim wines, situated eastward on the Main and not on the Rhine, share something with the Rheingaus, Rheinhessen, and Franconian wines, they are invariably classed with the Rheingaus. The name Hock, from Hochheim, has become the English name for all Rheingau and often all Rhine wines. Hochheim wines often succeed in poor years, since the grapes ripen one or two weeks earlier than in other parts of the Rheingau. The State Domain, Aschrott, Michel, Schönborn, and Werner are the largest growers and have the best parcels.

Vineyard area: 190 hectares (475 acres) white.

Grape variety: Riesling.

Important vineyards: Domdechaney (best vineyard—fruity, strong, full-bodied wines); Kirchenstück (lighter than Domdechaney, elegant); Stein; Hölle; and Viktoriaberg (a light and elegant wine from pure sand soil, named after Queen Victoria, whose favorite it was).

Other vineyards: Berg and Reichesthal (part of each is in the neighboring town of Kostheim); Herrnberg (part in Flörsheim); Hofmeister; Sommerheil; and Stielweg.

Johannisberg

The town is outstripped by the name of its great vineyard, Schloss Johannisberg. To the village of that name belong 190 hectares (475 acres) of the big vineyard—and Schloss Johannisberg itself owns 35 hectares (87 acres).

Schloss Johannisberg. Some Rheingau brokers and growers considered it to be consistently one of the best of the Rheingaus, even if its greatness did not justify its high price, highest in the Rheingau and often twice that of wines which almost equal it. Today, however, many German buyers feel that the neighboring vineyards are producing better wines. The huge block-form Schloss up on the hilltop above the countless rows of symmetrical vines is unquestionably the most imposing sight on the right bank of the Rhine. Originally called the Mons Episcopi, the hill was given to the Benedictine monks by the Archbishop of Mainz at the end of the eleventh century. The Benedictines built a monastery dedicated to John the Baptist, and the hill has ever since been called Johannisberg.

After the secularization decreed by Napoleon in 1803, the vineyard was in turn the property of the Prince of Orange, of Napoleon, and the Emperor of Austria—who gave it to Metternich in 1816 for services rendered at the

Congress of Vienna, and with the Metternich family it remains today. The castle was partially destroyed by bombs during the Second World War, but it has now been rebuilt.

Estate-bottled (*Erzeugerabfüllung*) Schloss Johannisberg *Qualitätswein* is sold with a yellow-seal label. The *Qualitätsweine mit Prädikat* (quality wines with special attributes) are classed and rated as follows: red seal, average-quality Kabinett; orange seal for better Kabinettweine; green seal, average Spätlese wines; white seal for high grade Spätlesen; pink seal, Auslese; sky-blue seal, better quality Auslese wine; gold seal for Beeren- and Trockenbeerenauslesen. In lesser years there will be none of the higher grades; therefore, sky-blue-seal Auslesen and gold-seal Beerenauslesen, for example, do not exist for every vintage. Sparkling wine is made in certain years from the lighter and less good Riesling wines; it is sold under the name Fürst von Metternich Prädikats-Sekt.

Important vineyards: Schloss Johannisberg (see above), Goldatzel, Hölle, and Vogelsang.

Other vineyards: Hansenberg, Mittelhölle, and Schwarzenstein.

Kiedrich

The vineyards lie high up at the foot of the Taunus Mountains behind Erbach. Some of the wines have undoubted distinction and character. Dr. R. Weil has the largest holdings in Kiedrich. The name Heiligenstock (which used to be that of a fair-quality Kiedrich vineyard) is now given to the *Grosslage* that includes the local properties listed below and part of the Sandgrub vineyard in Eltville. Heiligenstock will thus appear on bottles containing at least 85% wine from any combination of these vineyards. The other 15% of the wine must come from within the Bereich Johannisberg.

Vineyard area: 170 hectares (425 acres) white.

Grape varieties: Riesling and Sylvaner.

Important vineyards: Gräfenberg, in good years unquestionably one of the best Rheingaus; Sandgrub (or Sandgrube), a vineyard partly in Eltville, but the Kiedrich portion is the better; and Wasserrose (or Wasserros).

Other vineyard: Klosterberg.

Lorch

Not one of the largest quantity producers of the Rheingau, it only in the best years comes up to average quality. A characteristic *Bodenton* or *goût de terroir* is much-liked by some people, however. Count Kanitz has the largest holdings and produces by far the best wines.

Vineyard area: 187 hectares (467 acres) white.

Grape varieties: Riesling and Müller-Thurgau.

Vineyards: Bodenthal-Steinberg (best and largest); Kapellenberg; Krone; Pfaffenweis; and Schlossberg.

Martinsthal

Until forty years ago this was called Neudorf. The wines are rarely, if ever, exported.

Vineyard area: 78 hectares (195 acres) white.

Grape varieties: Riesling and Müller-Thurgau.

Vineyards: Langenberg, Rödchen, and Wildsau.

Mittelheim

Average-quality wines, adjoins Johannisberg on the east. The vineyards are divided among the *Grosslagen* of Erntebringer, Mehrhölzchen, and Honigberg.

Vineyard area: 167 hectares (417 acres) white.

Grape varieties: Riesling and Müller-Thurgau.

Vineyards: Edelmann (best), Goldberg, and St. Nikolaus.

Östrich

The wines here and in adjoining Mittelheim are disappointing in comparison with their great neighbors. The town may make more wine than any other in the Rheingau.

Vineyard area: 400 hectares (1,000 acres) white.

Grape varieties: Riesling, Sylvaner, and Müller-Thurgau.

Vineyards: Doosberg (has a fair name in Germany), Lenchen, and Klosterberg.

Rauenthal

With the exception of Schloss Johannisberg, these wines are the most expensive of the Rheingau; and, with Johannisberg, Steinberg, and the best parts of Hattenheim and Erbach, they are, in good years, some of the greatest. Generally throughout the Rheingau the best lands are held by the big wine estates; they have the best viticultural methods and go to the most pains, and they make the finest wines. It is a special characteristic of Rauenthal that even the small growers produce excellent wines. The largest holder is the State Domain (28 hectares—70 acres), followed by Frh. Langwerth von Simmern with 3 hectares (7 acres). On an average, the Rauenthal vineyards produce about one-third less wine per acre than is grown in other districts—but they gain in quality what they lose in quantity. The greatest section has always been the Rauenthalerberg, a slope under cultivation for seven hundred years; but wines may not now be sold under that name, although Rothenberg and Gehrn are well situated on this hill.

Vineyard area: 100 hectares (250 acres) white.

Grape variety: Riesling.

Important vineyards: Baiken, Gehrn, Rothenberg, and Langenstück.

Other vineyards: Wülfen and Nonnenberg.

Rüdesheim

The situation of the Rüdesheimer vines on the steep slopes rising from the Rhine makes the wines quite dependable in all but the worst years and inclined to be below the general high level in the best years. The slopes have maximum sun exposure, and the benefit of reflected rays from the river; the grapes are therefore riper than elsewhere in cool summers. On the other hand, the sun burns the slopes, which drain very quickly, and in a hot summer the wines will be lacking in fragrance and roundness. While Rüdesheim is a well-known Rhine wine town in Germany, it is less famous there than abroad, where it shares with Nierstein in the Rheinhessen the honor of being the most celebrated of all. It is a great haunt of tourists cruising along the Rhine; and the concentration of shippers in the town once meant that many a non-Rüdesheim wine carried "Rüdesheim" on the shipper's label. No other vineyards in Germany suffered so badly from the war; two hundred bomb craters were blasted in the 18-hectare (45-acre) area of the State Domain alone. A peculiarity of Rüdesheim viticulture is that a little Orleans vine, the variety brought originally to the Rheingau in the time of Charlemagne, can still be found there. Even on the well-exposed slopes of Rüdesheim, it is only in the best years that the variety ripens enough to give good wine. What is perhaps the world's best collection of drinking vessels is housed in a half-ruined castle called the Brömserburg, or Niederburg, the oldest castle of the whole Rhine area, dating in parts from the ninth, tenth, and twelfth centuries. You may see implements used in Rheingau viniculture at the time of Christ, tiny clay cups of the Stone Age and all their descendants, as the typical high-stemmed German drinking glasses evolve before your eyes. The evolution of the German bottle is also shown, reaching its present form about 1790.

Vineyard area: 320 hectares (800 acres) white.

Grape variety: Riesling.

Important vineyards: The *Einzellagen* on the Rüdesheimerberg are best—Berg Rottland, Berg Roseneck, Berg Schlossberg, Bischofsberg, and Klosterberg.

Other vineyards: Drachenstein, Kirchenpfad, Klosterlay, Magdalenenkreuz, and Rosengarten.

Winkel

The town on the bank of the Rhine, with its several excellent vineyards and the Grey House, said there to be the oldest house in Germany, cannot compete in interest with the famous estate lying within its boundaries, a five-minute drive up the vineyard slopes—the renowned Schloss Vollrads.

Schloss Vollrads. The actual castle, a five-story tower, stands out of a green sea of vineyards across the courtyard from the wine sheds. It is almost as inaccessible as it was until 1920, when the drawbridge was still in use. Today you may walk across a permanent bridge to the base of the tower and watch the swans in the moat; and if you are lucky you can go farther. Graf Matuschka-Greiffenclau keeps in the castle the private museum of the family, which has been arranged in the library of the ancient tower. It is not always possible to penetrate to the tower, but there is a good deal to be seen in the wine sheds and in the large house, built in the seventeenth century and partly rebuilt in 1908; and you may taste the superb wines too. The estate at Schloss Vollrads is one of the only unified tracts on the Rhine, where the vineyards tend to be so much parceled out. The Greiffenclau family has been at Vollrads since the fourteenth century and is the oldest of the wine clans of the Rhine. The late-gathered wines of Schloss Vollrads, heady and heavy with perfume, are always exquisite. The wines are entirely from the Riesling grape and the approximately 37 hectares (92 acres) where they are grown constitute one of the three

largest privately owned Rheingau vineyards. The best area, roughly a fourth of the total, is the Schlossberg-Marienberg plot.

Like Schloss Johannisberg, Schloss Vollrads distinguishes its different wines not only by name but also by a color code. The colors of the foil capsules covering the top of the bottle neck and cork vary with the quality of the wine inside the bottle. The typical *Qualitätswein* has a green capsule; slightly better quality wine has the green capsule with two gold stripes, two silver stripes for dry wines; and in special vintages, an even better wine will have a red capsule. For *Qualitätsweine mit Prädikat*, blue marks Kabinett wines; blue with two gold stripes for better quality Kabinett; pink and pink with the two stripes signify the two grades of Spätlesen; and the Auslesen wines have a white capsule, or a white capsule with the gold stripes if of a higher quality. Beerenauslesen are marked with a gold capsule, Trockenbeerenauslesen have this same gold capsule and a neckband showing the castle tower.

A sparkling wine (i.e., Sekt) is made from the lesser wine grown and sold as Schloss Vollradser.

Winkel vineyard area: 278 hectares (695 acres) white.

Grape varieties: Riesling and Sylvaner.

Important vineyards: Schloss Vollrads (see above); Hasensprung; and Jesuitengarten.

Other vineyards: Bienengarten; Dachsberg; Gutenberg; Schlossberg; and part of Klaus.

UNION OF RHEINGAU WINE-GROWERS
(one morgen = .25 hectare, or .6 acre)

Holding	Headquarters	Morgen
Verwaltung der Staatsweingüter	Eltville	456
Schloss Eltz Güterverwaltung	Eltville	148.5
Freiherrl. Langwerth v.Simmern'sches Rentamt	Eltville	140
Rentmeister Egon Mauer	Eltville	15
Weingut Oek.Rat Jak.Fischer Erben	Eltville	31
Weingut C. Belz Erben	Eltville	20.5
Weingut Richter-Boltendahl	Eltville	51
Weingut Freiherr zu Knyphausen	Erbach	55
Weingut Dr. Weil	Kiedrich	72
Robert v.Oetinger'sches Weingut	Erbach	14
Weingut Eberhard v.Oetinger	Erbach	14
Gräfl.von Schönborn'sches Rentamt	Hattenheim	163
Gemeinde-Weingut "Georg Müller Stiftung"	Hattenheim	19
Fürstl. Löwenstein-Wertheim-Rosenberg'sche Gutsverwaltung	Hallgarten	45
Weingut K.F. Engelmann	Hallgarten	16
Weingut Adam Nass	Hallgarten	16
Gutsverwaltung Geh.Rat Wegeler Erben	Östrich	120
Weingutsverwaltung Dr. Mülhens-Berna Erben	Östrich	10
Reitz'sches Weingut	Östrich	12
Graf Matuschka-Greiffenclau'sche Gutsverwaltung	Winkel	152
Weingut Jakob Hamm	Winkel	18
A.v. Brentano'sche Gutsverwaltung	Winkel	29
Geromont'sche Gutsverwaltung	Winkel	16

UNION OF RHEINGAU WINE-GROWERS
(one morgen = .25 hectare, or .6 acre)

Holding	Headquarters	Morgen
Fürst v.Metternich	Johannisberg	125
Landgräfl.Hess. Weingut	Johannisberg	104
Weingut Freiherr v.Zwierlein	Geisenheim	40
Erbslöh'sches Weingut	Geisenheim	27
Freiherr v.Ritter zu Groenesteyn	Kiedrich	120
Gräfl.v.Kanitz'sche Weingut	Lorch	60
Domdechant Werner'sches Weingut	Hochheim	52
Geh.Rat Aschrott'sche Gutsverwaltung	Hochheim	48
Weingut Dr. H. Nägler	Rüdesheim	23
August Eser	Mittelheim	35
H. Hupfeld Erben	Mittelheim	16
Adm. Schloss Reinhartshausen	Erbach	247
		2,580

Rheinhessen

German white and red wines.

Rheinhessen provides soft wines without pronounced character, the most obvious and easy to know of all German growths. Owing probably to their intense bouquet and their straightforwardness and sweetness, the best of them have always been popular abroad. They are not wines to lay down, for they improve very little in bottle and tend to fade after eight or ten years. With the exception of the tiny quantity of specially selected Auslese and Trockenbeerenauslese, a Rheinhessen over ten years of age will seldom be interesting.

The German province of Rheinhessen, which gives its name to the wines (all produced inside the province are Rheinhessens and none grown outside may claim the name), is the Hesse which provided the Hanoverian kings of England with their Hessian troops of mercenaries, and lies in the middle of the German wine country where the Rhine bends sharply at Mainz, and washes it on two sides. Westward, the region is bounded by the River Nahe; on the south, the border with the Palatinate is a purely arbitrary political division, the two areas flowing into each other without any perceptible change.

Going up the Rhine, however, through Rheinhessen and into the Palatinate, there is a visible difference. The Palatinate is more romantic, more open, and the timbered houses have an old-fashioned look. In the heart of Rheinhessen, at Nierstein and Oppenheim, the strangled grimy streets with their rows of brick houses might be in Pittsburgh or Newcastle. It is surprising that people who can build such towns and live in them should also make the lovely Niersteiner and Oppenheimer wines.

There is a saying in Rheinhessen: "If you are not a wine grower, then you're not a Rheinhessen man." For a thousand years wine has been produced in the district, and today 154 of the 157 towns have vineyards. Most are tiny. Except around Nierstein, Oppenheim, and Bingen, the choicest areas, there are no large holdings, and 80% of Rheinhessen growers have no more than a hectare (2.5-acre) plot each. They live partly by wine and partly by other farm pursuits—which is a fundamental strength of the Rheinhessen economy, enabling the district to offset bad vintage years. Making up for the weakness inevitable in vineyards cut up into such small parcels are the newly consolidated cooperatives. These large organizations have helped to create larger individual holdings, to increase plantings of successful hybrid vines, and to make the presently aromatic, penetratingly perfumed Rheinhessen wines popular throughout Germany and in countries abroad. Much of the expansion and improvement has come in the central sections, away from the traditional Rhine front. On the way upriver from Oppenheim toward Worms, each of the little villages in between the expanses of gently rolling vineyard has its clean new-looking cooperative.

The important wine centers stand at either side of the bent arm of the Rhine, at Bingen, Oppenheim, and Nierstein. Most of the best vineyards lie on what is called the Rhine front, a strip going back a mile or two from the river edge. The center of the inland area is the town of Alzey, focus of a district bearing the same name. The Alzey wines are good, clean-tasting, common wines, but they are seldom, if ever, exported. The 22,500 hectares (56,250 acres) of vineyard in the Rheinhessen *bestimmten Anbaugebiet*—quality wine producing area—are divided into three sub-regions or *Bereiche*: Bingen, Nierstein, and Wonnegau. Each is roughly the same size. Bereich Bingen is in the northwest third of the district and includes the town of Bingen opposite Rüdesheim in the Rheingau, Ingelheim, Gau-Algesheim, Sprendlingen, Pfaffen-Schwabenheim, Wörrstadt, Gau-Bickelheim, and Wollstein. Bereich Nierstein covers the northeast section from Mainz down the Rhine to Mettenheim and takes in Nackenheim, Nierstein, and Oppenheim. Bereich Wonnegau is the southern third of the Rheinhessen and includes Worms, Osthofen, Pfeddersheim, Dalsheim, and Alzey. The average annual production is large—2.5 million hectoliters (66,250,000 U.S. gallons, 55,000,000 imp.), of which 92% is white wine and the rest red. Most of the red is made around Ingelheim.

Soil, vine, weather, and man always combine to create the qualities of a wine. The climate in Rheinhessen is mild and dry, with a good deal of sunshine, and comparative freedom from the killing spring and autumn frosts which terrorize the neighboring growers, especially on the Mosel. The rule of nature being what it is, the wines lack the character they would develop in a more precarious climate where the vines would have to fight for their lives; instead, they reflect the comparative softness of Rheinhessen weather. Much of the wine comes from the Sylvaner grape variety, and this fortifies the tendency to a rich mildness which may find its highest expression in roundness and "full-mouthedness" (as they say in Rheinhessen) but never in "steel" (another excellent Rheinhessen expression) and distinction. The 6% of Rheinhessen wine from the Riesling grape, usually found on the south faces of hillside vineyards, provides the small quantity possessing *race* and steel. About 40% of the district is planted in Sylvaners. There is now about as much Müller-Thurgau as Sylvaner; and a trace of Gewürztraminer—a variety which used to be widespread but has died out and is being re-established here and there around Bingen and below Oppenheim. Red wines are

RHEINHESSEN

0   5   10 MILES

0   5   10 KILOMETRES

made from the Burgunder, Portugieser, and St. Laurent plants, the well-known reds from Ingelheim coming from the first two varieties.

The Rheinhessen soil, composed of chalk, marl, and quartz (often a chalk decking, with marl beneath), varies considerably. The facings along the Rhine around Bingen are slate, like the slate of the Mosel, while from Nackenheim to Nierstein, and a little farther on, a peculiar red sandstone is found, a deposit from the Ice Age. Its water-shedding property accounts for the fact that Niersteiners, Nackenheimers, and Schwabsburgers are likely to suffer less than most vines in very wet years.

THE IMPORTANT RHEINHESSEN VINEYARDS

The following are the most important Rheinhessen wines, including all that are to be found in England and the United States. The Rheinhessen quality-wine label identifies the wine by town or village (*Weinbauort*) and vineyard (*Lage*). As an example, wine of the Daubhaus vineyard in the township of Oppenheim is Oppenheimer Daubhaus. The town or village name as listed below, placed before the name of the vineyard, and with *-er* added, will always give the name of the wine as it appears on the label—except for the wines of Bingen, which are not Bingener but Binger wines.

Blended *Grosslagen* wines will have the name of the *Bereich* and the name of the *Grosslage*—the section of vineyards from which 85% of the wine must come. The other 15% must have been produced anywhere in the same *Bereich*. Liebfraumilch—though now by law the designation of a "quality" Rheinhessen wine, and not an umbrella-like term for nearly any light German wine—can come from anywhere in the vast district; it must bear a control number certifying its "authenticity" but in any case is still some of the least-distinguished Rheinhessen wine, and as such some of the most mediocre German wine found abroad.

For a complete list of the individual vineyard names (*Einzellagen*) arranged by town (*Weinbauort*), section of vineyards (*Grosslage*) and sub-region (*Bereich*), see Appendix B, p. 617.

The names of growers, running into many hundreds, cannot be listed here. In the better wines, however, the grower's name or name of the wine estate appears on the label, indicated by *Weingut* or a similar term. An attempt has been made to list some of the best growers, but the list is not exhaustive.

Grape varieties indicate the type of the wines. White: Sylvaner (soft), Riesling (more character), Müller-Thurgau (Riesling × Sylvaner), Gewürztraminer (spicy). Red: Burgunder (red aromatic). A bottle of white Rheinhessen wine without indication of the grape variety will almost certainly be Müller-Thurgau.

Alsheim

Situated on a low ridge of hills just over a kilometer from the Rhine, halfway between Worms and Oppenheim. The largest producer in its area, and among the four or so largest in the entire Rheinhessen. Much Riesling wine.

Vineyard area: white—342 hectares (845 acres); red—30 hectares (75 acres).

Grape varieties: Riesling, Sylvaner, Müller-Thurgau, Gewürztraminer, Portugieser, and St. Laurent.

Vineyards: Fischerpfad, Römerberg, Sonnenberg, Frühmesse, and Goldberg.

Bechtheim

Slope wines, 3 kilometers (just over 2 miles) back from low, vineless, flat land bulging into the Rhine.

Vineyard area: white—300 hectares (750 acres); red—24 hectares (60 acres).

Grape varieties: Riesling, Sylvaner, and Portugieser.

Vineyards: Geyersberg, Rosengarten, and Stein.

Wine estates: Dr. Blum'sches Weingut, Ferdinand Koehler, and Weingut Wilhelm Schoeneck.

Bingen

Lying directly across the Rhine from Rüdesheim and the Rheingau, at the point where the Nahe flows into the Rhine, Bingen sprawls up a mountain famous since Roman times for its vineyards. Bingen-Kempten, on the town's outskirts, and Bingen-Büdesheim, behind it, where rolling hills fringe the Nahe, form a unit with Bingen and can be considered as such. The connection with Rüdesheim is a ferry which whirls like a feather in the powerful current when it docks at either bank. Steep, tangled Bingen qualifies for its name Wine Town, Rhine Town: surviving the plague, the Thirty Years' War, and other disasters, it had provided its six thousand citizens with 130 wine bars and 120 wine merchants by the end of the last century. Population has tripled today, and the fun goes on. When a past bishop of Mainz, addressing the Bingen clergy, asked to borrow a pencil, everyone reached under his cassock and brought out a corkscrew, which was then dubbed the "Bingen pencil," a name which has stuck. Distinctly Rheinhessen wines, though separated from the Rheingaus only by the width of the river, Bingen wines derive a liveliness from the slate soil. Those grown right along the Rhine front sometimes have a smoky taste, once said to come from the smoke of the busy railway and the river boats, but with the use of electricity and diesel fuel, it is apparent that this quality comes from the soil.

Vineyard area: white—364 hectares (910 acres); red—60 hectares (150 acres).

Grape varieties: Riesling, Sylvaner, and Müller-Thurgau.

Vineyards: Bubenstück, Kapellenberg, Kirchberg, Osterberg, Pfarrgarten, Rosengarten, Schlemenstück, Schlossberg Schwätzerchen, Schwarzerberg, and Scharlachberg.

Wine estates: Villa Sachsen and Jung auf Junghof.

Bodenheim

Monastery holdings of the Middle Ages produce spicy, full wines with much bouquet, but they never reach the peaks attained by the Niersteiners and Oppenheimers a few kilometers to the south.

Vineyard area: white—200 hectares (500 acres); red—87 hectares (210 acres).

Grape varieties: Riesling, Sylvaner, Müller-Thurgau, and Portugieser.

Vineyards: Ebersberg, Burgberg, Hoch, Leidhecke, Silberberg, Westrum, Heiterbrünnchen, Kapelle, Kreuzberg, Mönchspfad, and Reichritterstift.

Wine estates: Peter Kerz III, Oberstleutnant Liebrecht'sche Weingutsverwaltung, and Anton Riffel.

Dalheim

Rather strong wines, quite clean-tasting.

Vineyard area: white—95 hectares (235 acres); red—2 hectares (5 acres).

Grape varieties: Sylvaner and Portugieser.

Vineyards: Altdörr, Kranzberg, and Steinberg.

Dalsheim (-Flörsheim)

A great deal of trouble with phylloxera caused extensive replanting with American vine-stocks at a tremendous cost. Sylvaner was always the main producer, but Müller-Thurgau has been introduced and suits the clayey soil. The wines are much improved, with many made from hybrids.

Vineyard area: white—186 hectares (460 acres); red—8 hectares (20 acres).

Grape varieties: Riesling, Sylvaner, Gewürztraminer, Müller-Thurgau, Spätburgunder, St. Laurent, and Portugieser.

Vineyards: Steig, Bürgel, Frauenberg, Hubacker, and Sauloch.

Wine estate: Dr. Becker H. Müller.

Dexheim

Since the Middle Ages, considered the equal of the Niersteiners and Oppenheimers, which it adjoins, but now it is not quite up to the peak wines of its famous neighbors.

Vineyard area: white—73 hectares (180 acres); with a trace of red.

Grape variety: Sylvaner.

Vineyard: Doktor.

Wine estates: Adolf Dahlheim, August Dahlheim, and Sander.

Dienheim

The village adjoins Oppenheim on the south, and the vineyards, on the Rhine front, produce first-quality wines.

Vineyard area: 357 hectares (875 acres) white.

Grape variety: Sylvaner.

Vineyards: Falkenberg, Herrenberg, Höhlchen, Kreuz, Siliusbrunnen, Tafelstein, Herrengarten, Paterhof, and Schloss.

Dromersheim

In a protected inner valley. One of the oldest wine areas in Rheinhessen, formerly a holding of Kloster Fulda.

Vineyard area: white—150 hectares (375 acres); red—50 hectares (125 acres).

Grape varieties: Sylvaner, Müller-Thurgau, and Portugieser.

Vineyards: Honigberg, Kapellenberg, Mainzweg, and Klosterweg.

Friesenheim

Vineyard area: 33 hectares (73 acres) white.

Grape varieties: Müller-Thurgau and Sylvaner.

Vineyards: Altdörr, Bergspfad, and Knopf.

Gau-Algesheim

On the Rhine front between Bingen and Ingelheim, facing the Rheingau. A famous New Wine Festival takes place during the second weekend in October in the historic marketplace, formerly the scene of one of the great annual wine markets in the Middle Ages.

Vineyard area: white—101 hectares (251 acres); red—51 hectares (126 acres).

Grape varieties: Sylvaner, Riesling, Portugieser, and Burgunder.

Vineyards: Rothenberg, Goldberg, Johannisberg, Steinert, and St. Laurenzikapelle.

Wine estate: Avenarius'sche Gutsverwaltung.

Gau-Bischofheim

South-facing on a hill slope just north of Nierstein.

Vineyard area: 60 hectares (150 acres) white.

Grape variety: Sylvaner.

Vineyards: Glockenberg, Herrnberg, Pfaffenweg, and Kellersberg.

Wine estate: Oberst Schultz H. Werner.

Guntersblum

Usually fruity wines. On the Rhine front; third largest producer in the Rheinhessen, with much small parceling in the shallow-slope vineyards, forming a solid stretch of vines extending about a kilometer on either side of the vineyard road.

Vineyard area: white—356 hectares (880 acres); with a trace of red.

Grape varieties: Sylvaner, Riesling, Müller-Thurgau, and Gewürztraminer.

Vineyards: Autental, Bornpfad, Himmelthal, Eiserne Hand, Steinberg, Sankt Julianenbrunnen, Kreuzkapelle, Steig-Terrassen, Sonnenberg, and Sonnenhang.

Wine estates: Emil Schätzel and Schlossgut Schmitt.

Hahnheim

South-facing slope vineyards in the center of Rheinhessen.

Vineyard area: white—97 hectares (240 acres); red—5 hectares (12 acres).

Grape varieties: Sylvaner, Riesling, Müller-Thurgau, Burgunder, Portugieser, and St. Laurent.

Vineyards: Knopf and Moosberg.

Wine estate: Walter Heinz.

Harxheim

Steep-slope wines from vineyards adjoining the Nierstein area, but not approaching the quality of the wines from the Rhine front hills at Nierstein.

Vineyard area: white—75 hectares (187 acres); red—5 hectares (12 acres).

Grape varieties: Sylvaner, Müller-Thurgau, and Portugieser.

Vineyards: Schlossberg, Lieth, and Börnchen.

Wine estates: August Böll and Peter Lotz.

Ingelheim

Here the red wines surpass the whites, the reverse of the usual order, both in Rheinhessen and in Germany generally. The white wines are good table wines but are not distinguished. The red wines from the Frühburgunder and Spätburgunder grape varieties have real quality; some experts say that the finest red growths are the best red wines of Germany and the only ones in a class with the world's great red wines. Nieder-Ingelheim, Ober-Ingelheim, Frei-Weinheim, and half a dozen other such names of small nearby communities or parts of Ingelheim are being absorbed into the single name Ingelheim, owing to its fame; and Ingelheim wines will be from anywhere in the hilly area of the medieval town overlooking the Rhine.

Vineyard area: white—214 hectares (530 acres); red—134 hectares (330 acres).

Grape varieties: Frühburgunder, Spätburgunder, Portugieser, Sylvaner, Riesling, and Müller-Thurgau.

Vineyards: Horn, Pares, and Rheinhöhe, among many others.

Wine estate: J. Neuss (reds).

Ludwigshöhe

By the time the tiny village below Oppenheim is reached, the slope has leveled to a broad plain. A good deal of Ludwigshöhe, and much wine from many of the other less well-known towns (most of which are not named here), goes in to Liebfraumilch.

Vineyard area: 57 hectares (140 acres) white.

Grape varieties: Sylvaner and Riesling.

Vineyards: Honigsberg and Teufelskopf.

Wine estates: Weingut Brüder Dr. Becker and Johann Graf.

Mettenheim

Wines grow on the edge of flat land in a wide bend of the Rhine, a little south of the excellent stretch from Bodenheim up to Guntersblum. Good average wines, without peak ones.

Vineyard area: white—108 hectares (266 acres); red—12 hectares (28 acres).

Grape variety: Sylvaner.

Vineyards: Michelsberg, Goldberg, and Schlossberg.

Wine estate: Gerhard Koch.

Nackenheim

On the red clay-and-slate soil just above Nierstein, some really first-class white wines are grown. Nackenheimers used to be used for blending, but their high quality has become recognized. In some years Nackenheim produces the lowest quantity yield per acre in Rheinhessen, always an index of high quality. The town, dominated by a baroque church, is pushed almost into the Rhine by the steep vine-covered mountain; the moderating influence of the river on the climate aids the wines. Nackenheim has the largest wine-bottle capsule factory in Europe.

Vineyard area: white—64 hectares (158 acres); red—5 hectares (12 acres).

Grape varieties: Riesling, Sylvaner, and Müller-Thurgau.

Vineyards: Engelsberg, Rothenberg (outstanding), and Schmitts-Kapelle.

Wine estates: Gunderloch-Lange and Gunderloch-Usinger.

Nierstein

The most important area, giving the best Rheinhessen wines. Everyone in Nierstein is an owner in the vineyards that have been famous for hundreds of years. Of some 550 parcels, about two dozen produce the soft, elegant, full-bodied, peak wines known around the world as Niersteiners. Look for Riesling on the label: the best Niersteiners are from the Riesling grape and are so identified. The wines have a marvelous bouquet. Nierstein derives its name from the mineral springs the Romans called Neri and from the boundary stone which once marked the division between German and Frankish territories. The town came to be called Neri am Stein, which was corrupted to Nierstein. Driving from Mainz with the Rhine on your left, you see the fairly steep *Weinberg*, solid with vine, sloping back from the road, the chief areas indicated by large white block letters spelling out HIPPING, KRANZBERG, etc. It is the largest wine *Weinbauort* on the Rhine, and much the largest in Rheinhessen.

Vineyard area: 760 hectares (1,900 acres) white.

Grape varieties: Riesling, Sylvaner. (A trace of the Orleans grape variety, once widespread in France but now vanished, is found here. It was brought to Germany in the Middle Ages from Orleans, then an important French wine zone, supposedly by Charlemagne.)

Vineyards: Best are Glöck, Heiligenbaum, Kranzberg, Ölberg, Orbel, Hipping, Pettenthal, Bildstock, Hölle, and Paterberg. Others are Bergkirche, Schloss Schwabsburg, Zehnmorgen, Pfaffenkappe, Brudersberg, Goldene Luft, Brückchen, Kirchplatte, Klostergarten, Rosenberg, and Schloss Hohenrechen.

Wine estates: Emil Förster, Frh. von Heyl zu Herrnsheim, Gustav Gessert, Weingut Louis Guntrum, Georg Harth, Fritz Hasselbach, Weingut Friedrich Kehl, Franz Karl Schmitt (widow of), Georg Schmitt'sches Weingut, Georg Albrecht Schneider, Reinhold Senfter, and Weingut Heinrich Schlamp Jr.

Ockenheim

Can be very good in years with plenty of sunshine, when quite a lot of Spätlese is made on the best south-facing slopes. The Müller-Thurgau grape variety is being used more and more, owing to the public taste for the aromatic wines produced.

Vineyard area: white—129 hectares (320 acres); red—65 hectares (160 acres).

Rheinriesling

Grape varieties: Sylvaner, Riesling, Müller-Thurgau, and Portugieser.

Vineyards: Hockenmühle, Klosterweg, Kreuz, Laberstall, St. Jakobsberg, and Schönhölle.

Wine estate: Wilhelm Merz.

Oppenheim

Generally, Oppenheimers are fuller and softer than Niersteiners, while Niersteiners have more elegance. In dry, hot years Oppenheimers are likely to surpass Niersteiners; in wet, cool years Niersteiners will be better. The Oppenheimer soil retains water, whereas the Niersteiner slope is steeper and water runs off. After two or three glasses of the splendid wine, the town may take on the virtue of its famous product. Seen coldly, it is an ugly scar of brick and dirty gray stucco along a sooty railway line. In the stark interior of St. Katherine's Church there are a few tombstones decorated with vineyard motifs from the fifteenth and sixteenth centuries.

Vineyard area: 287 hectares (710 acres) white.

Grape varieties: Sylvaner, Riesling, and Müller-Thurgau.

Vineyards: Daubhaus, Herrengarten, Paterhof, Herrenberg, Kreuz, Sackträger, Schlossberg, Zuckerberg, Schloss, Schützenhütte, and Gutleuthaus.

Wine estates: Friedrick Baumann, Adam Becker, Franz Josef Gallois, Louis Guntrum, J. A. Harth & Co., Ernst Jungkenn, Karl Koch (Erben), Franz Josef Senfter, Carl Sittmann, Weingut der Stadt Oppenheim, and Dr. L. Winter.

Osthofen

Vineyard area: white—234 hectares (580 acres); red—12 hectares (30 acres).

Grape varieties: Müller-Thurgau, Riesling, and Sylvaner.

Vineyards: Goldberg, Hasenbiss, Kirchberg, Klosterberg, Rheinberg, Neuberg, Leckzapfen, and Liebenberg.

Schwabsburg

With its windowless tower and castle built by Frederick Barbarossa, Schwabsburg is a pretty village and vineyard lying in a little valley a mile west of Nierstein. The vineyards have south and southwest exposure, and they share the reddish slate-and-clay soil of the usually greater vineyards on the Rhine front. Schwabsburg vineyards have become part of the *Weinbauort* Nierstein.

Selzen

Vineyard area: 90 hectares (222 acres) white.

Grape variety: Sylvaner.

Vineyards: Osterberg, Gottesgarten, and Rheinpforte.

Wine estate: Weingut Schätzel (Erben).

Ülversheim

Wines usually strong and full-bodied, grown almost entirely on the south face of the Rhine front.

Vineyard area: 95 hectares (235 acres) white.

Grape varieties: Sylvaner, Müller-Thurgau, and Riesling.

Vineyard: Schloss Aulenberg.

Westhofen

Vineyard area: 364 hectares (900 acres), nearly all white.

Grape varieties: Sylvaner, Riesling, Müller-Thurgau, Gewürztraminer, Portugieser, and St. Laurent.

Vineyards: Brunnenhäuschen, Kirchspiel, Benn, Aulerde, Morstein, Rotenstein, and Steingrube.

Worms

An occasional tiny vineyard may be found right in among the ancient buildings and war ruins of the city—one (a Valckenberg property) is in the shadow of the cathedral where Martin Luther was condemned as a heretic in 1521, but nothing in Worms is of real viticultural importance, except the Liebfrauenstift, one of the twenty *Einzellagen* in the large *Weinbauort*.

LIEBFRAUMILCH AND THE LIEBFRAUENSTIFT

On April 29, 1910, a fatal day in German wine history, the Chamber of Commerce of Worms ruled that the name Liebfraumilch could be used by any Rheinhessen wine of good quality. It was like staking out a tired old horse in the public park and saying that any child of good quality could mount it. Liebfraumilch today is allowed the name *Qualitätswein*—quality wine—and as such may come from anywhere in its area of origin, either the Rheinhessen, the Rheingau, or the Palatinate. The bottle will even carry a certification number awarded by a panel of local judges, but the wine inside is never anything more than a shipper's blend of innocuous wines. It can never have been very good, for the soil of the Liebfrauenstift vineyards around the tall, bleak church on the outskirts of Worms is flat river-deposit earth which gives a special taste to the wines. Nevertheless, arising in the sixteenth and seventeenth centuries, before vineyard placenames had come into being, the name Liebfraumilch gradually became world-famous. The production of the original vineyards around the Liebfrauenkirche, never more than 2,000 cases in the best years, was entirely inadequate for the demand, and the name spread over other wines. Most of the parcels behind 10-foot brick walls on all sides of the church are owned by the Valckenberg and the J. Langenbach estates, though small holdings are in the hands of Eberhard, W. Mahler, and E. Rieth.

Rheinriesling

Variety of Riesling cultivated in Austria.

Rhenish

English term formerly used for Rhine wines and extended to all German wines. It has dropped out of currency in favor of Hock.

Rhine wines

General name for wines grown along the River Rhine. *See* Rheingau; Rheinhessen; Mittelrhine; Palatinate.

Rhône (Côtes du Rhône)

Red, white, and rosé wines.
District: Southern France.

The Rhône is a river of wine; it drains vineyards on its broad delta plain, along the steep cliffs above Avignon, in the Cévennes and Jura mountains, and around the lake of Geneva. Yet the only wines to bear the name are those which come from the central section—the Côtes du Rhône.

Lyon, with its great gastronomic tradition, stands at the head of the Rhône Valley; east of the river is the land of the fat Bresse chickens; to the west, Périgord, rich in truffles and *foie gras;* from the south come the plentiful fruit and fish of the valley—and the great restaurants excel in *poulet en vessie,* in *quenelles Nantua,* and all the rest of the famous regional dishes and *charcuteries.* The inhabitants eat heartily and wash down their meals with the robust Rhône wine—and with Beaujolais.

The vineyards of the Côtes du Rhône extend for 220 kilometers (140 miles) from Lyon to Avignon, stretching precariously over sheer, high cliffs on both sides of the sun-baked river. Their touchstone is granite—the soil's dominant element. Drawing their character from the steep, sun-drenched granite cliffs they come from, the wines are not subtle; they are big, rough, and heady, with a strong, almost pungent perfume, and they are tamed only by long imprisonment in the bottle. They compare seldom in quality, never in quantity, with the greatest clarets and Burgundies; but at their best they can be superb. Yet it has been the fate of these distinctive wines often to be classed as Burgundies—a practice which does justice to neither region. The reason perhaps was the proximity of the upper Rhône vineyards to those of southern Burgundy; or the sturdy Burgundy bottle in which Rhône wines also are sold.

Except for Tavel, Châteauneuf-du-Pape, and Hermitage, Rhône wines have not hitherto been well known. The situation has changed, however. As a result of the efforts of the Baron LeRoy du Boiseaumarié the wines are often seen outside their own region. The Baron, one of the few men to have a statue erected to him during his own lifetime, was himself a grower in Châteauneuf-du-Pape and was president of the International Wine Office; he held the rank of Commandeur of the Légion d'Honneur and headed the syndicate of growers of the Côtes du Rhône. Baron LeRoy was instrumental in formulating and obtaining the controls that brought honest wines back into Châteauneuf-du-Pape, which had been fraud-ridden, and he later extended his activities to embrace first all Rhône wines, then all of France.

The area over which the Côtes du Rhône extend is long and narrow, and the wines produced there show considerable variation. Some sections of the Côtes are more advanced than are others and are apt, therefore, to produce better wines. Overall quality has risen enormously in recent years, but it is uneven; many growers still need help, especially those in the lesser-known districts. The entire region produces more than 1.5 million hectoliters (39.7 million U.S. gallons, 33 million imp.) of wine annually, some under the name Côtes du Rhône, some—superior in both quantity and quality—under more specific headings.

The better wines include:

AVERAGE PRODUCTION

Crus	Hectoliters	U.S. Gallons	Imperial Gallons	Wines
Châteauneuf-du-Pape	100,000	2,650,000	2,200,000	red, white, rosé
Condrieu	400	10,560	8,790	white
Cornas	2,600	68,900	57,200	red, white, rosé
Côte Rôtie	2,500	66,250	55,000	red, rosé
Crozes-Hermitage	22,000	583,000	484,000	red, white, rosé
Gigondas	35,000	927,500	770,000	red, rosé
Château-Grillet	65	1,723	1,430	white
Hermitage	5,000	132,500	110,000	red, white, rosé
Lirac	20,000	530,000	440,000	red, white, rosé
Saint-Péray	2,000	53,000	44,000	white
Saint-Joseph	4,000	106,000	88,000	red, white, rosé
Tavel	30,000	795,000	660,000	red, rosé
	223,565	5,924,433	4,918,420	

The region's lesser wines are sold either as Côtes du Rhône or with that name followed by some addition. While it is generally true in French wines that the more specific name denotes the better growth, this is not strictly so along the Rhône. When the general name is followed by that of one of the better communes—Vinsobres, Visan, Vacqueyas, Cairanne, or the white wine village Laudun—the wines will have met higher than normal standards and are often delightful. If, on the other hand, the general name is followed by the name of a department—Ardèche, Drôme, Loire, Rhône—the standards are more relaxed and the wines may be inferior. One important consideration in this question of standards is the minimum required alcoholic content—always stipulated for fine French wines. Although alcoholic content is always a question of importance, it is vital to Rhône wines. Alcohol adds body and strength, two characteristics that are closely identified with these wines. If the label says simply Côtes du Rhône, the wine must have at least 10.5% alcohol by volume. If this name is followed by the name of a department (Côtes du Rhône—Drôme, for example), only 9.5% is required, sapping the wine of some of its robust strength. Those wines that come from the communes mentioned above have alcoholic contents ranging from a minimum 12% to 12.5%. Just as Beaujolais produces Beaujolais Villages, the Côtes du Rhône also produces a lesser known Appellation Contrôlée called Côtes du Rhône Villages, the best ones coming from Cairanne, Vinsobre, Chusclan, and Sablet.

Most of the finer Côtes du Rhône wines are pressed from one kind of grape, sometimes two or three—with the exception of Châteauneuf-du-Pape, where thirteen are allowed. The principal variety is the Syrah, which gives firm, robust wines of fine color and bouquet, but is sometimes inclined to be hard. The introduction of the white Viognier imparts the qualities of softness and freshness. Other leading white-wine varieties are Roussanne which,

grown on a sunny slope, gives fine soft wines, and Marsanne, a sturdier and more productive grape planted more often than Roussanne. For the general name Côtes du Rhône, growers may include grapes from any or all of the following varieties: Grenache, Clairette, Syrah, Mourvèdre, Picpoule, Terret Noir, Counoise, Muscardin, Bourboulenc, Carignan, Ugni Blanc, Roussanne, Marsanne, and Viognier.

Rhône summers are long and consistently warm. As a result, there is not as much variation between the vintage years as elsewhere in France. There is, however, some difference. The best recent years were 1964, 1966, 1967, 1970, and 1973.

Characteristics of Rhône Wines

Châteauneuf-du-Pape. A full-bodied wine, deep in color, softer and quicker to mature than most Rhône growths. There is also a white wine, pleasant but of less importance.

Clairette de Die. A semi-sparkling white wine from the Clairette and Muscat grapes, made near the village of Die on the River Drôme.

Condrieu. White wine with a tinge of color; robust and perfumed. Both dry and semi-sweet styles are produced, and all are at their best when young and fresh. Condrieu is a favorite of the Lyonnais.

Cornas. Red wine, sometimes a bit hard to begin with, of a fine garnet color. It ages well, becoming soft and velvety in maturity but never so perfumed as Hermitage.

Côte Rôtie. These robust and heady red wines stand up well. The color is rich; there is a hint of violet in the bouquet—and, some say, of raspberry in the taste.

Crozes-Hermitage. Red wine with a rather violet tinge, not so deep in color as Hermitage, nor with so much softness. It has a faint *goût du terroir*.

Château Grillet. The white wine, which shows some resemblance to Condrieu, is robust and vigorous, with perhaps a little more finesse than the latter. Since the production is very small, this wine is not much seen outside its own district.

Hermitage. The red wine is full-bodied and vigorous, with a certain delicacy and softness in maturity, and a fragrance of iris-root in the bouquet. It ages well. The white wine has a golden tinge, is dry yet fruity, with a characteristic perfume. It will last a long time without oxidizing.

Saint-Joseph. The red wines are delicate and perfumed, with less body than the Hermitage, but of a fine ruby color. They are ready after a few years in bottle. The white wines are lighter than the white Hermitage.

Saint-Péray. White, spirited wines with body, a tinge of color, and a definite bouquet. In ageing, they sometimes maderize prematurely. Some of these wines make dry or semi-sweet *mousseux*.

Tavel. One of the best rosés of France, it comes mainly from the Grenache grape. It has a clear, pink color, without any trace of orange flaw. It is light, refreshing, and at its best when chilled.

Vaucluse and Gard. The wines, planted in a variety of soils in these two departments, are of widely varying types. In general, the terraced, gravelly, clayey vineyards are planted for rosé. Lirac and Chusclan produce pink wines which are not far behind those of Tavel. Laudun makes white as well as pink and red. Gigondas, Cairanne, and Vacqueyras wines are supple and rather high in alcohol; red, white, and rosé are made. Beaumes-de-Venise and Rasteau are dessert wines—*see under* Sweet fortified wines of France.

Ribeauvillé

Wine town in Alsace (*q.v.*).

Ricard

Very popular French licorice-flavored aperitif. Because of its strong taste and reasonably high alcoholic content, it is generally diluted with water before drinking, whereupon it turns milky and cloudy. This is a commercial pastis.

Rice wine

A Japanese fermented liquor made from rice. *See* Saké.

Riceys, Rosé de

A still, pink wine of Champagne (*q.v.*).

Richebourg

Burgundy red wine.
District: Côte de Nuits, France.
Commune: Vosne-Romanée.
Official Classification: Great Growth (Grand Cru).

Richebourg is one of the giants of its commune, partly since it is rated Great Growth (*Grand Cru*)—as high as a Burgundian vineyard can get—and partly since its 7.7 hectares or 19.8 acres (part in Richebourg, part in Les Verroilles) make it one of the largest of the great vineyards of Vosne. Only Romanée-Saint-Vivant, among the top vineyards of Vosne, is larger.

The vineyard lies well up the slope with La Romanée and La Romanée-Conti to the south of it and Romanée-Saint-Vivant just across the road and is considerably larger than its traditional size. In the 1930s, a decree of the Minister of Agriculture permitted the vineyard slightly above it on the slope, known as Verroilles or Richebourg, to be included in the controlled place-name. This made legal a practice that was actually a long-standing custom. It added, however, some 3 hectares (7.6 acres) to the *appellation* Richebourg. Unlike some of the other Great Growths of Vosne, this one is not a monopoly of any grower but is, at the time of writing, in the hands of eight different owners. Only three of these have sizable holdings: Domaine Louis Gros, Domaine de la Romanée-Conti, and Charles Noellat.

Needless to say, the fact that eight different growers make the wine means that there will be some variation between any two Richebourgs of a given year. In general

terms, however, it is the "velvet wine" of Vosne. All the commune's wines have this velvety quality, but in Richebourg it is more pronounced than in the others. Beneath this veneer is a robust fullness, and the wine acquires a superb perfume with age. The amount of wine averages about 300 hectoliters (7,950 U.S. gallons, 6,600 imp.) annually or the equivalent of some 3,500 cases.

See Vosne-Romanée.

Richon-le-Zion

One of the main wine centers in Israel (*q.v.*).

Riesling

A grape variety producing the most distinctive and noble wines of Alsace, the Mosel, and the Rhine. The fruit is small, yellowish, not very juicy; but it is one of the great grapes of the world. Alsatian Rieslings are generally sold as such and the varietal name usually, but not always, appears on the label of the great German Rhine and Mosel Rieslings. Riesling is also grown in Austria, California, Chile, and Switzerland.

Château Rieussec

Bordeaux white wine.
District: Sauternes, France.
Commune: Fargues.

After changing hands a number of times and acquiring sections which had formed adjoining small vineyards, Rieussec was consolidated in its present situation. Making a wine quite different from its neighbor, fuller-bodied but less subtle, it is contiguous with Château d'Yquem. The wine was officially classed a First Growth (*Premier Cru*) Sauternes in 1855, and the vineyard was purchased in 1971 by M. Vuiller, the owner of a large supermarket chain in southwest France.

Characteristics. Very *liquoreux* or rich in unconverted sugar, and one of the better First Growths.

Vineyard area: 46 hectares (115 acres).
Average production: 100 *tonneaux* (9,000 cases).

Río Negro

Wine-producing province of Argentina (*q.v.*).

Rioja

Red, white, and rosé wines.
District: Northern Spain.

Within the last half-century the best Riojas have established themselves as incontestably the best red table wines in Spain. Although a bottle from one of the better firms shows how outstanding the Rioja can be, equal to any red wine except the finest Bordeaux and Burgundies, and in spite of the fact that Riojas head Spanish wine lists and are fairly good value, they often tend to be only average wines. The trend among the large companies is to equalize quality; these companies dominate the market and comprise, with a few specified exceptions, the only firms allowed to produce those Rioja wines entitled to Certificates of Origin. On the other hand, the rise in overall quality can be expected to continue—although, unfortunately, the big firms actually making the wines which are exported are inclined to value age for its own sake, often keeping the wine too long in barrel and then selling it immediately after bottling; the result is that it loses much of the clarity, vigor, and freshness of wine allowed to mature in bottle. White wines, sometimes subjected to the same treatment, become flat and maderized. That the wine in the bottle may yet be younger than the vintage printed on the label may be due to this same reverence for age, to a casual disregard for exactitude, and also to the semi-*solera* system of adding, from time to time, a little very old wine from the reserve (*gran reserva*).

There are a few notable exceptions to this rule—for instance, at the *bodega* of the Marqués de Riscal at Elciego, where the wines are bottled after three years and aged in the bottle. Here, also, there have been new plantations of white grapes, and Dr. E. Peynaud, the Bordeaux oenologist, has been consulted about improved processes for making white wine. In general, however, Spaniards seem to feel that the weakened, over-oxidized, frail wines are more distinguished than the big, hard, more commonplace wines of the country. In any case, barrel-ageing is overdone, lasting sometimes as long as five or even ten years; when this practice is corrected—and there are signs that this is happening—the potentially splendid Rioja wines will come even more into their own.

The beginnings of the industry in this region along the River Ebro are obscure, and it can be assumed that the northerly climate of the region caused it to lag behind the more apparently vinous Mediterranean districts of Spain. Yet Rioja did take part, at least to some degree, in the flowering of Spanish wines during the period of the discovery of the Americas and the opening of vast markets to Spanish export. The first association of growers was founded in 1560.

A difficulty peculiar to Rioja was the lack of any good road by which the wines could be sent to the rest of Spain and to the world. For more than half a century, beginning in 1790, the achievement of this road was the goal of a wine industry which attempted to regain the splendor of the days of Spanish power.

The success story of Rioja starts with the founding, in 1892, of the viticultural station in Haro, heart of the vineyards along the Ebro; almost simultaneously the fight was begun to eliminate all outside wine from Rioja and prevent any other Spanish wines from using the name—a fight not yet completely won. Haro is now the important center, with a wine institute and college.

History has come full circle, and it is now generally recognized that Rioja owes its unique place among Spanish table wines to its geographical position. The region divides into three zones (Rioja Alta, Rioja Alavesa, and Rioja Baja) as it goes steeply downhill into the Ebro Valley, sheltered by the Sierra Cantabria. Upper Rioja—Rioja Alta—is northerly and Atlantic in type, producing the finest wines. Those of the Alava are heavier but still

good. Rioja Baja supplies mainly *vinos corrientes* (*vins ordinaires*). Figures for the wines granted Denominación de Origen were 50,000 hectares (125,000 acres) of vines producing 1 million hectoliters (26.5 million U.S. gallons, 22 million imp.) of wine, red, white, and rosé (*rosado*). It is significant that Rioja Baja produces nothing but common wines, never bottled and little exported.

DENOMINATIONS OF ORIGIN AND THE MAKING OF THE WINE

About twenty-five companies have the right to make Rioja—wine of Rioja entitled to the place-name, the Certificate of Origin, and the small, square, mill-edged stamp of authenticity on the bottle label. The number is not officially limited, but to qualify, a producer is supposed to have 400 hogsheads in his stores—this is a big investment, and the ordinary man cannot afford the price of the wood for so many barrels. The system is admittedly hit-and-miss, not devised to keep anyone out but to permit supervision and control in a developing and improving if still imperfect situation. Already a few growers and producers, not big enough to have the 400 barrels, have been allowed in because of the excellence of their wines.

The denomination Rioja, or the place-name of one of the villages within the zone, may only be used for wines combining certain specified characteristics and standards of quality. Where wines genuinely produced in the district do not quite come up to standard, the village name may appear on the label only according to this formula: "This wine was made in the village of X, but has not achieved the quality demanded for Rioja."

The legal zone for the production of Rioja falls within the limits of the province of Logroño, and in some areas of Alava and Navarre. Wines which have been aged or "elaborated" outside the zone are not allowed to carry the name Rioja.

The making of the wines follows traditional French methods—not surprisingly, since French hands and heads did the work some three-quarters of a century ago when phylloxera had destroyed the vineyards of Bordeaux but had not yet reached Rioja.

The flood of the French into Rioja in those days has left its mark: wines are vatted and fermented in much the same way as they used to be in France, and those not sold within a year as light, common wines are matured in oak casks, some of the Bordeaux size. They are kept in cellars which, in certain *bodegas* (wine-making establishments), resemble those of France to the last detail.

One great difference is that, whereas the good wines of Bordeaux are the products of a single vineyard-owner, Riojas are blends produced in the big *bodegas* from grapes grown partly, perhaps largely, by peasant farmers in the area—as is more the case in California and, in some instances, in the Rhône. As for the lesser, regional wine, much of this is now being made very successfully by village cooperatives and sold as *vinos corrientes* of good quality.

RIOJA WINE TYPES: BOTTLE LABELS

The Rioja wine district, officially delimited along the two sides of the River Ebro, is almost entirely in the province of Logroño in the north of Spain, a little east of Burgos. The small part not in Logroño province bulges like a bubble into the province of Alava—where the marked difference is that the Ebro, a narrowish thin stream at this point, cuts through the land, which now begins to rise. The important difference in the wines themselves is that here in Alava the Riojas are heavier and full-blooded, while in the plain of the Ebro they are lighter, more claret-like.

The region is finely subdivided for local purposes, but in the present state of the development of the wines, three divisions are important.

Rioja Alta

Upper Rioja, the northwest end of the zone, above and including the city of Logroño. The climate is much the same here as it is around the Basque coast and the Bay of Biscay, and so not unlike that of Bordeaux. The autumns, mild and long, are favorable to harvesting, and spring is pleasant. There are hard frosts and some snow in winter but the season is not violent. Yet two dangers challenge the vines: late spring frosts, usually occurring at the end of April or the beginning of May after warmer weather has brought the sap up the plant; and the *solano,* a roasting local wind coming out of the east. Even so, in the more reliable weather of Rioja, there is not so much difference in the vintages that *chaptalisation* is ever needed.

Alavesa

Wines in Alava are listed in the high-quality group, with those of Rioja Alta. Bottle labels sometimes state that the wine is an Alavesa. Generally, it will be heartier than Rioja Alta; it is habitually compared with Burgundies but, tasted on the spot, is reminiscent rather of a good Rhône wine.

Rioja Baja

Lower Rioja. The wines are rarely bottled. As the Río Ebro drops toward the Mediterranean, below the town of Logroño, the climate changes; here, it is more like Aragón than the Bay of Biscay. Autumns and springs are violent, the weather is hotter; while Rioja Alta is moderately dry, Rioja Baja is classified as arid. Because of the greater heat, the season here is always two weeks in advance, yet in the vast stretch of vineyard along the Ebro, the grapes are harvested later than they are upriver—and, as a result of this extra maturing time, they produce a wine markedly higher in alcoholic content, reaching up to 15% or 16% as compared with 11% or 12.5% in Rioja Alta. They are dark and often rather coarse, ordinary wines.

Riojas are sold for drinking in their second year, are sold in barrel, or are matured in American oak casks either of 600 liters (*bocoyes*) or 225 liters (*barricas bordelesas* or Bordeaux barrels). These more mature wines are the ones which generally reach both the foreign market and the better restaurants in Spain.

Vintage wines are labeled Cosecha (harvest) followed by the year (i.e., Cosecha 1969, Cosecha 1974), or Reserva or Reserva Especial, the latter designations sometimes followed by the year and sometimes not. Reserva is a wine which has been kept longer than a Cosecha (almost invariably in wood, not in bottle), and a Reserva Especial will generally have been kept longer still. It is not always easy to choose between them: the older wines are sometimes overaged and flat from too long a life in the wood; on the other hand, the best wines of the greatest years are usually the ones set aside for this maltreatment. Vintage date, it has been said before, is to be taken as an approximation. It is considered a certain vintage if "most" of the wine in the bottle or barrel is of that vintage. The greatest years of this century in Rioja are 1904, 1920, 1922, 1924, 1925, 1928, 1934, 1935, 1942, 1948, 1953, 1954, 1957, 1962, 1964, 1970, 1974, 1975, and 1978.

White wines are sweet (*dulce*) or dry (*seco*). The white wines cannot compete with the reds, and are too often *pasado* (maderized). Red wines are graded by age as Finos de Mesa (fine table wines) or Reservas, and by degree of color: *rosado, clarete, ojo de gallo,* and *tinto,* ranging from pale pink to deep red. *Clarete* and *tinto* are the types most often to be met with; *clarete* is an honest light red wine produced by short contact with the color-importing skin of the red grape from which it comes. *Tinto* is simply the Spanish word for red wine—which is never called *rojo,* although the literal word *blanco* is used for the white.

Here, as in California, the wines are usually known by the *bodega* names of the shippers and not by vineyards. It is freely admitted in Rioja that the various vineyards differ widely: it matters considerably whether the plot has a southern or a northern exposure; the soil naturally varies throughout the region, but on the whole, it is chalky, and this influences the wines. Nevertheless, separate vatting of musts according to vineyard is in its infancy. If a wine *does* carry the name of a vineyard—a few names, such as Viña Zaco, Viña Tondonia, and Viña Paceta have become widely known—this will be largely symbolic. Certain high-grade *bodegas,* such as those of the Marqués de Riscal, Marqués de Murríeta, and Compañía Vinícola del Norte de España, may use mainly grapes of their own planting, with a small quantity carefully selected from smaller growers; but most blend their wines from the harvests of numerous little vineyards.

In the past, Riojas were known as Cepa (vine variety) Sauternes, Cepa Chablis, Cepa Rhin, Cepa Barsac, Cepa Médoc, and so on; or sometimes as Estilo Sauternes, Especial Sauternes (or Graves, or Barsac), or even simply as Chablis, or Sauternes. This imitative labeling has recently been outlawed by an agreement with France.

VINE VARIETIES

The rolling Rioja Alta, sheltered from rough weather by high mountains—which are out of sight—has a khaki-colored, parched look, something like Arizona, or North Africa. The patchwork hills striped and quilted by the vine plots might be in Chablis.

Wine-making in the important growths is modernized.

Some *bodegas* and cooperatives have installed up-to-date machinery; and even the many small growers who produce the ordinary wines sold everywhere in the north of Spain (but not entitled to the place-name Rioja) now plow the earth instead of chopping it by hand. At the same time, the backward corners of the province are primitive and picturesque. The ancient villages tucked into the hills are all off the main roads—an isolation which has safeguarded their character—and countless houses are distinguished by ornate coats-of-arms in stone. The district taking its wine name from a slurred-over pronunciation of one of the little rivers tributary to the Ebro, the Río Oja, is poor; much of the landscape is arid and rocky, although there are fertile and beautiful spots. The look of poverty in Rioja has comparatively little to do with the wine, all of which, from the export point of view, is made at least in theory in the flourishing big *bodegas*.

The principal wine producers in the Rioja are:

La Rioja Alta, S.A.; R. López de Heredia, Viña Tondonia, S.A.; Bodegas Gómez Cruzado, S.A.; Carlos Serres, Hijo; De la Torre y Lapuerta, S.A.; Bodegas Martínez Lacuesta, Hnos., Ltda.; Bodegas Franco Españolas; Bodegas Ramón Bilbao; Rioja Santiago, S.A.; Compañía Vinícola del Norte de España; Bodegas Bilbainas; Bodegas Riojanas; Bodegas Montecillo; Vinos de los Herederos del Marqués de Riscal, S.A.; Federico Paternina, S.A.; Bodegas Berberana; AGE, Bodegas Unidas, S.A.; Bodegas Gurpegui; Bodegas Lagunilla, S.A.; Bodegas Marqués de Murríeta; Bodegas Muerza, S.A.; Bodegas Palacio, S.A.; Herederos de Enrique Bilbao—Bodegas Ramón Bilbao; Bodegas Faustino Martínez; Vinícola Vizcaina, Rojas y Cía., S.R.C.; Bodegas Campo Viejo de Savin, S.A.; Bodega Coop. Del Valle de Ocón; Bodega Coop. Nuestra Señora de la Anunciación; Bodega Coop. Nuestra Señora de Valvanera de Cuzcurrita, Tirjo y Sajazarra; Bodega Coop. Nuestra Señora de Vico; Bodega Coop. San Isidro; Bodega Coop. San Miguel; Bodega Coop. San Pedro Apóstol; Bodega Coop. Santa Daria; Bodega Coop. Sonsierra; Bodega Coop. Virgen de la Vega; Bodega Coop. La Bastida; Compañía Española Promotora de la Exportación, S.A.; Comercial Pirineos; Junta Provincial de Bodegas Cooperativas del Campo; and Vajda, S.L.

The red wines are made principally from the grape varieties Garnacha, Tempranillo, Graciano, and Mazuelo. No Rioja vine, either red or white, is capable of making a satisfactory wine alone; all lack some essential ingredient—acidity, richness, finesse—and all the good wines are blends.

Garnacha, which resembles French Grenache, is the big common producer, weak in bouquet, and not a variety which ripens fully in the Rioja Alta, except in the hottest years. It yields the mass of wine in Rioja Baja—and in other parts of Spain, especially around Madrid, where it is generally called Aragón or Tinto Aragones, because it came originally from Aragón. Its wide use in Rioja is due mainly to its ability to resist oïdium, which, with mildew, is the great menace there.

The must of the Tempranillo, high neither in sugar nor in acid, is quite neutral, and the other elements in a blend with this grape always inform the taste. But it matures quickly—although it does not keep particularly well—and it is valued for its contribution of color. Graciano has a marked and quite individual perfume; Mazuelo, a variety close to the Carignan of the Rhône and Provence in France, would be more widely grown if it were not for its susceptibility to oïdium.

The white wines are usually a blend of Malvasia, Viura, Calagraño, and Garnacha.

Château Ripeau

Bordeaux red wine.
District and Commune: Saint-Émilion, France.

Combined with Château Jean-Faure, adjoining it and long under the same ownership, Ripeau is now one of the large producers among the best Saint-Émilion vineyards. Lying next to Château Cheval-Blanc, near the boundary of Pomerol, the vineyard suffered as badly as Cheval-Blanc and the Pomerol vineyards did in the February 1956 freeze, and there was little 1956, 1957, 1958, or 1959 Château Ripeau wine. Other later vintages, however, are in the market in quantity. The property was once owned by Michel de Wilde, the son-in-law of Mme Loubat, who with her husband established both of the vineyards now combined. Today, Ripeau belongs to de Wilde's daughter and her husband, M. Janoueix, an owner and shipper in Libourne.

Characteristics. A generous wine with an individual bouquet. Typical of a good Saint-Émilion.

Vineyard area: 15 hectares (37.5 acres).

Average production: 75 *tonneaux* (6,000 cases).

Ripley

American hybrid grape developed by the New York State Agricultural Station to be used as a table grape and for wine. The wine is white and dry, but by itself tends to be flat; the grape might contribute to a very superior blend if the proper partner could be found.

Riquewihr

Wine town in Alsace (*q.v.*).

Riviera del Garda

Red or rosé wine from Lombardy (*q.v.*).

Rivesaltes

Sun-baked district of Haut-Roussillon, France, famous for its Muscat wines.

See Sweet fortified wines of France.

Robertson

Wine district in the Little Karoo region of the Cape province.

See South Africa.

Clos de la Roche

Burgundy red wine.
District: Côte de Nuits, France.
Commune: Morey-Saint-Denis.
Official Classification: Great Growth (Grand Cru).

Clos de la Roche is one of the least-known wines of this section of the Côte de Nuits and is thus often good, and sometimes exceptional, value. Throughout the centuries of its existence it has been overshadowed by Bonnes Mares, by the Clos de Tart and Clos des Lambrays and neglected because the wines of Morey were more often than not sold under the name of one of the two famous adjoining communes—Gevrey-Chambertin and Chambolle-Musigny—probably more to the advantage of the two neighbors than to their loss.

The vineyard is the largest of the important Growths of Morey, covering some 15 hectares (37 acres). It stands up the hill, above the road that goes through the vineyards, along the boundary between Gevrey and Morey. Its nobility is such that it is one of the rare Great Growths (*Grands Crus*) of Burgundy, and bottles are not labeled with both vineyard name and commune name—vineyard name alone is sufficient. To earn the name, of course, the wine must meet the rigorous Great Growth standards. Like most of the wines of Morey, it is sturdy and rich, yet curiously delicate, much like a Clos de Tart. On a curve from the sturdy nobility of the great Chambertin to the elegance of Musigny, Clos de la Roche lies perhaps just beside Chambertin, lacking some of its austere majesty but adding a beguiling grace.

As is the case with most Burgundian vineyards, this one is divided among a number of growers. All together, in an average year for quantity, they produce some 500 hectoliters (13,250 U.S. gallons, 11,000 imp.)—or about 5,000 cases.

Rochefort-sur-Loire

Wine commune in the Coteaux du Layon district of Anjou (*qq.v.*).

Roditis

One of the principal grape varieties used for Greek spirits.

Château Romer

Bordeaux white wine.
District: Sauternes, France.
Commune: Fargues.

The little-known château is situated in a wood in the commune whose wines are entitled to the place-name Sauternes. The wines tend to be heavy, and are an exclusivity of the Calvet shipping firm.
Vineyard area: 15 hectares (38 acres).
Average production: 40 *tonneaux* (3,800 cases).

Rosato

Italian term for pink wine or rosé.

Rosé

In French, pink or rose-colored wine. When properly made it comes from red grapes fermented for two or three days on the color-imparting skins and husks, but drawn off at the delicate moment when just enough color has been absorbed to give the wine its attractive pink cast. In France, the best rosé is from Tavel near the mouth of the Rhône, but some excellent ones are now being made in Bordeaux, in Anjou, and in most wine-producing regions. In America, where rosé is tremendously popular, some good examples come from California.

Rosé de Béarn

A fair quality V.D.Q.S. wine made in the French department of Basses-Pyrénées.

Rosé des Riceys

A still pink wine of Champagne (*q.v.*).

Rosette

White wines, semi-sweet and rarely distinguished, from Bergerac, France.
See Bergerac.

Rosolio

A red Italian liqueur with a taste of roses. The French used to make their own version of this liqueur, which they called Rossolis.

Rossese (Dolceacqua)

Red wine from Rossese grapes, grown along the Italian Riviera.
See Liguria.

Rosso

Red in Italian. In California the word now refers to a red wine that is just slightly sweet, but the common *vini rossi* of Italy are always dry.

Rosso Conero

A fruity but rather acid red wine from the Italian Marches (*q.v.*).

Rosso Piceno

Red Italian wine from the Piceno Hills, on the fringe of the Apennines.
See The Marches.

Rotgipfler

Grape variety cultivated in Austria.

Rouge

French term for red wine.

Rougeau (leaf reddening)

Vine disease, caused by a wound which prevents the sap returning to the roots.
See Chapter Eight, p. 29.

Château Rouget

Bordeaux red wine.
District and Commune: Pomerol, France.

The property, owned by M. Bertrand, is one of the oldest in the district and has made some very agreeable wines typical of Pomerol.
Vineyard area: 11 hectares (27 acres).
Average production: 35 *tonneaux* (3,400 cases).

Rough

A big red wine, with a considerable amount of tannin, will be rough before it has had time to mature, which in the biggest years may take well over a decade. This roughness is not to be confused with the coarseness of wines from poor grapes and poor vineyards—a common, harsh flavor which will never disappear with age.

Round

To be round, a wine must be harmonious but also big. It will be in perfect balance, and it gives a sense of "roundness" in the way it fills the mouth.

Roussette

The principal wine of Seyssel, in Haute-Savoie. It is white, flinty dry, and made from Roussette grapes.
See Seyssel.

Roussillon

See Grand Roussillon; Sweet fortified wines of France; Appendix G.

Rubino di Cantavenna

A light but full red wine from the Italian Piedmont (*q.v.*).

Ruby Port

A young, blended wood Port, rich in color, fruity and sweet.
See Port.

Ruchottes-Chambertin

Burgundy red wine.
District: Côte de Nuits, France.
Commune: Gevrey-Chambertin.
Official Classification: Great Growth (Grand Cru).

Many excellent and even outstanding bottles can be found, although this wine is one of the lesser of the Chambertin family. Some severe critics have called the wine common and lacking in breed, but while it is not generally the equal of the magnificent Chambertin, a well-made Ruchottes should be neither of these things.

The vineyard adjoins the Clos de Bèze, to the south of the village of Gevrey-Chambertin, and is fairly high on the slope for exceptionally great wines. It covers just over 3 hectares (7.9 acres), and production usually amounts to 100 or so hectoliters (2,650 U.S. gallons, 2,200 imp.), or the equivalent of about 1,100 cases.
See Gevrey-Chambertin.

Rüdesheimer Berg (Rüdesheimerberg)

The Rüdesheimerberg, or Rüdesheimer Mountain, a steep slope rising up from the Rhine, produces the best Rüdesheim wines. The label will carry Rüdesheimerberg, written as either one or two words, followed by the name of the actual vineyard spot, as Rüdesheimer Berg Bronnen, or Rüdesheimer Berg Rotland. Owing to the steepness of the clifflike vineyards, drainage is excellent, and in the wet years Rüdesheimer Berg wines are among the best Rheingaus. The grapes roast in the sun in the hot years, producing wine frequently below Rheingau average.
See Rheingau.

Rufina

A pretty, small Chianti town about 32 kilometers (20 miles) northeast of Florence in the Sieve River Valley. The wines are among the best not accorded the Classico designation.

Ruländer

Grayish-colored Burgundy grape (Pinot Gris) introduced into Germany by one Ruhland; it is also planted in Alsace and Switzerland. Also called Grauerburgunder or Tokaier.

Rully

A commune in the Chalon Slope of Burgundy which produces both red and white wines and has its own Appellation Contrôlée.
See Chalonnais.

Rum

Rum is the distillate of products of fermented sugarcane. Of all spirits, it retains the most of those natural taste factors which come to it from its product of origin.

Starch-derived spirits, such as vodka from potatoes, or whisky from grain, must be cooked, or malted. In the case of rum, based on sugar, the processes by which starch is turned into sugar are not necessary: rum does not have to be distilled at very high proof, as gin and vodka do; it receives the minimum of chemical treatment and can be aged in casks which have already been used for spirit-ageing, because it does not need the tannin which such a spirit as Cognac will absorb from the oak. Rum may be flavored or adulterated by other processes than the essential reduction of its proof strength with pure water—but it need not be; and if it is a decent rum, it should not be. Its color varies from water-white, the natural hue, through amber to mahogany. The only coloring matter used is sugar caramel, which does not affect the flavor. A rum's real character will be determined by the following factors:

The Material of Which It Is Made

Rum is made principally from molasses, which is the uncrystallizable mass remaining after the formation of sugar; sometimes directly from the sugar-cane juice, or from second-grade molasses and other residues. The last type is usually called tafia, not rum, and it is seldom worth exporting, or even bottling. The majority of fine rums come from molasses, but a few do not; one of the best of Haiti is made directly from cane juice; and the most famous rum of Martinique comes from cane juice concentrated into a syrup.

Changing Tastes in Rum

Full body and a distinctive richness of flavor used to be the qualities most appreciated in rum, but in the last twenty-five years tastes have been gradually changing. Many people now prefer a lighter rum, subtler in flavor and more delicate in aroma. The greater demand for the light style has led to a more general use of the continuous column patent still.

Slow or Rapid Fermentation

The rapid fermentation of *a rum of the light type* can be completed in as little as twelve hours, and a day to a day and a half is general practice. Although Jamaica and other countries are now making a good deal of this style, Puerto Rican and Cuban are the usual examples of typical light rums. Slow fermentation, reinforced by the addition of dunder (the residue left in the still after distillation), produces a heavier type; men who prefer their rum distinctive and pungent say that any other kind is like skimmed milk. Slow fermentation may take up to twelve days. The Wedderburn and Plummer types, traditional Jamaican rums of the old style, are identified with slow fermentation; and Martinique produces slowly-fermented heavy rums, of Grand Arôme. High-ester rums are made in much the same way as the Wedderburn rums, except that a much higher ester content is aimed at.

Yeast Types

The yeasts used in fermentation are cultured or natural. When they are cultured, it is said that they are likely to be bred in secret, like Derby runners, everything staked on their individuality. An important Haitian maker is convinced that the secret of his rum is in the harmony between cane and yeast, which come from the same place; whereas Puerto Rican distillers believe to a man that the taste of their product owes its virtue (very great, they say) to the private strain of yeast they cultivate.

Pot or Patent Still

As in the making of whisky, either the pot still or the continuous-operation patent still may be used. The patent still is more suitable for the increasingly popular light rums. Pot-still spirits retain more of their natural character; the rums are heavier and not, therefore, to all tastes. The old Jamaican-style rum is the prototype for pot-distilled rums of greater body.

Proof at Which Distilled

Lighter rums are distilled at higher proof. In Jamaica, for instance, distillation strength may rise to 96° (Gay-Lussac), whereas the fuller pot-still rums will be distilled at about 86° (Gay-Lussac).

Place of Origin

A somewhat confusing question. The U.S. Federal Alcohol Administration regulation puts it this way: "Puerto Rico, Cuba, Demerara, Barbados, St. Croix, St. Thomas, Virgin Islands, Jamaica, Martinique, Trinidad, Haiti, and Santo Domingo rums are not distinctive types of rum. Such names are not generic but retain their geographical significance. They may not be applied to rum produced in any other place than the particular region indicated in the name." The fact is that each main center makes differing types of rum, but the distinct rum types *are* identified with certain areas. Jamaica is even now associated with a heavy, pungent rum, although today it is producing lighter types; and conversely, light rums are attributed to Cuba or Puerto Rico, although each island makes a certain amount of rum in other styles. Differences in the rums are the result of differing methods of preparation and of the influences of soil, climate, and especially water.

ORIGIN OF RUM

Rum is initially the essentially West Indian product of cane and water—sugar-cane perhaps brought from the Azores by Columbus on his second voyage and the pure West Indian water which tumbles down from the mountains. First records of rum are from Barbados in 1600, and here is a description of a rum punch bowl of the West Indies in the spacious days of the eighteenth century:

"A marble basin, built in the middle of the garden especially for the occasion, served as the bowl. Into it were poured 1,200 bottles of rum, 1,200 bottles of Málaga wine, and 400 quarts of boiling water. Then 600 pounds of the best cane sugar and 200 powdered nutmegs were added. The juice of 2,600 lemons were squeezed into the liquor. Onto the surface was launched a handsome mahogany boat piloted by a boy of twelve, who rowed about a few moments, then coasted to the side and began to serve the assembled company of six hundred, which gradually drank up the ocean upon which he floated."

Rum was overwhelmingly popular in the American colonies before 1775: about 450,000 hectoliters (12 million U.S. gallons, 10 million imp.) a year were downed, four gallons (3 imp.) per person; whereas 1.25 gallons a year per person for all spirituous liquors combined is the best that can be done today. One historian declares that the British law of 1763, designed to make the Americans give up Spanish West Indian rums in favor of the British product, caused the Revolution—and a revolution might just as well be fought over rum as over tea.

An apparently authentic story about Paul Revere tells that he set out on his ride in morose silence and did not begin to shout that the English were coming until he had stopped at the home of a rum distiller—one Isaac Hall, Captain of the Minute Men—for two drafts of Medford rum. (Medford was the name for all the rum along the Atlantic Coast in those days.) George Washington, at any rate, was launched on rum. He was elected to the Virginia House of Burgesses in 1758 not by campaigning but by distributing among the voters 75 gallons of rum; and it was the Virginia House of Burgesses which later sent him to the Continental Congress.

Rum was used in the slave trade, boats loaded with the spirit going to Africa to trade, and bringing back Negroes. Dead Man's Chest, a tiny West Indian island, roistered its way into history—"Fifteen men on Dead Man's Chest—yo-ho-ho, and a bottle of rum." In the 1920s, rum revived a kind of piracy, when the speed launches were running rum from Cuba to the Florida Keys.

After Prohibition, the United States developed a fad for drinking concoctions of rum mixed with slices of fruit and chunks of ice. This still goes on, although excellent brands of rum are now available.

The distillation process is approximately the same for rum as for whisky—except that rum need not be malted. (See Distillation; Gin; Whiskey, Scotch; Whiskey, Bourbon; etc.)

By and large, the British drink West Indian rum, from the islands that were formerly their possessions, and the French the rums of the French West Indies. United States imports are principally from Puerto Rico, followed by the Virgin Islands, with Jamaica and Haiti a long way behind, and a still smaller amount from the French West Indies, Barbados, and other islands.

See Rum, Puerto Rican; Rum, Jamaican; Rum, West Indies; Rum, French West Indies; Rum, Haitian; Rum, Martinique, etc.

Rum, Barbados

The beautiful garden-like island of Barbados in the West Indies is composed largely of sandstone, coral, and volcanic ash deposits, a mixture which gives the soil a porous character very suitable to the cultivation of sugar-cane. Although the warm climate is ideal, the island has no rivers and all the water used for irrigation as well as for other purposes must be pumped from subterranean caverns.

Since sugar-cane is the island's major product, much

rum is made; production has been increasing slowly while export has been rising more rapidly. Latest figures show a jump upward in exports of one-third to about 720,000 proof gallons annually.

Barbados rum is distilled from molasses, the by-product of the sugar-cane; and distillation is carried out both in pot stills and in patent stills. Semi-light in body and color, Barbadian rums generally have a soft, almost smoky or leathery flavor. Only three distilleries operate on the island; the West India Rum Refinery, Barbados Distilleries, and Mt. Gay Distilleries. Certain of the old rums of the latter company can be drunk neat, like a fine brandy.

Rum, Cuban

The light, delectable rum of Cuba is the natural drink of the Cubans, to whom the lightness of the type is all-important—and the rum is distilled and aged with that end in view, and treated with charcoal to make it even lighter.

Cane sugar, yeast, and the crystalline torrent water of the volcanic West Indian islands are the dominant ingredients of good rums. The Cuban and Puerto Rican types are generally distilled from molasses—a by-product of refined cane sugar—and fermented with cultured yeast and pure water. Cuban rum is often processed by blending or transforming newer spirits with older ones and is sand-filtered during ageing.

There are two leading styles of rum in Cuba: Carta Blanca (White Label), which is the base for Daiquiris; and Carta Oro (Gold Label), to which some caramel is added to mellow the color—this is, therefore, a little darker as well as sweeter than the Carta Blanca. The best rums come from the vicinity of Santiago, at the south end of the island. The principal producers prior to Castro's takeover were: Compañía Ron Bacardi; Alvarez Camp y. Co., Santiago; Arechabaia; Cadenas; and Matanzas. Now all exports to the Western world have ceased. Much Cuban rum goes to Russia.

Rum, Demerara

The export rum of Guyana.
See Rum, Guyana.

Rum, French

Rum is rapidly increasing in popularity in France, imported mainly from the French West Indies and to a lesser extent from Réunion Island. The rums are not very often seen outside France and, except for two or three from Martinique, cannot be considered to figure in the world market.

French West Indies

A considerable quantity of full-bodied rum, some of it high grade, is made in the islands of Martinique and Guadeloupe. It must be remembered that the islands are not possessions or territories of France but are actual French departments, like the Gironde or Basses-Pyrénées.

In this preferential situation, it is natural that the rums gravitate to the French mainland, where they are widely sold. Of the two islands, Martinique is more important.

See Rum, Martinique.

Réunion Island

The sole spirituous product of this former French colony in the Indian Ocean off the coast of Madagascar is rum. Like Martinique and Guadeloupe, Réunion is actually a department of France. About 37,500 hectoliters (1,000,000 U.S. gallons, 833,000 imp.) annually are distilled from molasses. Most of this is white rum, very little aged; but a small quantity of cask-matured rum is also produced.

French Guiana

Prévot and Mirande, the two distilleries, produce annually a little less than 7,500 hectoliters (200,000 U.S. gallons, 165,000 imp.) of undistinguished white rum. No other spirit is made.

Rum, Guyana

Two types of rum are made, pot-still and continuous-still.

The distinguishing characteristic of Guyana rum is its exceedingly rapid fermentation—usually completed in from thirty-six to forty hours.

In addition to export rum, there is made for domestic consumption in this country of some 400,000 souls situated close to Venezuela a "fruit" rum made by steeping various spices and fruits in the distillation from Coffey continuous stills. The product is then lightly tinted with caramel and bottled at a strength of 24° under proof or 85.7° U.S. proof. The resulting rum is lighter-bodied than the better-known Demerara variety. Courantin, one of the "fruit" rums, is occasionally seen in England; it has a pleasant and quite noticeable scent of spices and fruit.

Demerara, named after the river along which the sugar-cane grows, is the important rum of Guyana. Most is exported. Both continuous and pot-still processes are used. Made from molasses, not directly from cane juice, the rum is fermented spontaneously in wooden vats. A trace of sulfuric acid is added to kill bacteria and a little ammonium sulfate to feed the yeast. The rum is generally quite darkly colored by the addition of caramel obtained by burning cane sugar. Demerara is not as heavy as might appear from its color. Because of the very rapid fermentation process, it is not likely to have quite the pronounced flavor of rums which are obtained by slower fermentation. Among Demeraran rums themselves, those distilled in pot stills will have up to a third more of the taste-giving esters than the Coffey-still varieties, and more than twice the amount of the higher alcohols. Demerara is exported at approximately 43° over proof, or 163.4° U.S. proof. Guyana leads the other British-influenced countries of the Caribbean in rum export.

Rum, Haitian

Although sugar-cane is grown on all parts of the island of Haiti, it is in the north, behind the small port of Cape Haitian, that the best cane for rum-making is found. A rim of mountains runs along the north coast, and behind, in the valleys, the rainfall is not as abundant as it is elsewhere. The mountain Citadelle of the Black Emperor, Henri Christophe, who went dramatically mad and killed himself with a silver bullet, soars into the sky, high above the cane-cutting crews rhythmically swinging their machetes while the chanter calls out his rising and falling phrases to set the pace.

Almost two centuries ago Haiti revolted and freed itself from France. Nevertheless, traditions, attitudes, and customs are still predominantly French; and the French skill in making fine brandy continues to influence the making of Haitian rum—which is double-distilled in pot stills, the first run, or raw rum, being redistilled. This is the same method used in the production of Cognac brandy. First-run Haitian rum, however, is often sold as a low-priced island product, although never exported. It is completely colorless: hence its name—clairin. On the Haitian feast days, this rum is sold raw by the glass from small folding stands placed along the streets and roadways, each stand lit with a flickering lamp which gleams like a yellow star. Clairin is considered to have the special virtue of propitiating the powerful gods of Voodoo. For this reason, or perhaps only because it is cheap, it is the libation spirit poured on the ground at the Voodoo ceremonies (90% of the country still worships in the religion brought by the slaves from Africa), and the gods have their taste before the celebrants begin to drink.

The best known of Haitian rum, and one of the fine rums of the world, is Rhum Barbancourt. This is medium-bodied and has an exquisite balance. According to M. Jean Gardère, maker of Barbancourt, this is to some extent due to the fact that a certain yeast found in the area where the cane grows is used to ferment the juice. This common origin, with the same soil ingredients and conditions, has a subtle influence on both yeast and cane juice, producing the harmony which does undoubtedly exist in the rum. The juice, which is pasteurized in order to seal in the natural vitamins throughout distillation, is processed as soon as it has been crushed from the cane, and there is no secondary fermentation. The Barbancourt plant, founded in 1862, now has a capacity of 25,000 hectoliters (658,000 U.S. gallons, 547,000 imp.). One-star, three-star, and five-star rums are made, the first originally limited to Haitian sale, but all are exported.

Until Haiti's independence, France was the market for Haitian rums, import of which sometimes reached 684,000 hectoliters (18 million U.S. gallons, 15 million imp.) a year. Today, Martinique rum dominates the French market. Jean Gardère says that the persistent link between France and Haiti is the kinship of soils; the calcareous soil underlaid with lime, which yields rum in Haiti, is practically identical with that which gives two of the greatest vinous products of France—brandy in Cognac and wine in Champagne.

The following are the principal rum distillers of Haiti:

Proprietor	Name of Rum	Distillery
Jean Gardère	Rhum Barbancourt	Damien (Port-au-Prince)
René Audain	Rhum Tropical	Manègue (Port-au-Prince)
Hermann Colas	Rhum Marie Colas	Cazeau (Port-au-Prince)
Guy Séjourné	Rhum Champion	Croix des Bouquets
Max Nazon	Rhum Nazon	Port-au-Prince
Armand Tesserot	Rhum Tesserot	Port-au-Prince

Rum, Jamaican

No center of rum-making has been so much affected by recent changes in taste as Jamaica. Traditionally, a heavy, rich-flavored, almost pungent rum was made here—slow-fermented, strengthened with dunder, and distilled in pot stills at low proof.

Now, although Jamaican rums still tend to have a more characteristic flavor and aroma than do most others, they are definitely lighter than they used to be, and the slow-fermentation method has been abandoned. The rums made can be divided into four types: light continuous-still rum—or common clean; light and medium-bodied pot-still rum; Wedderburn and Plummer heavier types; high-ester rum.

For the first type, molasses is the raw material, and distillation is carried out in a continuous still of two or three columns—distillation strength may be as high as 96° (Gay-Lussac). Great care is taken not to remove the true rum constituents of the fermented wash.

Light and medium pot-still rums are made from a wash obtained by mixing cane juice, high-grade molasses, water, and acid. In the pot still, characteristic taste and smell are retained.

Wedderburn and Plummer rums have more body than the previous types—in these the tradition of the past is preserved, and anyone who wants to sample an old robust Jamaica rum should taste one of them. Most of the pot-still rums are distilled at around 86° (Gay-Lussac).

High-ester rums are fermented and distilled in much the same way as are Wedderburn—but the ester content must be higher.

The bulk of the Jamaican (and of other West Indian) rum is taken to London to be aged and bottled there.

Rum, London Dock

West Indian rum taken in bulk to London and aged and bottled there.

Rum, Martinique

The large production of spirits (160,000 hectoliters or 4.24 million U.S. gallons, 3.52 million imp.) is divided, 55% for rum made from molasses and 45% for that made from sugar-cane juice.

There are nearly a hundred principal growers of cane sugar and about fifty rum-makers. The capital, Fort-de-France, is as much a town of rum as any other in the world. The dusty savannah with its statue of Josephine, who left the island to become in time the bride of Napoleon, is fringed all along one side by the dingy rum offices, piled up to the roofs with crates awaiting shipment. The port is at the side of the town, not along the main quay but on an inlet, where the transoceanic vessels rear over the houses, their stacks poking up incongruously along what appears to be a marine avenue, a little lazy smoke appearing as they get up steam to carry the rum out to the world. At one time, Martinique was the proud owner of a rum capital quite different from the rather tawdry and crowded town of Fort-de-France. This was St. Pierre, richest city of the Caribbean. The ruins may still be seen—handsome cobbled streets along the sides of which pure mountain water bubbles and sings. The buildings are crushed, empty skulls overgrown with wild banana, vine, and mango: in a few seconds, early in the century, a blast from the nearby volcano obliterated the town, killing forty thousand people. Despite the desolation, there are several rum companies established in the strip of St. Pierre, which is coming to life again along the coal-black volcanic beach; and one of the best-known of all the rums, Saint James, has its plantations nearby.

While about fifty proprietors make the rum, it is said in Martinique that at the head of the industry are ten families. This led, in the early fifties, to a strike probably unique in history—"the strike of the ten families." When the sugar-cane is ripe, it must be cut and treated at once. Since a Communist government was then in control of the island, the rum- and sugar-owners considered that they were being taxed out of existence. The cane ripened and the sole crop of the island was ready to be made. "Now," said the ten families to the Communist deputies, "we go on strike. We can hold out over a year of no profits. Do you think you can? Without sugar and rum there will be no crop to tax, and no income for you. Don't you think we ought to sit down and have a reasonable discussion?"

The rums made directly from cane juice are sometimes strengthened by the addition of dunder for the fermentation and sometimes not. (Dunder is the residue left in the still after distillation and is generally used in processes of slow fermentation.) When the rums are uncolored by cask-ageing and remain white they are called Grappe Blanche. Such spirits are mainly consumed on the island, forming the base for the inevitable Martinique Punch.

Punch Martiniquais, of early West Indian origin, is probably British. The recipe is: rum, cane-sugar syrup, and a slice of lemon peel. In the happy days just before inflation, the cost was 7 francs, and they gave a customer the sugar-syrup bottle, the rum bottle, a tumbler, and left him to himself. By bringing in a sugar-cane syrup usually made in Martinique, the firm of Duquesne has introduced the punch in France.

A single Martinique rum is made by the fermentation of dunder, about 60%, with concentrated cane-juice syrup. This is the well-known Rhum Saint James, sold in its squarish tall bottle. Its darkness and its aroma distinguish it from most other rums.

Rums made from molasses are fermented with dunder

and colored with caramelized sugar. The premium rums of this style are called Grand Arôme and are slow fermented over a period varying from eight to twelve days. The heavy, rich rums compare with the Wedderburn-type rums of Jamaica, the prototype for the style.

Many consider Rhum Clément, made both white and tawny, to be the aristocrat of Martinique rums. The distillery near the village of François is unpretentious. The canes are trundled on threading railway lines, pushed by the black workers or pulled by a tiny engine, and are then carried up into the jaws of the crushing rollers on belts like greatly enlarged tire-chains. Juice drips stickily into the vats; bled, smashed cane slides off down a chute. The juice achieved by this process is converted into several grades of rum, the finest of which, one is told by M. Charles Clément himself—small, dapper, and the most charming of men—are aged upward of a dozen years. Rhum Duquesne, another good type, is made in the south of the island. Part of the production is distilled as white rum, sold under the trademark Genippa; the rest is aged in warehouses, to be sold as Grand Case (silver label, three years old) and Val d'Or (gold label, ten years old). The whole enterprise is a family business managed by M. O. des Grottes.

Rums utilizing molasses are almost always made at distilleries connected with the large sugar refineries. There are not so many of these, the important ones being at Vive—run by Fernand Clerc, whose three hundred pounds make him in at least one sense the biggest rum man on the island—at Galion, Rivière Salée, François, and Lareinty. The distilleries making rum direct from cane juice are much more numerous.

Several other spirituous drinks are made in Martinique, some of them based on rum. They include the native rum punch, bottled by the firm of Dogue; anisette, triple sec, crème d'orange, and other liqueurs. Orange is the most common flavoring. Maduva, messica, and maitina are all concocted with essence or juice of orange.

Rum, New England

Rum of a particularly strong, heavy, and hearty sort was among the factors which shaped New England. Blackstrap molasses came in from the West Indies to Connecticut, Rhode Island, and Massachusetts, and went out again as rum—to the taverns of the northern colonies, by ship to the southern ones to be traded for cotton and tobacco, and to Europe for the goods the New World was not yet prepared to make for itself. The most important aspect of the rum business, however, was the "triangular trade" which made the fortune of many a New England sea captain. Rum, shipped from New England to Africa, bought slaves. Slaves, carried to the islands of the West Indies, filled the ships with molasses, and the molasses was brought back to New England to make rum. The unsuccessful efforts of George III to tax molasses added as much heat to the cause of the American Revolution as did the more renowned Stamp Tax, and "taxation without representation" was denounced over many a glass of New England rum in many a wayside tavern.

Perhaps the first of the important spirit industries of the United States, New England rum is still being made in Massachusetts, where about 7,500 hectoliters (200,000 U.S. gallons, 166,000 imp.) of it are sold each year. It is still a heavy rum, dark, pungent, and full-bodied. Distilled at no more than 160° proof, it is aged in charred oak barrels; and it is from this ageing that it takes its characteristic dark color. There are only three firms making New England rum today.

In addition to those still being made and sold, there are some superb old rums to be found in the private cellars of New Englanders—which, once tasted, stand with certain fine old American Bourbons in the same class as fine French Cognacs.

Although their populations are small, the New England states of Maine and New Hampshire have the highest present per capita consumption of rum in the United States.

Rum, Panay

See Rum, Philippine Islands.

Rum, Philippine Islands

Two leading brands of rum are made: Tanduay and Panay. These have different flavors and Tanduay is by far the better seller of the two; it is also the higher priced.

Rum, Puerto Rican

Puerto Rico is the foremost world producer of rums and its products dominate the United States market, accounting for 70% of the rum consumption there. The two main types are White Label (very light-bodied) and Gold Label (slightly less light). In the United States, White Label outsells the Gold by about three to one, while in Puerto Rico itself the proportion is reversed—although there is not such a large demand for it among the inhabitants of Puerto Rico as there is for such cheaper varieties as Palo Viejo and Ron Llave.

Cuba, the other island which is famous for its light rums, also produces White Label and Gold Label. (*See* Rum, Cuban.)

Puerto Rico has always depended on its rich and abundant crop of sugar-cane as a vital means of support, and it is from this sugar-cane that the rum industry draws its existence. Ponce de León, who headed the first government of the island, is known to have distilled the cane, and a dispatch writer in 1526 reports that the natives were getting tipsy on sugar-cane rum. Ponce de León was a commercially-minded man, and one authority goes so far as to state that his search for the fountain of youth was nothing more than a quest for a sound distillable water.

The refining of raw sugar-cane results in fine sugar and a by-product called blackstrap molasses. Puerto Rican rums are distilled from this molasses, fermented with cultured yeast and mountain water, aged under government control, and required to be shipped in bottle. During the war years when whiskey was short, rums of every description were made, and many a bad Puerto Rican rum or purported Puerto Rican rum found its way into the United States. After the war, these could no longer be sold and they remained a glut on the market; and Puerto Rico established strict export laws to assure high-quality rums under the island imprint. The government now operates a rum pilot plant through the University of Puerto Rico—the only instance in which a project of this nature is government sponsored.

Puerto Rican rum is a characteristic type and is usually light-bodied and dry in contrast to the thicker aromatic rums of Martinique. Generally, Puerto Rican-type rums are fermented with cultured yeast and distilled in patent stills.

Puerto Rican rums are made on widely scattered points of the island, which have sharp differences in climate, ranging from almost perpetual rainfall to almost constant drought. The soils vary too; and, finally, each distiller cultivates his own yeast from a single yeast cell, producing the type which is peculiarly identified with his own brand name. Yeast is continually manufactured by every distiller in order to provide a sufficent amount for the carrying on of fermentation from day to day, and the yeast strain is never allowed to die. It is considered in Puerto Rico to be the secret of the rum. Something in these yeasts and soil and climatic conditions indelibly marks the rums, and as there are intuitive wine-tasters, so there are rum connoisseurs who boast that when they taste a glass of rum they can say exactly where it comes from.

Many of the old distillers who made rum before Prohibition were forced out of business during that period. An exception is the Puerto Rican Distilling Company, maker of Ronrico, which is generally light, although some 151° heavier-bodied rum is made. Fourteen distiller permits are at present granted in Puerto Rico. The Destilería Bacardi claims to have the largest capacity of any distillery in the world. The principal exported brands (arranged alphabetically) are: Bacardi, Boca Chica Carioca, Don Q, Maraca, Merito, Ronrico.

Rum, Tanduay

One of the leading types made in the Philippine Islands.

See Rum, Philippine Islands.

Rum, Trinidad

The rums, which are medium-light in type, are distilled from molasses in continuous stills. Before fermentation, the molasses is diluted with water and clarified—which makes the subsequent fermentation easier to control. Yeast is added, and the quick fermentation will be over in anything from thirty-six to forty-eight hours. The resultant rums, clean but not as distinguished as some of the other styles, are distilled at strengths varying between 83° and 96° (Gay-Lussac).

Rum, Virgin Islands

The rums tend to be medium-style, generally somewhat heavier than the light rums of Puerto Rico. Much of the product is exported in bulk.

Of the three islands, St. Thomas, St. John, and St. Croix, the last is much more suited to the growing of sugar-cane and therefore to the production of rum. St. Thomas is small, hardly more than a few mountains rearing up out of the Caribbean Sea; while St. Croix is much more extensive, with many stretches of flat land, almost the whole of its surface consisting of beautiful beaches surrounding a vast field of cane. The rums of the Virgin Islands are called Cruzan (from a former reference to St. Croix rums) and Old St. Croix. Both labels are owned by Virgin Islands Rum Industries, Ltd.

Rum, West Indies

Barbados, Jamaica, British Guiana (Guyana), and Trinidad form this group in the Caribbean; the first, second, and fourth are islands, the third a small country on the northeast coast of South America. Together they produce about 7 million proof gallons of rum annually, Barbados and Jamaica making roughly 1.5 million gallons each, while Trinidad and British Guiana make some 2 million gallons each. The leading exporter, with about 1.5 million gallons, is British Guiana, followed by Jamaica with 1 million gallons, Barbados with 700,000 gallons, and Trinidad with 300,000 gallons.

Rum is the traditional drink of the British navy. There are records of the ship's crew of Sir George Summer taking refuge from a hurricane at Bermuda in 1609 and seeking consolation in drinking rum, referred to as "comfortable waters." Hundreds of thousands of gallons of rum were included in the British supplies during the American Revolution. From the eighteenth century to the present day, rum has been rationed out daily to the men of the Royal Navy.

See Rum, Jamaican; Rum, Barbados; Rum, Guyana; Rum, Trinidad.

Rumania

Vines were grown in Rumania long ago: there were vineyards in Scitia Minor (today's Dobrudja) even before the Greeks founded their Black Sea colonies, early in the seventh century B.C. And on the foothills of the Carpathians there long existed such large plantations as those at Cotnari and Uricani, Huşi, Odobeşti, Panciu, Nicoreşti, Dealul-Mare, and Drăgăşani. The Greeks sent the wine in amphorae throughout the civilized world of their day. Later on, the merchants of the northern ports carried away great casks of the wine to their big fairs, which would not have been complete without the barrels of Cotnari, Odobeşti, and Drăgăşani.

Rumania now produces 7 million hectoliters (185 million U.S. gallons, 154 million imp.), ranking her sixth in Europe, just behind Portugal and ahead of West Germany. The vineyards have been expanding and total almost 300,000 hectares (750,000 acres). Each Rumanian drinks about 33 liters of wine every year. The government has encouraged the wine industry and plans to increase the size of the vineyards over the next decade by 100,000 hectares. Even though the government plays an important role, only 20% of the grape plantings belongs to the state. More than half of the wine is made by large cooperatives, but individual plots still account for one-third of the production.

Planted recently, and now developing well, are the vineyards of Tîrnave, Sîmbureşti, and Segarcea. The extension of the vineyards over most of the country is due foremost to the fact that Rumania is situated almost entirely in the vine-growing zone (toward the northern limit), and the country has the favorable features of rolling hills, with sunny, sheltered slopes, and southern exposure, and a wide range of suitable soils.

PRINCIPAL REGIONS

The Cotnari Vineyard

In northeast Rumania, near the historic town of Iassy, these vineyards cover the lower slopes of the Carpathians and enjoy splendid conditions of climate, soil, and exposure. Cotnari is one of the oldest vineyards in the country—in 1646 it was mentioned by the Jesuit monk Marcus Bandinus in an account of his sojourn in Moldavia. Old as it is, the vineyard still flourishes. Its new plantations, the result of modern scientific knowledge, promise a great development in the near future.

Grape varieties: Grasă de Cotnari, Fetească Albă, Tămîioasa Romînească, Frîncuşa.

Type of wine. Cotnari is a natural dessert wine, with 13% to 15% alcohol and more than 50 grams in a liter of residual sugar. It is well balanced, with a particularly fine flavor and bouquet.

The Murfatlar Vineyard

Situated close to the Black Sea, on the Murfatlar Hills, the vineyard has a character all its own: more than 17,000 hectares (42,500 acres) form an unbroken vineyard on sunny slopes fanned by a mild sea breeze, and the wine-making plants are run according to up-to-date methods by qualified technicians. There exists, also, in this region, an experimental station of the Institute of Horticultural and Viticultural Research.

Grape varieties. The prevailing grape varieties here are Pinot Chardonnay and Pinot Gris. Other types, such as Muscat Ottonel, Pinot Noir, and Cabernet Sauvignon, are also grown, with satisfactory results.

Type of wine. Murfatlar is a dessert wine, with a fine bouquet in which a faint, unique nuance of orange-flower is detectable.

The Tîrnave Vineyard

Extending along the banks of the River Tîrnave, the vineyards are well known for the quality of their wines. The more important areas are: Blaj, Mediaş, Richiş, Jidvei, Seuca, Valea-Lungă, Aţel, Tigmandru—to mention only a few of the more outstanding.

Grape varieties to be found in the vineyard area are Italian Riesling, Fetească, Ruländer, Furmint, Traminer, Sauvignon, Neuburger, and Muscat Ottonel.

Type of wine. Tîrnave produces dry wines from the Fetească and Riesling grape varieties, demi-sec and sweet wines from the Traminer and Sauvignon, and a famous *vin liquoreux* from the Muscat Ottonel.

The Dealul-Mare Vineyard

Where the lower slopes of the Carpathian Hills imperceptibly meet the plain and the hillocks bask in the hot rays of the sun, the vines produce such Rumanian favorites as the wines of Valea Călugărească, Tohani, Săhăteni, Urlaţi, Istrita, and Pietroasele.

Grape varieties: Italian Riesling, Fetească Albă, Tămîioasa Romînească, Muscat Ottonel, Cabernet Sauvignon, Pinot Noir, and Merlot.

Types of wine. The pride of the Valea Călugărească vineyard is the red wines from the Pinot Noir and the Cabernet Sauvignon. These are big wines of a rich, dark color, with a pleasant flavor, harmonious and velvety, yet full of character.

The Vrancea Vineyard

This is the largest stretch of vineyard in Rumania, extending over such varied country and types of soil and subject to climatic conditions so diverse that the wines produced in the region are correspondingly various. The principal types are:

Odobeşti. White table and quality wines from Galbenăçt, Fetească, Muscat Ottonel, and Aligoté grapes.

Coteşti. White and red table wines and quality wines from Riesling, Fetească, Muscat, Pinot Noir, and Cabernet Sauvignon grapes.

Panciu. White table wines, especially appreciated for their freshness.

Nicoreşti. Red table wines and quality wines from Băbească de Nicoreşti and Fetească Neagră.

The Banat Vineyard

There are two centers of production: the vineyards of the plain—Teremia Mare, Tomnatec—which produce large quantities of pleasant table wines of a greenish-white color and of a consistent quality, and the hill vineyards, such as Buziaş, Recaş, Miniş, Ghioroc, Baratke, Pîncota, and Şiria.

Grape varieties used in the white wines of Teremia and Tomnatec are Creaţa (Riesling de Banat), Majărcă, and Steinschiller. The red wines of Miniş and Recaş are made from Kadarka and Cabernet grapes.

Type of wine. From the stony terraces of Miniş comes the famous Kadarka de Banat—a red wine appreciated for its characteristic flavor and aroma.

The Other Vineyards

The white wines of Drăgăşani (Stefaneşti, Jasi, Huşi, and Galati), the white and red wines of Segarcea (Mehedinti, Uricani, and Sîmbureşti), the semi-dry white wines of Alba Iulia, Aiud, Lechinţa, and Bistriţa complete the wide range of wine production in Rumania.

It has been estimated that by the development of the nurseries and by the application of modern scientific methods of viticulture and viniculture Rumania's vineyards should become the most up-to-date in Eastern Europe. The present plan is to plant large areas with varieties which will ensure the basic production necessary for the big vinicultural combines which are being created in order to turn the country's great wine potential to the best account.

WINE EXPORTS

Wine has become an important export only in recent years. In 1975 nearly 1,000,000 hectoliters (26.5 million U.S. gallons, 22 million imp.) were sent abroad—different varieties to suit the tastes of different markets. Thus, to the German Federal Republic are exported white and red table wines from Riesling, Fetească, Kadarka, Cabernet Sauvignon, and Rotburgunder grapes. To Austria, besides ordinary white wines, Rumania sells quality wines of the Riesling, Fetească, Ruländer, Muscat Ottonel, Tămîioasa Romînească varieties, as well as red wines such as Rotburgunder and Cabernet Sauvignon. Rumanian wines are also exported to Switzerland, Belgium, Holland, Sweden, Denmark, France, the United States, and Great Britain—and, of course, in great quantities to Poland, Czechoslovakia, and East Germany.

The following are the principal varieties of wine bottled for export by the "Vinexport":

WHITE TABLE WINES

Perla de Tîrnave	Sauvignon
Fetească de Tîrnave	Aligoté
Riesling de Tîrnave	Riesling de Dealul-Mare
Grünsilvaner	Ordinary white table wine
Rulända	Superior white table wine
Furmint	

WHITE DESSERT WINES
Cotnari	Murfatler

RED WINES
Pinot Noir	Cabinet
Cabernet	Băbească de Nicoreşti
Kadarka	

Recently, Rumania entered wines for the competition organized by the French at Montpellier. According to an enthusiastic French report these wines "were a pleasant surprise . . . a sumptuous Merlot de Nicoreşti, ruby-colored and with a delicate flavor . . . Cabinet de Ploieşti, light and with a pleasing finesse. The dry and semi-dry white wines of Coteşti remind one of our Alsatian growths, and can be classified among the best in the world. The Riesling, with its freshness, and the Fetească, with its delicate yet definite aroma, have met with unanimous approval. In the same group, the Fetească de Tîr-

nave lived up to its name—The Pearl of Tîrnave. . . .The thick Chardonnay de Murfatlar with its taste of honey . . . and the subtler Cotnar . . . delighted the tasters."

Rumbullion (rumbustion)

Two seventeenth-century English-West Indian terms for rum. The exact origin of the words is obscure, although it has been suggested that they come from the dialect of Devonshire.

Ruppertsberger

Good wines of Mittelhaardt in the German Palatinate. The best vineyards are Hoheburg, Gaisböhl, Linsenbusch, Nussbien.
See Palatinate.

Russia

The U.S.S.R. is the third largest wine-producing nation in the world—after Italy and France—and both volume and vineyard size are rapidly increasing. In the ten-year period before the devastation of the Second World War, production averaged only 5 million hectoliters (132 million U.S. gallons, 110 million imp.). Now, about 32 million hectoliters (846 million U.S. gallons, 704 million imp.) are made every year, roughly twice the amount produced in the United States.

While wine, especially on the borders of the Black Sea, has always been important in Russia, it was not until the 1930s that the government undertook a rapid expansion of viticulture in the naturally favored areas, particularly the Soviet Republics of Armenia, Azerbaijan, and Georgia (in the neck between the Black and Caspian seas) and in the Crimea. By 1948 the acreage in vine tripled the pre-Revolution figure and had passed a million acres; today there are 1,250,000 hectares (3,125,000 acres) of vineyards. Nearly 8 million hectoliters of wines are imported—most of it from Algeria—and more than 700,000 hectoliters (18.5 million U.S. gallons, 15.4 million imp.) are exported. Consumption is 15 liters per capita, and the state encourages wine-drinking to cut down on the tremendous quantities of spirits consumed. Russians on the average drink more liquor than anyone else in the world.

Increase of production is partly due to territorial acquisitions, notably in the present Moldavian Soviet Socialist Republic—formerly Bessarabia and a part of Rumania. Bessarabia has always produced a large quantity of wines, especially around Kishinev, now the capital of the Moldavian S.S.R.; much of this wine, formerly known as Bessarabian, also comes from around the mouth of the River Dniester, in the region of what is Belgorod Dnestrovskiy, but was Akkerman—a name by which the wines were frequently known. This district is now actually in the Ukraine.

Very important in the Soviet scheme of wine expansion is the making of sparkling wines. One hundred million bottles are made annually. Probably the best is Kaffia, from the Crimea. A close second, if not equal, is that made at the Abrau Dursso Collective at Krasnodar in the region of the Kuban Valley near the Sea of Azov, a section always important in Russian viticulture. The wine is the same as the white wine of Abran (sometimes wrongly attributed to the Crimea), which lies to the west.

Three-fourths of Russian wine is sweet—over 15% of sugar—with about 15% of alcohol. Oenologists at the Technical Wine Institute at Odessa and the Magarach Research Center in Yalta work with standard European varieties such as Cabernet Sauvignon and Riesling, but their experiments are not aimed at making dry table wines; they try instead to improve the quality of the sweet wines.

Russian viticulture must cope with one great problem: the winter cold, with temperatures as low as $-40°$F. ($-40°$C.). After the harvest, the vines are pruned and taken off the training wires to be bent down and covered with dirt as insulation against the cold. Then the following spring these same vines must be uncovered and re-mounted before the new canes start to grow. Much emphasis has been put on mechanization, and this once time-consuming task is now performed both spring and fall by large machines. Mechanical harvesting, however, is less developed, and most of the grapes are still hand-picked. Agricultural engineers will have a workable harvesting machine in the fields within a few years.

IMPORTANT DISTRICTS

With a few mediocre exceptions, all the wine of the Soviet Union is produced in the vast arc of southern Russia, beginning at the Rumanian border on the west and stretching across the north of the Black Sea, the Caucasus, the Caspian Sea, and finally the north of Iran and India to the frontiers of China and Mongolia. The whole of this huge region produces wines in larger or smaller quantities but all the important ones come from west of the Caspian Sea—from the lower River Don, from around the Sea of Azov, and especially from the Crimea. Good wines are produced in the Caucasian republics of Azerbaijan, Georgia, and Armenia.

From earliest times, vines flourished in these regions, and wines are known to have been made long before our era. Traces of viticulture have been found in the ancient kingdom of Van which, about a thousand years before Christ, extended as far as the Armenian plain and the southern part of Transcaucasia. By the time of Herodotus (*fl.* 460 B.C.), the wines of Armenia had won great renown. When, some 250 years earlier, the Assyrians descended on the cities of Van, they found and pillaged great cellars of wine. Sulfur was already in use, and some of the wine is believed to have been pressed from sun-dried grapes. The Georgians, also, learned very early to cultivate their vines. Archaeologists have discovered painted wine jars and large amphorae dating from, at latest, the second millennium B.C.; in the *Odyssey*, Homer praised the "perfumed, sprightly wines of Colchis [western Georgia], land of the golden grape." Xenophon related that the wines of the Black Sea shores were robust,

pleasant and aromatic when mixed with water.

Crimea

The sweet wines and the dessert wines, both red and white, are the most important, though dry wines and fortified wines are made, as well as sparkling wines, which include the good Kaffia. Production is not large, but the small area of the Crimean peninsula thrusting into the Black Sea is the finest wine region of Russia. The southern and eastern sections are best, and important vineyards lie along the coasts and near the cities of Sevastopol and Simferopol. Crimean viticulture was originally developed at the beginning of the last century, under the direction of a M. Pallas, a French expert who brought many workers and managers from France to create or improve the vineyards. The chief estate, which gave its name to the most famous wine, was Massandra, the property of Prince Woronzow. Today Massandra is the name used for a combine of a number of Crimean wine collectives, and there is a red Massandra and a dry white one. But the most famous of these wines, still being made, is the rich, amber, fortified Madeira-type, sometimes considered the best wine of Russia. Other outstanding Crimean wines are the white Livadia, made from the Muscat (there is also a red Livadia from the Cabernet grape); the dry white Sémillon Oreanda (usually called Orianda outside Russia); the Saperavi or, today, the Saperavi Massandra, a dry red wine not to be confused with the great golden dessert Massandra, but a very flavorful wine on its own account; the pink dessert Alupka, and the Ay-Danil dessert wines. A number of grape varieties known in Europe are used here—for example, Riesling, Cabernet, Pinot Gris, and, most extensively, Muscat.

River Don

The lower Don, as it descends to empty into the Sea of Azov below Rostov, produces red and white wines and a relatively small quantity of sparkling wine, the best-known of which is Donski. The viticultural centers are Tsimliansk, Constantinovka, and Novocherkassk. Grape varieties are of local type: Pletchistik, Krasnotop, and Pukhliakovski, all white wine grapes.

Moldavia

Formerly Bessarabia and part of Rumania, Moldavia produces the largest quantity of wine in the U.S.S.R. The region used to be planted in hybrid vines which gave ordinary wines. Today there are also some Pinot, Aligoté, Riesling, Traminer, and other European varieties. There are 250,000 hectares (625,000 acres) of vines, of which 180,000 are in production.

Ukraine

After the scourge of the vine louse phylloxera in the last century, a great percentage of the area was replanted in hybrids. These are now being systematically replaced. Centers are Odessa and Nikolayev on the Black Sea and Dniepropetrovsk on the Dnieper. The vineyards in all parts of the Ukraine total 260,000 hectares (650,000 acres).

Stavropol

Dry white wines (Riesling, Bechtau, and Sylvaner Bechtau) and Muscat-based dessert wines from the north slopes of the Caucasus Mountains.

Krasnodar

A region, and also its principal city, lying east of the Black Sea and the Sea of Azov. There are some very large cooperatives in this region. Good red and white dry wines are made along the Black Sea, near Anapa and Novorossiysk, from the Riesling and Cabernet grapes. The Kuban Valley produces large quantities of fortified and dessert wines. The Abrau-Dursso Collective, on the Black Sea, produces one of the best sparkling wines in the U.S.S.R. Two other sparkling wines that are exported from this area are Krasnodar and Isimljanskoje Ygristoje.

Georgia

With about 100,000 hectares (265,000 acres), the Georgian Republic is the largest producer among the first-quality wine districts, containing some of the oldest vineyard sites in Russia. Some Georgian wines seen abroad are white Myshako Riesling and Ghurdjurni. The Takhetia region is the best, producing the white Gourdjaani and Tsinandali; the red Mukuzani, Napuréouli, and Mzvane or Mtzvane. In this region, the must is fermented with the skins and stems in earthenware pots, giving the wine a particularly stringent taste. A good red is made from the Saperavi grape, which also produces one of the finest red table wines of the Crimea. Mzvane, making the white of the same name, is also a grape variety; another local type is the Rka-Ziteli. There is also abundant production of sparkling wines and brandy.

Azerbaijan

Table wines, fortified wines, and *eaux-de-vie* are produced in Russian Azerbaijan on the border of Iran. Matrassa, a table wine named after the grape variety, is the best of the region, which has only been growing vines since the 1960s. The principal centers are Kirovabad, Kurdamirsk, Chemakhinsk, and Geokchai. Dessert wines are also made in this region.

Armenia

Wine has always been a fundamental product in the Armenian economy and the region is called "Fatherland of the Vine." Natural wines, fortified wines, and brandy are made in large quantities. The wine centers are Echmiadzin, Achtarak, Vedin, and Oktemberian (35,000 hectares or 87,500 acres of vines).

In addition to the foregoing important districts, expanding wine production by means of irrigation is underway in Turkmenistan, where fortified wines, a so-called Tokay, and Yasman-salik and Kara-Isium are made. In Uzbekistan, north of Turkmenistan, three-quarters of the grape culture is devoted to the locally famous Iziun table grape, but the remainder goes principally to dessert wines; in Daghestan, adjoining Georgia and Azerbaijan, a certain amount of fairly good wine is made; in Tadzhikistan, on the north of Pakistan and Kashmir, dessert wine is now being produced from about 20,000 hectares; and in the vast stretches of Kazakhstan, which reaches from the Caspian Sea to Mongolia, vine planting has been introduced in recent years.

The chart opposite gives the authorized Soviet wine place-names or Appellations d'Origine. These were extracted from a bulletin of the International Wine Office, to which acknowledgment is also due for some of the other material on Soviet wines. Certain wines are designated by the Soviet wine industry as port, madeira, tokay, etc. *This can never be correct,* as only a wine from the banks of the Upper Douro River in Portugal can fulfill all the conditions necessary to Port; only a wine from the island of Madeira can fulfill the conditions for a Madeira, etc. But in the situation prevailing at the time of writing, of very limited information from the Soviet Union, the terms port-type, madeira-type, etc., will be used to indicate the approximate style of the wines.

SPIRITS

The Russian national drink is traditionally vodka, which has for some time now been most popular also west of the Iron Curtain. A large quantity of brandy is also made.
See Vodka.

Russian River Valley

Californian wine district in Sonoma County on the coast 50 miles north of San Francisco.
See United States: California.

Ruster Ausbruch

A very sweet Austrian wine, made from late-picked grapes in the vineyards of Rust, Burgenland.
See Austria.

Rutherglen

Celebrated region in Victoria, Australia, producing some of the best fortified and dessert wines, and some full, red table wines as well, now, however, all in smaller quantities than formerly.
See Australia.

Ruwer

See Mosel-Saar-Ruwer.

Wine District	Type	Grape Varieties and Place-Names
Crimea (Massandra Combine)	Dry white	Sémillon Oreanda, Riesling Massandra, Aligoté Ay-Danil
	Dry red	Cabernet Livadia, Saperavi Massandra, Bordo Ay-Danil
	Sweet dessert	White Muscat Massandra, White Muscat Livadia, Pink Muscat Gourzouf
	Red dessert	Black Muscat Kuchuk-Lambat, White Muscat Kastel
	Pink dessert	Pink Muscat Alupka
	Dessert	Tokay Ay-Danil, Tokay Alouchta, Pinot Gris Ay-Danil
	Red Muscat	Aiou-Dag
	White port-type	Sou-Dag, Alupka
	Red port-type	Livadia, Kuchuk-Lambat, Alouchta, Massandra
	Madeira-type	Kuchuk-Uzen, Massandra
Ukrainian S.S.R.	White	Riesling, Aligoté
	Red	Cabernet
Krasnodar (Abrau-Dursso Combine)	Dry white	Riesling Abrau, Riesling Anapa
	Dry red	Cabernet Abrau
Georgian S.S.R.	Dry white	Tsolikohouri, Sémillon, Kahouri, Tibaani
	Red	Téliani, Mukuzani, Napuréouli
	White dessert	Ousahelohouri, Tchkhavéri, Tvichi, Psou, Tetra, Ahméta
	Red dessert	Hvantchkara, Kindzmaraouli, Ahachéni
	Brandy	Eniséli, Gremi, Vartsihé, Tbilisi
Azerbaijan S.S.R.	Red	Matrassa
	White port-type	Akastafa
	White dessert	Kara-Tachanakh
	Red dessert	Chamakha, Kurdamir
Armenian S.S.R.	White	Etchmiadzine, Voskévaz
	Red	Aréni, Norachéne
	White sherry-type	Achtaraque
	Red port-type	Aigéchate
	Red fortified	Arévchate
	Brandy	Dvine, Erévan, Arménia, Nairi
Kazakhstanian S.S.R.	Sparkling white	Ak-Kainar
	White	Issik
	Fortified, dessert	Chirine, Kazakhstane, Tselinnoe, Ak-Boulak, Muscat Violet
Kirghizian S.S.R.	White dessert	Muscat of Kirghiz, Muscat Violet
	Red	Cabernet, Kirghizstan
	Red port-type	Ala-Too
Tadzhikistanian S.S.R.	Port-type	Taifi
	Red port-type	Tadzhikistan
	Red dessert	Vakche
	Dessert	Chirine, Gontchi, Guissare, Djaousse
Turkmenistanian S.S.R.	Dessert	Térbache
	Fortified	Yasman-Salik, Goulistane, Kopetdague
Uzbekistanian S.S.R.	Red	Uzbekistan
	White dessert	Aléatiko, Umalak, Bouaki
	Red port-type	Farkhad
Bessarabia Combine	White	Pinot, Aligoté
	Red	Bordo (presumably Cabernet)
Tempelhof Collective	White	Riesling, Sylvaner

S

Saar

See Mosel-Saar-Ruwer.

Sables-Saint-Émilion

Formerly a place-name; the wines have been incorporated into the better-known *appellation* Saint-Émilion.
See Saint-Émilion.

Saccharometer

See Mustimeter.

Saccharomyces Cereviseae

The yeast of wine, found on the skins of grapes.
See Yeasts; Chapter Nine, p. 38.

Sack

Early name for Sherry wine (see, for example, Shakespeare, *Henry IV, Part* 2, Act IV, Scene iii). It was believed at one time to come from the Spanish *seco* (dry); but because the wine at that time was probably sweet (not at all the Sherry we know) it is easy to accept Mr. H. Warner Allen's theory that the word came from the Spanish *sacar*—to take out, to export. The name of this sweet export wine was afterward attached to other, comparable wines, such as Canary Sack and Málaga Sack.

Sacramental wines

Used in the sacraments of the Christian Church. The need to keep up the supply of these wines caused the monasteries to take an active part in the viticulture of the Middle Ages. The term also applies to wines used during the Passover and other Jewish holidays.

Sacramento Valley

Californian wine region.
See United States: California.

Saint-Amour

Red wines of Beaujolais, in south Burgundy.
The vineyards are the farthest north in the region, touching the area of Pouilly-Fuissé in the Mâconnais. The red wine is one of the fullest of the Beaujolais.
See Beaujolais.

Saint-Aubin and Saint-Aubin-Côte de Beaune
Burgundy red and white wines.
District: Côte de Beaune, France.

Saint-Aubin stands back in the Côte d'Or hills behind Puligny-Montrachet and Chassagne-Montrachet, but its wines are not equal to those of its famous neighbors. For one thing, it is slightly too high above the favored strip of the slope's midsection for really first-rate wines. Because of the quality difference, the Saint-Aubins should be considerably less expensive than others of the Côte de Beaune and, if bought fairly young, can be excellent value.

Wines may be sold as Saint-Aubin, Saint-Aubin-Côte de Beaune, or, after blending with growths from other communes, as Côte de Beaune-Villages—any wine with the right to one of these names has the right to them all. Production in an average year for quantity is some 3,000 hectoliters (79,500 U.S. gallons, 66,000 imp.), about two-thirds of it white, and more is sold under the Villages name. Out of the 228 hectares (570 acres) of vineyard eligible for the name Saint-Aubin, 156 hectares (390 acres) are classified as First Growths.

FIRST GROWTHS (*Grands Crus*)

	Hectares	Acres
Champlot	8	19.8
En Remilly	2	4.9
La Chatenière	10	24.7
Les Combes	15	37.1
Les Frionnes	1	2.5
Les Murgers-des-Dents-de-Chien	3	7.4
Sur Gamay	14	34.6
Sur-le-Sentier-du-Clou	12	29.7

Saint-Aubin-de-Luigné

Dry white wines of the Coteaux du Layon district of Anjou (*q.v.*).

Saint-Denis

See Clos Saint-Denis; Morey-Saint-Denis.

Clos Saint-Denis
Burgundy red wine.
District: Côte de Nuits, France.
Commune: Morey-Saint-Denis.
Official Classification: Great Growth (Grand Cru).

The vineyards of the Clos Saint-Denis stand alongside the Route des Grands Crus, the road that threads through the middle of the Côte d'Or vineyards, slightly before you reach the village of Morey heading south. In

1927, the village chose to add the vineyard name to its own, although the Clos was not at that time classed among the topmost of the commune. This was remedied in 1937 when Clos Saint-Denis was ranked among the Great Growths (*Grands Crus*)—the thirty-one outstanding vineyards of the Côte d'Or.

The wine which starts its career in the vineyard of Clos Saint-Denis is among the lightest of the top-rated wines of the Côte de Nuits. In fine years, delicacy and finesse are the characteristics to look for, rather than the full robust strength of its peers, Clos de Tart, Clos de la Roche, and Clos des Lambrays. (This last is an outstanding wine despite its classification among the First Growths—*Premiers Crus*—instead of among the Great Growths.)

Within the 6.5 hectares (16.2 acres) of the vineyards there are a number of growers who together declare to the French government 200 hectoliters (5,300 U.S. gallons, 4,400 imp.) of wine in an average year for quantity—or about 2,200 cases.

Saint-Émilion

The vine, a variety of Ugni Blanc, which yields the greater part of the Charente wines used in making Cognac (*q.v.*). It is grown in other districts of France, where it is also known by such names as Clairette à Grains Ronds, Clairette de Vence, Graisse, Queue de Renard, and Roussan. In Italy, this grape is called Trebbiano; in Corsica, Rossola.

Saint-Émilion

Red wine.
District: Bordeaux, France.

The wine is the fullest and heartiest of the red wines of Bordeaux. Some of the vintages require a considerable amount of time to develop; the 1945, for example, was not ready to drink before 1965. (This, however, is exceptional, and the 1945 has been very slow-maturing throughout Bordeaux.)

The vineyards can be conveniently divided into two types: those of the plain and those of the slopes. But within the groups, and across them, there is considerable variation, owing to the differences in soil and the different exposures of a terrain which, rising up into a crown around the town of Saint-Émilion itself, is very hilly, except where it flattens out on the borders of the neighboring district of Pomerol. This distinction between plain and hill played a drastic role in late February 1956, when Bordeaux viticulture experienced its second most disastrous winter since 1709. The frost settled in the lowest areas and all the vineyards of the plain, including Château Cheval-Blanc, finest of the Saint-Émilions, lost their 1956 and 1957 crops, and in many cases crops for years after, since either the productive branches or the whole vines were frozen. (Three years later, various growers reported that vines were suddenly dying from the aftereffects of this frost.) Hill vineyards survived, and Château Ausone, probably the best of the slope wines, was, for example, unhurt.

Saint-Émilion itself is believed to be the oldest wine town in France, and certainly it is the most picturesque. Placed on a hill of soft, easily hewn stone, it is uniquely all of a piece; the wine cellars of many of the châteaux are the old quarries from which the rock itself was cut in the Middle Ages, and blocks of the rock provide the tawny, sun-ripened stone of which the town is built. There can be no more romantic setting for drinking a great wine than in sight of the vineyard where it is grown. The terrace of the town's leading restaurant, the Hostellerie de Plaisance, is erected on the dome of a church—the gray, dim Église Monolithe, hollowed out of the solid rock underneath the inn. This ninth-century chapel is the largest in the world to be cut out of a single rock. An unforgettable sight is a ceremonial installation of the wine society, the Jurade, conducted in guttering taper light in the crypt. From the Plaisance belvedere, sipping your wine, you have a view across the mellow, red roofs of the King's Tower, built by Louis VI in 1124, of the ruined arches over the Cloister of the Cordeliers and of vineyards spilling down the Saint-Émilion slopes and spreading out over the plain.

Ausonius, who wrote an epic poem about the Moselle, lived in a luxurious Roman villa which may or may not have been near the present site of Château Ausone. In his time, the third century, vineyards already girdled Saint-Émilion. The saint himself came in the eighth century, on his way to Santiago de Compostela in Spain, then an important goal of medieval pilgrims. If you go down into his hermitage near the church and stand by his bed and seat carved out of the stone, you will be told that he found the place a wilderness and, attracted by a miraculous spring, established a colony. It may not be irreligious to think this spring may have been Saint-Émilion wine, for the city was bustling and had already known and was forgetting the Roman grandeur. In any case, the saint lingered, and never went to Santiago de Compostela.

An Appellation Contrôlée, or legally controlled wine place-name in its own right, Saint-Émilion is also a Bordeaux, in the wine area of that name. The city of Bordeaux is about eighteen miles to the west.

In addition to Saint-Emilion itself, seven surrounding communes have the right to the place-name Saint-Émilion. They are Saint-Laurent-des-Combes, Saint-Christophe-des-Bardes, Saint-Hippolyte, Saint-Étienne-de-Lisse, Saint-Pey-d'Armens, Saint-Sulpice-de-Faleyrens, and Vignonet. Lying in a semicircle on the south and west of Saint-Émilion, none produces a wine of the high level of the first-rate growths; but Château Larcis-Ducasse in Saint-Laurent-des-Combes, which is a continuation of the slope beyond Pavie, is worthy of mention. Château Monbousquet, set back from a small country road across the Bordeaux-Bergerac road, on the flat land of Saint-Sulpice-de-Faleyrens, is an estate where wines were raised by Saint-Émilion's great promoter, Daniel Querre, certainly one of the largest growers of wine. He was a beaming man of 300 pounds, whose trumpet voice

ST-ÉMILION/POMEROL

issued the call to grape harvesting from the top of a twelfth-century tower each year during the Jurade ceremony of the Ban des Vendanges. His example is now followed by his son Alain Querre.

Five communes lying to the north of Saint-Émilion and to the east of Pomerol have the right to add Saint-Émilion to their names, the Appellations Contrôlées of this district being: Saint-Georges-Saint-Émilion, Montagne-Saint-Émilion, Lussac-Saint-Émilion, Puisseguin-Saint-Émilion, and Parsac-Saint-Émilion. Since 1975 wines of Parsac-Saint-Émilion have been sold as Saint-Émilion. Château Saint-Georges, and to a somewhat lesser extent the other wines of Saint-Georges-Saint-Émilion, are only divided from the Saint-Émilions proper by tradition. From the quality standpoint, they have the same characteristics of longevity and splendor developing after sufficient age in bottle.

Sables-Saint-Émilion was an Appellation Contrôlée given to the wines of a small district touching Saint-Émilion on one border, but lying between Pomerol and the River Dordogne. These wines have, since 1974, been sold as Saint-Émilions.

The wines of Saint-Émilion were officially classified in the summer of 1955 by the French Institut National des Appellations d'Origine, the body that controls wine place-names. Before that date, Château Cheval-Blanc and Château Ausone had always been considered as the leading and exceptional growths, with the others following after. In 1955 they were accorded the right to stand at the head of the First Great Growths (*Premiers Grands Crus*) but were not otherwise distinguished from ten more which were also rated Firsts and listed in alphabetical order after Ausone and Cheval-Blanc. Learning from the difficulties that had been encountered in the classification of Médoc wines exactly a century earlier, the officials who set up the Saint-Émilion Classification did not make the mistake of dividing the Classified Growths (*Crus*) into Firsts (*Premiers*), Seconds (*Seconds*), Thirds (*Troisièmes*), Fourths (*Quatrièmes*), and Fifths (*Cinquièmes*), thereby running the risk that a Third Growth might be mistaken for a third-rate wine. The vineyards of Saint-Émilion were placed in two groups only: First Great Growths (*Premiers Grands Crus*), of which there are twelve; and Great Growths (*Grands Crus*), which total about seventy.

FIRST GREAT GROWTHS (*Premiers Grands Crus*)

Château Ausone	Clos Fourtet
Château Cheval-Blanc	Château La
Château Beauséjour-Bécot	Gaffelière
Château Beauséjour-Duffau-Lagarrosse	Château La
Château Bel-Air	Magdelaine
Château Canon	Château Pavie
Château Figeac	Château Trottevieille

The entire classification will be found in Appendix A, p. 547. For the individual First Great Growths, see under their names. Cheval-Blanc is unanimously elected best of all Saint-Émilions and, with Château Pétrus in Pomerol, equal to the five Médoc Greats—Lafite, Latour, Margaux, Haut-Brion (Graves), and Mouton-Rothschild. The position of Château Ausone is not so secure, but most people feel it follows Cheval-Blanc and also deserves a place in the upper hierarchy. A few contend that, in recent years, La Gaffelière, just below it on the same slope, has equaled and sometimes surpassed Ausone.

Saint-Estèphe

Bordeaux red wine.
District: Haut-Médoc, France.

Saint-Estèphe is the northernmost and fourth in order of the great red wine communes on the famous Médoc peninsula jutting north from Bordeaux in southwest France. Of the annual 6,000,000 bottles (from 1,100 hectares; 2,775 acres) entitled to the official place-name (the largest volume of the communal wines), not all is of the very high average quality of the wines of Margaux, Pauillac, and Saint-Julien. Some of the lesser Saint-Estèphe wines are transitional between the Bas-Médocs and the more aristocratic Haut-Médocs. This is not surprising, since the village stands on the boundary of the two regions.

While the lesser wines may lack something in finesse, in Château Cos d'Estournel, Château Montrose, and Château Calon-Ségur Saint-Estèphe has three of the very distinguished Médoc vineyards. The span of the quality range is broader than in the other three famous communes, and a certain care is needed in selecting the wines.

Characteristically full and with a big nose, the wines vary within the region, and a Calon-Ségur at the northernmost extremity will be the most "Saint-Estèphe" of the Saint-Estèphes. At the opposite end of the scale from the delicate and feminine wines of Margaux, Saint-Estèphes are frequently likened in Bordeaux to Saint-Émilion wines, generally heavier than the Médocs. When young, they will be distinguished for their fruity fullness.

Saint-Estèphe has five vineyards rated as Classified Growths (*Crus*) in the 1855 Classification of Médoc wines, fewer by far than the other leading communes. They are:

SECOND GROWTHS (*Seconds Crus*)

Château Cos d'Estournel
Château Montrose

THIRD GROWTH (*Troisième Cru*)

Château Calon-Ségur

FOURTH GROWTH (*Quatrième Cru*)

Château Lafon-Rochet

FIFTH GROWTH (*Cinquième Cru*)

Château Cos-Labory

(For individual Classified Growths, *see* Chateau Cos d'Estournel, Château Montrose, Château Calon-Ségur, etc.)

Sainte-Foy-Bordeaux

Bordeaux white wine.
District: Southwest France.

Sweet white wines made according to the Sauternes method of select picking of overripe grapes and from the Sauternes varieties Sémillon, Sauvignon, and Muscadelle. The wines come from the easternmost part of the Bordeaux wine region and are more properly linked with the adjoining area of Monbazillac sweet white wines. A small quantity of red wine also bears the name, but it generally amounts only to about 3% of the production.

Saint Gall

Fortified French aperitif made from red wine.

Saint-Georges-Saint-Émilion

One of five communes in the north of Saint-Émilion which share the right to the Appellation Contrôlée Saint-Émilion (*q.v.*).

Saint-Jean-de-Minervois, Muscat de

See Sweet fortified wines of France.

Saint-Joseph

Red and white wines of the French Côtes du Rhône. *See* Rhône.

Saint-Julien

Bordeaux red wine.
District: Haut-Médoc, France.

One of the four leading Médoc red wine communes in the Bordeaux region in southwest France—the others are Pauillac, Margaux, and Saint-Estèphe—Saint-Julien is smallest in production, making about 3,500,000 bottles of wine a year from some 650 hectares (1,625 acres); the wine is entitled to the official place-name or Appellation Contrôlée. As a regional wine it is probably the best-known of the four in the world market.

The wine, from vines grown in a gravelly soil marked by the presence of a considerable amount of clay, has affinities with both those of Pauillac immediately to the north, and those of Margaux, grown about 13 kilometers (8 miles) to the south, the other side of a stretch of land too low and moist for fine wines. Slightly darker in color and fuller-bodied than the typical Margaux, the wines in this respect tend to resemble the Pauillacs; but they are less full and quicker to mature than a characteristic Pauillac and have more of the finesse, delicacy, and femininity identified with Margaux.

The community, a small village lying in among the famous Léovilles, on a curve of the vineyard road running north from Bordeaux, is also known as Saint-Julien-Beychevelle, signifying the link with the ancient Beychevelle estate. After crossing pasture-land, the vineyard road suddenly climbs, and on the higher ground Saint-Julien begins, with Château Beychevelle and then Château Ducru-Beaucaillou on the river side, and Château Branaire facing them across the road. At the turning, a rather large wine bottle, an eyesore in the corner of the vineyard of Beychevelle, takes the visitor's eye. Entering the region, a large billboard announces:

PASSERS-BY!
You are now entering the ancient
and celebrated vineyard of Saint-Julien.
Bow low!

The ancient fame of Saint-Julien has been revived by its mayor, M. Henri Martin, owner of Château Gloria, and in the late fifties and middle sixties the president of the C.I.V.B., the official Bordeaux wine association, and now head of the Commanderie du Bontemps.

In an average year, approximately sixty different wines carry the Saint-Julien place-name, to which they are entitled if grown in the delimited region, cared for according to certain quality restrictions, and approved in annual taste testings.

The Saint-Julien vineyards rated as Classified Growths (*Crus*) in the 1855 Classification of Médoc wines are:

SECOND GROWTHS (*Seconds Crus*)
Château Léoville-Las-Cases
Château Léoville-Poyferré
Château Léoville-Barton
Château Gruaud-Larose
Château Ducru-Beaucaillou

THIRD GROWTHS (*Troisièmes Crus*)
Château Lagrange
Château Langoa-Barton

FOURTH GROWTHS (*Quatrièmes Crus*)
Château Saint-Pierre
Château Talbot
Château Branaire
Château Beychevelle

Saint-Julien has neither First nor Fifth Growths.

(For individual Classified Growths, *see Château* Léoville-Las-Cases, *Château* Léoville-Poyferré, *Château* Léoville-Barton, etc.)

Saint-Lambert-du-Lattay

Commune making sweet white wines in the Coteaux du Layon district of Anjou (*q.v.*).

Saint-Laurent

Red wine grape used in Austria, Czechoslovakia, etc.

Saint Martin

Saint Martin (*c.* 345) was an early patron of wine in the Loire Valley, and to him is attributed the discovery that wines do better when they are pruned.
See Loire.

Saint-Nicholas-de-Bourgueil

Red and rosé wines from a sub-district of the Touraine in the French Loire Valley. The total area of 14,000 hectares (35,000 acres) is planted in Cabernet Franc.
See Bourgueil; Touraine.

Saint-Péray and Saint-Péray Mousseux

Dry and sweet still wine; also sparkling wine.
District: Rhône Valley, France.

The wines were highly appreciated in France during the Second Empire (1852–70) but fell from grace shortly afterward, and are only beginning to come back into favor. Now, as then, the full-bodied sparkling wine seems to be the more sought after.

The vines (Roussanne and Marsanne) are grown on cliffs overlooking the Rhône, on the river's right bank. Sometimes the growers will wait until the grapes are over-ripe and let the *pourriture noble,* or noble rot, form on them, drying the skin and leaving a sugar-rich grape for making an ultra-sweet wine. Generally, however, the grapes are picked at maturity and vinified into a dry wine. Much of the output is subjected to a secondary fermentation in the bottle to render the wine sparkling. About 80 hectares (200 acres) of vines exist, and production amounts to nearly 1,250 hectoliters (33,000 U.S. gallons, 27,000 imp.).

Château Saint-Pierre

Bordeaux red wine.
District: Haut-Médoc, France.
Commune: Saint-Julien.

About three and a half centuries old, the vineyard owes its name to a Baron St. Pierre, who bought it in 1767. In 1892 part of the vineyard was sold to M. Léon Sevaistre and named Château Saint-Pierre-Sevaistre, while the remainder of the estate became known as Château Saint-Pierre-Bontemps. The two sections were eventually reunited by the present Belgian owners, the Antwerp wine firm of Castelin et Van der Busshe Fils. The wines have been in need of some improvement. A few of the good sections of the vineyard were purchased by Henri Martin, who incorporated them into his Château Gloria.

Characteristics. Rather light and generally undistinguished. Improved vinification has helped the quality.
Vineyard area: 17 hectares (42 acres).
Average production: 60 *tonneaux* (5,000 cases).

Saint-Raphaël

Delicate, red, bitter-sweet French aperitif based on fortified red wine and flavored principally with quinine. It is highly advertised throughout France, where it is very popular.

Saint-Romain

Burgundy red and white wines.
District: Côte de Beaune, France.

Lying far back in the hills, behind Meursault and Auxey-Duresses, Saint-Romain makes a little wine, of reasonably little note, although it may often represent good value compared with other growths of the famous slope. Some of it—both red and white—is sold under the communal name, and some is blended with wines of other specified communes of the Côte de Beaune and sold as Côte de Beaune-Villages. There are about 100 hectares (250 acres) allowed for the growing of the finer vines, and production in a good year for quantity is about 2,000 hectoliters (53,000 U.S. gallons, 44,000 imp.), just more than half of it white, with an unspecified further amount sold as Côte de Beaune-Villages.

Saint Véran

Burgundy white wine.
District: Maconnais, France.

Not far in fact or intent from the more famous Appellation Contrôlée of Pouilly-Fuissé, this region also makes white wine from the Chardonnay grape. Some 15,000 hectoliters (397,500 U.S. gallons, 330,000 imp.) are produced annually on the region's 240 hectares (593 acres).

Saint Vincent

Patron saint of French wine-growers. According to legend, he became thirsty in Heaven and asked permission to return to earth for a while, so that he might taste the good wines of France again. He was granted leave of absence and no doubt he meant to go back when his time was up. But the red wine of Graves was his undoing; he was found in the cellar of La Mission-Haut-Brion, lost to the world and to his appointment in Heaven, and as a punishment he was turned to stone.

His statue is still to be seen there, clutching a dilapidated bunch of grapes and wearing his mitred cap awry. The Saint Vincent holiday is widely celebrated in Burgundy. Processions honoring this wine saint are held in many villages of the Côte d'Or on January 22 each year.

Sainte-Croix-du-Mont

Bordeaux white wine.
District: Southwest France.

A small district south of Bordeaux and divided from Sauternes by the River Garonne. The white wines are sweet and are very reminiscent of their neighbors across the river, made from the same grape varieties—Sémillon, Sauvignon, and some Muscadelle—and produced from late-picked and overripe grapes which have achieved a concentrated sweetness, as in Sauternes. If the wines lack the very great elegance and finesse of some Sauternes, they are nevertheless the best of the white sweet wines of the right bank of the Garonne and, priced far below the famous Sauternes, are excellent buys.

The bluff or slope of Sainte-Croix-du-Mont carries solid vine like a cape over its sloping shoulders. At the top thrusts out the church of Sainte-Croix-du-Mont with its delicate spire and, a hundred yards away, the medieval fortified castle; these landmarks are illuminated in the summer and they shine for miles over the Sauternes and Graves vineyards.

Production averages around 15,000 hectoliters (397,500 U.S. gallons, 330,000 imp.), about half that of Sauternes, and to achieve the place-name the wines must attain 13% of alcohol. In fact they frequently reach 15%. No better place for tasting them can exist than the outdoor terrace built just below the castle in 1955 and 1956. From the tables placed on the grassy ledge of the bluff, vineyard tumbles away in a rush below until it is checked by the low-lying land bordering the river. Across the river, shrouded with willows, is Sauternes, and on the horizon the outlines of Château d'Yquem can be dimly made out.

Saké

A Japanese fermented liquor, from 12% to 16% alcohol by volume. It is made from rice which is cleansed and steamed and allowed to ferment. Toward the end of the fermentation period more rice is added, then the saké is drawn off, filtered, and put into casks for maturing.

The saké is colorless and rather sweet, with a bitter aftertaste. The Japanese serve it warm, in porcelain cups. Natives of Okinawa also make a saké, but it is harsher and usually served cold. The more than one dozen different types of the wine fall roughly into three styles: *mirin*, for cooking; *toso*, spicy and sweet, drunk for New Year's celebrations; and *seishu*, the completely refined wine known in the West.

Salmanazar

A large glass bottle usually for display purposes. When filled it contains 9.6 liters or 325 U.S. fluid ounces (338 British). The equivalent of twelve regular bottles.

Salta

Wine-producing province of Argentina (*q.v.*).

Saltillo

Wine-producing town in Mexico, site of the Compañía Vinícola de Saltillo.
See Mexico.

Samogon

Bootleg vodka in Russia.

Samos

The Muscat of Samos is one of the best-known wines of Greece, and the place-name is controlled.
See Greece.

Sampigny-les-Maranges and Sampigny-les-Maranges-Côte de Beaune

Burgundy red and white wines.
District: Côte de Beaune, France.

Sampigny is a minor wine commune at the southern end of the Côte de Beaune. Its wines are normally blended with those from other Côte de Beaune communes and sold as Côte de Beaune-Villages but may also sometimes be found under their own name. The vineyards cover 44 hectares (108 acres), and wines from the 29-hectare heart may add the designation Côte de Beaune to the commune name. In exceptionally rare cases, wines may be seen with the label Sampigny-les-Maranges, or Sampigny-les-Maranges-Clos du Roi, in both cases the added names being those of the better vineyards within the commune. Les Maranges and the Clos du Roi are the only two that have this right.

Samshu

The Chinese saké (*q.v.*).

San Joaquin Valley

Warm Californian region producing raisins and sweet fortified wines. The principal districts are Madera, Fresno, Kings, Tulare, and Kern counties.
See United States: California.

San Juan

Province of Argentina extensively planted in vines.
See Argentina.

San Marino (Sangiovese)

The smallest country in the world, only 59 square kilometers (23 square miles), and half of that nearly perpendicular, produces a red table wine called Sangiovese and a sparkling sweet dessert Moscato. The total production of wine is some 20 hectoliters (530 U.S. gallons, 440 imp.) annually. Every drop of the rather hard Sangiovese, all of the Moscato, and a dessert liqueur named Titanium, are consumed by the approximately 1 million tourists who, every year, visit the toy state enclosed within Italy. Titanium takes its name from Monte Titano, the sheer peak that thrusts up from the Italian plain 16 kilometers (10 miles) inland from Rimini and the Adriatic. On top of this the town of San Marino is perched. The liqueur is made from the wildflowers of the mountain, as it has been for over a century. To sip it or drink the wine in an outdoor café in the spotless little stone town, looking out to the Adriatic or to the dim blue Apennines, is a bibulous experience never to be forgotten—and you are sure to hear from some native of how San Marino has kept its independence against such would-be conquerors as Cesare Borgia and Napoleon and remained a dot of freedom for 1,600 years.

Sancerre

Loire Valley white wine.
District: Loire Valley, France.

A small, well-known district of the Upper Loire producing an annual 40,000 hectoliters (1,040,000 U.S. gallons, 865,000 imp.) of very dry white and a small amount of red and rosé wine. The town from which the district takes its name commands a sweeping view of the river from the top of a hill, on the slopes of which (and on those of the hills of twelve surrounding towns) are planted about 280 hectares (700 acres) of Sauvignon vines. No other grape is allowed in wine labeled Sancerre. The best vineyards are Bué, Champtin, and Chavignol.

This wine derives a special flavor from the district's limestone soil—markedly dry and apt in wet summers to have too much acidity. In warm summers, however, this acidity is balanced by sufficient alcohol and the wine has a crisp and refreshing tang. Never great, Sancerre is nevertheless one of France's very pleasant and popular white wines. The reds and rosés, made from the Pinot Noir grape, account for about 10,000 hectoliters (260,000 U.S. gallons, 217,000 imp.).

Sandweine

The "Sand wines" of Burgenland in Austria get their name from the sandy soil in which the vines grow—soil which the phylloxera louse avoids. These wines are among the few in Europe which need not be grafted onto American root-stocks. They are labeled Seewinkel followed by the informing grape variety.
See Austria.

Sardinia

Sangiovese

Red wine grape used in Chianti, Montepulciano, and other Italian wines.

Sangría

A refreshing warm-weather Spanish wine punch made of red wine, citrus juice, sugar, soda or water, and sometimes garnished with berries, fruit slices, or other flavorings.

Sansevero

Dry white Italian wine.
See Apulia.

Santa Maddalena

Red wine of Alto Adige, sometimes referred to as Sankt Magdelener.
See Trentino-Alto Adige.

Santa Rosa

Center of Californian wine district in Sonoma County.
See United States: California.

Santarem-João Santarem

Blue-black grape used in the hill-slope wines of Colares, Portugal (*q.v.*).

Santenay and Santenay-Côte de Beaune

Burgundy red, and some white, wines.
District: Côte de Beaune.

Santenay is the last important wine commune of the Côte de Beaune before it tails off into the southernmost Cheilly-les-Maranges, Dezize-les-Maranges, and Sampigny-les-Maranges. The wines—which have equal right to the name of the commune or communal name with Côte de Beaune added—are predominantly red and are light, fast-maturing, sometimes extraordinarily fruity, and often very good if priced below those from some of the other Côte de Beaune wine communes. Authentic red Santenay of a good year often rivals wines from Chassagne-Montrachet or Volnay, although it never gets into a position to challenge the exceptionally great Burgundies. Some of it is blended with the output of other Côte de Beaune communes and sold as Côte de Beaune-Villages, and some is sold under the more specific commune names. Quantities go to Switzerland and the Low Countries where, being fairly low in price, the wine is highly appreciated. There are almost 400 hectares (1,000 acres) of vineyard within Santenay's boundaries, and in an average-quantity year production amounts to about 10,000 hectoliters (265,000 U.S. gallons, 220,000 imp.) of red wine.

Santorin

A Greek wine, from the island of the same name, which may also, when it is sweet, be labeled Vino Santo.
See Greece.

Sardinia

Red, white, and rosé wines.
District: Italian island.

The mountainous island of Sardinia, in the Tyrrhenian Sea, off the coast of central Italy is, after Sicily, the largest island in the Mediterranean. It has been inhabited since prehistoric days, and it is known that even the earliest dwellers cultivated the vine—since little else seems to grow easily there. The island has a strange, wild air and is populated by a short, individualistic people to whose mysterious origins huge stone monuments may be the undeciphered clues. Giants' tombs, witches' houses, and the even more inscrutable *nuraghi*—conical stone towers which seem to have served the early Sardinians as both shelters and defenses—pepper the island, and around them the inhabitants go about their business. Wine is a fairly big part of this business; nearly 2 million hectoliters (53 million U.S. gallons, 44 million imp.) are produced annually.

Since the 1960s, Sardinian wine production has undergone an oenological revolution. New grape varieties, early harvesting to preserve acidity, temperature-controlled fermentation, and early bottling are some of the features of the modern vinification which has transformed the style and quality of Sardinian wines. In place of the sweet fortified wines of yesteryear, the island now produces good, fresh, dry red and especially white wines. These light wines, with a slight prickle (CO_2), are favored by the numerous tourists who flock to Sardinia and, above all, to La Costa Smeralda, a vacationland built by the Aga Khan around Porto Corvo, Porto Rotondo, and Cala di Volpe. Costa Smeralda has become one of the best summer resorts in Europe.

Vernaccia di Oristano (D.O.C.)

Sardinia's best-known wine, made from the grape variety with the same name. Most of the vines, which were imported at the end of the fourteenth century, grow around Oristano in the Tirso River Valley, which runs from central Sardinia westward to the Gulf of Oristano, midway along the coast. The dry, amber-colored wine is high in alcohol (16% or higher), has a light bouquet, and a quick, sprightly, bitter aftertaste. Fortified Vernaccia *liquoroso* comes in two types: sweet with 16.5% and dry with 18% of alcohol by volume. If aged for four years in wood, these wines may be called Riserva.

Nuragus di Cagliari (D.O.C.)

Almost certainly the oldest wine of the island, this is also one of the better table wines, made from grapes of the same name grown around Cagliari. The straw-colored, heady wine annually amounts to about 10% of all Sardinian wine production.

Vermentino di Gallura (D.O.C.)

The wine comes from vineyards spreading south from Santa Teresa di Gallura, the northernmost town. From grapes grown on some of the most unpromising mountain slopes, about 600 hectoliters (15,900 U.S. gallons, 13,200 imp.) of wine are made annually. It is dry and amber-colored, has some 13% to 14% of alcohol, but lacks any real distinction.

Malvasia di Bosa (D.O.C.)

This is produced in very small quantities—just 150 or so hectoliters in an average year—from Malvasia and Seberu grapes grown near Bosa, on the west coast of the island, slightly to the north of center. The wine has a good, nutty flavor, and compared with Vernaccia has a deeper, richer color, and is somewhat less dry. Another wine from the same grape is Malvasia di Cagliari (D.O.C.), a wine with a bitter aftertaste of toasted almonds.

Oliena

The dryish, garnet-red wine is made from Cannonau and Monica grapes grown in the district of Nuoro.

Cannonau di Sardegna (D.O.C.)

A ruby-red wine, dry or semi-sweet, made of Cannonau grapes; a rosé is also made. When fortified, Cannonau makes an excellent dessert wine or can be had as an aperitif (liquoroso secco).

Dessert Wines

Girò di Cagliari (D.O.C.) is sweet and red, slightly reminiscent of Port, and is made from Girò grapes grown in the general vicinity of Cagliari. Monica di Sardegna (D.O.C.) and Monica di Cagliari (D.O.C.) are similar but deeper in color—almost a deep purple. Nasco di Cagliari (D.O.C.) is white, or rather a deep, golden color, and is famed partly for its bouquet (said to have the perfume of orange blossoms) and partly for its slightly bitter tang. Muscats may also be found, notably Moscato di Sorso-Sennori (D.O.C.) and Moscato di Cagliari (D.O.C.), both of which are often fortified.

See Italy.

Saumur and Coteaux de Saumur

Still, semi-sparkling, and particularly sparkling white wines, usually dry. Some rosé and red.
District: Anjou, France.

The difference between the two names has never been clearly established and may never be, and for the moment they have substantially the same meaning. The wines are red, white, and rosé (although in actual practice red wines are rarely, if ever, seen abroad) and may be either still or sparkling, the production of the latter taking up a goodly proportion of each year's harvest. Sparkling Saumur is slightly heavier and more common than sparkling Vouvray, but is no match for Champagne.

Most sparkling Saumur is vinified and aged in huge caves, which burrow back into the chalky cliffs surrounding the ancient city. French law insists that all such wines be made by the champagne process (see Champagne) of secondary fermentation in the bottle, and 40% of the wines must come from the juice of Chenin Blanc grapes; the rest is ordinarily made up of Groslot with some Cabernet. In recent years, the quality of the sparkling wine has improved due to the creation of a new appellation, "Crémant de Loire."

Non-sparkling white Saumur will sometimes be about the finest of its type in the region of Anjou. It is generally dry—sometimes, however, preserving a slight trace of sweetness—and often proves more robust than the dry wines from the rest of the district. Rosé (both ordinary and that made exclusively from Cabernet grapes) is quite frequently encountered, but it does not differ markedly from good Angevin rosés. Some of the whites are pétillants, or semi-sparkling. About 60,000 hectoliters (1.59 million U.S. gallons, 1.32 million imp.) are made annually.

Saumur-Champigny

Red wine.
District: Anjou, France.

On the chalky slopes downstream from the confluence of the Loire and the quiet River Vienne to just east of Saumur, Cabernet Franc grapes are grown to produce a fresh, generous wine with a deep ruby color. The wine has a perfume recalling the scent of violets. Since the Appellation Contrôlée of Saumur-Champigny is nearly as far north as the Cabernet Franc can be successfully cultivated, vintage years are quite important. In very bad years part of the crop does not ripen completely and must be vinified simply as Rosé d'Anjou. The average annual production of Appellation Contrôlée red wines is 10,000 hectoliters (260,550 U.S. gallons, 200,600 imp.).

Saussignac, Côtes de

White wines (not very important) of the Dordogne region in southwest France. Wine-producing villages are Gageac-et-Rouillac, Monestier, and Razac-de-Saussignac. Since 1955 the name Saussignac can be replaced by Bergerac, provided the wines come from the above-mentioned communes and attain the prescribed degrees of sugar and alcohol.

Sauternes

White wine.
District: Bordeaux, France.

The suspense in the final moment of harvesting a Sauternes is worthy of a Hitchcock film. To make the entirely natural sweet wine, the grape must achieve both a state of overripeness and the famed *pourriture noble*. Failing this, the wine will lack the extra richness, sugar, and alcohol sometimes reaching 16% and even 17% with 6% of sugar; in fact, it will not even be entitled to the legal designation of Sauternes. But if, on the other hand, the beneficial overripening is allowed to go too far, the bouquet is lost in the increased suavity and richness of the wine. Add to this the fact that the overripening occurs very late in the season, when frost may strike down the vines any day, and it is easy to understand the nervous pacing of the grower in Sauternes, inspecting his vines several times a day as he decides whether to pick or not.

No other wine in the world is made on such a scale by this delicate and nerve-racking process, though a portion of the crop from certain great vineyards along the Rhine and Mosel in Germany is produced identically. Trockenbeerenauslese, the German word for the process and the resultant wine, perhaps best describes it. "Dried-grapes-specially-selected"—a child's Erector-set word built up with German literalness.

The Sauternes process is the only one by which a wine of such richness may be produced without human interference in the form of extra sugar, of fermentation arrested by the addition of brandy, or any of the other methods used in the production of various wines. A mold or fungus, *Botrytis cinerea*—the French picturesquely, and with botanical correctness, call it a mushroom—attacks the grapes late in the autumn, and the skins shrivel. No sugar is *added* by this process, but the proportion of sugar becomes greater as the water grows less. At the same time, the mold causes transformation within the grapes, of a nature not yet defined, that increases the glycerins and pectins and gives the wine its suavity and smoothness. The "legs" of a great Sauternes are celebrated. They are the slow streams which descend with unctuous richness down the inner side of the glass after the wine has been tipped away.

The bunch of grapes, ready for the selected picking, is dried and folded and (while it is not a pleasant comparison) has a marked resemblance to the wizened, leathery, folded-in appearance of a hanging bat. Covered over with the *pourriture noble*, it hardly gives promise of the golden nectar it is to produce. With much of the juice dried out, the quantity is reduced. To this loss of volume must be added the greatly increased cost of picking. The mold develops haphazardly over a vineyard, and the rows must be picked through as many as six to eleven times. For these reasons, true Sauternes can never be cheap.

True Sauternes. For no other wine is more widely flattered by the theft of its name. "Sauternes" is not merely a white sweet wine, but the white sweet wine of Sauternes, France. The wines to be met with in many other places in the world which call themselves "sauternes"—or even "sauterne," as if to justify bad practice by bad spelling—are not what they claim to be.

The character of a wine is determined by several factors, among which are the influences of a specific soil and climate in a given geographical place; for grapevines do not behave in the same way in different soils and climates. When the right vine or vines have been found for a certain wine-favoring area, a famous wine will result, over decades of development. Nowhere else will exactly the right combination of factors exist to produce the same wine.

The Sauternes district is composed of five communes: Sauternes, Barsac, Bommes, Preignac, and Fargues. In all sections the wine is made identically, and mainly from the Sémillon and Sauvignon grapes. Muscadelle is used in very small amounts in the blends. Because a Sauternes vineyard is not picked section by section but according to the degree of overripeness, there is a difference in quality between early-season pickings and very late pickings. When brought in, the bunches first enter a long revolving tube. This *fouloir*, or beater, extracts the first juice. Then, after destalking, the grapes are pressed three times. In the past all these different grades of juice were made into separate wines; but around the end of the last century this practice largely ceased. Today the general custom is to mix the yield. This is done in large tanks, where the day's pick remains only a few hours and is then let off into casks, where it ferments and matures. Differences in the different days' harvesting cause differences in the wine in cask, and when it becomes apparent that a wine is not up to standard, it is the practice of every fine château to exclude it from that which will be bottled under its name. Instead, it is sold to the Bordeaux shippers, to be bottled simply as Sauternes. (In such cases, shippers are strictly forbidden to let it be known that the bottle is really from one of the Classified Growths [*Crus*], being sold at the much lower price for regional wine.)

Yielding on an average only 900 bottles to the hectare (380 bottles to the acre), the entire region produces the equivalent of 2.5 million bottles a year. Sauternes tend to differ from one vineyard to another, but the only generalization to be made is that the Barsacs, which are entitled to the separate name Barsac as well as that of Sauternes, are likely to be less sweet. They come from a flatter land and a less stony, more chalky soil in the northern portion (*see* Barsac). It is Sauternes proper, the rolling, hilly region around the tiny village of Sauternes and the towns of Bommes and Fargues, which is the most picturesque. The vineyard road, hardly more than a lane, runs between old stone walls. The great vineyards clothe the slopes, the crown of which will usually display the château. Lower-lying vineyards were severely damaged in the freeze of February 1956, and from these, and to a lesser degree the slope vineyards, no 1956 or 1957 vintage was seen, and very little of vintages for several subsequent years. Hail destroyed most of the 1973 harvest; and 74s are rare.

Sauternes should be served cold, but not so iced that the taste will be numbed. It can be brought to serving temperature in an ice bucket or in the refrigerator. Some French people will serve an old Sauternes which has oxidized as an aperitif; the oxidation will have reduced some of the sweetness but not all.

Sauternes are best served at the end of the meal, when they go well with a dessert and even better with fruit; and

some knowledgeable people serve a glass of sweet Sauternes *as* the dessert. Counter to all this, however, is the opinion of the owner of Château d'Yquem, who maintains the nineteenth-century tradition that Sauternes should be drunk not with the dessert only but also with certain fish, foie gras, and Roquefort.

CLASSIFIED VINEYARDS OF SAUTERNES AND BARSAC, 1855 CLASSIFICATION

FIRST GREAT GROWTH (*Premier Grand Cru*)

Château d'Yquem (Sauternes)

FIRST GROWTHS (*Premiers Crus*)

Château La Tour-Blanche (Bommes)	Château Climens (Barsac)
Château Lafaurie-Peyraguey (Bommes)	Château Guiraud (Sauternes)
Clos Haut-Peyraguey (Bommes)	Château Rieussec (Fargues)
Château de Rayne-Vigneau (Bommes)	Château Rabaud-Promis (Bommes)
Château Suduiraut (Preignac)	Château Sigalas-Rabaud (Bommes)
Château Coutet (Barsac)	

SECOND GROWTHS (*Seconds Crus*)

Château Doisy-Daëne (Barsac)	Château Caillou (Barsac)
Château Doisy-Védrines (Barsac)	Château Suau (Barsac)
Château d'Arche (Sauternes)	Château de Malle (Preignac)
Château Filhot (Sauternes)	Château Romer (Fargues)
Château Broustet (Barsac)	Château Lamothe (Sauternes)
Château Nairac (Barsac)	

Sauvignon Blanc

An exceptionally fine white grape used for some excellent white wines. With Sémillon (and some Muscadelle) it produces all of Bordeaux's finest whites, from the sweetest Sauternes to the driest Graves. Some marvelously pleasant Loire Valley white wines come solely from this grape, notably those of Sancerre, and the best wine is from Pouilly-sur-Loire, where the wine is known locally as Blanc Fumé (white smoke). In California the Sauvignon Blanc is considered among the finest grapes for white wine, especially in the Livermore, San Benito, and Santa Clara valleys. The wine varies, of course, according to the soil and climate of the vineyard and the manner in which grapes and wine are treated; but whenever conditions are favorable, the wine will have considerable breed and distinction. Among other names for this vine are Surin, in parts of the Loire Valley, and Muskat Sylvaner in Germany.

Sauvignon (Cabernet Sauvignon)

The finest of the claret grapes grown in the Médoc; small and blue-black in color, thick-skinned, and juicy. The wine they yield is very full and slow in maturing.

The other regional names for this grape include Bouchet and Vidure.

See Cabernet.

Savagnin

The dominant grape variety in the golden-white wines of Château-Châlon. Savagnin Rose is another name for the red Gewürztraminer of Alsace; Savagnin Noir is none other than the Pinot Noir.

Savatiano

One of the principal grape varieties used for Greek liqueurs and also for table wines—often those which have been doctored with resin—it is found in central Greece and in the Peloponnese.

Savennières

A wine region of the Anjou-Coteaux de la Loire district in France.

See Anjou.

Savigny-les-Beaune and Savigny-les-Beaune-Côte de Beaune

Burgundy red and white wines.
District: Côte de Beaune, France.

In the early Middle Ages the vineyards were owned by Cistercians and Carmelites, but the French people and many of the nobility were not far behind in establishing their claims. A great moated castle, built in 1340, totally destroyed in 1468, and rebuilt in 1672, still stands to the side of the main square, surrounded by a rambling and slightly disheveled park. During the eighteenth century this was the home of the Duchesse de Maine. Today its opulence has declined, its windows are closed, and a few chickens scratch in what was once the main court.

Within the confines of present-day Savigny there are about 360 hectares (900 acres) of vines, and production in an average year for quantity is 12,000 hectoliters (318,000 U.S. gallons, 264,000 imp.), all but a few hundred hectoliters red. This wine was greatly appreciated in the distant past (a Duke of Burgundy wanted to elevate one grower to the rank of a demi-god for the quality of his wine), but its reputation has diminished considerably. It is distinctly light and fragrant with considerable finesse but definitely not a wine to keep for any length of time.

The town stands between Pernand-Vergelesses and Beaune and the wines of all three are fairly similar, although those of Beaune are far and away the best. Savigny sells its wines either under the commune name or under commune name with Côte de Beaune added, but if a wine qualifies for either name it is qualified for both. Wines may also be blended with those from certain other communes along the slope and sold as Côte de Beaune-Villages. The best vineyards of the commune are rated

First Growths (*Premiers Crus*)—higher minimum standards and better wines—and their wines may be sold with both commune name and vineyard name. These vineyards are Vergelesses, Marconnets, Dominode, Jarrons, and Lavières.

Savoy (Haute-Savoie)

In this region of France, four white wines are permitted Appellations Contrôlées. These are Crépy, Seyssel, Seyssel Mousseux, and the Vins de Savoie (*qq.v.*).

Scharlachberg

Excellent white wine from near Bingen on the German Rhine.
See Rheinhessen.

Scharzhofberg

Generally the finest wines of the German Saar. These wines freqently attain an incomparable elegance.

Schaumwein

A German term for sparkling wine.

Schiave

A red grape grown in Italy, particularly in the vineyards of the Alto Adige.

Schiedam

Term sometimes used for Hollands gin because Schiedam in Holland is one of the chief places of its manufacture.

Schiller wine

A pinkish wine from red and white grapes which once comprised half the wine made in the German Württemberg district.

Schloss

Literally, "castle" in German, but with regard to wine, the counterpart of the French château, encompassing the building, vineyards, cellars, etc.

Schloss Böckelheimer Kupfergrube

Good wines of the Nahe Valley in Germany, grown on the slopes of the Kupfergrube, or "Copper mine."
See Nahe.

Schloss Johannisberg

Most expensive of the Rheingaus (German Rhine wine). The best-informed brokers and growers on the river consider it one of the finest Rheingaus consistently over the years, though not always first in any given year. (For a full explanation of the different types of capsuling, indicating the different grades and qualities of Schloss Johannisberg, *see* Rheingau: Johannisberg.)

Schloss Vollrads

Best of the wines of the Winkel section of the German Rhine, and one of the best Rhine wines, Schloss Vollrads is bottled and sold in six grades, or qualities differentiated by the colors of their capsules. For a full description of these grades and the wine, *see* Rheingau: Winkel.

Schlossabzug

The same as Originalabfüllung—a natural, unsugared wine, bottled on the estate; in this case a Schloss, or castle.
See Rheingau.

Schnapps

In Germany and Holland, any strong, dry spirit; in Scandinavia, usually aquavit. An aromatic schnapps is made from a base of Dutch-style gin flavored with aromatic herbs.

Schooner

A tall drinking glass most suitable for beer; usually about 15 fluid ounces.

Schwarzwalder

German name for kirsch, or cherry brandy.
See Kirsch.

Scion

A segment of a cane or shoot of one or more buds that is grafted onto a stock to make a complete plant. Scions of European *Vitis vinifera* vines were grafted onto American disease-resistant stocks after the phylloxera disaster in the late nineteenth century. When the correct stock is selected for the graft, it should impart none or very little of its own qualities to the fruit of the scion.

Scotch whisky

See Whisky, Scotch.

Sec

French for dry. This word appearing on the label of a bottle of Champagne does not, in fact, indicate a very dry wine, but rather one which is inclined toward sweetness.
See Champagne.

Secco

Italian term for dry wine; as French *sec.*

Séché

A term widely used in France for harsh, flat wines with an astringent aftertaste. This is usually the result of excessive oxidation.

Sediment

Lees or solid matter deposited by a wine while it is ageing. Such deposit does not necessarily affect the taste of the wine, but because of its bitter consistency and the fact that it spoils the look of the wine, it should be separated by decanting before serving.
See Chapter Nine.

Seeweine

Pleasant little wines of Lake Constance (or Bodensee) in the south of Germany.
See Baden.

Seewinkel

See Sandweine.

Seibel

French hybridizer who developed hundreds of vines of varying characteristics. Some of his most notable achievements were described by Philip Wagner in *A Wine-Grower's Guide.*

Sekt

German term for sparkling wine. Ludwig Devrient, a Berlin actor famous in the nineteenth century, invented a popular joke by calling for his Sekt—cup of Sack—when he played Shakespeare's Falstaff. He began to use the same term when calling for his favorite drink, Champagne, in restaurants and the name Sekt for German champagne-type wine was established.

Sémillon

White wine grape used in the Sauternes and Graves districts of Bordeaux, and fairly widely throughout the Dordogne and southwest France. It is grown also in California.

Seppeltsfield

Famous vineyard in Barossa Valley, South Australia.
See Australia.

Sercial

A white grape variety producing one of the best Madeira wines; dry, sometimes pale, sometimes golden, with a tremendous "nose."
See Madeira.

Sève

Literally, "sappy" (from the French word for sap). The term as used in France suggests a feminine charm, elegance, and a distinction which is graceful and not assertive in a masculine way. It is employed also to describe those Sauternes which have that deep, luscious quality.

Seyssel

White still and sparkling wines.
District: Upper Rhône Valley, France.

Near the source of the Rhône is the butterfly-shaped district of Seyssel, made up of the communes of Seyssel (department of Haute-Savoie), Seyssel (department of Ain), and Corbonod. The dividing line between the twin cities of Seyssel and between the two departments is the Rhône. The wines are white, and some of them are made sparkling.

The area consists of a series of hills and depressions cut out by some ancient glacier that also left in its path the flinty clay and flinty chalk deposits which compose the present soil. These hills provide a number of southerly and southeasterly slopes, on which the vines are planted. For the still Seyssel, the only grape planted is the Roussette. Whether or not this was the vine that was grown in antiquity at Saint-Cornas and Hermitage along the lower Rhône and transported to Seyssel by boats trading in salt; whether it was imported from Cyprus; or whether or not it is the Hungarian Furmint brought in by one of the Princes of Savoy is still a matter for discussion. Whatever its origin, the vine produces a light flinty-dry white wine that is best when drunk young and is, for that reason, usually bottled in the April following the harvest. The Roussette also goes into the sparkling Seyssel in a proportion of at least 10%, the rest being made up of Molette and Chasselas. This last vine is called, in Seyssel, Bon Blanc.

The delimited area of Seyssel has about 60 hectares (150 acres) planted in vines, and the average production is less than 2,500 hectoliters (66,250 U.S. gallons, 55,000 imp.) yearly.

Seyve-Villard

Contemporary French hybridizer who has developed a number of hybrid vines mostly for warm or hot climates, including some of the best available to the wine-maker. For red wines, S-V 13359, S-V 18315, and S-V 23657 have had a certain success, as have his white S-V 5276 and S-V 19287, which resembles the Muscat grape.

Shandy (Shandygaff)

A long drink popular in England; beer mixed with ginger beer or lemonade.

Shebeen

In Ireland and Scotland, a place where taxable liquors are sold without a license; also, a low tavern or public house.

Shekar

Hebrew term for an intoxicating drink, later applied only to cider.

Sherry

Sherry, celebrated since Shakespeare's time, tends to eclipse, for most people, the fame of all other Spanish wines. It is a fortified wine, a wine to which grape brandy has been added to bring up the alcoholic content to approximately 16% for the Finos and 18% for the Olorosos. Spaniards are much more fond of Sherry than are the Portuguese of Port; but the English drink a great deal more Sherry than do the Spaniards (though not quite as much as they once did), and exports to other European countries are increasing.

The Sherry vineyards lie around the town of Jerez de la Frontera, south of Seville, in the most romantic part of Spain. Here, a great horse-fair is held each spring: just as Seville is a city of wine and bulls, Jerez (which once traded in gold and in Barbary apes) is a town of wine and horses. The great bulls and bullfighters come here, too, from Seville, and young *caballeros* in gray Córdoba hats ride with beautiful girls on horseback or drive them around in open carriages.

Only a few years ago, Jerez, in spite of the activity in the Sherry *bodegas*, looked half asleep in the midday sun: a town of dignified white houses and wrought-iron balconies, withdrawn from the invading tide of commercialization. Today, a great highway roars near the town, and everyone is wide awake. There has been a real boom in the demand for Sherry; and, as exports and prices rise, some of the big firms tend to expand. Pedro Domecq, for instance, has set up a holding company, Domecq International, in Luxembourg, to manage its widespread interests—one of which is a joint investment with Seagrams in a large Rioja firm. In spite of the clamor for the product—and of the improvement in quality in certain sherry-style rivals in other countries—the Consejo Regulador, the official body which controls Sherry and its closely guarded Denominación de Origen, will not allow its stocks to be diminished by more than 40% in any year. The purpose is to prevent quantity from swamping quality. In one respect, the wine-makers of Jerez are fortunate: they still can increase the acreage of their vines. There are about 11,000 hectares of vineyards (27,500 acres) officially planted which produce nearly 800,000 hectoliters (21.2 million U.S. gallons, 17.6 million imp.) of the famous wine.

Yet the fascination of Sherry and the mystery of its ageing have not changed, and the *bodegas*, as much as the *feria*, draw visitors to Jerez. Sherry is an anglicized term taken from the name of the city, which has changed over the centuries from the Latin Xeres to the Moorish Sher-risch, and hence to the Spanish Jerez. Vines have grown in the region ever since the Phoenicians founded the town, over a thousand years before Christ. The Greeks came and then the Romans, who ruled the city for four hundred years. It was from the later invaders, the Vandals, that the whole province took the name Andalusia. Then, in 711, the Moors arrived. Until the reconquest of Jerez, about 1264, it lay on the border between the warring Christian and Moslem kingdoms and so was known as Jerez de la Frontera. Much later—in the nineteenth century—the export of Sherry wine reached its peak, and the town enjoyed great good fortune. Toward the end of the century, however, Sherry was declining in popularity, and in the 1890s phylloxera reached Andalusia. The vine disease (which at that period destroyed most of the vineyards of Europe) and the change in fashion menaced the prosperity of Jerez, and for some years exports were sadly reduced. Fortunately, the trade was to revive.

Sherry is known neither by vintage nor by vineyard. Vintage identity is lost in the *solera* system, by which a fine old Sherry is used to discipline a raw young one. Vineyard names do not exist for two reasons: (1) nearly all Sherry is blended from several different *pagos* (areas), and (2) the important *pagos* are divided into many different vineyards and therefore, between many owners, so that no one has the exclusive right to the name.

Nevertheless, place of origin is important. Forty per cent of the stocks of any firm may be purchased from the Zona de Jerez Superior (Zone of Superior Sherry), or "the triangle," as it is called—an irregular triangle lying inside the points of the three important towns, Jerez de la Frontera, Sanlúcar de Barrameda, and Puerto de Santa María. This zone is comprised of the finest soil, named *albariza*. The vineyards are composed of the white chalk soil which nourishes the vine with its lime content and protects it from summer heat by forming a baked crust beneath which moisture is retained. The famous *pagos* of Macharnudo, Carrascal, Añina, and Balbaina—and Miraflores in the east, producing the finest Manzanilla—are inside the triangle. Secondary soils are the *barro* and the *arena*. The former contains some chalk, with a considerable admixture of clay and sand; the latter is sandy, containing alumina and silica. These soils are found in other parts of the Sherry-producing zone, in which the Superior Zone produces the best wine. All Sherries are produced in the Sherry zone, which covers the towns of Jerez de la Frontera, Puerto de Santa María, Sanlúcar de Barrameda, Trebujena, Chipiona, Rota, Puerto Real, and Chiclana de la Frontera (all in the province of Cádiz).

VINEYARDS, VINES, AND VINTAGING

There is a saying in Jerez—*Niñas y viñas son malas de guardar*—which might be translated: "It's hard to keep watch over vineyards and young girls."

This is another way of saying that the Palomino, the grape which gives 90% of Sherry, is one of the few great wine grapes in the world which is also delicious to eat. A result is the curious *bien-te-veo* (which means "I can see you"), a small hut or lookout set up on stilts in the vineyards so that an overseer may watch out for whoever might steal the grapes.

There are other varieties of grape in Jerez (Pedro Ximénez, Mantúo, Albillo, Cañocaza), but the Palomino is predominant. An apparent abundance of varieties may confuse the amateur, because Palomino is known in the area by no less than seven other names. Listán is the most common of these and is in wide use in the Sanlúcar Manzanilla vineyards. Horgazuela is the name for Palomino in Puerto de Santa María, and elsewhere Tempranilla, Palomina, Ojo de Liebre, Temprana, and Albán are encountered. Whatever it is called, the vine produces thick clusters of pale, fat grapes, hanging like swarms of bees and ripening as much from the reflection of heat off the hard shield of the *albariza* as from the direct sunshine. Pruning removes all but a single branch of the vine, supported in a forked stick against the weight of fruit to come. The production of the vine is limited in order to

extend its life—which is two-thirds shorter (giving it a total of about thirty years) than it was before the post-phylloxera replanting onto grafted American roots. The effort to preserve the vines is based on the high cost of replanting. The vineyards themselves are patched here and there in rolling country otherwise given over to grain and cotton; but from the main roads and the railways they cannot be seen at all. The whitewashed houses up the narrow dirt tracks that lead from the vineyards are attached, like unimportant outbuildings, to the great sheds within which the vintaging is carried out. In the spring, when the plants are being treated against disease, the mules plod along the rows, their panniers burdened with earthen Arab urns stained brilliant blue by copper sulfate. At harvest time, the grapes are carried in the woven wicker *canastas* or wooden *tinetas* and dumped in gleaming heaps on esparto grass mats which resemble large round trays. In an hour or two the whole yard of the wine shed is given over to this sunning, which lasts until the sunshine has brought the sugar-content of the grapes into proper balance as bees and wasps drone over what appear to be mounds of molten honey.

Until quite recently, one could see the harvest as it had been carried out for centuries and the grapes trodden in the *lagares* (wide wooden troughs) by men wearing a special kind of nailed boot. Today, a token treading may be performed as a ritual and a tourist attraction; but in general, the old custom has given way to automatic pressing.

The first fermentation of Sherry, lasting three days to a week, is extremely violent. The barrel bungs foam over like the mouths of newly opened Champagne bottles. After this, there is a slow fermentation of about three months, during which time the bung stoppers are left loose so that the wine is in free contact with the air. At the end, the young wine is cleared of particles and is totally dry—i.e., every bit of fermentable sugar has been converted into alcohol. In January or February the wine is tested for quality (with the nose, not by tasting) and for the type it may finally become. A curious attribute of Sherry is that, without human intervention, it will soon show signs of assuming either the character of a light, dry Fino or of a fuller, darker Oloroso. The sign is the pale scum of microscopic yeasty flowers which develops on a Fino and is known as the *flor*. A wine destined to be an Oloroso has no *flor*, or very little (which can be killed by an injection of brandy). When a new wine has had its first, tentative classification, it is racked (drawn off the lees into another cask), tested for alcoholic content and, if this is below strength, will be slightly fortified with wine brandy—a potential Fino up to about 16%, an Oloroso to about 17% or 18% of alcohol by volume. This addition of brandy definitely separates the one style of Sherry from the other.

After a short rest, the wine is tested again and the cask marked with chalk. One downward stroke (*raya*) means that the wine is good, with a clean bouquet and sufficient body; two strokes, that the wine is quite good; three, there is some slight flaw; and two strokes with a cross-bar (grid) means that the wine is only fit for burning—i.e., distilling into brandy. For anywhere up to three years, the wine remains in the *añada* casks (*año* means "year") in the spacious, airy *bodega*, through which the air is allowed to circulate. The Sherry is always under the surveillance of the cellarmaster (*capataz*), and the examination marks chalked on the wood grow more precise: Y (*palma*, a delicate Fino); ⅄ (*palma cortada*, a fuller Fino); /-(*raya*, an oloroso style); //-(*dos rayas*, a less distinguished Oloroso). When it progresses beyond the *añada* stage, the wine enters the *criadera*, or nursery, which is the first stage in the *solera* system.

IN THE SHERRY BODEGAS

The wine is stored in dim, cool sanctuaries at ground level, all facing southeast to the sea. These are the *bodegas* of the great wine firms, to which visitors are welcome. Nothing is asked of the guest but a love for Sherry or the willingness to learn. He will be invited to taste a vast range of wines, and the *capataz*, or perhaps the owner himself, will take up and wield deftly the willowy *venencia*, or sherry dipper—a narrow silver cup at the end of a flexible whalebone spine. The guest is given a hint of the deep mystery of the *flor* as the *venencia* is plunged into the wine. The white scum of *flor* must be penetrated by a stabbing thrust, the bullet-like cup plunging through the creamy layer to reach the wine; the cup disappears into the barrel bung, and with a sudden motion that causes a distinct *pock* of sound, the whalebone wand is flicked sharply down. Pouring the wine, once it has been brought out in the silver *venencia* cup, is an art that looks simple—and is not. The expert grips the flexible shaft between his thumb and forefinger and, holding a glass with his free hand, he lets a long stream of wine cascade through the air and into the glass. The amateur tries it—and with unerring accuracy the Sherry goes up his sleeve.

The white *flor* magically increases at the budding of the vine in spring and at its ripening in the autumn. At first thin and flaky, like the snow in a glass paperweight, *flor* in time looks like a skin of old cream. After its period of flowering, which may continue for years, it dies and settles to the bottom of the wine.

Air turns most wine acid. Sherry—and the wines of the Jura in France—thrive, however, on air. Deprived of it, they do not produce their characteristic taste. The towering vaulted *bodegas* of Jerez are open to the passage of the air on which the *flor* feeds. Two different microscopic organisms feed on air (technically, they are a bacterium, *Acetobacter*, which turns wine into vinegar, and a yeast of the group responsible for fermentations). In normal (non-Sherry) situations, the *Acetobacter* will appear, and for this reason these wines deteriorate when they come in contact with the air. Somehow, in the region around Jerez (and in Jura), at a concentration of alcohol from 11.5% to 15.5% and at a temperature of 58° to 68°F. (14° to 20°C.), it is the fermenting yeast which succeeds, transforming the wine into that dry, light, crisp condition called Fino in Sherry. The Spaniards believe that the *Saccharomyces* is the yeast that forms a *flor* veil on the surface, consuming whatever sugar is left in the wine after fermentation.

SOLERA

The most interesting thing about Sherry (apart from the mysterious *flor*) is the peculiar system by which it is kept at its best. A very old, very fine Sherry has the power to educate and improve a younger one. Because of this, the old wines are kept in the oldest barrels of what the growers call a *solera*. This is a series of casks graduated by age. A series (or scale) is made up of identical butts. The oldest class in a *solera* is the one called the *solera*. The next oldest is the first *criadera*, the next the second *criadera*, and so on. When the wine is drawn from the *solera*, it is drawn in equal quantity from each butt. Then starts a progressive system by which the *solera* is refilled by the first *criadera* and that in turn by the second *criadera*, etc. The magic result of this system is that the oldest casks remain eternally the same in quality. A cask of 1888, for instance, may retain hardly a spoonful of its original vintage; but each replacement poured back into it over the years will have been educated to be 1888, and replacements still to come will be schooled to the same standard. By this system, it is possible not only to preserve the same quality and character of wine over the years, but also, by constantly refreshing the Fino types with younger wine, to keep these from losing their freshness.

TYPES OF SHERRY

All Sherries stem either from the Fino or the Oloroso type. Fino is Sherry on which *flor* has developed fully. Oloroso is a wine which has not shown a disposition to have much or any *flor* and the small or nearly nonexistent "flowering" of which has been suppressed by the addition of a stronger dose of fortifying wine brandy than that given a Fino. No one can influence this first basic decision taken by the wine itself, and no one knows why one cask wants to become Fino while a barrel of what appears to be the same wine, from the same harvest and vineyard, wants to become Oloroso. There is nothing to do but watch and wait, and when the wine has made up its mind, treat it accordingly.

Fino

This is a very pale, light gold wine; the lightest in color of the Sherries. The nose of the wine is not pronounced but characteristic—like the scent released by a freshly picked apple. There is a hint of almond too. Ideally, Fino should never be bottled—for when it is drunk from the wood it has always been only in beneficial contact with the air. Less fortified than Oloroso, Fino is more alive. Once bottled, it may keep up to two years—depending on weather and cellaring conditions—but it will not improve at all and will eventually lose its freshness. Because of its delicate constitution, Fino is exported at higher alcoholic strength to help it travel (18% to 20%, while domestic Fino is 16% to 17%), and this diminishes the bouquet.

There is no way of knowing just how old a bottle of Fino is when purchased, since the Sherry (which is always bottled just before shipping) is not dated, although some shippers feel that labels should bear the date of bottling.

Under the circumstances, Fino should be bought shortly before it is to be drunk, and from a supplier who can be trusted not to have kept it too long on the shelf. Once opened, Fino is inclined to fade away; and for this reason, the practice in Jerez is rather to buy the wine in half-bottles.

Manzanilla

Manzanilla is both a Sherry Fino—the Fino of Finos—and a separate and individual wine in its own right. This comes about because it is produced in *soleras*, develops *flor*, and comes from the Palomino grape grown on the same kind of chalky, limy soil which produces Fino; but it does these things about 19 kilometers (12 miles) from Jerez, around the seacoast town of Sanlúcar de Barrameda. The vintage is rather earlier here, before the grapes are quite ripe; nor are they usually laid out in the sun to develop extra sugar. The sea also makes a difference, giving the special tang or bitterness, especially in the aftertaste, which distinguishes Manzanilla. This is the palest of the Finos, a fresh, incredibly light, tart wine—usually sold from the barrel in Spain. It is an unchallenged favorite of many Spanish people, and at any bar, along with the inevitable *tapas*—onions, olives, shrimps speared on toothpicks—one will hear calls for Manzanilla.

A peculiar proof of the relationship between Manzanilla and Fino wines of Jerez is that if young Manzanilla is taken to a *bodega* in Jerez for storing, it becomes Jerez Fino; whereas, if a young Jerez Fino is taken to Sanlúcar de Barrameda and kept in the Manzanilla *bodegas*, it becomes Manzanilla. This mysterious behavior is explained by the influence of the sea air. Blowing through the Sanlúcar *bodegas*, it creates Manzanilla, with its own unmistakable, salt-sharp tang.

In the small, whitewashed town of Sanlúcar de Barrameda, Manzanillas are classified into five types: (1) Manzanilla Pasada (2) Manzanilla Olorosa (3) Manzanilla Fina (4) Manzanilla and (5) Amanzanillado. In fact, Manzanillas are graded in exactly the same way as Sherries are in Jerez. There are some 1,000 hectares (2,500 acres) in vines which produce approximately 50,000 hectoliters (1,325,000 U.S. gallons, 1,110,000 imp.).

Palma

A name often used for a distinguished, delicate Fino in Spain, Palma has recently come into use in export as a brand name. Palmas may be graded 1, 2, 3, or 4, the higher numbers usually indicating greater age; but different *bodegas* apply different meanings to the grades.

Amontillado

A darker-colored Sherry, from one to three degrees stronger in alcohol than a Fino. It averages 18% of alcohol by volume, though with age it may reach 24% and 25%. A Fino which is kept in cask and not refreshed from time to time by younger wine may become an Amontillado. Since there is a great demand for Amontillado, the practice is to watch for a darkening of the *flor* and an increasing nuttiness in the taste of Finos. If this is found, the cask is marked to indicate that it should not be refreshed: in one *bodega*, where English influence predominates, the simple word *no* is chalked on the barrelhead.

Amontillados as sold are by no means always pure Amontillado. Many of those seen abroad are sweetened mixtures. They may have Fino or other wines blended in, although there must be some Amontillado or the characteristic nuttiness of flavor will disappear. Generally speaking, the nuttier the taste, the truer the Amontillado. These wines should be dry, clean, and nutty both to the nose and palate. There are some Amontillado-Finos which lie on the borderline. It should be remembered that Sherry types shade into each other; the demarcations are somewhat arbitrary and necessitated by commercial considerations. In one of the largest Jerez *bodegas*, special visitors are sometimes shown a scale of thirty-four glasses in which are Sherries ranging in color from straw to mahogany, in alcohol from 15.2% to 22.8%, and in taste from light and fresh to pungent. Every one of these will be dry. No Sherry is sweet in its natural state.

Oloroso

A more full-bodied wine than Amontillado. As its name implies, the wine is strong in bouquet—nutty and pungent in the finest bottles. But its most distinctive characteristic is *gordura*, a rich vinosity and opulence that can literally be translated as "fatness." Oloroso leaves a lingering sensation of richness on the palate which produces an illusion of sweetness. In fact, while there are many sweetened Olorosos sold as such—or as Amoroso, Cream, and so on—the natural Oloroso, inside Spain, is dry.

It was not until about a century and a half ago that a taste began to develop with the public for the lighter Sherry derived from the *flor*. Previously, Oloroso was the only style shipped, and the *flor*, which must have existed as it does today, would have been dosed out of existence with brandy. The consequence of the taste for Fino was the division of the wines according to whether or not they showed a marked tendency to develop *flor*.

In a true Oloroso, the nose of the wine must be absolutely clean. The average alcoholic strength will be 18% to 20% of the volume, although with age 24% and 25% may be reached. The Olorosos are beautifully golden, the gold darkening with the years and indicating the wine's age in the barrel. Having more body than Finos, Olorosos will survive better in the bottle but, like other Sherries, they do not improve in glass.

Palo Cortado

This is a rare type: an Oloroso with the characteristics of the Fino group. In different *bodegas* Palo Cortado tends to mean different things. At one of the most important firms, a Palo Cortado is an Oloroso with a Fino nose. A true Palo Cortado is a vintage wine, very rare in Sherry, and something which simply "happens"—it cannot be achieved by blending. It is admitted, however, that the real thing must be matured for at least twenty years and is commercially not practicable, and that many wines of the style actually on the market are *like* Palo Cortado.

Raya

Very common in Jerez, this designation will not be found abroad. It means a lesser and coarser Oloroso.

Amoroso

A sweetened Oloroso, of a dark color. The style was created for the English taste and is unknown in Spain. (Although in Spain Sherry is taken dry, it is the practice to add sweetener before shipping for many export styles. The best of such sweeteners is Pedro Ximénez, or P.X.)

The full-bodied Amoroso, known as East India, gets its name from the practice in the days of sailing vessels of sending casks of Sherry aboard ship to the East Indies and back. The airing of the wine and the constant rolling at sea was considered beneficial, and the saying was that "the seasick wines of Jerez are worth double." Brown Sherry is a very dark, sweet Amoroso, likely to be cheaper than East India. Sherries are sometimes darkened by the addition of *color* (a blend of fresh and concentrated grape must) to produce styles demanded in certain markets. Brown Sherry is usually a blend of old Oloroso, P.X., and a touch of *color*.

Cream Sherry

A heavily sweetened Oloroso. It was developed in Bristol, England, and is now extremely popular in the United States also. Some Cream Sherries are bottled in Bristol from Oloroso sent in cask from Jerez; and Creams are now produced in Jerez also to meet the growing demand—although Bristol Cream and Bristol Milk are of course bottled in Bristol.

In England, dark, sweet Sherries may be served, not as aperitifs, but as alternatives to Port at the end of a meal.

Tio Pepe

This is not a type, but a brand name for a dry Sherry, just as Dry Sack is for a medium Sherry.

Most Sherry wine is served at a room temperature; but a dry Amontillado can be slightly cooled, and Finos and Manzanillas may be chilled.

Sherry butt (Bota)

This storage butt contains 600 liters. The shipping butt contains 500 liters. For buying purposes, the butt is reckoned as holding 516 liters, allowing 16 liters for evaporation, clarification, etc.
See Sherry.

Shiraz

A city in southwest Iran, near the Persian Gulf, which gave its name to the best-known Persian wines. Before the Mohammedan prohibition, wine was freely drunk in Persia; and viticulture persists on a small scale in the mountainous regions. Shiraz is mentioned by Marco Polo, and classical writings carry fabulous accounts of it, in one case telling how the vine was trained by pulleys and weights to grow up one side of the house and down the other.
See Iran.

Shot berries

The formation of grape clusters of varying size; this failure of the vine normally follows *coulure*, or dropping of the flower, in late spring and early summer.
See Chapter Eight, p. 29.

Sicily

Red and white wines.
Region: Italian island.

Sicily, divided from the toe of Italy by the Straits of Messina, is the largest and most romantic of the Mediterranean islands. It has beautiful beaches, the volcanic Mount Etna, and stretches of wild maquis. Oranges, lemons, and vines grow there; and in the nearly three thousand years of occupation, men have left classical ruins, baroque towns and palaces, sun-baked villages, and a few scabrous slums. Summers are hot and the vines prolific: Sicily's contribution to the total wine production of Italy is 9 million hectoliters a year (208 million U.S. gallons, 198 million imp.).

Phoenicians, Greeks, and Saracens have ruled Sicily, Norman and Spanish kings have reigned there. In 1860, Garibaldi arrived with a straggling troop of volunteers and freed the island from the Bourbons. He landed at Marsala and is said to have found the wine shop of an English merchant, Woodhouse, open, and to have refreshed himself with the sweet Marsala he preferred.

Recent developments in the Sicilian wine industry are covered in Appendix G.

TYPES OF WINE

Marsala (D.O.C.) is the most important—an aperitif and dessert wine in great favor all over Italy, and one which can be ordered by the glass in almost any café or bar. Marsala, dark amber in color, is a blended wine made from grape juice syrup (must), from aromatic white wine, and from *passito* of dried grapes, fermented with brandy. The wine is matured in a cask from two to five years. The Vergine type is usually made by the *solera* system.

Corvo di Casteldaccia. The best-known Sicilian red and especially white table wines.

Etna (D.O.C.). There are red, white, and rosé wines made from grapes grown on the slopes of the cone-shaped mountain. All are high in alcohol—the red a rich jewel-color, the white a pale-straw, and the rosé a dark pink, inclining to ruby.

Mamertino. None of the Sicilian wines is really dry, but this golden white wine from the slopes around Messina is semi-sweet and alcoholic, with an aromatic bouquet.

Moscato di Siracusa (D.O.C.). These vineyards yield a rich, sweet, dark golden wine from the Muscat grape.

Malvasia di Lipari (D.O.C.). A sweet yellow wine (perhaps the best Italian wine of its type) from sun-dried grapes, produced on the islands of Salina, Stromboli, and Lipari—part of the province of Messina. *Passito* and *liquoroso* types are made with the dried fruit.

Moscato di Pantelleria (*D.O.C.*). An amber-colored, perfumed dessert wine from the island of Pantelleria.

Faro. A red wine produced in the neighborhood of Messina; quite a good table wine, usually not too high in alcohol, but sometimes reaches 14%.

Eloro. The red and white wines made in the country around Ragusa and Noto are dryish and brilliantly colored; the white wine is a deep yellow.

Frappato di Vittoria. A cherry-red dessert wine, sometimes very sweet, sometimes not so sweet, but always alcoholic; produced near Ragusa.

Alcamo (*D.O.C.*). This wine, also known as Bianco d'Alcamo, is made from Catarratto and some Trebbiano grapes grown in northwestern Sicily, between Palermo and Trapani. It is dry, fresh, fruity, fragrant, with a pale straw-yellow color.

Cerasuolo di Vittoria (*D.O.C.*). A cherry-colored wine of particularly high alcoholic content, suitable for very long ageing, with a bouquet of pomegranates and jasmine. An excellent table wine.

Moscato di Noto (*D.O.C.*). Produced in the province of Siracusa, this is a pale yellow-colored wine with a deep scent of honey, made in small quantity near the area of production of Moscato di Siracusa. Di Noto is entirely different in style, mainly because of different viticultural and vinicultural techniques.

See Appendix G.

Château Sigalas-Rabaud

Bordeaux white wine.
District: Sauternes, France.
Commune: Bommes.

The property belongs to the Marquis and Marquise de Lambert. The Marquise is a member of the de Sigalas family, one of whose ancestors fought with La Fayette in the Revolutionary War. (*See* Château Rabaud-Promis *for the origins of the estate.*)

Characteristics. Better than its neighbor, very distinguished. One of the best Sauternes in good years.

Vineyard area: 14 hectares (35 acres).
Average production: 35 *tonneaux* (3,000 cases).

Silent spirit (Cologne spirit or neutral spirit)

British distillers' term for rectified spirit, colorless, odorless, and tasteless, used in making gin and other spirituous drinks.

Siller wine

A style of red wine made in central and southeastern Europe from red and white grapes mixed together before vinification begins. The fermenting juices are racked off the skins after a few days so that only a part of the coloring and the tannin present in the skins passes into the must, thereby making the rest of the winemaker's work easier and the wine drinkable much more quickly. Though the technique may seem at first just that of mak-

ing a rosé, a typical eastern European Siller is far deeper in color than the average French rosé.

A variation, the Schillerwein of Württemberg in Germany, is usually made from red and white grapes grown together in the same vineyard plot. In Styria, the same wine is called Schilscherwein.

See Schiller wine.

Silvestro

Italian liqueur into which go a number of different herbs, dominated by mint. It is said to have been invented by Fra San Silvestro.

Singlings

Brandy after the first disillation and before redistillation.

Šipon

Slovenian grape variety which may be found on the labels of Ljutomer (or Lutomer) white wines—e.g., Lutomer Šipon. The word is pronounced sheepon and is sometimes spelled Chipon.

See Yugoslavia.

Sirah

Red wine grape.
See Syrah; Petite-Sirah.

Château Siran

Bordeaux red wine.
District: Haut-Médoc, France.
Commune: Labarde-Margaux.

The name is said to go back to 1428, when a certain Guilhem de Siran swore allegiance to the Abbot of Saint Croix in the church of Macau.

The property was originally known as Saint-Siran. In 1809 the Comtesse de Toulouse-Lautrec-Moufa, grandmother of the painter, inherited the estate. Alain Miailhe, former proprietor of the adjoining Château Dauzac and present owner of Château Siran, has completely rebuilt the vatrooms and *chais*.

Characteristics. The wine deserves a better rank than Cru Bourgeois. In the author's personal classification, Château Siran is ranked higher than some Crus Classés. Made quite carefully, Siran has the finesse and character of a superior wine.

Vineyard area: 30 hectares (75 acres).
Average production: 120 *tonneaux* (11,000 cases).

Sizzano

Red wine from the Italian Piedmont (*q.v.*).

Skhou

Distilled koumiss (*q.v.*).

Sling

A mixed iced drink in a long glass. The ingredients are spirits (usually gin), cordials, and fruit juice.

Slivovitz

Slivovitz (pronounced shleevovitsa) is the most common name for Serbian and Bosnian plum brandy from Yugoslavia. Sometimes Slivovica, or Slivovitza, or Šljivovica (Šljiva means plum in Serbo-Croatian), it is made from Pořegača or Madjarka blue plums in the second largest plum-growing area in the world. Slivovitz is the national drink in Bosnian and Serbian Yugoslavia, where it is called rakija. The spirit is double-distilled; and in export, in Western Europe, Britain, the United States, Australia, and other countries, it is sold at 70° proof and 87° proof, in tall bottles or in round, flat bottles, the shape of the traditional Yugoslav wooden flask. Famous since the Middle Ages, it comes from the fruit of trees never less than twenty years old and is fermented three months in 75-hectoliter (2,000-U.S.-gallon, 1,665-imp.) casks. Distilled twice, it matures in the wood in 19-hectoliter (500-U.S.-gallon, 416-imp.) casks; when it is one year old, hand-selected fresh plums are added. The brandy is then bottled and should be given about five more years. Variants of slivovitz are made in other Balkan countries, but Yugoslavia is the most important producer.

Sloe gin

A cordial made from the small, bitter, black plumlike fruit of the blackthorn, steeped in gin (*q.v.*).

Smash

A long, iced drink made with spirits, sugar, and mint.

Château Smith-Haut-Lafitte

Bordeaux red wine.
District: Graves, France.
Commune: Martillac.

The magnificent château stands untenanted in the midst of beech woods. The red wine, classed one of the Firsts of Graves in 1953, is a monopoly of the Louis Eschenauer firm of Bordeaux. White wine has been made since 1968 entirely from Sauvignon Blanc grapes.

Characteristics. A red wine with less character than most of the Graves in the first class, but rewarding when it is allowed to mature fully. The white is clean and pleasant.

Vineyard area: red—34 hectares (85 acres); white—5 hectares (12.5 acres).

Average production: red—140 *tonneaux* (13,000 cases); white—20 *tonneaux* (1,900 cases).

Soave

Italian white wine grown around Verona. It is dry, with an agreeable bouquet and a smooth texture.
See Veneto.

Sochu

Chinese spirit distilled from saké.

Soft

A wine which is not firm, not hard, and not rough. Wine of certain grape varieties matures rapidly and quickly achieves softness; in other cases, age is the determining factor. Once softness is attained, it is unlikely that a wine will keep long.

Solera system

Method by which Sherry wine, Málaga wine, and some Spanish brandies are produced.
See Sherry.

Som

Most Rumanian wine is made from the Riesling, Leanyka, and Furmint (known in Rumania as Som).

Somlói Furmint

A white wine from Somló, near Lake Balaton.
See Hungary.

Sommelier

French term for wine waiter.

Sonnenglanz

Important vineyard at Beblenheim, Alsace, France.
See Alsace.

Sonoma

Californian wine region, north of San Francisco, which provides some excellent table and sparkling wines.
See United States: California.

Sorbino

Finnish cherry liqueur.

Sour

A wine which has nearly turned to vinegar and is not fit to drink. The opposite of a sweet wine is a dry wine, not a sour one.

An American mixed drink made with fruit juice (usually lemon), spirits, and ice—i.e., whiskey sour, brandy sour, etc.

South Africa

South Africa, with its dry, hot climate and its viticultural tradition of three centuries, is a wine-producing country, but unfortunately not yet a wine-drinking one, although, happily, the trend toward the civilized habit of taking a glass of wine with a meal becomes more general every day. The great improvement in the quality of sherry-type and table wines is no doubt contributing largely to the slow change for the better in drinking tendencies. Not so many years ago, the so-called sherries were extremely harsh, and the table wines rough and indistinguishable; but this is no longer the case. The sherry is closest to that produced in Jerez de la Frontera. There has, moreover, been a tremendous improvement in the presentation—that is, the labeling—of the better table wines, even in the last few years.

How long it will take to turn South Africans into beverage wine-drinkers, as distinct from those who drink to celebrate, is difficult to say; but the outlook is now hopeful. Ninety per cent of the production is consumed locally. Now that the cheap rough wine of early days is on its way out, growers are making table wines which are, in some cases, attaining a higher average quality than some of their European counterparts. The *vins ordinaires* are some of the best in the world. It is significant that the consumption of table wines in South Africa has, according to a reliable estimate, trebled since 1945 and is now 9.8 liters per capita annually. South African restaurants offer fine values and good selections of the local table wines.

The southwestern Cape is one of the most reliable wine-growing districts in the world. The climate is seldom erratic, and heavy rain just before the grape-picking is a rarity, so that there is scarcely ever a poor vintage. Depending on the area, the picking season, or vintage, begins in February or March, and when a farm has several grape varieties it may go on for as long as two months.

WINE HISTORY

In 1955 the South African wine industry celebrated its tercentenary. It was at the end of the year 1654 that the first cuttings from Holland arrived at the Cape, and probably they were short (three-inch-long) slips of young vines from the Rhineland. The following year another consignment was sent out from Holland, and they were probably all Muscat, Green Grape (Groendruif), Muscatel, and the Steen grape known as Steendruif in Afrikaans.

On February 2, 1659, wine was pressed for the first time at the Cape, and Johan van Riebeeck wrote in his diary: "Today, praised be the Lord, wine was made for the first time from Cape grapes."

Credit should be given to the Co-operative Wine Growers' Association of South Africa for a chronological history of events since, in 1679, Simon van der Stel became governor of the Cape of Good Hope, established his farm at Groot Constantia, and set an example to the colonists by making fine wines. Significant dates follow: *1688* French Huguenots arrived and settled in Franschoek, Paarl, Drakenstein, and Stellenbosch; they extended the vineyards and improved the quality of Cape wines. *1711* South African wines were becoming known, and an early traveler in his writings spoke of the "world-famed Constantia wines," which were then being made at Wynberg. These were sweet wines. *1805* The English took possession of the Cape and, because of the Napoleonic Wars, encouraged the export of South African wines to Great Britain. *1811* The first official wine-taster was appointed, by Sir John Cradock, to keep an eye on the quality of the wine exported. *1826* Export trade to Britain flourished and wine growers and merchants invested considerable capital in the industry. *1861* With the abolition of preferential tariffs by the Gladstone government, the export trade to Britain collapsed. *1885* Phylloxera ravaged Cape vineyards, and wine-growers faced complete ruin. To combat the disease, they grafted their vines onto disease-resistant American root-stocks. The vines flourished, but soon the industry was faced with an even greater danger—overproduction. *1917* Overproduction meant ridiculously low prices for wine, and the growers decided to form a central organization to look after their interests. This led to the founding in 1918 of the Co-operative Wine Growers' Association of South Africa Ltd., today better known as the K.W.V. *1924* Parliament passed Act 5 of 1924, the Wine and Spirit Control Act. The K.W.V., under its constitution, annually fixes the minimum price to be paid for distilling wine; this Act made the transactions of non-members subject to the same provisions as those of members and changed the face and character of the South African wine industry. *1926* The export trade with Britain and Holland was resumed. *1931* The South African Wine Farmers' Association (London) Ltd. was established in the United Kingdom, with the K.W.V. holding a half interest. The purpose of this company was to effect distribution, maintain continuity of supplies, uniformity of quality, and stability of prices. *1940* The Wine and Spirit Control Amendment Act, No. 23 of 1940, was passed and provided for the fixing of the price for good wine sold by producers; it also empowered the K.W.V. to limit the production of wine alcohol in the Cape. *1950* K.W.V. acquired full control of the South African Wine Farmers' Association (London) Ltd.

WINE REGIONS

As an important form of agriculture, viticulture is limited to the southwestern districts of the Cape, between latitudes 33° and 34°S. The areas with summer rainfall are not favorable for vine growing; but vines grown at a high altitude in the Transvaal and Northern Cape produce table grapes, raisins, and sultanas.

The viticultural area may be divided into two distinct regions, the Coastal Belt and the Little Karoo. The former stretches from the coast to the first mountain range, and the districts of Stellenbosch, Paarl, Malmesbury, Ceres, Tulbagh, and the Constantia Valley lie in this area. The latter extends from beyond the Drakenstein range to the Swartberg Mountains and embraces the dis-

445

tricts of Worcester, Robertson, Montagu, Oudtshoorn, and Ladismith.

The Cape Division (in which lie the wine farms to the southeast of the Table Mountain range that runs across the Cape Peninsula) is the oldest wine-growing area in the country. Since the legislation in 1972 on South Africa's "Wines of Origin" (details on p. 448), both Cape and Caledon districts come under Stellenbosch. The Stellenbosch vineyards are about 45 minutes by car north of Capetown, and Stellenbosch itself is a handsome old town with great flower gardens and trees. The university there works closely with the S.A. Wine Institute, a department of the Ministry of Agriculture.

The Coastal Belt vines are grown mainly on mountain slopes, the yield being 3 to 6 tons (3.36 to 6.72 short tons) per acre, from which dry white and red wines are produced, as are good sherry- and port-types. Due to the slight variation in climatic conditions, there is very little variation in the quality of these wines from year to year. The grape varieties grown are Hermitage, Steendruif (very like Sauvignon Blanc), Groendruif, Riesling, Cabernet Sauvignon, Clairette Blanche, and the Port varieties.

In the Little Karoo, where the rainfall is less than half that in the Coastal Belt and where the vines are grown under irrigation, the yield is 6 to 10 tons (6.72 to 11.2 short tons) per acre, and the grape varieties are Hermitage, Steendruif, Hanepoot, Muscadel, and Sultana, yielding sweet wines, sherry-types, and brandies.

In the Coastal Belt the soil varies from sandy to heavy loam, while in the Little Karoo the soils are deep, rich alluvial. Some wine-growers claim a considerable variation in origin of the soils on their farms; 62,869 morgen (1 morgen = 2.09 acres) of this region are planted to 142 million vines, while in the Little Karoo 40,000 morgen are planted to 125 million vines.

The seasons in South Africa are not as in Europe. Spring lasts from September to November, summer from December to February, autumn from March to May, and winter from June to August. The grapes reach full ripeness between February and April, and the harvesting begins before the onset of autumn.

TYPES OF WINE

The Constantia wines, already mentioned as being exported in the late eighteenth and early nineteenth centuries, were dessert wines, and these are still of good quality. They include port-type wines—Tawny, Ruby, White, and Vintage—produced from Hermitage and Portuguese variety grapes grown at Paarl, Stellenbosch, and adjoining areas, and made in the Portuguese manner; and Muscadel wines, produced from Muscadel grapes grown at Robertson, Montagu, Bonnievale, and the Nuy district of Worcester. The trend is to varietally labeled wines.

Sherry-type production in South Africa started about thirty years ago, and only as recently as 1942 were these wines produced by the *solera* system, the traditional method of Sherry manufacture in Spain. It is interesting to note the resemblance geographically and climatically between Paarl, center of the South African wine industry, and the Sherry-producing areas of Andalusia in Spain. Jerez de la Frontera has a latitude of 34°41′N. and Paarl is situated at 33°45′S.

Both light-bodied and full-bodied red natural wines are produced at the Cape—the light from Cabernet, Cinsault, and Shiraz grapes grown in the Constantia Valley, and in the districts of Stellenbosch and Somerset West nearest to the coast; the fuller wines from Cinsault, Shiraz, Pinotage and Gamay grapes grown at Paarl, Stellenbosch, and Durbanville. There is a shortage of Cabernet Sauvignon. Rosés have been produced at the Cape for some years now and are gaining in popularity. Reds are aged from one and a half to three years in vats or small cooperage.

Dry and semi-sweet white table wines, which must contain less than 2% sugar, are made from Riesling, Chenin Blanc, Traminer, Colombard, and Clairette Blanche grapes grown at Paarl, Stellenbosch, and Tulbagh. White wines make up 95% of the production. A bit watery, they are better than similar wines from Chile.

Sparkling wines are made from Riesling and Clairette Blanche grapes by natural fermentation, and also by artificial impregnation of the wine with carbon dioxide.

There is some difficulty in giving the total vintage return for South Africa, a figure that has to be compiled from the returns of growers which include both alcoholic products and non-alcoholic products such as table grapes and grapes for the making of raisins. They do not, however, include returns from the main sultana-producing areas. Based on the returns of growers as supplied by the Co-operative Wine Growers' Association, the wine production for the year 1972, district by district, was as follows:

District	Hectoliters
Caledon	70,000
Cape Peninsula	70,000
Ceres and Tulba	400,525
Malmesbury	833,500
Montagu	235,600
Paarl	623,100
Robertson	722,000
Stellenbosch	760,000
Worcester	997,000
Total	4,711,725

SPIRITS

Liqueurs with an alcoholic content of 55° to 78° proof spirit, or 32% to 44% by volume, are made in ever-increasing variety, based upon European counterparts; but the legendary liqueur named by early Cape settlers, Van der Hum, is typically South African. It was produced in days gone by in the Old Cape homes with a flavoring made from *nartjie* (tangerine) peel, but now, unfortunately, a synthetic flavoring is employed.

Brandy was first made in the Cape in the year 1672. It is now distilled and matured under strict government supervision. The alcoholic content is 75° proof spirit or 43% by volume. The grapes from which distilling wines are produced are the "French" and "Green" varieties grown in the areas around Worcester, Montagu, and Robertson. Only the best quality distilling wines are allowed to be used for distillation into brandy and these must be approved by the Government Brandy Board. All types of South African brandy must contain a minimum of 25% brandy distilled in a pot-still, matured for a minimum period of three years in casks of imported oak approved by a government commissioner. If certified by the Government Brandy Board to be pure wine brandy, it qualifies for an excise duty rebate of 43.7 cents per proof gallon, and provision has now been made for higher rebates for brandies matured for four and five years. Sixty-five per cent of all brandy is made by one corporation, controlled by Anton Rupert of Rothman's cigarettes.

ORGANIZATION OF THE WINE AND SPIRIT INDUSTRIES

At the producer's level, the wine industry is highly organized, largely as a result of the monopolistic powers of the Co-operative Growers' Association of South Africa—the K.W.V. already referred to. This was founded in 1918, its main object being: "To so direct, control and regulate the sale and disposal by its members of their produce, being that of the grape, as shall secure or tend to secure for them a continuously adequate return for such produce."

Early opposition from wine-growers who preferred to withhold support from this cooperative was overcome in 1924, when Parliament passed the Wine and Spirit Control Act in terms of which the transactions of non-members were made subject to the same conditions and obligations as were imposed by the Constitution of the K.W.V. Since that time, no person may sell, acquire, or utilize wine in the Cape province for distilling or conversion into spirits except through or with the consent of the Association; nor may any wine-grower sell or distill or otherwise dispose of brandy or spirits distilled from his own wine except through and with the consent of the K.W.V.

Under its constitution, the Association annually fixes a minimum price for distilling wine, declares the surplus (i.e., that portion of the vintage which it considers cannot be absorbed by the local market) and indicates what portion of a member's vintage must be held by him and delivered as a surplus, free of charge, to the Association. If the member cannot deliver the specified surplus, owing to his having sold his entire crop, then he must contribute cash instead. Cooperation is compulsory. The K.W.V. is debarred from selling its products for use in Africa south of the equator except to distilling cooperative societies, and to the wholesale trade. In the South African wine industry a clear distinction is made between what is called good wine and distilling wine. The former is intended for consumption as wine, while the latter is intended for distillation into brandy or wine spirits.

The Surplus Declaration by the Association under its

constitution for the year 1969 was 35% of the total crop, and in handling the surplus it found its greatest outlet in the Cape's traditional market, Great Britain. In South Africa, the K.W.V. has five wineries situated in Paarl, Stellenbosch, Robertson, Montagu, and Worcester, with a total storage capacity of almost 60 million U.S. gallons (40 million imp.). Membership of the Association increased from 4,444 in 1959 to 6,000 in 1974—evidence of successful organization under the cooperative system. Uncontrolled surpluses before 1918 resulted in wine-growers being barely able to obtain a penny per bottle for their best wines.

In the year 1978, South African exports of wine and brandy amounted to 100,000 hectoliters and 21,000 hectoliters respectively, while the total wine production amounted to 6.2 million hectoliters. The aggressive K.W.V. has the monopoly for export wines, but the giant Stellenbosch Farm Wineries has virtually the same for locally consumed wines. Since its great expansion in the 1950s, the winery makes 75% of all internal South African wine; most of the grapes come from the 60 cooperative growers associated with the winery.

No longer is South Africa's wine trade based on preferential tariffs but on quality. Cape wines have to pass a government quality control before they may be exported, and the excise control of brandy in the Republic is among the strictest in the world. All brandies shipped from South Africa carry with them certificates of age, method of maturation, and distillation.

Whereas the wine-growing countries of Europe have recognized for some time the importance of place of origin in the pedigree and identification of wines, South Africa was, until September 1973, without any system approximating the French Appellation d'Origine Contrôlée. But after investigation by a government committee under Dr. J. A. van Zyl, this system has now been adopted in South Africa and given the force of law with the introduction of the W.O. (Wines of Origin) seal—the truth on the label. The seal is awarded by the South African Wine and Spirits Board as its guarantee that "what is stated on the label will also be found in the bottle, insofar as it refers to place of origin, vine variety, and vintage year—or any combination of the three." The maintenance of the new regulation involves the usual complicated system of production records, sampling, testing, certification procedure, and a reasonable system of policing.

The W.O. seal now has to be applied to the capsule on bottled wines which bears the year of vintage or any one of the prescribed list of names of designated areas for the production of Wines of Origin, or of vine *cultivars* (varieties) approved by the Wine and Spirits Board. By the end of 1973, about fourteen areas had been defined formally in terms of the legislation as areas for Wines of Origin, and fourteen estates were approved for the production of "Estate Wines of Origin."

The geographic areas approved for Wines of Origin included Malmesbury, Paarl, Piketberg, Robertson, Stellenbosch (including Caledon and Cape), Tulbagh, Worcester, Swellendam, Constantia, Durbanville, Olifants River, the Little Karoo, and an area known as Bo-berg (Paarl and Tulbagh Divisional Council areas). The Boberg designation is limited to liqueur wines such as "sherries" and "ports." The best wines come from Malmesbury, Paarl, Stellenbosch, Tulbagh, Worcester, Constantia, and Durbanville, this last noted for reds.

The estates defined for the production of Estate Wines of Origin included Alto at Stellenbosch; Backsberg at Paarl; Groot Constantia and Meerendal in the Cape Town area; Middelvlei, Muratie, Neethlingshof, Overgaauw, Simonsig, Uiterwyk, and Verdun—all at Stellenbosch; and Montpellier, Theuniskraal, and Twee Jongegezellen at Tulbagh.

A number of estates which in the past were generally assumed to be estate wine-producers had not then applied for registration under the scheme, either because of technical problems or practical considerations. This does not imply that their wines are not up to the standard set, or that any stigma is attached to them.

Unfortified wines designated as Wines of Origin must be derived wholly (100%) from the grape variety indicated; fortified wines must be at least 80% products of the indicated variety.

An estate wine must comply with certain quality standards defined by the Board and must be produced or manufactured entirely in a cellar on the estate, from grapes grown on the estate. A distinction has been drawn between estate wines produced, manufactured, and bottled on a particular estate, and wine produced or manufactured on the estate but bottled elsewhere.

No wine may be sold or exported under the name of any wine *cultivar* allowed for the making of wine, unless 75% was produced or manufactured from vines of such a *cultivar*, and the wine is characteristic of the variety. Certain exceptions are listed.

Provision is made for "Wines of Origin Superior" (or W.O.S.), a rare distinction for a superior-quality wine made entirely from grapes of the specified *cultivar*.

Provision was also made for a transition period in the case of certain noble varieties, including Cabernet Sauvignon, Cabernet Franc, Pinotage, Riesling, Shiraz, or Sylvaner. This transition period comes to an end in December 1982.

So far as Cabernet, Pinotage, Shiraz, and Riesling are concerned, all wines bottled under the label of these *cultivars* must contain at least 30% of the variety up to 1976, 50% up to 1983, and thereafter, 75%. This must be certified by the Board.

In the case of varieties in plentiful supply, including Steen, Frans, Sultana, and Cinsault (Hermitage), 75% of the specified variety must be used, but the contents need not be certified specifically by the Board. In the case of Muscadel and Hanepoot the figure was 40% initially, increasing to 75% within five years.

The official record and control system facilitates control in detail of the production and handling of wine from the time of pressing until the wine is bottled, labeled, certified, and ready for marketing. This has obliged wineries to acquire additional equipment to deal with small batches of wine separately in all its stages. Not only do varieties have to be processed separately but vintages must be kept apart, and this is expected to add considerably to the cost of the end product.

With the introduction of any scheme involving control, teething troubles are to be expected. The opinions of producers and merchants may vary, but all in all, they agree that the dispensation holds benefits for all concerned with either production, marketing, or consumption of wine.

Southwest France

Apart from the great region of Bordeaux, there are several more wine-growing provinces in this part of France, stretching from the Dordogne to the Pyrenees. Some of these wines are entitled to Appellations Contrôlées and most will be found under individual headings: Béarn, Bergerac, Côtes de Duras, Côtes de Montravel, Côtes de Saussignac, Côtes du Buzet, Gaillac, Jurançon, Madiran, Monbazillac, Pacherenc de Vic Bilh, Pécharmant, etc.

A second group of lesser wines, agreeable to drink in their own part of the country, is listed under the Vins Délimités de Qualité Supérieure. These are: Cahors (Lot), red; Côtes du Marmandais (Lot-et-Garonne), red and white; Fronton (Haute-Garonne), red, white, and rosé; Laville-dieu (Tarn-et-Garonne), red and white; Rousselet de Béarn (Basses-Pyrénées); Villaudric (Haute-Garonne).

See V.D.Q.S.

Spain

Spain has the largest acreage of vineyard in Europe but not the highest yield; Italy and France make more wine. Nearly 30 million hectoliters (789.5 million U.S. gallons, 658 million imp.) are harvested every year from 1,720,000 hectares of vineyards (4,300,000 acres)—more than one-fifth of all the European vineyard land. Here, as elsewhere, the current expansion of viticulture and the gradual modernization of wine-making methods have been very marked in recent years. The country, with its extreme contrasts in climate, landscape, and soil, produces wines of all types: from delicate Fino Sherries to rich dessert wines, from frail wines of old vintage to strong hearty reds, to the delightful whites of Alella and the thin green wines of the northwest. From the central plain comes a great gush of ordinary wine (*vino corriente*) used for carafe wine and for blending both at home and abroad.

The greater part of the country is a vast tableland (*meseta*), with outbreaks of jagged mountain ranges and snow-covered peaks. Its climate is harsh and Continental with dry, torrid summers and biting winters. Seen from the air, Spain is like a brown relief map wrinkled into dry creeks and valleys, with sudden gleams of water. For the traveler by road or train, however, the monotony is broken: after an expanse of arid grass come umbrella pines, cork oaks, a sweet-smelling scrub of rosemary and lavender, or a patchwork of olive groves. Arriving at one of the great rivers, he is in a landscape of cornfields and poplar trees. Once through the Sierra Morena, into the province of Córdoba, the sharp air softens. In the spring, all Andalusia is green; figs, oranges, and lemons grow in season. The winters are mild here, and around the Mediterranean coast the weather is tempered by the sea, and the narrow strip of land bordering the shore is planted like a garden with fruit, olives, and vines—the last growing prolifically near the sea or on the sheltered slopes of some of the mountain valleys. The most productive areas are in La Mancha with New Castile, in Catalonia, and the Levante along the east coast. The best wines come not from these areas but from the Sherry region in West Andalusia, and from the Rioja vineyards in Logroño, Alava, and Navarre. The quantity of the prized wines of Jerez was, in 1971, little more than half that of La Mancha.

HISTORY

The vineyards of Andalusia are very old. In about 1100 B.C. the Phoenicians founded Gadir (Cádiz) and planted vines, presumably brought from the East. Then came Greeks, Carthaginians, and Romans, spreading both the vines and the science of viticulture through Spain. Wine was supplied to Rome, and Cicero praised the growths of Tarragona and Catalonia. When Rome fell, the barbarians invaded—Vandals, leaving their name to Andalusia, were followed by Goths. They must have trampled down the vineyards, but the vine persisted; and when the Arabs landed, in 711, they protected and increased the grapevines for the sake of the fruit. Gradually, the wine-drinking Christian kings won back the land until, in 1492, the last Moorish kingdom of Granada was retaken.

Early in the fourteenth century, Spanish wines were coming to England. By the time of Spain's ascendancy, when the Emperor Charles V was ruling the Netherlands from Spain, Sack (Sherry), Tent (Alicante), and Canary wines were familiar drinks in northern Europe.

At the beginning of this century, Spain, less affected by the phylloxera epidemic than were many European countries, was doing a flourishing export trade. But the French laws against the entry of foreign wines in the early 1930s and the crisis of overproduction, to which importations from Algeria into France contributed, hit Spain hard. Then came the Spanish Civil War. Neglected vines developed phylloxera; whole vineyards, especially those near Madrid and Toledo, were destroyed. Wine became scarce, and the price doubled. The Second World War made conditions worse, and in the 1940s there were outbreaks of mildew and a prolonged series of droughts to contend with. Not until 1952-53 did wine production really improve and prices begin to drop. Since 1959, the vineyard area has been spreading, mainly in New Castile.

The natural consequence has been an increase in export figures. In 1970, they were higher than in the six previous years; in 1976, this total rose again, by 90%, to 6,000,000 hectoliters (158,700,000 U.S. gallons, 132,000,000 imp.). This increase applies to all wines except the lighter, unfermented types with the Denominación de Origen. Spain's leading customers are the United Kingdom, Switzerland, the Netherlands, West Germany, Sweden, and Hungary—in that order. One imagines, from popular pictures of drinkers aiming the wine accurately into their mouths from spouted glass *porrones*, that the Spanish consume much of their own wine. In fact, their consumption is moderate: just under 92 liters a head in 1970, falling to 70 in 1978. The dark *bodega* with its wooden casks and stone floor is still frequented. But many people have taken to the big supermarkets, where they have a greater choice of bottled wines from farther afield than the neighboring villages. Many of these bottles are produced by the new agricultural cooperatives; but it is also possible to find on the shelves such finer wines as the Rioja of the Marqués de Riscal.

WINE LAWS

Spain is following the trend toward greater control of the complete wine-making process, from planting to bottling and labeling, although, in most districts, there is still a long way to go. Jerez is the shining exception, Rioja

second best. The program for establishing an efficient system of place-names (Denominación de Origen), with high standards and quality controls, is well in hand, and the following appellations are now functioning:

Andalusia. Jerez-Xeres-Sherry. Manzanilla-Sanlúcar de Barrameda (in Cadiz province). Huelva. Málaga. Montilla-Moriles (in Córdoba province).

Rioja. Rioja.

La Mancha and New Castile. Almansa. Mancha. Manchuela. Mentrida. Valdepeñas.

Levante. Cheste. Jumilla. Utiel-Requena. Valencia. Alicante. Yecla.

Catalonia. Alella. Panadés. Priorato. Tarragona. Ampurdán Costa Brava. Grandesa Terralta. Conca del Barbera.

Aragon. Carinena.

Navarre. Navarra.

Galicia. Ribero. Valdeorras. Valle de Monterrey.

Inside Spain, Rioja dominates every first-class wine

list—with the result that some of the sound Valdepeñas and other respectable wines are apt to be ignored. Customers have come to think of Rioja as being the only wine fit to accompany a good meal. In general, the white wines are not up to the standard of the red ones, although there are naturally exceptions to this rule—Alella, for one.

In spite of the wide variety of Spanish wines, individual characteristics are too often ironed out by the vintner's steady hand. Not only are crops from various vineyards vatted together within one area, but there is a good deal of blending across the country. The average goal is plateau, not peak—although this does not apply to the best of Rioja, to the sweet wines of Málaga, nor to the fine wines of Montilla-Moriles. While it is encouraging, the new Spanish wine law is in no way as complete as the French—or in a different way, the West German. The positive effects will be noticed from 1975 on, yet even then unscrupulous practices may continue, since virtually no strong enforcement is written into the law.

See separate entries for Málaga; Montilla-Moriles; Rioja; Sherry.

OTHER WINE REGIONS

Central Spain: La Mancha and New Castile

In La Mancha, a sea of short-pruned vines, miles of them, breaks the monotony of the plain. In the sun-roasted soil, vines are planted three meters apart, the occasional olive trees which grow among them casting a little shade. The land of Don Quixote has changed less than many parts of Spain. There is light industry now, and some modern improvements in farming; but mud-walled farmyards survive, as well as bell chimneys and outdoor ovens. It is a red-earth region of chalk or slatey soil, of wheat, windmills, and wine.

In the bitter winters, vines have to struggle—which has an invigorating effect on the wine; the grapes ripen well under the scorching summer sun; and after the harvest, wine flows, both red and white, into the carafes of Madrid's cafés, and over the borders to France. There is also a good deal of distillation. Long barrel-ageing is not practiced here. People like their wines young, brisk, bright, and fresh. The bulk is ordinary (*vino corriente*), some of it labeled, inaccurately, as Valdepeñas for the region's most distinguished wine.

La Mancha, merging with New Castile (which is centered around Madrid) divides into two areas, Upper and Lower: La Mancha Alta and Baja. The first includes the provinces of Albacete and Cuenca; the second, and larger, embraces Toledo and Ciudad Real. In the east, La Mancha borders on Valencia and Alicante; in the west, it touches Estremadura where most of the conquistadores came from; and southwards, it stretches as far as the Sierra Morena. What the Spanish writer José de Castillo has described as the heart of the red wine country is the area where the four districts of La Mancha, Levante, Murcia, and Albacete meet. Here they drink the "valient," alcoholic reds.

Valdepeñas, best and best-known of Manchega wines, is produced in the south of the region, 85 kilometers (136

miles) south of Madrid on the road to Granada. The town of Valdepeñas, with its innumerable *bodegas*, is dedicated to wine. In this part of the country, *pellejos* are still to be seen—wine-skins made from the whole hide of a pig. Slightly macabre though this appears, it makes a good, airtight container in which the wine keeps well. Some of this wine is still made in *tinajas*, the huge, bulbous terra-cotta jars molded from the clay and ocher-colored soil. The process is simple and traditional; the fermented red wine remains in the *tinaja*, deposits soon sink to the bottom, and the cleared wine is left where it is to mature until the following spring, when it will be pumped into barrels and sold. White and rosé (*rosado*) wines, however, are racked into another amphora after the first fermentation, in order to separate them from the skins. In Toboso and Villanobledo, towns where the legends of Dulcinea and Don Quixote are remembered, *tinajas* are made, many of them to be ornamental rather than useful, as the slow change to oak casks and even glass-lined fermenting vats gets under way.

The reds (*tintos*) have not the deep, blackish color of much of the Spanish wine; they are a clear ruby. A good red Valdepeñas should be smooth and well-balanced, with something of a northern character, though heavier. The name, protected by the Denominación de Origen, is still too often taken in vain. White wines of Valdepeñas are either a pale, greenish shade, or else a deep golden yellow.

The other Manchego wines granted the Denominación de Origen are Mancha in Albacete, making pale whites and *claretes* (light reds) of between 12° and 13° of alcohol; Manchuela, stretching from Albacete to Cuenca and the verge of Valencia, producing robust, rather strong, *tintos, claretes*, and *rosados;* Almansa, which joins the Meseta to the coastal area of Alicante, its strong wines (both *claretes* and blackish *tintos*) sometimes reaching 17° of alcohol; and Mentrida, near Toledo, producing strong, dry, rather ordinary reds.

Leading grapevines planted in La Mancha are: reds—Cencibel, Monastrel, Tinto Basto, Garnacha, Bobal, Aragón, and Castellana, with some other varieties; whites—principally Arién and Jaén, with Pardillo and Cirial. Cencibel mixed with Arién produces the good *claretes* of Valdepeñas, favored by the chalk and slatey soils. Acreage and production figures are as follows in 1971:

Almansa. 15,000 hectares (37,500 acres) producing 180,000 hectoliters (4.87 million U.S. gallons, 3.96 million imp.) of white and red wine.

Mancha. 200,000 hectares (500,000 acres) producing 2,900,000 hectoliters (76.9 million U.S. gallons, 63.8 million imp.) of red and white wine.

Manchuela. 60,000 hectares (150,000 acres) producing 1 million hectoliters (26.5 million U.S. gallons, 22 million imp.) of red and white wine.

Valdepeñas. 21,000 hectares (53,000 acres) producing 340,000 hectoliters (9 million U.S. gallons, 7.5 million imp.) of red and white wine.

Mentrida. 21,000 hectares (53,000 acres) producing 300,000 hectoliters (7.9 million U.S. gallons, 6.6 million imp.) of red and white wine.

The Levante and Alicante

On Spain's east coast, the fertile strip of irrigated land which borders the Mediterranean between Alicante and Benicarlo—the sunny Costa Blanca, with its *huerta*, the gardenland irrigated by the Arabs, where palms, figs, cotton, oranges, and rice-fields grow—forms only a part of this wine region and has the outlets of two busy ports, Alicante and Valencia. One of the driest districts of Spain, mild and fine in winter, it is a prolific producer of grapes, second only to La Mancha. Behind it is the more rugged zone of Cheste, where the climate is Continental; and this is backed by the steep, bleak mountain slopes of Utiel-Requena. The growths of these three Denominaciones de Origen (Valencia, Cheste, Utiel-Requena) appear to be vinous expressions of the terrain. It is a region of simple wines for quick drinking: more sweet than dry, more red than white; and they wash down the native paella, the fish and prawns, and the game, all plentiful here. Wine is big business, and everywhere new cooperatives with modern equipment are replacing small, individual cellars.

Valencia

Always famous for its sweet wines, Valencia makes sweet *tintos*, *blancos*, and *claretes* today, as well as amber-colored *mistelas*, from Muscatel and Malvasia, Planta Nova, Garnacha, Merseguera, Bobal, and other grapes. They are much relished in their own province. There is also a popular aperitif, scented with herbs and blended from old *soleras*. The sweetish, bright red wines of Valencia are robust and heady, with anything from 12° to 16° of alcohol. One of the most palatable is Fondillón, for which demand far exceeds the small supply. These reds, and the *rosados*, are taken with meals; at about two years of age, they have the character of vintage wines.

Cheste

In this central zone, vines grow around the towns of Chivas and Turia. Most of the wine is white—dry, sweet, or semi-sweet, either pale in color or deep gold. Merseguera and Planta Nova are leading grapes; 7,500 hectares (18,750 acres) are in vineyard.

Utiel-Requena

In the mountainous area where Valencia touches Castile, the wines—mostly red—are at once weaker, coarse, and more vivid in color than those of the plain. *Tintos*, *claretes*, and *rosados*, all range between 10° to 13° of alcohol; 50,000 hectares (125,000 acres) are planted in vines.

Jumilla

Another Denominación de Origen under Levante is actually in northern Murcia, where the hinterland is poor, though long ago the province was rich in mines. But toward the sea, this, too, has its *huerta*. These vineyards, sloping down to a long river valley, push their way into Valencia. The red wines are pleasantly ordinary, with a trace of sweetness, much of it from the Monastrel grape. Yecla is another flourishing wine town in the same dis-

trict. Jumilla has 25,000 hectares (62,500 acres) of vineyards.

Yecla

Now raised to the Denominación de Origen, Yecla lies in the same area as Jumilla, in the district of the Levante, bordering on northern Murcia. About 26,000 hectares (65,000 acres) of vineyard are planted mainly in Monastrel, which gives red wines. Like Jumilla, it is a town of *bodegas*, where the grapes from the adjoining vineyards are made into dark, strong wines.

Catalonia

As in the Levante, this region divides into the fertile, sunny land edging the coast of the Costa Brava, and the higher, rockier terrain inland. Vineyards were planted here in Graeco-Roman times; the wines were celebrated in the Middle Ages; and present-day production, both in bulk wines, and in better growths rating the Denominación de Origen, is high.

Tarragona

Encircling Priorato, a small area with its own Denominación, Tarragona is traditionally associated abroad with a coarse, strong, sweet red. This conception is out of date, since there is now a far greater variety in the vines, and in the wines—heavy and light, sweet and dry, in both whites and reds. Reus is the important center for Tarragona.

Ampurdán Costa Brava

Lately awarded the Denominación de Origen, these vineyards of northern Catalonia are planted in the province of Gerona, inland and near the French border. Quite pleasant white and *rosado* wines are made from 6,800 hectares (17,000 acres) of land planted in Cariñena and Garnacha grapes. In the district is the Castello de Perelada—with its wine library and museum—which produces reds, whites and roses, as well as the famous sparkling wine. After Perelada, the best-known labels are those of the Barón de Terrades.

Alella

The vineyards, about 12 kilometers (20 miles) north of Barcelona, dating back to Roman times, cover the slopes of a steep massif, one vineyard facing the sea, the other inland. The vines, grown in granitic soil around the town of Alella and several neighboring villages, combine well: those with a northern outlook are high in acidity, counteracting the low acidity of the south-facing grapes. A terrain of some 600 hectares (1,500 acres), planted principally in Garnacha, Picpoule, Macabeo, Pansa Blanca, and Red Sumoll grapes, produces white, *rosado*, and red wine. There is also a golden dessert type called Lacre Violeta. The wines of this small region are made in the traditional way (usually kept in oak for three years before bottling) and preserve their natural qualities. Most praised is the soft, fruity Marfil Blanco. The whites are light, with a very agreeable bouquet.

Priorato

Set against the backcloth of the Sierra de Montsant

and the ruins of the old priory of the holy mountain, the vineyards are stepped in terraces down to the red-earth valley of the River Ciurana. On the rocky, high ground, grapes and olives grow together, for oil as well as wine is important. Slate in the volcanic soil and the ticklish breezes of the mistral (known locally as *seré*) induce a rich harvest and wines strong in alcohol. In the surrounding villages, almost everybody works among the vines. The market towns are Gandesa and Falset; the wines they sell, both dry and sweet, are good but very strong and vividly red. Some of the common wines reach from 19° to 24° of alcohol. The whites are brilliantly clear, with a fruity scent. The highest vine patch in the district is the Conca del Barbara, climbing to the crest of a hill and making vigorous reds and spirited whites with a distinctive bouquet. Important among the red grapes of Priorato are Cariñena and Garnacha. The whites come from Macabeo and Pedro Ximénez.

Panadés

One of two classified names in the district of Barcelona. This, too, divides into a coastal strip (Baja), a central zone, and mountain vineyards (Alta) which are among the highest in Spain. Throughout the area, most of the soil is the excellent chalky *albariza*. Vineyards of the plain, around Sitges and Villafranca del Panadés, produce strong, dark, sweetish wines; one of the principal grapes is Malvasia. From the high ground comes a charming light white, from Perellada and Montonech vines. El Panadés Central specializes in the best sparkling wines of the country, known as *cavas* Codorníu. The extra-dry—probably most to the taste of Anglo-Saxons—is called Non Plus Ultra. Only cellars where wine is so made, by the *méthode champenoise*, are allowed the name *cavas*. One of the largest firms exporting Spanish wines is owned by the Torres family and has an assortment of good red and white wines, with a winery at Villafranca de Panadés.

Gandesa Terralta

Often mentioned with Priorato (above); now has its own Denominación. The bright red, alcoholic wines and the transparent white are obtained from 11,500 hectares (28,500 acres) of vineyard planted primarily in Garnacha, Macabeo, and Cariñena.

Conca del Barbera

The highest vine patch in the Priorato region, where the vines, climbing to the crest of the hill, yield vigorous reds and spirited whites with a distinctive bouquet. The name has recently been promoted to the Denominación de Origen. The grapes Macabeo, Perellada, Pansa, Sumoll Tinto, and Bobal are planted in 7,000 hectares (17,500 acres) of vineyards.

Aragón

The old royal province has an old reputation for its wines. The sun-baked vineyards, sheltered by the Sierra de la Muela and watered by the River Ebro, make wines of all shades and styles; in particular the Cariñena, which has the Denominación de Origen. Coming, as do the *co-rrientes*, in reds and whites, sweet and dry, these are wines of distinctive character which attain a high degree of alcohol, although some of them, light in body, provide pleasant, if heady, table wine, taken usually when young. Favored grapes are Garnacha, Cariñena, and Bobal.

Navarre

The Denominación Navarra covers four districts: Montaña, Valdizarbe, Ribera Alta, and Ribera Baja. With 22,500 hectares (56,500 acres) this is romantic country, stretching from the woods and mountain streams of the Pyrenees to the fiestas of Pamplona, enclosing rich farmland and old monasteries, and touching down to Logroño—where some of the wines are allowed the Denominación Rioja. In the north, they make tart, prickly *vinos verdes*. Those southern vineyards that do not merge with Logroño are planted either near Pamplona (where the *corrientes* are not unlike those of the French side of the mountains) or, more importantly, in the valleys of the Ebro and Ribera, where the wine is stronger and sometimes rather sharp. Leading grapes are Carasol and Secano.

Galicia

On the Atlantic coast, Spain has the greenness and moisture of the whole of that seaboard, where the temperate climate produces large crops of grapes and wine. Inland, vines are pruned low, in the Castilian manner; but nearer the sea, they climb up posts and along wires arranged to protect them from the wet earth—a system known as *parrales*. The region has three Denominaciones: Valdeorras, Valle de Monterrey, and Ribero. Valdeorras, with 6,500 hectares (11,200 acres) in the sheltered valley of the Sil, sticks to the old plan of vineyard plots; the Monterrey Valley, cutting through the south of Orense toward Portugal, has less rainfall than the rest of the region: the vine-covered slopes produce pleasant reds, from Alicante, Albarello, and other grapes, and whites from the Jerez vine. The white wines of Orense province are often stronger and more perfumed than the reds. Ribero wines are partly in Orense, partly in Avia—the latter highly regarded in their own country. The reds are successful but, again, weaker than the whites. Traditions of wine-making were handed down by the monasteries. Albariño, Treixadura, Palomino, and Alicante are among the grapes used. On this Atlantic shore, near Portugal, wines are often as light, sharp, fresh, and prickly as the Vinhos Verdes of the Minho area. In the Pontevedra district, vines are cultivated on *parrales* in the areas Condado, Albarino, and Rosal.

Huelva

Huelva borders with Portugal in the extreme south of Spain, with the River Guadalquivir threading between it and the province of Cádiz. This land of vines and *camargue*, of horses, bulls, and grapes, produces wines which have a great reputation in their own country. The Denominación Huelva embraces the district Condado de Niebla, where vines grow near the river. The vineyard area of 19,000 hectares (47,000 acres) produces about

650,000 hectoliters (17,160,000 U.S. gallons, 14,300,000 imp.) of wine. Famous names here are Palma del Condado, San Juan del Puerto, and Villalba del Alcor—with Manzanilla, which is said to have given its name to the wine of Sanlúcar de Barrameda.

Estremadura

The long, narrow province of green forests, deep valleys, and plentiful game bordering Portugal, has no Denominación de Origen but a good deal of wine, most of it pleasant, strong, and brilliant to the eye. Caceres makes full-bodied whites and "valiant" reds. The Almendraljo area also has a good production of average wines to drink with the porks and savory stews and solid gazpachos of the region.

León and Castile

There is not yet a Denominación de Origen in these provinces. The wines which are most familiar are those of Toro and Rueda. The first lives up to its name: a strong, vigorous red. The whites of Rueda, from the Verdejo Blanco grape, are heady, golden, aromatic. What is most interesting about the neighborhood is that, in Valbuena de Duero, near Valladolid, is the small vineyard of Vega Sicilia (only 60 hectares—150 acres) planted in grapes brought from Burgundy and Bordeaux by the landowner Don Eloy Lecarda, after the phylloxera had destroyed his original vines. The wine, made in the Bordeaux style, is aged in oak casks and has considerable fame. It is never less than five years old when bottled; the older, vintage type is labeled Reserva Especial Única.

Basque Provinces

Vizcaya and Guipzcoa, in the areas of Bilbao and San Sebastián, are of little interest in wine history, although the thin local Chiclas and cider are drunk with some pleasure by the inhabitants and visiting tourists.

The Islands

The Canaries. Canary Sack and Palma Sack (the latter from Las Palmas, port of Gran Canaria) made the Spanish islands off Africa famous in the Elizabethan Age. The color was named for the bird, the bird for the islands—and the islands were once overrun by dogs (*canes*). The coincidence provided many puns in old plays ("Never in your life . . . unless you see canary, put me down"—*Twelfth Night*).

The importance of Canary wine in the world diminished with the oïdium plague of over a century ago, although some 60,000 hectoliters (1.59 million U.S. gallons, 1.32 million imp.) of *corriente* are still produced for local consumption, most of it white, a little *clarete*. A great variety of grapes is grown. Some of the wines do very well: among them the white Vidueno, the dry white of Palma, the Muscatels, and the Tacorontes or Mountain Wines.

The Balearics. All of these islands grow grapes in small vineyard plots and make wine, mostly in the traditional way. In Majorca, the area of Benisalem produces dark, heavy reds, while Felanitx has lighter rather flat wines. In Ibiza and Formentor, where the wine is stronger, some modern cooperatives are being established.

Spanish earth

Silicate of aluminum—used in fining or clearing wines.

Sparkling Burgundy

Red, rosé, or white Burgundy wine rendered sparkling either in huge vats or in bottle, according to the champagne method. Since the region's fine wines are never used in its production, sparkling Burgundy, always white, is almost without exception undistinguished.
See Burgundy.

Sparkling wines

Wines made effervescent by the presence of carbon dioxide in the bottle. The best of these wines are made by the champagne method of secondary fermentation in bottles (*see* Champagne). The others are made either by the bulk process—fermenting the wine in big tanks and bottling under pressure (*see* Charmat); or by the less commendable method of adding carbon dioxide in much the same way as it is pumped into gassy fruit drinks (*see* Carbonated wines).

Spätburgunder

German descendant of the Pinot Noir grape, brought there from Burgundy. It comprises 60% of the vine in the Ahr Valley.
See Ahr.

Spätlesen

Late-selected, naturally sweet wines.
See Germany.

Spätrot (grape)

See Zierfandler.

Spent liquor

The leftover residue after distillation.

Spirits

Potable alcoholic liquids obtained through distillation—e.g., brandy, whisky, gin, vodka.
See Chapter Ten, p. 52.

Spiritus Vini Gallici

"Spirit of French wine"—British pharmaceutical term for brandy.

Spritzer

German term for Rhine wine and soda, one-third wine to two-thirds soda—i.e., the Byronic Hock and seltzer. It is a cool and refreshing summer drink when taken in a tall glass with plenty of ice. Any sound wine can be used, but white or rosé are the favorites.

Spritzig

German term for the light prickle caused by an excess of carbon dioxide.

Spruce beer

This black beer, sometimes called Danzig spruce beer, is fermented at Danzig from young shoots and sap of the spruce tree.

Spumante

Italian term for sparkling wine, of which the most celebrated example is Asti Spumante.

Stalky

Hardness in wine from the tannin in the stalks. Usually the stalk is separated from the grapes and pressed independently for the juice it yields. It is also used in the distillation of marc or grappa.
See Grappa; Marc.

Stein wines

Steinweine are the green-gold, "stone" wines of Franconia in Germany, and of Styria, Austria. In the famous oval, flat Franconian flask they are of such special character that they are generally destined for the connoisseur.
See Franconia; Austria; Bocksbeutel.

Steinberger

In the finest wine years along the German Rhine this is one of the best Rheingaus. A small quantity of superior wine produced along the surrounding wall on a higher rise is known as Steinberger Mauerwein. The vineyard lies not far from Wiesbaden, beyond the ancient Cistercian monastery Kloster Eberbach, renowned for its wines—sometimes the wine is spoken of as Kloster Eberbach. In fact, Steinberger is made in the Kloster Eberbach cellars, but there is no Kloster Eberbach wine as such.
See Rheingau.

Steinhaeger

A Westphalian (German) gin resembling Hollands.
See Hollands; Geneva.

Stellenbosch

Wine district in the Cape province.
See South Africa.

Stemming

In the making of wine, grapes are usually separated from their stalks before fermentation by a machine known in France as an *égrappoir* or *foulograppe*. Agreement with this practice, first adopted in the fine red wine regions of Burgundy and Bordeaux, is not unanimous, but there are strong arguments in its favor. In the case of red wines, separation increases the degree of alcohol by about 0.5 as a result of changes which take place between the must and the stalk. It makes the wine less astringent and gets rid of foreign substances. The wine will be clearer, suppler, and ready sooner than those which have absorbed extra alcohols and tannins from the stems; and the process saves labor, since the marc which remains after pressing will be less bulky if there are no stalks in it.

The *égrappoir* has not been used much in making white wines, but today it is often employed before the pressing of finer wines.

Still wines

Non-sparkling table or beverage wines. U.S. law stipulates that still wines must contain less than 14% of alcohol. The term is sometimes used for the non-sparkling wines of Champagne.

Stinger

An iced drink made with brandy and crème de menthe and flavored with a twist of lemon.

Stock

A cutting or entire vine onto which a section of another vine called a scion is grafted. The stock grows to provide the healthy and disease-resistant roots of the vine, and the scion matures and grows the fruit.

Stoup

An obsolete term for a drinking vessel, cup, flagon, or tankard—and also for a draught of wine.

Stout

A strong black, heavy, British beer.
See Beer.

Stravecchio

Italian term for very old wine.

Straw wines

Wines from grapes that have been picked at maturity and dried on straw mats in the sun or suspended in lofts before vinification. A notable example is the *vin de paille* from the Jura Mountains in France.

Strega

An Italian liqueur, sweet and yellow in color.

Stück

German Pfalz and Rheinhessen cask of 1,200 liters (317 U.S. gallons, 264 imp.), or 1,585 bottles. The usual Rheingau measure is the *Halbstück* or half *Stück*, containing 792 bottles.

Stuck wine

One which stopped fermenting before all the sugar had been converted to alcohol.

Sturdy

A self-explanatory wine-tasting term, less flattering than robust.

Styria

Wine region of Austria; not a large producer. White and rosé wines are made here; Graz, the capital, has, like Vienna, its *heurige*, or May wines; and another interesting growth is the pale gold Steinwein.

See Austria.

Château Suau

Bordeaux white wine.
District: Sauternes, France.
Commune: Barsac.

The wine is well made but little known.
Vineyard area: 7 hectares (17 acres).
Average production: 17 *tonneaux* (1,500 cases).

Château Suduiraut

Bordeaux white wine.
District: Sauternes, France.
Commune: Preignac.

Once famous and classed as a First Growth (*Premier Cru*) in 1855, the vineyard almost disappeared from existence in the first part of this century. It has been reconstituted, and in the last decade has produced good wines. Formerly known as Cru du Roy, the vineyard adjoins Château d'Yquem along one strip and is now owned by a M. Fonquernie.

Characteristics. A rather soft Sauternes—the wines have a lightness and balance which give them longevity.
Vineyard area: 60 hectares (150 acres).
Average production: 110 *tonneaux* (10,000 cases).

Sugar wine

"Wine" made by adding sugar and water to grape husks and allowing the mixture to ferment.

Sugaring

A "sugared" wine is one whose grapes received additional sugar before fermentation. Sugaring is usually done to compensate for under-ripeness in the grapes. Permitted sugaring during fermentation is in France called *chaptalisation*.

Sulfur dioxide

The use of sulfur to sterilize wine is almost as old as wine itself: in the *Iliad*, Achilles fumigates his cup with sulfur before pouring a libation to Zeus. In modern wine-making, sulfur dioxide (SO_2) is sprayed on newly picked grapes to stop premature fermentation, is added to newly fermenting wine, put into barrels in which wine will be stored, and is given in discreet doses to wine to keep it healthy. Used in moderation, it imparts no taste or aroma; but if overdone it is apt to produce both—a fairly frequent fault with mediocre sweet and semi-sweet white wines where massive doses are added to ensure that the unfermented sugar will not be attacked by yeasts after the wine is bottled.

The action of the sulfur is to kill unwanted yeasts. Those microbes and bacteria which are harmful to wine are the first affected, but *Saccharomyces* yeasts are only attacked if a considerable quantity of sulfur is present. The traditional method of releasing sulfur dioxide, which is a gas, is by burning sulfur wicks; but compressed liquid SO_2 is also available, and tablets of potassium metabisulfite ($K_2S_2O_5$) when dissolved in wine give sulfur dioxide, water, and unimportant quantities of cream of tartar, one of wine's normal constituents.

Sulfurization

The purpose of dosing must or wine with sulfur dioxide (SO_2) or sulfurous acid (H_2SO_3) is to slow down fermentation where necessary, to kill unwanted microorganisms, and to aid in the production of a sound wine. It is very important that sulfurization should not be overdone, a fault which leads, in carelessly made wines, to an unpleasant smell, and even a taste, of sulfur. The amount of sulfurous anhydride which will become bound will increase slightly with increasing sugar content, pH and temperature. The pH determines the amount of SO_2 in the active form (H_2SO_3). As the pH goes up, more SO_2 must be added to have an equivalent amount in the active form. The quantity which may be used is regulated by law, the maximum varying in each wine-making country, since the necessity for sulfurization depends to some extent upon the climate. Yeasts are most resistant to SO_2 when they are most active (which happens in the tumultuous fermentations which take place in very hot weather), and at such times an unusually high dose may

PURIFYING ACTION OF SULFUROUS ANHYDRIDE

Sulfurous acid per liter (in grams)	Volatile acidity (sulfuric acid in grams)	Condition at tasting	MICROSCOPIC EXAMINATION	
			Liquid	Deposit
trace	16.10	Sour and affected by *casse*	Bacteria of *tourne* and *aigre*	Yeast and bacteria
0.050	0.76	Yellow, brown, fairly clear, slight musty taste	Some bacteria	Fairly pure yeast
0.100	0.52	Slightly roseate, sparkling (*droit de goût*)	Free from bacteria	Pure yeast
0.150	0.47	bright pink,		
0.200	0.45	sparkling		
0.250	0.36	(*droit de goût*)		

be permissible—as it is also when there is some disorder in the wine or must. Where fermentation is slow (as when there have been heavy rains at the beginning of the harvest, or in a cold climate), less than 100 milligrams of sulfur dioxide per liter will be sufficient to sterilize the wine-making processes. Where the temperature of the atmosphere is 68°F. (10°C.) or over, the dose may be as high as 150 milligrams per liter. Sulfurous anhydride added to red wine grapes or to the must of white wine in carefully calculated doses helps to destroy biological disorders, while leaving the true alcoholic yeasts free to develop.

The above table shows how SO_2 acts as a purifier, how it kills the bacteria, and how it acts as a preventative of brown *casse* by destroying oxidases. Wines which have been treated with sulfur dioxide are apt to be better balanced and richer in certain elements than are those which have not been so treated. The alcoholic content may rise, the volatile acidity level may drop. This increase is the result of a purer fermentation and hence a better utilization of the sugar. The use of sulfur dioxide does not cause a permanent fading in color. In red wine, loss of color will be temporary, and the wine will regain its hue when action ceases. Under the right conditions, the final color will not only be improved but will be free of any brown or yellowish cast. When the time comes to rack the wine, it will be found that the quantity of SO_2 present will decrease with each racking.

See Sulfur Dioxide; Chapter Nine, p. 38.

Süssdruck

Swiss light red or rosé made from Pinot Noir.

Suze

Popular yellow, bitter, gentian-based French aperitif.

Sweden

Sweden's climate provides cold comfort for grapevines, and wines must be—and are—imported from elsewhere. Like her Scandinavian neighbors, Sweden manufactures various spirits, consumes most of what she distills, and imports even more. These imports and all other aspects of the wine and spirits trade are in the hands of the State Monopoly, the Aktiebolaget Vin & Spritcentralen.

The liquor industry was nationalized in 1917, in order to keep the country from "going dry." In the years leading up to that date, Swedish distillers—175,000 of them—were producing about 1 million hectoliters (26.5 million U.S. gallons, 22 million imp.) of spirits per year, and the scant population of 3 million was soaking it up with alarming results. The situation was nearly critical when the legislature began to search for a solution. Temperance advocates were pressuring the lawmakers, and only as a result of the foresight and ability of Dr. Ivan Bratt was the State Monopoly introduced as a compromise to control the sale of spirits on a rationed basis. The control was lifted in 1955.

Present sales of wine (imported) and spirits amount to about 1.4 million hectoliters (37.1 million U.S. gallons, 30.8 million imp.) yearly, but Sweden's population has nearly tripled since nationalization of the industry in 1917, so it is obvious that the drive to slow liquor consumption has had some success. In the past few years, more wine than liquor has been sold for the first time. Much of the wine comes from the extensive supplies the Monopoly has bought over the years. Still, the single most popular drink is the national spirit, aquavit, followed by Swedish punch (*q.v.*), a rice and sugar-cane liqueur. On the shelves of the three hundred or so Monopoly shops may be found more than 450 different wines and spirits.

Imported into Sweden annually are about 700,000 hectoliters (18,515,000 U.S. gallons, 15,400,000 imp.) of wine—well over half of it table wines, the rest fortified wines such as vermouth, Sherry, and Port. Ninety per cent of this wine is bottled in Sweden. The Monopoly imports wine in huge tankers which dock right at the quay next to the bottling plant in Stockholm. Everyday wines from Portugal, Spain, Algeria, and France are the most popular; they sell at reasonable prices, since the state organization as the largest single purchaser of wine and spirits in the world saves money with bulk shipments. The great wines of France are represented in the stores, but the selection is limited to a few from Bordeaux. Most of the wines are of vintages before the tremendous inflation of French wine prices, so some of these bottles are good values. Yet since the early 1970s less and less fine wine from Bordeaux and Burgundy—and virtually none from Champagne—is imported.

Swedish punch

A spicy cordial based on rum. It is sometimes drunk in a small glass as a liqueur, sometimes mixed with hot water to make a punch.

Sweet

High sugar content makes wines sweet. Sweetness may be added by sugaring or liqueuring, or by artificially halting fermentation before all sugar has been converted to alcohol. The great natural sweet wines are made from overripe grapes, in which the sugar has concentrated. These include the Sauternes and Barsacs of Bordeaux and the great Rhine and Mosel wines designated Auslese, Beerenauslese, or Trockenbeerenauslese (i.e., selected berries, individually picked, and overripe, dried almost to a raisin condition).

Sweet fortified wines of France

The sun-drenched Mediterranean coastline of France, particularly the corner next to the Spanish border, has long proved its suitability for growing those grape varieties that produce wines as sweet as they are potent. These wines, which are of little interest in countries where Port and Sherry are available, are known in France as *vins doux naturels* and *vins de liqueur*, or sweet natural wines and fortified wines. In both cases, the wines are strengthened by the addition of pure alcohol or brandy—a process known as "fortifying." The term "sweet natural wine" is apt to be confusing, since it could apply equally to these fortified wines and to sweet but unfortified wines like those made in the Sauternes district of Bordeaux. The difference between a *vin de liqueur* and a *vin doux naturel* is slight, and the terms are often used imprecisely and synonymously. The main difference is that in a *vin de liqueur* the fortifying spirit is added before any fermentation can take place, and the result is thus simply grape juice and spirits. As such, it is in the class of a high grade *mistelle*, except that the latter is used as a base for aperitifs and the former comes from better grapes and is designed to be drunk as it is. The *vin doux naturel* must be at least 90% from one grape variety, or be a blend of the varieties Muscat, Grenache, Maccabéo, or Malvoisie grapes, and the fortifying alcohol (5% to 10% of the volume to be treated) is added in the course of fermentation—not to prevent, but to arrest it. Both systems revolve around the fact that the sugar will not ferment after the wine has reached a certain strength; and both allow the wine to retain its sweetness, while providing it with a high alcoholic content. The legal alcoholic limits are 14% minimum and 21.5% maximum; and most of these wines are sold at about 18%. (These limits do not apply to the *vin de liqueur* made in the region of Cognac and known as Pineau des Charentes, where they are changed to 16% and 22%.)

The sweet wines are made in small and widely scattered areas, ranging from Grand Roussillon in the extreme southwest corner on the Mediterranean, eastward to Frontignan, Lunel, Mireval, and Saint-Jean-de-Minervois, and across the Rhône to Rasteau and Beaumes-de-Venise. Somehow the vines in these areas have managed to survive, in spite of the fact that they have been trampled on by armies—Romans, Arabs, French, and Spanish are among the many that have either crossed the area or settled in it—and in spite of the phylloxera epidemic. Modern economy seems to be succeeding where ancient armies and insects failed, however, and the present production of these wines is less than 600,000 hectoliters (15.9 million U.S. gallons, 13.2 million imp.) per year—a mere drop in the barrel.

AREAS PRODUCING FORTIFIED WINES

Grand Roussillon

Grand Roussillon is the former name for the wine region in southern France consisting of the districts of Banyuls, Maury, Rivesaltes, the Côtes d'Agly, and the Côte du Roussillon in the departments of Pyrénées-Orientales and Aude. The region was granted the Appellation d' Origine Controlée of Côtes du Roussillon in 1977. The vines grown in this area, principally the Muscat, Grenache, Maccabéo (or Maccabeu), and Malvoisie, produce a variety of wines, including red, white, and rosés of all types and a diminishing quantity, fortunately, of those known as *rancios*. Rarely will any two people agree on how to describe the taste of a *rancio*, but everyone seems to be able to identify it. The wine is, in a sense, "rancid," although it is not nearly so unpleasant as the word suggests. The French refer to this flavor as *goût de terroir*, or taste imparted by the soil—in fact it is only imparted by alluvial soil; and to get the taste, the wines must age for a long time and must become oxidized.

The credit for the introduction of wines into Grand Roussillon is given to the army of Hannibal, which passed through in 217 B.C. According to local legend, Hannibal left here his sick, tired, and straggling soldiers, who found the climate enough like their native Carthage in North Africa to settle down and plant vines. The vines were pulled up when the Arabs, with their Moslem prohibition against alcohol, moved in, but were replanted after the area had been reconquered. Hot and dry, mountainous and peppered with rocks, the land of Grand Roussillon is an arid, unwelcoming place, but vines often thrive in the most unlikely soil. Most of the holdings are small and so is production, and one sees everywhere that friend of the small grower, the cooperative cellar. Here the member-growers bring their grapes in the autumn, and here the wine is made. This system saves each grower the expense of buying individual presses and all the other equipment needed for making wine.

Banyuls

The wines of Banyuls in the extreme southeast corner of Roussillon are generally considered to be the best that the province has to offer. A desolate rocky land cut by steep ravines and baked by the hot sun that throws its early morning beams on the steep vine-covered slopes, Banyuls is known for its sweet heavy fortified wines, although it produces other wines as well. A natural red wine and a rosé, both called Grenache after the informing grape variety, have won some renown in their home country, but are rarely found elsewhere in France and are almost never exported. At harvest time (late in the autumn) the grapes are brought down the steep slopes on muleback, and about four-fifths of the production—total production averages 50,000 hectoliters (1,320,000 U.S. gallons, 1,100,000 imp.) each year—is taken to the nine cooperative cellars to be made into wine. The 2,800 hectares (7,000 acres) of vineyard are tended by some 1,600 growers and their workers.

Côtes du Roussillon

Adjoining Banyuls and lying slightly to the east and north of it is what is perhaps the most romantic section of the region. The history of the Côte du Roussillon can still be read today from the many ruins on its steep slopes—monasteries and hermitages as well as the fallen estates of the Knights Templars who, after the Crusades, established one of their headquarters in this area. However, as Roussillon's importance in international politics has declined, so did the reputation of its vineyards. What were once the favorite wines of kings were reduced to a small quantity, most of which were consumed locally. The *rancio* of Haut-Roussillon, once held in high esteem, was more or less abandoned, because the cost of storing the wine while it ages made it too expensive to produce. However, developments in the late 1960s and the 1970s have revitalized this wine-producing region which was granted an Appellation d'Origine Contrôlée for red and white wines in 1977. Red wines from the better Côtes du Roussillon Villages may qualify for the Côtes du Roussillon Villages appellation as well. In all, the Côtes du Roussillon, plus the "Villages," produce about 30,000 hectoliters (79.2 million U.S. gallons, 66 million imp.) of wine per year.

Rivesaltes

Farther away from the Spanish border, and lying next to the Côtes du Roussillon, is the area known as Rivesaltes. Here the sun-baked alluvial soil also produces wines that were better known in the past than they are today, and more honored. The famous wines of Rivesaltes have always come from the Muscat grape, made under the name "Muscat de Rivesaltes" and amounting to about 100,000 hectoliters (2,640,000 U.S. gallons, 2,200,000 imp.) per year. The simple appellation Rivesaltes may contain other grape varieties. In the past half-century or so the growers have been slowly neglecting the Muscat and replanting more and more in Grenache and Malvoisie. The reason for this is that the wine from the Muscat grape is one that must be tended with great care and the yield is very low. But the sweet, amber wine of the Malvoisie still thrives in Rivesaltes and is much appreciated by the inhabitants. Yearly production of "Rivesaltes" is

about 230,000 hectoliters (5,992,000 U.S. gallons, 5,060,000 imp.) per year, most of it made at the many cooperatives scattered throughout the region.

Côtes d'Agly

The harsh, gray, rocky soil of this large area, in the northeast of Roussillon, is cut by the upper arm of the River Agly, before it runs down through Rivesaltes. The land is also watered now and then by streams which run swiftly after the infrequent downpours and then dry up for the rest of the year. The most extensively grown vines are those of the Grenache variety. None of the wines used to be considered to equal those of the other sections of Roussillon, but recently they have improved.

Maury

The small area of Maury, in the northeast corner of Roussillon, has had the unfortunate destiny to be in a militarily strategic position and has thus been almost totally destroyed time after time. But whenever the new wave of conquerors settled down or left, the peasant growers would again replant their vines in the unpromising stony soil. The vines grow at the foot of Queribus, the last of the Catharian castles. Mostly planted in vines of the Grenache Noir variety, the wines are sweet, and the red ones are extremely dark in color. This darkness fades with age, and the wines of Maury take on the brownish tinge and a slightly maderised, or *rancio*, taste and may be sold as Maury Rancio. Maury accounts for an average of 50,000 hectoliters (1,320,000 U.S. gallons, 1,100,000 imp.) per year. Its 1,400 hectares (3,500 acres) are tended by about 530 growers and virtually all of the production is vinified in the three cooperative cellars.

Frontignan

Once again the origins of the vines here are lost in the mists of time, but growers in the Frontignan area—facing the Mediterranean Sea, some distance west of the delta of the River Rhône—say that the famous Muscat wines of Frontignan date from Roman times, or that the vines were brought back from the Crusades, or that they were planted to celebrate a royal marriage in 1204. It is widely believed that returning Crusaders did bring back grapevines from the Near East and so altered the course of viticulture in these regions and in the Pyrenees. At the present time, 20,000 hectoliters (530,000 U.S. gallons, 440,000 imp.) of wine are grown annually by some 350 growers on 350 hectares (875 acres) of land around the ancient city of Frontignan in the department of Hérault; 75% of the wine is made at one cooperative cellar.

The Muscat de Frontignan, so called because only the vine of that name is allowed, is made according to one of three methods. The first is for natural wine not enriched by any addition of alcohol, and it is the same as the process for any other natural wine, except for one stage, known as *passerillage*. This originated in Spain and was designed to increase sugar content: the stalks of the grapes are pinched just above the clusters, just before the grapes are picked in the late autumn. This cuts off the passage of sap between the grapes and the vine. The grapes are then allowed to ripen thoroughly in the hot Mediterranean sun, and, since no sap can get to them, they dry out, leaving the grapes extra-rich in natural sugar. This system allows the wine to attain the legal minimum of 15% alcohol.

The other two types of wine, *vin doux naturel* and *vin de liqueur*, are the more common, and the difference between the processes of production has already been explained. Both systems allow this powerful wine to retain at least a part of its natural sugar, and in both cases the wine must have an alcoholic content of at least 15%.

In an attempt to preserve the integrity of the wine, it has been decreed that all genuine Muscat de Frontignan must be sold in bottles bearing a special seal, which is given by a group of experts only after they have tasted a sample of the wine and approved its quality.

In the area adjacent to Frontignan a lesser-known Muscat is produced, called Muscat de Mireval.

Saint-Jean-de-Minervois (Muscat de)

A tiny pocket in the department of Hérault in southern France, Saint-Jean-de-Minervois makes *vin doux naturel* and *vin de liqueur* following the same customs and regulations as its neighbor, Frontignan. Production here is rarely as high as 500 hectoliters (13,250 U.S. gallons, 11,000 imp.) per year, however.

Lunel (Muscat de Lunel)

Like the Muscat wines of Frontignan, those of Lunel are made into *vin doux naturel* and *vin de liqueur*; no unfortified wines are produced here. Another district whose importance is more historical than contemporary, Lunel growers make some 3,300 hectoliters (87,120 U.S. gallons, 66,000 imp.) of wine a year.

Beaumes-de-Venise (Muscat de)

On the eastern side of the Rhône in the department of Vaucluse, Beaumes-de-Venise makes *vin doux naturel* and *vin de liqueur* exclusively from the Muscat grape, as does

Frontignan. The area produces only 3,000 hectoliters (79,500 U.S. gallons, 66,000 imp.) of wine per year.

Rasteau

Slightly to the north of the region of Beaumes-de-Venise is the delimited area known as Rasteau. This enjoys the peculiar advantage of being able to grow and sell fortified wines, made in the same way as those entitled to the name Grand Roussillon; and of also making other wines in the same manner as those wines entitled to the name Côtes du Rhône. The result is that the production varies from no fortified wines in one year to almost 3,000 hectoliters (79,500 U.S. gallons, 66,000 imp.) in another. The deciding factor is the weather—and which type of wine it happens to favor. The fortified wines of Rasteau must come at least 90% from the Grenache grape and the others from any vine allowed in the making of Côtes du Rhône. The 130 growers take virtually all of the harvest to the one cooperative cellar.

Pineau des Charentes

At some time toward the end of the sixteenth century, a worker in one of the cellars in the Cognac region of France made the mistake of putting some newly made wine into a barrel already containing a small amount of Cognac. The result of this error has come to be known as Pineau des Charentes. First produced in very small quantities, the output was increased after the First World War and the wine was put onto the commercial market.

Pineau des Charentes must be made by producers of Cognac in the two French departments of Charente and Charente-Maritime and only from their own grapes. The new wine is taken and, within twenty-four hours, a little Cognac, a year or two old, is added to it. The color may be either rosé or white; the rosé variety comes from the Cabernet Sauvignon, Cabernet Franc, Malbec, and Merlot Rouge grapes; the white from the Saint-Émilion, Folle Blanche, Colombard, Blanc Ramé, Jurançon Blanc, Montils, Sémillon, Sauvignon, or Merlot Blanc grapes. It can only be sold after receiving the seal of approval of a committee of tasters which has wide powers. These include the right to approve, to disapprove, to demand further ageing or blending with the same product from another part of the area and to specify the quantities to be used. This last rule was added to improve the quality of some wine from a seaside area that may, when unblended, have a slightly salty taste. Pineau des Charentes, a popular aperitif in France, must contain from 16.5% to 22% of alcohol. Over 20,000 hectoliters (660,000 U.S. gallons, 550,000 imp.) are made each year.

See Appendix G.

Switzerland

Switzerland is largely a wine-drinking, wine-growing country; and as it is divided into three parts—French-speaking, Italian-speaking, German-speaking—so the vineyards tend to follow, with vines of French, Italian, or German types. There are, however, a few notable excep-tions: Johannisberg is grown from the green Sylvaner grape in the French canton of the Valais, and the Bordeaux Merlot has been imported, very successfully, into the Ticino. So the striking general characteristic of Swiss wines is their infinite diversity—the vast difference, for instance, between the sunny Dézaley that grows on the slopes above Lake Geneva and the Vispertermin wines harvested up in the mountains of the Valais, not far from the Matterhorn and 1,100 meters (3,600 feet) above sea level. Hillside vineyards are steeply terraced, existing only by the hard labor of their owner; most of the vineyards are divided into small parcels whose proprietors now tend to join cooperatives and share equipment. In some regions, the wine is vinified by the brokers or cooperatives; in others, it is bottled directly on the property. Every November, there is a big auction of the year's vintage.

The total area of vineyards in Switzerland is 14,000 hectares (35,000 acres). Only three cantons out of the twenty-three plant no vines, but the most important wine-production is in the French parts—Vaud, Valais, Geneva, and Neuchâtel. Vines flourish on the shores of the lakes of Geneva and Neuchâtel, along the right bank of the Upper Rhône, and in the Italian Ticino or Tessin. Cultivation is sparser in east and central Switzerland, and here, as well as in the Ticino and around Geneva, most of the wines are drunk locally. The country produces about 1 million hectoliters (26.5 million U.S. gallons, 22 million imp.) of wine per year. The idea that Swiss wines do not travel is changing; they are seen in the windows of wine merchants in England and in other countries. It is generally agreed that these wines can be very agreeable but a bit short—i.e., not lasting on the palate. Compared to French wines, they are not cheap.

FRENCH SWITZERLAND

La Suisse Romande is a pleasant sunny country of orchards, castles, and hills sloping down to lake shores.

Vaud

For twenty years before Valais surpassed it, Vaud was the largest wine-producing canton in the country. About 40% of the entire production comes from the vineyards planted east and west of Lausanne, along the shores of Lake Geneva. The wine region divides into two sections—Lavaux to the east of the city, and La Côte to the west.

Lavaux

The region stretches for 16 kilometers (10 miles), from Lausanne to Montreux, with Vevey almost exactly in the center (see Vevey Festival). It faces south over the lake, getting the best exposure to the sun and protected from extremes of temperature. It is said that wines were made here in Roman times, and this is probably true. It is certain that the Bishop of Lausanne, who was active c. 1137, took a serious interest in the cultivation of the vine, commanded the Cistercian monks to tend the grapes and thus established them as the first important growers in the area—which begins at Lutry and ends at Pully. To the traveler, this is one of the most charming wine districts in Switzerland. The Castle of Chillon broods over the lake; the vineyards climb up from the shore in a progression of steep terraces; vines grow in every crevice of the rocks, and the grapes ripen in the double heat of the sun and of the sunshine reflected from the water. But the proprietors lead a hard life; machines cannot be taken up the steep inclines, harvesters have to climb precipitous paths with their *hottes* full of fruit, and when the soil is washed down the slopes by the rain, they must carry it up again on their backs.

Principal vineyards: Dézaley, which produces a golden, still growth, described by many of the Swiss as their finest wine; Saint-Saphorin, Rivaz, Epessés, Riex, Villette, Lutry, Cully. Around Lausanne are the Clos des Abbayes and the Clos des Moines, owned by the city and auctioned each December.

Grape variety: Principally, the Chasselas, which adapts itself well to the soil and climate, producing very dry robust white wines quite different from those grown in France.

La Côte

The pastoral charm of these vineyards on the western shore of Lake Geneva is unspoiled, in a country of orchards, fields, and of vines planted mainly on the upper slopes above the farmland. The wine road passes some charming villages—Féchy, Mont-sur-Rolle, Vinzel, Luins. Others of the lively, pleasant wines grown in this district are Bougy, Begnins, Bursins, and Perroy. Chasselas, Gamay, and Pinot Noir grapes produce some agreeable wines.

Chablais Vaudois

These rather heady, smooth white wines are produced in the district of Aigle, on the foothills of the Alps. The growths of Bex, Ollon, Yvorne, Villeneuve, and Aigle have race, acidity, tang, and the true gunflint flavor.

Northern Vaudois

In this little area, which stretches as far as Concise near the southern end of Lake Neuchâtel, grow the white and red wines of Orbe, Grandson, Bonvillars, and Concise. A few miles to the east, divided between the cantons of Fribourg and Vaud, the *pétillant* white wines of Vully are planted along the shore of the Murtensee. Some red wines, little known but quite drinkable, are also produced.

Neuchâtel

This is the most northerly part of French Switzerland. The wine region begins a little way up the lake, at Vaumarcus, and continues in an uninterrupted plantation as far as Le Landeron, at the opening of the neighboring Lake Bienne—a less important group of vineyards extends along the farther shores of this lake, their best growths the lively wines of Schafis and Twann. The Neuchâtel white wines, grown in a chalky soil, are light and sprightly. For over a century, vintners have been practicing French methods of secondary fermentation in bottle, and they say that a good Neuchâtel makes stars in the glass. The red wine made solely from Pinot Noir grapes is considered one of the best Swiss wines. Oeil de Perdrix, also made from the Pinot Noir and short-vatted, is a rosé with a special charm. The town of Neuchâtel, capital of the canton, stands at the northwest corner of the lake. Looking down at it from the hills, you see the formidable castle, and the church of "La Collegiale." Vines surround the town. Neuchâtel is the most widely exported wine of Switzerland.

Principal vineyards: Auvernier, Cormondrèche, Cortaillod, Cressier, St.-Blaise—the wines are sold sometimes under the label of a *clos* or village, oftener as Neuchâtel.

Grape varieties: Chasselas and Pinot Noir. Pinot Gris and Chardonnay produce some good wines.

Valais

This is the *vieux pays*—the old land—on the banks of the Rhône as it flows, from its source, between Italy and France. The river is bordered by fruit trees and, on its right bank, vineyards climb the mountainside. On the lower slopes, the sheltered terraces bask in the sun. Higher up, you may catch a glimpse of peasants perched at a dizzy height above the water, breaking up the soil by hand or tying vines to the tall stakes. Here, where the autumns are long, mild, and mellow, vines have been in cultivation since Roman days, and old traditions persist. At times, the peasants of Anniviers will come down from their mountains, with fife and drum, to enjoy a fête day between their long, hard spells in the vineyards. When the harvest is over and the new wine made, 8-gallon barrels are dragged up to these settlements above the clouds and stored in the cellars, for the wine to mature in its larchwood casks for ten or fifteen years. This is known as the Vin du Glacier, usually a rather hard white wine.

Between Loèche and Martigny, some 5,500 hectares (15,000 acres) are planted in vine, divided among about 20,000 proprietors—about one-third in red, the rest in white. Old vines and young ones march up the slopes and straggle into the gullies. Little aqueducts, or *bisses*, cut into the dry land, bring their glacier water, and walls separate the terraced vineyards. Most Valais wines take their names from the grape, not the place.

Principal growths and grape varieties: Despite appearances, the vine structure of the Valais vineyards is varied. Four grape varieties predominate: Fendant, the regional name for Chasselas; Sylvaner, which confusingly makes a wine called Johannisberg; Gamay, which is blended with Pinot Noir to create the wine of Dôle; and Pinot Noir. The first two produce white wines, the second two produce reds. There are also a number of other vines well known locally: Amigne, Arvine, Hermitage, Pinot Gris (Malvoisie), Paien, and Muscat. These are all white wine grapes, with the exception of Pinot Gris, which can produce a salmon-colored wine. Fendant, or Chasselas, is a lively thirst-quenching wine. It combines good fruit and acidity, and can be quite fine. The wine is dry without being hard. The best Fendants are a touch sweet and round. Fendants usually measure between 10.5 and 11.8% alcohol. The Chasselas vine may have been imported originally by mercenaries returning home from France—since the land was too poor to support all the inhabitants, many hired themselves out as soldiers abroad and later returned with money, honors, and vine plants. A general who fought for Louis XV is actually believed to have brought in the Fendant, with one of the king's gardeners to supervise its planting.

Dôle is produced from a blend of Pinot Noir and French Gamay. The grapes are vatted, vinified, and pressed together. In the blend, it is important that the Pinot Noir predominate. Dôle is a powerful, perfumed red wine, which some connoisseurs consider to be the best of all the Swiss vintages. It is a noble, generous wine of a fine ruby color. The Pinot plant was imported in 1848, and Dôle was first produced about 1851. Although more than half of the planting is Pinot Noir, it should be pointed out that only a small portion is actually vinified and bottled as such.

Johannisberg is the second most important white wine of the Valais, some 10 to 15% of the total production. It is made from Sylvaner, also called Rhine in the Valais. It is the only vintage that goes well with the local asparagus; and in years when the grapes are harvested late, it achieves a *pointe de douceur* and makes an agreeable dessert wine. Riesling, from the Rhine vine, is a pleasant little

wine, as is white Hermitage. Colonel Dénéréaz brought in the white grape about one hundred years ago; and quite recently, Dr. Wuilloud managed to acclimatize, in his domaine at Diolly, the red Syrah of Hermitage. The Pinot Gris, gathered late, makes, in the Valais, Malvoisie, a sweet soft dessert wine with a lingering aroma. Arvine, Amigne, and Rèze are the old vines of the Valais. Amigne may have been the *Vitis aminea* of the Romans and Muscat, which also grows here, their *Vitis apiana*. It is certain that Rèze was current at the beginning of the fourteenth century. Arvine is a noble, spirited wine, and Amigne is pleasantly perfumed. The Rèze has almost, but not quite, disappeared. Fendant is the wine that flows most plentifully. The red *vin de pays*, or Vieux Rouge du Valais, is gradually vanishing, and is well worth tasting before it is too late.

The last of the appellations in the Valais is Goron, which is, in fact, a declassified Dôle. Gamay and Pinot Noir lacking in sufficient alcohol are used to produce this popular carafe wine.

Geneva

The vineyards of this smallest canton in Switzerland, planted in a horseshoe around the city of Geneva, produce charming, light wines that are little known abroad. They are mostly rather dry and slightly *pétillants*, with a fine bouquet.

Principal vineyards: Best-known are the growths of the district of Mandement, on the western shore of the lake. The wine that bears this name is light and dry with a trace of hazelnut in the bouquet. Villages which give their names to Geneva wines are Peissy, Russin, and Satigny—in a small region, the largest Swiss wine parish. Here stands the Priory of Satigny, dating from A.D. 50. In the year 912, the Prior gained possession of the vineyards.

Grape varieties: Chasselas for white wines with a number of "specialty" vines, such as Aligoté, Chardonnay, and Pinot Gris. Lately there have also been plantings in Pinot and Gamay, since the soil reveals distinct potentialities for red wines.

ITALIAN SWITZERLAND

In the Ticino, the sun shines, the lakes are blue, the stalls in the arcaded streets of the towns are piled with ripe fruit and, although wine-making is not a major occupation, the vineyards bear well, both red and white wines. The native Nostrano, from Bondola and other grapes, are inclined to be harsh, yet, when they are drunk cool in the shade of an arbor—as Keats liked to drink claret—they have a distinctive, agreeable flavor. In the past few years, the Bordeaux Merlot has been planted here: it gives a soft, fruity red wine, sold under the official label Viti, and promises well for the future of Ticino wine-growing.

GERMAN SWITZERLAND

The principal wine-making cantons in German Switzerland are from the largest in area to the smallest: Zurich, Schaffhausen, Argovia, the Grisons, Thurgovia, Saint-Gallen, and Basle.

Zürich

The leading district in the wine-making of German Switzerland is not so favored in soil and climate as are the warmer western cantons, yet it produces some pleasant wines. Klevner (Pinot Noir) is now being planted and production has improved.

Principal vineyards: Herrliberg, Meilen, and Erlenbach produce rather sweet red wines. There are white wines, grown mainly along the shores of the lake of Zürich, and some red ones come from Weinland.

Grape varieties: Klevner, Riesling × Sylvaner, and Rauschling.

Schaffhausen

In this northern canton the most important district is Pettgau. There is a splendidly situated vineyard here, and a fresh and very agreeable wine is made from Klevner. A good deal is also made at Stein-am-Rhein. From Stein come the Blaurock and the Kefersteiner; and a good Malvoisie, from Pinot Gris, is made near the town of Schaffhausen.

Other cantons

Argovia, the Grisons, Thurgovia, Saint-Gallen, and Basle have a slightly less favorable climate than the southern part of the country. The wines are agreeable, rather light but fruity, and mainly consumed within the regions where they are produced.

Sylvaner

A productive white grape grown in Alsace, Austria, Switzerland, and Germany. The wines it gives are light and pleasant. It is also called Österreicher or Franken in German-speaking countries.

See Alsace; Austria; Germany; Switzerland.

Synthetic wine

A concoction of concentrated fruit-must, yeast, and water.

Syrah (Sirah)

The grape grown in the Rhône Valley for red Hermitage—it is said to have been brought back, either from the Middle East by Crusaders or to have come from Syracuse with the earlier legions of Probus. In any case, the grapes will flourish in warmer climates, and they have been transplanted to other parts of the world, such as Switzerland, California, Australia, and South Africa.

Syria and Lebanon

In ancient times vines flourished on the shores of the eastern Mediterranean, and this was probably the earliest wine-making region of the world. Damascus was a great center, mentioned in the Bible, and the wines of Helbon and the famous Chalybon were exported all over the then known continents. (*See* Chapter One.)

Nowadays, vineyards are found mainly in the mountainous country away from the coast. In Syria, apart from the district of Latakia, vines grow in the hilly regions of Aleppo, Homs, and Damascus—roughly 72,000 hectares (some 180,000 acres) in all. In Lebanon, the acreage, which has doubled in the past twenty years, is now about 24,000 hectares (60,000 acres). Three-quarters of the vineyard is planted in the valley of Bekaa. In both countries, the bulk of the harvest is intended for table grapes, dried raisins, and grape juice, leaving an inferior quantity of grapes to be pressed for wine. Arak also is made. Spirit-making is generally in the hands of Christians, and it is they who produce and use the wines—ordinary table wines with 9% to 10% of alcohol, from French grape varieties. A little sparkling wine is made as well.

During the Second World War, French troops stationed in Syria naturally demanded wine, and production increased and the wine-making processes improved. When the French troops left, production fell a great deal and is now lower in Syria than it is in Lebanon.

Szekszárdi Kadarka

One of the best of the full-bodied red wines of southern Hungary.

See Hungary.

Szemelt

Hungarian wine term for *auslese.*
See Auslese; Germany.

Table wine

In one sense, this is the ordinary wine commonly drunk at table. The term is being used more and more to describe still natural wines, differentiating them from sparkling and fortified wines, as well as from wines with a place-name. U.S. federal law specifies that the term table wine applies only to wines having less than 14% of alcohol per volume.

Tafia (taffea)

The early French West Indian Negro word for rum, and therefore one of the first names in general use for the spirit. Today tafia is a second-quality spirit made from impure molasses or cane leftovers, while rum proper is made from the first-grade molasses or cane sugar.

See Rum; Egypt.

Taglio

Italian term for blended wine.

Tahbilk

A vineyard in Victoria making mostly white, and a few red, table wines, all sold under the name of the informing grape variety.

See Australia.

Château Talbot

Bordeaux red wine.
District: Haut-Médoc, France.
Commune: Saint-Julien.

Classified a Fourth Growth (*Quatrième Cru*) in 1855, Talbot commands equal prices with some of the Second Growths (*Seconds Crus*). The wine is made mainly from the Cabernet Sauvignon and Petit-Verdot vines and takes its name from the English Lord Shrewsbury who was killed in 1453 in the region at the end of the Hundred Years' War; but it is uncertain whether Talbot himself ever owned the property. M. Jean Cordier, the present owner, has made a great success of his *chai*, which is dramatically modern, neat, and clean; big vats and huge barrels have taken the place of the traditional hogsheads, or *barriques*.

Considering its good wine, and the many less good wines with a better classification, Château Talbot can be said today to be definitely underclassified.

Characteristics. Big, full-bodied, and yet supple wines, which are usually well made.

Vineyard area: 85 hectares (213 acres).

Average production: 320 *tonneaux* (30,000 cases).

Tannat

Important grapevine in Madiran, in the French Pyrenees. This is considered to be the same as the Harriague, extensively used in Uruguayan viticulture.

Tannin

An important component of wine, drawn from grape skins, pips, and stems and dissolved in the liquid during fermentation. It is an essential constituent of wine, giving character and long-lasting quality. It also combines with the aldehydes to precipitate a deposit. Tannin is an astringent substance found also in tree bark and some nuts; it has certain antiseptic qualities.

See Chapter Nine, p. 38.

Tarragona

One of the dozen or so official wine place-names in Spain.

See Spain.

Tarragona Port

A thick, heavy, red wine, made near Tarragona south of Barcelona in Spain, which incorrectly professes to be Port wine. True Port wine comes only from specially delimited vineyards on the Douro in Portugal. This imitation port from Tarragona has been excluded by law from Britain since 1916. It is still sold in the United States and some other countries.

Clos de Tart

Burgundy red wine.
District: Côte de Nuits, France.
Commune: Morey-Saint-Denis.
Official Classification: Great Growth (Grand Cru).

The Clos de Tart received its present name in 1141 when the vineyard called Climat de la Forge was sold to the Bernardines de l'Abbaye de Notre-Dame de Tart, a feminine offshoot of the Cistercian order. A bull of Pope Lucius III confirmed the sale in 1184 and the vineyard has been the Clos de Tart ever since. The sisters cultivated the vineyard—expanding it slightly in 1240—until the French Revolution, when it was seized and sold by the state. Unlike most Burgundian vineyards, the Clos de Tart has been kept intact through the changes it has undergone since the Revolution, and today it is entirely in the hands of the shipping firm of J. Mommessin, whose headquarters are in Mâcon.

Clos de Tart lies just north of the village of Morey, to the right of the vineyard road as you go south, and between Bonnes Mares and the Clos des Lambrays. Its 7.5

Tartar

hectares (17.8 acres) are entirely enclosed within an ancient wall which borders the road along the midsection of the hill. The wine is often known as a "ladies' wine," but this is in deference to the distaff side of the Cistercians, for it is sturdy and big. To its Morey characteristic of robustness is added a special delicacy and subtlety, and it ages with great grace. The vineyard has been rated a Great Growth (*Grand Cru*) by the French wine authorities, the highest rank a Burgundian vineyard can receive; and while it may not have all the fiery strength of neighboring Clos des Lambrays—ranked only as *Premier Cru* (First Growth)—it sometimes merits the considerable renown it has received.

Production in an average-quantity year is 275 hectoliters (7,285 U.S. gallons, 6,050 imp.), or the equivalent of about 3,000 cases.

Tartar

This important by-product of wine comprises the greater part of the crystalline deposit left in wine casks and vats. In a relatively pure state, this is cream of tartar; but where there has been contact with lime, some neutral tartrate of calcium will be present also. Remedies against precipitation of tartars in the wine are antitartrates (such as citrate of sodium) and freezing.

Tartaric acid

The most important of the fixed acids found in wine, and one particularly associated with the grape rather than other fruits. COOH·CHOH·CHOH·COOH.
See Chapter Nine, p. 38.

Tartrates

Salts of tartaric acid; a component of wine.
See Chapter Nine, p. 38.

Tastevin

A small silver cup for tasting wine used principally in Burgundy but also in the Midi. It is flat, with raised indentations to reflect the color of the wine.

Tasting

Determining the quality and characteristics of wine simply by tasting and smelling it. A blind tasting is one in which the origin or identity of the wines is not previously disclosed to the tasters.

Tatachilla

Large vineyard in McLaren Vale, South Australia; its wines are sold in England as Keystone burgundy.
See Australia.

Taupette

Slang in the Cognac region for *preuve,* the little glass tube let down into the Cognac barrel on a chain in order to obtain some of the liquor to test or "prove" it.

Taurasi

Strong red wine from the Campania (*q.v.*).

Tavel

Rosé wine.
District: Rhône Valley, France.

Vintage years mean less along the Rhône than in other fine vineyard regions of France, and probably least of all at Tavel. The reason is that Tavel makes only rosé, and rosé owes far more to soil and grape variety than to weather. The ratio between alcohol and acidity will vary slightly over the years, but the skill of the *vigneron* in making wines from properly matured grapes—picking early in hot years, late in cool ones—does much to regulate it. Furthermore, vintage differences seldom mean a great deal until the wine has attained some age. By its very nature, rosé is a wine to be drunk in its first blush of youth—vintage years can therefore be overlooked (except to check the year marked on the bottle to tell whether or not the wine is still young and fresh; a one-year minimum, five-year maximum is a good rule).

As rosés go, Tavel is full-bodied and sturdy. It is also unquestionably the world's best-known pink wine. Legally, it must contain 11% of alcohol, but usually it reaches 12% or more. The dominant grape in its make-up is Grenache, but several others are also allowed in varying amounts. Grenache must not account for more than 60% of the wine, and there must be at least 15% Cinsault.

The vines grow in a varied soil made up predominantly of cretaceous marl and chalk. The permitted growing area, roughly 750 hectares (1,875 acres), includes almost the entire commune of Tavel—about 8 kilometers (5 miles) from Châteauneuf-du-Pape and the same distance from Avignon, on the right bank of the Rhône—and a tiny section of neighboring Roquemaure. Almost 25,000 hectoliters (662,500 U.S. gallons, 550,000 imp.) of wine are produced annually, and they are shipped not only throughout France but all over the world. Sixty per cent of the total volume is made by the cooperative Les Vignerons de Tavel.

Tawny Port

Port wine matured in wood for anything from four to ten years and blended before it is bottled. Not as heavy and splendid as a great Vintage Port, it will, however, have more finesse and, at its best, great elegance. Tawny Port should not be laid down but should be drunk soon after it is bottled.
See Port.

466

Tent

Spanish red wine from Alicante. The term was once common in England.

Tequila

Of the three drinks fermented from the juice of the Mexican century plant—tequila (distilled), mescal (distilled), and pulque—tequila is the most civilized. Colorless, tossed down in Mexican style after a lick of salt from the back of the hand, it is like liquid fire in the throat. Popular in the U.S.

See Pulque.

Terlaner (D.O.C.)

White wine of South Tyrol.
See Trentino-Alto Adige.

Château du Tertre

Bordeaux red wine.
District: Haut-Médoc, France.
Commune: Arsac-Margaux.

For some years, the château on the country lane running between Arsac and Margaux was abandoned. It has now been replanted by a Belgian group under the supervision of Philippe Gasqueton of Château Calon-Ségur. Along with the other wines made in Arsac, it has since 1955 enjoyed the right to the place-name Margaux. A Fifth Growth (*Cinquième Cru*) of the 1855 Classification, Château du Tertre was an indication that the old ranking does not always hold true.

Characteristics. The quality of the wine slipped almost out of sight, but in 1966 it made a small recovery and has continued to improve.

Vineyard area: 50 hectares (125 acres).
Average production: 200 *tonneaux* (18,000 cases).

Thermometer

No vat-house or *chai* should be without a thermometer and one is also invaluable in a cellar or any room where wine is stored. A *maître de chai* who constantly takes the temperature of the fermenting must will, in very hot weather, probably be able to moderate fermentation where it is excessive and so save the wine—hence, in an unusually hot summer, one vineyard will produce a better wine than another in the same district. A thermometer must be used too in conjunction with such instruments as mustimeters and alcoholmeters, in registering the degree of spirits. In Great Britain, Holland, and the United States, the Fahrenheit type is employed; in Germany, the Fahrenheit and the Réaumur; while in France

and most of South America, the thermometer in use is the Celsius, based on the Centigrade system.

The variations in their scales are as follows: Centigrade, or Celsius, shows the freezing-point of water as 0° and its boiling-point as 100°; Réaumur shows 0° as the freezing-point of water and its boiling-point as 80°; Fahrenheit shows 32° as the freezing-point of water and its boiling-point as 212°.

To ascertain the temperature of a liquid the thermometer should be kept in the liquid for some minutes; the thermometer is quick to respond and the division on the scale at which the mercury stops indicates the temperature of the liquid. Tables showing the respective scales of the three thermometers are given in Appendix D, p. 642, but below are shown the calculations necessary to convert from one scale to another.

To convert Centigrade into Réaumur, multiply the Centigrade temperature by $\frac{4}{5}$. To convert Réaumur into Centigrade, multiply by $\frac{5}{4}$.

To convert Centigrade into Fahrenheit, multiply the Centigrade temperature by 1.8 and add 32. To convert Fahrenheit into Centigrade subtract 32 from the Fahrenheit temperature and divide by 1.8.

To convert Fahrenheit into Réaumur, subtract 32 from the Fahrenheit temperature and multiply by $\frac{4}{9}$. To convert Réaumur into Fahrenheit multiply the Réaumur temperature by $\frac{9}{4}$ and add 32.

See Chapter Nine.

Thief

A *pipette*, or tube, for withdrawing wine or liquor from a cask or other container; usually made of glass, sometimes of silver.

Thin

A watery or poor wine, one that lacks alcohol, flavor, and body.

Three-Star

A designation used in Cognacs and Armagnacs and frequently believed to indicate an exact age of three, five, or some other number of years. Actually, Three-Star is a type, and while it may average roughly an age of five years in Armagnacs, and somewhat younger in Cognacs, it does not necessarily do so. The system was probably devised because of the ease of drawing a star symbol—at the time the use of stars arose in Cognac, the trick of drawing a star without lifting pen from paper was in vogue—and subsequently it became famous. While a Three-Star brandy need not be of any given age, it will always be younger than a V.S.O.P., X.O., or Reserve, and will be less expensive. Star styles and other designations are considered fully under Cognac (*q.v.*).

Tía María

A proprietary West Indian liqueur based on rum and flavored with Jamaican spices and coffee.

Tinta

A grapevine family—Tinta Cão, Tinta Francisca, etc.—used in making Port. Some of these Tintas have now been planted also in California.

Tintara

Vineyard in McLaren Vale, South Australia.
See Australia.

Tinto

In Spain, a *vino tinto* is a red wine.

Tirage

French term for the act of drawing wine from barrels.

Tischwein

German term for common wine, or *vin ordinaire*. Not to be confused with *Tafelwein*, or table wine.

Toddy

A hot drink made with spirits, sugar, lemon slices, cloves, and hot water. In certain tropical countries, it is also a cold drink, made from the liquor of the fermented sap of palm trees.

Tokaier

See Ruländer.

Tokaji

One of the label words for Tokay, followed by an indication of the type of Tokay—e.g., Tokaji Édes Szamorodni.
See Tokay.

Tokay (Tokaj)

Down into the Hungarian river town of Tokaj, the two streams Bodrog and Hernád rush from the Carpathian Mountains; they converge and flow to the Danube and thence into the Black Sea.

Nobody knows how long vines have grown on the volcanic soil in the fork of the rivers; they were already there when the Magyar (Hungarian) tribes arrived a thousand years ago. In the corner of Hungary near Slovakia and the Ukraine, the wine was famous at least by the time of the Crusades. The eighteenth-century writer Szirmay de

Szirma said that the real fame of Tokay arrived with the discovery of the *aszú* method only half a century before his time. Modern writers, however, date the discovery earlier. The real magic of Tokay Aszú was likely first realized in the middle of the seventeenth century by one Máté Laczkó, private secretary at the court of Lady Zsuzsánna Lórántffy, widow of György Rákóczi I, Prince of Transylvania. The prince owned extensive Tokay vineyards on Mount Oremus at Sárospatak. This was the beginning of the Aszú Tokay we know today.

There are people in Hungary who will say that the steely wines of great breed from Lake Balaton are the best in the country, but the world will not agree. Tokay, the most concentrated of all, seems to capture more than any other the romance of wine. Even Champagne cannot quite approach this golden aristocrat, once guarded by an entire troop of Cossacks for the table of Catherine the Great. The most superb Trockenbeerenauslese Rhine or Mosel, or a Château d'Yquem of the greatest year, will lack at least one of the elements that ennoble Tokay. Voltaire said of it: "This wine invigorates every fiber of the brain and brings forth an enchanting sparkle of wit and good cheer from the depths of the soul."

The Tokajhegyalja wine district in northeastern Hungary borders on Czechoslovakia and the Soviet Ukraine. There are some 6,500 hectares (16,250 acres) of vineyards which annually produce about 200,000 hectoliters (5.3 million U.S. gallons, 4.4 million imp.) of various Tokays.

Twenty-eight villages in this defined district have the right to the name for their wines—Tokaji, as it appears on the labels, "wine from Tokaj," the *i* indicating place of origin. All are grown on a volcanic soil with feldspar, porcelain clay, and porphyry in it, a fundamental contribution to the character of the wine. The topsoil is decayed lava and loess. All of the towns with the right to the name are in the southern foothills—Hegyalja means "foothill"—of the Eperjes-Tokaj range, protected to the north by the high Carpathian Mountains. The most important villages are Tállya, Tarcal, Tokaj, Olaszliszka, Erdőbénye, Tolcsva, Mád, Satoraljaujhely, and the cultural and political center of the district, Sárospatak. A small part of the producing area is in Czechoslovakia.

As with any great wine, the geographical location and soil are only two of the factors contributing to its originality. There are also the climate, grape, and the methods of winemaking to consider. In Tokaj the summers are hot and dry; the autumns are especially long, so that in good years there is plenty of sunshine to overripen the grapes. Only three grape varieties are permitted: Furmint, Hárslevelű, and Sárgamuskotály. The Furmint is by far the most important as it is most conducive to overripening and noble rot. Walloon wine-growers brought it to the region in the thirteenth century after a Tartar invasion.

The process by which the more concentrated grades are made has a good deal in common with the method used for Sauternes or the German Trockenbeerenauslesen wines, but in some ways it is unique. The Tokay-Furmint grape, a dull yellow fruit with a thick skin, becomes overripe in the warm rays of the autumn sun, and the parasitic fungus *Botrytis cinerea* (*q.v.*) begins under the right conditions to reduce the natural acids and concentrate the grape sugar. The Magyars called the grapes that had been blessed in this way *aszú,* which means "dried out," describing the weeping away of water from the fruit. In the days of the Habsburgs, when the wines were particularly popular, they were called *Ausbruch,* the German translation of the Hungarian term.

As in Sauternes or on the Rhineland slopes and Mosel terraces, a late-gathered, dried-berry wine will be made. In France and Germany the essential process is to pick over the vineyard repeatedly, selecting only the overripe or dried-up berries each time. In Hungary, the Furmint grape cluster too ripens unevenly, some berries being ready days before others. But the method devised for Tokay is different. In picking over a Tokay vineyard, the dried grapes are separated from the others and put into containers, the Hungarian name for which is *puttony.*

THE GREAT NAMES IN TOKAY

The berries that have been thus selected are vinified alone or mixed with other grapes and juice, each combination producing one of the famous Tokay wines. It is at this point in the wine-making process that the aszú method begins to differ from the techniques found in the Sauternes region of France or the Rheingau of Germany.

Tokaji Eszencia

Made exclusively from dried-up berries, this is the most treasured of essences used in the making of Tokay wine. The overripe berries and those in a state of noble rot are gathered one by one and are stored in vats until the end of the harvest. Only the weight of the piled-up fruit forces the syrup from the grapes. This immensely rich liquid is slowly fermented for years in the small casks called *gönci.* There is nothing else on earth remotely like this very heart of Tokay, and many stories of its magical life-giving and restorative powers have been told. Tokaji Eszencia made in the classic manner has not been available outside of Hungary for many years. The state cellars make very little of the fabulous wine, and when a bottle of Eszencia of a recent vintage does appear, it is most likely a blend of standard Aszú wine with a very small part of the essence.

Tokaji Aszú

The Aszú grapes, having yielded their small tribute of Eszencia, are trodden into a paste so that the pips remain whole and unbruised. The skins, on the other hand, almost dissolve. While this process goes on, the grapes not affected by the fungus are harvested and pressed in the usual way. Into this must some of the green and sappy stalks are stirred for a few hours of maceration. A blend of the must and the Aszú dough is then made and fermented in open vats for a few days. The solid pulp is filtered out, and the enriched must is poured into the *gönci* casks for the slow and final part of fermentation lasting four to seven years. This slow fermentation oxidizes the wine and gives it the fine and distinctive Tokay bouquet. So, as with certain Sherries and Château Chalon wine of Arbois in France, the special bouquet of the wine is due to controlled oxidation. Tokay cellars have a unique mold, characterized by the *Cladesporium cellare,* which forms a black, almost cottony film on the cellar walls. By microcondensation, it absorbs the ethers, volatile aldehydes, volatile acids, and alcohol vapors caused by wine evaporation that are in the air.

The character of a Tokaji Aszú will be indicated by the *puttonyos* content stated on the neck label. The buckets, or *puttonyos,* of raisin-dry, concentrated grapemash added to the fermentation of the pick-of-the-vineyard run are shown on each bottle of the vatting. Thus, the neck label on every bottle will state: 3 Puttonos, 4 Puttonos, or 5 Puttonos, etc. The more Aszú berries that have been put in, the more concentrated the wine will be. A wine labeled five or six *puttonyos* is one made almost entirely from the aszú mash, with little of the standard grape must added. The nature of the vintage depends on the stage of ripening of the vineyard on the day of picking.

Alcoholic content and other characteristics of course vary with the *puttonyos* content, but alcohol is generally between 14% and 15% by volume. The Furmint grape does not achieve the proper condition for making Aszú below an altitude of 100 meters (350 feet), and all the best wine is made on the slope vineyards ranging between an altitude of 125 and 250 meters (420 and 820 feet). It has been estimated that the Aszú berry proportion of the entire Tokay crop averages about one part in three thousand, although in many years no Aszú can be made at all.

Tokaji Szamorodni

Szamorodni is a Slavonic, not a Magyar word, evidence of the interest that the Russians and Poles have often had in Tokay wines. The word means "such as it was grown" and refers to wine made from grapes from which the Aszú berries have not been selected. Therefore, when the conditions of the vintage favor the full development of the *Botrytis cinerea,* few of the bunches are left untouched for Tokaji Szamorodni. Conversely, in a year when little Aszú can be made, there is much of this wine. The vinification resembles that of Aszú, since the fermentation is in two stages: the first for a few hours on the solids, just long enough, as the Hungarians say, "to wash the sweetness out of the Aszú berries"; then the second in the *gönci* barrels kept in the typical low rock cellars. It is more important to know the Tokay years for Szamorodni than for Aszú, since on the former there is no indication of *puttonyos* strength. On the other hand, considerable help has been given to British and American buyers by labeling export bottles of Szamorodni as either dry or sweet; the indications are given in English both on the body and neck label. Szamorodni Sweet will, of course, be from the pickings which included more Aszú berries and can have a tremendous nose. The designation Tokaji Édes Szamorodni also indicates that the Szamorodni is sweet.

Tokaji Aszú and Tokaji Szamorodni are sold only in white bottles of about a pint or half-liter, with long throats, shaped not unlike Indian clubs. The other varieties of Tokay wine are sold in the tall, slender Rhine-style bottle usual for Hungarian wines. By law, these bottles bear the government export mark.

Tokaji Máslás

After an Aszú or Szamorodni has been racked, plain Tokay wine is poured into the little 120-liter or 150-liter *gönci* barrel and for several months is left to stand on the lees. The result is Tokaji Máslás.

Tokaji Forditás

Tokaji Forditás is made by performing a second time the making of Aszú. The used pulp after the Aszú has been made is revived by the addition of fresh must, and a second fermentation is obtained.

OTHER TOKAY TERMS

Tokaji Pecsenyebor: Tokay wine of the lowest quality.
Tokaji Édes: sweet Tokay.
Tokaji Száraz: dry Tokay.
Monimpex: the state export monopoly.
Magyar Állami Pincegazdaság: Hungarian state cellars.

Tokay d'Alsace

Another name for the Pinot Gris grape.

Tom and Jerry

A drink made of eggs, hot milk or water, sugar, brandy, and rum.

Tom Collins

An iced drink made of gin and sugar mixed with lime and lemon juice and filled up with soda-water.

Tonneau

In France (1) Any large barrel. (2) The standard wine measure in Bordeaux. Although no container of this size actually exists, a Bordeaux *tonneau* is equal to four *barriques*, or barrels, and contains 900 liters, equivalent to 237 U.S. gallons or 198 imp. gallons. As of 1977 one *tonneau* no longer equals 96 cases of twelve 73-centiliter bottles each, but 100 cases of twelve 75-centiliter bottles each.

Toro

Red wine of Zamora.
See Spain.

Torgiano

Red or white wine from Umbria (*q.v.*) in Italy.

Toul

See Côtes de Toul; Lorraine.

Touraine and Coteaux de Touraine

White, red, and rosé wines.
District: Loire Valley, France.

The large district spreads over both banks of the Loire around Tours and is famous both as "the garden of France" and the "château country" of such magnificent palaces as Blois, Amboise, Chenonceaux, and Azay-le-Rideau. It is celebrated also as the region where the inhabitants speak the purest and clearest French of all. Over 250,000 hectoliters (6,625,000 U.S. gallons, 5,500,000 imp.) of wines are made annually in the Touraine, some fairly ordinary but a few in the front rank of French wines.

Tours is on the Loire's left bank, an old city not without charm. The best vineyards are across the river and slightly to the north, but you will hardly realize that Indre-et-Loire and Loir-et-Cher (the departments in which Touraine lies) is wine country until you leave the valley. The winding river road threads its way beneath high cliffs, and roadside advertisements inform you that wines may be obtained, but a vine is a rare sight indeed. Most of the vineyards are on the other side of the bluffs which rise steeply from the river, planted on the back sides. These slopes are important, for tunneling back into them are long cellars whose limestone walls maintain a constant temperature and humidity, where the wines age under excellent conditions. There is hardly a house without its deep cellar running back into the hill on which it stands, and hardly a cellar where wines are not quietly sleeping, waiting for the "moment of truth" when the cork is pulled and the wine turned gently into the clear glasses.

To most people, Touraine wines mean Vouvray, yet the district produces red and rosé wines as well as white. Touraine white is the finest. Still and sparkling wine, red, rosé, and white, stem from this rich and fertile section of the valley and some have the great vigor the others lack. Many, however, are too low in alcohol—in general the measure of a wine's stamina—to travel, but are decidedly pleasant when sipped in the shadow of a soaring castle wall overlooking the river.

A lot of the Touraine soil is too heavy with clay and too moist to be suitable for wine; but as you climb the slopes you find a coarse-grained limestone topped with a chalky clay, a formation known as *aubuis*, which Loire growers say is ideal for the Chenin Blanc vine, the most widespread variety here; and Vouvray is the best example of the wines it produces. In other localities, the soil is flintier and has less limestone; and Cabernet Franc and lesser amounts of Gamay, Cot, Pinot Noir and Pinot Gris, and a minute amount of Groslot are planted for rosé wines. This is the type of soil prevalent in Chinon.

Wine is named either from the district or from one of the more specific sub-districts. The general name is Touraine—Touraine Mousseux, if sparkling—applied to wines from the specified area which attain from 9% to 10.5% of alcohol and which have been harvested in no more than 45 hectoliters per hectare (468 U.S. gallons, 390 imp. per acre). Wines with more specific names meet

Map labels: Paris 119 m., Blois, Mesland, N 152, T O U R A I N E, N 10, N 152, Vouvray, Amboise, R. Loire, Tours, Montlouis, R. Cher, N, St. Nicolas-de-Bourgueil, N 751, Bourgueil, Azay-le-Rideau, N 152, TOURAINE, N 751, Saumur 10 m., R. Vienne, N 10, Chinon, Bordeaux 185 m., FRANCE

Scale: 0 5 10 15 20 MILES / 0 5 10 15 20 KILOMETRES

more stringent standards. The Touraine sub-districts (*see under individual headings*) are: Bourgueil, Saint-Nicolas-de-Bourgueil, Chinon, Montlouis, Touraine-Amboise, Touraine-Azay-le-Rideau, Touraine-Mesland, Vouvray.

Touraine-Amboise

Loire Valley red, white, and rosé wines.
District: Touraine, France.

A minor subdivision of the Touraine, making a small quantity of wine generally slightly better than that simply called Touraine but not in the class of the more famous Touraine sub-districts. Red and rosé wines come from Cabernet Franc, Cot, and Gamay grapes; white from Chenin Blanc. Red wines must have 9.5% of alcohol, rosé 10%, and white 10.5%.
See Touraine.

Touraine-Azay-le-Rideau

Loire Valley red, white, and rosé wines.
District: Touraine, France.

Azay-le-Rideau, with its magnificent château, was given the right in 1953 to sell its dry wines under its own name, one that applies equally to the output of the seven surrounding communes. The white wines must be made from Chenin Blanc grapes, must have at least 10% of alcohol, and are good but not exceptional Touraine wines. The red and rosé wines are made mostly from the Groslot grape.
See Touraine.

Touraine-Mesland

Loire Valley red, white, and rosé wines.
District: Touraine, France.

A minor subdivision of the Touraine given its own controlled place-name in 1955. Red and rosé wines come mainly from Gamay grapes; white from Chenin Blanc and Sauvignon. Rosé and white wines must have 10.5% alcohol, red only 10%.
See Touraine.

Touriga

Leading red grape in the Dão region of Portugal. It is also used in making Port.

Tourne

A disorder of wine, in which it becomes gassy and disagreeable to nose and taste, hazes, and loses color.
See Chapter Nine, p. 38.

Traben-Trarbach

White-wine villages on opposite banks of the German Mosel, each possessing some good vineyards.
See Mosel-Saar-Ruwer.

Traminer

Now known commonly as the Gewürztraminer, the Traminer appears frequently on the labels of the German wines derived from this grape. This grape is also planted in the South Tyrol.

See Alsace; Germany; Gewürztraminer.

Trappistine

A very pale yellow-green, herb-flavored, Armagnac-based liqueur made at the Abbaye de Grâce de Dieu in the French department of Doubs.

Trebbiano

The Italian name for Ugni Blanc, one of the most widespread white wine grapes from Italy. This vine also flourishes in France, where it is known by various names, notably Saint-Émilion des Charentes.

See Saint-Émilion.

Trebbiano di Abruzzo

Italian white wine.
See Abruzzi.

Trentino-Alto Adige (South Tyrol)

White and red wines.
District: Italian Tyrol. (Known also as Sud Tyrol.)

The Alto Adige is potentially Italy's finest growing area for dry white wines, but at present the potential is only realized in isolated instances. Soil, climate, and vines in this northeast alpine corner are capable of producing inexpensive wines to rival those of Austria or Alsace; but the 5,800 growers have been the inhibiting factor, generally preferring to stick to the traditional methods of making light traditional red wines between the light red wines of Germany and the fuller reds found farther south in Italy. Fortunately, modern cooperatives, especially in Trentino, are investing in modern technology and the wines have improved accordingly.

Before 1919 the Alto Adige was part of the Austrian Tyrol. The Treaty of Saint-Germain, at the end of the First World War, transferred it to Italy; but the inhabitants remain Germanic, and Austria continues to drink the wines. What the Austrians do not import goes mostly to Switzerland and Germany, and this division of the spoils predates the coming of the Italians by a considerable time. Just under 85% percent of the 650,000 hectoliters (17 million U.S. gallons, 14 million imp.) made annually are red; but good though some of them may be, they are sometimes outclassed by the best of the whites. It is a general rule that the finer whites are from the northern Alto Adige section, the reds from Trentino—extending south around the city of Trento to the sunny shores of Lake Garda.

GRAPEVINES

The vines cultivated in Trentino-Alto Adige are a cosmopolitan group. The Austrian influence is reflected in Rieslings and Traminers, the French in Pinots, Cabernets, and Merlots; and the Italians have introduced—among others—Schiave, Lambrusco, Deroldego, and Garganega (known locally as Terlano). Riesling is the most interesting vine. When cultivated on the chilly slopes, it gives grapes capable of fermenting into marvelous wine. Much the same can be said of Traminer, although it is a general rule that Riesling will always produce the finer fruit under the same conditions. Schiave is common in the northern part of the region, producing sound, sometimes thoroughly delightful red wines; and Merlot seems to be on the increase. The Italian discovery of the Merlot is an important event in modern viniculture, for the result is a wine in the hearty Italian manner but one with the rough edges considerably smoothed.

In Trentino, the most widespread vine is Deroldego (or sometimes Teroldico), producing largely red wines of ordinary quality. Lambruscos and Merlots are abundant also, but the grapes of these and other vines are usually crushed together or blended after crushing to give a wine with more balance than any one seems able to produce alone.

BEST WINES

Riesling del Trentino (D.O.C.)
Potentially the queen of the Alto Adige but today too often aged in cask until it is yellowish and oxidized. Some exceptions must be allowed (although not to the extent claimed by the Italians) and these give one reason to think that while the wines will never have all the breed of the finest German Rieslings, they could conceivably stand with anything below this level.

Santa Magdalener (D.O.C.)
Alto Adige red wine, sometimes referred to—even today—as Sankt Magdalener. It is made from Schiave grapes grown on slopes near Bolzano. Santa Magdalener is a clean, smooth, pleasant wine giving a slight aroma of almonds and is probably the finest red wine of the area, deeper in color and with more flavor than Caldaro.

Deroldego Rotaliano (D.O.C.)
This wine from Trentino is either ruby-red or rosé; both are dry and full-bodied, pungent and sturdy. The red may tend toward harshness, with a slight trace of tannic bitterness.

Traminer Aromatico del Trentino (D.O.C.)
The dry white Gewürztraminer wine is imbued with the typical spicy perfume. The best in Italy comes from the Alto Adige, and although it is not outstanding, it may well be an excellent, reasonably priced bargain.

Caldaro (Lago di Caldaro D.O.C.)
Pleasant garnet-red wine with a trace of almond in the bouquet; from Schiave and occasionally some Pinot and

Lagrein grapes grown around Lake Caldaro (formerly the Kaltersee) not far south of Bolzano. It is light and enjoyable but gains little with age. The best is called Classico Superiore.

Vino Santo del Trentino (D.O.C.)

Sweet dessert wine from white Pinot grapes which are dried before vinification. The wine is similar to Tuscan Vino Santo but without all the latter's excellence.

LESSER WINES

Cabernet del Trentino (D.O.C.)

Made of Cabernet Franc and Cabernet Sauvignon, the wine is dry, full, and slightly tannic but is certainly not one of the best products of these good grapes. The bouquet is reminiscent of grass.

Val d'Adige (Valdadige)

Red wine from Schiave, Lambrusco, Pinot, and Deroldego grapes grown on the banks of the lower Adige in the Trentino section of the region. The river is long and passes through a wide variety of soils, rendering the wines variable in the same measure. It is the common red wine of the area.

Colline di Caldaro

Red wine from Schiave and Pinot Noir, grown along slopes in the general vicinity of Lake Caldaro.

Küchelberger

Pleasant red wine from the Küchelberg, a mountain near Merano. Schiave grape vines predominate.

Lagarino Rosato

Pink wine from Lagrein grapes. Before 1919 it was called Lagreinkretzer.

Marzemino del Trentino (D.O.C.)

A dry, ruby-red, well-balanced wine with a somewhat bitter taste. Best when young.

Meranese di Collina (D.O.C.)

Light, red wine from Schiave grapes grown along the hills near Merano, north of Bolzano.

Merlot del Trentino (D.O.C.)

These Bordeaux grapes make a sound dry red wine that is pleasant enough but certainly not outstanding.

Moscato del Trentino (D.O.C.)

Neither so heavy nor so sweet as most Muscat wines and thus an interesting change for Muscat-lovers. A fortified Moscato Liquoroso is also produced.

Pinot Nero del Trentino (D.O.C.)

The Pinot Noir grapevine—sometimes called by its old Austrian name, Blauburgunder—is cultivated in scattered sections of the region. Its wine is bright red, sometimes even pink, and is pleasantly bitter.

Lagrein del Trentino (D.O.C.)

A red wine from the Lagrein grapes, very fruity and dry, usually with about 12% of alcohol.

Sorni

Red wine from Merlot, Deroldego, and several subvarieties of Schiave grapes. The town of Sorni is slightly north of Trento.

Sylvaner (D.O.C.)

A small dry white wine, but perfectly adequate in carafe at or near its source. Bressanone (formerly Brixen) is its headquarters.

Terlaner (D.O.C.)

A well-known and quite presentable greenish-white wine of the Alto Adige. Terlano is the local name for the Garganega vine, but the wine is more often a blend of Terlano, Riesling, and Pinot Noir.

Termeno d'Avio

Unspectacular rosé wine from southern Trentino. It is made from Lambrusco, Merlot, Deroldego, and Marzemino grapes.

Trier

Ancient wine city of the German Mosel. There is a famous museum here, and fair white wines are produced. *See* Mosel-Saar-Ruwer.

Trinidad rum

See Rum, Trinidad.

Triple sec

Triple sec white Curaçao was originally the name used by the makers of Cointreau, but so many other firms started using the designation that the originators ceased putting it on their labels and called their liqueur simply Cointreau. Triple sec is now used by a number of manufacturers in various countries for liqueurs of the Curaçao type.
See Curaçao.

Trittenheim

Wine town of the German Mosel. Among the good vineyards are Apotheke and Altärchen.
See Mosel-Saar-Ruwer.

Trockenbeerenauslese

Literally "dried-berry-selected" in the block-building German language, the elephantine word describes the process whereby the finest sweet wine of the Rhine and

Mosel and some of the most elegant wines in the world are obtained. The grapes are allowed to dry and shrivel on the vine until the ultimate in concentrated sugar-sweetness is achieved; the berries are then individually selected, in this state of super-maturity, by the pickers. Increasing labor costs in a prosperous post-war Germany are rapidly pricing this exquisite type of wine out of the market. Trockenbeerenauslese is the German equivalent of the Sauternes-style wine of France, with the difference that in the warmer southwestern France it is still possible to produce a naturally sweet wine by individual selection of grapes at a price which, though very high, is still not prohibitive.

Château Trotanoy

Bordeaux red wine.
District and Commune: Pomerol, France.

Jean-Pierre Moueix makes this especially rich and flavorful wine from old vines on a clay and gravel soil.
Vineyard area: 9 hectares (22 acres).
Average production: 30 *tonneaux* (2,500 cases).

Château Trottevieille

Bordeaux red wine.
District and Commune: Saint-Émilion, France.

Always one of the leading Saint-Émilions, it was rated a Premier Grand Cru when the vineyards were officially classified in 1955. Trottevieille sells well abroad, particularly in Belgium. The property belongs to M. Casteja, the son-in-law of the late Marcel Borie, who also owned Château Batailley, a classified vineyard in the Médoc.
Characteristics. A carefully made wine with body and bouquet and a fine color.
Vineyard area: 10 hectares (25 acres).
Average production: 50 *tonneaux* (4,800 cases).

Tuica

A plum spirit made in Rumania. It varies in color from greenish to yellow. It is sometimes taken hot with sugar and peppers.

Tun

A wine cask containing 954 liters (252 U.S. gallons, 210 imp.). A tun filled with water or wine weighs approximately one ton avoirdupois.

Tunisia

The vine was established, especially in the vicinity of Carthage, in Punic and Roman times. Afterward, under the rule of the Moslems, wine-making was forbidden for more than a thousand years. The modern history of wine in Tunisia, now an independent country, began when it came under French control.

Viniculture along French lines was developed in the Cape Bon region (on the peninsula enclosing the Gulf of Tunis on the east); around Tunis itself, and in the Medjerdah and Oued Miliane valleys. Wines were made in quantity, a peak of nearly 1,200,000 hectoliters (31,680,000 U.S. gallons, 26,375,000 imp.) annually being maintained in the 1930s. Phylloxera, the deadly vine louse which half a century earlier had ruined Europe's vineyards, reached Tunisia in 1936. In ten years the vineyard area had dropped by half and wine production by nearly two-thirds.

Replanted on grafted, phylloxera-immune American vine-stocks (as were the post-epidemic vineyards of Europe), the Tunisian vine plantation now covers some 38,000 hectares (95,000 acres), not all of which are yet in full production. Quantity stands at about 604,000 hectoliters (15.9 million U.S. gallons, 13 million imp.). The earlier peak production is now common, although when the vineyards were first reconstituted, an attempt was made to obtain quality at the expense of quantity.

Tunisia produces red, white, and rosé natural wines, fortified Muscat wines, and *eaux-de-vie.* All wine-growing is confined to a narrow area near the coast, forming a crescent around and behind Tunis but at some distance from the town. The leading districts are Grombalia and the section formed by the triangle Tunis-Mateur-Bordj-Toum, producing quantitatively more than 90% of the total. Growths (*Crus*) are not particularly important in the present state of Tunisian viticulture; however, names of some repute include Carthage, Tébourba, Coteaux du Khanguet, Saint-Cyprien, Cap Bon, and Sidi-Tabet. Important names of fortified wines are Byrsa and Rancio.

The traditional grape varieties in Tunisia have always been, for the red, Carignan, Alicante-Bouschet, and Cinsault; for white wines, Clairette de Provence, Beldi, and Ugni; and for the rosé, Alicante-Grenache. The wines have characteristically shown a tendency to maderize—particularly the reds, which are based exclusively on Alicante-Bouschet and which mature too rapidly in the climate, showing a feeble color and then quickly developing the onion-skin hue and a bitterish taste. In an attempt to correct this, Pedro Ximénez vines from Spain and Sémillon and Sauvignon from France have been introduced for the white wines; and for the red wines, the Nocera, Pinot Noir, and Cabernet varieties. The rosés, based on Alicante-Grenache, have proved the most successful of the types, making one of the best rosés of North Africa, provided that they are bottled as soon as they fall clear and are drunk young. Otherwise they will maderize.

A series of controls established between 1942 and 1957 acted as incentives to make wines of quality by guaranteeing that such wines would be identified and therefore command premium prices.

In 1942 the classification Vin Supérieur de Tunisie was established. It includes no restriction as to place of origin within Tunisia nor limitation as to grape varieties. Wines submitted by growers for the classification are analyzed chemically to establish their purity and are then tasted blind by a committee of experts chosen by the Commission of Classification. Vins Supérieurs de Tunisie are sold in bottle. The bottle dressing carries a numbered insignia showing that it belongs to a classed lot, and the vintage must be indicated. The wines must be at least one year old. (It is interesting that the technique parallels almost exactly that set up in 1955 in Bordeaux for wines to be exported to the U.S.)

In 1947, the Appellation Contrôlée Vin Muscat de Tunisie was established. In place of origin, wines are not restricted except to Tunisia, but they must be of the Alexandrian Muscat, Muscat de Frontignan, or Muscat de Terracina grape varieties. The wines are fortified by one of two means: tasteless, rectified spirit may be added before fermentation has begun, thus preventing fermentation and retaining the entire sugar content of the must as sugar; or the fermenting must may be stopped by the addition of either spirits of wine or completely rectified spirit, resulting in a wine of a minimum of 17% of alcohol and of 70 grams of sugar per liter. The wines made by the first method should properly be called mistelles, since they are actually grape juice with added alcohol, never having undergone fermentation. It is illegal to mix the two types. The better quality results from the use of wine spirits rather than of completely rectified spirit.

In 1957, a place-name system that defined the different wine-producing regions was established. This system also created a hierarchy of wines, broken down as Vins Supérieurs, Vins de Qualité Supérieure (V.D.Q.S.) and Appellation d'Origine Contrôlée (A.O.C.).

Turkey

At the turn of the century Turkish wines were seen in some quantity in Western Europe. But exports ceased with the First World War, and by the late twenties that war and the Turco-Greek conflict which followed had almost put an end to wine-making. The prolific, grape-producing regions of Thrace and the Aegean had been devastated, and most of the non-Islamic population had disappeared. The land was left to cultivators who liked eating grapes, were forbidden by their religion to drink wine, and were often persuaded that to sell their grapes to wine-making plants was sinful. It was the task of the new republic to revive the country's viniculture.

When, in 1927, the state monopolies wine industries were started, total production had fallen to some 20,000 hectoliters (about 528,000 U.S. gallons, 440,000 imp.) a

year. Since the middle thirties, however, it has been expanding gradually, and the state has been making a serious effort to raise quality as well as quantity without putting up prices: in order to win customers, Turkey must sell more cheaply than the established wine-producing countries. Up-to-date machinery has been installed in the government plants, employees have been trained in modern techniques of viticulture and viniculture, and the decree of 1928 that the Moslem faith was no longer the official religion has helped to overcome the scruples of some of the growers.

In comparison with the West, Turkey now seems to be a latecomer in wine production; yet the vine flourished in this region long before Greek colonists planted the first vineyards in Gaul. The earliest vines of all are believed to have grown wild in Anatolia and around the shores of the Caspian Sea; and in Mesopotamia the Sumerians are said to have been making wine as long ago as the third millennium B.C. This long start was lost in the Middle Ages when the Turks themselves (ardent converts to Islam) began their conquests, which culminated in the fall of Constantinople in 1453. Grapes went on growing, but most of them were (and are) kept for the table, or made into vinegar or the miel de raisin which many of the peasants use instead of sugar. In the early years of the Ottoman Empire there was a must tax on the production of wine in the vineyards of non-Moslems. In 1564 a new tax was levied on all alcoholic drinks—but this proved so difficult to enforce that it was afterward repealed. By the late nineteenth century, although indigenous wine-drinkers were still rare, something like 3.5 million hectoliters (924 million U.S. gallons, 77 imp.) of wine were produced, largely for export.

The types of wine made in Turkey are dry, semi-dry, sweet, fortified, and sparkling. The grapes for the sweet wine are late-picked; the fortified wines are sweet Muscatels; the sparkling wines are carbonated. The best growths come from central and southeastern Anatolia; others of very good to medium quality are produced in the Thracian and Aegean regions. Thrace and Marmara, the Aegean, Middle Anatolia, the Mediterranean, and Southeastern Anatolia are the only wine-producing regions. Officially approved grape varieties are listed on page 476.

METHODS OF WINE-MAKING

Turkish growers rarely make their own wine, although a few do so in places such as Bozcaada and Mürefte. They usually sell their grapes to the townsmen who operate the plants. These fall into two categories: on the one hand, the government-controlled monopolies established in 1927 and the Atatürk Farm Administration; on the other, private enterprises. The state wineries are operated with modern industrial machinery by technically qualified personnel; the private concern, often housed in a shop or shed, may be quite seedy and makeshift, the machinery is usually rather primitive and the makers are unlikely to be trained vinicultors. Some of these men make trouble with the peasants by offering for their grapes—already very cheap—a price which is absurdly low.

Region	Red Wine Grapes	Red Wine Vineyards
Thrace and Marmara	Clairette, Chardonnay, Yapincik	Tekirdag
	Riesling, Sémillon	Tekirdag-Canakkale
	Beylerce	Bilecik
	Vasilaki	Canakkale-Balikesir
Aegean	Sémillon	Manisa-Izmir
	Bornava Misketi	Manisa
Middle Anatolia	Emir	Nevsehir-Kayseri-Nigde
	Hasandede	Ankara
Mediterranean	Dökülgen	Hatay
South & East Anatolia	Dökülgen, Morozkaraso, Rumi	Gaziantep
	Kabarcik	Gaziantep-Urfa

Region	White Wine Grapes	White Wine Vineyards
Thrace and Marmara	Pinot Noir, Gamay, Karalâhana, Cinsaut	Tekirdag
	Adakarasi	Balikesir
	Papazkarasi	Edirne-Kirklareli
	Kuntra	Canakkale
Aegean	Carignan, Grenache, Merlot, Alicante-Bouschet	Izmir
	Calkarasi	Denizli
	Cabernet Sauvignon	Manisa-Izmir
Middle Anatolia	Kalecik Karasi	Ankara
	Papazkarasi	Eskisehir-Nevsehir
	Dimrit	Nevsehir-Kayseri
Mediterranean	Sergi Karasi	Adana-Hatay
	Burdur Dimitiri	Isparta-icel-Burdur
South & East Anatolia	Horozkarasi, Sergi Karasi	Gaziantep
	Okuzgozu, Bogazkere	Gaziantep-kilis

In pressing the fruit, both hand-operated and hydraulic basket presses are used—the latter in the big plants. The pomace is first pressed by hydraulic processes, afterward by hand presses; only in making wines of better quality is the must of the second pressing processed independently. In well-run plants, the juice ferments in concrete tanks in rooms where the temperature is kept low and is transferred after about a week to more concrete tanks for ageing. Most of the wines are rather light and are aged only from eight to twelve months; a few bigger wines will be left for two or three years. Since most Turkish wines are low in acidity, it is necessary to add sufficient sulfur dioxide—the quantity is controlled by the regulations drawn up in 1954—and to rack the wine earlier than is usual. The first racking generally takes place fifteen to twenty-one days after ageing begins, and then sulfur is added; the second racking comes in four to six months; the third, six months later. Those wines which are allowed longer ageing are afterward racked only once a year. The wine is fined before bottling, mainly with gelatin—blue finings are not permitted—and is always filtered. Most plants blend their wines to achieve consistency of style and sell it in bottle—but some is marketed in cask. The product of the state monopolies is generally cheaper than wine made by private firms.

PRODUCTION

In spite of the efforts of the state, output is still small. The habit of wine-drinking is being urged on the people, and as the old religion loses its hold the custom is indeed growing. Yet most Turks would rather eat their grapes—and these grow luxuriantly over most of the country and are cheaper to buy than most other fruits. Annual domestic consumption of wine is reckoned at barely one liter per head. In 1950 Turkey came fourth among the countries listed by the Office International du Vin for vineyard acreage—but wine production was by no means proportionate. About only 3% of the grapes were being diverted to this end. The situation improves slowly: today the Turks keep track of wine-grape area and report that there are now some 800,000 hectares (about 2,000,000 acres) devoted solely to growing grapes for wine. Production is probably about 400,000 hectoliters (10.6 million U.S. gallons, 8.8 million imp.), though it may vary widely from year to year.

The principal objective of the state wine industry is, naturally, to increase its export trade; 40,000 or so hectoliters (1,060,000 U.S. gallons, 880,000 imp.) are perhaps exported every year. Sweden, purchasing 50% of the exports, is the principal buyer of Turkish wines, followed by

Switzerland and West Germany. Before these figures can substantially be improved, the government department concerned is well aware that certain reforms must be made, primarily in standards of viniculture and the selection of grape varieties. In order to encourage halfhearted growers, regulations were at first only leniently enforced; now peasants must be made to learn modern methods of tending their vines and private manufacturers obliged to model themselves on the state monopolies. Moreover, Turkey is growing too many varieties of grapes, and although permissible vines for each region have been listed, standardization has not yet been enforced. Then, phylloxera, which reached Turkey toward the end of the last century, still lingers in some districts: cultivators have not yet mastered as thoroughly as have the *vignerons* of Western Europe the art of grafting their vines onto disease-resistant American root-stocks. Finally, the government is hoping to find domestic substitutes for the corks and wooden staves (for barrels) which are so expensive to import. With so many improvements planned, one may expect that Turkish wine will soon become familiar abroad.

Tuscany

Red and white wines.
District: Central Italy.

Tuscany is the home of Chianti, so famous that it is sometimes mistakenly assumed to be synonymous with Italian wine. It is perhaps superfluous to add that though several oceans of this renowned wine used to spring from elsewhere in Italy (and the world), all true Chianti comes only from Tuscany. And some of it is excellent.

CHIANTI D.O.C.

The Chianti district comprises about 70,000 hectares (175,000 acres) between Florence and Siena and is as steep, rocky, and unpromising a vineyard area as any. Leave Florence by the busy main road and the Porta Romana, pass the quiet, well-tended, American military cemetery, then turn off to the left and find yourself virtually in another world. The hills are bleak, low-lying but steep, peppered with vines, cypresses, and harsh rocks. The road is no longer a highway but a winding, narrow lane where few cars may be seen, only an occasional ox cart or horse ambling slowly along in the summer heat. Weatherbeaten signposts point the way to the historic but dusty and deserted-looking centers: Greve, Radda, Castellina, and Gaiole. From the tops of the higher hills frown massive fortresses; this is the area which once served as a buffer state between warring Florence and Siena. The castles were built by the Florentines to stop raiders from Siena; and in 1376 the châtelains combined to form the Chianti League to deal with attackers and hold them off long enough for Florence to arm. The conflicts of bygone times are the province of the historian, but the student of wine can also profit from a glance at this background: it is one of the claims of the area—now known as the Chianti Classico district—to have sole right to the name Chianti. Historically, the Chianti Classico growers say no one else within or without Tuscany is en-

titled to the name. They reinforce their historical argument by pointing out that geologically the district differs from surrounding areas. The ancient clay-schist soil, the layers of covering flint and limestone, and the thin top of pebbly sand are not duplicated elsewhere. Since soil is an essential—perhaps the most essential—factor in deciding the characteristics of any wine, it follows that nothing grown outside the Chianti Classico district is really Chianti. Logic to the contrary, most Chianti is grown outside.

Perhaps the name is too famous. Perhaps the gay round-bottomed flask—the ubiquitous *fiasco*—drew too much attention to it. The fact remains that growers in half a dozen surrounding areas became attracted by the sweet smell of success and began selling their wines as Chianti—admittedly qualifying it by some other term, but calling it Chianti nonetheless. Each, in addition, has formed its own *consorzio* to protect the name it has appropriated, and each arrogantly proclaims its right to go on using the name, as they all have for years.

It must be admitted that some of the subsidiary Chiantis are wonderful wines. Chianti Rufina (not Ruffino, which is a trademark) is often considered to be a better balanced wine than the Classico variety, but some of the other offerings are not in the same class. Fortunately, despite the confusion and proliferation of names, real Chianti is available and easily recognizable: the authenticity of any bottle, or *fiasco,* may be verified by checking to see if it has the seal of the Chianti Classico *consorzio* (Consorzio per la Difesa del Vino Tipico di Chianti) portraying a black cockerel on a gold background with a surrounding red circle bearing the name of the organization. The following wines are allowed the Appellation d'Origine: Chianti Colli Aretini, Chianti Colli Fiorentini, Chianti Colli Senesi, Chianti Colli Pisane, Chianti Montalbano, Chianti Rufina.

Contrary to popular conception, Chianti is apt to come either in the normal tall bottles or a *fiasco*—in general, the finest ones are run off in regular bottles, the better to age them. (The straw wrapping of a *fiasco* has a tendency to rot; and furthermore, this expensive style of bottle cannot be laid down easily: the cork will not remain in contact with the wine and will dry out, admitting air which spoils the wine.)

Some Chianti firms never put their finest wine in a *fiasco,* while others confound confusion by using both styles for both qualities; yet it can be accepted as a general rule that Chianti in *fiasco* must be drunk young, while in bottle it may be kept and aged. It is an interesting sidelight on the *fiasco* that today it is not as cheap in comparison with a bottle as it was fifty years ago. At that time it was possible to blow the round-bottomed flasks and hire women to weave straw around them for practically nothing. Today labor is more expensive and mass-produced bottles cost less per unit, even if they lack the customer appeal of a *fiasco.*

True Chianti, even after years of ageing, is never a very subtle wine. A great part of its charm lies in the heady strength, the sturdy vigor, and slight trace of bitterness—even harshness—which is so characteristic. In the better wines, this bitterness disappears to some extent and the wine mellows and softens; but it never goes entirely away. Some young Chianti may have a prickly, *frizzante,* semi-sparkling bite, caused by adding the fermenting juice of late-maturing grapes to the wine after it is made, and this heightens the refreshing characteristics and adds to its gaiety. This practice, called *governo,* increases the amount of glycerin in the wine, making it more round and supple. Only in the very rarest cases will Chianti be a great wine, but it can almost invariably be counted on to be pleasant.

The wine is traditionally made from five types of grapes used in a set formula. Sangiovese (50% to 80%) is said to impart body and alcoholic content; Canaiolo (10% to 30%) gives bouquet and tempers the hardness; and Trebbiano and Malvasia (10% to 30% combined)—both white grapes—lighten the intensity of the color. Finally, Colorino (about 5%) helps in giving true Chianti its usually bright ruby-red color.

Some large firms have unfortunately set a somewhat low standard of quality in the wines they export. As in most of Italy, the really outstanding wines are made in small quantities, and one is apt to find them only in some Italian hotels or restaurants where the proprietors are willing to pay the price for quality. In such a case it is a pleasure to drink Chianti—which is too often just an ordinary wine in a Chianti flask.

VIN SANTO D.O.C.

The name, it is said, means "wine for the Saints." Fortunately, some is reserved for sinners too, but it is doubtful if it will ever be enough. The real Vin Santo is a sweet golden wine made by farmers in Tuscany—in fact throughout Italy—but never in any quantity. Some firms in and around Florence are beginning to put small amounts on the market, but as yet good ones are rarely sent for export.

Vin Santo is a pleasant dessert wine, albeit one that is not as sweet as most others in this category. It is vinified (in Tuscany, at any rate) from carefully dried Trebbiano and Malvasia grapes—which are dried by suspending them from hooks along the rafters of a loft or attic. The drying takes several months, and at the end about two-thirds of the juice has gone, leaving the rest comparatively rich in sugar. This juice is then pressed and put in small barrels of never more than about 6 hectoliters (150 U.S. gallons, 125 imp.) capacity, which are filled about three-quarters full then closed and left in a warm place for four years. Heat, as a rule, is death to wine, but in this case a special maderization is wanted; the wine changes in color from white to deep amber and takes on a nutty, almost Sherry-like taste and aroma. At the end of its ageing, it is filtered and is then ready to drink. The grapes are selected more for taste than sugar content and the wine is distinctive—sweet, but the sweetness masked and balanced by its austere, elevated alcoholic content.

OTHER WINES OF TUSCANY

Aleatico di Portoferraio

Sweet red dessert wine from the capital of Elba, the island that was not quite big enough to contain Napoleon. Its Aleatico (made from grapes of that name) is a full, warm, rich wine and one that can be excellent. Its fame, however, seems to be outrunning it, and there are grounds for suspicion today that not all the wine so labeled is what it claims to be.

Elba (D.O.C.)

Two types are produced, a red and a white. The white is a light straw-colored wine made from Trebbiano-Toscano grapes, known locally as Procanico, grown on the Isle of Elba. Italian wine enthusiasts like to compare this to Chablis, but they should not be taken too seriously. The red is deep, dry, ruby wine with a slightly aromatic taste; it comes mostly from Sangiovese, with some Procanico and Canaiolo. The D.O.C. Elba can be applied to white and red naturally sparkling wines. Descriptions that recall Napoleonic times are allowed on the wine labels, provided they had been in use for ten years before July 1967.

Bianco Vergine Valdichiana (D.O.C.)

"Virgin white," partly on account of its color, partly since only free-run grape juice is used, not juice extracted in the press. About 11% of alcohol, dry, and pleasantly fresh, in consequence of an acidity slightly higher than is customary in Italy.

Brolio

An excellent Chianti Classico named after the huge medieval fortress where the wine is always made. The best is never put in *fiasco* and will not always have the name Chianti on the label.

Brunello di Montalcino (D.O.C.)

Red wine from the hillsides of Montalcino, a little south of Siena. One of the best wines of all Italy, certainly one of the longest-lived—supposedly up to half a century. Made from Brunello grapes (a variety of Sangiovese), this wine is often compared by enthusiastic Italians to the best Burgundies. The cork should be drawn twelve hours before serving.

Lacrima d'Arno

Literally "tear of the Arno River," the wine is a pleasant dry white wine made mostly from the Pinot grape.

Meleto

A good Chianti Classico.

Montecarlo Bianco (D.O.C.)

A good white from a town in eastern Tuscany, delicate and dry, made primarily from Trebbiano grapes.

Moscatello di Montalcino

Tuscan sparkling Muscat wine, but generally closer to *frizzante* (semi-sparkling) than *spumante* (sparkling). It is produced in small quantities by a cooperative cellar.

Vernaccia di San Gimignano (D.O.C.)

White wine from Vernaccia grapes usually vinified to be dry, more rarely sweet. The better-known dry variety is a light amber color with a small bouquet and a slightly bitter aftertaste, and the sweet is still much used as an altar wine—its original purpose.

Vino Nobile di Montepulciano (D.O.C.)

A red wine that achieved some literary fame in the eighteenth century when the poet Francesco Redi apostrophized it in his *Bacchus in Tuscany* as *Montepulciano d'ogni vini è il Re* (Montepulciano, of all wines it is king). Perhaps in deference to contemporary republican Italy, the "king" has become something of a commoner. Made mostly from the Sangiovese grape by the noble families of Montepulciano, a town 48 kilometers (30 miles) south of Siena, this wine was already exported at the beginning of the fourteenth century.

U

Ugni Blanc

Widespread vine giving grapes for dry white wine. It is cultivated in southern France—in the region of Cognac (where it is called Saint-Émilion) and elsewhere; also in California and throughout Italy where, under the name Trebbiano, it contributes to most of the better Italian dry white wines.

See Trebbiano; Saint-Émilion.

Ullage

Air space in a bottle or cask between the top and the level of the wine. In bottled wine it is usually brought about by a faulty cork or by overexposure to heat and should be approached with caution if not suspicion—the wine may well be bad.

See Ouillage.

Umbria

White and red wines.
District: Central Italy.

The vines are pruned short, their branches frequently draped over the lower limbs of small trees which are kept in shape and cut down to size simply for that purpose. Umbrian growers do not share the apparent lack of concern shown by cultivators in some Italian vineyards, and theirs are apt to be remarkably well kept.

This region, south of Florence and north of Rome, produces some 800,000 hectoliters (21.2 million U.S. gallons, 17.6 million imp.), of which Orvieto is the best known.

Orvieto is white, and one of Italy's most consistently delightful wines, some of it semi-sweet, some of it dry. The latter is the result of the modern taste for drier wines. Orvieto was early aware of the trend; many of the growers began to vinify their wine dry, and there was a great outcry. Conservative wine-drinkers, such as Tuscany's austere Baron Ricasoli, have felt that sweet Orvieto is one of the finest examples of Italian viniculture; vinified to be dry, it becomes a pleasant, reputable wine, but no longer Orvieto. The growers reply that the market for Orvieto *amabile* or *abboccato* (as the semi-sweet is designated) has fallen off to the point where it is no longer possible to specialize in it. "Our traditional wine is as good as it was," they maintain, "but, in addition, we are putting out a dry wine under the same name. It may have slightly different characteristics, but it is still of Orvieto quality."

Sweet Orvieto has a particular charm and special delicacy. The grapes are mainly Trebbiano, Malvasia, Verdicchio, Verdello, and Procanico. In the dry wine, Trebbiano is the dominant grape.

Orvieto is aged in deep cellars dug back into tufa rock cliffs resembling those found in Vouvray, and these play an important part (the growers say) in giving the wine its characteristics. Dry Orvieto is usually considerably higher in alcohol than the sweet type, in which some of the sugar has been prevented from fermenting (up to 13% as against 11%), but it manages to preserve the charm of its counterpart. It is rarely perfectly dry, but seems to balance a trace of residual sugar against a faintly tart aftertaste. About half of the 50,000 hectoliters (million-odd gallons) produced annually are dry.

Colli del Trasimeno (D.O.C.) is the name of white and red wines produced in an area surrounding Lake Trasimeno, near Perugia. The white has a straw-yellow color and a well-balanced taste; the red is rather dry and slightly tannic, with a fine scent of violets.

Torgiano (D.O.C.) wines are red and white. The red, the better of the two, is made with Sangiovese and is a full-bodied wine; the white is made from Trebbiano Toscano. Both come from an area south of Perugia adjacent to the medieval Turris Janis—the tower of Janus, the Roman two-faced god of doors.

United Kingdom

Vines are grown in England and wine made commercially—still on a limited scale, although cultivation has developed considerably in the past ten years. Some 400 hectares (1,000 acres) were under vine in 1980, and over 200 growers were selling their wine. Mr. Jack Ward and his partner Ian Howie of the Merrydown Company have established a cooperative with very up-to-date machinery, to which about 30 proprietors send their grapes for pressing; others have their own wine sheds. There is also a fair number of private vineyards, as there once were, cultivated as a hobby, on country estates in the eighteenth and nineteenth centuries. The last of these estates was at Castle Coch, Glamorgan, the property of the Marquis of Bute, which was abandoned during the First World War.

In Norman and early medieval times, the English produced much of their own wine. According to the Venerable Bede, vineyards already existed in his time (*c.* A.D.730); and one of the laws of Alfred the Great (849-901) decreed that growers should be compensated for damage to their vines. After the Norman Conquest, wine-making naturally spread, especially in the monasteries; vineyards were recorded in the west and south of England; in Wales, Essex, and Suffolk; and later as far north as Lincolnshire and York. But in the mid-fourteenth century, cultivation declined (though it did not cease altogether), mainly because so much wine was coming in from the Continent—especially from Plantagenet possessions in Gascony—that it was easier to import than to grow.

After the Second World War a new interest in wine-making developed, and vineyards were planted in Lincolnshire, East Anglia, southern England, and Wales. Among growers successfully producing and selling English wine has been Sir Guy Salisbury-Jones, who planted his vineyard at Hambledon, Hampshire, in 1952. Other well-known names are Mr. Nigel Godden, Pilton Manor, Somerset; Lady Montagu at Beaulieu; Mr. and Mrs. J. G. Barrett, Felsted, Essex; and Major Colin Gillespie of Wooton, Somerset, who won first prize in an international blind-tasting at Trier with his Schoenburger. Mr. Barlow, at Adgestone Vineyard on the Isle of Wight, harvested a Schreube dessert wine one New Year's Eve—the grapes were all in a state of noble rot. In 1966 the English Vineyards Association was founded for the encouragement of viticulture.

Particularly encouraging to present-day growers in what was once considered an unfavorable climate is the progress of new and more adaptable vine species. A little red wine is made from Pinot Noir, Wrotham Pinot, and Austrian Zweigeltrebe; but here, as in Germany, the climate is more suitable for white wines. Müller-Thurgau is the grape most widely used. There is still some Seyve-Villard, but this is losing ground and people are beginning to plant more Pinot Chardonnay and Pinot Blanc, with some Huxelrebe, Reichensteiner, Madeleine Angevine, and other German varieties. Many of the vines are trained by the *guyot* method; some by the *gobelet*.

Apart from 1972 (a singularly bad year), most seasons see a reasonably satisfactory harvest of English wines—light and dry—some of which are on sale in London stores, such as Harrods, or listed at restaurants. At Horam Manor, Sussex, Merrydown has a winery shop at which they sell the products of other leading growers.

The term British wine, as distinct from English wine, is used for certain strong, cheap, fortified mixtures of imported grape concentrate fermented in Britain, resulting in recognizable but uninspiring dessert-style wines.

See also Whisky, Scotch.

United States: Arkansas

Though the thought may seem unlikely, Arkansas produces nearly 1,060,000 U.S. gallons (40,000 hectoliters, 880,000 imp. gallons) of wine annually. Most of the vineyards are in Franklin County, Johnson County, and in the northwest corner of the state around Tontitown. There are some 5,000 acres (2,000 hectares) of vines.

Four of the important wineries—there are eleven in the state overall—are at the small town of Altus: Wiederkehr, Post, Sax, and Mount Bethel. The Altus area accounts for nearly all of the wine produced in the state. Table wines are made, but most of them tend to be rather sweet, though they may improve as the French-American hybrid and *vinifera* vines now replace the less good native varieties, which have been dominant since the latter part of the nineteenth century.

United States: California

In California, climate, soil, and other conditions conducive to the production of good wine are equal to those in most of the great vine-growing regions of the world. For nearly forty years after the repeal of Prohibition in 1933, the great handicap in the production of fine wines came from the enormous acreage of poor and mediocre grape varieties in the many districts.

Plantings of the finer vines were the minority until the late seventies, while such red-wine grapes as Carignane and Alicante-Bouschet, and white-wine grapes like Burger, French Colombard, and Thompson Seedless, all of which usually produce only ordinary wines, were the majority. Zinfandel, the fine grape of California, used to be wrongly regarded as a bulk producer, but when grown in the proper area it makes a distinctive red wine of better than average quality for a Californian wine and when properly aged can make a superior wine as such. For the most part, the cooler regions in north California—Napa, Sonoma, Livermore Valley, Santa Cruz, Santa Clara, Mendocino, northern Monterey—yield table wines, some of excellent distinction and flavor, and the warmer regions give dessert wines. It was unfortunate that for many years until 1965, 60% of California wines were the sweet, fortified variety, rather than the table wine type. Since then, table wines have far outsold the so-called ports and sherries and now constitute more than 80% of all the wines produced in the state. Figures from recent years indicate that sales of table wines are advancing at a rate two and a half times greater than that of dessert wines.

Today 70% of all the wine sold in the United States comes from California. The production of table, dessert, and sparkling wines in 1978 totaled 295 million U.S. gallons (about 11 million hectoliters, 240 million imp. gallons)—roughly the same amount produced by all the Appellation Contrôlée wines of France in an average year. (Of course, the Appellation Contrôlée wines comprise only the best one-sixth of all French production.) In 1979 table-wine sales reached 228 million U.S. gallons. Production of fortified wines declined by 3% from the previous year for a 15% share of the market. Sparkling wines produced totaled 20 million U.S. gallons, 6% of the whole; eight years earlier, "champagnes" had represented only about 2% of the volume. By 1985, when U.S. wine consumption will reach 650 million U.S. gallons (25 million hectoliters, 550 million imp. gallons), California wines will continue to make up about 70% of the market. Wines from other states will continue to account for about 10% of the total, but consumption of imported wines will amount to roughly 20% of all wines drunk in the United States.

In the United States, there are two types of vines, the indigenous American *Vitis labrusca*, found wild in the east, and the *Vitis vinifera*, or the European variety, imported into California. It is the *Vitis vinifera* which forms the basis of the wine industry throughout the world.

In California and the rest of the United States, the wine-maker talks in tons per acre, while in Bordeaux,

Burgundy, and the other vineyards of Europe, the yields are expressed in hectoliters per hectare.

WINE HISTORY

The history of California goes back to Cortez, the Spanish conqueror of Mexico who, in 1524, ordained that wine-making should become one of the industries of the New World. The vines were probably of Spanish origin, although it is not certain that cuttings or seeds were brought from Spain. In time, the new wines were competing with the wines of Spain, and the Spanish, like the Emperor Domitian before them, ordered that the colonial vineyards be uprooted. Wine-growing continued, however, and for many years the wine industry in Mexico and Baja California was carefully concealed from Spanish officials. A Jesuit priest, Father Juan Ugarte, planted what were probably the first wine grapes to be grown on the West Coast in about 1697 at Mission San Francisco Xavier in Baja California. This was a European variety, the only one to be planted by the Fathers, and it was named, appropriately enough, Mission—and still has that name today. While the Spanish missions were being established and spreading slowly northward, the Mission grapes made their appearance in the vineyards of Alta California. The Franciscans, led by Padre Junípero Serra, brought them into what is now California, planting them at Mission San Diego de Alcalá soon after its establishment in 1769. The vines prospered and the harvest was said to have been better than any known before in the New World. Padre Serra's Franciscan missionaries constructed twenty-one missions, most of them with vineyards, from San Diego to Sonoma, the northernmost point of the Camino Real, or King's Highway—a great thoroughfare today—but the missions were largely confined to southern California. Descendants of the vines they cultivated are still living. San Gabriel Arcangel Mission near Los Angeles was chosen as the site for their largest winery, and the mission still preserves the little adobe building where the Indians trampled the juice from the grapes. Today visitors still come to see the gnarled remains of the mission's old Trinity vine, which was planted more than a century ago.

Between 1770 and 1830, when the missions were flourishing, wine was produced according to the needs of the Fathers. In the 1830s the Mexican government secularized the missions and these vineyards were mostly abandoned; but it had now been established that wine and brandy could be produced in the state.

New Vineyard Owners

The downfall of the missions and the resulting ruin of the vineyards and wine presses roughly marks the beginning of the modern industry. Before 1830, private holdings of vineyards were rare. As early as 1824, however, Joseph Chapman, one of the first Americans to settle in Los Angeles, planted four thousand vines. He was followed by Jean-Louis Vignes, a Frenchman from Bordeaux, who started his commercial venture in wine-mak-

ing approximately where the Los Angeles Union Station now stands, and by 1833 his successful wine and brandy were acclaimed throughout the state. As others followed him, viniculture expanded and within a generation became the principal industry of the Los Angeles district. Vignes was one of the first to advocate the planting of noble grape varieties. In the early 1830s, he imported cuttings of choice European vines which were delicately packed and shipped from France to Boston and then around Cape Horn to California. The long journey did not damage the vines; they were planted and some bore fruit and were used in Californian wines. Another of the newcomers to Los Angeles who built up, also in the 1830s, an extensive business in grapes and wines was William Wolfskill, a Kentucky trapper. By 1858, two years before his death, Wolfskill had increased his holding to 145 acres (about 58 hectares) with 55,000 vines, and he had a wine cellar with a capacity of 60,000 to 100,000 U.S. gallons (2,300 to 3,800 hectoliters, 50,000 to 83,000 imp. gallons).

Along with Vignes and Wolfskill, the names of Charles Kohler and John Frohling are important in this pioneering record. These two partners of German descent purchased a vineyard of 3,000 vines near Los Angeles, and at the same time they opened a wine shop in a San Francisco basement, the first of its kind, starting with 500 U.S. gallons (416 imp.) in the cellars; by 1862, they had 500,000 U.S. gallons (416,340 imp.) of wine and 20,000 U.S. gallons (16,650 imp.) of brandy in storage vaults.

The Mission grape was introduced into the earliest commercial vineyards by Chapman, Vignes, and other pioneers who planted it first in southern, then in northern California. The vine was a rough, prolific producer, lacking character and ill-suited to the production of table wines; yet for more than eighty years it dominated Californian viticulture.

During the 1850s, each wine district was known by the kinds of wines it manufactured. Port-type came from Los Angeles; hock, "sauterne," and claret from Sonoma and Napa; "sherry" came from Sonoma and El Dorado counties. One contemporary writer on wine said: "But we shall not probably make our best wines till we cease to strive for foreign imitations and strike out boldly for the manufacture of new kinds of wine, which will bring out the excellence with which nature has no doubt enriched the grape in this peculiar climate." This is a point on which California vintners are still being attacked.

European Plantings Increased by Colonel Haraszthy

The great transition from the use of the Mission grape to fine European varieties was brought about by a new settler in California twelve years or so after Jean-Louis Vignes's success with foreign cuttings from France. The extraordinary newcomer on the scene was Ágoston Haraszthy, a Hungarian nobleman, who has since been recognized as the father of Californian viticulture. The first considerable importation of foreign vines began early in 1851, when Colonel Haraszthy introduced a hundred cuttings and six choice rooted vines which he planted in San Diego. Among these was the famous Zinfandel, which was later to be used in the making of a very popular dry red wine. At first, growers clung to the Mission grape and were slow to buy the new variety, believing that the colonel was only speculating on the cuttings, but by 1878 extensive acreages were planted with Zinfandel. Colonel Haraszthy, convinced that the finest foreign grapes could grow in California, experimented with his cuttings to determine the regions of the state best suited to the different kinds. He also believed that, to get the best and quickest results, many types should be introduced.

In 1861, he was assigned by Governor John G. Downey to conduct a viticultural expedition in Europe to gather all varieties that might prove satisfactory. During an extensive three-month sojourn, Haraszthy and his son Árpád visited parts of France, Germany, Switzerland, Italy, and Spain. They selected some 100,000 cuttings from 300 varieties and all were shipped to California in the course of one year. Some of these were planted in his Buena Vista vineyard at Sonoma, but the majority were sold to growers from all parts of the state. In 1863, Haraszthy organized the Buena Vista Vinicultural Society, to which he conveyed his 6,000-acre (2,400-hectare) farm in Sonoma Valley with its 400 acres (160 hectares) in vines; it was his gift of a wide assortment of grapes and his continual research that stimulated the great modern expansion of the industry. Most of the superior varieties of imported vines during this period were planted around San Francisco Bay, which was one of the areas to benefit enormously from Haraszthy's practical demonstration that superior wine can come from non-irrigated grapes.

The great plunge into the wine industry attracted the inexperienced farmers and seekers after immediate profits, indifferent to the choice of vine varieties, soil, or location. The realization of Haraszthy's ideal was postponed and even today it has not been fully achieved. In the 1860s, Los Angeles, Anaheim, and Sonoma stood out as the three major wine and grape districts, possessing more vineyards than any others.

It was the discovery of gold which originally brought the prosperity of the liquid gold—the wine—to California. The wine market prospered in proportion to the gold discovered, and wine from Los Angeles was a luxury even to the Forty-niners. When the gold rush was over, wine prices dropped drastically and the state legislature was forced to keep viticulture alive by exempting new vineyards from taxes. In 1870, the future looked brighter: the new European grape varieties, Haraszthy's success, and the beneficial legislation of the state and national government led to expansion and national recognition. Unfortunately, the national economic crisis between 1875 and 1877 caused the wine industry to slump. The depression did, however, frighten away amateurs and speculators, and by 1878 those who continued in the industry were producing better wines from finer grape varieties. They survived not only the depression but the phylloxera pest as well.

The Coming of Phylloxera

The phylloxera, a burrowing plant louse fatal to the vine, had appeared in California before 1870; but in 1876 it became a real plague, which went on for at least three years, ravaging vineyards in Sonoma, Napa, Yolo, El Dorado, and Placer counties, as it had been devastating most of the vineyards of Europe. The French were the first to succeed in combating the disease, by grafting their *vinifera* vines onto phylloxera-resistant eastern American vines; soon Californian growers did the same.

The Beginning of Legislation

Valuable aid in stamping out phylloxera came from the California State Board of Viticultural Commissioners. This organization was formed in 1880 and did much to stabilize the industry. The commission helped growers to find the best climates and soils for each grape variety and gave vital assistance in the control of vine maladies. An elaborate experimental grape-growing station under the College of Agriculture of the University of California also contributed to the progress of the industry. The college has continued the research and teaching of viticulture and oenology to this day; in recent times it was for many years under the capable guidance of Professors Emeritus A. H. Winkler, Maynard A. Amerine, and Harold Berg, and now under Professor A. Dinsmoor Webb, all of them noted researchers who have earned the respect of oenologists and viticulturists throughout the world. The commission sponsored state control laws which established California's earliest standards of quality in wine.

Between 1880 and 1895 viticultural ideas, conditions, and policies within the state were transformed. Tariff, taxation, and the fight for wine control laws were important matters to every grower and vintner in California. Before the turn of the century, the wines were taking prizes in international exhibitions, and California was competing with Europe for world markets.

Between 1900 and 1915 there was a further increase both in cultivation and in sales—but movements toward total abstinence were growing, and when the Prohibition law was passed, viticulture in California suffered a severe blow, and many of the new wineries stopped functioning. Production dropped from about 50 million U.S. gallons (1.9 million hectoliters, 42 million imp. gallons) of wine in 1912 to approximately 27 million U.S. gallons (1 million hectoliters, 22 million imp. gallons) in 1919. But Prohibition was not altogether disastrous: the law still allowed wine to be used for medicinal and sacramental purposes, thus enabling a part of the commercial wine industry to remain. When Prohibition was finally acknowledged a failure, and the Volstead Act was repealed in December 1933, those growers who had not given up were able to resume full-scale production almost immediately. For a time, the demand for wine far exceeded the supply, prices were exaggerated, and inferior wines were sold. Not until 1938 could the market be said to have settled down.

In 1934, standards of quality were laid down for Californian wines by the Californian Department of Public Health and the Federal Government. Federal regulations safeguarded the controls which ruled that all the wine, wherever sold, must meet Californian requirements.

Perhaps the most important step in the whole history of

Californian wines has been the effort of the vintners to improve varietal plantings and to produce good varietal wines—named after the grape variety (Cabernet Sauvignon, Chardonnay, etc.) from which they are produced. Unfortunately, the attempt to eliminate the Mission grape in the cooler regions and cut down the percentage of Alicante-Bouschet has not been entirely successful. The industry has never completely recovered from Prohibition. At that time the demand was for tough-skinned, very productive grapes which could be shipped to eastern markets. A vine of such high quality as the Cabernet Sauvignon, producing scarcely more than 3 to 6 tons to the acre (about 50 to 100 hectoliters per hectare), was overlooked in favor of Carignane and Alicante-Bouschet, which would yield as much as 15 short tons to the acre (almost 250 hectoliters per hectare). These impaired the quality of post-repeal wines and are still largely the cause of much legitimate criticism. Even today, in some years 40% to 50% of the grapes used for wine in California are varieties suited only for use as raisins or table grapes.

In general, however, the story since repeal has been one of improvement, as there have been numerous plantings of fine varietals which can produce the best white and red table wines. Producers who became known in the 1940s and 1950s included Louis M. Martini, the dean of Napa Valley wine-growers; Herman Wente; John Daniel, Jr., of Inglenook; Madame de Latour of Beaulieu Vineyards; and Chaffee Hall of Hallcrest. Peter Mondavi of Charles Krug, and Robert Mondavi; Martin Ray, who at one time owned Paul Masson Vineyards; and Louis Benoist, the former owner of Almadén, all brought skill and ingenuity to winegrowing in California. They likewise did much to maintain the quality of American wines, in spite of the pressure of "mass production." And the late Frank Schoonmaker, a New York wine merchant who, with the help of the author, introduced fine American wines east of the Rockies, is another among those who have fought for quality over quantity in the United States.

There are some 450 bonded wineries in California, but aside from a few dozen very large wineries, the greater percentage tend to produce and sell rather limited quantities of varietal wines, a laudable trend. It is a continually changing scene, especially in recent years, with the constant appearance of new wineries and wines. Some vineyards have become too commercialized, sacrificing quality for quantity. Paul Masson and Cresta Blanca, which formerly produced excellent wines, are examples of this, although they are now making a notable effort to achieve a higher standard. Only a few select wineries insist that Californian wines should be called by original Californian names; for this reason, the late Paul Rossigneux (president of Napa and Sonoma Wine Company), Robert Mondavi, and the late Carl Wente have always been respected for their uncompromisingly high standards.

Today Californian growers are faced with the task of getting the industry to the point at which it can compete on equal terms with the European market—and this can only be done with varietal wines, not with imitations. Sherry comes from Spain, Port from Portugal, Burgundy,

Chablis, and Sauternes from France, and to name a Californian wine for one of these is to admit its inferiority. Good grapes, aided by suitable soil and climate, will produce good wines. The planting of fine varietals in Californian soil certainly should result in wine worthy of being judged on its own merit.

RECENT DEVELOPMENTS

In California today grapes and wine have produced a billion-dollar industry. Plantings of grapes increased by more than 150% from 1970 to 1980. New grape-growing regions have been prepared to take the place of those areas lost to the spreading cities of the most populous state in the nation. The time may come when one-sixth of the vast acreage devoted to agriculture in the state will be vineyards. But today the total land area planted in grapes is approximately 675,000 acres (270,000 hectares), of which roughly half, or 325,000 acres, is planted exclusively in wine grapes. The development of winery facilities has also been great: millions of dollars are spent annually for new buildings, equipment, and research.

The expansion of the industry has not affected the range of size of the wineries in California; the very largest still exist side by side with the many small ones. The several producing great volume make more than 65% of California wines. Slightly smaller than these giants are three or four companies which also market a wide selection of wines across the country. The wineries which have become famous in the past ten years are primarily medium-sized with products of average price but above-average quality. It is from these producers and some of the small wineries that the very good California wines come. Though the range of varietal table wines produced by the state's wineries now can be bought in most metropolitan centers around the country, some of the best wines remain known—and indeed available—only in California.

Since the mid-1960s the California wine boom has attracted large corporations, huge food and beverage companies, and financial institutions. The investors include Heublein, Inc., which purchased United Vintners, (Inglenook, Italian Swiss Colony, Lejon, and Beaulieu); National Distillers, which bought Almadén Vineyards in 1967; Seagrams, which has expanded its Paul Masson property; Coca-Cola of Atlanta, which bought Sterling Vineyards and Monterey Vineyards in 1978; and Nestlé, the Swiss processors of chocolate, coffee, and milk products, which purchased Beringer Bros. in the early 1970s. And in 1973, Moët-Hennessy, a French Champagne and Cognac conglomerate, founded Domaine Chandon Vineyards. The company acquired 800 acres (320 hectares) of vineyard land in Napa and Sonoma counties and by 1975 was producing sparkling wines by the traditional *méthode champenoise*. Before the vineyards came into production Domaine Chandon bought grapes from local growers. Piper Heidsieck, another French Champagne producer, established a joint venture with Sonoma Vineyards in 1980. Several German companies have acquired California properties as well. These include the Peter Eckes Co., which bought Franciscan Vineyards in 1979, and the A. Racke Co., producers of Kupferberg sparkling wines, which bought Buena Vista Vineyards in 1979. In 1974, prices for the best wines began to fall as more good grape vine varieties came into production. In 1976 these prices dropped drastically, down 60% from 1971, but in 1978, Chardonnay prices broke all records.

Plantings

In 1969, after several years of decline, the number of new acres planted only in wine grapes began a steady rise. In 1972, 48,000 acres (19,000 hectares) were planted, more than for the entire period 1965-1970. With even greater acreage added in 1973 and 1974, there were more than 322,000 acres (129,000 hectares) of wine vineyards by the beginning of 1975. By 1980, 70,000 additional acres (28,000 hectares) were under cultivation, making the total vineyard area of California nearly equal to that of Bordeaux and Burgundy combined.

More significant than the fantastic increase in the sheer acreage of the vineyards is the trend for planting better wine grapes. For example, in 1959 the noble Cabernet Sauvignon grape of Bordeaux covered only 630 acres (250 hectares); by 1979 this figure increased to 27,000 acres (10,000 hectares). Chardonnay and Pinot Noir plantings have grown proportionately. Yet in spite of these gains, and those made by good but less famous wine grapes, the lamentable Thompson Seedless table grape makes more Californian wine than any other variety.

Much of the planting of both great and good wine stocks has been carried out in the newly developed areas of the state. San Benito, Monterey, San Luis Obispo, Lake, Mendocino, Amador, and Santa Barbara counties are some of the places into which vineyards have spread or have been expanded. Almadén Vineyards pioneered grape-growing in the San Benito area, including Paicines and Cienega. Paul Masson, Mirassou, and Wente Bros. started most of the Monterey vineyards in the 1960s. In San Luis Obispo vineyards have spread over 4,500 acres (1,800 hectares) in less than seven years. Wines are produced there from Cabernet Sauvignon, Zinfandel, Sauvignon Blanc, Chardonnay, Merlot, Pinot Blanc, and Gewürztraminer. Most of the vines grow near Paso Robles and the town of San Luis Obispo. Farther south in the state, close to Riverside and Temecula, these same good plants, plus Johannisberg Riesling and Chenin Blanc, thrive in a climate cooled by ocean breezes. Another southern California venture has begun in Kern County, 100 miles (160 kilometers) north of the city of Los Angeles. Both here and in the southern Salinas Valley in Monterey, many modern sprinkler and irrigation techniques are practiced. And at the opposite end of the state, beyond the famous North Coast vineyards, Zinfandel vines have been planted on the foothills near Mount Lassen.

Research

For almost a century, new plantings and the other aspects of wine-making in the state have been closely guided by the University of California. Its specialists have advised vintners in Australia, New Zealand, Spain, Portugal, Italy, Yugoslavia, Argentina, Brazil, Chile, South Africa, and even Japan. Students come to the branch campus at Davis, 70 miles (110 kilometers) northeast of San Francisco, to study viticulture and oenology or to do graduate work and research. Many of the projects are funded by California wine companies. The close liaison with local producers began in 1875, when the newly established university appointed E. W. Hilgard as Professor of Agriculture. Five years later the legislature decided to create a department for instruction in "the arts and sciences pertaining to viticulture, the theory and practice of fermentation, distillation, and rectification, and the management of cellars . . . to be illustrated by practical experiments."

Three internationally known scientists of the university have played major roles in improving Californian wines over the past three decades: H. P. Olmo, a plant pathologist and geneticist; Maynard A. Amerine, a world-traveling oenologist, researcher and writer; and Harold W. Berg, a consultant in wine problems whose advice has aided the wine-growers of many countries. Much of Dr. Olmo's work is readily seen in California vineyards, for he has spent forty years breeding new cross strains which will produce sound wine in many parts of the state. Dr. Amerine, respected around the world, has been the president of the American Society of Oenologists, has won awards from many foreign wine organizations, has written several fine books on wine and wine-making, and, most important, has done much to improve the quality of California wines. Professor Berg, recently retired chairman of the wine faculty, has done valuable research in grape processing, wine stabilization, and ageing.

One of the achievements of the men at Davis was the classification of the California viticultural districts into five temperature zones. In the 1930s Professors A. J. Winkler and Maynard Amerine studied the relation between climate and the quality of wine produced from different grape varieties in the various regions of California. They found that temperature is one of the most important climatic factors affecting the successful cultivation of wine grapes and that the summation of daily degree readings is of significant value for predicting the best varieties to be grown in any district. Their heat summation concept developed from the total of mean daily temperatures above 50°F. (10°C.) for the days from April 1 through October 31. 50°F. is the temperature above which most vine-shoot growth occurs; the time period corresponds to the vine-growing season. Thus, a day with an average temperature of 65°F is given a heat summation value of 15 "degree-days." Five climate regions were then defined according to the totals for the season:

Region I—less than 2,500 degree-days
Region II—2,501 to 3,000 degree-days
Region III—3,001 to 3,500 degree-days
Region IV—3,501 to 4,000 degree-days
Region V—more than 4,000 degree-days

Knowing the temperature region of his vineyard, a grape-grower can make a general prediction as to which vines will prove most successful. Where the total is less than 1,800 degree-days, most grape varieties will not ripen sufficiently to produce wine with the legal minimum degree of alcohol. In warmer districts the grapes mature quickly and yield huge crops, but the acidity, color, and aroma are too low to make good dry table wines. Dessert or fortified wine requiring much natural grape sugar and common table wines are made in these hot sections of the state. In the cooler vineyards, where a vine can bear only a limited crop, the fruit can ripen slowly, retain its high acidity, and concentrate those elements of color and aroma which make fine table wines.

The premium wine districts of California fall in Regions I, II, and III, while Regions IV and V produce mostly table grapes or the bulk and dessert—fortified—wines already mentioned. These zones are abstract temperature regions and do not necessarily define continuous or similar geographical areas. In the long and flat Central Valley both the northern and southern ends are Region V, yet the middle section is Region IV. In the foothills and coastal valleys distinct microclimates are created by the mountains. Locations with different temperature ratings may be miles apart, or separated only by a few hundred feet on the same hillside. Most of the Napa Valley, for example, is Region III, with a few scattered sections rated I and II. But the nearby Peachland section of Sonoma County is nearly all Region I.

Heat summation data are a useful tool for giving viticulturalists a rough idea of the vines which may be grown successfully in untried parts of the state. The concept can also help determine the approximate rate at which the fruit will ripen. Talk of the five temperature zones has become a part of everyday life in California wine districts. But since such information is only one simple expression of a single factor affecting vineyard climate, too much importance should not be placed on it. And though important, climate is still only one of the variables in the production of fine wine. Some growers in new areas cite a Region I, II, or III rating as synonymous with high grape quality. Such a thermal classification is perhaps a necessary, but certainly not a sufficient, condition for producing good wine grapes. The experience gained through trial and error—in a company with modern techniques—will in the end establish the spots where good wines can be made.

Technological Advances

Mechanical grape harvesting was born in California and plays a more important part in the industry there than in any other fine wine district in the world. The practice is most common in the great flat valleys and basins of the interior, where mainly bulk wines are made; but machine picking is used in some parts of the coastal counties, where the best California wines originate. The giant harvesters are of two types: one uses suction to pull the fruit, along with most of the leaves, from the vine, while the other shakes the plant and catches the falling grapes. Where harvesting is done by machine, oenologists think it vital that the grapes be crushed as soon as possible after picking. In more than one vineyard operation, the machines include apparatus for crushing and stemming the grapes in the field. Some have spotlights for work at night.

Another machine, though smaller than those that harvest the fruit, has been developed to perform another time-consuming human chore. To speed up production of sparkling wines at Korbel and other *méthode champenoise* champagne cellars, a new device gently shakes many bottles at once to dislodge the tartrate sediment in the bottle neck for removal. Taittinger and others in the Champagne district in France are converting to this method.

California viticulturalists have improved their techniques of irrigation and have invented new ones for using water in frost protection. The most common device used previously to counter the disastrous spring frosts—which can destroy 75% of the crop—was the old-fashioned smudge pot. It has been replaced in many vineyards by sprinklers which spray the vines during the early morning hours, when the cold takes its heaviest toll. The water on the tender leaves and shoots will freeze at 32°F. and in the process give off a modicum of heat that protects the vine. In addition, the mist in the air prevents the air temperature from falling too low. Since such systems need at least 50 gallons per minute for each acre to be protected, storage ponds and reservoirs have been dammed to guarantee the supply. But as the call is raised to leave the streams and valleys of many counties in a natural state, it has often been difficult for growers to find the water for frost protection programs.

Just as water for frost protection is not needed in every part of California, neither is it required for irrigation all across the state. In the North Coast districts, where annual rainfall is 30 to 40 inches, many vines are not irrigated, while others may have one deep soaking during the hottest part of the summer. For these plantations irrigation and frost control is often supplied by one sprinkler system. Other parts of the state have climates not so fortunate as some of the areas north of San Francisco. In the San Joaquin Valley, for instance, as much as three acre-feet (43,560 cubic feet) of water are needed each season to ensure good wine grape crops. In those places where it is required, the method of irrigation will vary. The new "drip" plan from Israel waters the plants with a light trickle of water from ground-level pipes. And those same sprinkler systems popular for frost control and irrigation in cooler parts of the state are also employed in the hot climates, where the fine mists help to keep temperatures down when the scorching sun may burn the grapes.

Since supplies of water for any purpose may be more expensive in the future, it is fortunate that not all of the new measures for warding off the spring and even autumn cold rely on it. Wind-machines are one such development. Ground-level models simply circulate the air over the vines to keep the temperature from dropping. Those mounted on towers mix the cool lower-level air with warmer air from above. Another new device is a sophisticated combination of the wind-machine and the smudge pot. Its propane heater first warms the air, then its blowers distribute the hot gas through the vine rows in a series of inflatable plastic ducts.

GRAPE VARIETIES

With the demand for good table wines increasing, more good varieties of *Vitis vinifera* are being planted in California than at any previous time. Unfortunately, however, some growers seeking fast profits from the high prices paid for the very best grapes are planting Cabernet Sauvignon, Pinot Noir, or other fine varieties in districts with climates much too hot for these vines to produce properly.

The largest single expansion of varietal plantings has occurred in Monterey, the lower end of the North Coast wine region. In the hot interior valleys such as the San Joaquin, there have also been improvements in the quality of the grapes. The attempt is being made to reduce the acreage of Thompson Seedless and other table grapes used regrettably for wine, in favor of sound *vinifera* or cross varieties.

The warmest parts of the state will never produce great wine from the classic European varieties, but with carefully selected vines—especially some of the crosses bred by the researchers at Davis—the average quality of much of the bulk wine can be raised.

As good wine grapes became more available, many California wines took on the name of the grape from which they were made. A "varietal wine," then, is one whose name is the same as the grape which makes up more than one-half of the wine. A law to come into effect in 1983 will prohibit a California wine from bearing a grape, or varietal, name unless the specified variety accounts for at least 75% of the wine. With the present rush to make varietal wines, it would be desirable to have some sort of enforcement for this statute. Over fifty wines with grape names are produced by hundreds of wineries around the state.

Many of these are experimental vintages, and even those named for one of the noble wine grapes may not be wines of distinction. But when made with skill and labeled in good faith by a reputable vintner, a wine called perhaps "Napa Valley Cabernet" or "Sonoma Pinot Noir" is a vast improvement over one named for some famous European wine district.

If California is to join the great quality wine-producing areas of the world—France, Germany, Italy, Spain—then good laws going beyond the "51%" rule must be adopted and enforced. No region on earth makes fine wine without protecting both the wine and the consumer with intelligent regulations. Certainly California aims to produce some great wine, but so far none of the attendant laws has been forthcoming. The good and conscientious wine-makers of Napa, Sonoma, and the other better districts want strict control not only of grape variety but of place-name as well. The North Coast valleys are still a long way from being divided in the remarkably precise manner of the French Appellation Contrôlée, but the Bureau of Alcohol, Tobacco and Firearms has held hearings that will eventually result in a similar system.

A few of the red-wine grape varieties successfully planted in California are the Cabernet Sauvignon (sometimes referred to simply as Cabernet but not to be confused with the Cabernet Franc), Pinot Noir, Gamay Beaujolais, Grenache, Barbera, and Zinfandel. Some of the recommended white grape varieties are the Chardonnay, Sauvignon Blanc, Sémillon, Chenin Blanc, Pinot Blanc, White or Johannisberg Riesling, Sylvaner or Franken Riesling (sometimes called Riesling), Gewürztraminer and Traminer (also called the Red Traminer).

Leading Red Wine Grapes

Cabernet Sauvignon. Of the large number of red wine grape varieties, very few have been recommended for planting in California. Of those that have passed rigorous tests, the Cabernet Sauvignon is still the most valuable: it is the best adapted to the cooler parts of the coastal valleys and usually ripens about mid-season; it matures more slowly than the same variety in the Bordeaux region and produces a fuller, heavier wine. In California, the Cabernet lacks bouquet and finesse but has produced, in limited quantities, some remarkably great wines which can compare with some of the better red wines anywhere in the world. The Cabernet Sauvignon from northern California has outproduced in terms of quality some of the best red wines of Italy, Spain, and Portugal and attains an even fuller wine than those made from the same variety in Chile. In the suitable coastal regions it gives a wine of pronounced varietal flavor and bouquet, high acidity, and good color, holding its own with some of the better Bordeaux. Cabernet Sauvignon attains its highest quality after ageing; but only recently have most Californian growers come to realize that their table wines improve with bottle age—and so more matured Cabernet Sauvignons are now appearing on the market. As the price goes up, the value goes down. As stated before, as of 1983 varietal wines can bear the name of a grape on the label provided that the wine is made of a minimum 75% of that particular variety. Producers of better varietal wines use a greater percentage of the specified grape, usually 75% to 100% and, as in France, the rest of a blend is a combination of complementary grapes such as Merlot or Malbec. A 100% Cabernet Sauvignon wine would be an oddity in Bordeaux; and 75%—such as at Château Mouton-Rothschild—is considered very high.

Pinot Noir. The outstanding red grape of Burgundy and major grape in the making of Champagne. In California, the Pinot Noir has the reputation of being a difficult varietal. It ripens early and is not always easy in fermentation and ageing. Though some very good wines have been made, they have not yet threatened the supremacy of the better Burgundies. Research on clonal variants better adapted to California conditions has brought some improvement. On the whole, they tend to be lightish, little suited to long ageing. The better California Pinot Noirs come from the cooler climates of southern Napa, Sonoma, Monterey, Mendocino, and Lake counties.

Gamay and Gamay Beaujolais. The first, confusingly, is the true Gamay of the Beaujolais region of France; when grown in the Napa Valley it goes by the name of Napa Gamay. The Gamay Beaujolais is not a true Gamay, but a clonal variant of the Pinot Noir, which may in fact be sold as a Pinot Noir if the winery so chooses. Though made from genetically distinct grapes, wines sold as Gamay (or Napa Gamay) and Gamay Beaujolais will be similarly light, fruity wines, successfully trading on the Beaujolais image of being short-vatted and easy drinking. They are generally low in tannin and high in grape-y aroma. In the parts of the Napa Valley where the late-ripening variety of the Gamay (the Napa Gamay) is produced, it differs from the Gamay Beaujolais in flavor and aroma. The Napa Gamay is also known by its French name, Gamay Noir.

Grenache. The Grenache is a good producer, strong and resistant to disease—a much-sought-after variety. The grape, which is successful in the making of Tavel rosé in the Rhône Valley, is often used for rosés in California also, because of its pinkish color. The Grenache Rosé from the Almadén Vineyards in the Santa Clara Valley was the first and most popular of its kind.

Barbera. In Italy, Barbera at its best is sometimes likened to the Nebbiolo and ages almost as well; in California, it is a high-acid variety of only average vigor and production. Blending is not recommended, but with ageing and special care Barbera may yet yield a wine comparable with some of those in Piedmont. It does best in the coastal valleys and the intermediate Central Valley region, where it produces a full-bodied, honest wine.

Zinfandel. This is the most widely planted good red-grape variety in California; its exact origin is unknown, and it is not grown extensively in any other country. It is subject to mildew, and any excessive humidity or irrigation may lead to rotting; generally it is harvested early and finds a growing place in practically all the regions of California, although the best dry wines of this variety are made in the cooler areas. Zinfandel, a very productive variety, produces some pleasant, straightforward wines, and its multiple appeal of bouquet, good color, and wholesome aroma and flavor account for its popularity. A well-made Zinfandel from a good winery is superior to many of the Cabernet Sauvignons found on the market today. This grape variety needs greater recognition and respect than it now has outside California. A red, a white, and a rosé wine can be made from the Zinfandel. This varietal is taking its well-deserved place as the pride of California.

Ruby Cabernet. This is a new hybrid developed by Dr. Olmo of the California Agricultural Experimental Station in Davis. It is a good producer with color and a high acid content.

Grignolino. This grape is one of the several Californian varieties which are native to Piedmont in Italy. It produces a highly characteristic wine ranging from orange-pink to orange-red in color, and it is sometimes bottled as a natural rosé. Grignolino has a unique aroma and an exceptionally high acid content and should be aged several years. The largest plantings of this grape are in Santa Clara and Cucamonga.

Less Important Red Wine Grapes

Some of the other red wine varieties that produce heavily but are not fine grapes are Alicante-Bouschet, Carignane, Petite-Sirah, and Rubired. The Alicante-Bouschet is a large producer of common wine; unfortunately, too much is still grown in California and finds its way into the so-called burgundies, clarets, and chiantis of the middle and southern regions. Carignane, which is not bad in a

good soil, is heavily produced in the warmer regions and often used in blending. Petite-Sirah, a superior variety, is favored in Napa as well as in Sonoma, Monterey, Kern, and San Joaquin counties.

Leading White Wine Grapes

Fine dry white wine varieties are found mainly in the northern coastal and cooler regions of California.

Chardonnay. This is not a large producer generally; it is the grape of French Chablis and other white Burgundies—among them, Meursault and Montrachet. The Chardonnay has all the virtues needed to produce good wine. It ripens well, particularly in the cooler regions, and attains an excellent balance of sugar and acid. Because it adapts itself so well in the cooler parts of Napa, San Benito, Sonoma, and Monterey, it makes the finest white wines of California. The cultivation of the Chardonnay is not an easy task, but the results seem to be worth the trouble. It produced a blander wine in California by not having the richness it has in France; however, the style of recent Chardonnays has been greatly enhanced through the use of small oak cooperage.

Sauvignon Blanc. This is the principal grape variety used in the production of the white Graves of France, and, with the Sémillon, it is the base of all the great Sauternes. It is used extensively in France for Pouilly-Fumé and Sancerre. In California, this variety thrives particularly well in the coastal regions. As in the French Sauternes, the Sauvignon Blanc is sometimes blended with Sémillon—plus Muscadelle of Bordelais—to produce a California-type sauterne. The variety is finding its way alone into bottles from small wineries as good-quality dry wine.

The Sauvignon Blanc should not be confused with the Sauvignon Vert (Colombard), an inferior grape variety.

Sémillon. This is another variety best suited to the North Coast region. During the late seventies, *botrytis* vinification suddenly became a wine-maker's fad. (This applies, with the possible exception of Phelps and Chateau St. Jean, to Riesling and Gewürztraminer grapes as well.) The expensive and laborious process is not justified when the wines are compared to fine Barsacs, Sauternes, and Anjous of France, and Trockenbeerenauslesen wines of Germany. (This is an excellent reason why wines made with Sémillon from California should not be called sauternes. Sémillon is one of the world's finest grapes and is quite capable of making an original dry or sweet wine in California.)

Pinot Blanc. This is the grape variety used in the making of many white French Burgundies and a few Alsatian wines. In California, it seems to preserve its ancestral virtues, although until now it has not been widely planted. It has a good quality, and is a strong, disease-resistant grape with a distinction of its own. Its productivity is rather higher than that of the Pinot Chardonnay, but it rarely exceeds 3 short tons (2.68 long tons) per acre. The Pinot Blanc has often been confused with the Chardonnay, but many experts consider the Chardonnay an entirely different variety and not a true Pinot at all. Tests have shown that the Pinot Blanc is beginning to do well in the slightly warmer regions as well as in the cooler districts.

Chenin Blanc. This variety was also known as the White Pinot and should not be confused with Pinot Blanc. The Chenin Blanc produces and adapts well to regions varying from slightly cool to warm. In France this variety, known as Pineau de la Loire as well as Chenin Blanc, produces delightful white wines of which Vouvray and Saumur are the most familiar. It is above average in quality but lacks the distinction of Pinot Blanc. Chenin Blanc is versatile, since it sometimes produces a fresh, light, fruity wine, slightly sparkling, and at other times it is apt to make a much sweeter wine, according to the whim of the vintner. The Chenin Blanc, as it is commonly called in California, has become quite popular in the past few years. It is now one of the most widely planted better white wine grapes.

Riesling. The Riesling, or White Riesling, or Johannisberg Riesling, is responsible for the outstanding reputation of all the famous wines of the Rhine and Mosel valleys as well as most of the fine Alsatian wines. It performs at its best under relatively cool conditions, which California's somewhat Mediterranean climate cannot quite give. The Riesling is one of the finest grape varieties in the world and produces throughout Europe (except in the Mediterranean region) a wine of excellent quality. The cooler parts of California produce a wine above average but lacking the balance and delicacy of the Riesling wines of Europe. In the North Coast region of California, it is a large producer and ripens late in the season.

Sylvaner. In California this variety is also known as the Franken Riesling. In the valleys of the Rhine and the Mosel, and in Alsace, it is grown only where the Riesling does not produce well. Its wine is generally of good character and balance and above average in California where it does better than the Riesling (Johannisberg Riesling) when planted in a slightly cool to warm district. Sylvaner is a delicate, early-maturing grape with a certain distinction of character and a good balance of sugar and acid. Light and dry, the wine is usually drunk when it is quite young.

Gewürztraminer. The "Red" Traminer is often favorably compared to the very best Rieslings when grown in the better parts of Alsace and the Jura Mountains in France. In the cooler parts of California it produces a wine with a distinctive delicate aroma and proper balance. It is also called the Red Traminer because of the red blush of the ripening grape. The Krug Winery of St. Helena in Napa Valley produced a small quantity of good Traminer wine. It has an unmistakable bouquet and spiciness. Stony Hill, Château St. Jean, and Hacienda also make good quality Gewürztraminers.

Less Important White Wine Grapes

Some of the other dry white wine grape varieties, some of which are widely produced but lacking in distinction, are the French Colombard, Folle Blanche, Burger, and Sauvignon Vert.

The Burger is extensively planted in California, chiefly for its high production and a supposedly neutral character which allows it to "stretch" other wines of superior quality. The Sauvignon Vert, another coarse heavy grape, is frequently substituted in blending for the Sauvignon Blanc. The Sauvignon Vert is sometimes called Colombard, which should not be confused with the French Colombard, a vigorous, highly productive grape of high acid content used for blending in the Chablis-type and Rhine-type of Californian wines. Sauvignon Vert, French Colombard, Burger, and Folle Blanche are favorably grown in the warmer inland valley regions.

Crosses

Just over 40,000 acres (14,500 hectares) are now planted in crosses, and these grapes represent an important aspect of future wine production in California. In accepting the American Oenologists' Society Award of Merit in 1973, Dr. Olmo of the Davis school declared: "There is great need for California to make wines that are uniquely Californian in origin. We cannot hope to duplicate the famous wines of other countries merely because we have imported their varieties and use their winemaking methods. Our soils and our climatic areas are not the same. But we can and should produce wines that are as good as those produced elsewhere—by the creation of new varieties that will give a product of high quality with genuine distinctness of type. The first step is to eliminate some of the defects of varieties that we already have. In the future we should not have to rely on varieties that were selected by the French, or the Germans, or the Italians, and have been found by centuries of experience to be suitable in certain regions. Their regions are not ours, and rather than imitate their types, the time will come to build our industry on varieties developed in and bred for California localities."

Two of the more important crosses developed at the University of California at Davis have been the white wine grape Emerald Riesling and the red Ruby Cabernet. At least three other promising crosses have been successfully grown—Rubired, Royalty, and the newest, a wine grape named Carnelian. The Ruby Cabernet is a cross between Cabernet Sauvignon and the tremendously productive Carignane. It produces well and tolerates warmer climates. The grape has some of the characteristics of Cabernet Sauvignon, although the wine will never achieve its status or distinction. The Emerald Riesling, a cross between the White or Johannisberg Riesling and the Muscadelle de Bordelais, yields a white table wine with some of the Riesling characteristics. Another hope for future sound wines is Professor Olmo's newest hybrid, the Carnelian. This cross of the Cabernet Sauvignon, Carignane, and Grenache produced a grape which gives high yields, makes reasonable wine, and grows well in warmer regions. Carnelian may yield as many as 11 tons to the acre (about 180 hectoliters per hectare). Wines produced from it have been medium-red in color, and light in body with good balance; they can be enjoyed young but mature well. Rubired and Royalty resulted from the need for grapes with good color and acidity and the ability to resist powdery mildew. A nineteenth-century cross called Alicante Gazin was crossed with the Port grape Tinta

Cão; the result was the Rubired. Rubired crossed with a little-known plant called Trousseau produced Royalty. Both were introduced in 1964. Of all the California crosses, Emerald Riesling and Ruby Cabernet are perhaps the most successful.

APERITIFS

Aperitifs or appetizer wines are technically classed as dessert wines because of their alcoholic content but are classified separately because they are drunk before instead of after meals. The two main aperitifs in California, as elsewhere, are sherry and vermouth. Californian sherry should, of course, not be confused with the real Sherry, which can come only from the region of Jerez de la Frontera in Spain.

Californian "Sherry"

The sherry-type wine has the characteristic nutty flavor obtained through processes of ageing and warm temperatures. In California many different regions are used to make these wines. The best quality grape for the purpose is the Palomino or Napa Golden Chasselas (not a real Chasselas). Authentic Spanish Sherry is made almost entirely from the Palomino. This grape has become a varietal in California and is used for the best sherries, although many growers continue with such varieties as the Flame Tokay, Mission, Thompson Seedless, and Fehér Szagos, which produce lesser wines of the type.

Three styles of sherry-type wines are produced in California: a dry aperitif with a sugar content of from 0% to 2.5%; Californian sherry, with 2.5% to 4% of sugar; and a sweet cream sherry with over 4%. All these wines range from not less than 17% of alcohol to about 20%.

Most of the Californian sherry is made by heating the fortified wine in wood, concrete, or steel tanks from two to six months, at temperatures varying from 120° to 140°F. (49° to 60°C.). It is then stored in small oak barrels, to be aged for six months—or longer, in the case of better-quality wines.

Scarcely any sherry is made by the Spanish "flor" method, although some is produced for blending purposes by a newly developed method known as the "submerged flor" technique. One exception is the Llords and Elwood winery near San José, where an authentic outdoor solera system is used to make a "flor" sherry.

Californian Vermouth

There are two kinds of vermouth—the dry French type (pale amber) and the sweet Italian type (dark amber). The first step in the making of Californian vermouth is to select and age neutral white wines. These are then flavored with herbs and other aromatic substances (usually imported) which are introduced into the wine—or an infusion of aromatic herbs is added to the basic fortified wine and the mixture is aged in barrel. Vermouth producers all have their secret formulas containing sometimes as many as fifty different herbs, roots, seeds, barks, flowers, dried fruit, wormwood, etc. Vermouth ranges

from 15% to 20% in alcoholic content—a very light type has recently become popular in California and elsewhere in the United States.

DESSERT WINES

California dessert wines have an alcoholic content of not less than 18% and range from medium-sweet to sweet. There are four distinct Californian dessert wines—"port," "white port," muscatel, and "tokay." Unfortunately, place-name controls are particularly negligent where Californian dessert wines are concerned; but there are a few bearing such varietal names as Muscat de Frontignan and Tinta port varieties which are usually of better quality. The hot interior valleys produce the best grapes for dessert wines.

Californian "Port"

This is made from many grapes—but rarely from those which go into genuine Port. Carignane, Petite-Sirah, Trousseau, Grenache, Valdepeñas, and Zinfandel are most commonly used in Californian ports; while Alicante-Bouschet, Alicante Gazin, and Salvador are added, for the dark color they contribute in blending. Californian port is usually deep red in color, fruity, and heavy-bodied. It ranges from 8% to 14% natural grape sugar content and is usually sweeter and darker in color than the Ports from Portugal. There is also a lighter-colored, lighter-bodied wine known as tawny port.

Californian ports, like other dessert wines, thrive best in the warmer regions. The better quality wines are made with Tinta Madeira, Tinta Cão, and Touriga (choice Portuguese grape varieties). A great deal of credit must go to the Ficklin Vineyards of Madera in Madera County, which is producing the best port-type wine in California, using the methods employed in Portugal (see Port).

White "Port"

This variety is made from such grapes as the Thompson Seedless, or any of the standard, light-colored wine grapes. It is sweet and straw-colored.

Californian Muscatel

This is a dessert wine made from Muscat grapes (which are used also for a light Muscat white table wine). Muscatels, which have an unmistakable aroma and flavor, are, on the whole, a drug on the market and are only rarely agreeable wines. They range in color from golden and dark amber to red, and in sweetness from 10% to 15% natural grape sugar content. These muscatels are sometimes sold as cheap substitutes for whiskey, especially in monopoly state stores.

The better varieties of grapes are used in the making of Muscats as table wines, which can be considered as finer wines. The white grapes used are the Muscat de Frontignan (sometimes called Muscat Canelli in California) and Malvasia Bianca, while the red grapes are Malvasia and Aleatico.

Most Muscatels are made from the Muscat of Alexandria (also a table grape) and have a golden color, but there are at least seven other Muscat grape varieties used in California. In the Central and San Joaquin valleys, the Black Muscat or Muscat Hamburg is grown. Californian Muscat varieties find their proper home in the warm climate of the San Joaquin Valley region, where the grapes attain a high sugar content.

Californian "Tokay"

This is made by blending other dessert wines, such as port, angelica, and sherry and bears no relationship to Hungarian Tokay wines, nor is it necessarily made from the Flame Tokay, a table grape planted extensively in the Lodi area. This tokay ranges from 7% to 10% natural grape sugar content, and has a slightly nutty flavor reminiscent of Sherry. The color of Californian tokay is amber-pink; it is a wine of less than average quality and is the lowest in production of the better-known dessert wines.

Angelica is an original Californian wine and is not one for Californians to be proud of. This white dessert wine, very sweet and straw-colored and blended with brandy, is more of a cordial than a wine. The Mission grape and the cheaper Grenache—the Spanish variety—go into the making of the highly fruity Angelica. "Winos" of the post-Repeal Era popularized Angelica, which is rarely seen today.

Aleatico wine has the spicy, fruity flavor of the Aleatico grape and resembles the red muscatels. There is also an Aleatico table wine, inferior and rarely to be found.

"Malaga" in California is just a name referring to a cordial wine of no particular distinction, and quite unconnected with the Málaga of Spain.

Berry wines in California have the distinct taste of the berries used and include such sweet, fruity wines as blackberry, raspberry, etc. The Sacramento Valley area near Elk Grove is a noted berry-wine-producing region.

Other dessert wines include Californian grenache, (made from the Grenache grape in the San Joaquin Valley); Californian marsala, rarely found on the market and having nothing in common with the Marsala from Sicily; and Californian madeira, which is usually a poor imitation of genuine Madeira.

One of the principal barriers to the production of even acceptable sherry-type wine in California was the old law that required a 19.5% alcoholic content in local sherries. As of 1971 it became legal to make sherry with 17% alcohol, the strength of the wine in Spain.

Special natural wines are not strictly a dessert wine type, but they seem to have grown from the recent boom in the berry wine industry. Dr. Maynard Amerine gives a kindly description of the origin of these wines: "The idea of flavored wines dates back in time to Greek and Roman civilizations. In these periods they resulted from attempts to mask bad odors and tastes. This then led naturally to the practice of adding desirable flavors, allowing the wine to serve as the 'vehicle' for the added flavor, just as spices and perfumes perform useful roles. The addition of botanicals to wine for medicinal and even mystical reasons also made such flavored wines popular in older civilizations;

after distillation was discovered, fortified wines and brandy became a favored base for flavored wines and liqueurs."

The California "special" wines are made from a base of wine. The additions may include herbs, spices, fruit juices, aromatics, essences, and other natural flavorings. However, no further alcohol or wine spirits are added. Such concoctions are not wines.

SPARKLING WINES

These may be red, pink, or white, and their alcoholic content ranges from 10% to 14% by volume. The most popular sparkling types in California are "champagne" and "sparkling burgundy." Although no wines outside France have any right to the title of Champagne, some of the Californian sparkling wines are made by the true champagne method in which secondary fermentation takes place in the bottle. When this happens, the wine is allowed to bear the label of bottle-fermented champagne, provided the words Californian or American are added, with a statement that it is a sparkling wine made by the champagne method in California, the state of New York, etc. The alternative method is the Charmat process, in which secondary fermentation takes place in bulk in huge glass-lined vats.

In France, however, only bottle-fermented sparkling wine is allowed to be authentic Champagne (*q.v.*) and only if it has been made in the Champagne region.

Californian "champagnes" are produced throughout the state, but the finest come from the cooler regions—the counties of Sonoma, Santa Clara, Napa, and Alameda. Sweeter types come from the Cucamonga district in southern California and the interior valleys; bulk-process types are made in both these regions, as well as in the inland valley. Bottle-fermented types are mostly found in the areas which produce good table wines: the Almadén Vineyards of Los Gatos, F. Korbel & Bros. of Guerneville, Weibel Champagne Vineyards of Mission San José, Hanns Kornell, Schramsberg, Beaulieu Vineyards, and Domaine Chandon (owned by the Moët-Hennessy group) are probably the best champagne producers in California. Piper-Heidsieck and Sonoma Vineyards formed a joint venture in 1980.

Pinot Noir and Pinot Chardonnay, the grapes that go into the making of French Champagnes, yield the best quality; other good grapes for Californian champagnes are the Pinot Blanc, Sémillon, Sauvignon Blanc, White Riesling, and Folle Blanche. Some of the inferior grape varieties are the Sauvignon Vert, Burger, French Colombard, and Green Hungarian. Californian champagnes range from dry to sweet and are dosed with sugar in the usual way; but a real *brut* champagne is rare in California.

Pink champagnes from California may be either bottle-fermented or bulk-processed (the government requires labels to designate bulk-process champagnes as well as the bottle-fermented types).

Of the sparkling wines, Sparkling California "burgundy," after champagne the most popular in the country, is red wine made sparkling by either of the two methods used for champagnes. It is usually semi-sweet or sweet, and produced from Pinot Noir, Carignane, Mondeuse, and Petite-Sirah. Of the sparkling wines, mosel- and sauternes-types are treated by the champagne method and are made from the table wines bearing the same names. Sparkling Muscats are made from light Muscat wines, usually Muscat Canelli (Muscat de Frontignan): they tend to be very sweet and are sometimes sold under the Italian name "Moscato Spumante." Another wine is made from the Malvasia Bianca which produces a sweet Muscat-flavored sparkling wine.

Californian carbonated wines are made to sparkle by artificial carbonation and under Californian law must be designated as such. Sometimes known as effervescent wines, they are mass-produced and much cheaper than the relatively better quality and naturally fermented sparkling wines.

VINE-GROWING REGIONS

There are six natural vine-growing regions in California—the North Coast, the Sacramento, the Central Valley, the San Joaquin Valley, the South Coast, and San Luis Obispo. Each has its well-known districts, and almost every grape and type of wine is produced in one or more of these.

North Coast

The North Coast region is north and south of San Francisco Bay in the many valleys which lie parallel to the coastal ranges and is generally characterized by warm summers and moderate annual rainfalls. The best dry table wines, both red and white, are grown here. The principal districts are Napa, Sonoma, Mendocino, Livermore, Santa Clara, San Benito, Santa Cruz, and Monterey.

(1) Napa

This is undoubtedly the most famous red wine district in California, with more than a hundred bonded wineries and some of the finest vineyards in the country. Napa is the Indian word for "plenty," and the valley abounds in rich, fertile land, while the hillsides are planted in fine grapes. There are approximately 24,000 acres (9,000 hectares) of vineyard, and in 1979, 59,000 tons of grapes were harvested. The average yield per acre was about 3 tons, or 50 hectoliters per hectare. This average is low, since much of the acreage was not bearing. The value of the crop exceeded $20 million, compared with $15 million for the Sonoma harvest.

Two-thirds of the production is in red wine. The Cabernet Sauvignon is the royal grape of Napa, producing better than the Pinot Noir. The Cabernet, the same variety used in the great red Bordeaux, is very slow to mature in the Napa region and the wine is sometimes left in casks to age for as long as four years.

The cooler parts of the valley produce some of the best

Cabernet Sauvignon wine in America. Since 1970, more than 3,800 acres (1,520 hectares) of this one variety have been added to the valley vineyards. With 5,700 acres (2,280 hectares) of Cabernet now growing in Napa, only Sonoma and Monterey can count more of this fine variety.

Napa is divided into the Upper Valley and the Lower Valley. The center of the Upper Napa Valley is the dignified town of St. Helena, but the district stretches 7 miles (11.3 kilometers) north toward Calistoga and in the south it goes as far as Rutherford and Oakville. The Lower Valley covers the area around the city of Napa, an hour's drive from San Francisco, and takes in the northwestern part of a wide valley bottom running up to the Sonoma County border. The soil in the southernmost part of Napa County is heavy and this region is the coolest, owing to its proximity to San Francisco Bay. The Upper Valley has a gravelly soil, and the mountains influence both the climate and the exposure.

It is a general opinion in Napa that if more grapes were planted on the slopes, better wine would be made—three-quarters of the vines are planted on the flats; and this is one of the few districts where the growers admit that they have good and bad years, so that some will be regarded as vintage years and others not. Another sign of progress in the valley has been the establishment of many group co-operatives; and since 1942 there has been a Vintner's Association to deal with recurrent problems.

Some of the most important vineyards are those of Beaulieu, Beringer, Robert Mondavi, Christian Brothers, Inglenook, Charles Krug, Louis Martini, Freemark Abbey, Sterling Vineyards, Schramsberg, Joseph Heitz, Chappellet, Cuvaison, Clos du Val, Trefethen, and Domaine Chandon, to name a few.

The Lower Napa Valley and Solano County are relatively small producers but the area has recently expanded into neighboring Chiles Valley. The Carneros area of the valley has recently proven to be a prime location.

Beaulieu Vineyard. Georges de Latour founded this beautiful estate and the vineyards in 1908. He imported many cuttings from his native France and found the ideal site for them near Rutherford, where the gravelly soil holds the annual rains without need of irrigation. Beaulieu has maintained a continuous operation right from its beginning: the winery made sacramental wines during Prohibition, and when Repeal followed, Beaulieu enjoyed a success it had never had before with a wide distribution of wines throughout the United States.

There are now four vineyards with about 1,000 acres (400 hectares) in active production, all of them in the center of Napa Valley, except for about 150 acres in the Carneros region, the southernmost part of the valley, where the bay breezes temper the climate. The principal varieties grown are the Pinot Noir, Chardonnay, and the Cabernet Sauvignon. The Muscat de Frontignan variety thrives abundantly and makes a fine varietal wine. In 1969, the vineyard was sold to the Heublein Corporation, which expanded the winery.

One of the great wine-makers of the Napa Valley, André Tchelistcheff, supervised production at Beaulieu from

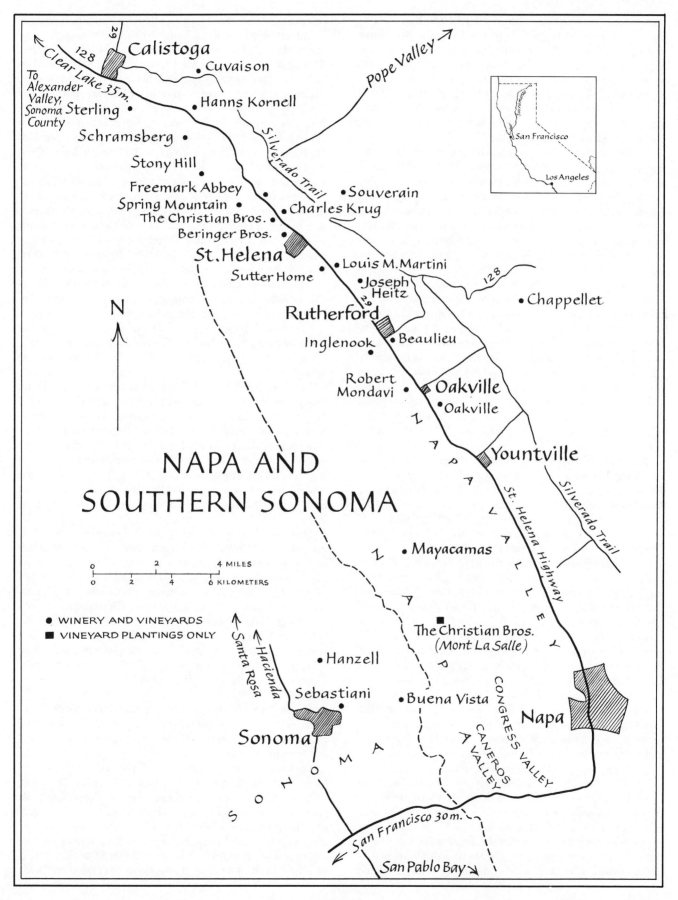

Calistoga

128
29

To Alexander Valley, Sonoma County

Clear Lake 35 m.

• Cuvaison

• Hanns Kornell

Sterling •

Schramsberg •

Silverado Trail

Stony Hill •

Freemark Abbey •

• Souverain

Spring Mountain •

The Christian Bros. •

Charles Krug •

Beringer Bros. •

St. Helena

Sutter Home

Louis M. Martini •

128

Joseph Heitz •

• Chappellet

Rutherford

29

Inglenook •

• Beaulieu

N

Robert Mondavi •

Oakville

• Oakville

NAPA AND SOUTHERN SONOMA

Yountville

St. Helena Highway

Silverado Trail

0   2   4 MILES
0   2   4   6 KILOMETERS

• Mayacamas

NAPA VALLEY

• WINERY AND VINEYARDS
■ VINEYARD PLANTINGS ONLY

■ The Christian Bros. (Mont La Salle)

Santa Rosa

Hacienda

• Hanzell

Sebastiani •

• Buena Vista

CONGRESS VALLEY

CANEROS VALLEY

Napa

Sonoma

SONOMA

San Francisco 30 m.

San Pablo Bay

493

1938 until his retirement in 1973. His BV Private Reserve Cabernet Sauvignon is one of the most distinctive red table wines in the country. Tchelistcheff started the tradition of making a Pinot Noir wine, and despite his relative successes with the Beaulieu Pinot Noirs, they are no substitute for the real Côte d'Or Burgundies.

For the past thirty-five years, the wines of Beaulieu, particularly the Private Reserve label, have been among the finest wines produced in the United States.

Beringer Brothers. Two German brothers, Frederick and Jacob Beringer, assured the success of this well-known winery founded in 1876 at St. Helena in the Napa Valley on the north coast of California. The entrance to the spacious and recently refurbished old "Rheinhaus" is just north of the city limits. The vineyard known as Los Hermanos has been active from the very beginning and even flourished during Prohibition by selling sacramental wines to the clergy throughout the country. After many years of operation by the Beringer family, the vineyard and winery were sold in 1970 to Nestlé International, the large food and beverage company. The beautiful tunnels excavated in the limestone hills behind the old winery were preserved, and the rest of the facilities were modernized in a three-year program. Myron Nightingale, one of the most respected wine masters in California, has been put in charge of the wines.

Vintage varietal wines include Cabernet Sauvignon, Pinot Noir, and Chardonnay. One of the most popular wines is "Bärenblut," a blend of Pinot Noir and Grignolino.

The original winery is one of the most picturesque in the Napa Valley and it is visited by thousands every year. Nestlé built a new winery directly across Highway 29 from the Rhine House. This facility handles the production of the 2,700 acres (1,080 hectares) of Napa and 1,300 acres (520 hectares) of Sonoma vineyards, plus that of the Carneros vineyards near San Pablo Bay.

Chappellet Vineyards. One of the most beautiful wineries constructed in the North Coast area is Chappellet, situated on Pritchard Hill 1,400 feet (425 meters) above the floor of the Napa Valley. It was planned and built by Donn Chappellet, a southern Californian who made a success in the automatic food vending business. The hillside land he purchased in 1967 included hundreds of acres of vineyards, much of which was replanted in Merlot, Chardonnay, Cabernet Sauvignon, Chenin Blanc, and Johannisberg Riesling.

The handsome pyramid-shaped winery, built into the side of a hill among oak trees, blends beautifully into the terrain. Its gleaming stainless steel fermenting vats contrast with the new wooden cooperage and the matte metal roof. The oenologist is Anthony Soter.

The Christian Brothers. Known in the United States as "The Brothers of the Christian Schools," these are members of a religious order founded in the seventeenth century, in France, by St. Jean-Baptiste de La Salle, primarily for teaching. The winery of the Brothers is now one of the most important producers in the North Coast region of California. The large vineyards are at Mont La Salle

on the edge of the Napa Valley and along Redwood Road in the Macayamas range, with new vineyard properties throughout the other sections of the Napa Valley. The grape plantations total more than 1,500 acres (600 hectares), mostly in Napa and the San Joaquin Valley, where the dessert wines and brandies are made. The Brothers control more vineyard land than any other Napa group, and in fact own half a dozen wineries, including the old "Greystone" ageing cellars just north of St. Helena near Charles Krug and Beringer Bros. Their mountain vineyard produces excellent Pinot Chardonnay and Pinot St. Georges. Two of the well-known Christian Brothers wines are Château La Salle, a light Muscat table wine, and Pineau de la Loire. Christian Brothers is one of the largest producers of well-made wines on the North Coast. Fromm and Sichel are worldwide distributors for their products. Christian Brothers sell more brandy than any other distiller in the United States.

The vice-president and cellarmaster is Brother Timothy, whose collection of antique wine accessories and illustrations has toured museums throughout the country.

Clos du Val. Deserving admiration and encouragement is Bernard Portet, who in 1972 produced his first wines, Cabernet Sauvignon and Zinfandel. A Chardonnay was added in 1977.

Cuvaison, Inc. This small winery is north of St. Helena along the Silverado Trail, which runs parallel to "wine" Highway 29. In 1970 two wine-lovers, Thomas Cottrell and Thomas Parkhill, established Cuvaison with the intention of making a limited number of 100% varietal, vintage-dated table wines. In 1973 a controlling interest was purchased by Oakleigh Thorne of New York, who in turn sold Cuvaison to a Swiss corporation in 1979. Cabernet Sauvignon, Zinfandel, and Chardonnay wines are produced.

Domaine Chandon. In May 1977 Domaine Chandon, owned by the French Moët-Hennessy combine, launched its first wines in the California market. Their major product is a sparkling wine, one that is laudably not labeled Champagne, since Moët adheres to the view that Champagne itself can come only from the Champagne district of France. Top wine-makers from the Moët et Chandon cellars in Épernay went to California to create this first wine and to train the staff who will produce succeeding vintages. Grapes are supplied by their own plantings in Carneros—mostly Pinot Noir and Chardonnay—and at one time from the Trefethen vineyards.

Jerome Draper Vineyards. Though no wine is made here, these vineyards have contributed fine quality wine grapes grown on the 105 acres (42 hectares) to some of the best wineries in the valley.

Franciscan Vineyards. Another of the small wineries of Napa, sold by Raymond Duncan and Justin Meyer in 1979 to the German beverage firm of Peter Eckes & Company, the world's largest producer of brandy, including the Maria Krön label. It has 500 acres (200 hectares) of vines and a medium-sized wine-making facility on the wine highway 6 miles (9.5 kilometers) south of St. Helena at Rutherford. The first grapes were harvested in 1973, and the first white wines were ready for sale the following year.

Freemark Abbey. Seven partners reorganized this winery, which is located a short distance north of St. Helena, the premier wine town of the Napa Valley. Freemark Abbey's modern and well-equipped wine-making facilities are in the lower levels of a handsome old brownstone building built in the late nineteenth century. The upper section of the large structure is a store devoted to candles, cookware, and specialized merchandise. Only varietal table wines such as Chardonnay, Johannisberg Riesling and Cabernet are produced. The partners have experimented extensively with ageing their wines in oak cooperage from a number of European countries. In a recent New York blind tasting with a distinguished panel of judges, a Freemark Chardonnay won top honors. The Freemark Abbey group purchased Rutherford Hill Winery, formerly known as Souverain of Rutherford, from Pillsbury Mills in 1976. This handsome winery, tucked into the hills east of the Silverado Trail, is one of the most beautiful sites in Napa and produces about 40,000 cases per year.

Heitz Wine Cellars. With but 45 acres (18 hectares) of home vineyards at his winery, Joseph Heitz looks to other growers in the Napa Valley for many of the grapes to be used in his good varietal table wines. Heitz, a former professor of oenology with a reputation as a master wine-blender, began his own operations in the early 1960s. He first bought the tiny property of Leon Brendel in St. Helena and then purchased an old stone winery with vineyards on Taplin Road a few miles east of the town. Within a decade, his wines had such a success that Heitz expanded his facilities. Production is projected to reach 40,000 cases by 1985. Heitz makes a wide variety of wines: Chardonnay, Cabernet, Pinot Noir, White Riesling, Zinfandel, Barbera, and Grignolino, plus "champagne," "port" and "sherry."

Inglenook Vineyards. This winery is just off Highway 29—called the Napa Valley Wine Road—at the crossroads town of Rutherford. The nearby vineyards were founded in 1879 by Captain Gustav F. Niebaum, on the slopes of Mount St. John. He kept up the vineyards until his death in 1908, when Inglenook was passed on to his nephew, the late John Daniel, Jr. Daniel directed its operation through Prohibition, and after Repeal successfully carried on the family tradition of growing fine grapes on the 225-acre (90-hectare) vineyard. The best were Cabernet Sauvignon, Pinot Noir, Sémillon, Chardonnay, Pinot Blanc, and Zinfandel, with some land planted in the Gamay of Beaujolais and the Merlot from Bordeaux. In 1964 the Inglenook organization was sold to United Vintners, which in turn became part of Heublein in 1968. Film director Francis Coppola, of *The Godfather* fame, purchased the Niebaum mansion in 1975, and established his own vineyard and winery, the Niebaum-Coppola Estate.

Though the production of generic wines was begun by the new owners, they have continued to make some of the fine vintage varietal wines which originally brought fame to the property. The great days of Inglenook started in the late 1930s, when the company became the first California winery to restrict its output to varietals. Bottles of Cabernet Sauvignon and "Cask Selection" wines from these vintages are rare and fetch very high prices at auctions.

Hanns Kornell Champagne Cellars. The Hanns Kornell cellars are 5 miles (8 kilometers) north of St. Helena east of the main Calistoga highway. German-born and -trained Kornell is one of the few remaining independent "champagne" producers in California, even though his winery on Larkmead Lane has been turning out sparkling wine for more than twenty years. The winery itself dates from the late nineteenth century. Kornell took it over after moving from Sonoma, where he had established his first winery in the early 1950s. Today he makes what he calls "Third Generation" champagnes—wines which have won numerous medals at international competitions. There are no vineyards, for Kornell buys still wine and then develops his sparkling *cuvées*. He has an inventory of more than 1.5 million individually processed bottles resting in his cellars. One of the new vintages is a "Sehr Trocken" wine in the style of the German Sekt. Kornell produces sparkling wines for other vintners lacking the skill or inclination to make their own.

Charles Krug Winery. Established in 1861, this is the oldest operating winery in Napa Valley. It is now owned and family operated by Peter Mondavi of C. Mondavi & Sons, who produce and bottle at Charles Krug Winery, St. Helena, fine generic and varietal wines. The old winery building trimmed in brown and gold is north of St. Helena along Highway 29, framed by nearby mountains.

Charles Krug, one of the great names in California wine history, was a worthy pupil of Colonel Haraszthy in Sonoma. In 1858 he made the first commercial wine in Napa County, using a small cider press. He built his first winery and planted his first vines on the present St. Helena site in 1861; and soon his wines were famous throughout America and in Europe. During his lifetime he trained C. H. Wente, Jacob Beringer, C. J. Wetmore, and many other leading Californian wine-makers, and was a prominent figure in California wine circles until his death in 1892.

Since 1943, when the Mondavis acquired the Krug winery buildings and vineyards, the size, scope, and efficiency of the cellars have been enlarged. They are among the best equipped and most efficient in California. The family has also pioneered wine-making innovations and techniques. Krug Chenin Blanc was the first varietal made from that grape in California.

In 1962 the Mondavis purchased approximately 500 acres in nearby Oakville of the historic To Kalon vineyard, considered one of the finest in all Napa Valley. Other sources of fine Napa Valley wine grapes contribute to the vineyard program.

The premium wines of C. Mondavi & Sons bear the labels Charles Krug and C. K. Mondavi. When, in the mid-1960s, Robert Mondavi left Krug to found his own Napa winery, the family's long-simmering feud almost

495

became a public issue. Peter Mondavi now again controls the winery and vineyard.

Louis M. Martini Company. Founder Louis M. Martini was born in Pietra Ligure, Italy, in 1887 and came to the United States at the turn of the century. For many years his dream had been to produce excellent wines, and when Prohibition was repealed in 1933, he built a large winery at St. Helena, some 65 miles (104 kilometers) north of San Francisco. Over the next ten years he acquired three important, well-situated vineyards and planted them with fine grape varieties. In 1941, the author and his then associate, Frank Schoonmaker (who deserves the gratitude of all California premium producers), started selling American wines under American names. It was then that Louis Martini wines, among others, were for the first time offered east of the Rockies.

The family vineyards today consist of 380 acres (152 hectares) in the Carneros district, 280 acres in the mountains near Sonoma, 200 acres in Healdsburg, and 280 acres near St. Helena, including the expansions carried out in the 1960s by the son, wine-maker Louis P. Martini.

The late Louis Martini at age 86 was the dean of Napa Valley wine-growers and certainly one of the most important figures in the California industry. His wines have a national reputation for quality and fair price.

A third Martini generation is now learning the family business in Napa.

Mayacamas Vineyards. The beautiful terraced Mayacamas vineyards are high on the crests of the Mayacamas Mountains, up the steep Lokoya Road and 1,000 feet (300 meters) above the Mont La Salle property of the Christian Brothers. They are about 12 miles (19 kilometers) from the town of Napa. The original owner, Jack F. M. Taylor, began to make wine there in 1945. He and his wife, Mary, were among the first new producers of good wine in Napa after the Second World War. Their output included seventeen red and white table wines, and a remarkable Zinfandel Rosé.

In 1969 Robert Travers and his wife, together with a few partners, bought the winery and the vineyards from the Taylors. The quality has remained high, but wisely, the selection of wines has been cut to vintage-dated varietals: Chardonnay, Cabernet Sauvignon, and some other wines.

There are 48 acres (24 hectares) of vines.

Robert Mondavi Winery. One of the leaders of the premium wine industry in California today is quality-minded Robert Mondavi. He and his sons Michael and Timothy and daughter Marcie produce some of the best varietal wines in the United States. Years of work as a partner in the Charles Krug Winery gave Mondavi the experience needed to launch a new operation of his own in 1966. The winery, northwest of the historic town of Yountville, is one of the most efficient and handsome in the state. Mondavi's philosophy is similar to that of the other conscientious North Coast vintners: "There is a place for a relatively small winery to produce, in a limited quantity, wines that will have the complexity and character to be found in the great growths of the world."

The Mondavi vineyards cover 800 acres (320 hectares). Once the winery had had its first harvest and began to grow, a share of the business was bought by the Rainier Brewing Company of Seattle, Washington.

Robert Mondavi was one of the first in California to experiment with barrels for ageing made from different types of oak. In 1979, Mondavi and Baron Philippe de Rothschild, proprietor of Château Mouton-Rothschild and other *Grands Crus* in Pauillac, formed a joint venture. A small part of Mondavi's vineyard is jointly owned and vinified. The Spanish-style winery with handsome paneling and spacious patios is used by groups for luncheons and wine tastings. The Mondavis also sponsor musical events.

Schramsberg Vineyards. Established by a German pioneer, Jacob Schram, the old winery had fallen upon bad days until Jack Davies, an energetic man from Los Angeles, bought the abandoned building and vineyards in 1965. He brought into the venture a group of partners, but Davies and his wife live at Schramsberg and produce its famous sparkling wines. Schramsberg makes only sparkling wines. Former president Nixon took Schramsberg wine (which is served at the White House) to China for his 1972 visit. Davies has replanted the 50 acres (20 hectares) of home vineyard with Pinot Noir and Pinot Chardonnay grapes, from which he makes Blanc de Blancs and a Blanc de Noir wine.

The winery is on a winding road off Highway 29, between St. Helena and Calistoga. The building dates from the middle of the nineteenth century and has been designated a state landmark.

Spring Mountain Vineyards. In 1976, Michael Robbins sold his vineyard and winery one mile north of St. Helena on Highway 29 (now the property of St. Clement Vineyards; see Appendix G) and relocated on the site of an 1885 vineyard, with an original 90-foot cave and tunnel still intact, farther up the hillside on Spring Mountain Road. A former engineer from Des Moines, Robbins and his wife, Shirley, have been making wines in Napa since 1967. Their 140 acres (56 hectares) in Rutherford and Napa provide grapes for Cabernet Sauvignon, Chardonnay, Sauvignon Blanc, and Pinot Noir wines, first crushed in the new winery in 1976. Their Chardonnays have won numerous awards and critical acclaim.

Sterling Vineyards. Sterling Vineyards, along with Monterey Vineyards, was acquired by Coca-Cola of Atlanta in 1978. The medium-sized and modern winery opened in 1973 is 4 miles (6.5 kilometers) north of St. Helena. The 400 acres (160 hectares) of vineyards were cleared in the early 1960s and are at present planted in Chardonnay, Chenin Blanc, Cabernet Sauvignon, Sauvignon Blanc, and Merlot. The Chardonnay wine is good and well known.

The winery is located high above the valley and is reached by an aerial tramway, making it a favorite attraction for the many Napa tourists.

Stony Hill Vineyard. Situated on a private road north of St. Helena, Stony Hill is small and secluded. The winery produces four wines: Chardonnay, White Riesling, Gewürztraminer, and Sémillon de Soleil. The late Frederick McCrea started the operation in 1951 and raised the buildings on the family's summer-home site. The 40 acres (16 hectares) of vines followed. The small-scale winery makes some of the best white wines in California; they have won awards at the State Fair; but unfortunately the very small supply is sold only by mailing list.

Sutter Home Winery. Driving north into the heart of the North Coast wine country, one can find Sutter Home just south of St. Helena near so many of the other best wineries. The wines are good and have been made by the Trichero family since 1946. They produce mostly Zinfandels, including a white one. The reds are made from Amador County grapes.

Many more newer Napa vineyards and wineries, established during the wine boom of the 1970s, are profiled in Appendix G.

(2) Sonoma

This district, which lies directly north of San Francisco, yields some excellent table wines and sparkling wines which rank with the very best in the state. Sonoma is one of the three top wine-producing counties in California, with an average total of 25,000 acres (10,000 hectares) planted in vines, and with over sixty it is second only to Napa in number of bonded wineries. The wines of Sonoma County come from the Sonoma Valley, Santa Rosa, and the Russian River Valley, as well as from a few select microclimates such as Alexander Valley and the Dry Creek area.

The Sonoma Valley runs parallel to the Napa Valley, separated from it by the high peaks of the Mayacamas Mountains; this is the original "Valley of the Moon" of Jack London, who wrote and died in this beautiful country. Chateau St. Jean, Hanzell, and Sebastiani make the best quality table wines. In north Sonoma County, Simi and Sonoma Vineyards have gained good reputations.

Santa Rosa is named for the Santa Rosa Creek which empties its waters into the Russian River, and is the site of the Fountaingrove Vineyard, founded in 1873. Uprooted, it is now a cattle ranch.

In the Russian River Valley are a number of the area's wineries. The most important of them is Korbel & Bros. champagne company, with vineyards on the hillsides along the river. The average yield for all the Sonoma region vineyards is about 2.5 tons per acre, a little more than 40 hectoliters per hectare. The average is low because of the many non-bearing acres included.

Buena Vista Vineyards. Situated on what has become "winery row" a mile from the historic town plaza of Sonoma, and 40 miles (64 kilometers) north of San Francisco, are these historic vineyards originally planted by the great Californian viticulturist, Colonel Ágoston Haraszthy, who wrote his classic *Report on Grapes and Wines of California* on the terrace of his Buena Vista house and advised growers from many parts of California on the cultivation of their vines. After his death in 1869, his win-

ery was carried on by his sons Attila and Árpád. The phylloxera plague destroyed many of the European vines at Buena Vista, and the final catastrophe came with the earthquake of 1906, when the winery and storage caves collapsed in ruins. Thereafter, viniculture at this famous vineyard remained at a standstill until 1943, when the two wineries were restored and more acreage was bought by Frank Bartholomew, the president of United Press International (*see* Hacienda Wine Cellars, below). The Young's Market company of Los Angeles bought Buena Vista in 1968 and purchased a 700–acre (330–hectare) tract in the Carneros Creek area (where a new winery was built), that fine region for the varietal wine grape which straddles the border between Sonoma and Napa.

In 1979, Buena Vista was purchased by A. Racke, the German producers of Kupferberg sparkling wines. Chilean René Lacasia is the wine-maker, and about 100,000 cases of wine are made annually.

Hacienda Wine Cellars. Former newspaper editor Frank H. Bartholomew founded Hacienda Wine Cellars in 1972 right in the heart of the Valley of the Moon, a mile and a half from the center of Sonoma. By 1977, A. Crawford Cooley, formerly in the electronics industry and manager of his family's Oak Valley vineyard, and wine-maker Steve MacRostle were managing Hacienda, with Bartholomew as consultant. Hacienda has 130 acres (60 hectares) and produces about 20,000 cases annually.

Hanzell Vineyards. When James D. Zellerbach retired as U. S. ambassador to Italy in the 1950s, he came to Sonoma wanting to make wines as good as the fine European ones he had come to know. He modeled his wines, vineyards, and the winery itself on a French original. The building and plantation attempted to resemble those of the Clos Vougeot, and the wines were made from only Burgundy grapes. In his close attention to every French detail, Mr. Zellerbach discovered that much of the complexity of European wines derives from the ageing in barrels made from oak common only to parts of Europe. He was the first to import French barrels, but today the practice is widespread. Hanzell is a combination of the ambassador's last name and his wife's first name, Hannah.

After Mr. Zellerbach's death, the property was bought by Douglas Day, whose widow Mary continued to make the same small number of fine wines until her death. The property now belongs to Countess Barbara de Brye and her husband Jacques. Bob Sessions is the wine-maker.

Italian Swiss Colony. This sprawling winery in the gently rolling hills of Asti, California, is the largest of the United Vintners operations, all owned by Heublein. The original Italian-Swiss colony was founded in 1881 as an agricultural haven for displaced citizens of those two nations. Even before the turn of the century, it counted more than 1,500 acres (600 hectares) of vineyards. Today, hundreds of grape-growers throughout the region supply the enormous winery, and United Vintners has 2,000 acres (800 hectares) of its own vineyards.

Andrea Sbaboro started the company and built the winery in 1887, but his first wines were failures. A young Italian pharmacist from San Francisco, Pietro Rossi, came to Asti and brought the wine-making skills he learned in Europe. Soon the wines were a success. The present generation of Rossis is still active in the company.

When Louis Petri ran Italian Swiss Colony from the 1940s through the 1960s, the winery organization became one of the largest in the world.

The capacity of the six Heublein wineries at Asti, Madera, Reedly, Oakville, and Stockton, combined with Inglenook at Rutherford, is 95 million gallons (1.146 million imp. gallons, 3.6 million hectoliters). They produce a wide range of table wines, dessert wines, "ports," "sherries," "champagnes," as well as brandy and flavored wines. Among the many national brands are Lejon, Petri, Bali Hai, and Annie Green Springs.

F. Korbel & Bros., Inc. The Korbel winery and vineyards are located in one of the most picturesque sections of California, alongside the winding Russian River at Guerneville. The Korbel brothers came from the small town of Behine in Czechoslovakia to settle down here, where they made their first "champagnes" in the nineties. After the Second World War they dropped their table wines and devoted their skill exclusively to the production of sparkling champagnes. Early in 1954 Anton and Leo Korbel sold the corporation to Adolph, Ben, and Paul Heck. Adolph and Paul Heck, originally from St. Louis, were formerly president and production manager of Italian Swiss Colony of Asti, California; Adolph became the president and wine-maker of Korbel and Paul Heck the executive vice-president.

Some of the important varieties used at the ranch for the production of sparkling wines are Pinot Noir, Pinot Blanc, Sémillon, and White Riesling. The winery produces Korbel Brut and Korbel Extra Dry (for eastern markets mainly), and Korbel Sec (medium dry), Korbel Rouge, and Korbel pink champagnes.

Although the Heck brothers continue to run the winery and vineyards, the Jack Daniels Distilling Company has owned Korbel and distributed the wines since 1966. The winery makes table wines as well as sparkling ones. Many of the grapes for the still wines come from the 700 acres (280 hectares) of varietal vineyards in the northwestern section of the county.

Martini & Prati Wines, Inc. Seven miles (11 kilometers) northwest of Santa Rosa on Laguna Road stands one of the oldest and largest wineries of Sonoma. From its 62 acres (25 hectares) of vine, Martini & Prati make generic wines, fruit wines, vermouth, and a pleasant Zinfandel. Most of these are shipped in bulk to bottlers in other parts of the country. The winery owns the Fountaingrove label, which at one time marked some of the best California wines.

J. Pedroncelli Winery. Though less well known than some of its neighbors, the Pedroncelli winery makes good wines: a fine Zinfandel, Chardonnay, Chenin Blanc, Cabernet Sauvignon, Pinot Noir, and Petite-Sirah. The vineyards and winery are a mile northwest of Geyserville along Highway 101. John Pedroncelli, Sr., chose the Canyon Road property in 1927 because the land and climate reminded him of his native Italy. There are today nearly 150 acres (60 hectares) of vineyard. Pedroncelli made the first, and one of the best, Zinfandel rosés in California.

Sebastiani Vineyards. The town plaza of Sonoma, where the State Bear Flag was briefly raised in the 1840s to mark the capital of California, sits in the midst of quite a few buildings that have the same name: Sebastiani. The reason for this is the Sebastiani Winery and vineyards, founded by Samuele Sebastiani in 1904. He had saved enough money in the eight years since his arrival from Italy to come to Sonoma and make wines. Soon the original bulk-wine business was profitable, and buildings with the family name started appearing around the town.

Twenty-five years ago the winery gave up making anonymous bulk wines and started to produce better ones under the family label. Their successes have been admirable, and include Cabernet Sauvignon, Zinfandel, Pinot Noir, and a surprisingly good Barbera. These wines are sold as "Proprietor's Reserve" wines.

The winery is still family-owned and -managed. Following his father August's death in 1980, Sam Sebastiani is president of the vineyards. There are about 700 acres (280 hectares) of vineyards.

Simi Winery, Inc. This winery, with a distinctive stone façade, is north of Healdsburg along the dramatic Redwood Highway. It was built in 1876 by the Simi brothers, two early San Francisco wine merchants. Russell Green bought the winery in 1970, rebuilt it and started to make good varietal wines from grapes grown on vineyards he had owned since 1958. The British beverage firm of Scottish & Newcastle briefly owned Simi from 1972 until 1976, when Schieffelin & Company, the New York-based beverage importing firm, established Simi as its subsidiary. Management and operation of the winery are totally independent of Schieffelin.

Sonoma Vineyards. Started in a tiny tasting room at Tiburon facing San Francisco Bay, Tiburon Vintners quickly grew into a large wine and grape enterprise and is now located in the town of Windsor off Highway 101 near Santa Rosa. The modern winery features an outdoor amphitheater for summer musical productions.

Rodney Strong, a dancer who had performed on Broadway and in Europe, sold generic and varietal wines with the Tiburon label throughout the Bay area. His business grew and became one of the largest quality vineyard operations in northern California. In 1976, Sonoma Vineyards became a public company owned by many individuals and managed by Mr. Strong. The 1,250 acres (500 hectares) of vines produce about 50% of the grapes used in their wines. In a joint venture with the French Champagne firm of Piper-Hiedsieck, a sparkling wine called Piper-Sonoma is marketed.

Many more newer Sonoma vineyards and wineries, established during the wine boom of the seventies, are profiled in Appendix G.

(3) Mendocino

Growers in this district have recently begun to cultivate finer wine grapes, and vineyard area has increased from 1,200 to about 10,000 acres (4,000 hectares) and is still growing. Hillsides once thought impossible to irrigate for frost control are now being watered from farm ponds filled by the run-off from the mountain rains. Cabernet Sauvignon and Gamay Beaujolais are the major grapes planted, but some interest is shown in Pinot Chardonnay and the reliable Zinfandel. Mendocino may have great potential as a fine-wine district, but until the beginning of the seventies it was somewhat ignored. Certain vineyards, especially those in the cooler micro-climate, will indeed produce some of the best wine from northern California. The best wineries in this county are found near Ukiah.

Cresta Blanca Winery. California's first premium winery, now north of Ukiah rather than in the Livermore Valley near San Francisco, has returned to the production of varietal wines.

Charles Wetmore, an early and innovative vintner, established Cresta Blanca in 1892. He had traveled in Europe for the state Viticultural Committee and brought back cuttings of fine vines from France. Remarkably, only one year after the estate was founded, Cresta Blanca wines won medals at the 1893 Paris Exhibition. After some poor vintages under Schenley ownership, the winery was bought by the Guild Wine Company in 1971. Fair wines from Petite-Sirah, Cabernet Sauvignon, Zinfandel, Grignolino, Sylvaner, and Pinot Chardonnay are produced, along with some dessert and sparkling wines.

Fetzer Vineyards. In the secluded Redwood Valley on Bel Arbes Road lies the 90-acre (36-hectare) vineyard and winery owned by Bernard and Kathleen Fetzer. Strictly a family enterprise, with John Fetzer the winemaker and James Fetzer the manager, Fetzer Vineyards make 100% varietal vintages, some of which are sold as Mendocino wines. The winery is one of the few in the area to use the county place-name. The Fetzers have been making good wine at their facility since 1968; vineyards planted in Zinfandel, Sauvignon, and Cabernet date from the late 1950s.

Parducci Winery. Three miles (about 5 kilometers) north of Ukiah are these fifty-year-old cellars, established after Repeal by Adolf Parducci. One of the better-known and more innovative North Coast wineries, Parducci makes most of its wines from vineyards in Mendocino and Lake counties. Although not an annual practice, since 1969 Cabernet Sauvignons vinified from grapes grown on scattered plots have been produced in an effort to try out new wine growing districts. John and George, Adolf's sons, now operate the winery. Their medium-priced Chenin Blanc is consistently good.

Profiles of newer Mendocino vineyards and wineries, established during the wine boom of the seventies, can be found in Appendix G.

(4) Livermore

This is a district noted for its production of many fine wines. Alameda County's Livermore Valley is known throughout the country for its good Sauternes-type, as well as for other outstanding white wines. The valley was named after pioneer Robert Livermore who, as early as 1848, had a vineyard near the town that bears his name.

The Livermore Valley (more of a basin than a valley) comprises two important wine-growing areas—the vineyards surrounding the town of Livermore, and the neighboring sector of Pleasanton. In 1887, Charles A. Wetmore said of the valley: "Here every condition known to be essential for the production of the highest grades of wines and brandies, approximating the noblest French types, exists." With cuttings he brought directly from the vineyards of Margaux and Château d'Yquem in Bordeaux, Wetmore founded in 1882 the concern which won renown as Cresta Blanca, now reopened in Mendocino. Today, the two outstanding wineries of Livermore Valley are Concannon Vineyard and Wente Bros.

The soil of most of the vineyards in this section is made up largely of coarse, arid-looking stones like that of the Châteauneuf-du-Pape vineyards of the Rhône Valley and the gravel of some of those in Graves and the Médoc. This soil is, in California, particularly adapted to the production of full-bodied white wines ranging from very dry to sweet. Recent attempts to make the wines lighter have been successful, and early bottling has done much to improve these wines which only in 1968 were considered by many to be very heavy. Because of the climate and the nature of the soil, it is doubtful if the Pinot Noir will ever be successfully cultivated in Livermore. In the past dec-

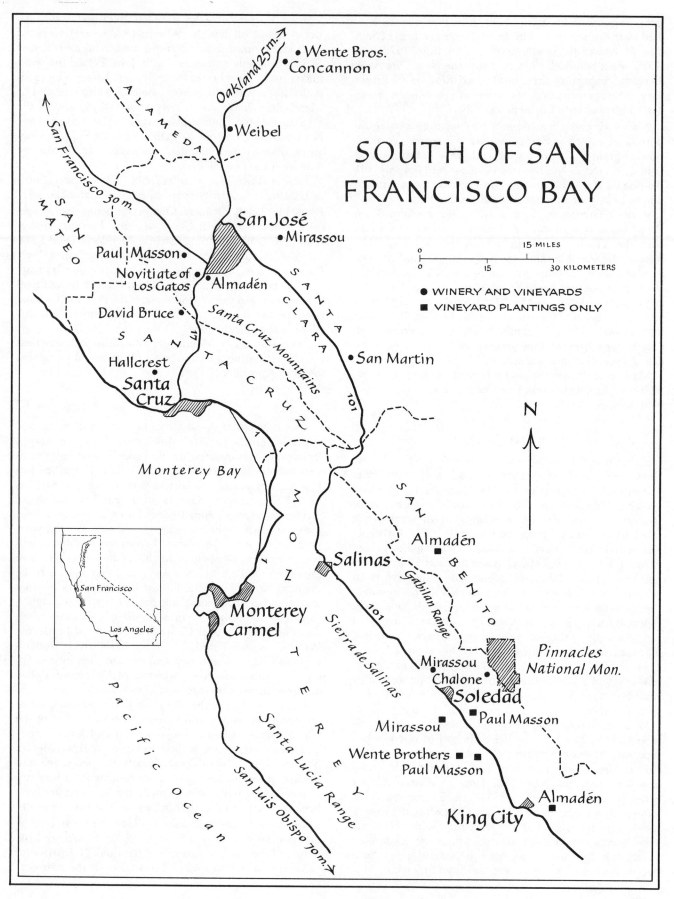

SOUTH OF SAN
FRANCISCO BAY

ALAMEDA

Oakland 25 m.

• Wente Bros.
Concannon

• Weibel

San Francisco 30 m.

SAN MATEO

San José
• Mirassou

Paul Masson •

Novitiate of
Los Gatos •
Almadén •

SANTA CLARA

15 MILES
0   15
0   30 KILOMETERS

● WINERY AND VINEYARDS
■ VINEYARD PLANTINGS ONLY

David Bruce •

Santa Cruz Mountains

SANTA CRUZ

• San Martin

101

Hallcrest •
Santa
Cruz •

N

Monterey Bay

1

MONTEREY

SAN BENITO

Almadén ■

Salinas

Gabilan Range

101

Pinnacles
National Mon.

Monterey
Carmel

Sierra de Salinas

Mirassou
Chalone •
Soledad ■

Pacific Ocean

Santa Lucia Range

San Luis Obispo 70 m.

1

Paul Masson •

Mirassou ■

Wente Brothers ■
Paul Masson ■

Almadén

King City

San Francisco
Sacramento
Los Angeles

ade, however, some good red wines have come from the valley, including a Concannon vintage Cabernet Sauvignon and Wente Gamay Beaujolais from Monterey County.

Southwest of Livermore and very close to the tip of San Francisco Bay are the wine-growing centers of Mission San José and Irvington, extending almost to Santa Clara County. In this southern Alameda district the red wines are almost as successful as the white; and sparkling wines, aperitifs, and dessert wines are all produced here too. The most important wineries are Weibel Champagne Vineyards and Llords & Elwood. Alameda's vineyards have decreased in size to only about 2,000 acres (800 hectares). However, Almadén has purchased 260 acres (104 hectares) in Pleasanton and planted the vineyards in ten sound grape varieties. South of Pleasanton, the Sunol Valley is now flourishing in vine.

Bynum Winery. Wine-maker Davis Bynum used to make wines in a small Alameda winery along San Pablo Avenue north of Berkeley, and continues to do so at his new one on an old hops ranch in Sonoma County near Healdsburg. Bynum's Petite-Sirah, Traminer, and Charbono won medals at the 1972 Los Angeles Fair. Bynum also has a small vineyard in Napa close to Rutherford.

Concannon Vineyard. This winery produces red and white table wines, and also a Muscat de Frontignan dessert wine. It was founded by James Concannon in 1883 when 47 acres (19 hectares) of land of gravelly composition were purchased in the heart of the Livermore Valley. Then, in 1889, he convinced President Porfirio Díaz of Mexico that viticulture should be established in that country on a commercial basis. Hence the Irishman from Livermore was able to ship cuttings from his vineyards to be planted in suitable areas in Mexico. In 1980, the 350-acre (140-hectare) Concannon Vineyard was sold to Augustin Huneeus, former president of Paul Masson. Jim Concannon remains involved in the vineyard management.

Concannon's Petite Sirah and Zinfandel Rosé (made from Amador County grapes) are noteworthy, as is the unusual white wine made from the Rkatsitelli grape, a Russian variety. The Livermore Valley was long known only for its white wines. But the Wente and Concannon families, neighbors for more than a century, have done much to improve the red wines of the region.

Llords & Elwood Winery. The late Julius "Mike" Elwood and his son Richard started this winery in 1955 with plants at Fremont and Mission San José, where space was leased from Weibel. They purchase grapes from nearby Alameda vineyards, and their wines bear such names as Dry Wit Sherry, Ancient Proverb Port, and Velvet Hill Pinot Noir.

Weibel Champagne Vineyards. A company specializing in champagne-type wines; a latecomer among the finer Californian wineries. Rudolph Weibel, Sr., had worked with wines in Switzerland and with Champagnes in France since 1906 and afterward settled in San Francisco in the wine importing business. He and his son, Frederick, founded the Weibel Champagne Vineyards in 1939 at Mission San José in southern Alameda County. The property was once owned by Josiah and Leland Stanford, and wine was sold under the label of Stanford.

The Weibels specialize in bottle-fermented champagne-type wines and for their Grand Cru Select they use a blend of the very fine Pinot Chardonnay.

After the death of his father, Frederick Weibel expanded the property with purchases in Mendocino. Construction of a new winery began near Ukiah in 1972.

In addition to sparkling wines, Weibel now makes vintage-dated Pinot Noir, Chardonnay, and Green Hungarian. These wines are often a pleasant surprise for those who have known the winery only for "champagne." A flor-type "sherry" has recently gained attention.

Wente Bros. An old-established property in the Livermore Valley producing good varietal wines—in particular, some of the finest Graves-type and Sauternes-type in America. The late Carl Wente, the founder, came to the U.S. from Germany in 1880 and owed his early training in Californian wines to Charles Krug of Napa Valley. Wente put his experience into practice when he purchased, in the latter part of 1883, a few vineyards in the Livermore Valley. The firm has long specialized in top-quality table wines—thanks partly to the excellent soil. The original winery and vineyards are located on Tesla Road outside Livermore.

Carl Wente enlarged his property, and his two sons, the late Herman and Ernest, added to it the valuable El Mocho Vineyards. On the El Mocho property, Louis Mel, the former owner, planted cuttings of Sémillon, Sauvignon Blanc, and Muscadelle du Bordelais from the famous Sauternes vineyard of Château d'Yquem. Today, these fine properties are in the capable hands of the Wente growers and their Château Wente sauterne is recognized for its quality.

At the present time the estate has 800 acres (320 hectares) of vineyard, of which 90% is planted in such choice white varieties.

Most of the Wente wines are labeled with varietal names rather than the misused place-names borrowed from Europe. Because of the increasing urbanization of the Livermore Valley, the former head of the winery, Karl L. Wente, continued the expansion in Monterey begun by his father, Ernest. His widow and sons, Eric and Philip, manage the vineyards. Today some of the best Wente wines come from this 300-acre (120-hectare) vineyard planted in Pinot Noir and Gamay Beaujolais, among other varieties. The Wentes make much use of machine harvesting at this plantation near Greenfield.

Profiles of new wineries and vineyards in the Livermore area, established during the wine boom of the seventies, can be found in Appendix G.

(5) Santa Clara–San Benito–Santa Cruz–Santa Barbara

The district centralizes most of its wine-growing in Santa Clara County, where there are some forty bonded wineries. This county consists of three vineyard areas. West of the Santa Clara Valley and at the foothills of the Santa Cruz Mountains lies Los Gatos, and a little to the northwest and higher up the mountain slopes, Saratoga.

This Los Gatos-Saratoga area produces some of the finest table wines and sparkling "champagnes" of California. The principal vineyards are those of Almadén, Mount Eden, Ridge, Mirassou, and Paul Masson.

The second area of Santa Clara lies to the east of San José and the vineyards of the Evergreen area stretch onto the slopes of Mount Hamilton. Although this district does not produce heavily, the wines are generally superior. The hundred-year-old home winery and vineyards of the Mirassou family are here.

The third area is in the southern part of Santa Clara County near the towns of Madrone, San Martin, and Gilroy. One of the largest in this area is San Martin, and there are many small wineries making good average wine and catering to the local trade. Santa Clara County is one of the world's greatest fruit-growing districts, and its viticultural past goes back to the days of the Spanish padres who planted the valley's first domestic grapes.

Santa Cruz County is separated from Santa Clara only by the bordering Santa Cruz Mountains. There are eight bonded wineries, and the vineyards produce good sound grapes. In the past fifteen years, this county has become more important because of its good varietal vineyards. It is gaining greater recognition, although there are only about 125 acres (50 hectares) of grapevines; most of these are at higher and cooler elevations.

The counties of San Benito and San Luis Obispo lie south of Santa Clara and Santa Cruz, and their output of table wines is improving and increasing. Largely because of Almadén, San Benito counts 5,800 acres (2,320 hectares) of varietal grapes, plus four bonded wine cellars. The producers in San Luis Obispo are grouped around the quiet town of Paso Robles.

Almadén Vineyards. These vineyards produce large quantities of jug and varietal wines. About 8 miles (13 kilometers) south of San José and between Los Gatos and the former quicksilver mining town of Almadén stands the California State Historical Landmark No. 505. "In 1852 Charles Le Franc made the first commercial planting of fine European wine grapes in Santa Clara County and founded Almadén Vineyards." Whether Le Franc or Étienne Thée, his French compatriot from Bordeaux, was the original founder, is open to debate, but it was undeniably Charles Le Franc who planted choice European grape varieties at the foot of the Santa Cruz Mountains, where the heat of the constant Californian sun is tempered by cool evening breezes from the Pacific. The rocky soil is not fertile enough for large yields, but the hillsides of Almadén offer grapes of special quality.

Almadén wines are almost all varietal wines, bearing the grape name on the label. The Pinot Chardonnay is a good American white wine; and the local Cabernet Sauvignon is a red wine of distinction. The pride of this winery is probably its particularly fine rosé—the Almadén Grenache Rosé, a really delightful pink wine.

Louis Benoist, a San Francisco businessman, bought the vineyards in 1941 and increased the acreage in varietals by securing, under the recommendation of soil experts, two vineyard tracts totaling 300 acres (120 hectares). One of these, in the Santa Cruz Mountains near Eagle Rock, is planted entirely with Johannisberg Riesling; the other, the Foothill Vineyard, lies 2 miles south of the main ranch, and its principal growths are Cabernet Sauvignon and Pinot Chardonnay.

In 1959 the 3,500-acre (1,400-hectare) Rancho Paicines, 150 miles (240 kilometers) south of San Francisco in San Benito County, was purchased by Almadén Vineyards, and grapes were planted in hillside land—among them Pinot Noir, Cabernet Sauvignon, Johannisberg Riesling, Gewürztraminer, Sémillon, and Pinot Chardonnay. The property, classified as a mountain vineyard with elevation ranging from 700 to 1,000 feet (200 to 300 meters), includes several soil types and climate exposures, particularly adapted to the cultivation of fine varietal wine grapes. Almadén later leased and then purchased the winery and 500 acres (200 hectares) of vines on the old Valliant property of the W. A. Taylor Company. This land, 4.5 miles (7.2 kilometers) south of Paicines, has become the Almadén Cienega branch. Still other new vineyards are in Alameda and Monterey. National Distillers bought Almadén in 1967; today it is one of the fastest-growing wineries in the state and is one of the largest owners of varietal wines in California.

David Bruce Winery. Located along Bear Creek Road in the peninsula town of Los Gatos, David Bruce's winery includes a small cellar and some varietal grape vineyards planted with Zinfandel, White Riesling, Pinot Noir, Chardonnay, and Cabernet Sauvignon. Dr. Bruce, a physician, has been producing wines in California since 1964. Unfortunately, the wines are often too concentrated and too alcoholic for pleasurable drinking.

Paul Masson Vineyards. Begun in Santa Clara in the 1880s, the Paul Masson operations were for many years confined to that region. Only in the late sixties did the large company move into Monterey, where the soil and climate encourage good varietal wines. The main table wine and "champagne" cellars remain at Saratoga, about 15 miles (24 kilometers) from San José.

The winery is named for a Burgundian who came around the Horn to San Francisco in 1878. Masson carried an introduction to a fellow Frenchman, Charles Le Franc, and soon the two were making a popular "champagne." Masson became Le Franc's partner, son-in-law, and when Le Franc died in 1892, his successor. In 1905 Masson built a hillside "château" and winery in the midst of his Santa Cruz mountain vineyards. Martin Ray took charge in 1936 but later established his own winery. Since 1942 Paul Masson has been owned by the Seagram distillers.

Five thousand acres (2,000 hectares) of good vineyards have been planted in the Gilroy and promising Pinnacles sections of Monterey. In addition to a selection of varietal wines, fortified wines, "champagnes," and brandies, much of the Paul Masson production consists of "proprietary" blends using grapes developed by the University of California. Examples are Rubion, Baroque, and Emerald Dry.

Mirassou Vineyards. The vineyards of Mirassou are in the

Evergreen district 5 miles (8 kilometers) east of San José and 75 miles (125 kilometers) south near Soledad in Monterey. Mirassou wines are made at Evergreen, where they may be sampled in a new tasting room.

The Mirassou wine business started in Gold Rush days. When the daughter of Pierre Pellier, himself a wine-grower, married Pierre Mirassou, the winery began to prosper. In the 1960s a fifth generation took over the company and started to sell the wines under the family name instead of in bulk as had been done before. Within a few years wines from Mirassou were known throughout the state. Auctions of varietal wines are held at the winery several times during the year.

Novitiate Winery. The Jesuit order has operated a winery in California since 1888. The present winery overlooks the town of Los Gatos and can be reached by a circuitous road from the village below. Most of the surrounding vineyards have been sold to developers, and the grapes for the wines come from 600 acres (280 hectares) in San Benito. A few are shipped from the interior valleys. Novitiate is known for its fortified dessert wines and "sherries," but has recently made good table wines. Eighty percent of the production used to be sacramental wine, and churches are still major customers.

Ridge Vineyards. Begun as an experiment by a group of Stanford University scientists, Ridge Vineyards is located high in the Santa Cruz Mountains at Cupertino. The wines made by David Bennion and three friends were such a success that he left the University to devote full time to viticulture. The abandoned nearby Montebello winery was taken over in 1970. Ridge produces annually about 20,000 cases. An excellent Zinfandel, fermented with wild yeasts, accounts for about three-quarters of the Vineyards' production. Some of the Zinfandel grapes come from Amador County.

San Martin Vineyards Co. A producer of fine varietal wines from throughout California. Since 1973, winemaster Ed Friedrich has supervised the construction of a modern production facility and has produced wines which have won nine international honors. Among the winery's unusual products are Montonico, a 100% varietal dessert wine, and several low-alcohol (10%) wines, including Chenin Blanc and Johannisberg Riesling, which are made in the German style and are known as "soft wines." San Martin also makes an elegant Zinfandel from Amador County grapes. San Martin is part of the Somerset Wine Company and is owned by Norton Simon, Inc., of New York.

(6) Monterey

This district south of San Francisco may become the largest varietal wine-growing region in California. The principal vineyards are in the Salinas Valley and foothills around Soledad and in the region of the Pinnacles National Monument. The valley runs from Monterey Bay 130 miles (210 kilometers) southeast into San Luis Obispo County. The soil is decomposed granite. After a period of intense planting (vineyard acreage tripled from 1972 to 1977) Monterey now has 34,000 acres (13,600 hectares) of

vineyard. Within the next decade the area will further overtake both Napa and Sonoma in total acres in vines.

Thirty years ago, scientists at the University of California declared that Monterey County had great potential for fine wine-growing.

The climate zones are I, II, and III. Mirassou and Paul Masson, when faced with the spreading towns of Santa Clara County, took the word of the university experts and in the early 1960s planted vines in the new district. Now at least twenty varieties of the best wine grapes grow in Monterey. The major ones are Cabernet Sauvignon, Chenin Blanc, Pinot Noir, Zinfandel, and Johannisberg Riesling.

The rich benchlands surrounding the floor of the Salinas Valley are seldom bothered by frost. They have abundant water from underground sources, including the great underground Salinas River.

Chalone Vineyards. High in the Gavilán Mountains on the eastern edge of Salinas Valley is Chalone Vineyards, founded in 1966. Owner Richard Graff hauls water by tank truck and irrigates with the Israeli "drip" system. The Chardonnay, Pinot Noir, Chenin Blanc, and Pinot Blanc are well-made regional wines.

Monterey Vineyard. Owned by Coca-Cola of Atlanta, this vineyard is one of the most northerly in the Monterey region, with a 2.2-million-gallon-capacity winery at Gonzales. Dr. Richard Peterson, who suceeded André Tchelistcheff as wine-maker at Beaulieu Vineyards, is responsible for the winery, which is backed by extensive plantings of fine varietals.

Sacramento Valley

This region extends from the northern part of San Joaquin County up as far as Oroville in Butte County and comprises Sacramento, Placer, Yolo, Amador, Butte, and northern San Joaquin counties. The Sacramento Valley is merely an extension of one great inland valley region marking the heart of Californian agriculture, but with its variations in soil, contour, and climate it is one of four important subdivisions. This region is somewhat affected by the moderating influence of San Francisco Bay, and consequently the summers become slowly hotter and the winters cooler. Some parts of the valley, particularly where the winter frosts are negligible and the summers mild, may eventually prove to be the home of better wines. Much of the land to the north is broken and irregular and entirely unsuitable to the planting of wine grapes. Butte County shows some promise, and wine grapes are grown there in increasing numbers. The whole valley produced few good grapes for many years, but a total of 3,000 acres (1,200 hectares) is now planted.

Most of the region's vineyards are found in the northern section of San Joaquin County and in Sacramento County. The majority go in for mass production, and ordinary table wines and dessert wines abound. If any of the wineries located in the Sacramento, Central, and San Joaquin valleys intend to make better wines, they must go to far-distant counties outside of these hot valleys to obtain quality grapes.

The major district of the Sacramento Valley region is

the Lodi-Sacramento, which dominates the better part of the region's wine-growing area. From the state capital of Sacramento southward to the town of Elk Grove, table and dessert wines are bulk-produced and types of "burgundies" and "ports" are made from inferior as well as from good grape varieties grown elsewhere. At Elk Grove in Sacramento County many fruit, dessert, and berry wines are produced, as well as aperitifs and table wines.

In northern San Joaquin County, the lively little city of Lodi is noted for its wineries given over to dessert wines, although table wines are also produced. However, the Lodi area, which branches out in all directions from the city, produces substantial amounts of table wine. Most is vinified from Zinfandel and Tokay grapes. San Joaquin County counts nearly 25,000 acres (10,000 hectares) of wine grapes and has one of the highest per-acre yields in the state. As might be expected, the wines are some of the least good that California can produce. There are twenty-three bonded wineries and fourteen distilleries. San Joaquin makes a great deal of brandy.

Barengo Vineyards. Known for years as Acampo Winery and Distilleries, this property was once owned by the Mondavis of Charles Krug. Dino Barengo bought it in 1944 and changed the name to Barengo Vineyards twenty years later. When in 1973 he sold the company to Marvin Adler of Los Angeles, Barengo remained as part of the management. In 1976 Ira Kirkorian and his son Kent, grape growers in the San Joaquin region, acquired Barengo. Barengo Vineyards produced the first Ruby Cabernet wine in the San Joaquin County region and is known for its German-style "May Wine," "marsala," "sherries," and "ports." Barengo also makes wine vinegar. The winery is on Highway 99, 3 miles (4.8 kilometers) north of Lodi.

East-Side Winery. Located in the eastern section of Lodi, this is a cooperative which makes and bottles many table and dessert wines, brandies and vermouths under seven different labels. A 50,000-gallon redwood barrel has been converted into a tasting room. The winery experiments with Ruby Cabernet and Emerald Riesling. Much of the East-Side brandy is sold to other firms for bottling under their own names.

Franzia Brothers. Franzia Brothers annually makes more than 8 million gallons of wine, mostly generic, at its winery situated along Highway 120, about two hours from San Francisco. In 1973, 60% of the company shares were purchased by the Coca-Cola Bottling Company of New York City, leaving the remaining shares with the Franzia family. There are nearly 1,200 acres (480 hectares) of vineyards. These were begun in 1906, the year of the San Francisco earthquake; the first Franzia winery was built in 1915. Today Franzia sells a half a dozen dessert, table, and sparkling wines under different labels. The wines are consistently improving but not high-quality. Franzia is fighting for a share of the market largely controlled by Gallo.

Guild Wineries & Distilleries. Known in California as Guild Wine Company, it is the third largest producer in the state. The headquarters on "Winemasters' Way" are within walking distance of the center of Lodi; executive offices are in San Francisco. Nine Guild wineries are spread around the state but most are grouped around Lodi and Fresno. The late Lawrence Marshall organized the cooperative in the late 1930s. Thirty years later Guild purchased Alta, Garrett, and Cribari & Sons, then bought out the Schenley subsidiaries Roma and Cresta Blanca. Guild may be best known for Vino da Tavola, a low-priced red table wine. There are fifty other products and twenty different labels.

Central Valley

The major district in the Central Valley, known as the Escalon-Modesto, contains some of the largest distributing Californian wineries. Escalon and Manteca are south of Stockton in the southern part of San Joaquin County, and the vineyards mostly lie in an east-west direction between these two small cities. The Central Valley region covers the southern San Joaquin and Stanislaus counties and takes in northern Merced County in the vicinity of Livingston. It is a large producer of table grapes—Flame Tokay, Thompson Seedless and Sultanina—and unfortunately too many of them are used in the making of wines. However, good Zinfandel plantings are increasing. The important wineries in Stanislaus County are in Modesto and Salida.

The largest winery in the world, the E. & J. Gallo Company, is in Modesto. The Central Valley produces enormous quantities of mediocre to good wines—mostly dessert wines and a few ordinary table and sparkling wines made from grape varieties that are considered heavy producers and even from table grape varieties producing a substandard quality. Approximately 500,000 short tons (445,000 long tons) of grapes are crushed yearly in this region. The area has a marked resemblance to the lesser areas of southern France and to a lesser degree Algeria, not only in climate but in wines produced. More wine grapes are being planted in the Central Valley. Today, of the 90,000 acres (36,000 hectares) in vines, two-thirds are planted with grapes that will yield fairly decent wines.

E. & J. Gallo Winery. Ernest and Julio Gallo are two of the best-known names in the American wine business. Their main winery in Modesto is the largest of its kind in the world. Other facilities are at Fresno, Cucamonga, and Livingston. Gallo has a fermenting capacity of 50 million U.S. gallons (1.8 million hectoliters, 41.5 million imp. gallons) and can bottle 150,000 cases a day. Railroad spurs run directly through the Modesto shipping area. Gallo makes its own wine bottles.

A combination of astute merchandising and a product that suits the average American taste has made Gallo wines recognized everywhere. There is obviously expertise involved in producing inexpensive but sound wines on such a huge scale. The company experiments with new wines and its staff of Ph.D.s trained in chemistry, oenology, and microbiology is the largest in California.

The best Gallo red wine grapes come from large cooperatives in Napa, Sonoma, and a few other coastal regions. Several thousand acres are farmed in the Atwater-Modesto-Livingston section of the San Joaquin Valley.

Only recently have visitors been allowed at the wineries. Today Gallo tries to put less emphasis on dessert wines and more on such table wines as "Hearty Burgundy" and "Chablis Blanc." Yet tremendous quantities of ordinary bulk table wines, apple, berry, and flavored wines are still made.

San Joaquin Valley

The region forms the southern branch of the great inland valley. It is the warmest area, a typical valley climate, with a lack of moderating sea breezes. The annual rainfall is negligible and irrigation is necessary; daytime temperatures in July and August average from 80°F to over 100°F (27°C-34°C). The San Joaquin is a great raisin area, and it produces sweet fortified wines of better than average quality. Dry table wines are also made, but they lack quality, mainly on account of the poor balance between sugar and acid in the grape varieties grown.

The principal district of the region is the Fresno-San Joaquin Valley, comprising five counties. From north to south they are: Madera (lying south of Merced County), Fresno, Kings, Tulare, and Kern counties.

Madera County vineyards surround the city of Madera, the most important in quantity being Papagni (*see* Appendix G).

Fresno County, with the city of Fresno as its center, has twenty-four bonded wineries, many of them producing wines misnamed port, sherry, sauternes, etc.—handicaps to a promising industry. The wines of the inland valley regions may be improved by the planting of better varieties. Around Fresno there are many towns with large wineries—Fowler, Selma, Reedley, Parlier, and Sanger.

Kings County's vineyards are near Hanford, while Tulare has its centers in Tulare and Cutler.

Kern County's large acreage of vineyards stretches from Delano to Arvin, outside the city of Bakersfield. There are seven wineries in Kern, and although they do not produce directly to the public, they play a considerable role in supplying wine to major firms in other areas. Approximately 1.5 million short tons (1.34 million long tons) of grapes are crushed annually in the San Joaquin Valley. More than half of the 90,000 acres (36,000 hectares) of wine grapes have been planted in the last six years.

Bear Mountain Winery. Bear Mountain is a farmer-owned cooperative in the heart of the lower San Joaquin Valley, much closer to Los Angeles than to the North Coast area. It was organized in 1966 around old winery facilities owned by the Di Giorgio farming group. Within five years Bear Mountain was harvesting more than 100,000 tons of grapes. The storage capacity of the winery at Di Giorgio in Kern County is 23 million U.S. gallons (870,000 hectoliters, 19.1 million imp. gallons).

California Growers Winery. Arpaxat Setrakian, an Armenian, founded this winery at the small town of Cutler, southeast of Fresno, in 1936. He had been for many years a leader in the raisin industry. His son Robert took charge in 1972 and has changed the production from bulk to varietal wines.

California Wine Association. This is the survivor of what was once almost a wine monopoly in California: the "Eleven Cellars" group of cooperatives. Before Prohibition the association owned more than sixty wineries. Today the one that remains is that of the Perelli-Minetti family; it is 70 miles (110 kilometers) south of Fresno on Highway 99. The head of the company was the late Antonio Perelli-Minetti, who studied wine-making in Italy and made wines for Italian Swiss Colony when he came to the U.S. in 1902. By 1970, the once large group had lost its last affiliated cellar and had to consolidate the operation in Delano. The wines are fairly sound and are sold under many of the fine old names of the California wine business, all that remains from the period when the association was an important force in the state's wine industry.

Ficklin Vineyards. Californian winery specializing in good port-type wine made from the choicest Portuguese grapes. Five of the finest varieties are used: Tinta Cão, Tinta Madeira, Alvarelhão, Souzão, and Touriga. Exceptional care goes into the making of Ficklin port, and with the help of the Davis Oenological Station, they are producing matured wines somewhat comparable with those of Portugal.

David Ficklin and Walter Ficklin, Jr., make a very small quantity of Emerald Riesling and Ruby Cabernet table wines. These two grapes were crossed especially for use in such warm regions as the one in which Ficklin is located. The small winery is in the heart of San Joaquin Valley, near the town of Madera, 22 miles (about 35 kilometers) north of Fresno.

South Coast

This region is a combination of three districts—Los Angeles County, San Diego, and Cucamonga-Ontario districts. Los Angeles and San Diego counties, lying in the southern coastal valley region, are cooled by sea breezes, while the inland district of Cucamonga-Ontario—synonymous with San Bernardino County—is an extension of the desert area, and its summers are comparable with those of the San Joaquin Valley. This warmer area is less suitable for the production of good table wines, although quite good fortified wines are made.

In the Escondido district in San Diego County, an area which once devoted most of its wine-growing to muscatels, new vineyards are producing some better-quality wines.

The most famous district in southern California is around Cucamonga. Light wines which are produced in large quantities here should be consumed early because the warm climate is not conducive to the production of full-bodied, lasting growths. Red table wine made from grape varieties which go into so-called chiantis, clarets, and burgundies is a specialty. There are a few vineyards in this area which make a fair Grignolino Rosé. Wines of all natures are produced in the Cucamonga-Ontario district, ranging from red table wines and sparkling "champagne"-types to aperitifs and dessert wines. Quality in this sun-parched region depends on the grower's integrity and his willingness to substitute quality for quantity. Grapes grown in the warmer parts of the hot desert region—such as the Coachella and Imperial valleys—are not suitable for wine and not used for such, although this area does well with its early-maturing table grapes.

Southern California is of little importance in the over-all production of wine in the state. Less than 5% of the total is made in the area. There are, however, over twenty-five wineries, six of them belonging to Brookside Vineyards. Some parts of San Diego and Santa Barbara counties are having a revival of grape and wine production. San Bernardino leads the area with 12,500 acres (5,000 hectares) of wine grapes; Santa Barbara counts about 6,000; and San Diego has about 500 acres.

Brookside Vineyard Company. Brookside, known for its Assumption Abbey label, has done much to bring wine-growing back to the southern part of the state. Beatrice Foods of Chicago owns the entire operation and has planted extensive vineyards away from the urbanized areas where certainly no good wine could be produced. The headquarters remains in Cucamonga, south of the San Bernardino Freeway on Archibald Avenue, but the new plantations are in Temecula. The company was started by two immigrants, Théophile Vaché and Marius Biane, with vineyards planted in the 1850s near Redlands. The present generation of Bianes opened retail outlets on major highways throughout southern California and parts of Arizona. Brookside holds a San Bernardino vintage festival each year.

(7) San Luis Obispo

South of Monterey, at the source of the Salinas River, San Luis Obispo County is today regaining its former reputation as an important vine-growing region. Endowed with a favorable microclimate, its wine-producing future looks promising. Paso Robles is the capital of the region, and the area near the cities of Shandon and Templeton, and the Edna Valley, are most important to the wine industry.

Hoffman Mountain Ranch Vineyards. Dr. Stanley Hoffman, a cardiologist from Beverly Hills, has had his vineyards at the foot of the Santa Lucia Mountains, 6½ miles (10 kilometers) west of Paso Robles, since 1965, when he and his wife, Theresa, and their sons David and Michael left the city to become vine-growers and winemakers. Guided by the great oenologist André Tchelistcheff, the Hoffmans have planted mostly Pinot Noir and Chardonnay grape varieties, which grow well in the chalky soil. They also produce an excellent Zinfandel.

York Mountain Winery. Far off the beaten wine track, York Mountain is at the town of Templeton, halfway between Los Angeles and San Francisco. The vineyards are on the eastern slopes of the Santa Lucia Mountains in San Luis Obispo County. In 1881 Andrew York and his three sons built a small stone winery where family members operated until the early 1970s, when it was sold to Max Goldman.

More information on San Luis Obispo vineyards can be found in Appendix G.

United States: Maryland

Maryland's climate is eminently suited to the culture of the grapevine, but few have taken advantage of it. One exception is the admirably run Boordy Vineyard in Riderwood, near Baltimore, which produces about 7,000 cases annually (three-fifths of the entire state's produc-tion). Mr. and Mrs. Philip Wagner, who introduced French hybrids commercially to the United States, founded Boordy Vineyard in 1945. Apart from their extensive experimentation with different types of grapes, the Wagners also demonstrated, with the wines they made, how good eastern American wines from hybrid grapes can be, if properly handled. Their contributions to American wine-making are enormous. Although the Wagners continue to grow grapes and operate their nursery, which features a wide variety of hybrid vines, the Deford family acquired the Boordy Vineyard in 1980.

There are several small wineries of interest in Maryland, including Montbray Wine Cellars, where America's first Riesling "Ice Wine" was made in 1974. See Appendix G for further information.

United States: Michigan

The grapes are grown in the southern part of the state at Benton Harbor and Paw Paw, near Lake Michigan. Concord grapevines take up most of the vineyard space, with some Catawba and Delaware, but the dry, sweet, and sparkling wines—all three types are made—are inferior to those produced elsewhere in the United States.

The most important winery from the standpoint of quantity is Warner Vineyards, formerly Michigan Wineries, which produces wines from native and hybrid grape varieties. But in Berrien County, not far from the lake, is the Tabor Hill vineyard, where the owners make sound table wine and experiment with plantings of *Vitis vinifera*, such as the Chardonnay and Riesling. Here, as elsewhere, the *vinifera* varieties, along with hybrids, will spell the future of good table wines.

See Appendix G for more information on wine-growing in Michigan.

United States: New York

With an annual production of nearly 112 million U.S. gallons (4.5 million hectoliters, 93 million imp. gallons) New York makes more wine than any other state except California, which makes almost ten times as much. Yet of greater significance than the vast disparity of volumes are the two fundamentally different grapevine species at the heart of New York and California wines. Most California vines are *Vitis vinifera*, the classic European grape varieties, with certain French and American hybrids and table grapes also producing wine. In New York the hybrids are perhaps even more important, but the soul of most New York State wines was the vine species *Vitis labrusca*, the native American variety (*see* Chapter Eight).

Eastern American wines have had little in common with those made in Europe or California. This difference, however, should not be taken as an immediate sign of inferiority. The native wines of any country in the world have their own merits and their own occasions, and when the grower realizes his function and produces wines that fulfill their proper part, such wines cannot be replaced by the product of other lands. Some growers, of course, understand their role better than do others. This explains the rivalry between those who are realistically trying to adapt their vineyards to the existing conditions of soil and climate and those who try to reproduce wines of Europe or California. To confound the confusion, there is a further rivalry among America's more realistic growers—a struggle between those who advocate the use of native American vines and others who are tending more and more toward the use of hybrid vines. At present, native American vines have the larger following, but hybrids and *Vitis vinifera* are the vines of the future.

WINE HISTORY OF NEW YORK AND EASTERN U.S.

The Vikings are said to have made the first trip from Europe to the New World. What they saw, apparently, was vines, for they named the new country Vineland. History neglects North America for several centuries thereafter, but conditions on the continent remained so far unchanged that early settlers almost to a man were fired by the prospect of making wine in their new territory. The first wines were produced from wild grapes—and were found to be thoroughly unsatisfactory. European vines were imported—and speedily died. The first grape that has come down to us as being even remotely suitable for making palatable wine is the Alexander, an accidental cross between an American (perhaps *Vitis labrusca*) and a European vine. It is named for its discoverer, John Alexander, the gardener of William Penn.

With the example of the Alexander before them, the workers in the vineyards made various attempts to develop a grapevine more suitable to the wine-maker. Numerous grapes were brought forward, most of which flourished briefly, if at all, then fell into a well-deserved oblivion. Some have continued. Catawba, Concord, Delaware, Elvira, and smaller amounts of Diana, Dutchess, Noah, and a few other early crossings may still be found here and there, but with the exception of Concord, the amount of land devoted to them is small and getting smaller. Concord is enjoying new life, thanks to its adaptability for making sweet "strictly kosher" wine, and for reasons not connected with the making of wine. Its potential for use in table wines is nil.

All of these grapes were technically hybrids, the result of crossing different vines. But in all cases they were crossings of two or more native American vines and had no European blood. Later hybridizers have been crossing European with American vines, aiming at some combination of European grape quality and American vine hardiness. The search for the better vine continues, but a significant number of these "French hybrids" have been tested and set out in American vineyards. In many cases the results have been remarkably good.

With certain exceptions, the blending of wine from native grapes with that from hybrids infuriates the hybrid advocates. Even a small addition of native juice gives the characteristic "foxiness" of American vines, and this foxiness is the crux of the problem. The expression has nothing to do with foxes. Probably it came from the pronounced taste and pungent aroma of the wild ("fox") grape. Wine-drinkers who do not like this characteristic—and many do not—insist that it must be eliminated before eastern America can produce any wines it can put forward with pride. Those drinkers who are not disturbed by

foxiness—and again many are not—feel that it is the traditional mark of eastern American vines and that to do away with it would be to rob them of their most distinctive heritage. History alone will judge between them.

VINE-GROWING REGIONS

The more than 40,000 acres (16,000 hectares) of wine vineyards are grouped in four distinct regions. By far the most famous is the Finger Lakes area, then the up-and-coming Hudson River Valley, followed by Chautauqua and the United States portion of the Niagara Peninsula. Wine grapes are now planted, too, on eastern Long Island.

(1) Finger Lakes

The important vineyards border lakes Keuka and Canandaigua, and to a lesser extent, Seneca and Cayuga. The Finger Lakes form a series of slits gouged out by an ancient glacier and extending like outstretched fingers into the gently rolling countryside. Upper New York's normally harsh climate is tempered by the waters into something nearly ideal for grapevines. The stony, volcanic earth is rich with minerals and the vine roots can penetrate far below the winter frost-level, where underground water lies to feed the vines in the dry summer months. Though the first vines were planted in Hammondsport by the Episcopal Reverend James Bostwick in 1829, wine-making was not begun on a large scale until several decades later. And when many wineries did build in the area after the Civil War, sparkling wines were the most important products. Sparkling wines of different types are, as ever, dominant, but still wines are by no means overlooked.

The firms in the Hammondsport–Pleasant Valley section, at the southern end of Lake Keuka, include the large Taylor Wine Company and its subsidiary, the Pleasant Valley Wine Company—home of the well-known Great Western New York State champagne-type wine. Pleasant Valley and Taylor blend wines from more than thirty grape varieties, half of them hybrids. The grapes are grown at vineyards as far away as 120 miles (190 kilometers) from the wineries, which stand side by side in the town of Hammondsport.

A few miles north of these two is the Gold Seal Winery, pleasantly situated on the western shore of Lake Keuka. Gold Seal, formerly the Urbana Wine Company, is best known for its Charles Fournier brand of sparkling wines. Most Finger Lakes sparkling wines are still made from Catawba, Delaware, Elvira, and some Isabella grapes, with, in most cases, neutral or flat-tasting wines from California. This blending with Californian wines is necessary to reduce the overbearing taste of foxiness of the eastern varieties. Most of these sparkling wines are fermented in the bottle. Mr. Fournier was once the head of Gold Seal and should be noted for having hired one of the most interesting wine men in the United States, Dr. Konstantin Frank, and for implementing some of Frank's ideas.

Dr. Frank, a Russian immigrant and now a septuagenarian, proudly and somewhat fiercely makes wines from European grape varieties at his Vinifera Vineyards not

NEW YORK STATE

```
0    20    40    60    80    100 MILES
0      40      80      120      160 KILOMETRES
```

far from the Gold Seal Winery. He had worked at vineyards in many parts of Europe before coming to the United States and eventually to the Finger Lakes region, where the plantings of native vines and hybrids puzzled him. Having successfully cultivated the sensitive *vinifera* vines in the Russian cold, he refused to believe that the same vines could not survive the milder—though still quite chilly—New York winters. Frank finally convinced Charles Fournier that the great European vines would do well at Hammondsport, and Riesling and Chardonnay vines were planted in an experimental Gold Seal vineyard. (These wines are now, for the most part, blended with other Gold Seal products.) Frank now has his own 80-acre (30-hectare) estate run with the help of his son and son-in-law. His best wines are white, made from Riesling, Chardonnay, or Gewürztraminer grapes, including a few rare examples of late- or selected-picking Riesling wines in the style of German Spätlesen or Beerenauslesen wines. Konstantin Frank is, with another Russian immigrant, André Tchelistcheff in northern California, one of the most dedicated men making wine in America today.

Another winery north of Hammondsport is owned by Walter S. Taylor, perhaps the most publicized New York

vintner after Dr. Frank. Taylor is the grandson of the founder of the Taylor Wine Company, from which he was parted in 1970 after publicly criticizing the production methods of the family company itself and those of other eastern winemakers. His sloping Bully Hill Vineyards above Keuka Lake have a good mixture of gravel, clay, and minerals in the soil, which supports abundant growth for better *labrusca* vines, French-American hybrids, and some *viniferas*. Baco Noir, Chelois, Seyval Blanc, Foch, Aurora, Diamond, and a few Riesling and Pinot Chardonnay vines are planted on the 250 acres (100 hectares) of vineyards. Most of the land faces southeast. Bully Hill wines generally have varietal names and vintage dates. The production of both Bully Hill and Vinifera Vineyards is tiny compared with that of the giant local wineries.

Naples, on Lake Canandaigua, is the headquarters of Widmer's Wine Cellars, owned by the R. T. French Company of Rochester. The late Will Widmer, son of the founder, was trained in Germany at the Geisenheim wine school and produced light table wines which represented the best that could be made from the native grapes of eastern America. Many Widmer wines are vintage-dated varietals, perhaps the only ones made from *labrusca* grapes. The company makes a quantity of fortified sherry-type wine that is aged dramatically for several years in casks lying on the winery roof. Widmer also grows *vinifera* grapes and makes wine in the Alexander Valley in Sonoma County, California.

(2) Hudson River Valley

The region extends from Newburgh (71 miles [28.4 kilometers] from New York City) northward for roughly 15 miles (6 kilometers). It is actually more of a center for table grapes than wine grapes, although many growers sell their Concord grapes to be made into kosher wine.

One of the best-known vineyards is unquestionably High Tor, situated on the famous hill from which it derives its name—the hill immortalized by Maxwell Anderson. The former owner and radio writer, Everett Crosby, experimented both with native American vines and with hybrids. Crosby has continued as a consultant to Richard Voigt, the present proprietor, whose wines bear the names High Tor or Rockland. The white table wines, for example, are produced mostly from Delaware grapes, while the reds and rosés come from hybrids.

Another important Hudson Valley wine is made slightly upriver near Highland, on a bluff overlooking the great valley. The Hudson Valley Wine Company was founded by the Bolognesi family and is now owned by Herbert Feinberg, who with his two brothers was a partner in the Monsieur Henri wine importing firm, sold to Pepsi-Cola in the seventies. It is regrettable that more of the *Vitis labrusca* vines have not been replaced by *Vitis vinifera* and French-American hybrids.

In Ulster County at Marlboro is the Benmarl Wine Company—the name comes from the Gaelic words meaning "slate hill." Mark Miller, an illustrator who lived in the Burgundy district of France for six years, bought the well-situated vineyard estate, where in the nineteenth century the *labrusca* hybrid Dutchess was developed. Since the purchase in 1957, Miller and his family have replanted the site with the help of Dr. Konstantin Frank, who advocates *vinifera* vines, and Philip Wagner, who champions the French-American hybrids. Most of the vines are made from hybrids, but a sizable percentage of the vineyard will be in *viniferas* when the full expansion is realized. A remarkable Seyval-Blanc from Benmarl has impressed French and American wine experts. The owners and advisers of Benmarl Wine Company have joined with other producers in the area to promote the Mid-Hudson Valley as a place-name to identify the local wines, as Napa or Sonoma Valley does for those northern California wines. And indeed, the Hudson Valley may well become for New York City what the Napa Valley is for San Francisco. Benmarl can be reached in a little over an hour from New York City and promises to be among the better vineyards in the nation.

(3) Chautauqua

The Chautauqua "belt" starts west of Buffalo, skirts along to the south of Lake Erie, cuts a path through a piece of Pennsylvania, and ends up at last in Ohio. Its vineyards abound in Concord grapes, most of which are for use as table grapes. Chautauqua's wine is "kosher."

Grapes were planted here by 1818, before the start of the first Finger Lakes vineyard. Again, a minister set out the vines, and again, it was many years before a winery was built. Those wineries that were producing at the end of the nineteenth century were harried by temperance movements and by the Welch brothers, who made Chautauqua the Concord grape juice center of the nation, and indeed the world, at the turn of the century. Today the Frederick Johnson winery in Westfield is the only one of importance.

(4) Niagara

The vineyards stand on both sides of the Niagara River between Lake Erie and Lake Ontario, partly in New York State and partly in Canada. On the American side, considerable quantities of table wine are made, partly from hybrids and partly from the native grapes which are grown generally east of Buffalo. (*See also* Canada.) The Niagara Falls Wine Cellar is at Lewiston, not far from the town of Niagara Falls.

NATIVE WINE GRAPES OF NEW YORK AND EASTERN U.S.

A large number of grapevines have been developed in the United States, but most have, for one reason or another, proved themselves unsuitable for the production of wine grapes. A few have been satisfactory and are still under cultivation. Some of the more important are:

Concord. This blue-black grape is the most widely planted in the eastern United States. It is adaptable to a wide variety of soils and climates, has several uses, and is hardy and productive. However, it is useless for the purposes of the wine-maker, because of its strong foxy attributes. In recent years it has enjoyed a considerable vogue, thanks to its suitability for making very sweet kosher wines.

Fredonia. A close relative of the Concord. Fredonia is planted in New Jersey but is rare elsewhere. It is of little interest to the informed wine-drinker.

Isabella. A dark-red, almost black grape now found in the New York Finger Lakes region. It is often used with Catawba and Delaware for the New York State sparkling wines.

Norton. A poor producer, and easily killed in a bad winter. Its grapes are red and extremely high in acidity.

Catawba. The most ubiquitous white-grape-producing vine. It is used both for still white wines and for sparkling wines, notably in New York State and Ohio.

Delaware. One of the better *Vitis labruscas*. A light producer, handicapped with a foxy taste, this Eastern *Vitis labrusca* was once extensively planted. Fortunately, it is on its way out.

Diana. A delicate vine producing white grapes. Its culture is almost entirely confined to the vineyards of Widmer's Wine Cellars in New York State.

Diamond. Not an outstanding wine grape, but one still to be found in the New York Finger Lakes region.

Dutchess. An "average" grape found today, as is Diana, almost entirely in New York.

Elvira. Produces grapes for white wine but has almost disappeared from the American scene because of its low sugar content and the consequent low alcoholic content of the wine that comes from it.

Noah. Another white grape which is slowly dying out. A few plantations may still be found in New Jersey.

HYBRID WINE GRAPES

Every country has experimented with hybrids. American hybrids are given names, whereas the French (these two being of the most importance in American viticulture) carry only the name of the hybridizer and a number. Some outstanding grapes are:

Alpha. An American hybrid for red wine grapes. It is praised for its ability to withstand ferociously cold winters, but its wine is extraordinarily high in acid.

Baco 1. A French hybrid for red wines. It is far more satisfactory in the northern United States than it is in its native France. Wine made from this grape is often called Baco Noir.

Foch. An early-ripening red wine grape, originally from Alsace. It is vigorous and easy to handle.

Seibel 5455. A good, steady, red wine variety, making a sound, well-balanced wine.

Seibel 7053. A heavily-producing vine giving grapes that make a sound, ordinary red wine.

Seibel 13053. A vigorous vine for grapes which make either a light attractive red wine or a good rosé. The wines are known as Cascade.

Seibel 5279. A French hybrid giving a pale, light wine bearing some resemblance to the wines of Alsace.

Seibel 9110. Gives a white grape that is particularly suitable as a table grape but can be used to make a perfumed white wine.

Seyve-Villard 5276. A productive vine. Gives a white wine that is clean and fresh and generally excellent. One of the most promising of the French hybrids. Well known as Seyval-Blanc.

Seyve-Villard 12375. Gives a white grape that can be used either as a table grape or to make a sound white wine.

United States: Ohio

Ohio's largest wine district borders Lake Erie, running roughly from Vermillion westward to Port Clinton, with Sandusky as its geographical and vinicultural center. The most important vineyards are on Middle Bass Island—although of almost the same importance are those at Kelley—and on North Bass and South Bass (or Put-in-Bay) islands. The Catawba grape is the traditional favorite, although recently other native varieties and some hybrids have replaced it in a number of instances.

The wines may be either red or white and mostly still, although there are some good sparkling wines. For the most part, the still wines are treated with sugar, a practice that raises alcoholic content but generally does little for quality. They are also often blended with neutral Californian wines, with the result that quantity is increased and some of the wine's wild foxiness is toned down. It might be thought that these practices would destroy any intrinsic Ohio characteristics the wines might have, and such is certainly the case with many of them. But at their best,

they have a forthright individuality of character and are sound and presentable table wines. The best still wines are white, but the sparkling wines outshine them.

Meiers Wines Cellars is the leading firm, with wineries at Sandusky and the principal establishment at Silverton, a suburb of Cincinnati. Most of the state's wine is produced by this company, which makes over 2.5 million gallons (94,000 hectoliters, 2 million imp. gallons). Meiers has a quite successful vineyard overlooking the Ohio River at New Richmond, 20 miles (36 kilometers) east of Cincinnati. This part of the state was once the most important vineyard in the country and gained the title Rhineland of America. It was here that Nicholas Longworth planted extensive vineyards and made his famous sparkling Catawba wine in the nineteenth century.

Though black rot, oïdium, and phylloxera have attacked the Ohio vineyards since Longworth's time, recent wines from this picturesque site (called Jac-Jan Vineyard) give some idea of the qualities that made Ohio River wines dear in Europe and America 150 years ago. The Jac-Jan Vineyard is planted in French-American hybrid vines.

Other wineries in the state include Heineman, Lonz, Steuk's, and Markko—all in the area of the Lake Erie Islands or Sandusky. Also noteworthy is the *Vitis vinifera*-planted Grand River Winery in Madison.

For more on wine in Ohio, *see* Appendix G.

United States: Oregon

As in neighboring Washington State, the potential of wine-growing in Oregon is rapidly being realized. Parts of the state have the same cool climate found in wine-producing areas in Washington and California, but the number and size of the vineyards remain quite small; some 1,000 acres (400 hectares) is now under vine.

The Hillcrest Vineyard at Roseburg is the pioneer wine-making enterprise in the state. Its owner learned viniculture from Maynard Amerine at the University of California and has experimented with vineyard sites since 1963. Hillcrest and several other wineries have formed a wine-growers' association.

See Appendix G for further information.

United States: Pennsylvania, Rhode Island, Tennessee, Texas

See Appendix G.

United States: Virginia

The vineyards in this state are few in number but the wine is good. The plantings are situated principally in Albemarle and Clarke counties.

One large winery in Petersburg makes quantities of Scuppernong wine—a contemporary cousin of what was probably the first wine made in the eastern United States.

See Appendix G.

United States: Washington

Within only a few years, Washington may produce more grapes than any other state except California.

Large, fertile, irrigated vineyards are being developed in the southern part of the state and in the Yakima River Valley in the east; these plantations count more than 20,000 acres (8,000 hectares) of vines, and the vineyard is rapidly expanding.

The climate of the Washington vine-growing districts is at least as good as the weather in the best California regions. The valleys are cool, with relatively little frost, and the growing season is usually sufficient to produce well-ripened wine grapes with an acceptable balance of sugar and acidity. These conditions make Washington State vineyards particularly suitable to the best varieties of *Vitis vinifera*, the species of classic European wine grapes. Pinot Noir, Cabernet Sauvignon, Gewürztraminer, Riesling, Sémillon, and Chardonnay are planted both in test plots at the state agricultural experiment stations and in the many new private vineyards recently set out.

Grape production is preceding the making of wine: Washington supplies grapes to wineries in northern California, southern British Columbia, and Canada. The American Wine Growers make wine in Washington from Washington-grown grapes (the wines are called Ste. Michelle), as does Associated Vintners of Kirkland. More information on new Washington State wineries can be found in Appendix G.

United States: Wisconsin

See Appendix G.

Upper Moselle

See Mosel-Saar-Ruwer.

Uruguay

The smallest of the South American countries achieves a vinous importance incommensurate with its size by producing some 1,000,000 hectoliters (26.45 million U.S. gallons, 22.0 million imp.) of wine annually; but the Uruguayan is a wine-drinking man and little of it is exported. Small amounts sometimes trickle into neighboring Brazil, but, in general, if you want to drink Uruguayan wines you must go to Uruguay.

Red, white, and rosé wines are made. The pink is considerably deeper in color than is usual, verging more toward Spanish *clarete* than French rosé. Vermouth is also produced, and some fortified and sparkling wines. Contrary to the general rule, fortified wines are often sold as port and sparkling wines as champagne, but in other respects, Uruguayans tend to prefer wines with local names; or wines named from the dominant or informing grape used. The most widespread vine is Harriague, and it is reasonably established that this is the Tannat of Madiran in the French Pyrenees. Vidiella, of obscure origin, and Cabernet from the Bordeaux region of France are also fairly widely planted; and when wine from the two is blended together the result is well balanced and

agreeable. Some Barbera and Nebbiolo—imported from Italy and keeping their original names—are also to be found. White wines are made, notably from Sémillon and Pinot Blanc grapes. Some hybrids and the American Isabella vine are planted, but the increased production of these varieties is accompanied—as it always is—by a marked decrease in quality.

Uruguayan viticulture was established in the 1890s near Montevideo and today extends over the low hills and plains of the departments of Montevideo, Canelones, San José, and Maldonado (along the River Plate), Soriano and Paysandú (next to Argentina), and Florida (in central Uruguay). The country is actually an extension of the Brazilian plain, and the gently rolling, volcanic hills—*cuchillas*—never rise above 600 meters (2,000 feet). Climate is temperate and mild—maintaining an average high of 71°F. (22°C.) in the summer months of January and February, and an average low of 50°F. (10°C.) in the winter months of July—and rainfall is sufficient but not excessive. The vineyards cover about 22,000 hectares (55,000 acres).

SPIRITS

The Uruguayans distill quantities of brandy—most of which is miscalled cognac—and some grappa, distilled from pomace after the grapes have been pressed. Caña—a type of rum—is popular, as is amara (or amargo), an aperitif. Anisette, gin, and guindado (fermented cherries reinforced with alcohol) are also fairly common. A popular Vino Seco is made by adding a large quantity of white wine to red, then enriching the mixture with wine alcohol and letting the whole maderize in the sun, a process which sounds somewhat distressing to conservative amateurs of wine. All wines and spirits are controlled by the state, and various schools at the University of Uruguay are attempting to improve knowledge, and thus wines, by sending students to study abroad, particularly in Italy and France.

Ürziger Würzgarten

White wine.
Middle Mosel.

The best wine-producing vineyard of Ürzig produces a spicy and fruity wine, from volcanic and slate soil of such steepness that vintaging becomes a death-defying mountain sport.

See Mosel-Saar-Ruwer.

Usquebaugh

The anglicized form of *uisge beatha*, original Celtic name for whisky.

U.S.S.R.

See Russia.

V

Vacqueyras

One of the best communes of the Côtes du Rhône, producing white, red, and rosé wines.
See Rhône.

Vaduzer

Red wine of Liechtenstein.

Two-thirds of the wine which is grown in the little principality on the Swiss-Austrian border is called Vaduzer, after Vaduz, the capital. The remaining third is produced in Schaan, Triesen and Balzers and known as Schaaner, Triesner and Balzner.

Vineyards were probably established in Liechtenstein by Roman invaders and later by monks in the first centuries of the Christian era. At this time the country was not Liechtenstein but a part of the Roman Empire (and later of Germany). In 1699 and 1712, the Princes of Liechtenstein purchased the Rhine plains and towering mountains, over which they have ruled ever since. All the vines were cultivated by monks until 150 years ago, when the vineyards were secularized. Today, some 800 hectoliters (20,000 U.S. gallons, 17,000 imp.) are made annually.

Vaduzer is a light wine, bordering on a rosé. It is made exclusively from the Blauburgunder grape, although in earlier times white Elbling was the dominating grape there. Riesling-Sylvaner was tried too; but both varieties were abandoned. The small growers have a cooperative, and a single domain, Bockwingert, comprises about half the vineyard area in Vaduz. The most interesting estate is the Abtwingert, the vineyard of the Rotes Haus.

In 1525, this Red House already belonged to the Benedictines of the order of Saint Johann in Toggenberg. It was probably a hundred or more years old then. A visit to the massive Gothic wine press still in operation in the cellars shows why the Rotes Haus is classed second to the castle of the Prince of Liechtenstein among the sights of the principality. In the middle of the nineteenth century, Alois Rheinberger—the Rheinbergers are the present owners—took the methods of Vaduzer wine-making to Illinois and planted the well-known vineyard of Masberg Mansion at Nauvoo.

Val d'Adige

Common red wine grown on the banks of the River Adige, in Trentino.
See Trentino-Alto Adige.

Valais

The dramatic alpine vineyard region on either narrow bank of the upper Rhône River east of Geneva in Switzerland (*q.v.*).

Valdepeñas

Favorite wine of the cafés of Madrid, grown in vineyards south of the capital in La Mancha. Strong red wines and dry white wines. Until the great popularity of Rioja, this was the best-known Spanish non-fortified wine.
See Spain.

Valgella

Red wines of Valtellina, Italy, made from the Nebbiolo grape.
See Lombardy.

Valpantena

A wine somewhat similar to Valpolicella.
See Veneto.

Valpolicella

The best wines of Veneto, in Italy—ruby red, fragrant and fruity, with a delicate bouquet and a rich texture.
See Veneto.

Valtellina

Name of a series of red Italian wines made from Nebbiolo grapes.
See Lombardy.

Van der Hum

A South African liqueur of which the principal ingredient is the peel of the *nartjie,* a type of South African orange. The subsidiary ingredients vary according to the producer, each one of whom has his own closely guarded formula. The liqueur is tawny in color and has a strong taste of orange. Van der Hum means "what's his name"; a variation, known as Brandy-Hum, is made by diluting Van der Hum to half quantity with brandy, thus reducing the sweetness.
See South Africa.

Varietal wine

American term for wine made wholly or predominantly from the grape variety named on the label, such as California Pinot Noir, New York State Riesling, etc. Legally, such wine must be made of at least 51% wine from the grape named. The rule was established in an attempt to break away from meaningless generic names such as Californian burgundy and is now followed by most of the best wine-makers. The day when American producers cease entirely to use misappropriated and misapplied European place-names and adopt varietal names for wines that are strictly American will be a bright day indeed for American wine-lovers.

Vat

A container for wine, varying in size; the name is derived from the Dutch word for 100 liters (1 hectoliter—or 26.4 U.S. gallons, 22 imp.). It is the usual translation for the French *cuve*—a vessel of oak, stainless steel, or cement (sometimes lined with glass) in which wines are fermented and blended.

V.D.P.V. (Verband Deutscher Prädikatswein-Versteigerer)

The most important association of wine-growers in Germany. In German, a *Versteigerer* is an auctioneer, and the name of the organization reflects that time when many of the important individual estates held auctions for the sales of their wines. Today only a small number of the vineyard owners of Germany belong, but many of the very best producers do. As a group, their purpose is to maintain the quality of and promote the cause of fine German wines. Quite often the label of the member estate will include the emblem of the association: a black eagle with grapes on its breast surrounded by the letters V.D.P.V. Until the passage of the 1971 West German Wine Law, the name was Verband Deutscher Naturwein-Versteigerer, but the new title was adopted to conform to the ruling abolishing the use of the word *Natur* with regard to wine.
See Germany.

V.D.Q.S.

These letters stand for Vins Délimités de Qualité Supérieure, or delimited wines of superior quality. They are found on wines from certain sections of France—wines which are considered good enough to be quality-controlled, but not of the caliber of the wines of Appellation d'Origine Contrôlée. In effect, they make up a secondary classification of the better wines of France.

Although the classification only dates back to 1949, it includes a number of wines, some of them extremely good. Many of the better—but none of the best—wines of France are included, and previously all the best wines of Algeria. In the decrees covering the various V.D.Q.S. wines, the growing area, the vines permitted, and the minimum limits of alcohol are always stipulated. In most cases, the wines must be tasted by a committee of experts set up for that purpose and only after approval has been given have they the right to the name. V.D.Q.S. wines carry these initials as well as the name of the place of origin on their labels, and in the case of estate-bottled wines, the name of the grower will also be included. They are likely to be good buys, if they can be found, and provided most of the price goes for the wine and not for duties and transportation, for they are sound and do not carry the high price that may go with a greater reputation.

V.D.Q.S. Place-Name Wines

Auvergne	Gros Plant du Pays Nantais
Cabrières	La Clape
Châteaumeillant	Minervois
Châtillon-en-Diois	Montpeyroux
Cheverny	Pic-Saint-Loup
Corbières	Picpoule de Pinet
Corbières Supérieures	Quatourze
Costières du Gard	Rosé de Béarn
Coteaux d'Aix-en-Provence	Rousselet de Béarn
Coteaux d'Ancenis	Roussette de Bugey
Coteaux des Baux-en-Provence	Saint-Chinian
Coteaux du Giennois	Saint-Drézéry
Coteaux du Languedoc	Saint-Georges-d'Orques
Coteaux du Luberon	Saint-Saturnin
Coteaux de la Méjanelle	Sauvignon de Saint-Bris
Coteaux de Pierrevert	Valençay
Coteaux de Saint-Christol	Vin d'Entraygues
Coteaux de Vérargues	Vin d'Estaing
Coteaux du Vendômois	Vin du Haut-Poitou
Côtes d'Auvergne	Vin de Lavilledieu
Côtes de Cabardès et de l'Orbiel	Vin de Marcillac
Côtes de Forez	Vin de la Moselle
Côtes de Frontonnais	Vin Noble du Minervois
Côtes de la Malepere	Vin de l'Orleánais
Côtes-du-Marmandais	Vin de Saint-Pourçain-sur-Sioule
Côtes Roannaises	Vin du Thoursais
Côtes de Toul	Vin du Tursan
Côtes du Vivarais	Vins de Bugey
Faugères	Vins du Lyonnais
Fronton	

(V.D.Q.S. wines are treated in this book either under their own proper names—Corbières, Minervois, for example—or under regional headings: e.g., Provence.)

Veldt

One-time unit of measure used in Cognac, now extinct: 27 veldts equaled a Cognac cask of 205 liters, 35 veldts equaled 72 U.S. gallons, 60 imp.

Velletri

Red or white D.O.C. wines from Latium (*q.v.*).

Veltliner

White wine grape grown in Austria and Czechoslovakia, and also to a small extent in California.

Velvety

Used of a wine which, through ageing, has reached sufficient maturity to conserve body, yet produces a sensation of great smoothness.

Vendange

French term for the grape harvesting; also the vintage season.

Venencia

In Spain, especially Jerez de la Frontera, a bullet-shaped silver cup on a pliable whalebone handle usually about two and a half feet long. This is used for taking samples from Sherry casks.

Veneto (Venetia)

Red and white wines.
District: Northeast Italy.

The wines of Veneto are about the most charming and consistently good in Italy, although rarely if ever could one of them be classified as great. The region around Venice produces some 8.5 million hectoliters (225 million U.S. gallons, 187 million imp.) per year and is considered third in importance among Italian wine districts. Soave is dry, white, and—as the name implies—distinctly suave, while Valpolicella, Valpantena, and Bardolino perform graceful variations on a theme, the dominant notes of which are dry, red, and light. The typically Italian pungency and harshness seem to be absent from these wines, which come from the vineyards around Verona, city of Romeo and Juliet. Wander round Verona's Roman amphitheater or listen to the opera on a summer evening; amble through the ancient streets or into one of the medieval courtyards—and the Veronese wines, pleasant to drink anywhere, here seem perfectly delicious. It is true that wines always taste best in their own district; but these, fortunately, are able to travel—and seem to carry a bit of Verona with them.

THE BEST WINES OF VENETO

Valpolicella and Recioto della Valpolicella (D.O.C.)

This is unquestionably the best. It is ruby-red, of medium alcoholic content (perhaps 10% to 13%), has a delicate bouquet and a rich, mouth-filling texture. Every now and then a bottle will emerge with a slight trace of residual sugar, which will start working in the bottle, giving the wine a *frizzante* or prickling taste that is by no means unpleasant. As is the case with other Veronese wines, the best bottles can be expected to come from the smaller houses—because of the unfortunate predilection many firms have for labeling wines according to demand rather than supply.

The principal grapevines cultivated in the vineyards of Valpolicella are Corvina, Rondinella, Rossignola, Negrara, and Molinara; Barbera and Sangiovese vines may also be found in the area.

Valpantena, the name of a valley within the district, is a good example of the local wine, and its labels will carry the valley name following the word *Valpolicella*. Recioto della Valpolicella (D.O.C.) is produced in nineteen communes from partly dried, selected grapes—the result is a

particularly interesting sort of Veneto wine. The name derives from the word *recia*, which means "ear" in the local dialect, and it is from the "ear" or uppermost part of the grape bunch that the ripest fruit is selected to make this wine. Recioto may be dry, semi-sweet, or sweet and sparkling. The dry wine is called Amarone (D.O.C.).

Bardolino (D.O.C.)

This is grown in the place of that name, and in the neighboring territories on the southeastern shore of Lake Garda: a dry wine, clear ruby-red in color. When very young, it has a beguiling charm, which it tends to lose after a very short time. The "new look" in Italian viniculture is very much in evidence here, for Bardolino is now being fermented a considerably shorter time than is traditional, resulting in a wine which is lighter, fresher, cleaner, and distinctly more pleasant than it would otherwise be, with an alcoholic content of 10.5% to 13%. It is made from a variety of grapes, with Corvina, Molinara, Rondinella, and Negrara in the lead.

Soave and Recioto di Soave (D.O.C.)

Like its red counterparts, Soave is not great but almost always good for an Italian wine. It has, at its best, a light straw color with greenish highlights, a small but pleasant bouquet, and a dry, very slightly acid taste. Like so many Italian white wines it comes from the Trebbiano grapevine (although Garganega is also important), in this instance cultivated in the towns of Soave and Monteforte d'Alpone, about 16 kilometers (10 miles) east of Verona. Care should be taken when buying the wine because its increasing popularity has not been accompanied by a comparable increase in output. A Recioto di Soave Spumante (sparkling) is very occasionally seen, but it has little to offer and its export future is dubious. The high iron content of Soave's soil leads to problems in wine clarification which are increased when the wine is made sparkling.

Prosecco di Conegliano di Valdobbiadene (D.O.C.)

A pleasant wine made from Prosecco grapes in the province of Treviso, some 48 kilometers (30 miles) due north of Venice, it is known either as Prosecco di Coneglia or Prosecco di Valdobbiadene. By any name the wine is delicately dry and very fruity, and sparkling and semi-sparkling types are also made.

MINOR WINES OF VENETO

Colli Euganei (D.O.C.)

Small red and white wines from the Euganean Hills in the province of Padua, 32 kilometers (20 miles) southeast of Soave. It is often used as a carafe wine in better dining places.

Breganze (D.O.C.)

Red and white wines made at Vicenza, the town of the great sixteenth-century architect Andrea Palladio. White Berganze is of Tocai, Pinot, and some Riesling grapes;

the red, of Merlot and Cabernet. When only one grape variety is used, the D.O.C. name may be followed by the name of that strain: thus, Breganze Cabernet, etc.

Cabernet di Pramaggiore (D.O.C.)

Not far from Venice, this full-bodied red table wine is made from Cabernet Franc and some Merlot grapes. It is dry, and with a bouquet almost recalling the scent of sweet grass. When aged for more than three years, the wine may be called Riserva.

Gambellara and Recioto di Gambellara Spumante (D.O.C.)

Gambellara is a light, dry white wine resembling Soave, although Soave is higher in alcohol. Garganega and some Trebbiano grapes go into the wine, which is made not far east of the town of Soave. Recioto di Gambellara Spumante is a sweet sparkling wine made in the same manner as the other similar wines of the region.

Merlot di Pramaggiore (D.O.C.)

A rather dry but full red table wine made near Venice from Merlot and Cabernet grapes.

South of Vicenza, the Berici Hills produce light red and white wines. Red wines are made principally from Cabernet Franc and Merlot; white wines from Tocai, Pinot Blanc, Garganega, and Sauvignon Blanc. Similar wines from the same vines are made in the River Piave district (D.O.C.).

Venezuela

Venezuela has no vineyards. The country does produce spirits, but not many of them and only in small quantities.

The leading spirit is probably cocui (sometimes cocuy) from the agave cocui plant, the equivalent of the Mexican tequila/mescal spirits. It varies in proof from 80° to 100°, depending upon the still used and the purity desired, and is drunk neat rather than complemented with lime and salt, as tequila is. The taste of cocui is a special one, somewhat similar to that of tequila but slightly harsher.

Rums—and some excellent ones are made—are popular, as are *aguardientes;* beer is on the increase and a few liqueurs are produced in the vicinity of Caracas. In addition to these, a beverage fermented from corn and called *chicha* is popular with the Indians. *Chicha* is coarse, acid, unusually high in alcohol and altogether far too rough to be widely appreciated. About 35,000 hectoliters (927,000 U.S. gallons, 770,000 imp.) of wine are imported annually.

Vente sur souches

French term for advance sale of wines made before the harvest, "on the vinestock." When the agreement is based on a certain degree of alcohol in the wine, the price can be fixed under a reserve for an increase or decrease of this

price, according to whether the wine, when it is made, has an unexpectedly higher or lower degree of alcohol. Every contract for a *vente sur souches* must include a declaration that the consenting parties are aware of this rule (art. 320-332, Code du Vin). Any infraction of the law is subject to indirect taxation and to a fine (art. 1760, Code du Vin). Sometimes in recent years there have been advance sales of Classified Growths of Bordeaux. The quotations have then been given in *tonneaux*, or tons.

Véraison

French term for the maturing of the grape, when it changes from green to a reddish hue or to a translucent greenish-white.
See Chapter Eight, p. 29.

Verdelho

A leading grape variety used in Portugal in making White Port and grown elsewhere—in Australia, for example.

Also the designation of a sweet, soft Madeira wine.

Verdicchio dei Castelli di Jesi

Light, dry or semi-sweet, white Italian wine.
See The Marches.

Verdot

The grape, also known as Petit Verdot, is used plentifully in the ordinary red wines of Bordeaux and sparingly in the better Médocs.

Vergennes

American grapevine whose fruit yields a pleasant, light, dry wine. Originally from Vermont, the vine is most widely cultivated in New York State.

Verjus

In French, grapes resulting from a late or second flowering of the vine. Such grapes do not mature and they retain a high acid content; they are used by the winemaker in very hot summers when the ripe grapes are deficient in acid.

Vermentino

This grape produces a good white wine in Liguria, the Italian Riviera, and is grown also in Corsica.

Vermentino Ligure

Thin, light, white Italian wines, sometimes slightly sparkling.
See Liguria.

Vermouth

Vermouth is not a wine. It is wine-based, but it undergoes so many additions and manipulations that it ceases to be recognizable as the product of the vine. It is, however, a popular and excellent aperitif and is indispensable in some cocktails—principally, of course, in the Dry Martini.

The name is thought to derive from either the German *Wermut* or the Anglo-Saxon *wermod*, both meaning "wormwood." Vermouth was certainly being made in Italy in the seventeenth century, and now it is produced all over the world; the two main types are "French" and "Italian." Vermouth is also made in California and many wine-producing countries.

Vermouth-making is a complicated but not a great art. It requires wine, sugar syrup or mistelle (unfermented grape juice fortified with brandy), alcohol, assorted herbs and plants, a pasteurizer, refrigerating vats, vast filters, and a table of ingredients, weights, and measures. When these essentials are collected, the process becomes a production-line affair.

The essential matter is the wine, usually white and fairly insipid. The transformations in taste will be such that the use of distinctive or fine wine would be a needless expense; and much Italian vermouth is based on the product of the southern Italian plains, that of France on the output of the Midi. Next in importance are the herbs and flavorings. These will include wormwood, hyssop, quinine, coriander, juniper, cloves, camomile, orange-peel, and sometimes even rose petals, but the exact ingredients and their proportions are jealously guarded by each manufacturer. The wine may be aged as much as two years or it may not be aged; but the first step will be the addition of sugar syrup, or mistelle. After this come alcohol and flavorings.

The flavoring herbs which give vermouth its character are macerated and steeped in alcohol. They are sometimes heated, so that the flavor may pass into the spirit in the same manner as in an infusion of tea. When the alcohol is sufficiently flavored, it is added to the sweetened wine and the whole mixture agitated to blend it together. Even in the most modern plants, wooden paddles are generally used for blending, so that any extraneous tastes may be kept out of the eventual vermouth. Tannin is added, then gelatin to clarify it; and, finally, the mixture is pasteurized. After pasteurization, it is refrigerated, falling sometimes as low as 14°F. (−10°C.) for a period of two weeks or so. During this time any tartrates in the wine form crystals and drop to the bottom of the vats, and from there the vermouth is put through a huge Seitz filter to remove any last impurities and tartrate particles that might remain. After this rigorous treatment, the vermouth is stored for a few months, bottled, and shipped. It can now be reasonably expected to survive in tropical heat or arctic cold; but manufacturers say that prolonged periods of excessive temperature will turn even this hardy creature, oxidizing it and giving it a musty and unpleasant taste. Such an occurrence, however, takes considerable heat.

French vermouths are generally held to be dry, Italian sweet. This is to some extent true, but both types are made in each country, although the very sweet are all Italian. The very dry French Chambéry is allowed the Appellation d'Origine. This is a special type, lighter than those from Sète in southern France. Chambéry is made from lighter wines, many coming from surrounding alpine hillsides—the herbs are not the same as those used by the manufacturers of the heavier vermouths. Another popular dry type is Noilly-Prat. The Italian Cinzano may be red or white, sweet or fairly dry—as also may Martini and Gancia.

Vernaccia

White-wine grape used in Italy for wines of The Marches, Sardinia, etc.

Vernaccia di Sardegna (Dicampidano)

One of the best-known wines of Sardinia (*q.v.*).

Verveine du Vélay

French liqueur made in Puy, central France, on a brandy base, flavored with herbs. There are two varieties, one yellow and one green; the green is the stronger.

Verzenay

Village near Reims producing a First-Growth Champagne.
See Champagne.

Verzy

Commune of the mountain of Reims district producing a First-Growth Champagne.
See Champagne.

Vevey Festival

The world's most important wine festival, given since the seventeenth century, in the town of Vevey, Switzerland, a development of the activities of the medieval Wine-Growers Guild. The official name is Fête des Vignerons. The fête has taken place in this century in 1905, 1927, and 1955. The 1955 festival, which took five years to prepare, was one of Europe's biggest tourist events that year. The performances, sometimes by as many as 3,300 participants including 950 children, celebrated the wine before daily audiences of 15,000 for two weeks.

See Switzerland.

La Vieille Cure

A very popular French liqueur made at Cenons near Bordeaux according to a formula which includes various brandies and fifty-two different herbs. It is golden in color and somewhat similar to Benedictine.

Vieux-Château-Certan

Bordeaux red wine.
District and Commune: Pomerol, France.

The Thienpoint brothers, Belgian wine merchants, make this subtle, velvety, full-bodied wine.

Vineyard area: 14 hectares (35 acres).
Average production: 60 *tonneaux* (5,800 cases).

Vigne

In France, an individual grapevine, but in wine-growers' parlance, a small parcel of a vineyard.

Vigneron

French term for a wine-maker and wine-grower; a skilled vineyard worker.

Vignoble

French term for vineyard.

Vila Nova de Gaia

A village lying opposite the city of Oporto, on the River Douro in northern Portugal. Most of the Port lodges, or warehouses, are in Vila Nova de Gaia and all Port wine which is legally Port is shipped from Oporto.

See Port.

Villafranca del Panadés

Wines from the province of Barcelona. The best types are dry.

See Spain.

Vin

French term for wine.

Vin blanc

French for white wine.

Vin bourru

French term for wine still on the original lees, or just drawn from the barrel. It is a term of praise when applied to such wines as Beaujolais, which are to be drunk young.

Vin de coule

French term for wine from first pressing.

Vin de cuvée

Term used in Champagne for wine of first pressing.

Vin doux naturel

In France, sweet wine which has been fortified with brandy, added to stop fermentation and ensure both a high alcoholic content and a residue of unfermented sugar. The yeasts cease their activity when approximately 17% of alcohol is present. Most of the French *vins doux naturels* come from the Grand Roussillon region on the Mediterranean near the Spanish border; the bulk of the rest, from Frontignan nearer the mouth of the Rhône. This may be red or white and contains from 14% to 17½% of alcohol by volume (although the great bulk is sold at 18%) and has little attraction for wine-drinkers where Sherry and Port—to which it bears some small resemblance—are available.

See also Vin de Liqueur; Sweet fortified wines of France.

Vin fin

A much-abused French term meaning "wine of quality." The inference is that the wine so called is superior. This is sometimes true—as in the case of Vins Fins de la Côte de Nuits—but is much too loosely used when it appears on a label with a commercial trade name.

Vin de garde

A great French wine with high alcoholic content and much tannin. Worth laying down until maturity has subdued all early excesses.

Vin du Glacier

Hard white wine of Valais, so named because after the harvest it is stored in high alpine villages.

See Switzerland.

Vin de goutte

French wine from last pressing.

Vin gris

Pink wine frequently attributed to Alsace but really pertaining to nearby Lorraine.

See Lorraine; Alsace.

Vin d'honneur

French for wine of honor. Since, from earliest times, wine has been poured in libation to the gods and has graced the tables of kings, it was natural that men should serve it to those whom they wished to honor. Even today, *vins d'honneur* are offered on certain occasions. Historic wine ceremonies recalled by Mssrs Renouil and Traversay in their *Dictionnaire du vin* are:

Vin de bourgeoisie—offered in the Middle Ages to the mayor and any citizen who was made burgher of a town.

Vin de coucher (nuptial wine)—offered before they retired by newly married couples to the guests who had honored their wedding feast.

Vin de l'étrier (stirrup cup)—offered to a parting guest.

Vin du curé—offered to the priest after baptism.

Vin de veille (night-cap)—courtiers used to place this beside the king's bed in case he should want a drink in the night.

Vin du clerc—offered by defendants to the clerk of the tribunal after a verdict in their favor.

Vin jaune

Yellow wine of the Jura region in France. This is made from late-picked grapes and kept for an unusually long time; when it is in the barrel it forms a white film, known in Sherry-making as *flor*.

See Jura.

Vin de liqueur

This French term has two meanings: (1) a very sweet wine, such as a rich Sauternes; (2) wine of approximately 18% of alcohol caused by the addition of brandy and added to Champagne prior to shipment.

Vin de marc

Wines made in France from a pressing of the residues with added water and sugar.

Vin mousseux

Sparkling wine.

Vin ordinaire

The French term for common wine.

Vin de paille

"Straw wine," made in the Jura region of France, and elsewhere. It derives its name from the time-honored process of drying the grapes on beds of straw before pressing, as well as from the color of the wine.

See Jura.

Vin de presse

In France, wine made from the pressing of the residues after the regular wine has been made. Taken by itself, it is very harsh.

Vin de primeur

In French, young wine. Often used as a synonym for Vin bourru (*q.v.*).

Vin de queue

French term for inferior wine made from the pressing of the stalks.

Vin rosé

French term for pink wine, made from red grapes by fermenting the juice on the skins (which give the color) a shorter time than is taken for red wine. Rosé should never be a mixture of red and white wines—although it sometimes is; it should be served quite cool.

Vin rouge

French for red wine.

Vin Santo

See Tuscany.

Vin de tête

In Sauternes, wine from the first crushing; the best. Château d'Yquem, 1921, had a *crème de tête*.

Vinage

French term for adding alcohol to wine to raise its strength. In some districts, and for cheap wines, a moderate addition of alcohol improves the product; but the practice can only be condemned in the case of fine wines.

Vinasse

Residual liquor. In French, the residue of wines and fermented liquors after distillation, also a derogatory term for ordinary wine.

Vine

Woody-stemmed climbing plant of the *Ampelidaceae* family, which includes Virginia creeper and other varieties as well as the grape-producing *Vitis* (with its subgenera *Euvites* and *Muscadiniae*), which alone is of importance to the wine-maker.

See Chapter Eight, p. 29.

Vine species

For classification of the species of genus *Vitis*, *see* Chapter Eight, p. 29.

Vinello (vinettino)

Forms of the diminutive applied to the Italian word for wine to express contempt for a wine's poorness or thinness. Therefore, a little, thin wine.

Vineyard

An area planted in grapevines.

Vinho liquoroso

Portuguese for fortified wine.

Vinho do rodo

Portuguese for sparkling wine.

Vinho trasfugado

Portuguese term for Madeira, after it has been racked, or drawn off its lees.

Vinhos Verdes

Light and crackling or slightly sparkling, these "green" and slightly acid wines from the north of Portugal, just below Spanish Galicia, are extremely popular in their homeland and make charming hot-weather drinks.
See Portugal.

Viniculture

The series of varied operations included in the making and maturing of wine.

Oenology usually refers to the more scientific aspects of wine production and study, while viniculture relates to the more practical considerations.

Vinifera

Species of genus *Vitis* (sub-genus *Euvites*) which embraces those native European vines responsible for the greatest wines of the world. *Vitis vinifera* has been transplanted to Australia, South Africa, California, and South America.
See Chapter Eight, p. 29.

Vinification

Wine-making.

Vino da arrosto

Italian term for wine of breed.

Vino de color

In Spain, concentrated grape juice for coloring and sweetening wines.

Vino corriente

Spanish term for common wine.

Vino dulce

In Spain, very sweet wine for blending.

Vino espumoso

Spanish for sparkling wine.

Vino de pasto

Spanish for table wine. It is also a type of Sherry of no great distinction.

Vino Santo

Sweet white dessert wine made in Greece and in the Venetian region of Italy, where the golden wine comes from white grapes left to dry on the plant.

Vino tierno

Spanish term for heavy, sweet wine, used in blending.

Vino de la tierra

Spanish term for *vin de pays*, or ordinary wine of the region.

Vino tinto

Spanish term for red wine.

Vinosity

The essential quality or heart of the wine, a strong personality achieved by the accentuation of the best characteristics of the particular type. The term is often used to suggest high alcoholic content, an error arising from the failure to realize that alcohol is only one among the ingredients contributing to the character of the wine.

Vinprom

The State Enterprise for handling wine-growing and the wine trade in Bulgaria (*q.v.*).

Vins Délimités de Qualité Supérieure

See V.D.Q.S.

Vins de la Moselle

One of the two controlled place-names in the Lorraine area in France. The growths are classed Vins Délimités de Qualité Supérieure (delimited wines of superior quality). Some are rosés, some white.

Vins Natures de la Champagne

See Champagne.

Vins de pays

A controlled class of wines made in various regions in France. In the hierarchy of French wines, they are technically a step above the least distinguished category, *vins de consommation courante*. But their level of quality is far below that of most V.D.Q.S. wines. *Vins de pays* are grown and made in specific areas with certain grape variations and methods of production, which are specified by the Ministry of Agriculture and controlled by local growers associations. Typically, they will bear the name of the *pays* in which they were grown, as in Vins du Pays des Vals d'Agly in the Pyrénées Orientales, or Vins du Pays de Haut Rive, in the Aude. Their quality can vary from the pleasant-if-unexceptional to downright poor. The greatest producer of *vins de pays* in France is the Languedoc-Roussillon region, with over forty different varieties.

These regional wines often have a low alcoholic content and so are sometimes not fit to travel; yet, drunk young and in the region where they are made, they may be very pleasant. For example, a restaurant in the Savoie recommends a Roussette d'Apremont, the *vin de pays*. This small white wine is taken by at least 70% of the customers—and they are quite right. The same may be said of many of the small wines of Anjou and the Jura (particularly around the region of Arbois), although the same wines would be disappointing if they had to undergo ageing and shipment.

Vins de Savoie

Red, white, and sparkling wines.
District: Southeast France.

Wines of this Appellation Contrôlée may be labeled Vin de Savoie or Roussette de Savoie. These two names are applied to wines made throughout the French foothills of the Alps in the Savoie, Haute-Savoie, Ain, and Isère departments. Nearly all of the 70,000 hectoliters (1,855,000 U.S. gallons, 1,540,000 imp.) produced each year is white wine made from the Altesse, Jacquère, or Roussette grapes. Mondeuse-Noir and Gamay, along with a few local varieties, are used for the small quantity of red wine.

Vintage and vintage charts

The vintage is the *vendange*, or gathering, of the grapes, and hence the wine from grapes of a specific harvest, the date of which will be shown on the label.

Champagne and Port have given the word *vintage* a special connotation, namely, "a very good year." The lesser years are blended to give a non-vintage wine, and it is only in the great years that a vintage is stated on the label. Bordeaux, Burgundies, Rhine wines—any wine from a good vineyard—will bear a vintage date on the label irrespective of whether the year was good or poor.

The vintages of different years are rated on a scale (usually from 1 to 10); the system is a useful one in countries of temperate climate where in spite of careful viticulture, variations in the weather may so affect the harvest that one year's yield may be excellent, the next only average, and the third quite poor. But these ratings, printed on charts and circulated among consumers, may lead to a certain amount of confusion, because they do not tell enough.

Charts are based on the fact that wine-makers can judge, roughly, at the time of the harvest how good the wine is going to be. The statisticians then come along and summarize the consensus of opinion into ratings. But these estimates of its quality apply to the wine at its peak, which may be in five years' time, or in fifteen. The charts stated that 1945, for instance, was a great year; but not that a slow-maturing red wine, such as Bordeaux, would not reach perfection for some twenty years because an excess of tannin makes it slow to mature, and so a great deal of this wine was drunk prematurely.

For the same reason, of two young wines, the pleasanter to drink now may very well be the one which has received the lower vintage mark, simply because it is not going to last so long, and will therefore have developed better in its first two or three years than the wine of the greater vintage.

Moreover, there are endless exceptions to vintage ratings. Several poor red wines were made in Burgundy in the great year of 1947, but the chart cannot tell you this. On the other hand, there is always a vineyard which comes up with something magnificent, even in the worst years. These wines will be good bargains, because they cannot be so highly priced as an equal wine of a "good" year. On the whole, red wines from leading vineyards in the finest districts seldom fall below a certain standard, even in a poor summer.

In countries where the summers are always unbearably hot, the weather will not seriously affect the quality of the wine, and vintage ratings are, therefore, of little importance.

Vintage Port

Along the River Douro in Portugal, where the only true Port wine is made, not every year is considered worthy of being called a vintage year. The last quarter of a century has seen some half a dozen great vintages, but a vintage may be declared by an individual Port wine-maker for his wine, and so the practice is not uniform. Vintage Port, selected from the best years, is always the wine of a single year, which will be indicated. Any Vintage Port should be aged in bottle at least a decade; it goes on improving in glass for many, many years.

See Port.

Vintage wines

Of a particular vintage or year, which is marked on the label.

Virginia

Wine-producing region in the United States. The vineyards, few but good, are situated principally in Albemarle and Clarke counties, with Charlottesville at the center.

See United States.

Viticulteur

A French vine-grower, usually one with his own vineyard. A *vigneron* is almost the same, but more often is the name of a sharecropper.

Viticultural ecology

The study of the relationship of the vine and the climate and soil in which it grows, and the quality of wine which its fruit produces.

Viticulture

The science and art of grape-growing.

Vitis vinifera

The species of vine from which most of the wine in the world is made. For a fuller account of this and other types of vine (*Vitis*)—for example, *Vitis labrusca, Vitis riparia, Vitis coignetiae*—*see* Chapter Eight, p. 29.

Vitiviniculture

The study and practice which encompasses all grape-growing and wine-making activities.

Vodka

Vodka, once the traditional Russian drink, taken neat and tossed off quickly before, during, and after meals, is now an international drink consumed and indeed made over most of the Western world. (It still shows at its best with caviar.) The neutrality of the spirit has made it popular: many people who like to drink do not really care for the taste of alcohol. The lack of smell is another virtue. The fashion for vodka-drinking in the West started in California and soon spread over America and then Europe. Some people like to dilute it with mineral water or tomato juice, others to take neat vodka and follow it with a chaser. And it is, of course, a remarkably good base for Martinis and other cocktails.

Vodka, which was native to Poland, Latvia, Lithuania, and Estonia, as well as Russia, was popularly assumed to be a spirit made from potatoes. Now it is more likely to be produced from grain. Like gin, it is distilled at very high proof, rectified into a spirit with neither the taste nor the aroma of the materials used. Unlike gin, it remains unflavored—although some individual vodkas are infused with herbs and aged for more than three years—sometimes in barrels that have contained wine.

Different vodkas range from about 65° proof to more powerful types at 98° proof.

Volatile acidity

In wine, the state caused by the presence of acetic acid (the acid of vinegar), which is produced by aerobic spoilage bacteria and is the principal cause of vinegary wine. Such acidity commonly occurs when first-year ageing casks are left incompletely filled; as the wine evaporates, the casks must be "topped up" every two weeks or so.

See Chapter Nine.

Volnay

Burgundy red wine.
District: Côte de Beaune, France.

The Volnays are rather delicate wines for Burgundy, quick to mature, with less depth of color than the Beaunes and Pommards and greater elegance. They are suave, rounded, well balanced, with a particularly fine bouquet. The commune lies south of Pommard, on rather high ground. Some of the vineyards are more exposed than others, and as a measure against the disasters of frost and hail, they are much parceled out. The total area is about 213 hectares (527 acres); the average yield, approximately 8,000 hectoliters (212,000 U.S. gallons, 176,000 imp.).

In the Middle Ages, Volnay had a light, *oeil de perdrix* color which was much relished and the wine was popular. The dukes of Burgundy made presents of Beaune and Volnay to kings and to the papal court at Avignon. Louis XI, who kept his prisoners in cages, defeated the Burgundian dukes, annexed their land, and got possession also of the vines of which they were so proud. Volnay seems to have been a special favorite: the entire harvest of 1477 was taken, by his orders, to his château at Plessis-les-Tours.

Volnay is only a jump away from Meursault, and the white wines must be sold as Meursault. There is an old jingle which runs:

Entre Pommard et Meursault
C'est toujours Volnay le plus haut.

Topographically, this is indisputable. Set between two hills, the village dominates its vineyards and is itself dominated by the church—most of the vineyard paths lead down, the village streets climb up, to the church. Caillerets, the highest of the vineyards, close to the cemetery, is also the best. Up the slopes, you can see across the great Burgundian valley, sometimes as far as the snow-capped Jura peaks. Just south of Volnay, off to the right and up a lane, is the small village of Monthélie. Its wines, lesser and less known than the Volnays, are also less expensive.

Another local jingle is:

Qui n'a pas de vignes en Caillerets
Ne sait ce que vaut le Vollenay,

which means that no *vigneron* can really know what Volnay means unless he owns a strip of vines in Caillerets, *les cailles du roi.* The Volnay vineyards are as follows:

FIRST GREAT GROWTHS (*Premiers Grands Crus*)

Vineyard	Hectares	Acres
Les Caillerets	2.7	6.7
Les Caillerets-dessus	14.7	36.6
Clos des Ducs	2.4	6
Les Brouillards	6.5	16.2
Les Mitans	4	9.9
L'Ormeau	4.3	10.7
Les Angles	3.5	8.7
Les Pointes d'Angles	1.5	3.7
Les Fremiets	6.5	16.2
Les Champans	11.3	28.2
Les Chevrets	6	14.9
Le Clos des Chênes	16.9	42.1
La Barre	2	4.9
La Bousse d'Or	1.9	4.8

Vöslau

One of the regions near Baden producing red wines and Roten Sekt (red sparkling wine).

See Austria.

Vosne-Romanée

Burgundy red wine.
District: Côte de Nuits, France.

No vineyards have ever been praised so highly and so consistently as the best of Vosne-Romanée. In good years the wines are unquestionably magnificent and are among the most expensive in the world.

The five greatest vineyards of Vosne are minuscule, even by Burgundian standards. Their combined area is barely 26 hectares (65 acres) and the annual output is only slightly more than 525 hectoliters (14,000 U.S. gallons, 11,600 imp.), the equivalent of less than 6,000 cases. Demand for the largest of them—Romanée Saint-Vivant—is so insistent that the grower could never hope to approach it, and wines from La Romanée and Romanée-Conti are so rare that drinking one of them must always be an event.

Romanée-Conti is the great wine of the commune in spite of the small size of the vineyard—just 1.8 hectares (4.5 acres). The pre-war vintages—hardly more than a memory now—were the most magnificent, for replanting and the large number of young vines in the vineyard have, since the fifties, brought the quality slightly down from its former height. While the Romanée-Conti is the "central jewel in the necklace of Burgundian wines," La

Romanée, La Tâche, Richebourg, and Romanée Saint-Vivant are worthy companions for it. (*See under separate headings.*)

The great unifying factor in the wines of Vosne is their velvety softness and finesse. All of the wines of the commune share these characteristics, and in addition they are light and delicate and beautifully balanced; they are feminine wines, not assertive, and they age most gracefully. This is true not only of the greatest vineyards, but also of those classed just slightly below—such as Grande Rue, Gaudichots, Beaumonts, and Malconsorts, all of which produce wonderful wines.

The vineyards which produce the wines that go to market with the words Vosne-Romanée on the label are mostly in that commune, but some are in adjoining Flagey-Échezeaux. Wines from Flagey's two greatest vineyards—Grands-Échezeaux and Échezeaux—may carry their own names or may be declassed into First Growth of Vosne-Romanée (Vosne-Romanée *Premier Cru*). Since the names are not well known and rather difficult for the non-Gallic tongue to pronounce, growers often use the lesser name for these wines despite the general rule that the more specific the name the better the wine and therefore the higher the price. These two vineyards alone increase the Vosne-Romanée vineyard area by 72 hectares (180 acres) and there are 51 more acres in Flagey, producing wines that carry the name Vosne-Romanée, geography to the contrary. Vineyard acreage actually within Vosne amounts to about 172 hectares (425 acres), and the combined amount of wine made in an average year for quantity amounts to 6,500 hectoliters (172,500 U.S. gallons, 143,000 imp.). The classified vineyards of Vosne are:

In Vosne-Romanée

GREAT GROWTHS (*Grands Crus*)

Vineyard	Hectares	Acres
La Romanée-Conti	1.8	4.5
La Tâche	6	14.9
Les Richebourg	8	19.8
La Romanée	.83	2
La Romanée Saint-Vivant	8.5	21.3

FIRST GROWTHS (*Premiers Crus*)

Vineyard	Hectares	Acres
Les Gaudichots	5.8	14.3
Les Malconsorts	5.9	14.7
La Grande Rue	1.3	3.3
Les Beaux-Monts	2.4	6
Les Suchots	13.1	32.4
Clos des Réas	2.1	5.3
Aux Brûlées	3.8	9.6
Aux Petits-Monts	3.7	9.2
Aux Reignots	1.7	4.2
La Chaume	7.4	17.9

In Flagey-Échezeaux

GREAT GROWTHS (*Grands Crus*)

Vineyard	Hectares	Acres
Grands-Échezeaux	9.2	23
Échezeaux	30	75

Vougeot

Burgundy red and white wines.
District: Côte de Nuits, France.

Stand on the vineyard road on the bluff to the south of Chambolle-Musigny and you can see the land pitch sharply down in front of you, revealing on the plateau below the famous castle of the Clos de Vougeot (*q.v.*) surrounded by vineyards, the whole enclosed by a weather-beaten stone wall.

Excepting the Clos—the largest single vineyard in Burgundy and one of the most famous in the world—there is not a great deal to Vougeot. A tiny settlement nestles to one side of the low wall with its small arched entries, and outside this wall lie several vineyards whose wines are sold—if they conform to the proper minimum standards—as Vougeot, followed by the name of the vineyard.

Commune and Clos take their name from the River Vouge, a tiny stream that comes bubbling down the hill separating Vougeot from Chambolle-Musigny. The settlement is an ancient one and its vineyards have been in continuous cultivation for centuries, for when the Cistercians arrived at the beginning of the twelfth century these were among the lands given to them by local squires. The monks pieced together the vineyard which lies within the walls of the Clos, built the château, and made the name famous; and they left their stamp on the other vineyards of the area as well. No single group in history has done so much for the cause of fine wines as the Cistercians, and their crowning achievements are the Clos de Vougeot and Kloster Eberbach in the Rheingau. The vineyards outside the walls are Les Petits-Vougeots and Les Cras (both planted in Pinot Noir and producing red wines) and La Vigne-Blanche, or Clos Blanc de Vougeot (planted in Chardonnay and Pinot Blanc and giving white wine). The Clos Blanc is owned entirely by the Dijon shipping firm of Héritiers Guyot.

The Clos is, of course, the great wine of the commune. The others, however, are pleasant and often entrancing. Red Vougeot is generally full-bodied, filling the mouth, yet it always manages to preserve a certain delicacy and often has an assertive bouquet all its own. The white is dry, sometimes quite fruity, and very much like one of the white wines from Aloxe-Corton on the Côte de Beaune, without having all the great breed of the finest from Aloxe.

Within the walls of the Clos are 50 hectares (124 acres) of vines, but outside are only some 12 hectares (30 acres). From these twelve, approximately 360 hectoliters, (10,000 U.S. gallons, 8,000 imp.) of red wine and 45 hectoliters (1,200 U.S. gallons, 1,000 imp.) of white are produced in an average year for quantity.

GREAT GROWTH (*Grand Cru*)

Vineyard	Hectares	Acres
Clos de Vougeot	50	124

FIRST GROWTHS (*Premiers Crus*)

Vineyard	Hectares	Acres
Clos Blanc de Vougeot	1.8	4.6
Les Petits-Vougeots	5.8	14.4
Les Cras	4.2	10.6

Clos de Vougeot

Burgundy red wine.
District: Côte de Nuits, France.
Commune: Vougeot.
Official Classification: Great Growth (Grand Cru).

The 50 hectares (124 acres) of the Clos de Vougeot (or Clos Vougeot) are so famous that the vineyard is practically a national asset of France; it was a tradition for passing regiments of the French army to salute the vines. Started in the twelfth century by Cistercian monks, on the slopes above their monastery, it remained in the hands of the clergy until the French Revolution, when the state confiscated church property. The monks did not plant the entire vineyard—some of it they accepted as a gift from early Burgundians with names such as Hugues le Blanc, Eudes-le-Vert, and Wallo Gile, but they consolidated the holding and built a wall around it.

In the sixteenth century the vineyard was so big that it was felt that a château and a house for the wine-press should be added to the buildings inside the wall. The drawing-up of the plans for this building was entrusted to a young and zealous monk, and he went to work with fervor but made the mistake of signing the completed blueprint with his own name. The abbot informed him that he had committed the deadly sin of pride and ordered that the plans should be given to other monks to complete. These new hands botched them hopelessly. Legend has it that the original architect, following the strict code of the Middle Ages, repented his sin and died of chagrin, and the Clos was built complete with all its structural faults as a monument to his sinful pride and fall from grace.

Since its foundation, the building has undergone repeated additions and renovations. The last—although this is almost a continuous process—was at the hands of the Confrérie des Chevaliers du Tastevin de Bourgogne, the society which makes sure that the rest of the world does not forget the wines of Burgundy. The members of the order, who are mostly shippers, growers, and visiting dignitaries interested in wines, meet every month or so in the great dining room of the château, and the halls which once resounded with the plainsong of the Church now reverberate with the noise and tumult of the Chevaliers singing the songs—and the praises—of Burgundy. The great dinning hall can seat five hundred people, and the towering stone pillars are decorated with coats of arms, with baskets which once were used to carry in the grapes, and with the dates of the most famous vintage years, dating back to 1108.

Since the vineyard was confiscated, after the Revolution, it has seldom been under one ownership—the last proprietor lived in the nineteenth century, and his grave lies beside the terraced drive leading up to the forbidding gates of the château. Since his death the ownership has become more and more diverse and today there are about a hundred people with holdings within the walls.

Each one of the owners has his own plot. His vines will be of varying ages, and age has a direct effect on quality. The vines will be tended as each owner desires, the grapes will be picked when he feels that it is time, and wine-making procedures will vary according to his talent, conscience, and ability. Once made, the wines will be sold to different people, some in barrel to shippers and some bottled by the growers. Apart from all else, the vineyard itself is divided into three different sections and the wines will vary accordingly. As a result, drawing a common set of taste characteristics which are distinctly Clos de Vougeot is extremely difficult. If such a summation had to be made, it would be fair to say that in a good year a characteristic Clos de Vougeot is relatively full-bodied and with a big nose, which does not have all the austere majesty of a Chambertin nor the delicate grace of a Musigny or a Romanée-Saint-Vivant but inclines toward the latter. In any case, it is a mouth-filling wine, and the aftertastes are glorious and lingering.

Average yearly production for the whole 50 hectares (124 acres) is about 2,000 hectoliters (53,000 U.S. gallons, 44,000 imp.).

Of the three sections of the Clos set up by the early monks, that just behind the château, leading up to the wall, is traditionally the best part, with the middle section just behind it; and the bottom, close to the Route Nationale (national highway), distinctly inferior. The difference is partly in the pitch of the slope—very flat at the bottom, becoming steeper toward the château—and partly in the soil. Chalky clay, reddish-brown in color and rich in pebbles, makes up the top parts; and the bottom, more brown than red, has more humus and fewer pebbles. The land at the bottom is prone to hold moisture, and only in dry years do the vines produce comparably with those planted higher up.

At one time the vineyard was divided into plots, and despite the divided ownership many of these still retain their traditional identity. In the uppermost part are Musigny de Clos de Vougeot (closest to Chambolle-Musigny), Garenne, Plante Chamel, Plante Abbé, Montiottes Hautes, Chioures, Quartier de Marci Haut, Grand Maupertuis, and Petit Maupertuis. The middle is made up of Dix Journaux, Baudes Bas, and Baudes Saint-Martin; and the bottom, where the wine is generally inferior but commands nevertheless the same high price, has Montiottes Bas, Quatorze Journaux, and the bottom portions of Baudes Bas and Baudes Saint-Martin.

Some white wine is made in the little commune of Vougeot. This is not entitled to the name Clos de Vougeot but is sold as Clos Blanc de Vougeot.

Vouvray

Loire Valley dry white wine; still, semi-sparkling, or sparkling. District: Touraine, France.

Vouvray is the famous wine of Touraine, the peaceful, parklike Loire Valley region in the heart of the château country. The vineyards climb the slopes, upstream and across the river from Tours, once the center of the courtly life of the Valois. The best vineyards are the ones above the cliffs, where the cellars have been dug out of the hillsides. There are only 700 growers in Vouvray, and the wine is produced by eight communes—Chançay, Noizay, Parçay-Meslay, Reugny, Rochecorbon, Sainte-Radegonde, Vernou, and Vouvray itself—and even in lesser years it is a light, delightful wine, excellent to drink with the local blood sausage and *rillettes* (little pots of pork *pâté*) on the terrace of the restaurant of Pont de Cisse, which looks out over the sloping vineyards.

These vineyards date from the eighth century, and they have been in continuous production, except for a few years at the end of the last century, when they were devastated by phylloxera. The vines were reconstituted with grafts from sturdy phylloxera-resistant American rootstocks, and the first harvest from the new plants was gathered about 1900. In 1936 it was laid down that the bearing portions of the vine must be Chenin Blanc or Arbois, and no other grapes are legally permitted.

The vines thrive in a clay and limestone *aubuis* soil on the chalky hills of the district, which also provide cellars in which the wines mature. The casks are stored in caves cut into the cliff—caves in which people also lead a troglodyte existence. Driving along the river bank toward Vouvray, you can see houses which often are merely façades, with rooms dug back into the hillside. The high-vaulted, deep caverns make splendid cellars; in Marc Bredif's, there is a vast circular tasting room, with an old grindstone set in the middle as a table, and niches cut out of the chalky walls for the bottles.

The wines are characteristically soft and dry, but with a tendency toward sweetness which may become pronounced in a year when the sun has been strong or the picking late: the extra sunshine generates more grape sugar, which ferments into a higher alcoholic content. The sweet wines keep longer than their drier counterparts and usually travel better; but both types are found abroad. Although Vouvray rarely suffers a poor vintage, the wines are apt to have an acid finish when there has been insufficient sun. Once or twice in a decade, there is a great vintage year, and then the sweet, sunny wines are produced in abundance. Yet most Vouvrays, whether still, sparkling, or *pétillants*, are dry, although the driest usually conserves a trace of sugar; unlike the Sauternes, most of the Vouvrays produced from the Chenin grape are short-lived and their chief characteristic is a fruity freshness, although, in the few rich years, exceptions can be found. Some of the more sugary wines are made *mousseux* (sparkling) or *pétillants* (semi-sparkling or crackling); and to many drinkers *pétillants* is synonymous with Vouvray, although a much greater quantity of still table wine is produced.

Vouvray labels rarely carry vineyard names, because wines are generally blended by local firms and sold under their names, although the town or commune of origin is sometimes included. The better bottles, of course, carry the vintage year, the best of which are 1947, 1949, 1955, 1957, 1959, 1961, 1964, 1966, 1967, 1969, 1970, 1973, and 1976. Most of the older vintages, belonging to the occasional great years, are unobtainable today.

All Vouvray must contain at least 11% alcohol (9.5% if it is sparkling); and sparkling wine must be made by the champagne process (*see* Champagne). On an average, 60,000 hectoliters (1.59 million U.S. gallons, 1.32 million imp.) of wine are produced annually in this region.

Vrac

Wine sold *en vrac* includes the price of the wine bottle and cork, and may or may not include the capsule and label, but never the price of the case.

V.S.O.

Of Cognacs, this means Very Special Old.

V.S.O.P.

Very Superior Old Pale. This designation used in Cognacs and Armagnacs indicates a brandy in type—but not in actual vintage in the sense of wines—about twelve years old. Market demands being greater in Cognacs, the V.S.O.P.s are sold more quickly, and are now on an average younger than V.S.O.P. Armagnacs. Age in brandy is fully discussed under Cognac (*q.v.*).

V.V.S.O.P.

Of Cognacs, Very Very Special Old Pale.

W

Wachau

Important wine zone in Lower Austria. Among the wines from this district are Kremser and Dürnsteiner. *See* Austria.

Wachenheim

Good wine town of the German Palatinate. The best vineyards are Gerümpel, Altenburg, Rechbächel, Goldbächel, Rennacker, Luginsland, and Mandelgarten. *See* Palatinate.

Wacholder

German beverage resembling gin.

Wachstum

In German, this means the same as Kreszenz (*q.v.*).

Waldmeister

German name for woodruff, a wild herb which is essential in May wine—a popular wine punch made in Germany from a young wine base.

Walluf

Oldest wine-producing town in the Rheingau. *See* Rheingau; Germany.

Walporzheim

Region of the German Ahr Valley producing red wine. *See* Ahr.

Wash

Whisky after fermentation and before distillation.

Washington

Wine-growing state in the U.S., one of the few regions outside California where the *Vitis vinifera* flourishes. *See* United States.

Wassail

English traditional custom of preparing a special punch for Christmas Eve. The name comes from the Anglo-Saxon *wes hál,* "be in good health."

Wawern

German white wine of the Saar region. *See* Mosel-Saar-Ruwer.

Wedderburn

Pot-distilled and slow-fermented, this heaviest style of West Indian rum used to be identified with Jamaica, in contrast to the lighter rums of Puerto Rico and Cuba. Today the different centers make rums of both types. Jamaica is producing an increasing quantity of the lighter style in addition to Wedderburn and Plummer. *See* Rum, West Indies; Rum, Jamaican.

Weeper

British term for leaker (*q.v.*).

Wehlener Sonnenuhr

German wine experts are unanimous in naming Wehlener Sonnenuhr as the best Mosel wine, in spite of the fact that Bernkasteler Doctor is better known. No other Mosel has greater elegance or finesse than Sonnenuhr at its best. J. J. Prüm is the greatest name in this wine. *See* Mosel-Saar-Ruwer.

Wein

German term for wine.

Weinbauer

German term for wine-grower.

Weinberg

German term for a hillside vineyard.

Weingut

German term for wine estate.

Weinviertel

Important valley and region north of the Danube. *See* Austria.

Weissbier

German name for a sour beer popular in Berlin.

Weissburgunder

The chief grape variety cultivated in Styria, Austria.

Welschriesling

The chief grape variety cultivated in Burgenland, Austria.

Whiskey, American

American whiskey and the American people grew up together. The pioneer needed a drink as sturdy as himself, as rugged as the land he grappled with; something to cure snakebite, ward off disease, something to enjoy when he returned from the lonely plains and forests to the honkytonk saloons. Young whiskey, rough and "green," helped to sustain the men who conquered the young American continent and still holds undisputed sway over the tastes of their descendants. Sixteen bottles a year pour down the throat of the average American adult; altogether more than 60 million cases of whiskey, ranging from well-matured, often magnificent spirit to harsher "spirit blends," are consumed. Even "moonshine" and "bootleg" can be found. One out of every four drinks of hard liquor consumed in the United States is bootleg—the untamed spirit of the plains still prevails.

Whiskey was originally spelled whisky and was made in the mists and moors of Scotland. Probably at the same time it was whiskey among the peat bogs and lake country of Ireland. Today it is spelled whiskey in the United States and in Ireland. It is made in various parts of the world, but the largest single producer is the United States. American whiskeys differ from their European counterparts not only in taste and aroma but in general nature. They are not regional in character; Scotch whisky is inimitably Scotch, Irish whiskey the unique product of Ireland, but American whiskeys are classed by type, not origin. Bourbon, rye, or other styles can be made anywhere in America, and as long as they meet the government's specifications and pay their taxes, they have the government's blessing.

WHISKEY'S RISE TO POPULARITY

The Founding Fathers of the American republic were not whiskey-drinkers. The pilgrims of the North and the Virginia gentlemen of the South had tastes which turned toward beer and wine, rum and applejack. Whiskey had to await the settlement of Pennsylvania by Scotch-Irish immigrants and the great surge of Westering; and its original production owed much—as is the case with applejack—to poor roads and lack of communication. The settlers had brought over with them the secrets of distilling, and the land was fertile—perfect for grain, the base of whiskey. But transport was another problem. The roads that existed were poor, and in rainy seasons impassable, and if the farmer failed to get his crop to market he was ruined. But if he let the grain ferment, distilled it either at his own home in small pot stills or in those of a neighbor, the problem was solved. With the grain turned into whiskey, he had a less bulky cargo and a lighter one—a product that was easier to sell. In Pennsylvania and over in Kentucky, distilling was built up at the small farms into an important industry. The rum-makers of

New York tried to have the spirit banned from the state, but in spite of their efforts whiskey won the competition and replaced rum as the common drink. The industry grew and prospered until a famous commotion forced it to move farther west.

In 1791 the government of President Washington was having financial difficulties. To raise money, it established an excise tax on whiskey—and the makers protested. The violence of the Whiskey Rebellion, or insurrection, has been greatly exaggerated, although the President felt called upon to send troops of the militia to ensure the maintaining of peace and order—and the proper collection of excise taxes. The farmers grumbled, declared the government was meddling in their private affairs, and moved west, to southern Indiana and Illinois, deeper into Kentucky and farther west in Pennsylvania. Hostile Indians were easier to face than friendly tax collectors. What the farmers looked for—and found—in these areas was pure, clear, distiller's water, with little organic material but rich in sulfate of lime and earthy carbonates; the kind of water found over veins of chalk or limestone. In the eastern United States, a deep base of limestone runs through western Pennsylvania, through Kentucky, Indiana, and southern Illinois, then ducks underground and reappears in Maryland. Today 80% of America's licensed distillers are to be found in these five states, where American distilling came of age.

From these early beginnings, whiskey became a business—and big business at that. In 1911 the nation produced over 100 million U.S. gallons (83 million imp.), a figure which was not to be exceeded until 1935. Between these dates fell the Dark Age of American spirits, when distilleries were closed and padlocked, and bootlegger and smuggler reigned. On November 16, 1920 the Volstead Act became the Eighteenth Amendment to the Constitution of the United States, thus proclaiming Prohibition; and not until December 5, 1933 was the politician ready to admit officially that the noble experiment was in reality a dismal failure. It took the distillers a little while to dust their equipment and get back into production, but by 1935 they were in full swing. Since Repeal—excepting the years of the Second World War—the industry has followed a strong albeit slightly erratic course. Peak production was in 1951, when the amount distilled was over 205 million U.S. gallons (170,600,000 imp.). Since then the industry has stabilized, producing approximately 100 million U.S. gallons (83 million imp.) annually and withdrawing about the same amount from the warehouses where the spirit ages.

WHISKEY-MAKING

Whiskey is made from grain. Any grain may be used, but in America the important ones are corn (maize) and rye with some millet, sorghum, and barley. The grain is "mashed" (diluted with water and cooked in huge pressure cookers) then left to ferment into "beer" or "distiller's beer." Sweet mash whiskey is made by adding selected yeasts to start the fermentation; sour mash by triggering it with some leftover "spent beer" or "draff"—

527

the residue of a previous fermentation. Both "beer" and "draff" are then pumped into huge patent stills for distillation and rectification. By American law, all whiskey must be distilled at less than 190° proof U.S. (166° British), or about 95% alcohol. Above that figure, the spirit loses all the characteristics or congeners of the grain used and becomes merely neutral or "silent" spirit. Most whiskey is distilled from 140° to 160° proof, and some as low as 125°, notably some of the better Bourbons and ryes. After distillation, it is diluted and aged (the Bourbon in new, charred oak barrels), is diluted again—to between 80° and 100° proof—and bottled.

The origin of the charred barrel for ageing whiskey is unknown. According to one legend, it began in the West Indies in the making of rum. A fire in a warehouse charred some of the barrels which were used as they were, and the spirit was so improved by the experience that it became general practice to use charred barrels for rum, and later for whiskey. Another story attributes the origin to Kentucky: here the practice of steaming barrel staves to make them bend more easily was overdone and the wood charred; but it is hard to believe that a Kentuckian would be so careless in a matter so important as whiskey. Whatever the origin, the practice improves and softens the taste of the spirit and imparts body and color to it.

WHISKEY TYPES

American whiskey types are fairly rigidly defined by law. Some definitions have little interest for the consumer, since the types concerned are never on sale and serve merely as the base from which others are developed. The more important are:

Bourbon Whiskey

Originally the corn whiskey made in Bourbon County, Kentucky; now any whiskey distilled at no more than 160° proof, stemming from a mash of at least 51% corn, and aged for not less than two years in new charred oak barrels—most stays in the barrels for four years. It may be made by the sour mash process, and most bottles will be Straight Bourbon.

Corn Whiskey

Different from Bourbon, corn whiskey must be made from a mash of at least 80% corn, and may be aged in used or uncharred barrels.

Rye Whiskey

The mash must contain at least 51% rye, distillation must be no higher proof than 160°, and ageing accomplished in new charred oak barrels. Some Straight Rye and Blended Straight Rye are found, but not to the same extent as in Bourbon.

Other definitions include:

Whiskey

The most general name of all, never found alone on bottles. A label which carries any other term—Straight, Blended, Bourbon, etc.—must, of course, fulfill the requirements for whiskey as well as for the other terms it carries. According to the government, whiskey is "an alcoholic distillate from a fermented mash of grain distilled at less than 190° proof in such a manner that the distillate will have the taste, aroma, and characteristics generally attributed to whiskey, and withdrawn from the cistern room of the distillery at not more than 110° proof and not less than 80° proof and is further reduced before bottling to not less than 80° proof." Since no ageing period is specified, a bottle simply labeled whiskey would be reasonably raw and undrinkable.

Straight Whiskey

Whiskey distilled at no more than 160° proof and aged at least two years in new charred oak barrels. Straight corn whiskey may be aged in used or uncharred barrels. Straight whiskeys found on the market are usually Straight Bourbon or Straight Rye; they comprise about 27% of total whiskey sales.

See Whiskey, Light.

Blended Straight Whiskey

A blend of two or more straight whiskeys. This type makes up only about 1% of whiskey sales, but serves as a base for one of several blended whiskeys.

Blended Whiskey

A blend made of at least 20% 100°-proof straight whiskey, either with other whiskey or neutral spirit or both, bottled at no less than 80° proof. About 25% of all whiskeys sold are blended. The advantage is that they are lighter and less expensive than straights, and the leeway of 80% (which can be made up of any combination of whiskeys or plain spirit) allows the distiller to make a consistent standard whiskey, one that will not vary from year to year. It also permits the making of some very poor excuses for whiskey. One to which a large proportion of neutral spirit is added is known as a spirit blend and offers little to the civilized palate. The secret of a blended whiskey at any distillery is in the art of a master blender, who can distinguish what characteristics are needed to produce the replica of the firm's previous whiskey, determine the amounts of each component, and ensure that all the ingredients blend or "marry" properly. A small amount of Sherry—up to 2.5%—may be added as a blending agent.

Bottled-in-Bond Whiskey

The words do not necessarily guarantee a superior whiskey, but in fact this is what is usually indicated. The term is allowed only for straight whiskeys, at least four years old, bottled at 100° proof, the product of a single distillery by the same distiller and from a single season or year. The whiskey is aged in government-controlled warehouses (although control is fiscal, not qualitative) and taxes are paid on withdrawal.

Whiskey, Bourbon

Early in the colonial history of America, a Baptist minister, Elijah Craig, established a still in Georgetown, Kentucky and began producing whiskey from a base of corn.

The still is said to have been one of the first in Kentucky and customers in neighboring towns christened his product Bourbon County Whiskey, from the county of origin. It was considerably later that Kentucky became the unchallenged headquarters of the American whiskey industry.

Kentucky today has more than half of the nation's licensed distilleries and remains the major source for Bourbon, but the whiskey has long since jumped the county lines. By American regulation the name applies to any whiskey distilled from a fermented mash of grain containing at least 51% corn (the other grains vary, but a good balance is achieved with corn, rye, and malt) distilled at not more than 160° proof (in practice somewhere between 125° and 140° is more common) and aged in new charred oak barrels. Whiskey aged two years in wood and unblended is Straight Bourbon Whiskey; blended only with other Straight Bourbons, it is Blended Straight Bourbon, or Bourbon—A Blend of Straights.

Blended Bourbon is a mixture of Bourbon and other spirit, either whiskey or grain neutral spirit. A Straight Bourbon is usually a heavy, dry, mellow and full-bodied spirit, while a blended one will be lighter, from the addition of neutral spirit. In the United States, Straight Bourbon and Blended Straight Bourbon are the largest selling whiskeys, with some 80 million U.S. gallons (306.8 million imp.) or approximately 30 million cases sold annually, mostly in the South and West.

When the ground corn has been weighed and prepared for mashing, it is mixed with limestone water and steamed. The other ingredients (rye and barley malt) are then added. The yeast, sour wine in character, takes about five days to grow; this, with the mash, is pumped through coolers into the fermenters at a temperature of about 70°F. (21°C.) and left for the necessary period, while the yeast is being nourished by maltose sugars—and so the whiskey is made. Part of the mixture produced while the temperature rises is called new beer, and in distillation this has to be separated from the whiskey by heating—alcohol has a lower boiling point than new beer, therefore the whiskey forms vapors, which are condensed for further distillation. The new whiskey passes into a cistern where the proof is reduced, and is then poured into barrels to mature in a government bonded warehouse. Every six months characteristics are tested and graded. When it is ready for bottling, it is checked against standard samples of its brand, regauged for tax payment, and then bottled.

Whiskey, Corn

Whiskey distilled from a mash of fermented grain containing at least 80% corn. It is aged, if at all, in used containers, but usually gets little ageing, since the demand for it is in rural areas where fiery, young "corn likker" sets standards of taste. Corn whiskey, unaged, is raw, colorless, and—to say the least—unsubtle. It differs from Bourbon in many respects: legally, in that Bourbon must be from a mash 51% of which is corn, and must be aged in new, charred cooperage.

See also Whiskey, American.

Whiskey, Irish

"Of all wine, Irish wine is the best" was the ingenuous statement of Peter the Great of Russia; and it simply confirmed what generations of Irish had always believed. Just how many generations is a disputed point, for some maintain that the making of whiskey goes back at least a thousand years; others put it at a mere five hundred or so. Unquestionably, long before either whiskey or brandy was commercially remunerative, the Gael—both Irish and Scot—was distilling his fermented barley malt for his own pleasure. The Irish claim that brandy—a comparative newcomer—came about thanks to Irish missionaries taking the secret of distillation into France. How else, they ask, can you explain the similarities in the methods of distilling and the coincidence of *uisge beatha* and *eau-de-vie*, both of which mean "water of life"?

Until a century ago, Scotch whisky was for Scotsmen and Irish was the stuff which enjoyed popular favor. Then the Scots learned how to blend their brews and still keep them inimitably Scotch and made them known with brilliant salesmanship. After a period of doubt as to whether these blends could in fact be legally called whisky, these doubts were resolved by a Royal Commission and the world clamored for them. The world is still there, and the Irish, in spite of improving prospects and faithful adherents all over the globe, are having some trouble in finding an expansion of the markets for their austerely dry pot-still, unblended spirit of distinctive flavor. A further burden on the Irish distiller is high taxation, so that the Irishman cannot afford a fair share of his natural drink, and the moonshiner is attempting to provide a beverage made without the benefit of the excise officials. The popular name for this beverage is poteen—illegal whiskey named from the little—and easily dismantled—pot still in which it is made. Back in the bogs and around the lakes, poteen-making is popular and profitable, and the police rarely catch up with a bootlegger before he has packed up and moved on. If, in his hurry, he were to leave some behind him, the lucky finder would be saved more than one pound ($2.40) a bottle.

In spite of taxes, the Irishman loves his whiskey. Even horses, they say, hardly know how to leave the stuff alone. It happened some time ago, but they still talk about it in Dublin. Back in a small agricultural town a farmer, after a long night journey, stopped to water his horse at the local trough. The horse drank deep, and when his thirst was quenched, he moved away from the trough, staggered slightly and collapsed—dead drunk. The trough was found to be full of fine old whiskey, pure and ready to drink. Rejoicing was general until someone called the police who, in turn, called in the local excise people. Their inquiries showed that a nearby distillery was using convenient local waterpipes to drain its whiskey out of an excise-free warehouse for bottling, but someone had got it on the wrong circuit. The fine was large, and horses are staying sober in that part of Ireland now.

The excise officials are not always so fortunate. In spite of their efforts, poteen-making persists in certain areas, and in those parts, it is said that no self-respecting cattle or sheep dealer would consider doing business with a man who didn't offer him a small *deoch* to ward off early morning chill in the winter animal fairs. This may or may not have an effect upon the price, depending presumably upon the quality of poteen offered.

The making of quality Irish whiskey, such as Old Bushmills', follows much the same principles as the making of Scotch. (*For full details of the distilling process, see* Whisky, Scotch.) There are, however, some important differences in procedure. The popular and prestige Irish whiskeys are pure pot-still, containing no grain whiskeys as in the average Scotch. Also, they are three times distilled against twice in Scotland. Next, the mash is all of Irish grain—mostly barley, malted and unmalted, with a little wheat, oats, and rye. The malted barley is not, as it is in Scotland, dried directly over peat, so it lacks the "smoky" or "peaty" taste so common in Scotch. The wash, or whiskey before distillation, is placed in great stills, much larger than the Scottish type, sometimes capable of holding up to 750 hectoliters (20,000 U.S. gallons, 16,600 imp.); and distilling is done to bring out the whiskey at about 50° over proof (roughly 86% alcohol by volume or 172° by American standards) instead of 20° over proof (70% or 140° American) preferred by the Scot. As in all pot-still spirits, the middle section of the distillate is the only part drawn off, and the "heads" and "tails" are held over to be redistilled. The Irish calculate that a mere 10% of the wash comes over as whiskey, and much of this will evaporate as the spirit ages.

An Irishman, writing of his native whiskey, says it takes seven days of a man's time to make whiskey and seven years of its own. The man may spend a greater or lesser amount of time making the preparations, but the whiskey will not really be worth the name unless it gets the full time, although by Irish law it is mature at five. Some is aged for ten years, and the very best for twelve or fifteen—always in the wood; for once out of the cask whiskey will age no more.

Scotch whisky is a blend of heavy malt whisky with grain whisky, which changes the character of both ingredients and produces what the world knows as Scotch. On the other hand, Irish whiskey blends, in the mash, the ingredients of malt and grain and, after pot-still distillation, the addition of grain whiskey or grain spirit has no syllogistic effect but merely weakens the flavor. Irish whiskey will have caramel added—to give it the proper color—and water, so that it will be within reasonable limits. Most is sold at 30° under proof in Britain and Ireland (80° proof American), but this is subject to minor variations. Furthermore, most of the whiskey is the traditional pot-still whiskey. Irishmen have been pushing Irish punch (Irish whiskey, lemon peel, sugar, and boiling water) and Irish coffee (Irish whiskey, coffee, and sugar with a layer of cream floating over the top) in promoting their product—and there are now several blended whiskeys on the market. While they have been criticized for not adapting their ideas earlier to the changing world taste, their critics are perhaps unaware of the true nature of the product. There can be no doubt that a characteristic pot-still Irish whiskey properly aged is a magnificent spirit.

Whiskey, Light

As Scotch and Canadian whiskies became more popular in the United States in the early 1960s, American distillers grew eager to produce a lighter whiskey, but one could not be made due to the U.S. federal laws controlling the alcoholic strength at which American-made whiskeys were distilled. The regulations stipulated that American whiskeys—such as Bourbon and rye—must be distilled at less than 160° proof, or below an alcoholic content of 80%. And the lower the percent of alcohol at production, the more whiskey flavor is retained by the spirits. To make "light whiskey," then, the American companies had to be able to distill their spirit at more than 160° proof. As the proof rises toward 200°, the whiskey becomes a grain alcohol spirit with no taste, like vodka.

Federal laws held another obstacle to the new liquor: that all American-made whiskeys (except corn) should be aged in new, charred oak barrels.

In 1967, the necessary changes in the laws were effected, and Light Whiskey was defined as "a grain distillate produced in the United States on or after January 26, 1968 at a proof of over 160° and less than 190° and stored in used charred or uncharred new oak barrels." Further, "if Light Whiskey is mixed with less than 20% of straight whiskey on a proof gallon basis, the mixture is designated Blended Light Whiskey or Light Whiskey—A Blend." The products have not been all that successful.

Whiskey, rye

Most American rye whiskey is made in the states of Pennsylvania and Maryland and is consumed generally in that region. Straight rye accounts for less than 23,000 hectoliters (500,000 U.S. gallons, 332,000 imp.) of whiskey per year, and many consumers switched from it during and after the war, when several well-known brands changed from making straight to making blended whiskey.

According to government regulations, rye must be distilled from a mash of fermented grain containing at least 51% rye, at a proof not to exceed 160°, and must be aged in new charred oak barrels. Straight Rye has at least two years' barrel-age and is unblended; Blended Straight Rye—as the name implies—is a blend of two or more Straight Ryes. Bottles labeled simply Blended Rye will have neutral spirit or sometimes other whiskeys added, resulting in a lighter, less distinctive, less expensive spirit. Ryes are generally heavier and slightly more austere than Bourbons, with some affinity to Irish whiskey, although they are made in patent instead of Irish-style pot stills.

Whisky, Canadian

The most distinctive characteristic of Canadian whisky, generally speaking, is its lightness of body. All Canadian whisky, Canadian rye whisky, must, by law, be produced from cereal grain only. The combination of grains used, their treatment, and the special and rigid control exercised by the distiller during the entire production process, set Canadian whisky apart from any other grain distillate.

Canadian whisky is well known outside its own country, and its good reputation has been built up over 130 years by one company, over 100 years by each of four others, and by several distillers not so long established who are yet maintaining the traditions of their elders.

This is how Canadian whisky is made:

The Grain

No amount of ageing will make good whisky out of an inferior batch of grain. Therefore, when the grain is moved to the distillery, none is accepted until it has been thoroughly tested and approved by the distiller's chemist. When the grain, which consists of corn and rye and barley malt, has been milled into a fine meal or coarse flour, it is fed into a large cooker containing a fixed amount of water. This mash is heated with live steam in order to get the starch into solution, and when this has been accomplished barley malt is added to convert the starch into grain sugar. This step, saccharification, produces the grain sugar which is later fermented into alcohol by the introduction of yeast.

The Yeast

The culture and development of the yeast is a full-length story in itself. Each distillery carefully develops in test-tube bottles an isolated, pampered culture. One of the most critical points of control is the development of the living yeast cells. Since these *are* alive, sterile techniques and extreme caution are employed to prevent contamination.

Fermentation

The mash which has been saccharified is pumped from the cookers through large cooling coils into fermentation vats or tanks, which are then inoculated with the living yeast cells. The cells convert the sugar in the mash into alcohol and carbon dioxide, and this process takes about three to four days.

Distillation

When fermentation is complete the fermented mash is pumped into a continuous-operation, temperature-controlled, multiple-column patent still, usually cylindrical in shape and several stories high. This complex modern equipment allows many variations in the distilling procedure and consequently many variations in the final product. Thus the distiller is able to control the concentration of those components which contribute the flavor to the whisky.

Ageing

The next major step is the ageing of the whisky. Canadian distillers have found nothing that can do the job of mellowing and maturing their product better than nature itself. The unmatured whisky from the still is reduced to barreling strength and put into wood casks or barrels which may be charred on the inside, and this young whisky now faces a four-, six-, eight-, or twelve-year wait,

in temperature-controlled warehouses. During the ageing process, a number of slow chemical reactions occur, the more volatile components of the whisky evaporate and the wood brings out a mellowing process. Certain wood sugars and tannin are extracted from the wood, and it is these extracts which give the whisky its golden coloring. When sufficiently aged, various batches of whisky are "married"—an art in itself. The resulting product is tasted and tested for quality, and when approved the whisky is filtered many times, bottled, labeled, and ready for the market.

Canadian whisky for consumption in Canada is bottled at 70° proof (Sikes) or 39.9% of absolute alcohol by volume. Canadian whisky bottled in Canada for export is usually bottled at the proof strength permitted or used in the country of destination. It is exported to 154 different countries and territories throughout the world.

The Canadian distiller is subject to more government supervision and control than any other manufacturer or privately-owned enterprise in the nation. Some two hundred excise officers are stationed in Canadian distilleries, and their control extends from the receipt of grain at the distillery all through the production process, bottling, and shipment, and terminates with the payment of excise duty.

There is no government interference, however, with the distilling techniques employed by individual distillers. Each has complete control over the quality and character of his products.

The label on a bottle of Canadian whisky, which states distilled, aged, blended, bottled under Canadian government supervision is no idle boast, it is a statement of fact.

Whisky, malt

This is Scotch whisky made in Scotland entirely from malted barley (with yeast and water), to be distinguished from grain whiskies in which some maize (corn), wheat, oats, or rye will be used.

Malt whisky is distilled in pot stills, grain whisky in patent stills. For this reason, grain whisky distilleries can turn out many times more than malt whisky distilleries in the same length of time.

There are three types of Scotch malt whisky: Highland Malt, West Highland Malt (now known as Islay malt), and Lowland Malt. The first is produced widely throughout the Highlands in some eighty distilleries, half of them in the vicinity of the River Spey. This is considered the best. West Highland, from Islay in the Inner Hebrides and the peninsula of Kintyre, is usually stronger-flavored. The comparatively few distilleries in the south making Lowland Malt Whisky produce it generally for blending. West Highland Malts are often referred to as Islay or Campbeltown. There are seven distilleries on the island of Islay and one on the island of Jura producing Islay malts with the characteristic "smokiness" which has made them famous. They are Ardbeg, Eowmore, Bruichladdich, Bunnahabhain, Caol Ila, Lagavulin and Laphroaig, and Isle of Jura.

See Whisky, Scotch.

Whisky, Scotch

Scotch whisky is imitated everywhere. At one time the Japanese made it in a town they renamed Aberdeen for the benefit of their bottle labels. The Germans, thorough if not successful, imported the actual water from Speyside in Scotland, but they did not get Scotch, which was, and remains, inimitable.

Just why it is that Scotch can be made only in Scotland is one of the mysteries—akin to the unanalyzable combination of known ingredients that is the true virtue of great wines. Supposedly, Scotch is merely the product of barley, yeast, Scottish water, and Scottish air, and a distilling process which holds no mystery at all.

The barley, it appears, can come from anywhere. It has been imported from as far away as Australia and California, or grown at home in Scotland and England. The foreign barley used to be considered the better, because it was drier—an important factor—but now, most of it is domestically grown. What makes Scotch "Scotch" is another matter. Blending—these days—has something to do with it. Until a century ago, Scotch was for Scotsmen, a straight, high-proof beverage. Blending began, and it is this trick which has carried the fame of the drink around the world—only in Scotland is unblended "singles" Scotch whisky to be found in any quantity. The secret of the blending lies in the fact that all the components are Scottish, with Scotch malt whisky as the irreplaceable base. To produce their unique malt whiskies, the Scottish distillers themselves rely on techniques which are more like magic than science. It is an authentic story that the actual physical shape of the pot still can have something to do with the whisky distilled in it; and one distiller, having built a new still and never being able to recapture the lost beauty of his spirit, was compelled to have his worn-out still recopied—including the patches.

The whisky runs through quite a history—and several identities—before it becomes the Scotch we know. Arrived at the distillery, barley is screened to get rid of extraneous seeds, etc. Following, generally, a period of storage, there is the steeping: the barley is plunged into water in large vats and left for a predetermined saturation period. Then it goes to the broad cement floors where the maltmen spread and tend it. In two to three days it germinates; rootlets spring forth, and when, four or five days later, these wither and the grain becomes modified, the maltmen consider that the barley is "malted."

The malt is conveyed to the kiln floor, where it lies on sheets of perforated metal until thoroughly dried by warm air from peat fires burning below. Toward the end of this process, when it is considered that the green malt has absorbed so much of the peaty flavor that it will retain it till liquor meets palate, coke or anthracite is added to bring the temperature to 160°F. (71°C.). Devised to let the controlled heat pass off, the kiln roofs are cowled with "pagoda tops," the air escaping under the ruffled eaves aided today by extractor fans which lend a strange Chinese grace to the sturdy, blunt, Scottish stone buildings.

After its trial by fire, the malt is allowed to rest for about two months, then it is screened and the withered rootlets, or malt culms, are strained off to become useful cattle food. The malt itself is ground or crushed in a roller mill of appropriate design.

The ground malt is then poured into the mash tun, a great claw-armed, circular tub with a sprocket rod splashing endlessly around, stirring the crushed malt through the seething water. Four waters, each hotter than the one before, are used in this extracting of the solubles from the malt. This solution is called wort—pronounced wurt. The first two waters, which have been saved from an earlier extraction, are known as the sparge. The infused waters passing off from the tun stream through the cooling machine, which cools them down by 72% to 75°F. (24°C.), an appropriate temperature for adding yeast. After this, they are lodged in the fermenting vats, usually called the backs. The third and fourth washings of waters become the new sparge, to be saved and used as first and second waters in a later extraction. The residue after the wort is drawn is the draff, or cattle food.

Yeast is added to the wort in the backs—fermenting vats sometimes of larch or pine, but today often of steel—and fermentation begins. The active element of the yeast changes the sugary wort into alcohol and carbon dioxide; the carbon dioxide escapes into the air and the alcohol remains at about a gallon of proof spirit per 10 gallons of wort. Once again the name of this product we are following through its conversion from barley to whisky changes. What was once malt, and then wort, is now wash.

The wash flows into the copper pot stills—dully-gleaming affairs which in the great distilleries can dwarf the size of a man—and is distilled. It passes through a phase after the first distillation when it carries still another name, "low wines" (because it has not yet reached the height of full strength); but during redistillation the clear and stronger fractions are collected in the spirit receiver vat and are now classified as whisky. This new whisky will be about 16° over proof or about 58% alcohol by volume and will require to be reduced a little by pure spring water. At around 11° over proof or 55.5% alcohol by volume, it enters the cask. The distiller will have expected to get a range of from 2.5 to 3 gallons from his bushel of barley, but he will lose something of both strength and volume while his whisky lies for the maturation period in cask. In a damp climate he will lose more strength and in a dry one more volume. It is something to think about that each year 11 million liters (3 million U.S. gallons, 2.5 million imp.) of Scotch whisky evaporate into the soft Scottish air.

The cask itself is the final contribution to the beauty of the whisky. This improves greatly with age—in barrel, not in bottle—and it matures usually in casks made from American oak. The casks must be oak. When wine-steeped casks are not obtainable, the distiller will have to add a little caramel or burnt-sugar coloring to give his whisky the tawny tinge the public expects.

Whisky casks are known as butts if they hold more than 364 liters (96 U.S. gallons, 80 imp.); as hogsheads if they hold from 205 to 364 liters (54 to 96 U.S. gallons, 45 to 80 imp.); barrels if they hold 160 to 205 liters (42 to 54 U.S. gallons, 35 to 45 imp.); and as quarters if their capacity is less than 136 liters (36 U.S. gallons, 30 imp.). Octaves hold between 41 and 68 liters (11 and 18 U.S. gallons, 9 and 15 imp.). The butts are of three different types, varying in shape: puncheons, pipes, and one called simply a butt.

The blenders are the great artists of the whisky trade, and it is fascinating to see these men at their work, going more by sense of smell than taste, their nostrils dilating sensitively in the tall, narrow, tulip-shaped, noseing glasses with their short two-finger-wide stems. When a blender has made his selections, the ingredients are mixed together by paddle stirrers in colossal vats, then left to "marry." The proportions will be about 40% malt whisky and 60% grain whisky, though occasionally these will be approximately reversed. It is the blending which creates the infinite scale of whiskies; it is not uncommon for a blend to be made up from as many as fifty types. Most experts agree that the best Scotch blends usually consist of about half Highland and Lowland malts, a little Islay or Campbeltown, and the remainder, unmalted grain whisky. On the whole, the Highland malts are light in body and full-flavored; the Lowland malts are also light, but less distinctly smoky; while the Campbeltowns and Islays are noted for heavy body and plenty of smoke.

Before bottling, whisky is reduced by the addition of soft water from the Scottish lochs—and it is filtered.

The shortage of Scotch in the 1940s was mainly the result of the wartime ban on distilling and the limited ration of barley allowed the industry in the first years after the war (the quota of barley 1945-50 covered one year's distillation), combining with the long period necessary for ageing. Another factor has been the great increase in world sales, especially in the United States. At the present time, when supplies are fortunately adequate, Americans are drinking 13 million—or more—cases a year of this most popular of all the grain spirits—which has now become the most fashionable aperitif and nightcap drink in France and other European countries. The present trend shows an increase in the consumption of single malts.

The rise in excise on Scotch whisky has been astronomical. A hundred years ago it was 10s. ($1.40) a proof gallon. The two great upward leaps were after the two world wars—to £1 10s. ($4.20) after the First; and to £11 11s. 11d. ($32.47) after the Second. It is now some $50 U.S. the proof gallon.

White Port

Port wine (Oporto, Portugal) made from white grapes. Generally, it inclines to be a little sweeter than red Port and finds its great market in France; but there is a growing tendency also to manufacture a dry White Port which is served as an aperitif in Portugal and is beginning to be known and appreciated abroad.
See Port.

White rot

A blight of vines.
See Chapter Eight, p. 29.

Wienerwald-Steinfeld

A good vineyard region in Austria, embracing Gumpoldskirchen and Baden.
See Austria.

Wiltingen

A town in the Saar Valley, southwest of Trier. The 140 hectares (350 acres) of surrounding vineyards produce excellent white wines of which the best-known is Scharzhofberg.
See Mosel-Saar-Ruwer.

Wine

The word should apply only to the naturally fermented juice of the grape, although it is extended too often to "wines" made from vegetables, berries, and other fruits. The term is abused especially in reference to drinks made from cherries. True wine produced from grapes can be divided into three main types:

(1) Still beverage, or table wines to accompany a meal. These divide again into red, white, and rosé (according to the grapes used and the length of time the skins have been left to ferment with the juice); and into dry or sweet wines, depending on whether all the grape sugar has been allowed to ferment into alcohol, or whether some residual sugar has been left.
(2) Sparkling wines, of which Champagne, made by the process of secondary fermentation in bottle, is the finest example.
(3) Fortified wines, such as Port, Sherry, and Madeira, to which brandy has been added.

The different wine-growing countries make, from a variety of grapes, numerous wines in each category—every one of importance is to be found under its own heading.

For an analysis of the nature of wine and an account of how it is made, *see* Chapter Nine, p. 39.

Wine counterfeiters and grape thieves

Throughout history the growers of the grape have not dealt lightly with those who pilfered or tampered with their products. In Germany, grape thieves were led through the villages with their hands held up before them and locked in a fiddle-shaped wooden vise. This was equipped with a bell which clanged above their heads, so that all the villagers might turn out to mock them. Alternatively, the thief might be forced to ride backward through the town on a donkey, the stolen goods in his hands, the legend emblazoned on his back and breast: "He stole grapes!" It was in Germany also that wine counterfeiters and wine adulterators were severely punished during the Middle Ages, being sentenced to death for falsifying the honest product of the grape.

Wine fountains

For hundreds of years the wine fountains, from which wine flowed in place of water, brightened the scene at harvest and other festivals in many countries. Old German chronicles tell of the wine fountain of Urach (claiming to be the oldest in Germany with its date of 1474), where the wine flowed for three days and nights in alternating jets of red and white, to celebrate a royal wedding. Wine fountains were known to the Egyptians, the Greeks, and the Romans. Today the custom has been revived and the wine fountains flow at many European harvest festivals.

Wine gallon

A gallon of 128 U.S. (160 British) fluid ounces of wine or spirits irrespective of proof or alcoholic strength; also known as bulk gallon.

See Proof gallon.

Wine societies

Different wine-making districts of France have each their own society or *confrérie*, part medieval relic, part sales promotion. Growers and shippers take part, dressed in the historic costumes with which they have been invested at a long ceremony of inauguration, followed by a feast. Among the more famous of these associations are the Commanderie du Bontemps du Médoc et de Graves (*q.v.*), La Connétablie de Guyenne, La Jurade de Saint-Émilion, Les Chevaliers du Tastevin at Nuits-Saint-Georges, Les Compagnons du Beaujolais, La Commanderie de Champagne de l'Ordre des Coteaux, La Confrérie des Chevaliers de la Chantepleure de Vouvray, and La Confrérie Saint-Étienne in Alsace. Others are La Confrérie des Compagnons de la Capucine at Toul, Les Compagnons Hauts-Normands du Gouste-Vin, La Conseil des Echansons de France in Paris, La Commanderie des Vins et Spiriteux de France (also in Paris), the Nouvel Ordre Hospitalier, Curieux et Courtois des Chevaliers de Saint-Bacchus in Paris, the Ordre Bachiques et Epicurien du Gay Savoir en Bien Mangier et Bien Boire, Les Compagnons du Pintou in Auvergne, La Confrérie Vineuse des Piliers Chablisiens, La Confrérie des Troi Ceps in the Yonne, Le Cousinerie de Bourgogne, La Confrérie des Vignerons de Saint-Vincent in Macon, La Confrérie du Gosier-Sec de Clochemerle in the Beaujolais, La Confrérie des Chevaliers de la Syrah et Roussette for the Rhône Valley, l'Ordre Illustre des Chevaliers de Meduse in the Côtes de Provence, La Confrérie des Echansons de Vidauban, La Confrérie des Comtes de Nice et de Provence, l'Echansonnerie des Papes at Châteauneuf-du-Pape, Le Commanderie de Tavel, l'Ordre de la Boisson de la Stricte Observance des Costières du Gard, Antica Confraria de Saint-Andu de la Galiniera for the Hérault, le Consulat de Septimanie of the Coteaux du Languedoc, l'Illustre Cour des Seigneurs de la Corbière, La Commende Majeure de Roussillon pour Garder le Devoir et le Droit de la Vigne et du Vin, l'Ordre de la Dive Bouteille in Gaillac, La Confrérie du Vin de Cahors, La Viguerie Royale du Jurançon, La Viguerie du Madiran, La Commanderie des Chevaliers de Tursan, Le Grand Conseil de Bordeaux, l'Académie du Vin de Bordeaux, Les Compagnons de Bordeaux, le Club des Amis du Vin de Bordeaux, La Commanderie du Bontemps de Sauternes et Barsac, La Commanderie de Bontemps de Sainte-Croix-du-Mont, La Connétablie de Guyenne, Les Compagnons du Loupiac, La Confrérie des Hospitaliers de Pomerol, Les Gentilshommes de Fronsac, le Consulat de la Vinée de Bergerac, Le Principauté de Franc-Pineau in Charentes, l'Ordre des Chevaliers Bretvins, La Confrérie des Chevaliers du Sacavin in Anjou, La Confrérie des Vignerons de la Canette in Bouille-Loretz (Deux-Sèvres), La Confrérie des Vin Gousiers d'Anjou, La Commanderie du Taste-Saumur, La Confrérie des Hume-Piot du Loudonois, La Confrérie Vineuse de Tiré-Douzils in Poitou, Les Entonneurs Rabelaisiens in Chinon, La Confrérie des Fripe-Douzils in Bourgueil, La Confrérie des Chevaliers des Cuers du Baril in the Touraine, La Coterie des Closiers de Montlouis, La Commanderie des Grands Vins d'Amboise, La Confrérie des Compagnons de Grandgousier, La Confrérie des Baillis de Pouilly-sur-Loire, le Collège des Chanoines de Tannay, Les Chevaliers de Sancerre, La Compagnie des Vignerons d'Honneur, La Compagnie d'Honneur des Sorciers et Birettes for Anjou, La Confrérie de Chevaliers du Cep in Verdigny, l'Ordre des Chevaliers du Paissiau, La Maîtrise des Echansons in Reuilly, Le Cercle des Chevaliers du Cep in Châteauroux, l'Ordre des Vins Palais in Saint-Pourcain, La Confrérie des Compagnons du Bousset d'Auvergne, La Confrérie de Saint-Verny, La Confrérie de Bacchus et d'Icare in Lyon, La Compagnie du Sarto for the Savoie, La Commanderie des Nobles Vins du Jura et Gruyère de Comte, and La Pairie des Vins d'Arbois. There are societies, also, in honor of the great French brandies: La Confrérie des Alambics Charentais at Cognac; and La Compagnie des Mousquetaires d'Armagnac at Condom.

In Switzerland there is the Confrérie des Vignolants de Neuchâtel, l'Ordre de la Channe, and La Confrérie de Guillon. Belgium has the Gilde de Saint-Vincent de Belgique and the Confrérie des Chevaliers Rabelaisiens de Belgique. In Italy the societies are the Confraternità della Cheer, the Cavaliers d'Asti et de Montferrato, and the Confraternità d'la Tripa. The United States too has at least one group: the Universal Order of the Knights of the Vine of California.

Winery

The American name for an establishment where wine is made.

Winkel

Town with several good vineyards, on the bank of the Rhine.

See Rheingau.

Wintrich

Good white wine district of the German Middle Mosel. *See* Mosel-Saar-Ruwer.

Winzer

German term for wine-grower. Winzerverein on a label indicates that the wine has been produced by a cooperative.

Wood

The cask. Wine is "in the wood" when it is in the cask.

Woody

This can indicate two conditions in a wine or spirit, usually curable: (1) a smell from wholesome oak when the liquor has been too long in the cask; (2) a taint from defective wood.

Worcester

Wine district of the Cape province. *See* South Africa.

Wort

The extract from malt which is fermented to make malt whisky. The word is pronounced wurt. *See* Whisky, Scotch.

Württemberg

German red and white wines.
District: Neckar River Valley.

The Württemberg *Gebiet* is one of the eleven designated quality wine producing regions in West Germany. It is the one region which produces more red than white wine; the total harvest is about 500,000 hectoliters (13.25 million U.S. gallons, 11 million imp.). The area is officially divided into three *Bereiche*, or sub-regions; in the south, Remstal-Stuttgart; in the central section, Württembergisch Unterland; and in the north, Kocher-Jagst-Taubertal. For a complete list of the vineyards, arranged by these sections, see Appendix B, p. 625.

The Württemberg region is the valley of the River Neckar, flowing north and then northwest from above Stuttgart to its confluence with the Rhine at Mannheim and the valleys of the six smaller rivers that enter it. These are the Rems, Enz, Murr, Kocher, Jagst, and Tauber.

After numerous setbacks, Württemberg wines began to improve in quality during the last century, mainly under the influence of the Association for the Betterment of the Wine founded in 1824 and later the basis of the cooperatives; and by means of the replanting of the vineyards with Riesling and other noble vines. Although Württemberg is still one of the largest German producers, replanting, conversion of vineyards to other farm uses, the invasion of the vine louse phylloxera at the end of the last century, and the expansion of city and industrial areas, have reduced the total vine plantation considerably. The wines are not among the most interesting in Germany, and in at least one way Württemberg seems unsuited for wine production: the area is a meeting point for the warmth coming from the sea zones and for the Continental land-mass cold. This causes sudden and violent changes of weather, storms and, worst of all for the wine, sharp, unexpected frosts in spring and autumn. Offsetting the generally unfavorable weather to some extent is the warming influence of the rivers along which most of the vineyards are situated.

The important red wine grape variety from the point of view of quantity is the Trollinger, which gives a rather harsh wine from exceptionally large grapes. Better red wines, as elsewhere in Germany, come from the Spätburgunder plant, originally the Pinot Noir of Burgundy.

Best white wines are Riesling, followed by Sylvaner, and to a lesser extent Traminer and Ruländer (an adaptation of the French Pinot Gris). Much success has been achieved with wines made from some of the new hybrid grape varieties. The large cooperatives, which control most of the vineyard land, seem to encourage plantings of these new stocks.

Certainly the most popular product of the Württemberg wine-growers is the light pink, aromatic Schillerwein. Though rosé in color, it is not vinified in the manner of many of the other rosé wines made in Europe. To make the Schillerwein, red and white grapes are mixed before crushing, and the whole fermented together. Often the red and white varieties grow side by side in the same vineyard plots, so that the mixture is made by the pickers as they work through the fields. The wine is well known and much demanded in the production region.

Würzburg

Center of the German Steinwein of Franconia (*q.v.*).

Wynberg

First district in Cape province to produce wine. *See* South Africa.

Xérès

French for Sherry (*q.v.*). Xeres was the name given by the ancient Romans to the Sherry city of Jerez.

X.O.

The oldest style of Cognac found on the general market. The designation is used mainly by the Cognac firm of Hennessy. While, except in the exceedingly rare vintage brandies, age designations in brandy indicate a style rather than an exact number of years, X.O.s often claim, and frequently have, about forty years of barrel-age. (Brandies, like other spirits, do not age in bottle.) Age in brandy is fully discussed under Cognac (*q.v.*).

Xynisteri

One of the dominating grapes in Commandaria, the famous dessert wine of Cyprus. The other is the Mavron.

Y

Yakima Valley

Wine region in Washington State, one of the rare districts outside California where European grapevines have flourished.

See United States.

Yalumba

Famous vineyard in Eden Valley, South Australia, from which comes a dry white wine called Carte d'Or.
See Australia.

Yam wine

Beverage fermented from yam roots in Africa and South America.

Yamanashi

One of the main vine-growing districts of Japan (*q.v.*).

Yawa

West African palm wine.

Yayin

Biblical term for wine, evidently related to *vinum*, *Wein*, etc.

Yeasts

Natural, microscopic, unicellular organisms found on the skins of grapes, and responsible for alcoholic fermentation. One of these, *Saccharomyces cereviseae*, is the true wine-maker which gives the wine its character and its main constitution. As the last grams of sugar are fermented out, this yeast disappears and dies. A lesser variety, *Saccharomyces bayanus*, important in the white wines of Bordeaux, as well as in the Pomerols and Saint-Émilions, is more resistant to alcohol than *S. cereviseae* and increases as fermentation advances. *Saccharomyces acidifaciens,* yet another variety of fermenting yeast, is often found to be a cause of trouble in white wines. In many modern wineries yeast selections or cultures are chosen with great care.

Undesirable yeasts may also be found in ripe grapes. These can be destroyed by sulfuring of the must and by adding cultured yeasts.

See Chapter Nine, p. 38.

Yeso

In Spain, gypsum-rich dust used for "plastering" (*q.v.*).

Château d'Yquem

Bordeaux white wine.
District and Commune: Sauternes, France.

Château d'Yquem is the greatest natural sweet white wine, the only wine which can always, without fear of argument, be claimed to be the best of its kind—although a few Trockenbeerenauslesen of Germany may in great years be compared with it. This was recognized in ratings of Bordeaux in the eighteenth century; and in 1855, when Sauternes and Médoc were classified on the basis of their known excellence and sales, d'Yquem was the only wine classed a First Great Growth (*Premier Grand Cru*).

Distinguished even among the finest of the other Sauternes by an extra suavity and full richness and vinous luscious depth, and a more beautiful gold in color, d'Yquem is the result partly of the highest possible wine-making standards, partly of the magnificent exposure of the terrain on a hill commanding the whole Sauternes district, and also of something almost magical which must be in the soil itself. In every great wine zone there are one or two plots which somehow manage, year in and year out, to produce wines better even than those of vineyards touching their borders. There is no more remarkable example of this than Château d'Yquem.

The property, which had produced wine for at least two or three centuries, came into the family of the Marquis de Lur-Saluces by marriage in 1885. It is owned and directed today by Count Alexandre de Lur-Saluces, an heir of Marquis Bertrand de Lur-Saluces, who was a great campaigner for all French wines and was the head both of the French wine promotional organization and the Association of the Classified Growths of Bordeaux. More than a century and a half ago Thomas Jefferson had already written: "Sauterne. This is the best white wine of France and the best of it is made by Monsieur de Lur-Saluces." Add an *s* to Sauterne, and place the word "sweet" in front of white wine to avoid controversy about the excellence of some dry whites, and the statement is true today.

Château d'Yquem is and always has been expensive. Today, it is generally sold to Bordeaux shippers bottled —that is to say, at the château with no charges added for casing, etc.—at about 100 francs (approximately £7 or $20) per bottle. It achieved what was probably the highest price paid for any wine in the last century when the brother of the Emperor of Russia bought four barrels of the 1847 vintage for 20,000 francs (about £3,646 or $10,200 now). Costly as it is, the high price of the wine is justified not only by market demand, but by two special factors. About 1847, Château d'Yquem, first of all the Sauternes vineyards, introduced the practice of using only hyper-rich, half-rotted grapes attacked by the so-called noble rot (*pourriture noble*). This process—requiring the vineyard to be picked over many times, because the bunches reached the desired maturity at different intervals—has made the production of all Sauternes expensive and is now the practice in all Sauternes vineyards. Château d'Yquem, in addition to this, sells under its own name only the best; the wine of poor years or from lesser sections in mediocre years is sold to the trade simply as Sauternes, at a financial loss. In 1954, for example, the vineyard declared 336 barrels of fine wine and 172 barrels of district Sauternes; and in 1955, 480 barrels with 100 barrels of Sauternes. "All the wines of Château d'Yquem are château bottled. But the vineyard gives its name only to wines very rigorously selected . . ."—Marquis Bertrand de Lur-Saluces. Until 1876, different segments of the pressing were sold separately in differing grades, but since that date the harvest has been equalized by the vatting together of the pick of different days. The wine is aged for three years in new wooden barrels, or *barriques*. The wine has an extremely long life, and bottles of a hundred years and older can still be found in excellent condition, if they have been properly kept. Although this great sweet wine is properly appreciated, the present fashion for dry wines is so irresistible that Château d'Yquem is now making some fair dry white wine called Y (Y Grec).

The castle itself, a turreted and walled château-fort on its high hill, is one of the landmarks of southwestern France; and one of the most charming evenings to be spent in Europe is at the annual concert given in the great courtyard by some internationally known string quartet as part of the May Bordeaux Music Festival. The floodlit château gleams like a fairy-tale castle, its battlements and towers visible over miles of the dark Sauternes countryside.

Hail is the great enemy of the vineyard, and in 1951, 1952, and 1973 the crop was wiped out. No d'Yquem was produced in 1964, 1972 or 1974.

Characteristics. Full-bodied and luscious, with superb finesse, this expensive wine is well worth the price. It ages exceedingly well, for maderization acquired through ageing becomes an asset and is not offensive. The great sweetness offsets any overlay of excessive oxidation.

Vineyard area: 100 hectares (250 acres).

Average production: 80 *tonneaux* (6,500 cases of d'Yquem, some 2,000 cases of Y—both quantities vary greatly).

Yugoslavia

Yugoslavia, the state of the Southern Slavs, which now embraces the Croatian and Slovene provinces of the Austro-Hungarian Empire, Serbia, Montenegro, Macedonia, Bosnia, and Herzegovina, has the eighth largest vineyard area in Europe.

In few places does wine better fulfill the truism that it never tastes as good as where it is grown. In Macedonia and Montenegro, almost self-contained and inaccessible parts of the world which have kept their native characteristics even today, the wines, when you drink them there, are enhanced by the local costumes, the hardy romance of the surroundings, and sometimes by the very vessels in which they are kept. The carved, round, wooden brandy-

and wine-flasks, ornate canteens with their leather bindings and carrying straps of braid, are among the most attractive in the world. It is not necessary to visit the rugged regions to experience the charm of Yugoslav wines. Many thousands of tourists taste the red wines of Dalmatia in the white, walled city of Dubrovnik. A very different experience from drinking such full, red, alcoholic (13% to 14%) southern wines as Dingač (pronounced Dingach) or Bol in their place of origin is that of drinking the white wines of Slovenia in the alpine north.

At the present time, Dalmatian wines are probably not at their potential best, and the wines of Slovenia are more fully realized. Slovenian white wines, Serbian white, red, and rosé, some of the wines of Istria, and lately the dry white wines and red wines of Macedonia are frequently to be met with in Great Britain and the United States. The countries to which Yugoslavia chiefly exports her wines are Germany, both East and West, Czechoslovakia, Poland, and Britain.

HISTORY

Wine is of very ancient origin in Yugoslavia, as it is in all the Mediterranean and Balkan countries. Some historians say it came from Thrace, up through the Macedonian mountains and into what is now Yugoslavia, about four thousand years ago. It is certainly true that the Dalmatian and Istrian wines flourished under the Greeks, and Slovenian wines under the Romans. Slovenia and the Danube Plain (Croatia) are full of Roman remains, decorated very often with wine and grape motifs; the several languages of Yugoslavia have common words for various aspects of vine care and wine-making, taken direct from the Latin; and the museums in towns as far apart as Dubrovnik in Dalmatia and Ptuj in Slovenia, not 80 kilometers (50 miles) south of the Austrian border, have many Greek and Roman wine amphorae and implements dug up in the environs.

Here as in other countries of Europe, wine culture was carried on by the feudal lords and the great monasteries in the Middle Ages. We hear of the wines of Ohrid, far in the south, and of Albania, being in great favor in Europe at the time of the Crusades.

It must be remembered, however, that for centuries part of Yugoslavia was overrun by the Turks. Sarajevo, in the center of the country, is even today the most Turkish city west of Istanbul. The needle-minarets of its seventy or eighty mosques remind us of the Moslem influence; and the Moslem is forbidden to drink wine. Thus where the Turk dominated, viticulture was abandoned until these regions were liberated from Moslem influence—a slow process of emancipation lasting from 1804 until 1912.

On the other hand parts of what is now Yugoslavia belonged to Austria. Ljutomer, for instance, was for centuries in Styria and thus was Austrian. The consequence was that northern Yugoslav wines and methods of viticulture are typically Austrian. Even today, confusion is caused by the fact that certain of these wines gained a world reputation under German names, which are now being replaced by Yugoslav appellations. Ljutomer, one of Yugoslavia's most famous wines, named after the town near which it grows in the northernmost tip pressed into Austria and Hungary, first became known as Luttenberger, its Austrian name, and was frequently supposed to be a wine from Austria. It is seldom realized that Luttenberger and Ljutomer are different names for the same wine.

VINES AND STATISTICS

Yugoslavia has something over 250,000 hectares (625,000 acres) of vineyards and makes each year roughly 6.5 million hectoliters of table wine (162.5 million U.S. gallons, 143 million imp.). The quantity produced is approximately the same as the amounts made each year in the neighboring countries of Greece, Rumania, and Hungary. Much wine is drunk—the average consumption is some 27 liters per head annually, four times the U.S. rate. The export trade has grown in recent years; now about 740,000 hectoliters (19.5 million U.S. gallons, 16.2 million imp.) are shipped abroad. Very little wine is imported.

The vines grown are numerous and varied. Particularly in the north of the country, where the Austrian influence was most felt, there are imported vines such as Riesling, Traminer, Sylvaner, Merlot, and Sauvignon. However, a number of native vines are also used—as are hybrids, many of which were planted at the time of the phylloxera crisis which hit Yugoslavia about the turn of the century.

WINE-GROWING DISTRICTS

Yugoslavia was created just after the First World War out of six separate Slavonic-speaking states: Serbia, Croatia, Slovenia, Bosnia-Herzegovina, Montenegro, and the northern part of Macedonia. While they make up a harmonious whole, each state still clings to its ancient habits and customs, and the wines grown in each are different from the others. The proportional amounts of wine by state are as follows: Serbia 45%; Croatia 35%; Slovenia 9%; Macedonia 9%; Bosnia-Herzegovina 2%; Montenegro negligible.

Serbia

Serbia is the great bulk-wine producing section of Yugoslavia and until recently most of the wines grown there were more likely to be served in the place of their origin, often as carafe wines, than found abroad. They are named after the general district from which they come (example: wines from the huge region of Župa will sell as Župa Red). Most of the Serbian wines are made from the Prokupac vine, which is commonly known as the "national vine of Serbia." Some of the following names are the best known:

Župa (pronounced Zhoopa). Here, in the center of Serbia, the warm, sun-bathed hills produce a vast amount of red wine which is full, heavy, and rich, but not particularly noted for its breed or distinction. A pink, or rosé, wine is also made, and both types stem from the Prokupac vine. The vineyards are extensive, with the city of Alek-

sandrovac the central wine town.

Krajina (pronounced Krayina). Centered around the city of Negotin, this district lies on the borders of Rumania and Bulgaria. The wines are almost entirely red, made from a blend of the Prokupac, Skadarka, and Začinak vines. They were once fairly well known in France, where they were sent at the time of the worst of the phylloxera crisis at the end of the last century. A white wine named Bagrina of Krajina, after the vine, is also made.

Vlasotinci (pronounced Vlasotinsi). From the south of Serbia. Most of the wines are pink and are made from the Prokupac and Plovdina vines.

Venčac-Oplenac (pronounced Ventchats-Oplenats). Up the Morava River from Župa, this region is the heart of the part of Serbia called Šumadija (Shumadiya), where the insurrection against Turkish rule started at the beginning of the last century. Wines are grown—the main headquarters being the city of Topola—mainly from the Prokupac, Pinot Noir, Gamay, and most recently Chardonnay vines; both red and rosé wines are made. The rosé of Oplenac is well known.

Smederevo. An enormous region lying on the rolling hills on the south side of the Danube near the Rumanian border. A good white wine is produced here from the Smerdervka and Wälschriesling grapes.

Vojvodina (25,000 hectares—62,500 acres—of vineyards). An autonomous province of Serbia, east of Croatian Slavonia and bordering on Hungary and Rumania. The region is an important agricultural center, growing grapes for wine as well as for the table, and many of the big new plantations have replaced the older native varieties with better Western strains. There are three districts: Fruška Gora is a gentle wooded mountain between the Sava and the Danube, where there are vast vineyards and giant modern wineries. They grow Wälschriesling, Sémillon, Traminer, White Pinot, and Sauvignon Blanc. The best areas are Erdevik, Vrdnik, and Sremski Karlovici, which in the last century—when this was part of Hungary—made a red wine called Carlowitz (Karlovice Rothwein), popular in Great Britain, Austria, and the Netherlands. Sound white wines are produced there now, comparable to the high quality of those from the Maribor area of Slovenia. This was formerly a good district for red wines, growing Skadarka and other native grape varieties. The policy of the government is now to replant the white wine-producing vines, and to replace the native red varieties with the Burgundian Gamay and Pinot Noir, since the emphasis is not on red wine production. Bermet was a local vermouth, formerly made at Sremski Karlovici.

The second of the Vojvodinian districts, Subotička Peščara, between the Danube and the Tisza rivers, is reclaimed sand land, an extension of the Hungarian Alföld—the Great Plain. Planting has been somewhat improved here and now includes Austrian Grüner Veltliner, Wälschriesling, the Hungarian Ezerjó and Muscat Ottonel, plus a good local variety called Kevedinka for white wines. Kadarka, Blaufränkisch, and Pinot Noir produce the red wines. No high-quality wines are made here, and it will be interesting to see how this region with

YUGOSLAVIA

N

| 0 | 20 | | 100 | MILES | | 200 |
| 0 | 20 | | 100 | 200 KILOMETRES 300 | | |

© CASSELL & CO LTD 1967

its new plantings, some of them necessarily experimental, will develop.

The third and the largest of the Vojvodinian regions is the small part of the Banat that is not Rumanian. Bits of it are deep, sandy land unsuitable for cultivation, but two-thirds of the vineyard area of Vojvodina is in this area, although the majority of the grapes grown are for the table rather than for wine. The Banat has its own peculiar climate; it is in the extreme southeastern corner of the Pannonian Plain, where the foothills rise to become the Transylvanian Alps. Vršac is in the foothills and is still a center of wine production; some of the wine is said to be of good quality. It is primarily a white wine area and the same vines are grown as in Fruška Gora, but with the addition of a local Riesling-type called Banatski Rizling Kreaca. The small amount of red wine also comes from Merlot, Cabernet Sauvignon, Gamay, and Pinot Noir grapes.

Kosmet. Another autonomous province of Serbia, bordering on Albania and Macedonia. The ancient Greeks first grew vines here on the foothills of the mountains. The modern vineyards were only replanted ten years ago, decades after the phylloxera devastation at the end of the last century, using Cabernet Sauvignon, Cabernet Franc, Gamay, and Pinot Noir. These red wines are rather pleasant and popular in several Western European countries. A little white wine is made from Žilavka and Wälschriesling. The Kosmet region joins with Macedonia to form one great wine district. There are 150,000 hectares (375,000 acres) of vines in Serbia, Kosmet, and Macedonia combined.

Croatia

The wines of Croatia can most conveniently be divided into two major types: those which are grown in the inland section stretching from the broad Danubian plain to the mountains above Zagreb, between the Drava and Sava rivers; and those which come from the Adriatic coast, including the wines of the once Italian portion of the Istrian Peninsula and of the fabulous Dalmatian coast.

540

The inland vine-growing districts include the valleys of the Danube, Drava, and Sava rivers and extend to the alpine slopes which lead into Slovenia, adjoining the famous wine district of Ljutomer, perhaps the best in Yugoslavia. The flatter vineyards produce wines more like those in Serbia, however; most of them are light, slightly acid but agreeable wines with no particular breed but without pretense. The wines most frequently encountered include those from Plješevica (pronounced Plyeshivitsa), Vinica (Vinitsa), Varaždin (Varajdeen), and Medjugorica (Mejugoritsa).

In the northeast part of Croatia, the vineyards start climbing the slopes and the Austrian influence begins to make itself felt. Traminers and Rieslings, Sauvignons and Sémillons make their appearance in the vineyards and these white wines, when they are well made, are numbered among the best of the country, having a richness in alcohol, a trace of unfermented sugar and a perfume that may be expected in wines from such vines. The important vine-growing towns are Kutjevo (pronounced Kutyevo), Erdut, Ilok, Vukovar, Belji, Djakoro, and Slavonski Brod.

Along the coast are the vineyards of Istria and Dalmatia. The most famous vineyards in this region are on the islands of Vis, Hvar, Brač, and Korčula, and the Istrian Peninsula. Hills recede inland from the broken coastline and the land is covered with huge rocks. The hills themselves are shaved bare by the constant Adriatic wind, the *borra*. Yet in spite of this, vines grow and produce wines of the Mediterranean style—typically big, full, and deep red, with lots of tannin and very little acid. Often the Dalmatians cut them with water before drinking—in much the manner of the French with the heady wines of Algeria. White wines are also made.

The vines are various. There appear to be some not known as named varieties elsewhere. This would seem to indicate a very early introduction of the vine into the region. In fact, some Yugoslavian viticulturists believe that one type of vine is native to Yugoslavia.

Among the least "Dalmatian" of the wines grown are those of Polja (pronounced Polya), which form a bridge between the wines of the inland vineyards and those grown along the coast. Lighter and lighter-colored than most Dalmatian wines, the white wines of Imotski and Promina are the most typical.

Most of the red Dalmatian wines (red wines lead white by a ratio of about two to one) are grown from the Mali Plavac vine, a native Yugoslav variety. The best are cultivated around the regions of Bol, Pitovske Plaže (pronounced Pitovsky Plaza), Sveta Nedelja (Sveta Nedelya), Vis, Brela, Lastovo, Postup, and Dingač (Dingach). The wines are often sold with the name of the vine and the place of origin (Plavac of Vis, wine from the Plavac grown around Vis). Sometimes they carry only the place-name.

Some pink, or rosé wines grown along the coast go under the name of Opol, and the best are found around the villages of Vis, Šibenik, and Kaštel.

The better white wines of Dalmatia resemble the reds in that they are heavy, deep in color, and are distinctly mouth-filling wines. The best-known come from the Grk (pronounced Gerk), Pošip (Poship), Bogdanuša (Bogdanoosha), Vugava, and Maraština (Marashtina) vines. Grk is pale-yellow and dry, with an odd aftertaste all its own, and is grown mostly on the island of Korčula, as is Pošip, and near the city of Split. The other vines are most successfully cultivated on the islands of Hvar and of Vis near Šibenik and Žadar respectively.

A curious type of sweet wine called Prošek (pronounced Proshek) is made from semi-dry grapes, or by use of concentrated wine and grape juice, or by cooking the must; this is mostly for the Dalmatian palate.

The wines of the Istrian Peninsula are grown more in the Italian manner than the Yugoslavian. Various other plants are found in the same plots of land growing alongside the vines, which are often trellised or draped over trees. Teran accounts for a small part of the production here and extends into the Slovenian part of the Istrian Peninsula, where it is better known. One of the better-known wines is the Malvazÿa, grown from the vine called Malvasia in Italy, Malvoisie in France, and Monemvasia in its native Greece. It makes some of the more agreeable wines of Yugoslavia. Also grown are Cabernets, the vine of France's Bordeaux region, Merlots, and some members of the Pinot family imported from Burgundy.

Slovenia (Ljutomer)

The whole wine region of Slovenia is influenced by the nearness of the Adriatic on the west and the enormous Danube plain on the east, moderating the alpine climate and providing fairly mild, moist winters and temperate summers. The Atlantic winds, blowing through "the Viennese Gate," an Alpine mountain pass, help to maintain the temperate climate. The towering mountains of the Julian Alps break up into limestone *karst* toward the Adriatic, and this is the characteristic stony vineyard soil. Fifteen thousand hectares (37,000 acres) are in vines.

The region can be broken down into three parts: the Adriatic shore, the basin of the River Drava, and the basin of the River Sava. The most important is the basin of the Drava, with the famous Ljutomer. Important growths here include Ormož (pronounced Ormoj), Pohorje (Pohorye), Kozjak (Kozyak), Slovenske, Gorice (Goritze), and Gornie Radgona (Gornye Radgona).

The Ljutomer white table wines are readily available in England, the United States, and other markets. Often spelled Lutomer, the wines are identified by the regional name followed by the informing grape variety: i.e., Lutomer Riesling, Lutomer Sylvaner, Lutomer Sauvignon, Lutomer Traminer, Lutomer Šipon (pronounced Sheepon). The Sauvignons and Rieslings are dry, the Sylvaner has a slight sweet tendency, the Traminer is fairly sweet—with, of course, the spiciness always characterizing the wines of that grape variety. The color varies in the wines from a full gold to one tinged with green; while German—and sometimes French, according to the grape variety—in style, the wines are never as subtle and delicate as the comparable German and French wines; they are less highly developed and individual. On the other hand, they can have a very full bouquet and distinctive taste that may be just a little excessive. The Riesling often achieves 14% to 15% of alcohol, and most of the others are only a little less strong. Šipon—also sometimes spelled Chipon—is a native grape variety. The wine is either dry or sweet, depending upon how it has been vinified, and tends to keep a light freshness even when aged a considerable time. Barbera, Merlot, and Cabernet Sauvignon grapes are currently used to produce most of the wines in this region.

The other two wine sections of Slovenia are of lesser importance. The best-known wine of the River Sava is the pink Cviček (pronounced Tsveechek), a light, fresh rosé that is much sought after by local Yugoslavs during the heat of the summer. The most important of the Adriatic wines is the red Kraški Teran (Krashki Tayran) from the northern part of Istria, a wine with a wide and ancient reputation for having curative powers, perhaps because of its richness in lactic acid, in iron, and in tannin. But it is an acquired taste.

Macedonia

Red, white, and pink wines are grown in Macedonia and a certain amount of dessert wine as well. Macedonia is now one of Yugoslavia's important wine regions. The Turkish invasion was responsible for practically doing away with the vineyards for a considerable period, and these were never reconstituted after the phylloxera epidemic. However, the Yugoslav government has made a great and successful effort to rebuild the vineyards since the end of the Second World War; and a large amount of wine intermediate in character between the Mediterranean and the more northerly type is grown. The Vranac (pronounced Vranats) vines are important for red wines, Žilavartea and Smederevka for white. Districts growing wines today include Tikveš (pronounced Tikvesh), Demir Kapija (Demeer Kapiya), and such towns as Tetovo, Ohrid, Bitola, Štip, Djeudyjelÿa, and others. Yugoslav wine experts are watching the progress of Macedonian wine with satisfaction.

OTHER YUGOSLAV WINES

Bosnia-Herzegovina and Montenegro are the smallest of the wine-producers of Yugoslavia, together accounting for hardly more than 2% of the wines produced. Montenegrin wines are almost entirely confined to those grown from the Vranac vine. Of the wines of Bosnia-Herzegovina two are better known: Žilavka and Blatina. The best is white Žilavka, and particularly the Žilavka grown around the city of Mostar, a big, rich, alcoholic (13% to 14%) wine with a profound perfume. It is generally made by vinifying grapes from the native Yugoslav Žilavka vine with about 30% of other varieties.

Today, vine cultivation is increasing in Herzegovina and Montenegro.

VINTAGES

According to the Institute of Viniculture in Maribor there were only two outstanding vintages in the 1800s, those of 1834 and 1890. In general, vintage is of small importance in Yugoslavia, owing to the fact that most of the wine is blended. While it is true that export is restricted to a few authorized exporters and there are some large domaines and cooperatives, the actual grape-growing is, astonishingly, still 95% in the hands of the peasant-growers—each at present limited by law to owning a maximum of about 10 hectares (25 acres). The fortunes of the Yugoslav grower have been varied since 1950. In 1954, for example, up to two-thirds of the crop was destroyed by vine disease in certain parts of Serbia and elsewhere; while in Istria, and along the Adriatic, in the best wine areas the production was above average. But since then his lot has generally improved, and with it so has the quality of the wine. As more Yugoslavian wine goes to Western consumers, the trend has been to make fewer blended ones and more varietal wines—wines labeled and sold featuring the grape variety rather than the name of the district.

SPIRITS

See Maraschino; Slivovitz.

Zagarolo

White wine from near Rome.
See Latium.

Zamora

Spanish province, north of Salamanca. Here the thick, dark Toro vines are grown; and, at Quintanella de Abajo, the Vaga Sicilia.
See Spain.

Zeller Schwarze Katz

The "Black Cat" wine of Zell on the German Mosel is a good deal more famous than it deserves to be. This is due to the name and the publicity, but not the wine, which is often a blend of poor wines.
See Mosel-Saar-Ruwer.

Zeltinger Sonnenuhr

A lovely feminine Mosel, frequently the best in the district of Zeltingen, where wines run a wide gamut of variety for Mosels.
See Mosel-Saar-Ruwer.

Zierfandler

Grape variety cultivated in Austria. It is also known as Spätrot.

Zikhron Yaacov

Important center of Israel's wine industry.
See Israel.

Žilavka

Native Yugoslav grape from which a white wine of this name is grown near Mostar in Bosnia-Herzegovina: it is big, rich, and alcoholic, with a distinctive perfume.
See Yugoslavia.

Zinfandel

One of the most popular and best red wine grapes in California, where it produces good, sound wines. The grape may be the Primitivo from the region of Bari in Italy.
See United States: California.

Żubrówka (Zubrovka)

A type of Polish vodka much appreciated abroad. Pale green in color, it is flavored with a wild grass that is a favorite food of the *żubra*, or Polish bison, which figures on the label. In each bottle of genuine Żubrówka a blade of the grass is enclosed.
See Poland.

Župa

Prolific region for red and pink wines in the Serbian part of Yugoslavia (*q.v.*).

Zwack

A proprietary brand of liqueurs formerly made in Hungary and now produced in Austria and Italy. Zwack liqueurs, and especially the apricot brandy known as Barack Pálinka, were one of the most popular brands in the U.S. before the Second World War.

Zwicker

On an Alsatian bottle label, the term indicates the blending of noble and common wines. Alsatian wines bearing trade-names are usually Zwickers.

Zymase

The complex of enzymes found in yeasts which ferments alcohol and carbon dioxide gas from sugars.

Zymotechnology

The technology of fermentation, and more particularly yeast fermentations.

Appendixes

According to the French government's decree of June 21, 1973, granting a new official and legal Classification to the First Growths of the red Médoc wines, the listing and presenting of the Classification should read as follows:

MÉDOC
1973 CLASSIFICATION
FIRST GROWTHS
(in alphabetical order)

Château Lafite-Rothschild
Château Latour
Château Margaux
Château Mouton Rothschild
Graves: Château Haut-Brion

1855 CLASSIFICATION
Second, Third, Fourth, and Fifth Growths*

---

*Not modified by the governmental decree.

APPENDIX A
Bordeaux Wines

I THE OFFICIAL CLASSIFICATION OF THE GREAT GROWTHS OF THE GIRONDE: CLASSIFICATION OF 1855

The official production is given in tons (*tonneaux*), the Bordeaux standard measure, consisting of 4 barrels. A *tonneau* averages around 96 cases when it is bottled.

The following figures of production are approximate, varying from year to year, and an estimate has been attempted by deducting the ullage, or evaporation, which usually consists of 15%.

HAUT-MÉDOC WINES
FIRST GROWTHS (*Premiers Crus*)

	Commune	Hectares	Tonneaux	Average Production Cases (12 bottles)
Château Lafite	Pauillac	88	250	22,000
Château Latour	Pauillac	70	250	22,000
Château Mouton-Rothschild*	Pauillac	70	250	22,000
Château Margaux	Margaux	66	200	18,000
Château Haut-Brion**	Pessac. Graves	40	130	11,500

* Decreed a First Growth in 1973.

** This wine, although a Graves, is universally recognized and classified as one of the five First Growths of the Médoc.

SECOND GROWTHS (*Deuxièmes Crus*)

	Commune	Hectares	Tonneaux	Average Production Cases
Château Rausan-Ségla	Margaux	23	140	11,000
Château Rauzan-Gassies	Margaux	27	100	9,000
Château Léoville-Las-Cases	St.-Julien	62	250	22,000
Château Léoville-Poyferré	St.-Julien	55	125	10,500
Château Léoville-Barton	St.-Julien	46	200	18,000
Château Durfort-Vivens	Margaux	50	225	20,000
Château Lascombes	Margaux	110	375	35,000
Château Gruaud-Larose	St.-Julien	76	320	30,000
Château Brane-Cantenac	Cantenac-Margaux	115	375	35,000
Château Pichon-Longueville-Baron	Pauillac	27	90	8,000
Château Pichon-Lalande	Pauillac	49	200	20,000
Château Ducru-Beaucaillou	St.-Julien	45	170	15,000
Château Cos-d'Estournel	St.-Estèphe	60	300	27,000
Château Montrose	St.-Estèphe	49	230	12,000

THIRD GROWTHS (*Troisièmes Crus*)

	Commune	Hectares	Tonneaux	Average Production Cases
Château Giscours	Labarde-Margaux	78	350	33,000
Château Kirwan	Cantenac-Margaux	23	100	8,000
Château d'Issan	Cantenac-Margaux	35	100	9,000
Château Lagrange	St.-Julien	55	220	20,000
Château Langoa-Barton	St.-Julien	17	50	4,500
Château Malescot-Saint-Exupéry	Margaux	32	140	12,000
Château Cantenac-Brown	Cantenac-Margaux	32	150	13,000

	Commune	Hectares	Tonneaux	Average Production Cases (12 bottles)
Château Palmer	Cantenac-Margaux	40	140	12,500
Château La Lagune	Ludon	60	220	20,000
Château Desmirail	Margaux	0	0	0
Château Calon-Ségur	St.-Estèphe	55	260	24,000
Château Ferrière	Margaux	—	10	900
Château Marquis-d'Alesme	Margaux	15	75	7,200
Château Boyd-Cantenac	Margaux	18	60	4,500

FOURTH GROWTHS (Quatrièmes Crus)

	Commune	Hectares	Tonneaux	Average Production Cases (12 bottles)
Château Saint-Pierre-Sevaistre	St.-Julien	17	60	6,000
Château Branaire	St.-Julien	49	200	14,000
Château Talbot	St.-Julien	85	340	32,000
Château Duhart-Milon-Rothschild	Pauillac	40	150	15,000
Château Pouget	Cantenac-Margaux	8	30	3,000
Château La Tour-Carnet	St.-Laurent	30	120	11,000
Château Lafon-Rochet	St.-Estèphe	45	130	10,000
Château Beychevelle	St.-Julien	61	225	20,000
Château Prieuré-Lichine	Cantenac-Margaux	55	260	22,000
Château Marquis-de-Terme	Margaux	42	170	15,000

FIFTH GROWTHS (Cinquièmes Crus)

	Commune	Hectares	Tonneaux	Average Production Cases (12 bottles)
Château Pontet-Canet	Pauillac	76	400	40,000
Château Batailley	Pauillac	50	250	23,000
Château Grand-Puy-Lacoste	Pauillac	40	125	14,000
Château Grand-Puy-Ducasse	Pauillac	26	125	10,500
Château Haut-Batailley	Pauillac	22	60	6,000
Château Lynch-Bages	Pauillac	65	250	24,000
Château Lynch-Moussas	Pauillac	35	175	16,000
Château Dauzac-Lynch	Labarde-Margaux	40	160	15,000
Château Mouton-Baronne-Phillippe (formerly known as Mouton Baron Phillippe)	Pauillac	50	180	16,200
Château du Tertre	Arsac-Margaux	45	120	9,500
Château Haut-Bages-Libéral	Pauillac	19	80	7,000
Château Pédesclaux	Pauillac	15	60	7,000
Château Belgrave	St.-Laurent	35	100	8,000
Château Camensac	St.-Laurent	59	260	24,000
Château Cos Labory	St.-Estèphe	15	65	5,200
Château Clerc-Milon	Pauillac	27	100	8,000
Château Croizet-Bages	Pauillac	22	90	7,000
Château Cantemerle	Macau	21	90	8,000

EXCEPTIONAL GROWTHS (Crus Exceptionnels)

	Commune		Commune
Château Villegeorge	Avensan	Château la Couronne	Pauillac
Château Angludet	Cantenac-Margaux	Château Moulin-Riche	St.-Julien
Château Chasse-Spleen	Moulis	Château Bel-Air-Marquis d'Aligre	Soussans-Margaux
Château Poujeaux-Theil	Moulis		

See author's suggested revised classification on pp. 117–121.

II   THE CRUS BOURGEOIS AND CRUS ARTISANS OF THE MÉDOC

The following figures of production are approximate and indicate average annual output, as given by the communes and taken from their Déclarations de Récoltes records.

MINOR GROWTHS OF THE HAUT-MÉDOC

	Commune	Hectares	Acres	Tonneaux
Château l'Abbégorsse-de-Gorsse	Margaux	4	10	11
Château d'Agassac	Ludon	33	83	80
Château Andron-Blanquet, Château St.-Roch	St.-Estèphe	15	37.5	75
Château Angludet	Cantenac-Margaux	30	75	120
Château Antonic	Moulis	5	12.5	13
Château d'Arches	Ludon	4	10	17
Château d'Arcins	Arcins	73	180	340
Château Arnauld	Arcins	9	22	18
Château Balac	St.-Laurent	11	27	50
Château Balogues-Haut-Bages	Pauillac	6	15	7
Château Barateau	St.-Laurent	7	17.3	31
Cru Barraillot	Margaux	3	7.5	9
Château Barreyres	Arcins	62	153	300
Château Beaumont	Cussac	95	238	400
Château Beauregard	St.-Julien	4	10	19
Château Beauséjour, Château Picard	St.-Estèphe	23	57	110
Château Beau-Site-Haut-Vignoble	St.-Estèphe	19	47	80
Château Beau-Site-St.-Estèphe	St.-Estèphe	25	62	135
Château Bel-Air	St.-Estèphe	4	10	14
Château Bel-Air Lagrave	Moulis	12	30	46
Château Bel-Air-Marquis d'Aligre	Soussans-Margaux	17	42	50
Château Bellegrave	Listrac	9	22	33
Château Bellevue	Cussac	1	2.5	3
Château Bel-Orme	St.-Seurin-de-Cadourne	25	62	130
Cru Bibian Darriet	Listrac	2	5	9
Château Biston Brillette	Moulis	10	25	50
Château Bonneau	St.-Seurin-de-Cadourne	5	12.5	9
Château Borie-Lalande	St.-Julien	18	45	45
Château Bouqueyran	Moulis	2	5	8
Château Bourgade de La Chapelle (see Château Rosemont)				
Château Bournac	St.-Estèphe	3	7.5	8
Château Branas	Moulis	3	7.5	12
Château du Brassat (see Cru Arnaud)				
Château du Breuil	Cissac	19	47	100
Château Brillette	Moulis	27	67	40
Château Cambon	Blanquefort	5	12.5	20
Château Cambon-La-Pelouse	Macau	40	100	180
Château Canteloup	St.-Estèphe	15	37.5	50
Château Cap du Haut	Moulis	7	17.3	35
Château Capbern, Château Capbern-Gasqueton, Château La Rose-Capbern, Château Grand Village Capbern, Château Moulin-de-Calon	St.-Estèphe	36	89	75
Château Capbern-Gasqueton (see Château Capbern)				
Château Capléon-Veyrin	Listrac	5	12.5	23
Château Caronne	St.-Laurent	36	89	180
Château du Cartillon	Lamarque	20	50	85
Château Charmail	St.-Seurin-de-Cadourne	12	30	50
Cru Charmant	Margaux	6	15	20
Château Chasse-Spleen	Moulis	42	105	210
Château Châteaufort de Vauban	Cussac	3	7.5	12
Château Chevalier d'Ars (Coopérative)	Arcins	25	62.5	100
Château Cissac	Cissac	26	65	100

	Commune	Hectares	Acres	Tonneaux
Château Citran	Avensan	53	130	130
Château Clairefont	Margaux	8	20	35
Château Clarke	Listrac	75	185	300
Château Clauzet	St.-Estèphe	3	7.5	15
Château de Côme	St.-Estèphe	2	5	10
Coopérative (Cru Cantereyne)	St.-Sauveur	—	—	varies
Coopérative (Grand Listrac)	Listrac	110	275	550
Coopérative "Marquis de St. Estèphe"	St.-Estèphe	500	1,235	1,500
Coopérative "Cru La Paroisse St.-Seurin-de-Cadourne"	St.-Seurin-de-Cadourne	110	275	550
Coopérative "La Rose Pauillac"	Pauillac	110	275	400
Château Coutelin-Merville	St.-Estèphe	11	27.5	41
Domaine de la Croix	Ordonnac	16	40	80
Château Deyrem-Valentin	Soussans-Margaux	7	17.3	30
Château Dillon	Blanquefort	15	37	70
Château Domeyne	St.-Estèphe	2	5	9
Château Donissan-Veyrin	Listrac	6	15	25
Château Duplessis Hauchecorne	Moulis	16	40	70
Château Dutruch Grand Poujeaux	Moulis	18	45	85
Domaine d'Esteau (see Château Fontesteau)				
Château Eyquem (see Château Haut Marbuzet)	St.-Estèphe			
Château Fatin (see Château Le Crock)				
Château Fellonneau	Macau	1	2.5	4
Château Fonbadet	Pauillac	30	75	100
Château Fonréaud	Listrac	39	97.5	180
Château Fontesteau, Domaine d'Esteau	Cissac	12	30	50
Château Fourcas-Dupré	Listrac	32	35	38
Château Fourcas-Hosten	Listrac	44	110	180
Château Franquet (see Château Chasse-Spleen)				
Château Gaciot	Avensan	5	12.5	18
Château Glana	St.-Julien	71	175	300
Château Gloria, Château Haut Beychevelle Gloria	St.-Julien	44	110	200
Château Gobineau-Graves-de-Lafon	Listrac	8	20	12
Château du Grand-Clapeau	Blanquefort	11	27.5	35
Château Grand-Jaugueyron	Cantenac-Margaux	3	7.5	7
Château Grand-Soussans	Soussans-Margaux	3	7.5	6
Château Grandis	St.-Seurin-de-Cadourne	5	12	24
Château Graves-Richeboh	Moulis	2	5	6
Cru des Graves	Moulis	2	5	7
Château Cru du Gravier	Arsac-Margaux	4	10	18
Cru des Gravières	Cussac	10	25	16
Château Gressier Grand Poujeaux	Moulis	13	32	50
Château Hanteillan	Cissac	30	75	150
Château Haut-Bages-Averous	Pauillac	1	2.5	4
Château Haut Beychevelle Gloria (see Château Gloria)				
Château Haut Bellevue	Lamarque	3	7.5	10
Château Haut-Carmail	St.-Seurin-de-Cadourne	5	12	25
Cru Haut Coutelin	St.-Estèphe	4	10	12
Château Haut Marbuzet	St.-Estèphe	40	100	200
Château Haut Plantey	Listrac	3	7.5	7
Château Haut-Tayac	Soussans	6	15	25
Cru Hennebelle, Cru Landarey	Lamarque	4	10	14
Château Hostein	St.-Estèphe	3	7.5	9
Château Houissant	St.-Estèphe	20	50	85
Château Hourbanon	Prignac	6	15	32
Château La Bécade	Listrac	28	70	140
Cru La-Bécasse	St.-Julien	4	10	20

	Commune	Hectares	Acres	Tonneaux
Château La Clare	Bégadan	18	45	90
Château La Closerie	Moulis	7	17.5	23
Château La Couronne	Pauillac	3	7.5	7
Château La Croix (see Château Phélan-Ségur)				
Château La Dame Blanche (The white wine of Château du Taillan, which has only the Appellation Bordeaux Blanc Supérieur)	Le Taillan	12	30	50
Château La Fleur Milon	Pauillac	13	32	50
Château La Galiane	Soussans-Margaux	4	10	9
Château La Gurgue	Margaux	10	25	35
Château La Haye	St.-Estèphe	6	15	20
Château La Mouline	Moulis	45	112	200
"Cru La Paroisse St.-Seurin-de-Cadourne" (see Coopérative)				
Château La Rivière	Blaignac	12	30	60
Château La Rose-Capbern (see Château Capbern)				
Château La Rose de France	St.-Julien	2	5	8
Château La Tour l'Aspic	Pauillac	4	10	7
Château La Tour-de-Bessan (see Château La Tour-de-Mons)				
Château La Tour du Haut Moulin	Cussac	24	60	100
Château La Tour Haut Vignoble	St.-Estèphe	12	30	52
Château La Tour de Leyssac	St.-Estèphe	4	10	20
Château La Tour Lichine (see Château Capbern)				
Château La Tour de Malescasse	Lamarque	5	12.5	9
Château La Tour Marcillannet	St.-Laurent	6	15	9
Château La Tour-de-Mons, Château Richeterre, Château La Tour-de-Bessan	Soussans-Margaux	25	62.5	100
Château La Tour Pibran	Pauillac	7	17	25
Château La Tour du Roc	Arcins	9	22	30
Château La Tour du Roch Milon	Pauillac	18	45	20
Château La Tour des Ternes	St.-Estèphe	12	30	13
Château Labégorce	Margaux	20	49	100
Château Labégorce-Zédé	Soussans-Margaux	19	47	60
Château Laconfourque	St.-Julien	1	2.5	4
Château Ladouys	St.-Estèphe	4	10	10
Château Laffitte-Carcasset	St.-Estèphe	20	50	48
Château Lafon	Listrac	7	17.5	30
Château Lagorce	Moulis	3	7.5	7
Château Lagravette-Peyredon	Listrac	5	12.5	10
Château Lalande (see Château Tronquoy-Lalande)				
Château Lamarque, Château Cap de Haut	Lamarque	47	117	250
Château Lamothe	Cissac-Médoc	29	71.5	150
Château Lamothe-de-Bergeron	Cussac	10	25	21
Château Lamothe et Grands Moulins	St.-Seurin-de-Cadourne	30	74	150
Château de Lamourous	Le Pian	4	10	16
Château de Lamouroux	Margaux	7	17	20
Cru Landarey (see Cru Hennebelle)				
Château Lanessan	Cussac	30	75	125
Cru Langa	Cussac	3	7.5	4
Château Larose Trintaudon	St.-Laurent	157	390	750
Château de Laroze	Margaux	2	5	7
Cru Larragay	Listrac	2	5	6
Château Larrieu-Terrefort-Graves	Macau	3	7.5	5
Château Larrivaux	Cissac	5	12.5	19
Château Lartique	St.-Estèphe	2	5	13
Château Latour-Dumirsil	Cissac	10	25	16
Château Latour Prignac	Prignac	115	287	600
Cru Le Bécassé du Ferrey (see Château Ferrey Gros Caillou)				
Château Le Boscq	St.-Estèphe	13	32.5	39

	Commune	Hectares	Acres	Tonneaux
Château Le Bourdieu	Vertheuil	51	126	250
Château Le Crock, Château Fatin, Château St.-Estèphe "La Croix"	St.-Estèphe	27	67.5	97
Château Le Fournas	St.-Sauveur	6	15	20
Château Le Fournas Bernadotte	St.-Sauveur	20	50	120
Château Le Meynieu	Vertheuil	6	15	30
Château Le Raux	Cussac	4	10	7
Château Le Roc	St.-Estèphe	1	2.5	5
Château Lemoyne-Lafon-Rochet	Le Pian	6	15	15
Château Les Graves de Germignan	Le Taillan	3	7.5	8
Château Les Ormes-de-Pez, Château La Tour Haut Vignoble	St.-Estèphe	21	52.5	80
Château Lescarjeau	St.-Sauveur	5	12.5	13
Cru Lescourt	Listrac	2	5	5
Château Lestage	Listrac	40	99	180
Château Lestage	St.-Seurin-de-Cadourne	1	2.5	5
Château Lestage Darquier	Moulis	4	10	8
Château Lestage Darquier Grand Poujeaux	Moulis	5	12.5	20
Château L'Hôpital	St.-Estèphe	5	12.5	17
Château Liversan	St.-Sauveur	32	80	130
Château Loquey	St.-Seurin-de-Cadourne	12	30	50
Domaine du Lucrabey	Cissac	5	12.5	7
Château Mac-Carthy	St.-Estèphe	4	10	12
Château MacCarthy Moula	St.-Estèphe	6	15	12
Domaine de Magnol	Blanquefort	9	22	40
Château Malécot	Pauillac	7	17.5	21
Château Malescasse	Lamarque	32	80	100
Château Malleret	Le Pian Médoc	22	55	100
Château Malmaison	Moulis	4	10	5
Château Marbuzet	St.-Estèphe	12	30	50
Château Marque	St.-Seurin-de-Cadourne	1	2.5	6
Clos du Marquis	St.-Julien	8	20	11
Château Marsac-Seguineau	Soussans-Margaux	7	17	30
Château Martinens	Cantenac-Margaux	20	49	50
Clos du Mas	Listrac	5	12.5	9
Château Maucaillou	Moulis	45	112	230
Château Maucamps	Macau	3	7.5	8
Château Médrac	Moulis	1	12.5	2
Château Meyney	St.-Estèphe	50	109	240
Château Monpelou	Pauillac	8	20	5
Château Montbrun	Cantenac-Margaux	9	22	40
Château Morin	St.-Estèphe	10	25	45
Clos du Moulin	St.-Estèphe	5	12.5	7
Château Moulin-à-Vent	Moulis	20	49	90
Château du Moulin du Bourg	Listrac	7	17	35
Château Moulin de la Bridane	Pauillac	2.5	6	13
Château Moulin Joli (see Château Les Ormes-de-Pez)				
Cru du Moulin de Laborde	Listrac	7	17	35
Château Moulin Rose	Lamarque	3	7.5	9
Château Moulin de la Rose	St.-Julien	4	10	14
Château du Moulin Rouge	Cussac	6	15	30
Château Moulis	Moulis	7	17.5	30
Château Nexon-Lemoyne	Ludon	16	40	75
Château Pabeau	St.-Seurin-de-Cadourne	10	25	38
Château Paveil	Soussans-Margaux	18	43	55
Château Peyrabon	St.-Sauveur	29	72	100
Château Peyredon	Moulis	3	7.5	9
Château de Pez	St.-Estèphe	40	100	150
Château Phélan-Ségur, Château La Croix	St.-Estèphe	48	118	200

	Commune	Hectares	Acres	Tonneaux
Château Pibran	Pauillac	7	17.5	22
Château Picard (see Château Beauséjour)				
Château Pichon	Parempuyre	3	7.5	10
Château Pierre Bibian	Listrac	14	35	60
Château Pomeys	Moulis	7	17	25
Château Pomys	St.-Estèphe	15	37	70
Cru Pontet-Chappez	Arsac-Margaux	4	10	20
Château Pontoise-Cabarrus	St.-Seurin-de-Cadourne	18	17.5	90
Château Poujeaux	Moulis	35	86	125
Château Ramage La Batisse	St. Sauveur	44	110	200
Château Renouil Franquet	Moulis	4	10	8
Château Reverdi	Listrac	4	10	18
Château Reysson	Vertheuil	46	115	200
Château Richeterre (see Château La Tour-de-Mons)				
Château Robert Franquet	Moulis	4	10	20
Château Roland	Pauillac	5	12.5	19
Château Rose Ste.-Croix	Listrac	6	15	16
Château Ruat	Moulis	6	15	25
Château St.-Estèphe "La Croix" (see Château Le Crock)				
Château St. Haon	Blanquefort	13	32	50
Château St.-Martin	Listrac	2	5	8
Château St.-Paul	St.-Seurin-de-Cadourne	19	47	100
Château St.-Roch (see Château Andron-Blanquet)				
Château St.-Seurin (see Clos Castets)				
Château Saransot-Dupré	Listrac	4	10	15
Château Ségur	Parempuyre	30	75	140
Château Sémeillan	Listrac	12	30	50
Château Sénéjac	Le Pian	16	40	70
Château Siran	Labarde-Margaux	30	75	120
Château Sociando-Mallet	St.-Seurin-de-Cadourne	22	55	100
Château du Taillan (The white wine is called Château La Dame Blanche)	Le Taillan	5	12.5	10
Château Tayac	Soussans-Margaux	18	44	75
Château Terrey-Gros-Caillou	St.-Julien	14	35	80
Château Teynac	St.-Julien	5	13	19
Château Teynac, Clos St.-Julien	St.-Julien	4	10	12
Château Tronquoy-Lalande	St.-Estèphe	13	32.5	60
Cru du Troupian	St.-Estèphe	2	5	5
Château Verdignan	St.-Seurin-de-Cadourne	40	100	150
Château Villegeorge	Avensan	9	22	40
Château Vincent	Cantenac-Margaux	1	2.5	4

MINOR GROWTHS OF THE MÉDOC (OR BAS-MÉDOC)

	Commune	Hectares	Acres	Tonneaux
Domaine des Anguilleys (Château Vieux Robin)	Bégadan	8	20	45
Clos Beau Rivage de By	Bégadan	5	12.5	25
Château Bégadanet	Bégadan	4	10	12
Cru Bel-Air Mareil	Ordonnac-et-Potensac	3	7.5	12
Château Bellerive	Valeyrac	9	22.5	50
Château Bellevue	Valeyrac	9	22.5	45
Château Bensse (see Coopérative de Prignac)				
Château Blaignan	Blaignan	45	112	200
Château de By (Château Greysac)	Bégadan	8	20	40
Domaine de By	Bégadan	31	77	145
Cru Canteloup	Blaignan	2	5	6

	Commune	Hectares	Acres	Tonneaux
Château Carcanieux-les-Graves	Queyrac	16	40	80
Château Castéra	St.-Germain-d'Esteuil	30	75	145
Cave Coopérative "Belle Vue"	Ordonnac-et-Potensac	130	322	700
Cave Coopérative "St.-Jean"	Bégadan	500	1,250	2,300
Château Chantelys	Prignac	4	10	11
Château des Combes	Bégadan	4	10	20
Domaine de la Croix	Ordonnac	16	40	80
Coopérative ("La Chatellenie")	Vertheuil	——	——	300
Coopérative de Prignac, Château Bensse	Prignac	200	494	950
Coopérative de Queyrac, Château St.-Roch	Queyrac	56	138	300
Coopérative de St.-Yzans, Cave St.-Brice	St.-Yzans	140	346	1,000
Château Côtes de Blaignan, Cru Hontane	Blaignan	5	12.5	14
Cru des Deux-Moulins	St.-Christoly	13	32.5	48
Château Gallais-Bellevue (see Château Potensac)				
Château Greysac (Chateau Bertins)	Bégadan	52	125	250
Château Haut-Blaignan	Blaignan	7	17	42
Cru Hontane (see Château Côtes de Blaignan)				
Château Hourbanon	Prignac	6	15	32
Château La Cardonne	Blaignan	55	133	300
Château La Clare	Bégadan	18	45	90
Château La France	Blaignan	6	15	30
Château La Gore	Bégadan	7	17	40
Château La Rivière	Blaignac	12	30	60
Château La Rose Garamay (see Château Livran)				
Château La Tour-Blanche	St.-Christoly	26	64	150
Château La Tour de By	Bégadan	60	148	300
Château La Tour du Haut-Caussan	Blaignan	6	15	35
Château La Tour-St.-Bonnet	St.-Christoly	40	99	215
Domaine de Lafon	Prignac	3	7.5	7
Clos Laforest	St.-Christoly	4	10	20
Domaine de la Lagune	Bégadan	5	12.5	25
Château Latour Prignac	Prignac	115	287	600
Château Laujac	Bégadan	4	10	19
Château Le Tréhon	Bégadan	13	32	55
Clos Les Moines	Couquéques	10	25	50
Château Les Ormes-Sorbet	Couquéques	15	37	80
Cru Les Tourelles	Blaignan	15	37	80
Château L'Hermitage	Couquéques	6	15	15
Château Livran, Château La Rose Garamay	St.-Germain-d'Esteuil	40	100	200
Château Loudenne	St.-Yzans	28	68	150
Château Lugagnac	Vertheuil			
Clos Mandillot	St.-Christoly			
Château Monthil	Bégadan	15	37	70
Clos Morteil	Bégadan	4	10	15
Clos du Moulin	St.-Christoly	8	20	40
Château Panigon	Civrac	20	20	90
Domaine de Patache	Bégadan	36	62.5	200
Château Pay-de-Lalo	St.-Germain-d'Esteuil	2	5	7
Château Peymartin	Ordonnac	15	37	80
Château Plagnac	Bégadan	25	62	125
Château Potensac, Château Gallais-Bellevue	Ordonnac-et-Potensac	40	100	200
Château Preuilhac	Lesparre	26	65	125
Château Reysson	Vertheuil	34	85	65
Cru du Roc	Couquéques	2	5	6
Château Roquegrave	Valeyrac	25	62	100
Château de Roquetaillade	Ordonnac-et-Potensac	3	7.5	12

	Commune	Hectares	Acres	Tonneaux
Château St.-Anne	St.-Christoly	4	10	7
Château St.-Bonnet	St.-Christoly	30	75	150
Cave St.-Brice (see Coopérative de St.-Yzans)				
Château St.-Christoly	St.-Christoly	4	10	20
Château St.-Germain	St.-Germain-d'Esteuil	2	5	8
Cru St.-Louis	Conquéques	3	7.5	11
Château St.-Roch (see Coopérative de Queyrac)				
Château St.-Saturnin	Bégadan	8	20	25
Château Sigognac	St.-Yzans	40	100	180
Cru Verdon	Valeyrac	3	7.5	12
Château Vernous	Lesparre	15	37	70
Cru du Vieux-Château Landon	Bégadan	20	49	100
Château Vieux Robin, Domaine des Anguilleys	Bégadan	5	12	30

III   SAINT-ÉMILION: 1955 OFFICIAL CLASSIFICATION

In 1955 the best Saint-Émilion wines were officially classified by the French Institut National des Appellations d'Origine as First Great Growths and Great Growths. Since 1955 there have been official revisions in 1958 and 1969. Those growths listed in italics are considered superior in their class.

The following figures of production are approximate and indicate average annual output, as given by the communes and taken from their Déclarations de Récoltes records, minus approx. 15% in ullage.

FIRST GREAT GROWTHS (St.-Émilion—Premiers Grands Crus Classés)

		Hectares	Acres	Tonneaux	Cases
A)	Château Ausone	7	17.5	35	2,800
	Château Cheval Blanc	35	88	160	14,000
B)	Château Beauséjour-Bécot	7.6	19	35	3,000
	Château Beauséjour-Duffau-Lagarrosse	6	15	25	2,000
	Château Bel-Air	13	33	50	4,000
	Château Canon	20	50	100	9,000
	Château Figeac	34	85	180	15,000
	Clos Fourtet	20	50	80	6,700
	Château La Gaffelière	20	50	110	9,400
	Château La Magdelaine	11	27	40	3,700
	Château Pavie	35	88	200	16,200
	Château Trottevieille	10	25	50	4,000

GREAT GROWTHS (St.-Émilion—Grand Crus Classés)

	Hectares	Acres	Tonneaux
Château l'Angélus	25	62.5	150
Château l'Arrosée	25	62.5	150
Château Baleau	16	40	80
Château Balestard-la-Tonnelle	8	20	40
Château Bellevue	6.5	16	35
Château Bergat	4	10	20
Château Cadet-Bon	3	7.5	10
Château Cadet-Piola	18	45	75
Château Canon-la-Gaffelière	22.5	45	125
Château Cap de Mourlin	9	22.5	50
Château Cap de Mourlin	6.5	16	40
Château Chapelle Madeleine	1	2.5	1
Château-le-Chatelet	2.5	7	7
Château Chauvin	9.5	24	35

555

	Hectares	Acres	Tonneaux
Château Coûtet	12	30	35
Château Couvent-des-Jacobins	8	20	40
Château Croque-Michotte	10	25	50
Château Curé-Bon	5	12.5	20
Château Dassault	18	45	70
Château Faurie-de-Souchard	8.5	21	45
Château Fonplégade	7	17.5	45
Château Fonroque	18	45	60
Château Franc-Mayne	6.5	16	35
Château Grand-Barrail-Lamarzelle-Figeac	23.5	58	150
Château Grand-Corbin	13.5	33	65
Château Grand Corbin-Despagne	25.5	63	160
Château Grand-Mayne	17.5	44	70
Château Grand-Pontet	14	32.5	60
Château Grandes-Murailles	2	5	8
Château Guadet-St.-Julien	5.5	13	25
Château Haut-Corbin	3.5	9	15
Clos des Jacobins	8	20	45
Château Jean Faure	9	22.5	40
Château La Carte	4.5	11	25
Château La Clotte	4.5	11	25
Château La Cluzière	3	7.5	12
Château La Couspaude	4.5	11	20
Château La Dominique	17	42.5	70
Clos La Madeleine	1	2.5	4
Château La Marzelle	5.5	12	35
Château La Tour-Figeac	16	40	100
Château La Tour-du-Pin-Figeac	8.5	21	65
Château La Tour-du-Pin-Figeac	7	17.5	45
Château Laniotte, Château Chapelle-de-la-Trinité	5	12.5	25
Château Larcis-Ducasse	11	25	60
Château Larmande	8.5	21	50
Château Laroze	28	70	100
Château Lasserre	7	17.5	40
Château Le Couvent	.6	1	3
Château Le Prieuré	4.5	11	25
Château Matras	8.5	21	35
Château Mauvezin	2	5	10
Château Moulin du Cadet	5	12.5	30
Château l'Oratoire	6	15	35
Château Pavie-Decesse	8.5	21	40
Château Pavie-Macquin	12	30	50
Château Pavillon-Cadet	3.5	9	15
Château Petit-Faurie-de-Souchard	9	22.5	50
Château Ripeau	30	75	150
Château St.-Georges-Côte-Pavie	6	15	21
Clos St.-Martin	2.5	6	10
Château Sansonnet	6.5	16	30
Château Soutard	18	37.5	70
Château Tertre-Daugay	16.5	41	65
Château Trimoulet	16	40	70
Château Trois-Moulins	4.5	11	25
Château Troplong-Mondot	25	62.5	150
Château Villemaurine	6.5	16	35
Château Yon-Figeac	21	52.5	120

PRINCIPAL GROWTHS OF SAINT-ÉMILION

	Hectares	Acres	Tonneaux
Domaine Allée-de-Lescours	4	10	11
Clos d'Armens	2	5	7
Château d'Arthus	5	12.5	13
Clos d'Arthus	12	30	23
Château Badette	8	20	23
Château Badon (see Château Vieux-Ceps)			
Domaine de Badon-Patarabet	2	5	12
Château Barbey	2	5	9
Château Barbeyron	4	10	13
Château Barde-Haut	12	30	43
Château Bardoulet	2	5	7
Domaine de Bardoulet	3	7.5	15
Château du Basque	8	20	35
Château Béard	5	12.5	22
Château Beau-Mazerat (see Château Grand-Mayne)			
Château Beausite	4	10	15
Château Bel-Horizon	2	5	5
Château Belair-Sarthou	5	12.5	19
Château Belle-Assise	5	12.5	22
Château Bellefond-Belcier Guillier	11	27.7	42
Château Bellegrave	11	27	55
Château Belles-Plantes	3	7.5	9
Clos Bellevue-Figeac	3	7.5	12
Cru Bellevue-Mondotte	2	5	7
Clos Bellevue-Peyblanquet	3	7.5	7
Château Bellile-Mondotte	4	10	11
Clos Bernachot	2	5	8
Clos Berthoneau (see Château Du Roy)			
Château Bézineau	13	32.5	53
Cru Bibey	6	15	18
Château Bicasse-Lartigue	3	7.5	11
Château Bigaroux	5	12.5	11
Château Billeron	8	20	27
Cru Biquet	4	10	19
Château Bois-Grouley	3	7.5	14
Château Bois-Rond-Grand-Corbin	4	10	16
Château Bord-Fonrazade	4	10	14
Château Bord-Lartigue	2	5	11
Château Boulerne	9	22.5	32
Château Bouquey	4	10	19
Domaine du Bourg	2	5	13
Château Boutisse	16	40	77
Château Brisson	4	10	13
Château Brisson, Château Destieux	9	22.5	30
Château Brun	6	15	20
Clos Brun	3	7.5	13
Château du Calvaire	6	15	23
Clos du Calvaire	2	5	7
Château Cantenac	7	17.5	42
Clos Cantenac	13	32	65
Château Canteranne	6	15	26
Château Caperot (see Château Monbousquet)			

Saint-Émilion: Principal Growths

	Hectares	Acres	Tonneaux
Clos Caperot	3	7.5	10
Château Capet-Guiller	12	30	50
Château Cardinal Villemaurine	12	30	60
Château Carteau-Bas-Daugay	4	10	18
Château Carteau-Côte-Daugay	8	20	40
Château Carteau-Pin-de-Fleurs	3	7.5	16
Château Cassevert (see Château Grand-Mayne)			
Clos Castelot	10	25	43
Domaine de la Cateau	3	7.5	11
Château Cauzin	4	10	23
Clos de la Cavaille-Lescours	1	2.5	7
Cave Coopérative, Royal St.-Émilion, Côtes Rocheuses			1,760
	775	1,920	450
			270
Château Champion	5	12.5	16
Château Chante-Alouette	6	15	23
Clos Chante-l'Alouette, Domaine Haut-Patarabet	4	10	24
Château Chantecaille	3	7.5	17
Château Chantegrive	5	12.5	20
Domaine de la Chapelle	3	7.5	15
Château Chatelet (*see* Château Larques)			
Château Cheval-Brun	5	12.5	14
Château Cheval-Noir	4	10	11
Château du Clocher	3	7.5	13
Domaine de la Clotte	5	12.5	15
Château du Comte	3	7.5	5
Clos Cormey	7	17.5	29
Château Cormey-Figeac	10	25	43
Château Côte-Migon-la-Gaffelière	1	2.5	6
Château Côte de Rol-Valentin	3	7.3	9
Château Côtes-Bernateau	8	20	50
Cru Côtes-Pressac	2	5	8
Cru Côtes-Roland	2	5	9
Clos Côtes-Roland-de-Pressac	2	5	9
Cru Côtes-Veyrac	2	7.5	19
Château Coudert	3	7.5	12
Château Coudert-Pelletan	9	22.5	36
Château Croix-Figeac	3	7.5	12
Domaine de la Croix-Mazerat	2	5	5
Château Croix-du-Merle	3	7.5	8
Château Croix-Peyblanquet	4	10	9
Château de la Croix-Simard	1	2.5	7
Château Croix-Villemaurine	1	2.5	5
Clos Daupin	2	5	10
Château des Demoiselles	1	2.5	5
Domaine des Dépendances Cru Jaugueblanc	3	7.5	13
Domaine Despagne	7	17.5	15
Château Despagnet	3	7.5	13
Château Destieu	4	10	15
Château Destieux	9	22.5	30
Château Destieux	7	17.5	25
Château Destieux (*see* Château Brisson)			
Château Destieux-Verac	11	27.5	36

	Hectares	Acres	Tonneaux
Château l'Étoile-Pourret (see Château La Grâce-Dieu)			
Domaine des Escardos	7	17.5	12
Château Fagouet-Jean-Voisin	6	15	35
Château Faleyrens	5	12.5	12
Château de Ferrand	30	75	148
Château Ferrandat	4	10	16
Cru Ferrandat	1	2.5	9
Château Pont-de-Figeac, Château Grangeneuve	25	62.5	79
Petit Clos Figeac	3	7.5	15
Clos Fleurus	1	2.5	8
Clos Fleurus	1	2.5	5
Château Fombrauge	38	94	150
Château Fond-Razade	4	10	8
Château Fond-de-Rol	1	2.5	5
Château Fonrazade	4	10	14
Clos Fonrazade	4	10	25
Clos Fontelle	1	2.5	5
Château Fougères	9	22.5	45
Château Fougueyrat, Château La Tour-Laroze, Cru Le Châtelet	19	47.5	87
Domaine de Fouquet	6	15	5
Clos Fourney	4	10	14
Château Fourney (*see* Château Vieux-Guinot)			
Château Franc (*see* Château Franc-Patarabet)			
Château Franc-Beau-Mazerat	3	7.5	11
Château Franc-Cantenac	1	2.5	5
Château Franc-Cormey	2	5	4
Château Franc-Cros	4	10	14
Château Franc-Laporte	9	22.5	50
Clos Franc-Larmande	3	7.5	9
Cru Franc-Mazerat	2	5	8
Château Franc-Patarabet, Château Franc	4	10	20
Château Franc Peilhan	3	7.5	9
Château Franc-Petit-Figeac	3	7.5	22
Château Franc Pipeau	3	7.5	17
Château Franc Pourret	11	27.5	49
Château Franc-la-Rose	4	10	20
Cru Franc-Rozier	3	7.5	15
Domaine de la Gaffelière	2	5	9
Château Gaillard	8	20	11
Château Gaillard-de-Gorse	3	7.5	10
Château Gastebourse (*see* Château Pontet Clauzure)			
Château Gaubert, Clos des Moines	16	40	55
Clos Gerbaud	1	2.5	7
Château Godeau	3	7.5	8
Clos Gontey	2	5	13
Château Grand-Berc	4	10	13
Domaine du Grand-Bigaroux	2	5	9
Château Grand-Caillou-Noir	3	7.5	16
Château Grand-Corbin-Manuel	8	20	40
Clos Grand-Faurie	4	10	24
Domaine du Grand-Faurie	4	10	17
Château Grand-Gontey	4	10	16
Clos Grand-Gontey	4	10	17
Domaine du Grand-Gontey	2	5	9
Château Grand Jacques	11	27.5	46

Saint-Émilion: Principal Growths

	Hectares	Acres	Tonneaux
Château Cassevert, Château Beau-Mazerat, Château Grand-Mazerat	17	42.5	85
Château Grand-Mazerat (see Château Grand-Mayne)			
Château Grand-Mirande	6	15	32
Château Grand-Peilhan-Blanc	7	17.5	34
Château Grand Pey-de-Lescours	24	60	112
Château Grand-Rivallon	3	7.5	9
Château Grangeneuve (see Château Figeac)			
Château Grangey	5	12.5	22
Château des Graves	4	10	24
Cru des Graves	2	5	6
Château Graves-d'Armens	3	7.5	5
Château Graves d'Arthus	5	12.5	21
Château des Graves-de-Mondou	4	10	14
Château Gravet	12	30	60
Clos Gravet	11	27.5	51
Clos du Gros	1	2.5	6
Château Gros-Caillou	12	30	60
Clos Gros-Caillou	3	7.5	8
Clos des Gros-Chênes	5	12.5	27
Cru Grotte-d'Arcis	3	7.5	14
Château Guadet-le-Franc-Grâce-Dieu	8	20	40
Château Gueyrot	6	15	27
Château Guillemot	7	17.5	17
Château Guinot	4	10	16
Clos Guinot	6	15	40
Domaine du Haut-Badon	3	7.5	8
Domaine de Haut-Barbey	2	5	7
Château Haut-Barbeyron	4	10	5
Château Haut-Benitey	5	12.5	13
Château Haut-Berthonneau	1	2.5	7
Clos Haut-Bibey	2	5	11
Clos Haut-Cabanne	1	2.5	6
Château Haut-Cadet	13	32.5	36
Château Haut-Fonrazade, Cru La Tour-Fonrazade	11	27.5	43
Château Haut-Grâce-Dieu (see Château Peyrelongue)			
Château Haut-Grand-Faurie	4	10	21
Cru Haut-Grand-Faurie	1	2.5	5
Château Haut-Gueyrot	2	5	6
Clos Haut-Jaugueblanc	1	2.5	5
Château Haut-Jean-Faure, Clos La Fleur-Figeac, Clos La Bourrue, Château Tauzinat-l'Hermitage	7	17.5	49
Château Haut-Jeanguillot	4	10	17
Château Haut-Lartigue	3	7.5	15
Château Haut-Lavallade	4	10	23
Château Haut-Mauvinon	8	20	28
Clos Haut-Mazerat, Vieux Château Mazerat	8	20	35
Château Haut-Panet-Pineuilh	2	5	9
Domaine Haut-Patarabet (see Clos Chante-l'Alouette)			
Château Haut-Peyroutas	2	5	6
Château Haut-Pontet	5	12.5	25
Château Haut-Pourret	5	12.5	30
Château Haut-Rabion	5	12.5	17
Château Haut-Renaissance	3	7.5	19
Domaine Haut-Trimoulet	5	12.5	20
Clos Haut-Robin	4	10	14

	Hectares	Acres	Tonneaux
Château Haut-Rocher	5	12.5	15
Château Haut-Segotte	7	17.5	42
Château Haut-Simard	20	50	150
Château Haut-Touran	3	7.5	8
Château Haut-Troquart	4	10	19
Domaine Haut-Vachon	4	10	18
Château Haut-Veyrac	7	17.5	30
Château Haute-Nauve	3	7.5	8
Domaine Haute-Rouchonne	4	10	16
Château Hautes-Graves-d'Arthus	9	22.5	47
Château l'Hermitage-Mazerat	4	10	17
Château Jacqueblanc	20	50	100
Clos Jacquemeau	1	2.5	5
Château Jacqueminot	4	10	15
Château Jacquenoir	4	10	20
Château Jaubert-Peyblanquet	5	12.5	11
Château Jaugueblanc	5	12.5	21
Clos Jaumard	2	5	8
Château Jean Blanc	6	15	33
Clos Jean Guillot	1	2.5	5
Cru Jeanguillot	2	5	8
Domaine de Jean-Marie	2	5	6
Château Jean-Marie-Cheval-Brun	2	5	8
Château Jean-Voisin	15	37	60
Clos Jean-Voisin	3	7.5	9
Grand Domaine Jean-Voisin	2	5	7
Château Joly	6	15	27
Cru Jubilé	2	5	9
Château Jupille	2	5	5
Château Justice	3	7.5	15
Château La Barde	3	7.5	6
Clos La Barde	4	10	13
Château La Barthe	4	10	17
Domaine La Beillonne	2	5	14
Clos La Bourrue (*see* Château Haut-Jean-Faure)			
Château La Bouygue	3	7.5	17
Château La Chapelle	4	10	20
Château La Chapelle-Lescours	3	7.5	18
Château La Clotte-Grande-Côte	4	10	11
Château La Côte-Daugay	1	2.5	6
Clos La Croix	9	22.5	49
Château La Croix-Chantecaille	6	15	32
Clos La Croix-Figeac	3	7.5	18
Château La Croizille	4	10	9
Château La Fagnouse	5	12.5	37
Château La Fleur	5	12.5	28
Château La Fleur-Cadet	4	10	14
Clos La Fleur-Figeac (*see* Château Haut-Jean-Faure)			
Château La Fleur-Pourret	3	7.5	6
Château La Fortine	2	5	6
Château La Garelle	12	30	48
Cru La Garelle	1	2.5	8
Clos La Glaye	4	10	17
Château La Gomerie	2	5	12
Château La Grâce-Dieu, Château l'Étoile-Pourret	13	32.5	35

Saint-Émilion: Principal Growths

	Hectares	Acres	Tonneaux
Château La Grâce-Dieu-les-Menuts	10	25	51
Château La Mauléone (*see* Château Pontet Clauzure)			
Château La Mélissière	10	25	11
Château La Mélissière	9	22.5	9
Domaine La Mélissière	1	2.5	6
Château La Mouleyre	7	17.5	19
Château La Nauve	9	22.5	31
Clos La Nauve	2	5	5
Château La Rose-Côte-Rol	4	10	19
Château La Rose-Rol	4	10	19
Château La Rouchonne	4	10	8
Château La Sablière	6	15	28
Château La Sablonnerie	10	25	35
Château La Tour	7	17.5	27
Château La Tour-Baladoz	3	7.5	12
Château La Tour-Berthoneau	2	5	8
Château La Tour-des-Combes	12	30	60
Château La Tour-Cravignac	3	7.5	16
Château La Tour-Fonrazade	8	20	40
Cru La Tour-Fonrazade (*see* Château Haut-Fonrazade)			
Château La Tour-Laroze (*see* Château Fougueyrat)			
Château La Tour-Peyblanquet	6	14	21
Château La Tour-St.-Émilion	4	10	18
Château La Tour-St. Pierre	11	275	55
Château La Tour-Vachon	4	10	21
Clos Labrit	3	7.5	19
Château Lagaborite	2	5	8
Château Lagrave-Figeac	3	7.5	17
Château Lapelletrie	9	22.5	54
Château Lapeyre	8	20	35
Château Larcis-Bergey	1	2.5	8
Château Lardon-Jacqueminot	15	37.5	74
Clos Larmande	4	10	15
Château Laroque	44	110	200
Domaine Laroque, Château Nardon	3	7.5	19
Clos Larose	2	5	10
Château Larques, Château Chatelet	19	47.5	36
Château Lartigue	3	7.5	9
Clos Lartigue	1	2.5	5
Cru Lartigue	3	7.5	11
Clos Lartigues	2	5	8
Château Lassègue	20	50	100
Château Latour Blanche	1	2.5	4
Château Latour-Pourret	6	15	16
Château Lavallade	11	27.5	56
Château Lavergne	2	5	15
Clos Lavergne	9	22.5	46
Château Le Basque	18	45	47
Château Le Bon-Pasteur	3	7.5	9
Clos Le Bregnet	5	12.5	22
Château Le Castelot	5	12.5	21
Château Le Cauze	20	50	130
Cru Le Châtelet (*see* Château Fougueyrat)			
Château Le Freyche	4	10	13

	Hectares	Acres	Tonneaux
Clos Le Freyche	4	10	9
Château Le Grand-Barrail	3	7.5	11
Château Le Grand-Faurie	4	10	17
Château Le Gueyrot	4	10	15
Château Le Jurat	9	22	39
Clos Le Loup	6	15	5
Château Le Merle	6	15	12
Château Le Peillan	13	32.5	20
Château Le Poteau	4	10	17
Château Le Rocher	3	7.5	10
Château Le Sable-Villebout	4	10	11
Château Le Tertre	4	10	13
Château Le Thibaut	9	22.5	33
Château Le Thibaut-Bordas	3	7.5	13
Cru Le Vignot	1	2.5	7
Château Les Bazilliques	6	15	30
Château Haut-Sarpe, Clos du Vieux, Château Les Grandes-Plantes-Haut Béard	10	25	50
Clos Les Graves	4	10	12
Domaine Les Jouans	3	7.5	15
Château Les Moulins	4	10	19
Château Les Moureaux	4	10	23
Château Les Roquettes-Mondottes	3	7.5	10
Château Les Templiers	3	7.5	14
Château Les Tuileries	3	7.5	18
Château Les Vieilles-Nauves	2	5	7
Château Les-Vieilles-Souches-La-Marzelle	4	10	18
Château Lescours	32	80	160
Château Lespinasse	4	10	19
Domaine de Liamet	2	5	8
Château de Lisse	13	32.5	32
Domaine du Logis-de-Moureaux	1	2.5	6
Domaine de Longat	3	7.5	6
Château de Long-Champ	4	10	26
Château Magnan-la-Gaffelière	8	20	40
Clos du Maine	2	5	10
Château Malineau	4	10	14
Château Mangot	20	50	66
Château Marrin	6	15	33
Château Maurillon	1	2.5	7
Château Mayne-Vieux	5	12.5	17
Château Menichot	5	12.5	18
Clos des Menuts	2	5	8
Domaine des Menuts	1	2.5	5
Château du Merle	6	15	18
Clos Meylet-la-Gomerie	2	5	10
Château Millery-Lapelletrie	2	5	10
Château Milon-Feuillat	3	7.5	10
Château Mitrotte	1	2.5	6
Château des Moines	4	10	21
Château des Moines	4	10	23
Clos des Moines (*see* Château Gaubert)			
Château Monbousquet, Château Caperot	31	77.5	144
Château Mondotte-Bellisle	6	15	16
Château Mondou	4	10	16
Clos Mondou	2	5	9

	Hectares	Acres	Tonneaux
Château Monlot-Capet	8	20	37
Clos Monplaisir	2	5	8
Château Montbelair	2	5	8
Château Montlabert	10	25	40
Domaine de Montlabert	2	5	10
Château Montremblant	5	12.5	25
Château Morillon	2	5	8
Domaine de la Mouleyre	5	12.5	19
Château Moulin-Bellegrave	5	12.5	13
Château Moulin de Cantelaube	3	7.5	6
Château Moulin-de-Pierrefitte	3	7.5	14
Château Moulin-St.-Georges	11	27.5	48
Château Moulin-St.-Georges, Château Pin-du-Fleur	13	32.5	65
Cru Mourens	2	5	7
Château Myosotis	3	7.5	10
Cru Napoléon	2	5	7
Château Nardon (*see* Domaine Laroque)			
Clos de Naudin	2	5	6
Château de Neuville	1	2.5	7
Château Pailhas	12	30	51
Clos Pailhas	3	7.5	8
Clos du Palais-Cardinal	5	12.5	6
Château Panet	22	55	80
Château Paradis	5	12.5	28
Château Paradis, Château Patarabet	19	47.5	64
Château Parans	7	17.5	35
Clos Pasquette	3	7.5	15
Domaine de Pasquette	5	12.5	26
Château Patarabet	3	7.5	11
Château Patarabet (*see* Château Paradis)			
Clos Patarabet	1	2.5	5
Cru Patarabet	1	2.5	4
Domaine Patarabet-la-Gaffelière	2	5	8
Clos Patarabet-Lartigue	2	5	9
Château Patris	5	12.5	29
Clos Patris	1	2.5	5
Château Pavillon-Figeac	4	10	9
Château Peillan-St.-Clair	6	15	18
Château Pelletan	5	12.5	16
Château Pérey	8	20	30
Domaine de Pérey	2	5	10
Domaine Petit-Basque	2	5	6
Château Petit-Bigaroux	5	12.5	15
Château Petit-Bois-la-Garelle	3	7.5	14
Château Petit Bord	1	2.5	4
Domaine du Petit Clos	4	10	18
Château Petit-Cormey	6	15	25
Château Petit-Faurie	1	2.5	5
Château Petit-Faurie-Trocard	4	10	21
Clos Petit-Figeac, Clos Pourret	3	7.5	16
Château Petit-Fombrauge	2	5	6
Cru Petit-Gontey	2	5	9
Domaine du Petit-Gontey	3	7.5	9
Château Petit-Gravet	5	12.5	10
Domaine du Petit-Gueyrot	2	5	12

	Hectares	Acres	Tonneaux
Château Petit-Mangot	5	12.5	33
Château Petit-Val	5	12.5	27
Château Peygenestou	2	5	10
Château Peymouton	3	7.5	10
Château Peyreau	18	45	75
Château Peyrelongue, Château Haut-Grâce-Dieu	11	27.5	52
Château Peyrouquet	1	2.5	7
Château Peyroutas	8	20	42
Clos Pezat	1	2.5	6
Château Picon-Gravignac	4	10	12
Château Pidoux	2	5	10
Clos Piganeau	1	2.5	8
Château Pindefleurs (see Château Moulin-St.-Georges)	6	15	30
Château Piney	6	15	13
Cru Piney	1	2.5	4
Château Pipeau	19	47.5	112
Château Pipeau-Menichot	6	15	22
Château Plaisance	6	15	29
Cru Plaisance	4	10	20
Cru Plateau-Jappeloup	3	7.5	6
Château Pointe-Bouquey	4	10	19
Château du Pont de Bouquey	3	7.5	11
Château Pont-de-Mouquet	12	30	40
Château Pontet	4	10	17
Château du Pontet	3	7.5	12
Château Pontet Clauzure, Château La Mauléone, Château Gastebourse	8	20	43
Clos Pourret (*see* Clos Petit-Figeac)			
Château Pressac	24	60	90
Clos Pressac	7	17.5	32
Château Puy-Blanquet	25	62.5	84
Château Quentin	35	87	93
Château Quercy	4	10	22
Château Queyron	4	10	17
Château Queyron-Pin-de-Fleurs	4	10	27
Château Rabat	3	7.5	10
Château Rabion	5	12.5	19
Domaine Rabion-Pailhas	4	10	14
Château Régent	4	10	20
Château Reine-Blanche	5	12.5	16
Château des Religieuses	2	5	9
Château Renaissance	5	12.5	24
Domaine de Rey	4	10	19
Château Reynard	4	10	14
Château Rivallon	8	20	24
Domaine de Rivière	5	12.5	21
Château Robin	4	10	14
Château Robin-des-Moines	5	12.5	7
Château Roc	4	10	20
Clos du Roc	3	7.5	8
Château Roc-St.-Michel	4	10	18
Château Rochebelle	3	7.5	7
Château du Rocher	9	22.5	39
Château Rocher-Bellevue-Figeac	8	20	14
Côtes Rocheuses (*see* Cave Coopérative)			
Château de Rol	5	12.5	24

	Hectares	Acres	Tonneaux
Côtes de Rol	4	10	26
Domaine de Rol	3	7.5	13
Château Rol-de-Fombrauge	4	10	20
Clos Rol-de-Fombrauge	5	12.5	23
Cru Rol-de-Fombrauge	4	10	15
Château aux Roquettes	2	5	7
Domaine de la Rose	2	5	12
Château Roucheyron	6	15	28
Clos Roucheyron	1	2.5	5
Domaine du Rouy	2	5	9
Château du Roy, Clos Berthoneau	3	7.5	20
Royal St.-Émilion (*see* Cave Coopérative)			
Château Roylland-Matras	8	20	34
Château Rozier	10	25	43
Château Rozier	3	7.5	17
Château Rozier-Béard	6	15	22
Clos du Sable	2	5	5
Château St.-Christophe	7	17.5	29
Clos St.-Émilion	8	20	44
Domaine St.-Jean-de-Béard	4	10	11
Château St.-Julien	3	7.5	9
Château St.-Lô	8	20	38
Château St.-Martial	2	5	9
Château St.-Pey	9	22.5	59
Château St.-Pierre	4	10	11
Château St.-Roch	3	7.5	9
Clos St.-Valéry	3	7.5	13
Château de Sarenceau	5	12.5	26
Château de Sarpe, Château Vieux-Sarpe	6	15	12
Clos de Sarpe	3	7.5	10
Clos des Sarrazins	6	15	14
Château Saupiquet	1	2.5	9
Domaine Saupiquet	2	5	8
Domaine de Sème	4	10	20
Clos Sicard	4	10	15
Château Simard	15	37.5	74
Clos Simard	3	7.5	13
Château Soutard-Cadet	3	7.5	11
Château Tarreyre	2	5	11
Château Tauzinat	3	7.5	5
Domaine Tauzinat	3	7.5	10
Château Tauzinat-l'Hermitage (*see* Château Haut-Jean-Faure)			
Château Teyssier	4	10	16
Château Toinet-Fombrauge	8	20	36
Château Tonneret	2	5	10
Château du Touran	4	10	25
Château Touzinat	7	17.5	40
Château Trapaud	11	27.5	94
Château Trapeau	8	20	47
Domaine de Trapeau	3	7.5	20
Château Trianon	5	12.5	21
Clos Trimoulet	4	10	21
Château Troquart (*see* Château Ripeau)			
Château Truquet	4	10	18
Domaine Vachon	3	7.5	16

	Hectares	Acres	Tonneaux
Château du Val-d'Or	3	7.5	19
Clos Valentin	4	10	21
Clos Verdet-Monbousquet	5	12.5	11
Clos Vert-Bois	4	10	10
Château Veyrac	3	7.5	25
Domaine de la Vieille-Cloche	4	10	20
Château Vieille-Tour-La-Rose	3	7.5	16
Clos du Vieux (*see* Château Les Eyguires)			
Château Vieux-Castel-Robin	4	10	17
Château Vieux-Ceps, Château Badon	6	15	28
Vieux-Château-Chauvin	4	10	18
Vieux-Château-Fortin	5	12.5	16
Château Vieux Garouilh	5	12.5	27
Château Vieux-Guinot, Château Fourney	5	12.5	32
Château Vieux-Larmande	4	10	11
Vieux Château Mazerat (*see* Clos Haut-Mazerat)			
Vieux-Domaine-Menuts	3	7.5	13
Château Vieux-Moulin-du-Cadet	3	7.5	16
Vieux-Château-Peymouton	9	22.5	37
Vieux-Château-Peyrou	1	2.5	7
Clos Vieux-Pontet	2	5	6
Château Vieux-Pourret	4	10	19
Château Vieux-Sarpe (*see* Château de Sarpe)			

LESSER GROWTHS OF SAINT-ÉMILION AND SURROUNDING VILLAGES

	Commune	Hectares	Acres	Tonneaux
Château Ambois	St.-Georges-St.-Émilion	1	2.5	4
Domaine d'Arriailh	Montagne-St.-Émilion	4	10	6
Château Austerlitz	Sables-St.-Émilion	5	12.5	18
Château Barbe-Blanche	Lussac-St.-Émilion	8	20	22
Château Barraud	Montagne-St.-Émilion	4	10	21
Domaine de Barraud	Montagne-St.-Émilion	4	10	11
Château Bayard	Montagne-St.-Émilion	7	17.5	39
Clos Bayard	Montagne-St.-Émilion	5	12.5	22
Domaine de Bayard	Montagne-St.-Émilion	8	20	19
Clos Beaufort-Mazerat	St.-Émilion	2	5	9
Château Beauséjour	Montagne-St.-Émilion	6	15	30
Château Beauséjour	Puisseguin-St.-Émilion	14	35	58
Château Beausite	Lussac-St.-Émilion	3	7.5	10
Château Bel-Air	Montagne-St.-Émilion	8	20	29
Château Bel-Air	Puisseguin-St.-Émilion	11	27.5	55
Château Bel-Air-Lussac	Lussac-St.-Émilion	12	30	46
Château Bellevue	Lussac-St.-Émilion	11	27.5	32
Château Bellevue	Montagne-St.-Émilion	4	10	19
Château Béouran	St.-Émilion	1	2.5	7
Cru Berlière	Parsac-St.-Émilion	4	10	15
Domaine de Berlière	Parsac-St.-Émilion	3	7.5	5
Château Berliquet	St.-Émilion	7	17.5	19
Château Bertineau-Goby	Montagne-St.-Émilion	9	22.5	28
Château Binet	Parsac-St.-Émilion	9	22.5	19
Château Bonneau, Château des Rochers	Montagne-St.-Émilion	9	22.5	43
Domaine de Bonneau	Montagne-St.-Émilion	4	10	12
Château Branne	Montagne-St.-Émilion	6	15	35
Château Calon	Montagne-St.-Émilion	20	50	71
Château Calon-Montagne	St.-Georges-St.-Émilion	3	7.5	11
Château Calon-St.-Georges	St.-Georges-St.-Émilion	3	7.5	12

	Commune	Hectares	Acres	Tonneaux
Château Cap-d'Or	St.-Georges-St.-Émilion	5	12.5	26
Domaine de Cassah	Puisseguin-St.-Émilion	6	15	12
Cave Coopérative des Côtes-de-Castillon	St.-Étienne-de-Lisse	3	7.5	14
Cave Vinicole de Puisseguin	Puisseguin-St.-Émilion	570	1,408	3,200
Domaine du Chatain	Montagne-St.-Émilion	3	7.5	10
Cru Chêne-Vert	Parsac-St.-Émilion	7	17.5	32
Château Chêne-Vieux	Parsac-St.-Émilion	8	20	34
Domaine de la Clotte	Montagne-St.-Émilion	5	12.5	14
Coopérative de Montagne	Montagne-St.-Émilion	145	358	706
Clos des Corbières	Montagne-St.-Émilion	2	5	8
Château Corbin	Montagne-St.-Émilion	13	32.5	65
Domaine de Corniaud	Montagne-St.-Émilion	5	12.5	15
Domaine de Corniaud-Lussac	Lussac-St.-Émilion	3	7.5	10
Château Côte de Bonde	Montagne-St.-Émilion	7	17.5	14
Cru Côtes-du-Fayan	Puisseguin-St.-Émilion	8	20	23
Château Coucy	Montagne-St.-Émilion	11	27.5	45
Château du Courlat	Lussac-St.-Émilion	9	22.5	40
Domaine Croix-de-Grézard	Lussac-St.-Émilion	2	5	9
Château Croix-de-Justice	Puisseguin-St.-Émilion	5	12.5	14
Château Cruzeau	Sables-St.-Émilion	3	7.5	14
Clos Daviaud	Parsac-St.-Émilion	5	12.5	13
Château Divon	St.-Georges-St.-Émilion	4	10	19
Clos l'Église	Montagne-St.-Émilion	4	10	17
Clos de l'Église	Montagne-St.-Émilion	13	32.5	46
Clos de l'Église (see Château St.-Georges)				
Château Faizeau	Montagne-St.-Émilion	7	17.5	32
Château Fongaban (see Château Mouchet)				
Château Fontmurée	Montagne-St.-Émilion	8	20	40
Domaine de Fontmurée	Montagne-St.-Émilion	10	25	39
Domaine Franc-Baudron	Montagne-St.-Émilion	6	15	20
Château Froquard	St.-Georges-St.-Émilion	3	7.5	15
Château Gadet-Plaisance	Montagne-St.-Émilion	4	10	12
Château Gaillard	Sables-St.-Émilion	4	10	16
Château Garderose	Sables-St.-Émilion	5	12.5	20
Château Gay-Moulins	Montagne-St.-Émilion	7	17.5	27
Clos Gilet	Montagne-St.-Émilion	3	7.5	13
Château Gironde	Puisseguin-St.-Émilion	4	10	5
Château Goujon	Montagne-St.-Émilion	3	7.5	5
Domaine du Gourdins	Sables-St.-Émilion	1	2.5	6
Domaine des Grands-Champs	Montagne-St.-Émilion	4	10	10
Domaine des Grands-Pairs	Lussac-St.-Émilion	2	5	8
Domaine de Grimon	St.-Georges-St.-Émilion	5	12.5	20
Château Gueyrosse	Sables-St.-Émilion	4	10	15
Château Guibeau	Puisseguin-St.-Émilion	25	62	125
Château Guillou	St.-Georges-St.-Émilion	13	32.5	59
Château Haut-Bastienne	Montagne-St.-Émilion	4	10	20
Domaine Haut-Caillate	St.-Georges-St.-Émilion	2	5	10
Château Haut-Chéreau	Lussac-St.-Émilion	2	5	5
Domaine Haut-Corbière	Sables-St.-Émilion	2	5	11
Domaine Haut-Guillennay	Sables-St.-Émilion	2	5	10
Château Haut-Guitard	Montagne-St.-Émilion	4	10	20
Château Haut-Langlade	Parsac-St.-Émilion	4	10	14
Château Haut-Larose	Lussac-St.-Émilion	5	12.5	19
Clos Haut-Listrac	Puisseguin-St.-Émilion	4	10	14
Domaine de Haut-Marchand	Montagne-St.-Émilion	4	10	6

	Commune	Hectares	Acres	Tonneaux
Clos Haut-Montaiguillon	St.-Georges-St.-Émilion	5	12.5	24
Château Haut-Musset	Parsac-St.-Émilion	5	12.5	17
Château Haut-Piquat	Lussac-St.-Émilion	9	22.5	34
Château Haut-Plaisance	Montagne-St.-Émilion	7	17.5	29
Château Haut-Poitou	Lussac-St.-Émilion	2	5	9
Château Haut-Pourteau	Lussac-St.-Émilion	2	5	8
Château Haut-St.-Georges	St.-Georges-St.-Émilion	2	5	9
Château Haut-Sarpe	St.-Christophe-des-Bardes	9	22.5	50
Château Haut-Troquard	St.-Georges-St.-Émilion	3	7.5	16
Clos Haut-Troquard	St.-Georges-St.-Émilion	1	2.5	6
Domaine de la Haute-Faucherie	Montagne-St.-Émilion	3	7.5	12
Château l'Hermitage	Montagne-St.-Émilion	6	15	26
Château Jura-Plaisance	Montagne-St.-Émilion	8	20	34
Clos-Domaine-Château-La-Bastienne	Montagne-St.-Émilion	12	30	54
Clos La Cabanne	Puisseguin-St.-Émilion	4	10	22
Cru La Chapelle	Parsac-St.-Émilion	7	17.5	13
Château La Clotte	Puisseguin-St.-Émilion	2	5	4
Château La Couronne	Montagne-St.-Émilion	4	10	21
Château La Croix-de-la-Bastienne	Montagne-St.-Émilion	2	5	12
Cru La Croix-Blanche	Montagne-St.-Émilion	2	5	7
Château La Croix-de-Blanchon	Lussac-St.-Émilion	5	12.5	16
Château La Faucherie	Montagne-St.-Émilion	3	7.5	6
Château La Fleur-Perruchon	Lussac-St.-Émilion	5	12.5	17
Château La Fleur-St.-Georges (*see* Château St.-Georges)				
Château La Grande-Clotte	Lussac-St.-Émilion	5	12.5	19
Château La Grenière	Lussac-St.-Émilion	5	12.5	16
Château La Mayne	Sables-St.-Émilion	3	7.5	8
Château La Paillette	Sables-St.-Émilion	3	7.5	10
Château La Papeterie	Montagne-St.-Émilion	9	22.5	55
Château La Perrière	Lussac-St.-Émilion	5	12.5	20
Château La Picherie	Montagne-St.-Émilion	6	15	13
Château La Plante	Sables-St.-Émilion	1	2.5	5
Cru La Rose	Puisseguin-St.-Émilion	5	12.5	17
Château La Roseraie-du-Mont	Puisseguin-St.-Émilion	4	10	9
Château La Tête-du-Cerf	Montagne-St.-Émilion	6	15	15
Château La Tour-Ballet	Montagne-St.-Émilion	1	2.5	5
Château La Tour-Blanche	Parsac-St.-Émilion	3	7.5	19
Château La Tour-Gilet	Montagne-St.-Émilion	6	15	34
Château La Tour-de-Grenet	Lussac-St.-Émilion	30	75	150
Château La Tour-Guillotin	Puisseguin-St.-Émilion	6	15	24
Château La Tour-Paquillon	Montagne-St.-Émilion	8	20	35
Château La Tour-St.-Georges (*see* Château St.-Georges)				
Château La Tour-de-Ségur	Lussac-St.-Émilion	12	30	60
Château La Vaisinerie	Puisseguin-St.-Émilion	8	20	27
Clos La Vallée-du-Roi	Montagne-St.-Émilion	3	7.5	8
Domaine de Lamaçonne	Montagne-St.-Émilion	3	7.5	12
Château Langlande	Parsac-St.-Émilion	6	15	12
Domaine de Laplaigne	Puisseguin-St.-Émilion	7	17.5	31
Château Larue	Parsac-St.-Émilion	4	10	13
Château Latour	Montagne-St.-Émilion	5	12.5	21
Château Latour-Musset	Parsac-St.-Émilion	10	25	35
Château Latour-de-Ségur	Lussac-St.-Émilion	8	20	9
Château Le Chay	Puisseguin-St.-Émilion	13	32.5	58
Cru Le Franc-Rival	Lussac-St.-Émilion	2	5	9
Château Le Gravier-Gueyrosse	Sables-St.-Émilion	3	7.5	12

Saint-Émilion: Lesser Growths

	Commune	Hectares	Acres	Tonneaux
Château Le Mayne	Puisseguin-St.-Émilion	3	7.5	9
Clos Le Pas-St.-Georges	St.-Georges-St.-Émilion	6	15	31
Château le Pont-de-Pierre	Lussac-St.-Émilion	3	7.5	15
Château Le Puy-St.-Georges (see Château St.-Georges)				
Château Le Roc-de-Troquard	St.-Georges-St.-Émilion	3	7.5	10
Château Le-Tertre-de-Perruchon	Lussac-St.-Émilion	3	7.5	7
Château Lenoir	Sables-St.-Émilion	4	10	13
Domaine du Léonard	Puisseguin-St.-Émilion	9	22.5	40
Château Lépine	Sables-St.-Émilion	2	5	7
Château Les Bardes	Montagne-St.-Émilion	3	7.5	13
Château Les Carrières	Montagne-St.-Émilion	2	5	5
Château Les Côtes-de-Gardat	Montagne-St.-Émilion	5	12.5	24
Château Les Eyguires	St.-Christophe-des-Bardes			
Domaine Les Genêts	Montagne-St.-Émilion	3	7.5	9
Château Les Grandes-Vignes	Montagne-St.-Émilion	2	5	10
Château Les Jacquets	St.-Georges-St.-Émilion	5	12.5	22
Château Les Laurets	Puisseguin-St.-Émilion	75	185	375
Château Les Renardières	St.-Georges-St.-Émilion	4	10	14
Château Les Tuileries-de-Bayard	Montagne-St.-Émilion	8	20	29
Château Les Vieux-Rocs	Lussac-St.-Émilion	3	7.5	5
Château Lestage	Parsac-St.-Émilion	8	20	47
Château L'Ormeau-Vieux	Puisseguin-St.-Émilion	7	17.5	23
Château Lucas	Lussac-St.-Émilion	9	22.5	37
Château de Lussac	Lussac-St.-Émilion	20	50	88
Château Lyonnat	Lussac-St.-Émilion	49	121	218
Château Lyon-Perruchon	Lussac-St.-Émilion	4	10	11
Château Macureau	Montagne-St.-Émilion	6	15	26
Clos des Magrines	Puisseguin-St.-Émilion	3	7.5	6
Château Maison-Blanche	Montagne-St.-Émilion	30	75	150
Château Maisonneuve	Parsac-St.-Émilion	7	17.5	6
Clos Maisonneuve	Parsac-St.-Émilion	2	5	8
Domaine de Maisonneuve, Château St.-Georges-Macquin	St.-Georges-St.-Émilion	17	42.5	54
Château Martinet	Sables-St.-Émilion	12	30	56
Clos Maurice	St.-Sulpice-de-Faleyrens	1	2.5	6
Château Meynard	Sables-St.-Émilion	6	15	11
Château Montaiguillon	Montagne-St.-Émilion	23	57.5	128
Château Montaiguillon	St.-Georges-St.-Émilion	3	7.5	16
Château Montesquieu	Puisseguin-St.-Émilion	14	35	63
Clos Montesquieu	Montagne-St.-Émilion	3	7.5	12
Château Mouchet, Château Fongaban	Puisseguin-St.-Émilion	10	25	35
Château Mouchique	Puisseguin-St.-Émilion	4	10	17
Château du Moulin	Puisseguin-St.-Émilion	6	15	30
Château Moulin-du-Jura	Montagne-St.-Émilion	3	7.5	10
Château Musset	Parsac-St.-Émilion	7	17.5	28
Château Naguet-La-Grande	Parsac-St.-Émilion	5	12.5	12
Château Négrit	Montagne-St.-Émilion	9	22.5	41
Château Pavillon-Fougailles	St.-Émilion	1	2.5	5
Château Petit-Clos	Montagne-St.-Émilion	8	20	27
Château Petit-Refuge	Lussac-St.-Émilion	4	10	13
Château Peyrou	St.-Étienne-de-Lisse	5	12.5	24
Château Piron	Parsac-St.-Émilion	6	15	17
Château Plaisance	Montagne-St.-Émilion	20	50	46
Clos Plaisance	Parsac-St.-Émilion	9	22.5	28
Clos Plince	Sables-St.-Émilion	1	2.5	6
Château du Puy	Parsac-St.-Émilion	6	15	24

	Commune	Hectares	Acres	Tonneaux
Château Puy-Bonnet	*Parsac-St.-Émilion*	5	12.5	10
Château du Puynormond	*Parsac-St.-Émilion*	7	17.5	24
Domaine du Puynormond	*Parsac-St.-Émilion*	5	12.5	21
Château Quinault	*Sables-St.-Émilion*	12	30	58
Domaine de Rambaud	*Lussac-St.-Émilion*	3	7.5	6
Clos des Religieuses	*Puisseguin-St.-Émilion*	8	20	40
Château Rigaud	*Puisseguin-St.-Émilion*	3	7.5	10
Château Roc-de-Puynormond	*Parsac-St.-Émilion*	6	15	10
Château Rocher-Corbin	*Montagne-St.-Émilion*	6	15	37
Château des Rochers (*see* Château Bonneau)				
Domaine des Rocs	*Lussac-St.-Émilion*	8	20	40
Château Rocs-Marchand	*Montagne-St.-Émilion*	9	22.5	9
Château Roudier	*Montagne-St.-Émilion*	30	75	150
Château Roudier	*St.-Georges-St.-Émilion*	3	7.5	17
Domaine de Roudier	*Montagne-St.-Émilion*	7	17.5	9
Château des Roziers	*Montagne-St.-Émilion*	4	10	14
Château Sablons	*Montagne-St.-Émilion*	5	12.5	20
Château St.-Georges, Château La Tour-St.-Georges,	*St.-Georges-St.-Émilion*	35	87	140
Château Le Puy-St.-Georges,				
Château La Fleur-St.-Georges, Clos de l'Église				
Château St.-Georges-Macquin (*see* Domaine de Maisonneuve)		15	37.5	75
Château St.-Jacques-Calon	*Montagne-St.-Émilion*	6	15	22
Château St.-Louis	*St.-Georges-St.-Émilion*	4	10	18
Château St.-Michel	*Montagne-St.-Émilion*	2	5	9
Château St.-Paul	*Montagne-St.-Émilion*	5	12.5	23
Château Samion	*St.-Georges-St.-Émilion*	9	22.5	35
Château Soleil	*Puisseguin-St.-Émilion*	5	12.5	21
Château Taureau	*Lussac-St.-Émilion*	3	7.5	11
Château Teillac	*Puisseguin-St.-Émilion*	7	17.5	31
Château Terrien	*Lussac-St.-Émilion*	3	7.5	11
Château Tetre-de-la-Mouleyre	*Parsac-St.-Émilion*	2	5	8
Clos Teynac-Rival	*Lussac-St.-Émilion*	3	7.5	14
Château Teyssier	*Puisseguin-St.-Émilion*	28	70	120
Château des Tours	*Montagne-St.-Émilion*	59	147.5	275
Château Vieux-Bonneau	*Montagne-St.-Émilion*	4	10	14
Vieux-Château-Calon	*Montagne-St.-Émilion*	5	12.5	24
Vieux-Château-Goujon	*Montagne-St.-Émilion*	2	5	7
Château Vieux-Guillou	*St.-Georges-St.-Émilion*	4	10	17
Vieux-Château-La-Beysse	*Puisseguin-St.-Émilion*	4	10	6
Château Vieux-Logis-de-Cazelon	*Montagne-St.-Émilion*	2	5	8
Château Vieux Montaiguillon	*St.-Georges-St.-Émilion*	3	7.5	13
Château Vieux-Mouchet	*Montagne-St.-Émilion*	1	2.5	6
Domaine du Vieux-Moulin-de-Calon	*Montagne-St.-Émilion*	1	2.5	6
Vieux-Château-Négrit	*Montagne-St.-Émilion*	10	25	54
Vieux-Château-Palon	*Montagne-St.-Émilion*	5	12.5	17

IV POMEROL

The wines of Pomerol are not officially classified. Château Pétrus is recognized as being the outstanding Great Growth, followed by other wines italicized below, which are considered superior in their class.

The following figures of production are approximate, and indicate average annual output, as given by the communes and taken from their Déclarations de Récoltes records.

PRINCIPAL GROWTHS

	Hectares	Acres	Tonneaux
Clos des Amandiers	2	5	11
Clos Barrail-du-Milieu, Clos du Pellerin	2	5	5
Château Beauchêne (*see* Clos Mazeyres)			

Pomerol: Principal Growths

	Hectares	Acres	Tonneaux
Château Beaulieu	1	2.5	7
Château Beauregard	13	32	51
			(4,500 cases)
Clos Beauregard (*see* Château Taillefer)			
Château Beauséjour	2	5	6
Château Beau-Soleil	3	7.5	15
Château Bel-Air, Vieux-Château-Boënot	10	25	35
Clos Bel-Air (*see* Domaine La Pointe)			
Château Bellegraves	4	10	24
Château Bellevue	5	12.5	23
Château Boënot, Château Trintin	4	10	19
Clos Bonalgue	3	7.5	11
Château Le Bon-Pasteur	6	15	25
Château Bourgneuf-Vayron	9	22.5	36
Domaine de Bourg-Neuf	1	2.5	6
Château Brun-Mazeyres	3	7.5	13
Domaine de Cantereau	1	2.5	6
Château du Casse	2	5	8
Clos du Castel	2	5	9
Château Certan-Giraud	2	5	12
			(1,150 cases)
Château Certan-Marzelle	4	10	15
Château Certan-de-May	4	10	18
			(1,500 cases)
Château Clinet	6	15	39
Clos du Clocher, Château Monregard-Lacroix	5	12.5	28
Domaine des Clones	2	5	7
Clos du Commandeur	1	2.5	5
Cru Côte-Gazin	1	2.5	5
Clos du Fagnard	2	5	9
Château Ferrand	11	27.5	45
Château Feytit-Clinet	6	15	15
Château Franc-Maillet	4	10	22
Château Gazin	25	62	80
			(7,500 cases)
Château Gombaude-Guillot, *Château Grandes-Vignes-Clinet*	6	15	30
Château Gouprie	3	7.5	15
Cru Grand-Mazeyres	2	5	7
Château Grand-Moulinet	1	2.5	5
Château Grandes-Vignes-Clinet (*see* Château Gombaude-Guillot)			
Clos des Grands Sillons	3	7.5	20
Château Grange Neuve	4	10	16
Château Grate-Cap	4	10	19
Château Guillot (*see* Clos Les Grands-Champs)			
Château Haut-Cloquet	2	5	11
Domaine du Haut-Cloquet	1	2.5	5
Cru Haut-Groupey	2	5	6
Château Haut-Maillet	5	12.5	19
Clos Haut-Mazeyres	9	22.5	27
Domaine de Haut-Pignon	2	5	7
Domaine de Haut-Tropchaud	1	2.5	6
Château des Jacobins	1	2.5	5
Château La Cabane	9	22.5	35
Château La Chichonne	2	5	5
Clos Lacombe	2	5	6
Château La Commanderie	5	12.5	20
Château La Conseillante	11	28	40
			(3,500 cases)

	Hectares	Acres	Tonneaux
Château La Croix	8	20	23
			(2,000 cases)
Château La Croix-de-Gay	6	15	34
Château Lacroix-St.-Georges	4	10	21
Château La Croix-Taillefer	2	5	7
Château Lacroix-Toulifaut	1	2.5	11
Château Lafleur	4	10	14
			(1,200 cases)
Château Lafleur-Gazin	4	10	13
Château Lafleur-Pétrus	9	22	35
			(3,200 cases)
Château La Fleur-des-Rouzes	4	10	13
Château La Ganne	5	12.5	15
Château Lagrange	8	20	30
			(2,500 cases)
Château Lagrave	7	17.5	16
Château l'Angélus	1	2.5	5
Château La Patache	2	5	6
Château La Pointe	20	50	80
			(7,500 cases)
Domaine La Pointe, Clos Bel-Air	4	10	9
Château La Renaissance	1	2.5	5
Clos La Rose	3	7.5	13
Clos La Soulatte	2	5	8
Château Latour-Pomerol	9	22	40
			(3,500 cases)
Château La Violette	2	5	10
Château Le Caillou	5	12.5	30
Château Le Carillon	4	10	22
Château Le Gay	8	20	25
Clos l'Église	5	12.5	24
Domaine de l'Église	7	17.5	35
Clos de l'Église-Clinet	4	10	21
			(1,700 cases)
Château l'Enclos	7	17.5	34
Château Les Bordes	2	5	13
Château Les Grandes-Vignes	1	2.5	5
Clos Les Grands-Champs, Château Guillot	5	12.5	23
Château Les Grands-Sillons	2	5	14
Château Les Hautes-Rouzes	2	5	9
Château l'Évangile	13	32.5	36
			(3,450 cases)
Château Margot	1	2.5	5
Château Mayne	3	7.5	11
Château du Mayne	2	5	11
Château Mazeyres	10	25	47
Clos Mazeyres, Château Beauchêne	6	15	26
Château Monregard-Lacroix (see Clos du Clocher)			
Château Moulinet	13	32.5	50
Château Nénin	20	50	76
			(7,300 cases)
Cru de la Nouvelle-Église	2	5	6
Clos du Pellerin (see Clos Barrail-du-Milieu)			
Château du Petit-Moulinet	3	7.5	12
Château Petit-Village	9	22.5	42
			(4,030 cases)

Pomerol: Lalande de Pomerol

	Hectares	Acres	Tonneaux
Château Pétrus	12	30	40
			(3,800 cases)
Château Pignon-de-Gay	2	5	10
Clos Pleville	1	2.5	5
Château Plince	7	17.5	34
Château Plincette	1	2.5	5
Château La Providence	3	7.5	7
Clos René	10	25	55
Domaine de René	3	7.5	8
Château Rève-d'Or	5	12.5	19
Domaine de Robert	4	10	13
Château Rocher-Beauregard	2	5	8
Château Rouget	11	27	35
			(3,400 cases)
Clos du Roy	3	7.5	12
Clos St.-André	2	5	12
Clos St.-Anne (*see* Château Taillefer)			
Château de Sales	31	77.5	110
Château Tailhas	9	22.5	54
Château Taillefer, Clos Beauregard, Château Toulifaut, Clos Toulifaut, Clos St.-Anne	21	52.5	102
Château des Templiers	3	7.5	17
Clos des Templiers	1	2.5	10
Château Thibéaud-Maillet	2	5	16
Château Toulifaut (*see* Château Taillefer)			
Clos Toulifaut (*see* Château Taillefer)			
Château Trintin (*see* Château Boënot)			
Château Tristan	1	2.5	5
Château Trotanoy	9	22.5	30
			(2,500 cases)
Château de Valois	6	15	28
Domaine de la Vieille-École	1	2.5	5
Vieux-Château-Boënot (*see* Château Bel-Air)			
Vieux-Château-Bourgueneuf	3	7.5	18
Vieux-Château-Certan	14	35	60
			(5,800 cases)
Vieux-Château-Cloquet	2	5	7
Vieux-Château-l'Angélus	1	2.5	10
Vieux-Château-Tropchaud	2	5	6
Château Vieux-Maillet	1	2.5	5
Clos Vieux-Maillet	2	5	7
Château Vraye-Croix-de-Gay	6	20	15

APPELLATION LALANDE DE POMEROL

COMMUNE DE LALANDE DE POMEROL

Clos des Arnaud
Château de Bel Air
Château Bourseau
Petit Clos de Brouard
Château de la Commanderie
Château les Cruzelles

Château Laborde
Château des Moines
Château Templiers
Clos de Moines
Château de Musset
Château Perron

Clos de l'Église
Clos l'Étoile
Domaine de Grand Moine
Château Grand Ormeau
Clos Haut Cavujon

Château Perron
Sabloire du Grand Moine
Château de Viaud
Domaine de Viaud
Clos de la Vieille Forge

COMMUNE DE NÉAC

Domaine du Bourg
Château Canon Chaigneau
Clos du Casrel
Château Chatain
Clos du Chatain
Domaine du Chatain
Château les Chaumes
Château Chevrol Bel Air
Château Drouilleau Belles Graves
Château Fougeailles
Château Gachet
Château Garraud
Domaine des Grands Bois Chagneau

Domaine du Grand Ormeau
Château Haut Ballet
Château Haut Chaigneau
Château Lafaurie
Château Lavinot la Chapelle
Château Les Grandes Versaines
Château Moncets
Château Moulin à Vent
Château Siaurac
Domaine de Surget
Château de Teysson
Château Tournefeuille

V CÔTES DE FRONSAC

The following figures of production are approximate, and indicate average annual output, as given by the communes and taken from their Déclarations de Récoltes records.

PRINCIPAL GROWTHS

	Commune	Hectares	Acres	Tonneaux
Clos du Alem	*Saillans*	10	25	24
Château Arnauton	*Fronsac*	11	27.5	20
Château Bardon-Ferrand	*St.-Aignan*	2	5	7
Château Bicot (Lambert)	*St.-Aignan*	1	2.5	3
Château Bicot (Rodier)	*Fronsac*	3	7.5	6
Château Bicot Latour	*St.-Aignan*	3	7.5	16
Château Cantelouve	*Fronsac*	10	25	25
Cru Cardeneau (Durand)	*Saillans*	4	10	12
Cru Cardeneau (Godicheau)	*Saillans*	6	15	15
Domaine du Cardneau (Barraud)	*Saillans*	4	10	8
Domaine du Cardneau (Boussaye)	*Saillans*	2	5	7
Château du Carles	*Saillans*	13	32.5	28
Château Chadène	*St.-Aignan*	6	15	36
Domaine du Couprat	*Saillans*	5	12.5	9
Château du Fronsac	*Fronsac*	4	10	8
Château Gagnard	*Fronsac*	11	27.5	20
Château Gros Jean	*St.-Aignan*	4	10	22
Château Hauchat	*St.-Aignan*	1	2.5	5
Château Haut Rey	*Fronsac*	8	20	17
Château Jendeman	*St.-Aignan*	9	22.5	52
Domaine La Borie	*Saillans*	6	15	10
Domaine du Labrande	*Saillans*	5	12.5	12
Château La Croix	*Fronsac*	11	27.5	33
Château La Croix Gandineau	*Fronsac*	5	12.5	12
Château La Dauphine	*Fronsac*	6	15	14
Château La Faure	*Saillans*	13	32.5	27
Château La Fontaine	*Fronsac*	9	22.5	24
Château La Graves	*Fronsac*	3	7.5	7

	Commune	Hectares	Acres	Tonneaux
Château Lague Bourdieu	Fronsac	4	10	14
Château Lambert	St.-Aignan	3	7.5	15
Château La Valade (Rupied)	Fronsac	11	27.5	20
Château La Valade (Roux)	Fronsac	4	10	13
Château La Venelle	Fronsac	4	10	13
Château La Vieille Curé	Saillans	14	35	32
Domaine Les Bernard	Saillans	4	10	12
Château Les Troix Croix	Fronsac	12	30	36
Château Magondeau	Saillans	9	22.5	38
Château de Malgarni	Saillans	3	7.5	6
Château Mayne-Vieille	Galgon	16	40	40
Château Moulins	Saillans	16	40	35
Château Musseau de Haut	St.-Aignan	2	5	12
Domaine Normand	Saillans	13	32.5	26
Château Pay de Pie	Fronsac	4	10	10
Château Peguilhem	Saillans	7	17.5	21
Château Peychez	Fronsac	4	10	8
Domaine Pillebourse	Saillans	3	7.5	6
Château Placette du Rey	Fronsac	4	10	7
Château Plainpoint	St.-Aignan	12	30	45
Château Richautey le Haut	St.-Aignan	2	5	6
Château Richodey	St.-Aignan	3	7.5	26
Château du Tasta	St.-Aignan	12	30	45
Château des Tonnelles	St.-Aignan	6	15	46
Clos des Tonnelles	St.-Aignan	4	10	18
Cru des Tonnelles	St.-Aignan	3	7.5	12
Clos Vieux Capot	Fronsac	2	5	5
Château Vieux Moulin	Fronsac	5	12.5	19
Château Vignes	Fronsac	2	5	5
Château Villars	Saillans	12	30	43
Château Vincent	St.-Aignan	4	10	27
Château Vincent (Rigaud)	St.-Aignan	3	7.5	9
Château Vincent (Sudra)	St.-Aignan	5	12.5	32
Domaine de Vincent	St.-Aignan	4	10	17
Château Vincent La Mouleyre	St.-Aignan	2	5	14

VI CÔTES CANON FRONSAC

The following figures of production are approximate, and indicate average annual output, as given by the communes and taken from their Déclarations de Récoltes records.

PRINCIPAL GROWTHS

	Commune	Hectares	Acres	Tonneaux
Château Barrabaque	Fronsac	7	17.5	14
Château Belloy	Fronsac	5	12.5	10
Château Bodet	Fronsac	10	25	38
Château Canon	Fronsac	5	12.5	10
Château Capet-Bégaud	Fronsac	3	7.5	7
Château Cassagne	St.-Michel	4	10	15
Château des Combes-Canon	St.-Michel	2	5	7
Château Coustolle	Fronsac	12	30	37
Château Gaby	Fronsac	6	15	12
Château du Gazin	St.-Michel	25	62.5	58
Château Gombeau	Fronsac	4	10	13
Château Grand Renouilh	St.-Michel	6	15	11

	Commune	Hectares	Acres	Tonneaux
Château Haut-Caillou	Fronsac	3	7.5	9
Clos Haut-Caillou	Fronsac	3	7.5	8
Château Haut-Mazeris	St.-Michel	6	15	16
Château Junayme	Fronsac	13	32.5	34
Château La Chapelle-Lariveau	St.-Michel	5	12.5	16
Château La Marche	Fronsac	27	67.5	58
Clos La Marche	Fronsac	2	5	4
Château La Mausse	St.-Michel	7	17.5	17
Château Larchevêque	Fronsac	5	12.5	10
Château Lariveau	St.-Michel	7	17.5	18
Château Les Vignes	Fronsac	2	5	5
Château Mazeris	St.-Michel	7	17.5	15
Château Mazeris Bellevue	St.-Michel	6	15	12
Domaine du Mouchez	Fronsac	7	17.5	14
Château Moulin-à-Vent	St.-Michel	6	15	18
Château Moulin-Pey-Labrie	Fronsac	4	10	13
Clos Nardin	St.-Michel	1	2.5	4
Château Panet	Fronsac	4	10	8
Château Perron	Fronsac	3	7.5	4
Château Pichelebre	Fronsac	5	12.5	15
Château Roulet	Fronsac	3	7.5	5
Château Roullet	Fronsac	3	7.5	7
Château du Tasta	St.-Aignan	2	5	11
Clos de Toumalin	Fronsac	2	5	5
Domaine de Toumalin	Fronsac	6	15	12
Domaine de Trepesson	St.-Michel	2	5	6
Château Vincent	St.-Aignan	7	17.5	12
Château Vrai Canon Bouché	Fronsac	5	12.5	13
Château Vrai Canon Bourret	Fronsac	2	5	6
Château Vrai Canon Boyer	St.-Michel	7	17.5	22

VII GRAVES: 1959 OFFICIAL CLASSIFICATION

The vineyards of the Graves district were officially classified in 1953 and in 1959. Château Haut-Brion, the greatest of all Graves, is also officially classified with the great Médocs.

The following figures of production are approximate, and indicate average annual output, as given by the communes and taken from their Déclarations de Récoltes records.

CLASSIFIED RED WINES OF GRAVES

	Commune	Tonneaux	Cases
Château Haut-Brion	Pessac	130	12,000
Château Bouscaut	Cadaujac	120	10,000
Château Carbonnieux	Léognan	120	12,000
Domaine de Chevalier	Léognan	50	4,500
Château Fieuzal	Léognan	60	5,500
Château Haut-Bailly	Léognan	55	5,000
Château La Mission-Haut-Brion	Pessac	70	6,000
Château La Tour-Haut-Brion	Talence	18	1,500
Château La Tour-Martillac (Kressmann La Tour)	Martillac	92	9,200
Château Malartic-Lagravière	Léognan	45	4,000
Château Olivier	Léognan	10	900
Château Pape-Clément	Pessac	120	11,000
Château Smith-Haut-Lafitte	Martillac	160	15,000

CLASSIFIED WHITE WINES OF GRAVES

	Commune	Tonneaux	Cases
Château Bouscaut	Cadaujac	18	1,500
Château Carbonnieux	Léognan	150	14,000
Domaine de Chevalier	Léognan	8	950
Château Couhins	Villenave-d'Ornon	40	3,800
Château La Tour-Martillac (Kressmann La Tour)	Martillac	6	500
Château Laville-Haut-Brion	Talence	20	1,800
Château Malartic-Lagravière	Léognan	6	500
Château Olivier	Léognan	80	7,000
Château Haut-Brion*	Pessac	16	1,500

* Added to the list in 1960.

OTHER PRINCIPAL GROWTHS

wh = WHITE; r = RED

	Commune		Hectares	Acres	Tonneaux
Château André-Lamothe	Portets	wh	2	5	11
		r	4	10	15
Domaine Andron	St.-Selve	wh	3	7.5	5
Château d'Arbanats	Arbanats	wh	6	15	10
Clos d'Armajan	Budos	r	2	5	4
Château d'Arricaud	Landiras	wh	12	30	49
Château des Arrocs	Langon	wh	3	7.5	10
Domaine Arzac	St.-Selve	wh	2	5	5
Clos l'Avocat	Cérons	wh	3	7.5	10
Château Bahans (minor growth of Château Haut-Brion)	Pessac	r	—	—	22
Château Bardins	Cadaujac	wh	2	5	2
		r			5
Château Baret	Villenave-d'Ornon	wh	40	60	25
		r			20
Domaine du Barque	St.-Selve	r	6	15	20
Clos Barreyre	Virelade	wh	3	7.5	8
Cru Barrouet	Pujols	wh	3	7.5	7
Domaine du Basque	Pujols	wh	3	7.5	12
Château Batsères	Landiras	wh	4	10	15
Château Beauchêne	Beautiran	wh	3	7.5	7
		r	2	5	5
Domaine du Beau-Site	Portets	wh	0.3	0.8	2
		r	3	7.5	9
Château Bel-Air	Portets	wh	2	5	6
Château Bel-Air	St.-Morillon	wh	3	10	10
Château Bellefontaine	St.-Pierre-de-Mons	wh	3	7.5	7
Domaine Bellevue	Toulenne	wh	1	2.5	7
Domaine de Bellevue	St.-Selve	wh	4	10	13
Château Belon	St.-Morillon	wh	3	7.5	6
Domaine de Bequin	Portets	wh	5	12.5	11
		r	3	7.5	7
Château Bernard-Raymond	Portets	wh	3	7.5	13
		r	2	5	11
Cru du Bérot	Arbanats	wh	2	5	6

	Commune		Hectares	Acres	Tonneaux
Cru Bichons	La Brède	wh			11
			5	12.5	
		r			2
Domaine de Biot	Arbanats	wh	2	5	5
		r	2	5	4
Domaine de la Blancherie	La Brède	wh	10	25	30
Château Boiresse	Ayguemortes	wh	4	10	15
Domaine du Bonat	St.-Selve	wh	5	12.5	14
Clos de la Bonneterie	Portets	wh	2	5	6
		r	2	5	4
Cru de Borderie	Portets	wh	3	7.5	9
		r	2	5	8
Cru Boritz	St.-Pierre-de-Mons	wh	4	10	12
Domaine du Boscq	St.-Morillon	wh	2	5	5
Cru Bouyon	Pujols	wh	2	5	5
Château Boyrin	Roaillan	wh	6	15	16
Domaine de Brochon	Arbanats	wh	3	7.5	7
		r	2	5	3
Domaine de Brondelle	Langon	wh	2	5	4
Domaine de Brouillaud	St.-Médard-d'Eyrans	wh	7	17.5	19
Château Bruhaut	St.-Pierre-de-Mons	wh	2	5	4
Château de Budos	Budos	r	9	22.5	31
Clos Cabanes	St.-Pierre-de-Mons	wh	4	10	11
Clos Cabannes	St.-Pierre-de-Mons	wh	1	2.5	5
Château Cabannieux	Portets	wh	3	7.5	7
		r	3	7.5	6
Cru de Cadenne	Pujols	wh	5	12.5	12
Cru du Caladis	Portets	r	3	7.5	9
		wh	4	10	10
Cru Calens	Beautiran	r	6	17.5	20
Cru Camegaye	Landiras	wh	2	5	9
Château Cantalot	St.-Pierre-de-Mons	wh	7	17.5	22
Cru de Cap-de-Hé	Pujols	wh	2	5	6
Château Carmes-Haut-Brion	Pessac	r	2	5	8
Domaine Carros	St.-Selve	wh	2	5	9
Domaine de Casseuil	Langon	wh	4	10	6
Cru Castagnet	Virelade	wh	3	7.5	9
Domaine Castelnaud	St.-Pierre-de-Mons	wh	2	5	5
Château Catalas	Pujols	wh	6	15	17
Château Cazebonne	St.-Pierre-de-Mons	wh	7	17.5	12
Clos Chantegrive	Podensac	wh	10	25	50
		r	5	12.5	25
Cru Chanteloiseau	Langon	wh	5	12.5	12
Château Chaviran	Martillac	r	4	10	16
Clos Cherchy	Pujols	wh	4	10	11
Cru Cherchy	Pujols	wh	2	5	9
Château Chicane	Toulenne	wh	3	7.5	12
Domaine du Ciron	Pujols	wh	5	12.5	19
Domaine de Clare	Landiras	wh	3	7.5	8
Cru du Couet	St.-Pierre-de-Mons	wh	2	5	5

Graves: Principal Growths

	Commune		Hectares	Acres	Tonneaux
Domaine de Courbon	*Toulenne*	wh	4	10	11
Domaine du Courreau	*St.-Médard-d'Eyrans*	wh			5
			3	7.5	
		r			3
Domaine du Courreau	*St.-Morillon*	wh	3	7.5	11
Château Crabitey	*Portets*	wh	7	17.5	7
		r	8	20	13
Domaine de la Croix	*Langon*	wh	4	10	10
Château Cruzeau	*St.-Médard-d'Eyrans*	wh + r	30	75	100
Clos Darches	*St.-Pierre-de-Mons*	wh	4	10	9
Clos Darrouban	*Portets*	wh			3
			2	5	
		r			3
Domaine de Darrouban	*Portets*	wh	3	7.5	15
		r	2	5	3
Château Despagne	*St.-Pierre-de-Mons*	wh	4	10	14
Clos Despagne	*St.-Pierre-de-Mons*	wh	4	10	16
Château Doms et Clos du Monastère	*Portets*	wh			29
			15	37.5	
		r			12
Domaine du Druc	*Landiras*	wh	2	5	6
Domaine de Durce, Domaine de Papoula	*Portets*	wh	2	5	7
		r	1	2.5	7
Domaine Étienne	*St.-Morillon*	wh	2	5	6
Cru Eyquem	*La Brède*	wh	5	12.5	12
Domaine de Faye	*Portets*	wh	1	2.5	6
		r	2	5	7
Château Fernon	*Langon*	wh + r	40	100	120
Château Ferran	*Martillac*	wh	3	7.5	11
		r	0.5	1.2	1
Château Ferrande	*Castres*	wh	10	25	33
Château Fieuzal	*Léognan*	wh	1	2.5	4
Château Foncla	*Castres*	wh			21
			13	32.5	
		r			3
Château Foncroise	*St.-Selve*	wh			10
			7	17.5	
		r			4
Château des Fougères	*La Brède*	wh	2	5	5
Clos des Fougères	*Virelade*	wh	4	10	11
Château de France	*Léognan*	r	20	50	80
Domaine des Gaillardins	*St.-Selve*	wh	4	10	8
Cru Galand	*Cérons*	wh	1	2.5	4
Clos du Gars	*La Brède*	wh	2	5	5
Château Gazin	*Léognan*	wh			1
			7	17.5	
		r			28
Clos de Gensac	*Pujols*	wh	4	10	16
Domaine de la Girafe	*Portets*	wh	5	12.5	22
		r	2	5	11
Domaine de la Gleyre	*Pujols*	wh	2	5	9
Cru de Gonthier	*Portets*	wh	1	2.5	5
		r	2	5	7
Château Gorre	*Martillac*	wh	1	2.5	1
		r	2	5	3

	Commune		Hectares	Acres	Tonneaux
Domaine du Grand-Abord	Portets	wh	5	12.5	18
		r	2	5	6
Château Grand Chemin	Cérons	wh	2	5	8
Château Grandmaison	Léognan	r	2	5	8
Domaine de la Grave	St.-Selve	wh	3	7.5	6
Cru des Graves	Portets	wh	3	7.5	6
		r	1	2.5	4
Domaine de Gravette	St.-Morillon	wh	15	37.5	33
Château Graveyron	Portets	wh	6	15	18
		r	4	10	13
Château de la Gravière	Toulenne	wh	7	17.5	25
Château des Gravières	Portets	wh	3	7.5	12
		r	2	5	10
Clos des Gravières	Portets	wh	2	5	5
		r	1	2.5	5
Domaine des Gravières	Portets	r	2	5	6
Domaine de Guérin	Castres	r	4	10	6
Château Guillaumot	La Brède	wh + r	13	32.5	41
Château des Guillemins	Langon	wh	8	20	28
Domaine de Guirauton	St.-Morillon	wh + r	6	15	12
Cru des Guizats	Pujols	wh	2	5	8
Clos Harquey	Langon	wh	4	10	7
Château Haut-Bergey	Léognan	wh			2
		{ 4	10	
		r			16
Cru du Haut-Blanc	Pujols	wh	1	2.5	4
Domaine du Haut-Blanc	Pujols	wh	4	10	12
Domaine Haut-Callens	Beautiran	r	3	7.5	12
Cru du Haut-Claron	St.-Morillon	wh	3	7.5	7
Domaine de Haut-Courneau	Portets	wh	5	12.5	13
		r	5	12.5	13
Cru Haut-Gravette	St.-Morillon	wh	3	7.5	6
Château Haut-Madère	Villenave-d'Ornon	r	2	5	3
Château Haut-Nouchet	Martillac	wh			9
		{ 9	22.5	
		r			6
Cru Hautes Plantes	Landiras	wh	3	7.5	8
Cru Haut-Reys	La-Brède	wh + r	3	7.5	7
Château Jamnets	St.-Pierre-de-Mons	wh			5
		{ 2	5	
		r			4
Clos Jamnet	La Brède	wh	4	10	15
Cru Janot-Bayle	Budos	r	8	20	16
Domaine du Jau	St.-Morillon	wh	3	7.5	5
Château des Jaubertes	St.-Pierre-de-Mons	wh	6	15	15
Clos Jean Dubos	Pujols	wh	2	5	4
Château Jean-Gervais, Clos Puyjalon	Portets	wh			100
		{ 25	62	
		r			
Clos Jean-de-Maye	Portets	wh			6
		{ 5	12.5	
		r			11
Clos de l'Abbaye-de-la-Rame	Mazères	wh	6	15	12
Domaine de Labeillon	St.-Pierre-de-Mons	wh	2	5	5
Cru La Cabane	Pujols	wh	4	10	11

Graves: Principal Growths

	Commune		Hectares	Acres	Tonneaux
Château Côtes de Lacapère	Landiras	wh	2	5	6
Cru Lacapère	Landiras	wh	4	10	15
Domaine de Lacapère	Landiras	wh	2	5	7
Cru Lafon	St.-Pierre-de-Mons	wh	2	5	9
Château La Garde	Martillac	r	13	32.5	40
Château Lagueloup	Portets	wh + r	2	5	6
Cru La Hounade	Pujols	wh	2	5	9
Château La Louvière	Léognan	wh	20	50	45
		r	30	75	19
Clos Lamagine	St.-Pierre-de-Mons	wh	6	15	14
Cru La Mainionce	Pujols	wh	3	7.5	13
Cru La Médecine	St.-Pierre-de-Mons	wh	2	5	5
Cru de Lamoigon	Pujols	wh	3	7.5	5
Château Lamothe	Cadaujac	r + wh	4	10	10
Clos Lamothe	Portets	wh	3	7.5	9
		r	2	5	11
Château Lamouroux	Cérons	wh	8	20	37
Château Laouilley	Roaillan	wh	3	7.5	3
Domaine La Payrère	St.-Selve	wh	5	12.5	8
		r			2
Cru Lardite	Arbanats	wh	2	5	13
		r	2	5	5
Domaine de Larnavey	St.-Selve	r	2	5	8
Château Larrivet-Haut-Brion	Léognan	r	14	35	56
Cru Larroucat	Pujols	wh	2	5	8
Château La Salle	Martillac	wh + r	3	7.5	8
Domaine La Solitude	Martillac	wh	2	5	4
		r	4	10	7
Domaine de Lassalle	La Brède	wh + r	6	15	26
Cru La Terce	Budos	r	2	5	3
Château La Tour	Léognan	wh	4	10	9
		r			16
Château La Tour Bicheau	Portets	wh	4	7.5	12
		r	6	12.5	25
Château La Tour-de-Boyrin	Langon	wh	13	32.5	20
Clos La-Tour-Cluchon	Portets	wh	2	5	3
		r	2	5	5
Château La Tourte	Toulenne	wh	6	15	16
Cru Le Bourut	Pujols	wh	2	5	9
Château Le Brouillaud	St.-Médard-d'Eyrans	wh	5	12.5	16
Cru de l'Église	Virelade	wh	2	5	5
Clos Léhoul	Langon	wh	4	10	8
Château Le Mayne	Preignac	wh			9
Château Le Pape	Léognan	wh	4	10	3
		r			2
Château Les Charmettes	Budos	wh	2	5	4
Domaine Les Cluchets	Langon	wh	4	10	12

	Commune		Hectares	Acres	Tonneaux
Cru Les Graves	Toulenne	wh	4	10	12
Cru Les Guizats	Pujols	wh	2	5	4
Cru Les Mengets	Pujols	wh	2	5	4
Château Lespault	Martillac	wh	4	10	3
		r	0.5	1.2	2
Château de l'Espérance	La Brède	wh	4	10	10
		r	8	20	25
Cru Les Pinsas	Pujols	wh	2	5	5
Cru Les Rocs	Pujols	wh	2	5	5
Cru Lestage	Landiras	wh	4	10	9
Domaine Lestang	St.-Selve	wh + r	5	12.5	16
Château Le Thil	Léognan	r	3	7.5	4
Cru de l'Hermitage	Budos	r	8	20	12
Domaine de l'Hôpital	Castres	r	3	7.5	10
Château de l'Hospital	Portets	wh }	8	20	25
		r }			
Clos Liché	St.-Pardon-de-Conques	wh	3	7.5	7
Château Limbourg	Villenave-d'Ornon	wh }	10	25	5
		r }			6
Château Liot-Moros	Pujols	wh	5	12.5	15
Cru Lioy	Budos	r	3	7.5	4
Château Lognac	Castres	r	5	12.5	15
Domaine de Louisot	Virelade	wh	4	10	13
Clos Louloumet	Toulenne	wh	3	7.5	8
Cru de Lubat	St.-Pierre-de-Mons	wh	8	20	14
Château des Lucques	Portets	wh }	5	12.5	12
		r }			6
Domaine des Lucques	Portets	wh }	7	17.5	7
		r }			6
Château Ludeman-Lacôte	Langon	wh	7	17.5	20
Château Lusseau	Ayguemortes	r	4	10	10
Château Madélis	Portets	wh	2	5	6
		r	2	5	12
Château Madran	Pessac	r	3	7.5	4
Château Magence	St.-Pierre-de-Mons	wh	11	27.5	27
Cru Magnaud	La Brède	wh + r	5	12.5	11
Château Maillard	Mazères	wh	5	12.5	13
Clos de la Maison Blanche	Budos	wh	2	5	5
Château Malleprat	Martillac	wh	3	7.5	5
Domaine de Maron	Landiras	r	2	5	9
Domaine Martin	Roaillan	wh	2	5	6
Cru Massiot	Martillac	wh	2	5	6
Château de Mauves	Podensac	r	1	2.5	4
Domaine du May	Portets	wh	3	7.5	6
		r	2	5	5
Domaine du Mayne	Langon	wh	3	7.5	8
Cru Mayne d'Eyquen	La Brède	wh + r	5	12.5	14
Château Mayne-Levêque	Podensac	wh	10	25	50
		r	5	12.5	25

	Commune		Hectares	Acres	Tonneaux
Domaine de Metivier	Ayguemortes	wh	3	7.5	6
Château Millet	Portets	wh}			17
			10	25	
		r }			20
Château Mirabel	Pujols	wh	3	7.5	14
Château du Mirail	Portets	wh	5	12.5	16
		r	10	25	30
Château Moderis	Virelade	wh + r	5	12.5	10
Domaine de Mongenan	Portets	wh}			13
			5	12.5	
		r }			2
Clos de Mons	La Brède	wh + r	3	7.5	8
Cru Morange	Virelade	wh + r	2	5	7
Clos du Moulin-à-Vent	St.-Pierre-de-Mons	wh	5	12.5	18
Cru du Moulin-à-Vent	Cérons	wh	3	7.5	12
Cru du Moulin-à-Vent	Landiras	wh	3	7.5	10
Château Mouteou	Portets	wh	2	5	6
		r	1	2.5	4
Château Moutin	Portets	r	1	2.5	5
Château Mouyet	Budos	r	2	5	11
Cru Nodoy	Virelade	wh + r	5	12.5	20
Clos Nouchet	Castres	r	3	7.5	10
Château de Nouguey	Langon	wh	2	5	6
Clos du Pape	La Brède	wh	6	15	19
Domaine de Papoula (see Domaine de Durce)					
Cru Patiras	Toulenne	wh	2	5	4
Château du Pavillon	Roaillan	wh	6	15	8
Château Pédebayle	St.-Pierre-de-Mons	wh	8	20	20
Château Péran	Langon	wh	8	20	17
Cru Perran	Landiras	wh	3	7.5	12
Domaine Perrin de Naudine	Castres	r	5	12.5	15
Château Perron	Roaillan	wh	14	35	37
Château Pesilla	Landiras	wh	4	10	16
Château Pessan	Portets	wh	6	15	14
		r	6	15	12
Château Péyran	Landiras	wh	4	10	11
Château des Peyrères	Landiras		4	10	14
Cru Pezeau	Beautiran	r	3	7.5	10
Cru Pinaud	Cérons	wh	2	5	5
Château Pingoy	Portets	wh	5	12.5	21
		r	3	7.5	12
Château Pique-Cailloux	Mérignac	wh	7	17.5	13
Château Piron	St.-Morillon	wh + r	15	37.5	50
Clos de Places	Arbanats	wh + r	1	2.5	4

	Commune		Hectares	Acres	Tonneaux
Domaine des Places	Arbanats	wh	2	5	9
		r	1	2.5	6
Domaine de Plantat	St.-Morillon	wh + r	9	22.5	16
Cru des Plantes	Landiras	wh	14	35	56
Domaine des Plantes	Landiras	wh	4	10	11
Domaine du Plantey	Castres	wh	2	5	2
		r			7
Château Pommarède	Castres	r	3	7.5	10
Château Pommarède-de-Bas	Castres	wh	5	12.5	11
		r			4
Château Pontac	Villenave-d'Ornon	wh	14	35	20
		r			15
Cru du Portail	Landiras	wh	2	5	7
Château de Portets	Portets	wh	7	17.5	18
		r	35	87.5	100
Cru de la Poste	Virelade	wh	4	10	6
Château Poumey	Gradignan	wh	4	10	4
		r			12
Clos Puyjalon (see Château Jean-Gervais)					
Château Queyrats, Clos d'Uza, Château St. Pierre	St.-Pierre-de-Mons	wh	34	85	77
Château Rahoul	Portets	wh	2	5	5
		r	5	12.5	26
Château Respide	Langon	wh	34	85	55
		r			15
Château Respide	St.-Pierre-de-Mons	wh	4	10	5
Château Respide	Toulenne	wh	5	12.5	13
Château La Rocaille	Virelade	wh + r	9	22.5	13
Domaine Roland	Langon	wh	3	7.5	6
Château Roquetaillade	Mazères	wh	3	7.5	9
Château Roquetaillade-la-Grange	Mazères	wh	5	12.5	20
		r	10	25	40
Château Rosario	Eyzines	wh	1	2.5	4
Château Rostang-Haut-Carré	Talence	wh	1	2	2
		r	3	7.5	6
Château Roubinet	Pujols	wh	8	20	32
Cru Roudet	Pujols	wh	5	12.5	17
Cru Sadout	Virelade	wh + r	6	15	19
Château Saige-Fort-Manoir	Pessac	r	5	12.5	11
Château St.-Gérôme	Ayguemortes	wh + r	4	10	7
Clos St.-Hilaire	Portets	wh	3	7.5	12
		r	3	7.5	8
Clos St.-Jean	Pujols	wh	8	20	23
Château St.-Pierre (see Château Queyrats)					
Clos St.-Robert	Pujols	wh	26	65	54
		r	4	10	8
Domaine du Sapeur	Portets	wh	4	10	9
		r			10
Cru Sarraguey	Virelade	wh + r	5	12.5	20
Domaine des Sarrots	St.-Pierre-de-Mons	wh	2	5	5
Clos Sentouary	St.-Pierre-de-Mons	wh	2	5	5
Cru Terrefort	Pujols	wh	3	7.5	10

	Commune		Hectares	Acres	Tonneaux
Domaine de Teycheney	*Virelade*	wh	2	5	4
Domaine de Teychon	*Arbanats*	wh	4	10	16
Château Toumilon	*St.-Pierre-de-Mons*	wh	5	12.5	9
Cru Toumilon	*St.-Pierre-de-Mons*	wh	2	5	4
Château Tourteau-Cholet	*Arbanats*	wh + r	13	32.5	30
Clos de la Tuilerie	*Portets*	wh	3	7.5	10
		r	2	5	10
Cru La Tuilerie	*Landiras*	wh	2	5	7
Château des Tuileries	*Virelade*	wh	3	7.5	14
		r	7	17.5	19
Château Le Tuquet	*Beautiran*	wh ⎫			70
		⎬ 26	65	
		r ⎭			20
Château Tustoc	*Toulenne*	wh	8	20	26
Clos d'Uza (*see* Château Queyrats)					
Domaine des Vergnes	*Portets*	wh	2	5	4
		r	1	2.5	4
Clos Viaut	*St.-Pardon-de-Conques*	wh	2	5	4
Clos Viaut	*St.-Pierre-de-Mons*	wh	9	22.5	25
Cru Videau	*Pujols*	wh	6	15	25
Château La Vieille-France	*Portets*	wh ⎫			16
		⎬ 8	20	
		r ⎭			7
Château de Virelade	*Arbanats*	wh	3	7.5	9
		r	10	25	30

VIII SAUTERNES AND BARSAC

As in the Médoc, the Sauternes vineyards were officially classified in 1855. This classification is known as the Official Classification of the Great Growths of the Gironde.

The total production from these vineyards represents approximately 25 per cent of the total Sauternes production, amounting roughly to 350,000 cases per year.

The following figures of production are approximate, and indicate average annual output, as given by the communes and taken from their Déclarations de Récoltes records.

FIRST GREAT GROWTH

	Tonneaux	Cases
Château d'Yquem	200	20,000

FIRST GROWTHS

Château Guiraud	120	11,000
Château La Tour-Blanche	60	4,800
Château Lafaurie-Peyraguey	50	4,800
Château de Rayne-Vigneau	150	11,000
Château Sigalas-Rabaud	35	3,000
Château Rabaud-Promis	65	7,000
Clos Haut-Peyraguey	25	2,200
Château Coutet	75	6,500
Château Climens	65	6,000
Château Suduiraut	110	10,000
Château Rieussec	100	8,500

SECOND GROWTHS

Château d'Arche	80	7,500
Château Filhot	100	10,000
Château Lamothe	25	2,000

	Tonneaux	Cases
Château Myrat (no longer producing wine)	—	—
Château Doisy-Védrines	60	5,700
Château Doisy-Daëne	20	1,900
Château Suau	15	1,300
Château Broustet	30	2,700
Château Caillou	40	3,700
Château Nairac	25	2,000
Château de Malle	40	3,700
Château Romer	15	1,300

MINOR GROWTHS

	Commune	Hectares	Acres	Tonneaux
Château d'Arche-Lafaurie	Sauternes	19	47.5	48
Cru d'Arche-Pugnau, Château Peyraguey-le-Rousset	Preignac	15	37.5	32
Château d'Arches, Château Lamothe	Sauternes	15	37.5	40
Château d'Arche-Vimeney	Sauternes	5	12.5	11
Château d'Armajan-des-Ormes	Preignac	7	17.5	18
Cru d'Arrançon	Preignac	5	12.5	10
Cru Arrançon-Boutoc	Preignac	3	7.5	9
Château Augey	Bommes	10	25	26
Cru Baboye	Fargues	2	5	5
Château Barbier	Fargues	6	15	16
Cru de Barboye	Bommes	2	5	4
Cru Barjumeau	Sauternes	3	7.5	6
Château Barjumeau-Chauvin	Sauternes	3	7.5	9
Clos Barreau	Fargues	1	2.5	4
Château Barrette	Sauternes	5	12.5	14
Cru Barrette	Fargues	1	2.5	2
Cru Bas-Peyraguey	Preignac	2	5	4
Château Bastor-Lamontagne	Preignac	38	95	90
Château Batsalle	Fargues	4	10	9
Cru Batsalle	Fargues	1	2.5	3
Château Baulac-Dodigeos	Barsac	5	12.5	12
Cru Baylieu	Fargues	7	17.5	13
Château Béchereau	Bommes	12	30	22
Cru Bel-Air	Preignac	2	5	4
Château Bergeron	Bommes	5	12.5	15
Cru Bergeron	Preignac	4	10	11
Château Bernisse	Barsac	3	7.5	8
Cru Bernisse	Barsac	1	2.5	4
Cru Bignon	Bommes	1	2.5	3
Cru Bordesoulles	Preignac	3	7.5	7
Château Bousclas	Barsac	3	7.5	8
Cru Bousclas	Barsac	4	10	12
Cru Boutoc	Preignac	5	12.5	10
Cru Boutoc	Sauternes	2	5	5
Château Bouyot	Barsac	6	15	15
Cru Bouyreou	Preignac	1	2.5	2
Château Brassens-Guitteronde	Barsac	5	12.5	14
Cru Camelong	Bommes	1	2.5	2
Château Cameron et Raymond-Louis	Bommes	9	22.5	35
Château Camperos, Château Montalivet, Château Mayne-Bert	Barsac	12	30	27
Château Cantegril	Barsac	14	35	38
Cru Caplane	Bommes	2	5	5
Cru Caplane	Sauternes	5	12.5	16
Domaine de Caplane	Sauternes	5	12.5	25
Cru Carbonnieu	Bommes	6	15	23
Château de Carles	Barsac	6	15	16

	Commune	*Hectares*	*Acres*	*Tonneaux*
Cru du Carrefour	*Sauternes*	1	2.5	2
Cru de la Cave	*Preignac*	2	5	5
Cru du Chalet	*Barsac*	2	5	5
Cru du Chalet	*Preignac*	1	2.5	3
Domaine de la Chapelle	*Preignac*	2	5	4
Château de la Chartreuse	*Preignac*	5	12.5	10
Cru Chauvin	*Sauternes*	2	5	4
Cru Claverie	*Fargues*	2	5	6
Château Closiot	*Barsac*	5	12.5	11
Clos Cloziot	*Barsac*	1	2.5	2
Cru Cluziot	*Barsac*	1	2.5	2
Château Commarque	*Sauternes*	4	10	10
Cru Commarque	*Bommes*	1	2.5	3
Cru Commarque	*Sauternes*	6	15	11
Cru Commet-Magey	*Preignac*	4	10	8
Cru Commet-Magey-Briatte	*Preignac*	4	10	11
Domaine Cosse	*Fargues*	6	15	12
Domaine de Couite	*Preignac*	3	7.5	8
Cru Coussères	*Fargues*	1	2.5	2
Château Coustet	*Barsac*	6	15	21
Cru Coustet	*Barsac*	1	2.5	2
Domaine du Coy	*Sauternes*	3	7.5	8
Château de Coye	*Sauternes*	1	2.5	3
Cru Druenn	*Bommes*	2	5	4
Château Ducasse	*Barsac*	5	12.5	12
Cru Ducasse	*Fargues*	2	5	5
Château Dudon	*Barsac*	8	20	20
Domaine Duperneau	*Bommes*	3	7.5	9
Cru Duzan	*Barsac*	1	2.5	3
Clos d'Espagnet (*see* Château Esterlin)				
Château Esterlin, Clos d'Espagnet	*Sauternes*	3	7.5	7
Château de Fargues	*Fargues*	7	17.5	16
Château Farluret	*Barsac*	4	10	11
Cru Fillau	*Fargues*	4	10	10
Château Fleury, Château Terre-Noble	*Barsac*	2	5	4
Clos Fontaine	*Fargues*	2	5	6
Château Fontebride	*Preignac*	2	5	7
Domaine de la Forêt	*Preignac*	21	52.5	61
Cru Gavach	*Fargues*	3	7.5	7
Château Gilette, Domaine des Justices, Château Les Rochers, Château Les Remparts, Château Lamothe	*Preignac*	14	35	30
Clos Girautin	*Barsac*	1	2.5	3
Château Grand-Carretey	*Barsac*	1	2.5	2
Cru Grand-Carretey	*Barsac*	6	15	16
Cru Grand-Jauga	*Barsac*	2	5	6
Château Grand-Mayne-Qui-Né-Marc	*Barsac*	1	2.5	3
Cru Gravailles	*Preignac*	2	5	4
Château Gravas	*Barsac*	8	20	20
Château Grillon	*Barsac*	6	15	18
Cru Guillem-du-Rey	*Preignac*	7	17.5	22
Château Guimbalet	*Preignac*	1	2.5	4
Cru Guitteronde	*Barsac*	1	2.5	3
Château Guitteronde-Bert	*Barsac*	9	22.5	22
Château Guitteronde-Sarraute	*Barsac*	4	10	10
Château du Haire	*Preignac*	4	10	9
Cru du Haire	*Preignac*	6	15	18
Château Hallet	*Barsac*	10	25	24
Château Haut-Bergeron	*Preignac*	4	10	13

	Commune	Hectares	Acres	Tonneaux
Château Haut-Bommes	Bommes	7	17.5	14
Château Haut-Claverie	Fargues	4	10	8
Cru Haut-Lagueritte	Bommes	2	5	4
Château Haut-Mayne	Fargues	2	5	5
Cru Haut-Piquan	Sauternes	1	2.5	3
Cru du Hère	Preignac	2	5	2
Château Hourmalas (*see* Château St.-Marc)				
Cru Hourmalas	Barsac	2	5	6
Château Jany	Barsac	2	5	6
Clos Jauguet	Barsac	1	2.5	3
Cru Jauguet	Barsac	5	12.5	14
Château Jean-Galant	Bommes	2	5	7
Château Jean-Laive	Barsac	4	10	11
Clos de Jeanlaive	Barsac	5	12.5	11
Cru Jeannonier	Bommes	3	7.5	4
Domaine Jean-Robert	Preignac	1	2.5	3
Château du Juge	Preignac	4	10	10
Cru Junka	Preignac	3	7.5	4
Château Les Justices	Preignac	3	7.5	6
Domaine des Justices (*see* Château Gilette)				
Cru La Bernisse	Barsac	3	7.5	7
Château La Bouade	Barsac	12	30	31
Clos La Bouade	Barsac	3	7.5	8
Domaine de Labouade-Rambaud	Barsac	1	2.5	3
Cru La Bouchette	Bommes	1	2.5	2
Cru Labouchette	Preignac	2	5	5
Château La Brouillère	Bommes	4	10	9
Cru Labrousse	Barsac	2	5	5
Château La Chapelle-St.-Aubin	Bommes	3	7.5	6
Château La Clotte	Barsac	5	12.5	12
Cru Lacoste	Barsac	2	5	4
Cru La Côte	Fargues	5	12.5	9
Château Lafon, Château Le Mayne	Sauternes	6	15	19
Château Lafon-Laroze	Sauternes	3	7.5	5
Cru Lagardan	Bommes	3	7.5	10
Cru l'Agnet	Bommes	2	5	3
Château Lagravette	Bommes	2	5	5
Cru La Gravière	Preignac	2	5	5
Cru Lahonade-Peyraguey	Bommes	2	5	6
Château Lahouilley	Barsac	3	7.5	9
Château La Hourcade	Preignac	4	10	13
Cru Lalot	Preignac	6	15	16
Cru La Maringue	Bommes	4	10	8
Château Lamothe (*see* Château d'Arches)				
Château Lamothe (*see* Château Gilette)				
Cru Lamothe	Sauternes	6	15	14
Château La Mourette	Bommes	3	7.5	8
Cru Lanère	Sauternes	11	27.5	21
Château Lange	Bommes	5	12.5	12
Cru Lanusquet	Fargues	2	5	5
Clos Lapachère	Barsac	4	10	10
Château Lapelou	Barsac	6	15	16
Château Lapinesse	Barsac	16	40	44
Cru Lapinesse	Barsac	7	17.5	19
Cru La Pinesse	Barsac	2	5	5
Domaine de Laraude	Sauternes	2	5	5
Château Laribotte	Preignac	5	12.5	9
Domaine de l'Arieste	Preignac	8	20	21
Clos l'Arieste	Preignac	3	7.5	8

	Commune	Hectares	Acres	Tonneaux
Cru Larode	Sauternes	1	2.5	2
Château La Tour	Barsac	2	5	4
Château Latrezotte	Barsac	7	17.5	20
Cru l'Aubépin	Bommes	10	25	26
Cru l'Aubépine	Bommes	2	5	4
Cru l'Aubépins	Sauternes	3	7.5	6
Château Lauvignac	Preignac	3	7.5	6
Château Laville	Preignac	11	27.5	22
Château Le Coustet	Barsac	5	12.5	10
Cru Le Haut Bommes	Bommes	0.5	1.2	2
Château Le Hère	Bommes	6	15	10
Château Le Mayne	Preignac	13	32.5	34
Château Le Mayne (see Château Lafon)				
Château Le Mouret	Fargues	6	15	6
Cru Le Pageot	Bommes	2	5	4
Château l'Ermitage	Preignac	7	17.5	13
Cru Le Roc	Preignac	1	2.5	3
Château Le Rose-et-Monteil	Preignac	5	12.5	14
Cru Le Rousseau	Bommes	2	5	3
Château Le Arrieux	Preignac	5	12.5	15
Château Le Sahuc	Preignac	3	7.5	9
Cru Les Cailloux	Bommes	2	5	4
Cru Les Gravilles	Barsac	1	2.5	2
Château Les Plantes	Barsac	5	12.5	14
Cru Les Quints	Barsac	1	2.5	2
Château Les Remparts (see Château Gilette)				
Château Les Rochers	Preignac	7	17.5	18
Château Les Rochers (see Château Gilette)				
Cru Les Rochers	Preignac	2	5	4
Cru Les Tuileries	Fargues	1	2.5	3
Château Liot	Barsac	11	27.5	29
Château de Luzies	Barsac	3	7.5	9
Cru Mahon	Bommes	1	2.5	4
Cru Mahon	Preignac	2	5	6
Cru de Mahon	Preignac	2	5	3
Clos des Maraings	Preignac	3	7.5	6
Château Masereau	Barsac	7	17.5	15
Château Mathalin	Barsac	11	27.5	35
Domaine de Mathalin	Barsac	1	2.5	3
Château Mauras	Bommes	13	32.5	36
Cru Mauras	Bommes	3	7.5	5
Cru Mauvin	Preignac	6	15	16
Château du Mayne	Barsac	7	17.5	17
Château du Mayne	Preignac	2	5	5
Château Mayne-Bert (see Château Camperos)				
Clos Mayne-Lamouroux	Barsac	2	5	5
Cru Menate	Barsac	1	2.5	2
Château Menota, Château Menota-Labat	Barsac	17	42.5	54
Château Menota-Labat (see Château Menota)				
Château Mercier	Barsac	2	5	4
Clos Mercier	Barsac	3	7.5	8
Cru Mercier	Barsac	1	2.5	4
Clos de Miaille	Barsac	1	2.5	2
Cru Miaille	Barsac	1	2.5	3
Cru Miselle	Preignac	3	7.5	7
Château du Mont	Preignac	4	10	11
Château Montalivet (see Château Camperos)				
Château Monteau	Preignac	9	22.5	21
Cru Monteil	Bommes	3	7.5	7

	Commune	*Hectares*	*Acres*	*Tonneaux*
Cru Monteils	*Preignac*	1	2.5	2
Domaine de Monteils	*Preignac*	7	17.5	19
Cru Montjoie	*Preignac*	2	5	4
Château Montjou (*see* Château Terre Noble)				
Cru Mothes	*Fargues*	8	20	13
Cru du Moulin Neuf	*Preignac*	1	2.5	2
Château Mounic	*Fargues*	1	2.5	2
Domaine de Mounic	*Fargues*	1	2.5	2
Château Moura	*Barsac*	1	2.5	4
Cru Mouret	*Fargues*	3	7.5	7
Cru Mussotte	*Fargues*	1	2.5	3
Clos de Nauton	*Fargues*	4	10	7
Château Padouen-Terre-Noble	*Barsac*	7	17.5	10
Château Pageot	*Sauternes*	5	12.5	12
Cru du Pajeot	*Bommes*	4	10	7
Château Paloumat	*Fargues*	2	5	2
Château du Pape	*Preignac*	3	7.5	12
Clos du Pape	*Fargues*	5	12.5	11
Château Partarrieu	*Fargues*	8	20	9
Cru Passérieux	*Barsac*	3	7.5	7
Château Pébayle	*Barsac*	5	12.5	15
Château Peillon-Claverie	*Fargues*	9	22.5	26
Château Pechon-Terre-Noble	*Barsac*	3	7.5	9
Château Pernaud	*Barsac*	17	42.5	35
Cru du Perret	*Bommes*	2	5	6
Château Perroy-Jean-Blanc	*Bommes*	7	17.5	17
Cru Petit-Grillon	*Barsac*	2	5	5
Cru Peyraguey	*Preignac*	8	20	22
Château Peyraguey-le-Rousset (*see* Cru d'Arche-Pugnau)				
Château de Peyre	*Fargues*	1	2.5	3
Cru de Peyre	*Fargues*	1	2.5	3
Clos Peyret	*Preignac*	1	2.5	3
Château Peyron	*Fargues*	4	10	17
Château Piada, Clos du Roy	*Barsac*	11	27.5	29
Cru Pian	*Barsac*	2	5	7
Château Piaut	*Barsac*	9	22.5	22
Château du Pick	*Preignac*	23	57.5	59
Clos de Pierrefeu	*Preignac*	4	10	10
Cru Pilote	*Fargues*	3	7.5	8
Cru Piquey	*Bommes*	1	2.5	2
Cru de Pistoulet-Peyraguey	*Bommes*	2	5	4
Cru du Placey	*Barsac*	1	2.5	3
Cru Planton	*Barsac*	1	2.5	3
Château Pleytegeat	*Preignac*	12	30	51
Cru Pouteau	*Fargues*	2	5	4
Cru Pouton	*Preignac*	2	5	6
Clos des Princes	*Barsac*	2	5	6
Château Prost	*Barsac*	8	20	21
Château Pugnau	*Preignac*	3	7.5	8
Cru Puydomine	*Bommes*	2	5	4
Château Raspide	*Barsac*	5	12.5	16
Château Raymond-Lafon	*Sauternes*	3	7.5	4
Château des Remparts	*Preignac*	1	2.5	4
Cru Richard Barbe	*Bommes*	2	5	5
Cru Ripaille	*Preignac*	1	2.5	2
Château du Roc	*Barsac*	2	5	5
Château des Rocs	*Preignac*	1	2.5	3
Château de Rolland	*Barsac*	14	35	39
Domaine de la Roudette	*Sauternes*	2	5	6

	Commune	Hectares	Acres	Tonneaux
Château Roumieu	Barsac	18	45	46
Château Roumieu-Lacoste	Barsac	5	12.5	14
Clos Rouquette	Preignac	6	15	17
Clos du Roy (see Château Piada)				
Château Sahuc	Preignac	2	5	5
Château Sahuc-Latour	Preignac	4	10	8
Château St.-Amand	Preignac	7	17.5	20
Château St.-Marc, Château Hourmalas	Barsac	6	15	14
Château St.-Michel	Barsac	1	2.5	3
Cru St.-Michel	Barsac	1	2.5	3
Clos St.-Robert	Barsac	1	2.5	3
Cru St.-Sardeau	Fargues	2	5	6
Cru Saubade-Terrefort	Sauternes	2	5	3
Château Simon	Barsac	4	10	12
Château Simon-Carretey	Barsac	4	10	7
Château Solon	Preignac	4	10	13
Cru Soula	Fargues	4	10	9
Château Suau	Barsac	5	12.5	14
Domaine Tchit	Fargues	1	2.5	3
Cru Terrefort	Bommes	4	10	11
Domaine de Terrefort	Sauternes	3	7.5	6
Château Terre Noble, Château Montjou	Barsac	9	22.5	24
Château Terre-Noble (see Château Fleury)				
Cru des Terres Rouges	Barsac	2	5	4
Château Thibaut	Fargues	2	5	4
Cru Thibaut	Fargues	7	17.5	15
Château de Touilla	Fargues	3	7.5	4
Château Trillon	Sauternes	8	20	20
Cru Tucan	Barsac	2	5	3
Château Tucau	Barsac	3	7.5	9
Cru Tucou	Preignac	1	2.5	2
Château Valmont-Mayne	Barsac	2	5	4
Château Veyres	Preignac	10	25	30
Cru Vigne-Vieille	Barsac	3	7.5	8
Château Villefranche	Barsac	6	15	13
Château du Violet	Preignac	7	17.5	24
Cru du Violet	Preignac	1	2.5	5
Cru du Violet-et-Lamothe	Preignac	5	12.5	12
Château Voigny	Preignac	6	15	18

IX CÉRONS

The following figures of production are approximate, and indicate average annual output, as given by the communes and taken from their Déclarations de Récoltes records.

PRINCIPAL GROWTHS

	Commune	Hectares	Acres	Tonneaux
Château d'Anice	Podensac	12	30	50
Château Archambeau	Illats	4	10	34
Clos Avocat	Cérons	4	10	8
Clos de l'Avocat	Cérons	3	7.5	9
Château Balestey	Cérons	10	25	20
Clos de Barial	Illats	9	22.5	22
Clos du Barrail	Cérons	8	20	19
Château Beaulac	Illats	3	7.5	7

	Commune	Hectares	Acres	Tonneaux
Cru Bel-Air	Illats	3	7.5	12
Clos de Bos-Lancon	Illats	4	10	12
Cru de Bouley	Illats	4	10	8
Domaine de Bourdac	Illats	7	17.5	40
Clos Bourgelet	Cérons	7	17.5	15
Cru de Boutec	Illats	5	12.5	20
Cru de Braze	Illats	7	17.5	18
Cru Brouillaou	Podensac	11	27.5	28
Cru de Cabiro	Illats	3	7.5	11
Château Cages	Illats	5	12.5	17
Domaine du Caillou	Cérons	5	12.5	10
Domaine Caillou Rouley	Podensac	8	20	15
Château Cantau	Illats	4	10	9
Clos Cantemerle	Cérons	3	7.5	7
Château de Cérons	Cérons	15	37.5	28
Domaine de la Citadelle	Illats	4	10	14
Cru Cleyrac	Cérons	5	12.5	15
Cru des Deux Moulins	Illats	4	10	8
Cru Ducas	Illats	2	5	6
Domaine du Freyron	Cérons	3	7.5	5
Domaine de Gardennes	Illats	3	7.5	6
Château Grand Chemin	Cérons	4	10	8
Cru du Grand-Chênes	Cérons	3	7.5	6
Grand Enclos du Château de Cérons	Cérons	11	27.5	30
Château Hauret	Illats	4	10	9
Cru Haut-Buhan	Illats	7	17.5	18
Château du Haut-Gravier	Illats	11	27.5	22
Cru Haut La Hountasse (P. Banos)	Illats	3	7.5	6
Cru Haut La Hountasse (R. Banos, J. Banos)	Illats	5	12.5	15
Château Haut-Mayne	Cérons	5	12.5	10
Cru Haut-Mayne	Cérons	2	5	5
Cru de Haut-Mayne	Cérons	3	7.5	6
Château Haut-Rat	Illats	16	40	40
Château Huradin, Domaine du Salut	Cérons	8	20	30
Clos du Jaugua	Illats	4	10	8
Domaine de Jaussans	Illats	8	20	20
Château LaLanette Ferbos	Cérons	5	12.5	22
Château Lamouroux	Cérons	10	25	22
Château Lanette	Cérons	5	12.5	12
Cru Larrouquey	Cérons	7	17.5	18
Domaine Larrouquey	Cérons	5	12.5	12
Château La Salette	Cérons	5	12.5	12
Domaine Le Cossu	Podensac	5	12.5	11
Château Le Huzet	Illats	7	17.5	18
Château de l'Émigré	Cérons	2	5	5
Cru Le Tinan	Illats	3	7.5	6
Cru de Lionne	Illats	7	17.5	18
Château Madère	Podensac	12	30	28
Cru Madérot (Édouard Sterlin)	Podensac	9	22.5	18
Cru Madérot (Étienne Sterlin)	Podensac	2	5	6
Cru Majans	Cérons	3	7.5	6
Cru Marc	Illats	5	12.5	16
Château des Mauves	Podensac	7	17.5	16
Château Mayne d'Anice	Podensac	4	10	9
Cru Maynine	Illats	3	7.5	10
Domaine de Menaut Larrouquey	Cérons	12	30	32
Cru de Menjon	Illats	3	7.5	9
Cru Moulin de la Glorie	Illats	2	5	7
Château Moulin-à-Vent	Cérons	4	10	12

Loupiac: Principal Growths

	Commune	Hectares	Acres	Tonneaux
Cru du Moulin-à-Vent (Baron)	*Illats*	2	5	6
Cru Moulin-à-Vent (Biarnes)	*Illats*	16	40	51
Clos des Moulins-à-Vent	*Cérons*	5	12.5	14
Cru des Moulins-à-Vent (Lafond)	*Cérons*	3	7.5	6
Cru des Moulins-à-Vent (Lapujade, Despujols)	*Cérons*	9	22.5	14
Domaine des Moulins-à-Vent	*Illats*	9	22.5	21
Cru du Noulin	*Cérons*	3	7.5	6
Cru des Parrajots	*Illats*	3	7.5	8
Cru du Perliques	*Illats*	3	7.5	8
Château du Peyrat	*Cérons*	8	20	21
Cru Peyroutene	*Cérons*	4	10	9
Cru Pinaud	*Cérons*	4	10	10
Domaine de Prouzet	*Illats*	7	17.5	13
Château du Roc	*Cérons*	5	12.5	8
Clos des Roches	*Illats*	2	5	6
Cru St.-Roch	*Illats*	2	5	5
Domaine du Salut (*see* Château Huradin)				
Château du Seuil	*Cérons*	3	7.5	13
Château Sylvain	*Cérons*	11	27.5	28
Château Thomé-Brousterot	*Illats*	8	20	18
Château Uferic	*Cérons*	6	15	14
Cru Voltaire	*Cérons*	4	10	7

X LOUPIAC

The following figures of production are approximate, and indicate average annual output, as given by the communes and taken from their Déclarations de Récoltes records.

PRINCIPAL GROWTHS

	Hectares	Acres	Tonneaux
Château Barbe Morin	5	12.5	16
Cru Barberousse	4	10	15
Château Bel-Air	5	12.5	16
Château Bertranon	2	5	5
Château Bouchoc	2	5	4
Château Caudiet	10	25	36
Domaine du Chay	12	30	29
Château Chichoye	2	5	7
Clos de Ciron	4	10	9
Château Clos Jean	12	30	40
Château Couloumet	5	12.5	12
Château du Cros	21	52.5	56
Château Dauphine Rondillon	15	37.5	55
Château de l'Ermitage	2	5	7
Château La Nève	9	22.5	40
Château Le Tarey	5	12.5	13
Château Le Pavillon	4	10	14
Château Loupiac-Gaudiet	10	25	45
Château de Malendure	3	7.5	6
Cru Marges Dusseau	4	10	17
Château Mazarin	16	40	42
Côtes de Mossac	2	5	7
Château Moulin Neuf	10	25	40
Cru du Moulin Vieux	5	12.5	18
Château du Noble	7	17.5	15

	Hectares	Acres	Tonneaux
Château Peyruchet	12	30	34
Cru du Plainier	5	12.5	14
Château Pontac	10	25	36
Château Ricaud	36	90	78
Domaine de Roby	5	12.5	20
Château Rondillon	12	30	40
Cru de Rouquette	8	20	18
Cru de la Sablière	4	10	13
Cru St.-Romain	4	10	11
Château Terrefort	8	20	34
Clos de Terrefort	3	7.5	6
Cru de Terrefort	4	10	16
Cru de Terrefort Pierre Noire	3	7.5	11
Château Turon Lanère (Dalas)	3	7.5	10
Château Turon Lanère (David)	5	12.5	18
Château du Vieux-Moulin	9	22.5	40

XI SAINTE-CROIX-DU-MONT

The following figures of production are approximate, and indicate average annual output, as given by the communes and taken from their Déclarations de Récoltes records.

PRINCIPAL GROWTHS

	Hectares	Acres	Tonneaux
Cru Abraham	4	10	15
Cru Baret-les-Arrivaux	3	7.5	12
Château Bel-Air	12	30	46
Clos Belle-Vue	4	10	17
Château de Bertranon	2	5	9
Château Bouchoc	3	7.5	13
Domaine du Bougan	3	7.5	6
Domaine du Bugat	3	7.5	14
Cru du Canet	3	7.5	6
Château des Coulinats	3	7.5	13
Château Coullac	5	12.5	26
Domaine de Coullander	1	2.5	5
Clos du Crabitan	5	12.5	21
Domaine Damanieu	3	7.5	12
Domaine de l'Escaley	2	5	9
Domaine du Gaël	2	5	10
Cru de Gaillardet	1	2.5	4
Château Gensonne	2	5	5
Cru de Guerisson	3	7.5	7
Château Haut de Baritault	5	12.5	15
Cru Haut-Larrivat	3	7.5	12
Cru Haut-Medouc	3	7.5	15
Domaine de l'If	3	7.5	15
Château Jean-Lamat	4	10	16
Château Laborie	6	15	24
Château La Caussade	5	12.5	20
Domaine de Lacoste	2	5	9
Cru de La Côte Doré	2	5	8
Château Lafuë	10	25	35
Château La Grave	6	15	17
Cru La Grave	2	5	6

	Hectares	Acres	Tonneaux
Château La Gravière	11	27.5	51
Château La Graville	4	10	19
Château Lamarque	15	37.5	60
Château La Mouleyre	4	10	8
Clos La Mouleyre	4	10	16
Cru La Mouleyre	3	7.5	12
Château Lapeyrère	5	12.5	26
Clos l'Arabey	2	5	7
Château La Rame	5	12.5	20
Cru La Rame	6	15	27
Clos Larrivat	3	7.5	13
Château Laurette	15	37.5	66
Château Le Grand Peyrot	5	12.5	11
Clos Le Haut-Crabitan	2	5	8
Château Le Pin	3	7.5	13
Château l'Escaley	5	12.5	23
Clos Les Arrivaux	3	7.5	11
Cru Les Arroucats	2	5	7
Domaine Les Marcottes	4	10	20
Cru Le Tarey	5	12.5	23
Château Loubens	10	25	34
Domaine de Louqsor	1	2.5	5
Château Lousteau Vieil	7	17.5	33
Château des Mailles	6	15	24
Cru Medouc	4	10	8
Clos du Medouc	2	5	7
Cru Medouc La Grave	2	5	8
Château Megnien	3	7.5	13
Château du Mont	7	17.5	30
Cru de Montagne	5	12.5	19
Domaine des Noyers	7	17.5	25
Clos du Palmiers	3	7.5	12
Domaine de Pampelune	3	7.5	15
Domaine de Parenteau	4	10	19
Château du Pavillon	4	10	17
Cru Peillot	2	5	9
Cru du Pin	2	5	6
Château de la Princesse	2	5	9
Château Roustit	9	22.5	40
Château de Tastes	6	15	18
Château Terfort	3	7.5	11
Cru du Terrefort	2	5	9
Château Vertheuil	10	25	25
Domaine du Vignots	2	5	7

XII BOURG

The following is a list of some of the more important of the many hundreds of wine châteaux in the region.

Name	Commune	Name	Commune
Domaine des Augiers	*Comps*	Château Berthou	*Comps*
Château de Barbe	*Villeneuve*	Château de Blissa	*Bayon*
Château Barrieux	*Samonac*	Domaine de Bonne	*Gauriac*
Château Bégot	*Lansac*	Domaine de Bouche	*Samonac*
Domaine de Bel-Air	*Samonac*	Château de Bousquet	*Bourg*
Château Belleroque	*Bourg*	Domaine de Bujan	*Gauriac*

Name	Commune	Name	Commune
Château Cambes-Kermovan	*Bourg*	Château La Tour-Seguy	*St.-Ciers-de-Canesse*
Château Caruel	*Bourg*	Château Laurensanne	*St.-Seurin-Bourg*
Domaine de Christoly	*Prignac-Marcamps*	Château Le Mugron	*Prignac-Marcamps*
Château Colbert	*Comps*	Château Macay	*Samonac*
Château Cottière	*Teuillac*	Château de Maco	*Tauriac*
Château de la Croix (Millorit)	*Bayon*	Domaine de Marquisat	*Lansac*
Château Croûte-Charlus	*Bourg*	Château Mendoce	*Villeneuve*
Château Croûte-Mallard	*Bourg*	Château Mille-Secousses	*Bourg*
Château du Domaine de Descazeaux	*Gauriac*	Château de la Monge	*Bourg*
Château Eyquem	*Bayon*	Château Nodoz	*Tauriac*
Château Falfas	*Bayon*	Domaine de Noriou-Lalibarde	*Bourg*
Domaine de Fonbonne	*Teuillac*	Château Peychaud	*Teuillac*
Château Grand-Jour	*Prignac-Marcamps*	Domaine de Peyror	*Gauriac*
Château de la Grave	*Bourg*	Château Poyanne	*Gauriac*
Château de Grissac	*Prignac-Marcamps*	Château Rebeymond-Lalibard	*Bourg*
Château Gros-Moulin	*Bourg*	Château Rebeymont	*Bourg*
Domaine de Guerrit	*Tauriac*	Château des Richards	*Mombrier*
Château Guienne	*Lansac*	Château Rider	*Bourg*
Château Guiraud	*St.-Ciers-de-Canesse*	Domaine de Ribereau	*Pugnac*
Château de Haut-Gravat	*Bourg*	Château Rousselle	*St.-Ciers-de-Canesse*
Château La Barde	*Tauriac*	Château Rousset	*Samonac*
Château Lagrange	*Bourg*	Clos de Seillas	*Gauriac*
Château La Grolet	*St.-Ciers-de-Canesse*	Château de Taste	*Lansac*
Château Lalibarde	*Bourg*	Château Tayac	*Bayon*
Domaine de Lalibarde	*Bourg*	Château de Thau	*Gauriac*
Château Lamothe	*Lansac*	Domaine de Viaud	*Pugnac*

XIII BLAYE

Following are a few of the more important wine properties.

Name	Commune	Name	Commune
Château Barbet	*Cars*	Château Lafont	*Cartelègue*
Château Bellevue	*Cars*	Château La Garde	*St.-Seurin-Cursac*
Château Berthenon	*St.-Paul*	Château La Garde Roland	*St.-Seurin-Cursac*
Château Chaillou	*St.-Paul*	Château La Girouette	*Fours*
Château Breuil	*St.-Martin-Caussade*	Château Lagrange	*Blaye*
Château Cantemerle	*St.-Genès*	Château La Hargue	*Plassac*
Château Cazeaux	*St.-Paul*	Château Lamothe	*St.-Paul*
Domaine du Chai	*Fours*	Château La Perotte	*Eyrons*
Château Charron	*St.-Martin*	Château Lassale	*St.-Genès*
Château Chasselauds	*Cartelègue*	Château La Taure Ste.-Luce	*Blaye*
Château Clos d'Amières	*Cartelègue*	Château La Tour Gayet	*St.-Androny*
Château Crusquet de Lagarcie	*Cars*	Château Le Cone Moreau	*Blaye*
Château Crusquet Sabourin	*Cars*	Château Le Cone Sebilleau	*Blaye*
Château Dupeyrat	*St.-Paul*	Château Le Cone Taillasson	*Blaye*
Château Gadeau	*Plassac*	Château Le Menaudat	*St.-Androny*
Château Gigault	*Mazion*	Château Les Alberts	*Mazion*
Château Gontier	*Blaye*	Château Les Bavolliers	*St.-Christ-de-Blaye*
Château Gontier	*Blaye-Plassac*	Château Lescadre	*Cadres*
Domaine de Graulet	*Plassac*	Château Les Chaumes	*Fours*
Château Guillonnet	*Anglade*	Château Les Moines	*Blaye*
Château Haut-Cabat	*Anglade*	Château Les Pts Arnauds	*Cars*
Château Haut-Sociondo	*Cars*	Château Les Ricards	*Cars*
Château La Bertonnière	*Plassac*	Château Le Virou	*St.-Girons*
Château La Brousse	*St. Martin-Caussade*	Château Mayence	*Mazion*
Château La Cabane	*St. Martin-Caussade*	Château Mazerolles	*Cars*
Château La Cave	*Blaye*	Château Monconseil	*Plassac*
Château La Cure	*Cars*	Moulin de la Pitance	*St.-Girons*

Blaye

Name	Commune	Name	Commune
Château Pardaillan	Cars	Château Puy Beney	Mazion
Château Perrein	Mazion	Château Puy Beney Lafitte	Mazion
Château Peyrebrune	Cartelègue	Château Rebouquet	Berson
Château Pinet	Berson	Château Ricadet	Cartelègue
Château Pinet La Roquete	Berson	Château Segonzac	St.-Genès-de-Blaye

NOTE. In addition to all the châteaux listed in this Appendix there are approximately 1,500 others in the communes of Bordeaux which do not have separate listings.

German Wines

The *Bestimmtes Anbaugebiet* is a designated region carrying the official name of each of the eleven German wine-producing areas. Each of these largest regions is divided into one or more sub-regions, or districts, called a *Bereich*. Within the *Bereich* are found the separate villages and the vineyards associated with them. These towns or communes may be variously called *Weinbauort, Gemeinde,* or *Gemarkung.* As for the vineyards themselves, an individual plot is called an *Einzellage;* but all of the *Einzellagen* are officially grouped into sections of vineyards named *Grosslagen. See* Germany.

I ANBAUGEBIET (region): AHR

BEREICH (sub-region): WALPORZHEIM/AHRTAL

GROSSLAGE (SECTION OF VINEYARDS): KLOSTERBERG

Weinbauort (village)	Einzellage (vineyard)	Weinbauort (village)	Einzellage (vineyard)
Ahrweiler	Daubhaus	Heppingen	Berg
	Forstberg	Marienthal	Jesuitengarten
	Riegelfeld		Klostergarten
	Rosenthal		Rosenberg
	Silberberg		Stiftsberg
	Ursulinengarten		Trotzenberg
Altenahr	Eck	Mayschoss	Burgberg
	Übigberg		Laacherberg
Bachem	Karlskopf		Lochmühlerley
	Sonnenschein		Mönchberg
	Steinkaul		Schieferley
Bad Neuenahr	Kirchtürmchen		Silberberg
	Schieferley	Rech	Blume
	Sonnenberg		Hardtberg
Dernau	Burggarten		Herrenberg
	Goldkaul	Walporzheim	Alte Lay
	Hardtberg		Domlay
	Pfarrwingert		Gärkammer
	Schieferlay		Himmelchen
Heimersheim	Burggarten		Kräuterberg
	Kapellenberg		Pfaffenberg
	Landskrone		

II ANBAUGEBIET (region): BADEN

BEREICH (sub-region): BADISCHE BERGSTRASSE/KRAICHGAU

GROSSLAGE (SECTION OF VINEYARDS): HOHENBERG

Weinbauort (village)	Einzellage (vineyard)	Weinbauort (village)	Einzellage (vineyard)
Berghausen	Sonnenberg	Grötzingen	Lichtenberg
Bilfingen	Klepberg		Turmberg
Dietlingen	Keulebuckel	Hohenwettersbach	Rosengarten
	Klepberg	Karlsruhe-Durlach	Turmberg
Dürrn	Eichelberg	Söllingen	Rotenbusch
Ellmendingen	Keulebuckel	Walzbachtal (Ortsteil Jöhlingen)	Hasensprung
Eisingen	Klepberg	Weingarten	Katzenberg
	Steig		Petersberg
Ersingen	Klepberg	Wöschbach	Steinwengert

GROSSLAGE (SECTION OF VINEYARDS): MANNABERG

Weinbauort (village)	Einzellage (vineyard)
Bad Mingolsheim-Langenbrücken, Ortsteil Bad Langenbrücken, Ortsteil Bad Mingolsheim	Goldberg
Bruchsal (Stadtteil Obergrombach)	Burgwingert
Bruchsal	Klosterberg
Bruchsal (Stadtteil Untergrombach)	Michaelsberg
	Weinhecke
Dielheim	Rosenberg
	Teufelskopf
Heidelberg	Burg
	Dachsbuckel
	Herrenberg
Heidelsheim	Altenberg
Helmsheim	Burgwingert
Horrenberg	Osterberg
Kraichtal (Stadtteil Oberöwisheim, Stadtteil Unteröwisheim)	Kirchberg
Leimen	Herrenberg
	Kreuzweg
Malsch	Ölbaum
	Rotsteig
Malschenberg	Ölbaum
Mühlhausen	Heiligenstein
Nussloch	Wilhelmsberg
Östringen	Hummelberg
	Rosenkranzweg
	Ulrichsberg
Rauenberg	Burggraf
Rettigheim	Ölbaum
Rotenberg	Schlossberg
Tairnbach	Rosenberg
Ubstadt-Weiher (Ortsteil Stettfeld)	Himmelreich
Ubstadt-Weiher (Ortsteil Ubstadt)	Weinhecke
Wiesloch	Bergwäldle
	Hägenich
	Spitzenberg
Zeutern	Himmelreich

GROSSLAGE (SECTION OF VINEYARDS): STIFTSBERG

Weinbauort (village)	Einzellage (vineyard)
Bauerbach	Lerchenberg
Binau	Herzogsberg
Diedesheim	Herzogsberg
Eberbach	Schollerbuckel
Eichelberg	Kapellenberg
Eichtersheim	Sonnenberg
Elsenz	Spiegelberg
Eppingen	Lerchenberg
Eschelbach	Sonnenberg
Flehingen	Lerchenberg
Gemmingen	Vogelsang
Hassmersheim	Kirchweinberg
Heinsheim	Burg Ehrenberg
Herbolzheim	Berg
Kirchardt (Ortsteil Berwangen)	Vogelsang
Kraichtal (Stadtteil Bahnbrücken, Stadtteil Gochsheim, Stadtteil Oberacker)	Lerchenberg

Weinbauort (village)	Einzellage (vineyard)
Kraichtal (Stadtteil Neuenbürg, Stadtteil Menzingen, Stadtteil Münzesheim)	Silberberg
Kraichtal (Stadtteil Landshausen, Stadtteil Menzingen)	Spiegelberg
Kürnbach	Lerchenberg
Michelfeld	Himmelberg
	Sonnenberg
Mühlbach	Lerchenberg
Neckarmühlbach	Hohberg
Neckarzimmern	Götzhalde
	Kirchweinberg
	Wallmauer
Neudenau	Berg
Odenheim	Königsbecher
Rohrbach a. G.	Lerchenberg
Sinsheim (Stadtteil Hilsbach)	Eichelberg
Sinsheim (Stadtteil Weiler)	Goldberg
	Steinsberg
Steinsfurt	Steinsberg
Sulzfeld	Burg Ravensburger Dicker Franz
	Burg Ravensburger Husarenkappe
	Burg Ravensburger Löchle
	Lerchenberg
Tiefenbach	Schellenbrunnen
	Spiegelberg
Waldangelloch	Sonnenberg
Zaisenhausen	Lerchenberg

GROSSLAGE (SECTION OF VINEYARDS): RITTERSBERG

Weinbauort (village)	Einzellage (vineyard)
Dossenheim	Ölberg
Grossachsen	Sandrocken
Heidelberg	Heiligenberg
	Sonnenseite ob der Bruck
Hemsbach	Herrnwingert
Hohensachsen	Stephansberg
Laudenbach	Sonnberg
Leutershausen	Kahlberg
	Staudenberg
Lützelsachsen	Stephansberg
Schriesheim	Kuhberg
	Madonnenberg
	Schlossberg
	Staudenberg
Sulzbach	Herrnwingert
Weinheim	Hubberg
	Wüstberg

BEREICH (sub-region): BADISCHES FRANKENLAND
GROSSLAGE (SECTION OF VINEYARDS): TAUBERKLINGE

Weinbauort (village)	Einzellage (vineyard)
Beckstein	Kirchberg
	Nonnenberg
Boxberg (Stadtteil Unterschüpf)	Mühlberg
Dertingen	Mandelberg
	Sonnenberg

Weinbauort (village)	Einzellage (vineyard)
Gerlachsheim	Herrenberg
Grossrinderfeld	Beilberg
Höhefeld	Kemelrain
Kembach	Sonnenberg
Königheim	Kirchberg
Königshofen	Kirchberg
	Turmberg
	Walterstal
Krautheim	Heiligenberg
Krautheim (Stadtteil Klepsau)	Heiligenberg
Külsheim	Hoher Herrgott
Lauda	Altenberg
	Frankenberg
	Nonnenberg
Lindelbach	Ebenrain
Marbach	Frankenberg
Oberlauda	Altenberg
	Steinklinge
Oberschüpf	Altenberg
	Herrenberg
Reicholzheim	First
	Kemelrain
	Satzenberg
Sachsenflur	Kailberg
Tauberbischofsheim	Edelberg
Tauberbischofsheim	Silberquell
(Ortsteil Impfingen)	
Uissigheim	Stahlberg
Werbach	Beilberg
	Hirschberg
Wertheim	Schlossberg

BEREICH (sub-region): BODENSEE
GROSSLAGE (SECTION OF VINEYARDS): SONNENUFER

Weinbauort (village)	Einzellage (vineyard)
Bermatingen	Leopoldsberg
Bodman	Königsweingarten
Hagnau	Burgstall
Hilzingen	Elisabethenberg
Immenstaad	Burgstall
Kippenhausen	Burgstall
Konstanz	Sonnenhalde
Markdorf	Burgstall
	Sängerhalde
Meersburg	Bengel
	Chorherrnhalde
	Fohrenberg
	Haltnau
	Jungfernstieg
	Lerchenberg
	Rieschen
	Sängerhalde
Oberuhldingen	Kirchhalde
Reichenau	Hochwart
Salem (Ortsteil Kirchberg)	Schlossberg
Singen	Elisabethenberg
	Olgaberg
Stetten	Fohrenberg
	Lerchenberg
	Sängerhalde

Weinbauort (village)	Einzellage (vineyard)
Überlingen	Felsengarten

Not yet assigned a *Grosslage* (section of vineyards):

Weinbauort (village)	Einzellage (vineyard)
Klettgau (Ortsteil Erzingen)	Kapellenberg
Klettgau (Ortsteil Rechberg)	Kapellenberg
Lottstetten (Ortsteil Nack)	Steinler

BEREICH (sub-region): MARKGRÄFLERLAND
GROSSLAGE (SECTION OF VINEYARDS): VOGTEI RÖTTELN

Weinbauort (village)	Einzellage (vineyard)
Bamlach	Kapellenberg
Binzen	Sonnhohle
Blansingen	Wolfer
Efringen-Kirchen	Kirchberg
	Oelberg
	Sonnhohle
	Steingässle
Egringen	Sonnhohle
Eimeldingen	Sonnhohle
Feuerbach	Steingässle
Fischingen	Sonnhohle
Grenzach	Hornfelsen
Haltingen	Stiege
Herten	Steinacker
Hertingen	Sonnhohle
Holzen	Steingässle
Huttingen	Kirchberg
Istein	Kirchberg
Kleinkems	Wolfer
Lörrach	Sonnenbrunnen
Ötlingen	Sonnhohle
	Stiege
Rheinweiler	Kapellenberg
Riedlingen	Steingässle
Rümmingen	Sonnhohle
Schallbach	Sonnhohle
Tannenkirch	Steingässle
Weil am Rhein	Schlipf
	Stiege
Welmlingen	Steingässle
Wintersweiler	Steingässle
Wollbach	Steingässle

GROSSLAGE (SECTION OF VINEYARDS): BURG NEUENFELS

Weinbauort (village)	Einzellage (vineyard)
Auggen	Letten
	Schäf
Bad Bellingen	Sonnenstück
Badenweiler	Römerberg
Ballrechten-Dottingen	Altenberg
	Castellberg
Britzingen	Altenberg
	Rosenberg
	Sonnhohle
Britzingen (Ortsteil Dattingen)	Altenberg
	Rosenberg
	Sonnhohle
Feldberg	Paradies

Weinbauort (village)	Einzellage (vineyard)
Hügelheim	Gottesacker
	Höllberg
	Schlossgarten
Laufen	Altenberg
Liel	Sonnenstück
Lipburg	Kirchberg
Mauchen	Frauenberg
	Sonnenstück
Müllheim	Pfaffenstück
	Reggenhag
	Sonnhalde
Niedereggenen	Röthen
	Sonnenstück
Neiderweiler	Römerberg
Obereggenen	Röthen
Schliengen	Sonnenstück
Steinenstadt	Schäf
	Sonnenstück
Sulzburg	Altenberg
Zunzingen	Rosenberg

GROSSLAGE (SECTION OF VINEYARDS): LORETTOBERG

Weinbauort (village)	Einzellage (vineyard)
Bad Krotzingen	Steingrüble
Biengen	Maltesergarten
Bollschweil	Steinberg
Buggingen	Höllberg
	Maltesergarten
Ebringen	Sommerberg
Ehrenstetten	Oelberg
	Rosenberg
Eschbach	Maltesergarten
Freiburg i. Br.	Jesuitenschloss
	Steinler
Grunern	Altenberg
	Schlossberg
Heitersheim	Maltesergarten
	Sonnhohle
Kirchhofen	Batzenberg
	Höllhagen
	Kirchberg
Mengen	Alemannenbuck
Merzhausen	Jesuitenschloss
Norsingen	Batzenberg
Pfaffenweiler	Batzenberg
	Oberdürrenberg
Schallstadt-Wolfenweile	Batzenberg
	Dürrenberg
Scherzingen	Batzenberg
Schlatt	Maltesergarten
	Steingrüble
Seefelden	Maltesergarten
Staufen	Schlossberg
Staufen (Ortsteil Wettelbrunn)	Maltesergarten
Tunsel	Maltesergarten
Wittnau	Kapuzinerbuck

BEREICH (sub-region): KAISERSTUHL-TUNIBERG
GROSSLAGE (SECTION OF VINEYARDS): ATTILAFELSEN

Weinbauort (village)	Einzellage (vineyard)
Gottenheim	Kirchberg
Merdingen	Bühl
Munzingen	Kapellenberg
Niederrimsingen	Rotgrund
Oberrimsingen	Franziskaner
Opfingen	Sonnenberg
Tiengen	Rebtal
Waltershofen	Steinmauer

GROSSLAGE (SECTION OF VINEYARDS): VULKANFELSEN

Weinbauort (village)	Einzellage (vineyard)
Achkarren	Castellberg
	Schlossberg
Amoltern	Steinhalde
Bahlingen	Silberberg
Bickensohl	Herrenstück
	Steinfelsen
Bischoffingen	Enselberg
	Rosenkranz
	Steinbuck
Bötzingen	Eckberg
	Lasenberg
Breisach a. Rh.	Augustinerberg
	Eckartsberg
Burkheim	Feuerberg
	Schlossgarten
Endingen	Engelsberg
	Steingrube
	Tannacker
Eichstetten	Herrenbuck
	Lerchenberg
Ihringen	Castellberg
	Fohrenberg
	Kreuzhalde
	Schlossberg
	Steinfelsen
	Winklerberg
Ihringen (Ortsteil Blankenhornsberg)	Doktorgarten
Jechtingen	Eichert
	Enselberg
	Gestühl
	Hochberg
	Steingrube
Kiechlinsbergen	Ölberg
	Teufelsburg
Königschaffhausen	Hasenberg
	Steingrüble
Leiselheim	Gestühl
Neuershausen	Steingrube
Nimburg	Steingrube
Oberbergen	Bassgeige
	Pulverbuck

Weinbauort (village)	Einzellage (vineyard)
Oberrotweil	Eichberg
	Henkenberg
	Käsleberg
	Kirchberg
	Schlossberg
Riegel	St. Michaelsberg
Sasbach	Limburg
	Lützelberg
	Rote Halde
	Scheibenbuck
Schelingen	Kirchberg
Wasenweiler	Kreuzhalde
	Lotberg

BEREICH (sub-region): BREISGAU

GROSSLAGE (SECTION OF VINEYARDS): BURG ZÄHRINGEN

Weinbauort (village)	Einzellage (vineyard)
Buchholz	Sonnhalde
Denzlingen	Eichberg
	Sonnhalde
Emmendingen (Ortsteil Hochburg)	Halde
Freiburg i. Br. (Ortsteil Lehen)	Bergle
	Schlossberg
Glottertal	Eichberg
	Roter Bur
Heuweiler	Eichberg
Sexau	Sonnhalde
Wildtal	Sonnenberg

GROSSLAGE (SECTION OF VINEYARDS): BURG LICHTENECK

Weinbauort (village)	Einzellage (vineyard)
Altdorf	Kaiserberg
Bleichheim	Kaiserberg
Bombach	Sommerhalde
Broggingen	Kaiserberg
Ettenheim	Kaiserberg
Hecklingen	Schlossberg
Heimbach	Bienenberg
Herbolzheim	Kaiserberg
Kenzingen	Hummelberg
	Roter Berg
Köndringen	Alte Burg
Malterdingen	Bienenberg
Mundingen	Alte Burg
Nordweil	Herrenberg
Ringsheim	Kaiserberg
Tutschfelden	Kaiserberg
Wagenstadt	Hummelberg

GROSSLAGE (SECTION OF VINEYARDS): SCHUTTERLINDENBERG

Weinbauort (village)	Einzellage (vineyard)
Ettenheim (Ortsteil Wallburg)	Kirchberg
Friesenheim	Kronenbühl
Heiligenzell	Kronenbühl
Hugsweier	Kronenbühl
Kippenheim	Haselstaude
Lahr	Herrentisch
	Kronenbühl
Mahlberg	Haselstaude
Mietersheim	Kronenbühl
Münchweiler	Kirchberg
Oberschopfheim	Kronenbühl
Oberweier	Kronenbühl
Schmieheim	Kirchberg
Sulz	Haselstaude

BEREICH (sub-region): ORTENAU

GROSSLAGE (SECTION OF VINEYARDS): FÜRSTENECK

Weinbauort (village)	Einzellage (vineyard)
Berghaupten	Kinzigtäler
Bermersbach	Kinzigtäler
Bottenau	Renchtäler
Diersburg	Kinzigtäler
	Schlossberg
Durbach	Bienengarten
	Josephsberg
	Kapellenberg
	Kasselberg
	Kochberg
	Ölberg
	Plauelrain
	Schlossberg
	Schloss Grohl
	Steinberg
Erlach	Renchtäler
Gengenbach	Kinzigtäler
	Nollenköpfle
Hofweier	Kinzigtäler
Lautenbach	Renchtäler
Nesselried	Renchtäler
	Schlossberg
Niederschopfheim	Kinzigtäler
Nussbach	Renchtäler
Offenburg (Ortsteil Zell-Weierbach)	Abtsberg
Offenburg (Ortsteil Fessenbach)	Bergle
	Franzensberger
Oberkirch	Renchtäler
Oberkirch (Ortsteil Haslach)	Renchtäler
Ödsbach	Renchtäler
Ohlsbach	Kinzigtäler
Ortenberg	Andreasberg
	Franzensberger
	Freudental
	Schlossberg
Rammersweier	Kreuzberg
Reichenbach	Amselberg
	Kinzigtäler
Ringelbach	Renchtäler
Stadelhofen	Renchtäler
Tiergarten	Renchtäler
Ulm	Renchtäler
Zunsweier	Kinzigtäler

GROSSLAGE (SECTION OF VINEYARDS): SCHLOSS RODECK

Weinbauort (village)	Einzellage (vineyard)
Achern (Ortsteil Oberachern)	Alter Gott
	Bienenberg
Altschweier	Sternenberg
Baden-Baden	Eckberg
	Sätzler
Bühl (Ortsteil Neusatz)	Burg Windeck
	Kastanienhalde
	Sternenberg
	Wolfhag
Bühlertal	Engelsfelsen
	Klotzberg
Eisental	Betschgräbler
	Sommerhalde
Kappelrodeck	Hex vom Dasenstein
Lauf	Alter Gott
	Gut Alsenhof
	Schloss Neu-Windeck
Mösbach	Kreuzberg
Neuweier	Altenberg
	Gänsberg
	Heiligenstein
	Mauerberg
	Schlossberg

Weinbauort (village)	Einzellage (vineyard)
Obersasbach	Alter Gott
	Eichwäldele
Obertsrot	Grafensprung
Ottersweier	Althof
	Wolfhag
Renchen	Kreuzberg
Sasbachwalden	Alter Gott
	Klostergut Schelzberg
Sinzheim	Frühmessler
	Fremersberger
	Feigenwäldchen
	Klostergut
	Sätzler
	Sonnenberg
Steinbach	Stich den Buben
	Yburgberg
Varnhalt	Klosterbergfelsen
	Sonnenberg
	Steingrübler
Waldulm	Kreuzberg
	Pfarrberg
Weisenbach	Kestelberg

III   ANBAUGEBIET (region): HESSISCHE BERGSTRASSE

BEREICH (sub-region): STARKENBURG

GROSSLAGE (SECTION OF VINEYARDS): SCHLOSSBERG

Weinbauort (village)	Einzellage (vineyard)
Heppenheim (including Erbach and Hambach)	Eckweg
	Guldenzoll
	Maiberg
	Steinkopf
	Stemmler
	Zentgericht

GROSSLAGE (SECTION OF VINEYARDS): WOLFSMAGEN

Weinbauort (village)	Einzellage (vineyard)
Bensheim	Hemsberg
	Kalkgasse
	Kirchberg
	Paulus
	Streichling

GROSSLAGE (SECTION OF VINEYARDS): ROTT

Weinbauort (village)	Einzellage (vineyard)
Auerbach	Fürstenlager
	Höllberg
Schönberg	Herrnwingert

Not yet assigned a Grosslage (section of vineyards):

Seeheim	Mundklingen
Zwingenberg	Alte Burg
	Steingeröll

BEREICH (sub-region): UMSTADT

Weinbauort (village)	Einzellage (vineyard)
Dietzenbach	Wingertsberg
Gross Umstadt	Herrnberg
	Stachelberg
	Steingerück
Klein-Umstadt	
Rossdorf	Rossberg

IV ANBAUGEBIET (region): FRANKEN

BEREICH (sub-region): MAINVIERECK

GROSSLAGE (SECTION OF VINEYARDS): REUSCHBERG

Weinbauort (village)	Einzellage (vineyard)
Hörstein	Abtsberg

GROSSLAGE (SECTION OF VINEYARDS): HEILIGENTHAL

Weinbauort (village)	Einzellage (vineyard)
Grossostheim	Reischklingeberg
	Harstell
Wenigumstadt	Residual vineyards

Not yet assigned a *Grosslage* (section of vineyards):

Weinbauort (village)	Einzellage (vineyard)
Aschaffenburg	Pompejaner
Bürgstadt	Centgrafenberg
	Mainhölle
Dorfprozelten	Predigtstuhl
Engelsberg	Klostergarten
Erlenbach a. Main	Hochberg
Grossheubach	Bischofsberg
Grosswallstadt	Lützeltalerberg
Klingenberg	Hochberg
	Schlossberg
Kreuzwertheim	Kaffelstein
Michelbach	Apostelgarten
	Steinberg
Miltenberg	Steingrübler
Rück	Jesuitenberg
	Johannisberg
Wasserlos	Schlossberg

BEREICH (sub-region): MAINDREIECK

GROSSLAGE (SECTION OF VINEYARDS): KIRCHBERG

Weinbauort (village)	Einzellage (vineyard)
Astheim	Karthäuser
Escherndorf	Berg
	Fürstenberg
	Lump
Fahr	Residual vineyards
Köhler	Residual vineyards
Krautheim	Sonnenleite
Neuses	Glatzen
Neusetz	Residual vineyards
Nordheim	Kreuzberg
	Vögelein
Obereisenheim	Höll
Obervolkach	Landsknecht
Sommerach	Katzenkopf
	Rosenberg
Stammheim	Eselsberg
Untereisenheim	Sonnenberg
Volkach	Ratsherr
Wipfeld	Zehntgraf

GROSSLAGE (SECTION OF VINEYARDS): BURG

Weinbauort (village)	Einzellage (vineyard)
Hammelburg	Heroldsberg
	Trautlestal
Ramsthal	St. Klausen
Saaleck	Schlossberg
Wirmsthal	Scheinberg

GROSSLAGE (SECTION OF VINEYARDS): ROSSTAL

Weinbauort (village)	Einzellage (vineyard)
Arnstein	Residual vineyards
Eussenheim	First
Gambach	Kalbenstein
Gössenheim	Arnberg
Himmelstadt	Kelter
Karlburg	Residual vineyards
Karlstadt	Im Stein
Laudenbach	Residual vineyards
Mühlbach	Residual vineyards
Retzstadt	Langenberg
Stetten	Stein

GROSSLAGE (SECTION OF VINEYARDS): HONIGBERG

Weinbauort (village)	Einzellage (vineyard)
Dettelbach	Berg-Rondell
	Sonnenleite

GROSSLAGE (SECTION OF VINEYARDS): HOFRAT

Weinbauort (village)	Einzellage (vineyard)
Buchbrunn	Heisser Stein
Kitzingen	Wilhelmsberg
Mainstockheim	Hofstück
Marktbreit	Sonnenberg
Repperndorf	Kaiser Karl
Segnitz	Pfaffensteig
	Zobelsberg
Sulzfeld	Cyriakusberg
	Maustal

GROSSLAGE (SECTION OF VINEYARDS): EWIG LEBEN

Weinbauort (village)	Einzellage (vineyard)
Randersacker	Marsberg
	Pfülben
	Sonnenstuhl
	Teufelskeller

GROSSLAGE (SECTION OF VINEYARDS): RAVENSBURG

Weinbauort (village)	Einzellage (vineyard)
Erlabrunn	Weinsteig
Güntersleben	Sommerstuhl
Retzbach	Benediktusberg
Thüngersheim	Johannisberg
	Scharlachberg
Veitshöchheim	Wölflein

Not yet assigned a *Grosslage* (section of vineyards):

Weinbauort (village)	Einzellage (vineyard)
Böttigheim	Wurmberg
Eibelstadt	Kapellenberg
	Mönchsleite
Erlenbach bei Marktheidenfeld	Krähenschnabel
Frankenwinheim	Rosenberg
Frickenhausen am Main	Fischer
	Kapellenberg
	Markgraf Babenberg
Hallburg	Schlossberg
Homburg	Edelfrau
	Kallmuth
Lengfurt	Alter Berg
	Oberrot

Weinbauort (village)	Einzellage (vineyard)
Randersacker	Dabug
Rimpar	Kobersberg
Röttingen	Feuerstein
Schweinfurt	Mainleite
	Peterstirn
Sommerhausen	Reifenstein
	Steinbach
Tauberrettersheim	Königin
Veitshöchheim	Sonnenschein
Würzburg	Abtsleite
	Innere Leiste
	Kirchberg
	Pfaffenberg
	Schlossberg
	Stein
	Stein/Harfe

BEREICH (sub-region): STEIGERWALD

GROSSLAGE (SECTION OF VINEYARDS): SCHILD

Weinbauort (village)	Einzellage (vineyard)
Abtswind	Altenberg
Castell	Bausch
	Kirchberg
Greuth	Bastel

GROSSLAGE (SECTION OF VINEYARDS): HERRENBERG

Weinbauort (village)	Einzellage (vineyard)
Castell	Bausch
	Feuerbach
	Hohnart
	Kirchberg
	Kugelspiel
	Reitsteig
	Schlossberg
	Trautberg

GROSSLAGE (SECTION OF VINEYARDS): KAPELLENBERG

Weinbauort (village)	Einzellage (vineyard)
Schmachtenberg	Eulengrund
Steinbach	Nonnenberg
Zeil	Kronberg
Ziegelanger	Ölschnabel

GROSSLAGE (SECTION OF VINEYARDS): SCHLOSSBERG

Weinbauort (village)	Einzellage (vineyard)
Grosslangheim	Kiliansberg
Rödelsee	Küchenmeister
	Schwanleite
Sickershausen	Storchenbrünnle
Wiesenbronn	Wachhügel

GROSSLAGE (SECTION OF VINEYARDS): BURGWEG

Weinbauort (village)	Einzellage (vineyard)
Iphofen	Julius-Echter-Berg
	Kalb
	Kronsberg
Markt Einersheim	Vogelsang
Possenheim	Residual vineyards

GROSSLAGE (SECTION OF VINEYARDS): SCHLOSSTÜCK

Weinbauort (village)	Einzellage (vineyard)
Bullenheim	Paradies
Ergersheim	Altenberg
Frankenberg	Herrschaftsberg
Hüttenheim	Tannenberg
Ippesheim	Herrschaftsberg
Seinsheim	Hohenbühl
Weimersheim	Roter Berg

Not yet assigned a *Grosslage* (section of vineyards):

Weinbauort (village)	Einzellage (vineyard)
Altmannsdorf	Sonnenwinkel
Handthal	Stollberg
Kammerforst	Teufel
Kleinlangheim	Wutschenberg
Martinsheim	Langenstein
Michelau i. Steigerwald	Vollburg
Oberschwarzach	Herrenberg
Zeil a. Main	Mönchshang

BEREICH (sub-region): BAYER. BODENSEE

Weinbauort (village)	Einzellage (vineyard)
Nonnenhorn	Seehalde
	Sonnenbüchel

V ANBAUGEBIET (region): MITTELRHEIN

BEREICH (sub-region): BACHARACH

GROSSLAGE (SECTION OF VINEYARDS): SCHLOSS REICHENSTEIN

Weinbauort (village)	Einzellage (vineyard)
Niederheimbach	Froher Weingarten
	Reifersley
	Schloss Hohneck
	Soonecker Schlossberg
Oberheimbach	Klosterberg
	Römerberg
	Sonne
	Wahrheit
Trechtingshausen	Morgenbachtaler

GROSSLAGE (SECTION OF VINEYARDS): SCHLOSS STAHLECK

Weinbauort (village)	Einzellage (vineyard)
Bacharach	Hahn
	Insel Heylesern Wert
	Kloster Fürstental
	Mathias Weingarten
	Posten
	Wolfshöhle
Bacharach/Steeg	Hambusch
	Lennenborn
	St. Jost
	Schloss Stahlberg

Weinbauort (village)	Einzellage (vineyard)
Manubach	Heilgarten
	Langgarten
	Mönchwingert
	St. Oswald
Oberdiebach	Bischofshub
	Fürstenberg
	Kräuterberg
	Rheinberg

BEREICH (sub-region): RHEINBURGENGAU

GROSSLAGE (SECTION OF VINEYARDS): BURG HAMMERSTEIN

Weinbauort (village)	Einzellage (vineyard)
Bad Hönningen	Schlossberg
Dattenberg	Gertrudenberg
Hammerstein	Hölle
	In den Layfelsen
	Schlossberg
Kasbach	Stehlerberg
Leubsdorf	Weisses Kreuz
Leutesdorf	Forstberg
	Gartenlay
	Rosenberg
Linz	Rheinhöller
Rheinbrohl	Monte Jup
	Römerberg
Unkel	Berg
	Sonnenberg

GROSSLAGE (SECTION OF VINEYARDS): BURG RHEINFELS

Weinbauort (village)	Einzellage (vineyard)
St. Goar-Werlau	Ameisenberg
	Frohwingert
	Kuhstall
	Rosenberg

GROSSLAGE (SECTION OF VINEYARDS): GEDEONSECK

Weinbauort (village)	Einzellage (vineyard)
Boppard	Elfenlay
	Engelstein
	Fässerlay
	Feuerlay
	Mandelstein
	Ohlenberg
	Weingrube
Brey	Hämmchen
Rhens	König Wenzel
	Sonnenlay
Spay	Engelstein

GROSSLAGE (SECTION OF VINEYARDS): HERRENBERG

Weinbauort (village)	Einzellage (vineyard)
Dörscheid	Kupferflöz
	Wolfsnack
Kaub	Backofen
	Blüchertal
	Burg Gutenfels
	Pfalzgrafenstein
	Rauschelay
	Rosstein

GROSSLAGE (SECTION OF VINEYARDS): LORELEYFELSEN

Weinbauort (village)	Einzellage (vineyard)
Bornich	Rothenack
Kamp-Bornhofen-Kestert	Liebenstein-Sterrenberg
	Pilgerpfad
Nochern	Brünnchen
Patersberg	Teufelstein
St. Goarshausen	Burg Katz
	Burg Maus
	Hessern
	Loreley-Edel

GROSSLAGE (SECTION OF VINEYARDS): MARKSBURG

Weinbauort (village)	Einzellage (vineyard)
Braubach	Marmorberg
	Mühlberg
	Koppelstein
Filsen	Pfarrgarten
Koblenz-Ehrenbreitstein	Kreuzberg
Lahnstein	Koppelstein
Osterspai	Liebeneck-Sonnenlay
Urbar	Rheinnieder
Vallendar	Rheinnieder

GROSSLAGE (SECTION OF VINEYARDS): LAHNTAL

Weinbauort (village)	Einzellage (vineyard)
Bad Ems	Hasenberg
Dausenau	Hasenberg
Fachbach	Sites not chosen
Nassau	Schlossberg
Obernhof	Goetheberg
Weinähr	Giebelhöll

GROSSLAGE (SECTION OF VINEYARDS): SCHLOSS SCHÖNBURG

Weinbauort (village)	Einzellage (vineyard)
Damscheid	Frankenhell
	Goldemund
	Sonnenstock
Dellhofen	Römerkrug
	St. Wernerberg
Langscheid	Hundert
Niederburg	Bienenberg
	Rheingoldberg
Oberwesel	Bernstein
	Bienenberg
	Goldemund
	Ölsberg
	Römerkrug
	St. Martinsberg
	Sieben Jungfrauen
Perscheid	Rosental
Urbar b. St. Goar	Beulsberg

Not yet assigned a *Grosslage* (section of vineyards):

Weinbauort (village)	Einzellage (vineyard)
Hirzenach	Probsteiberg

VI ANBAUGEBIET (region): MOSEL–SAAR–RUWER

BEREICH (sub-region): BERNKASTEL

GROSSLAGE (SECTION OF VINEYARDS): BADSTUBE

Weinbauort (village)	Einzellage (vineyard)
Bernkastel-Kues	Bratenhöfchen
	Doctor
	Graben
	Lay
	Matheisbildchen

GROSSLAGE (SECTION OF VINEYARDS): BEERENLAY

Weinbauort (village)	Einzellage (vineyard)
Lieser	Niederberg-Helden
	Rosenlay
	Süssenberg

GROSSLAGE (SECTION OF VINEYARDS): KURFÜRSTLAY

Weinbauort (village)	Einzellage (vineyard)
Andel	Schlossberg
Bernkastel-Kues	Johannisbrünnchen
	Kardinalsberg
	Rosenberg
	Schlossberg
	Stephanus-Rosengärtchen
	Weissenstein
Brauneberg	Hasenläufer
	Juffer
	Juffer-Sonnenuhr
	Kammer
	Klostergarten
	Mandelgraben
Burgen	Hasenläufer
	Kirchberg
	Römerberg
Kesten	Herrenberg
	Paulinsberg
	Paulinushofberger
Lieser	Schlossberg
Maring-Noviand	Honigberg
	Kirchberg
	Klosterberg
	Römerpfad
	Sonnenuhr
Mülheim	Amtsgarten
	Elisenberg
	Helenenkloster
	Sonnenlay
Osann-Monzel	Kätzchen
	Kirchlay
	Paulinslay
	Rosenberg
Veldenz	Carlsberg
	Elisenberg
	Grafschafter Sonnenberg
	Kirchberg
	Mühlberg
Wintrich	Grosser Herrgott
	Ohligsberg
	Sonnenseite
	Stefanslay

GROSSLAGE (SECTION OF VINEYARDS): MICHELSBERG

Weinbauort (village)	Einzellage (vineyard)
Hetzerath	Brauneberg
Minheim	Burglay
	Günterslay
	Kapellchen
	Rosenberg
Neumagen-Dhron	Engelgrube
	Grafenberg
	Grosser Hengelberg
	Hofberger
	Laudamusberg
	Rosengärtchen
	Roterd
	Sonnenuhr
Piesport	Domherr
	Falkenberg
	Gärtchen
	Goldtröpfchen
	Günterslay
	Schubertslay
	Treppchen
Rivenich	Brauneberg
	Geisberg
	Niederberg
	Rosenberg
Sehlem	Rotlay
Trittenheim	Altärchen
	Apotheke
	Felsenkopf
	Leiterchen

GROSSLAGE (SECTION OF VINEYARDS): MÜNZLAY

Weinbauort (village)	Einzellage (vineyard)
Graach	Abtsberg
	Domprobst
	Himmelreich
	Josephshöfer
Wehlen	Klosterberg
	Nonnenberg
	Sonnenuhr
Zeltingen-Rachtig	Deutschherrenberg
	Himmelreich
	Schlossberg
	Sonnenuhr

GROSSLAGE (SECTION OF VINEYARDS): NACKTARSCH

Weinbauort (village)	Einzellage (vineyard)
Kröv	Burglay
	Herrenberg
	Kirchlay
	Letterlay
	Paradies
	Steffensberg

GROSSLAGE (SECTION OF VINEYARDS): PROBSTBERG

Weinbauort (village)	Einzellage (vineyard)
Fell	Maximiner Burgberg
Kenn	Held
	Maximiner Hofgarten

Weinbauort (village)	Einzellage (vineyard)
Longuich	Hirschlay
	Maximiner Herrenberg
Mehring	Vineyards on the right side of the Mosel
Riol	Römerberg
Schweich	Annaberg
	Burgmauer
	Herrenberg

GROSSLAGE (SECTION OF VINEYARDS): SANKT MICHAEL

Weinbauort (village)	Einzellage (vineyard)
Bekond	Brauneberg
	Schlossberg
Detzem	Maximiner Klosterlay
	Würzgarten
Ensch	Mühlenberg
	St. Martin
	Sonnenlay
Klüsserath	Bruderschaft
	Königsberg
Köwerich	Held
	Laurentiuslay
Leiwen	Klostergarten
	Laurentiuslay
Longen	Goldkupp
	Zellerberg
Lörsch	Goldkupp
	Zellerberg
Mehring	Blattenberg
	Goldkupp
	Zellerberg
Pölich	Held
	Südlay
Schleich	Klosterberg
	Sonnenberg
Thörnich	Enggass
	Ritsch

GROSSLAGE (SECTION OF VINEYARDS): SCHWARZLAY

Weinbauort (village)	Einzellage (vineyard)
Bausendorf	Herzlay
	Hubertuslay
Bengel	Sites not chosen
Burg	Falklay
	Hahnenschrittchen
	Schlossberg
	Thomasberg
	Wendelstück
Dreis	Johannisberg
Enkirch	Batterieberg
	Edelberg
	Ellergrub
	Herrenberg
	Monteneubel
	Steffensberg
	Weinkammer
	Zeppwingert
Erden	Busslay
	Herrenberg
	Prälat
	Treppchen

Weinbauort (village)	Einzellage (vineyard)
Flussbach	Reichelberg
Hupperath	Klosterweg
Kinheim	Hubertuslay
	Rosenberg
Lösnich	Burgberg
	Försterlay
Platten	Klosterberg
	Rotlay
Traben-Trarbach	Burgweg
	Gaispfad
	Hühnerberg
	Königsberg
	Kräuterhaus
	Kreuzberg
	Schlossberg
	Taubenhaus
	Ungsberg
	Würzgarten
	Zollturm
Traben-Trarbach (Ortsteil Starkenburg)	Rosengarten
Traben-Trarbach (Ortsteil Wolf)	Auf der Heide
	Goldgrube
	Klosterberg
	Schatzgarten
	Sonnenlay
Ürzig	Würzgarten
	Goldwingert
Wittlich	Bottchen
	Felsentreppchen
	Klosterweg
	Kupp
	Lay
	Portnersberg
	Rosenberg

GROSSLAGE (SECTION OF VINEYARDS): VOM HEISSEN STEIN

Weinbauort (village)	Einzellage (vineyard)
Briedel	Herzchen
	Nonnengarten
	Schäferlay
	Schelm
	Weisserberg
Pünderich	Goldlay
	Marienburg
	Nonnengarten
	Rosenberg
Reil	Falklay
	Goldlay
	Moullay-Hofberg
	Sorentberg

BEREICH (sub-region): OBERMOSEL

GROSSLAGE (SECTION OF VINEYARDS): GIPFEL

Weinbauort (village)	Einzellage (vineyard)
Bitzingen	Sites not chosen
Fellerich	Schleidberg
Fisch	Sites not chosen
Helfant-Esingen	Kapellenberg
Kirf	Sites not chosen
Köllig	Rochusfels
Kreuzweiler	Schloss Thorner Kupp

Weinbauort (village)	Einzellage (vineyard)	Weinbauort (village)	Einzellage (vineyard)
Meurich	Sites not chosen	Sommerau	Schlossberg
Nittel	Blümchen	Trier	Altenberg
	Hubertusberg		Andreasberg
	Leiterchen		Augenscheiner
	Rochusfels		Benediktinerberg
Oberbillig	Hirtengarten		Burgberg
	Römerberg		Deutschherrenberg
Onsdorf	Hubertusberg		Deutschherrenköpfchen
Palzem	Karlsfelsen		Domherrenberg
	Lay		Hammerstein
Portz	Sites not chosen		Herrenberg
Rehlingen	Kapellenberg		Jesuitenwingert
Soest	Sites not chosen		Karthäuserhofberg Burgberg
Tawern	Sites not chosen		Karthäuserhofberg Kronenberg
Temmels	Münsterstatt		Karthäuserhofberg Orthsberg
	St. Georgshof		Karthäuserhofberg Sang
Wasserliesch	Albachtaler		Karthäuserhofberg Stirn
	Reinig auf der Burg		Kupp
Wehr	Rosenberg		Kurfürstenhofberg
Wellen	Altenberg		Leikaul
Wincheringen	Burg Warsberg		Marienholz
	Fuchsloch		Maximiner

GROSSLAGE (SECTION OF VINEYARDS): KÖNIGSBERG

Weinbauort (village)	Einzellage (vineyard)	Weinbauort (village)	Einzellage (vineyard)
Edingen	Sites not chosen		Rotlay
Godendorf	Sites not chosen		St. Martiner Hofberg
Grewenich	Sites not chosen		St. Matheiser
Igel	Dullgärten		St. Maximiner Kreuzberg
Langsur	Brüderberg		St. Petrusberg
Liersberg	Pilgerberg		Sonnenberg
Mesenich	Held		Thiergarten Felsköpfchen
Metzdorf	Sites not chosen		Thiergarten Unterm Kreuz
Ralingen	Sites not chosen	Waldrach	Doktorberg
Winterdorf	Sites not chosen		Ehrenberg

BEREICH (sub-region): SAAR-RUWER

GROSSLAGE (SECTION OF VINEYARDS): RÖMERLAY

Weinbauort (village)	Einzellage (vineyard)	Weinbauort (village)	Einzellage (vineyard)
Franzenheim	Johannisberg		Heiligenhäuschen
Hockweiler	Sites not chosen		Hubertusberg
Kasel	Dominikanerberg		Jesuitengarten
	Herrenberg		Jungfernberg
	Hitzlay		Krone
	Kehrnagel		Kurfürstenberg
	Nieschen		Laurentiusberg
	Paulinsberg		Meisenberg
	Timpert		Sonnenberg

GROSSLAGE (SECTION OF VINEYARDS): SCHARZBERG

Weinbauort (village)	Einzellage (vineyard)	Weinbauort (village)	Einzellage (vineyard)
Korlingen	Laykaul	Ayl	Herrenberger
Mertesdorf	Felslay		Kupp
	Johannisberg		Scheidterberger
	Mäuerchen	Filzen	Altenberg
Mertesdorf (Ortsteil Maximin Grünhaus)	Abtsberg		Herrenberg
	Bruderberg		Liebfrauenberg
	Herrenberg		Pulchen
Morscheid	Dominikanerberg		Steinberger
	Heiligenhäuschen		Unterberg
Riveris	Heiligenhäuschen		Urbelt
	Kuhnchen	Hamm	Altenberg

610

Weinbauort (village)	*Einzellage (vineyard)*
Irsch	Hubertusberg
	Sonnenberg
	Vogelsang
Kanzem	Altenberg
	Hörecker
	Schlossberg
	Sonnenberg
Kastel-Staadt	König Johann Berg
	Maximin Staadt
Könen	Fels
	Kirchberg
Konz	Auf der Kupp
	Brauneberg
	Euchariusberg
	Falkensteiner Hofberg
	Klosterberg
	Sprung
Mennig	Altenberg
	Euchariusberg
	Herrenberg
	Sonnenberg
Oberemmel	Agritiusberg
	Altenberg
	Hütte
	Karlsberg
	Raul
	Rosenberg
Ockfen	Bockstein
	Geisberg
	Heppenstein
	Herrenberg
	Kupp
	Neuwies
	Zickelgarten
Pellingen	Herrgottsrock
	Jesuitengarten
Saarburg	Antoniusbrunnen
	Bergschlösschen
	Fuchs
	Klosterberg
	Kupp
	Laurentiusberg
	Rausch
	Schlossberg
	Stirn
Schoden	Geisberg
	Herrenberg
	Saarfeilser Marienberg
Serrig	Antoniusberg
	Helligenborn
	Herrenberg
	Hoeppslei
	König Johann Berg
	Kupp
	Schloss Saarsteiner
	Schloss Saarfelser
	Schlossberg
	Vogelsang
	Würtzberg

Weinbauort (village)	*Einzellage (vineyard)*
Wawern	Goldberg
	Herrenberger
	Jesuitenberg
	Ritterpfad
Wiltingen	Braune Kupp
	Braunfels
	Gottesfuss
	Hölle
	Klosterberg
	Kupp
	Rosenberg
	Sandberg
Estate	Scharzhofberger
	Schlagengraben
	Schlossberg

BEREICH (sub-region): ZELL/MOSEL

GROSSLAGE (SECTION OF VINEYARDS): GOLDBÄUMCHEN

Weinbauort (village)	*Einzellage (vineyard)*
Briedern	Rüberberger
	Domherrenberg
Bruttig-Fankel	Götterlay
Cochem	Bischofstuhl
	Herrenberg
	Hochlay
	Klostergarten
	Pinnerkreuzberg
	Schlossberg
	Sonnenberg
Ellenz-Poltersdorf	Altarberg
	Kurfürst
	Rüberberger
	Domherrenberg
Ernst	Feuerberg
	Kirchlay
Klotten	Brauneberg
	Burg Coreidelsteiner
	Rosenberg
	Sonnengold
Moselkern	Kirchberg
	Rosenberg
	Übereltzer
Müden	Funkenberg
	Grosslay
	Leckmauer
	St. Castorhöhle
	Sonnenring
Pommern	Goldberg
	Rosenberg
	Sonnenuhr
	Zeisel
Senheim	Römerberg
	Rüberberger
	Domherrenberg
Treis-Karden	Dechantsberg
	Juffermauer
	Münsterberg

GROSSLAGE (SECTION OF VINEYARDS): GRAFSCHAFT

Weinbauort (village)	Einzellage (vineyard)
Alf	Arrasburg-Schlossberg
	Burggraf
	Herrenberg
	Hölle
	Kapellenberg
	Katzenkopf
	Kronenberg
Beuren	Pelzerberger
Bremm	Calmont
	Frauenberg
	Laurentiusberg
	Schlemmertröpfchen
Bullay	Brautrock
	Graf Beyssel-Herrenberg
	Kirchweingarten
	Kroneberg
	Sonneck
Ediger-Eller	Bienenlay
	Calmont
	Elzogberg
	Engelströpfchen
	Feuerberg
	Höll
	Osterlämmchen
	Pfaffenberg
	Pfirsichgarten
	Schützenlay
Neef	Frauenberg
	Petersberg
	Rosenberg
Nehren	Römerberg
St. Aldegund	Himmelreich
	Klosterkammer
	Palmberg-Terrassen
Zell-Merl	Sites not chosen
Senheim	Bienengarten
	Rosenberg
	Vogteiberg
	Wahrsager
Treis-Karden	Greth
	Kapellenberg
	Treppchen
Valwig	Herrenberg
	Palmberg
	Schwarzenberg

GROSSLAGE (SECTION OF VINEYARDS): ROSENHANG

Weinbauort (village)	Einzellage (vineyard)
Beilstein	Schlossberg
Bremm	Abtei
	Kloster Stuben
Briedern	Herrenberg
	Kapellenberg
	Römergarten
	Servatiusberg
Bruttig-Fankel	Kapellenberg
	Layenberg
	Martinsborn
	Pfarrgarten
	Rathausberg
	Rosenberg
Cochem	Arzlay
	Nikolausberg
	Rosenberg
Ellenz-Poltersdorf	Silberberg
	Woogberg
Mesenich	Abteiberg
	Deuslay
	Goldgrübchen

GROSSLAGE (SECTION OF VINEYARDS): SCHWARZE KATZ

Weinbauort (village)	Einzellage (vineyard)
Senheim	Rüberberger Domherrenberg
Zell	Burglay-Felsen
	Domherrenberg
	Geisberg
	Kreuzlay
	Nussberg
	Petersborn-Kabertchen
	Pommerell
Zell-Kaimt	Marienburger
	Römerquelle
	Rosenborn
Zell-Merl	Adler
	Fettgarten
	Klosterberg
	Königslay-Terrassen
	Stefansberg
	Sonneck

GROSSLAGE (SECTION OF VINEYARDS): WEINHEX

Weinbauort (village)	Einzellage (vineyard)
Alken	Bleidenberg
	Burgberg
	Hunnenstein
Burgen	Bischofstein
Dieblich	Heilgraben
Güls	Bienengarten
	Im Röttgen
	Königsfels
	Marienberg
Hatzenport	Burg Bischofsteiner
	Kirchberg
	Stolzenberg
Kattenes	Fahrberg
	Steinchen
Kobern-Gondorf	Fahrberg
	Fuchshöhle
	Gäns
	Kehrberg
	Schlossberg
	Uhlen
	Weissenberg
Koblenz, Ortsteil Moselweiss	Hamm
Koblenz, Ortsteil Lay	Hubertsborn
Lehmen	Ausoniusstein
	Klosterberg
	Lay
	Würzlay

Weinbauort (village)	Einzellage (vineyard)	Weinbauort (village)	Einzellage (vineyard)
Löf	Goldblume	Winningen	Brückstück
	Sonnenring		Domgarten
Moselsürsch	Fahrberg		Hamm
Niederfell	Fächern		Im Röttgen
	Goldlay		Uhlen
	Kahllay		

Not yet assigned a *Grosslage* (section of vineyards):

Weinbauort (village)	Einzellage (vineyard)
Oberfell	Brauneberg
	Goldlay
	Rosenberg

Weinbauort (village)	Einzellage (vineyard)
Senheim	Lay

VII ANBAUGEBIET (region): NAHE

BEREICH (sub-region): KREUZNACH

GROSSLAGE (SECTION OF VINEYARDS): KRONENBERG

Weinbauort (village)	Einzellage (vineyard)
Bad Kreuznach	Agnesienberg
	Berg
	Breitenweg
	Brückes
	Forst
	Galgenberg
	Gutental
	Himmelgarten
	Hinkelstein
	Hirtenhain
	Hofgarten
	Höllenbrand
	Honigberg
	Hungriger Wolf
	In den Mauern
	In den 17 Morgen
	Junker
	Kahlenberg
	Kapellenpfad
	Katzenhölle
	Krötenpfuhl
	Mollenbrunnen
	Mönchberg
	Monhard
	Narrenkappe
	Nonnengarten
	Osterhöll
	Paradies
	Römerhalde
	Rosenberg
	Rosenheck
	Rosenhügel
	Schloss Kauzenberg
	St. Martin
	Steinberg
	Steinweg
	Tilgesbrunnen
	Vogelsang
Bretzenheim	Felsenköpfchen
	Hofgut
	Pastorei
	Schlossgarten
	Vogelsang
Hargesheim	Mollenbrunnen
	Straussberg

GROSSLAGE (SECTION OF VINEYARDS): PFARRGARTEN

Weinbauort (village)	Einzellage (vineyard)
Dalberg	Ritterhölle
	Schlossberg
	Sonnenberg
Gutenberg	Felseneck
	Römerberg
	St. Ruppertsberg
	Schlossberg
	Schloss Gutenburg
	Sonnenlauf
Hergenfeld	Herrschaftsgarten
	Mönchberg
	Sonnenberg
Schöneberg	Schäfersley
	Sonnenberg
Sommerloch	Birkenberg
	Ratsgrund
	Sonnenberg
	Steinrossel
Spabrücken	Höll
Wallhausen	Backöfchen
	Felseneck
	Hasensprung
	Höllenpfad
	Hörnchen
	Johannisberg
	Kirschheck
	Laurentiusberg
	Mühlenberg
	Pastorenberg
	Sonnenweg

GROSSLAGE (SECTION OF VINEYARDS): SCHLOSSKAPELLE

Weinbauort (village)	Einzellage (vineyard)
Bingen-Bingerbrück	Abtei Ruppertsberg
	Hildegardisbrünnchen
	Klostergarten
	Römerberg
Burg Layen	Hölle
	Johannisberg
	Rothenberg
	Schlossberg

Nahe: Schloss Böckelheim

Weinbauort (village)	Einzellage (vineyard)
Dorsheim	Burgberg
	Goldloch
	Honigberg
	Jungbrunnen
	Klosterpfad
	Laurenziweg
	Nixenberg
	Pittermännchen
	Trollberg
Eckenroth	Felsenberg
	Hölle
Genheim	Rossel
Guldental	Apostelberg
	Hipperich
	Hölle
	Honigberg
	Rosenteich
	St. Martin
	Sonnenberg
	Teufelsküche
Laubenheim	Fuchsen
	Hörnchen
	Junker
	Karthäuser
	Krone
	St. Remigiusberg
	Vogelsang
Münster-Sarmsheim	Dautenpflänzer
	Kapellenberg
	Königsschloss
	Liebehöll
	Pittersberg
	Rheinberg
	Römerberg
	Steinkopf
	Trollberg
Rümmelsheim	Hölle
	Johannisberg
	Rothenberg
	Schlossberg
	Steinköpfchen
Schweppenhausen	Schlossgarten
	Steyerberg
Waldlaubersheim	Alteburg
	Bingerweg
	Domberg
	Hörnchen
	Lieseberg
	Otterberg
Weiler	Abtei Ruppertsberg
	Klostergarten
	Römerberg
Windesheim	Breiselberg
	Fels
	Hausgiebel
	Hölle
	Römerberg
	Rosenberg
	Saukopf
	Schäfchen
	Sonnenmorgen

GROSSLAGE (SECTION OF VINEYARDS): SONNENBORN

Weinbauort (village)	Einzellage (vineyard)
Langenlonsheim	Bergborn
	Königsschild
	Lauerweg
	Löhrer Berg
	Rothenberg
	St. Antoniusweg
	Steinchen

BEREICH (sub-region): SCHLOSS BÖCKELHEIM

GROSSLAGE (SECTION OF VINEYARDS): BURGWEG

Weinbauort (village)	Einzellage (vineyard)
Altenbamberg	Kehrenberg
	Laurentiusberg
	Rotenberg
	Schlossberg
	Treuenfels
Bad Münster a. St.-Ebernburg	Erzgrupe
	Felseneck
	Feuerberg
	Götzenfels
	Höll
	Köhler-Köpfchen
	Königsgarten
	Luisengarten
	Rotenfelser im Winkel
	Schlossberg
	Steigerdell
	Stephansberg
Duchroth	Felsenberg
	Feuerberg
	Kaiserberg
	Königsfels
	Rothenberg
	Vogelschlag
Niederhausen an der Nahe	Felsensteyer
	Hermannshöhle
	Kertz
	Klamm
	Pfaffenstein
	Pflingstweide
	Rosenberg
	Rosenheck
	Steinberg
	Steinwingert
	Stollenberg
	Herrmannsberg
Norheim	Dellchen
	Götzenfels
	Kafels
	Kirschheck
	Klosterberg
	Oberberg
	Onkelchen
	Sonnenberg
Oberhausen an der Nahe	Felsenberg
	Kieselberg
	Leistenberg
	Rotenberg

Weinbauort (village)	Einzellage (vineyard)
Schlossböckelheim	Felsenberg
	Heimberg
	In den Felsen
	Königsfels
	Kupfergrube
	Mühlberg
Traisen	Bastei
	Kickelskopf
	Nonnengarten
	Rotenfels
Waldböckelheim	Drachenbrunnen
	Hamm
	Kirchberg
	Kronenfels
	Marienpforter Klosterberg
	Muckerhölle
	Mühlberg
	Römerberg

GROSSLAGE (SECTION OF VINEYARDS): PARADIESGARTEN

Weinbauort (village)	Einzellage (vineyard)
Alsenz	Elkersberg
	Falkenberg
	Hölle
	Pfaffenpfad
Auen	Kaulenberg
	Römerstich
Bayerfeld-Steckweiler	Adelsberg
	Aspenberg
	Mittelberg
	Schloss Stolzenberg
Boos	Herrenberg
	Kastell
Desloch	Hengstberg
	Vor der Hölle
Feilbingert	Bocksberg
	Feuerberg
	Höchstes Kreuz
	Kahlenberg
	Königsgarten
Gaugrehweiler	Graukatz
Hochstätten	Liebesbrunnen
Kalkofen	Graukatz
Kirschroth	Lump
	Wildgrafenberg
Lauschied	Edelberg
Lettweiler	Inkelhöll
	Rheingasse
Mannweiler-Coelln	Rosenberg
	Schloss Randeck
	Seidenberg
	Weissenstein
Martinstein	Schlossberg
Meddersheim	Altenberg
	Edelberg
	Liebfrauenberg
	Präsent
	Rheingrafenberg
Meisenheim	Obere Heimbach

Weinbauort (village)	Einzellage (vineyard)
Merxheim	Hunolsteiner
	Römerberg
	Vogelsang
Monzingen	Frühlingsplätzchen
	Halenberg
	Rosenberg
Münsterappel	Graukatz
Niederhausen an der Nahe	Graukatz
Niedermoschel	Geissenkopf
	Hahnhölle
	Layenberg
	Silberberg
Nussbaum	Höllenberg
	Rotfeld
	Sonnenberg
Oberhausen an der Nahe	Graukatz
Obermoschel	Geissenkopf
	Langhölle
	Schlossberg
	Silberberg
	Sonnenplätzchen
Oberndorf	Aspenberg
	Beutelstein
	Feuersteinrossel
	Weissenstein
Oberstreit	Auf dem Zimmerberg
Odernheim	Disibodenberg
	Hessweg
	Kapellenberg
	Kloster
	Monfort
	Weinsack
Raumbach	Schlossberg
	Schwalbennest
Rehborn	Hahn
	Herrenberg
	Schikanenbuckel
Sobernheim	Domberg
	Marbach
Sobernheim-Steinhardt	Johannesberg
	Spitalberg
Staudernheim	Goldgrube
	Herrenberg
Unkenbach	Römerpfad
	Würzhölle
Waldböckelheim	Johannesberg
	Kastell
Weiler bei Monzingen	Heiligenberg
	Herrenzehntel
Winterborn	Graukatz

GROSSLAGE (SECTION OF VINEYARDS): ROSENGARTEN

Weinbauort (village)	Einzellage (vineyard)
Bockenau	Geisberg
	Im Felseneck
	Im Neuberg
	Stromberg
Braunweiler	Hellenpfad
	Michaeliskapelle
	Schlossberg
	Wetterkreuz

Weinbauort (village)	Einzellage (vineyard)	Weinbauort (village)	Einzellage (vineyard)
Burgsponheim	Höllenpfad	Rüdesheim	Goldgrube
	Pfaffenberg		Wiesberg
	Schlossberg	St. Katharinen	Fels
Hüffelsheim	Gutenhölle		Klostergarten
	Mönchberg		Steinkreuz
	Steyer	Sponheim	Abtei
Mandel	Alte Römerstrasse		Grafenberg
	Becherbrunnen		Klostergarten
	Dellchen		Mühlberg
	Palmengarten	Weinsheim	Katergrube
	Schlossberg		Kellerberg
Roxheim	Berg		Steinkaut
	Birkenberg		
	Höllenpfad		
	Hüttenberg		
	Mühlenberg		
	Sonnenberg		

VIII ANBAUGEBIET (region): RHEINGAU

BEREICH (sub-region): JOHANNISBERG

GROSSLAGE (SECTION OF VINEYARDS): BURGWEG

Weinbauort (village)	Einzellage (vineyard)	Weinbauort (village)	Einzellage (vineyard)
Assmannshausen-Aulhausen	Berg Kaisersteinfels	Johannisberg	Goldatzel
Geisenheim	Fuchsberg		Hansenberg
	Mäuerchen		Hölle
	Mönchspfad		Mittelhölle
	Rothenberg	Estate	Schwarzenstein
Lorch	Bodental-Steinberg		Vogelsang
	Kapellenberg		Schloss Johannisberg
	Krone	Mittelheim	Edelmann (divisible)
	Pfaffenwies		Goldberg
	Schlossberg		St. Nikolaus (divisible)
Lorchhausen	Rosenberg	Winkel	Dachsberg
	Seligmacher		
Rüdesheim	Berg Roseneck		

GROSSLAGE (SECTION OF VINEYARDS): GOTTESTHAL

Weinbauort (village)	Einzellage (vineyard)
(Rüdesheim) Berg Rottland	
Berg Schlossberg	
Bischofsberg	Oestrich → Doosberg
Drachenstein	
Kirchenpfad	
Klosterberg	→ Klosterberg (divisible)
Klosterlay	→ Lenchen
Magdalenenkreuz	Estate → Schloss Reichartshausen
Rosengarten	

GROSSLAGE (SECTION OF VINEYARDS): GOTTESTHAL

Weinbauort (village)	Einzellage (vineyard)
Oestrich	Doosberg
	Klosterberg (divisible)
	Lenchen
Estate	Schloss Reichartshausen

GROSSLAGE (SECTION OF VINEYARDS): STEIL

Weinbauort (village)	Einzellage (vineyard)
Assmannshausen	Frankenthal
Assmannshausen-Aulhausen	Hinterkirch
	Höllenberg

GROSSLAGE (SECTION OF VINEYARDS): MEHRHÖLZCHEN

Weinbauort (village)	Einzellage (vineyard)
Hallgarten	Hendelberg
	Jungfer
	Schönhell
	Würzgarten
Oestrich	Klosterberg (divisible)

GROSSLAGE (SECTION OF VINEYARDS): ERNTEBRINGER

Weinbauort (village)	Einzellage (vineyard)
Geisenheim	Kilzberg
	Klaus
	Kläuserweg
	Schlossgarten

GROSSLAGE (SECTION OF VINEYARDS): HONIGBERG

Weinbauort (village)	Einzellage (vineyard)
Mittelheim	Edelmann (divisible)
	St. Nikolaus (divisible)
Estate	Schloss Vollrads

Weinbauort (village)	Einzellage (vineyard)
Winkel	Bienengarten
	Gutenberg
	Hasensprung
	Klaus (divisible)
	Schlossberg
	Jesuitengarten

GROSSLAGE (SECTION OF VINEYARDS): DEUTELSBERG

Weinbauort (village)	Einzellage (vineyard)
Erbach	Hohenrain
	Honigberg
	Marcobrunn
	Michelmark
	Schlossberg
	Siegelsberg
	Steinmorgen
Hattenheim	Engelmannsberg
	Hassel
	Heiligenberg
	Mannberg
	Nussbrunnen
	Pfaffenberg
	Schützenhaus
	Wisselbrunnen
Estate	Steinberg

GROSSLAGE (SECTION OF VINEYARDS): HEILIGENSTOCK

Weinbauort (village)	Einzellage (vineyard)
Eltville	Sandgrub (divisible)
Kiedrich	Gräfenberg
	Klosterberg
	Sandgrub (divisible)
	Wasseros

GROSSLAGE (SECTION OF VINEYARDS): STEINMÄCHER

Weinbauort (village)	Einzellage (vineyard)
Dotzheim	Judenkirch
Eltville	Langenstück
	Rheinberg
	Sandgrub (divisible)
	Sonnenberg
	Taubenberg
Frauenstein	Herrenberg
	Homberg
	Marschall

Weinbauort (village)	Einzellage (vineyard)
Martinsthal	Langenberg
	Rödchen
	Wildsau
Niederwalluf	Berg Bildstock
	Oberberg
	Walkenberg
Oberwalluf	Langenstück
	Fitusberg
Rauenthal	Baiken
	Gehrn
	Langenstück
	Nonnenberg
	Rothenberg
	Wülfen
Schierstein	Dachsberg
	Hölle

GROSSLAGE (SECTION OF VINEYARDS): DAUBHAUS

Weinbauort (village)	Einzellage (vineyard)
Flörsheim	Herrnberg (divisible)
Hochheim	Berg (divisible)
	Domdechaney
	Herrnberg (divisible)
	Hofmeister
	Hölle
	Kirchenstück
	Königin Viktoriaberg
	Reichesthal (divisible)
	Sommerheil
	Stein
	Stielweg
Kostheim	Berg (divisible)
	Reichesthal (divisible)
	Steig
	Weiss Erd
Wicker	Goldene Luft
	König Wilhelmsberg
	Nonnberg
	Stein

Not yet assigned a Grosslage (section of vineyards):

Weinbauort (village)	Einzellage (vineyard)
Frankfurt/Main	Lohberger Hang

REGION OF MELSUNGEN

Weinbauort (village)	Einzellage (vineyard)
Böddiger	Berg

IX ANBAUGEBIET (region): RHEINHESSEN

BEREICH (sub-region): BINGEN

GROSSLAGE (SECTION OF VINEYARDS): ABTEI

Weinbauort (village)	Einzellage (vineyard)	Weinbauort (village)	Einzellage (vineyard)
Appenheim	Daubhaus	Gau-Algesheim	Goldberg
	Drosselborn		Johannesberg
	Eselspfad		Rothenberg
	Hundertgulden		St. Laurenzikapelle
			Steinert

Weinbauort (village)	Einzellage (vineyard)	Weinbauort (village)	Einzellage (vineyard)
Nieder-Hilbersheim	Honigberg	Heidesheim	Geissberg
	Steinacker		Höllenberg
Ober-Hilbersheim	Mönchpforte		Steinacker
Partenheim	Sankt Georgen	Ingelheim	Burgberg
	Steinberg		Höllenweg
Sankt Johann	Geyersberg		Horn
	Klostergarten		Kirchenstück
	Steinberg		Lottenstück
Sprendlingen	Hölle		Pares
	Honigberg		Rabenkopf
	Klostergarten		Rheinhöhe
	Sonnenberg		Rotes Kreuz
	Wissberg		Sonnenberg
Wolfsheim	Götzenborn		Sonnenhang
	Osterberg		Schlossberg
	Sankt Kathrin		Schloss Westerhaus
			Steinacker
			Täuscherspfad
		Jugenheim	Goldberg

GROSSLAGE (SECTION OF VINEYARDS): ADELBERG

Weinbauort (village)	Einzellage (vineyard)		
			Hasensprung
			Heiligenhäuschen
			St. Georgenberg
Armsheim	Geiersberg	Schwabenheim	Klostergarten
	Goldstückchen		Sonnenberg
	Leckerberg		Schlossberg
Bermersheim v. d. H.	Hildegardisberg	Wackernheim	Rabenkopf
	Klosterberg		Schwalben
Bornheim	Hähnchen		Steinberg
	Hütte-Terrassen		
	Kirchenstück		
	Schönberg		

GROSSLAGE (SECTION OF VINEYARDS): KURFÜRSTENSTÜCK

Weinbauort (village)	Einzellage (vineyard)	Weinbauort (village)	Einzellage (vineyard)
Ensheim	Kachelberg	Gau-Bickelheim	Bockshaut
Erbes-Bürdesheim	Geisterberg		Kapelle
	Vogelsang		Saukopf
Flonheim	Bingerberg	Gau-Weinheim	Geyersberg
	Klostergarten		Kaisergarten
	La Roche		Wissberg
	Pfaffenberg	Gumbsheim	Schlosshölle
	Rotenpfad	Vendersheim	Goldberg
Lonsheim	Mandelberg		Sonnenberg
	Schönberg	Wallertheim	Heil
Nack	Ahrenberg		Vogelsang
Nieder-Weisen	Wingertsberg		
Sulzheim	Greifenberg		

GROSSLAGE (SECTION OF VINEYARDS): RHEINGRAFENSTEIN

Weinbauort (village)	Einzellage (vineyard)	Weinbauort (village)	Einzellage (vineyard)
	Honigberg	Eckelsheim	Eselstreiber
	Schildberg		Kirchberg
Wendelsheim	Heiligenpfad		Sonnenköpfchen
	Steigerberg	Frei-Laubersheim	Fels
Wörrstadt	Kachelberg		Kirchberg
	Rheingrafenberg		Reichskeller
			Rheingrafenberg

GROSSLAGE (SECTION OF VINEYARDS): KAISERPFALZ

Weinbauort (village)	Einzellage (vineyard)		
		Fürfeld	Eichelberg
			Kapellenberg
			Steige
Bubenheim	Honigberg	Hackenheim	Galgenberg
	Kallenberg		Gewürzgarten
Engelstadt	Adelpfad		Kirchberg
	Römerberg		Klostergarten
Gross-Winternheim	Bockstein		Sonnenberg
	Heilighäuschen		
	Klosterbruder		
	Schlossberg		

Weinbauort (village)	Einzellage (vineyard)
Neu-Bamberg	Eichelberg
	Heerkretz
	Kirschwingert
	Kletterberg
Pleitersheim	Sternberg
Siefersheim	Goldenes Horn
	Heerkretz
	Höllberg
	Martinsberg
Stein-Bockenheim	Sonnenberg
Tiefenthal	Graukatz
Volxheim	Alte Römerstrasse
	Liebfrau
	Mönchberg
Wöllstein	Äffchen
	Haarberg-Katzensteg
	Hölle
	Ölberg
Wonsheim	Hölle
	Sonnenberg

GROSSLAGE (SECTION OF VINEYARDS): SANKT ROCHUSKAPELLE

Weinbauort (village)	Einzellage (vineyard)
Aspisheim	Johannisberg
	Sonnenberg
Badenheim	Galgenberg
	Römerberg
Biebelsheim	Honigberg
	Kieselberg
Bingen	Bubenstück
	Kapellenberg
	Kirchberg
	Osterberg
	Pfarrgarten
	Rosengarten
	Scharlachberg
	Schelmenstück
	Schlossberg-Schwätzerchen
	Schwarzenberg
Dromersheim	Honigberg
	Kapellenberg
	Klosterweg
	Mainzerweg
Gensingen	Goldberg
Grolsheim	Ölberg
Horrweiler	Gewürzgärtchen
	Goldberg
Ockenheim	Hockenmühle
	Klosterweg
	Kreuz
	Laberstall
	St. Jakobsberg
	Schönhölle
Pfaffen-Schwabenheim	Hölle
	Mandelbaum
	Sonnenberg
Sponsheim	Palmenstein
Welgesheim	Kirchgärtchen

Weinbauort (village)	Einzellage (vineyard)
Zotzenheim	Johannisberg
	Klostergarten

BEREICH (sub-region): NIERSTEIN

GROSSLAGE (SECTION OF VINEYARDS): AUFLANGEN

Weinbauort (village)	Einzellage (vineyard)
Nierstein	Bergkirche
	Glöck
	Heiligenbaum
	Kranzberg
	Ölberg
	Orbel
	Schloss Schwabsburg
	Zehnmorgen

GROSSLAGE (SECTION OF VINEYARDS): DOMHERR

Weinbauort (village)	Einzellage (vineyard)
Budenheim	Sites not chosen
Essenheim	Römerberg
	Teufelspfad
Gabsheim	Dornpfad
	Kirchberg
	Rosengarten
Klein-Winternheim	Geiershöll
	Herrgottshaus
	Villenkeller
Mainz-Finthen	Sites not chosen
Mainz-Drais	Sites not chosen
Ober-Olm	Kapellenberg
Saulheim	Haubenberg
	Heiligenhaus
	Hölle
	Pfaffengarten
	Probstey
	Schlossberg
Schornsheim	Mönchspfad
	Ritterberg
	Sonnenhang
Stadecken-Elsheim	Blume
	Bockstein
	Lenchen
	Spitzberg
	Tempelchen
Udenheim	Goldberg
	Kirchberg
	Sonnenberg

GROSSLAGE (SECTION OF VINEYARDS): GÜLDENMORGEN

Weinbauort (village)	Einzellage (vineyard)
Dienheim	Falkenberg
	Herrenberg
	Höhlchen
	Kreuz
	Siliusbrunnen
	Tafelstein
Oppenheim	Daubhaus
	Gutleuthaus
	Herrenberg
	Kreuz

Weinbauort (village)	Einzellage (vineyard)
	Sackträger
	Schützenhütte
	Zuckerberg

GROSSLAGE (SECTION OF VINEYARDS): GUTES DOMTAL

Weinbauort (village)	Einzellage (vineyard)
Dalheim	Altdörr
	Kranzberg
	Steinberg
Dexheim	Doktor
Friesenheim	Altdörr
	Bergpfad
	Knopf
Hahnheim	Knopf
	Moosberg
Köngernheim	Goldgrube
Lörzweiler	Königstuhl
Mommenheim	Kloppenberg
	Osterberg
	Silbergrube
Nackenheim	Schmittskapellchen
Nieder-Olm	Goldberg
	Klosterberg
	Sonnenberg
Nierstein	Pfaffenkappe
Selzen	Gottesgarten
	Osterberg
	Rheinpforte
Sörgenloch	Moosberg
Undenheim	Goldberg
Weinolsheim	Hohberg
	Kehr
Zornheim	Dachgewann
	Güldenmorgen
	Mönchbäumchen
	Pilgerweg
	Vogelsang

GROSSLAGE (SECTION OF VINEYARDS): KRÖTENBRUNNEN

Weinbauort (village)	Einzellage (vineyard)
Alsheim	Goldberg
Dienheim	Herrengarten
	Paterhof
	Schloss
Dolgesheim	Kreuzberg
	Schützenhütte
Eich	Goldberg
Eimsheim	Hexelberg
	Römerschanze
	Sonnenhang
Gimbsheim	Liebfrauenthal
	Sonnenweg
Guntersblum	Eiserne Hand
	Sankt Julianenbrunnen
	Sonnenberg
	Sonnenhang
	Steinberg
Hillesheim	Altenberg
	Sonnheil

Weinbauort (village)	Einzellage (vineyard)
Ludwigshöhe	Honigberg
Mettenheim	Goldberg
Oppenheim	Herrengarten
	Paterhof
	Schloss
	Schlossberg
Ülversheim	Aulenberg
	Schloss
Wintersheim	Frauengarten

GROSSLAGE (SECTION OF VINEYARDS): PETERSBERG

Weinbauort (village)	Einzellage (vineyard)
Albig	Homberg
	Hundskopf
	Schloss Hammerstein
Bechtolsheim	Homberg
	Klosterberg
	Sonnenberg
	Wingertstor
Biebelnheim	Pilgerstein
	Rosenberg
Framersheim	Hornberg
	Kreuzweg
	Zechberg
Gau-Heppenheim	Pfarrgarten
	Schlossberg
Gau-Odernheim	Fuchsloch
	Herrgottspfad
	Ölberg
	Vogelsang
Spiesheim	Osterberg

GROSSLAGE (SECTION OF VINEYARDS): REHBACH

Weinbauort (village)	Einzellage (vineyard)
Nackenheim	Rothenberg
Nierstein	Brudersberg
	Goldene Luft
	Hipping
	Pettenthal

GROSSLAGE (SECTION OF VINEYARDS): RHEINBLICK

Weinbauort (village)	Einzellage (vineyard)
Alsheim	Fischerpfad
	Frühmesse
	Römerberg
	Sonnenberg
Dorn-Dürkheim	Hasensprung
	Römerberg
Mettenheim	Michelsberg
	Schlossberg

GROSSLAGE (SECTION OF VINEYARDS): SANKT ALBAN

Weinbauort (village)	Einzellage (vineyard)
Bodenheim	Burgweg
	Ebersberg
	Heitersbrünnchen
	Hoch
	Kapelle
	Kreuzberg
	Leidhecke

Weinbauort (village)	Einzellage (vineyard)	Weinbauort (village)	Einzellage (vineyard)
	Mönchspfad	Westhofen	Aulerde
	Reichsritterstift		Benn
	Silberberg		Brunnenhäuschen
	Westrum		Kirchspiel
Gau-Bischofsheim	Glockenberg		Morstein
	Herrnberg		Rotenstein
	Kellersberg		Steingrube
	Pfaffenweg		
Harxheim	Börnchen		
	Lieth		
	Schlossberg		
Lörzweiler	Hohberg		
	Ölgild		
Mainz	Edelmann		
	Hüttberg		
	Johannisberg		
	Kirchenstück		
	Klosterberg		
	Sand		
	Weinkeller		

GROSSLAGE (SECTION OF VINEYARDS): SPIEGELBERG

GROSSLAGE (SECTION OF VINEYARDS): BURG RODENSTEIN

Weinbauort (village)	Einzellage (vineyard)	Weinbauort (village)	Einzellage (vineyard)
Nackenheim	Engelsberg	Bermersheim/Worms	Seilgarten
Nierstein	Bildstock	Flörsheim-Dalsheim	Bürgel
	Brückchen		Frauenberg
	Ebersberg		Goldberg
	Findling		Hubacker
	Hölle		Sauloch
	Kirchplatte		Steig
	Klostergarten	Mörstadt	Katzebuckel
	Paterberg		Nonnengarten
	Rosenberg	Ober-Flörsheim	Blücherpfad
	Schloss Hohenrechen		Herrenberg

GROSSLAGE (SECTION OF VINEYARDS): VOGELSGÄRTEN

GROSSLAGE (SECTION OF VINEYARDS): DOMBLICK

Weinbauort (village)	Einzellage (vineyard)	Weinbauort (village)	Einzellage (vineyard)
Guntersblum	Authental	Hohen-Sülzen	Kirchenstück
	Bornpfad		Sonnenberg
	Himmelthal	Mölsheim	Silberberg
	Kreuzkapelle		Zellerweg am schw. Herrgott
	Steig-Terrassen	Monsheim	Rosengarten
	Teufelskopf		Silberberg
Ludwigshöhe		Offstein	Engelsberg
			Schlossgarten
		Wachenheim	Horn
			Rotenberg

BEREICH (sub-region): WONNEGAU

GROSSLAGE (SECTION OF VINEYARDS): GOTTESHILFE

GROSSLAGE (SECTION OF VINEYARDS): BERGKLOSTER

Weinbauort (village)	Einzellage (vineyard)	Weinbauort (village)	Einzellage (vineyard)
Bermersheim	Hasenlauf	Bechtheim	Geyersberg
Eppelsheim	Felsen		Rosengarten
Esselborn	Goldberg		Stein
Flomborn	Feuerberg	Osthofen	Goldberg
	Goldberg		Hasenbiss
Gundersheim	Höllenbrand		Leckzapfen
	Königstuhl		Neuberg
Gundheim	Hungerbiene		
	Mandelbrunnen		
	Sonnenberg		
Hangen-Weisheim	Sommerwende		

GROSSLAGE (SECTION OF VINEYARDS): LIEBFRAUENMORGEN

Weinbauort (village)	Einzellage (vineyard)
Worms	Affenberg
	Am Heiligen Häuschen
	Bildstock
	Burgweg
	Goldberg
	Goldpfad
	Hochberg
	Kapellenstück
	Klausenberg
	Kreuzblick
	Lerchelsberg

621

Weinbauort (village)	Einzellage (vineyard)
	Liebfrauenstift-Kirchenstück
	Nonnenwingert
	Remeyerhof
	Rheinberg
	Römersteg
	Sankt Annaberg
	St. Cyriakusstift
	St. Georgenberg
	Schneckenberg

GROSSLAGE (SECTION OF VINEYARDS): PILGERPFAD

Weinbauort (village)	Einzellage (vineyard)
Bechtheim	Hasensprung
	Heiligkreuz
Dittelsheim-Hessloch	Edle Weingärten
	Geiersberg
	Kloppberg
	Leckerberg
	Liebfrauenberg
	Mönchhube
	Mondschein
	Pfaffenmütze
Frettenheim	Heil
Monzernheim	Goldberg
	Steinböhl

Weinbauort (village)	Einzellage (vineyard)
Osthofen	Kirchberg
	Klosterberg
	Liebenberg
	Rheinberg

GROSSLAGE (SECTION OF VINEYARDS): SYBILLENSTEIN

Weinbauort (village)	Einzellage (vineyard)
Alzey	Kapellenberg
	Pfaffenhalde
	Römerberg
	Rotenfels
	Wartberg
Bechenheim	Fröhlich
Dautenheim	Himmelacker
Freimersheim	Frankenstein
Heimersheim	Sonnenberg
Mauchenheim	Sioner Klosterberg
Offenheim	Mandelberg
Wahlheim	Schelmen
Weinheim	Heiliger Blutberg
	Hölle
	Kapellenberg
	Kirchenstück
	Mandelberg

X ANBAUGEBIET (region): RHEINPFALZ (PALATINATE)

BEREICH (sub-region): SÜDLICHE WEINSTRASSE

GROSSLAGE (SECTION OF VINEYARDS): BISCHOFSKREUZ

Weinbauort (village)	Einzellage (vineyard)
Böchingen	Rosenkranz
Burrweiler	Altenforst
	St. Annaberg
	Schäwer
	Schlossgarten
Dammheim	Höhe
Flemlingen	Herrenbuckel
	Vogelsprung
	Zechpeter
Gleisweiler	Hölle
Knöringen	Hohenrain
Nussdorf	Herrenberg
	Kaiserberg
	Kirchenstück
Roschbach	Rosenkränzel
	Simonsgarten
Walsheim	Forstweg
	Silberberg

Weinbauort (village)	Einzellage (vineyard)
Kapsweyher	Lerchenberg
Minfeld	Herrenberg
Niederotterbach	Eselsbuckel
Oberotterbach	Sonnenberg[2]
Schweigen-Rechtenbach	Sonnenberg[2]
Schweighofen	Sonnenberg[2]
	Wolfsberg
Steinfeld	Herrenwingert
Vollmersweiler	Krapfenberg

GROSSLAGE (SECTION OF VINEYARDS): KLOSTER LIEBFRAUENBERG

Weinbauort (village)	Einzellage (vineyard)
Bad Bergzabern	Altenberg
Barbelroth	Kirchberg
Billigheim-Ingenheim	Mandelpfad[3]
	Pfaffenberg
	Rosenberg[4]
	Sauschwänzel
	Steingebiss
	Venusbuckel
Gleiszellen-Gleishorbach	Frühmess
	Kirchberg
Göcklingen	Herrenpfad[6]
Hergersweiler	Narrenberg[5]
Heuchelheim-Klingen	Herrenpfad[6]
Kapellen-Drusweiler	Rosengarten

GROSSLAGE (SECTION OF VINEYARDS): GUTTENBERG

Weinbauort (village)	Einzellage (vineyard)
Bad Bergzabern	Wonneberg[1]
Dierbach	Kirchhöh
Dörrenbach	Wonneberg[1]
Freckenfeld	Gräfenberg
Kandel	Galgenberg

NOTE: Numbers following a vineyard name indicate that the plot is divided between two (or more) villages.

Weinbauort (village)	Einzellage (vineyard)
Klingenmünster	Maria Magdalena
Niederhorbach	Silberberg
Oberhausen	Frohnwingert
Pleisweiler-Oberhofen	Schlossberg
Rohrbach	Mandelpfad[3]
Steinweiler	Rosenberg[4]
Winden	Narrenberg[5]

GROSSLAGE (SECTION OF VINEYARDS): KÖNIGSGARTEN

Weinbauort (village)	Einzellage (vineyard)
Albersweiler	Kirchberg
	Latt
Arzheim	Rosenberg
	Seligmacher[7]
Birkweiler	Rosenberg[8]
	Kastanienbusch
	Mandelberg
Frankweiler	Biengarten
	Kalkgrube
Godramstein	Klostergarten
	Münzberg
Landau	Altes Löhl
Ranschbach	Seligmacher[7]
Siebeldingen	Im Sonnenschein
	Mönchspfad
	Rosenberg[8]

GROSSLAGE (SECTION OF VINEYARDS): MANDELHÖHE

Weinbauort (village)	Einzellage (vineyard)
Kirrweiler	Mandelberg
	Oberschloss
	Römerweg
Maikammer	Heiligenberg
	Immengarten
	Kirchenstück
Maikammer-Alsterweiler	Kapellenberg

GROSSLAGE (SECTION OF VINEYARDS): ORDENSGUT

Weinbauort (village)	Einzellage (vineyard)
Edesheim	Forst
	Mandelhang
	Rosengarten
	Schloss
Hainfeld	Kapelle
	Kirchenstück
	Letten
Rhodt	Klosterpfad
	Rosengarten
	Schlossberg
Weyher	Heide
	Michelsberg

GROSSLAGE (SECTION OF VINEYARDS): HERRLICH

Weinbauort (village)	Einzellage (vineyard)
Eschbach	Hasen
Göcklingen	Kaiserberg
Herxheim bei Landau	Engelsberg
Herxheimweyher	Am Gaisberg
Ilbesheim	Rittersberg
	Sonnenberg[9]

Weinbauort (village)	Einzellage (vineyard)
Impflingen	Abtsberg
Insheim	Schäfergarten[10]
Leinsweiler	Sonnenberg[9]
Mörzheim	Pfaffenberg
Rohrbach	Schäfergarten[10]
Wollmesheim	Mütterle

GROSSLAGE (SECTION OF VINEYARDS): SCHLOSS LUDWIGSHÖHE

Weinbauort (village)	Einzellage (vineyard)
Edenkoben	Bergel
	Blücherhöhe
	Heidegarten
	Heilig Kreuz
	Kastaniengarten
	Kirchberg
	Klostergarten
	Mühlberg
	Schwarzer Letten
St. Martin	Baron
	Kirchberg
	Zitadelle

GROSSLAGE (SECTION OF VINEYARDS): TRAPPENBERG

Weinbauort (village)	Einzellage (vineyard)
Altdorf	Gottesacker
	Hochgericht
Bellheim	Gollenberg[11]
Böbingen	Ortelberg
Bornheim	Neuberg
Essingen	Osterberg
	Rossberg
	Sonnenberg
Freimersheim	Bildberg
Gross-u. Kleinfischlingen	Kirchberg
Hochstadt	Rotenberg
Knittelsheim	Gollenberg[11]
Lustadt	Klostergarten[12]
Ottersheim	Kahlenberg
Römerberg	Alter Berg
	Narrenberg
	Schlittberg
Schwegenheim	Bründelsberg
Venningen	Doktor
Weingarten	Schlossberg
Zeiskam	Klostergarten[12]

BEREICH (sub-region):
MITTELHAARDT-DEUTSCHE WEINSTRASSE

GROSSLAGE (SECTION OF VINEYARDS): FEUERBERG

Weinbauort (village)	Einzellage (vineyard)
Bad Dürkheim	Herrenmorgen
	Nonnengarten
	Steinberg
Bobenheim am Berg	Kieselberg
	Ohligpfad
Ellerstadt	Bubeneck
	Dickkopp
	Sonnenberg
Gönnheim	Martinshöhe

Weinbauort (village)	Einzellage (vineyard)
Kallstadt	Annaberg
	Kreidkeller
Weisenheim am Berg	Vogelsang

GROSSLAGE (SECTION OF VINEYARDS): GRAFENSTÜCK

Weinbauort (village)	Einzellage (vineyard)
Bockenheim	Burggarten
	Goldgrube
	Hassmannsberg
	Heiligenkirche
	Klosterschaffnerei
	Schlossberg
	Sonnenberg[14]
	Vogelsang[13]
Kindenheim	Burgweg
	Katzenstein
	Sonnenberg[14]
	Vogelsang[13]
Obrigheim	Benn
	Hochgericht
	Mandelpfad
	Rosengarten
	Schloss
	Sonnenberg[14]

GROSSLAGE (SECTION OF VINEYARDS): HOCHMESS

Weinbauort (village)	Einzellage (vineyard)
Bad Dürkheim	Hochbenn
	Michelsberg[15]
	Rittergarten
	Spielberg
Ungstein	Michelsberg[15]

GROSSLAGE (SECTION OF VINEYARDS): HÖLLENPFAD

Weinbauort (village)	Einzellage (vineyard)
Battenberg	Schlossberg
Grünstadt	Bergel
	Goldberg
	Honigsack
	Hütt
	Klostergarten
	Röth
	St. Stephan
	Schloss
Kleinkarlbach	Frauenländchen
	Herrenberg
	Herrgottsacker
	Kieselberg
	Senn
Mertesheim	St. Martinskreuz
Neuleiningen	Feuermännchen
	Schlossberg
	Sonnenberg

GROSSLAGE (SECTION OF VINEYARDS): HOFSTÜCK

Weinbauort (village)	Einzellage (vineyard)
Deidesheim	Nonnenstück
Ellerstadt	Kirchenstück
Friedelsheim	Gerümpel
	Rosengarten

Weinbauort (village)	Einzellage (vineyard)
Gönnheim	Klostergarten
	Mandelgarten
	Sonnenberg
Hochdorf-Assenheim	Fuchsloch[16]
Meckenheim	Neuberg
	Spielberg
	Wolfsdarm
Niederkirchen	Klostergarten
	Osterbrunnen
	Schlossberg
Rödersheim-Gronau	Fuchsloch[16]
Ruppertsberg	Gaisböhl
	Hoheburg
	Linsenbusch
	Nussbien
	Reiterpfad
	Spiess

GROSSLAGE (SECTION OF VINEYARDS): HONIGSÄCKEL

Weinbauort (village)	Einzellage (vineyard)
Ungstein	Herrenberg
	Nussriegel
	Weilberg

GROSSLAGE (SECTION OF VINEYARDS): KOBNERT

Weinbauort (village)	Einzellage (vineyard)
Dackenheim	Kapellgarten
	Liebesbrunnen
	Mandelröth
Erpolzheim	Kirschgarten
Freinsheim	Musikantenbuckel
	Oschelskopf
	Schwarzes Kreuz
Herxheim/Berg	Himmelreich
	Honigsack
	Kirchenstück
Kallstadt	Kronenberg
	Steinacker
Leistadt	Herzfeld
	Kalkofen
	Kirchenstück
Ungstein	Bettelhaus
	Osterberg
Weisenheim am Berg	Mandelgarten
	Sonnenberg

GROSSLAGE (SECTION OF VINEYARDS): MARIENGARTEN

Weinbauort (village)	Einzellage (vineyard)
Deidesheim	Grainhübel
	Herrgottsacker
	Hohenmorgen
	Kalkofen
	Kieselberg
	Langenmorgen
	Leinhöhle
	Mäushöhle
	Paradiesgarten

Weinbauort (village)	Einzellage (vineyard)
Forst	Elster
	Freundstück
	Jesuitengarten
	Kirchenstück
	Musenhang
	Pechstein
	Ungeheuer
Wachenheim	Altenburg
	Belz
	Böhlig
	Gerümpel
	Goldbächel
	Rechbächel

GROSSLAGE (SECTION OF VINEYARDS): MEERSPINNE

Weinbauort (village)	Einzellage (vineyard)
Gimmeldingen	Biengarten
	Kapellenberg
	Mandelgarten
	Schlössel
Haardt	Bürgergarten
	Herrenletten
	Herzog
	Mandelring
Königsbach	Idig
	Jesuitengarten
	Ölberg
	Reiterpfad
Mussbach	Bischofsweg
	Eselshaut
	Glockenzehnt
	Johannitergarten
	Kurfürst
	Spiegel
Neustadt an der Weinstrasse	Mönchgarten

GROSSLAGE (SECTION OF VINEYARDS): PFAFFENGRUND

Weinbauort (village)	Einzellage (vineyard)
Diedesfeld	Berg
Duttweiler	Kalkberg
	Kreuzberg
	Mandelberg
Geinsheim	Gässel
Hambach	Römerbrunnen
Lachen-Speyerdorf	Kroatenpfad
	Langenstein
	Lerchenböhl

GROSSLAGE (SECTION OF VINEYARDS): REBSTÖCKEL

Weinbauort (village)	Einzellage (vineyard)
Diedesfeld	Johanniskirchel
	Ölgässel
	Paradies
Hambach	Feuer
	Kaiserstuhl
	Kirchberg
	Schlossberg
Neustadt an der Weinstrasse	Erkenbrecht
	Grain

GROSSLAGE (SECTION OF VINEYARDS): ROSENBÜHL

Weinbauort (village)	Einzellage (vineyard)
Erpolzheim	Goldberg
	Kieselberg
Freinsheim	Goldberg[17]
Lambsheim	Burgweg[18]
Weisenheim/Sand	Altenberg
	Burgweg[18]
	Goldberg[17]
	Hahnen
	Halde
	Hasenzeile

GROSSLAGE (SECTION OF VINEYARDS): SAUMAGEN

Weinbauort (village)	Einzellage (vineyard)
Kallstadt	Horn
	Kirchenstück
	Nill

GROSSLAGE (SECTION OF VINEYARDS): SCHENKENBÖHL

Weinbauort (village)	Einzellage (vineyard)
Bad Dürkheim	Abtsfronhof
	Fronhof
	Fuchsmantel[19]
Wachenheim	Fuchsmantel[19]
	Königswingert
	Mandelgarten
	Odinstal
	Schlossberg

GROSSLAGE (SECTION OF VINEYARDS): SCHNEPFENFLUG VOM ZELLERTAL

Weinbauort (village)	Einzellage (vineyard)
Albisheim	Heiligenborn
Bolanden	Schlossberg
Bubenheim	Hahnenkamm
Einselthum	Kreuzberg[20]
	Klosterstüch[21]
Gauersheim	Goldloch
Immesheim	Sonnenstück
Kerzenheim	Esper
Kirchheimbolanden	Schlossgarten
Morschheim	Im Heubusch
Niefernheim	Königsweg[22]
	Kreuzberg[20]
Ottersheim/Zellerthal	Bräunersberg
Rittersheim	Am hohen Stein
Rüssingen	Breinsberg
Stetten	Heilighäuschen
Zell	Klosterstück[21]
	Königsweg[22]
	Kreuzberg[20]
	Schwarzer Herrgott

GROSSLAGE (SECTION OF VINEYARDS): SCHNEPFENFLUG AN DER WEINSTRASSE

Weinbauort (village)	Einzellage (vineyard)
Deidesheim	Letten
Forst	Stift
	Süsskopf
	Bischofsgarten[23]

Weinbauort (village)	Einzellage (vineyard)	Weinbauort (village)	Einzellage (vineyard)
Friedelsheim	Bischofsgarten[23]	Grosskarlbach	Burgweg
	Kreuz		Osterberg
	Schlossgarten	Grossniedesheim	Schafberg
Wachenheim	Bischofsgarten[23]	Hessheim	Lange Els
	Luginsland	Heuchelheim/Frankenthal	Steinkopf
		Kirchheim	Geisskopf

GROSSLAGE (SECTION OF VINEYARDS): SCHWARZERDE

Weinbauort (village)	Einzellage (vineyard)	Weinbauort (village)	Einzellage (vineyard)
Bissersheim	Goldberg		Kreuz
	Held		Römerstrasse
	Orlenberg		Steinacker
	Steig	Kleinniedesheim	Schlossgarten
Dirmstein	Herrgottsacker		Vorderberg
	Jesuitenhofgarten	Laumersheim	Kirschgarten
	Mandelpfad		Mandelberg
Gerolsheim	Klosterweg		Sonnengarten
	Lerchenspiel	Obersülzen	Schnepp

XI ANBAUGEBIET (region): WÜRTTEMBERG

BEREICH (sub-region): REMSTAL-STUTTGART

GROSSLAGE (SECTION OF VINEYARDS): HOHENNEUFFEN

Weinbauort (village)	Einzellage (vineyard)	Weinbauort (village)	Einzellage (vineyard)
Beuren	Schlossteige	(Ortsteile Bad Cannstatt, Untertürkheim)	Herzogenberg
Frickenhausen	Schlossteige		
Kappishäusern	Schlossteige	(Orteil Obertürkheim)	Kirchberg
Kohlberg	Schlossteige	(Ortsteile Hedelfingen, Rohracker)	Lenzenberg
Linsenhofen	Schlossteige		
Metzingen	Hofsteige	(Ortsteile Bad Cannstatt, Untertürkheim)	Mönchberg
	Schlossteige		
Neuffen	Schlossteige	(Ortsteil Degerloch)	Scharrenberg
Weilheim	Schlossteige	(Ortsteile Rotenberg, Uhlbach, Untertürkheim)	Schlossberg

GROSSLAGE (SECTION OF VINEYARDS): WEINSTEIGE

Weinbauort (village)	Einzellage (vineyard)	Weinbauort (village)	Einzellage (vineyard)
Esslingen	Ailenberg	(Ortsteil Uhlbach)	Steingrube
	Kirchberg	(Ortsteile Bad Cannstatt, Mühlhausen, Münster)	Steinhalde
	Lerchenberg		
	Schenkenberg	(Ortsteil Untertürkheim)	Wetzstein
Fellbach	Gips	(Ortsteile Bad Cannstatt, Hofen, Mühlhausen, Münster)	Zuckerle
	Goldberg		
	Herzogenberg		
	Hinterer Berg		

GROSSLAGE (SECTION OF VINEYARDS): SONNENBÜHL

Weinbauort (village)	Einzellage (vineyard)
Beutelsbach	
Schnait i. R.	Burghalde
Endersbach	Hintere Klinge
Rommelshausen	
Stetten i. R.	Mönchhalde
Strümpfelbach	Altenberg

Weinbauort (village)	Einzellage (vineyard)
	Lämmler
	Mönchberg
	Wetzstein
Gerlingen	Bopser
Stuttgart	Kriegsberg
	Mönchberg
(Ortsteil Gaisburg)	Abelsberg
(Ortsteil Untertürkheim)	Gips
(Ortsteil Uhlbach)	Götzenberg
(Ortsteil Obertürkheim)	Ailenberg
(Ortsteil Untertürkheim)	Altenberg
(Ortsteile Bad Cannstatt, Feuerbach, Münster, Wangen, Zuffenhausen)	Berg
(Ortsteil Bad Cannstatt)	Halde

GROSSLAGE (SECTION OF VINEYARDS): KOPF

Weinbauort (village)	Einzellage (vineyard)
Beinstein	Grossmulde
Breuningsweiler	Holzenberg
Bürg	Schlossberg
Grossheppach	Wanne
Grunbach	Berghalde
Hanweiler	Berg
Kleinheppach	Greiner

Weinbauort (village)	Einzellage (vineyard)
Korb	Berg
	Hörnle
	Sommerhalde
Neustadt	Söhrenberg
Schorndorf	Grafenberg
Waiblingen	Hörnle
Winnenden	Berg
	Holzenberg
	Rossberg
Winterbach	Hungerberg

GROSSLAGE (SECTION OF VINEYARDS): WARTBÜHL

Weinbauort (village)	Einzellage (vineyard)
Aichelberg	Luginsland
Baach	Himmelreich
Beutelsbach	Altenberg
	Käppele
	Sonnenberg
Breuningsweiler	Haselstein
Endersbach	Happenhalde
	Wetzstein
Geradstetten	Lichtenberg
	Sonnenberg
Grossheppach	Steingrüble
	Zügernberg
Grunbach	Klingle
Hanweiler	Maien
Hebsack	Lichtenberg
Hertmannsweiler	Himmelreich
Kleinheppach	Sonnenberg
	Steingrüble
Korb	Steingrüble
Rommelshausen	Häder
Schnait i. R.	Altenberg
	Sonnenberg
Stetten i. R.	Brotwasser
	Häder
	Lindhälder
	Puvermächer
Strümpfelbach	Gastenklinge
	Nonnenberg
Waiblingen	Steingrüble
Winnenden	Haselstein

BEREICH (sub-region):
WÜRTTEMBERGISCH UNTERLAND

GROSSLAGE (SECTION OF VINEYARDS): SCHALKSTEIN

Weinbauort (village)	Einzellage (vineyard)
Allmersbach a.W.	Alter Berg
Affalterbach	Neckarhälde
Asperg	Berg
Beihingen	Neckarhälde
Benningen	Neckarhälde
Besigheim	Felsengarten
	Katzenöhrle
	Neckarberg
	Wurmberg
Bietigheim	Neckarberg
Bissingen	Neckarberg

Weinbauort (village)	Einzellage (vineyard)
Erdmannhausen	Neckarhälde
Gemmrigheim	Neckarberg
	Wurmberg
Grossingersheim	Schlossberg
Hessigheim	Felsengarten
	Käsberg
	Katzenöhrle
Höpfigheim	Königsberg
Kirchberg	Kelterberg
Kleinaspach	Kelterberg
Kleiningersheim	Schlossberg
Löchgau	Neckarberg
Ludwigsburg (Ortsteil Hoheneck)	Neckarhälde
Marbach	Neckarhälde
Markgröningen	Berg
	Sankt Johännser
Mundelsheim	Käsberg
	Katzenöhrle
	Mühlbächer
	Rozenberg
Murr	Neckarhälde
Neckarweihingen	Neckarhälde
Poppenweiler	Neckarhälde
Rielinghausen	Kelterberg
Rietenau	Güldenkern
Steinheim/Murr	Burgberg
Walheim	Neckarberg
	Wurmberg

GROSSLAGE (SECTION OF VINEYARDS): STROMBERG

Weinbauort (village)	Einzellage (vineyard)
Bönnigheim	Kirchberg
	Sonnenberg
Diefenbach	König
Ensingen	Schanzreiter
Erligheim	Lerchenberg
Freudenstein	Reichshalde
Freudental	Kirchberg
Gründelbach	Steinbachhof
	Wachtkopf
Häfnerhaslach	Heiligenberg
Hofen	Lerchenberg
Hohenhaslach	Kirchberg
	Klosterberg
Hohenstein	Kirchberg
Horrheim	Klosterberg
Illingen	Forstgrube
	Halde
	Lichtenberg
	Schanzreiter
Kirchheim	Kirchberg
Kleinsachsenheim	Kirchberg
Knittlingen	Reichshalde
Lienzingen	Eichelberg
Maulbronn	Eilfingerberg Klosterstück
	Reichshalde
Mühlhausen	Halde
Obererdingen	Kupferhalde
Ochsenbach	Liebenberg

Weinbauort (*village*)	Einzellage (*vineyard*)
Ötisheim	Sauberg
Riet	Kirchberg
Rosswag	Forstgrube
	Halde
	Lichtenberg
Schützingen	Heiligenberg
Spielberg	Liebenberg
Sternenfels	König
Vaihingen	Höllisch Feuer

GROSSLAGE (SECTION OF VINEYARDS): HEUCHELBERG

Weinbauort (*village*)	Einzellage (*vineyard*)
Brackenheim	Dachsberg
	Mönchsberg
	Schlossberg
	Wolfsaugen
	Zweifelberg
(Ortsteil Botenheim)	Ochsenberg
Burgbronn	Hahnenberg
Cleebronn	Michaelsberg
Dürrenzimmern	Mönchsberg
Eibensbach	Michaelsberg
Frauenzimmern	Kaiserberg
	Michaelsberg
Güglingen	Kaiserberg
	Michaelsberg
Haberschlacht	Dachsberg
Hausen/Z.	Jupiterberg
	Vogelsang
	Staig
Heilbronn (Ortsteil Klingenberg)	Schlossberg
	Sonntagsberg
Kleingartach	Grafenberg
	Vogelsang
Leingarten	Grafenberg
	Leiersberg
	Vogelsang
Massenbachhausen	Krähenberg
Meimsheim	Katzenöhrle
Neipperg	Grafenberg
	Steingrube
	Vogelsang
	Schlossberg
Niederhofen	Grafenberg
	Vogelsang
Nordhausen	Sonntagsberg
Nordheim	Grafenberg
	Gräfenberg
	Ruthe
	Sonntagsberg
Pfaffenhofen	Hohenberg
Schwaigern	Grafenberg
	Ruthe
	Sonnenberg
	Vogelsang
Stetten a. H.	Sonnenberg
Stockheim	Altenberg
Weiler/Z.	Hohenberg
Zaberfeld	Hohenberg

GROSSLAGE (SECTION OF VINEYARDS): WUNNENSTEIN

Weinbauort (*village*)	Einzellage (*vineyard*)
Beilstein	Schlosswengert
	Steinberg
	Wartberg
Gronau	Forstberg
Grossbottwar	Harzberg
	Lichtenberg
Hof und Lembach	Harzberg
	Lichtenberg
Ilsfeld	Lichtenberg
Kleinbottwar	Götzenberg
	Lichtenberg
	Oberer Berg
	Süssmund
Ludwigsburg (Ortsteil Hoheneck)	Oberer Berg
Oberstenfeld	Forstberg
	Harzberg
	Lichtenberg
Steinheim	Lichtenberg
Winzerhausen	Harzberg
	Lichtenberg

GROSSLAGE (SECTION OF VINEYARDS): SCHOZACHTAL

Weinbauort (*village*)	Einzellage (*vineyard*)
Abstatt	Burgberg
	Burg Wildeck
	Sommerberg
Auenstein	Burgberg
	Schlossberg
Ilsfeld	Rappen
Löwenstein	Sommerberg
Unterheinriet	Sommerberg

GROSSLAGE (SECTION OF VINEYARDS): KIRCHENWEINBERG

Weinbauort (*village*)	Einzellage (*vineyard*)
Flein	Altenberg
	Eselsberg
	Sonnenberg
Heilbronn	Altenberg
	Sonnenberg
Ilsfeld (Ortsteil Schozach)	Mühlberg
	Roter Berg
	Schelmenklinge
Lauffen	Jungfer
	Katzenbeisser
	Nonnenberg
	Riedersbückele
Neckarwestheim	Herrlesberg
Talheim	Hohe Eiche
	Schlossberg
	Sonnenberg
Untergruppenbach	Schlossberg

GROSSLAGE (SECTION OF VINEYARDS): STAUFENBERG

Weinbauort (*village*)	Einzellage (*vineyard*)
Brettach	Berg
Cleversulzbach	Berg
Duttenberg	Schön
Erlenbach	Kayberg

Weinbauort (village)	Einzellage (vineyard)
Gundelsheim	Himmelreich
Heilbronn	Stahlbühl
	Stiftsberg
	Wartberg
Horkheim	Stiftsberg
Neckarsulm	Scheuerberg
Oedheim	Kayberg
Offenau	Schön
Talheim	Stiftsberg
Untereisesheim	Vogelsang

GROSSLAGE (SECTION OF VINEYARDS): SALZBERG

Weinbauort (village)	Einzellage (vineyard)
Affaltrach	Dieblesberg
	Zeilberg
Eberstadt	Dezberg
	Eberfürst
	Sommerhalde
Eichelberg	Hundsberg
Ellhofen	Altenberg
	Althälde
	Ranzenberg
Eschenau	Paradies
Gellmersbach	Dezberg
Grantschen	Wildenberg
Lehrensteinsfeld	Althälde
	Frauenzimmer
	Steinacker
Löwenstein	Altenberg
	Nonnenrain
	Wohlfahrtsberg
Löwenstein (Ortsteil Hösslinsülz)	Dieblesberg
	Zeilberg
Sülzbach	Altenberg
Weiler/Weinsberg	Hundsberg
	Schlierbach
Weinsberg	Althälde
	Ranzenberg
	Schemelsberg
Wimmental	Altenberg
Willsbach	Dieblesberg
	Zeilberg

GROSSLAGE (SECTION OF VINEYARDS): LINDELBERG

Weinbauort (village)	Einzellage (vineyard)
Adolzfurt	Schneckenhof
Bretzfeld	Goldberg
Dimbach	Schlossberg
Eschelbach	Schwobajörgle
Geddelsbach	Schneckenhof
Harsberg (Ortsteil Neuholz)	Dachsteiger
	Spielbühl
Kesselfeld	Schwobajörgle
Langenbeutingen	Himmelreich
Michelbach a. W.	Dachsteiger
	Margarete
Maienfels	Schneckenhof
Obersöllbach	Margarete

Weinbauort (village)	Einzellage (vineyard)
Pfedelbach	Goldberg
Siebeneich	Himmelreich
	Schlossberg
Schwabbach	Schlossberg
Unterheimbach	Schneckenhof
Untersteinbach	Dachsteiger
Verrenberg	Goldberg
	Verenberg
Waldbach	Schlossberg
Windischenbach	Goldberg

BEREICH (sub-region): KOCHER-JAGST-TAUBER

GROSSLAGE (SECTION OF VINEYARDS): KOCHERBERG

Weinbauort (village)	Einzellage (vineyard)
Belsenberg	Heilig Kreuz
Bieringen	Schlüsselberg
Criesbach	Burgstall
	Hoher Berg
	Sommerberg
Dörzbach	Altenberg
Ernsbach	Flatterberg
Forchtenberg	Flatterberg
Ingelfingen	Hoher Berg
Künzelsau	Hoher Berg
Möckmühl	Ammerlanden
	Hofberg
Niedernhall	Burgstall
	Engweg
	Hoher Berg
Siglingen	Hofberg
Weissbach	Altenberg
	Engweg
Widdern	Hofberg

GROSSLAGE (SECTION OF VINEYARDS): TAUBERBERG

Weinbauort (village)	Einzellage (vineyard)
Elpersheim	Mönchsberg
	Probstberg
Wermutshausen	Schafsteige

Not yet assigned a Grosslage (section of vineyards):

Weinbauort (village)	Einzellage (vineyard)
Kressbronn am Bodensee	Berghalde
Tübingen (Ortsteile Hirschau, Unterjesingen)	Sonnenhalden
Haagen	Schafsteige
Laudenbach	Schafsteige
Markelsheim	Mönchsberg
	Probstberg
Niederstetten	Schafsteige
Oberstetten	Schafsteige
Reinsbronn	Röde
Vorbachzimmern	Schafsteige
Weikersheim	Hardt
	Karlsberg
	Schmecker

APPENDIX C

Containers and Measures

I BOTTLE SIZES

Wine	Bottles	Metric capacity	U.S. ounces	British ounces	U.S. EQUIVALENT				BRITISH EQUIVALENT			
					Gal.	Qt.	Pt.	Oz.	Gal.	Qt.	Pt.	Oz.
ALSACE	½ bottle	36.00 cl.	12.17	12.67				12				13
	bottle	72.00 cl.	24.34	25.34			1	8			1	5
ANJOU	½ bottle	37.50 cl.	12.68	13.20				13				13
	bottle	75.00 cl.	25.36	26.40			1	9			1	6
BEAUJOLAIS	½ bottle	37.50 cl.	12.68	13.20				13				13
'Pot'	⅔ bottle	50.00 cl.	16.90	17.60			1	1				18
	bottle	75.00 cl.	25.36	26.40			1	9			1	6
BORDEAUX												
Fillette	½ bottle	37.50 cl.	12.68	13.20				13				13
	bottle	75.00 cl.	25.36	26.40			1	9			1	6
Magnum	2 bottles	1.50 l.	50.71	52.79		1	1	3		1	–	13
Marie-Jeanne	3 bottles (approx.)	2.50 l.	84.53	88.00		2	1	4		2	1	8
Double Magnum	4 bottles	3.00 l.	101.42	105.59		3	–	5		2	1	6
Jeroboam	6 bottles	4.50 l.	152.16	158.40	1	–	1	8		3	1	18
Imperial	8 bottles	6.00 l.	202.85	211.18	1	2	–	11	1	1	–	11
BURGUNDY	½ bottle	37.50 cl.	12.68	13.20				13				13
	bottle	75.00 cl.	25.36	26.40			1	9			1	6
Magnum	2 bottles	1.50 l.	50.71	52.79		1	1	3		1	–	13
CHAMPAGNE												
Split	¼ bottle	20.00 cl.	6.76	7.04				7				7
Pint	½ bottle	40.00 cl.	13.52	14.08				14				14
Quart	bottle	80.00 cl.	27.05	28.16			1	11			1	8
Magnum	2 bottles	1.60 l.	54.09	56.31		1	1	6		1	–	16
Jeroboam	4 bottles	3.20 l.	108.19	112.63		3	–	12		2	1	13
Rehoboam	6 bottles	4.80 l.	162.28	168.94	1	1	–	2	1	–	–	9
Methuselah	8 bottles	6.40 l.	216.37	225.25	1	2	1	8	1	1	1	5
Salmanazar	12 bottles	9.60 l.	324.46	337.88	2	2	–	4	2	–	–	18
Balthazar	16 bottles	12.80 l.	432.74	450.51	3	1	1	1	2	3	–	10
Nebuchadnezzar	20 bottles	16.00 l.	540.93	563.14	4	–	1	13	3	2	–	3
MOSELLE	½ bottle	35.00 cl.	11.83	12.32				12				12
	bottle	70.00 cl.	23.67	24.63			1	8			1	5
PORT												
Quart	bottle	75.75 cl.	25.61	26.66			1	10			1	7
Magnum	2 bottles	1.51 l.	51.20	53.15		1	1	3		1	–	13
Tappit Hen	3 bottles	2.27 l.	76.84	79.89		2	–	13		2	–	–
Jeroboam	4 bottles	3.03 l.	102.45	106.64		3	–	6		2	1	7
RHINE	½ bottle	35.00 cl.	11.83	12.32				12				12
	bottle	70.00 cl.	23.67	24.63			1	8			1	5

Wine	Bottles	Metric capacity	U.S. ounces	British ounces	U.S. EQUIVALENT				BRITISH EQUIVALENT			
					Gal.	Qt.	Pt.	Oz.	Gal.	Qt.	Pt.	Oz.
SHERRY												
Pint	½ bottle	37.86 cl.	12.80	13.32				13				13
Quart	bottle	75.75 cl.	25.61	26.66		1		10			1	7
U.S.												
Tenth	½ bottle	37.86 cl.	12.80	13.32				13				13
Fifth	bottle	75.72 cl.	25.60	26.65		1		10			1	7
Magnum	2 bottles	1.51 l.	51.20	53.15	1	1		3	1	–		13

NOTE: Basic metric capacities, and in some cases ounces, upon which most figures in this table are based, are those fixed by law. Actual contents will almost always vary because of differences in corking space.

II COOPERAGE

	Cask or barrel	Description	Metric capacity liters	U.S. equivalent U.S. gallons	British equivalent imp. gallons
FRANCE					
Alsace	Foudre	As in Germany, a huge barrel for sales and storage purposes	1,000 liters or any other size. No standard size is adhered to	264.2	220.0
	Aume	Used principally for shipping. Same size as Burgundy feuillette		30.1	25.1
Beaujolais	Pièce		216	57.1	47.5
	Feuillette	One-half pièce	108	28.5	23.7
	Quartaut	One-quarter pièce	54	14.3	11.9
Bordeaux	Barrique	Hogshead—so-called. Most common Bordeaux cask. Yields 25 cases of 12 bottles each	225	59.4	49.5
	Tonneau	A measure equivalent to 4 barriques. No actual barrel this size. Château production and price quotations stated in tonneaux. Yields 100 cases of 12 bottles each	900	237.8	197.9
	Demi-Barrique or Feuillette	One-half barrique	112	29.6	24.6
	Quartaut	One-quarter barrique	56	14.8	12.3
Burgundy	Pièce	Regular Burgundy barrel. When bottled, yields 24–25 cases of 12 bottles each	228	60.2	50.1
	Queue	Old French measure consisting of 2 pièces. No actual cask this size. Sales by Hospices de Beaune made in terms of queues	456	120.5	100.3
	Feuillette	One-half pièce	114	30.1	25.1
	Quartaut	One-quarter pièce	57	15.1	12.6
Chablis	Feuillette	Standard Chablis barrel. Larger than feuillette of Côte d'Or	132	34.9	29.0
Champagne		Regular Champagne cask. Also called a pièce	205	54.2	45.1
			108	28.5	23.7
Loire Valley					
Anjou Layon Saumur	Pièce	Capacity variable	220	58.1	48.4
Vouvray	Pièce	Capacity same as Bordeaux hogshead	225	59.4	49.5
Mâconnais	Pièce	Nearly the same size as the Beaujolais pièce	215	56.8	47.3
The Midi and Algeria	Demi-Muid	Storage barrel	600–700 (approx.)	171.7 (approx.)	143.0 (approx.)
Rhône Valley	Pièce	Standard barrel in the area of Châteauneuf-du-Pape. Slightly smaller than pièce of Côte d'Or	225	59.4	49.5

	Cask or barrel	Description	Metric capacity liters	U.S. equivalent U.S. gallons	British equivalent imp. gallons
GERMANY					
Rhine and Mosel	*Ohm*	An old Hock or Rhine measure which is now obsolete and is no longer used	150	39.6	33.0
	Doppelohm	Double *ohm* equal to a quarter *stück*	300	79.2	66.0
	Fuder (Mosel)	Large storage cask	1,000	264.2	219.9
	Stück (Rhine)	Huge storage cask	1,200	317.0	264.0
	Doppelstück (Rhine)	Double *stück*	2,400	634.0	527.8
	Halbstück (Rhine)	One-half *stück*	600	158.4	132.0
	Viertelstück (Rhine)	One-quarter *stück*	300	79.2	66.0
AUSTRALIA AND SOUTH AFRICA	*Hogshead*		295.3	78.0	64.9
LISBON	*Pipe*		531.4	140.4	117.0
MADEIRA	*Pipe*	Standard Madeira shipping cask. Yields on average 44½ cases of 12 bottles each	418.0	110.4	92.0
	Hogshead	One-half Madeira *pipe*	209.0	55.2	46.0
MARSALA	*Pipe*	Slightly larger than Madeira *pipe*. Yields 45 cases of 12 bottles each	422.6	111.6	93.0
	Hogshead	Same size as Madeira *hogshead*	209.0	55.2	46.0
PORT	*Pipe*	Standard Port cask. Average yield is 56 dozen reputed quarts	522.5	138.0	115.0
	Hogshead		259.0	68.4	57.0
	Quarter Cask	One-quarter standard	127.2	33.6	28.0
SHERRY	*Butt*	Standard Sherry cask. Yields, when bottled, 52 cases of 12 bottles each	490.7	129.6	108.0
	Hogshead	One-half *butt*, yields 26 cases of 12 bottles each	245.4	64.8	54.0
	Quarter Cask	One-quarter standard, or one-half *hogshead*	122.7	32.4	27.0
	Octave	One-eighth standard	61.4	16.2	13.5
TARRAGONA	*Pipe*	Same capacity as *pipe* of Port	350	92.5	77.0
	Hogshead		400	105.8	88.1
COGNAC	*Hogshead*	Most commonly used brandy cask	545.2	144.0	120.0
ARMAGNAC	*Hogshead*		272.6	72.0	60.0
RUM	*Puncheon*	Size varies considerably	422.6–518.0	111.6–136.8	92.9–113.9
	Hogshead	Equally variable in size	245.4–272.6	64.8–72.0	54.0–59.9
WHISKY—SCOTCH	*Butt*	Standard distillery cask. Sometimes a rum *puncheon*, made from oak, cut down to the *butt* length of stave and gallonage	491.0 (approx.)	129.7 (approx.)	108.0 (approx.)
	Puncheon	Capacity varies between 95 and 120 imp. gallons	431.9–545.5	114.1–144.1	95.0–120.0
WHISKEY—U.S.	*Barrel*	Standard new barrel for either Rye or Bourbon whiskey as required by law	181.7	48.0	40.0
WHISKY—CANADIAN	*Barrel*	Capacity variable. Usually exceeds slightly the standard U.S. 48-gallon barrel	181.7 (approx.)	48.0 (approx.)	40.0 (approx.)

	Cask or barrel	Description	Metric capacity liters	U.S. equivalent U.S. gallons	British equivalent imp. gallons
SPIRITS (*Aged*) U.S.	*Barrel*	Used cooperage: same U.S. barrel and size as for whiskey	181.7	48.0	40.0
	Hogshead	Cask holding between 45 and 80 imp. gals.		54.0-96.0	45.0-80.0
	Barrel	Cask holding between 35 and 45 imp. gals.		42.0-54.0	35.0-45.0
	Quarter	Cask holding between 15 and 30 imp. gals.		18.0-36.0	15.0-30.0
	Octave	Cask holding between 9 and 15 imp. gals.		10.8-18.0	9.0-15.0

CASE

Bordeaux and Burgundy			8.52	2.25	1.87
Champagne			9.23	2.4375	2.0304

APPENDIX D

Comparative Table of Spirit Strength

Sikes (British) U.P. (Under proof)	American	Gay-Lussac and Tralles	Sikes (British) U.P. (Under proof)	American	Gay-Lussac and Tralles
60.0°	45.7°	22.9°	39.6°	69.0°	34.5°
59.8	46.0	23.0	39.0	69.7	34.9
59.0	46.9	23.4	38.8	70.0	35.0
58.9	47.0	23.5	38.0	70.9	35.4
58.0	48.0	24.0	37.9	71.0	35.5
57.1	49.0	24.5	37.0	72.0	36.0
57.0	49.1	24.6	36.1	73.0	36.5
56.3	50.0	25.0	36.0	73.1	36.6
56.0	50.3	25.1	35.3	74.0	37.0
55.4	51.0	25.5	35.0	74.3	37.1
55.0	51.4	25.7	34.4	75.0	37.5
54.5	52.0	26.0	34.0	75.4	37.7
54.0	52.6	26.3	33.5	76.0	38.0
53.6	53.0	26.5	33.0	76.6	38.3
53.0	53.7	26.9	32.6	77.0	38.5
52.8	54.0	27.0	32.0	77.7	38.9
52.0	54.9	27.4	31.8	78.0	39.0
51.9	55.0	27.5	31.0	78.9	39.4
51.0	56.0	28.0	30.9	79.0	39.5
50.1	57.0	28.5	30.0	80.0	40.0
50.0	57.1	28.6	29.1	81.0	40.5
49.3	58.0	29.0	29.0	81.1	40.6
49.0	58.3	29.1	28.3	82.0	41.0
48.4	59.0	29.5	28.0	82.3	41.1
48.0	59.4	29.7	27.4	83.0	41.5
47.5	60.0	30.0	27.0	83.4	41.7
47.0	60.6	30.3	26.5	84.0	42.0
46.6	61.0	30.5	26.0	84.6	42.3
46.0	61.7	30.9	25.6	85.0	42.5
45.8	62.0	31.0	25.0	85.7	42.9
45.0	62.9	31.4	24.8	86.0	43.0
44.9	63.0	31.5	24.0	86.9	43.4
44.0	64.0	32.0	23.9	87.0	43.5
43.1	65.0	32.5	23.0	88.0	44.0
43.0	65.1	32.6	22.1	89.0	44.5
42.3	66.0	33.0	22.0	89.1	44.6
42.0	66.3	33.1	21.3	90.0	45.0
41.4	67.0	33.5	21.0	90.3	45.1
41.0	67.4	33.7	20.4	91.0	45.5
40.5	68.0	34.0	20.0	91.4	45.7
40.0	68.6	34.3			

Sikes (British)	American	Gay-Lussac and Tralles	Sikes (British)	American	Gay-Lussac and Tralles
19.5°	92.0°	46.0°	8.5°	124.0°	62.0°
19.0	92.6	46.3	9.0	124.6	62.3
18.6	93.0	46.5	9.4	125.0	62.5
18.0	93.7	46.9	10.0	125.7	62.9
17.8	94.0	47.0	10.3	126.0	63.0
17.0	94.9	47.4	11.0	126.9	63.4
16.9	95.0	47.5	11.1	127.0	63.5
16.0	96.0	48.0	12.0	128.0	64.0
15.1	97.0	48.5	12.9	129.0	64.5
15.0	97.1	48.6	13.0	129.1	64.6
14.3	98.0	49.0	13.8	130.0	65.0
14.0	98.3	49.1	14.0	130.3	65.1
13.4	99.0	49.5	14.6	131.0	65.5
13.0	99.4	49.7	15.0	131.4	65.7
12.5	Proof	50.0	15.5	132.0	66.0
12.0	100.6	50.3	16.0	132.6	66.3
11.6	101.0	50.5	16.4	133.0	66.5
11.0	101.7	50.9	17.0	133.7	66.9
10.8	102.0	51.0	17.3	134.0	67.0
10.0	102.9	51.4	18.0	134.9	67.4
9.9	103.0	51.5	18.1	135.0	67.5
9.0	104.0	52.0	19.0	136.0	68.0
8.1	105.0	52.5	19.9	137.0	68.5
8.0	105.1	52.6	20.0	137.1	68.6
7.3	106.0	53.0	20.8	138.0	69.0
7.0	106.3	53.1	21.0	138.3	69.1
6.4	107.0	53.5	21.6	139.0	69.5
6.0	107.4	53.7	22.0	139.4	69.7
5.5	108.0	54.0	22.5	140.0	70.0
5.0	108.6	54.3	23.0	140.6	70.3
4.6	109.0	54.5	23.4	141.0	70.5
4.0	109.7	54.9	24.0	141.7	70.9
3.8	110.0	55.0	24.3	142.0	71.0
3.0	110.9	55.4	25.0	142.9	71.4
2.9	111.0	55.5	25.1	143.0	71.5
2.0	112.0	56.0	26.0	144.0	72.0
1.1	113.0	56.5	26.9	145.0	72.5
1.0	113.1	56.6	27.0	145.1	72.6
0.3	114.0	57.0	27.8	146.0	73.0
Proof	114.29	57.14	28.0	146.3	73.1
O.P.			28.6	147.0	73.5
(Over proof)			29.0	147.4	73.7
0.6	115.0	57.5	29.5	148.0	74.0
1.0	115.4	57.7	30.0	148.6	74.3
1.5	116.0	58.0	30.4	149.0	74.5
2.0	116.6	58.3	31.0	149.7	74.9
2.4	117.0	58.5	31.3	150.0	75.0
3.0	117.7	58.9	32.0	150.9	75.4
3.3	118.0	59.0	32.1	151.0	75.5
4.0	118.9	59.4	33.0	152.0	76.0
4.1	119.0	59.5	33.9	153.0	76.5
5.0	120.0	60.0	34.0	153.1	76.6
5.9	121.0	60.5	34.8	154.0	77.0
6.0	121.1	60.6	35.0	154.3	77.1
6.8	122.0	61.0	35.6	155.0	77.5
7.0	122.3	61.1	36.0	155.4	77.7
7.6	123.0	61.5	36.5	156.0	78.0
8.0	123.4	61.7			

Comparative Table of Spirit Strength

Sikes (British)	American	Gay-Lussac and Tralles	Sikes (British)	American	Gay-Lussac and Tralles
37.0°	156.6°	78.3°	56.6°	179.0°	89.5°
37.4	157.0	78.5	57.0	179.4	89.7
38.0	157.7	78.9	57.5	180.0	90.0
38.3	158.0	79.0	58.0	180.6	90.3
39.0	158.9	79.4	58.4	181.0	90.5
39.1	159.0	79.5	50.9	181.7	90.9
40.0	160.0	80.0	59.3	182.0	91.0
40.9	161.0	80.5	60.0	182.9	91.4
41.0	161.1	80.6	60.1	183.0	91.5
41.8	162.0	81.0	61.0	184.0	92.0
42.0	162.3	81.1	61.9	185.0	92.5
42.6	163.0	81.5	62.0	185.1	92.6
43.0	163.4	81.7	62.8	186.0	93.0
43.5	164.0	82.0	63.0	186.3	93.1
44.0	164.6	82.3	63.6	187.0	93.5
44.4	165.0	82.5	64.0	187.4	93.7
45.0	165.7	82.9	64.5	188.0	94.0
45.3	166.0	83.0	65.0	188.6	94.3
46.0	166.9	83.4	65.4	189.0	94.5
46.1	167.0	83.5	66.0	189.7	94.9
47.0	168.0	84.0	66.3	190.0	95.0
47.9	169.0	84.5	67.0	190.9	95.4
48.0	169.1	84.6	67.1	191.0	95.5
48.8	170.0	85.0	68.0	192.0	96.0
49.0	170.3	85.1	68.9	193.0	96.5
49.6	171.0	85.5	69.0	193.1	96.6
50.0	171.4	85.7	69.8	194.0	97.0
50.5	172.0	86.0	70.0	194.3	97.1
51.0	172.6	86.3	70.6	195.0	97.5
51.4	173.0	86.5	71.0	195.4	97.7
52.0	173.7	86.9	71.5	196.0	98.0
52.3	174.0	87.0	72.0	196.6	98.3
53.0	174.9	87.4	72.4	197.0	98.5
53.1	175.0	87.5	73.0	197.7	98.9
54.0	176.0	88.0	73.3	198.0	99.0
54.9	177.0	88.5	74.0	198.9	99.4
55.0	177.1	88.6	74.1	199.0	99.5
55.8	178.0	89.0	75.0	200.0	100.0
56.0	178.3	89.1			

Conversion Tables

I MEASUREMENT OF LENGTH

Centimeters	Inches	Ft.	Ins.		Meters	Ft.	Yds.	Ft.	Ins.	Yds.		Kilometers	Miles
1	0.394		$\frac{2}{5}$		1	3.281	1		$3\frac{2}{5}$	1.094		1	0.621
2	0.787		$\frac{4}{5}$		2	6.562	2		$6\frac{7}{10}$	2.187		2	1.243
3	1.181		$1\frac{1}{5}$		3	9.843	3		$10\frac{1}{10}$	3.281		3	1.864
4	1.575		$1\frac{3}{5}$		4	13.123	4	1	$1\frac{1}{2}$	4.374		4	2.486
5	1.969		2		5	16.404	5	1	$4\frac{4}{5}$	5.468		5	3.107
6	2.362		$2\frac{2}{5}$		6	19.685	6	1	$8\frac{1}{5}$	6.562		6	3.728
7	2.756		$2\frac{4}{5}$		7	22.966	7	1	$11\frac{3}{5}$	7.655		7	4.350
8	3.150		$3\frac{1}{5}$		8	26.247	8	2	3	8.749		8	4.971
9	3.543		$3\frac{1}{2}$		9	29.528	9	2	$6\frac{3}{10}$	9.843		9	5.592
10	3.937		$3\frac{9}{10}$		10	32.808	10	2	$9\frac{7}{10}$	10.936		10	6.214
20	7.874		$7\frac{9}{10}$		20	65.617	21	2	$7\frac{2}{5}$	21.872		20	12.427
30	11.811		$11\frac{4}{5}$		30	98.425	32	2	$5\frac{1}{10}$	32.808		30	18.641
40	15.748	1	$3\frac{7}{10}$		40	131.234	43	2	$2\frac{4}{5}$	43.745		40	24.855
50	19.685	1	$7\frac{7}{10}$		50	164.042	54	2	$\frac{1}{2}$	54.681		50	31.069
60	23.622	1	$11\frac{3}{5}$		60	196.850	65	1	$10\frac{1}{5}$	65.617		60	37.282
70	27.559	2	$3\frac{3}{5}$		70	229.659	76	1	$7\frac{9}{10}$	76.553		70	43.496
80	31.496	2	$7\frac{1}{2}$		80	262.467	87	1	$5\frac{3}{5}$	87.489		80	49.710
90	35.433	2	$11\frac{2}{5}$		90	295.276	98	1	$3\frac{3}{10}$	98.425		90	55.923
100 = 1 meter	39.370	3	$3\frac{2}{5}$		100	328.084	109	1	1	109.361		100	62.137

10 millimeters = 1 centimeter	10 decimeters = 1 meter	10 dekameters = 1 hectometer
10 centimeters = 1 decimeter	10 meters = 1 dekameter	10 hectometers = 1 kilometer

MEASUREMENT OF LENGTH (continued)

Inches	Centimeters		Feet	Meters		Yards	Meters		Miles	Kilometers
1	2.540		1	0.305		1	0.914		1	1.609
2	5.080		2	0.610		2	1.829		2	3.219
3	7.620		3 = 1 yard	0.914		3	2.743		3	4.828
4	10.160		4	1.219		4	3.658		4	6.437
5	12.700		5	1.524		5	4.572		5	8.047
6	15.240		6	1.829		6	5.486		6	9.656
7	17.780		7	2.134		7	6.401		7	11.265
8	20.320		8	2.438		8	7.315		8	12.875
9	22.860		9	2.743		9	8.230		9	14.484
10	25.400		10	3.048		10	9.144		10	16.093
11	27.940		20	6.096		20	18.288		20	32.187
12 = 1 foot	30.480		30	9.144		30	27.432		30	40.280
20	50.800		40	12.192		40	36.576		40	64.374
30	76.200		50	15.240		50	45.720		50	80.467
40	101.600		60	18.288		60	54.864		60	96.561
50	127.000		70	21.336		70	64.008		70	112.654
60	152.400		80	24.384		80	73.152		80	128.748
70	177.800		90	27.432		90	82.296		90	144.841
80	203.200		100	30.480		100	91.440		100	160.934
90	228.600									
100	254.000									

12 inches (in.) = 1 foot (ft.)	3 feet = 1 yard (yd.)	1,760 yards = 1 mile

II SQUARE MEASURE

Square centimeters	Square inches		Square meters	Square feet		Hectares	Acres		Square kilometers	Square miles
1	0.155		1	10.764		1	2.471		1	0.368
2	0.310		2	21.528		2	4.942		2	0.722
3	0.465		3	32.292		3	7.413		3	1.158
4	0.620		4	43.056		4	9.884		4	1.544
5	0.775		5	53.820		5	12.355		5	1.931
6	0.930		6	64.583		6	14.826		6	2.317
7	1.085		7	75.347		7	17.297		7	2.703
8	1.240		8	86.111		8	19.768		8	3.089
9	1.395		9	96.875		9	22.239		9	3.475
10	1.550		10	107.639		10	24.711		10	3.861
20	3.100		20	215.278		20	49.421		20	7.722
30	4.650		30	322.917		30	74.132		30	11.583
40	6.200		40	430.556		40	98.842		40	15.444
50	7.750		50	538.196		50	123.553		50	19.305
60	9.300		60	645.835		60	148.263		60	23.166
70	10.850		70	753.474		70	172.974		70	27.027
80	12.400		80	861.113		80	197.684		80	30.888
90	13.950		90	968.752		90	222.395		90	34.749
100	15.500		100	1,076.391		100 = 1 square kilometer	247.105		100	38.610

10,000 square centimeters = 1 square meter   10,000 square meters = 1 hectare   100 hectares = 1 square kilometer

II SQUARE MEASURE (continued)

Square inches	Square centimeters		Square feet	Square meters		Acres	Hectares		Square miles	Square kilometers
1	6.452		1	0.093		1	0.405		1	2.590
2	12.903		2	0.186		2	0.809		2	5.180
3	19.355		3	0.279		3	1.214		3	7.770
4	25.806		4	0.372		4	1.619		4	10.360
5	32.258		5	0.465		5	2.023		5	12.950
6	38.710		6	0.557		6	2.428		6	15.540
7	45.161		7	0.650		7	2.833		7	18.130
8	51.613		8	0.743		8	3.238		8	20.720
9	58.064		9 = 1 sq. yd.	0.836		9	3.642		9	23.310
10	64.516		10	0.929		10	4.047		10	25.900
20	129.032		20	1.858		20	8.094		20	51.800
30	193.548		30	2.787		30	12.141		30	77.700
40	258.064		40	3.716		40	16.187		40	103.600
50	322.580		50	4.645		50	20.234		50	129.499
60	387.096		60	5.574		60	24.281		60	155.399
70	451.612		70	6.503		70	28.328		70	181.299
80	516.128		80	7.432		80	32.375		80	207.199
90	580.644		90	8.361		90	36.422		90	233.099
100	645.160		100	9.290		100	40.469		100	258.999

144 square inches = 1 square foot   4,840 square yards = 1 acre
9 square feet   = 1 square yard   640 acres   = 1 square mile

III   CUBIC MEASURE

Cubic centimeters	Cubic inches		Cubic decimeters	Cubic feet		Cubic meters	Cubic yards
1	0.061		1	0.035		1	1.308
2	0.122		2	0.071		2	2.616
3	0.183		3	0.106		3	3.924
4	0.244		4	0.141		4	5.232
5	0.305		5	0.177		5	6.540
6	0.366		6	0.212		6	7.848
7	0.427		7	0.247		7	9.156
8	0.488		8	0.283		8	10.464
9	0.549		9	0.318		9	11.772
10	0.610		10	0.353		10	13.080
20	1.220		20	0.706		20	26.159
30	1.831		30	1.059		30	39.239
40	2.441		40	1.413		40	52.318
50	3.051		50	1.766		50	65.398
60	3.661		60	2.119		60	78.477
70	4.272		70	2.472		70	91.557
80	4.882		80	2.825		80	104.636
90	5.492		90	3.178		90	117.716
100	6.102		100	3.531		100	130.795

1,000 cubic centimeters = 1 cubic decimeter
1,000 cubic decimeters = 1 cubic meter = 1 stere

III   CUBIC MEASURE (*continued*)

Cubic inches	Cubic centimeters		Cubic feet	Cubic decimeters		Cubic yards	Cubic meters
1	16.387		1	28.317		1	0.765
2	32.774		2	56.633		2	1.529
3	49.161		3	84.951		3	2.294
4	65.548		4	113.267		4	3.058
5	81.935		5	141.584		5	3.823
6	98.322		6	169.901		6	4.587
7	114.709		7	198.218		7	5.352
8	131.097		8	226.535		8	6.116
9	147.484		9	254.852		9	6.881
10	163.871		10	283.168		10	7.646
20	327.741		20	566.337		20	15.291
30	491.612		30	849.505		30	22.937
40	655.483		40	1,132.674		40	30.582
50	819.353		50	1,415.842		50	38.228
60	983.224		60	1,699.011		60	45.873
70	1,147.094		70	1,982.179		70	53.519
80	1,310.965		80	2,265.348		80	61.164
90	1,474.836		90	2,548.516		90	68.810
100	1,638.706		100	2,831.685		100	76.455

1,728 cubic inches = 1 cubic foot
27 cubic feet   = 1 cubic yard

IV WEIGHTS

Grams	Avoirdupois ounces	Lb.	Oz.	Kilograms	Avoirdupois pounds	Cwts.	Qtrs.	Sts.	Lb.	Oz.
1	0.035		–	1	2.205				2	3
2	0.071		–	2	4.409				4	7
3	0.106		–	3	6.614				6	10
4	0.141		–	4	8.818				8	13
5	0.176		–	5	11.023				11	–
6	0.212		–	6	13.228				13	4
7	0.247		–	7	15.432			1	1	7
8	0.282		–	8	17.637			1	3	10
9	0.317		–	9	19.842			1	5	13
10	0.353		–	10	22.046			1	8	1
20	0.705		–	20	44.092		1	1	2	1
30	1.058		1	30	66.139		2	–	10	2
40	1.411		1½	40	88.185		3	–	4	3
50	1.764		1¾	50	110.231		3	1	12	4
60	2.116		2	60	132.277	1	–	1	6	4
70	2.469		2½	70	154.324	1	1	1	–	5
80	2.822		2¾	80	176.370	1	2	–	8	6
90	3.175		3¼	90	198.416	1	3	–	2	7
100	3.527		3½	100	220.463	1	3	1	10	7
150	5.291		5¼	150	330.69	2	3	1	8	11
200	7.055		7	200	440.92	3	3	1	6	15
250	8.818		8¾	250	551.16	4	3	1	5	3
300	10.592		10½	300	661.39	5	3	1	3	6
350	12.346		12½	350	771.62	6	3	1	1	10
400	14.110		14	400	881.85	7	3	–	13	14
450	15.873		15¾	450	992.08	8	3	–	12	1
500	17.637	1	1¾	500	1,102.31	9	3	–	10	5
550	19.401	1	3½	550	1,212.54	10	3	–	8	9
600	21.164	1	5¼	600	1,322.77	11	3	–	6	12
650	22.928	1	7	650	1,433.00	12	3	–	4	–
700	24.691	1	8¾	700	1,543.24	13	3	–	3	4
750	26.455	1	10½	750	1,653.47	14	3	–	1	7
800	28.219	1	12¼	800	1,763.70	15	2	1	13	11
850	29.983	1	14	850	1,873.93	16	2	1	11	15
900	31.746	1	15¾	900	1,984.16	17	2	1	10	2
950	33.510	2	1½	950	2,094.39	18	2	1	8	6
1,000 = 1 kilogram	35.274	2	3¼	1,000 = 1 ton (metric)	2,204.63	19	2	1	6	10

IV   WEIGHTS (*continued*)

Metric tons	Long or gross tons	Tons	Cwts.	Qtrs.	Sts.	Lb.	Oz.
1	0.984	–	19	2	1	6	9¾
2	1.968	1	19	1	–	13	3½
3	2.953	2	19	–	–	5	13¼
4	3.937	3	18	2	1	12	7
5	4.921	4	18	1	1	5	¾
6	5.905	5	18	–	–	11	10¼
7	6.889	6	17	3	–	4	4
8	7.874	7	17	1	1	11	1½
9	8.858	8	17	–	1	3	11¼
10	9.842	9	16	3	–	10	4¾
20	19.684	19	13	2	1	6	6¼
30	29.526	29	10	2	–	2	11
40	39.368	39	7	1	–	12	15¾
50	49.210	49	4	–	1	9	1¼
60	59.052	59	1	–	–	5	6
70	68.895	68	17	3	1	1	11
80	78.737	78	14	2	1	11	12¼
90	88.579	88	11	2	–	8	1
100	98.421	98	8	1	1	4	6

IV   WEIGHTS (*continued*)

Avoirdupois ounces	Grams	Avoirdupois pounds	Kilograms	Long or gross tons	Metric tons
1	28.350	1	0.454	1	1.016
2	56.699	2	0.907	2	2.032
3	85.049	3	1.361	3	3.048
4	113.398	4	1.814	4	4.064
5	141.748	5	2.268	5	5.080
6	170.097	6	2.722	6	6.096
7	198.447	7	3.175	7	7.112
8	226.796	8	3.629	8	8.128
9	255.146	9	4.082	9	9.144
10	283.495	10	4.536	10	10.161
16 = 1 pound	453.592	14 = 1 stone	6.350	20	20.321
20	566.990	20	9.072	30	30.481
30	850.486	28 = 1 quarter	12.701	40	40.642
40	1,133.981	30	13.608	50	50.802
50	1,417.476	40	18.144	60	60.963
60	1,700.971	50	22.680	70	71.123
70	1,984.467	60	27.216	80	81.284
80	2,267.962	70	31.751	90	91.444
90	2,551.457	80	36.287	100	101.605
100	2,834.952	90	40.823		
		100	45.359		
		112 = 1 hundredweight	50.802		

16 ounces (oz.)	= 1 pound (lb.)
14 pounds	= 1 stone (st.)
28 pounds	= 1 quarter (qtr.)
112 pounds	= 1 hundredweight (cwt.)
20 hundredweight	= 2,240 lb. = 1 ton (long)
2,000 pounds	= 1 ton (short)

V CAPACITY

Centiliters	Ounces (U.S.)	U.S. equivalent			Ounces (British)	British equivalent	
		Qts.	Pts.	Oz.		Pts.	Oz.
20	6.763			6¾	7.039		7
25	8.454			6½	8.799		8¾
30	10.144			10¼	10.599		10½
35	11.835			11¾	12.319		12¼
36	12.173			12¼	12.671		12¾
37.5	12.681			12¾	13.199		13¼
40	13.526			13½	14.078		14
45	15.217			15¼	15.838		15¾
50	16.907		1	1	17.598		17½
55	18.598		1	2½	19.358		19¼
60	20.289		1	4¼	21.118	1	1
65	21.980		1	6	22.877	1	2¾
70	23.670		1	7¾	24.637	1	4¾
75	25.361		1	9¼	26.397	1	6½
80	27.052		1	11	28.175	1	8¼
85	28.742		1	12¾	29.917	1	10
90	30.433		1	14½	31.676	1	11¾
95	32.124	1	–	–	33.436	1	13½
100 = 1 liter	33.814	1	–	1¾	35.196	1	15¼

100 centiliters = 1 liter

V CAPACITY (continued)

Liters	Pints (U.S.)	Gallons (U.S.)	U.S. equivalent				Pints (British)	Gallons (British)	British equivalent			
			Gals.	Qts.	Pts.	Oz.			Gals.	Qts.	Pts.	Oz.
1	2.113	0.264		1	–	1¾	1.760	0.220			1	15¼
2	4.227	0.528		2	–	3½	3.520	0.440		1	1	10½
3	6.340	0.793		3	–	5½	5.279	0.660		2	1	5½
4	8.454	1.057	1	–	–	7¼	7.039	0.880		3	1	¾
5	10.567	1.321	1	1	–	9	8.799	1.100	1	–	–	16
6	12.681	1.585	1	2	–	11	10.559	1.320	1	1	–	11¼
7	14.794	1.849	1	3	–	12¾	12.319	1.540	1	2	–	6½
8	16.908	2.113	2	–	–	14½	14.078	1.760	1	3	–	1½
9	19.021	2.378	2	1	1	¼	15.838	1.980	1	3	1	16¾
10	21.134	2.642	2	2	1	2¼	17.598	2.200	2	–	1	12
11	23.248	2.906	2	3	1	4	19.358	2.420	2	1	1	7¼
12	25.361	3.170	3	–	1	5¾	21.118	2.640	2	2	1	2½
13	27.475	3.434	3	1	1	7½	22.877	2.860	2	3	–	17½
14	29.588	3.699	3	2	1	9½	24.637	3.080	3	–	–	12¾
15	31.702	3.963	3	3	1	11¼	26.397	3.300	3	1	–	8
16	33.815	4.227	4	–	1	13	28.157	3.520	3	2	–	3¼
17	35.928	4.491	4	1	1	14¾	29.917	3.740	3	2	1	18½
18	38.042	4.755	4	3	–	¾	31.676	3.960	3	3	1	13½
19	40.155	5.019	5	–	–	2½	33.436	4.180	4	–	1	8¾
20	42.269	5.284	5	1	–	4¼	35.196	4.400	4	1	1	3¾
30	63.403	7.925	7	3	1	6½	52.794	6.599	6	2	–	15¾
40	84.538	10.567	10	2	–	8½	70.392	8.799	8	3	–	7¾
50	105.672	13.209	13	–	1	10¾	87.990	10.999	10	3	1	19¾
60	126.806	15.851	15	3	–	13	105.588	13.199	13	–	1	11¾
70	147.941	18.493	18	1	1	15	123.186	15.398	15	1	1	3¾
80	169.075	21.134	21	–	1	1¼	140.784	17.598	17	2	–	15¾
90	190.210	23.776	23	3	–	3¼	158.382	19.798	19	3	–	7¾
100 = 1 hectoliter	211.344	26.418	26	1	1	5½	175.980	21.998	21	3	1	19¾

V CAPACITY (continued)

Centiliters	Fluid ounces (U.S.)	U.S. equivalent Qts.	Pts.	Oz.	Fluid ounces (British)
17.047	5.765			5¾	6
19.889	6.725			6¾	7
22.730	7.686			7¾	8
25.571	8.647			8¾	9
28.412	9.608			9½	10
31.253	10.568			10½	11
34.095	11.529			11½	12
36.936	12.490			12½	13
39.777	13.451			13½	14
42.618	14.411			14½	15
45.460	15.372			15¼	16
48.301	16.333		1	¼	17
51.142	17.294		1	1¼	18
53.983	18.254		1	2¼	19
56.824	19.215		1	3¼	20 = 1 pt.
85.237	28.823		1	12¾	30
113.649	38.430	1	-	6½	40 = 1 qt.
142.061	48.038	1	1	—	50
170.473	57.646	1	1	9¾	60
198.885	67.253	2	-	3¼	70
227.298	76.861	2	-	12¾	80 = 2 qts.
255.710	86.469	2	1	6½	90
284.122	96.076	3	-	—	100

Liters	Pints (U.S.)	Gals.	U.S. equivalent Qts.	Pts.	Oz.	Pints (British)
0.568	1.201			1	3¼	1
1.136	2.402		1	-	6½	2 = 1 qt.
1.705	3.603		1	1	9¾	3
2.273	4.804		2	-	12¾	4 = 2 qts.
2.841	6.005		3	-	—	5
3.409	7.206		3	1	3¼	6 = 3 qts.
3.978	8.407	1	-	-	6½	7
4.546	9.608	1	-	1	9¾	8 = 1 gal.
5.114	10.809	1	1	-	13	9
5.682	12.010	1	2	-	¼	10
11.365	24.019	3	-	-	¼	20
17.047	36.029	4	2	-	½	30
22.730	48.038	6	-	-	½	40
28.412	60.048	7	2	-	¾	50
34.095	72.057	9	-	-	1	60
39.777	84.067	10	2	-	1	70
45.460	96.076	12	-	-	1¼	80 = 10 gals.
51.142	108.086	13	2	-	1½	90
56.825	120.095	15	-	-	1½	100

Centiliters	Fluid ounces (U.S.)	Fluid ounces (British)	British equivalent Qts.	Pts.	Oz.
17.744	6	6.245			6¼
20.701	7	7.286			7¼
23.658	8	8.327			8¼
26.615	9	9.368			9¼
29.573	10	10.408			10½
32.530	11	11.449			11½
35.487	12	12.490			12½
38.445	13	13.531			13½
41.402	14	14.572			14½
44.359	15	15.613			15½
47.316	16 = 1 pt.	16.653			16¾
50.274	17	17.694			17¾
53.231	18	18.735			18¾
56.188	19	19.776			19¾
59.145	20	20.817		1	¾
88.718	30	31.225		1	11¼
118.291	40	41.634	1	-	1¾
147.864	50	52.042	1	-	12
177.436	60	62.450	1	1	2½
207.009	70	72.859	1	1	12¾
236.582	80	83.267	2	-	3¼
266.154	90	93.676	2	-	13¾
295.727	100	104.084	2	1	4

Liters	Pints (U.S.)	Pints (British)	Gals.	British equivalent Qts.	Pts.	Oz.
0.473	1	0.833				16¾
0.946	2 = 1 qt.	1.665			1	13¼
1.419	3	2.498		1	-	10
1.893	4 = 2 qts.	3.331		1	1	6½
2.366	5	4.163		2	-	3¼
2.839	6 = 3 qts.	4.996		2	1	-
3.312	7	5.829		2	1	16½
3.785	8 = 1 gal.	6.661		3	-	13¼
4.258	9	7.494		3	1	10
4.732	10	8.327	1	-	-	6½
9.463	20	16.653	2	-	-	13
14.195	30	24.980	3	-	-	19½
18.927	40	33.307	4	-	1	6¼
23.658	50	41.634	5	-	1	12¾
28.390	60	49.960	6	-	1	19¼
33.121	70	58.287	7	1	-	5¾
37.853	80 = 10 gals.	66.614	8	1	-	12¼
42.585	90	74.940	9	1	-	18¾
47.316	100	83.267	10	1	1	5¼

V CAPACITY (continued)

Liters	Gallons (U.S.)	American equivalent				Gallons (British Imperial)
		Gals.	Qts.	Pts.	Oz.	
4.546	1.201	1	–	1	9¾	1
9.092	2.402	2	1	1	3½	2
13.638	3.603	3	2	–	13¼	3
18.184	4.804	4	3	–	7	4
22.730	6.005	6	–	–	¾	5
27.276	7.206	7	–	1	10¼	6
31.822	8.407	8	1	1	4	7
36.368	9.608	9	2	–	13¾	8
40.914	10.809	10	3	–	7½	9
45.460	12.010	12	–	–	1¼	10
90.919	24.019	24	–	–	2½	20
136.379	36.029	36	–	–	3¾	30
181.838	48.038	48	–	–	4¾	40
227.298	60.048	60	–	–	6¼	50
272.758	72.057	72	–	–	7¼	60
318.217	84.067	84	–	–	8½	70
363.677	96.076	96	–	–	9¾	80
409.136	108.086	108	–	–	11	90
454.596	120.095	120	–	–	12¼	100

Liters	Gallons (U.S.)	Gallons (Imperial)	British equivalent			
			Gals.	Qts.	Pts.	Oz.
3.785	1	0.833		3	–	13¼
7.571	2	1.665	1	2	1	6½
11.356	3	2.498	2	3	–	19¾
15.141	4	3.331	3	1	–	13
18.927	5	4.163	4	–	1	6
22.712	6	4.996	4	3	1	19¼
26.497	7	5.829	5	3	–	12¾
30.282	8	6.661	6	2	1	5¾
34.068	9	7.494	7	1	1	19
37.853	10	8.327	8	1	–	12¼
75.706	20	16.653	16	2	1	4½
113.559	30	24.980	24	3	1	16¾
151.412	40	33.307	33	1	–	9
189.265	50	41.634	41	2	1	1½
227.118	60	49.960	49	3	1	13½
264.971	70	58.287	58	1	–	6
302.824	80	66.614	66	2	–	18¼
340.678	90	74.940	74	3	1	10½
378.531	100	83.267	83	1	–	2¾

VI TEMPERATURE

Centigrade degrees	Fahrenheit degrees		Centigrade degrees	Fahrenheit degrees
100.0	212.0		40.0	104.0
97.2	207.0		38.9	102.0
95.0	203.0		36.1	97.0
94.4	202.0		35.0	95.0
91.7	197.0		33.3	92.0
90.0	194.0		30.5	87.0
88.9	192.0		30.0	86.0
86.1	187.0		27.8	82.0
85.0	185.0		25.0	77.0
83.3	182.0		22.2	72.0
80.5	177.0		20.0	68.0
80.0	176.0		19.4	67.0
77.8	172.0		16.7	62.0
75.0	167.0		15.0	59.0
72.2	162.0		13.9	57.0
70.0	158.0		11.1	52.0
69.4	157.0		10.0	50.0
66.7	152.0		8.3	47.0
65.0	149.0		5.5	42.0
63.9	147.0		5.0	41.0
61.1	142.0		2.8	37.0
60.0	140.0		0.0	32.0
58.3	137.0		—2.8	27.0
55.5	132.0		—5.0	23.0
55.0	131.0		—5.5	22.0
52.8	127.0		—8.3	17.0
50.0	122.0		—10.0	14.0
47.2	117.0		—11.1	12.0
45.0	113.0		—13.9	7.0
44.4	112.0		—15.0	5.0
41.7	107.0			

Vintage Chart

No vintage chart is a sure guide to the wines rated, for great wines cannot be standardized. Wines are a product of inconstant nature and fallible man. There will be enough enjoyable bottles in any one district in any off year to make exceptions invalidating anything so dogmatic as a vintage chart. Often overlooked, nevertheless a major factor in the purchase of wines, is the proper selection of wines that are sufficiently mature for present-day consumption. Very great years are often slow in maturing, hence your consideration of whether the wines will be consumed immediately or laid away for future consumption should be a determining factor in your selections.

EXPLANATION OF RATINGS

20, 19—exceptionally great	14, 13, 12—very good	7, 6—low average
18, 17—very great	11, 10—good	5, 4—poor
16, 15—great	9, 8—fair	3, 2, 1—very poor

N.B.:   Many dry white wines as well as many reds may be too old for present-day consumption. All such wines are indicated by *italic figures*. All white Bordeaux older than 1964 which are not Sauternes, Barsac, or Ste. Croix-du-Mont should be considered as possibly being maderized.

Vintage	Red Bordeaux	White Bordeaux	Red Burgundy (Côte d'Or)	White Burgundy	Red Burgundy (Beaujolais)	Rhône	Loire	Alsace	Champagne
1926	13	*14*	12	*12*	*11*	12	*11*	12	*12*
1927	*2*	*6*	*2*	*2*	*3*	7	*5*	*3*	*3*
1928	19.5	*18*	18	*15*	*17*	16	*15*	15	*20*
1929	20	*19*	19	*19*	*19*	19	*16*	17	*17*
1930	0	*0*	*4*	*4*	*4*	9	*6*	*4*	*4*
1931	*3*	*2*	*4*	*4*	*3*	10	*7*	*5*	*6*
1932	*1*	*1*	*3*	*4*	*5*	*11*	*7*	*5*	*6*
1933	10	*6*	*17*	*16*	*17*	*14*	*14*	12	*15*
1934	17	*16*	17	*17*	*17*	16	*13*	14	*15*
1935	*5*	*6*	*12*	*13*	*12*	9	*12*	14	*11*
1936	*8*	*8*	*8*	*6*	*9*	14	*9*	*10*	*10*
1937	15	*18*	17	*16*	*13*	16	*14*	15	*16*
1938	9	*8*	*14*	*13*	*10*	13	*9*	*10*	*12*
1939	*5*	*6*	*3*	*3*	*8*	10	*8*	*4*	*8*
1940	8	*9*	*9*	*9*	*8*	9	*8*	*11*	*8*
1941	*2*	*1*	*4*	*4*	*5*	9	*7*	*8*	*12*
1942	12	*15*	*12*	*15*	*14*	15	*11*	*13*	*15*
1943	15	*15*	*14*	*15*	*15*	15	*14*	*15*	*18*
1944	*11*	*9*	*4*	*5*	*7*	9	*7*	*5*	*9*
1945	20	*19*	19	*16*	*20*	19	*18*	17	*16*
1946	*8*	*7*	*12*	*9*	*10*	15	*10*	*10*	*11*
1947	19	*19*	19	*20*	*19*	19	*19*	*19*	*19*
1948	13	*13*	*14*	*15*	*9*	9	*10*	*12*	*11*
1949	18	*18*	19	*17*	*19*	16	*13*	16	*17*
1950	14	*15*	*12*	*18*	*12*	15	*10*	*8*	*9*
1951	*9*	*6*	*8*	*8*	*7*	9	*7*	*9*	*7*
1952	17	*16*	16	*16*	*16*	18	*14*	*14*	*18*
1953	19	*17*	19	*17*	*19*	13	*17*	*17*	*17*

Vintage	Red Bordeaux	White Bordeaux	Red Burgundy (Côte d'Or)	White Burgundy	Red Burgundy (Beaujolais)	Rhône	Loire	Alsace	Champagne
1954	12	9	10	11	10	16	10	11	10
1955	18-19	17	17	18	17	18	18	15	19
1956	12	10	10	14	9	14	12	13	12
1957	17	16	17	18	18	18	18	17	11
1958	11	13	9	17	13	16	15	16	12
1959	18	18	19	18	18	17	19	19	19
1960	13	13	8	15	10	19	14	13	15
1961	20	19	19	19	20	18	17	17	18
1962	17	13	15	16	17	12	16	16	16
1963	8	6	9	11	9	11	9	11	7
1964	17	*	15	15	17	13	15	15	17
1965	11	10	6	11	11	15	10	10	6
1966	18	19	15	16	16	17	15	14	18
1967	16	14	13	15	14	15	14	14	16
1968	9	7	5	6	11	10	10	11	9
1969	13	13	18	16	15	13	15	14	14
1970	18	15	15	17	14	18	16	14	16
1971	17	**	15	16	16	16	16	17	17
1972	12	11	16	11	12	12	12	12	13
1973	15.5	13	14	15	13	11	13	13	14
1974	15	†	14	15	13	13	14	13	13.5
1975	19	+	11	15	11	11	13	15	16
1976	18	15	18	15	19	14	16	16	16
1977	15	‡	12	15	12	16	15	14	15
1978	18.5	16	17	17	19	18	16	15	14
1979	18	17	14.5	15.5	13	15	13	14	14
1980	16.5	**	13	15	13	15	13	13	13

* 10 dry   13 sweet   † 13 dry   7 sweet   + 13 dry   19 sweet   ‡ 18 dry   13 sweet   **17 dry   18 sweet

NOTE: Figures for subsequent years will be obtainable on application to the publishers.

Recent Developments

The last decade-and-a-half has witnessed great changes and developments in the world of wine. Both Europe and America began to reap the fruits of the post-World War II economy—greater amounts of leisure time and discretionary income—and turned their attention as never before to the appreciation of fine wine. In the United States, where average per capita consumption of wine has lagged behind that of Europe, this meant a great increase in the production and consumption of good-quality table wines. For America, the seventies represented a kind of vinous coming of age. Consumption and connoisseurship of wines became widespread and accepted on a national scale. The enlarged wine-drinking public showed enthusiastic curiosity and willingness to experiment with new wines and the newly emerging wineries. In France and Italy, traditionally the largest producers and consumers of wine, the new attitudes meant not an increase in production or consumption (if anything, the contrary), but a dramatic improvement in the average quality of the wines produced. Wine drinkers of Italy and France showed a greater readiness to spend a higher average price for their daily table wines, with the result that the market share of the lowest-quality wines decreased. New investments of research and money in the pursuit of quality resulted in the emergence of new vineyard areas and appellations in France and Italy, as well as the improvement of previously marginal regions. Such efforts bore fruit, most notably, in the previously maligned vineyards of the Languedoc-Roussillon in France, and in Sicily and Sardinia among Italian wines. The single most dramatic change among the wines of America was the spectacular increase in the number of wineries in operation throughout the country, supplying American wine drinkers with a constantly improving standard and selection of wines.

This encyclopedia, begun in the 1950s, has evolved and changed as the world of wine has changed. The need for updating and revision is dictated not only by each year's new vintage, but also by the developments in viniculture and viticulture throughout the world that have opened new regions of world vines and wines, and the inevitable evolution of even the tradition-bound vineyard areas.

In addition to bringing all the information within the body of the encyclopedia up to date, I have therefore felt obliged to add an extra section to treat in greater depth the areas where the most change has taken place.

France: Languedoc-Roussillon

Of all the wine-producing areas of France, the Languedoc-Roussillon, the world's largest vineyard area, has undergone the most notable changes. A small portion of the huge volume of wine that flows from the region annually has shown significant improvement, from some of the *vins de pays* class wines up to a number of the grower collectives making Appellation Contrôlée wines.

The greatest improvement has been felt in the departments of the Aude and the Pyrénées-Orientales. In the latter, the Côtes du Roussillon and Côtes du Roussillon-Villages have been awarded Appellation d'Origine Contrôlée status, France's highest wine category. It is thought by many that portions of the Corbières and Minervois V.D.Q.S. vineyards will be the next in line for promotion to A.O.C.

The improvement in these wines has been due largely to a small number of dedicated growers' cooperatives, which have employed enthusiastic and dedicated oenologists. Under their guidance, the growers' associations have installed new equipment and practiced up-to-date vatroom techniques. In the vineyards, they have made an effort to match better grape varieties, often not traditionally of the region, with more suitable slatey soils, which have produced better wines.

Languedoc

The Languedoc is the largest vineyard area of France. With its sister region to the south, the Roussillon, it covers 435,000 hectares (1,087,500 acres), 35% of France's entire vineyard area. It is the largest and most intensively cultivated strip of vineyard in the world.

Viticulturally speaking, the Languedoc begins where the Côtes du Rhone and the Côtes du Provence leave off: at the juncture of the Gard and Rhône rivers about 15 kilometers (9.5 miles) south of Avignon. It sweeps around the Mediterranean departments of the Gard (in part), the Hérault, and the Aude, ending in the south where the Corbières hills taper into the Roussillon, in the department of the Pyrénées-Orientales.

In recent years, great strides have been made toward improving the Languedoc wines. Local *sociétés d'intérêt collective agricole* (S.I.C.A.s) have assembled groups of producers, both cooperative and independent, who are replanting vineyards in better grapes, introducing better oenological techniques (carbonic maceration among many), and modernizing equipment. The effects of these changes are most noticeable in the southern Hérault and Aude, especially in the Fitou, Corbières, and Minervois regions. If the Languedoc has a future, it is certainly in these *appellations* in the south.

Of the great quantity of wine that the Languedoc produces, under 10% is classified as Appellation d'Origine Contrôlée (A.O.C.), and most of this percentage is not table wine, but *vins doux naturels*. The three classifications of wine below this represent the bulk of the region's production: Vin Délimité de Qualité Supérieure (V.D.Q.S.), vin de pays, and vin de consommation courante (V.C.C.).

Appellation d'Origine Contrôlée Wines of the Languedoc

Blanquette de Limoux is a sparkling wine from vineyards south of Carcassonne around the town of Limoux. Of the 1,950 hectares (4,875 acres) planted in vines, 1,800 (4,500 acres) are in production, resulting in an average of 50,000 hectoliters (1,325,000 U.S. gallons, 1,100,000 imp.) per year. It is certainly one of the best white-wine products of the Languedoc. Contrary to the general rule of the Languedoc, that white wines tend to be overendowed with alcohol and quick to maderize due to a lack of sufficient acidity, Blanquette de Limoux and the still wine Limoux Nature are generally fresh and well made. Their main fault is a lack of sufficient character to hold the drinker's attention for very long. At its best, the sparkling wine resembles a lesser non-vintage Champagne.

Fitou is perhaps the best dry red wine of the Languedoc. The tendency in the past was to produce rather heavy, herbaceous wines, a practice which continues in the production of the poorer Fitous. Better vinification methods and more care have resulted in an increasing number of fine, well-rounded, and satisfying Fitou wines.

Clairette de Bellegarde is a very small white-wine *appellation* located between Nîmes and Arles. The grape used is the local Clairette, and the wines are dry. Some claim that they are at their best when old and without freshness. Over the last decade, production has dwindled to less than 1,000 hectoliters (26,400 U.S. gallons, 22,000 imp.) per year.

Clairette du Languedoc is similiar in style to and made with the same grape as the Clairette de Bellegarde, in an area southwest of Nîmes, centered on the town of Aspiran. Production averages around 8,000 hectoliters (211,200 U.S. gallons, 176,000 imp.) of white wine per year.

Vins Doux Naturels are the fortified sweet aperitif wines made from the Muscat grape, which is allowed to grow into a state of overripeness. During fermentation, before all the sugar is converted to alcohol, *eaux-de-vie* are added to arrest the fermentation, leaving the wine with a high alcoholic content (17 to 20%) and much residual sugar. There are four V.D.N. in the Languedoc, all located in the department of the Hérault. They are Muscat de Frontignan, Muscat de Lunel, Muscat de Saint-Jean de Minervois, and Muscat de Mireval.

See Sweet Fortified Wines.

Vins Délimités de Qualité Supérieure of the Languedoc

Although they represent less than 10% of its total production, the Languedoc's twenty-one V.D.Q.S. wines account for nearly half of all the V.D.Q.S. wines produced annually in France. The most important of these are Corbières, Costières du Gard, Minervois, the Coteaux de Languedoc (which comprises a number of regional V.D.Q.S.), and Picpoul de Pinet and Côtes du Cabardès et de l'Orbiel.

Corbières (*see* page 187) is France's largest and most important V.D.Q.S. red-wine vineyard area. It divides itself into two types of vineyard terrain: the broad flat plain, located north and west of Narbonne on either side of the Carcassonne highway and elsewhere in the south, which is the source of the poorest wines of the region; and the hilly *coteaux* region south and southwest of Narbonne, which has lighter soils and cooler microclimates than the plain vineyards, and thus wines that are correspondingly superior. The slate-rich soils of the vineyard villages such as Castelmaure, Cascastel, Tuchen, Bizanet, Embres-et-Castelmaure, and Cucugnan, make full-bodied, round wines far superior to the region's average.

Some of the best villages have made strenuous efforts, through the local agricultural collectives, to improve quality by replacing the poorer grape varieties, such as Aramond, and perfecting the clones of the predominant Carignan grape. Experiments with better grapes not typical of the Languedoc have also made a great contribution to the quality of the Corbières wines. Syrah of the Rhône, Mourvèdre, and Merlot have given good results and account for much of the improvement in the wines. Carbonic maceration, a technique used to enhance the aromas and vinosity of the wines, has also done much to raise quality.

Certain villages have secured government subsidies to improve methods of production and vinification. Improvements would include combining disparate vineyard parcels for greater mechanization and efficiency, and improving vat-room equipment and technique.

Another development likely to change the profile of the Corbières is the growth of small domains held by growers who have made high-quality Corbières their mission. Limited yield, expert vinification, and in some rare cases barrel-aging before bottling, have produced a number of full-bodied wines with notable fruit. Some of the better domains include Château Beauregard, Domaines Fontsainte, Domaine des Ollieux, Domaine Saint-Maurice, Domaine Montjoie, Domaines de Villemajou, Domaine de la Voulte, Le Prieuré de Saint-Amand, Château des Palais, Château de Cabriac, and Domaine Saint Joseph.

Costières du Gard (*see* page 189). Red, white, and rosé wines come from this range of hills and plains between Nîmes and Arles. The wines tend to be light and less interesting than those of the southern Languedoc. Most of the wine is vinified at Vauvert, Générac, and Beauvoisin. Production averages around 250,000 hectoliters (6,625,000 U.S. gallons, 5,500,00 imp.) per year.

Minervois (*see* page 319) wines are second only to Corbières wines in importance in the Languedoc, both for their quantity (300,000 hectoliters, 7,950,000 U.S. gallons, 6,600,000 imp. per year), and for the good quality they can attain. Making red, white, and rosé wines, the Minervois lies on the Hérault-Aude border well inland from the Mediterranean, and the Montagne Noir lies to its west. The poorer, and more typical, Minervois are rather astringent and lacking in charm, with a very pronounced earthy taste. Better examples, however, are becoming more frequent from some of the better cooperatives. These wines will be generous, mouth-filling, and pleasantly, noticeably fruity. Even at their best, however, these wines are not as good as those of their southern neighbor, Corbières.

Coteaux du Languedoc (*see* page 198) is a general *appellation* covering only the red and rosé wines from thirteen different V.D.Q.S. *appellation* areas. In recent years, Grenache Noir, Cinsault, Mourvèdre, and Syrah have been encouraged as "*cépages améliorateurs*," or literally, "grape variety improvers." Production averages 100,000 hectoliters (2,650,000 U.S. gallons, 2,200,000 imp.) per year. The wines that have earned V.D.Q.S status are:

Pic-Saint-Loup, a small region of red, rosé, and a few white wines named for the peak about 25 kilometers (15.5 miles) northwest of Montpellier. Production averages about 35,000 hectoliters (927,500 U.S. gallons, 770,000 imp.) per year.

Cabrières, an area between Pézenas and Clermont-l'Hérault, especially known for the white Clairette du Languedoc, an A.O.C. wine.

Coteaux de la Méjanelle, an area located between Montpellier and the coast. Of the 8,000 hectoliters (212,000 U.S. gallons, 176,000 imp.), a tiny amount of white wine is produced.

Coteaux de Saint-Christol is a small region of *vin de café* red wines between Montpellier and Nîmes.

Coteaux de Verargues, bordering Saint-Christol, is a region that produces about 20,000 hectoliters (530,000 U.S. gallons, 440,000 imp.) of light red wine per year.

Faugères is a hilly region northwest of Béziers whose red wines have a marked earthy taste.

Saint-Chinian is a large region of red wines also northwest of Béziers.

Saint-Saturnin is a small red-wine region east of Lodève.

Montpeyroux neighbors Saint-Saturnin to the east and produces a similiar type of red wine.

Saint-Drézéry is a small region of red wines southeast of Pic-Saint-Loup.

Saint-Georges-d'Orques is a red-wine region west of Montpellier.

La Clape and *Quatourze* are red and rosé regions in the Aude. La Clape also produces some white wine. These wines are probably the best of the Coteaux du Languedoc V.D.Q.S. *appellations*.

Slate-rich soil, which is ideal for vine-growing, is found in Faugères and in parts of La Clape.

The name Cabrières applies only to rosé wine. The reds and rosés are made mostly from a blend of Carignan, Cinsault, Grenache Noir, and Aramon. Since the soil, climate, and style of vinification are nearly the same for each of these wines, it is the blend of grapes which distinguishes one from another.

La Clape, Côtes de Cabardès et de l'Orbiel (see below), and Quatourze lie in the neighboring departments of the Aude, but are considered part of the Coteaux du Languedoc.

The maximum legal yield for all of the V.D.Q.S. wines in the Coteaux du Languedoc is 50 hectoliters per hec-

tare, or about 3 tons to the acre. Even in this most productive of French vineyards, where the vines are those varieties that can give huge crops, the permissible yield is far below the level harvested in the "premium" wine districts of California. If the French can take steps to control the quality of some of their least-known wines, certainly the growers and legislators in the United States could do the same for the most famous American ones.

Picpoul de Pinet and Côtes du Cabardès et de l'Orbiel produce white and red wines, respectively, sold mostly to *vermouthiers* in Sète and Marseille.

Vins de Pays of the Languedoc

Below the V.D.Q.S. in quality but far outstripping them in production are the *vins de pays*. There are forty *vins de pays* in the Languedoc, producing on the average just under 4 million hectoliters (105.6 million U.S. gallons, 88 million imp.), which represents 10 to 15% of the total Languedoc harvest. They are usually named for the valley, or slope, where they are grown, e.g., Vins de pays du Val de Cesse (Aude) or Vins de pays des Coteaux Cevenols. The quality of these wines (and the quantity produced) in any one "*pays*" can vary enormously, from pleasant if undistinguished local wines meant for immediate consumption to the downright poor and badly made. The *vin de pays* production of the Languedoc represents more than 60% of all the *vins de pays* produced in France.

Vins de Consommation Courante of the Languedoc

The final category of wine produced in the Languedoc is the *vin de consommation courante* (V.C.C.), formerly known as *vin de table*. Of the 36 million hectoliters (950.4 million U.S. gallons, 792 million imp.) produced in the Languedoc annually, the V.C.C. wines amount to about 30 million hectoliters (792 million U.S. gallons, 660 million imp.) or about 4.2. billion bottles. The overproduction of the V.C.C. wines in the Languedoc has had a crippling effect on the region. Thousands of hectares of unsuitable land are planted in poor grape varieties; there is little economic incentive to produce better wines. Conversion to fruit and vegetable crops has been slowed by the expense and scarcity of water for irrigation.

Vin de Sables is a rather well-made *vin de consommation courante* grown on the sandy coast of the Mediterranean from the Camargue to Cap d'Agde. The largest producer of these wines is the Salins du Midi Company with their Listel *vin de marque* wines.

Roussillon

The Roussillon is the southernmost wine region of France, located in the department of the Pyrénées-Orientales. Despite the beauty of the country—the snow-covered peaks of the Pyrénées, the wild foothills cut through with mountain streams—the Roussillon has only recently taken a significant place on the wine map of France.

Until the mid-1960s, the Roussillon wines were of two types: *vins doux naturels* (V.D.N.), and rather lackluster dry red wines. The V.D.N. have always been immensely popular in France as aperitif wines, though having little appeal outside France. Until the dry red wines of the

Côtes du Roussillon came to prominence, the V.D.N. allowed the wine-growers to make a living in an otherwise arid region.

The V.D.N. Appellation Contrôlée of the Roussillon are Maury, Banyuls (and Banyuls Grand Cru), Rivesaltes, and Muscat de Rivesaltes.

With the exception of the A.O.C. Collioure, the dry red wines of the Roussillon were employed largely as blending wines. An intense effort begun in the 1960s to upgrade the wine resulted in 1977 in the new Appellation Contrôlée of Côtes du Roussillon, red and white wines. Production was restricted to 50 hectoliters per hectare (125 U.S. gallons per acre); minimum alcoholic content was set at 11.5% for reds, 10.5% for whites. Red wines from the better Côtes du Roussillon villages may qualify for the Côtes du Roussillon-Villages *appellation*. Some of the best of these villages are Caramany, Montner, Latour de France, Vingrau, and Estagel. Caramany and Latour de France may indicate their village name on the label.

The major grape of the region has always been the Carignan, which produces its best wines in the slate-rich hills of the north Roussillon along the Côte d'Agly and the villages named above. Other major grapes for the Côtes du Roussillon are Grenache, which lends vinosity; Syrah, the Rhône grape; and the Mourvèdre. Carbonic maceration, a technique used to enchance the aromas and vinosity of the wines, is also increasingly employed.

The best examples of the Côtes du Roussillon have an engaging berrylike aroma, rich agreeable tannic structure, and sustained fruit. In better years, the best of these improve in the bottle for up to three years. Côtes du Roussillon white and very good rosé wines are also made in small quantities. One of the best sources of rosé is the cooperative in the village of Rasiguères. White-wine production totals only 6,000 hectoliters (158,400 U.S. gallons, 145,200 imp.) and its quality is not as high as that of the red and rosé. Experiments are under way using the Sauvignon Blanc grape to upgrade the quality.

In all, the Côtes du Roussillon, plus the "-Villages," produce about 3 million cases of wine per year.

See Vins Doux Naturels.

Italy

No European country has benefited more from the increased world demand for improved-quality drinking wines than Italy. Beginning in the late 1960s, both within and without Italy, wine consumers looked to these vineyards for reliable, moderately priced wines. Intelligent Italian wine-makers, helped by Common Market financing and trade laws, improved vinification equipment and technique, which has resulted in longer-lived, fresher wines in the international marketplace. Under the pressure for improved quality, many Italian vineyard regions were able to elevate themselves from mere country wines into full-fledged D.O.C. (Denominazione di Origine Controllata) wines. The increased prosperity of the Italian wine industry has also allowed the formation of many modern *cantinas*, or growers' cooperatives, which have

availed themselves of up-to-date vineyard and vat-room techniques.

The main entries for Italian wines in the *Encyclopedia*, "Italy" as well as the provinces, have been updated and revised. Sicily and Sardinia, however, needed greater expansion to reflect the recent revolution in Italian wines that is especially evident in these regions.

Italy: Sicily

Today, Sicily accounts for close to a quarter of all Italian wine exports, a huge amount by any standard; a large part of the red, alcoholic wines are exported in bulk to France to be added to many of the lower-alcohol French wines.

In the past, fortified wines such as the famous Marsala predominated in Sicily's production, and grape plantings for Marsala, primarily the Grillo grape, covered much of the western part of the island. Since 1960, however, Sicily has become a large producer of dry red and white table wines. Vineyards once devoted to the Grillo grape have been replanted with Trebbiano, Catarratto, and Inzolia for whites; and Sangiovese, Nero Mascalise, Perricone, and Calabrese for dry reds.

Much of the improvement in Sicilian wines is due to the efforts of oenologists and to cooperative wine-making. To preserve freshness and fruit, oenologists have convinced growers to harvest their grapes earlier, around the beginning of September. Thus, despite hot summers, the wines are able to retain fruit and acidity and do not suffer from excessive alcohol. Also, wines are bottled earlier (in December following the harvest) rather than remaining in the vat for 10 to 14 months. Cooperatives have provided technology and commercial knowledge to support the improvement in Sicilian wine production. Among the largest exporters of bottled wines are Corvo, near Palermo, and the Settesòli cooperative in Menfi, near Agrigento. (The city of Agrigento itself is a showplace of Greek temples from the 6th and 5th centuries B.C.) Other good producers are the Enocarboj cooperative in Sciassa; Regaleali, belonging to Count Giuseppi Tasca; Sclafani near Palermo; and Villa Grande near Etna.

Corvo di Casteldaccia: The red and especially the white wines of this name are the best known of the Sicilian table wines. Started by the Duke of Salaparuta in the early 18th century, the firm is now owned by the Sicilian government. The greatly improved dry, fresh white wine has some of the hardness of the Trebbiano grape. The red, made from Nero Mascalise, Perricone, and Calabrese, is well vinified, strong, and long-lasting on the palate.

Italy: Sardinia

Since the 1960s, Sardinian wine production has undergone an oenological revolution. New grape varieties, early harvesting to preserve acidity, temperature-controlled fermentation, and early bottling are some of the features of the modern vinification techniques which have transformed the style and quality of Sardinian wines. In place of the sweet fortified wines of yesteryear, the island now produces good, fresh, dry red and especially white wines. These light wines, with a slight prickle (CO_2), are favored by the numerous tourists who flock to Sardinia and, above all, to La Costa Smeralda, a vacationland built by the Aga Khan around Porto Cervo, Porto Rotondo, and Cala di Volpe. Costa Smeralda has become one of the best summer resorts in Europe.

United States

The predicted American wine boom is by now an established fact. The burgeoning American interest in drinking and discussing fine American wines has led to a dramatic growth in the American wine industry. Per capita consumption has grown steadily from year to year. In California alone, creation of new wineries has brought the total to approximately 470, nearly a 100% increase since 1973. This increase in wine-making has affected all levels of the market, from the simplest jug wines to the finest varietals. Fine-quality wines were given a particular boost by the dramatic increase in prices among fine French wines in 1973 and 1974. American consumers increasingly turned their backs on the European market, in particular French wines, and began to investigate their own "grands crus." A few well-publicized comparative blind tastings between the wines of California and those of France confirmed the American consumer's belief in the fine quality of American wines.

A diverse group of individualists, drawn by the romance of wine from all walks of life, greatly contributed to the formation of many of the new wineries established in the seventies. Doctors, architects, engineers, industrialists, airline pilots, advertising executives, as individuals and as groups of investors, cleared land, planted vines, built vat rooms, and began to make wine. Their energy and dedication, along with American wine-drinkers' great curiosity and receptivity to new wines, spearheaded a general overall improvement in American wines. The largest wineries, such as Gallo, Almadén, and Paul Masson, which had previously specialized in brand-name jug wines and generics, placed more and more emphasis on varietals in their product lines.

The American wine industry is still feeling the effect of this sudden infusion of new blood and new talent. It will be a while before the long-range results are clear. However, some comments are in order now.

The diversity of background, training, and temperament of the new wine-makers has led to a fecund period of experimentation in wine-making and vine-tending methods. The decade of the seventies will be remembered as the period of great American oenological creativity, where new and often daring attempts were made to match grape varieties (and their clones and hybrids) with the vicissitudes of climate and soil in regions of California and other states that had never before been exploited for vine-growing and wine-making.

Some of the results were highly fruitful, and the full benefits will take years to assess. Clones were selected and developed out of an urgent need to find slower-ripening vines in the California heat. Highly sophisticated meth-

ods for controlling fermentation came into use. In small wineries, scrupulous (sometimes overly so) distinction of vinification vats became the practice. In other instances, these advanced techniques proved to be blind alleys— nothing more than tinkering for its own sake, producing rather eccentric wines of limited appeal: late-harvest Chardonnays; inky, concentrated, 100% Cabernet Sauvignons; and late-harvest Zinfandels.

There was a certain tendency as well, with the dramatic increase in the demand for wine, for growers and wineries to plant varietals in unsuitable soils without the patient experimentation needed to obtain the best match of grape variety, soil, temperature zone, and microclimate.

These mistakes and excesses are insignificant when compared with the pioneering strides the California wine industry made in the 1970s. In efforts to understand and master practices in oenology, certain winery owners and their wine-makers explored and exploited these techniques to their fullest extent, occasionally to the detriment of the wines being made. The reasoning among some was that they would never know how much was enough if they did not know how much was too much.

Once the techniques were mastered, wine-makers moved ahead to explore other advances in oenology. Cool, slow fermentation temperatures became cooler than ever; carbonic maceration (a fermentation technique; q.v.) was employed more intensively and on more grape varieties than was beneficial to the wine concerned; a vogue for the late-harvest wines and botrytised wines (see Botrytis cinerea) resulted in bottles that were more curious than palatable; overly long barrel-aging occasionally left wines excessively woody and unbalanced.

The coming years will show these excesses to have been minor, the small price paid by a vineyard region and a people in a hurry to produce the best wines possible.

Problems susceptible to straightforward technological solutions have been the easiest to solve. For this reason, white wines (by nature less complex and more dependent on enlightened vat-room technique than red wines), and particularly the Chardonnays, have reached a relatively higher level of quality than that achieved so far by most of the reds.

The problems that face wine-making in California will be solved only by patient experimentation in the future. A chronic problem among the finest red and white wines is that the California climate is *too* sunny and clement, ripening grapes too quickly for them to attain the complex secondary aromatic elements that distinguish the great wines from the merely good. More often than not, sugar levels in the grapes push the alcohol level in the wines beyond 13 and 14%, which is too much for the proper balance and finesse to be achieved. Only trial and error in the selection of varietal clones and different microclimates within the proper temperature zones will solve this problem.

Finally, as this new generation of American wine enthusiasm comes of age, the other remaining task is to standardize and codify American wine laws, and to name American wines only by American names. Once this has been accomplished, one will be able to say that American wines have passed through the lingering adolescent insecurity vis-à-vis their vinous European elders and have declared themselves a full-fledged force in the world of wine.

United States: Alabama

Although native grapes were domestically grown in Alabama as early as 1840, eventually yielding more than 400,000 gallons in 1880, Prohibition set in and the industry died out. Finally, in 1978, the last remnants of the dry laws were scrapped and small-winery licenses were made available.

To date, Perdido Vineyard, in the southern part of the state 50 miles northeast of Mobile, is the only bonded winery in Alabama. Most of Perdido's 50 acres (20 hectares) are devoted to Muscadine grapes, although small amounts of French hybrids have been successfully grown. In other parts of Alabama, particularly in the north, experiments with hybrids planted in strip-mined soil are being conducted.

United States: Arizona

Ranking eighth in table-grape production, the Arizona deserts are for the most part too hot for wine-grape growing. However, cooler regions found in the eastern mountains are under investigation as possible sites for vinifera and varietal vine cultivation. Experiments conducted in this area by the University of Arizona have been encouraging.

United States: Arkansas

See page 481.

United States: California

Although the BATF (Bureau of Alcohol, Tobacco and Firearms), a United States Federal Government body, is only in the beginning stages of recognizing a system similar to the European appellation laws, whose uniformity was necessitated by the Common Market, it is hoped that a future American counterpart will incorporate the same standards of clarity and precision. By establishing quality standards in the European tradition, appellations recognizing exceptional soils and microclimates will emerge in every state where wine is grown.

In California, where the evolution of wines is most rapidly progressing, the need for these laws is most obviously evident. By 1980, approximately 470 bonded wineries existed in California, as opposed to 240 in 1970. Total wine production leaped from 211 million gallons in 1970 to 383 million gallons in 1979.

Following is a list of the more prominent of the new California wineries, supplementing those covered on pages 492 through 506. Efforts have been made, in quoting production figures, to estimate the likely amounts the wineries will produce in the 1980s.

North Coast

(1) Napa

Burgess Cellars. Formerly Souverain Cellars, built in 1943 by J. Leland Stewart, Burgess Cellars is located at about 1,000 feet (300 meters) elevation on the western slopes of Howell Mountain northeast of St. Helena. Since 1972, when they bought these 22 acres (9 hectares), former airline pilot Tom Burgess and his wife, Linda, one-time New Yorkers, have made seven wines whose quality continues to improve. Bill Sorenson is the wine-maker behind the 20,000-case annual production. The Burgess white wines are fermented in oak barrels. Exceptionally good wines are the Chenin Blanc and Cabernet Sauvignon.

Cakebread Cellars. While still maintaining his commercial photography, auto repair, and agricultural businesses, Jack Cakebread, along with his wife, Dolores, and his three sons, added wine-making to his many careers in 1973. Twenty-two acres (9 hectares) of vines surrounding the St. Helena winery (designed by Cakebread), plus grapes from local vineyards, provide enough fruit for an annual 10,000 cases. The wines to date have been of average quality.

Carneros Creek Winery. Balfour Gibson (previously part-owner of San Francisco's Connoisseur Wine Imports), his wife, Anita, and Francis Mahoney form the three-person wine-making team at their 10-acre (4-hectare) Carneros Creek Winery, established in 1973. They are concentrating on growing Pinot Noir, whose young vines have begun to mature, resulting in top-quality wines in 1977 and 1978. Carneros Creek also produces a good tannic and full-bodied Zinfandel made from grapes grown 100 miles (160 kilometers) to the east in Amador County. Relatively close to San Pablo Bay, beneath the slopes of Miliken Peak, Carneros Creek is the southernmost winery in the Napa Valley. The cooler temperatures and fog in this area enable the grapes to mature longer on the wine; hence, the Chardonnay can be picked later, ensuring a good balance between sugar and acidity. Carneros Creek produces about 11,000 cases a year.

Caymus Vineyards. Located on Conn Creek Road in Rutherford, off the Silverado Trail, Caymus Vineyards is the domain of longtime Napa Valley grape-grower Charles Wagner, whose French relatives produce wine in the Alsace region. Wagner made his first Cabernet Sauvignon and Pinot Noir in 1972, and now, with the assistance of his son Chuck, six wines are sold under the Caymus and secondary Liberty School labels, including a first-rate Cabernet Sauvignon and a good Fumé Blanc. The 72 acres (30 hectares) of vines yield an average of 20,000 cases annually.

Chateau Chevalier. Gregory Bissonette, a stockbroker, and his wife, Kathy, bought this abandoned winery in 1969 and restored it, retaining the name given it by the 1891 founder, George Chevalier. The magnificent Victorian-style mansion, also brought back to life by the Bissonettes, is located outside of St. Helena on the steep hillsides off Spring Mountain Road. Of the 60 acres (25 hectares) planted in grapes, 65% are Cabernet Sauvignon and 30%

653

are Chardonnay. About 10,000 cases are produced annually. One hopes that the wines will improve in the 1980s.

Chateau Montelena. Ever since this winery's 1973 Chardonnay surpassed four top French white Burgundies and five other California Chardonnays in a blind tasting held by a panel of experts in Paris in 1976, its wines have continued to live up to their reputation. Owned by James L. Barrett, Lee Paschich, and Ernest Hahn since 1968, Chateau Montelena produces four wines; their making is under the direction of Jerry Luper, formerly wine-maker at Freemark Abbey. One hundred acres (40 hectares) of grapes yield about 20,000 cases of wine per year. The Chardonnays are consistently good. Located on Spring Mountain at the eastern end of Calistoga, Chateau Montelena features the five-acre (2-hectare) man-made Jade Lake.

Conn Creek Winery. Formerly off Highway 29 between St. Helena and Calistoga, Conn Creek moved to its new Silverado Trail location near Rutherford in 1979. Jointly owned by longtime Napa Valley grape-growers Bill and Kathy Collins, former airline pilot Koerner Rombauer and his wife, Joan, and the English firm of Ropner and Willow, Conn Creek wines are made by John Henderson, who at one time worked under Leland Stewart at Souverain Cellars. Growing about half their own grapes north of St. Helena in Yountville and purchasing the rest, Conn Creek has made three wines since 1975, averaging about 20,000 cases per year.

Diamond Creek Vineyards. Situated high up on Diamond Mountain, due west of Sterling Vineyards and minutes from Schramsberg and Calistoga, this secluded 20-acre (8-hectare) vineyard was founded in 1969 and makes three Cabernet Sauvignon wines, based on three different soil types, from 90% Cabernet Sauvignon grapes and 10% Merlot. One-time wine-marketing man Al Brounstein and his wife, Boots, are the proprietors; they aim to make tannic concentrated wines that require a long aging period. Their limited production, 2,500 cases annually, is exclusively Cabernet Sauvignon. So far, since their 1972 debut, the wines have been excessively tannic and their quality is questionable in the long run. The three Diamond Creek Vineyards appellations are Volcanic Hill, Gravelly Meadows, and Red Rock Terrace.

Forman Winery. In 1979, Sterling's former wine-master, Richard Forman, built a winery on St. Helena's Spring Mountain amid his 50 acres (20 hectares) of vines. Forman aims to gradually produce both a Merlot-Cabernet blend and a Sauvignon Blanc–Semillon blend at an ultimate average rate of 8,000 cases per year.

Grgich Hills Cellars. Mike Grgich, formerly wine-maker at Chateau Montelena, who worked with André Tchelistcheff, joined forces in 1977 with Austin Hills, of the Hills Brothers coffee family, to establish this winery near the intersection of Highway 29 and Rutherford Road. It was Mike Grgich who made the 1973 Chateau Montelena Chardonnay which surpassed four French white Burgundies in a 1976 Paris tasting. Now, he makes wines from grapes grown on Hills's two properties, one in cooler southern Napa and the other near Rutherford. Total acreage of vines is 140 (56 hectares). Annual production is around 15,000 cases. Current emphasis is on Johannis-

berg Riesling and Chardonnay; Zinfandel and Cabernet will be made as well.

Keenan Winery. The 45 acres (18 hectares) of steep, terraced vineyards on the slopes of Spring Mountain that surround the Keenan Winery, originally built by Peter Conradi in 1904, are planted exclusively in Chardonnay and Cabernet Sauvignon varieties. Wine-maker Joe Cafaro, previously with Charles Krug and Chappellet, produced the first Keenan wines in 1977. Proprietor Robert Keenan, a former San Francisco insurance executive, is limiting production of his wines, made in the traditional French method of small cooperage to a maximum of 7,000 cases per year. Keenan made a couple of very good Chardonnays in 1978, and the young vines promise to yield more good Chardonnays in the future.

Long Vineyards. Robert and Zelma Long's grapes, grown on their 14 acres (5½ hectares) of vines on the steep slopes of Pritchard Hill in St. Helena, have provided neighboring wineries with some exceptional wines (Mount Veeder's Chardonnays are one example). As of 1977, the Longs have been making small quantities (no more than 2,000 cases annually) under the Long Vineyards label. Zelma Long was formerly oenologist at Mondavi and now holds that position at Simi in Sonoma.

Mount Veeder Winery. Attorney Michael and photographer Arlene Bernstein, who began planting grapes in 1968, soon transformed what was originally their summer retreat from San Francisco into a winery. Their 20 acres (8 hectares) in the Mayacamas Mountains, about 1,000 to 1,400 feet (300 to 425 meters) in elevation on Mount Veeder, are planted almost entirely in red Bordeaux varietals. Their wines are deep in color and rich in tannin. About 4,500 cases are made annually. One of the wines Mount Veeder produces is a big, intense Zinfandel made from grapes grown 100 miles (160 kilometers) east in Amador County.

Nichelini Vineyards. Eleven miles (18 kilometers) east of Rutherford, and high up on a hill (985 feet or 300 meters in altitude), Nichelini Vineyards' 50 acres (20 hectares) of vines benefit from their intriguing elevated microclimate. Proprietor Jim Nichelini, a third-generation California wine-maker, currently makes six fairly average wines in large wooden vats in the so-called old Italian-Swiss tradition, at the rate of about 6,000 cases a year. None of the Nichelini wines carry a vintage date.

Niebaum-Coppola Estates. Francis Ford Coppola, the film director, entered into the wine business in 1975 with the purchase of the Niebaum estate, one-time home of millionaire sea captain and Inglenook founder Gustav Niebaum. Located in Rutherford, Niebaum-Coppola Estates consists of 120 acres (48 hectares) of vines yielding an annual 7,000 cases. Production will eventually peak at 20,000 cases. Russ Turner oversees the wine-making and winery management. Emphasis is on achieving a premium red wine by blending three varietals.

Robert Pecota. Constructed in 1978, this Calistoga winery offers three wines. Forty acres (16 hectares) of vines adjacent to the winery provide grapes for about 8,000 cases per year. The Gamay Beaujolais and Sauvignon Blanc look promising.

Joseph Phelps Vineyards. After building two neighboring

wineries, Joseph Phelps, president of a Colorado-based construction company, decided to establish his own vineyards on this former ranch on the Silverado Trail, not far from St. Helena, next door to Heitz Wine Cellars. Since 1973, he has been producing four wines, known for their elegance and balance. These include a Sauvignon Blanc he can be proud of, from grapes grown on his 128 acres (52 hectares) and grapes purchased locally. Walter Schug, the wine-maker, was trained in Geisenheim, Germany, and his well-balanced white wines bring to mind wines of the Rheingau. Production is about 50,000 cases a year. Phelps has planted some experimental Syrah vines (as opposed to Petite Sirah) that are imported from France's Rhône Valley. He also makes some excellent botrytised or late-harvest Rieslings.

Pope Valley Winery. Sixty-five acres (26 hectares) of this older vineyard across the hills from Napa Valley, owned and operated since 1972 by ex-electrical engineer James Devitt and his wife, Arlene, produce some red and white wines. Often high in acid, the wines have so far been only mediocre. Built into the side of a slate hill off Howell Mountain Road, this gravity-flow winery is the northernmost establishment in Napa County. Annual production is approximately 4,000 cases.

Raymond Vineyards and Cellars. When the Nestlé Company bought Beringer Winery in 1970, the Raymond family (father Roy Senior and sons Roy Junior and Walter), all part-owners of Beringer, purchased and planted 90 acres (36 hectares) south of St. Helena, with plans to establish their own winery. In 1974, the Raymonds' first wines, a Cabernet Sauvignon and a Zinfandel, were crushed. The family-run operation turns out about 20,000 cases annually. The wines are made from eight different grape varieties and are all vintage-dated and claim to be estate-bottled. The quality varies, but the wines are generally good. The Raymonds make a fine Chenin Blanc.

Saint Clement Vineyards. Dr. William Casey, a San Francisco ophthalmologist and his wife, Alexandra, both wine enthusiasts and gourmets, purchased their winery and restored Victorian mansion on the lower slopes of Spring Mountain in St. Helena in 1975 from Mike and Shirley Robbins, who moved their Spring Mountain Vineyards farther up the hill. Wine-making has become a second career for Casey, whose new gravity-flow, hydraulically equipped winery was completed in 1979. Small quantities of Cabernet Sauvignon (about 7,000 cases per year) and very good Chardonnay wines have been sold under the Saint Clement label since 1975. Casey grows only 2 acres (less than 1 hectare) of grapes and purchases the best quality he can find.

Silver Oak Cellars. About half of Silver Oak Cellars' 1,000 acres (400 hectares) in Napa, Sonoma, and Lake counties are planted in Cabernet Sauvignon. Owners Raymond Duncan, creative Denver oilman-turned-viticulturist, and Justin Meyer, also the wine-maker, owned Franciscan Winery and Vineyards until 1979. Meyer continues as an advisor at Franciscan. At Silver Oak, they make an excellent Cabernet Sauvignon wine that is aged three years in oak casks and two years in bottles before being sold. Their cellars are located three miles (5 kilometers) southeast of Rutherford off of Oak-

ville Cross Road. About 4,000 cases are sold annually under the Silver Oak Cellars label; most of their grapes are sold to other wineries.

Smith-Madrone Vineyards. The Smith brothers, Stuart and Charles, began planting vines at this Spring Mountain location in 1971. They crushed their first vintage in 1977 and made some good wines in their handmade winery, which features underground cellars and a sod roof. The output of Smith-Madrone will remain under 3,000 cases per year. Thirty-eight acres (15 hectares) are planted in predominantly Cabernet Sauvignon and Chardonnay vines.

Stag's Leap Vineyard. Former residents of Los Angeles, Carl and Joanne Doumani founded their winery in 1970, located on the Silverado Trail about a mile south of Yountville Cross Road. The Doumanis converted the abandoned, run-down Stag's Leap Hotel on their property into a home, and the neighboring stone buildings into a winery. They produce about 10,000 cases of excellent wine annually from grapes grown on their 100 acres (40 hectares) of vines. The vineyard operates as a small corporation of four partners, presided over by Doumani. Their Napa Valley Petite Sirah is notably rich and intense without being too tannic.

Stag's Leap Wine Cellars (not to be confused with the previous entry). Warren Winiarski surprised everyone when his 1973 Cabernet Sauvignon won first prize in a Parisian blind tasting in 1976. Consequently, his wines, known for their fruitiness and elegance, and for being characteristic of their grape varieties, are much in demand. Stag's Leap Wine Cellars, a family-run operation whose first wines appeared in 1972, is located on the Silverado Trail a mile south of the Yountville Cross Road. In addition to the Cabernet Sauvignon, which accounts for roughly half of the yearly 15,000-case production, Winiarski makes a very creditable Merlot varietal.

Stonegate Winery. James Spaulding, Dean of Journalism at the University of California at Berkeley, and his wife, Barbara, owners of Stonegate, planted some vines on the steep slopes west of Calistoga in 1969. Located just off Highway 29 on Dunaweal Lane (the road to Sterling Vineyards), Stonegate was bonded in 1973, when the Spauldings produced their first wines. Made from grapes grown on their own 35 acres (14 hectares) and from purchased grapes, Stonegate makes three wines—Sauvignon Blanc, Chenin Blanc, and Pinot Noir—at the rate of about 13,000 cases annually. David Spaulding and Michael Fallow are co-wine-makers.

Trefethen Vineyards. A family operation since 1968, owned by Gene Trefethen and currently run by son John and daughter-in-law Janet, Trefethen Vineyards is known for its white wines. Generally, all of them are full of finesse and elegance. Their very clean fruity Chardonnay could well be the pride of Napa, and the Trefethen Riesling is of a dry Alsatian style. Five wines of overall good quality are produced from Trefethen's 600 acres (245 hectares) at the limited rate of about 10,000 cases per year. From 1973 to 1976, Moët-Hennessy shared the Trefethen cellars to make their first California "champagnes" while their Yountville winery, Domaine Chandon, was under construction. In addition, Trefethen makes excellent inexpensive generic red and white wines under the Eshcol label.

Veedercrest Vineyards. The demand for the good wines of Veedercrest Vineyards at one point far exceeded its supply, especially when its Chardonnay was the preferred wine (over some Puligny-Montrachets) at Maxim's restaurant in Paris in 1972. Since then, the wines have been decent and drinkable, but without any distinction. The vineyard belongs to A. W. Baxter—a former college professor who also serves as wine-maker—and to Ed Ring and others, and is located at the intersection of Mount Veeder and Lokoya roads. Grapes from the 100-acre (40-hectare) vineyard are crushed and made into wine in a new facility. Production will peak at 20,000 cases annually.

Villa Mount Eden. Bought in 1970 by San Francisco financier James McWilliams and his wife, Anne, of the Bank of America Giannini family, Villa Mount Eden is a peaceful site at the foot of Mount Eden where the Oakville Cross Road meets the Silverado Trail. The wines are good, made from estate-grown grapes (from 90 acres, or 37 hectares, of vines) and field-crushing and cold-fermenting practices account for the fruitiness of the wines. Davis-educated Nils Venge, son of importer Per Venge, worked at Charles Krug and Sterling wineries before coming to Villa Mount Eden. In addition to the first wines, Chardonnay and Cabernet Sauvignon, made in 1974, Villa Mount Eden also makes several other wines, including a richly flavored Gamay and a well-balanced Gewürztraminer.

ZD Wines. Previously located in Sonoma County, engineers Gino Zeppone and Norman de Leuze moved their 6,000-case operation to the Napa Valley in 1969. Four acres (1½ hectares) in the cooler Carneros district yield a portion of the grapes needed for their wines. Other than some success with Chardonnays and big, powerful Pinot Noirs, ZD's quality has been inconsistent.

(2) Sonoma

Alexander Valley Vineyards. In 1963, Hank Wetzel, Jr., previously an executive with the Garrett Corporation in Los Angeles, and Russel Green, Jr., bought this acreage in the Alexander Valley, site of settler Cyrus Alexander's adobe house and gravesite, and an 1886 schoolhouse. While gradually restoring the Victorian mansion on the property, Wetzel planted the former grazing lands in vines and sold the grapes to neighboring wineries in the sixties and early seventies. Meanwhile, his son, Hank Wetzel III, and daughter, Katie Wetzel, completed their educations at Davis and became wine-maker and sales manager, respectively, for the family corporation established in 1975. That same year, the first Alexander Valley Vineyards wines were produced. Currently, five wines are made from eight grape varieties grown on 240 acres (98 hectares) and production will eventually reach 20,000 cases annually. Although on the whole the wines are rather undistinguished, a Chardonnay shows some promise.

Chateau Saint Jean. Located near Kenwood northwest of the town of Sonoma and southeast of Santa Rosa, beautiful grounds surround the French Mediterranean-style mansion of Chateau Saint Jean, which was founded in 1973 by three valley grape-growers, Robert Merzoian, Edward Merzoian, and Kenneth Sheffield. Seven grape varieties are planted on 105 acres (46 hectares) and yield 30% of the 70,000-case annual production. Overly precise Dick Arrowood, Saint Jean's energetic wine-master, has succeeded in unnecessarily producing some seven Chardonnays of the same vintage, eight Rieslings varying in flavor, four Cabernet and Zinfandel reds, and even more in certain vintages, all from different vineyards, which are usually identified on the labels. Botrytised wines (from both Riesling and Gewürztraminer grapes) seem to temporarily command Arrowood's major interest. Some of his best efforts to date, however, have been with Chardonnay and Riesling grapes purchased from the Robert Young Vineyard. One hopes that time, and trial and error, will pare down the present assortment to those few wines that represent the best quality the specific soil and microclimate can produce. Nevertheless, the wines are good and have been winning medals since their 1974 debut.

Clos du Bois. Clos du Bois wines, made from quality grapes grown on about 200 acres (80 hectares) in both the Dry Creek and Alexander valleys, was founded by Frank Woods in 1974. Tom Hobart, wine-master, supervises the crushing and bottling of the wines, which takes place at Souverain of Alexander Valley in cooperation with Bill Bonetti. The wines are innovatively marketed by Woods, whose expertise is also reflected in the successful River Oaks Vineyards operation, which produces larger quantities of fairly priced lesser wines from grapes grown on plots adjacent to those of Clos du Bois. About 25,000 cases are released annually under the Clos du Bois label. Although quality is inconsistent, Clos du Bois is capable of making a very good Gewürztraminer; the Chardonnay and Pinot Noir (from mountainside vineyards) also show a lot of promise.

Dehlinger Winery. Klaus Dehlinger, a Berkeley radiologist, and son Tom, who used to be wine-maker at Hanzell Vineyards, have made some very good wines since the founding of the Dehlinger Winery in 1976. Growing some grapes on 14 acres (5½ hectares) and buying the rest from other Sonoma vineyards, the Dehlingers have limited their production to four varietals best suited to their relatively cool region: Cabernet Sauvignon, Chardonnay, Zinfandel, and Pinot Noir. Located at the intersection of Guerneville and Vine Hill roads in the hills of Sebastopol, this winery produces an average of 6,000 cases per year. Particularly noteworthy are the Chardonnay and Cabernet Sauvignon.

Dry Creek Vineyard. A few miles northwest of Healdsburg, Dry Creek Vineyard was founded by David Stare in 1972. Ever since a 1970 visit to the Médoc, Stare has pursued vine-growing and wine-making instead of civil engineering. Stare's efforts have resulted in a wide range of good wines, including a very fine Chardonnay. Stare grows about half of his own grapes on 50 acres (20 hectares) and makes about 20,000 cases of crisp and elegantly styled wines per year.

Field Stone Winery. Known for its original and innovative wine-making techniques involving the use of a mechanical harvester and mobile press developed by the winery's late founder, Wallace Johnson, Field Stone also has the distinction of being the only underground winery built in this century. At one time mayor of Berkeley, Johnson owned the property surrounding Field Stone, Redwood Ranch, for many years, and in 1965 began growing grapes as well as raising cattle. Johnson sold his grapes to other Napa and Sonoma vineyards, and in 1976, with the help of his inventions, made his own wines under the Field Stone label. Production from the 800-acre (325-hectare) ranch and vineyards is expected to reach a maximum of 25,000 cases.

Foppiano Winery. Founded by Italian immigrant John Foppiano in 1864, this vineyard, south of Healdsburg between the Old Redwood Highway and the Russian River, is now run by his great-grandson, Louis Joseph Foppiano. Rod Foppiano, another member of the fourth generation, is the wine-maker. Good medium-priced wines are still produced by Foppiano, and the full-flavored varietals have shown excellent progress. Grapes grown from Foppiano's 200 acres (80 hectares), plus locally purchased produce, yield an average of 200,000 cases per year, much of which is of average quality.

Geyser Peak Winery. Owned by the Joseph Schlitz Brewing Company of Milwaukee since 1972, this huge winery (600 acres or 245 hectares), on a hill just north of Geyserville, produces everything from vintage wines, sold under its Geyser Peak label, to Summit brand table wines, available in bag-in-box containers. A bottle-fermented "champagne" was introduced in 1979, and an Amador County Zinfandel debuted in 1980. The 1978 Gewürztraminer (under the Geyser Peak label only) showed superb balance and flavor. Unfortunately, not many of the other varietals can match it; most of them lack elegance. Dante Bagnani, son of the previous owner, is in charge of operations, and Armand Bussone is wine-maker. Geyser Peak and Summit production totals about 450,000 cases per year.

Gundlach-Bundschu Winery. Four generations later, the Bundschu family has set out to reestablish the wine-making reputation earned by two of the original 1858 founders, Jacob Gundlach and Charles Bundschu. Although the 1906 earthquake and fire wiped out their prosperous wine business, the Rhinefarm vineyard, at that time the site for Julius Dresel's grafting experiments, continued to produce grapes for commercial purposes. Half of the production of the 350-acre (140-hectare) vineyard, an expansion of the original Rhinefarm, is retained to make about 24,000 cases annually. Wine-maker John Merritt has made a good Cabernet Sauvignon.

Grand Cru Vineyards. In 1970, Robert Magnani and Allen Ferrara founded Grand Cru Vineyards in Sonoma's Valley of the Moon, near Glen Ellen. Built on the site of an 1896 winery, Grand Cru produces some interesting wines, results of the innovative techniques of wine-maker Magnani and viticulturist Ferrara, former engineering partners. The 20,000-case winery specializes in German-style wines. Their artificially induced Botrytis Gewürz-

traminer and one of California's first white Zinfandels are the best-known examples of their efforts. Sauvignon Blanc and Semillon grapes grow on 30 acres (12 hectares); other grapes are purchased.

Hop Kiln Winery. As its name indicates, this winery is housed in a remnant of Sonoma County's once active hop-growing industry, now preserved as a state historical landmark. Owner Dr. Martin Griffin began making wines here in 1975, after 14 years of grape-growing and home wine-making. Part of the yield of 65 acres (25 hectares) of Russian River vineyards is used to make about 3,000 cases a year of several wines, including a Zinfandel from vines planted in 1880.

J. J. Haraszthy & Son. Descendants of Colonel Agoston Haraszthy, one of the more colorful figures of California's wine past and founder of Buena Vista, began making wines from purchased grapes in 1977. About 8,000 cases of wine a year, mostly Zinfandel, are made at the Glen Ellen site.

Iron Horse Vineyards. Owned by attorney Barry Sterling and his wife, Audrey, who decided to enter the wine business after living in France for several years, this property is located in the Sebastopol foothills. Starting out with 7,000 cases in 1979, including a noteworthy Chardonnay, the Sterlings hope to eventually produce 20,000 cases of wine from predominantly Chardonnay and Pinot Noir grapes grown on their 140 acres (55 hectares).

Johnson's Alexander Valley Wines. James Johnson, a San Francisco lawyer, bought this 70-acre (30-hectare) ranch in 1952 and cultivated pears, prunes, and grapes for many years. By 1975, most of the land was converted into vineyards. The three Johnson sons became joint owners of the property and crushed their first grapes that year. Nine wines are now made, and according to wine-maker Tom Johnson, the 10,000-case average production will eventually consist of 100% varietal wines made from grapes grown exclusively on the family's property.

Jordan Vineyard and Winery. Tom Jordan, Jr., formerly a Denver-based oilman who moved his business to Santa Rosa, bought this beautiful property in 1972 and with his wife, Sally, has created from scratch a French-style wine-producing chateau in the Alexander Valley. The winery, the home, the vineyards, the wine—every aspect of the Jordans' establishment is modeled after the traditional Bordeaux châteaux, whose wines the Jordans have greatly admired for years. A well-balanced and elegant Cabernet Sauvignon is the fruit of their efforts; it will eventually be produced at the rate of 60,000 cases annually. First released in 1979, the Jordan Cabernet shows great promise. The Jordans' 240 acres (98 hectares) are planted primarily in Cabernet Sauvignon, with small quantities of Chardonnay. A top winery.

Kenwood Vineyards. Quality, not quantity, is the goal at Kenwood Vineyards, formerly the bulk-wine-producing Julius Pagani Winery. Six partners have been responsible for this turnaround since 1970, when they bought the property located in the Sugarloaf Ridge foothills in Kenwood. Offering three wines from five grape varieties, some of which are grown at their 20-acre (8-hectare) vineyard, others purchased locally, the Kenwood team plans to produce not more than 40,000 cases per year. Their Zinfandel has so far been their most successful wine.

Landmark Vineyards. Landmark, which started out as a ranch in the 19th century and became a prune farm in the 1900s, has been transformed into a vineyard by its new owners, the Mabry family, who bought the property in 1974. An elegant arcade of tall cypresses leads the way to the Spanish-style hacienda and winery located in Windsor, not far from the highway exit. The Mabrys have cultivated vines on 80 acres (32 hectares) of vineyards in the Alexander and Sonoma valleys since 1972, and now grow an additional 60 acres (25 hectares) adjacent to the winery. They make about 25,000 cases per year. Although most wines have been of only average quality, the Chardonnay and Pinot Noir show some promise.

Lambert Bridge. Gerard Lambert, of the St. Louis pharmaceutical firm family, bought this Dry Creek Valley property in 1969 and named it after the nearby landmark that coincidentally bore his name. Specializing in Chardonnay and Cabernet Sauvignon, Lambert's wines are made by Nick Martin and managed by Dave Rafanelli (whose father runs a neighboring winery, *q.v.*). The wines debuted in 1975. Although 80 acres (32 hectares) of vines are cultivated, Lambert uses his best-quality Chardonnay and Cabernet grapes from 45 acres for his own wines and sells three other varieties from the remaining 35 acres (14 hectares). The Lambert Bridge Chardonnay shows potential.

Lytton Springs Winery. Grapes grown on these hillside vineyards near Healdsburg have been sold to many wineries since 1970; in fact, the famed Zinfandels made by the Ridge Vineyards in Cupertino, south of San Francisco Bay, were made largely from the fruit of Lytton Springs' 80-year-old vines. Since the completion of the winery in 1977, one of California's best Zinfandels has been made under the Lytton Springs Winery label. Owners Dee Sindt (publisher of *Wine World* magazine) and Bura Walters (wine-maker) make up to 30,000 cases annually, from their 50 acres (20 hectares) of Zinfandel grapes and from those they purchase outside.

Matanzas Creek Winery. Sandra MacIver—daughter of Edgar Stern, the New Orleans realtor and part-owner of San Francisco's magnificent Stanford Court Hotel—began growing grapes here in 1971, and with former Mount Eden wine-maker Meredith Edwards has managed to produce some consistently good wines. Located in two different microclimates between Glen Ellen and Santa Rosa, Matanzas Creek's 60 acres (25 hectares) are planted in three different grape varieties, whose fruit is fermented and vinified in a renovated dairy barn. The Chardonnay is outstanding and the fine Gewürztraminer is made in a full-bodied, dry Alsatian style. The winery anticipates reaching a total annual production of 8,000 cases.

Mill Creek Vineyards. The Kreck family started out in the 1950s as ranchers and cattle raisers at this property bordering the Russian River west of Healdsburg. Starting in 1965, the Krecks gradually planted vines, and they now have 70 acres (28 hectares). At first, grapes were sold commercially; now, since the 1976 completion of the Mill Creek winery, about 10,000 cases of 4 different wines are made annually. The wines are of overall average quality, although the Cabernet Sauvignon and Chardonnay show some promise.

Souverain of Alexander Valley. Built in 1972 and originally bought by the Pillsbury Company of Minneapolis, Souverain, as of 1975, belongs to a group of 180 grape-growers in Sonoma, Napa, and Mendocino counties. William Bonetti, wine-maker at Souverain, has not been hampered by ownership changes; made from the grower's best grapes, whose origins are indicated on the bottles, he succeeds in making excellent wines at the rate of about 500,000 cases annually. Souverain of Alexander Valley, situated in Geyserville, with its buildings designed after old hop kilns still seen in some parts of Sonoma County, is a showcase of winery architecture.

Joseph Swan Vineyards. From his 10 acres (4 hectares) 10 miles (16 kilometers) northeast of Santa Rosa, which are planted mostly in Pinot Noir and Chardonnay grapes, former Western Airlines pilot Joe Swan has been making some very good wines since 1969. His estate-bottled Pinot Noir tries to resemble some of the Côte d'Or Burgundies, but Swan is primarily known for his fine and concentrated Zinfandel. Maximum production is 2,500 cases per year, all of which is sold to a private mailing list of customers.

Preston Vineyards. Louis Preston and his wife, Susan, established their Dry Creek vineyard in 1975, making wines in the converted prune dehydrator that is surrounded by their 75 acres (30 hectares). The Prestons' selected vines produce about 3,500 cases per year. After experimenting with some other varieties, Preston is now devoting most of his wine-making expertise, from vine to bottle, into the production of Zinfandel and Sauvignon Blanc wines, the two grape varieties Preston has found to grow particularly successfully on his rich hillside soils.

A. Rafanelli Winery. Most of Americo Rafanelli's 25 acres (10 hectares) of Dry Creek vineyards produces grapes that are sold to other wineries, but the cream of the crop is reserved for his Zinfandel and Gamay Beaujolais wines. Having learned wine-making from his father, who made wines in Healdsburg in the forties, Americo carries on the family tradition by making full-bodied, old-style California wines that are not filtered or processed. His wines are produced at the rate of about 3,000 cases per year.

Trentadue Vineyards. Evelyn and Leo Trentadue have been supplying grapes to many wineries, including Ridge Vineyards, since 1969, when they left their Santa Clara Valley orchards to cultivate vines here in the Alexander Valley. As of 1973, the Trentadues have been wine-makers as well as growers, retaining enough of their grapes from 200 acres (80 hectares) of vines to make an annual average of 15,000 cases. So far, the wines have been undistinguished, with the reds slightly better than the whites.

Woodbury Winery. This port-style wine producer is located in Marin County, southeast of Sonoma. Woodbury, established in 1979, aims to produce 5,000 cases maximum per year. Proprietors Russell and Linda Woodbury are specializing in vintage wines from top-quality North Coast grapes, primarily blending Petite Sirah, Cabernet Sauvignon, and Zinfandel.

(3) Mendocino

Edmeades Vineyards. Deron Edmeades inherited this cool and wet 35-acre (14-hectare) property, as well as the determination to successfully cultivate it, from his late father, Dr. Donald Edmeades, in 1972. Yound Edmeades's efforts, along with those of wine-maker Jed Steele, have finally begun to pay off; their Cabernet Sauvignon, Zinfandel, and Gewürztraminer are quite satisfactory. Produce from the Anderson Valley vineyard is supplemented with purchased grapes, yielding an average of 30,000 cases of wine per year.

Husch Vineyards. Self-taught wine-makers Tony and Gretchen Husch started planting vines in the Anderson Valley in 1968, making theirs the oldest in that cool Region I location. The Husch wines, especially Chardonnay and Pinot Noir, have shown great progress since they first appeared in 1971. The 23-acre (9-hectare) vineyard provides all the grapes necessary to make a maximum of 4,000 cases annually.

Milano Winery. A renovated hop kiln in Hopland, in southeastern Mendocino County, is the site for the Milano Winery. It is owned and operated by two young wine-masters, James Milone and Gregory Graziano, who make their wines from hillside grapes grown on small lots. A peak production of about 12,000 cases a year is anticipated. The Milano Chenin Blanc shows potential.

(4) Livermore

The wine boom of the 1970s had little effect on the Livermore Valley region of Alameda County. Wente Brothers and Concannon (sold to Augustin Huneeus, former president of Paul Masson, in 1980) remain the leaders in wine production. Urban sprawl, a serious threat to agriculture in the valley, is being controlled by stricter zoning regulations. Increasing numbers of home wine-makers, especially in the East Bay area, are opening small businesses; this trend could develop into an important new phase in Alameda's wine trade.

(5) Santa Clara-San Benito-Santa Cruz

Following in the footsteps of the founding wineries in this section of the California coast—Paul Masson, Almadèn, Mirassou—a number of new wineries were either formed or re-formed during the 1960s and 1970s.

The push to explore new vineyard areas was particularly felt in Santa Cruz County, which underwent the most significant expansion in vineyard space in the 1970s. The good quality achieved by vineyards in the Santa Cruz Mountains, especially Ridge and Martin Ray, incited people to make further attempts to cultivate vines in this hilly dry region.

It is now generally recognized that the Santa Cruz hill vineyards divide into two sectors. The ocean-side slopes, the so-called Chaine d'Or, are cooled by temperate ocean breezes. This microclimate (Regions I and II) has made the Gewürztraminer and Riesling among the preferred grapes. The slopes with a northeastern exposure are a bit warmer and are preferred by growers for the planting of Pinot Noir, Chardonnay, Cabernet Sauvignon, and Pinot Blanc. The soils are light, serpentine-based and have a gravelly shale crust, which keeps the vines well drained of the little rain they receive.

The following wineries in Santa Clara, San Benito, and Santa Cruz counties represent the changes that have occurred and continue to occur in this area.

Bargetto Winery. A family enterprise since 1887, the Bargetto Winery, now run by brothers Lawrence and Ralph Bargetto, makes some good fruity wines at the rate of about 40,000 cases per year. Bargetto owns no vineyards. The winery is located about three miles north of the town in Soquel in the cool coastal region above the northern rim of Monterey Bay in Santa Cruz County.

Calera Wine. Purchased Zinfandel grapes were the first crushed in this gravity-flow winery near Hollister, opened in 1977. High up on the slopes of the Gavilan Mountains of San Benito County, 24 acres (10 hectares) of Pinot Noir bear grapes that, as of 1980, are made into a promising wine. Production is limited to 4,000 cases per year.

Felton-Empire Vineyards. Known as Hallcrest Vineyards under the former owner, attorney Chaffee Hall, the wines from this 45-acre (18½-hectare) vineyard in Felton, north of Santa Cruz in Santa Cruz County, are considered the best in the area. After Mr. Hall's death in 1969, his choice Riesling and Cabernet grapes went to the Concannon Winery in Livermore. Then, in 1976, oenologist Leo McCloskey, grower Jim Beauregard, and former pilot John Pollard joined forces, leased the property, renamed it Felton-Empire Vineyards, and within a year presented a complete range of wines that have lived up to and surpassed the Hallcrest reputation. Particularly successful is a fully botrytised Riesling, hinting at a German Rheingau Auslese wine, which should be pleasing to those seeking sweet wines. Felton-Empire produces about 10,000 cases per year.

Gemello Winery. In the town of Mountain View, north of San Jose in Santa Clara County, Gemello Winery was established in 1934 by the Piedmontese father of the present owner, Mario Gemello. The Gemellos have no vines of their own, buying grapes from several other regions, including Zinfandels from Amador County. The Gemello reputation was built on full-bodied red wines, which were often too heavy with wood, including Cabernet Sauvignon and Petite Sirah. Wine is produced at the average annual rate of 20,000 cases.

Martin Ray Vineyards. Peter Martin Ray, a Stanford professor, owns and manages this Saratoga establishment left to him by his innovative father, Martin Ray. Output is about 1,000 cases a year. Grapes from Ray's small vineyards supplement purchases of local grapes. It is hoped that Ray will meet with more success in the 1980s. His Chardonnay and Merlot show the most potential.

Mount Eden Vineyards. Established by the controversial pioneering vintner Martin Ray, Mount Eden Vineyards is situated high on the slopes of Table Mountain above the town of Saratoga in Santa Clara County. Ray claimed his were the only fine American wines and priced them accordingly. Outrageously expensive for the times (the 1950s), this created quite an uproar in the California wine community. Nevertheless, his exceptional Pinot Noir was one of the best wines made in the state. Since his death in 1976, a group of investors has managed the 22-acre (9-hectare) Mount Eden, whose hard-to-find, good-quality wines are treasured by connoisseurs. About 2,000 cases are produced annually.

Roudon-Smith Vineyards. Two electronics engineers, Robert Roudon and Jim Smith, revived this pre-Prohibition winery site in 1972. Purchased grapes from Santa Cruz, as well as from neighboring counties, account for the major bulk of the 6,000-case annual production. Roudon-Smith features Cabernet Sauvignon, Zinfandel, and Chardonnay wines. The reds have met with some success.

Sycamore Creek Vineyards. Terry and Mary Kaye Parks both left the teaching profession to revive vine-growing and wine-making on the site of the pre-Prohibition Marchetti Winery in 1976. Located in the Uvas Valley outside of Kirigin in Santa Clara County, Sycamore Creek has 16 acres (6½ hectares) of vines, which provide about half the fruit needed for the 3,000 cases made annually. None of the seven wines have been outstanding so far.

(6) Monterey

After a great burst of vineyard planting in the early 1970s. it is only a decade later that the Monterey region has settled down. From a high of 34,000 acres (13,600 hectares) planted in 1978, the vineyard area has dropped to 30,000 acres (12,000 hectares). Unsuitable plantings were pulled out and a greater effort to match proper grape varieties with the diverse soils and microclimates was made. It is now generally recognized that Monterey falls into two distinct growing zones. Upper Monterey, the northwest section of the county, is characterized by light soils and cool microclimates (officially Regions I and II) best suited to cultivating Riesling, Gewürztraminer, and Pinot Noir vines. The southeastern part of the county has slightly heavier soils and warmer temperatures (Region III), and some Monterey growers claim it is better suited to Cabernet Sauvignon, Zinfandel, Merlot, and Sauvignon Blanc.

Although most of the great planting of vines in Monterey was done by large wineries based outside the county, or by those already established in the region, the following new wineries, founded in the 1970s, deserve to be recognized.

Durney Vineyards. This Carmel Valley establishment is owned by Los Angeles businessman W. W. Durney. Eighty acres (32 hectares) of vines yield a portion of the grapes vinified at the 20,000-case winery. If the quality of Durney's wines continues at its present rate of improvement, some good wines may result.

Jekel Vineyards. Brothers William and August Jekel own and head this family venture begun in 1972. From their 140-acre (56-hectare) vineyard in the western Salinas Valley (known as the Arroyo Seco district), the Jekels have succeeded in making some very good Chardonnays and Rieslings. All wines are made from the produce of the Jekel Vineyards surrounding the 35,000-case-capacity winery.

Monterey Peninsula Winery. Fans of "pure" wines, neither filtered nor clarified, are the most likely devotees of this winery's products. Each bottle bears the name of the plot of land from which it originates. Dentists-turned-wine-makers Deryck Nuckton and Roy Thomas have been purchasing grapes and making wines of inconsistent quality since 1974. Some inky, intense wines have been made from Zinfandel, Cabernet Sauvignon, and Barbera, as well as Chardonnay grapes.

Turgeon & Lohr. Home-building business partners Bernie Turgeon and Jerry Lohr switched tracks in 1972 and entered the wine business. Although their winery is located in the heart of San Jose, Turgeon & Lohr's 280 acres (112 hectares) of vineyard are in Monterey County's Salinas Valley. Roughly three-quarters of the 110,000 cases produced yearly are derived from those grapes. Peter Stern, a Napa Valley native, is wine-maker.

Sacramento Valley

Three counties surrounding Sacramento on the north and east have been singled out as among California's most prized sectors for the growing of Zinfandel grapes. Amador County in particular has experienced great development in this regard. Its Shenandoah Valley and Fiddletown vineyards are especially prized for their cool nights, warm days, and red volcanic soil. These attributes are shared to a greater or lesser degree by various sites throughout the three counties, allowing a wide range of Zinfandel styles to be made, from the pleasantly light and flowery to the long-vatted and slow-to-mature. The potential of other varietals is also being explored.

D'Agostini Winery. Swiss immigrant Adam Uhlinger founded D'Agostini Winery in 1856, making it the oldest wine establishment in Amador County. Enrico D'Agostini bought the property, 8 miles (13 kilometers) northeast of Plymouth, in 1911. His four sons run the family business today, and are particularly recognized for their rather average Zinfandels made from Amador County grapes. The grapes from their 125 acres (51 hectares) and purchased grapes produce about 80,000 cases of wine per year.

Monteviña Vineyards. Three miles from Plymouth in the Shenandoah Valley, Monteviña Vineyards was opened in 1973 and is owned by retired banker Walker Field, his daughter Vicki, and her husband, Cary Gott, who serves as wine-maker. Most of the grapes grown on Monteviña's 160 acres (64 hectares) are sold, a portion being retained to make an average of 6,000 cases annually. Located in Amador County, Monteviña makes particularly successful Zinfandels, which grow well in the dry and intense heat of the region. Small amounts of Barbera, Cabernet Sauvignon, and Sauvignon Blanc are also produced.

San Joaquin Valley

JFJ Bronco Winery. After the Franzia Winery was bought by the Coca-Cola Bottling Company of New York in 1972, two Franzia brothers and one cousin founded this huge 60-million-gallon-capacity winery, where they receive, blend, finish, and bottle some fair inexpensive table wines from other wineries. Bronco is located 6 miles (10 kilometers) south of Modesto.

Giumarra Vineyards. "Papa Joe" Giumarra, a Sicilian immigrant, founded this huge 8,000-acre (3,250-hectare) vineyard, of which 5,000 acres (2,000 hectares) are now planted in grapes, in 1946. Defying the near-tropical climatic conditions of the Central Valley, generally believed to be unsuitable for the growing of noble grape varieties, Giumarra succeeds in cultivating six grape varieties and vinifying them well, resulting in some good wines. The average annual production at Giumarra is over 1½ million cases.

Robert Mondavi. A sub-winery in Woodbridge, near Lodi, vinifies over half-a-million cases of generic wines—mostly in jugs sold under the Robert Mondavi labels.

Papagni Vineyards. Located in the heart of the Central Valley, 9 miles (15 kilometers) south of Madera, Angelo Papagni's winery has been producing wines since 1973. Papagni's father, Demetrio, an immigrant from Bari in southwestern Italy, grew grapes in the region for many years. John Daddino is the wine-maker behind the approximately 80,000 cases per year made under the Papagni Vineyards label. Around 3,000 acres (1,200 hectares) of vines are under cultivation. The Papagni wines have done surprisingly well in some local and European blind tastings. Varietal wines include Chardonnay, Barbera, Zinfandel, Muscat (both still and sparkling), and Alicante-Bouschet. The Chardonnay and Alicante-Bouschet are almost textbook-defying in quality, especially considering the region where they are grown.

Quady Winery. Andrew Quady, an engineer at the United Vintners winery in Madera, makes small amounts (about 3,000 cases per year) of wine in his winery constructed in 1977. Quady's specialty is Vintage Port–style wine made from Amador County Zinfandel grapes.

South Coast Mountains

All the South Coast Mountain region vineyards are planted in ungrafted vinifera vines. This is contrary to the practice in the rest of California (with the exception of half of Monterey County).

Callaway Vineyard and Winery. Endowed with good humidity, mild heat, and a long growing season, Callaway's 150 acres (60 hectares) on a hill near Temecula, in Rancho California, north of San Diego, are in what has turned out to be an unexpectedly good vine-growing microclimate; few people recognized it as such when Ely Callaway first planted grapes there in 1969. Callaway's diligence and talents, which earned him the rank of major by age 24 and eventually made him president of the Burlington Mills textile firm, are reflected in his vine-growing and wine-making success. Under the direction of Karl Werner, formerly of the Schloss Vollrads Rheingau domain, Callaway wines are made in the traditional dry German manner, resulting in a good White Riesling and a botrytised Chenin Blanc, named Sweet Nancy after Callaway's wife. A drier Chenin Blanc is considered one of his best wines. Callaway's production is about 70,000 cases annually.

Mount Palomar Winery. Founded by Los Angeles radio-station owner John Poole in 1975, Mount Palomar is located 5 miles (8 kilometers) from Temecula in Rancho California. Mario Moramarco, whose family owned the

Old Mission Winery in Los Angeles, manages the vineyards and Joe Cherpin, whose family runs the Cherpin Winery in Fontana, is wine-maker. The vineyards cover 160 acres (60 hectares), yielding roughly 12,000 cases a year. Mount Palomar makes dry table wines and sherry-type wines.

San Pasqual Winery. Judge Charles Froehlich and attorney Milton Friedman began planting grapes 20 miles (32 kilometers) northeast of San Diego in 1973. Presently 100 acres (40 hectares) are planted in vines and an average of 25,000 cases are made yearly, with plans for expansion in the 1980s. Kerry Damsky is wine-maker. San Pasqual's specialty is an unusual Gamay wine.

San Luis Obispo-Santa Barbara

Although they have known wine-making for over a century, San Luis Obispo and Santa Barbara counties have experienced a renaissance of expanded varietal plantings and establishment of new wineries. Located 250 miles (415 kilometers) south of San Francisco, and about 100 miles (165 kilometers) north of Los Angeles, these two counties have grown from three or four wineries in the late 1960s to over two dozen today, with certainly more to come.

Vineyard plantings now total over 5,000 acres (2,000 hectares) in San Luis Obispo and over 6,000 (2,400 hectares) in Santa Barbara. Much of this new acreage is taken up by fine varietals such as Chardonnay, Cabernet Sauvignon, Zinfandel, and Riesling. Pinot Noir vines have been surprisingly successfully cultivated in certain pockets of these counties. The best areas of each county are those cooled by ocean breezes, which temper the effect of the warm daytime temperatures and allow the grapes to retain the high acidity levels necessary and too often lacking in southern California wines.

The principal growing areas in San Luis Obispo County center around Shandon to the north, the Edna Valley to the south, and Paso Robles and Templeton to the west. The Santa Ynez and Santa Maria valleys are Santa Barbara County's major vine-growing regions.

Estrella River Winery. Six miles east of Paso Robles, bounded by the Gavilan Mountains to the east and the Santa Lucia Mountains to the west, 500 acres (200 hectares) of rolling hills provide the family-run Estrella River Winery with about a quarter of the grapes needed for its 45,000 annual cases. Director Cliff Giacobine operates Estrella River with the assistance of his two brothers, James Giacobine and Gary Eberle, who serves as wine-maker. Their first crush took place in 1977 at their spectacular new winery. Altogether, nine varieties are grown and made into satisfactory table wines.

The Firestone Vineyard. Kate and Brooks Firestone, and Brooks's father, Leonard, of the famous tire family, have a majority share of this Santa Ynez Valley operation, with the minority share held by Suntory Ltd., a Japanese distillery. Their 300 acres (122 hectares), planted in 6 different grape varieties, have been producing nearly 65,000 cases a year since 1975. The Riesling and a good Pinot Noir are among the more notable of the Firestone wines. Located 5 miles (8½ kilometers) north of Los Olivos, near Santa Barbara, the Firestone Vineyard enjoys a unique microclimate cooled by ocean fogs. The Firestones pioneered vine-growing and wine-making in this area.

Hale Cellars. Owned and run by Los Angeles attorney Sam Hale and his wife, Donna, the former Los Alamos Winery covers about 350 acres (142 hectares) in the Los Alamos Valley. Encompassing a variety of microclimates, these vineyards have produced a wide range of varietals, at an average annual rate of 3,000 cases per year since 1972.

Lawrence Winery. About 7 miles (11½ kilometers) south of San Luis Obispo in the Edna Valley is the Lawrence Winery. Co-owner and wine-maker James Lawrence, who also designed the winery, which was constructed in 1977, was at one time wine-maker at Giumarra. Lawrence Winery can handle up to 200,000 cases annually of 16 different wines, too large a range to achieve greatness.

Sanford & Benedict Vineyards. J. P. Sanford and Michael Benedict, a former television executive and a biology professor at the University of California–Santa Barbara respectively, issued their first wines in 1976. Their 110 acres (44 hectares), planted in 1972, will eventually yield about 10,000 cases per year. The Sanford & Benedict Vineyards Pinot Noir is of particularly good quality.

Santa Ynez Valley Winery. Two vineyards, one of 100 acres (40 hectares) planted in the cooler Santa Ynez Valley and owned by the Bettencourt and Davide families, the other of 40 acres (16 hectares) in the Los Olivos area and owned by the Brander family, combine about half their respective harvests to make six wines. Boyd Bettencourt (a longtime agriculturist) and Erik Brander (an ex-industrial machinery man) formed their corporation in 1976. Brander's Davis-trained son Fred is wine-maker. The output of the winery, a renovated dairy barn, is roughly 10,000 cases of fairly average wines per year.

Zaca Mesa Winery. Not far from Los Olivos in the Santa Ynez Valley, Zaca Mesa is owned by former Atlantic Richfield executive Louis Ream. His Zaca Mesa Winery, completed in 1978, will hopefully smooth out the quality of his wines. Previous vintages made elsewhere were inconsistent.

United States: Colorado

Winters in the Rocky Mountains and its foothills are generally too rough for vine-growing, but in Golden, Colorado, a group of wine enthusiasts has successfully cultivated 20 acres (8 hectares) of Riesling, Chardonnay, and Gewürztraminer vines since 1973. Supplemented with California grapes, the group's Colorado Mountain Vineyards has produced about 3,000 cases a year since 1978 when the winery opened.

United States: Connecticut

Encouraged by revised farm winery and licensing laws that came into effect in 1978, a number of wine-growers in Connecticut have transformed their backyard vineyards into commercial enterprises. As a result, the 1980s will most likely see an expansion of the state's grape-growing and wine-making industry, once a part of colonial life.

Wineries, most of them still in the early and experimental stages, are scattered all over the state. In the mid-1980s, one can look to those wineries specializing in French hybrids for quality wines. Setting a good example is Haight Wineries, located in Litchfield in the northwestern corner of the state. Twenty acres (8 hectares) of Chardonnay, Riesling, and Foch grapes have yielded about 3,000 cases per year to date, with more planned for the future. Erbacher Vineyards in Roxbury, Hamlet Hill Vineyard in Pomfret, Springdale Winery in Granby, Stonecrop Vineyards in Stonington, and St. Hillary Winery in North Grosvenor are establishments that show promise as good producers.

United States: Delaware

Richard Becker owns and operates Delaware's only winery, the Northminster Winery in Wilmington.

United States: Florida

The produce of Florida's 400 acres (160 hectares) of Muscadine and other vines is primarily destined for the fresh-fruit market. Midulla Vineyards, north of Tampa, with 52 acres (21 hectares), accounts for more than a quarter of the state's production. The Bartels Winery in Pensacola and Foster Burgess's establishment in Freeport make Muscadine wines. Malinda's Vineyards in Ocala, and three other enterprises, one each in Tampa, Groveland, and Defuniak Springs, anticipate going into wine production in the 1980s. Research sponsored by the University of Florida is directed toward developing hybrid grapes that will grow in Florida's nearly tropical climate.

United States: Georgia

Small amounts of grapes from Muscadine, Concord, and other vines, blended with California concentrates, make Georgia's only wines. They are manufactured by the Monarch Wine Company of Georgia, in Atlanta, whose main products are peach "wines" and "brandies."

The Happy "B" Farm Winery in Forsyth opened in 1980.

United States: Hawaii

Bonded in 1977, the Tedeschi Vineyard on Maui is the property of Emil Tedeschi, a native of California's Napa Valley. Twenty acres (8 hectares) of Carnelian grapes will be made into wines in the 1980s when the vines reach maturity. In the meantime, Tedeschi is making dry and sparkling pineapple "wines."

United States: Idaho

Despite several encouraging experimental successes sponsored by the University of Idaho in the early 1970s, wine-growing is just beginning to gain momentum in this state in the early 1980s. For the most part, Idaho's winters are too cold for viticulture, but the Sunny Slope area near Boise in the southwestern corner of the state and the Clearwater River Valley near Lewiston have proven to be suitable growing areas for vinifera varietals.

Sainte Chapelle Vineyards, in the Sunny Slope area near Caldwell, is the only Idaho wine establishment of any commercial importance to date. Nearly 150 acres (60 hectares) of varietal vines thrive in these vineyards owned by Richard Symms (who planted them in 1971), winemaker Bill Broich (who has grown apples in the area for years), and partner Jim Mertz. Ste. Chapelle is about a half-hour's drive from Boise at an elevation of 2,500 feet (750 meters). The winery, named after the Gothic chapel in Paris, crushed its first grapes in 1976, and since that time has turned out some very good wines whose quality is backed up with a string of medals. The Chardonnays and Rieslings have been particularly successful. Ste. Chapelle wines are produced at the rate of about 45,000 cases annually, and more than 50% of the grapes needed to make them come from leased and owned vineyards in neighboring Washington State.

Perhaps Ste. Chapelle's most valuable contribution is the proof it offers that quality wines can be successfully and profitably made in this state.

United States: Illinois

The Mogen David Corporation, owned by the Coca-Cola Bottling Company of New York, makes an annual 8 million gallons of sweet sacramental wines (mostly from frozen California concentrates) in their Chicago plant, thereby making Illinois the nation's third leading wine producer. In the 1950s and 1960s, when America was just learning about wines, Mogen David's products acted as introductory and transition wines for many people who later switched to natural table wines as they became more wine-selective. Now, more and more small wineries are taking advantage of the suitable vine-growing conditions found in various parts of Illinois.

Nauvoo, a town on the Mississippi River near the western border of the state, has vineyards dating back to 1851, when a group of Swiss and Liechtensteiner immigrants settled there. At the Nauvoo State Historic Site and Park Vineyard, two of the original acres of labrusca vines survive, although their produce is not made into wine. Also in Nauvoo, the Gem City Vineland Company dates back to 1857 and makes labrusca wines. There are hopes that efforts will be made to replace the inferior labrusca with vinifera and hybrid varieties in the Nauvoo area. At present, the local cheese is better known than the wines.

In Monee, 40 miles (64 kilometers) outside of Chicago, the Monee Thompson Vineyard, owned by nutritionist John Thompson, is known for its rosé and white sparkling wines made according to the *méthode champenoise*. About 5,000 cases are made annually from the 30-acre (12-hectare) vineyard. The Lynfred Winery in Roselle, owned and operated by Fred Koehler, has produced some red and white wines. French hybrid, vinifera, and native grapes are all grown at both places.

United States: Indiana

New state laws, passed in Indiana in 1971, lifted most of the restraints left over from the Prohibition era and enabled many wine-growing hobbyists to go commercial. Consequently, Indiana is enjoying a renaissance of its once colorful and prosperous wine past. Between 1800 and 1830, Indiana was America's foremost wine-growing area.

Bill Oliver, a law professor at the University of Indiana in Bloomington can be given much credit for pushing the new laws through the state legislature. His vineyards, consisting of 40 acres (16 hectares) of French hybrids planted on strip-mined plots in Bloomington, yield more than 10,000 cases of wine per year. He started plantations in 1966. Also in the central part of the state, south of Indianapolis in Unionville, is Ben and Lee Sparks's Possum Trot Vineyards. The Sparkses planted their first vines in 1967 and since then have been promoting wine-growing in the Midwest, organizing an annual Indiana Grape Wine symposium. The Sparkses have a tiny 6-acre (2½ hectare) vineyard and turn out very small amounts of French hybrids annually. A bit farther north, Easley Winery in Indianapolis makes several wines from grapes grown in their vineyard along the Ohio River.

Near the shores of Lake Michigan in the north in New Carlisle, Banholzer Wine Cellars features the state's largest vineyard, 72 acres (29 hectares), planted primarily in French hybrids, with some viniferas. Established in 1972 by Carl and Janet Banholzer, Indiana's first, and so far only, Cabernet Sauvignon appeared in 1975 under the Banholzer Wine Cellars label. The Banholzers' fame was brief, however, due to three exceptionally brutal winters that killed the vinifera vines. Their French hybrid blends, however, show some potential. About 7,000 cases, under proprietary names, are made annually.

Also in the north, in the Notre Dame University town of South Bend, Rauner & Sons winery has been in operation since 1977. Three acres (1¼ hectares) of hybrid vines are grown. Matzke's Boulder Hill Vineyard, owned by Jim and Helen Matzke, is in nearby Laporte.

Along the Ohio River, Indiana's southern border, several wineries opened up in the 1970s. The town of Vevay was named by the Swiss immigrant Jean Dufour, who founded it in the early 1800s. Hampered by frosts and diseases that destroyed his Kentucky vineyards, Dufour successfully grew a labrusca hybrid in Vevay until his death in 1826. More than 100 years later, wine-making in this area has been revived by the Meyer family. The Meyers make tiny amounts of French hybrid wines, sold under their Swiss Valley label, from their 3 acres (1¼ hectares) of vines. The Villa Medeo Vineyards in Madison, a bit downriver from Vevay, has also produced French hybrids since 1974. Michael and Elizabeth Mancuso, Villa Medeo's owners, have 11 acres (4½ hectares) of vines, yielding 2,500 cases a year.

Finally, in the southwest, where the Wabash and Ohio rivers converge, is the Golden Rain Tree Winery in Wadesville. A group of wine enthusiasts founded the winery in 1975; they produce hybrid blends at the rate of about 10,000 cases a year. A dry red, "Director's Choice," is their best wine.

United States: Iowa

A century ago, Iowa made nearly 350,000 gallons of native grape wine, as opposed to 26,000 gallons of mostly fruit "wines" today. Long preoccupied with the production of a peculiar "rhubarb wine," Iowa is slowly reinstating its grape-wine production.

Amana, originally founded as a German religious group's communist utopia, continues to make the locally popular beverages, although several wineries (Ackerman, Colony Village, Ehrle Brothers, and Sandstone) have added native grape wines to their product lines. Christina Wine Cellars in McGregor, Okoboji Winery in Okoboji, Private Stock Winery in Boone, and the Waukon Corporation in Waukon are others.

If Iowa wine-makers plant more and more French hybrid and vinifera vines in the future, they have a good chance of turning their state into an important wine-producer.

United States: Kentucky

Like so many of its neighbors, Kentucky's 19th-century wine business was a victim of Prohibition. Finally, in 1976, fully revised state laws came into effect.

The Colcord Winery in Paris was the first small winery to take advantage of the laws. Owner Carlton Colcord has made wines since 1977. Prior to that time, he sold the yield from his 35 acres (14 hectares) of French-American hybrids and vinifera vineyards to wineries in Indiana and Ohio. One of his buyers was Bill Oliver of the Oliver Winery in Bloomington, Indiana (q.v.), who now grows his own vines in Kentucky, most of them on former strip-mining sites. Studies conducted by the University of Kentucky are exploring in depth the possibilities of transforming such lands into wine-grape-producing vineyards.

The Kentucky River Products Winery is another establishment pursuing a similiar land-reclamation program. It is located outside of Frankfort. The Laine Vineyards and Winery in Fulton makes French hybrid wines.

United States: Louisiana

Altar wines were made in the mid-18th century in Louisiana, followed by Scuppernongs and fruit "wines" until Prohibition. Today, oranges are fermented and sold as "orange wine." It will be some time before wine-grape growing will have any importance in Louisiana.

United States: Maryland

Wine-grape-growing in Maryland, started by the Wagners of Boordy Vineyards (see page 506), picked up slightly in the 1970s, although the state's vineyards still cover only about 60 acres (24 hectares). Although basically suitable for wine-grape-growing, the climate in Maryland can be erratic, with severe winters, excessive humidity, and irregular rainfall during the growing sea-

son; nevertheless, some small wineries have come up with some decent wines.

In addition to producing America's first "ice wine" in 1974, the wine-maker–proprietor of Montbray Wine Cellars in Westminster, Hamilton Mowbray, has also been responsible for Maryland's first Cabernet, Riesling, and Chardonnay wines. These accomplishments have convinced Mowbray to increase his vinifera plantings, to eventually total 25 acres (10 hectares). Currently, he makes about 3,000 cases a year. Mowbray has grown grapes and made wine in Maryland since 1966.

Byrd Vineyards in Meyersville, a family-run operation, has been making vinifera and hybrid wines since 1977 at the rate of about 2,500 cases per year. Fifteen acres planted in Chardonnay, Sauvignon Blanc, Cabernet Sauvignon, Gewürztraminer, and others have been under cultivation since 1972.

In addition to hay production and livestock raising, the Aellen family grows about 6 acres (2½ hectares) of French hybrids in Mount Airy, Maryland. Berrywine Plantation is the name of their operation.

Provenza Vineyards, not too far from Washington in Brookeville, is owned and run by orthodontist Provenza and his wife, Barbara. Provenza tends 15 acres (6 hectares) of hybrids, planted between 1970 and 1973, and has made wines since 1974.

Bon Spuronza Vineyards in Westminster, Ziem Vineyards in Fairplay, Blythe Vineyards in La Plata, and Burkittsville Vineyards in Burkittsville are other up-and-coming small wineries in Maryland.

United States: Massachusetts

For better or for worse, Massachusetts bears the dubious distinction of developing the Concord grape and introducing it to America's wine industry. Ephraim Bull and others conducted their horticultural experiments in the 1840s. Home wine-makers have grown Concords and other native grapes in Massachusetts since that time. Now, interest in cultivating hybrid grapes is on the rise, as is evidenced by the gradual appearance of small wineries.

One of these is Chicama Vineyards on Martha's Vineyard Island. California transplants George and Cathy Mathiesen have succeeded in growing 35 acres (14 hectares) of vinifera grapes here, yielding almost 5,000 cases of wines per year, made in Massachusetts's first bonded winery. Chicama has been in operation since 1971.

Commonwealth Winery in historic Plymouth is owned by David Tower, who planted small amounts of viniferas and hybrids in 1978. While waiting for those vines to mature, Tower has made some decent-quality wines from hybrid grapes purchased locally.

The Nashoba Valley Winery opened in Somerville in 1980.

United States: Michigan

Although Michigan's vine-growing history is short and uneventful, mainly revolving around grape juice and jam production, its future looks bright. A great deal of expansion is underway, and labrusca vineyards are being replaced with better hybrid and vinifera varieties at a rapid pace. The shores of Lakes Michigan and Erie are the prime growing regions, and Riesling and Chardonnay vines grown in these areas have yielded some surprisingly good wines. More and more small wineries are opening up (17 are currently in operation) and if proper care continues to be taken in matching appropriate soils, vinifera vines, and specific microclimates, Michigan wines may offer some competition, in terms of quality, to those of California.

The vinifera and hybrid vines of Tabor Hill Vineyards in southwestern Michigan (*see* page 506) came into maturity in the 1970s. As a result, some good Chardonnays and Rieslings form part of their annual 36,000-case output. Gerald Ford found some of Tabor Hill's wines so good that he served them in the White House.

Warner Vineyards (*see* page 506) is still the largest winery in Michigan, with a 3-million-gallon capacity. The Warner wines remain only mediocre in quality, but some viniferas have been planted.

Other wineries in the Paw Paw area include the St. Julian Wine Company, Michigan's oldest, which produces up to 1.5 million gallons of average-quality wines annually; the Frontenac Vineyards, which produces 40 varieties of fermented beverages, including some native grape wines, per year; the Bronte Winery, a 1-million-gallon facility in operation since 1933; Vendramino Vineyards, maker of some good table wines since 1977; and Fenn Valley Vineyards in Fennsville, where Doug Welsch, whose family owns the property, is making some good Rieslings and other wines.

Up north, activity in the Grand Traverse region best illustrates the changing face of Michigan's wine industry. Regulated by nearby Lake Michigan, the temperate winters and cool summers form a microclimate suitable to French hybrids, Riesling, Chardonnay, and other vinifera vines.

Bernard Rink, of Boskydel Vineyards, after extensive experimentation now grows 6 hybrids on his 20 acres (6 hectares). He makes about 8,000 cases a year, the blended generics and varietal hybrids being the most promising.

Thanks to 45 acres (18 hectares) of Chardonnay and Riesling grapes, plus German-educated Karl Werner's wine-making abilities, Chateau Grand Travers has already gained itself a reputation for quality. Canadian brewery millionaire Edward O'Keefe owns the property, and 12,000 cases a year have been made at the extravagant Traverse City winery since it opened in 1974.

Other potential good-quality wine-producers in Michigan are the Lakeside Winery in Harbert, the Fink Winery in Dundee, the Mawby Vineyards in Suttons Bay, and Milan Wines in Detroit.

United States: Minnesota

Despite the infamously cold winters common in Minnesota, two wine-producing vineyards do exist in the state. Sturdy hybrids, handled with care, can give some decent grapes; more than 100 acres (40 hectares) of vineyards are planted, and two bonded wineries exist in Minnesota.

David MacGregor of Lake Sylvia Vineyard can be partially credited with developing several hardy hybrid breeds, as well as the techniques (e.g., burial, mulching, removal from the trellis) needed to cultivate them. MacGregor has 7 acres (3 hectares) of vines, whose grapes were first crushed in 1976.

Alexis Bailly Vineyard is the domain of wine-maker David Bailly, whose ancestors made wines in the town of Hastings in 1834. Bailly revived the family tradition by planting vineyards in 1973 (now totaling more than 10 acres or 4 hectares) and making hybrid wines in a log-

United States: Mississippi

Mississippi's wine history traces a typically Southern pattern: its 19th-century Muscadine wine-making roots were destroyed by Prohibition, and a late Repeal (1966), accompanied by stiff winery taxes (eventually reduced by a vine-growing senator), delayed wine production in the state. Now four licensed wineries are in operation.

The Winery Rushing in Merigold, in the Delta region, is owned by the Rushing family, the first Mississippians to take advantage of the state's new laws. Since 1977, the average annual production from 22 acres (9 hectares) of Muscadines has been 15,000 cases.

The Old South Winery in Natchez has a 10,000-gallon-capacity winery for 13 acres (5½ hectares) of Muscadines. Dr. Scott Galbreath is the proprietor.

The Thousand Oaks Vineyard and Winery in Starkville belongs to the wine-conscious Senator Robert Burgin. He has a total of 25 acres (10 hectares), half of which are French-American hybrids. Native, Muscadine, and experimental viniferas (red and white varieties) are also grown. Burgin's winery opened in 1978.

Almarla Vineyards, in Matherville in southeastern Mississippi, covers 20 acres (8 hectares). Dr. Alex Mathers is testing American and French hybrids on a small scale. This winery opened in 1979.

United States: Missouri

As recently as 100 years ago, Missouri's wine business was a flourishing affair. Wines from Missouri's wineries, thriving in 48 counties, won prizes across the nation. Viticulturists from Missouri sent shiploads of phylloxera-resistant root stocks to Europe. St. Louis was hailed as the oenological research center of the Midwest. But with Prohibition all of this prosperity slowly faded away, and it wasn't until the 1960s that Missouri's wine industry began to regain some of its former vigor.

In 1980, the Bureau of Alcohol, Tobacco and Firearms granted America's first "appellation" to the tiny Missouri River community of Augusta, once a booming wine town. This distinction marks the beginning of a new wine-making era for Missouri, and if proper caution is exercised in planting appropriate grape varieties, the state may have a good chance of recapturing some part of its 19th-century reputation for quality.

Montelle Vineyards and Mount Pleasant Vineyards are the first two Augusta appellations, meaning their wines are made from at least 85% Augusta grapes.

Montelle Vineyards was founded by Clayton Byers and Robert Slifer in 1969. Grapes grown on Augusta's hillsides are used to make an exorbitant 40 versions of French and American hybrid and vinifera wines. The 1973 vintage was Montelle's first; the whites were better than the reds.

Mount Pleasant is owned by Lucian and Eva Dressel, leaders in Missouri's wine revival. Since 1968, they have made French hybrid and native American table wines, growing grapes on about 30 acres (12 hectares) and putting out about 10,000 cases annually.

Cuba, Missouri, is the site of the Dressels' latest venture, a joint ownership of the Winery of the Abbey, founded in 1979. Ziegler Winery, a Concord-grape producer, and Ozark Vineyards, a French-American hybrid producer since 1976, are also in the Cuba of Missouri.

Four wineries are clustered around St. James, a town in Missouri's Ozark Plateau. The St. James Winery makes some of its approximately 20,000 cases partially from 22 acres (9 hectares) of native grapes, French hybrids, and vinifera vines. Jim and Pat Hofherr opened the St. James Winery in 1970. Stoltz Vineyards and Winery, 132 acres (52 hectares), has a 6,000-gallon winery, bonded in 1967; Stoltz makes more than 100 different wines each year, a ridiculously staggering amount. The Rosati Winery, associated with the Ashby Vineyards, makes 11 different wines, most of them Concord-based. The fourth and newest winery in the St. James area, Heinrichhaus, opened in 1979.

The Peaceful Bend Vineyards in Steelville, not far from St. James, bottled its first wines, French-American hybrids, in 1972. Dr. Arneson, owner and wine-maker, is capable of making good wines.

Hermann, once said to have exported more wines than any other American town, now features two wineries. The Held family's Stone Hill Wine Company has 40 acres (16 hectares) of primarily native grapes, and produces fruit and berry "wines" as well as some mediocre generics, and sparkling wines. Total production is around 9,000 cases. Jim Dierberg's Hermannhof Winery opened in 1979. Not far from Hermann is Green Valley Vineyards, Nicolas Lamb's property.

Kruger's Winery, in Nelson, is run by Harold Kruger, who has been carrying on his German family's wine-making traditions since the early 1970s. Bowman Wine Cellars in Weston, and Carver Wine Cellars in Rolla are additional Missouri wine-producers.

In the city of St. Louis, Bardenheim Wine Cellars is run by descendants of the original 1873 founders. They have recently added Missouri-grown wines to their line of California blends. Jack Cohen's Garco Wine Company is also in St. Louis.

On the western border, in Lone Jack, George Gale and Dutton Biggs have a tiny establishment, Midi Vineyards, devoted to the production of hybrid vines, and McCormick Distilling in Kansas City started making wine in 1979.

United States: Montana

To date, only one adventurous soul has challenged Montana's cold stormy winters with wine-grape-growing. Dr. Jay Winship has harvested a few tiny amounts of grapes, and may open a winery in the future.

United States: New Hampshire

The Canepa family pioneered vine-growing in New Hampshire in 1969, initially blending the produce of their hardy French hybrids with California wines. Their White Mountain Vineyards varietals have been available since 1975. The Canepas are aiming for an annual production of 25,000 cases. Despite its success, White Mountain Vineyards is the only wine-grower in the state.

United States: New Jersey

Despite the fact that the Welch's Grape Juice Company, a major juice and jam producer in at least six states, was founded in New Jersey in 1870 by the teetotaling dentist Dr. Welch, this state has managed to maintain a respectable wine-making tradition over the years. Excluding large amounts of fermented apple juice, which account for the bulk of New Jersey's total "wine" production, some wines are made in the Atlantic City area to the south, as well as in the western portion of the state.

The Renault Winery in Egg Harbor is the matriarch of New Jersey's wineries, being the oldest (established in 1864) and the largest (1,400 acres, or 520 hectares, with a 500,000-gallon capacity). By putting out a "Wine Tonic" that was sold in drugstores, Renault stayed alive during Prohibition and now sells an overly wide selection of wines from, unfortunately, mainly native grapes, as well as some hybrid and vinifera varieties. Renault's wine-glass museum, not its wines, attracts the many tourists from nearby Atlantic City.

Renault's fellow Egg Harbor wine establishment is John Schuster & Son, dating back to 1868. The Gross Highland Winery, founded in neighboring Absecon in 1934, makes about 40,000 cases a year, its Charmat-process sparkling wines being the most noteworthy. The Tomasello Winery in Hammonton has about 100 acres (40 hectares) and has been in operation since 1933. Balic Winery in Mays Landing opened in 1974.

The Jacob Lee Winery in Bordentown, the B & B Vineyards in Stockton, the Polito Vineyard in Vincentown, and Antuzzi's Winery, with a 20,000-gallon capacity, in Delran, represent the core of western New Jersey's wine producers.

United States: New Mexico

One of the duties of the Franciscan missionaries who settled in New Mexico in the early 1600s was, of course, the making of sacramental wines. By 1880, New Mexico was the nation's fifth-largest wine-producer. Wine-growing dropped, but continued, during Prohibition, peaked in 1945, and only recently has begun to pick up again. New Mexican vines, especially the hardier French-

American hybrid varieties, benefit from the cool nights and warm dry growing season, but drastic contrasts in day- and nighttime temperatures, water shortages, and soils high in lime content complicate vine cultivation in this state. Small wineries began to emerge in the late 1970s, however, and the 1980s will most likely see a continuation of this trend.

Near Roswell, in southern New Mexico's Mesilla Valley, the state's largest vineyard (50 acres, or 20 hectares, with a 5,000-gallon capacity) is owned by Clarence Cooper, a university physics professor. His property is called La Vina. The neighboring Vina Madre, property of the Hinkle brothers, has 40 acres (16 hectares) of Barbera, Napa Gamay, Ruby Cabernet, Zinfandel, Cabernet Sauvignon, and other grapes. Dan Estrada grows a tiny amount of grapes for table wines made at his Estrada Winery. Other producers are the Corrales Winery in Corrales and Miguel Gonzales in Dona Ana.

Formerly of Stony Ridge in California's Livermore Valley, Len Rosingana anticipates opening a Santa Fe winery in the 1980s, as does Arturo Jaramillo. If New York investment banker Lee Elman goes through with his plans for a 1,000-acre (400-hectare) vineyard in the aptly named town of Truth or Consequences, it will be by far the largest in the state.

United States: New York

Like so many other states, New York enjoyed a burst of enthusiastic vine-planting, and the birth of a new generation of small wineries, in the 1970s. In fact, wine-growing in New York has in many ways presented more possibilities for improvement and expansion than in California.

Not only is New York's wine industry expanding (vineyards covered more than 40,000 acres or 16,000 hectares in 1980, as opposed to 10,000 acres or 4,000 hectares in 1970), it is also undergoing some important changes. First and foremost of these changes is the large-scale replacement of labrusca vines with hybrids and vinifera. Prior to the development of better grape varieties, the native labrusca vines were the only plants strong enough to withstand the cold eastern winters. The taste for "foxy" labrusca wines was, at best, an acquired one, and their gradual disappearance from the marketplace will be no great loss. Pioneers like Philip Wagner (who founded Boordy Vineyards in Maryland in the 1940s and who is largely responsible for the development of the French-American hybrids now widely grown in the East) and Dr. Konstantin Frank (whose successful cultivation of vinifera vines throughout the East has inspired many wine-growers to follow his example) have demonstrated that good-quality non-labrusca wines can be grown in favorable microclimates in New York and other eastern states.

In addition to switching over to more palatable wines, New York State wine-makers are realizing that the obstacles to making satisfactory red wines are very great, whereas good-quality whites can be produced with relative ease. Red-wine production is best left in the hands of researchers, backyard vintners, and other hobbyists.

More conscientious matching of white hybrid and vinifera grape varieties with specific microclimates, a procedure in part supported by New York State's appellation laws requiring that 75% of the wine's volume is from state-grown grapes, spells the future for New York's wines.

(1) Finger Lakes

New York's oldest and most famous wine-growing region underwent extensive expansion in the 1970s, and although still outnumbered by labrusca vineyards, the increasing acreage of hybrid and vinifera vines is most encouraging.

The Taylor Wine Company and its subsidiaries, Pleasant Valley Wine Company and Great Western Vineyards, are now owned by Coca-Cola of Atlanta, who has finally initiated a labrusca-replacement program. This Taylor trio, along with Gold Seal Vineyards (now owned by Seagram's) and Widmer's Wine Cellars, still forms the core of the Finger Lakes wine industry. Dr. Konstantin Frank & Sons, with its accompanying Vinifera Vineyards, maintains its high-quality standards and serves as a model establishment to many new smaller wineries that are appearing in the area. Bully Hill Vineyards, owned by rebellious members of the Taylor Wine Company family, is another quality producer whose output has reached about 25,000 cases per year.

Glenora Wine Cellars, perched on the hillsides of one of the Finger Lakes (Lake Seneca), is owned by Ray Spencer. Although established in 1973 and thus a newcomer to the region, Glenora has earned a good name for itself, mainly due to its Rieslings and Chardonnays. Production, presently at about 10,000 cases annually, will increase when the 250 acres (100 hectares) of vines reach maturity.

Also in Dundee is Glenora's neighbor, the Villa D'Ingianni Winery, opened in 1972. One hundred fifty acres (60 hectares) of grapes are grown and wine is made in a 140,000-gallon-capacity winery. Another Dundee establishment is the Hermann J. Wiemer Winery, founded in 1979.

Peter Johnstone's Heron Hill Vineyards is a 30-acre (12 hectare), 5,000-case operation that has produced consistently good white Chardonnays and Rieslings since its inception in 1977. Heron Hill Vineyards wines are some of New York State's more promising ones.

The Hammondsport Wine Company, owned by Canandaigua Wine Company and dating back to 1870, makes some bottle-fermented sparkling wines.

Frenchman Serge Demay makes tiny amounts of native and hybrid vines at his Demay Wine Cellars in Hammondsport.

The Barry Wine Company, originally a sacramental-wine producer, on the western shores of Hemlock Lake, has 150 acres (60 hectares) of various grapes. The owners, the Cribari brothers, are concentrating on developing their hybrid and vinifera and thus may be a good source for satisfactory table wines in the 1980s.

The Colaruotolo family makes small amounts of Gewürztraminer, Riesling, and Chardonnay wines from their 12 acres (5 hectares) of vines near Rochester. Wines are sold under their Casa Larga label.

(2) Hudson Valley

Concord grape and kosher wine production is losing its grip on the Hudson Valley wine-growing market as more and more small, quality-oriented wineries come into being, following in the footsteps of such examples as the Benmarl Wine Company and High Tor Vineyards (see page 509). Within a 90-minute drive from downtown Manhattan, more than 1,500 acres (600 hectares) of this historic valley are planted in French-American hybrids and vinifera vines.

Typical examples of the new breed of Hudson Valley wineries are Cascade Mountain Vineyards, Clinton Vineyards, Walker Valley Vineyards (all 15 acres, or 6 hectares, in size) and Northeast Vineyards. Cascade Mountain, owned by writer William Wetmore, has rapidly made a name for itself through its light red wines. Ben and Kathy Feder have achieved their best results with a Seyval Blanc, a French-American hybrid grape, at their Clinton Vineyards. Walker Valley Vineyards, under the care of owner and wine-maker Gary Dross, has produced some white hybrids, insignificant in quantity but impressive in quality, since the late 1970s. On a much smaller scale, Dr. George Green, a world-famous heart surgeon, puts out tiny amounts of good hybrid wines under his Northeast Vineyards label.

Some older Hudson Valley producers are changing their images and entering into the production of better-quality wines. These include the Brotherhood Winery, which has expanded its line of altar and sparkling wines to include hybrids, and the Great River Winery, known for its Marlboro sparkling wines, which now offers vintage French hybrids as well.

Cagnassó Winery and Cottage Vineyards in Marlboro, El Paso Winery in Ulster Park, and North Salem Vineyards in North Salem are Hudson Valley wineries whose quality is improving.

(3) Chautauqua

As in the rest of the state, Chautauqua wineries are moving away from kosher wine production and are realizing that their future lies in hybrid and vinifera wine production.

The Johnson Estate Winery (see page 509) remains the Lake Erie area's major producer, putting out close to 10,000 cases annually.

A newcomer with potential is Woodbury Vineyards, whose 10-year-old Chardonnay and Riesling vines are producing some good wines. Page Woodbury, who owns the vineyard, opened his winery in 1979.

(4) Niagara

No major changes have occurred in the Niagara area's wine industry in recent years. See page 509.

(5) Long Island

Since 1979, Alex and Louisa Hargrave have been proving that wine-growing on Long Island's tip, particularly the northern fork, can meet with success. Their 50 acres (20 hectares) of vinifera vines, planted in 1973, yield about 5,000 cases of Hargrave Vineyard wines, most notably Cabernet Sauvignon, Chardonnay, and Sauvignon Blanc. If other wine-growers follow the Hargraves' initiative, this section of Long Island could become an important wine-growing region.

United States: North Carolina

Wines made from Scuppernong grapes, which can withstand the heat of the South, dominate North Carolina's wine scene. Before Prohibition, Paul Garrett developed his Scuppernong empire in his home state of North Carolina and eventually expanded into other parts of the South. His Virginia Dare brand, of doubtful quality, was especially well known, immediately after Repeal.

Today, a few wineries making Scuppernong wines are in operation, among them Deerfield Wine Cellars in Edenton and John Dockery's Winery in Rockingham. The Biltmore Company in Asheville and Duplin Wine Cellars in Rose Hill are two establishments experimenting with French-American hybrids.

United States: Ohio

Ohio's wine industry experienced a revitalization during the 1970s similar to that enjoyed by many other states. Fortunately, Concord grape cultivation dropped to 65% of the total grape acreage by 1978, and its gradual decline continues (much too slowly) today; the labruscas are slowly being replaced by mostly Catawba, French-American hybrids, and some vinifera grapes. Older wineries have expanded their facilities and many new wineries have been established, bringing the present count to nearly 50.

The regions east and west of Cleveland along the shores of Lake Erie (including Sandusky and the Lake Erie Islands) still form the wine-growing heartland of Ohio. Although the Concord grape reigns, quality-oriented growers and wine-makers are replanting them with non-labrusca varieties. Meier's Wine Cellars (see page 510) remains the largest producer and is increasing its plantations of French hybrids on its Isle Saint George in Lake Erie.

The Cedar Hill Wine Company, located in the basement of a French restaurant in Cleveland Heights, produces about 2,500 cases of French-American hybrids and a tiny amount of vinifera wines from Lake Erie grapes. The quality of these wines, called Chateau Lagniappe, is quite good.

East of Cleveland, along the lakeshore, are several more of the newer, quality-conscious establishments. The Grand River Wine Company in Madison, with 20 acres (8 hectares) of vinifera and French hybrid grapes, has an annual production of approximately 7,000 cases. Also in Madison is Chalet Debonné Vineyards. Although much of Chalet Debonné's 40-acre (16-hectare) vineyard is planted in labruscas, the most successful wines of the 8,000-case production are the French hybrids.

Farther east, in Conneaut, the Markko Vineyards specializes in vinifera wines, producing Riesling, Chardonnay, and Cabernet Sauvignon grapes on 10 acres (4 hectares). Production is small (1,000 cases a year), but the quality of the Markko wines is promising. Another Conneaut winery, Buccia Vineyard, features French hybrid wines of satisfactory quality.

West of Cleveland, several smaller wineries unfortunately still concentrate on making Concord wines. These include Dover Vineyards in Westlake and John Christ Winery and Klingshirn Winery, both in Avon Lake. The Steuk Wine Company, Mantey's Vineyard, and E & K Wine Company (once Ohio's industry leader), all in Sandusky, now offer small amounts of French-American hybrids and vinifera wines in addition to their native American products.

Middle Bass Island and South Bass Island (or Put-in-Bay), not far offshore from Sandusky, enjoy a unique microclimate with an exceptionally long growing season. The Lonz Winery and the Bretz Winery on Middle Bass are potential quality producers. The Heineman Winery on Put-in-Bay has made primarily native American wines for nearly a century.

The Ohio River Valley near Cincinnati in south-central Ohio is regaining the wine-growing reputation it earned in the 1800s. The poet Longfellow wrote his "Ode to Catawba Wines" in honor of the once-famed wines from this region. Today, in downtown Cincinnati, Meier's (see page 510) has its 2.5-million-gallon winery, and the Warren Sublette Winery, a much smaller operation, makes some good French hybrid wines. Southeast of the city, right on the Ohio River, Moyer Vineyards has been known to produce some decent hybrid wines, including a dry bottle-fermented sparkling one, since 1973.

Brushcreek Vineyards in Peebles, due east of Cincinnati, makes native and French-American hybrid wines in small amounts.

Valley Vineyards in Morrow, northeast of Cincinnati, features a 40-acre (16 hectare) vineyard and offers a variety of native and hybrid wines. Relatively nearby is Tarula Farms in Clarksville, which offers similar wines.

Other wineries scattered throughout the state are: Heritage Vineyards in West Milton, Stone Quarry Vineyards Winery in Waterford, and Hafle Vineyards, with vineyards and wineries in Springfield and Columbus. All three offer a variety of native American and French-American hybrid wines.

United States: Oregon

Oregon is fast becoming a noteworthy wine-producing state. Fortunate microclimates (particularly in the northern part of the state) feature wet and snowy winters appropriate for the cultivation of certain European grape varieties. Refreshingly well-made state labeling laws, forbidding the use of European generic names (e.g., "chablis," "burgundy," "rhine," etc.) and requiring that varietal wines contain a minimum of 90% of the grape variety named on the label, serve as effective quality controls. While many Oregon wine-growers are still experimenting with numerous grape varieties in hopes of finding the perfect grape/soil match, and while many others still rely on grapes imported from Washington State, steadily increasing numbers of new plantings of the top varieties assure Oregon's future as a major quality wine-producer.

Some 30-odd small wineries and over 200 growers are the force behind Oregon's developing wine industry. Protected by the Coast Range Mountains to the west and the Cascade Mountains to the east, the vineyards are concentrated in two valleys: the Willamette in the northwest near Portland and the Umpqua in the southwest.

The Willamette Valley features the greatest number of wineries in the state. Many wine-growers have found its cool Region I microclimate and ideal hilly terrain particularly well suited to the Riesling grape. One of the leaders in this area, in quality as well as quantity, is the 25,000-case-capacity Sokol Blosser Vineyards. Forty acres (16 hectares) of vines in Dundee, southwest of Portland, yield 10 varietals. The Sokol and Blosser families opened their joint operation in 1974; the vineyards were planted in 1971. The neighboring Knudsen Erath Winery, also in Dundee, is owned by Cal Knudsen and Dick Erath, who make about 12,000 cases a year from half the total production of their 94-acre (38-hectare) vineyard. They stress the Chardonnay, Pinot Noir, and Riesling grape varieties. Knudsen Erath was established in 1967.

Adelsheim Vineyard, north of Dundee, has made vinifera wines blended from Oregon and Washington State grapes since 1978. Eventually, the 20-acre (8-hectare) vineyard, owned by Ginny and Dave Adelsheim, will be the exclusive source for an anticipated annual production of 5,000 cases. Chateau Benoit, set on a hillside in Lafayette, west of Dundee, is the property of Mary and Fred Benoit. Their wines, from 8-year-old vinifera vines, debuted in 1980. David and Diana Lett have made promising Chardonnays and Pinot Noirs from their 20-acre (8-hectare) Dundee vineyard since 1966. Their winery, the Eyrie Vineyards, is located in neighboring McMinnville; output is about 4,000 cases a year. Amity Vineyards, owned by Myron Redford, is outside of McMinnville. About 4,000 cases a year are made in the winery, built in 1976. Amity Vineyards' vinifera grapes come from a 15-acre (3½-hectare) vineyard.

More small wineries are clustered in the northerly and westerly stretch of the Willamette Valley between Portland and Salem. This extension is called Tualatin, which is also the name of the area's largest producer. Tualatin Vineyards (maximum capacity 25,000 cases) has 70 acres (27½ hectares) of vines that are coming of age. Tualatin Vineyards has already established a name for itself with varietals made from Washington and Idaho grapes. Wine-maker William Fuller, who formerly held that position at Louis Martini in California, has made wines at this Forest Grove location since 1973. Reuter's Hill Vineyard, incorporating the Charles Coury Vineyards since 1978, is also in Forest Grove. About 12,000 cases of vinifera wines of inconsistent quality are made annually from grapes grown on 60 acres (24 hectares). Owners of the nearby Cote des Colombes, in Banks, are presently doubling the size of their 10-acre (4-hectare) vinifera vineyard. Production, not to exceed 10,000 cases, should be of good quality. Shaler Vineyard Cellars is one of the newer wineries in the area and its viniferas, to appear in the early 1980s, will contribute, it is hoped, to the growing reputation of the Tualatin Valley.

South of Forest Grove, in Gaston, the Elk Cove Vineyards, whose 21 acres (8 hectares) of viniferas will eventually be the sole source for an anticipated production of 5,000 cases, has made some good blends from Washington State grapes since 1977. In neighboring Hillsboro, the Oak Knoll Winery is wisely adding varietal grape wines to their fruit and berry "wine" lines. The Ponzi Vineyards make a good Riesling, the best of their several viniferas, from their 10-acre (4-hectare) Beaverton vineyard planted in 1970.

Farther down the Willamette Valley, west of Eugene in Elmira, wine-growing pioneers George and Linda Smith courageously planted 25 acres (10 hectares) of vinifera vines in this cold-climate area in 1970. They have made wines at their Forgeron Vineyard winery (on a magnificent site overlooking Fern Ridge Lake) since 1977. Wines so far have been promising, and good results should be forthcoming by the mid-1980s.

Continuing south from Eugene, a number of wineries have sprung up in the Umpqua River Valley around Roseburg. These wine-growers were inspired by the success of Richard Sommer's Hillcrest Vineyard (*see* page 510), whose experimental plantings of the 1960s proved that viniferas could be cultivated in the area. Hillcrest now has 30 acres (12 hectares) in production, yielding about 9,000 cases of wine per year. Jonicole Vineyards, with plantings dating back to 1968, makes four wines in small quantities (3,000 cases annually) in their Roseburg winery, completed in 1976.

Vine-growing has been pursued in other parts of Oregon outside of the main valleys, particularly in the southwest. Valley View Vineyard specializes in viniferas grown on 30 acres (12 hectares) and vinified in the Wisnovsky family's Jacksonville winery. Siskiyou Vineyards, at the foot of southern Oregon's Siskiyou National Forest, was founded in the late 1970s with 12 acres (5 hectares) of vinifera vines.

United States: Pennsylvania

Although Concord grapes account for most of Pennsylvania's 14,000 acres (5,600 hectares) of vines, making it the nation's fifth-leading grape-producer, decent wine-grape plantations are gradually increasing. The state's Farm Winery Bill, passed in 1968, prevents wineries from producing more than 100,000 gallons of wine per year (hence they are called "limited wineries"). Archaic distribution laws, however, require that Pennsylvania wines be sold only at restaurants, wineries, or state-controlled liquor stores; this has discouraged many fledgling wine-growers from going commercial.

Pennsylvania's one-time wine-growing tradition has been recently revived in the 1960s and 1970s with the appearance of numerous small wineries, especially in the southeastern part of the state. Conestoga Vineyards, in

Birchrunville, opened in 1963; its founders can be credited with overcoming some of the bureaucratic red tape that eventually led to the 1968 revision of the state's wine laws. Conestoga makes small amounts of wines from French hybrid and labrusca grapes. Buckingham Valley Vineyards in Buckingham, founded in 1966, has gained a reputation as a reliable French hybrid producer; 10 acres (4 hectares) of vines provide some of the grapes necessary for the 5,000 yearly cases. Bucks County Vineyards in New Hope, founded in 1973, purchases most of the French hybrid, Chardonnay, and Riesling varietal grapes necessary for their annual 20,000 cases. Since 1974, the Adams County Winery in Orrtanna has offered white hybrid and vinifera varietals, made at the rate of about 3,000 cases a year. The Nissley Vineyards in Bainbridge, a 27-acre (11-hectare), 8,000-case operation, is run by the Nissley family. They began making French hybrids, their specialty, in 1978. The Dutch County Wine Cellars in Lenhartsville, the County Creek Vineyard and Winery in Telford, Wilmont Wines in Schwenksville, Tucquan Vineyards in Holtwood, Naylor Wine Cellars in York, York Springs Winery in York Springs, Lancaster County Winery and Pequea Valley Vineyard and Winery, both in Willow Street, and Mt. Hope Estate and Winery in Cornwall, to name a few, represent the new breed of Pennsylvania wine-makers in the southeast.

Pennsylvania's Erie County, in the northwestern corner of the state, forms part of the wine belt that stretches along the lake from Ohio to Chautauqua. As in the other regions bordering Lake Erie, this is unfortunately predominantly Concord country, but recent plantings of hybrid and vinifera vines have confirmed that the prospects for better-quality vine-growing and wine-making in this area are good. The founders of the Presque Isle Wine Cellars, located in North East near Erie, motivated others to follow their example when they presented some drinkable Pennsylvania-grown hybrid and vinifera wines in 1968. Wines are currently produced at the rate of about 2,000 cases a year, partially from their 20-acre (8-hectare) vineyard planted in 1958. Neighboring Penn Shore Vineyards, also in North East, unfortunately still specializes in Concord and native wines, although they are slowly adding more non-labruscas to their list. Penn Shore has been in operation since 1969. Mazza Vineyards has its headquarters in North East with some vineyards at other locations, but most of their 10,000-case production is from locally purchased grapes. Mazza offers several vinifera wines along with their French hybrid and native American types.

Wineries also operate in central Pennsylvania (Buffalo Valley Winery in Lewisburg, Doerflinger Wine Cellars in Bloomsburg, Kolln Vineyards in Bellefonte, Lembo Vineyards in Lewistown) and in the southwestern part of the state (Lapic Winery in New Brighton).

United States: Rhode Island

Even this tiny temperate state boasts four wineries to date. Sakonnet Vineyards, with 35 acres (14 hectares) of varietal hybrids and some vinifera, will eventually reach its maximum output of 10,000 cases. Prudence Island with 20 acres (8 hectares), is in the middle of Narragansett Bay and grows exclusively vinifera vines. South County Vineyards in Slocum has offered tiny amounts of vinifera since 1974, and Wickford Vineyards in North Kingstown will debut its first wines in the early 1980s.

United States: South Carolina

South Carolina is a very small grape-growing state, with the Concord, Muscadine, and Catawba varieties virtually the only wines cultivated. The 371-acre (148-hectare) Oakview Plantations in Woodruff specializes in making concentrates of those varieties. Tenner Brothers Winery in Patrick is owned by New York's Canandaigua Wine Company and makes similar products from local grapes. However, one exception to the labrusca rule is Dr. James Truluck, who has made French hybrid and vinifera wines from local plantings at his Truluck Winery in Lake City since 1976, proving that these varieties can thrive in South Carolina's climate.

United States: Tennessee

An estimated 150 acres (60 hectares) of vines are under cultivation in Tennessee. The Tiegs Winery in Lenoir City outside of Knoxville grows primarily French hybrid grapes. The Highland Manor Winery in Jamestown, between Nashville and Knoxville, unfortunately grows primarily American varieties. Both wineries had their first crushes in 1980.

United States: Texas

Franciscan missionaries came to Texas in the mid-1600s, equipped with European vine-stocks to make their sacramental wines. Unable to survive the harsh weather and many insects, the European plants were replaced with native vines, and Texas enjoyed a wine-growing spurt until Prohibition. Since Repeal, especially in the 1960s and 1970s, there has been a renewed interest in wine-growing in Texas, and approximately 350 acres (140 hectares) of this state's vast area are planted in vines. Unlike many of its neighbors, most of the fruit of these vines is used for wine. French-American hybrids, vinifera varieties (Chenin Blanc and the new cross Ruby Cabernet), and some Muscadines are grown. Cold winters, insects, intense heat, drought, and hail are problems that hamper grape-growing in certain parts of Texas.

Gretchen Glasscock, heiress to a Texas oil fortune, has a thriving 40-acre (16-hectare) vineyard on mile-high Blue Mountain in west Texas. Her property, 7 miles (4½ kilometers) south of Fort Davis, has a microclimate similar to California's coastal valleys.

Llano Estacado at Lubbock (also in west Texas), a 15-acre (6-hectare) vineyard, is jointly owned and operated by three Texas Technological University professors, who are experimenting with more than 100 grape varieties. Their 1980 crop was destroyed by a springtime hailstorm,

but the possibilities of good grape-growing exist in this region.

The Val Verde Winery, 300 miles (480 kilometers) south of Lubbock, has been run by the Qualia family for three generations. If the Qualias replace their South Carolinian vines with vinifera and hybrid varieties suitable to the hot, moist microclimate of Del Rio, they may come up with some decent wines.

La Buena Vida Vineyards in Springtown (central Texas), Fall Creek Vineyards in Tow, and Guadalupe Valley Winery in New Braunfels (southwestern Texas) are additional promising establishments.

United States: Virginia

Wine-growing has its place in Virginia's colorful history: the first settlers in Roanoke cultivated native vines, George Washington and Thomas Jefferson both grew grapes on their Virginia plantations, and Virginian wines won medals in Vienna and Paris in the late 1800s. The industry faded with Prohibition, and in recent years has been revived. Today, about 75% of Virginia's vines are vinifera, the remainder being primarily French hybrids with unfortunately some Scuppernong still being cultivated.

The Middleburg area has been the center for new developments in the state's wine-growing industry. Highbury, near The Plains, is an experimental vineyard and winery for the Vinifera Wine Grower's Association. Since its 1967 opening, it has inspired the establishment of several small commercial wineries in and around Middleburg. To name a few, there is the Piedmont Vineyard with 25 acres (10 hectares) of Chardonnay and Semillon grapes, the Meredyth Vineyard with 45 acres (18 hectares) of vinifera and French hybrids, and the Melrose Vineyard.

The Barboursville Vineyard, in the town of Barboursville 20 miles (32 kilometers) north of Charlottesville, may someday be Virginia's largest vineyards. According to owner Gabriele Rausse, up to 250 acres (100 hectares) will be planted in viniferas by the mid-1980s. So far, Barboursville can be credited with producing the state's first Cabernet Sauvignon made wholly from Virginia grapes.

The 13-acre (5-hectare) Farfelu Vineyard in Flint Hill (Rappahannock County), the La Abra Farm and Winery in Lovingston (in the Blue Ridge foothills), the Schiehallion Vineyards in Keysville (the Southern Piedmont region), the Morland Vineyard in King George (on the Potomac shore) and the Guilford Farm Vineyard in Stanley have all emphasized the cultivation of French hybrids since their beginnings in the 1970s. The Rosebower Vineyard in Hampton-Sydney grows approximately 3 acres (a little more than 1 hectare) each of French hybrids and viniferas.

Many other wineries are scattered all over the state, and as long as the new generation of wine-growers concentrates its efforts on cultivating the most suitable French hybrids and vinifera vines on the most suitable soils, Virginia can look forward to earning a reputation as a quality wine-producer in the 1980s.

United States: Washington

Although gradually dropping, about 20,000 acres (8,000 hectares) of Washington's 25,000 acres (10,000 hectares) of vineyards of still remain planted in Concord vines. Responding to the demand for quality wines, and aware of Washington's natural wine-growing gifts, many growers are slowly transforming their labrusca plots into vinifera and hybrid vineyards.

The Yakima River Valley and the South Columbia River Basin in the south-central part of the state are endowed with a soil and climate ideally suited to growing vinifera grapes. Sandy loam soil, over a rocky volcanic base, is moistened by irrigation, and the warm days and cool nights combine to produce well-balanced grapes, heavy with sugar and high in acid. The area lies just north of latitude 46 degrees, the same latitude that cuts across the Bordeaux and Burgundy regions.

Chateau Ste. Michelle, a 2,000-acre (800-hectare), 300,000-case operation, is the principal wine-grower in the Yakima Valley. Grapes grown in the Yakima and Columbia valleys are made into wines in either their suburban Seattle facility (for white wines) or their Yakima Valley facility (for red wines). The United States Tobacco Company owns Chateau Ste. Michelle and anticipates producing 1 million cases a year by the mid-1980s. Their Riesling and Grenache Rosé are the most successful wines, and occasional vintages of Gewürztraminer, Chardonnay, and Cabernet Sauvignon have been quite drinkable.

Preston Wine Cellars, with a capacity for 60,000 annual cases, made its quality reputation with Chardonnay and Fumé Blanc wines. Preston has some 200 acres (80 hectares) of vines in the Yakima Valley; the winery is located in Pasco, near the conjunction of the Yakima, Columbia, and Snake rivers.

Nearby, Leonetti Cellar, on the eastern edge of the Walla Walla Valley (in the city of the same name), is a tiny quality-oriented producer devoted to Cabernet Sauvignon and Riesling wines. Gary Figgins, wine-maker, limits his production to a mere 300 cases per year.

West of Pasco, farther up the Yakima River, the town of Prosser now boasts several wineries, as of the late 1970s. Hinzerling Vineyards had their first crush, of Riesling, Gewürztraminer, Chardonnay, and Cabernet Sauvignon grapes, grown on 22 acres (almost 9 hectares) in 1976. Hinzerling's production, according to wine-maker Mike Wallace, will eventually reach 8,000 cases annually. The Yakima River Winery, whose first vintage was in 1979, grows primarily white wines. The Rauner family, owners and managers, aims to produce about 12,000 cases by 1985.

Associated Vintners, a partnership of three wine lovers formed in 1963, has 32 acres (13 hectares) in the Yakima Valley. They make six vinifera wines in their suburban Seattle winery (located in Redwood), of which the Gewürztraminer is the most successful. In Seattle itself, the E. B. Foote Winery, founded in 1978 by the Foote family, makes about 5,000 cases a year from Yakima and other purchased grapes.

Formerly the Bingen Wine Cellars, Mount Elise Vineyards is located in the Columbia River gorge in Bingen at Washington's southern border. The Henderson family has made viniferas there since 1975 and anticipates producing 11,000 cases by the mid-1980s. At present, the Hendersons have some 30 acres (12 hectares) of vines.

Although making no wines of their own, the sizable 500-acre (200-hectare) Sagemoor Farms vineyards, also in the South Columbia River Basin, has sold many of its top-quality grapes to wine-makers in Washington and other states.

Western Washington is fast becoming a good viticultural region, as witnessed by the success of the Manfred Vierthaler Winery in Sumner and the Salishan Vineyards in La Center. Manfred Vierthaler is in the Puyallup River Valley and has made about 10,000 cases of German-style wines per year since 1976, from about 30 acres (12 hectares) of vines. Salishan Vineyards is owned by Lincoln and Joan Wolverton, who have made wines since 1976. From a dozen acres (about 5 hectares) of vines, they make close to 2,000 cases a year, emphasizing Pinot Noir.

United States: Wisconsin

Although several fruit and berry "wineries" thrive in Wisconsin, only one of any importance makes grape wines. The Wollersheim Winery at Prairie du Sac, founded in 1857, was revived in 1976. On a hill above the Wisconsin River, near Madison, the Wollersheim family grows 20 acres (8 hectares) of more successful French hybrids and some viniferas; they also sell hybrid rootstocks to local hobbyists. Although Wisconsin is far from becoming a major wine-producer (considering the current emphasis on fruit products), the Wollersheims have proven that the potential is there.

Select Bibliography

Aaron, Sam, and Beard, James. *How to Eat Better for Less Money.* New York: 1970.

Aaron, Sam, and Fadiman, Clifton. *The Joys of Wine.* New York: 1975.

Abel, Dominick. *Guide to the Wines of the United States.* New York: 1979.

Adams, Leon D. *The Wines of America.* 2d ed., rev. New York: 1978.

Allen. H. Warner. *Claret.* London: 1924.

    A Contemplation of Wine. London: 1951.

    A History of Wine. London: 1961.

    Natural Red Wines. London: 1951.

    Rum. London: 1931.

    Sherry and Port. London: 1954.

    White Wines and Cognac. 1952.

    The Wines of Portugal. London: 1963.

Ambrosi, Hans. *Wo grosse Weine Wachsen.* Munich: 1973.

    Deutscher Wein-Atlas. Bielefeld: 1973.

Amerine, Maynard A., and Joslyn, Maynard A. *Commercial Production of Table Wines.* Berkeley: 1940.

    Dessert Appetizer & Related Flavored Wines, Berkeley: 1964.

    Table Wines: The Technology of Their Production in California. rev. ed. Berkeley and Los Angeles and London: 1970.

Amerine, Maynard A., Berg, Harold W.; and Cruess, William V. *The Technology of Wine Making.* 2d ed. Westport, Connecticut: 1967.

Amerine, Maynard A., and Singleton, Vernon L, *Wine: An Introduction for Americans.* Berkeley and Los Angeles: 1966.

Balzer, Robert Lawrence, *The Pleasures of Wine.* New York: 1964.

    Wines of California. New York: 1978.

Barbadillo, Manuel. *El vino de la alegría.* Jerez de la Frontera: 1951.

Barry, (Sir) Edward. *Wines of the Ancients.* London: 1775.

Benvegnin, Lucien Capt. Émile, and Piquet, Gustave. *Traité de vinification.* Lausanne: 1951.

Berry, Charles W. *In Search of Wine.* London: 1935.

Bert, Pierre, *In vino veritas.* Paris: 1975.

Bertall,—. *La Vigne: voyage autour des vins de France.* Paris: 1878.

Bespaloff, Alexis. *Signed Book of Wine.* New York: 1971.

    Guide to Inexpensive Wines. New York: 1973.

Bijur, George. *Wines with Long Noses.* London: 1951.

Bode, Charles G. *Wines of Italy.* London and New York: 1956.

Bourke, Arthur. *Winecraft: The Encyclopedia of Wines and Spirits.* London: 1935.

Bradford, Sarah. *The Englishman's Wine.* London: 1969.

Bréjoux, Pierre. *Les Vins de Loire.* Paris; 1956.

    Les Vins de Bourgogne. Paris.

Broadbent, Michael. *The Great Vintage Wine Book.* London and New York: 1980.

Brunet, R. *Dictionnaire d'oenologie et de viticulture.* Paris: 1946.

Bürklin, Albert; Schultz, F. R.; von Bassermann-Jordan; von Diersburg, Roeder; and Weingarth, Otto, eds. *Verband deutscher Naturwein versteigerer.* 1953.

Butler, Frank Hedges. *Wine and the Wine Lands of the World.* London: 1926.

Capus, Joseph. *L'Évolution de la législation sur les appellations d'origine et la genèse des appellations contrôlées.* Paris: 1947.

Carling, T. E. *The Complete Book of Drink.* London: 1951.

    Wine Lore. London: 1974.

Carosso, Vincent P. *The California Wine Industry, 1830-1895.* Berkeley and Los Angeles: 1951.

Carter, Youngman. *Drinking Bordeaux.* New York and London: 1966.

Casabianca, A. *Guida storica del Chianti.* Florence: 1957.

Cassagnac, Paul de. *French Wines.* Translated by Guy Knowles. London: 1930.

Chappaz, Georges, *Le Vignoble et le vin de Champagne.* Paris: 1951.

Chidgey, Graham. *Guide to the Wines of Burgundy.* London: 1977.

Churchill, Creighton. *The World of Wines.* New York: 1964.

Ciais, Afrien; Quittanson, Charles; and Vanhoutte, René. *La Protection des appellations d'origine des vins et eaux-de-vie et le commerce des vins.* Montpellier: 1949.

Cocks, Charles, and Féret, Eduard. *Bordeaux et ses vins, classés par ordre de mérite.* 12th ed. Bordeaux: 1969.

Corato. Ricardo di. *Vini d'Italia.* Milan: 1978.

Cornelssen, F. A., ed. *Das Buch vom deutschen Wein.* Mainz: 1954.

Croft-Cooke, Rupert. *Madeira.* London: 1961.

    Port. London: 1957.

    Sherry. London: 1955; New York: 1956.

Crosby, Everett. *The Vintage Years.* New York: 1973.

Dallas, Philip. *Italian Wines.* London: 1974.

De Bosdari, C. *Wines of the Cape.* 3d ed. Cape Town; Amsterdam: 1967.

De Kerdéland, Jean. *Historique des vins de France.* Paris: 1964.

Delamain, Robert. *Histoire de Cognac.* Paris: 1935.

Del Castillo, José, and Hallett, David R. *The Wines of Spain.* Bilbao: 1972.

Desgraves, Louis. *Bordeaux au cours des siècles.* Bordeaux: 1954.

Dettori, Renato G. *Italian Wines and Liqueurs.* Rome: 1953.

Dion, Roger. *Histoire de la vigne et du vin de France.* Paris: 1959.

Doléris, J. A. *Les Vignobles et vins de Béarn.* Pau: 1935.

Dopson, Betty, and Topolos, Michael. *Napa Valley Wine Tour.* St. Helena, Cal.: 1978.

Doutrelant, Pierre-Marie. *Les bons vins et les autres.* Paris: 1976.

Dumay, Raymond. *Guide du vin.* Paris: 1968.

Engel, Ferdinand. *Wirtschaftssicherung des österreichischen Weinbaus.* Vienna: 1946.

Enjalbert, Henri. *Histoire de la vigne et du vin.* Paris: 1975.

Evans, Len. *The Australia and New Zealand Complete Book of Wine.* Sydney: 1973.

Eyland, J. M. *Ma Muse en vendanges.* Montpellier: 1960.

Faes, H., ed. *Lexique viti-vinicole international: français, italien, espagnol, allemand.* Paris: 1940.

Faith, Nicholas. *The Wine-masters.* London: 1978.

    Château Margaux. London: 1980.

Ferré, Louis. *Traité d'oenologie bourguignonne.* Paris: 1958.

Fisher, M. I. *Liqueurs: Dictionary and Survey.* London: 1959.

Foillard, David. *Le pays du Beaujolais.* Villefranche: 1929.

Francisque, Michel. *Histoire du commerce et de la navigation à Bordeaux.* Bordeaux: 1867-70.

Select Bibliography

Frolov-Begreev, Anton M. *Ampelografia S.S.S.R.* 7 Vols. Moscow: 1946-62.

Galet, P. *Cépages et vignobles de France.* 4 Vols. Montpellier: 1956-64.

Dinestet, Bernard. *La Bouillie Bordelaise.* Paris: 1975.

Gold, Alec, ed. *Wines and Spirits of the World.* Coulsdon: 1972.

Goldschmidt, Eduard, ed. *Deutschlands Wienbauorte und Weinbergslagen.* 6th ed. Mainz: 1951.

González Gordon, Manuel M. *Sherry: The Noble Wine.* London: 1972.

Got, Armand. *Monbazillac.* Bordeaux: 1947.

Grossman, Harold J. *Grossman's Guide to Wines, Spirits and Beers.* rev. ed. New York: 1980.

Gunyon, R. E. H. *The Wines of Central and Southeastern Europe.* New York: 1971.

György, Paul. *The Fine Wines of Germany and all the World's Wine Lore* Berlin: 1965.

Halásx, Zoltán. *Hungarian Wines Through the Ages.* Budapest: 1962.

Hallgarten, S. F. *Rhineland, Wineland.* London: 1951.

Alsace and Its Wine Gardens. rev. ed. London: 1965.

Harrison, Godfrey. *Bristol Cream.* London: 1955.

Healy, Maurice. *Stay Me with Flagons.* London: 1963.

Hedrick, Ulysses P. *The Grapes of New York.* Albany: 1908.

Grapes and Wines from Home Vineyards. New York: 1945.

Henderson, Alexander L. *The History of Ancient and Modern Wines.* London: 1824.

Higounet, Charles. *Histoire de l'Aquitaine.* Toulouse: 1973.

Hinkle, Richard Paul. *Central Coast Wine Book.* St. Helena, Cal.: 1980.

Hornickel, Ernst. *The Great Wines of Europe.* London: 1965.

Hyams, Edward. *Dionysos, A Social History of the Wine Vine.* London: 1965.

Isnard, Hildebert. *La Vigne en Algérie.* 2 Vols. Gap: 1951-54.

Jacquelin, Louis, and Poulain, René. *The Wines and Vineyards of France.* Translated by T. A. Layton. London and New York: 1962.

Jacques-Petit, F. *Les Appellations des vins et eaux-de-vie de France.* Angers: 1957.

James, Walter. *Wine in Australia.* rev.ed. Melbourne: 1963.

A Word Book of Wine. London: 1961.

Jeffs, Julian. *Sherry.* London: 1961.

The Wines of Europe. London: 1971.

Johnson, Frank E. *The Professional Wine Reference.* New York: 1978.

Johnson, Hugh. *Wine.* London: 1966.

World Atlas of Wine. London: 1977; New York: 1979.

Jones, Idwal. *Vines in the Sun.* New York: 1949.

Jung, Hermann. *Wein in der Kunst.* Munich: 1961.

Kaufman, William. *Champagne.* New York: 1973.

The Traveler's Guide to the Vineyards of North America. New York: 1980.

Keller, D. Josef, ed. *Pfalzwein Almanach.* Neustadt: 1953.

Kittel, J. B., and Breider, Hans. *Das Buch vom Frankenweine.* Wüzburg: 1958.

Kraemer, Ado. *Im Lande des Bocksbeutels.* 3d ed. Würzburg: 1961.

Krug, Henri and Rémi. *L'Art de Champagne.* Paris: 1972.

Laffer, H. E. *The Wine Industry of Australia.* Adelaide: 1949.

Lafforgue, Germain. *Le Vignoble girondin.* Paris: 1947.

Lafon, René; Lafon, Jean; and Couillaud, Pierre. *Le Cognac: sa distillation.* 4th ed. Paris: 1964.

Langenbach, Alfred. *German Wines and Vines.* London: 1962.

The Wines of Germany. London: 1951.

Larmat, Louis, ed. *Atlas de la France vinicole.* Paris:1949.

Vignobles et routes du vin. Paris: 1979.

Les vins de Bourgogne. Paris:1953.

Les vins des Côtes du Rhone. Pairs: 1943.

Latimer, Patricia. *Sonoma & Mendocino Wine Book.* St. Helena, Cal.: 1979.

Layton. T. A. *Wines of Italy.* London:1961.

Lebensfreude aus Rheinhessen. Mainz: 1954.

Léon-Gauthier, Pierre. *Les Clos de Bourgogne.* Beaune: 1931.

Leonhardt, George. *Das Weinbuch; Werden des Weines von der Reb bis zum Glase.* 2d ed. Leipzig: 1963.

Lichine, Alexis. *Alexis Lichine's Guide to the Wines and Vineyards of France.* New York: 1979.

Wines of France. rev. ed. New York: 1970.

Lucia, Salvatore P. *Wine as Food and Medicine.* New York and Toronto: 1954.

A History of Wine as Therapy. Philadelphia and Montreal: 1963.

Lutz, H. F. *Viticulture and Brewing in the Ancient Orient.* Leipzig and New York: 1922.

Magistocchi, Gaudencio. *Tratado de enología adaptado a la república Argentina.* Buenos Aires: 1955.

Malvezin, F. *Histoire de la vigne et du vin en Aquitaine.* Bordeaux: 1919.

Marchou, Gaston. *Bordeaux sur la règne de la vigne.* Bordeaux: 1947.

Le Vin de Bordeaux cet inconnu. Montpellier: 1973.

Marrison, L. W. *Wines and Spirits.* London: 1957.

Massee, William E. *Wines and Spirits, a Complete Buying Guide.* New York: 1961.

Meinhard, Heinrich. *German Wines.* London: 1971.

Melville, John. *Guide to California Wines.* 2d ed. San Carlos, California: 1960.

Mendelsohn, Oscar A. *The Earnest Drinker.* London: 1950.

The Dictionary of Drink and Drinking. London: 1965.

Morris, Dennis. *The French Vineyards.* London: 1958.

Mouillefert, P. *Les Vignobles et les vines de France et de l'etranger.* Paris: 1891.

Muir, Augustus, ed. *How to Choose and Enjoy Wine.* London: 1953.

Müller, Karl. *Weinbau-Lexikon für Winzer, Weinhändler, Küfer und Gastwirte.* Berlin: 1930.

Office International de la Vigne et du Vin. *Lexique de la vigne et du vin: Français, Italiano, Español, Deutsch, Portugues, English, Ruskii.* Paris: 1963.

Olken, Charles E., Singer, Earl G., and Roby, Norman S. *The Connoisseurs' Handbook of California Wines.* New York: 1980.

Orizet, Louis. *Le livre du vin.* Paris: 1968.

Vignobles et vins d'Aquitaine. Bordeaux: 1970.

Pacottet, Paul, and Guittonneau, L. *Vins de Champagne et vins mousseux.* Paris: 1930.

Penning-Rowsell, Edmund. *The Wines of Bordeaux.* rev. ed. London: 1979.

Perold, A. I. *A Treatise on Viticulture.* London: 1927.

Pestel, H. *Les Vins dt eaux-de-vie á appellations d'origine contrôlées en France.* Mâcon: 1959.

Peynaud, Émile. *Le goût du vin.* Paris: 1980.

Ponsot, Maurice, ed. *Vins, alcools et spirituex de France.* 3d ed. Paris: 1949.

Postgate, Raymond. *An Alphabet of Choosing and Serving Wine.* London: 1955.

The Plain Man's Guide to Wine. London: 1951.

Portuguese Wine. London: 1969.

Poupon, Pierre, and Forgeot, Pierre. *Les Vins de Bourgogne.* rev. ed. Paris: 1977.

Quelques Aspects du problème viti-vinicole luxembourgeois. A pamphlet. Luxembourg: 1956.

Rainbird, George. *Sherry and the Wines of Spain.* London:1966.

Ray, Cyril. *The Wines of Italy*. rev. ed. London and New York: 1979.

Lafite. New York: 1969.

Compleat Imbibers. London: 1952-64.

Mouton-Rothschild. rev. ed. London: 1980.

Reboux, Paul. *L'Algérie et ses vins*. Algiers: 1945.

Redding, Cyrus. *A History and Description of Modern Wines*. London: 1833.

French Wines and Vineyards. London: 1860.

Rendu, Victor. *Ampélographie française*. Paris: 1857.

Renouil, Yves, and de Traversay, Paul. *Dictionnaire du vin*. Bordeaux: 1962.

La Revue du Vin de France. Paris.

Ribéreau-Gayon, Jean, and Peynaud, Émile. *Traité d'oenologie*. 2 Vols. Paris: 1960.

Robb, J. Marshall. *Scotch Whisky*. London, Edinburgh, and New York: 1950.

Rodier, Camille. *Le Vin de Bourgogne*. 3d ed. Dijon: 1948.

Wine Lore. Dijon: 1931.

Roger, J. R. *The Wines of Bordeaux*. New York: 1960.

Roncarati, Bruno. *D.O.C. The New Image for Italian Wines*. London: 1971.

Roudie, Philippe. *Le Vignoble bordelais*. Toulouse: 1973.

Roupnel, Gaston. *La Bourgogne*. Paris: 1946.

Rozet, Georges. *La Bourgogne tastevin au main*. Paris: 1949.

Rudd, Hugh R. *Hocks and Moselles*. Constable's Wine Library; London: 1935.

Saintsbury, George. *Notes on a Cellar-Book*. London: 1920, 1963; New York: 1933.

Samalens, Jean and Georges. *Armagnac*. London: 1980.

Sandeman, Sons & Company, Ltd., George G. *Port and Sherry*. London: 1955.

Schoenman, Theodore, ed. *Father of California Wine: Agoston Haraszathy*. Santa Barbara, Cal.: 1979.

Schoonmaker, Frank. *Encyclopedia of Wine*. rev. ed. New York: 1980.

The Wines of Germany. rev. ed. New York: 1966.

Schoonmaker, Frank, and Marvel, Tom. *American Wines*. New York: 1941.

The Complete Wine Book. New York: 1934; London: 1935.

Scott, J. M. *Vineyards of France*. London: 1950.

Seltman, Charles, *Wine in the Ancient World*. London: 1957.

Shand, P. Morton. *A Book of French Wines*. London: 1960.

A Book of Other Wines than French. London: 1929.

Sichel, Peter. *Frank Schoonmaker's Classic: The Wines of Germany*. New York: 1980.

Sichel, Peter, and Ley, Judy: *Which Wine?* New York: 1977.

Simon, André L. *Champagne*. London and New York: 1962.

The Commonsense of Wine. London: 1966.

Concise Encyclopaedia of Gastronomy, Section VIII. London: 1946.

A Dictionary of Wines, Spirits, and Liqueurs. London: 1958.

Know Your Wines. London: 1956.

A Wine Primer. London: 1946.

The Wines of the World. London: 1949.

Simon, André L., and Hallgarten, S. E. *The Great Wines of Germany*. London and New York: 1963.

Stein, Gottfried. *Reise durch die deutschen Weingärten*. Munich: 1957.

Street, Julian L. *Wines*. 3d ed. New York: 1961.

Thompson, Robert, ed. *California Wine*. Menlo Park: 1973.

Thorpy, Frank T. *Wine in New Zealand*. Auckland: 1971.

Thudichum, John L. W., and Dupré, August. *A Treatise on the Origin, Nature and Varieties of Wine*. London and New York: 1872.

Time-Life Foods of the World: Wines and Spirits. New York: 1968.

Todd, W. J. *Port*. London: 1926.

Tovey, Charles. *Wine and Wine Countries*. London: 1862.

Tucker, T. G. *Life in Ancient Athens*. London: 1912.

Union Générale de syndicats pour la Défense des Grands Vins de Bourgogne. *Décrets définissant les vins à appellation d'origine contrôlée de la région de Bourgogne*. Nuits-Saint-Georges: 1944.

Valente-Perfeito, J. C. *Let's Talk about Port*. Oporto: 1948.

Veronelli, Luigi. *I Vini d'Italia*. London: 1964.

Viala, Pierre, and Vermorel, Victor. *Traité général de viticulture*. 7 Vols. Paris: 1901-1910.

Wagner, Philip M. *American Wines and Wine-Making*. New York: 1956.

A Wine-Grower's Guide. rev. ed. New York: 1965.

Waugh, Alec. *In Praise of Wine*. London: 1959.

Waugh, Harry. *Harry Waugh's Wine Diary*. 8 Vols. London: 1975-1978.

Weeks, C. C. *Modern Science and Alcoholic Beverages*. Manchester: 1921.

Weiss, Harry B. *The History of Applejack or Apple Brandy in New Jersey from Colonial Times to the Present*. Trenton: 1954.

Wilkinson, P. W. *First Steps in Ampelography*. Sydney: 1900.

Nomenclature of Australian Wines. Sydney: 1919.

Wilson, Rev. A. M. *Wines of the Bible*. London: 1877.

A Brief Discourse on Wines. London: 1861.

Wine and Spirit Trade Record. *Clarets and Sauternes*. London: 1920.

Winkler, Albert J. *General Viticulture*.

Acknowledgments

A work of this scope could not have become a reality without the knowledgeable and willing assistance of persons, institutions, and associations identified in many ways with the wines and spirits of the world.

First, I want to thank my assistants for their continued helpfulness: in particular, the Hon. Julian Grenfell, Peter C. Handler, Philip I. Togni, Pierre Gauthier, Anthony Wood, Harold Jurgenson, Paul Zuckerman, Parker R. Reis, Katie Philson, Martin Sinkoff, and Professor Lucio P. Ruotola.

To those listed below and to all the other unnamed people who furnished indispensable data and information through pamphlets and brochures I am deeply grateful.

Introductory Chapters

Dr. Maynard A. Amerine, Department of Viticulture and Enology, University of California, Davis, California.

James A. Beard, of New York, author of *The Fireside Cookbook* and *Fish Cookery.*

Dr. Herbert L. Gould, New York.

Dr. Charles P. Mathé, of San Francisco, Chairman of Board of Governors, The Society of Medical Friends of Wine.

Dr. E. Peynaud, of the Station Oenologique de Bordeaux.

Senator Professor Georges Portmann, of Bordeaux.

General

Sam Aaron, of Sherry-Lehmann, New York.

Leon Adams, of Sausalito.

Rafael Aguilar, Spanish Embassy Commercial Office.

José Duarte Amaral, President, Junta Nacional do Vinho, Lisbon.

E. T. Andersen, Vineland Station, Ontario.

José Ramón García de Angulo, President of the Consejo Regulador, Jerez.

Luigi Artusio, of the Stabilimento Fontanafredda.

Gerald Asher, Monterey Vineyard, San Francisco.

Mizuo Aso, of Sanraku-Ocean, Tokyo.

Australian Wine Board.

Raul Azparren, President, Camara de Comercio del Estado Lara, Barquisimeto.

Jeff Baker, of Davis, California.

John Baker, Managing Director, Walter Symons and Hedges & Butler, London.

André Balaresque, wine-broker, of Bordeaux.

Fernando Augusto Bandeira, of the Casa do Douro, Regua.

Dr. Lajos Bánlaki, Legation of the Hungarian People's Republic, Washington, D.C.

Manuel Barbadillo, of Sanlúcar de Barrameda.

Mr. & Mrs. J. G. Barrett, of Felsted, Essex.

Dr. Friedrich von Bassermann-Jordan, of Deidesheim.

Joe Baum, of New York.

The late Joseph Bavard, of Puligny-Montrachet.

Ed Beard, of St. Helena, California.

Comte Hubert de Beaumont, of Château Latour, Pauillac.

Jean Beliard, of Paris and New York.

Dr. Amos Becciolini, of the Consorzio of Chianti, Florence.

The Right Honourable Joseph Bech, former Prime Minister, Grand Duchy of Luxembourg.

Alexis Bespaloff, of New York.

The late E. Besserat de Bellefon, of Ay.

V. Besserat de Bellefon, of Ay.

Louis Benoist, of Almadén Vineyards, San Francisco.

M. V. Benzi, of Provence.

Lennart Berenmark, of the Company Aktiebolaget Vin-Sprit-centralen, Stockholm.

Paul Bergweiler, of Bernkastel-Kues.

Cavalier Guglielmo Bertani, of Verona.

G. Biehler, of Málaga.

Jochen G. Bielefeld, Deutsche Wein-Information, Mainz.

R. Bigot, of Noyers-sur-Cher.

Max Bilan, Union of Chambers of Commerce and Industry, Ankara.

Henri Binaud, former President, Syndicat des Négociants en Vins, Bordeaux.

Alain Blanchy, of Bordeaux.

H. Blechner, Austrian Embassy, London.

Anthony Dias Blue, San Francisco.

R. E. Boillot, of Volnay.

D. I. Bonarjee, High Commission of India, London.

André Bonin, Fédération Internationale des Confréries Bachiques, Paris.

E. Bonvin, Swiss Growers' Association, London.

Sr. Bosch, President, Compañía Ron Bacardi, S.A., Santiago de Cuba.

P. J. Botha, of Zuider-Paarl, South Africa.

The late J. Bouteiller, of Château Pichon-Longueville (Baron), Pauillac.

Julian Boyd, of Princeton, New Jersey.

Lloyd H. Brandon, Managing Director, H. M. Brandon and Company, Ltd., Jamaica, B.W.I.

Marc Bredif, of Vouvray.

Pierre Bréjoux, of the I.N.A.O., Paris.

Giovanni Bressano, of the Stabilimento Fontanafredda.

Toni Bromser, Diplom Weinbauinspektor, Staatsweinkellerei, of Kloster-Eberbach.

David Bruce, of New York City and Peking, China.

Bernard Brun, Bureau Balaresque, Bordeaux.

Dr. A. Bürklin-Wolf, of Wachenheim, Vice-President of the German Wine Association.

W. D. Burnet, Distillers' Co. Ltd., Edinburgh.

676

Joseph Burrier, of Beauregard and Moulin-à-Vent, President of the Cave Coopérative, Chénas.

Ely Callaway, of Temecula, California.
Eng. Vieira de Campos, of Colares.
Inspector Canal, of the Institut National des Appellations d'Origine des Vins et Eaux-de-Vie, Armagnac.
Daniel F. Canning, Press Officer, Mexican National Tourist Council, New York.
Peter L. Carp, of Naples, New York.
R. E. Dejean de Castillo, Argentine Embassy, London.
Dr. J. Cavadias, of the Royal Greek Embassy, Paris, Delegate to the Office International du Vin.
André Cazes, Mayor of Pauillac.
Jean-Michel Cazes, Château Lynch-Bages, Pauillac.
Mlle Chabert, President of the Cave Coopérative, Fleurie.
Georges S. Chappaz, of the Institut National des Appellations d'Origine des Vins et Eaux-de-Vie, Paris.
Pierre Chauveau, of Cognac.
Pierre Chauvot, of Bordeaux.
M. André Chavagnac, of Bordeaux.
Miss M. Clark, of F. & E. May, London.
John A. Clarke, of David Sandeman and Son, Ltd., London.
Ralph H. Cobbold, Director, Justerini and Brooks, Ltd., London.
H. K. H. Cook, Australian Government Trade Commission, New York.
Henri Coquillaud, Director, Bureau National Interprofessionel du Cognac.
Darryl Corti, of Sacramento, California.
Philippe Cottin, of Pauillac.
Pierre Couillaud, of the Viticultural Station, Cognac.
The late Emmanuel Cruse, of Château d'Issan, Margaux.
F. Jiménez Cuende, of Madrid.

Prof. Dalmasso, of the University of Turin, and Vice-President of the International Wine Office.
Paul Damiens, Technical Adviser of the I.N.A.O.
The late Pierre Damoy, of Gevrey-Chambertin.
Virgilio Augusto Dantas, of Lisbon.
J. Dargent, of the Comité Interprofessionel du Vin de Champagne, Épernay.
Horace J. Davis, U.S. Embassy, New Delhi.
C. V. Dayns, New Zealand House, London.
Kenneth Dean, of New York.
Jean Delamain, of Jarnac.
Jean Delmas, Ex-President of the Syndicat des Vins de Graves, of Château Haut-Brion.
Leonard A. T. Dennis, Director, Grants of St. James's, London.
Stanley Dennis, Director, Grants of St. James's, London.
A. Devlétian, of the Institut National des Appellations d'Origine des Vins et Eaux-de-Vie, Paris.
Jorge D. Dias, Casa de Portugal, London.
Mauricio González Diez, of Jerez.
J. Diris, Director, Bureau National Interprofessionel de l'Armagnac, Eauze.
J. Dolezal, Pilsner Urquell Co. Ltd., London.
Beltrán Domecq, of Williams & Humbert, Jerez de la Frontera.
José Ignacio Domecq, of Pedro Domecq, Jerez de la Frontera.
Matthew W. Downer, Public and Trade Relations Department, Brown-Forman Distillers Corporation, Louisville, Kentucky.
Georges Duboeuf, of Romanèche-Thorins.
Jean Dubois-Challon, of Château Ausone, Saint-Émilion.
Pierre J. Dubos, of Château Cantemerle, Macau-Médoc.
Jean Ducamin, Secretary General, Union des Coopératives de Bas-Armagnac, Réans.

S. Dumer, Turkish Embassy, Washington, D.C.
Albert J. Durante, Bourbon Institute, New York.
Comte Bertrand Duvivier, of Bordeaux.

Clay Easterly, Tennessee Viticultural and Oenological Society.
José M. Elizalde, of José M. Elizalde and Company, San Francisco.
Jakob Graf zu Eltz, of Eltville.
F. O. Emery, of London.
René Engel, of Vosne-Romanée.
Mogador Empson, of London.
M. R. Eritokritos, Cyprus Trade Centre, London.
H. B. Estrada, President, Bacardi Imports, Inc., New York.
R. L. Exshaw, of John Jameson and Son, Ltd., Dublin.

Aldo J. Fabrini, Beaulieu Vineyard Company, San Francisco.
Julio Faesler, Mexican Embassy, London.
Frederic L. Felton, President, Felton and Son, Distillers, South Boston, Massachusetts.
Robert E. Fillet, U.S.–China Chamber of Commerce, Washington, D.C.
Robert C. Finigan, Editor, *Finigan's Private Guide to Wines.*
R. W. Finlayson, President, Toronto Wine and Food Society.
Don A. Fisher, Distilled Spirits Institute, New York.
Sir Guy Fison, of Courage & Barclay, London.
Peter Fleck, of Zuider-Paarl, South Africa.
Armand Achille Fould, owner of Château Beychevelle, Saint-Julien.
G. S. Foulds, Australian Wine Centre, London.
Georges Fouquier, of Bordeaux.
J. Fourcaud-Laussac, of Château Cheval Blanc, Saint-Émilion.
M. Franchini-Netto, Brazilian Embassy, London.
Lord Fraser of Lonsdale, ex-Chairman of the Board of Charrington Vintners, London.
H. A. S. Fraser, Association of Canadian Distillers, Montreal.
M. Friedas, Office International de la Vigne et du Vin, Paris.

James Gallander, Ohio Research and Development Center.
Edoardo Gancia, Director of Gancia and Company, Canelli.
Jean-Paul Gardère, of Château Latour.
Rudolf Gareis, retired Weinbaudirektor, of Eltville.
Prof. Pier G. Garoglio, of the Istituto di Industrie Agrarie, University of Florence.
William Garrett, Great Falls, Virginia.
Dr. E. Ercole Garrone, Director of the Consorzio, Asti.
The late Edouard Gasqueton, proprietor, Château Calon-Ségur, Saint-Estèphe.
Philippe Gasqueton, manager, Château Calon-Ségur, Saint-Estèphe.
The late Claude Geoffray, of Château Thivin, Côtes de Brouilly.
Gerald de Geoffre, of Cognac.
Whitney Gerard, of Boston and New York.
Bernard Ginestet, of Margaux.
Pierre Ginestet, ex-co-proprietor of Château Margaux, Margaux.
Pierre Giovetti, wine-broker, of Bordeaux.
Jean Godet, of La Rochelle.
Pierre Goffre-Viaud, Controller of the I.N.A.O.
Mrs. Goldschmidt, Israeli Embassy, London.
Manuel González Gordon, of Jerez.
Henri Gouges, President of the Burgundy Growers Association, Nuits-Saint-Georges.
M. Graffé, Luxembourg Embassy, London.
G. Maxwell A. Graham, of Oporto.
John A. Grant, of Dumbarton, Scotland.

Acknowledgments

A. O. Grass, Canadian Wine Institute, Ontario.
Count Matuschka V. Greiffenclau, of Schloss Vollrads, former President of the German Wine Growers' Association.
The late Franz Greis, of Bernkastel-Kues.
Lord Grenfell, of London.
Louis Gros and Sons, of Vosne-Romanée.
Lester Gruber, of Detroit.
Sydney Gruson, of Paris.
M. de la Guignaraye, of Dusquene Rhums, Bordeaux.
Herman Guntrum, of Weingut Louis Guntrum, Nierstein.
R. E. H. Gunyon, of Sandwich, Kent.
Francis G. Guth, of Mexico City and Vienna.

Carl Haessler, Pennsylvania State University, North East, Pennsylvania.
Bernard Haramboure, of Pauillac.
Fritzi Haskell, of Minneapolis, Minnesota.
A. J. Hasslacher, M.C., Madeira Association, London.
J. Hastings-Trew, formerly of the Cyprus Viticultural Board, London.
Thomas Heeter, of Château Nairac, in Sauternes.
C. P. Hegwood, Jr., Mississippi State University.
Maurice Hennessy, of Cognac.
E. Hiitonen, of O.Y. Alkoholilike, Helsinki.
François Hine, of Jarnac.
Robert Hine, of Jarnac.
S. Hirano, Japan Trade Center, New York City.
H. Hjorth-Nielsen, Royal Danish Consulate General, London.
P. M. P. Hodsoll, formerly Chairman, Grierson, Oldham and Company, Ltd., London.
P. Höhl, of the Section de la Viticulture et de l'Économie vinicole, Division de l'Agriculture, Berne.
J. H. Hopkins, John Jameson & Son, Ltd., Dublin.
Herbert E. Horowitz, U.S. Liaison Office, Peking.
G. Horumba, Rumanian Legation, London.
Gordon S. Howell, Jr., Michigan State University, East Lansing.
Jean Hugel, of Riquewihr, Alsace.
Anthony Hughes, Cyprus Viticultural Board, London.

Dot. Augusto Ippoliti, of Florence.
Dr. Lorenzetto B. R. Luigi Ispettore, of the Consorzio of Chianti, Florence.
Italian·Institute for Foreign Trade, London.
Carlos García Izquierdo, Instituto Nacional de Denominaciones de Origen, Madrid.

Michel Jaboulet-Vercherre, of Pommard.
Julius L. Jacobs, of San Francisco.
Pierre Janneau, of Condom.
Guy Jarach, of Bordeaux.
Douglas Jooste, Deputy Chairman, J. Sedgwick & Co. Ltd., Cape Town, S. Africa.
Peter Jurgens, Ex-President, Almadén Vineyards, San Francisco.

Gabriel Kallay, of New York.
Gaetano Kano, of Montevideo, Uruguay.
The Honorable Kenneth Keating, U.S. Embassy, Tel Aviv.
R. H. King, Board of Trade, London.
Alfred A. Knopf, of New York.
Charles K. Knox, Minnesota Grape Growers Association, St. Paul.
Professor Kosinsky, Professor of Viticulture, University of Agriculture, Budapest.
Paul C. Kovi.

Henrik Kraft, Public Relations Officer, Tuborg Breweries, Ltd., Copenhagen.
Edouard Kressmann, of Bordeaux.
René Kuehn, of Ammerschwihr.

Comte Durieu de Lacarelle, of Château Filhot, Sauternes.
Henry Lacoste, President, Syndicat Régional des Courtiers des Vins et Spiritueux de Bordeaux, de la Gironde et du Sud-Ouest.
Jean Lafon, Director of the Viticultural Station, Cognac.
M. Lahlon, Moroccan Office for Control and Export.
John W. Laird, of New York.
Cathy Laloubère, of Bordeaux.
Harry Lanser, Connecticut Grape Growers Association.
Don Antonio Larrea, Chief of the Viticultural Station at Haro, Rioja.
Paul Lasserre and Mme Lasserre, of the Domaine de Micquer.
L. Lavadoux, of the Centre de Recherches Agronomiques, Bordeaux.
R. de Treville Lawrence, Sr., The Plains, Virginia.
Daniel Lawton, of Bordeaux.
Hughes Lawton, of Bordeaux.
Jerome J. Lehrer, Swiss Wine Bureau, New York.
The late Baron LeRoy de Boiseaumarié, of Châteauneuf-du-Pape, President of the Institut National des Appellations d'Origine des Vins et Eaux-de-Vie.
Raymond LeSauvage, President of the Bordeaux Brokers Association.
Henri Levèque, wine-broker, Podensac, Gironde.
José Joaquim da Costa Lima, Director of the Port Wine Institute, Oporto.
O. Lindo, J. Wray & Nephew, Ltd., Kingston, Jamaica.
Brett T. Lineham, New Zealand Trade Commission, New York City.
The late Madame Edmond Loubat, of Château Pétrus, Pomerol.
Jean-Pierre Lucquiaud
Mlle Gesa Lundemann, of Madrid.
The late Marquis de Lur-Saluces, of Château d'Yquem, Sauternes.
Lucien Lurton, of Margaux.

Alexander McNally, of New York and Connecticut.
M. Maby.
M. S. Mallia, Malta High Commission, London.
Miss Eleanor C. Maloney, Washington, D.C.
Karel Masek, North American Director, Cedok Czechoslovak Travel Bureau, New York.
Cavaliere Capurso Marino, of the Consorzio of Verona.
Ed. Marjary, manager, Château Mouton-Rothschild, Pauillac.
Michel Firino Martell, of Cognac.
Henri Martin, President, Comité Interprofessionel des Vins de Bordeaux, and Mayor of Saint-Julien.
John G. Martin, of Heublein, Inc., Hartford, Connecticut.
Gil Pires Martins, Vice-President, Junta Nacional do Vinho, Lisbon.
J. P. Mas, of the I.N.A.O. in Bordeaux.
Diana Masieri, of New York City.
Egon Mauer, manager of the Langwerth von Simmern Estate, Eltville.
F. & E. May, of London.
Abel Médard, Director, Comité Interprofessionnel du Vin de Champagne, Épernay.
D. Homen de Mello, of Lisbon.
Pierre F. Mendes, Casa de Portugal, London.
A. B. Meslier, régisseur of Château d'Yquem, Sauternes.

Prince P. von Metternich, of Schloss Johannisberg.

Dr. Franz Werner Michel, of Mainz.

Harald Svane Midttun, Royal Norwegian Information Service, New York City.

S. H. Miller, London Manager, John Jameson and Son, Ltd.

Brigitta Moberg, Royal Swedish Embassy, Washington, D.C.

Robert Mondavi, of St. Helena, California.

Monimpex, Budapest.

Duc Pierre de Montesquiou-Fezensac, Château de Marsan, Auch.

Miss Marcia Moore, Swiss Wine Bureau, New York.

John Mortenson, University of Florida, Leesburg, Florida.

Jean-Pierre Moueix, of Libourne.

Christian Moueix, of Libourne.

Dr. Antonio Niederbacher, of the Unione Italiana Vini, Milan.

Milos Nikolic, Yugoslav Information Center, New York.

Tom J. Noonan, Director, Grierson, Oldham and Company, Ltd., Dublin.

Dr. Giorgio Odero, proprietor, Frecciarosso Vineyards, Casteggio.

President de Oliveira, of the Junta Nacional do Vinho, Lisbon.

Alan Olson, German Wine Information Bureau, New York City.

Julio Saro Diez Ordonez, Instituto Nacional de Denominaciones de Origen, Madrid.

Frank W. Packard, of New York.

Raymond-Julien Pagès, President, Fédération d'Auvergne des Vins et Spiritueux, Clermont-Ferrand.

H. F. M. Palmer, Secretary, Australian Wine Board, Adelaide.

Peter Palmer, London.

Arthur Palombo, of San Francisco.

M. Paran, Israeli Embassy, London.

Andrés de Blas Pardilla, of Madrid.

Anne-Marie Pargade, of Bordeaux.

John Parkinson, of New York.

Pierre Perromat, President of the I.N.A.O., Paris.

Sp. Phylaktis, Cyprus High Commission, London.

Karel Pichl, Embassy of the Czechoslovak Socialist Republic, Washington, D.C.

Claudio R. Porrero, Spanish Embassy, London.

Bruno Prats, President of the Committee of Classified Growths and owner of Château Cos d'Estournel, St.-Estèphe.

Jimmie Pridmore, Clemson University, York, South Carolina.

R. Protin, Director, Office International du Vin, Paris.

The late Sebastian Prüm, of the Johann Josef Prüm Estate, Wehlen.

Manfred Prüm, of Wehlen.

Charles Quittanson, Inspector of Fraud, Institut National des Appellations d'Origine des Vins et Eaux-de-Vie, Dijon.

Claude Ramonet, of Chassagne-Montrachet.

Jean de Premio Real, of Mexico City.

H. Parks Redwine, Atlanta, Georgia.

Joachim Ress, of Winkel.

Theodor Rettinger, and son, of Wachenheim.

Peter Reynier, of J. B. Reynier, London.

Dr. Guglielmo Ricaldone, Director General, Stabilimento Cinzano, S. Vittoria d'Alba.

Bettino Ricasoli, of Florence.

Pedro Rivero, of Jerez.

Bertrand de Rivoyre, Ambares and Bordeaux.

J. Bernard Robb, of the Virginia Alcoholic Beverage Control Board, Richmond, Va.

Gaspar Roca, Puerto Rico.

Comte E. de Rohan-Chabot, Château de Saint-Martin, Taradeau, President of the Syndicat de Défense des Côtes de Provence.

Ed. Rolland, of the Académie des Vins de Bordeaux, and Château Coutet, Barsac.

Dr. Bruno Roncarati, of London.

Baron Philippe de Rothschild.

Jean-Pierre Rouff.

I. M. Roushdy, United Arab Republic.

Armand Rousseau, of Gevrey-Chambertin.

E. J. Rozier, President, Fédération Méridionale du Commerce en Gros des Vins et Spiritueux, Béziers.

Professor Lucio P. Ruotola, of Stanford University.

Brian St. Pierre, Wine Institute, San Francisco.

Tadashi Sakuda, Suntory, Ltd., Osaka.

Francisco Salamero, of Rioja.

Maj. General Guy Salisbury-Jones, Hambledon, Hampshire, England.

The late Joseph Salzmann, of Kaysersberg.

Jean Samalens, of Laujuzan.

Étienne Sauzet, of Puligny-Montrachet.

Noël Sauzet, of Jarnac.

Miss Elliseva Sayers, Portuguese Information Trade Office, New York.

D. V. Schiazzano, Italian Chamber of Commerce, London.

Guy Schyler, of Château Lafite, Pauillac.

M. D. L. Scott, Vice-President, Public Relations Division, Heublein, Inc., Hartford, Connecticut.

R. I. C. Scott-Hayward, Johannesburg.

Tom Seabrook, W. & J. Seabrook, Melbourne.

Philip Seldon, *Vintage* Magazine, New York.

Fernand Sentou, of Eauze.

Marcel Servin, of Chablis.

Pierre Sevez, President, Société du Vermouth Dolin, Chambéry.

The late Allan H. Sichel, Director, Sichel and Company, Bordeaux and London.

Peter M. F. Sichel, of New York City.

Freiherr Langwerth von Simmern, of Eltville.

Werner Sitzmann, of Málaga.

S. Sklar, London.

Luis Solari, Peruvian Embassy, London.

Prof. Dr. Steinberg, Director, Viticultural School and Research Station, Geisenheim.

Jane Stockwood, of London.

John Symms, Director, Charrington Vintners, Procurement.

Claude Taittinger, of Rheims.

Dr. Clemente Tarantola, Turin University.

Pierre Tari, Comité des Grands Crus Classés du Médoc.

André Tchelistcheff, of Napa.

Dmitri Tchelistcheff, Bodegas de Santo Tomás, Ensenada.

Tomás López Tello, of Valdepeñas.

Richard & William Teltscher, London.

Jacques Théo, Managing Director, Alexis Lichine & Co., Bordeaux.

H. Gregory Thomas, Grand Master, Commanderie de Bordeaux, New York.

Theodore M. Thomas, Michigan State University, Paw Paw.

Carmel J. Tintle, Schenley Industries, Inc., New York.

Dr. K. S. Tiwari, Directorate General of Technical Development, New Delhi.

Acknowledgments

Brigadier C. E. Tryon-Wilson, former Chairman, Associated Wine and Spirit Traders, London.
Mario Carlo Tucci, of Florence and New York.

The Ulster Magazine, Belfast.

Ramiro Valadão, Director, Portuguese Information Trade Office, New York.
H. Vella, of Pauillac.
Jean Vermorel, of Vaux-en-Beaujolais.
André-Jacques Vernaison, President, Fédération du Sud-Est, Lyon.
Maître Jacques Vivez, of Bordeaux.
D. Toledano, Israel Wine Institute, Rehovot.
Nicolas Trambitsky, of Paris.
Louis Trapet, of Gevrey-Chambertin.
John and Janet Trefethen, Rutherford, California.
Philip Wagner, proprietor, Boordy Vineyard, Riderwood, Maryland.
D. D. Ward, Managing Director, Mount Gay Distilleries Ltd., Barbados, B.W.I.

Jack L. Ward, Horam Manor, Sussex.
Harry H. Waugh, Director, John Harvey and Sons, Ltd., Bristol and London, and ex-director of Château Latour, Pauillac.
Odile Welfert, New York and Lyon.
H. Seymour Weller, Château Haut-Brion, Pessac.
Jan Wells, of San Francisco.
The late William Widmer, Widmer's Wine Cellars, Naples, New York.
Stanley Williams, Managing Director of Charrington Vintners Ltd.
Prof. Albert J. Winkler, of the College of Agriculture, University of California, Davis, California.
Basil J. Winston, of New York.

The late Georges Yard, of Beaune.

The Honorable Ardeshir Zahedi, Embassy of Iran, Washington, D.C.
V. Zanko, of the Poduzeče Industrijskih Vinarija, Zagreb.
Carlos J. Zitta, Centro de Vitacultores del Uruguay.

Index

In place names beginning with the word Château, abbreviated Ch., the abbreviation is disregarded in alphabetizing; thus Ch. Margaux will be found under Margaux. Alphabetization is word by word; a short word precedes a longer one beginning with the same letters. Prepositions and conjunctions within a name are not alphabetized. For example, entries appear in this order: Clos du Roi, Clos Saint-Pierre, Clos du Verger, Clos de Vougeot, Closeau. When an item has its own entry in the alphabetical text the page number for this entry precedes all other page references.

ABBREVIATIONS:

Fr. = French	Ch., Chx = Château, Châteaux
Germ. = German	comm. = commune
Gk = Greek	dept. = department
Hung. = Hungarian	dist. = district
Ital. = Italian	prov. = province
Portug. = Portuguese	vd = vineyard
Sp. = Spanish	

A

Aalborg Export, Aalborg Taffel, Danish brands of akvavit, 77
Abadir-Dukem, Ethiopia, 218
abboccato, Ita, term for semi-sweet wine, 57, 480
Abbott's Aged Bitters, U.S.A., 109
abocado, Sp. term for semi-sweet wine, 57
Abrau-Dursso wines, Krasnodar, 421-3
abricotine, Fr. apricot liqueur, 57
Abruzzi, prov. Cent. Italy, 57, 270
absinthe, 57, 358
Abstatt, Württemberg, 628
Abtei, Grosslage, Bingen, 617
Abtei, vd Zell-Mosel, 331
Abtsberg, vd Bernkastel, 329, 334, 335
Abtsberg, vd Franconia, 230
Abtsfronhof, vd Palatinate, 354
Abtsleite, vd Franconia, 230
Abtswind, Franconia, 230, 606
acariose (Fr.), acariosis, mite on vines, 57, 37
acescence (acetification, *piqûre*), disorder of wine, 57, 50
acetaldehyde in wine, 44, 49
acetic acid, 57; in distilled liquors, 53; in wine, 26, 46, 48-50, 57, 58
Acetobacter, bacterium, 50, 57, 440
Achaea, prov. Greece, 57
Achaia-Clauss, Gk wine firm, 249, 250
Achern, Baden, 604
Achille-Fould family, owners of Ch. Beycheville, 108
Achkarren, Baden, 94, 602
Achtarak, Armenia, 422
acidification of wines (addition of acids), 45, 48
acidity: fixed, 222, 46 48, 58; total, 46, 48; volatile, 46, 48, 49, 58
acid (acids), 57-8, in distilled liquors, 53; in grapes and wine 57-8, 39, 45-9
Aconcagua Valley, Chile, 58, 167, 169
acquavite, Ital. spelling of *aqua vitae*, 58
acqui-à-caution, document with shipments of Fr. wines, 58
Acquit Jaune d'Or, document with shipments of Cognac, 184-5
Adakarasi, Turkish grape, 476
Adam, ———, inventor of rectified spirits, 6, 7
Adams County Winery, Pennsylvania, 670
adega (Portug.), wine-store, wine-shop, 58
Adelaide, S. Australia, 88
Adelberg, Grosslage, Rheinhessen, 617-18
Adelsheim Vineyard, Oregon, 669
Adissan, comm. Languedoc, 173
Adolzfurt, Württemberg, 628
Adom Atic wine, Israel, 58
Advocat, Dutch brandy and egg drink, 58, 344
Aegean, dist. Turkey, 475, 476
Aellen family, owners of Berrywine Plantation, 664
Afames, Cyprus, 205
Affalterbach, Württemberg, 626
Affaltrach, Württemberg, 628
Affile (Ceasanes di Affile), Latuim, 286
agave (century plant), source of cocui, tequila, pulque, and mescal, 58, 316, 319, 387, 515
Agawam, Canadian grape, 141
age of wine, 12
ageing of distilled spirits, brandy, 53, 180-2, 184
ageing of wine: ancient Roman methods, 175; in barrels, 41, 43, 44; in bottles, 43, 44
Aghioghitico, Gk grape, 250

Aglianico, Ital. grape, 139, 140, 270
Aglianico del Vulture, Basilicata, 58, 97, 270
agrafe, agraffe (Fr.), clamp for first Champagne cork, 58
Agritiusberg, vd Saar-Ruwer, 332, 334
aguardiente, Sp. name for spirits, 58; in Mexico, 318, 319
Aguascalientes, Mexico, 317
Águeda, Portugal, 379
Aguilar de la Frontera, Montilla, 322
Agulha, Portugal, 377
Ahn, Luxembourg, 299
Ahr Valley, N.W. Germany, 58-9, 237-9; towns and vds, list, 599
Ahrweiler, Ahr Valley, 59, 237, 599
Aichelberg, Württemberg, 626
Aigrots, Les, vd Côte de Beaune, 103
Aiguebelle, Fr. liqueur, 59
Ain-Bessem-Bouira, Algeria, 62
Aiou-Dag, Crimea, 423
Aisne, Champagne, 157
Aiud, vd Rumania, 420
aiven, Tartar spirit from fermented milk, 59
Aix-en-Provence, comm. Provence, 59, 385
Ajaccio. Corsica, 188
Akastafa, Azerbaijan, 423
akevit, *see* aquavit
akvavit, *see* aquavit
Alabama, state U.S.A., 653
alambrado (Sp.), bottle in wire netting, 59
Alameda County, California, 292, 491, 499, 501
alasch, *see* allasch
Alavesa, Rioja, 59, 408, 409
Alba Flora, Majorca, 59
Alba Iulia, vd Rumania, 420
Albacete, La Mancha, 451
Alban, ancient Roman wine, 178
Albana di Romagna, Emilia-Romagna, 59, 217, 270
Albarello, Sp. grape, 453
Albariño, Sp. grape, 453
albariza (Sp.), chalky soil, 59, 439, 453
Albersweiler, Palatinate, 622
Albig, Rheinhessen, 620
Albillo, Sp. grape, 439
Albisheim, Palatinate, 625
Alcaeus, on wine, 59
Alcamo (D.O.C.), Sicily, 59, 443
Alcobaça, Portugal, 379-80
alcohol (ethanol, ethyl alcohol), 59; in distilled spirits, 52-3; effects on body, 26; origin of word, 6; in wine, 25-8, 45
alcoholic content of wines and spirits, 60, 214; Fr. laws on, 73; proof spirit, 383; specific gravity and, tables, 78-9; strength, comparative table, 634-6
alcohols, higher (propyl, isoamyl, isobutyl, etc.): in distilled spirits, 53; in wine, 39, 45
Aldegund, Zell-Mosel, 331
aldehydes, 60; in distilled spirits, 53; in wine, 44, 49
ale, 60, 105
Aleatico, Muscat grape: in California, 490, 491; in Corsica, 188; in Italy, 60, 76, 287, 478
Aleatico di Gradoli (D.O.C.), 287
Aleatico di Portoferraio, Elba, 60, 478
Aleatico di Puglia, Apulia, 60, 76
Aleksandrovac, Serbia, 539
Alella, Catalonia, 60, 450, 451
Alenquer, Portugal, 380
Alexander, American grape, 507

Alexander Valley, Sonoma dist., California, 497, 509
Alexander Valley Vineyards, Sonoma, California, 656
Alexandrakis, Ethiopian winery, 218
Aleyor, Majorca, 60
Alf, Zell-Mosel, 331, 612
Alföld, dist. Hungary, 260, 261
Algarve, Portugal, 375
Alger, dept. Algeria, 61-2
Algeria, 60-2; acidification procedures, 48; map, 62
Alicante (Alicantina, Grenache), grape: in Israel, 266, 267; in Spain, 453; in Tunisia, 474; *see also* Grenache
Alicante (Tent), S.E. Spain, 62, 450
Alicante-Bouschet, grape, 62: in Algeria, 61; in California, 481 484, 488, 490, 661; in Morocco, 325; in Tunisia, 474
Alicante Gazin, California hybrid grape, 489-90
Aligoté, grape, 62, 189; in Burgundy, 132, 135, 193; in Lorraine, 297; in Rumania, 419, 420; in Russia, 421, 423; in Switzerland, 464
Aligoté Ay-Danil, Crimea, 423
Alken, Zell-Mosel, 612
alkermes, cordial from kermes insect, 62
Allas-Champagne, comm. Cognac, 183
allasch (alasch), kümmel liqueur, 62, 278
Allegro, Portugal, 379
Allen, H. Warner, writer on wine, 424
Allmersbach a.W., Württemberg; 626
Allobrogian, ancient Roman grape, 175
Almadén Vineyards, Santa Clara County, California, 484, 485, 491, 501, 502; in Brazil, 125: Grenache Rosé, 488, 502
Almagro, Diego de, expedition to Chile, 169
Almansa, La Mancha, 450, 451
Almarla Vineyards, Mississippi, 665
Almendraljo, Estremadura, 454
almond: gin flavored with, 243; liqueur flavored with, 202, 347; wine flavored with, 138
Alonzo, David and Filemon, Mexican wine-makers, 318
Alouchta, Crimea, 423
Aloxe-Corton, comm. Côte de Beaune, 62-3, 128, 133, 188, 190, 191, 259, 282
Alpha, American hybrid grape, 510
Alsace, prov. E. France, 63-8, 24, 229; history of wine in, 3, 64-5; map, 65; spirits (*eaux-de-vie*), 68; vintage chart, 21; wine laws and labels, 15, 65-6
Alsatian Vins d'Origine, 65
Alsenz, Nahe, 343, 615
Alsheim, Rheinhessen, 401, 620
altar wine, *see* sacramental wines
Altärchen, vd Bernkastel, 330, 334
Altavilla, Ethiopian winery, 218
Altdorf, Baden, 603
Altdorf, Palatinate, 623
Altdörr, vds Rheinhessen: (Dalheim), 402; (Friesenheim), 402
Altenahr, Ahr Valley, 599
Altenbamber, Nahe, 614
Altenberg, vd Franconia, 230
Altenberg, Nahe, 343
Altenberg, vd Palatinate, 354
Altenberg, vds Saar-Ruwer, 332-5
Alter Berg, Palatinate, 623
Altesse, grape, 520
Altintas, Turkish grape, 476

Neuwies, vd Saar-Ruwer, 334
Neveu, Freiherr von, vd owner, Baden, 94
Nevşehir-Ürgüp, Turkey, 476
New Castile, Cent. Spain, 449-51
New England rum, 417, 75, 311, 414
New Hampshire, state U.S.A., 666
New Jersey, state U.S.A., 344, 509, 666; applejack, 76
New Mexico, state U.S.A., 666-7
New South Wales, state Australia, 85-7
New York, state U.S.A., 264, 265, 506-10; conditions for noble rot in, 122; grape varieties and hybrids, 509-10; kosher wine, 277, 509; map, 508; recent developments in, 667-8; wine areas and vds, 507-9
New Zealand, 344-6
Neyret, grape, 366
Niagara, American grape, 346; in Brazil, 125; in Canada, 141
Niagara, dist. Canada and New York, 346, 509
Niagara Falls Wine Cellar, Lewiston, New York, 509
Niagara peninsula, Ontario, 140-1
Nichelini Vineyards, Napa Valley, California, 654
Nicholas, Austrian wine, 89
Nicoreşti, vd Rumania, 419, 420
Niebaum-Coppola Estates, Napa Valley, California, 495; 654
Nieder-Hilbersheim, Rheinhessen, 617
Nieder-Olm, Rheinhessen, 619
Nieder-Weisen, Rheinhessen, 618
Niederberg-Helden, vd Bernkastel, 329
Niederburg, Mittelrhein, 607
Niedereggenen, Baden, 602
Niederemmel, vd Bernkastel, 334, 335
Niederfell, Zell-Mosel, 613
Niederhausen an der Nahe, Nahe, 342, 614, 615
Niederhauser Hermannshöhle, Nahe, 346, 342
Niederheimbach, Mittelrhein, 606
Niederhofen, Württemberg, 627
Niederhorbach, Palatinate, 622
Niederkirchen, Palatinate, 623
Niedermennig, Saar-Ruwer, 332
Niedermoschel, Nahe, 615
Niedernhall, Württemberg, 628
Niederrimsingen, Baden, 602
Niederrotterbach, Palatinate, 622
Niederschopfheim, Baden, 603
Niederstetten, Württemberg, 629
Niederwalluf, Rheingau, 392, 393, 617
Niederweiler, Baden, 602
Niefernheim, Palatinate, 625
Nielluco, grape in Corsica, 188
Nierstein, Bereich, Rheinhessen, 619-20
Nierstein, town, Rheinhessen, 24, 399, 403, 619-20
Niesgen, vd Saar-Ruwer, 334
Niğde, Turkey, 476
Nightingale, Myron, of Beringer vds, California, 494
Nikolausberg, vd Zell-Mosel, 331
Nikolayev, Ukrainian wine center, 421
Nill, vd Palatinate, 355
Nimburg, Baden, 602
nip, quarter-bottle, 346
Nirosan, insecticide, 179
Nissley Vineyards, Pennsylvania, 670
Nittel, Obermosel, 325, 331, 610
Noah, American grape, 346, 510; hybrid with Folle Blanche, see Baco 22A
noble, term, 346
Noble (Pinot Noir, Pinot Meunier), grape, in Loire Valley, 70, 294; see also Pinot Meunier
noble rot (Edelfäule, pourriture noble), 346, 15, 34, 36, 42, 47, 122, 381; in Anjou, 71, 122, 198, 199; in Bergerac, 107; in Germany, 122, 235, 240; on Isle of Wight, 481; in Jurançon, 275; in Portugal, 246; in Rheingau, 392; in Rhône Valley, 428; in Sauternes, 122, 433, 537; of Tokay, 468-9; see also Botrytis cinerea
Noblejas, Toledo, 346
Nocera, grape, in Tunisia, 474
Nochern, Mittelrhein, 607
Noellat, Charles, wine estate, Côte de Nuits, 407
Nogent-l'Abbesse, Champagne, 154
noggin, quarter-pint, 346
nohelik, American Indian liquor, 7
Noirien, see Pinot Noir
Noirots, Les, vd Côte de Nuits, 153
Noizay, comm. Touraine, 524
Nomentane, ancient Roman grape, 175
Non Plus Ultra, Panadés, 453
Nonaville, comm. Cognac, 183
Nonnenberg, vd Bernkastel, 330, 334-5
Nonnenberg, vd Rheingau, 397

Nonnengarten, vd Palatinate, 354
Nonnenhorn, Franconia, 606
Nonnenstück, vd Palatinate, 354
Nordhausen, Württemberg, 627
Nordheim, Franconia, 605
Nordheim, Württemberg, 627
Nordweil, Baden, 603
Norheim, Nahe, 346, 342, 343, 614
Norsingen, Baden, 602
Norte, Argentina, 80
North Carolina, state U.S.A., 668
North Coast region, California, 486, 489, 492, 494-503
Northeast Vineyards, New York, 668
Northland, New Zealand, 345
Northminster Winery, Delaware, 662
Norton, American grape, 346, 509
Norway, 346-7; aquavit, 77, 346-7
Norwegian punch, 387
nose, bouquet of wine, 347
Nostrano, Ticino, 464
Notre-Dame du Raisin, Brouilly, pilgrimage to, 102
Novitiate Winery, Los Gatos, California, 503
Novocherkassk, Russia, 421
Noyau (crème de noyau), liqueur, 347, 202
nu (Fr.), price of wine without container, 347
Nuckton, Deryck, owner of Monterey Peninsula Winery, 660
Nuits-Prémeaux, comm. Côte de Nuits, 197; see also Prémeaux
Nuits-Saint-Georges, comm. Côte de Nuits, 347-8, 24, 133, 192, 195, 197
Nuragus di Cagliari (D.O.C.), Sardinia, 431-2
Nussbach, Baden, 603
Nussbaum, Nahe, 615
Nussbien, vd Palatinate, 354, 356
Nussbrunnen, vd Rheingau, 396
Nussdorf, Palatinate, 622
Nussdorf, nr. Vienna, 89, 92
Nussloch, Baden, 600
Nussriegel, vd Palatinate, 355
nylon powder for fining white wine, 43

O

oak for barrels, 349, 364; Limousin, 53, 83, 117, 124, 180, 184; for whisky, 528, 530, 532
Oak Knoll Winery, Oregon, 670
Oakview Plantations, South Carolina, 671
Oakville, vds, Napa Valley, California, 495
oast house, 349
Ober-Flörsheim, Rheinhessen, 621
Ober-Hilbersheim, Rheinhessen, 617
Ober-Olm, Rheinhessen, 619
Oberberg, vd Nahe, 343
Oberbergen, Baden, 602
Oberbillig, Obermosel, 610
Oberdiebach, Mittelrhein, 320, 607
Oberdingen, Württemberg, 627
Obereggenen, Baden, 602
Obereisenheim, Franconia, 605
Oberemmel, Saar-Ruwer, 332-5, 349, 611
Oberfell, Zell-Mosel, 613
Oberhausen, Palatinate, 622
Oberhausen an der Nahe, Nahe, 614, 615
Oberheimbach, Mittelrhein, 606
Oberkirch, Baden, 603
Oberlauda, Baden, 601
Oberlin Wine Institute, Colmar, 65
Obermoschel, Nahe, 615
Obermosel, Bereich, Mosel-Saar-Ruwer, 238, 325, 327, 331; towns and vds, list, 609-10
Obernai Alsace, 66
Oberndorf, Nahe, 615
Obernhof, Mittelrhein, 607
Oberrhein, dist. Germany, 238, 239
Oberrimsingen, Baden, 602
Oberrotterbach, Palatinate, 622
Oberrotweil, Baden, 603
Obersasbach, Baden, 604
Oberschopfheim, Baden, 603
Oberschüpf, Baden, 601
Oberschwarzach, Franconia, 606
Obersöllbach, Württemberg, 628
Oberstenfeld, Württemberg, 627
Oberstetten, Württemberg, 629
Oberstreit, Nahe, 615
Obersülzen, Palatinate, 625
Obertsrot, Baden, 604
Oberuhldingen, Baden, 601
Obervolkach, Franconia, 605
Oberwalluf, Rheingau, 393, 617
Oberweier, Baden, 603
Oberwessel, Mittelrhein, 320, 607

Obrigheim, Palatinate, 623
obscuration, in alcoholic strength of brandy, 349
Occidente, Argentina, 80
Ochagavia, Silvestre, founder of Chilean viniculture, 169
Ockenheim, Rheinhessen, 403, 619
Ockfen, Saar-Ruwer, 332-5, 611
Ockfener Bockstein, Saar-Ruwer, 349
octave, small cask, 349, 532-3
Ödakra Taffel Aquavit, Swedish, 77
Odenas, Beaujolais-Villages, 101, 102
Odenheim, Baden, 600
Odernheim, Nahe, 615
Odessa, 421; Technical Wine Institute, 421
Odinstal, vd Palatinate, 356
Odobeşti, vd Rumania, 419
odors, wine contaminated by, 51
Ödsbach, Baden, 603
Odysseus, 174, 177
Oechslé degrees, 349; alcoholic content and specific gravity, Baumé equivalents, table, 79
Oedheim, Württemberg, 628
oeil de perdrix (Fr.), pinkish tint in white wines, 349, 462, 521
oenology, science of wine, 349, 519
Oesterreichischer (Sylvaner, Franken Riesling), grape, 349; see also Sylvaner
Oestrich (Östrich), Rheingau, 393, 397, 616
Oetinger, Freiherr von, wine estate, Rheingau, 395, 398
Oeuilly, Champagne, 156
off-license, English, 349
Offenau, Württemberg, 628
Offenburg, Baden, 94, 603
Offenheim, Rheinhessen, 621
Office International du Vin, 5
Oger, Champagne, 156
Oggau, Burgenland, 349, 89, 90, 128
Ohio, state U.S.A., 510, 668-9
Ohligsberg, vd Bernkastel, 330
Ohlsbach, Baden, 603
Ohrid, Macedonia, 538, 542
oidium, powdery mildew, 349, 5, 36, 122, 381; in Beaujolais, 102; in Bordeaux, 247; in Canary Islands, 454; in Japan, 272; in Madeira, 302, 303; in New Zealand, 345; in Spain, 410
Oiry, Champagne, 156
Okanagan Valley, British Columbia, 140-1
Okayama, dist. Japan, 272
O'Keefe, Edward, owner of Ch. Grand Travers, 665
okolehao (oke), Hawaiian spirit, 350
Oktemberian, Armenia, 422
Öküz Gözü, Turkish grape, 476
Olaszrisling, Hung. grape, 260, 261
Ölberg, vd Palatinate, 354
Ölberg, vd Rheinhessen, 403
Old South Winery, Mississippi, 665
Old Tom gin, 350, 243
oldest bottled wine, 350
Oleron's disease (bacterial blight of vines), 350, 36
Oliena, Sardinia, 432
Olifants River, S. Africa, 448
Oliver, Bill, vd. owner, 663, 664
Oliver Winery, Indiana, 663
Ch. Olivier, Graves, 350, 24, 248, 577, 578
Olizy-Violaine, Champagne, 155
Ollioules, comm. Provence, 384
Olmo, Dr. H. P., of University of California College of Agriculture, 485, 488, 489
Oloroso, Sherry without flor, 350, 322, 439-41
Oltrepò Pavese (D.O.C.), Lombardy, 350, 296
Omar Khayyam, 264
Ondenc, grape, 107, 233
Onsdorf, Obermosel, 610
Ontario, prov. Canada, 140-1
Opfingen, Baden, 602
Ophthalma, Cypriot grape, 205
Opimian, Roman vintage wine of 121 B.C., 350, 176, 177
Opol, Dalmatia, 541
Oporto, Hungarian grape, 261
Oporto, Portugal, 350, 372; Factory House, 220, 375; Port shipped from, 4
Oppenheim, Rheinhessen, 350, 399, 619, 620
Oppenheim, Weingut der Stadt, 404
Oran, dept. Algeria, 61-2
orange, bitter, as flavoring for aquavit, 77
orange bitters, 350, 109
orange brandy, 350
orange liqueurs, 204, 245, 316, 417
orange peel as flavoring for gin, 243
orange wine: Brazil, 350; Louisiana, 664
Ch. l'Oratoire, Saint-Émilion, 556
Orbe, Vaud, 462

Index

A NOTE ABOUT THE AUTHOR

ALEXIS LICHINE is a wine grower and wine merchant. He owns Château Prieuré-Lichine in the village of Margaux in the Médoc area near Bordeaux, and was for many years part-owner of Château Lascombes and three vineyards in Burgundy. His experience in selecting and purchasing wines for shippers began before World War II, and in 1955 he established his own firm, Alexis Lichine and Company, first in Margaux and then in Bordeaux. By the time he sold it in 1965, it had become one of the leaders in its field. Mr. Lichine subsequently continued in business with interests in the United States, Europe, and Africa, and in 1975 became an active wine merchant again as a director of and consultant to a major wine-importing firm in New York. He has produced a dramatized record album, *The Joys of Wine*. A new version of his classic *Wines of France*, first published in 1951, was issued under the title *Alexis Lichine's Guide to the Wines and Vineyards of France* in 1979.

Born in Moscow, Alexis Lichine went with his family to France after the Revolution, and came to the United States in 1934. During the war he served with U.S. Army Intelligence in North Africa and Europe, reaching the rank of major. He is an Officer of the Legion of Honor and a member of the prestigious Académie des Vins de Bordeaux. Mr. Lichine now divides his time between New York City and his château in the Médoc, with frequent trips through the vineyards of France, where he has probably spent more time than any other writer on wines.

A NOTE ON THE TYPE

The text for this book was electronically composed in Baskerville by Rocappi/ Lehigh, utilizing modern computerized photocomposition technology with type generated on a Fototronic cathode ray tube device. Book design by Irving Perkins with calligraphy by Alice Koeth; production supervision by Helen Barrow.

Printed by The Murray Printing Company, Forge Village, Massachusetts. Bound by American Book-Stratford Press, Inc., Saddle Brook, New Jersey.